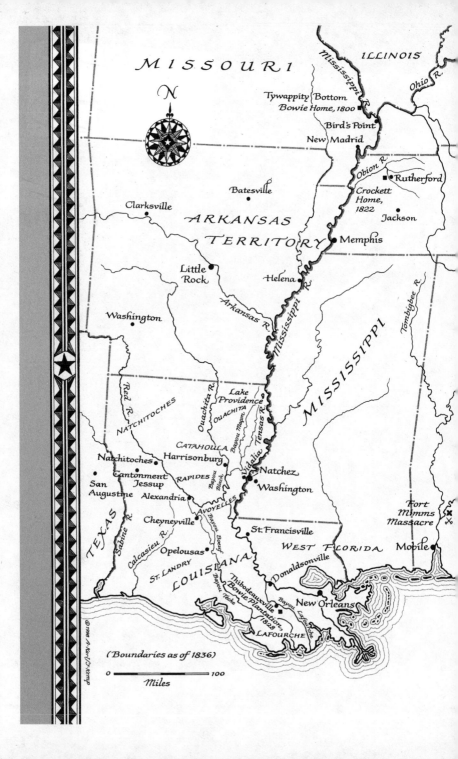

MISSOURI

N

ILLINOIS

Mississippi R.

Ohio R.

Tywappity Bottom
Bowie Home, 1800
Bird's Point
New Madrid

Obion R.

Rutherford

Batesville

Crockett
Home,
1822

Jackson

Clarksville

ARKANSAS

TERRITORY

Memphis

Little
Rock

Helena

Mississippi R.

Arkansas R.

Washington

Tombigbee R.

MISSISSIPPI

Red R.

Ouachita R.

Lake
Providence

OUACHITA

Bayou Macon

Tensas R.

NATCHITOCHES

CATAHOULA

Harrisonburg

Natchitoches

RAPIDES

Bayou Black

Vidalia

Natchez

Cantonment
Jessup

Washington

San
Augustine

Alexandria

AVOYELLES

Bayou Boeuf

Fort
Mimms
Massacre

Cheyneyville

St. Francisville

WEST FLORIDA

Mobile

Sabine R.

TEXAS

Calcasieu R.

Opelousas

ST. LANDRY

LOUISIANA

Donaldsonville

Thibodeauxville
Bowie Plantation,
1828

Bayou Lafourche

New Orleans

Bayou Teche

LAFOURCHE

©1998 A. Karl/J. Kemp

(Boundaries as of 1836)

0   100
Miles

KENTUCKY

VIRGINIA

Bowie Birthplace,
1796

Cumberland R.

Cumberland
Gap

Elliott
Springs • ■ Bowie
Home, 1788

Rogersville

Holston R.

Crockett Birthplace,
1786

Crockett Tavern

Nashville   Murfreesboro   Knoxville •

Nolichucky

NORTH
CAROLINA

TENNESSEE

Crockett Mill, 1820
■ Lawrenceburg   Bean's
• Creek

Elk R.

■ Crockett Home,
1813

Tennessee R.

Huntsville

SOUTH
CAROLINA

Saluda R.

EDGEFIELD
DISTRICT

Ninety
Six •   • Red
Bank • ■ Travis
Birthplace,
1809
Edgefield

Black Warrior R.

Chattahoochie R.

Battle of
Tallusahatchee

✘ Fort
Talladega

ALABAMA

GEORGIA

Ebenezer
■
Bowie
Home,
1760

Savannah R.

Alabama R.

Savannah

Burnt Corn
• Claiborne
• Sparta

The World of
CROCKETT, BOWIE,
and TRAVIS

1786~1836

Pensacola •

FLORIDA

Gulf of Mexico

THREE ROADS
TO THE ALAMO

Books by William C. Davis

The Cause Lost: Myths and Realities of the Confederacy

Civil War Journal

*A Way Through the Wilderness: The Natchez Trace and
the Civilization of the Southern Frontier*

"A Government of Our Own": The Making of the Confederacy

Jefferson Davis: The Man and His Hour

Diary of a Confederate Soldier

Touched by Fire (2 volumes)

The Image of War (6 volumes)

The Imperiled Union (2 volumes)

*The Orphan Brigade: The Kentucky Confederates
Who Couldn't Go Home*

Battle at Bull Run

Duel Between the First Ironclads

The Battle of New Market

Breckinridge: Statesman, Soldier, Symbol

THREE ROADS TO THE ALAMO

THE LIVES AND FORTUNES OF DAVID CROCKETT, JAMES BOWIE, AND WILLIAM BARRET TRAVIS

WILLIAM C. DAVIS

HarperPerennial

A Division of HarperCollinsPublishers

First HarperPerennial edition published 1999.

Designed by Interrobang Design Studio
Maps copyright © 1998 by Anita Karl and Jim Kemp

The Library of Congress has catalogued the hardcover edition as follows:

Davis, William C., 1946–
    Three roads to the Alamo : the lives and fortunes of David Crockett, James Bowie, and William Barret Travis / Wiliam C. Davis. — 1st ed.
        p.   cm.
    Includes biographical references and index.
    ISBN 0-06-017334-3
    1. Pioneers—Texas—Biography. 2. Alamo (San Antonio, Tex.)—Siege. 1836. 3. Crockett, David. 1786–1836. 4. Bowie, James d. 1836. 5. Travis, William Barret, 1809–1836. I. Title.
    F390.D276   1998
    976.4'009'9—dc21   97–43815

ISBN 0-06-093094-2 (pbk.)

  00 01 02 03 ❖/RRD 10 9 8 7 6 5 4 3

We can no longer say there is nothing new under the sun. For this whole history of man is new. The great extent of our republic is new.

THOMAS JEFFERSON, 1801

What is the American, this new man? He is an American, who leaving behind him all his ancient prejudices and manners, receives new ones from the new mode of life he has embraced, the new government he obeys, and the new rank he holds. He becomes an American by being received in the broad lap of our great Alma Mater.

MICHEL-GUILLAUME-JEAN DE CRÈVECOEUR
(J. HECTOR ST. JOHN)
Letters from an American Farmer

Millions of men are all marching together toward the same point on the horizon; their languages, religions, and mores are different, but they have one common aim. They have been told that fortune is to be found somewhere toward the west, and they hasten to seek it.

ALEXIS DE TOCQUEVILLE, *Democracy in America*

CONTENTS

Maps appear at front and back of book.
Illustrations follow page 206.

ACKNOWLEDGMENTS

There is a fair bit of irony about the writing of this book. The portion describing the deaths of the protagonists was finished in a hotel room in Jackson, Mississippi, just blocks from the Alamo Theater. The last chapter was finished in the Emily Morgan Hotel in San Antonio, in a room overlooking the Alamo itself, on March 6, 1997, the anniversary of the battle. Through one window I could see the building that now rests where once the north wall of the compound stood, where Travis fell. Through another I could see across today's Alamo Plaza to the site of Bowie's room near the main gate, and the spot where he died. And somewhere within reach of my gaze, Crockett met his end. Though, alas, there was no sense of "connection" in writing at that place, on that date, of those men, there was about it, certainly, a sense of having ended where I began.

This book was a long time in coming. Its origins go back to a youth in the 1950s, an introduction to the Alamo story in the celebrated Disney Davy Crockett films, and a teenage reading of Walter Lord's still wonderful *A Time to Stand.* When I first began writing professionally, while still in college in 1968, my second published article was an outline of the Alamo story. There it rested until 1993, when a chance conversation there in San Antonio with Texan historian Kevin Young led to brief thoughts of doing a life of James Bowie, a notion soon abandoned because of a presumption that there would be insufficient source material to write a true biography. Yet the idea fermented awhile, and two years later resulted in the concept of this combined biography of all three of the major Alamo icons: Bowie, David Crockett, and William Barret Travis. Now, thirty years after that initial article appeared, my involvement with these men comes full circle, and ironically the result reveals among other things that my fear about insufficient Bowie sources was quite unfounded.

Not surprisingly the effort to produce this book has led to involvement with innumerable friends, archivists, and fellow historians, and at least one rather remarkable—and somewhat pioneering—adventure in the course of my research. Archivists at scores of institutions gave the kind of aid that these unsung heroes and heroines—too numerous to mention individually—always offer. The services of a few do require some special mention, however, especially old friends Rickie Brunner at the Department of Archives and History, Montgomery, Alabama; Anne Lipscomb-Webster at the Mississippi Department of Archives and History in Jackson; Warren Stricker at the Daughters of the Republic of Texas Library in San Antonio; Ken Nelson of the Family History Library, Church of Jesus Christ of Latter Day Saints, Salt Lake City, Utah; Richard Shrader at the Southern Historical Collection, University of North Carolina; Sally K. Reeves of the New Orleans Notarial Archives, and Aaron Marr at the Palo Alto Battlefield National Historic Site, Brownsville, Texas. The skilled staff at the Center for American History, University of Texas, Austin—especially Kate Adams, Ralph Elder, Trudy Croes, and John Wheat—offered unstinting help in the face of repeated demands on their time. And at the National Archives in Washington, D.C., Michael Musick, Rick Peuser, Richard Fusick, and John K. Vandereedt gave invaluable aid with the splendid treasures in the still largely unplumbed depths of its holdings.

County and parish court clerks throughout Louisiana, Alabama, Arkansas, and Texas—again too many to thank by name—also proved most helpful, though Keith Fontenot of the St. Landry Parish Courthouse in Opelousas, himself a fine historian, was especially helpful. James Leslie of Little Rock lent valuable assistance with material from the Arkansas History Commission. Robert Bowie of Little Rock also provided some helpful information, and Dr. Ralph Caldroney of Lexington, Kentucky, offered some very useful insights on James Bowie's last illness. Mrs. Richard Rod, a descendant of Rezin Bowie, and her husband were most gracious and cooperative on questions relating to surviving family relics. Numerous historians—and old friends—sent sources and tracked down references for me, especially Dale K. Phillips, Glenn LaFantasie, Robert K. Krick, Richard J. Sommers, James I. Robertson, and Joseph Glatthaar. Margaret Henson offered a lot of sound counsel from her intimate acquaintance with Samuel May Williams and Juan Davis Bradburn; and Texas and Alamo historians William R. Chemerka, J. R. Edmondson, Joan Headley, Alan Huffines, and Gary Zaboly proved nothing but generous in sharing their insights and sources. Meanwhile a number of friends scattered around the nation took time out from their own activities to visit an archive or library for me in search of an elusive source or two, especially Jennifer Davis, Melissa M. Delcour, Sylvia Frank, Bobby Horton, Steven Stedman, and Meredith Swentor. Deborah Hardin provided me with a marvelous historical map of early Texas that proved to be one of the most useful references in the whole project. Randy Roberts, embarking on his own detailed study of the Alamo and its role in American culture, gave the finished manuscript a careful reading. Hearty thanks are due all of them.

In a special category are four friends and distinguished historians in Texas, without whose encouragement and aid I could not have attempted such a book. In addition to playing a role in its inception, Kevin Young offered unlimited help with sources and references to other scholars throughout the research for this work. Stephen L. Hardin of Victoria College did the same, helping provide an outsider a guide through the intricacies of early Texas history. Thomas R. Lindley, an indefatigable researcher, shared a wealth of material from his pioneering work on Travis and obscure sources in the state archives. Lindley, Hardin, and Young have also read the manuscript of this work and prevented many an error or omission from slipping through. And my old friend Michael Parrish of Austin sent a constant stream of source documents from old manuscript catalogs, as well as providing accommodation and delightful company on my several visits to Texas.

Then there was the adventure. It has long been assumed that when the Alamo fell on March 6, 1836, the victorious Mexican army captured whatever official papers remained there, as well as possibly some personal papers in the effects of the dead defenders. This was confirmed a few years ago, when Thomas Lindley found a broadside published in Mexico a few weeks after the battle, containing the text of a March 1 letter to Travis found in the Alamo. The assumption since then has been that any such captured papers—which could include daily muster rolls, copybooks of official correspondence, even personal letters and diaries—would be in the Mexican military archives if they still existed. Unfortunately, access to those archives has been denied to North American researchers—and apparently to many Mexican historians—for generations, for very understandable reasons, given the Mexican view that the Texas rebellion and the later 1846–48 war with the United States were blatant land grabs. The Texas historian Eugene C. Barker got to look at them early in this century, and at least one or two others have since been granted limited permission to do research there, but otherwise all requests have been denied. Even though this present work is not in the main about the Alamo or even the Texan revolution, still the remote possibility that some papers of Travis, Bowie, or Crockett might have found their way to Mexico City suggested making an effort to find them, despite the discouraging prospect of success.

An old friend and noted Civil War historian, Peter Cozzens is a Latin American specialist currently with the United States Consulate at Tijuana. He put me in touch with Donald R. Hamilton, Minister-Counselor for Public Affairs for the United States Information Service (USIS) at our embassy in Mexico City. Through the generous efforts of Mr. Hamilton and his assistant Bertha Cea, an approach was made to the Mexican military authorities, initiated by Ambassador James R. Jones, and coordinated by Col. Daniel O. Mason, military attaché at the embassy. Happily their approach bore fruit, and Gen. Enrique Cervantes Aguirre, secretario de la defensa nacional, cordially granted permission for me to visit and work in the Archivo Historico Militar Mexicano without restriction.

Inevitably in any international dealing there are bound to be missteps and misunderstandings, but thanks to the efforts of Colonel Mason and his counterpart at Defensa, Teniente Colonel Gerardo Wolburg, my visit came off almost without a hitch. Once I was in the archives, the staff, headed by General Mendoza and Captain López, was most cordial and cooperative. Mrs. Guadalupe Escalante, who served wonderfully as translator and interpreter, contributed vitally to the success of my visit and proved to be a delightful guide to the charms of Mexico City itself. There is nothing like writing a part of a chapter on early Texas and Mexico on a sultry July evening in a room at the lovely Maria Cristina Hotel on the Río Lerma, with the music and fragrance of the historic Zona Rosa in the background.

I did not find any lost Travis, Crockett, or Bowie papers. It was always a remote possibility in any event. I did find, however, some startling and previously unknown documents relating to the Alamo itself that rewrite significant portions of what we have known, or thought we knew, about the siege and fall of the garrison. Those findings appear in this volume, no doubt destined either to refuel old controversies or else start new ones of their own. Perhaps more important, I became aware of the stunning quality and extent of the military archives held by Defensa. The real story of the Texan revolution, our sad war with Mexico in 1846–48, and much of the early history of what today we call the Southwest cannot be fully understood or written without extensive recourse to those records. And on a personal note, having gone to Mexico City rather apprehensive about the reception I would find, I came away having had perhaps the most enjoyable research experience in a long and wide-ranging career. The cordiality of General Mendoza and his staff, even to the point of providing coffee and cookies every day at noon, was completely disarming, while the introduction that Mrs. Escalante gave me to the rich and hospitable culture of Mexico was in its own way just as eye-opening. To everyone involved in bringing me to Mexico and Defensa, I owe a surfeit of gratitude; in offering it here I want to add the fervent desire that our two neighboring nations, so often at odds through prejudice and misunderstanding, will one day become, as they should be, the best of friends.

A final word about approach. This is a book about three men, what they knew, what they did, and how they epitomized their time. But it is not a work of "lives and times," and as a result it does not devote a great deal of space to more background than is necessary to put their actions in context. Furthermore, however controversial their lives may have been, the sources from which those lives can be—and have been—constructed are subject to even more controversy. In many cases extensive discussion is necessary to establish why a source is used, or rejected, or to defend some statement of events. Unfortunately all this is necessary thanks to the extensive mythology and fabrication that has dogged their biographies in the past. In order not to clog the narrative with such extended discourse, I have confined these discussions to the notes, and would urge anyone who is interested in the controversies surrounding these men to read the notes carefully in order to learn where my conclusions have come from and what some of the alternatives are. Here, too, I will mention one other stylistic practice: Spelling and punctuation were idiosyncratic and ad hoc in this era. Nevertheless I have left the words of the people as they wrote them, without correcting spelling or adding or altering punctuation. Neither have I inserted the scholar's "[*sic*]" after every misspelling. Only in cases where meaning might be clouded have I intruded by bracketed corrections.

As always, special thanks are due my editor, M. S. Wyeth, for having the confidence to attempt this somewhat unconventional approach to the story, as well as to Susan H. Llewellyn for able and appreciated assistance in copyediting and catching some of the embarrassing number of mistakes and contradictions that even the best intentioned of historians may add to the story.

THREE ROADS
TO THE ALAMO

MEN AND LEGENDS

Stranger! should in some distant day,
By chance your wandering footsteps stray
To where those heroes fought and fell,
And some old garrulous crone should tell
The story of a nation's birth,
Of human ashes mixed with earth—
The bodies of the bold and free,
Who bled and died for liberty—

FALL OF THE ALAMO, *The Knickerbocker,* SEPTEMBER 1836

The three first met at the American Theater in New Orleans on January 10, 1828. Andrew Jackson, his eyes set on the presidency, came to the Crescent City to be honored by a grand ball on the anniversary of his defeat of the British in 1815. Every political and social light in the region was there to shine, with Stephen Austin, the great colonizer of Texas, presiding as host. Sitting at Austin's side was an honored veteran of the Battle of New Orleans, James Bowie of Louisiana, while others on the dais were Congressman David Crockett of Tennessee and young William Barret Travis of Alabama.

What each thought of the others at this first meeting, no one can say, though Bowie was already well known in the region as a man of audacious bravery, Travis was a youthful lawyer and political writer of note, and Crockett had a national reputation as a daring hunter and larger-than-life folk character. They came as a committee to go to Texas in advance of a host of future colonists, to spread American civilization and what would become Jacksonian democracy to the new Southwest. All three made speeches, Crockett extolling the transcendent virtues of Old Hickory, the man who would be the first people's president, and Travis saying much the same. Bowie added his mote to the praise of Jackson, then turned his words toward Texas. They were going to have to fight the Mexicans for possession of the new country, he warned. They might even have to die in defense of Texan and American liberty. If so, they were ready, and legions would follow them to glory.

They were last together on February 25, 1837. A carpenter, his name lost to history, labored over a small coffin that morning. No ordinary casket, this box was to hold remains more symbolic than real, its burden not the body of a single man but a smattering of the ashes of two hundred or more. It was just nine days short of a year since they had died, their battered corpses immolated in one huge funeral pyre and two smaller ones. In the intervening twelve months the piles of ashes and charred bones just sat out in the open, blown by the prairie winds, picked over by foraging rodents, scattered by the passage of men and animals. The men those ashes once had been became truly a part of the soil they had died for. Still, more remained than the small casket could hold, and so only ashes from the two smaller piles went into the box. On the inside of its lid the carpenter carved three names—"Travis"— "Bowie"—"Crockett"—three to stand for them all, and now to rest forever together in this casket, united in eternity as they had been united in their deaths.

And yet it is all illusion: On the one hand fiction become fact, and on the other misconception turned into history. Not one of them, not Crockett or Bowie or Travis (or Austin, for that matter) attended the Jackson dinner. There were no speeches of Texas and dying for liberty. The whole story is an invention.[1] As for their burial together nine years later, it is quite possible—even probable—that not an atom of the onetime bodies of any of the three found its way into the coffin that bore their names.[2]

They would become accustomed to not being where posterity supposed them to be. Near Morristown, Tennessee, there stands a Crockett Tavern, a twentieth-century building in which he never set foot, that may or may not be on the actual site of his boyhood home. In Opelousas, Louisiana, visitors tour the Jim Bowie House, a building he never owned or lived in and that has nothing whatever to do with him. At Perdue Hill, Alabama, restoration continues on the William Barret Travis House, for which not a scrap of evidence exists to establish it as his onetime home. No one is trying to fool anyone here. The Travis House sponsors admit that only local tradition associates him with the cottage. Opelousas forthrightly declares that the Bowie House is merely named after a famous former resident. The Crockett Tavern managers openly confess that their reconstruction and siting are conjectural. Certainly all three dwellings represent what these men *could* have lived in at some moment in their lives.

And that in itself is significant, for in the eight score years since their deaths, their stories have been usurped by what they *might* have done, where they *could* have been, and even how they *might* have died. Such a vacuum of information dominates the major portions of their histories that supposition, fabrication, and myth have filled the empty spaces and are so oft-repeated that falsehood and legend stand side by side with fact in the canon of their biographies. The single instance of that famous January 1828 dinner in New Orleans shows how far from the truth their admirers have strayed. Demonstrably Crockett was at that moment a thousand miles to the east in Washington; Travis was an unknown eighteen-year-old student in rural Alabama who would hardly be invited to share a dais with anyone, let alone the next president; and Bowie, though the only one who *might* have been in New Orleans at the time, was by all associations opposed to Jackson. Whereas the story says that he was invited to speak in honor of his prominent role in the 1815 Battle of New Orleans, in fact he was nowhere near the battle and saw no action at all in the War of 1812. This first meeting of the three whose names would be forever linked by their deaths at the Alamo simply never happened.

Ignorance has been the curse of their posterity, and it still flourishes. Even while this book was being written Sen. J. Strom Thurmond of South Carolina boasted of his fellow Carolinian Travis as the man who commanded the Alamo "with 3,000 *Russians* threatening to attack."[3] (Perhaps the aged Cold Warrior was simply confused, but then, he is almost old enough to have *been* at the Alamo.) More dangerous than carelessness or senility, both of which have affected the record of Travis and the others, has been willful ignorance. Anyone could have looked into the 1828 dinner story and easily discovered the impossibility of any of the three attending, much less making prophetic speeches about Texas. Anyone could have found the myriad contradictions and impossibilities that disprove all but one of the fabled Bowie duels and fights. Anyone could have disproved the myth and found the real reason why young Travis fled Alabama, abandoning wife and child. Anyone could have discerned the weaknesses that call into question, if not negate, the several supposed accounts of Crockett's death.

Yet no one did, and in most instances those limning these lives have not looked. Like Americans in general, perhaps they were too enamored of the myth to want to supplant it with a reality that might be prosaic rather than lurid or heroic. We all part reluctantly with our myths, and the more so when by removing the fable, we leave a hole in the story that we cannot fill with fact, for in proving that something did not happen, we do not automatically establish what did. The biographies of all three of these men have been slim in the past. Remove everything founded in legend and hearsay and falsehood, and those lives would have been thinner yet. The biographers, just as much as their readers, have needed the myths to give some flesh to these dimly seen and still scarcely fathomed icons.

James Bowie is an exaggerated example that speaks for all three. Much of what we might have known of the personal side of the man supposedly disappeared when two trunks of family papers were destroyed through carelessness. Perhaps it happened, perhaps not. Many a family has a cherished fable about the trunk filled with "old papers" that sat ignored in an attic, prey to mice and prowling children. Real or not—and it may not matter, since in any case Bowie does not seem to have been much of a correspondent—the absence of any such cache of family archives left the field almost entirely to the creators of folklore. "There have been many, many anecdotes published of the prowess of the Bowies," said his brother Rezin's grandson John Seyborne Moore in 1875, "some of which have a little truth, but the most of which are fiction, out and out."[4] He was right, but having said that, Moore himself and other Bowie family members contributed their own full share to the growing corpus of fiction about their ancestor, producing in the main the most unreliable single body of information available on him. James Bowie left no direct descendants, and not one of Rezin's grandchildren who wrote about him ever met him, much less knew him firsthand, or ever really knew their own grandfather, who would have been their best source.

Instead, in the late 1800s and early 1900s they produced as "family stories" amalgamations of what they read in the press, heard from

friends, and dim thirdhand recollections. They became defensive, as
family understandably will, when anything unflattering was said of
Bowie, and actually dismissed as a fabrication the most accurate and
authentic single personal source on him, his brother John's 1852 family
memoir, chiefly because it connected him with the slave trade. They
accepted the fictitious 1828 Jackson dinner fable, and 140 years and
more after his death were still defending him against any critical comment, now basing their case on grossly fictionalized twentieth-century
biographies that are little more than compendiums of mythology. One
of the most prolific defenders of all was not even a member of the family, but the sister of Moore's wife, who not only never knew or met
James Bowie or his brother but never knew anyone who did. Yet she
produced letters and newspaper interviews that added immeasurable
confusion to the Bowie saga.[5]

It did not stop there. So great are the holes in Bowie's life that students have gone to extraordinary lengths to fill them. One tried the
highly questionable technique of handwriting analysis to attempt to get
some idea of his personality and state of mind, while another even
engaged a widely known—and thoroughly discredited—self-
proclaimed psychic, the late Peter Hurkos, to try to establish the ownership of a certain knife that he hoped had been Bowie's. Needless to say,
Hurkos provided a wealth of information as he held and "read" the
knife, and told the owner everything he wanted to hear, including
episodes known by everyone but Hurkos to be fictional and drawn
from published accounts that he had obviously researched beforehand.[6]

It is almost as bad for Travis and Crockett. In 1834 the Monroe County,
Alabama, courthouse burned to the ground, destroying almost all the
records that could have told much of his life in Alabama prior to his
departure for Texas. Moreover, when he left, in 1831, his remaining sib-
lings were for the most part too young to have known him well, and
they never saw him again. More than sixty years later, when they started
producing statements about his life, they were writing about a man who
to them was all but a stranger, making them just as susceptible to incorporating myths into their "recollections" as the Bowie family. Crockett,
of course, became legendary while yet alive, meaning that his biography
was clouded by fabrication and myth even before his death.

But for their dramatic ends on March 6, 1836, at the Alamo, perhaps only Crockett of the three would have attracted enough attention either for the creation or the dispelling of myth, since he was already a celebrity. It is their deaths that made their lives matters of interest; and, more fascinating still, in looking at their days prior to that chilly March dawn, they emerge as metaphors for their entire generation. This book was never conceived as an "Alamo book," though inevitably that epochal event figures largely at the close, and looms over the whole with an ever-darkening shadow. Rather, this is a representative look at the three distinctive kinds of men who were responsible for pushing white American civilization west of the Mississippi, and at the same time of those sorts who ever appeared at the forefront of the move across the continent. Their involvement in Texas settlement and revolution, and their apotheosis at the Alamo, only magnified them as exaggerated portraits of hundreds of thousands of others. They were all products of the Scots-Irish migration; they were all the kind of men the French observer Alexis de Tocqueville had in mind when he wrote in the 1830s of the American penchant for "improvisations of fortune." Crockett stood for the thousands who were always on the edge of the wilderness—the men for whom no home was ever permanent, not itinerants so much as seekers, their gaze always cast westward. Bowie epitomized those who invariably followed the Crocketts, the entrepreneurs and exploiters—the men who came and profited, often outside the law, and moved on to the next potential bonanza, their addresses almost as temporary as Crockett's. And then arrived Travis, the man of community and society, the lawgiver, town builder, even founder of a state or nation—one of the millions who came and stayed to create.

They were, in their way, the new Elizabethans, and Tocqueville did not fail to observe that "the present-day American republics are like companies of merchants formed to exploit the empty lands of the New World, and prosperous commerce is their occupation."[7] Confronted with a seemingly limitless new frontier of inexhaustible resources, they saw in it the remaking of themselves, as each left the life in which he had failed east of the Mississippi and the Sabine, just as those earlier adventurers crossed the Atlantic to rebuild their fortunes. They came as rapacious consumers of land and wildlife, and with limited regard for those who already inhabited the new world they coveted. Yet they made something of what they took. Despite the mess their generation usually left behind, they were builders as well as destroyers. The lives and fortunes of Crockett, Bowie, and Travis reveal the full complexity of a people who were at once plunderers and patriots, and offer a stark repudiation to any who would see them or their era in a single dimension.

"Life consists with wildness. The most alive is the wildest," said Henry David Thoreau. "One who pressed forward incessantly and never rested from his labors, who grew fast and made infinite demands on life, would always find himself in a new country or wilderness, and surrounded by the raw material of life."[8] That is where Crockett, Bowie, and Travis wanted to be—in that "new country"—where the wilderness gave them the freedom to make their fortunes out of the raw material around them. And that is what drew their generation with them. For those three the road west stopped at the Alamo. For those who followed, the horizon had no limit.

CROCKETT

> *I never had six months education in my life I was raised in obs[c]urity without*
> *either wealth or education I have made myself to every station in life that I*
> *ever filled through my own exertions . . .*
>
> ĐAVID CROCKETT, AUGUST 18, 1831

When he wrote his autobiography in the winter of 1833–34, David Crockett insisted that it should run at least 200 pages. That, to him, was a real book. As he wrote he studied other books, counted the words on their pages, and compared the tally with his own growing manuscript. As a result, when published his narrative spanned 211 pages, and he was content. By that time in his life he had been a state legislator, three times elected to Congress, the subject of a book, the thinly disguised hero of an acclaimed play, a popular phenomenon in the eastern press, and touted for the presidency. Yet he devoted more than one-fourth of his own work to his youth: a time when his "own exertions" availed him nothing. He remembered youthful pranks, a few adventures, and vicissitudes that should have made him wise but only left him gullible. Repeatedly he returned to three things he remembered from his first eighteen years: that the father whom he loved was a stern disciplinarian and could be violent; that he wept easily as a child and as a young man; and that he was poor. Certainly it took no stretch of memory to recall the last in particular. For David Crockett poverty was never yesterday.

His was the story of a whole population of the poor who started moving from the British Isles in the 1700s and simply never stopped. Despite the misnomer "Scots-Irish," they were almost all Scots, as surely were Crockett's ancestors.[1] Like so many who grew up ignorant and illiterate on the fringes of young America, he knew little of his forebears, and some of what he believed was erroneous. Indeed, that father whom he loved yet feared knew little himself, or else chose not to speak of it. Perhaps the child David did not listen or kept his distance, especially when John Crockett had been at the drink and felt ill-tempered and prone to reach for the birch.

The man David did not even know where his own father had been born, and believed it was either in Ireland or during the ocean passage to the colonies.[2] More likely it was his grandfather, for whom he was named, who first set foot on American soil. When he came is lost among the thousands of anonymous arrivals in the generations before the Revolution, but he probably landed in Pennsylvania and migrated west to the Susquehanna before turning southwest through the Cumberland Valley along with the rest of the tide of Scottish immigrants, reaching Virginia's lower Shenandoah Valley by 1755. The first David Crockett farmed there near Berryville, by then a married man with a new son, Robert, born there that August, and another son, John, probably already a few years old and perhaps born in Pennsylvania.

The tide of migration did not willingly yield any of the flotsam that rode its crest. The immigrants who first reached a new region took up the best land, and those like David Crockett who came after often had to keep moving until it seemingly became a habit. By 1771 he had moved his family, now including two boys in their later teens, to Tryon County, North Carolina, settling on the south side of the Catawba River. It was to be a brief stop, for by 1776 the Crocketts were over the western mountains into the valley of the Holston River. There was confusion about just which colony—North Carolina or Virginia—owned the region, and for a time the inhabitants simply governed themselves under the articles of what they called the Watauga Association. But then on July 5, 1776, aware of the revolt that had commenced the year before in Massachusetts but unaware of the momentous event of the day before in Philadelphia, David Crockett and other Wataugans petitioned the legislature of North Carolina to assume dominion and responsibility over the region. With the continent seemingly in upheaval, they sought some order, especially as the local aboriginal population launched occasional attacks on isolated settlers. North Carolina annexed the area that same year, but, perhaps because of the hostile natives, the Crocketts moved northwest of the Holston to

It seemed easy after the hard work of the building was finished, and these men were always looking for an easy livelihood. Instead of laboring all the hours of the day in his own fields, the miller could charge his neighbors to grind their grain, and the river did the work for him. Yet most who tried it failed, in part because there were so many others at the milling trade, and also because they were all hostages to nature. Cove Creek reminded John Crockett of that fact when it rose out of its banks before the mill was even completed. It washed away all the construction done thus far and drove the Crocketts out of their cabin.

Characteristically, when a disaster or loss hit one of these people, they moved away not only from the event but from its locality. John Crockett already held title to a three-hundred-acre parcel on the south side of the Main Holston Road connecting Knoxville with Abingdon, Virginia, about thirty miles from Cove Creek. Now he moved his family there and set himself up in the other mainstay occupation of the frontiersman with business aspirations: tavern keeping. On the south side of the road, on the slope that led down to a spring, he dug out a cellar, lined it with a stone foundation, and on that built a small log structure that served as home and inn.[9]

Prosperity always eluded John Crockett—probably due to a combination of hard times for everyone, bad luck, and a certain unwillingness or inability to commit himself to one thing and stay with it in the face of adversity. Then, too, he may have been overardent at his own barrel, an unfortunate and unprofitable weakness for a tavern owner. Certainly he either made an insufficient living by his trade or else mishandled what he took in receipts, for in barely a year he found himself four hundred dollars or more in debt. The sheriff of Jefferson County seized his property and on November 4, 1795, sold it at public auction to William Line for forty dollars.[10] David was old enough by now to know what was happening and to remember as well as to be embarrassed by it, for though he told of many hardships in his autobiography, and even spoke with the poor white's typical assertive pride in youthful poverty, he made no mention of his family losing the tavern.

He did admit, however, that in these years "I began to make up my acquaintance with hard times, and a plenty of them."[11] William Line may have profited by John Crockett's misfortune, but either he

Carter's Valley, another area of disputed sovereignty, and there David joined with neighbors in 1776 and again on November 6, 1777, in petitioning Virginia to annex the locality.[3]

By now three of his sons, John, William, and Joseph, were grown and had their own homes nearby, and Robert was probably already off serving in the revolutionary forces. Indeed, that is in part what saved them, for David Crockett's days of wandering were done. He had but one last move in store, and it was the Creek or Chickamauga who sent him and his wife on their way. Already incensed at the influx of unwelcome settlers on their ancestral territory, the Indians had agreed to treaties that established definite boundaries protecting their land. But they reckoned without the rapacious appetite of settlers and the speculators, who even now saw the promise of profit on the bow wave of settlement. In an act that would be the hallmark of the push west to the Mississippi and beyond, unscrupulous entrepreneurs ignored the existing occupants and began selling vast quantities of Indian land to incoming settlers. The strain became intolerable, and the affronted victims struck back, often not at the speculators but at any isolated and convenient target. One day in the summer of 1778 they chose the Crockett homestead.

David and his wife were at home, along with Joseph and their youngest, James. The raid almost certainly took them by surprise. David and his older son were probably in their field tending crops, their rifles out of immediate reach. The attackers fired a ragged volley that brought Joseph down with a broken arm. His father fell either to bullets or swift tomahawk blows. James may have been with them, but he was both deaf and mute and knew little of what was happening until it was all over. His mother probably met death alone in the cabin. As quickly as they had come, the attackers left. In their idiosyncratic way, having killed the parents, they took the boy James with them and kept him for nearly eighteen years before returning him to white society. The wounded Joseph either played or looked dead or simply no longer interested the raiders, who left him behind. With him they left a memory that would become a legacy of hatred between the Crockett family and the Creek nation.[4]

At least John Crockett had someone to share his grief. He was living in his own home some three miles away when tragedy struck. Perhaps as little as a year earlier he had married Rebecca Hawkins, a young woman born in Maryland who came south with her father, Nathan, to the settlements north of the Holston.[5] But he barely had time to start a family before the war with Britain began to take him away from home for extended periods of time. He went to Lincoln County to join its militia, but by 1780 was back home in what was now Washington County, North Carolina. That October he was one of the "over-mountain men" who took their rifles and walked through the mountain passes to rendezvous with regulars to form an army that defeated the British and helped turn the tide of the war in the southern colonies at the Battle of King's Mountain. While his son David lost all recollection of anything else his father did in the Revolution, he never forgot John Crockett's role at King's Mountain, or that image of the citizen volunteer, his deer rifle on his shoulder, riding off on his own accord to join other men who answered no authority but their own, in common defense of their notion of liberty.[6]

After 1781 the war dwindled to occasional skirmishes in the South, and John Crockett could concentrate on making a place for himself. In 1783, the year of the peace, he became a constable in Greene County, which was split from Washington. He also succumbed to the lure of speculation, buying land at sixpence an acre and selling it for twenty times that four years later. But more often than not speculators bought land in exchange for their personal promissory note and sold it for much the same, and where little or no hard coin changed hands there was no real wealth to be gained. Indeed, even as he sought to make a killing in land, Crockett saw debts against him registered in the county court records. Whatever may have been his dreams of prosperity, the reality was that he occupied a page in the annals of the poor and always would.[7]

At least his family grew. By 1786 he had four sons and had moved yet again, to the bank of Big Limestone Creek where it flowed into the Nolichucky River on the eastern edge of Greene County. There on August 17, 1786, Rebecca produced another child. Interestingly John waited until this fifth baby boy before honoring his own father with a namesake. The infant David Crockett would have almost no recollection of the Limestone Creek homestead, however, or of the events then exciting his father and others. Already a strong streak of independence

and resistance to authority characterized these Scots and Iri[ ] As soon as they moved—which was often—they formed a[ ] giance, at first to some distant authority like Virginia [ ] Carolina that could protect them; and when protection seen[ ] issue, their loyalties speedily became more local. At the mon[ ] Crockett was born, the settlers in Greene and Washingto[ ] and elsewhere were trying to form their own new state. At[ ] the Revolution, North Carolina ceded much of its wester[ ] back to the new United States, and in the fall of 1784 settle[ ] at Jonesboro, scarcely five miles from Crockett's birthpla[ ] nize and declare the new state of Franklin. John Crocket[ ] the Franklin movement, and young David might well have[ ] be a native of this new state. It did not last, however, a[ ] North Carolina had resumed sovereignty. It would not be [ ] David Crockett's fortunes were entwined with those of [ ] seeking independence.

In later years he remembered just two incidents from hi[ ] neither of them distinctly, but both involving that ever-[ ] panion on the frontier, mortal danger. He was not yet v[ ] breeches when he and his older brothers and a friend p[ ] Nolichucky, and one of the boys got all but David to t[ ] John Crockett's canoe. Once in the stream, they lost [ ] drifted toward a dangerous falls, when the timely arriva[ ] neighbor saved them from possible drowning. He reme[ ] his uncle Joseph Hawkins accidentally shooting a man[ ] grapes, and how his father passed a handkerchief throug[ ] the fortunate survivor's body, front to back. Imminer[ ] everywhere, feared, and yet as well a subject of morbid c[ ]

When David was no more than seven years old, the fi[ ] ily moved once more, a few miles to Cove Creek. There [ ] entered partnership with Thomas Galbreath in building [ ] one time or another, almost every settler on the frontier [ ] a hand at milling. It was the only industry on the edge [ ] other than smithing. A man could build the mill hin[ ] proper stones in the streambeds, and shape them with h[ ] allowed him to stay on at the tavern trade, by leasing the property or as an employee, or else Crockett managed to build another tavern not far away and resume his business. In any case for the next three years he continued providing room, board, and drink for the wagoneers passing through what had finally become the new state of Tennessee in 1796. Times were still strained, and young David was now old enough to contribute his mote to the family's survival. Using a wooden maul and wedge, he split fence rails for the father of a playmate, no doubt turning his meager earnings over to his own father.[12]

That was not enough. One of the travelers passing through the tavern in late 1798 was Jacob Siler, a German then driving a herd of cattle to Rockbridge, Virginia, some 225 miles northeast. "Being hard run every way," as David recalled, John Crockett hired out his son to go with Siler to help with the cows, despite the fact that David, who was only twelve, would have to make the return trip by himself. Of course the boy had no say in the matter. He knew better than to dispute his father and risk the birch. "I had been taught so many lessons of obedience," he recalled, that resistance did not occur to him, despite his child's terror at being taken away from home, spending weeks with a man he did not know, and having to risk the 225 miles back on his own.[13]

The trip took two weeks or more before they reached the vicinity of Natural Bridge, Virginia, yet it seemed so long to David that he almost doubled the distance in memory, recalling 225 miles as 400. Siler treated him kindly, and at the end of the road gave him a few dollars above what had been paid to his father. Indeed, he liked David enough to try to persuade him to stay on rather than go home. The boy felt torn. He was more than homesick, and yet, as he admitted later, his father's discipline had so ingrained in him the habit of obedience that he was afraid to resist or openly disobey any adult male. And so he agreed, feigning delight but secretly miserable and lonely.

He stayed hardly longer than a month, all the time striving to convince the Siler family that he liked the arrangement. Though barely a teenager, young Crockett already had winning manners. Those evenings in the family tavern had exposed him to many a traveler brimming with tales of the road, some of them no doubt told the better for a few drams. Learned young, and practiced and honed in maturing

years, easy manners and conviviality lubricated frontier life. It would
have been unusual if David had not already acquired some natural bent
for storytelling and theatricality. He already had a few experiences of
his own to spin into stories—his days on the road, the characters he
had seen in the tavern, some of whose speech and expressions he could
mimic. Added to the rosy hue of his cheeks and his good honest looks,
his genuine personality made him a winning character even at first
acquaintance. Despite his unhappiness at Natural Bridge, he would
still speak with scarcely concealed pride years later of how thoroughly
"I got the family all to believe I was fully satisfied." It was a kind of
acting. He was playing a character.[14]

But when the opportunity came to leave, he took it. He had seen his
father pull up stakes in the face of adversity enough times that he felt no
compunction about leaving the Silers by stealth rather than facing them
with his unhappiness. One Sabbath night, as a winter snow started to
fall, he went to bed, but not before bundling his few belongings and his
precious dollars. Then he lay awake until halfway through the night,
when he stole out of the house and started to trudge through the deepening snow to a tavern several miles distant, where he was to meet
some teamsters he knew who were moving south to Knoxville. In their
company he traveled some thirty miles until his impatience got the better of the slow progress of the wagons, and he set off alone on foot.
Fortunately he did not walk far before a man with several horses over-
took him. As before and so many times after, David's winning manners
impressed the horseman enough that he invited the boy to ride one of
his animals and accompany him on the road. The miles now passed
quickly, and in a few days, when they parted company, David was but a
good morning's walk from his father's tavern.

It was a happy homecoming, and through the balance of the winter
and the two seasons to follow his life was as before—some work,
some play, and always learning. Indeed, though Crockett had not yet
set foot in a schoolroom, he was already acquiring knowledge. He had
traveled the open road and gone distances and seen places that most of
his playmates had not. He learned the ways of the road and the wilderness from the teamsters who stopped for a meal and a night at the tavern. He certainly learned from his father. John Crockett may have been
a failure at business, but he had at least some rudiments of literacy.

Certainly he could sign his name. As a constable he needed to know the rudiments of law, and he would also serve as a magistrate. Even his doomed efforts as a miller and tavern keeper offered lessons he could pass on in the matter of building, of wooden gears and frontier mechanics, of currency and counting and trade. Much of this his sons learned simply by living with him.[15]

Yet whatever his other failings as a provider or even as a father, John Crockett must have grasped the value of more formal education, perhaps seeing in it the missing element that left his own efforts so dogged by failure. Schoolteachers of the time were hired by the community, and customarily the parents gave lodging and board as well as a modest income from subscription. As a man of some standing—if minor—in the community, Crockett probably had a hand in hiring Benjamin Kitchen to commence a school nearby in the fall of 1799. Having done that, he naturally decided that his sons should attend.[16]

David Crockett, now thirteen, knew nothing more of formal learning than perhaps a few letters. After the first four days in Kitchen's school, he found himself just acquiring some familiarity with the alphabet when he ran afoul of the school bully and ambushed him with fists the fourth day after class. For some reason Crockett thought that his extracurricular fight would cause him trouble with master Kitchen, and so the next morning, though he set off for school as usual, he spent the day hiding in the woods and then came home at the proper time. Afraid of his father's wrath, he persuaded his brothers to lie for him and claim he had been in class. The charade continued thereafter until Kitchen sent home a note. Why had David not been in school the past several days? he asked.

The question caught John Crockett at a very bad moment for David. He had been drinking. He yelled for the truant to come to him. "I knew very well that I was in a devil of a hobble," David recalled more than thirty years later, "for my father had been taking a few *horns*, and was in a good condition to make the fur fly."[17] His plea that he feared to face master Kitchen lest he be whipped only prompted John Crockett to growl that there would be whipping aplenty here at home unless he returned to school. When the boy seemed hesitant, his father's anger erupted. He grabbed a two-year-old hickory stick that was more cudgel than cane, and came at the lad, who quickly fled.

There followed a chase, in which David had the advantage of being young and sober. He outdistanced his father, hid in a thicket for a time, and then—hurt, angry, and frightened—went to the home of a friend. One thing he knew now was that he could go neither to the school nor to his home. All that remained to him was the road.

He never suspected how much time would pass before again he crossed his father's threshold. Wandering seemed to come somewhat naturally to young David, as did hardship. First he hired himself to his friend, Jesse Cheek, for a cattle drive to Virginia. He went back over the road he knew now to Abingdon, on to the Roanoke River crossing, then east to Lynchburg, and on through Charlottesville.

These days before the turn of the century were interesting ones for anyone passing through Charlottesville, for there was the rural seat of *the* Virginian, Vice-President Thomas Jefferson. He would still have been at his hillside Monticello when David passed through, preparing to return to the capital in Philadelphia for his last session as president of the Senate. Crockett may not have seen him, but Jefferson's presence was strong in Charlottesville. The term of President John Adams was coming to an end; George Washington had but a few weeks to live; and the influence of their Federalist Party was waning with them. Jefferson would probably be chosen president in a few months, and with him would come a renewed adherence to the Enlightenment and a new commitment to democracy. Yet it would be deceptive, for Jefferson's was a middle-class democracy, founded on the landed, the educated, and most of all the successful. David Crockett and his kind were not part of the coming Jeffersonianism. All he could do was aspire to it.

The drive ended at Front Royal, 375 miles from where it began, a long trip indeed for a thirteen-year-old on foot. With the herd sold, Crockett started on the road back, this time in company with one of the other drovers. With only a horse between them, which the other never seemed to share, they parted company, and with four dollars in his pocket Crockett continued by himself. The road made for easy acquaintance and alliances, and when Crockett met Adam Myers, he agreed to accompany him even though he was heading north. That errand done, however, Myers promised that he was then returning to Tennessee and would take David with him. The weeks on the road had softened his hurt and his anger but not his fear. "I often thought of home, and, indeed, wished bad enough to be there," he later recalled, but he also remembered "my father, and the big hickory he carried." He had not forgotten the "storm of wrath" that ruled John Crockett when last he saw him. "I knew my father's nature so well, that I was certain his anger would hang on him." Better to stay away awhile longer, he thought.[18]

One road led to another, though, and none of them seemed to take him home. David's was a trusting and gullible nature. When not acting he spoke plainly and truthfully, saying what he felt or believed without thought or artifice; and he took others at their word and as a result was often deceived. Moreover his habitual acquiescence in the expectations of adult males—expected of all youths—made it difficult for him to refuse even if he did suspect deceit, and more inclined to run than to stand up for himself. And so, even though often moved to tears by his homesickness, he spent three largely unhappy years as a teamster and vagabond. Myers never seemed to get around to going back to Tennessee, instead making runs to Baltimore while David worked as a day laborer at twenty-five cents a day. In the spring of 1800 he went to Baltimore with Myers, giving the man his little hoard of seven dollars for safekeeping on the journey. Never before had he seen a real city, much less something like the Chesapeake Bay. Crockett went down to the wharf to marvel at the great sailing ships, and when he ventured to walk aboard one he encountered the master of the vessel. The winning way that won him instant friends on the road worked for David on the deck of a schooner as well, and shortly the captain offered him a job and a berth for a voyage to England. At age fourteen or nearly so he would have been a bit old for a cabin boy, but hard labor had made him firm and fit, and his stature, probably no more than a few inches over five feet by then, would suit him well for the cramped lower decks. He could make a good deckhand, and his cheerful manner would always be welcome during the long weeks at sea.

But Myers refused to let him go, and kept him all but confined until they were several days into their return journey, more than once threatening to use his wagon whip on the boy. Finally Crockett simply escaped in the night, taking his clothes but unable to get at his seven dollars. Dejectedly he took to the road, only to encounter yet another in the succession of men who would befriend him. This time Crockett broke down in tears at his misfortune, and the samaritan promised to confront Myers and get his money back. It was to no avail, though, for Myers had already spent it. David moved on with his new friend for a few days, and then set off for Tennessee once more, no longer fearful of his father's wrath after experiencing the deceit and violence of the larger world. As if to soften his disillusionment with humankind, several wagoneers who heard his story took up a collection among themselves and gave him three dollars for the journey. By then it cannot have escaped David Crockett's notice that something in him could win the affection and the trust of others.

The money (and his legs) got him just over halfway home, across the Roanoke, before it gave out. He took a month's job to earn five dollars, and then bound himself by an indenture to work four years for a hatmaker who would provide room and board, some small income, and undoubtedly teach him the hatter's trade as well. It would be a useful skill to have, make him independent of his father, and perhaps promise a good living as the Tennessee frontier matured and men craved some headgear more sophisticated than animal skins. But the hatter went broke after a year and a half and left David with nothing for his time. All he could do was take a few odd jobs to earn a little money, and then try once more for Tennessee.

The spring rains in 1802 had swelled many of the streams, and when Crockett reached the New River just a few miles after starting, the water ran so rough that no ferryman would cross. Determined not to be stopped, he got the use of a canoe and set off by himself, brave if unwise. The raging current and cold wind carried him two miles downstream and soaked him thoroughly before he reached the other side. His clothing almost froze on him as he walked nearly an hour before he came to a house where he stopped and begged a seat by the fire. Better yet, his host offered "a leetle of the creater" to warm the inner man. Liquor was nothing new to a tavern keeper's son and a young man who had been on the high road with the wagoneers. This probably was not David Crockett's first drink, nor was it to be his last, but it is the only one of his life that he thought significant enough to rhapsodize over in his autobiography thirty years later.

Another ninety miles, and he crossed the line into Tennessee at last, but there he stopped in Sullivan County to visit with an uncle and one of his brothers for several weeks. Finally, as the weather warmed and the days grew longer, he took the road for the final fifty miles to home. He could do it in two days, and well after dark the second evening he saw the familiar Crockett tavern on its slope on the south side of the road. Now the imp in him took over. He had been away for three years, almost. He had surely grown by several inches and filled out. A youthful sprout of whiskers may well have dulled the ruddy cheeks. Would his family know him? He entered and took a place on the fringes of the dim and crowded room of travelers, spoke little, and just watched. When his mother called the guests to the communal table for supper, he sat down, and was just eating when his oldest sister, Betsy, looked hard at him, burst into a smile, and jumped from her stool to grasp his neck, yelling: "Here is my lost brother."

Even John Crockett was delighted, and the much-feared birch rod stayed in the corner. The son had traveled widely now, more widely than the father, and had experienced more of the world than any of his brothers. At sixteen he was a man so far as the frontier was concerned. John could not hold him or dictate to him much longer, but although he forgave him, he still expected obedience and one last service. A son's labor belonged to his father by right until that son went off on his own. The old specter of debt never left John Crockett, as it never would, and now he made a bargain with his son. If David would work off a thirty-six-dollar note due another man, his father would thereafter release him from all responsibility, and as well relieve himself from having to provide for him. Young Crockett agreed and spent the next six months redeeming the note, even though the workplace put him in the objectionable company of coarse men who gambled and drank far too much. Though never in later years a prude, still David Crockett seemed from his early years to carry with him a rude frontier gentility of good manners and relatively chaste speech. He loved a good story, and by now surely told them toe to toe with the older men, but he stopped short of the obscenity common to the road. Certainly he could and did drink, but as with gambling, there was simply never enough money to indulge to regular excess. He had seen enough of the rougher tavern crowd by now to know that this was not the company he craved. Consequently, when his employer asked him to stay on even after the debt was paid, he declined.

Crockett took a job with a Quaker instead, a job that started to earn him some cash of his own. But a few days into the effort the man informed him that he, too, held a note against John Crockett, this one for forty dollars. He suggested that if David would work for him for six months, he would sign the note over to him, in effect making David his father's creditor. David knew his father too well for that. "I was certain enough that I should never get any part of the note," he said later. Nevertheless, perhaps out of guilt for the three years of uncertainty he had put the family through during his disappearance, he agreed, and toiled away until the Quaker presented him with the debt. Then young Crockett went to the Crockett tavern and handed his father the note, not in presentation for payment but as a present, and this time it was John Crockett who broke into tears. The act was more than a gift, however. It was David Crockett's declaration of independence. There would never be another caning, no more appropriation of his labor, no more fear. His debt to his father, in every sense, was paid. He was nearly seventeen. Now he was a man.

No sooner did Crockett take another job than he decided that it was time for him to take a wife as well. His first infatuation was with the Quaker's niece, and it hit him powerfully. "I have heard people talk about hard loving," he confessed, "yet I reckon no poor devil in this world was ever cursed with such hard love as mine has always been, when it came on me."[19] Overcome by his feeling, and no doubt as well inhibited by his humble circumstances, he could barely speak to her. After several false starts he told her how he felt, only to find out that she was already engaged to another.

Though he thought himself heartbroken, still Crockett took it well enough to realize that his prospects for finding a wife—not to mention his prospects in the world—would improve if he had some education. It took more than riding a wagon or walking behind a herd of cattle to make one a man of the world. He needed schooling, and a better effort than he had made of it during those four days several years before. Education cost money, of which he had none, and so Crockett turned to the only currency he had, his labor. He struck a bargain with a schoolmaster to work for him one or two days a week, in exchange for receiving lessons on the other days.

It proved to be a felicitous arrangement. Thanks to his age, Crockett would have been placed with the other older boys, there being no other divisions or grades among the pupils. The master taught them chiefly by repetition of their lessons, aloud, over and over until they knew them by rote, with the result that some called it a "blab" school. Yet once he mastered the alphabet and the beginnings of a vocabulary, Crockett could find the lessons of some interest. Textbooks were few, but regardless of the age of the intended pupils, they were written for adults, with no differentiation by age or grade. The reading books, such as they were, came from New England, mostly, and were often just compilations of biblical sayings, anecdotal stories about animals, some encyclopedia entries, newspaper articles, and of special interest to Crockett, excerpts from the *Autobiography of Benjamin Franklin.* The selections taught moral and civic examples, as well as the reading itself, and there was also some elementary mathematics, history, geography, grammar, of course, and even bits of art and music. There was probably also a spelling primer, though spelling in England and America—not yet standardized—was idiosyncratic, its chief goal comprehension rather than uniformity. There being no dictionaries, Crockett, like most other nonuniversity students of his time, learned to spell phonetically, writing as he spoke, and thus unconsciously incorporating his East Tennessee drawl into his written words.[20]

Crockett later played down his education, but in fact in six months he learned enough of sums and multiplication that he could calculate his own almost constant debt, and he learned to read well enough that in the years ahead he expanded his education on his own. By the measure of his time and place, he was now a literate man, and some considerable distance ahead of his friends and associates in learning. He would have continued his program further but for the now burning desire to have a wife, and quite consciously he shopped about the neighborhood for a suitable mate. He soon found one in Margaret Elder, and paid court to her with much the same application that he invested in his schooling— and nearly as long. By October 1805, with Crockett now nineteen, she accepted his suit and he proudly appeared before the clerk of the court at Dandridge, Jefferson County, to obtain his marriage license.[21]

Nothing seemed to pass easily for young Crockett. With the wedding arrangements set, he took his proudest new possession, a rifle, to a shooting match just five days before the intended nuptials. He shot well at the meet, having a good eye and an apparent natural skill with the weapon, and won the prize of a whole beef, which he sold immediately for five dollars. That only buoyed his step as he walked to Margaret's home, where he intended to observe the previously neglected formality of asking her parents for their permission to wed. On the way he met her sister, who tearfully told him that he was deceived, and that his betrothed planned to marry another on the morrow. "It was the cap-stone of all the afflictions I had ever met with," he confessed. As he sadly turned his face homeward, dejection almost overcame him, and he concluded that "I was only born for hardships, misery, and disappointment." For several weeks, in an almost universal experience that at the moment seemed uniquely his own, he neither ate nor slept, unable to free his mind of the torment of his lost love and her deception. "It was the worst kind of sickness," he said, "a sickness of the heart."[22]

But it passed. Indeed, as young hearts heal rapidly, so did his, and within a few months he courted again. At a frolic one evening he met Polly Finley, "and I must confess, I was plaguy well pleased with her from the word go." David wooed both mother and daughter, seeing in the former an ally in his campaign. He soon discovered that he had a rival, but Polly preferred young Crockett, and in time, with the mother's objections being their chief obstacle, they came to an understanding. Once more Crockett went to the court clerk in Dandridge, where on August 12, 1806, now aged twenty, he took out another marriage license. Two days later he and his brothers and a few friends approached the Finley home. In an old frontier custom, he sent the others to the house with an empty jug. If William Finley filled it with drink, it was a sign that David and his wedding party were welcome and the match approved. His friends came back with a brimming container, David sent for the preacher, and the match was made.[23]

The couple spent their first few days living with her parents and his, and then, with the wedding gift of two cows with calves, Crockett rented a small farm near Finley Spring on Bay's Mountain in Jefferson County and commenced making his own way. He quickly came to a sobering realization: "Having a wife, I wanted every thing else; and, worse than all, I had nothing to give for it." What he got was the almost immediate start of a family. On July 10, 1807, Polly gave birth to John Wesley, and two years later to William. Polly made them a comfortable home within their meager means, and David could at least feed them from his hunting in the wilderness, but he simply could not provide enough to pay even their rent, much less anything for the necessities they could not make themselves. Years later a friend of the time could only recall Crockett as "a poor man." Faced with the problem, he did as his family before him, and as his people had done for generations. He moved on.[24]

In the next four years the Crocketts moved twice. First, sometime in the fall of 1811, he took them a grueling 150 miles west past Knoxville, across the Tennessee River, over the Cumberland Plateau, and then south to Lincoln County, almost to the Alabama Territory line. There, on the Mulberry fork of the Elk River, he marked his initials on a beech tree for a reference point, and laid out a five-acre claim on state land, built a cabin, and several months later received a warrant for title to the property. The hunting was good in the area, better than in the home he had left, and perhaps Crockett indulged too much his passion for taking the deer and other game, for once more he failed to prosper on the land. He entered a claim for fifteen more acres next to his first holding, but lost both tracts in the end for delinquency on his taxes. By then he had already removed his family anyhow, to Bean's Creek, a few miles south, and just above the Alabama border. Arriving sometime in 1813, for some reason he chose to call his new home "Kentuck," which, given his itinerant nature, might just as well have signaled his next intended destination if this claim did not show profit.[25]

If ever David Crockett had any awareness of politics or of national affairs on a sphere greater than his immediate neighborhood in these years, he gave no indication, but now outside events compelled his attention. The United States was at war with Great Britain again, as he well knew, but that was a faraway war. However, from the Canadian border to the Gulf Coast, the British were enlisting native allies to distract the Americans, capitalizing on relations already strained by the

pressure of white westward expansion. Anticipating the need for a pre-
emptive strike, some whites that summer attacked a party of Creek at
Burnt Corn Creek in southern Alabama Territory, inaugurating what
would be called the First Creek War. The Creek were not long in
retaliating. White settlers and a couple of companies of Mississippi
volunteers occupied a stockade at Fort Mims, about thirty miles up the
Alabama River from Mobile, and on August 30, 1813, the Creek struck
by surprise. The whites never even got the gates to the fort closed.
After several hours of brutal and largely one-sided fighting, nearly five
hundred lay dead in the stockade. No more than fifty escaped to
spread the news of the massacre through the shocked frontier. The
British might be hundreds of miles away, but now there was war right
here on their hearths.

"I, for one, had often thought about war," said Crockett in after
years, "and I did verily believe in my own mind, that I couldn't fight in
that way at all." Unlike many of his peers, David Crockett had no real
instinct for fighting. His was a nature too cheerful, too even-tempered.
Though certainly he felt the prejudices of his time, he bore no man ill.
He preferred fun to feuding, bragging to brawling. But self-defense
was something else, and when word of Fort Mims reached Bean's
Creek, he told Polly that he would have to join the local militia. "My
dander was up, and nothing but war could bring it right again," he
told her. Despite all his protestations that he had to go, that it was better to fight and stop the Creek in Alabama than have them appear at
his doorstep in Tennessee, she could not accept his leaving her alone
in a country still strange and new to her, where she had neither family
nor friends. In the end she stopped arguing and wept, then went to her
spinning wheel. David Crockett never knew if she accepted his decision or simply resigned herself to it, but for the rest of his life he carried with him the mental portrait of her sad, tear-streaked face as she
turned to her housework while he went off to war.[26]

Early on September 24 he shouldered his rifle and rode the ten
miles to Winchester, where the volunteers gathered. There Capt.
Francis Jones organized the Tennessee Volunteer Mounted Riflemen.
For the rest of his life Crockett would be proud that "I was one of the
first men that ever crossed the Tennessee river into the Creek war."[27]
Along with the rest he enlisted for ninety days' service, and two days

later, after getting in a supply of firewood and stores for Polly and the children, Crockett and the company set off south for the war.

Rapidly they rode first to Huntsville and then on to a nearby springs that was to be the rendezvous for several companies of militia that would soon be reorganized into the Second Regiment of Volunteer Mounted Riflemen. In the end almost thirteen hundred of them mustered, to join the cavalry division of Col. John Coffee. Meanwhile in Nashville Maj. Gen. Andrew Jackson was organizing the infantry division of militia before bringing it south. He already had some experience, having made a frustrating and fruitless expedition to Natchez, Mississippi, the previous winter, but his standing in Tennessee was undimmed, and he would command the campaign to avenge Fort Mims.

Until Jackson and the infantry arrived, however, the cavalry had to cover Tennessee from hostile incursion and also to find out what the Creek were doing. When a request went out for good woodsmen skilled with the rifle to ride deep into Alabama to seek the foe, Crockett's captain suggested him, and the next day he and a dozen others set out on their scout. They crossed the Tennessee below Huntsville, then separated into two groups, a major leading one and Crockett detailed to command the other. Within two days they began crossing the paths of small bands of Creek warriors, sometimes missing them by no more than an hour as they made their way southeast toward Ten Islands on the Coosa River. Finally on October 6 he learned of a large band crossing the river, on their way north to meet the advancing Jackson. Crockett and his party rode all night by moonlight the fifty miles or more back to the rendezvous to carry the warning. It was with no little chagrin, then, that Crockett found Colonel Coffee unimpressed by his intelligence, made the worse the next day when a major came in from a scout with much the same news, which Coffee then took seriously. Whether intended or not, the message that Crockett got from Coffee's attitude was that officers had little or no regard for anything that did not come from a fellow officer. To a poor white like Crockett it was exactly the sort of slight that he expected from the smug, the better educated, the affluent—the classes that did their best to suppress the poor. It was, he said, "one of the hateful ways of the world," and he did not forget it.[28]

The next day Jackson himself arrived, having pushed his command doggedly after getting Coffee's anxious report of what Crockett and the officer had learned. By then the cavalry had moved down to the Tennessee to watch its crossings, and south, scouting to the headwaters of the Black Warrior River. They saw plenty of sign of recent Creek activity, and once or twice came across their camps only recently vacated. Thanks to the haste with which the militia had mustered and the inefficiency of Jackson's commissary, none of the volunteers came well supplied. They lived largely on parched corn, and after a few days their meat ran out. Crockett himself volunteered to go into the woods alone to hunt, and one day actually came across a freshly killed and dressed deer carcass, eloquent testimony that the foe were almost within earshot of the main column.

The hardship of the long scout seemed wasted when the volunteers finally discovered that the report of Creek crossing the Coosa several days before had all been mistaken. There was nothing for them to do but go back to Ten Islands. There Coffee's division camped and built a stockade, Fort Strother, and started sending out scouting parties. Within a few days they learned positively that a band of Creek sat camped at Tallusahatchee, no more than eight or ten miles distant. Coffee immediately mounted the division, nine hundred strong, and sent them out well before dawn on the morning of November 3. They divided into two parties, approaching the camp from opposite sides, and then joined their flanks to surround the still unsuspecting Creek completely.

The fight opened shortly after sunrise, when a company of rangers advanced on the sleeping village and a shout of alarm awoke the foe. At first the Creek saw only the rangers, and rushed out at them as the whites purposely withdrew to their main line. Suddenly the volunteers opened fire, forcing them back into their camps, and then began inexorably to close in on them, tightening a circle from which there was no escape. This was to be the white man's repayment for Fort Mims, as everyone knew, and Crockett felt no more compunction than the rest at firing into the teeming mass of trapped natives before him. Seeing themselves hopelessly surrounded, about eighty women and children in the camp ran out to surrender themselves, and some were taken alive. But for the rest, once the killing fire started, only their blood could quench the flame. When one woman loosed an arrow that struck a militiaman, Crockett himself felt no hesitation at joining twenty others in answering with a fatal volley. "We now shot them like dogs," he recalled without remorse. Two score warriors took shelter in one wooden house, and the volunteers set it alight and burned them alive. He never forgot the image of one boy no more than twelve, a leg and arm broken by rifle fire, trying fruitlessly to crawl away from the blazing hut. Crockett said apparently with no touch of compassion that "he was so near the burning house that the grease was stewing out of him." Any dead Creek, even a child, redeemed the debt for Fort Mims, and was one more that would never threaten his own home and family. It was a part of the brutal but inevitable law of the frontier.

In the end the massacre—it could hardly be called a battle—left 186 natives dead. Not one adult male escaped. Only five of the volunteers died of their wounds, but without waiting the Tennesseans mounted and rode back to Fort Strother, mindful that there could be more and larger parties of Creek in the vicinity and not wanting to be caught out in the open. Hunger still welcomed them, however, for Jackson's commissary remained inept at best, and discontent among the volunteers rose in chorus with their grumbling bellies. So hungry were they that the next day they rode back to Tallusahatchee, remembering beef and potatoes in some of the burning houses. Crockett surveyed a battleground strewn with bloating and half-burned corpses, but then he and others found a large store of potatoes beneath the ruins of the great house that they had burned with forty warriors inside. "Hunger compelled us to eat them, though I had a little rather not," he said, "for the oil of the Indians we had burned up on the day before had run down on them, and they looked like they had been stewed with fat meat."[29]

It gave only a brief respite from starvation, however, and a few days later they boiled and ate beef hides. On November 7 word came that Creek were besieging Fort Talladega, just over thirty miles south of them, and Jackson put his small army on the march in the night. Once again he hoped to surround and annihilate the foe, and divided Coffee's cavalry into the two wings of his advance, expecting them to swing around the foe and link on the other side. It all worked as before, and with the encirclement complete, Jackson sent two companies of rangers to initiate the fight and lure the Creek into rushing against his lines. But the rangers themselves almost fell into a trap and had to abandon their horses and flee into the fort, whereupon the Creek then turned and charged Jackson's lines. When one line of riflemen loosed a volley, the Creek fell back in disorder and then rushed another side of the surrounding wall of militia, only to be repelled yet again. Before it was done, well over three hundred of them lay dead, and more would have fallen had they not finally escaped through a gap left by some militia who broke ranks.

Crockett and the rest returned to Fort Strother, and to starvation and discontent. Tallusahatchee and Fort Talladega may have vented their anger at the Creek, but increasingly now they turned it on their own authorities who showed no signs of relieving their distress. Winter's cold approached, their clothing wore thin, and their mounts approached collapse. Some of the officers importuned Jackson to allow the men to take their horses back to Tennessee to replenish both men and beasts, promising—apparently without consulting their men— that when they returned they would serve out the campaign even beyond their enlistment. Jackson agreed to a two-week furlough, starting November 22, ordering that they rendezvous at Huntsville on December 8 to return to the army. It suited his purpose to have his cavalry fit and equipped for a winter campaign, and at the same time the furlough might quell or at least dampen some of the now mutinous spirit among the volunteers.

Though barely a hundred miles from home, it probably took the weak and weary men and horses several days before Crockett saw the familiar rude cabin at Bean's Creek. Still he must have had a good two weeks to replenish Polly's firewood, kill and salt or smoke some more game for her table, and trade or work for enough to purchase some vegetables to fill out her diet after he left again, and grain to refit his horse. He must have eaten ravenously himself. Of course he expected he would not have to be away long when his furlough ended, for his ninety-day enlistment itself would expire by the end of December, and he apparently knew nothing of his officers' promise. What he could not expect was that his active service was already over for the time being.

Back at Fort Strother the unrest and incipient mutiny finally erupted when infantry volunteers confronted Jackson himself and announced that they were leaving, regardless of their unexpired enlistment. The general single-handedly quelled the insubordination, though it was a temporary victory. Early in December some of their enlistments actually did expire, and he could not hold them longer. Just as Crockett and other mounted men returned to Huntsville on December 8 for their rendezvous, large groups of these released volunteers passed through, and the infection for home spread to Coffee's men. Crockett and others reasoned that with their own enlistment expiring December 24, just over two weeks hence, it was pointless to proceed. Some of the men refused to go any farther toward the Tennessee, while several hundred did cross the river but halted immovably on the other side, Crockett probably among them. Many turned ugly, plundering the army grain supplies and frightening the local population. Given his mild nature, Crockett was not likely to have been among of the riotous element, but he shared their enthusiasm for going home enlistment or none. The promise to serve out the campaign after their furloughs meant nothing to them for they had not given it, and now they demanded to return to Tennessee. Coffee drew them up in formation and harangued them about their duty, reading letters from Jackson reminding them of their pledge. The general called them deserters and "luke-warm patriots indeed, who, in the moment of danger and necessity, can halt in the discharge of their duty, to argue and quibble," strong words hardly calculated to endear him to them. Many a man who would come to hate Jackson dated his animosity from those days. A minister even appealed to their duty to their God and their honor, but it availed him nothing. A few officers and half a dozen enlisted men agreed to go on to Fort Strother, but all the rest, Crockett certainly included, stuck to their demand to be dismissed, and so they were.[30] A few weeks later, on December 24, Private Crockett was discharged and paid $65.59. Through a calculating error, he was actually underpaid six cents, but since this was already more money than David Crockett had ever seen in his life, he probably neither noticed nor cared.[31]

However reasonable it may have seemed at the time, Crockett later took no pride in his action, and in future years—with very definite purpose—he distorted the story of what happened that December. A sense of guilt may well have begun to plague him not long after he returned to Polly, as he heard stories of the battles at Emuckfau Creek and Enotachopco Creek, and the decisive battle of the campaign at Horseshoe Bend on the Tallapoosa in March 1814. The Creek War was won, and he had not been there to take part. When he gathered with his neighbors in the local tavern to trade war stories, he could hardly compete by matching his participation in two one-sided massacres with their tales of winning the war. Yet there was his family to tend, a spring crop to plant, and always hunting to be done. By the fall, however, his shame, or his adventurous spirit, the enthusiasm of the moment, or the need for more hard cash propelled him once more into the war.

The authorities called for volunteers to form an army to march south and drive the British out of Pensacola, and despite Polly's entreaties David stepped forward to enlist on September 28 as a "mounted gunman." Perhaps because of his previous experience as a scout—and in spite of his behavior in December—he was soon raised to third sergeant in Capt. John Cowan's company of scouts and set off once more to serve under Jackson. Their mission now was not only the British, but a portion of the Creek nation that refused to accept the treaty that followed Horseshoe Bend, and at a leisurely pace they rode far south of the scene of their earlier operations, down to the confluence of the Tombigbee with the Alabama, not far from Fort Mims, and only a few miles north of Mobile.

Lacking forage for their horses, the volunteers set off on foot for Pensacola, about sixty miles southeast, but they arrived on November 8 to find that the town had fallen to Jackson the day before. Crockett came just in time to see British ships in the harbor evacuating their soldiers, and to go into town that night for a "few horns" with his messmates. Jackson and the main army left almost at once, marching east for Mobile and New Orleans. A few days later Crockett's volunteers retraced their steps toward Fort Mims, and near there they camped for several weeks to fill their knapsacks for another winter campaign. Their mission now would be to keep the Creek at bay while Jackson dealt with the British regulars.

It would be a season of long scouts and little action. In time they moved back toward Pensacola, then turned east and crossed the

Escambia. Crockett heard occasional skirmishes on the fringes of the advance, and made a few scouts on his own, especially to find food for the once more undersupplied volunteers. By the New Year they camped near the Chattahoochee River, thirty-four days out from their base and having taken only twenty days' rations of flour and even less of beef. Crockett himself mainly subsisted on coffee he had bought back near Pensacola. In desperation they even attacked a Creek town that promised a stiff resistance, all with the hope of capturing food. But the town had been burned and abandoned, and not a morsel remained.

Part of the command just left, marching for Baton Rouge on the Mississippi, while Crockett's regiment returned to central Alabama and Fort Decatur on the Tallapoosa. Along the way, as they pushed through virgin wilderness, Crockett left the column every day to hunt game, but the farther they went the more scarce became the deer and squirrels. Finally Crockett went absent without leave, feeling that nothing worse could happen to him on his own than if he stayed with the regiment. It was, he said, "root hog or die." After three days he got three squirrels and a couple of turkeys, and finally had a full meal, followed by fresh honey from a nearby bees' nest. A few deer followed, and when the main column caught up with Crockett, it quickly forgot his absence in the small bonanza of meat he presented.

Arrival at Fort Decatur revealed not the provisions they had expected but only a single ration of meat and no bread. Crockett traded some of his powder and shot for two hatfuls of corn from a friendly native, and then set out for another fifty miles to Fort Williams. Nothing but a ration of pork met them there to get them the remaining forty miles to Fort Strother. It was February by then, and the farther north they marched, the more they felt the winter. None of them even knew that the month before Jackson had defeated the British decisively at New Orleans, or that the conflict with Britain was already over anyhow. Crockett's war now was with cold and starvation, his campaign simply one of getting home alive. Happily Fort Strother proved abundantly supplied, and he stayed several days to recoup himself. Then, despite having still a month of his six months' enlistment outstanding, he simply repeated what he had done a year before. He left the army and went home. Polly was overjoyed to see him, for certainly there had been no news of him since he left the previous September. And when, a few days after his return, he got orders to leave again on a scout, he decided that he had done enough. He found a young man in the neighborhood and hired him to serve as a substitute for the last month of his enlistment. On March 27, 1815, Coffee gave Crockett his discharge, with praise for his good conduct and an apparent demotion to fourth sergeant either as a clerical error or else a mild rebuke for David's penchant for doing as he pleased.[32]

Crockett took pride in his war service, even if later he glossed over his desertions and exaggerated his participation, to the extent of claiming he had been in battles fought while he was home between enlistments. Certainly it was important enough to him that in his later autobiography he devoted even more space to it than to his youth, giving a third of those precious 211 pages over to his war exploits, real and fabricated. He had seen new country, much of it unsettled and ripe for men like himself to exploit. He had seen and served with Andrew Jackson and taken some measure of the man, most of it favorable. He had seen and shot at an enemy. He knew the face of battle. It was a fitting climax to the schooling of a frontiersman, and like so much else, self-taught. Yet even now, as he chained himself once more to the ceaseless routine of the soil and the care of his family, the real education of David Crockett was only just begun.

BOWIE

1796–1820

. . . an extended and organized system of enterprise, of ingenuity, of indefatigability, and of audacity . . .

BEVERLY CHEW, AUGUST 1, 1817

Thousands of men like David Crockett, coming home that spring of 1815, experienced only the fringe of the War of 1812 without seeing a real battle. Two such, brothers, trudged westward across the bayous and prairies of Louisiana toward Opelousas. From earliest youth they did everything together, as their father had before them with his own twin brother. In fact, they belonged to a family whose males knitted themselves so closely together in everything that any woman marrying one might have felt more like a visitor than a hostess in her own home. They felt a loyalty to the family that was intense beyond almost every other consideration. But that was natural: They were Scots, and the clan was in their blood.

If Crockett did not even know with certainty where his father had been born, these brothers at least had inklings of their tribe's origin. More than two centuries before, in 1581, King James VI of Scotland granted a tenement and garden in Cowper to his master of the wine cellar, Jerome, who probably traced his surname back even farther to the ancient Mac Ghille-bhuidhe. By Jerome's time, however, it had been shortened simply to Bowy and was pronounced to rhyme with the French *Louis*.[1] Like so many Scots, Jerome called his son James for his king, a name repeated generation after generation until John Bowie crossed the ocean to Maryland in about 1705 and settled on the Patuxent River in Prince Georges County.

Being a generation earlier than the Crocketts, the Bowies missed the traditional migration of the Scots-Irish, but still they moved. John's grandson James Bowie left home when he was about twenty-one and settled in South Carolina in 1760, married, and soon moved on to Ebenezer, Georgia, near the Savannah River. He was probably a squatter for his first year or two. There in 1762 his wife bore him twin sons, Rezin Pleasant and Rhesa, with two more children to follow, but then in September 1766 he petitioned the colonial administration for 300 acres on the north side of the Ogeechee River. As the family grew, he petitioned for additional land, and by 1772 his holdings had increased to 750 acres. His livestock throve to the extent that he registered an earmark for his cattle and pigs, a slash on the left ear and a hole in the right. His standing in the community grew apace, making him a magistrate for Richmond County by the time of the Revolution. His sons could write at least their names, if they did not read and write anything more.[2]

When Georgia joined the other twelve colonies in revolt, the twins, Rezin and Rhesa (despite their almost Arabic sound, the names were in fact Scottish in derivation), were just thirteen and far too young to serve, but their father, James, enlisted. Eventually, as the conflict lingered on and shifted to the south, the boys grew into the war. In 1779, now seventeen, Rezin joined Col. Francis Marion's mounted partisans and with them attacked Savannah on October 9. The attack failed, and a British saber slash nearly cost Rezin Bowie his hand, leaving him prostrate in a prison-camp hospital for some time. Elve ap Catesby Jones, a girl of Welsh background, joined the volunteer nurses tending the American wounded, and soon found herself devoting more than normal care to young Bowie. For his part the nurse attracted him despite her abrupt and candid manner. Behind her uncultured exterior—she was illiterate and unable to do more with a pen than make her mark—lay a powerful intellect. Scarcely more than two years later, with the war not yet over, they married, and in 1784, after independence, his service earned him a grant of 287.5 acres in Washington County, where the couple began housekeeping.[3]

The young Bowies added to their new farm and their family. Their first children, twin girls, died while yet infants, but in 1785 they welcomed John, the first of many sons. As his family grew, so did Rezin's aspirations. After daughter Sarah came in 1787, he turned his gaze toward new land in that part of western North Carolina soon to become Tennessee. They made the long trek nearly three hundred miles northwest, almost to the Kentucky border, to Sumner County. Near Elliott Springs he bought a few hundred acres, where Elve gave birth to daughter Mary in 1789 and Martha two years later. Then on September 8, 1793, came another son, a second Rezin Pleasant. With his family growing, the father Rezin acquired another 640 acres on Station Camp Creek two months after his new son's birth, but after another two months sold it all and decided to move thirty miles north, across the Kentucky line to Logan County. There with his wife, four children, five horses, and three black slaves, he settled 200 acres on Terrapin Creek.[4]

The Bowies did well in Kentucky. Within a year of landing in Logan, Rezin more than doubled his string of horses, including a breeding stud. He acquired a small herd of twenty-three cattle and increased his slave holdings to eight to help work the property. He paid taxes, secured the surveys and permission to build the inevitable mill on the creek, and before long the wagon path crossing his property to the creek became known as Bowie's Mill Road.[5] Elve had a third son there in the spring of 1796. Inevitably with the Bowies there had to be a James sooner or later, and this boy was the one.[6]

The family prospered and grew in the ensuing years. They added another 200 acres to their holdings. Yet another son, Stephen, came the year after James, and Rezin's brothers Rhesa and John moved to Kentucky.[7] Indeed, not only did the Bowies expand but so did Logan itself—and that presented a problem. Rezin senior may have enjoyed the company of other Logan settlers like Adam and Margaret Kuykendall or the Smiths, whose infant son Benjamin Fort Smith was only a few weeks older than James,[8] but he did not care for the growing population. Like so many of his wandering kind he craved the wilder regions on the outer edge of the frontier. His son John was already old enough to recognize that his father was "passionately fond of the adventures and excitements of a woodsman's life."[9] Rezin Bowie must have seen the handbill.

There were already stories of wonderful new lands to be had just for the asking. In 1795 the Treaty of San Lorenzo adjusted major differences between the United States and Spain, and the Spaniards, who owned the vast Louisiana Territory west of the Mississippi River, decided to invite American settlers into the region. The very year of James Bowie's birth, they distributed handbills throughout the Ohio River Valley settlements, offering liberal grants and no taxes to those who would come to their part of the New World. The only requirement was that settlers convert to Catholicism. The Bowies resisted the temptation at first, but so many others rushed west, ignoring the religious requirement, that in 1798 Madrid halted the immigration temporarily. It soon commenced again, however, and in October 1799 the best known of all Kentuckians, Daniel Boone, crossed the great river. The Spaniards made him an *empresario*, his task to persuade others to follow—and follow they did.

A generation later Tocqueville marveled at the exodus. "At the end of the last century a few bold adventurers began to penetrate into the Mississippi valley," he wrote. "It was like a new discovery of America; soon most of those who were immigrating went there; previously unheard of communities suddenly sprang up in the wilderness." And there one could find what he called "democracy in its most extreme form." In those new lands, "in some sense improvisations of fortune, the inhabitants have arrived only yesterday in the land where they dwell. They hardly know one another, and each man is ignorant of his nearest neighbor's history."[10]

It was that kind of solitude, that sort of "extreme" democracy, that Rezin Bowie could not resist.[11] On February 19, 1800, he sold his Logan County property, packed his family, including brothers Rhesa, John, and the youngest David, and their sister Elsie, and set off west to pick up the old road that led from Nashville, Tennessee, northwest through Kentucky to the Ohio River.[12] When they reached Livingston County on the river, the Bowie clan apparently liked what they saw and briefly changed their minds about Missouri. They settled on a parcel of land in Livingston, but scarcely had the family gotten settled before they moved again, this time probably by "broad horn," one of the self-made flatboats that took tens of thousands down the rivers to new land. With them they took all the seed needed to plant a new crop, several hundred seedlings for fruit trees, and perhaps even some livestock. If not sold before the journey, their eight slaves went with them.[13] Just where the Ohio flowed into the Mississippi, at a spot known as Bird's Point, they made landing and came ashore onto an extensive alluvial plain called the Tywappity Bottom. They found an area scarcely settled, no more than forty or fifty families scattered about, and many of them congregated in the small village of Ze-wa-pe-ta some thirty miles north. In 1789 the Spaniards had opened a river road—designated *El Camino Real*, or royal highway—that passed through the bottom and ran south to New Madrid and north to St. Genevieve. The bottom itself constituted a dividing line between the Cape Girardeau District to the north and the New Madrid District to the south, and in August 1800 the Bowies wasted little time in establishing themselves.[14]

They selected a plot beside the Marias des Peches in the New Madrid District and immediately began building two cabins, one for Rezin's family and the other for his brothers and sister. Other than Charles Findlay and Abraham Bird, who had been there two years, their only neighbors were the honeybees and the mosquitoes, and the deer, turkey, beaver, and even bears that inhabited the dense and seemingly impenetrable forests that lined the bottom.[15]

Rezin cleared fifty acres and started the family planting turnips and laying out and planting an orchard of eight hundred or more fruit trees. He applied to Henry Peyroux, commandant of the New Madrid District, for a formal concession of land and got it on December 19, allowing him a total of 380 *arpents*, the French measurement equivalent to just more than five-sixths of an acre.[16] Here they would stay for two years, and here James Bowie undoubtedly placed his earliest recollections. As a child of four growing to six, his work was slight. There was abundant time for play in those foreboding woods that seemed always to hold more lure than fright for the Bowie men. All around him were associations from the now gone Apple Creek band of the Shawnee. Their old abandoned encampments dotted the bottom. The name "Tywappity" had probably been left by them, but if so this oddest of all place names in the Missouri country was so old that its origin or meaning had been completely lost.[17] There was time to be spent learning, for Elve had acquired enough literacy by now to teach her children the alphabet. Thanks to the Spanish stipulation of Catholicism, there were no Protestant congregations in the Tywappity. Still, like

many of the other Protestant settlers, the Bowies evaded the conversion requirement, though if and when they attended a church service it
was Catholic, and they developed a comfortable tolerance for the faith.
At home Rezin was a Presbyterian, naturally, and Elve a very devout
Methodist, and she took on herself the religious instruction of her
children.[18]

Rezin Bowie prospered in Missouri, for there was some money to be
made from clearing and selling the extensive timber that covered so
much of the land.[19] He became close to Abraham Bird, who would
marry his sister Martha a few years later. Brother Rhesa took out a
claim of his own, as did David, and their sister Elsie married a local
man. Rezin was often in New Madrid to act as witness for the transactions of his friends and neighbors as they sold property to new
arrivals. It was the success of Logan County all over again, and therein
lay the problem.[20] In the short span of two years, Tywappity lost that
frontier edge that Bowie craved. Rezin was thirty-eight now. He had
always liked being on the road. In March 1802 he went back to Logan
County on business, but that hardly satisfied his itch for new vistas.[21]
His oldest son, John, was seventeen, nearly a man, and though his
youngest, David, born in Missouri, was an infant, still Rezin could feel
the onset of middle age.[22] It was time for one more move.

International events reached deep into the North American continent. The concession that Rezin got on October 1, 1800, was one of
the very first acts of a new administration, for that very day Spain
agreed to return the Louisiana Territory to France by the Treaty of San
Ildefonso. No doubt it took months for the news to reach the
Tywappity, and in any event it meant little or no difference in life for
the settlers in that stretch of the domain. Awaiting a transfer of officials
that never came, Spanish administrators continued to run the region.
However, the return of French rule to the Lower Mississippi promised
a regime friendlier to American settlers, if only because they had been
common allies against Britain in the last war, and France was at war
with the British even now. Besides, there was already a sense of
inevitability about the spread of settlement westward across the continent. The Bowies themselves were a part of the vanguard that crossed

the Mississippi, if only by a few miles. If someday all of this vastness would be a part of the United States, then the first on the scene stood to gain the most.

Rezin may have anticipated the move as early as April 6, 1802, when he gave Abraham Bird his power of attorney to act for him in the sale of some of his land to neighbor Charles Findlay. The sale of part of the Marias des Peches land came in October, and Rezin was in New Madrid on business as late as November 16, but within a few weeks, or months at the most, even though he still owned at least one parcel that he held for another six years, he quit Missouri for good.[23]

The Bowies no doubt built another broad horn, or else paid for a passage on a downbound flatboat, this time on a several days' voyage of 350 miles south to the bluff city of Natchez. Across the river lay the Territory of Orleans, all of later Louisiana except that part south and east of the Mississippi then known as the Isle de Orleans, in which lay the city of New Orleans, and Spanish-held West Florida. Thirty miles west of Natchez a stream called Bushley Bayou flowed northeasterly into the Ouachita River. There Rezin applied for and received a grant of eight hundred *arpents* near a place called Big Prairie on the bayou, and that summer began once more the business of making a success in the wilderness.[24]

It was 1803, and even as President Thomas Jefferson was in the act of purchasing the Louisiana Territory from France, Rezin erected a whisky distillery on the Bushley.[25] Over the next several years he acquired more property, sold a parcel to his son-in-law Bird who had moved south, and sold another to his brother John, for once more the whole extended family were a part of the move. Young Rezin, though a mere fifteen years old in 1808, got 640 acres on the Ouachita nearby.[26] With the perennial shortage of hard currency that always plagued the frontier, they established credit with the local traders.[27]

Following the purchase and the beginning of American administration, the Bushley Bayou land became a part of Rapides County, though the French practice of calling such jurisdictions parishes was so habitual with the largely Creole population that in practice the word "county" was almost never used. No sooner did his address officially change, however, than Rezin decided to switch it again. His brother Rhesa had gone on south into Opelousas Parish, settling on a bayou near the town of Opelousas itself, and in 1809 Rezin's family followed. By now the parish had been renamed St. Landry, and there Rezin settled at last and for good. He planted cotton on the broad prairies, cut timber to send south to the boatyards at New Orleans, and distilled his whiskey to ship along with the lumber.[28]

Now at last the Bowie clan began to disperse, though they all remained in Louisiana. Brother John J. Bowie acquired more property not far from Bushley Bayou at a place called Sicily Island, in what in 1808 became Catahoula Parish.[29] Though he was no more than twenty-six years old, he was by now known as John senior, to distinguish him from Rezin's son John, now John junior, who was in fact only a year younger. John Junior, too, stayed in Catahoula, and so did a cousin named Rhesa.[30] Not only did the Bowies stick together; their penchant for repeating the same names and their proliferation of sons caused no little confusion.

Around 1812 Rezin and Elve laid out a claim for 640 *arpents* on Bayou Vermilion in Attakapas Parish just south of Opelousas, and there he continued the timber-cutting business, at the same time selling the remainder of his Catahoula property to his brother John.[31] The boys were more than old enough to take a real part in the work now, especially Rezin junior, James, and Stephen. The older two grew up inseparable, typical of their clan. Their inclinations and interests were much they same. Both loved all manner of outdoor sport, especially riding and hunting with their hounds, even after bear. They grew up tall and muscular, with James now sixteen and Rezin three years older. Rezin especially was keenly intelligent, hazel-eyed, with chestnut hair. If James did not completely share his brother's intellect, still his was an agile and inventive mind, and both boys were said to take after their mother, Elve, as had their older brother John. Only Stephen seemed less gifted intellectually, though some thought him the handsomest of them all.[32] What education of the formal variety they got came from her, largely self-taught herself. From their father they learned the example of ingenuity, hard work, and the instinct to exploit the frontier's abundant opportunity.

Other kinds of education awaited James and Rezin in their teen years. Even after the start of substantial settlement, dangers loomed. Following the purchase of Louisiana, almost all the region was public land, unavailable for purchase until it was properly surveyed and townships and ranges were laid out. That would be the work of years to come. The only more immediate ways to take possession of a tract were either to buy it from a confirmed occupant or else to acquire a Spanish grant owned by a grantee who never actually took possession. No matter how the land was obtained, however, when the buyer arrived on the scene he might find the property already inhabited by squatters. Eviction required the law, and sometimes force, as Rezin and Elve apparently discovered when squatters on one of their properties tried to resist being displaced.[33]

The boys also learned about life with slavery. Their grandfather John owned a few, and so certainly did their father, Rezin. Though hardly planters on even a modest scale, the Bowies still worked enough land that they needed a few field hands. Moreover, Rezin's timber-cutting enterprise required substantial cheap labor. Typically for land owned by small farmer–slaveholders, Bowie plantations enjoyed benign, even familial, relations between blacks and whites. They certainly were for Uncle Rhesa, who never married but who fathered a son named James by a slave mistress sometime around 1790 and thereafter openly acknowledged him, gave him his freedom and the family name, and brought him to Louisiana with the rest of the clan. The black James Bowie remained in Catahoula when the rest moved south. For years to come he steadily did land and loan business with both Johns, senior and junior, even buying and selling slaves himself, and achieved some minor position in the community near Sicily Island.[34] Wherever the Bowie blood flowed, the clan loyalty followed. In later years the family remembered as well stories of Rezin's young James's closeness to an old slave woman named Mandy, of the little kindnesses he did for her, and of the advice she passed on to the boy.[35] There was never any question that the Bowie slaves were property, though, and with the exception of a few favorites like old Mandy, they were usually sold with the land whenever a Bowie moved on.

Mostly James Bowie looked up to his brothers, especially nineteen-year-old Rezin, and it must have upset him in the late summer of 1812 when Rezin left home and went northwest one hundred miles, along the Red River past Alexandria, to the frontier outpost at Natchitoches, and James could not follow. Louisiana became a state that year, its western boundary at the Sabine River. Many Americans believed that the Louisiana Purchase had rightfully included the province of Texas beyond, but Spain held firmly to the territory as a part of its Mexican possession, even in the face of a frequently rebellious population. That led to a series of uprisings by Mexican officials—with North American collaborators or instigators—to wrest away the province of Texas. José Bernardo Gutiérrez and Augustus Magee raised a small contingent of adventurers, including Rezin Bowie, at Natchitoches in August 1812, and marched on Nacogdoches, Texas immediately. A few months later when Magee died, Samuel Kemper took over. He was already a veteran of an uprising in West Florida in 1804, and another in 1810 when he and his brothers Reuben and Nathan helped lead ragtag planters and adventurers in taking control of Spanish territory from Baton Rouge to Mobile. The independent republic of West Florida lasted just ten weeks before the United States took possession and added all but the eastern bit of it to Louisiana. Now, with revolution seemingly in his blood, Kemper led the small but growing company of filibusters (a term derived from "freebooter," a name for pirates; land pirates is largely what the filibusters were) in capturing the capital of Texas itself, San Antonio de Béxar, on April 1, 1813. But for Kemper, as for many of the Anglo-Americans with him, Gutiérrez spoiled the victory and shamed their efforts when he allowed the surrendered Spanish commander and his staff to be executed. Kemper and more than one hundred of the men who had come with him left in disgust and returned to Louisiana, Rezin Bowie presumably among them.[36] Still, it was the first time a Bowie had seen Texas and its abundant promise, a first taste of filibustering, a first promise that the frontier did not end at Louisiana.

By the time of Rezin's return more than enough had happened east of the Sabine to occupy Bowie attention. There was family news, some good, more bad. On his return to St. Landry, Rezin courted Margaret Neville, and on September 15, 1814, they wed.[37] John senior had also married in 1806, but his fortunes turned against him in February 1812, when Catahoula's sheriff had to seize his goods and chattels to redeem unpaid debt.[38] Sometime in this period James's brother David, aged only seventeen, drowned in the Mississippi. And Rhesa Bowie, though just in his early fifties, was ailing, and would die in a few months.[39]

If those blows to the family were not enough in themselves, by late 1814 the war with the British finally came to the Lower Mississippi Valley. Prior to that time it had been as if there were no war at all. General Jackson did lead a small army south in 1813, intending to fortify the mouth of the Mississippi below New Orleans, but he got no farther than Natchez. The subsequent Creek War was too distant to involve western Louisiana. Only in November 1814, when the British gathered an expedition to strike at New Orleans, did the war finally arrive. Jackson was already in Mobile, and as soon as he learned of the enemy plans he marched for the Crescent City. Now it was Louisiana's war at last.

And this time James went with Rezin. The younger brother was well on the way to nineteen when the call came for volunteers to assemble in Opelousas and march to defend New Orleans. While James described brother Rezin as "a perfect rowdy" at this age, he was if anything an even rougher sort himself, less thoughtful and more instinctive in his actions.[40] It was already time to leave his father's house, as Rezin had on his marriage. The call to the war provided the perfect opportunity.[41]

Men from all over western Louisiana, but especially Rapides, Natchitoches, and St. Landry Parishes, mustered in or near Opelousas as the new year dawned. Rezin left with his wife, Margaret, already three months pregnant. He and James both enlisted on January 8, 1815, as privates in Capt. Coleman A. Martin's company, which soon merged with a number of others from the region to form the Seventeenth, Eighteenth, and Nineteenth Consolidated Louisiana Militia Regiment, commanded by prominent Alexandria attorney Josiah S. Johnston.[42] James saw some familiar faces there to serve with him, men like his uncle Abraham Bird, and there were plenty of new faces as well. The consolidated regiment was a polyglot of nationalities, like Louisiana itself, and side by side with the Bowies were men of Spanish, French, Portuguese, Acadian, and apparently even African backgrounds. There were Sgt. Samuel Wells of Alexandria and Capt. Jean Bruard, commanding a company in the Eighteenth. José Domingo Losoya, who had fled San Antonio after its fall to Kemper in 1813, was there as a private, along with a number of other *bexareños*, some of whom may have been known to Rezin. John Davis Bradburn, whose path he would cross in years to come, joined the same company as James and Rezin but soon took a commission as a third lieutenant under Bruard.[43]

Once organized they left almost immediately for New Orleans, but it was already too late. In a misty dawn battle on the very day that James Bowie enlisted, General Jackson turned back the British attack, and within days word would come that the warring nations had made peace. Rezin never gave up his disappointment at missing the great battle, and always treasured his enlistment papers in the regiment as a memento. No doubt James felt the same. It would have been one of the great moments of their generation.[44]

They did not reach New Orleans until January 24—James Bowie's first visit to the great city, with all its exotic flavors of Europe and the Caribbean—and even then they were not allowed to remain long. Assigned to the Second Brigade of Louisiana Militia, their regiment went upriver to Donaldsonville, almost halfway back to Opelousas, and there they remained for more than two weeks. Colonel Johnston found the garrison duty so tedious that he simply went home three days before they were ordered back to New Orleans. There James and Rezin spent more than a month, now really having time to experience the city, as well as to meet soldiers from other units who had seen action in the battle. Dr. James Long, a surgeon at the battle, was in town then, and they may well have met. Certainly they became acquainted with an even more interesting character, a North Carolinian just five years older than Rezin, whom he may already have known. Warren D. C. Hall lived in Natchitoches prior to the Gutiérrez-Magee expedition, and went with them to San Antonio, where he too was repelled by the executions that followed. Here was a true adventurer, and though he served in another unit at the time of the Battle of New Orleans, he transferred to the Bowies' regiment early in March. A friendship between Hall and James especially blossomed, as each felt some kindred in the other.[45]

Together they all mustered out in New Orleans on March 31, 1815, and James and Rezin each received $21.93 for their two months and twenty-three days' service.[46] There remained the long walk back to Opelousas, the disappointment of missing all the action, and yet a certain eye-opening after the visit to New Orleans and the exposure to so many new faces. James had been away from his father's house for three months, largely on his own, living in the company of other ambitious young men, and with the example of fellow soldiers who were older and who had made their way in the world—some of them, like Hall and Bradburn, rather dramatically. After that experience going back home to the family timber business held little luster.

James Bowie was full grown to six feet or nearly so, raw-boned, a stoutly built 180 pounds. Above his fair complexion sat sandy hair, not quite red. His deep-set blue eyes, the more pronounced because of his high cheekbones, were so pale as to appear gray, and sitting shadowed deep within their sockets gave them a penetrating look heightened by his manner of gazing directly into another's eyes when speaking. "Taken altogether, he was a manly, fine-looking person," his brother John believed, "and by many of the fair ones he was called handsome." Much more to the point at this juncture in his life, John saw that brother James was "young, proud, poor, and ambitious, without any rich family connections, or influential friends to aid him in the battle of life."[47] James Bowie had met some men in New Orleans who might be good connections in time, but for now his ambition and $21.93 were all that he had to start life on his own.

Once he reached Opelousas, James did not remain long at home before coming to the decision to strike out on his own. Poverty was not necessarily a handicap. He had his discharge money, and, while hardly a rich man, still his father was comfortable by rural Louisiana standards and could offer modest help. And for as little as $100.00 or even less, a man could buy a piece of unimproved land along one of the more remote bayous. A standard measure of forty *arpents* frontage, by forty *arpents* in depth back from the bayou to where the land sloped down into swamp, yielded 1,350 acres, and the timber on such a parcel would more than pay for it when cut, sawed into planks, and sent down to the markets. Moreover, Bowie did not even need to buy the land.

With the exception of its one city at New Orleans, and a few small towns and villages like Opelousas and Alexandria, Louisiana was thinly settled when it passed into American hands. When it became a state, the government recognized as lawful all the valid existing land claims from Spanish grants, but as much as 90 percent of the state remained public domain. It would take decades for the slow wheels of bureaucracy to survey all that and offer it at public auction. Meanwhile, until such survey, or until the holder of a valid Spanish grant appeared to claim a parcel, squatters could and did move in. They built their cabins, cleared the timber, planted crops, and treated the land in every way as their own until evicted by a grant holder or offered the opportunity to buy the grant and keep their place. Consequently, with virtually no money and little other wherewithal but an ax and a gun, a man could make a home for himself.

Most likely James Bowie squatted when he left home again sometime in 1815. Commencing just a few miles above Opelousas, Bayou Boeuf meandered in a northwesterly direction to Alexandria, along the way cutting across the southwestern corner of Avoyelles Parish. It was sparsely settled country, with just a lonely woodcutter's cabin now and then standing beside the swamp. What was not heavily timbered was grassy prairie where Creole squatters raised cattle—a wild country, full of game, and much of it as yet unclaimed or settled, where the reach of civil law was almost unknown.[48] In short, it was ideal for a young man starting out on his own with little but ambition, and determined to provide for himself. He chose a piece of unoccupied land close to the border between Avoyelles and Rapides, and began to clear it of timber.[49] There for the next few years he worked to build his plantation. For money he cut the cypress, whipsawing them into planks, then floating the loads down Bayou Boeuf to sell in Opelousas. That made him enough for food, clothing, and powder and shot with which to hunt for his meat, with money to save besides.[50] Within two years he had put by three hundred dollars to purchase his land and improvements from the claimed owner on April 3, 1817. At the same time he bought a small family of four slaves from his father, offering in payment his note for $1,700.[51]

Gradually Bowie expanded his smallholding, needing more adjacent timberland as his own was cleared. In October 1818 he acquired two more parcels on Bayou Boeuf in Avoyelles, handing over cash or personal notes for $700.[52] Two months later, in December, Bowie gave notes totaling $1,040 for three more parcels, one on the Red River that flowed through Avoyelles, and two others on nearby Elm Bayou.[53] And in February 1819 he added yet more Bayou Boeuf property, for another $500.[54] All or most of these transactions involved promissory notes rather than hard cash in payment. Bowie was clearly learning that an enterprising man willing to take risks could acquire property with little more than his word, trusting that the returns from exploiting the land would provide the cash to meet the notes. It was the beginning of speculation, the lesson not slow in impressing him. Indeed, in October 1818, still only twenty-two, he went into his first business venture, buying another Bayou Boeuf property in partnership with John Stafford for $1,000, with the intention of making a profit from it by subdivision and speculation. The owner, John D. Reeves, was unable to give them absolute proof that he held a clear title to the property, but they took him at his word.[55] In the informal and uncertain legal world of the frontier, where even the wealthy had limited actual hard cash and there were no banks, a handshake and a promise had to be enough.

Meanwhile James Bowie enjoyed his youth, the freedom of living on his own, and the opportunity to indulge what John Bowie called "the innate love of excitement" that he inherited from his father. He hunted and fished and explored in the rugged bayou wilderness. No manner of backwoods sport found him reluctant to participate, and he acquired something of a local reputation for daring to the point of recklessness. In the forest he roped deer and wild horses, and occasionally on a bet or a dare even roped and rode alligators. The woods had plenty of bears that came out into the clearings in the summers to eat planters' green corn, and Bowie devised a rude trap made of a hollowed cypress knee. He put honey in the bottom or pointed end of the knee, then drove nails from the outside through to the hollow, inclined toward the point, and left the trap in a corn patch. When the bear shoved his snout in to get the honey, the spikes held it fast and prevented him from pulling it out, and in that helpless condition he became easy prey for Bowie's gun.[56]

Bowie occasionally went to Cheyneyville on Bayou Boeuf, a settlement a few miles from his plantation, where he traded at Bennet's store for sundries and materials to mend his clothes, or a quart of wine from time to time.[57] There too he saw the occasional newspaper, received mail from family, and sat with neighbors in a tavern for gossip and conviviality. In Cheyneyville he could find music and amusement, a game of cards, and a merry glass to soften the hard life of the frontier. Society was important to James Bowie. He loved company, and his open, frank manner and even temper attracted others to him. He was also ambitious and knew it to be in his interest to cultivate friendships with what John Bowie called "the better class of the people." And there, on rare occasion, when there were too many glasses and the merriment turned to harsh words, his other side might emerge. "The displays of his anger were terrible," brother John recalled, "and frequently terminated in some tragical scene." He would not abide an insult. When enraged, James Bowie became entirely single-minded in his determination to vent his anger on a foe. What observers took for fearlessness was as much an entire forgetfulness of his own safety in the grips of his fury. He soon acquired a reputation as a man both to respect and to fear.[58]

He also gained standing as one who was game for adventure. By the summer of 1819 echoes of Rezin's earlier Texas flirtation with Kemper beckoned, and now James Bowie met another of the adventurers with their eyes perennially fixed on Texas. "Never was a more propitious moment for effecting their purpose," said the Natchez press of the filibusters. "Should New-Mexico and Texas unite in the great cause, the consumation of the independence of all America will be soon and certain."[59] Texas, as usual, was in a lawless, leaderless state of ferment. Hoping to capitalize on that, and on resentment that in the recent Adams-Onís Treaty the United States had yielded the claim that Texas was rightfully included in the Louisiana Purchase, Dr. James Long, Ben Milam, and seventy-five others gathered in Natchez in June 1819 intent on invasion and liberation.

Word of the planned expedition was in all the Natchez newspapers and certainly reached as far as Avoyelles. Moreover, Long's route of march to Natchitoches took him through Rapides Parish, perhaps as close to Bowie as Alexandria, and men joined him all along the way. It would have been very difficult indeed for James Bowie to resist the temptation to emulate his brother, especially since his friend from their old regiment, Warren D. C. Hall, was involved. By the time Long reached Nacogdoches, west of the Sabine, his numbers had swelled to three hundred, Bowie no doubt among them. There in late June they declared a new government, began enacting laws, and Long proclaimed that he would sell land in Texas at a dollar an acre as a lure to more adventurers to join him, something that would especially have appealed to Bowie.[60]

Meanwhile James himself soon became a favorite among the filibusters, especially with Hall and Long's lieutenant, Col. James Gaines. He may even have engaged in one or two of the little skirmishes in July and August as Long spread his reach into Texas, for Gaines recalled Bowie being "a very devil" in a fight, though this would have been Bowie's first taste of mortal combat. Yet it was obvious to most that Long was outmanned and outclassed by the Spanish authorities, and on October 28, 1819, they drove him out of Nacogdoches, and within a month the expedition was a shambles. James Bowie was not there to see it happen. By October 2 he was already back in Avoyelles. He may simply have lost interest in the ill organized and haphazardly led expedition. Equally if not more likely, in Texas he encountered something that appealed to him much more than the promise of cheap land tied to a tottering revolution.[61]

The other Bowie brothers had grown apace, with varying fortunes. Rezin's firstborn appeared in June 1815 shortly after his return from the war but died a few months later. But then in October 1817, as James was setting up his plantation, Margaret gave birth to a son whom they named, predictably, James.[62] Rezin—who endured seeing his name appear as everything from "Reason" to "Recision"—established himself in his own right in St. Landry Parish as a businessman, and then in Avoyelles, where James had settled. He was appointed an officer of the Avoyelles Mounted Riflemen militia and rose rapidly to a position of respect in the community. While James acquired a smattering of Spanish, Rezin learned to read and speak both Spanish and French. A friend, William H. Sparks, found him "a man of most exalted genius, wonderful originality and high attainments." Moreover, Rezin was "eminently social and genial in his nature, fond of adventure, as careless of the present as indifferent to the future." Sparks concluded that he was "little in nothing, but noble even in his vices."[63] In short, he

seemed the near-mirror image of brother James, though more thoughtful and less impulsive. Already, however, Rezin suffered the signs of
poor eyesight that plagued many of the Bowie men, but that happily
seems to have missed James.[64]

Brother Stephen now was past his twenty-first birthday, and out on
his own like the rest. Just recently he had married Mary Ann Compton,
whose family moved to Rapides from Maryland. She was already
expecting their first child, and the new family needed a home.[65] The
eldest, John, also prospered, though he, too, suffered from severe near-
sightedness that kept him from participating in some of the wilder
escapades James and Rezin indulged in.[66] But when it came to business
ventures that required daring brains as much as physical prowess, John
stood very much side by side with his brothers, and now, in late 1819,
a new opportunity in a very old business beckoned.

For almost two hundred years slavery had been an increasingly important factor in the economy and society of the United States. By the
turn of the nineteenth century it was confined to the agrarian South
and what was called the Old Southwest—Alabama, Mississippi, and
Louisiana. Of course it was an important source of labor for the great
planters as well as the small farmers like the Bowies, and in its modest
way it had been a part of Bowie family life for three generations or
more. Undeniably, and especially in a region like Louisiana, where
there was no established aristocracy of old families, the ownership of
slaves brought to the newer men a species of social equality that they
craved.[67] The Bowies, too, sought that, though in James's case at least,
it was not so much for social station for its own sake as for the opportunity to enhance his fortunes afforded by access to the upper strata of
society.

Slaves also meant money. Congress abolished the African slave
trade just a decade earlier in 1808, partly in the mistaken expectation
that domestic supply of bondsmen would be equal to future demand.
But it reckoned without the growth and expansion into the Old
Southwest, where plantation farming required vast cheap labor. The
demand for slaves in Louisiana west of the Mississippi far outstripped
the supply, sending prices ever higher and sending planters seeking

other sources. Smuggling of slaves commenced as soon as Congress abolished the foreign trade, most of them coming into the country through the Caribbean and the Gulf Coast. The federal government made only halting efforts to contain smuggling or to capture the smugglers themselves, and since Congress had failed to provide a policy on how to handle any contraband slaves seized, the several states devised their own means. One thing they would not do was send them back to Africa, or to the South American countries from whose slave ships many of them had been captured in the first place. The states needed slaves despite the law. The best solution seemed to be to sell them at auction, with the proceeds going into the federal treasury. The slaves thus sold henceforward acquired legal status, and the government at least derived some good from those breaking its laws. Some states, Louisiana among them, provided an added incentive by promising half the auction proceeds to the person or persons turning in smuggled slaves or on whose information they were taken.[68]

By 1819 one source dominated the illicit slave business in Louisiana, ironically a man much credited with having helped to save New Orleans during the battle of January 8, 1815. Mystery and myth surrounded Jean Laffite even in his own time, but no doubt existed that his principal trade for years had been all manner of smuggling, much of it the cargoes he took as a privateer from Spanish hulls captured in the Caribbean and the Gulf of Mexico. Following the victory at New Orleans, he continued for a time to operate out of his remote fastness in the Barataria region forty miles south of the city. By 1817, however, his presence had become an increasing irritant to local and national authorities, and he scouted for a new base of operations. As so often in the affairs of the region in this era, his gaze turned inevitably toward Texas.

The Magee-Gutiérrez expedition was only one in a succession of poorly planned and ill-led filibustering attempts to wrest Texas from Spain, sometimes loosely coordinated with efforts for independence elsewhere in Mexico. Col. Henry Perry served with Kemper in Texas in 1813 but returned to the United States when the expedition ended in repulse after Kemper and others abandoned the enterprise in disgust. But two years later he was back on another campaign, raising three hundred volunteers at Belle Isle in the swampy coastal plain southwest of New Orleans, and in November taking them west to Galveston Bay. Settling first on the mainland beside the Trinity River, Perry moved across the bay in the winter of 1816 to what some in the area called Snake Island, thanks to its serpent population. By then another adventurer and revolutionary, Louis Michel Aury, made his own armed camp in a few shacks on the island, using it as a base for his ships to prey on Spanish vessels. When Perry arrived, accompanied now by the Bowies' old companions in arms John Davis Bradburn and Warren D. C. Hall, he refused to subordinate himself to Aury, and the two maintained separate and none-too-friendly camps until November, when yet another revolutionary, Francisco Xavier Mina, arrived with more men and sufficient authority to exert command over Perry and to achieve an uneasy cooperation with Aury. Finally in April 1817 Aury convoyed Mina and Perry in his ships in an attack on the Mexican coast. The expedition broke down in predictable squabbling, and Aury left the others and sailed back to Snake Island. When he got there, however, he found new occupants and new rulers. The Laffites had come.[69]

Jean and his brother Pierre Laffite knew Snake Island well. In addition to their smuggling activities, they operated as legitimate importers of wine and spirits from Bordeaux to New Orleans, as well as consumer goods like vinegar and hard merchandise. Shortly after Mina's arrival, the Laffites began loading wine by the cask and the bottle aboard their ship *Devorador* and shipping it to the uneasy community of filibusters at what they then called "Galveztown." The *Devorador* made one voyage in January 1817 and two in March, and when its captain returned from these trips he no doubt brought word of Mina's advancing preparations to depart for Mexico. Indeed, so good was his information that when Jean Laffite registered the *Devorador's* next outgoing cargo of wine on April 4, he almost certainly knew that three days later the Mina expedition would depart, leaving the island almost abandoned.[70] That was his opportunity. Perhaps on that very same April 4, with the casks of vinegar and the cases of bottles of red and white wine, Jean Laffite boarded forty or fifty of his own men, knowing that they would be the ones drinking that wine as the new rulers of Galveztown.

By April 15 Laffite was firmly in control on Snake Island, and before long his Baratarians built a larger settlement atop Aury's old shantytown. In time Laffite commanded three hundred or more men in the

village he named Campeachy. He built himself a substantial house, the
Maison Rouge, and for his men he erected a tavern, a billiard room,
and several "groggeries" to keep them happy when they were not at
sea preying on Spanish vessels.[71] By the time Aury returned with his
ships in July, he found the Campeachy establishment too strong to
challenge and had no choice but to move elsewhere.

But Aury left Laffite a small legacy, one that may have been part of
Galveztown's original lure. While operating from the island as a privateer against Spanish shipping, Aury found a number of slaves among
his prizes. He did not need them, the revolutionaries in Mexico were
definitely opposed to slavery; the only other way to dispose of them
was to import them into Louisiana in spite of the abolition of the slave
trade. Aury opted for the last and shipped the blacks overland to the
Sabine and on to Alexandria, to an eager market.[72] Where slaves had
been a nuisance to Aury, however, they meant profit to Laffite. Snake
Island sat outside the border of the United States, and Mexico was in
turmoil, meaning that neither jurisdiction could threaten him, yet
Campeachy lay close enough to Louisiana that the distance to his buyers was not prohibitive. Moreover, rather than risk his own skin by
importing the slaves into Louisiana—for which penalties up to death
awaited—he could simply establish a slave mart there and let the
Louisiana buyers come to him.

It worked perfectly. The very month that he occupied the island,
Laffite brought in two prizes with 287 slaves, and by August the collector of customs in New Orleans complained of "the most shameful
violations of the slave act" by the Laffites and, worse, that "a great proportion of the population are disposed to countenance them." Laffite
built a large barracks for the slaves on the west bank of the Sabine, by
the fall filled with more than 650 of them, and left all risk for smuggling the blacks into Louisiana to the planters "whose eagerness to
procure them will induce them to run every hazard." Men went to
Campeachy or the Sabine barracks with large sums of cash to buy
slaves for themselves and others in what the collector called "an
extended and organized system of enterprise, of ingenuity, of indefatigability, and of audacity," and despite the occasional successes of revenue cutters in capturing small boatloads of contraband slaves, the
impact was minuscule.[73]

If enterprise, ingenuity, indefatigability, and audacity were what it required, then the business ideally suited the temperament of the Bowie brothers. They must have known at least in a general way about the slave smuggling by Laffite from Barataria in earlier years, and the arrival of the slaves sent by Aury to Alexandria was certainly common knowledge in the interior of Louisiana. Moreover, Rezin at least already had some limited experience in the business. While Laffite established himself at Galveztown, Rezin had helped a New Orleans trader who brought in sixty illegal slaves from Cuba with an elaborate ruse to recover the blacks when seized by authorities.[74] To young men of ambition who did not scruple at violating federal law, the profits could be considerable. In the more remote parishes a young adult male slave brought $650 or more, while in the New Orleans markets legal domestic slaves commanded as much as $1,500.[75]

The opportunity would not wait long before the government did something about Laffite, but while it lasted the potential was dazzling. Moreover, by the fall of 1819 the Bowies needed money, especially James. A hurricane that swept through the region that summer caused widespread damage, and on top of that a financial depression seized all of western Louisiana in 1819 and lasted for two years.[76] James felt the financial embarrassment keenly. In February he had bought a mulatto slave woman from Judge Jesse Andrus of the parish court at Opelousas for $1,200, giving his note due June 1. The date came and went with no payment, and when Andrus started demanding his money, Bowie refused to pay. Moreover, he used a technicality when Andrus got a summons for him to appear at Opelousas. He lived in Avoyelles Parish, Bowie argued, and was not subject to a St. Landry summons. Andrus continued trying to get Bowie to court throughout the summer of 1819, to no avail, and when James went off with Long it may in part have been in the hope of evading him, as well as in the expectation of finding something that would change his fortunes.[77]

All it took was Warren Hall. He had returned to Snake Island with Aury and decided to stay on, establishing himself at the west end of the island, where he soon became friendly with Laffite. Sometime in 1818 or 1819 Hall had made a brief visit to Rapides Parish, and while there saw his old friends James and Rezin Bowie and gave them all the details of Campeachy and of the opportunity awaiting. Hall more than sufficiently piqued their interest so that James—and possibly Rezin— later accompanied him on a visit to Galveztown, probably on the same trip that Hall and Gaines made as envoys for Long that summer of 1819. Hall introduced him to Laffite, and James and the smuggler struck up an instant friendship. He spent some time at Campeachy and learned the manner of Laffite's operation. Laffite sold slaves like any other merchandise, by weight, at one dollar a pound, the average healthy male costing $140. He had also a supply of weak and ill blacks that he could not sell and that he did not care for overmuch, but still he kept them rather than turn them out or simply kill them.

Campeachy was a bustling place in its way, something of a cross-roads for that milling jumble of shadowy figures whose past, present, and future aspirations for Texas and for profit kept them ever at the edge of the frontier awaiting the next scheme, the next opportunity. Besides Hall and Bradburn, there was the Irish sailor John McHenry, and J. Randal Jones of Nacogdoches, and a number of the earliest set-tlers of the Brazoria region of Texas, a few miles inland and to the west. Freebooters, filibusters, adventurers, and all the flotsam of the frontier passed this way, and while Laffite cordially entertained Bowie at Maison Rouge for several days, men like these filled his head with the stories of the huge forests, the vast fertile plains, the lost Spanish silver mines, and more of the riches of Texas there for the taking. Mexico would be independent from Spain soon, and Texas was far enough from Mexico City that men of enterprise could profit there with a minimum of governmental interference. It was something to ponder.

More immediately, though, the Bowies got a concession from Laffite. They, too, tendered a dollar a pound, but they also offered to buy the infirm blacks as well, though for a reduced price.[78] The deal struck, the Bowies returned to Louisiana, for there was still much to be done on the scheme and their own twist to put to it. They would buy directly from Laffite themselves, of that they were certain, and their brother John would join them in the venture. They had then to get the blacks to a market, and that presented a challenge. The rev-enue cutters made bringing the slaves by boat along the coast dangerous, especially since additional vessels had been assigned to the patrol just the past August.[79]

Fortunately the Bowies had some familiarity with the interior of western Louisiana. In May 1817 John and their father bought property and a sawmill on Bayou Nezpique, some thirty miles west of Opelousas, and they would have known that its sources lay only a few miles from the Calcasieu River.[80] That stream flowed southwest to Calcasieu Lake on the Gulf Coast just thirty miles from the Sabine. Thus the slaves could be marched from the Sabine to Calcasieu Lake, and from there taken upriver by boat. A two-day overland march from the stream could take them either to Opelousas or Alexandria, with the latter the preferred destination. But if they wanted, they could also take them to the mouth of Bayou Lafourche, a coastal passage from Galveztown of 250 miles—in a good westerly breeze a matter of only two days.[81] Once on the bayou, they could sail or row upstream to its meeting with the Mississippi at the French and Acadian settlement of La Fourche des Chitimachas in Ascension Parish. It was sixty miles above New Orleans and thirty miles below Baton Rouge, deep into Louisiana and close to buyers but a safe distance from state or federal agents, and Laffite had a man there named Martin who handled his smuggled imports and might help with slaves.[82]

However they got the blacks into the Louisiana interior, it was at this point that the Bowies' ingenuity changed the old pattern. They would not sell the slaves to planters themselves. Doing so ran them the risk of being caught and charged, with potentially deadly consequences, and also some planters could be reluctant to buy, knowing that the slaves would be confiscated if discovered. The Bowies wanted something that was as risk free as possible, and they hit on a brilliantly simple scheme: They would themselves turn the slaves in to a state or federal official as illegal imports, while concealing their own roles as the conveyors of the blacks. The slaves thus seized would be sold at auction, and the Bowies would outbid other buyers, secure in the knowledge that they could afford to do so because half of the purchase price would be paid to them for having turned in the slaves in the first place. If a slave sold at auction for $1,000, the Bowies really only paid a net of $500 after receiving their reward. Add the $140 they paid Laffite for the slave, and they had an investment of $640. But with the sale came a clear and legal title to the slave. The black had been effectively "laundered" and could now be sold anywhere to anyone without fear. If he went for $1,000 again, they had a clear profit of $360 on their investment, more than 50 percent.[83]

It only required that they find an official or officials who would not show much curiosity at the Bowies' seemingly remarkable civic spirit as they repeatedly turned in large numbers of slaves and then engaged successfully in the bidding at auction. Ironically Pierre Laffite himself had been a deputy U.S. marshal in Ascension Parish a few years earlier, charged with enforcing the slave trade laws.[84] No doubt he still had connections there, or one of his successors was sufficiently susceptible to bribery to ask no questions. Better yet, the Bowies' sister Martha had married Alexander Sterrett, whose brother James was an attorney in New Orleans and would soon be appointed customs officer for the Mississippi district.[85] If anything, the Bowies' connections were almost too easy.

The last remaining obstacle was cash. Laffite took no promissory notes. The Bowies needed real currency, and James for one was already dodging at least one creditor. The only way for him to raise his share of the investment capital was to sell his Bayou Boeuf plantation.[86] His need coincided with Stephen's, and on October 2 James sold his newly married brother the 480-acre parcel on which he then lived, along with the family of slaves purchased from their father— now increased to six—and the mulatto woman he had bought from Andrus the previous February. Almost a third of the sale price of $17,000 reflected the value of the slaves, while the balance showed what could be done with land speculation.[87] James had assembled his plantation from four separately purchased parcels at a total expense of $1,500. The synergy of building them into one larger tract, with improvements of a house and clearing the land, multiplied their value several times over. A few days later Bowie sold his remaining Bayou Boeuf land for an additional $500 in hand.[88] How much actual cash he got in the transactions is uncertain, for Stephen Bowie, barely twenty-two, would never be good with money and surely did not have anything like $17,000 in cash. More likely he borrowed a small part of the amount to hand over, and for the rest gave his notes. Certainly, even after the sale of all his Bayou Boeuf land, James Bowie did not have enough to pay Andrus the $1,200 still owed for the slave woman now sold to Stephen. He never would pay it, and a year later Andrus finally gave up and dismissed the suit.[89]

Nevertheless James put together enough for his share in buying the first group of forty slaves, about $1,850. Further, the brothers may have divided the responsibilities of the enterprise. John, who suffered the worst eyesight, stayed at home and helped with the disposal of the slaves, perhaps as far away as Mobile. Rezin went on one or two of the expeditions and thereafter disposed of more of the blacks in Mississippi.[90] James himself did the most dangerous work of convoying the contrabands through the swamps and bayous, bringing them in lots of forty at a time, as many as one or two men could handle. Although the blacks were chained, Bowie found little need for fetters: The frightened Africans knew nothing of the country and had nowhere to go, while they were told enough of alligators, snakes, and hostile natives to know that safety, if not happiness, lay with the Bowies. On one trip a few slaves may have escaped, not to be found again, but for the rest James Bowie felt secure that they would not run.[91] He even told Laffite on one of his visits to Campeachy that he rarely lost a slave because he was armed and he knew they feared him. Instilling fear in others was something James Bowie did with ease.[92]

Over the ensuing months in 1819 and early 1820, James, and sometimes Rezin, made at least four trips to Campeachy or the Sabine barracks, smuggling a total of as many as 180 or more slaves in the process. James formed more close friendships with a few of Laffite's men and reportedly became somewhat close with Laffite himself, one member of the commune even believing that the two clean-shaven men looked alike.[93] He may have seen the remaining damage from the late-summer hurricane in 1818 that wrecked Campeachy, forcing him to meet Laffite in his impromptu residence on an anchored brig while the village was rebuilt. He would have missed one important visitor at the smuggler's headquarters, though. George Graham, in addition to being president of the Washington branch of the Bank of the United States, had also until recently been interim secretary of war for President James Monroe. In the fall of 1818 he came to Galveztown as part of a mission to keep an eye on the activities of Americans in Texas, as well as to persuade Laffite to abandon his Campeachy enterprises. He saw for himself that men like Bowie were buying slaves from Laffite, made an official protest, and secured Laffite's disingenuous promise to give up the place in a few months.[94]

In fact Laffite remained until early 1821, but the Bowies ceased their involvement months earlier. By John Bowie's reckoning they made $65,000 from their slave smuggling. Divided three ways between James, Rezin, and John, that meant more than $21,000 apiece. If Stephen participated, or if the Bowie blood ran true to form and they cut him in, the share of each would still have been over $16,000. Yet the numbers may be deceptive, for chances are that while they had to pay cash to buy the slaves at auction themselves—plus any bribe or cut required by Sterrett and others—their own buyers were very likely to pay with a combination of cash and promissory notes, especially in a depressed economy. Thus they may only have realized a fraction of that $65,000 immediately, and some of the balance they probably never got, for James Bowie was not the only man in Louisiana to renege on a note. Whatever they actually realized, John Bowie quite candidly admitted that they "soon spent all our earnings."[95]

They could have stayed at the business longer, but other imperatives drew them away. John had political ambitions, and being a smuggler would hardly advance them. Rezin, too, had some political interests, and his growing plantations and community station required his complete attention at home. Stephen, if he was ever involved more than peripherally, had a daughter by the summer of 1820, and now a plantation of his own to manage. Only James was free of ties and obligations. The slave business had brought some travel and adventure, and certainly some profit, even if he had to wait for much of it. It also showed him a species of crime easy on the conscience because it left no victim yet still offered considerable profit. He stole from no one when he smuggled slaves. The federal government profited, the planters who needed slaves got a good product at fair market price, and he made money in the bargain.

As for the law, if the breaking of it ever bothered him at all, he could always comfort himself that many thought it a bad law in the first place. But then, as evidenced by his evasion of the debt to Jesse Andrus, conscience in his business dealings—so long as they were not with family or friends—did not overburden James Bowie. Moreover, the fact that he chose to default and then renege on a debt to a judge revealed that he was none too thoughtful either. When he saw an opportunity, he lunged at it, stopping neither for careful reflection and planning nor for consideration of consequences. Where it concerned making money, he showed even at this age that he mirrored Tocqueville's observation of Southern men that "they feel that they are getting poor because they are not getting rich as quickly as their neighbors."[96] Impatience for profit was a part of his nature, and by the latter months of 1820 other opportunities at home in Louisiana called that dwarfed the slave business for a nature like his. Owning neither plantation nor home of his own now, at the age of twenty-four he was going to make a bid to be the biggest land speculator the Southwest had ever seen.[97]

CROCKETT

1815–1824

> *It now became necessary that I should tell the people something about the government, and an eternal sight of other things that I knowed nothing more about than I did about Latin.*

DAVID CROCKETT, 1834

David Crockett saw more than enough of death during his service with the volunteers to become quite inured to the sight of suffering, but those had been Creek, his enemies, on faraway battlefields. Within a few months, however, death called at his own modest cabin on Bean's Creek and would not be denied. That summer his wife, Polly, fell ill, her problem undiagnosed. It could have been any one of the several frontier killers like typhoid, cholera, or the so-called milksick, which came in epidemics. She did not die quickly but lingered and suffered somewhere between two days and two weeks before she expired. When Crockett buried her near the cabin, he laid to rest as well much of the romance within him. There would be another woman, perhaps several, but only Polly Finley seems to have captured his heart. He ever after held the memory of the death of his "tender and loving wife" as "the hardest trial which ever falls to the lot of man."¹

Crockett always displayed a fair pragmatism in his character. When he needed something, he went after it purposefully. When he decided as a young man that he needed a wife, he looked and tried until he found one. Now he was nearly thirty, with three small children, one of them still an infant, all of them needing care and he with a failing farm to work. In like circumstances men often broke up their families, placing the children in the homes of friends and relatives, but Crockett felt too attached to his sons John and William, and to baby Margaret. "I couldn't bear the thought of scattering my children," he confessed, showing once more that tender and sentimental side that often countered the image of the rough backwoodsman. He tried having his brother's family live with him, but he found that his sister-in-law did not favor his children as he thought she should. And he missed the company of a wife for himself. Nothing would do but that he should find another.

Not far from Bean's Creek, Crockett knew of a widow named Elizabeth Patton. She had lost her husband, James, to something much more dramatic than the milksick or cholera: The Creeks slaughtered him at Fort Mims. Losing a man in so traumatic a fashion as a massacre might have discouraged some women from marrying again, but Elizabeth had two small children to care for, besides which her luck with almost any second husband seemed bound to be better than with her first. To David she looked a likely prospect. Moreover, she owned her own farm, came of a comparatively affluent family, and was rumored to have eight hundred dollars in cash of her own, an almost princely sum in this backwoods settlement. An alliance with her promised to better not only his present condition but also to bode well for his future prospects and those of his children. In the winter and spring of 1816 he saw her occasionally at social affairs and started to apply the smile in his ruddy cheeks and all the winning manners that came so naturally to him. Yet it was more negotiation than courtship, and even when he began calling on her specifically to further his suit, he confessed that he was "as sly about it as a fox when he is going to rob a hen-roost." This was no courtship based on love but on present and future necessity. Perhaps Elizabeth Patton was not fooled. Crockett himself praised her industry, and she seemed quite sensible enough not only to see through any guise of ardent lover on his part but also to realize that he and she did share mutual needs and, as Crockett put it, "that we could do something for each other."[2]

"We soon bargained," said Crockett, and sometime in the summer of 1816 they went to the home of Elizabeth's father in Franklin County, where they engaged Pastor Richard Calloway to perform the ceremony. Nothing could have been less suited to the solemnity of the occasion, or offered a greater opportunity for Crockett's yarn spinning in future years, than the unscheduled entrance of a pig through the house door when the bride was supposed to enter for the ceremony. Unruffled, Crockett arose from his seat and calmly led the snorting animal back outside, as he did so addressing the beast: "Old Hook, from now on, *I'll* do the grunting around here."[3] Crockett soon there- after met his friend James Gowen, who teased him about Elizabeth's eight hundred dollars. Crockett only grinned and replied with the old folk saying that what was "sauce for the goose" became equally "sauce for the gander": What was hers was now his too.[4]

Crockett had plans for that "sauce," for the itch was on him to move again. His small Bean's Creek place was worth very little. Elizabeth's home would bring more, and with what they could get in selling the two, plus his gander's "nest egg," they could retire his debts and buy something more promising in new country. And there was plenty of new country waiting. During his travels in the Creek War he had seen much of fertile Alabama, and in the wake of the Creek defeat a lot of that territory now came open to settlement as public domain. With three friends he set out in the fall of 1816, across the Tennessee River, and south to Jones Valley, then on to the Black Warrior. The trip seemed cursed from the start. This was a warm season, and wherever they came near water they contended with myriad mosquitoes that bit men and animals. Scarcely were they across the Tennessee when one of Crockett's friends stepped too near a poisonous snake and took a bad bite that forced him to leave the party. Once on the Black Warrior, their horses wandered off in the night and David set off on foot in pursuit. All day he walked, wading creeks and swamps, and when he called at cabins along the way he got reports that his horses had passed by earlier, obviously intent on retracing their steps home.

Crockett believed he walked fifty miles that day, and in the end, exhausted, he gave up and stopped to pass the night with a settler's family. When he awoke the next morning he felt almost too sore to walk but set out to rejoin his companions, only to stop in the early afternoon, dizzy, nauseous, with terrible aches in his head and back. He found his rifle too heavy to carry and himself too weak to walk farther. He just lay down by the side of the trace and waited for the spell to pass. What he did not yet know was that one or more of those mosquitoes that bit him a few days before had left a poison of its own in his system—malaria. Two passing natives stopped and tried to give him some fruit, but he could not eat, and they told him in their frank way that he would surely die. Fearing the same thing himself, he made to stand again but found himself too disoriented, and only covered the mile or so back to a house with their aid. He spent the next several days in delirious fever, taking only warm tea, and then felt well enough to accompany two passing friends back to where he left his original companions. He found them healthy, but Crockett only got worse, and once more had to be left at a nearby house for care while his friends bought horses and returned home, carrying with them the news that he was dying. Behind them Crockett lay speechless in his fever for almost two weeks before it finally broke and he started to mend.

It was well into the fall when Elizabeth Crockett, resigned to being a widow once more, saw in her doorway an emaciated, hollow-eyed, almost unrecognizable man who proved to be her husband. Crockett discovered to his amusement that rumor said not only that he was dead but that two men actually testified to having seen him buried. "I know'd this was a whapper of a lie, as soon as I heard it," he ever after declared. Yet death had come close enough, and if he knew anything of malaria, he knew that it would come again. Moving his family could never make him escape that cold hand, but even as he slowly recovered he determined anew to take them from the farm that he found as "sickly" as himself.[5]

Crockett worked his place for nearly a year after his recovery, but his Alabama experience seems to have put him off returning there to look for cheap land. However, several months earlier the Chickasaw ceded some of their land in south central Tennessee to the United States, and by 1817 it lay open to settlers. Crockett left in the summer of 1817 to explore the region, only to suffer a recurrence of malaria that confined him for some time in the area of Shoal Creek. He recovered, and when he returned to Bean's Creek he announced to his family that they were moving, and at once. Early in the fall they made the eighty-mile trek westward, locating themselves on 160 acres at the head of Shoal Creek about three miles west of the tiny village of Lawrenceburg. In October, within weeks of their arrival, the state officially decreed the area Lawrence County, and about the same time the inhabitants sent a list of nominees for justices of the peace for the new jurisdiction to the legislature. Crockett's name was on the list, and

on November 25 the legislature confirmed him. It was to be his very
first public office.[6]

A certain logic suggested Crockett for the position, though a minor
one to be sure. Despite his protestations later that he knew nothing of
the law and had never read a page of a legal text, the fact remained
that he must have learned at least something from his father's service
as a constable and magistrate. Moreover, unlike most of his fellow citizens in the new county, Crockett could read and write with increasing
facility. And he came to the county with the added cachet of experience in the Creek War and a lieutenant's commission in the Franklin
County militia, given him in May 1815. Such things offered no guarantees of administrative ability, but they made him more than qualified to
be a justice of the peace.[7]

Something else may have encouraged the people of Lawrence to
entrust adjudication of their affairs to Crockett. For all the play and
sham about him as he told his stories and played the odd prank, there
was no true guile in the man. He was exactly as he seemed: He said
what he thought and meant what he said, a truly honest man. Years
later, as he looked back on these days, he took pride in the fact that
"my judgments were never appealed from, and if they had been they
would have stuck like wax." Of course, the judgments were not his
alone, but those of a court of magistrates like himself. Mostly they
decided in disputes about debt, such as how much one man owed
another in a questioned sale of pork. In his role as an individual justice
of the peace Crockett also certified bills of sale of slaves and sometimes
adjudicated damages in suits. Occasionally he had to issue a warrant to
the constable to bring a debtor before the magistrates, or for someone
accused of theft or changing the earmarks on another party's hogs. If
Crockett and his peers found such malefactors guilty, they could even
impose a sentence of whipping.[8]

His magisterial duties occupied little of Crockett's time, in fact, but
his entry into public awareness brought him to the attention of other
community leaders, who suggested in the winter of 1818 that the lieutenant from the Franklin County militia seek a higher office in the
militia being organized for Lawrence. State law required every county
to enlist one or more regiments and to elect their officers, and a man
named Matthews approached Crockett with the suggestion that he

announce himself as a candidate for major and at the same time support Matthews for the lieutenant-colonelcy. The proposition itself suggests that within only a few months of moving to the county, Crockett
enjoyed sufficient public esteem that his support was something worth
having. Crockett announced himself as a candidate, but when
Matthews held a cornhusking frolic to be attended by most of the settlers in the area, intending to do a little electioneering himself, the
Crockett family also came and David learned that he would be running against Matthews's son, who would obviously get his father's
support regardless of any promise made to Crockett. He confronted
Matthews with the story, and Matthews confessed, adding—as if it
would mitigate things in some way—that his boy "hated worse to run
against me than any man in the county." Typically Crockett resorted to
wit and irony for his revenge. He said that Matthews need have no
fear: Crockett would not run against his son but would run against *him*
for the colonelcy instead. With wonderful good grace, Matthews
offered his hand, they shook, and then both returned to the frolic to
make speeches—for Crockett probably his first public address. He
kept it short, announced why he had changed his sights from major to
colonel, and then quipped that "as I had the whole family to run
against any way, I was determined to levy on the head of the mess."[9]

    That speech typified virtually every electioneering address he would
make for the rest of his life—a bit of self-deprecation, a bit of prankish
frontier wit in which the tables were turned on an opponent, and a
modest protestation that he did not seek the office but rather that it
sought him. In fact his contest itself set a pattern, at least in the way
Crockett saw his public service. When someone else suggested or
offered that he should seek office, he accepted out of naive belief in the
integrity of the offer. Then he found himself deceived, but rather than
withdraw, he confronted his deceivers and exposed their actions in
defense of his own, winning the election by gaining the sympathy of
the voters.[10] Indeed, for the rest of his public life, Crockett perceived—
and presented—himself as the honest man put upon by deceivers, yet
who triumphed through virtue—his own and the public's.

    Crockett won the election, and on March 27, 1818, he took office as
lieutenant colonel of the Fifty-seventh Regiment of Militia. Though
Crockett held the commission no more than a year or so, the title of

"Colonel" stayed with him the rest of his life. Soon he added to it other titles in Lawrence County, including town commissioner of Lawrenceburg, court referee, and road commissioner. For the next two years he adjudicated in land disputes, took censuses of voters and tax-payers, oversaw the improvement of county roads, and performed whatever small tasks came the way of a rural functionary. None of it paid him much, nor did it take onerous amounts of time from the working of his farm, though he would hardly have minded if it had.

Despite his repeated attempts to find more and better land, David Crockett never had a taste for farming. The monotony of the plow and the soil wearied him. He needed the excitement of the hunt, whether for new land, deer and bear, or elective office. Interestingly in a man so guilelessly truthful with others, he seems never to have been honest with himself about his nature. To the end of his days he would keep seeking new land. It was always the *next* farm that he would content-edly settle and work, never the one he was on. In his defense, he was hardly unique. "An American will build a house in which to pass his old age and sell it before the roof is on," observed Tocqueville a few years later.

> He will plant a garden and rent it just as the trees are coming into bearing; he will clear a field and leave others to reap the harvest; he will take up a profes-sion and leave it, settle in one place and soon go off elsewhere with his changing desires. If his private business allows him a moment's relaxation, he will plunge at once into the whirlpool of politics. Then, if at the end of a year crammed with work he has a little spare leisure, his restless curiosity goes with him traveling up and down the vast territories of the United States. Thus he will travel five hundred miles in a few days as a distraction from his happi-ness.[11]

Crockett was simply one of a generation of men with a spirit in their feet telling them: "Go."

In Lawrence County, Crockett did at least try to drive some roots deeper than a plowshare. No doubt using Elizabeth's eight hundred dollars and borrowing more, he began building a kind of rural indus-trial complex on Shoal Creek, including a water-powered gristmill, a whiskey distillery, and another mill for grinding charcoal, sulfur, and saltpeter to manufacture gunpowder. The whole cost of the concern ran to nearly three thousand dollars, but the work proceeded slowly, hampered by his own short funds. By October 1820 he was already in debt, with the mill not yet in operation, but he expected to start grinding in the coming spring.[12] Moreover, by the measure of this backwoods community, Crockett, poor as he was, enjoyed some measure of prominence thanks to his several small offices and his very visible, if slowly growing, mills and distillery. In 1821 the voters would go to the polls to elect an assemblyman, representing Lawrence and neighboring Hickman Counties, to the legislature. Friends urged Crockett to seek the seat. Certainly he could use the income. Better yet, if he could not admit to himself that he was no farmer, he unhesitatingly confessed that he enjoyed the bustle of the hustings, entertaining the voters with his brand of wit and repartee, and the approbation of the voters when they gave him their ballots. He agreed to run and thereafter looked back on late 1820 as the moment when "I just now began to take a rise."[13]

Crockett had resigned his post as justice of the peace the year before, and in January 1821 he gave up his office as a town commissioner in Lawrenceburg, all to concentrate on his bid for the legislature.[14] In February he announced his candidacy but then left for almost three months, driving a herd of horses to North Carolina when he should have been at home electioneering. Only in late May or June did he return and begin to canvass the district. It was, he said, "a bran-fire new business to me," but regardless of his protestations he obviously relished taking the stump. "It now became necessary that I should tell the people something about the government, and an eternal sight of other things that I knowed nothing more about than I did about Latin."

He went first to Hickman County, and there learned that the hottest issue at the moment was a drive to move the county seat from Vernon to Centreville. If there was any doubt that Crockett possessed some of the skills of the politician, he soon showed himself gifted with a native grasp of the statesman's art when he avoided taking a stand on either side of the issue. In fact, through much of his early political career Crockett studiously avoided committing himself on most issues, and as he showed at the first big stump speaking meeting of the campaign, he even went so far as to declare himself utterly ignorant of anything connected with government.

People of the frontier mixed their politics with their fun, the two being inseparable in any case, since campaigning often afforded the best entertainment in the backwoods. Organizers announced a squirrel hunt on the Duck River in Hickman, a competition between Crockett's supporters and those backing his opponent, in which the side returning with fewer scalps had to pay for the general dinner and drink. Crockett himself put his gun to work, and at the end of the hunt his side counted the majority of pelts. They all gathered at Centreville for the festivities.

After the eating, but before the drinking got into full sway, the candidates spoke, and when Crockett rose he tried to present himself as a complete novice, notwithstanding that he had spoken at least once when campaigning for the militia commission in Lawrence. In fact he pretended that he did not want to speak at all, though he undoubtedly knew from the outset that this was the very purpose of the event. He well understood the prevailing ethic of American politics and easily adopted the disingenuous guise of the reluctant candidate. When he did stand to speak, he told the audience that he wanted their votes, and then began to expound on his position on the issues confronting them, when he either realized that he actually had nothing to say or more likely decided to continue declining to take any stand at all for fear of losing as many votes as he won. As he would do for years to come, he resorted to wit and stratagem to divert the crowd. He went silent "as bad as if my mouth had been jam'd and cram'd chock full of dry mush." The voters stared at him in wide-eyed, open-mouthed wonder as he struggled to speak. Finally he told them his problem. He felt like the man found thumping the top of a barrel, who said there had been some cider in it a few days before, and he was trying to see if any remained but couldn't get to it. Well, there had been a "little bit of a speech" in him a few days earlier, said Crockett, but now he could not seem to get to it.

The ruse worked perfectly. The crowd roared with laughter, and that gave him confidence to go on to other rough stories that only won the listeners even more. Knowing that his opponent would get to speak after him, though, and worried that the man would show up the complete lack of substance in his speech, Crockett concluded by saying that he felt keenly thirsty and suggested that the voters join him at the whiskey stand. Most of them did, leaving his opponent speaking to a largely empty field while Crockett continued his storytelling at the liquor barrel. In the entire episode Crockett sold *himself* to the voters, while never risking alienating one of them with an unwelcome opinion on the subject of the county seat.

The next day, Sunday, Crockett went to Vernon, whose residents felt rather differently on the courthouse issue than did his audience in Centreville. Again he simply dodged. "I found I could get either party by agreeing with them," he said, "but I told them I didn't know whether it would be right or not, and so couldn't promise either way." When asked to speak the following day along with candidates for Congress and the governorship, Crockett had to agree, but though he later claimed that his nerves nearly got the best of him, in fact he already knew exactly what to do. The candidates for the bigger offices spoke first, and at considerable length, so that when it came time for the legislative aspirants to make their mark, the crowd had grown restive and jaded. Crockett sensed their mood and gave a repeat of his Centreville performance. He said not a syllable about politics but simply told amusing stories, then quickly finished. "I found I was safe in those parts," he said, and never bothered to campaign in Hickman County again.[15]

Crockett learned more than just how to duck the issues in his earliest stump meetings. He also became acquainted for the first time with leaders of real prominence. At the Vernon meeting he met William Carroll and Edward Ward, both seeking the governorship. Each stood close to Jackson, though Old Hickory and Carroll were especially so, and Crockett would have found the latter especially to his liking. Ward lived the life of an aristocrat, but Carroll came of modest antecedents and played them for all they were worth in his campaign. He had made rather than inherited his money, he had fought in the Creek War, and he knew how not to assume airs when face to face with the common man. In short, he was Crockett, only with a higher reach. Moreover, in 1821 the common man was beginning his rise, like Crockett himself, as an expanding, newly franchised electorate reacted against the aristocratic and moneyed classes that had dominated state houses and Washington alike until then. Carroll and Crockett were a part of the same phenomenon, as hundreds of thousands of new voters across the South and Southwest sought candidates like themselves.

When voters went to the polls in August, they gave Crockett a two-to-one majority against his forgotten opponent. That fall, early in September, he set out for Murfreesboro, then the state capital. The road took him east first to Pulaski, in neighboring Giles County, where he met a man nine years his junior whom he already knew as an attorney occasionally practicing in Lawrence County. James Knox Polk was seemingly everything that Crockett was not. He came of a good family, had a university education, and boasted a prosperous practice. The two decided to ride together to Murfreesboro, as Polk had secured appointment as clerk to the state senate, and possibly another assemblyman from Giles accompanied them. Along the way Polk, a true politician with a considerable command of issues and current affairs, expressed to Crockett an opinion that the coming session of the legislature might likely make some considerable changes in the state's judiciary. The comment took Crockett by surprise. "Now so help me God," he later said, "I knew no more what a 'radical change' and a 'judiciary' meant than my horse, but looking straight into Mr. Polk's face as though I understood all about it, I replied, 'I presume so.'" That said, he took pains to keep his distance from Polk for fear he would be forced to reveal his ignorance, or so he claimed. In fact he may have told the story later chiefly to use as a metaphor for his quite genuine departure from Polk on substantive issues a few years later.[16]

David Crockett took his seat in an elected assembly for the first time on September 17, 1821, and the next day found himself assigned to the Committee of Propositions and Grievances, one of the glamorless minor assignments that went to freshmen legislators. He would make little impression in the ensuing weeks of the session, but when he cast his votes he finally revealed some bedrock policy beliefs, and not surprisingly they proved to be very close to home. A week after taking his seat he cast his first vote in favor of relieving delinquent citizens in his region from owing heavy penalties for overdue property taxes. Three days later, and despite all his protestations of ignorance of the law and government, he introduced a preamble and resolutions to reform the manner of issuing land-grant surveys in order to prevent a few men from monopolizing the best property, and in the following weeks carefully guided it into the form of a bill in both House and Senate that eventually became law. However much the pose of bumpkin suited his purpose when seeking votes from those who were truly ignorant of the forms of governing—and suspicious of those who knew too much—he revealed a ready grasp of parliamentary procedure. At the same time, by his bill and his votes he showed that making public land available to the poor like himself was already a firmly rooted idea with him when he took office. Like his honesty and frank manner, and his inborn views as a poor white, such a position, once adopted, he could never yield.

In fact Crockett almost certainly came to Murfreesboro with his land reform resolutions already well thought out and perhaps even drafted, evidence that despite his claim that he had never read a newspaper, he certainly knew something of public affairs. The public lands in western Tennessee had been an issue for some years, actually dating back to the time when the state itself belonged to North Carolina. During the Revolution the Old North State incurred heavy debts and afterward issued land warrants to its veterans to reward them for their service. In ceding Tennessee to the United States, North Carolina required that all those warrants be honored when presented. In 1806, with Tennessee now a state, Congress started meeting those warrants in its eastern half, reserving the western part where Crockett lived as public domain. But the warrants outstripped the available land in the east, and that, combined with fraud and forgery, quickly made a confused mess of affairs. Finally the Congress opened the west, too, to satisfy the warrants. By this time, however, quite a number of squatters already lived on some of this land, with improvements made at their own expense, yet a warrant holder could present his claim, have it surveyed on the squatter's land, and order his eviction.

Crockett was equally interested in occupancy claims, for under old law in Tennessee if a man lived without disturbance as a squatter on a claim for seven years, he could declare it his if he could provide any sort of legal claim, such as a bill of sale, even if the seller himself had not owned proper title. In 1816 the state supreme court ruled that the occupant must have an unbroken chain of pure title back to the original grant, but in 1819 the legislature overrode that. Crockett himself tried to acquire three hundred acres in 1820 when he bought two occupants' claims in Lawrence County, and in this session he must have watched with keen interest as the state supreme court reviewed the legislature's 1819 action, early in 1822 deciding in favor of the rights of the occupant.[17] Ironically David Crockett never felt much attachment to any of his several smallholdings, and left them seemingly without reservation, but the idea of anyone being forcibly removed from property, even if it was not theirs, aroused his ire. His bill to reform surveying would be only his first volley at land practices.[18]

Scarcely did Crockett commence his term at the Fourteenth General Assembly before he got devastating news from Lawrence County. His mill was finally in operation on Shoal Creek, though with Crockett so much absent either hunting, electioneering, or as now in the legislature, Elizabeth Crockett oversaw most of the real work. Being a large woman, she could handle the task, and having a good business sense, she managed the enterprise better than her husband anyhow. But now late summer storms swelled the banks of the Tennessee River and its tributaries, including Shoal Creek, and in a sudden flash flood, the waters carried away both the grist- and powder mills, leaving only part of his dam, the millrace, and the twenty-by-twenty-four-foot log house where the Crocketts lived.[19] The message from Elizabeth, when Crockett received it, stunned him. "I may say," he recalled, "that the misfortune just made a complete mash of me." With his gristmill gone, he could not even continue to operate the distillery, which depended on corn from the mill.

On September 29 he secured a leave of absence from the legislature and hurried back to Lawrence to survey the damage, but there was nothing to be done. Elizabeth pragmatically told him they should simply settle their debts as best they could from their surviving property and start over. Debt was an old acquaintance to Crockett, of course, but his rigid innate honesty would not let him do as so many others in his situation had done for generations. He could not simply pack his family and what money he had and move on. To Crockett any debt became a matter of honor. When he left his former home in Jefferson County in 1811 and moved west, Crockett owed John Jacobs one dollar, yet throughout the ensuing years he never forgot that obligation.

In the spring of 1821, when he took that string of horses to North Carolina for sale before commencing his stump campaign, Crockett and the herd passed through Jefferson, and he stopped at the Jacobs house on Mossy Creek. Ten years had passed, but after introducing himself to Mrs. Jacobs, he gave her a silver dollar, in spite of her efforts to refuse the money. "I owed it and you have got to take it," he told her.[20] Now he would do the same. He would sell his remaining property and use the proceeds to redeem the debts left by the mill. He believed it "better to keep a good conscience with an empty purse, than to get a bad opinion of myself."[21] David Crockett always valued that "good opinion" of himself highly, sometimes above all other things, regardless of the personal cost.

Crockett returned to Murfreesboro on October 9 to finish out the session, and despite his anguish over his misfortune, he remained active and engaged. Even before going home to Lawrence, he voted for Carroll in the legislature's ballot for the governorship, and Crockett's support may in some way indicate that he also favored the movement to nominate Jackson for the presidency in 1824, since Carroll promoted Old Hickory's candidacy. He also joined other Carroll supporters in voting to call a constitutional convention. Though it failed, consistently thereafter he supported every successive attempt, his hope no doubt being that among other reforms, the underrepresented western half of the state would receive a proper apportionment of assemblymen, and that tax reform would mean levies on the value of land rather than on simple acreage. A revised constitution might also attempt to deal with the matter of vacant lands, though the decision on that issue lay chiefly in Washington.

In his day-to-day votes on the assembly floor, Crockett gave little real indication of being either a party or a policy man, though whatever position he took, whether against the suppression of gambling or in opposition to divorce, he assumed it forcefully. And he did show that he could take a position on an issue when it no longer stood to affect him. He actually introduced a bill to define the boundaries of Hickman County and permanently fix the county seat in Vernon, and months later presented a petition from the citizens of Hickman to the same end. The legislature decided differently, voting to move the seat to Centreville, but Crockett emerged from the ballot a winner in both camps. He had finally sided with Vernon, appeasing its supporters, but the verdict of the legislature made Centreville happy and inclined not to hold his opposition against him. Had Vernon won with his support, he might have lost his Centreville following entirely.[22]

The first session of the Fourteenth General Assembly adjourned on November 17, and Crockett could look back on his service in it with some pleasure. For a freshman assemblyman he had been active and outspoken, and if he took with him any agenda at all, he certainly made efforts to represent the interests of men like himself, the poor white settlers of western Tennessee. Indeed, as a result of that, he encountered in Murfreesboro probably for the first time in his life a substantial and considered condescension from the more moneyed and propertied men of central Tennessee. He probably always bore something of a grudge against the affluent, the educated, the aristocrats from the old established families, the kind of men who had run state and local government in the United States for a generation. These were the prejudices of his class, and he would have been unusual not to share them. The behavior of some of the other legislators in the assembly only reinforced his feelings.

No nickname or sobriquet seems to have applied itself to Crockett as yet, and in his own transactions he invariably signed himself as "David," a small formality at best, but perhaps a sign that he could stand on his dignity as well as the next man, regardless of his station in life. Anyone who ridiculed that station invited Crockett's wrath or, worse, his wit. In debate one day Crockett made his point and sat down, only to see James C. Mitchell, a well-to-do lawyer from McMinn County, arise to speak in opposition. In doing so he referred to Crockett not by name but rather as "the gentleman from the cane," meaning the sparsely settled hardscrabble canebreak country of western Tennessee. Mitchell intended nothing at all by the remark, but when others in the house chuckled at the reference, Crockett saw in it a slur on the lowly station of himself and his constituents, and immediately his hackles rose. He tried but failed to pursue the point in debate, and then confronted Mitchell outside the chamber and demanded an apology. Mitchell earnestly denied any wish to insult or offend Crockett. He had simply referred to Crockett as being from the cane in the way he would refer to another member as being from the mountains,

or from across the Tennessee, but the explanation did not erase
Crockett's wounded pride. He knew his poverty, the rudeness of his
life, and his own unpolished speech and manners. Indeed, he made
capital of them, taking an almost aggressive pride in the fact that however modest his attainments, they came without benefit of name or
wealth but entirely from his own hard work. Yet beneath that veneer
of pride he concealed a lifelong embarrassment and frustration, and a
compelling desire to be accepted as a gentleman—in short, to rise very
close to the station of those whom he appeared to despise. It was the
eternal frustration of the poor, and in Crockett it left a sensitive spot so
touchy that any irritation, real or imagined, inevitably begged a
response.

In the assembly hall Crockett dressed in what he had, nothing better than homespun shirt and trousers, and perhaps a leather hunting
jacket or at best a modest woolen coat. Mitchell and most of the more
affluent members, by contrast, dressed like lawyers, in pantaloons or
knee breeches, waistcoats, cutaway coats, and shirts with fancy cuffs
and cotton ruffles at their collars. The contrast between them and the
poorer members like Crockett was stark enough to embarrass without
words. Following his encounter with Mitchell, Crockett happened on
a lost ruffle dropped in the street in Murfreesboro. It matched the style
worn by Mitchell almost exactly, and Crockett's revenge quickly came
to mind. The next time Mitchell spoke in the House, Crockett arose
immediately afterward. At his neck he wore the ruffle, and the stark
contrast of the stylish bit of foppery topping his rough country garb
sent the assembly into an uproar of laughter. Mitchell himself simply
left the room, and thereafter Crockett eschewed the ruffle but accepted
the sobriquet of "the gentleman from the cane" as a badge of honor for
himself and his rude backwoods constituents.[23]

If Crockett relished his victory over Mitchell, the thrill dissipated
quickly enough when he returned to Lawrence County and the reality
of having to start his home all over again. Joined by his son John
Wesley and a neighbor, he started off west to look for yet another
place to make yet another new start. During his session in the legislature Crockett had helped give birth to new counties in the western
part of the state, including massive Carroll County, extending from the
Tennessee to the Mississippi. Now he rode nearly 150 miles northwest

to the Rutherford fork of the Obion River, and there he saw a patch of ground that looked likely. No neighbors would crowd him, the nearest being seven miles distant. He found the wilderness so untouched that he had to fell trees across some of the swollen creeks in order to cross by holding fast to the trunk while he waded. Ten years before, it had been a normal deep forest, but the massive New Madrid earthquakes of 1811–13 inundated the area, creating Reelfoot Lake and making some of the ground impassable. Yet the country all around teemed with game, and he could not resist turning his exploration for land into a hunting trip.

It was country made for Crockett. Here in this wilderness there were no aristocrats, and wealth meant nothing. Moreover, this was the environment in which his natural gifts flourished. Here *he* felt like an aristocrat. With the exception of his stiff pride in spite of his poverty, Crockett took nothing so seriously as he did his prowess at hunting. Indeed, he showed considerable particularity just in the manner of his dress for the hunt. He wore a linsey-woolsey hunting shirt, dyed a faded brown by soaking in boiled nutshells. Moccasins on his feet quieted his tread, while leggings above them kept his trousers from flapping or catching on brush as he silently stalked prey. At his belt he wore everything that he needed, and assigned a specific place for each article. A tomahawk rested on his left hip, while a sheathed butcher knife balanced it on the other, within easy grasp for his right hand. His bullet pouch and powder horn hung from straps over his left shoulder, dangling beside the knife. Crockett took great care to make certain that no article could get in the way of speedy access to any of the others.

About his actual weapons "the gentleman from the cane" showed just as much particularity. He wanted no ornamentation, no brass or silver inlays on the stock of his rifle, for such things could cause an unwelcome reflection of sunlight that might spook game. As for the knife, he set great store by it. "A single bullet may settle up a buck or bear into a right sort of fix to finish him with a 'butcher' and give no sign, as the rifle does by crack and smoke, of your whereabouts," he explained, "especially if some skulking red-skin or vagabond should be upon your tracks for mischief." The knife, he averred, "did its work as noiselessly and surely, as well as being a mighty saver of lead and powder."[24]

However else he might fail in life, on the hunt he was always a success. In fact his entry into politics was only a sort of extension of his ventures into the wilderness, for bagging an office was in its way a hunt, just like bagging a bear. Moreover, Crockett did not walk alone in his endless stalks in the woods and the ever greater number of his kills on this and other trips. A whole generation of poor men like him at the edge of the frontier hunted continually, not just for food but for the satisfaction, the validation, of the kill. They lived in a society with no established aristocracy, in which skill at the craft of the frontier established its own hierarchy—with no skill more decisive than hunting. The man who killed the most deer or bear or wolves achieved a station above his peers. Men boasted of taking staggering numbers of animals, killed solely for the sake of the killing and its enhancement of their social standing.

In fact Crockett and the hunters were not unlike the land speculators. Each sought to exploit the wilderness for their own betterment. A speculator rose by using stealth to capture more land than his peers, just as Crockett's harvest of the wildlife of the forests elevated his prestige. One bested other men and the government; the other conquered nature. The land mattered no more to a speculator, who would never live on it, than the deer and bear meat did to Crockett, who could never eat all that he killed. The United States of the time was a nation at war, pitting the common man against the forces of privilege and preferment on the one hand and the resources of the continent on the other. With game as with land, enough to live on was not enough. With his extensive kills Crockett seemed to need more than just enough, for each one reaffirmed his prowess, and that in turn assured his sense of himself as a man. When he looked through the cloud of smoke from his rifle and saw the deer fall in the glade or the bear from a tree, he knew he was a success. It is just possible that for Crockett the moment of the kill erased for a few minutes the memory of poverty, misfortune, debt, and all his life's failures, whether by chance or his own doing. If so, then like a narcotic the hunt briefly erased memories of what he preferred to forget, yet as with a narcotic the effect did not last and had to be repeated again and again. Winning an election gave the same thrill, and the same temporary relief, and better yet, on the hustings Crockett could see the approval in the faces and the votes of the crowd. Crockett—like the hundreds of thousands in his wake—needed the conquest itself and for its own sake in order to feel whole.[25]

In his trek in the Obion country, Crockett killed deer and elk in abundance, leaving them behind to be collected later as he continued his stalk. Though adept with his rifle, his success lay more in his woodcraft than his accuracy, for the best hunter got close enough to his game without detection that even an indifferent shot must strike home.[26] So enamored was Crockett of this wilderness experience that he stayed through the winter, though such may have been his intent from the time he left Lawrence County. When he finished with his initial hunt, he returned to the land he liked and began building a cabin and clearing fields, though he held no title to the property. He would simply be an occupant for the time being, hoping in time to acquire title either through purchase or simply by squatting long enough. He planted corn in his field but found he had no time to enclose it with a rail fence—though there seemed plenty of time for more hunting. "During that spring I killed ten bears, and a great abundance of deer," he later recalled. Indeed, for the rest of his life he exhibited a prodigious memory of almost every kill: where and when and what he shot. While speculators made tavern boasts of their extensive titles, Crockett expounded the tally of his kills.[27]

Finally he had no choice but to leave this scene of his success and return to the Lawrence of debt and failure. In his absence the creditors had set in motion that relentless and universal litigation found all across the spreading American West. He must have paid some of his accounts beforehand, but still nearly three hundred dollars in outstanding suits awaited him, and though he challenged a few, the court found in favor of the creditors on most.[28] In the end the court ordered his land seized and sold to satisfy the judgments, adding humiliation to failure. Perhaps, then, Crockett felt relieved on his return to Lawrence to find a summons to a special session of the legislature called by Governor Carroll. That, at least, would take him from this scene of woe and back to Murfreesboro on July 22, when the session convened.

Once again in the capital, Crockett revealed that he took the business of being a representative seriously, and if he did not stand out among his peers, certainly he should have given his constituents every satisfaction. Much of the session was spent on minor matters, boundary issues and the like, and Crockett cast his vote time after time in favor of relief for the poor like himself, even on a bill he introduced to provide relief for a free black. He consistently favored reform of abuse, whether in his support of the continuing—but unsuccessful—attempts to call a constitutional convention or in his opposition to a bill that would have reversed the prohibition of fees paid to justices of the peace for certain actions. He had seen the latter abuse in action before he became himself a justice of the peace. The victims called it "fee-grabbing," and so far as Crockett was concerned "there is no evil so great in society—among the poor people—as the management and intrigue of meddling justices and dirty constables."[29]

The reform Crockett really wanted to see related to the land, of course. In fact Carroll called this special session in part to push for an extension of the deadline for holders of the old North Carolina warrants to present their claims, but Crockett vigorously opposed such a measure and only voted for it in the end after the Senate passed the extension and it became evident that the House must follow. His motive was transparent, of course. Any North Carolina warrant disallowed because of a passed deadline meant that much more western Tennessee land available to poor squatters like himself by their occupancy claims. It seems not to have occurred to him that the warrant holder might also be a poor man in need of cheap land, or else his view of the plight of the poor did not extend beyond himself and Tennesseans like him. This state's land, like its game, was foremost for Tennesseans to capitalize on. North Carolina should take care of its own.

If there was any doubt of this, his stand for the August 21 report of the education committee clearly defined his position. The committee proposed that the legislature call on the state's congressional delegation in Washington to press for an act giving this assembly power to sell vacant land in the eastern half of the state to raise money for education. It was not, of course, the education that interested him, for he may already have felt suspicious of state-supported schools and colleges. He wanted to see that vacant land put on the market, at bargain prices, for the poor and landless, and he happily voted along with the majority for the resolution, though nothing came of it. Interestingly

enough, Crockett also supported the use of state funds to encourage
the establishment of ironworks and manufacturing concerns. Having
tried his hand at industry in a small way, it seemed consistent to him
that government should assist the small rural manufacturer. Moreover,
given the nature of the mineral deposits in Tennessee, most of the
ironworks would be in his part of the state.[30]

As soon as the session adjourned on August 24, Crockett went back
to Lawrence and moved his family to the new Obion claim. He had
cleared about twenty-five acres or less, now growing corn, and the
family moved into a typical "dogtrot" house, two sixteen-by-eighteen-
foot hewn-poplar-log cabins connected by an eight-foot open pas-
sageway in the center. A fireplace and chimney of branches and twigs
plastered with mud heated each cabin, and about forty feet south of
the house he had dug a shallow well. In time he would cover the logs
with split-log siding and lay a wooden floor inside the living cabin,
but there would be little more beautification than that. Given time, he
would also plant a few dozen peach trees and some apples in a small
orchard.[31]

Once there, he stayed only long enough to harvest the corn remaining that had not been ruined by deer, then left once more to roam the
woods on what now became for him an annual fall hunt. He hunted
until Christmas, when he ran out of powder for his flintlock rifle, then
nearly froze to death crossing icy expanses of water trying to reach
more powder to continue the hunt.[32]

Once more he was gone so long Elizabeth believed him dead, and
by now she must have begun to wonder if, with her husband's
repeated lengthy absences, he had married her only to have someone
to look after his children. Certainly a wife was a necessity for a frontiersman, but increasingly it appeared that to Crockett, Elizabeth was
only that.

He kept right on hunting through the winter, proud that he kept his
family supplied with meat, and proud as well of all those long-remem-
bered kills.[33] He also kept his sights polished for any wolves he came
across, for the county paid a three-dollar bounty for a wolf pelt. That
winter of 1823 those bounties and what he got for his deer and bear
hides was the only money Crockett earned. He had to take them all
the way to Jackson, nearly forty miles south, and there he bought the

few supplies like coffee and sugar, and of course powder and lead, that
he could not harvest from the land in Carroll. There he could also
"take a horn" occasionally, even meeting old friends from his time in
the Creek War and reliving with them stories of earlier days. At least
once Crockett even let the drink, or the frustration of his poverty, or
some other provocation get the better of his usually pacific nature, and
he struck a man, earning an indictment for simple assault.[34]

Happily politics saved him from anything worse, for on a February
1823 trip to Jackson he spent an evening in a tavern with Jackson's
nephew by marriage, Dr. William E. Butler, and local politicos Maj.
Joseph Lynn and Duncan McIver. Despite their conviviality with one
another, each of the three intended to seek the seat in the legislature for
the new county, and during the ensuing conversation someone jokingly
suggested to Crockett that he ought to run as well. Living a good two
days from Jackson or any other settlement, Crockett said the idea was
preposterous and dismissed it, apparently without further thought. But
a few weeks later at home, a passerby showed him an issue of the new
Jackson Pioneer, containing an announcement of his candidacy.

It may have been accident or, as Crockett later maintained, a prank
at his expense. He may even have been behind it himself but unwilling
to tell Elizabeth that he wanted to leave yet again for months at a time
for politicking. He expressed chagrin, whether real or pretended, at
seeing his name in the paper, and announced that he would not be
made fun of. Whoever was responsible for this, Crockett told his wife,
he would make the man pay. No one would have fun with his name at
his expense. He would go to Jackson and campaign and turn the jest
around on its anonymous author by winning the election. Once again
David Crockett was the reluctant candidate. He neither sought nor
wanted the office. It had come looking for him, in the guise of deceit
and ridicule. Now he must win it to repudiate a trickster and defend
his honor.[35]

His campaign proved to be a virtual repeat of his first bid for office,
for, having found a winning formula for capturing votes, Crockett was
sensible enough not to change it. He capitalized on both his local reputation as a bear hunter and the small notoriety given his "gentleman
from the cane" sobriquet, both of which sat well with these rough voters.
His three opponents soon agreed that only one should oppose him,

and Butler got the nod, in part because even Crockett confessed that he was clever, and almost certainly because his family connection to Jackson gave him considerable clout. At the first opportunity, Crockett accosted Butler at a stump meeting for the district congressional candidates and, quite conscious of the crowd listening to him, good-naturedly warned the doctor how he would use him in the canvass. He threatened to wear a special hunting shirt with two ludicrously big pockets, one for twists of tobacco and the other for a jug of spirits, and he would give a chew from one and a drink from the other to every man he met, at the same time asking for his vote.[36] Moreover, to combat Butler's clear advantage in funds, Crockett promised to depopulate the forests of Obion of their wolves to sell their pelts, if he had to, to buy his whiskey and tobacco. Crockett left Butler slightly bemused, and the crowd of onlookers thoroughly amused.

Once the electioneering commenced in earnest, Crockett aimed more of his tricks at Butler. When the doctor invited David to his home in Jackson for a small frolic after one of their debates, Crockett made an elaborate point of leaping from the floor to a chair without stepping on the carpet, and kept his feet on the chair rungs while sitting rather than touch them to the rug. If any present missed the point, he soon gave it to them in a speech chiding Butler for the fact that he walked on finer materials than the wives and daughters of the poor voters could afford to wear. And during a series of meetings in which both candidates gave substantially the same address time after time, Crockett arose to speak first one day and took advantage of his keen ear for mimicry and his retentive memory to give Butler's talk almost word for word, effectively rendering the doctor speechless.[37]

Crockett certainly did not know it, but his electioneering practices, especially as he and others remembered them in later years, unconsciously cast him firmly in the mold of an ancient folk hero, the so-called Trickster. The character—dating back to the semimythical Merlin and beyond in Western culture—had his counterparts in other societies, including among the native populations of America. He was an outward buffoon, yet inwardly calculating for effect. He played outlandish pranks, some of them mean, and took pleasure in fooling others,

though he seemed often to be easily fooled himself. He knew good
from evil, could do both at will, yet at times seemed wittingly or
unwittingly to trust his fortunes to the dictates of others. He both
molded events and lived as the hostage of fortune. Above all he combined a mischievous nature with an unbending sense of justice, and
saw himself—and wanted others to see him—as an example to the
common people. He was never entirely assimilated into society, but
always on its edges, where freedom from restraint gave scope to his
extrahuman appetites.[38] Scores of real and mythologized folk heroes
through the ages fit that mold, each slightly sculpted to fit the culture
of the moment, and each generally needing only a popular movement
of some sort among the lowly masses to come to the fore. In 1823
Americans had no folk heroes as yet. They were too new a people,
their only household gods the Founding Fathers, men too lofty and
remote to become the stuff of legend. But the common man was rising
now, and he would want one of his own for an icon. The recently
deceased Daniel Boone nearly fit the requirement, yet he was too con-
templative, brave but quiet, with none of the roughness and out-
landishness, tinged with violence, that resonated with the common
folk. They admired Boone, but he lacked the stuff of a human talis-
man.[39] The ancestral practices of their culture for millennia, and seemingly human instinct itself, would compel them when the time came to
look for the Trickster. And out in West Tennessee a man pranked and
played and spread his little mayhem, all the while pressing for the freedom of his kind, even as he acted as the prisoner of the prejudices and
fears of his class. In David Crockett, though yet he knew it not, there
were the makings of a folk hero.

When two more late entries came into the legislative race, they only
took votes away from Dr. Butler, and Crockett won handily with a
majority of nearly 250. In its way the election represented a triumph for
one resident in the district barely more than a year; now a seasoned legislative veteran, he made the long journey to Murfreesboro for the
opening of the session in September 1823. His prospects looked excellent as now he found himself placed on three committees: military
affairs, one overseeing drawing new county lines, and best of all, the
one charged with addressing his pet interest, the vacant lands. He
should have been greatly pleased, and indeed, perhaps he felt a bit too

pleased with himself, or rather cockier than was wise in a lonely representative from the far west of the state, for almost immediately his prideful independence revealed his limitations as an effective statesman.

Politics was about playing the game, a hand washing a hand, and mutual scratching of backs, and all the other euphemisms that party and machine politicians used to express the simple idea that a man got ahead by integrity, tempered with loyalty and compromise. The road ahead in Murfreesboro just now lay open to the followers of Andrew Jackson, who expected to see him nominated for the presidency in 1824. Meanwhile Sen. John Williams's term had just expired, and he announced his intention to seek reelection. Since he and Jackson bitterly disliked each other, Old Hickory wanted to see another incumbent replace him, but in the end Williams appeared so strong that Jackson himself had to agree to run at the very last moment. The contest in the legislature—which chose senators—proved to be embarrassingly close, and Crockett repeatedly took a lead in supporting Williams. Jackson won with a margin of just six votes—he later declined the office—and Crockett, though friendly to Jackson's presidential aspirations, made no effort to downplay his opposition. Williams had done a good job and deserved reelection, and that was enough for him, he said. Unstated, perhaps, was his resentment at the less-than-devoted interest of some of the Jackson supporters in the western land issue. "It was the best vote I ever gave," he said later. "I had supported the public interest, and cleared my conscience in giving it, instead of gratifying the private ambition of a man."[40]

Yet Crockett was disingenuous with himself if he believed that, for he knew as well as any that Jackson really did not want the office and had no "private ambition" in that direction. Jackson and his supporters wanted the office denied to Williams, who could be an embarrassment in Washington two years hence. However, even though he favored Jackson for the presidency, Crockett could not bend his pride in his independence. He would not go along with the group when they expected him to do so, even if he shared their ultimate goal. In that self-righteous pride of the poor man who, ironically, could afford to be independent because he thought he had nothing to lose, Crockett was dangerously prone to be independent solely for its own sake. He called it obeying "my conscience," but now and thereafter David Crockett would repeatedly confuse his conscience with his pride. It cost him now and would cost him more in an arena in which men needed the support of their peers to accomplish anything, and in which they won that support through loyalty and the inevitable tradeoffs of politics. Crockett's love affair with his conscience may have made him admirable as a man, but it completely unsuited him for the world of politics. He would make his independence his personal religion, recklessly unmindful that religions have a way of creating martyrs.[41]

While Jackson's friends in the legislature went on their guard with Crockett thanks to his stiff-necked support of Williams, he spent the rest of his legislative session and the one to follow addressing the same kind of issues he had encountered the term before. Without fail he supported those bills and resolutions that might in any way relieve or benefit men like himself. He opposed using prison labor on state projects, knowing that not a few men in Tennessee jails had committed no crime other than debt. He spoke in favor of the state Bank of Tennessee and the plan to establish branches in every county, believing that it would make loans available to the poor so they could buy their farms and start their businesses. Ironically, considering his own electioneering techniques, he favored a bill to prohibit selling liquor near polling places to prevent candidates from buying votes with drinks, yet he argued against an attempt to place other restrictions on taverns. Revealing his frequent inability to recognize a conflict of interest, he even introduced a bill to provide monetary relief for widows and encouragement for men to marry them, something he had done himself. If there was a bit of self-serving in many of his votes, it was largely due to the fact that the constituents whose interests he served were chiefly people like himself. He saw himself as a champion of the poor and did his best to live up to the image.[42]

Of course Crockett also had his bit of fun, as now he felt increasingly comfortable speaking from the floor. He kept the pose of the ignorant bumpkin when it suited him, and made no attempt to broadcast the fact that—for his time and place—he had a better-than-average education, or that he read much of the news of the state and nation in the local press.[43] Even when substantive arguments could be launched on an issue, more often than not he chose to wear the armor of the bumpkin's naive wit into battle. When another member introduced a resolution to move the capital from Murfreesboro to Nashville—a thinly veiled gesture for Jackson, who lived in the latter town—Crockett could not resist responding when one of the transparent arguments in the case was the poor food and housing in Murfreesboro and the unfriendliness of its people. He arose and declared in opposition to the measure that for his part he had never lived so well in his life as he did there in the capital. At his boardinghouse they had turkeys and pies and puddings every night, and he suggested that it would be much cheaper to move the poor man who introduced the resolution over to where Crockett lived than to move the government to Nashville. And as for the people not being polite, why, in Murfreesboro even the blacks took off their hats to him when he passed, something the white people certainly did not do for him at home.[44]

When it came to the matter of land, however, he was deadly earnest. In the amorphous allegiances in the legislature, with no firm parties taking shape, almost everyone backed Jackson for the presidency, and that provided the nearly universal basis of loyalty that Crockett had peripherally challenged. Within the legislature two factions followed different Jackson adherents, one led by Polk, and the other by Felix Grundy. Thus even a very sophisticated assemblyman had to step carefully lest he offend the wrong faction. When Grundy proposed to sell vacant state land for cash, Crockett broke with Polk and opposed the measure, arguing that it would price the poor out of contention, and that especially in districts like his where no one had any money, the land would be bought and monopolized by speculators from outside the district who would not actually settle the land, thus retarding population growth. He wanted the land sold on credit in whole or part, and declared that he had not come to Murfreesboro to "legislate for ready-money men." He then sided with Polk in opposition to the presentation of a bank of warrants from the University of North Carolina, all of them unclaimed warrants owed to the state's soldiers and now passed on by its legislature. They would evict hundreds if not thousands of squatters, and Crockett demanded that those occupants be given first chance to buy their land. In the end he and Polk got them a preemption right to buy their smallholdings, but the North Carolina claims remained unresolved. Thus, too, his support for the state bank as a means of occupants getting loans to buy their land. But then he broke with Polk once more when he voted in favor of widows—always a favorite topic with Crockett—being allowed to keep land on which they squatted. Moreover, he and Polk now revealed a fundamental difference that would dog them in the future. Polk favored selling public land to raise money for colleges and universities; Crockett only wanted the proceeds spent on common schools. He could not countenance the sons of the wealthy—the only ones who would attend a university—having their education subsidized by money the hard-pressed poor labored to pay for their pitiful quarter sections.

Having ardently favored instructing the Tennessee congressional delegation to ask Congress to authorize selling the vacant land in the eastern half of the state, Crockett even more enthusiastically backed a similar petition now calling for the sale of the vacant land in the western half. Moreover, he continued his efforts to reform the manner of surveys on land warrants, and to protect occupants from being victimized by unscrupulous speculators in warrants. He also addressed taxation, trying to reduce the burden on the small landholder, and when Governor Carroll yet again tried to get a vote to call a convention to revise the state's constitution, it finally passed, Crockett's vote being one of the vital two-thirds majority.[45]

In sum, by the time Crockett left Murfreesboro at the end of his second term on October 22, 1824, he could look back on his record with pride—of which he sometimes possessed too much. He stood up for the needs and concerns of his constituents, who by now spread across a ten-county expanse thanks to the new counties created in part through his efforts. If the common man of western Tennessee sought a champion, he found him in Crockett, and though he actually passed very few bills of his own, and none of real consequence, still he stood up for his people. He gave them what they wanted and expected from their elected representative. At the same time, and at first without knowing it, he also began to give them something they needed spiritually, something even Jackson could not give them. He gave them distinction and—even if it came in a bumptious and often self-deprecating manner—self-esteem, a powerful and heady feeling to those who for generations had been the unseen, unheard, and ignored bottom drawer of society. The aphrodisiac lure of that newfound regard could well lead them, and him, untold distances from the boggy canebrakes of the Obion.

BOWIE

*They despised a petty thief, but admired Lafitte; despised a man who would
defraud a neighbor or deceive a friend, but would without hesitation co-operate with a man or party who or which aspired to any stupendous scheme or
daring enterprise without inquiring as to its morality.*

WILLIAM H. SPARKS, CA. 1880

The business of Louisiana in 1820 was the acquisition of wealth. Men
lived on the expectation of fortune, hoping each new day for the
bonanza that awaited in the trading houses of New Orleans or out in
the vast soil. They were a culture of men seeking the big sale or the
windfall crop to redeem all those notes that they traded like currency,
and leave money besides to parlay into real riches. As a result this frontier was as much economic as geographical, and the relaxed restraints
of civilization on the one loosened inhibitions on the other. This was a
frontier for exploitation, and just as ruthlessness and individualism and
relentlessness were acceptable means of conquering the wilderness, so
were they part of the currency of ambition in the courthouses and
counting houses. At the same time they redefined notions of public
and private honesty and morality. Moreover, personal and civic ambitions became mixed to the point that political office was a prize sought
just like wealth, and often coveted because it afforded a better opportunity to realize personal gain. Men fought for the right to rule rather
than to serve. At this, the dawning of the era of the rise of the common
man, these Louisianians wanted to be anything but common, and
James Bowie was nothing if not a man of his time.[1]

The speediest road to riches lay in the soil, and for men willing to
blindfold themselves to the law, it could be there for the taking. Vast
portions of Louisiana land floated somewhere in the legal shadows

between Spanish grant and public domain. No one knew for certain
how many grants the Dons had given along the bayous, and though
the United States received registers of grants made by the several
Spanish governors at the time of the Louisiana Purchase, still they
were not necessarily complete. The Spaniards surveyed many of the
grants, but the surveyor took the surveys—called plats—with him
when he moved to Cuba. Many—perhaps hundreds—of grantees
failed to claim their tracts. Moreover, some of those awards had been
"floating" grants, tied to no specific tract, but intended to allow the
recipient to locate the land to his choosing within a specified area or
along a certain stream. And many of the Spanish and French Creoles
who received the grants never set foot on their lands but subsequently
sold them to American settlers, leaving it to them to register and
occupy the property. Squatters abounded, and until the General Land
Office could register, locate, survey, and issue patents on all of the
Spanish grants, the survey and sale of the remaining public domain
would be impeded, at no small cost to the treasury.

Such a state of confusion offered ripe opportunity for profit, and the
less scrupulous in western Louisiana speedily seized the chance. No
sooner did Louisiana become a state in 1812 than the fraud commenced. The next year, at the very northeast corner of the state, John
Millikin held a Spanish claim he purchased but could not prove to be
genuine, when two locals came forward and offered for one hundred
dollars each to swear as his witnesses that they had seen him buy it
from the original grantee. "By those two men I could have proved my
own claim, and, if necessary, a *thousand* others," he warned the General
Land Office. "Thus you can see what a system has been pursued to
monopolize all the lands of this State." One need not even furnish an
original Spanish grant. The perpetrator had merely to forge a deed of
conveyance of the property from the fictitious original grantee and
then pay some indigent squatters to swear as witnesses, sign by mark,
and then he could come forward to claim the land. They were not even
very careful in their forgery. In one 1813 case a conveyance stipulated a
grant supposedly given by Gov. Bernardo de Gálvez in 1776 for property on Lake Providence, yet that body of water had been known as
Stock Island Lake until Millikin himself renamed it in 1813, thirty-
seven years *after* that name appeared in the supposed grant.[2]

"If one claim can be forged and sworn to, hundreds may be, and no doubt are," warned Millikin, and he was right.³ Moreover, it could turn ugly. The next year in Catahoula Parish a group of men combined in a scheme in which one created and registered the fraudulent conveyances, two others acted as witnesses to their purchase from fictitious original grantees, and a fourth in some position of authority approved the sales and issued title. It got messy when the conspirators fell out over a division of the proceeds from the property, and one of them killed another. Josiah S. Johnston of Alexandria was practicing in the Catahoula court when it happened, and came away impressed with the extent of the land fraud being practiced. He, too, warned the government: "It may be strongly suspected," he wrote in March 1814, "if any individual is conducting an unusual number of claims without written titles, that there is something wrong, or if they are proven by the same witness."⁴

This sort of practice was widely known in Louisiana, and would certainly have come to James Bowie's attention. His brother John lived in Catahoula at the time of the well publicized murder, and of course Johnston himself had commanded the Bowies in the War of 1812. Even though James sold his Bayou Boeuf plantation to Stephen, he needed someplace to return to from his slaving expeditions, and apparently an unwritten part of the agreement with his brother was that he could continue to live there. Thus he certainly kept abreast of the local news, and in daily association with neighbors like his friend Caiaphas Ham and the three Martin brothers, Robert, John, and William.⁵ The Martins, especially, closely observed the land fraud schemes.

But even if Bowie knew little of the means of fraud from other sources, he soon learned it at infuriating firsthand. When he and his partner, John Stafford, bought a Bayou Boeuf parcel from John D. Reeves in October 1818, they intended to profit by it, and soon. Each spent some money in improving the land, but by April 1819 they had yet made nothing from it and were unable to pay Reeves the note due. That resulted in another summons to the court in St. Landry, and another plea from James that, not being a resident of that parish, he was not bound by its courts. They continued to try to sell the property, however, and by 1820 Bowie discovered something mortifying: Reeves had sold them a property with a faulty title and had not told them. They had been stung by much the same sort of fraud that

Johnston and Millikin foretold. Within twenty-four hours Bowie and Stafford went to Opelousas and posted at the courthouse and other public places a statement of what Reeves had done, and thereby repudiated their notes to him and warned others not to take those notes in exchange for goods or payment of debt, as was common. Then they set about trying to find Reeves himself, and it was well for the culprit that, though known to be in Opelousas, he had secreted himself well.[6]

By now James Bowie's character and temper stood fully developed, and even his friends confessed that his qualities were mixed. Caiaphas Ham, his friend and neighbor from Bayou Boeuf, admired Bowie's courage and his loyalty to friends. "He was a clever, polite gentleman," said Ham. "He was a true, constant, and generous friend; an open, bitter enemy, who scorned concealment, and any unfair advantage. He was a foe no one dared to undervalue, and many feared. When unexcited there was a calm seriousness shadowing his countenance which gave assurance of great will power, unbending firmness of purpose, and unflinching courage. When fired by anger his face bore the semblance of an enraged tiger."[]

William Sparks saw the same traits and more. He found Rezin cool and anxious to avoid violence, but James was quick and "always belligerent in the presence of his enemies." Where Rezin concealed his feelings for his own ends, "with James the deeper ardor of his nature forbade this equanimity." A gleam in his eye, the clenching of his jaw, and the pursing of his thin lips, gave certain signals that Bowie was on the boil and that whoever had offended him should beware. "It was his habit to settle all difficulties without regard to time or place, and it was the same whether he met one or many," said Sparks. Otherwise cool and self-possessed, James Bowie was relentless when enraged, and then in the height of his fury his demeanor could suddenly change to a seeming coolness that some mistook for fear or second thought. "It was then," said Sparks, "that he was terribly dangerous to an over-confidant foe."[7]If Bowie had found John Reeves in Opelousas that day, or anytime soon thereafter, it would have been much the worse for Reeves. But he did not, and it may be just as well, for in a perverse way Bowie should have thanked him. In the event, since he never paid the notes due, Bowie lost nothing out of pocket other than what he and Stafford invested in time and labor to improve the property. Far more important, however, Reeves showed him at embarrassing firsthand how to practice a land fraud. He either secured a bogus title to the tract or else persuaded Bowie and Stafford that he could furnish such title if necessary, and on that basis they agreed to buy. If it had worked completely, Reeves would have had his money, Bowie and Stafford their land, and only the government would have been the poorer for the loss of a piece of what was rightfully public domain. Like the slave smuggling, it was another crime from which everyone profited, and seemingly without a victim other than a faceless bureaucracy in Washington.

The lure proved irresistible. "I know no other country where love of money has such a grip on men's hearts," Tocqueville said of the Bowies' generation.[8] Sparks observed of James and Rezin specifically that in personal relations they were truthful and frank, sincere in their conduct. "They held in contempt all little men and all little meanness," he said. But there was something else in their nature: "They despised a petty thief, but admired Lafitte; despised a man who would defraud a neighbor or deceive a friend, but would without hesitation co-operate with a man or party who or which aspired to any stupendous scheme or daring enterprise without inquiring as to its morality."[9] With the lesson learned from Reeves, and fired by the lure of easy money that he could never resist, just such a "stupendous scheme" now came to James Bowie.

In an effort finally to clear the way to the surveying and sale of the public domain in Louisiana, Congress passed an act on May 11, 1820, authorizing all claimants to Spanish land grants in Louisiana to file their claims prior to December 31. It required that all such claims, with any supporting evidence, were to be turned over to the "registers"—registrars—of the district land offices, and those officers in turn should immediately file reports to the General Land Office in Washington, D.C., with recommendations on each of the claims presented.[10] There were just three districts at the time. The New Orleans, or South Eastern, District, covered all of Louisiana east of the Atchafalaya and south of the former West Florida parishes. The land office in Opelousas handled everything west of the Atchafalaya and south of the Red River, while the District North of Red River, or "Ouachita District," had its office in Natchitoches and covered the balance of the state.

It was this last region that especially interested James Bowie, for it was the least settled, and attractive soil rimmed long rivers and bayous. In the main the land along the bayous sat well above the waterline and sloped gradually back until it disappeared in forested swamps. For productive harvesting of timber or planting of crops, a distance of forty *arpents*, or 6,600 feet back from the bayou, was all that was practical. The old Spanish grants typically specified this distance, and a bayou frontage of fifteen, twenty, forty, or even sixty *arpents*. Moreover, the old grants often included the same measure on both sides of a bayou, making in all a considerable grant of land. The Ouachita, or Red River, District possessed another benefit, as well: The government surveyor's office lay right across the Mississippi in Washington, just outside Natchez, and readily accessible, an important feature since every claim, once recommended by the local register, still must be properly surveyed before a patent was granted and ownership confirmed.

All over western Louisiana men scrambled to get their claims—most of them quite legitimate—filed. But James Bowie followed a different course. He traveled north for several days, or even weeks, scouting the country along Bayou Maçon, which flowed into the Tensas River in the northeastern part of the state. He looked a few miles west at Deer Creek, in Catahoula, and from there turned his eyes fifteen miles farther west to Horseshoe Lake, an isolated former bend of the Ouachita River now in Ouachita Parish. He turned southwest to the Red River and its tributaries Bayou Darrow, Bayou Toreau, Bayou Marteau, and the Rigolet de Bon Dieu, concentrated in an area fifteen miles northwest of Alexandria in Rapides Parish. All but the Rapides locations lay in or close to Catahoula, where his brother John and perhaps even his mulatto cousin James could no doubt be of some help. The ground close to Alexandria was only forty-five miles—a good day's ride— from Stephen's plantation, where he lived, so James could look after affairs there himself.

He followed the scheme exposed by Millikin and Johnston several years earlier. James himself had enough familiarity with Spanish to essay forging the land grants, probably using a genuine one as an example for wording and style. Though there is no suspicion whatever that Rezin took part in the scheme with him, he was even better at the language and had already had some experience at faking Spanish documents in his earlier involvement with the Cuban slaves.[11] Brother John, too, had some Spanish. Any of the three of them could have done the penwork, but the scheme was entirely James's. He needed identities for the fictional grantees, and created names wholly consistent with the early Spanish and French settlers of Louisiana, but quite fictitious. His imagination gave life to Antonio Vaca and Francois Leclair, Juan Bulgar and Pedro Himenes, Jacques Dupui, Louis Hernando, Juan de Lion, Juan Mansol, Jacques Pecendon, Baptista Garza, and twenty more. As evidence that John at least played some very minor role, one forged grant (to Santiago del Rio) would be his. James's pen became that of Spanish governors from Gálvez in 1776 to Manuel Gayoso de Lemos in 1799, and in his hand it granted tracts of ten, fifteen, twenty, thirty, forty, and even sixty *arpents'* frontage on those bayous. In the process—and evidence of Bowie's tendency to rush without thinking everything through carefully—he made no attempt to prevent the handwriting in all of the grants from appearing the same, even though they were supposed to have been written by a number of secretaries for three different governors. Neither was he very careful about giving some of the common names of the grantees their customary spelling. And lurking within some of the grants he left glaring telltale giveaways—had he but thought.[12]

He was not yet done with penmanship. Having created the grants, Bowie next forged deeds of sale by which he could show himself as purchaser. Obviously they bore dates prior to the December 31, 1820, congressional submission deadline, and in the interest of security placed the location of the sales far enough away from the Ouachita District and Natchez that it would be difficult to verify any of the sellers' names. Some variety in dates and places of sale lent added verisimilitude. He headed some of the documents April 1817 in St. Martinville, St. Martin Parish, in the southern part of the state, and the rest out of state in Mobile in November 1818, in Pensacola the following month, and in San Augustine, Texas, in December 1819. Although the purchase prices, being a fiction, were immaterial, he kept them reasonable, ranging from $35 to $150.

Only at this point did Bowie probably spend any money remaining with him from the slave smuggling. He needed two men to attest by their signatures or marks to having witnessed in person his purchase of each of the grants. At the going rate for perjured witness of $100 per man per document, it could have cost Bowie $6,000 or more, though by locating the sites of his purchases anywhere from 100 to 250 miles away, he put verification of the witnesses at a sufficient distance to risk forging their signatures or marks as well.[13] As a result his "purchases" now carried signed witness by men like Francois De Leon, Pedro Gonzales, Baptista Garza—one of the fictitious sellers—and more, but the one name used more than any other as a witness was that historically ubiquitous character "John Smith."[14] Thus it was done. All he now had to do was take his documents to Daniel J. Sutton, registrar of the land office for the District North of Red River. Wisely Bowie waited until almost the last moment, ensuring that Sutton would already be swamped with other genuine—and forged—land claims, and would not have time to give his documents careful scrutiny before filing his required report on January 1, 1821.

Nor was this all of Bowie's enterprise, for he did exactly the same thing on a smaller scale in what was called the Lafourche Interior, for plots along Bayous Black and Caillou and another Bayou Boeuf, all in the Eastern District some fifteen miles south of the newly founded hamlet of Thibodeauxville, the first trading post between New Orleans and Bayou Teche. Again they were based on forged grants dated from 1775 to 1798, from Gálvez, Esteban Miró, and Gayoso, and this time given to names like Francois Flores, Miguel Saturneno, Antoine Pilbero, and five others. In an added wrinkle, rather than present forged documents of sale to himself, Bowie had his "grantees" assign all of the grants but one "for the use of" his Avoyelles friend and neighbor Robert Martin, and the other to William Wilson. The effect, if confirmed, would be that the land officially belonged to the grantee, but the application and all dealings with Samuel H. Harper, the land register in New Orleans, would be by Martin and Wilson. Bowie could then create a deed of sale from the grantee to himself as before, and pay Martin and Wilson something for their trouble. These documents, too, Martin and Wilson filed at the very last minute with an already harassed Harper.[15]

The audacity of Bowie's scheme was stunning. In the Lafourche he laid claim to almost nineteen miles of bayou frontage, containing more than twenty-thousand acres of prime land. North of the Red River his ambition was even greater, where more than a fourth of all claims filed were his, and of the class of claims that submitted original Spanish grants, his constituted twenty-nine out of fifty-one. There he claimed forty-two miles of waterfront and 45,700 acres. In all, if his scheme succeeded, he would own more than 65,000 acres, just over one hundred square miles of Louisiana, and all at almost no expense other than the surveying.[16] Moreover, he made his forged grants general in nature, specifying only a certain bayou or river or lake without further identifying the property. That kind of floating grant would allow Bowie to pick the best available plots to locate his surveys, and in some cases he already had buyers—squatters happy to act as perjured witnesses in order to get a preferential price for title to their land. He would become one of the largest landowners in the state. His intent was not to own land, however, but to sell it, and at the going rate of anywhere from $2 to $5 or more per *arpent*, he stood to make as much as $250,000 which would make him what he really wanted to be—one of the richest men in the Southwest.

James Bowie was hardly alone in forging fraudulent grants, though he worked on an almost industrial scale compared to others. The land registrars soon recognized the falsity of much of the paper coming across their tables. First to spot the problem was Levin Wailes, the registrar at Opelousas. On the very day of the filing of reports, January 1, 1821, and within hours of the deadline just past, he complained of "a most disgraceful scene of speculation." He believed that as many as half the claims filed with him would prove to be fraudulent, yet he still took them in at his office, in order to keep them from being sold to unsuspecting buyers.[17]

Bowie filed no immediate claims in the Opelousas District, but Samuel Harper quickly identified nine suspicious claims filed with him, eight of them Bowie's. When his clerk and translator started working with the grants and accompanying papers, he found the handwriting on all of them virtually the same and the signatures of several supposed

individuals to be identical. He gave them to a couple of the former secretaries of the Spanish governors who were still in New Orleans, and
who would know the governors' signatures, and they pronounced the
documents forgeries. Harper immediately ordered his clerk to stop
entering the grants in the official record books, so that in any future
dispute about the grants, no certified copy could be taken from his
records, and Martin and Wilson would have to produce the original
grants. By March 9 he felt sure enough of the swindle to take action.

But then a phenomenal stroke of luck bought Bowie valuable time.
Harper applied to the U.S. district attorney and to the attorney general
of Louisiana to see if any existing statutes allowed him to initiate criminal prosecution, though at the time he did not yet know that Bowie
himself lay behind the forgeries. Incredibly the attorneys informed
him that no law on the books, either state or federal, applied. This
kind of fraud was simply too new. Harper still hoped to head off the
scheme, though, when he wrote to Washington on March 9 to inform
Secretary of the Treasury William H. Crawford that though he had
passed favorably on the Bowie claims in his January 6 report, he now
believed that "the whole of the claims above mentioned are feigned
and fraudulent." Since Congress had to pass a formal act accepting his
report before surveying and granting of patents could proceed, he
urged that Crawford take steps to remedy the mistake. What Harper
could hardly anticipate, however, was that through pure accident his
letter would never reach Washington. Three years passed before the
Treasury Department finally heard of his warning.[18]

Having gotten his claims past the land registrars and into their
reports, Bowie had to wait until Congress approved them before he
could start the surveying. He could expect that it would take a long
time, and impatient though he was, he could not rush Congress.
Besides, in the interim other matters required attention. From 1820
onward he divided his time between New Orleans during the winters
and Avoyelles the rest of the year, with frequent visits to Alexandria
and perhaps Natchez. He went about the business he always practiced
of cultivating acquaintances with influential men, and as well of enjoying himself. All who knew him testified to his prodigality: "His style of
living was like a man who had plenty of money," one recalled, and his
friend the Natchez attorney Angus McNeil agreed that Bowie "was

exceedingly lavish in the expenditure of money."[19] Whatever he actually made from the slave smuggling he soon spent, and by May 1821 creditors once again went to court for judgments against him for debt.[20] Living with Stephen on the Bayou Boeuf plantation kept his expenses to a minimum, at least. Unable as yet to sell any of his land claims, with no other apparent source of income, and to recoup his finances, it is quite possible that Bowie undertook another slave venture or two, for Laffite still clung to his perch at Galveztown as late as June or even October 1821, and cargoes of captured Spanish slave ships continued to come in to meet Louisiana smugglers.[21] When all else failed—and sometimes in preference to all else—James Bowie's winning and persuasive manner always elicited loans. He had, said McNeil, "an extraordinary Capacity in getting money from his friends."[22]

Meanwhile there were the affairs of Louisiana to watch, and even broader aspects to claim his attention. In May 1821 his old friend Warren Hall found himself in some trouble with the law, and surrendered to the sheriff in Alexandria for a trial that ended in acquittal. The episode attracted some attention and engendered bitterness in a frontier town already torn by political, social, and economic rivalries. Despite his acquittal, Hall formed a grudge against the judge in the case, and wrote and then circulated a libelous pamphlet reflecting not only on the judge but also on attorney Josiah Johnston. Tempers flared, and the judge responded to Hall that "he will fight the d—d rascal over a rail with a butcher's knife," a popular idiom in frontier dueling in which the antagonists sat—or were even nailed by their pants—facing each other on a log or rail, and then fought to the death with long knives. In reality it may never have happened, but the threat of it showed a man's grit.[23]

The duel never came to pass, but there were others, for Alexandria became increasingly a violent place. Robert Crain fought a duel in May 1821 and wounded his opponent with his "stick sword," or sword cane.[24] A few months later Henry Blanchard accosted a physician in the streets in anger over a land deal gone sour, and killed him with a sword cane, the sort of fate that could well have met John Reeves if Bowie had caught him. Influential men complained that "the most bloody deeds may go unpunished."[25] Being often in Alexandria, and well acquainted with Hall at least, Bowie missed none of this, and by

mid–1822 already knew men like Blanchard and Crain at least by reputation if not in person, for it was a small and complex, and increasingly polarized, community.[26]

Then there were the political distractions. In 1822 a bitter contest
for the congressional seat for western Louisiana took place between
the current representative, Josiah Johnston, and William Brent, a former federal deputy attorney general for the area. He was a Marylander
who came to Louisiana in 1809, backed by powerful friends like
Henry Clay of Kentucky. Yet even some of his supporters disliked and
distrusted him, and when he married a local woman that winter, her
father disowned her and refused ever to see her again.[27] The campaign
turned vicious, involving largely personal attacks by Brent on
Johnston's honesty, and predictably over the issue of land. Brent
accused Johnston of favoring and pushing the survey and confirmation
of large grants for himself and his friends at the expense of the smaller
grant holders, and there may have been something to it, since both
Johnston and his partner, none other than George Graham, both
received large tracts in partnership on Bayou Lafourche. Such a charge
struck a chord with the average voter, himself a small landholder.
Brent argued in favor of speedy land settlements, and for the use of
"preemption rights," whereby for a small sum a man could effectively
take a plot off the market by purchasing the first option to buy it at a
later date when he had sufficient money. One of James Bowie's very
first property deals back in 1818 had been a preemption right. It was
how the poor man got started.

Brent also promised men appointments if he was elected, even
though they would be to offices a congressman had no power to fill;
one of Johnston's friends admitted that some influential men "were
completely *bamboozled* by him." And then, as a sop to Johnston's
friends, Brent hinted that if elected, he would himself support a move
to elect Johnston to the Senate. The governor supported him, and gave
him a militia appointment that allowed Brent to appear on the hustings in uniform, always a sure vote winner on the frontier. He bent
every effort to win the support of Reuben Kemper, now a resident of
Rapides, old and infirm but still a man who commanded enormous
respect and influence. Johnston's brother John reminded him that
Kemper "is indefatigable when he interests himself in the service of

another," and another friend predicted that whichever way Kemper went, so too would Rapides.[28] Brent won the election, but at the expense of an even more divided Alexandria.

James Bowie seemed to own no real property at the time, other than a nineteen-year-old slave named Henry, whom he sold the next year to his mulatto cousin James.[29] As a result he did not vote, but there is little question that his sentiments lay with Brent. He knew Johnston, at least by reputation, but Brent was the kind of man with whom Bowie could do business and ask favors if the time and need came.

Attractions loomed beyond the Louisiana horizon to vie for Bowie's attention. Dr. James Long had not given up his dream of empire. For more than a year he built a new force at Point Bolivar, opposite Galveztown, but even onetime supporters like John Sibley, now parish judge at Natchitoches, saw that Long was now an anachronism, and predicted that he "will be troublesome." Indeed he was. Leaving behind rumors that he had been condemned to hang for killing a man with a dirk in a tavern duel, Long set sail in September with only a handful of men for La Bahía, whence he marched overland a few miles to capture a settlement of the same name, but also called Goliad. A few days later they were themselves captured and sent to Mexico City for trial. Long never returned. In a few months he was shot under mysterious circumstances, and the day of the filibuster in Texas came to an end.[30]

Yet the end of Long was only the beginning for Texas settlement. Mexico won its complete independence from Spain in August 1821, and encouraged limited settlement of its province of Coahuila y Tejas by *norteamericanos* in order that they form a buffer between the Mexican interior and the marauding Comanche and other tribes. That same month Sibley wrote from Natchitoches that "the Province of Texas is fast filling up by American settlers," and complained that "the Road by Nackitosh is full." By the late winter of 1822 four steamboats made regular passage from New Orleans up the Red River to Natchitoches laden with freight for the Texas trade. Several other vessels ran regularly between New Orleans and what was now more commonly called Galveston with passengers, lumber, tools, and provisions, all bound for the settlement of *empresario* Stephen F. Austin.[31] Texas was the talk of the frontier, and for a man with an appetite for land

and opportunity—especially one like James Bowie, who had heard and even seen some of it firsthand—such talk held promise for the future.

The winter of 1823 was the coldest in years. It killed father Rezin Bowie's fruit trees, froze the bayous, and for a time even chilled the rising fever tempers in Alexandria.[32] Bowie, as was his custom, wintered in New Orleans that year, and again in 1824, where the century-old Creole custom of the *Boeuf Gras* on Shrove Tuesday had by now become an annual festival. Oxen pulled a huge bull's head on a cart down the Rue Royale and the Rue Dauphin in the Old Quarter, as masked celebrants followed in train, drinking, singing, and dancing. The Carnival, or Mardi Gras, in early March 1824 was the biggest and best since the one that celebrated the victory over the British in 1815.[33] The alluring city offered many other enticements as well. There was theater, for example. Bowie could well have seen a few performances in Natchez before its theater burned in 1821, and even after that traveling troupes occasionally came down the Mississippi to perform at inns. New Orleans, of course, had several playhouses, where broad farces ran cheek by jowl with Shakespeare, and the leading names of the eastern stage sometimes played. The noted tragedian Edwin Forrest appeared here this winter season and he and Bowie became at least passingly acquainted.[34] He may even have performed his signature role in *Metamora*, in which he played a fierce character armed with a great terrifying knife.

There were also the taverns and the gaming tables. Bowie liked gambling, especially faro and something called "bucking the tiger," and it was one of the ways that money easily made just as easily left his purse. He relished the comradeship and bustle of the grog house. Wine, beer, rum, and a "mean" whiskey were the social beverages of the time and place. Milk was for children, and thanks to the danger of typhoid fever, few people drank water. The quantities that even sober men consumed sometimes startled foreigners, and if Bowie occasionally had more than he should—well, so did almost everyone else.[35] Certainly there were women, too. New Orleans abounded with American, French, Spanish, and mixed nationality women, and at any

level of the social strata that would suit a man's taste or mood. Bowie
left not an atom of a record of his love life for these years, but surely
there was one, if only casual and certainly not of any lasting nature,
but at least enough to spawn future rumors and myths, that often terminated with jealous fights and violent death.[36]

In 1823 James may well have accompanied Rezin on a voyage to
Havana, where his brother made a substantial purchase of a genuine
grant on Bayou Caillou from the Spanish owner. At the same time he
almost certainly called on Capitán Vicente Pintado, once the chief surveyor in the Florida parishes until the rebellion and annexation left
him without a position, who had moved to Havana in 1817. Pintado
and Kemper were old enemies, and Rezin may well have known of
him in that connection. More likely, however, Rezin wanted to see
Pintado because the Spaniard had taken all his land surveys of Spanish
grants with him. Using them for reference, he continued to issue
certificates of survey for the property he had located, and Rezin would
need one for the grant he had just purchased. The certificate cost him,
but it was worth it, for this was the best possible confirmation of a
grant's authenticity. Pintado's papers were of no positive use to James,
of course, for there could not be anything there to confirm forged
grants. Nevertheless, if he took the time to make a careful examination
of all of Pintado's papers, he would have seen where genuine surveys
lay, and made certain that he did not conflict with them when he tried
to get his own claims surveyed. Such conflicts only slowed the process
of surveying and, worse, signaled to land registrars that when two
grants vied for the same land, one was a fake.[37]

All of this merely provided diversion. Bowie's continuing fixed purpose was the land claims. In 1821 he cultivated an acquaintance with
Isaac Thomas, an influential planter near Alexandria who began writing letters on his behalf to men of influence in Washington trying to
hurry the confirmation of the claims, and continued to do so into 1823.[38]
When Josiah Johnston was in fact elected to the U.S. Senate, Thomas
urged him, too, late in 1822 to get speedy congressional action, especially on the claims in the District North of Red River, where lay most
of Bowie's claims. "Ouachita is restless, and unsettled," Thomas
warned, and the men there had nothing else on their minds.[39] Certainly
Johnston took an interest in the matter, the more so thanks to his

partnership with Graham in a plantation on Bayou Boeuf that itself rested in part on claims quite near some of Bowie's Martin and Wilson tracts.

That Johnston had some special influence—and a conflict of interest—in the matter is evident from the fact that in 1823 a new commissioner took charge of the General Land Office in Washington—none other than his partner, George Graham. Typical of the labyrinthine nature of Louisiana politics and society at the time, Graham himself was a first cousin of William Brent.[40] The connections between them all were even more complex than family ties or business relations. Virtually no formal political parties existed at the time, though the disintegrating old Federalist Party still anxiously tried to protect the propertied interests. Instead factions orbited around a number of candidates who stepped forward in the coming presidential election of 1824, representing constituencies more regional than ideological, and only three were real contenders: The Federalist John Quincy Adams spoke for the northeast and for business, Henry Clay for the burgeoning West, and Andrew Jackson attracted the most numerous and least prosperous everywhere, the men like Crockett who saw themselves as the sinews of the young nation. Johnston and Brent, though opposed to each other, stood closely allied with Clay, while Graham favored Clay and Adams alike. Thus, despite their bitter animosity, Johnston and Brent had shared ties to Clay and Graham, and shared interest in the claims. Applicants close to either Johnston or Brent expected their man's support when it came to getting claims confirmed, and both of them assumed Graham's support. When it came to exercising his duties, the land commissioner himself could be torn between kinship on the one hand and his own business interests on the other, though Graham appeared to be more of a stickler for propriety and the rule of law than many other public officials. Land, blood, and politics all combined to produce a seething and confused ferment in Louisiana.

The news Bowie had awaited so long finally came in March 1823. On February 28 Congress voted to confirm both the Sutton and Harper reports. A major milestone passed, and Bowie wasted no time in racing for the next. He already knew Milo Johnson, the deputy surveyor working out of the Washington, Mississippi, land office. Johnson lived near him in Avoyelles, and now Bowie hired him at the

standard rate of one dollar a mile to begin surveying his claims along
Bayou Maçon and elsewhere. The work occupied much of the next
year, and occupied Bowie himself, since he had now to select the
actual tracts on which he wanted to locate his floating grants.[41] As
Johnson completed each survey he sent it to the land office at
Washington for the registrar to handle. Once that official approved the
supporting documents filed by Bowie, and entered the survey in his
plat book, the deed would be done. He need only issue a land patent
to Bowie, and the land was his.

Problems began to appear almost as soon as the first surveys
reached Washington, Mississippi, for the register there now was
Edmund Wailes, son of Levin Wailes, who had already spotted so
many fraudulent claims in the Opelousas district. When Bowie's documents arrived, Wailes smelled the same scheme at work and simply let
the papers accumulate in his office without acting on them. Months
later his successor, George Davis, found them when he came to take
over as surveyor of public lands south of Tennessee.[42] But Bowie may
not have known this for some time, since he rode out with Johnson
overseeing the surveys and actually making his first sales. In June 1823
he sold a tract in Catahoula, and another in October, and then in
December he sold four of the Bayou Maçon parcels, totaling altogether 6,431 acres, for which he received on paper $6,018. While he
did not yet have his patents in hand, he sold the tracts on the basis of
his personal bond for sums up to $20,000 that he would provide good
and sufficient title on demand. He realized no money right away from
the Bayou Maçon parcels, but took notes that would start to come due
in February 1824. The only real cash to enter his pocket was $900 for
the Catahoula ground.[43] Still, it was a start.

In the process he made more mistakes. Even though his forged
grants specified Bayou Maçon, he persuaded Johnson to locate the
actual surveys on more desirable Bayou Tensas, which ran parallel and
a few miles closer to the Mississippi. To do so Bowie got Hiram Burch
and Hugh White, two local squatters, to go before Justice of the Peace
William B. Prince on December 5 to swear that locals regarded Bayou
Tensas as a "leading fork" of Bayou Maçon and always had, and that
thus the name applied to both. Bowie already knew Burch and White,
and there was no difficulty in securing their marks to the statements.

As for the justice of the peace, two days earlier Prince himself had bought 1,015 acres of that Bayou Tensas property from Bowie, which made it very much in his interest to help establish an explanation for the conflict in names. In fact, Prince, Burch, and White and all of Bowie's other purchasers in the area were squatters, now buying from Bowie what they hoped to be legitimate title to the land they lived on, and at a preferential price. Bowie profited, they profited, and only the government suffered. If the later suspicions of his superiors were correct, Milo Johnson also profited from knowingly locating surveys on the wrong bayou. Bowie simply bought his complicity with an outright bribe.[44]

From the beginning of 1824 onward, the pace of activity on Bowie's claims accelerated, but so did the mounting suspicions of the officials in the Washington, Mississippi, land office. Kenneth McCrummon, a surveyor with Wailes, saw by February 1 that Bowie's practices—though he was not yet certain that Bowie was the forger—went beyond just fraud, actually hindering settlement. No sooner did a legitimate settler choose a piece of what he presumed to be the public domain and make application for purchase, than "a promising nest of Tittle makers, preemption provers &c &c" came forward, presented a false Spanish grant, "and he is obliged to move as there is no way for him to combat a fraudulent tittle." Some discouraged settlers simply gave up on Louisiana and went west, putting Bowie in the ironic position of unknowingly encouraging the settlement of Texas.[45]

By spring news of what was happening, especially with claims on the Sutton report, got to Graham in Washington, D.C. He ordered Principal Deputy Surveyor John Wilson not to perform surveys for anyone who could not show that the property they wanted surveyed was the specific land covered in their grants. There would be no more floating claims like Bowie's Bayou Maçon–Tensas grants.[46] By October, as more information came into the land office at Washington, Mississippi, George Davis was thoroughly onto Bowie's fraud. "The manner in which the confirmation of many or most of those claims have been obtained," he complained to Wailes, "as well as in relation to the testimony offered to influence, in some instances, their location, are both shocking and astonishing."[47] On October 21 Davis sent Wailes out into the field to survey more of the public lands, as well as to keep his eyes open for fraud. Meanwhile, the more Davis delved into the papers in his own office, the worse the situation looked. He now saw that land north of the Red River was definitely being converted to private ownership with no benefit to the government whatever. McCrummon reported to him that his own investigation of Bowie's actual grants had revealed serious anomalies. For one thing, he spoke with many residents who had lived for decades in the region, yet not one of them had ever heard of any of the supposed grantees. Moreover, it seemed highly suspicious that the grants covered the best land in the region, yet in the 1770s–1790s those areas were unknown and virtually unexplored. How, then, did the old Spanish governors miraculously manage to specify what would be decades later the most desirable locations?

By mid-October McCrummon advised Davis that from Rapides to Natchitoches, the best informed people regarded the Bowie grants as frauds. "It is possible, and barely possible, that there may be some few valid and honest claims among them; but it is my opinion," he said, "that the far greater part of these documents are base counterfeits." Moreover, with a tendency to boastfulness that caused him problems more than once, James Bowie proudly exhibited some of his grants in the area, and men who saw them "speak publicly of them, not only as counterfeits, but very bungling counterfeits." McCrummon warned that "the whole thing is ridiculed and contemned [sic] by every honest man in the northern district as a base attempt to defraud the government." He strongly advised Davis to send all grants and title documents to Graham in Washington for careful scrutiny before issuing any patents, and Davis in turn advised Graham that "if all that I daily hear upon the subject be not mere idle stories, it will require but a little further indulgence by Congress to the persons for filing notices of claims to wrest from the government all the lands in that interesting district of Louisiana worth being surveyed."[48]

Bowie had been careless and overconfident. Just when he first realized his problem is uncertain, but by the last week of October, when he still had not been issued any patents despite having sent in a number of Johnson's surveys, he went to Washington, Mississippi, himself and confronted Davis. For two or three successive days he planted himself in Davis's office, at first no doubt polite but as time went on increasingly belligerent. When Bowie could not achieve his ends by charm and persuasion, he resorted to bullying and intimidation instead, a side of his nature noted by more than one man. Davis, however, stood his ground. He found Bowie "extremely anxious to obtain my approval of Johnson's locations in order to facilitate the sale of the lands." Bowie's mode of operation was to find squatters already on good land, "and after the parties come to an understanding on the subject, the squatters are found ready to assist in the most iniquitous means of defrauding the Government—or so says report." The squatters, "who seem to stand in the same relation to him that the Jackall does to the Lion," were only too happy to give any manner of false witness that would secure them cheap land as their scraps from Bowie's feast.

When Bowie showed his squatters' statements that Bayou Tensas was really called Bayou Maçon, and had been for some years, Davis pulled out a map that very clearly labeled it as Tensas, adding that his own familiarity with the population of the area convinced him that virtually all inhabitants knew it as such. Moreover, he said, standing firm, he refused to approve Johnson's survey and issue a patent "while a doubt remained in my mind." He said he would refer the case, and all the documents on file, to Graham in Washington, D.C. That stopped Bowie momentarily. The less Washington knew of his dealings, the better. He did not even know that Harper's letter about his Lafourche frauds had gone astray, but he certainly did not want suspicion of his other grants to go abroad. Seeking a different route than bullying, and thinking to overawe Davis and still contain the problem locally, he went to Natchez and returned the next day with the young John A. Quitman, junior law partner of the widely influential William Griffith. Quitman sailed into Davis as if arguing a case before a jury, and Davis finally got them both to leave only by declaring that even an order from President James Monroe himself would not induce him to approve the surveys until he was satisfied of their propriety.[49]

The situation rapidly got out of control, and then only a day or two later, Davis discovered the fatal error that James Bowie himself had unwittingly introduced into his documents. Studying two grants in particular, one to Francisco Adante from Miró in 1788, and another to Juan Gonzales from Miró the following year, something finally connected in Davis's mind. He remembered both from his own recollection and from talks with longtime residents of the district, that Bayou Maçon was really French for Bayou *Mason,* so called because the noted frontier outlaw Samuel Mason, whose dark deeds were still told and retold, supposedly lived on it for a time around 1803. The problem was, if Bayou Maçon only got its name subsequent to 1803, how could it have been named in a Spanish grant in 1788, fifteen years earlier? Whether the location of the grants was Bayou Maçon or Bayou Tensas no longer mattered. Here was proof absolute of rank forgery. Moreover, despite the fact that the grants were in the names of Gonzales and Adante, Davis now informed Graham that "the real claimant is, however, named Bowie."[50]

This smelled of disaster. In the Sutton report six claims totaling nearly 8,500 acres, almost a fifth of his hoped-for domain, made specific mention of Bayou Maçon in the forged grants. The obvious dis-qualification of the Adante and Gonzales claims equally revealed the others as forged as well. Worse, the suspicion that he lay behind them jeopardized all the rest of his claims, and the name "James Bowie" at last came to the attention of the big authorities in Washington. He could forget ever having the Maçon surveys confirmed now, and maybe the others, too. On a wider front, the exposure of land fraud throughout Louisiana was becoming public. Even as Bowie remonstrated and bullied Davis in his office, Wailes reported from Alexandria the discovery of "a certain class of land claims, founded on the basest and most palpa-bly fraudulent documents of title, embracing immense tracts of the most valuable public lands in the State." He had seen many of their documents, some of them no doubt Bowie's for the land near Alexandria, and found the Spanish grants to be almost laughable in their clumsi-ness. "There is a certain combination of individuals in the State, com-posed of persons whose characters have ever been suspicious, and who have suddenly risen from indigence to the possession of titles for immense bodies of valuable lands." He advised Graham to make very careful inquiry before Congress acted on any more reports from any of the land registrars in Louisiana.[51]

The best Bowie could do now was to try to contain the damage. Sutton still held office as land registrar. If the surveyor Davis insisted on sending his papers to Graham for adjudication, then the only thing to do was to remove all originals from Sutton's files, leaving him with nothing but clerk's copies, from which no one could make any comparisons of handwriting.[52] Sometime in the next few months, either without Sutton's knowledge or with his active connivance, Bowie got all of his original papers out of the Washington, Mississippi, land office. It was too late to halt suspicion of the balance of his claims, but at least the move erected an impassable roadblock to further investigation of his documents. And after all, Congress had approved all his claims on the Sutton report more than a year before, and as long as his other forged grants contained no obvious anomalies like the Bayou Maçon slipup, then he might still be able to proceed with surveys on the rest and save the bulk of his scheme. James Bowie was not beaten yet.

But it was time for a move all the same. Avoyelles had always been a backwater. It was convenient to his oversight of the surveys on Bayou Tensas and his Catahoula claims, but that work was almost finished now, with most of those properties virtually lost anyhow. After four years of living with his brother Stephen's family, he was ready to be out on his own once more. It was time for a change, and for a man of business and ambition in that region, there was only one place to go: Alexandria. Rapides led all the other western parishes in population, capital, and manufactures. The most influential men lived there— Johnston, Isaac Thomas, the Wells family, Kemper, and more, men whose company Bowie needed to cultivate. A recently completed brick courthouse and a new bank, the first in the region, had just opened in the city, evidence that Rapides was moving out of the recent depression. Bowie would need access to cash loans and credit if he hoped to expand his operations.[53] Most important, the major share of his claims north of the Red River sat on the bayous just a few miles upriver from the city. He must watch over and nurture their progress and try to avoid the mistakes of the past. On October 20, 1824, he went to the Avoyelles courthouse in Marksville and registered a formal change of domicile to Rapides.[54] His plans for himself were still big, and it was time to move in circles in which opportunity equaled his ambitions, for already his vision had begun to extend beyond the horizons of Louisiana.

CROCKETT

Jackson is a hero, but *Crockett is a* horse. *Here is to General Jackson in the
next presidents chair, loco Crockett in his seat in Congress, and loco
Alexander in the corn field.*

ĐAVID CROCKETT, 1827

What Crockett needed to do when he came home from that last session
of the legislature was stay put, work his farm, and try somehow to put
his personal affairs in order. His Rutherford Fork place was now in the
newly formed Gibson County. In April he leased another tract of land
on the south fork of the Obion, not far from his original squat, and that
only doubled the acreage he needed to tend.[1] His family's poverty left
them wholly dependent upon his hunting for meat and the produce of
their land for fruit and vegetables, and for the next year and more only
the wolf bounties and animal hides brought any real money into the
rude dogtrot. Circumstances denied them even the most modest luxuries, and instead of pewter or iron cutlery, when they sat at table the
Crocketts dined with rough forks that he made from split cane.[2]

It was no time to run for Congress. The sitting representative from
western Tennessee, Adam Alexander, wrong-footed himself in 1824
when he voted in support of the tariff law that actually increased the
already controversial rates of the 1816 law. Unfortunately both laws
heavily favored manufacturers, which did absolutely nothing for the
rural occupants of Alexander's district and, if anything, only resulted in
their paying higher prices for anything they bought that had to be
imported. Along with many others that year, Alexander's vote made
him vulnerable, and Crockett's friends urged him to challenge the
incumbent. In fact Crockett needed little coaxing. He actually
announced his candidacy months before the campaign began, issuing a

circular letter in the district sometime in 1824, perhaps even before the end of his legislative term. He had tasted politics and public approbation and liked them every bit as much as a good chase for bear. There is no reason to suppose that the idea of seeking a larger preserve in which to continue the hunt did not occur to him well before any friends asked him to run. Besides the repudiation that his election to Congress would deliver to those who looked down on his poverty and lowly origins, a seat in the national legislature would also put him right where his pet issue of vacant land must ultimately be decided.[3]

All his pro forma protestations to the contrary, Crockett would not have been Crockett had he not hungered for the office long before being offered the plate. He later protested that he resisted all entreaties for some time, and perhaps he did, though he might just as well have been practicing the prevailing ethic that called for a public pose of modesty and reluctance. Moreover, such a pose suited Crockett's own view of himself as a man pulled into public affairs by the acclamation of his people rather than by any ambitions of his own, of which he surely possessed an abundance. "I know'd nothing about Congress matters," he claimed. If he had any inclination to seek reelection to the legislature, he decided to put that off in favor of the congressional race, implying that in the end, and against his will, "I was obliged to agree to run."[4]

It might have been better had he declined. A race for Congress needed money, far more than he had ever spent on his assembly seat and abundantly more than he could command now. Popular as he may have been in his assembly area, he was largely unknown in much of the rest of the eighteen-county congressional district. Moreover, Alexander showed skill as a local politician, enjoyed influential friendships, and had good connections to the seemingly all-powerful Jackson. Then, too, Crockett brought certain liabilities to the contest, most notably a bill he had introduced in the last legislature to change the meeting days of the county courts in West Tennessee, and also a suggestion that a brigade of East Tennessee militia be shifted to west Tennessee, apparently instead of raising an additional militia brigade in the west. Moreover, by his independence he had in some degree offended both Jackson and his law partner Judge John Overton, and their leader in the legislature, Felix Grundy. Crockett was about to get a lesson in what happened when a new boy on the block tried to play by his own rules, though whether or not he would *learn* that lesson was an entirely different matter.

When the campaign began in the summer of 1825, Crockett no doubt trusted to his tried and proved electioneering style for a time, though he soon found that he did not have the money to buy the drinks and the twists of tobacco, or the wherewithal to afford appearances in eighteen county towns. Neither did he as yet have any influence with the sparse press in the district, chiefly the two papers in Jackson. In addition, cotton prices ran unusually high that year, and the profit realized by the growers in his area helped to alleviate their previous anger at Alexander over his tariff vote, for the high tariff also protected cotton. Alexander did not fail to take credit for the windfall.[5]

Then, in the June 18 *Jackson Gazette*, Overton came out against Crockett. Writing under the pseudonym "Aristides," he challenged David for seeking to change the court days without considering the interests of his constituents, most of whom took some trouble to make a day to come to the seat to do their legal business. At the same time Crockett's stand on the militia brigade attracted his fire, for it would have denied West Tennesseans whatever positions and benefit came from having a brigade enlisted in their own population. For all the effort Crockett invested in the legislature to serve his constituents, Overton was able to make a case from these two measures that the "gentleman from the cane" paid little mind to their interests.[6] Crockett tried to respond by pointing out that the militia matter was not his fault, and in fact that a clerical error explained his failure to oppose the bill, but the explanation did not stick. Indeed, for three months he attempted to counter the "Aristides" charges, an effort that seemed to have little impact on the voters.[7]

In fact, nothing did. "I might as well have sung *salms* over a dead horse," he later said of his arguments against Alexander and Overton. In the end Alexander "rather made a mash of me," he said, though in fact the vote showed a close race, Crockett polling just 267 fewer votes than Alexander, out of 5,465 cast. It made a very creditable showing for a first attempt, especially considering Crockett's financial handicap and the opposition of the Overton forces. But the defeat stung bitterly, and more than he was ready to admit. Years later he claimed that he lost by only 2 votes instead of 267, which he certainly knew to be untrue, and implied that his loss by even that tiny margin might have been due to a dishonest count.[8] Clearly Crockett's skin was far too thin for politics, and moreover in this first defeat, as in others to follow, he compounded being a poor loser with the insecurity of his class. Alexander's victory was just one more page in the long history of conspiracy and corruption among the upper classes as they tried to grind the upright, honest, and *independent* yeoman into subservience. Crockett could never see personal slight or defeat in any other light.

Typically he needed victories to assuage his loss; to salve his own wounds he must inflict wounds on others, and the bears of West Tennessee paid. He briefly worked at building two flatboats, intending to fill them with barrel staves that he would take to market, but as soon as the bears were fat he took to the wilderness, and after a good series of kills tried to return to his other work but found that "I at length couldn't stand it any longer without another hunt." In the end the long hunt lasted almost without interruption into the spring of 1826, and Crockett claimed to have single-handedly killed 105 bears, 47 of them in the last month alone.[9] It was a savage tally, even though Crockett exaggerated the number. In fact he took closer to 80 bears that season, and not by himself but in company with a party of several.[10]

Certainly they did not waste the bears, for Crockett's vivid recollection of every kill included salting the meat and packing it home for consumption. Still, no other hunt of his life resulted in such a degree of killing, and no other remained so vividly in his memory. When he wrote his autobiography eight years later in 1833, he devoted fully one-tenth of it to this winter hunt, as if somehow to erase the painful memory contained in the two sparse paragraphs he gave to his failed congressional campaign. It took several tons of bear meat hanging in the smokehouses of Crockett and his friends to restore the wounded pride caused by his rejection at the polls.

Only in the spring did Crockett really concentrate on his barrel stave project. Somehow he had hired a couple of men to do the work of splitting and finishing the staves while he was at his hunt, and by spring nearly thirty thousand of them lay packed on the flatboats. As soon as the flow of the rivers allowed, Crockett and his associates put off into the Obion. On each of the flats, or "broadhorns," as they were called, they built a small cabin in the center where the off-watch man could eat and rest out of the elements, and the trip proved to be not unpleasant for a time. Crockett always delighted in new country, a bit of exploration and adventure, and, it seemed, an excuse to get away from home. But he bargained without the broad Mississippi. When the Obion emptied into the great river, Crockett saw something that stunned him and terrified some of his hands, for none of them had ever beheld such a stream, and none knew how to manage the flats on something that big and powerful.

He decided to lash his two flats together, but it only made them more difficult to handle, and when they tried to make land on their first night out they could not. Other experienced boatmen they passed urged them simply to keep on through the night, and so they did. With the river high, the current took them along at something around eight miles an hour, so that a few hours before dawn, they were only a few miles above Memphis. Crockett himself was off watch, having decided they could do nothing but let the current take them as it pleased, and went into one of the cabins to warm himself at a fire. Ruminating there over what appeared to be yet another bad turn in his fortune, he did not hear the distant sound of a rhythmic crashing in the water. Ahead of them lay what boatmen called a sawyer, a huge driftwood tree snagged in the bottom mud, its trunk pointing upstream. Sawyers rose out of the water in response to the current until their weight in the air countered the water's resistance, and then they crashed down again, repeating the process endlessly until eventually they washed away.

Crockett did hear his hands outside running to the sweeps when they spied the sawyer, but it was too late. The trunk came down right in the middle of the joined flats, breaking them apart, and then he felt another great shudder as the boat he was on ran broadside into a raft of driftwood caught at the head of an island just beyond the sawyer. The swift current pushed the flat with Crockett on it under the driftwood, and as he struggled to get out of the cabin hatch, the water came pouring in. The only other exit was a small window on the side of the cabin, too small to crawl through, but he stuck out his arms and yelled for his friends, and they dragged him out—though the tug ripped away his clothing and a fair bit of his skin in the bargain—and then leaped for safety onto the driftwood.

"I was in a pretty pickle," Crockett later recalled. The two rafts passed down either side of the island locals called the "Old Hen" or "Paddy's Hen-and-Chickens," and then Crockett saw the one he had been on simply disappear for good beneath the driftwood. They sat out the night there in the middle of the river, cold, hungry, and with Crockett bleeding from several serious abrasions. Worse, all their work, and his prospects for some immediate substantial cash, disappeared with the current. Yet somehow his salvation from certain death put not only this loss but the defeat at the polls in a new perspective. "I felt happier and better off than I ever had in my life," he remembered, "for I had just made such a marvellous escape, that I had forgot almost every thing else." To his eternal credit, and despite the unseemly pique and small-mindedness that he could show when hurt or disappointed, David Crockett never lost his essential good cheer and natural gentility for long. He would always be an optimist.

The next morning a passing boat saw the miserable, shivering Tennesseans on their island and picked them up. Apparently word of the mishap had reached Memphis earlier that morning, for when the boat with a nearly naked Crockett and friends pulled up to the wharf at the foot of the city, scores of spectators lined the bluff. Among them stood Maj. Marcus B. Winchester, who ran a clothing and dry goods store. Seeing Crockett's special plight, Winchester ran to his store and returned with a pair of trousers to spare the foundling's modesty, taking him back to his store later and fully outfitting him. Within minutes Crockett wore a new suit of clothes and warmed himself beside a welcoming fire after a hearty meal. In a couple of hours, fired inside by a little of the "creater," he appeared on the streets of Memphis, where he and his companions found themselves rather lionized for having survived their ordeal. Gratitude meant a lot to Crockett, and he never afterward forgot Winchester's generosity or spoke of him in any but admiring terms.

He should have been grateful, for in its way this accident, which Crockett would have regarded as providential, proved to be the remaking of him. Indeed, more than once in his life he found a kind of rebirth in disaster. In this case it was the meeting with Winchester, who took an instant liking to the bruised and shivering fellow huddled by his fire. Crockett soon began to entertain him with his jokes and stories, some of them no doubt of his pranks during his election campaigns, and he and Winchester parted a few days later as fast friends. Likewise, Crockett achieved a species of popularity in Memphis itself, thanks both to his wit and good humor, and also the entrée that Winchester could provide to other men of influence. When Crockett left, Winchester sent him on his way with some money in his pocket, and Memphis sent him off with his confidence in his ability to win friends renewed.[11]

Before going home, Crockett and a companion boarded a steam-boat—the first he ever rode—and went downriver as far as Natchez, hoping to find some remnant of the flats and the thirty thousand staves, but all he found were reports that one of the boats had been seen drifting by. He may even have been coincidentally on the same boat that brought James Bowie back that spring from his first trip to Washington, but if so neither took notice of the other. Finding his errand a fruitless one, Crockett gave up and returned upriver, finally reaching the Obion and Gibson County in late spring or early summer, after almost nine months of nearly constant absence.

Once more the land and Elizabeth could not hold him. His revelation on the driftwood raft, followed by his reception in Memphis, may have changed his mood after his humiliation the year before, but in his renewed good spirits he only fastened his resolve more steadfastly on redeeming himself by erasing the injustice of defeat at the polls with a victory. Major Winchester probably encouraged Crockett to make another try against Alexander in the 1827 election, and that support made it easier for David to do what he surely always wished anyhow: He would run again. His decision in the matter already made, the quandary over funding evaporated when Winchester sent for him to come to Memphis early in 1827, and there made Crockett the loan of one hundred dollars or more to meet the costs of the drinks and the circulars and the many nights' lodging at inns during the campaign. Moreover, Winchester frequently did business in a number of the courthouses in the district, and he promised to speak in Crockett's behalf with his influential friends at every opportunity, as well as to advance him more money as needed.[12] His help could be crucial, for the Ninth Congressional District was the second largest in the entire United States, with well over twenty thousand voters and a huge expanse of territory for a candidate to cover.

Given that boost, Crockett went into the contest with a confidence that he lacked in 1825, and spurred by the extra advantage that Gen. William Arnold of Jackson also entered the lists, far more likely to take votes from Alexander than from Crockett. A veteran of three stump races now, Crockett was undeniably a skilled campaigner. He took onto the platform with him not only a well-honed arsenal of jokes and stories and tricks, but also an understanding gained by experience of which issues to evade and which to address. He squarely positioned himself as the friend of the poor and repeatedly hammered on his vacant-land stand. He played on his own lack of education, even exaggerating his ignorance, and thereby catering to his own and the voters' latent suspicion of high learning when he stressed his opposition to using public funds from those lands to build colleges for the sons of the rich, and his support for the common-school movement. Over and over he made the contest not one of candidates or ideologies but of poor against rich. By voting for him, the men of West Tennessee would be expressing loyalty to their class; in endorsing his independent spirit they would be asserting their own. It was an approach being seen elsewhere in the late 1820s as the expanded franchise finally opened almost universal white male suffrage, and with it the accumulated aspirations of the common man. Though neither Crockett nor anyone else at the time would have recognized the concept, he was establishing himself as a pioneer populist in America, a position heavily weighted with latent power.[13]

Crockett also further developed his own persona, entirely conscious that as much by accident as design, he had cast himself earlier in a role that attracted the voters. He spoke the speech of his people, with a drawl and a way of chewing words that turned "crop" into "crap." He took advantage of his ear for frontier vernacular and liberally larded his speeches with quaint expressions like "horn" for a glass of liquor, and "stand up to my lick-log, salt or no salt," as a way of saying that he did his duty. He even began to embellish his pronunciation, intentionally using ungrammatical words, like "know'd" instead of "known," when he saw that they drew a smile from the voters. He had always had a

good ear, and had traveled more than enough in his youth and manhood to acquire a host of idioms and expressions that salted his speech.

Then there was his affability. However much he may have adopted
an exaggerated pose on the stand, he projected a basic and genuine
gentility. People liked him, and he adapted with ease to the tenor of
those around him. He could sense their expectations of him, smoothly
catch their mood on introduction, and then succeed, said one, in "agree-
ably confirming preentertained opinions in reference to himself."[14] He
calculated what he said carefully for effect, and more by instinct than
by cunning seemed to know that these backwoods voters were looking for a new type: an identity springing from themselves that represented the new America; a generation that, like a child, was ready to
move out on its own and declare its independence from its Founding
Father parents. Washington, Jefferson, and John Adams had been the
types of their time, but the last of their ilk, James Monroe, left the presidency early in 1825, and Jefferson and Adams both died in 1826, just
months before this canvass. Their era died with them, and so did
Yankee Doodle, and these new Americans sought a replacement in
their own image of themselves. Andrew Jackson fitted the mold in
large degree, yet even he was tainted by a kind of frontier aristocracy,
as well as by his stunning ability to create mortal enemies through a
willfulness that exceeded even Crockett's. But by the time of this canvass in the backwoods of West Tennessee in 1827, David Crockett was
coming to realize that he made rather a nice fit indeed.

Crockett gave the appearance of quite firmly aligning himself with
Jackson during the canvass, endorsing his candidacy for the presidency
in 1828. "I was," he said later, "without disguise, the friend and supporter of General Jackson, upon his principles as he laid them down."[15]
At a Fourth of July stump meeting, he was more than outspoken.
"Jackson is a hero, *but* Crockett is a *horse*," he toasted. "Here is to
General Jackson in the next presidents chair, loco Crockett in his seat
in Congress, and loco Alexander in the corn field."[16] Crockett's "loco"
was an extremely early, perhaps even seminal, usage of a term that
years later came to define more radical Jackson supporters, and others
who observed this campaign applied it to him as liberally as he did
himself, though its origin is lost.[17] "You have heard of the celebrated
Loco Crockett," an observer of the campaign wrote to a friend in

North Carolina, "'who can whip his weight in wild cats,' 'jump higher, fall down lower and drink more *liquors* than any man in the State.'"[18]

Quite evidently Crockett had added something else to his campaign arsenal, for now he adopted the outlandish hyperbolic brag-and-boast of the Mississippi flatboatman as part of his personal idiom. Not only did he make the voters smile with his claims of whipping wildcats, but he may have gone further, claiming he could "wade the Mississippi," even "carry a steam-boat on his back."[19] He did not originate such expressions as these and other like claims to being "half-horse and half-alligator," for they had been commonplace among the Kentucky flatboatmen on the Mississippi and Ohio Rivers for twenty years or more. Crockett quite probably heard such during his 1826 river trip, if not before, and simply brought them inland and added them now to the character he consciously constructed to entertain his audiences and cajole their votes.[20]

Of course there were the usual pranks and jokes on the stump. For one thing Crockett amused himself by keeping the source of his money for drinks a secret, which no doubt put his opponents off guard. For another, he took full advantage of the tendency of his opponents to ignore him as being of no consequence, while they flayed at each other. That gave Crockett the opportunity to dodge issues—on which Alexander and Arnold surfeited their audiences— and instead make points with his wit. He never tired of telling of the meeting at which a flock of clucking guinea fowl interrupted Arnold again and again, until he stopped his speech to shoo them away, giving Crockett the opening to comment to the crowd afterward that while Arnold may have ignored him in his speech, certainly the birds did not, for they were chanting "Crockett, Crockett, Crockett" until he quieted them.[21] Crockett's son John accompanied him on at least one stump tour in March, and confidently told friends at home in a flurry of slang that "the old hook is a going ahead electioneering. I think the old fellow will come out in the gunter."[22]

Crockett did come out "in the gunter," by which his son meant the "full measure." On the polling day late that summer, Arnold took 2,417 and Alexander 3,647, but Crockett throttled them both with 5,868 votes.[23] Crockett more than doubled his vote of two years before, while Alexander's only grew by 800. More important, almost twelve thousand of the eligible voters turned out on election day, more than double the number who voted in 1825, and at least half of the new voters went for Crockett. The perceptive observer could have seen a phenomenon in operation. Something was happening in West Tennessee—mirrored across the nation—that brought thousands of new men to the polls to vote perhaps for the first time, and they liked what they saw in David Crockett. A new and stunning dynamic was entering American politics.

There is no question that his election surprised many, perhaps not least Crockett himself. A few years later he told a friend that "he never knew why the people of his district elected him to Congress, as it was a matter he knew precious little about at the time and had no idea what he would be called on to do when he arrived in Washington."[24] That, of course, may just have been Crockett's old pretended pose of ignorance and naïveté, but others were quite genuinely taken aback. A friend wrote to Henry Clay just days after the balloting that "Crockett the bear hunter who voted for Colo. Williams, in opposition to Genl J[ackson], is elected 2 to 1."[25] Significantly, among politicians at large Crockett, if known at all at that moment, was remembered only for being the man who killed bears and who opposed Jackson's election to the Senate in 1825, and the two acts may have been viewed as somewhat synonymous. Far more significant, however, even though Henry Clay had undoubtedly never heard of Crockett before, Clay's son-in-law, James Erwin, now regarded this election result as sufficiently important to relate it to him in detail. He was already Jackson's archrival, and the man around whom an organization called National Republicans was starting to form as an opposition to Jackson's new Democratic Party.

A few weeks after the election Crockett called on Erwin in Nashville and asked for an introduction to his father-in-law. Clay was the acknowledged leader of western statesmen in Washington, had been Speaker of the House, and now filled the post of secretary of state, and that alone made such a request understandable for an incoming freshman representative. Though he was not yet public on the matter, Clay shared at least some of Crockett's concerns over sale of public lands, and Crockett also agreed at least in part with some of Clay's advocacy of federally funded internal improvements. Yet at the same time, Crockett's wish to see Clay betrayed either a striking failure to sense the prevailing political breezes—or else an even less admirable evolution of his old policy of not taking any stand at all into one of trying to ingratiate himself with all parties so that no matter who lost, he would be on the winning side.

Everyone in the nation knew that Clay loathed Jackson by now, suffering a near obsession with seeing Old Hickory defeated for the presidency in 1828. Though Clay and President John Quincy Adams formed a coalition at the moment, it was clear that after 1828 Clay would be the party leader no matter what happened. Thus for Crockett, on the record as an ardent Jackson man, to seek out Clay could in itself be suspicious, and how much more so when he told Erwin that when he arrived in Washington he intended "to pursue his own Course." That certainly sounded like Crockett. But then he said that when the House organized and elected its Speaker, he intended to vote for John W. Taylor of New York, a prominent opponent of Jackson and a man all too closely associated with Clay. More startling yet, he suggested to Erwin that if Clay thought Taylor a bad choice, Crockett would vote for anyone Clay suggested, "as he is more willing to trust your experience than his own." Was Crockett trying to ingratiate himself with Clay as a fellow westerner with shared interests, or was there something more sinister in his offer? If Jackson lost in 1828, Clay might be the winner, or even if Adams were elected, still Clay would be the man of the future. Could Crockett really have entertained a calculating notion of currying favor just in case? Or worst of all—and far more likely—was he simply so naive that he believed that a professional career politician like Clay would give an honest opinion uninfluenced by party concerns; that because Crockett himself would "pursue his Course" without reference to partisanship, Clay would too?

Erwin made no mistake in delineating Crockett for Henry Clay. "Col. Crockett is perhaps the most illiterate Man, that you have ever met in Congress Hall," he said. "He is not only illiterate but he is rough & uncouth, talks much & loudly, and is by far, more in his proper place, when hunting a Bear, in a Cane Break, than he will be in the Capital." Yet it would be worth the great Clay's time to be mindful of Crockett and perhaps to court him. "He is independant and fearless & has a popularity at home that is unaccountable," added Erwin, and then he threw in the essential element. "He is the only man that I now know in Tennessee that Could openly oppose Genl. Jackson in his District & be elected to Congress."[26] The message was clear enough: Crockett had confronted the Jackson bear in his own Tennessee lair and still emerged a vote winner. He would need watching. If he proved to be a sensible man, or even a foolish one who could be managed—as his offer on the speakership suggested—he might be a potential convert to the Clay-Adams party, and a potent weapon to use wittingly or unwittingly against Old Hickory.

Crockett did something seemingly unusual after his election victory. He spent time with his family, and even took them to western North Carolina for a visit with Elizabeth's relatives. They stopped first in Nashville in the third week of September, where the congressman-elect made his call on Erwin. As they traveled east, he suffered another recurrence of malaria, severe enough that though he continued on his way, once Crockett reached Swannanoa, near Asheville, he remained bedridden four weeks recuperating.[27] While there he found himself unintentionally involved in a feud between two local politicians that grew out of their own recent congressional election. Insults flew, and a challenge to a duel ensued, resulting in a meeting on November 6, several miles south of Swannanoa in Saluda. One of the principals, Samuel Carson, had been Crockett's friend, and now David accompanied him to the dueling field, where he saw Carson's opponent take an apparently fatal bullet. Crockett was never a man quick to violence. He had a temper but generally kept it well governed unless highly provoked. Moreover, he was more prone to ridicule dueling than to participate, but typically his sense of loyalty to a friend overrode any opposition in principle, and the next that was seen of him he was riding back to Carson's home for all his poor horse was worth, flailing his hat almost to tatters against the animal's flank to get more speed, and yelling "the Victory is Ours." It had been a season of victory.[28]

There was no time to take his family back to Tennessee now, for Congress was due to start its session on December 3. Elizabeth would have to get home on her own. By November 15, after allowing a physician to "bleed" him sufficiently to satisfy conventional wisdom about treating his illness, he rallied strength despite his weakness and, in company with Congressman Carson and his colleague Lewis Williams, left for Washington.[29] Crockett was no doubt glad of the company of these two experienced men, especially the ten-year veteran Williams. He felt uneasy and uncertain about how he would fare when thrown into the House with what he called "the great men of the nation," and they must have passed the time on the long journey educating Crockett on procedures and customs.[30] At the same time Williams, like Erwin, watched Crockett on Clay's behalf and let Clay know of their progress.[31]

The trip itself may have come close to killing Crockett, for he was hardly in any condition to make a grueling overland journey. "I have thought that I was never to See my family any more," he confessed a few weeks later, "tho thanks be to god I hope that I am Recovering."[32] The long hours in the saddle, and the poor beds and indifferent fare at the inns along the way did not help. Offered rabbit for dinner at one stop, he declared that he would "rather eat a paper of pins" than a bunny.[33] They traveled by way of Richmond, Virginia, and while there Crockett learned that the Jacksonians intended to run Andrew Stevenson for the Speakership, a choice he found acceptable enough.[34] On reaching Washington he rented a room at Mrs. Ball's boarding-house, and there met surely for the first time his fellow boarders Thomas Chilton of Kentucky, Nathaniel Claiborne of Virginia, and William Clark of Pennsylvania.[35] Even here his company was potentially dangerous, for Clark and Chilton were about to break with Jackson in favor of Adams and Clay, and Claiborne was already in their camp. Of course Crockett may have had no idea of the leanings of his fellow boarders when he took lodging at Mrs. Ball's. He just needed a place to live. But it is also just possible that Williams or Erwin directed him to a house populated by Clay's friends, where their influence might be subtly applied. Certain it is that from the day of his election to the moment he walked into the chamber of the House of Representatives for the first time, the interested eyes of Jackson's enemies were on him, and he was scarcely in Washington before his companion Williams introduced him to President Adams himself on November 27.[36]

Crockett's fellow delegates from Tennessee included James K. Polk, John Bell, John Blair, Robert Desha, Jacob Isacks, Pryor Lea, John H.

Marable, and James Mitchell, the very man who had dubbed him "gentleman from the cane." Almost to a man they backed Jackson, and most of them Crockett would have known in person or by reputation. When they all took their seats on December 3, the first order of business was organization of the House, and it became speedily apparent that the Democrats held more than enough of a majority to deny Taylor the speakership. As Polk saw it, the contest was a referendum on the coming presidential contest itself, and Andrew Stevenson of Pennsylvania was the Jackson candidate. The Clay-Adams men ran Taylor but simply never had the votes. Polk did note that in the voting there had been some "undisciplined militia against well drilled regulars," a metaphor indicating that some supposed Jackson men tried to act independently rather than follow the party line, but he may have been referring to Crockett in particular, thanks to his militia title of "colonel."[37] If Crockett still intended to vote for Taylor, he finally came around and voted with his delegation, though his original adherence to Taylor remains puzzling, the only apparent explanation being that, though friendly to Clay, Taylor had the reputation of being his own man.

At the same time they reelected Matthew St. Clair Clarke of Pennsylvania to be clerk. Crockett did not know Clarke, but he soon would. When the House gave one of its principal patronage jobs, the office of public printer, it also went to a Democrat, Duff Green, though his allegiance was to his kinsman John C. Calhoun much more than to Jackson. Unaware of this, Crockett actually crowed over the appointment, because it displaced Joseph Gales as publisher of the daily *Congressional Debates* and returned him to his editorship of the Washington *National Intelligencer*. Without knowing Gales, apparently, Crockett called him a "treasury pap Sucking Editor," apparently holding it against him that the Clay-Adams coalition that defeated Jackson in 1824 had given Gales his post. In short, his resentment was not for Gales the man but for the seeming "corrupt bargain" that had gotten him his job.[38]

Crockett commenced his days in Congress as befitted a new man, keeping quiet and watching and learning. He joined the rest of his delegation in petitioning President Adams not to interfere with a current appointee in West Tennessee, presented a petition to establish a new mail route in his district, and paid a call on the postmaster general to urge the appointment of his friend James Gibson to a postmastership, only to be told that he could name whomever he pleased and the cabinet official would approve.³⁹ It went slightly to Crockett's head, for never before in his life had he experienced such deference, especially from such quarters. "I find a representative have powar to appoint who they pleas," he wrote a friend.⁴⁰ What Crockett did not realize was that Postmaster General John McLean, having broken with the administration, was distributing as much patronage to the Jacksonian opposition as he could. Thus, even though Crockett got what he wanted, his pride in his new influence was misplaced. McLean simply used him unwittingly to a different end. These were murky waters in Washington.

Crockett waited exactly three days before trying to make his mark. His ego boost from McLean may have helped propel him to some extent, but in the main it was simply like him not to observe the conventions of being seen but not heard for awhile as a freshman. Besides, he epitomized one of the phenomena of American politics that Tocqueville would witness just three years later. "In America a deputy is generally a nobody apart from his position in the assembly," said the visiting French observer, and certainly that applied to Crockett. "He is therefore perpetually stung by the need to acquire importance there, and he has a petulant longing to air his ideas in and out of season. He is pushed in that direction not only by his own vanity but also by that of his electors, whom he is always bound to gratify."⁴¹ Add to that the fact that for Crockett, the shortest distance toward any destination was always straight ahead, and he had neither the time nor the finesse to play conventional games toward that end. He had come there to get that vacant land issue settled, and on December 6 he introduced a bill to effect his goal. Moreover, based apparently on little more than his own naive optimism and, thanks to McLean, perhaps a mistaken notion of his "powar," he believed confidently that he would see the bill passed that session, and even sent open letters to editors in his district telling constituents what he was accomplishing for them.⁴²

Very quickly reality began to confront him. Congress did not move speedily on anything unless it was a highly charged partisan issue, which hardly applied to West Tennessee acreage. After two weeks Crockett's enthusiasm began to wane as he found nothing being done, and little inclination to do anything until after Christmas. The House sometimes sat barely an hour a day.[43] More than two months after he introduced his bill, there was still no movement, and no chance of hurrying it as there had been when he sat in the state legislature. "Thare is such a disposition here to show Eloquience that this will be a long Session and do no good," he concluded by February 1828. He still expected to get his bill passed somehow, though, predicting that "in a few weeks you will find that I have been successful."[44]

Instead the speeches just droned on. He soon found that the most irksome thing about being a representative was having to listen to all those endless attempts at eloquence, especially since so many were aimed not at the business of the House but toward the coming election. He began ducking out whenever he thought a speaker had gone on long enough, and some days when there was no likelihood of anything else being done, he did not attend at all.[45] "There's too much talk," he complained. "Many men seem to be proud they can say so much about nothing. Their tongues keep working, whether they've got any grist to grind or not." Noting that some men simply sat without ever saying a word, Crockett concluded that they still earned their eight dollars a day in salary just by listening, "provided they don't go to sleep." For his own part he found the thought of splitting stringy gumwood on a hot August day far less daunting than trying to keep awake in the House.[46] It was all what Crockett called "one of my plaguy botherations."[47]

While he waited in what amounted to a triumph of hope over experience for the House to do something with his land bill, Crockett at least took pleasure in seeing the advance of Jackson's presidential prospects. It troubled him to see so much time wasted on the floor of Congress in partisan squabbling, but Jackson himself appeared to be above it all. He thought Old Hickory like the rough diamond in the soil, and of course that was just how Crockett saw himself. The gem had no value until polished, and the more Jackson's enemies tried to rub him, the brighter he sparkled. By early February he felt no doubt of Jackson's election. "Old hickory is rising," he told his constituents. "The die is cast."[48]

As the session wore on and spring came, Crockett's optimism for action on his land bill dipped even lower. When the House bogged down in debate on the tariff in March, he looked on in dismay as a largely partisan element tried to reshape the duties in a way that would align the

West, the South, and the mid-Atlantic states against New England, the home of President Adams. Critics charged that the House was concerned not with protecting manufacturers but manufacturing a president, and Crockett became so frustrated that he determined to vote against every single tariff amendment and against the tariff bill itself. The faster they got rid of the issue, the sooner they might come to his land bill. Moreover, the maneuvering of the public's business for such obvious partisan ends rankled him, and while he placed no blame on Jackson—who may not have approved the tariff manipulation—the behavior of Old Hickory's adherents, including Polk, increased Crockett's suspicion of party machines and of the men like Polk who ran them.[49]

There was still no action on the land bill. In time Crockett gained confidence in himself and his deportment, and believed: "I am getting along very well with the great men of the nation much better than I expected."[50] So he was, but there were undercurrents that escaped him. Polk, always difficult to read, no doubt felt some suspicion, before the session commenced, of both Crockett's depth as a statesman and his soundness for Jackson. Then, too, when he received a letter from a constituent asking him to help collect a modest $12.75 debt owed by Crockett that was more than five years overdue, he had to wonder just how responsible his colorful colleague might be. Perhaps most disturbing of all, well-meaning West Tennesseans confirmed for him what he may have feared privately: "Should that bill pass Relinquishing those lands to the State," said an enthusiastic Crockett supporter from near Jackson, "Crockett will be invincible, whether he aids in the cause or not."[51] If there was one thing the Jackson men in Tennessee had to guard against, it was someone who could not be counted on to follow the Jackson line becoming invincible.

As acknowledged leader of the House delegation, Polk patiently dealt with Crockett as he pressed for action and support on his bill. The bill approved by the Tennessee legislature that Crockett proposed provided that the United States would relinquish all its remaining unoccupied public domain in Tennessee to the state, with the proviso that such land was to be sold to raise money for education, a common policy followed in Alabama, Mississippi, and several other new states formed out of former territories. Increasingly David came to doubt that the state would handle the land fairly. He became convinced that it would try to keep the price on the land too high for the existing occupants to purchase their squats, or for the poor to move into the area and buy property. Polk certainly understood Crockett's point of view, regardless of his own sympathies, and inquired on his own into the actual sales potential of the land. He sought an opinion from Crockett's recent opponent Alexander, who responded that at least half of the vacant land would not bring more than twelve and one-half cents to the acre. Moreover, even if all of it sold for that price, the proceeds still would not make up the existing deficit in the state's common-school fund. In short, they could not realize enough to meet existing commitments, let alone fund colleges and universities.[52]

Interestingly enough, Polk could no doubt have heard this same conclusion from Crockett, but he preferred to get it from someone whose judgment he trusted more, which shows just how little confidence Crockett may have enjoyed among his peers from the very first, despite his touching belief that he was "getting along very well" with them. The Tennessee delegation met frequently in planning its approach when the bill should finally come up for debate, and Polk allowed Crockett to take center stage in the discussion. When Blair proposed that they amend the bill to stipulate that proceeds from land sales should endow a university in Nashville, Crockett led the way in defeating the idea. Instead the delegation agreed to amend the bill to provide that proceeds should go only to the common-school fund.[53]

On April 24 Polk finally took the floor to speak in behalf of the bill when the House took it up. He argued that Tennessee had been shortchanged. It was supposed to have gotten 444,000 acres of lands for its public schools' benefit in the 1806 cession from North Carolina, but the North Carolina warrants then claimed all but 22,000 acres of that, and it was only right that the deficiency be made up from federal land remaining in the western half of the state, and even then the North Carolina warrant holders had already claimed all of the best land there too. What remained would not pay Congress the expenses of establishing its land offices or running the surveys to sell it publicly. Crockett stood to second him, averring that much of it would bring scarcely one cent an acre, let alone Alexander's figure. As he could testify

from his own explorations, much of the country lay underwater anyhow. He went on to urge that this bill would enable the poor people
of the district to own their own property, and at the same time the
money they paid would help to educate their children, not in the colleges that scarcely one in a thousand would ever see but in the common schools that could prepare them for life. He knew the advantage
of educational opportunities, he said, "from having experienced the
want of them," and he wanted what he had missed in life to be
afforded to those who came after him.[54]

In the face of some opposition, and an anticipated amendment from
Ohio, the House voted 131 to 64 to table the bill on May 1, much to
Crockett's chagrin. It would not come up again in the remaining three
weeks of the session, and the disappointment only added to Crockett's
misery. Three times after taking his seat in the House he suffered
relapses, no doubt indications that he had never really recovered from
the previous fall's malaria bout and had pushed himself too hard. He
came down with what he thought to be pleurisy, but may have been
pneumonia allied to his general debility, and a physician taking prodigious quantities of blood from him in "treatment" only made the condition worse. He lost weight, lost the color in his cheeks, and nearly lost
hope of recovery.[55] No wonder he had little heart for regular attendance.

Yet while the Tennessean's health declined, his standing in
Washington seemed to climb, though it had little to do with real
influence. With every passing day his character—both by nature and
his own conscious assembly—came closer and closer to coincidence
with a national mood and hunger. By March reports had him uttering
his rural campaign boasts in Washington itself, to the delight of its
nabobs.[56] No doubt Crockett played to that intentionally, meeting and
leaving prominent men with an exaggeratedly vigorous handshake
and a quaint invitation to "come out to Tennessee for a riproarious bar-
hunt."[57] The eastern press began to report his movements and sayings,
and just as often to engraft rustic stereotypes onto him regardless of
fact. Jackson sheets presented him as Poor Richard, a comparison not
lost on Crockett, who soon bought, if he did not already have, a copy
of Benjamin Franklin's *Autobiography*. The administration press, meanwhile, pictured him as a bumpkin and lout.[58] In fact there were some
already tiring of the exaggerated stereotyping of the western character,

the overwhelming Jacksonian image of the rapacious conqueror measuring his success in land acquired or animals shot, the exploitive man on the make. Such men were a reality, embodied in James Bowie for one.[59] Yet defenders of the West argued that the old Jeffersonian yeoman farmer still most truly represented the region: sober, industrious, and responsible, if rustic.[60] Crockett himself would have agreed, for however much he began to appreciate the advantages of being regarded as some sort of original "character," he retained as well the aspiration to be a gentleman. He wore the best clothes he could afford, observed the formal niceties so far as possible, and tried to speak in the House as befitted a dignified statesman, even if he did feel the need to apologize for his accent and unfamiliarity with grammar.[61] Ironically, like so many poor whites, he desperately aspired to be that which he affected to despise the most, a middle-class gentleman. Now, as he experienced the kind of attention—and possible influence—that the rather embarrassing role of bumpkin gained him, versus the realization that as a gentleman he lacked either the lure or the skill to win such notoriety, he faced perhaps for the first time the struggle between the real man he felt himself to be and the "gentleman from the cane" that the public wanted. They expected—indeed hungered for—an original American type belonging to them and to no other, a character who thought, talked, and acted big, "the genius of the New World."[62] Such a heavy expectation exacted heavy demands. Torn between Jefferson and Jackson, Crockett may have sensed even before becoming a certified icon that the view from the pedestal would be distorted, and that from such a perch, whichever way he looked, there was a long way to fall.

Even though Congress adjourned on May 26, Crockett's health kept him in Washington well into the summer before he felt well enough to return home, and by then there was little time to accomplish much. Money was always tight, though he managed enough from his salary as a representative to repay Winchester the $250 he had borrowed. But that almost exhausted his funds, forcing him to go heavily into debt now when he acquired 225 acres in new Weakley County, north of Gibson, and spent the balance of the summer and fall building a

new gristmill. When he needed a young slave boy to help with the
work, he was even willing to trade a horse and colt and $150 in the
bargain before finding he could not raise even that much money.[63]
Meanwhile the debts continued to accumulate.[64] And there was mounting trouble with Elizabeth, who by now felt thoroughly tired of
Crockett's unwillingness or inability to settle on something to support
the family and stick to it. A religious woman, she remonstrated with
him for his complete lack of interest in church, and may have added
venom to her barbs when she nagged him for his drinking. Though
never known to be intemperate, Crockett certainly grew up with the
example of a father who took too many horns from time to time, and it
appears that by the fall of 1828 David himself may have taken to
drowning his worldly misfortunes in occasional overindulgence, a
habit he could just as easily have picked up at Mrs. Ball's boarding-
house in Washington.[65] Perhaps the only good news this fall was
Jackson's easy victory over Adams. Crockett certainly gave him his
vote, and predicted that Old Hickory would "shine conspicuous when
his enemies will stand before the world unnoticed by every Honist
American Citizen."[66]

   With all of his woes at home, Crockett probably welcomed the day
when he left to go via Nashville to Washington for the second session
of his term. The House convened on December 1, 1828, and Crockett
quickly found that the apparent antagonism of the opposition press
remained strong. During the first session of Congress, Crockett
received an invitation to dine at the Executive Mansion with President
Adams and four others. It may have been innocent enough, a courtesy
extended to new representatives, or the National Republicans may
have been continuing what seems to have been a desultory but as yet
uncoordinated effort to stay close to Crockett. Gulian Verplank and
James Clark, close adherents of Clay's—Clark currently held the seat
from Clay's own Kentucky district—went with Crockett, adding to
the possibility that the dinner may have been as much courting as
courtesy. No sooner did Crockett return to Washington for this new
session, however, than he read a Nashville newspaper account published while he was on his way east, saying that he had behaved with
unforgivable boorishness at the meal, demanding more food when his
plate was removed, even licking his fingers, and drinking out of all six

cups attached to the punchbowl. The report incensed Crockett when he finally saw it just after New Year's, and he got Clark and Verplank to publish open letters attesting to his "perfectly becoming and proper" conduct in refutation of the obvious fabrication.[67] Viewed in the light of immediately subsequent events, it was a revealing incident. Since there were at least six people at that dinner—there being six punch cups—any one of the other five attendees, including the president, could have put the lie to the story. In short, too many people knew the truth of the matter for one of those in attendance to get away with fabricating the tale. Moreover, since neither Adams nor the other two guests ever gainsaid Clark's and Verplank's denials, the story must have been groundless, and Crockett certainly felt comfortable in asking two members of the opposition for their supporting statements. The story had to be a lie made up by someone who knew the dinner took place and who gave it to the Clay-Adams press, yet who must surely have known that at least half the guests present who could refute the tale were themselves National Republicans. In other words, a fantasy concocted to embarrass Crockett must inevitably be embarrassing to the National Republicans as well, when the truth came out and men like Clark and Verplank were forced to refute what appeared in their own party organs. Moreover, as the opposition, headed by Clay, kept a covetous eye on Crockett, it could hardly hope to encourage his defection by making a fool of him in its press. The Clay-Adams men simply stood nothing to gain by printing such a lie—yet if they did not, then who did?

Jackson—or someone very close to him. There is no evidence that Crockett and Old Hickory had ever met up to this time, or even that Jackson knew of David as anything other than the Democrat who had voted against him for the Senate a few years before. Yet for Jackson, who interpreted any opposition to his aims as betrayal, that would have been enough to mark Crockett, and all the representative's many public avowals of support would thereafter mean nothing. Moreover, as Jackson and his managers met during the campaign that summer and fall, Polk exerted a strong influence on the nominee, and enjoyed his trust as much as any man. No doubt some state issues, including the vacant land bill, entered their conversations, and it would have been very strange if at least once or twice their conversation did not turn to

Crockett, the Democrat who already appeared to be too friendly with
the Republicans, the Democrat who refused to follow the party
machine, the man spoken of as becoming "invincible."

On top of it all, Polk and the rest of the Tennessee delegation probably knew weeks before the meeting of the new session that Crockett
intended to make a dramatic change in the land bill that the rest of
them opposed. He was quite simply too independent, too unmanage-
able, and in danger of becoming an embarrassment to Jackson and the
party right in Old Hickory's home base, Tennessee. He needed to be
disciplined, reined in, taken down a peg. Thus, in all probability, it
was a *Democrat*, though surely not Jackson and probably not Polk, who
gave the false story to the press. Significantly, he waited until after
Jackson's election victory, so that the embarrassment of one Democrat
could not hurt a much greater one. Even more significant, the newspaper that broke the story was not in some National Republican
stronghold like Kentucky or Massachusetts, but the *National Banner*,
right in Old Hickory's capital, Nashville.[68]

Certainly the David Crockett who took his seat in the second session
was a man in transition. For one thing he had sworn off liquor, and
resolved never again to taste anything stronger than cider. For another,
he seemed to be struggling with the acquisition of some faith. "I have
never made a pretention to Religion in my life," he confessed. "I have
Run a long Rail tho I trust that I was called in good time." News of the
tragic death of a niece whose head was crushed in an accident at his
mill may have helped turn his thoughts to mortality and salvation. "I
have been Reproved many times for my wickedness by my Dear wife,"
he recalled, then thought with his usual wry wit that she would be "no
little astonished when she gets infermation of my determination."[69]

More important still was the sea change that Polk and the rest of the
delegation noticed, and probably knew of even before the session
commenced. Crockett was going out on his own on the land bill in
direct opposition to their otherwise unanimous wishes and the instructions of their legislature, instructions he had himself approved when
he sat in the assembly. Sometime prior to the convening of the House,
Crockett showed Polk an amendment that would eliminate the provision for the state to sell the land to raise money for the common
schools, and that instead would make outright donations of 160 acres

to every existing squatter who could show that he actually occupied the land and had made improvements. Polk and the others told him not to do it, but Crockett refused to listen, saying he would rather kill the bill as it now stood if he could not carry his amendment. Even when the delegation agreed to alter the bill to provide for current occupants to have first option at their plots, still Crockett remained adamant, even publishing his intention in the press in his district. Knowing his colleagues to be unanimous against him, he said he preferred to "obey my constituents, who have placed me in office and whose servant I am."[70]

Polk suspected that David may have been obeying someone else. By his own observation he saw prior to the session that Crockett was "estranged from his colleagues, and associated much with our political enemies." The whole delegation had treated Crockett with kindness, he thought, "and was more disposed to conceal than to expose his folly." In that veiled evidence of condescension may be found at least some of the origin of Crockett's break with them. Besides being parts of the machine and subject to its will, which alone would have impelled David to stand aside from them, he may also have sensed that they did not fully accept him, that their courtesy to him was patronizing and insincere, and certainly that came to apply to Polk, who by February 1829 declared that "I have no other feelings towards Col. Crockett, than those of pity for his folly and regret that he had not consulted *better advisers*."[71] Just when Polk found out that Crockett intended to go his own course, and came to the belief that David listened to "*advisers*" from the opposition, is unclear, though it could have come as early as the previous September when Crockett was in Nashville and could have met with Polk during his visit. However, his admission that he preferred to "conceal than to expose" Crockett's folly is tacit testimony that he felt Crockett could be exposed, and perhaps even deserved it. Whoever gave the Adams dinner story to the *National Banner* obviously was of like mind.

Set on his course, on January 5 when debate on the bill commenced, Crockett arose and made his position clear. He distrusted the legislature's promise to spend the land proceeds on common schools, and feared the money would go to universities instead. "The children of my people never saw the inside of a college in their lives," he argued, "and never are likely to do so." Their parents could hardly afford even twelve and one-half cents an acre, let alone the fifty cents per acre fee for surveying federal public land. They deserved their land free in payment for their hardships and dangers in settling the raw frontier. Already many had been pushed off previous squats by the imposition of the North Carolina warrants, and it was all too much, and too unfair. "If their little all is to be wrested from them, for the purpose of State speculation; if a swindling machine is to be set up to strip them of what little the surveyors, and the colleges, and the warrant holders, have left them, it shall never be said that I sat by in silence."[72]

It was typical Crockett, with all the virtue of simple honesty, and lacking utterly in practical sense and finesse; a bulldog approach loaded equally with earnestness and his longtime resentment of the wealthy, the educated, and the professional; seasoned with the suspicion of a class that often saw itself as victimized. It was the sort of approach that made him his own most effective foe, and so it proved now, for the opposition forces smelled the fresh blood of a small wound in the Jackson flanks and set about opening it further. Polk and his colleagues felt humiliated at the things Crockett said about the Tennessee legislature. Then, to add to their embarrassment, in successive debates prominent Clay and Adams men backed Crockett's amendment. Polk saw all too clearly what Crockett could not, however. David believed he was seeing evidence of bipartisan support, honest men favoring an honest measure, but the more subtle Polk recognized that they were taking the "opportunity to use *Crockett*, and to operate upon him through this measure, for their own political purposes."

If the amendment could have come to a vote that first day, it might have passed. But in nine subsequent days of debate Blair and Isacks openly denounced him, and every other member of his own delegation spoke to oppose his amendment. As the talk dragged on and on, Crockett even made the either desperate or frivolous statement that he would vote for any measure any other member asked him to support, in return for a vote in favor of his amendment. Obviously he had learned that politics involved bargaining, but not as blatant as this. On January 14, with everyone in the House thoroughly tired of the subject, a vote to table the bill and the amendment carried by 103 to 65. To his constituents Crockett actually applauded the failure of the Polk bill, for now he could introduce a new one of his own. Worse, he reiterated for the Tennessee press his distrust of its own legislature. "If I am whipped," he promised, "I will not stay whipped."[73]

"You may suppose that such a man under no circumstances could do us much harm," Polk fumed two days after the tabling motion carried. "Rely upon it he can be and has been opperated upon by our enemies. We cant trust him an inch." The Tennessee delegation talked of preparing a statement to be signed by all of them repudiating Crockett's conduct, and one loyal Democrat back in Shelby County referred to "*Davy Crockett*" and fumed to Polk that "it is a misfortune to the state that such a man should be one of her delegates."[74]

In his fury Polk made another accusation that may have had some foundation, and if so, it showed just how effectively the opposition had "opperated" on Crockett, and how naive he could be in the face of more skilled politicians. During the course of the debates he believed that he saw some of the National Republicans helping Crockett with his speeches and parliamentary procedure, most notably that same Joseph Gales whom Crockett had denounced the year before, yet who now Polk saw "nursing him, and dressing up and reporting speeches for him" in the *National Intelligencer*, even though Polk and others would swear that Crockett never delivered those speeches as reported. There appeared to be a good possibility that when it came time to vote anew for a House printer, Crockett might side with Gales and his partner, William Seaton, against the Democratic candidate, Duff Green.[75] So incensed was Polk at Crockett's action that he sent full explanatory letters of the whole episode, including his suspicions, to several prominent men in Tennessee. It was evident that he felt that Crockett had declared war on his own delegation, and Polk and the rest were ready to fight back.

It is not hard to fathom what was happening to Crockett. He never felt truly accepted as a member of his own delegation. From the moment of his departure for the first session of the House, members of the opposition had been at least as friendly as his own party, and perhaps more so, and certainly anxious to accommodate, right up to Henry Clay and President Adams. Now when he simply tried to do what he knew to be right, his colleagues all abandoned him, and suddenly the only friends he seemed to have were men like Gales and other Republicans. A man of the world might have seen their motives as questionable, but a simple man of the canebrakes, a man who said and meant what he thought and felt, and who took others likewise at their word, saw only open hands of friendship from men whose agreement with his amendment only proved that he was right to go ahead. Besides, whom was he to represent, his fellow delegates, whom he knew in his pure heart to be wrong, or the people who had sent him here? Moreover, this had nothing to do with Jackson. Crockett's loyalty there was as iron fast as ever, it seemed. His dispute was with some of Jackson's supporters such as Polk, who appeared to have abandoned the interests of the common man, but certainly that was a different matter: Surely there was no disloyalty in being right?

Suddenly Crockett felt out of place and isolated in Washington. His colleagues rebuffed or ignored him, the bill was dead for the balance of this Congress, and his only friends seemed to be men he should not befriend. When he learned that Elizabeth's father intended to visit in Weakley County in the winter, he wished he could be there, and fell into a nostalgic reverie for home that he seemed never to have felt before. When he walked down the streets of Washington and saw dogs yapping after the farmers' carts on market days, he felt a sudden homesickness for his own hounds and the long hunts of winters before.[76] In the unusual cold of this season in the East, he remembered the suffering of his poor neighbors in Tennessee. When a fire broke out across the Potomac in Alexandria, he watched it from the Capitol steps for a time, then joined others in a cab to rush over and help fight the flames for hours as families struggled to save their homes; and when discussion arose in the House the next day proposing to appropriate relief for the homeless, he supported the bill.[77]

Crockett decided to leave Washington the very day after the session ended, so anxious was he to be at home among friends and the people he understood. He became all the more anxious when the Tennessee delegation counterattack started with Pryor Lea's unsigned open letter in the Washington press on St. Valentine's Day. Without naming Crockett, Lea accused a representative of abandoning his delegation and courting the opposition, adding that "he has openly set himself up in market, offering to vote for any thing in order to get votes by it." Lea reiterated Polk's charge that Crockett was getting cozy with Gales, and even that Crockett admitted on one occasion that Gales had "made me a much better speech than I made in the House, or ever could make." Crockett took up the fight in the press, and replied in temper that Lea was a "*poltroon, a scoundrel* and *a puppy*," suggesting that if Lea would identify himself, Crockett would "resent" the insults with a challenge. Lea did identify himself in responding, declining the invitation to duel but repeating his charge that his colleague had made himself the "willing instrument of political, sectional and personal malignities" opposed to the interests of Tennessee, on the part of men who wished to "induce him to act with them in future."[78] The correspondence went back and forth in the press for several days, with Crockett, by his intemperate language, giving Lea the best of it. Crockett himself termed the episode "unfortunate" and sought to get statements from several members of Congress attesting that there had been nothing underhanded in his conduct or the discharge of his duties. Not everyone responded.[79]

There seemed but one bright moment that winter in Washington. On March 4 Andrew Jackson took office as seventh president of the United States, and Crockett for one felt what he believed to be joy on the occasion, and vindication for the common man whom both he and Old Hickory championed. Jackson actually arrived in Washington unexpectedly early before his supporters were ready for him, and in order to avoid too much pomp, leading Crockett to quip that he had "stolen a march upon his friends, as he always had done upon his enemies."[80] No doubt Crockett called on Old Hickory prior to the inauguration if he was able, and certainly he felt no hesitation in making his first request of the president-elect when he joined Chilton and six other representatives, all Democrats, in requesting an appointment for another Jackson supporter.[81] It was well for the applicant that Jackson regarded him favorably, for Crockett's name on the application would likely have produced no action. Old Hickory felt that he owed no patronage to the canebrake upstart.

6

BOWIE

1824–1826

He has acquired an influence since you left us that astonishes those that have witnessed its Progress; his success in these land titles have led the mob to believe that he is endowed with more than human energy & ability.

WALTER OVERTON, 1826

Alexandria and western Louisiana were reeling with political excitement in the fall of 1824, when James Bowie moved to his new home in a room at Bailey's Hotel. There were still no real parties. More and more now, with a presidential election imminent, factions in the region gelled into two, those supporting Henry Clay and those favoring Jackson. Each candidate enjoyed strong personal ties to the region's influential men, as Clay did with Johnston and Brent, while Jackson commanded widespread popular loyalty thanks to his victory at New Orleans. Clay had strong support among the French-Creole population, whom Jackson had offended with his high-handedness in 1815. Clay also favored a high protective tariff on sugar, which endeared him to planters. Jackson, on the other hand, came free of the taint of the professional politicians who many thought had run the country for their own benefit long enough. Some of the old Jeffersonians looked to him as well.

Certainly James Bowie favored Clay, for "Harry of the West" represented most of the interests that concerned him, and Bowie's close associates were Clay supporters as well. Being opportunists rather than ideologues, they all favored Clay's stand on a sugar tariff, but they opposed his equally firm support of tariffs that protected other industries than their own. In the end, though, the presidential contest was for Bowie what it was for everyone else—a matter of distant interest at best. An electoral college composed of delegates chosen by popular

ballot still elected presidents. Louisianans in 1824 would not see the
names of Clay, Adams, or Jackson on their ballots, but only those of
nominated electors pledged to one of the candidates. As a result state
and local politics commanded far more attention, and raised much
greater excitement. With no fixed political ideology in sway in the
region, voters still looked at matters through the lens of immediate
and personal importance. Loyalty, like partisanship, was local.[1]

The gubernatorial contest attracted only passing attention that year.
For some time now common custom had alternated governors from the
American and the French communities, and "by due rotation" the Creoles
expected and got the chair for one of their own that year.[2] The real attention went to even more local races. At least seven prominent men entered
the contest for the Rapides seat in the legislature, including Johnston's
brother John, Bowie's friend from the Seventeenth–Nineteenth Louisiana,
Samuel L. Wells, Gen. Walter H. Overton of the state militia, and more.
The partisans of Wells and Overton especially laid on each other with a
heavy hand, arousing some high feeling. Arbiters watched the polling
places carefully for fraud on election day in July, making certain to speak
with every voter to ensure eligibility. Overton won by the narrow margin
of five votes, and by the time Bowie arrived, partisans on all sides were
trying to cool the feelings aroused by the campaign.[3]

William Brent's contest for reelection generated the most heat.
Many in the parishes of Rapides, Opelousas, Attakapas, Natchitoches,
Ouachita, and Concordia, which made up the Third Congressional
District, still felt bitter toward Brent for his slanderous campaign
against Johnston in the last race. Now he ran against Henry Bullard of
Rapides, a Jacksonian, and the campaign quickly turned nasty.
Bullard's supporters circulated rumors that Brent himself had filed
forged papers to secure his property in the district.

Some charged Brent with "indelicate character" flaws, and only a
few concentrated on issues, like Brent's break with Clay on the tariff
issue. For his part Brent wisely stayed in Washington the entire time
and allowed surrogates to campaign for him. He announced himself in
favor of renewing the United States claim for Texas as a part of the
Louisiana Purchase, saying it should be annexed, a position bound to
appeal to men like Bowie. He used his congressional franking privilege so blatantly in sending out his own campaign material that the

local postmasters complained about the volume of his mail, but among the voters at large it gradually came to appear that Brent was an absent victim, in Congress doing his job while men attacked him at home where he could not defend himself in person.[4] In the end the backlash from the Bullard campaign largely reelected Brent, but behind it yet more bitterness was added to the Wells-Overton animosity. "Electioneering is warm," Johnston's brother John warned him just before the voting; "it may produce some unpleasant results if they should indulge in their passions."[5]

The congressional election was just past when Bowie moved to Alexandria, but by then Brent had engendered even more hostility. Josiah Johnston took his seat in the U.S. Senate early in 1824 to fill out the unexpired term of another. The office went up for election again that fall, and when Johnston sought it, Brent reneged on his former promise of support and campaigned against him, circulating charges that Johnston's close personal alignment with Clay included full support of all the tariffs, not just the one on sugar. Johnston responded with accusations of his own, and by the time Bowie took up his rented residence in Alexandria, Brent was publicly accusing Johnston of being "mean, scurrilous and cowardly." All that prevented a duel was Brent's refusal to accept Johnston's challenge.[6] Within a few weeks Brent further enraged many in Louisiana when the presidential election went to the House of Representatives after neither Jackson, Adams, nor Clay received sufficient votes in the electoral college. Jackson had the plurality in the college and was expected to win in the House, but Clay threw his support to Adams. Even though Louisiana at large favored Jackson, its delegation was divided. One man voted for Jackson, but Brent and the third went for Adams, giving him the state. The result led to charges of a "corrupt bargain" when Adams made Clay his secretary of state, while men in Louisiana predicted that it would be unsafe for Brent ever to return home.[7]

All this served as background for the Bowie family's just completed first venture into politics, and James Bowie's first taste of what it could be like. His brother John served as justice of the peace in Catahoula in 1821-22, and was a frequent fixture at the parish courthouse, whether taking the payment of parish taxes or buying land at a sheriff's sale.[8] In the spring of 1824 he decided to seek Catahoula's seat in the legislature, running against James G. Taliaferro, a man with whom he had done business selling some slaves just the year before.[9] John Bowie kept his reasons for seeking office to himself, but obviously having a voice in the legislature in Baton Rouge would not hurt any of the family's enterprises, including James's land deals. "Squire Bowie," as some called him, campaigned actively, and by coincidence spent much of his time in the Bayou Maçon area, where his brother's claims were being surveyed. He spread sufficient mischief that Taliaferro was forced to abandon his determination not to campaign—but too late.[10]

The result smelled bad from the day of the election in July. Of the five polling places in the district, somehow only two of them received their regulation ballot boxes. As a result, in three locations no voting took place. At the other two Taliaferro charged that "votes were taken and counted which were illegal." Some voters appeared to be under age, while others may not have owned sufficient real property to qualify, which suggested purchased votes. Moreover, the two ballot boxes furnished did not have proper locks and keys for security. Even worse, Taliaferro complained that "the most violent and unfair exertions were made to compromit the interest of the opposing candidate," meaning himself. Those "violent and unfair exertions" seemed to smack of intimidation, something that was much more James Bowie's game than his nearsighted brother John's.[11] When John emerged the victor with a majority of a mere three votes, Taliaferro contested the result, but it may have been preordained against him. So prominent was John Bowie and so wide were his contacts in some areas of Catahoula that when Taliaferro took depositions relating to the voting, it had to be done in the home of John's mulatto cousin James on Bayou Bushley.[12] Taliaferro's charges may have been nothing more than spite at being defeated in what just happened to be an extremely ineptly run election, something not uncommon in Louisiana. But the humid aroma of a fix clung to the result like a stale dew all the same.

James Bowie might well need a good connection, not so much in Baton Rouge as in Washington. He may have left Avoyelles behind when he moved to Alexandria, but the suspicions of the General Land Office followed him.[13] In March, George Graham—already devoting increased scrutiny—finally saw the lost Harper letter and stated that at least nine claims—including all of Martin's and Wilson's—were false.[14]

By December he established that "Bowie was concerned in all of them."[15] That winter Graham counterattacked, warning his agents against false claims, stirring the press against forgers, and replacing Sutton with John Hughes.[16] However, the new man found all of Bowie's documents mysteriously missing, quite possibly removed at James's behest by John Wilson, a surveyor recently fired for extortion.[17] After the scare over the Bayou Maçon grants, Bowie knew not to leave any originals of his forgeries on file. And meanwhile he was creating more, again churning out titles using Robert Martin and his brother William, recording the titles in several parishes.[18] He was anxious to get surveys and patents so he could sell the land for good money in the current boom for cotton land, but Graham stymied him with delays while waiting to bring the matter to Congress in December 1825.[19] George Davis also suspected Milo Johnson, and when he performed some Catahoula surveys without authorization, including a claim for John Bowie, Davis stopped him. "I had not expected to find the name of *Bowie* among the claimants there," Davis told Graham.[20] Seemingly it was impossible to escape that name, a name soon to become known in important circles as a synonym for fraud.

Bowie did nothing to help. In the fall of 1825 he registered at least six new bogus claims for 8,100 acres or more in the Southwest District headquartered at Opelousas, using two of the fictitious grantee names from his Sutton claims, and having a third presented by Martin Despallier of Rapides, a man so transparently a front that it was soon known to land officials that "Despallier is the person who has the reputation of having made the claims known in our state as the Bowie claims."[21] If Bowie's audacity commanded admiration, his prudence did not, for this was no time to be handing the land offices more forged papers. Information of widespread fraud flooded Washington, attended by stories of the eviction of good settlers thanks to frauds like Bowie's, some claiming his activities to be worse than burglary or horse theft.[22] At this very time Bowie was evicting squatters from his Terrebonne claims.[23]

As Bowie kept on laying a paper trail of copies of his false titles, Graham ordered Hughes to provide every scrap of available information on what everyone now referred to as "the Bowie claims." By January 1826 Hughes had examined the documents in his office, gathered what information he could in the locality, and knew the general mode of Bowie's operations. The question was how to remedy the situation. The only solution he could suggest was to decline to give a patent to anyone but the legal representatives through power of attorney of the original grantees—who were, of course, imaginary, "and where the *legal* Representatives of Vaca, Llano, Gonzales, De Santo & fifty others are to come from is more than I can tell, but I presume efforts will be made to find substitutes for them."[24]

All that Bowie knew with certainty was that his surveys were not being ordered and that his patents were not being issued. Characteristically he decided to go to Washington and confront Graham himself. Leaving Rezin his power of attorney to handle affairs in his absence, James went to New Orleans in late January.[25] Bowie spent some time in the city before he booked passage, and then on the evening of February 13 he stepped aboard the ship *Virginia* bound for New York, with the expectation of a short voyage. He had seen much of Louisiana and a bit of Texas. Ahead of him lay a wholly new part of the nation, and the real seats of power.[26]

Following the voyage through the Gulf and up the Atlantic coast, Bowie traveled by post road from New York to Washington, reaching the capital before the end of February. Certainly the General Land Office claimed one of his first visits, and he found George Graham ready for him. The commissioner refused to be either cajoled or bullied. He may even have confronted Bowie with the evidence amassed to date to prove his claims fraudulent. Certainly Bowie left the office with nothing but a bitter resentment toward Graham.[27] Moreover, if Bowie did not already know of the alliance between Graham and Johnston, he surely knew of it by now. Graham entertained Johnston for dinner at his home while Bowie was in Washington, and when conversation turned inevitably to news from Louisiana, Graham must have told Johnston of Bowie's visit. The senator already had cause to regard Bowie as a character to suspect, thanks to correspondence from Louisiana, and after talking with Graham he must have watched him carefully from then on, especially considering that some of Bowie's Robert Martin claims adjoined the Terrebonne plantation that he operated in partnership with Graham.[28]

As for Bowie, he probably did not bother visiting Johnston while in Washington. Instead he called on Representative Brent, with whom he already had much in common. Of course, more than one suspicious land claim attached to Brent himself. He had some influence in Washington, and as one of the Louisiana representatives who cast the state's vote against Jackson in the 1825 House election, he could be expected to have access to President Adams's ear. Bowie understood things like influence and how to cultivate relations with those who possessed it. Moreover, Brent loathed Johnston, and sensing now that the senator was his foe as well as Graham, Bowie could use Brent's hatred to his own advantage. Brent also favored a change in the incumbent at the surveyor general's office, and that would certainly benefit the fortunes of Bowie's claims, for a new man might not regard them with the prejudice that now permeated the General Land Office.[29] Thus their combined antipathies and mutual interests made them natural allies. Through Brent, Bowie may even have gotten an interview with Secretary of State Henry Clay, whose counsel would be important in another scheme then gestating in Bowie's fertile brain.[30] When Bowie left Washington that spring to return to Louisiana, he brought with him Brent's warm friendship and support. Brent may not have known it, but Bowie also came away from the capital with a taste for the kind of power to be wielded there, and an idea of where he could get it.[31]

Once back in Alexandria, James Bowie redoubled his efforts. For several weeks that summer he rode through the parishes west and north of town, still pressing to get his surveys done, displaying his forged papers and—regardless of what Graham may have told him—announcing that he would soon be able to sell the land.[32] At the same time, he carefully ingratiated himself with the men of property in Catahoula, Avoyelles, and Ouachita Parishes, with an end in mind that he did not as yet reveal. He had already made good inroads into the Rapides community. Alexandria was a pleasant, compact village on the edge of a live oak forest just back from the Red River, its whitewashed houses rimmed with verandas and piazzas, and shaded by China and Catalpa trees. The nearby falls on the river made a constant, not-unpleasant hum in the ears of the inhabitants. Several professional men, doctors and lawyers, practiced there, and the new College of Rapides admitted tuition students into its large, ugly edifice. The weekly *Louisiana Herald* provided some semblance of regional news, and a new bank made fitful starts at encouraging the economy of the

region.³³ Unfortunately the bank only opened in 1824, secured capitalization slowly, and by the following year so selectively limited the risk
on its loans that one disgruntled man complained that "it appears to
me that the Establishment is only intended to help those who dont
stand in need of it & for the accommodation of speculators &
swindlers."³⁴ Bowie himself may have been one of those speculators
seeking loans, but since he was in the business of forging titles rather
than buying them, he hardly had need of bank loans, while he secured
enough from personal advances from friends and an occasional land
sale to support himself.³⁵

Besides, James Bowie already had a line on a small fortune even if
his land deals all fell through. He discussed more than land claims with
Brent and others in Washington, hence his other stops almost certainly
included the Treasury and Henry Clay's State Department to look into
another matter. Charles Mulhollan—one of his near neighbors on
Bayou Boeuf and probably an acquaintance from the Laffite days,
when Mulhollan illegally imported slaves—put Bowie onto an opportunity that naturally appealed to him. Perhaps everyone in Rapides
knew of the long-standing claims of old Reuben Kemper. The man
was an undeniable hero in the southwestern mode. A leader in the successful West Florida rebellion that eventually saw the Florida parishes
annexed to Louisiana, he then fought with his brother in Texas before
the War of 1812 and played a vital part in securing Jackson's victory at
New Orleans.³⁶ Certainly Bowie cultivated his acquaintance, even
though Kemper was known to be friendly with George Graham, and
in the last election had opposed Brent.³⁷ Kemper commanded tremendous respect in the parish despite his declining years.

In the West Florida enterprise, Henri de la Français—usually referred
to as Enrique de la Francia, the Spanish version—provided the insurgents arms and ammunition worth $11,850, and Kemper took personal
responsibility. Kemper believed that those arms later went to American
forces in the War of 1812, and in April 1814, when the U.S. government
assumed the debts of the Florida republic, Kemper presumed that this
would include the de la Français matter. In January 1817 de la Français
gave Kemper his power of attorney to collect the debt for him, and
being in poor health himself transferred authority to receive the claim
to Kemper's close friend William Johnson of Mississippi. Two years

later de la Français died of fever, the claim still unpaid. Kemper himself had fed and lodged the man for several years, and from his own funds advanced him more than $4,000 against the claim.[38]

Following de la Français's death, Mulhollan, the curator of his estate, secured a judgment in November 1822 against Kemper for the debt plus 10 percent interest a year, while Kemper himself kept steadily pressing the claim. By 1824 he had enlisted the aid of Josiah Johnston and repeatedly urged him to serve his interests in Washington.[39] Further muddying the matter, at some point William Johnson was believed to have transferred the claim back to Kemper, but the curator, Mulhollan, who had been a neighbor of de la Français at Bayou Sara in his last years, thought otherwise. No written transfer existed, which meant that de la Français's heirs—or those purporting to be his heirs—might have a chance at staking the claim themselves.[40]

Mulhollan, apparently a kindred spirit, approached Bowie, and the upshot was that in mid-May 1826 Bowie called on Kemper and informed him that he had acquired the claim from de la Français's heirs at the instigation of Mulhollan. He showed the old man a document of transfer, of course, but Kemper was not convinced. "I am sorry to say it is done by them by an unfair contrivance," he complained to Johnston.[41] As usual with Bowie, that "contrivance" was forgery and perjury, with probably a bit of bribery in the mix. During his visit to New Orleans in February, prior to sailing for Washington, he appeared before local notary Felix De Armas, with a man in tow who swore on oath that he was the brother and sole heir of de la Français, one Jose de la Francia of Matanzas, Cuba. While the notary copied his statement, de la Francia attested that he had appointed Bowie "his true and lawful attorney" to collect the $11,850 plus interest from Kemper. Further, he empowered Bowie to receive also the 10 percent a year on the debt, which by now amounted to $17,775, making the total debt $29,625. In default of payment by Kemper, de la Francia authorized Bowie to take all lawful means necessary to collect the debt.[42]

Kemper could only plead with Josiah Johnston for protection. "I pray you to be on the alert," he said a few days after Bowie called, and at the same time appointed Johnston as his agent in Washington for all his affairs, for Kemper also had nearly $40,000 in claims and accrued interest of his own due him for funds he had advanced the West

Florida insurgents.[43] Johnston did look into Kemper's problem, but what he found was embarrassing to Kemper and positively disconcerting to Bowie. When West Florida submitted to the Treasury Department a certificate listing all the claims that it recognized to be transferred to the United States, the de la Français claim did not appear. It turned out that a Spanish officer had turned the arms over to de la Français for safekeeping when he thought his post threatened by the Florida rebels, but instead of transporting the weaponry to another Spanish post, de la Français sold them to Kemper, taking his personal note in payment. Soon afterward the Spanish commander appeared on the scene and forcibly retrieved the cache. The Treasury Department took the position that since de la Français had stolen the arms in the first place, and since the Spanish took them back later, the government had derived no benefit from the arms and no money was due.[44] That meant not only that Kemper was owed nothing, but also that in forging the power of attorney, Bowie had acquired title to nothing.

When Johnston notified Kemper of his findings in a letter on July 6, the old man may have been chagrined, but the news startled Bowie. In frustration he said he would never take another step in the matter. "I hope he has been as good as his word," said Kemper, "yet I have my doubts of his sincerity." Before leaving Kemper's, Bowie railed against Senator Johnston "and made some very unjust remarks," in which he tried to turn Kemper against Johnston, saying that the man to depend on in Washington was Brent. But there, seemingly, they left the matter. Bowie had nothing, but honest old Kemper somehow felt that he was still personally responsible to the de la Français heirs—if any— once again, even though the man had spent not a cent for the arms, and they never saw use in the War of 1812. All he could do was urge Johnston anew to press his personal claim of forty thousand dollars plus interest with the government. Payment of that would allow him to settle with Bowie.[45]

Bowie probably drowned some of his frustration at the Rapides Inn, where he could find a game of cards and a convivial glass, as well as reflect on how to recover the Kemper situation, for he rarely let even major setbacks deter him from an enterprise. Meanwhile the inn was an important place to meet the men he needed to know, and his brother John saw that James was "very successful in securing a fair portion of the friendship of the better class of the people."[46] It was a kind of society that suited his ambitions and pretensions. Travelers found the planters of this area "reckless of the value of money," a people who "live more in sensation, than in reflection," and that certainly described James Bowie.[47] "His extreme politeness and fascinating manners were captivating," confessed one friend, "and he was much esteemed by his friends, and those who knew him best." He also paid very careful attention to his appearance. "James Bowie always dressed with good taste," said his friend Sparks.[48] A successful and ambitious man of business must look successful and use money lavishly, even if he wasted it at the gaming tables. "Money gotten easily, and without labor," commented the disapproving master of the College of Rapides, "is easily lost."[49]

Other associations in the community were also important. Alexandria had as yet no Masonic lodge of its own, but Bowie became a Freemason either at Natchez or in one of the new lodges at Natchitoches or Opelousas.[50] Such fraternal organizations wielded enormous social and business as well as political importance on the frontier, and no man of Bowie's aspirations could afford not to be a Mason, though there was a burgeoning anti-Masonic political movement among the National Republicans and other groups, so he might need to be wary of being too closely tied to the order. Masonry gave him further entrée into the most influential parlors and counting houses. Meanwhile, he gained acquaintance with the Cuny family, led by its scion Gen. Samuel Cuny and his physician brother, Richard. Connection to the Cunys naturally led to the Wellses, and James was already a friend of Samuel L. Wells III, an aspiring local attorney and politician exactly his own age, whose brother Montfort had run for the legislature two years before and who himself had sought the office of sheriff in 1824, only to lose to the land speculator and reputed duelist Maj. Norris Wright, in part because of several forged ballots. In the way of Rapides society, becoming a friend of the Wellses automatically made one an enemy of Wright, but then that was Bowie's nature anyhow. "He loved his friends with all the ardor of youth," said brother John, "and hated his enemies and their friends with all the rancor of the Indian."[51]

Knowing the prominent Alexandria men also introduced Bowie to their sisters and daughters. He was thirty years old when he returned from Washington, still unmarried and apparently unentangled romantically. It is unlikely that he remained entirely a stranger to female company, however. Vague stories later surfaced of dalliances with a Creole girl named Judalon de Bornay in New Orleans, an Acadian woman named Sibil Cade, and even the former quadroon mistress of Laffite, Catherine Villars. A young Spanish noblewoman in New Orleans named Montejo was also rumored to be involved, but her parents' intractable disapproval of Bowie led her in the end to enter a convent.[52]

In Alexandria, however, Samuel Wells had an orphaned cousin named Cecilia, just turning twenty-one when Bowie returned from his Washington trip, and in her he may have taken a more serious interest, quite possibly with the encouragement of the Wells brothers, who looked on her as a sister. Setting aside any possible romantic attractions Bowie may have felt for her, such an alliance with one of Rapides' most influential families would have been very much to his purpose. If indeed he did court Cecilia Wells, though, he did it with a leisurely pace and deliberation that never characterized any of his other actions.[53]

These associations inevitably drew Bowie into the family and political squalls that swirled constantly in Rapides. Alexandria sat isolated from the rest of the state, with few roads and bridges connecting it to other communities. A man could only travel overland to the Mississippi in the fall and winter; for the rest of the year the roads became swamps. This isolation, compounded by slow and indifferent mail service that took eight days just to get a letter from New Orleans, turned the community in on itself, compounding its natural preoccupation with local matters. Every event, no matter how insignificant, seemed enlarged in importance by boredom, isolation, and the ever-present ambition and avarice. The hostility of the factions in the area became notorious throughout Louisiana.[54]

In May 1826, not long after Bowie's return from Washington, John Johnston complained that Alexandria "is a dull place and it affords nothing—much idleness, much distress, and no prospect of a change. I am afraid it is on the decline." Despite the recovery from the depression, prosperity did not wait around the corner. "The cry of *hard times* is raised with a louder voice than ever known in this country," he told his brother, and that only infused more pollution into the already volatile climate.[55] By June the decline in crop prices, the bankruptcy of some of the inhabitants, and the static or declining population, led him to fear that Rapides was in a permanent slump. Worse was the effect on the populace. "Society here, if I do not now abase the term, stands on a trembling point, beyond which if but little pressed by its enemies, it will be viewed, in its unreclaimable state," he warned the senator. "A feeling of hostility seems to seize every mind, to enter every Bosom." He saw all around him "more fighting, menacing, abusing than I have ever before known." Many families went to homes in the cool pine woods to escape the summer heat, and he could only hope that their seething passions might cool with their bodies.[56]

Such calm was hardly likely in an election year, however. Brent stood for reelection again, and the campaign proved if anything even more bitter than those before. Charges swirled of Brent's heavy engagement in forged Spanish grant business, and that in Washington he received money for claims on behalf of his constituents but failed to turn it over. Others said that Brent was bankrupt and reneging on his debts in the district. In Natchitoches he was roundly detested.[57] For his part, as before, Brent wisely stayed in the East at his new estate, Pamonky, on the Potomac. Everyone expected him to be easy prey after his part in electing Adams the year before, but the Jacksonians in Louisiana fell apart this year and fielded two candidates, dividing the opposition vote. As the day for the voting approached in late July, Brent once again expected to win, and so he did by a majority of more than five hundred votes.[58]

Once more it came at the expense of high feeling, and this time, even though Brent won, the influential men of the district had wearied of him. Though victorious, he appeared wounded fatally so far as future electability was concerned. Within three months of the balloting, men in Rapides looked about for another Adams-Clay man to run in Brent's place in 1828, even if such a candidate must run against Brent himself as well as a Jacksonian candidate. "I think any diligent man of popular habits who will take the pains can effect it," an observer told Johnston in October. Surprisingly, the "diligent man" that some of them looked toward was James Bowie.[59]

So successful had he been at cultivating the friendship of leading men in Alexandria that, despite the growing unsavory aroma of fraud attached to his name, some very important people considered putting him forward. Certainly there is no doubt that the nature of his land dealings was now common knowledge, and becoming more so all the time. His forgery, careless and not intelligently thought out, fooled few if any of the local population. Even the family friend William Sparks, who admired James, asserted that he lacked Rezin's ability to plan carefully and think things through, "and was without a particle of his genius."[60] Moreover, James Bowie boasted too much of his slow but steady success at hoodwinking the authorities. Longtime residents almost saw his land schemes thrown in their faces as Bowie exhibited them publicly, old Kemper referring casually to his "fraudulent claims."[61] One of the first things recent settlers to the area learned was Bowie's reputation. When Washington Bastian and his son Samuel arrived from Philadelphia around this time, they almost immediately heard stories of how Bowie "devoted himself to the forging of land titles," of how land registrars refused to record his claims for confirmation, and even dark rumors of his waylaying and stabbing a man who had threatened to take him to court after buying a bogus claim.[62] The last was hardly Bowie's style, but it did speak, even in rumor, to his ability to intimidate. The old hero Kemper, veteran of many a battle, confessed that fall that to some degree he feared James Bowie.[63]

Yet none of this necessarily disqualified Bowie from being considered for Congress. After all, Brent walked under a cloud of suspicion of dishonesty scarcely less substantial than Bowie's. As for bullying and intimidation, while hardly savory traits, they could have their uses in frontier politics. Moreover, Bowie established the right connections with men like the Wells family, Isaac Thomas, General Cuny, and more. They would overlook his weaknesses since he stood on their side in the local squabbles of the day. In short, their support in sending him to Washington would earn them a useful quid pro quo when they needed favors from Washington. After all, Bowie was not the only shady land speculator; he simply did it on a vastly greater scale. If he could take on Graham successfully, it would be good for all of them. In fact, Bowie's success thus far with the General Land Office already attracted to him a certain aura of inevitability, as if he could accomplish anything. It stunned some. "Mr Bowie notorious for his land titles, came from Washington the warm & devoted friend of Brent," Overton told

Johnston in August. "He has been riding through Catahoula Washita & other Parishes ever since his return & he has acquired an influence since you left us that astonishes those that have witnessed its Progress; his success in these land titles have led the mob to believe that he is endowed with more than human energy & ability."[64]

Bowie recognized Brent's vulnerability before he saw him in Washington. Brent may have told him that he was considering making this next term his last. The two being of like mind and interests, Brent may even have promised Bowie his support should he choose to seek the seat in 1828. Setting aside the proven worthlessness of Brent's word, when Bowie returned to Louisiana and made what was now clearly revealed to be a politically motivated trip through the parishes of the district, he did not hesitate to let planters assume that Brent intended to back him. Already that summer Rezin won a seat in the legislature from Avoyelles, and John was reelected from Catahoula. The potential for advancement of the family's enterprises—and especially his own—by having two brothers in Baton Rouge and himself in Washington would be powerful.

Moreover, Bowie counted on powerful support in Rapides. The Cunys and the Wellses backed him, and even Kemper was rumored to favor him, certainly in preference to Brent, suggesting that Bowie won his support either through intimidation or perhaps by the promise of being able to advance the de la Français matter if elected. "Jim Bowie of Rapides is the only man in the District who can turn Brent out," Kemper reportedly told a friend, while Overton groaned to Johnston that "the Wells, Bowie & the Kempers have formed an alliance which if not holy will be sufficiently violent & from one of those named there will be a candidate for every office either in the gift of the people or of the executive."[65]

Bowie may even have announced his candidacy informally by August, with the election itself almost two years distant. From the first, however, men commented on the possibility with distaste. Speaking of Bowie's candidacy, Overton lamented: "[T]hus you see the unfortunate changes on our moral & political horison; men of independence who cannot stoop to low & dirty intrigue, are shunned as being out of fashion." His implication, of course, was that Bowie *would* stoop to "low & dirty intrigue." "What a state of things," he exclaimed. "The most corrupt & daring are the most successful."[66]

Nor was Overton's suggestion that there might be violence entirely out of order. A renewed fight between Wright and Wells for sheriff promised fireworks. "The contest will be hard," one man predicted. "It seems as if we now always demand to have our little society cut up by parties." Wright, having offended many during his tenure as sheriff, now tried to make up with his old foes. Some of Senator Johnston's opponents, meanwhile, sought to damage Wright by associating the two, even though the senator came out staunchly for Wells. Manufacturers of rumors tried to divide all houses against themselves, and it appeared likely that the race would give birth to some surprising new amalgamations of factions, but none stranger than Kemper supporting Bowie.[67]

By October, with the campaigning under way, passions and tempers rose. "The Country is again in a high state of excitement," said Overton.[68] The pages of the *Red River Herald* and the *Lafourche Gazette* echoed the furor for all to see. Renewed charges of voting fraud against Wright came from the Wells camp, and in the end they gave the ballot to Wells. "I have seen some faces in town as long as Don Quixottes," Judge Bullard told Johnston when he saw Wright's backers a day or two after the election in early January 1827.[69] Wright, for one, did not take the defeat with equanimity. Henceforward the Wellses and the Cunys were not just his political opponents but personal foes. And to their number he added James Bowie, who had naturally backed Wells in his successful bid.[70] Moreover, it is not unlikely that, in his habitual vociferousness, Bowie may have said intemperate things about Wright. Wells was a friend, and Bowie entertained a fierce loyalty to his friends. "When he gave his friend his hand it was a pledge of fidelity never to be broken by him," said Archibald Hotchkiss, an acquaintance from these days. "When he espoused the cause of a friend he would adhere to him to the bitter end."[71] If Norris Wright was Samuel Wells's enemy, then he was James Bowie's as well. Certainly the disgruntled Wright saw it that way.

His new ambitions and the course of local politics seldom diverted Bowie from his true interest. He still pressed his fictitious claims in Lafourche.[72] It characterized both Bowie's boldness and his poor judgment that he continued pushing the Martin claims even when Josiah Johnston and Graham became partners in a neighboring plantation. Who but James Bowie would press a bogus title next door to the commissioner of the General Land Office, the man even then trying to expose him? Johnston and Graham's overseer, C. Beaman, informed them of plantation affairs, including the frequently unpleasant relations with the Martins, who squatted on the Bowies' claims. In August he told Johnston that "the Martins & myself will continue friendly we ar so at present & I no it best to keep so," but he did not deny that "they have no friendship for you." Whatever the Martins did, said Beaman, they only acted as tools of "the head man *James Bouy* that . . . is the enemy of Geo Graham."[73]

And who but James Bowie, already under heavy scrutiny and suspicion for fraud, and actually trying to steal property virtually next door to his most dangerous enemy, would have the audacity to repeat the whole scheme yet again? This time his brother John joined him as partner and front, their aim set on Arkansas.[74] The Spaniards had given few "floating" grants in the area because it was barely explored before it left their hands. Moreover, as part of the Louisiana Purchase, it had become a federal territory in 1819 and was as yet sparsely settled, conditions ripe for a harvest in bogus land claims. James Bowie knew how to pick the fruit. On May 26, 1824, Congress passed the first act calling for the presentation of land claims under Spanish grants, following it with another on May 22, 1826. As early as late 1825 James Bowie decided to go after land there, and whatever the precise nature of the brothers' arrangement, the plan was a repeat of James's Louisiana frauds. It helped that John Bowie knew some of the country and some influential men who might help. James would forge the Spanish grants and the transfers to his brother, and John Bowie would do all the actual selling, with the proceeds to be split between them.[75]

James created the grants themselves in late 1825 or early 1826, and followed with more after the act of May 22, making some of the same mistakes he had made earlier. Gayoso always wrote his signature with a fine hand, but Bowie's forgeries were "but miserably imitated," according to one observer; Miró's signature was free, rounded, and careless, while Bowie evidently wrote his imitation slowly, and with pointed letters. He made other equally serious errors. This time he also forged Spanish *requétes* or applications supposedly written and signed entirely by the original grantees, and yet it was evident that they were all in the handwriting of as few as two, and no more than four, different men. Moreover, while Bowie used the names of real men like Joseph Talbo, Juan Morian, Juan Toledano, and Bernardo Sampeyrac, they were known locally to be indigent hunters who could scarcely write their names, let alone a full document. Worse, Bowie wrote in an American script rather than Spanish calligraphy, used the same pen and ink and even the same paper for all of the documents, and wrote them all in the same handwriting, consistently misspelling the same common Spanish words. Yet in their content they purported to have been written over a thirteen-year period by dozens of different men. He also botched an attempt to age the papers by soaking them in water. In his ambition, the impatience that often characterized Bowie's dealings led him to become even more careless than before. He was bound to be caught.[76]

He made the grants for tracts of 360, 400, 480, 520, and 560 *arpents*, which according to the acts could be entered in any land office in the territory, and he produced them in startling abundance, numbering more than 300 in all. Though the individual grants were less ambitious than his Louisiana forgeries, he and John and perhaps one or two others in the scheme produced enough false documents to lay claim to more than sixty thousand acres in Arkansas, nearly equal to the one hundred square miles of Louisiana that he had tried to gain. Anticipating the May 1826 congressional act, Bowie started making transfers of the *requétes* to his brother dating from April, and continued with them sporadically through the next several months. The same men witnessed all the conveyances to John, chiefly two squatters named Henry Hobb and John Cook.[77]

With the hopeful prospect before him of confirmation of the claims by Congress, Bowie decided shortly before the Wells-Wright election to travel north into Arkansas in person to start inspecting the areas where he hoped to lay his locations once the claims were approved, and then he expected to go on to Washington once more to renew his campaign to get his Louisiana claims confirmed.[78] Most likely accompanied by his brother John, he rode north in November and December and looked at the land in Hempstead County in the southwestern part of the territory, around Clarkesville in the northwest, near the future capital at Little Rock in the center, surrounding Batesville in the northeast, and around Helena on the Mississippi shore.[79] This kind of wide-ranging expedition was what he enjoyed most, and John easily saw the pleasure his brother took in scouting the wilderness "where natural inclination also gave the employment a charm peculiarly pleasant to him."[80] It could be dangerous work, of course. Even in Louisiana, when surveying the lands he claimed, Bowie rode armed. His friend Madison Wells recalled that "Bowie was constantly in danger of his life," especially from squatters whose presence he did not welcome and whom he had to evict.[81]

Like most men of the time, he probably carried a sword cane when in Alexandria, and perhaps a small pistol in his belt or pocket. Out in the backwoods, however, he would have carried two handguns or more. They were unreliable at best, their flintlock mechanisms prone to misfire and the powder loads themselves often apt to absorb so much moisture from the humid climate that they would not ignite. He would also carry a knife, useful for marking a trail, skinning game, and as a last resort should his pistols fail him. He was past his thirtieth birthday when he rode into Arkansas and back, but while he must have had more than one rough-and-tumble tavern brawl or disagreement with a squatter, to date no serious violence attached to his name. If he ever drew those pistols or that knife against another man, posterity preserved not an inkling of the incident. That was about to change.[82]

For some reason Bowie canceled his plans for the trip to Washington and instead unexpectedly took passage on a steamboat from Helena, his final land stop, down the Mississippi and thence up the Red River, reaching Rapides around December 12. True to form, he injudiciously boasted about the land he expected soon to acquire. Indeed, his Arkansas forgeries were known to Kemper and a few others even before Bowie made the trip.[83] Kemper himself may have played a part in Bowie's decision to come back early. Somehow Bowie learned that Kemper, faced with undeniable proof of the invalidity of the de la Français claim, had gone ahead and signed a treaty with the presumed heirs to transfer to them those claims of his own amounting to nearly $32,948, plus enough interest to bring the total close to $40,000. The U.S. Treasury had issued warrants approving all those claims as far back as 1818–20, and now the only obstacle to payment was securing an appropriation from Congress.[84] It was far more than he owed them, but he was old and ailing and well knew that he might not live to see his warrants paid. This way at least he could assure that he had honored what he insistently regarded as an obligation. For Bowie, meanwhile, it meant a sudden reversal of fortune. The spurious de la Français claim that had been worthless the past summer was suddenly worth several times its face amount. If he could prove that *he* had lawfully acquired title to the debt, then Kemper's $40,000 was his.[85]

Perhaps he also felt that, with the election imminent, his friend Samuel Wells needed him near at hand. John Bowie, too, had to be back now, because he was due to take his seat in the state house for the first session of the Eighth Legislature on January 1, the same day that Rezin would take his seat for the first time, and James's friend Montfort Wells was now going to Baton Rouge to represent Rapides.[86] Bowie's own future political interests may also have required him to come home. If he had been injudicious in what he said against Wright during the campaign for sheriff, so, too, did Wright respond in kind. Bowie's old friend Ham recalled that Wright "made statements derogatory to Col. Bowie's character." Given Bowie's already widespread reputation for questionable land dealings, as well as the knowledge of what he was doing in Arkansas at the moment, it is not hard to guess the sort of things Wright said, charges against Bowie that could damage Wells, thanks to their close association. Worse, such things could compromise his congressional chances in 1828, and worst of all Wright said them with Bowie absent and unable to defend himself. It was exactly the sort of action designed to transform Bowie into a vengeful fury.

It is just possible that he got word of it all while in Arkansas, but if not he certainly learned soon enough on his return. The very day that he stepped off the boat in Alexandria on December 13 or 14, friends—possibly including his brother Rezin—met him at the wharf and told him what Wright had been saying. That was all Bowie needed to hear. His rough traveling gear was packed in his baggage—on the boat he would have dressed in his town clothes, which did not provide a convenient place to carry a hunting knife—but he may have had a pistol in his pocket, and a clasp knife, and that was enough. Bowie marched up the riverbank and through the town streets to Bailey's Hotel. There he found Wright among his friends and without hesitation demanded to know if what he had heard was true.

It was a moment of confrontation not uncommon on the frontier, and all too common in Rapides. "The men are 'sudden and quick in quarrel,'" lamented the master of the College of Rapides. "The dirk or pistol is always at hand."[87] In fact the political, speculative, and family feuds made violence of this sort so prevalent in Alexandria that the governor had just recently appointed a new judge to deal with it: "The commission of murders, riots and offences against the laws of the state have become so frequent," complained the town's *Louisiana Messenger* only a few weeks earlier, "that few men are assured of safety."[88]

Wright responded to the moment without a word. He quickly drew and cocked a pistol and pointed it at Bowie's chest, and Bowie in almost the same instant grabbed a chair and held it in front of him to take the anticipated blast. They were at a standoff for a few moments, and then Bowie raised the chair over his head to strike at Wright. The other took advantage of the action and fired his pistol into Bowie's unprotected chest, striking him in the left side. The impact knocked the chair from Bowie's hands but failed to move him from his feet, and now he leaped on Wright, threw him to the floor, and began beating him furiously with his fists. If he had a pistol of his own, he may have forgotten it or it may have misfired. Instead Bowie used one hand and his knees to hold Wright immobile while he reached into a pocket with his other hand and drew out the clasp knife. He had raised it to his mouth and was pulling out the blade with his teeth when Wright's friends recovered from their shock and swarmed on Bowie, pulling him away. Dropping the knife, he sank his teeth into one of Wright's hands, biting down with such force that when the men roughly dragged him off, he left one of his teeth in Wright's finger. All that saved Bowie was the arrival now of friends of his own, who interposed themselves between him and Wright's people and carried Bowie upstairs to the room he usually occupied when in town. Once they regrouped, however, Wright and the others started to follow, but when they saw the trail of blood on the stairs, they concluded that Wright had wounded Bowie mortally and left the hotel. What they saw in fact was blood from Bowie's mouth where the tooth came out.

On examination, Bowie discovered just how lucky he had been, though the fiery pain in his jaw suggested otherwise. Wright's pistol was either too small or improperly loaded to inflict more than a painful wound. Moreover, the bullet may have been deflected by coins in his vest pocket, leaving little else than a very severe bruise and perhaps a fractured rib. It confined him to his room for a few days, but that was all. Out on the streets of Alexandria, Wright and his friends cooled down, and in any case sentiment ran against him for drawing and firing on a man who was initially unarmed. The *Louisiana Messenger* expressed one more time its outrage on the way men went about armed and so speedily resorted to dirks, knives, and pistols when anger exploded. Meanwhile, in his room at Bailey's, James Bowie nursed his pains and reflected bitterly on the unreliability of pistols and the fact that his cowardly foe lived only because the time it took to open his clasp knife with his teeth gave Wright's friends their opportunity. He resolved that he would never again lose those precious moments in a fight, nor would he allow his fondness for fine dress to leave him unarmed. He would make a leather scabbard for his hunting knife and keep it on his belt, and he told his brothers that he would "wear it as long as he lived." Having skirted the periphery of violence for so long, even threatening it on others, at last Bowie felt it himself. If ever there was a next time, he would be ready.[89]

CROCKETT

All his friends admit that he is somewhat eccentric, and that from a deficit in education, his stump speeches are not famous for polish and refinement—yet they are plain, forcible and generally respectful.

Jackson Gazette, AUGUST 15, 1829

At least one thing remained constant in David's life: He had to borrow seven hundred dollars to settle his accounts and get home from Washington.[1] At least some of the money he no doubt intended to apply to his reelection campaign, for no sooner did he set foot in Tennessee again than he took to the hustings, and this time somewhat on the defensive. He had failed to get his land bill through as he had boasted. Worse, the colleagues he had alienated in his own delegation now openly charged him with being the agent of the bill's death on the table. Somewhat disingenuously Crockett began trying to counter that charge with his constituents the very day of the tabling motion, sending an open letter for publication in which he argued that he had hoped that the death of the Polk version of the bill would have brought his colleagues around to his own. The fact was, of course, that events moved out of his control and left him looking very much like his own worst enemy, and by extension an enemy of the interests of the poor people of West Tennessee.[2]

Moreover, the only real accomplishment of his term in Congress had been getting a new postal route established in his district, a small achievement at best.[3] At least he did wisely keep his district advised of what he was doing, even when there was really nothing to tell, and in common with all representatives he took advantage of the free frank to send copies of his speeches—the printed, not spoken, versions—for circulation among his constituents.[4] On arriving in Weakley County on March 15, he remained scarcely two weeks before setting off on an almost monthlong sweep through the district.[5] Already the Polk forces sought to damage him with the same kind of ridicule used in the anonymous *National Banner* story about the Adams dinner, now hammering him for breaking with the convention of waiting to be asked to run. They ran in the Jackson press an announcement lampooning Crockett, over the signature of "Dennis Bruldrugery." In it a caricature of Crockett nominates himself to run, since no one else would back him—which was true so far as the Jackson Democrats now were concerned. "I can offer without any solicitation, as many others do, and pretend that every body has persuaded them," said the item. "I shall always find a set of veteran topers, who will sell both body and soul for good liquor. Let alone their votes."[6]

The prospect of a hard campaign did not daunt him in the least. Crockett was back on home soil now, among people whose ways he understood. Bolstered by the best health he had enjoyed in years, he thundered through the district day after day, his performances on the stump almost immediately forcing out one would-be opponent. That gave the Polk forces to understand that it would take a more concerted effort to beat him, and so they put up Pleasant Miller, a former U.S. representative and strong supporter of preemption rights for occupants on the vacant lands. But Miller almost immediately broke with them and with Jackson himself, and pulled out. John W. Cooke took Miller's place, and took full advantage of the ammunition no doubt put out by the Polk machine to paint Crockett as a man sleeping with the enemy and abandoning the interests of Tennessee. During one of their meetings on the stump, Crockett responded in kind by laying some heavy—and fictitious—charges against Cooke, who bristled and told the crowd he could prove Crockett a liar and would do so at their next meeting. When they appeared before a crowd again, Crockett saw the men Cooke had brought to refute his charges, and when he arose to speak first pointed out the witnesses and said Cooke really did not need to bring them, for he freely admitted that all his charges had been lies. "Fellow citizens, I did lie," he said. "They told stories on me, and I wanted to show them, if it came to that, that I could tell a bigger lie than they could. Yes, fellow citizens, I can run faster, walk longer, leap higher, speak better, and tell more and bigger lies than my competitor, and all his friends, any day of his life." The crowd roared with laughter and applause, and Cooke, both enraged and deflated, simply decided to drop out of the race, muttering that "if a man can get five hundred votes for telling a lie, and one thousand for acknowledging the fact, an honest man may well be off!"[7]

By the middle of April, when Crockett visited Nashville, all three opponents had evaporated, and in their place, and no doubt at the urging of Polk and others, Colonel Alexander entered the lists once more. The prospect did not daunt Crockett, so inflated with his success thus far that he expected he would "back out" Alexander too, or else beat him by a five-thousand-vote majority. "So say the people," he averred, an expression he sometimes used to mask his own expectations. Moreover, from the way Crockett freely used Polk's name in reference to the land bill, he made it clear that he felt his real opponent was not Alexander but Polk, and in mid-April in Huntington he forthrightly charged on the stump that Polk had presumed to speak and act for the district in spite of Crockett's being its elected representative, suggesting even that Alexander had been in collusion with him following his defeat by Crockett in 1827.[8] Though James K. Polk was a man certainly not reluctant to scheme, Crockett always seemed to see conspiracy in any opposition, especially if it succeeded.

This time he was right, however, for the Jackson forces, unquestionably led or abetted by Polk, Lea, and others, used every trick available. Besides the "Bruldrugery" lampoon, they sent the press fictitious letters from supposed district residents avowing a preference for Polk's version of the land bill. Going further, they slurred Crockett at every opportunity, and from the stump and in the broadsheets accused him of drunkenness, adultery, gambling, and worse—the same sort of charges apparently wielded by the hapless Cooke.[9] Of course, when it came to rough-and-tumble campaigning, they were playing Crockett's game, as Cooke learned to his sorrow, and the more outlandish charges refused to stick.

Crockett also wisely kept his attacks confined to Alexander and, by extension, his presumed managers like Polk. All the while he continued to campaign as an ardent supporter of Andrew Jackson himself, and there is little to suggest that Crockett was being disingenuous. All of his problems were with Polk, the Tennessee delegation, and the state legislature. He and Jackson had never crossed words, Old

Hickory to date had done nothing to break faith with him, and Crockett saw a very clear distinction between attacking Jackson's machine and striking at Jackson himself. David Crockett grew to political awareness during the so-called Era of Good Feeling, when there were no real parties with national platforms, but only loose factions, often coalitions, centered around leaders. The loyalty was to a man, not a faction, and he did not recognize that now with the coalescence of many of those factions into a powerful new movement, things had changed. Loyalty to a leader was not enough. To survive, a politician must be loyal to the group as well, including swallowing some unpalatable men and ideas for the greater good of the whole.

The growing discipline and organization of the Democrats gave them the White House in 1828, and very soon the Clay and Adams factions of the National Republicans, and anti-Jackson forces from the Democrats, would learn the lesson of that discipline by forming their own new party, soon to be called the Whigs. Just then the Jackson forces were trying their best to make Crockett an object lesson—the first in American politics—of the price to be paid for the sin of breaking ranks. Crockett seemingly felt no anger at Jackson for letting it happen, any more than he expected that Old Hickory held against him his dispute with Polk. In Crockett's mind his follower-leader relationship with Jackson was an altogether different issue from his split with the legislature and the congressional delegation of Jackson's own state. With almost childlike naïveté, he simply did not grasp that the two were inevitably a part of the same dynamic. Soon enough Jackson himself would show him that they were.

As usual, Crockett charmed the people on the stump. There were the same pranks and jokes, the same speeches larded with peculiar expressions that brought a laugh. His awakening to religion—never sufficiently developed to be called a conversion or rebirth—made him the more attuned to the deep simple convictions of many of the people, and to their expectations of sobriety and reverence in their elected officials. One night a lay preacher read him the Twenty-third Psalm, with its resonant verses of shepherds, green pastures, and the valley of the shadow of death. Its reference to a table prepared "in the presence of mine enemies" may have struck Crockett as a particularly apt description of his position in the Democratic Party just then, for when he heard it he felt deeply moved. "He did not make a very good Christian of me, as you know," David said afterward, "but he has wrought upon my mind a conviction of the truth of Christianity, and upon my feelings a reverence for its purifying and elevating power such as I had never before felt."[10]

Crockett seemed to know instinctively the right combination of backwoods persona and gentleman politician to adopt with his constituents, so that he always seemed respectable, as a statesman should be, yet never ceased to be quite recognizably one of them. When he appeared at a corn shucking at his friend James Blackburn's home, the crowd there saw "a fine gentleman" ride up, dressed in a good broadcloth suit. But when he dismounted he took off his jacket, rolled up his shirtsleeves, and commenced shucking corn and kept at it until the call for dinner.[11] As he put it himself, he needed to show his people that "Congress had not made me too proud to go to see them." He always had several twists of tobacco in one saddlebag, though if his determination to give up liquor still held, the other bag may not have contained a jug as in days gone by. Sometimes he met with a constituent who put up an argument, or who had voted for him last time but broke with him now over the land bill or other matters. Crockett remonstrated politely and used every trick of cajolery to change his mind. Faced with one adamant voter, he realized that if "this man should go to talking he would set others to talking, and in that district I was a gone fawn-skin." His solution was to admit his error in whatever the matter might be and confess it and his conversion in his stump speeches in that vicinity.[12] The admission cost him little and may not necessarily have been disingenuous in every case, but it would have the effect of confining talk on the subject to that locality—or even of bringing it to a complete stop.

Crockett even launched a modest counterattack against his real foes. In April he observed signs that Polk, Lea, and Marable might face stiff competition for reelection themselves, and it gave him joy. To pay them back for the trouble they sought to cause him, he made a brief trip through Marable's district, no doubt speaking on behalf of the challenger, Cave Johnson, and then visited Polk's district, where he boasted

sarcastically that he had "done what little I could for him." Of course to
Polk and the others this only further confirmed Crockett's apostasy,
and their conviction of his treason would have been cemented if they
had known that during the campaign he corresponded with Gales and
Seaton to keep them abreast of affairs in the Tennessee canvass. One
additional matter he reported to them was his visit with Tennessee governor Sam Houston in Nashville on April 16, the very day that Houston
resigned after a humiliating estrangement from his wife. The two were
at least passingly acquainted already, and now Houston confided to
Crockett that he intended to go west to the Arkansas Territory and live
among the Cherokee who had raised him.[13]

Crockett remained confident throughout the campaign. By late May
he still expected to trounce Alexander by 5,000 votes, and though he
proved to be over-optimistic, still the actual returns in August gave
him 6,773 to Alexander's 3,641.[14] Crockett quite rightly looked on it as
a vindication of his behavior, and an utter repudiation of the Polk
forces and their vindictive campaign against him. Certainly he looked,
if anything, stronger than before. Two years earlier almost 12,000 men
voted for the three candidates, and 49 percent of them went for
Crockett. In 1829, however, there were 1,400 fewer voters, only two
candidates, and yet David garnered 64 percent of the tally. While
Alexander's count remained virtually the same, Crockett picked up
nearly a thousand voters. News almost as good came when he learned
that Johnson had beaten Marable, and that Pryor Lea's contest was so
close that it required a recount, though Lea narrowly won in the end.
Polk, however, handily held his seat. Thus, while Crockett seemed
stronger than before, the polling wounded his enemies, not mortally to
be sure, but enough to convince him that his was the true course as
ratified by the people. The message seemed clear: He had but to continue in his honest, independent path, redouble his assaults on Polk
and the rest, and he must surely prevail.

There is no question that people—Whig and Democrat alike—kept
an eye on this Tennessee race. In his district it was seen as a vindication
of his essential decency and character. "All his friends admit that he is
somewhat eccentric," said his local press, "and that from a deficit in education, his stump speeches are not famous for polish and refinement—
yet they are plain, forcible and generally respectful."[15] During the cam-

paign, when Crockett called on Ephraim Foster, onetime private secretary to Jackson during the Creek War and now a legislator starting to drift toward the Whigs, he left the impression of "a pleasant, courteous, and interesting man, who, though uneducated in books, was a man of fine instincts and intellect, and entertained a laudable ambition to make his mark in the world." Foster's son recalled on those visits that "he was a man of a high sense of honor, of good morals, not intemperate, nor a gambler. I never saw him attired in a garb that could be regarded as differing from that worn by gentlemen of his day."[16]

Crockett's election attracted sufficient nationwide notice that two years later it was still being spoken of when Tocqueville came to the United States. "Two years ago the inhabitants of the district of which Memphis is the capital sent to the House of Representatives in Congress an individual named David Crockett," he wrote, "who has no education, can read with difficulty, has no property, no fixed residence, but passes his life hunting, selling his game to live, and dwelling continuously in the woods."[17] Yet the image Tocqueville depicted was misshapen, elements of truth exaggerated into fiction. Crockett had some education, he certainly could read, and he had both property and a fixed residence. As for dwelling in the woods and selling pelts to live, his days of the long hunt were over and had been for several years when the Frenchman wrote in 1831. Clearly the people who talked to that foreign visitor told him of a different David Crockett than the man in the broadcloth suit who proved himself a competent legislator in Murfreesboro, ran—or at least owned—a gristmill in Weakley County, and managed, however foolishly, to stymie even the powerful forces of Polk.

Something beyond his control was happening to Crockett. In January 1829 William Moncrieff brought out a new play called *Monsieur Mallett; or, My Daughter's Letter.* Its most memorable character was Jeremiah Kentucky, portrayed to great popularity by the actor James Hackett. Moncrieff wrote the character in 1828, describing a bold, bragging frontiersman, a dynamic stump speaker and a U.S. representative, and of course "half-horse, half-alligator, with a touch of the steamboat, and a small taste of the snapping turtle."[18] At the time of writing Moncrieff may not even have known of Crockett or had him in mind. More likely he was influenced by the earlier tales of John

Wesley Jarvis, who wrote stories of outlandish frontiersmen for popular amusement, and to feed the growing appetite for western characters. That same appetite accounted for the success of Moncrieff's play, which only whetted the public's taste for more. But then the distant reports in the South and the East and elsewhere of the stump campaign out in West Tennessee began striking a resonant chord. Perhaps there was more to Hackett's character than acting. A real, live Jeremiah Kentucky appeared to be stumping the canebrakes out there, a man who could feed the American hunger for its own distinctive character not on the theater boards but on the living stage of the world.

Real life of another kind faced Crockett after his election. The months before the first session of the new Congress were filled with the usual round of acting as witness in petty civil matters at the Weakley court and fighting his own perpetual battle with debt. Three suits from creditors sat on the docket that fall, none of them resolved. Moreover, the gristmill seemed not to be working, and the marriage with Elizabeth was definitely breaking down. Once again the departure for Washington must have come as a relief, especially since for Crockett it amounted to a triumphal return after his defeat of the Polk forces.[19] Now if only he could take that victory march to the House floor and carry the land bill with him.

Typically Crockett wasted little time and went about his task the only way he knew how, head-on. The Twenty-first Congress convened on December 7, 1829, and through the entire course of the session Crockett struggled and maneuvered. At first he succeeded in getting the land bill removed from the Public Lands Committee, headed by Polk, and referred instead to a special committee that Crockett himself chaired, something he could not have achieved without the votes of the anti-Jacksonians in the House. The move to put Crockett in a position on the committee superior to Polk was obviously designed further to embarrass the squabbling Democrats. Crockett's committee debated for several weeks before it reported a revised version of the bill in January 1830, and meanwhile the Tennessee delegation's internecine fighting continued almost daily on the House floor as David tried repeatedly to get his original bill off the table for discussion, only to fail. Polk himself may have realized that he and his followers were going too far, and backed off slightly in the tenor of his opposition in order not to give the appearance that this whole business was no longer about the vacant land but about punishing Crockett. But it was too late for that, as almost every observer realized what really lay at the root of the argument: The *fight* over the bill had taken on a life of its own, becoming more important than the bill itself.[20]

The revised bill that Crockett reported out of his committee made concessions he had been unwilling to countenance before, showing that he may have begun to realize the value of half loaves and compromise. They proposed to guarantee to the state enough of the vacant land to sell at a minimum of twelve and one-half cents per acre to make up the deficiency in the common-school fund. Those already occupying and improving squats would receive a preemption right for 160 acres at the same cost per acre, but with one year's credit to raise the money. And, perhaps most galling of all, the bill would recognize the claims of North Carolina warrant holders, even though it risked the displacement of not a few current occupants. Crockett made no secret of his disappointment in the final draft. "This is the Best provision I could make for the occupints placed as I was in the powar of a majority of the Committee against me," he told his friends. "I was compeld to put up a claim and urge the propriety of it." At least he believed that whole Tennessee delegation now backed the revised bill, with a fair chance of its passage. Still there was a note of sadness and defeat in his admission to his constituents that "this is the best that I could do for them."[21] Even then his foes in the Polk camp put out the story that Crockett tampered with the wording of the bill between what the committee agreed upon, and the final printed version.[22]

In the end it was not enough. Discussion on the bill was postponed in April, and on May 3 it met defeat by 90 to 69. Crockett immediately moved for reconsideration, suggesting a revision of the occupants' terms, but in the process he almost alienated North Carolina's representatives by attacking their state's motives. In the end he was fortunate not to see his motion for reconsideration defeated but only laid on the table, where it would have to wait for the fall session. Yet the support of his delegation evaporated. In the tabling motion, only Cave Johnson stood with Crockett in opposition. It was a sobering conclusion, and

Crockett wasted no time in letting his constituents know what had happened—and why, as he saw it. On May 7 he sent an open letter to the *Jackson Gazette* and made it clear that henceforth he declared his independence from the Tennessee delegation entirely. He would "set up shop" on his own.[23]

Adding to his discomfiture, Crockett found his voice to be without influence on other matters of importance to him. One of the things that he shared with Henry Clay was an advocacy—though more restrained—of internal improvements, of the judicious expenditure of federal money on roads and canals to encourage interstate commerce, though like so many others he was really only interested in improvements that might benefit his own region. Crockett supported the bill for a National Road from Washington to New Orleans, proposing an amendment that it should terminate instead at Memphis in his own district, so that his constituents could "come in for snacks" at the pork barrel, but the House rejected his amendment and the bill.[24] And when Jackson rejected a bill to build the Maysville Road in Kentucky, Crockett vainly voted to override a veto clearly aimed as a partisan blow at Clay. Though David's commitment to internal improvements was only lukewarm at best, it is not hard to see in the override his own reproach to Jackson for denying the will of the House. Moreover, Crockett seems not to have recognized the nuance in the president's position on improvements. Before his election Jackson favored them so long as they were chiefly for defense. Now, however, he had to reduce the national debt, and any expense not vital to security only deepened the nation's deficit. Crockett could see only that Old Hickory had reneged, assuming he had lied in order to curry votes.

Crockett also did not understand the vital interconnection between internal improvements and the tariff, for it was tariff revenue that chiefly financed the government.[25] He even proposed the abolition of the Military Academy at West Point because it, like the rest of the government, was funded chiefly by tariffs levied on goods that the poor like him had no alternative but to buy. Since only the sons of the wealthy and influential seemed to secure appointments to the academy, he charged that the tariff was a means to "pick the pockets of the poor to educate the sons of the rich."[26] Yet in supporting tariff-funded internal improvements, in effect he contradicted his own tariff position, which can only be interpreted as spiting himself to strike at Jackson. In March he had reaffirmed his support for the president: "To GEN JACKSON I am a firm and undeviating friend," he declared. "I have fought under his command—and am proud to own that he has been my commander. I have loved him, and in the sincerity of my heart I say that I still love '*him*'; but to be compelled to love every one who for purposes of self-aggrandizement *pretend* to rally round the 'Jackson Standard,' is what I never can submit to. The people of this country, like the humble boatsman on the Mississippi, ought to begin to look out for *Breakers!*" he warned. "The *fox* is about: let the *roost* be guarded."[27] This last was a thinly veiled reference to the new secretary of state, Martin Van Buren, the "*fox*." Crockett detested the slick, pragmatic, cynical machine politician for whom winning an election justified any means. Now he held the cabinet position widely regarded as the last step before the presidency. At every turn since taking office, Jackson had dug the bedrock of Crockett's support from beneath his feet. By May and the vote on the veto override, Crockett no longer stood apart just from the leaders in Jackson's party. Now he labored in the throes of a break with Jackson himself, and feeling with it all the hurt, disillusionment, and even betrayal of a deceived lover.[28] And like a suitor spurned, his pain slowly began to turn to resentment and then anger.

It flared the brighter over Jackson's Indian Removal Bill, introduced on February 24. Crockett took no part in the debate on the issue, which proposed appropriating five hundred thousand dollars for the relocation west of the Mississippi River of several of the peaceful tribes from Mississippi, Alabama, Tennessee, and Georgia. Crockett said not a word on it during the debate when it began on May 15, though by now his disillusionment with Jackson was well under way. The Clay forces savaged the bill and nearly defeated it, yet when it came to a vote on May 24 it passed by the narrow margin of 102 to 97. Crockett was the only man in his delegation to vote against the bill, standing alone now against his colleagues and his president, and even, as he well knew, against the wishes of many of his constituents, who viewed the Cherokee and allied tribes as a menace, and their tribal lands as fair game for squatter settlement.

In fact the Indian Bill was so controversial that many a representative felt compelled to explain his vote, especially the several Democrats who opposed it, and Crockett was no exception, yet what he issued amounted more to a capsule biography and a vindication of his career. Quite possibly with the assistance of some of his new anti-Jackson friends, especially Gales and Seaton, Crockett penned a defense that showed very definite signs of being aimed at eastern opposition men as much as his own constituents. Granting that he knew no one within five hundred miles of his home who agreed with his vote, he justified it on the basis that the bill gave Jackson half a million dollars with no oversight or accountability. Moreover, in contrast to most of his constituents, he felt sympathy for "the poor remnants of a once powerful people" now being forced from their homes. However warlike the Creek and allied tribes may have been, as he well knew, those who survived were largely of the peaceful factions; and the Chickasaw of northern Mississippi and Alabama, who bordered his district, had always been the pacific friends of the white man and in treaty after treaty made way without violent complaint for the advance of American settlement. His conscience demanded that he stand for the right, even if it pitted him against his constituents, he said. He even appealed to a higher law and repeatedly proclaimed that though he stood in defiance of White House, Congress, and constituents, he could do naught else, because what he did was right. Someone, probably Crockett himself, sent a copy to the *Jackson Gazette*, hoping at least that it might contain the damage his vote would do him there. Significantly the copy indicated that Crockett delivered the speech in the House on May 24, the day of the vote. Within a few months it also appeared in a compilation of Indian Bill speeches published in Boston, but this time dated as if delivered on May 19.

He never gave the speech at all, however. From first to last it was an obvious attempt to mollify his voters on the one hand and on the other to appeal to the Democrats, chiefly in the North, who voted in opposition with him. Some of them could be useful when his land bill came up again in the next session. And it cannot be denied that Crockett's vote, and naturally his apologia, would enhance his standing with those who seemed to be his true friends now, the embryonic Whigs. Besides all the political implications of the business, he also seems to have felt some genuine sympathy for the plight of the Indians. After all, he knew their situation: poor, despised, friendless, and now to be landless. The Indian Bill would do to them what the North Carolina warrants did to the Tennessee squatters, and while he undoubtedly entertained all the prejudices of his time and place, he could never fail to empathize with anyone who was poor, downtrodden, and helpless. That was in the simple generosity of his nature, one of those kinder elements that led so many to see in him a "natural" gentleman.[29] Ever the egalitarian, David refused to countenance that one class enjoyed more entitlement than another.[30]

Crockett was starting to find himself a growing celebrity in this session. His notoriety as an outspoken foe of the Jackson machines, in spite of his protestations of support for Old Hickory himself, made him an object of interest. In addition, as Jackson now revealed sides of his personality and attitudes unseen prior to this election, an increasing number of his old followers crossed the aisle to side with the Adams and Clay people in a new coalition. Crockett did not publicly proclaim a new allegiance, and of course he would have maintained in any case that he paid homage to no party, but people now widely saw him as having crossed the aisle as well. When he spoke the galleries in the House responded. "Crockett was then the lion of Washington," said a man who listened to him speak against a relief bill for the widow of war hero Stephen Decatur. "I was fascinated with him." Callers at Mrs. Ball's, where he continued to lodge, were likely to find him writing or franking large piles of letters as his correspondence grew.[31] "To return from the capitol without having seen Col. Crockett, betrayed a total destitution of curiosity," proclaimed an 1831 newspaper, "and a perfect insensibility to the Lions of the West."[32] Something in the attention actually seemed to buoy him. Always preoccupied with his health, he felt better during this session than he had for some time.

When Crockett went home at the recess, his Clay associations became increasingly apparent, just as the antiadministration forces showed growing awareness of his potential. For more than two years now he had enjoyed some acquaintance with Matthew St. Clair Clarke. There was nothing at all unusual or unseemly about it, for as clerk of the House, Clarke knew every one of the members. That he had close Clay-Adams connections meant nothing in itself. Outside the House debates, members of all sides freely and cordially enjoyed one another's company. Still, for nearly a year now Crockett had been close enough to Clarke to send regards to him when writing to Clarke's friends, so the acquaintance was growing, and Clarke was close to Gales and Seaton and other antiadministration men, and especially to Nicholas Biddle, president of the federally chartered Second Bank of the United States.[33] Then, too, Bowie's old nemesis Sen. Josiah S. Johnston watched Crockett's progress in Washington with interest. Johnston, as thorough an adherent as Henry Clay ever had, paid particular mind to David's modest break with Jackson on internal improvements. During the summer he proposed to Clay that if Tennessee governor William Carroll, who also appeared to be a possible convert, and Jackson's foe former senator John Williams, could be united with Crockett to advocate internal improvements and Clay's protective tariff, "they may shake the state."[34] Getting any state behind Clay boded well for his so-called "American System" and his own presidential prospects in 1832, but getting Jackon's own home state to break with him on policy would be trebly damaging. Johnston undoubtedly met Crockett during the sessions, though nothing suggests that they became friends or that he made any special attempts to woo him. Interestingly, though, Johnston did have dealings and an acquaintance in 1830 with a Philadelphia publisher named Edward Carey, who took a special interest in books by and about public men.[35]

Crockett returned for the second session by traveling overland, through Nashville and Knoxville, the Cumberland Gap, and north down the Shenandoah. He stopped along the way staying chiefly with anti-Jacksonian hosts, itself a sign of where he felt comfortable now.[36] In Staunton, Virginia, he visited with Henry McClung, a friend of Houston's and himself an outspoken Adams-Clay man. No doubt they talked of the sad downturn in Houston's fortunes, and certainly money came up, for Crockett had to borrow five dollars to get him on his journey to Washington. Yet they also talked politics, and especially the "State of party" as Crockett called it. With all the realignment of the Clay and Adams factions, now being joined by disillusioned Jacksonians, Crockett believed that the forces backing Clay stood virtually even with Old Hickory's. He may not have said that he counted himself now as actually anti-Jackson the president, but his break with the Jacksonians was clear. It only awaited a real test in Congress to see where the strength lay.[37]

Crockett missed the opening of the session by a week and might as well have missed the whole sitting. In the first three weeks he tried twice to get the House to reconsider the land bill tabled in the last session and failed both times, though only by 92 to 89 on the second attempt. The forces did appear evenly divided now, for a shift of only two votes would have given him a majority (91 to 90). Crockett found hope in the narrow loss. Just hours later he predicted that "I do believe I will be able to get it up and pass it in spite of all their opposition before I leave here."[38] Meanwhile, all around him he saw change that looked more and more like the work of Jackson himself, prodded by the evil genius of Van Buren. When the Cherokee mounted a challenge to the Indian Bill in the Supreme Court, Jackson forces got up a bill to repeal part of the 1789 Judiciary Act so that the Court could not actually sit on the matter. Such tampering with the basic law of the land, and the balance of power, incensed Crockett. For the first time he now actually believed that he perceived Jackson himself behind the maneuvering, and moreover that it appeared to be a movement toward personal aggrandizement, a reach for dictatorial authority. "This is what we call going the whole hogg to nullify the whole powar of the Supreme Court of the united states," Crockett fumed. "I do believe it is a political manuver of this adminestration," he said, "which will destroy the whole powar of the genl government." If that happened, he warned a friend, "thin we are no more a united states." He believed that secession and even civil war could follow.[39]

A few weeks later Crockett finally acknowledged that he was at war himself. Jackson had campaigned against corruption and for fiscal responsibility, his catchphrases being "retrenchment and reform." Yet everywhere David looked he saw the opposite. In the Post Office Department huge deficits appeared despite the promises to correct former abuses, and he prepared an open letter to send to his constituents on the matter. He also condemned Jackson's use of the spoils system. "This is high times in this best land of liberty," he said sarcastically. "This is the effect of this glorious sistem of retrenchment & reform this is the effect of turning out men that knows their duty to accomodate a set of Jackson worshippers."

"Can any honist people have the like of this put upon them," he pondered. "I for one cannot nor will not I would see the whole of them hung up at the devil before I will submit to such carryings on as this." As all his frustration of the last three years came pouring out, Crockett finally admitted what he had appeared to resist for so long. Whenever he failed or was frustrated, there was always someone behind it, someone of malignant purpose who must bear the blame. Dark men of evil design conspired to hold him down, just as they did all of the poor from whom he sprang, and those same men sought now to pervert the government of the nation he loved. He saw what the president wanted and had schemed to get, but he would not be duped. "I have not got a collar Round my neck marked my dog with the name of Andrew Jackson on it." As a result, "because I would not take the collar round my neck I was hurld from their party."[40] He liked that aphorism about the dog collar. From now on he would use it again and again.[41]

Crockett had come to his epiphany. The enemy was not just Polk and had never been Polk and the others. They were merely instruments. The foe was Jackson himself. He even feared that Jackson might bring on a foreign war, just as a means of assuming the same kind of dictatorial power he had exercised in Florida when still a general.[42] That being the case, there was only one way to meet an enemy, the manly way, straight on, out in the open. Crockett never deceived anyone about where he stood in the past, and now he felt it vital that he proclaim his break openly.

He did so in the House, on February 24, during yet another debate on internal improvements, this time Crockett's unsuccessful advocacy of an appropriation for navigation work on the Ohio and Mississippi Rivers. "Although our great man at the head of the nation, has changed his course, I will not change mine," he proclaimed. "I am yet a Jackson man in principles, but not in name," he asserted. "I shall insist upon it that I am still a Jackson man, but General Jackson is not; he has become a Van Buren man." He punctuated his position with yet another new phrase that he would use again and again with variations: "I would rather be politically dead than hypocritically immortalized." His conscience meant more to him than any elective office.[43] Four days later he refined what would become his watchword in his own campaign to come: "I thought with him, as he thought before he was

President: he has altered his opinion—I have not changed mine. I have not left the principles which led me to support General Jackson: he has left them and *me*." As for his stalled land bill, Jackson's managers were to blame for that. They, even those from Tennessee, had set aside the interests of his constituents in their campaign to drive him out of Congress to replace him with someone who "would run at their bidding and do as they direct." Let them try.[44]

The rest of the session realized Crockett's prediction in January that Congress would accomplish little in the face of the partisan warfare.[45] He never got the land bill off the table again, and when Congress adjourned on March 3, he must have been glad to see the doors of the chamber close behind him. He had been powerless to do more than annoy the administration. A friend said that he was utterly "without influence" in Congress, and the painful truth of that had been made all too evident to him.[46] Yet he remained in Washington for several weeks, part of the time posing for a portrait and also trying to attend to his ever-perilous financial affairs. There was no question of his de facto alliance with the Clay-Adams men now, though he did not consider himself a member of their party. Undoubtedly they counseled him on what all knew would be a desperate election battle for his seat.

It was no secret that the Jackson forces were determined to defeat him. Adam Alexander reported to Polk from the district that he heard constituents' rumblings that sounded "decidedly unfavourable to the Western David."[47] Even before the commencement of this last session, they started publishing accusations that Crockett was a bolter and a traitor to Jacksonian democracy and the common man, harping especially on his Indian Bill vote, and the Jackson *Gazette*, which had been neutral, came out against Crockett in December 1830. When the Jacksonians selected William Fitzgerald of Weakley County to oppose the incumbent, the *Gazette* endorsed him. "He can't 'whip his weight in wild cats,' nor 'leap the Mississippi,' nor 'mount a rainbow and slide off into eternity and back at pleasure,'" said one correspondent, parodying Crockett's own vernacular, "but this we believe, that Mr. Fitzgerald will make a better legislator; that he will as far excel Col. Crockett upon the floor of Congress, as the Col. does him in the character of a *mounte-bank*."[48] Jackson himself broke his silence on Crockett in April, writing directly to friends in Madison County to say that "I trust for the honor

of the state, your Congressional District will not disgrace themselves
longer by sending that profligate man Crockett back to Congress."[49]
For both men, now, the contest had become personal.

Before he left for home, Crockett borrowed five hundred dollars from
William Seaton, Gales's partner, and of course a prominent Clay supporter. Whether it was for debts, to pay for the portrait, or to help fund
his campaign he did not say, but clearly Whigs were now willing to make
money available to him. Yet in order to pay it back he had to borrow
another six hundred dollars from a fellow representative when the debt
came due.[50] He did not actually leave for Tennessee until the first of May,
going by coach along the old National Road through western Maryland
to Wheeling, Virginia, where he took passage on the steamboat *Courier*
for the trip down the Ohio. Along the way he accidentally left behind his
new portrait, hardly an auspicious way to begin his race for reelection.
Worse, he did not reach home until the middle of May, meaning he had
already lost fully two months of potential campaign time.[51]

He returned to Tennessee an embattled figure and yet a folk hero in
the making, and surely that would aid him in his race. That newspaper
reference to him as one of the "Lions of the West" was no accidental
turn of phrase. Thanks to the fact that his independence and his colorful vernacular made him good copy, and thanks to the hunger of the
people now for a truly original American character like him, he was
known throughout the nation, and especially in the East, where there
was always a half-patronizing taste for bumpkins in their literature.
James Fenimore Cooper and Washington Irving were supplying the
literary need quite nicely now, but Crockett was the only man in the
country who fitted the evolving stereotype in the flesh. His storytelling was already becoming legend. "No matter what we may say of
the merits of a story," said one of his listeners in February 1830, "it is a
very rare production which does not derive its interest more from the
manner than the matter."[52] Those who sat in the House gallery to listen
to him saw "a true frontiersman, with a small dash of civilization and a
great deal of shrewdness transplanted in political life," said Ben Poore
of Washington. "He was neither grammatical nor graceful, but no
rudeness of language can disguise strong sense and shrewdness."[53]

He had become the image of the new American ideal, as he put it
himself, a "self-taught man," part legend and part reality. He declared

during the coming canvass that "I never had six months education in my life I was raised in obs[c]urity without either wealth or education I have made myself to every station in life that I ever filled through my own exertions."[54] Unwittingly—or perhaps with a bit of self-awareness—he defined the very essence of the aspiration of the age of Jackson, of this new man, this American. He was Cooper's Natty Bumppo, Sir Walter Scott's Rob Roy McGregor, and Irving's Brom Bones of Sleepy Hollow. Literature idealized the free man, the independent frontiersman, and here was Crockett, the living incarnation. He possessed every asset for the role—humble birth, poverty, lack of schooling, experience as a hunter and warrior, an original—which could mean singular, odd, or eccentric—manner of speech and repartee, and the rise to prominence in national affairs. His life represented the triumph of liberty and democracy, for nowhere else on the planet could such a man live such a life. The public did not see his private aspirations, his constant struggle to rise to the middle class, to look, act, and be taken for a gentleman, and did not want to see that man. They preferred the Crockett who was, like the idealized image of the westerner then sweeping the salons of America, a *natural* aristocrat, a truly new character on the world stage, the first truly and uniquely original *American* character.[55]

Inevitably, that lost portrait was not the only likeness of him abroad in 1831 as he prepared to face Fitzgerald. The actor Hackett, who had portrayed Jeremiah Kentucky the year before, enjoyed such success with the part that he craved a play in which he could limn such a character not in a supporting role, but as the star. He urged his friend James Kirke Paulding to write such a play for him, and Paulding knew where to go for material. Why make it all up when he had but to portray a living man. He asked his friend the writer Jarvis to send him "a few sketches, short stories, and incidents, of Kentucky or Tennessee manners, and especially some of their peculiar phrases and comparisons." Even more specifically Paulding suggested that "if you can add, or *invent*, a few ludicrous Scenes of Col. Crockett at Washington, you will be sure of my everlasting gratitude."[56]

By the latter part of 1830, when it became known that Paulding was writing a new play to be titled *The Lion of the West; or, A Trip to*

Washington, there was no doubt in the public mind that its leading character, the outlandish Colonel Nimrod Wildfire, was not just similar to Crockett but in large measure based on him. Paulding actually wrote to Crockett disingenuously to assure him that Wildfire was really a general character of the western sort, and Crockett, who of course had neither read nor seen the as-yet-unperformed play, took him at his word that the character simply represented "many who fill offices and who are as untaught as I am."[57] And so, even before *The Lion of the West* made its debut in November 1831, many Americans knew of and anxiously awaited its appearance, and knew as well from rumors that Paulding's buckskin-clad Wildfire, marching about the stage wearing a wildcat-skin hat, would be neither wholly fact nor wholly fiction, but rather Crockett as seen in a mirror skewed out of shape, and thus distorting the image.

Crockett needed all the positive notoriety he could get, even at the risk of becoming a folk or literary hero, for others were distorting his image for different ends when he went out on the stump. "I was hunted down like a wild varment," he said later, "and in this hunt every little newspaper in the district, and every little pin-hook lawyer was engaged."[58] The Jackson forces portrayed him as a Henry Clay man, reviled him as the "coon killer" and "the authorized Whig jester." Fitzgerald's friends furnished him, and the *Gazette*, with copies of Crockett's votes, and as well with listings of the number of votes he had missed. Certainly Crockett had given his opponents more than enough material to throw at him, especially on the Indian Bill, and then he overtly helped them himself with his announced repudiation of Jackson.[59]

Crockett knew he was beleaguered from the start. Despite his mounting debts, he needed even more money for the canvass, and what he got from the bank was not enough. On May 19, just days after returning to Weakley County, he sold his property there to Elizabeth's brother George Patton, selling a slave woman in the bargain. By making himself a man without property, Crockett actually became one of the landless whose cause he championed. It must have been a very difficult choice for him to make, and no doubt further strained relations with Elizabeth, but Crockett decided he had no choice: The greater goal justified the sacrifice. As if to reinforce his own determination that he was doing the proper thing, he scribbled across the bottoms of the two sales documents a simple phrase: "Be allways sure you are right then Go, ahead."[60] Crockett liked certain aphorisms when he coined them himself, and those that were his own he used repeatedly. He liked this one. Perhaps he would use it in the future.

As the stump campaign wore on through the summer, Crockett tried to drive home his theme of independence; that Jackson had left him, not the other way around; and that the Jackson machine cared nothing for the poor people of West Tennessee. Even if these charges were true, the trouble was that his new friends in the Clay camp offered even less, for they were largely on record as being opposed to preemption rights or cheap land for the poor. Crockett advocated the rechartering of the Bank of the United States, due soon for renewal, in spite of Jackson's opposition.[61] Tennesseans wanted the Cherokee and Chickasaw removed, and they did not share Crockett's enthusiasm for internal improvements that had to come from high Whig tariffs. As for Jackson, Crockett could be nothing but honest. He would never support him or vote for him for reelection. Again and again he sang the old refrain of having been one of the first to volunteer to fight the Creek with Old Hickory, but the Jackson in the White House now was not the same man. "I never did support men and forsake principles," he said, "nor I never will." He "always parsued one straight forward corse and I ever expect to."[62] "I have acted fearless and independant and I never will regret my course."[63]

The campaign had the usual spate of trickery, but there was a grimness to it this time that showed more malice than fun. Fitzgerald's handlers went far and wide through the large district making appointments for Crockett to speak—about which he knew nothing, of course. When the day for the speeches arrived, Crockett naturally did not appear, but Fitzgerald and his supporters did, haranguing the crowds with Crockett's record when he could not defend himself.[64] As for Fitzgerald himself, Crockett regarded him as "a little county court lawyer with verry little standing he is what we call here a perfect lick spittle." He believed Fitzgerald had authorized the libels and falsehoods that appeared in the newspapers. Meanwhile, when the two did meet on the stump, Fitzgerald came with a chorus of those same "little pin hook county court lawyers" who attested vociferously to anything he said. "The truth is the Jackson worshippers became desperate and had to resort to any and every thing," said Crockett.[65] They even tried to use the very quaintness and "eccentricity" that made Crockett a celebrity in the East by turning it against him in ridicule. Adam Huntsman, one of those "pin hook" lawyers, was something of a writer himself, and in the Jackson press began to publish vernacular letters promoting Fitzgerald. "I air oppose to Kirnil Krokets lection," he wrote. "I think he air not fit to go to Kongress." Crockett responded in kind, signing himself as Jacob Van Spetts and saying that "my hatvice to you is to jine Crockett."[66] The letters went back and forth, only getting worse, until the editor apologized for the mockery of journalism produced by the canvass.[67]

Crockett never exhibited the confidence in this campaign that had characterized his two previous runs, and the Jacksonians smelled victory three weeks before the polling. One reported to Polk that Crockett would be beaten, predicting that "the name of David the mighty man in the River Country will no longer Disgrace the Western District in the National Legislature."[68] Even before the results came in from the polls, Crockett knew himself to be bested. "I expect I am beaten," he told a friend on August 22. "I have one consolation I would rather be beaten and be a man than to be elected and be a little puppy dog."[69] The actual count was not as bad as it could have been, considering all the effort the Jacksonians had thrown at him, and revealed the bedrock reserve of support Crockett enjoyed in his district. Some 16,482 voters cast ballots, a dramatic increase over 1829, showing just how much interest the contest excited, and Fitzgerald won by only 8,534 to 7,948, a margin of just 586. Crockett took seventeen of the eighteen counties, including Weakley, where both he and Fitzgerald lived, but in Madison County his opponent heavily trounced him, and that decided the issue. Had his mood allowed him, David might have found pride in the fact that his vote significantly outstripped his winning totals in his two previous elections.[70] Instead, unwilling to accept defeat gracefully, and convinced as always that any defeat represented dishonesty and conspiracy, he ascribed his loss to "managemint and rascality," and attempted to challenge the result, charging fraud, but Congress refused.[71] As for Fitzgerald, Crockett could not find it in himself to accept defeat with grace. He would refer to his opponent only as "the thing that had the name of beating me," and receded into self-righteous self-pity, saying: "I have been made a political marter of for being an honest man." There was no doubt that he would run again.[72] "I have always believed I was an honist man," he proclaimed, "and if the world will do me justice they will find it to be the case."[73] Two years later he would give the voters that chance.

TRAVIS

1809–1831

I Travers by birth a Norman
To gain victorious conquest
With Wm Conqueror I came
As one Chief rol'd among the rest

EPITAPH, PRESTON FREERY, ELEVENTH CENTURY

When twelve-year-old Berwick Travis found himself an indentured servant in Loudon County, Virginia, in 1763, unsuccessfully petitioning for release from his master, those proud words of his presumed ancestor nearly seven centuries before seemed at best ironic, for he was neither chief nor conqueror. Nearly a decade later, however, he had worked out his period of servitude and at once traveled south, along the Shenandoah Valley route taken by Crockett's grandfather just the year before, into and across North Carolina, and down to the Saluda River in what colonists then called the Ninety-Six District. It was fairly remote country, its only real community the village of Ninety-Six itself, and when Travis got a grant of 100 acres on the north side of the river, beside Mine Creek, his circumstances looked if anything even more removed from the splendors of Tulketh Castle in Preston, England, where the boastful Travers dwelled. This home was no castle.[1]

While working his farm Travis kept a tavern for a time, marrying Ann Smallwood the year after he arrived, and there they carved out a living for the next forty years and raised their children. After the Revolution, which Berwick Travis seems to have missed, South Carolina became a state, and the old Ninety-Six District divided, leaving Travis in the new Edgefield District or County. When he died in 1812, he left an estate valued at $4,232.12, nothing to put him on a par with Travers of Tulketh, but a very respectable testament to his hard work. He also left seven heirs besides his wife—four daughters and three sons. Two of those men were already out on their own, and one at least was on the way to making himself a man of note.[2]

Alexander Travis, just twenty-two when his father died, had already embraced his life's calling. Three years before, in 1809, he succumbed to the religious revival that swept the backwoods country of North and South Carolina, and ever after drew people to him with his fervid sermons in the millennial tradition of Lorenzo Dow, the great frontier Methodist evangelist. Yet Travis was more scrupulous, and less eccentric, than "Crazy Dow," and drew attention by his faith rather than any oddity. The other son, Mark Travis, was born September 6, 1783, and was nearly thirty when their father died, and more in Berwick's mold, a farmer and carpenter.[3] Yet both brothers shared a regard for education that they passed on in later years, and a mutual devotion to the church, each adhering to the missionary Baptist faith.[4]

Mark Travis may also have been a bit of a rogue, for he apparently fathered an illegitimate son named Taliaferro sometime prior to 1807. But he was not a man to shirk responsibility. On June 1, 1808 he married Jemima Stallworth, whose brother was already married to Mark's sister, and soon thereafter he took young Taliaferro into his home, acknowledging him as his son, though whether Jemima was herself the boy's mother is a mystery.[5] There was no question about the subsequent outpouring of children that came to the Travises, however. Starting in 1809 Jemima gave birth to ten more in the next two decades, the last being born almost twenty years to the day from the appearance of the first.[6] The first of those born in wedlock was William Barret Travis, who came into his parents' home a few miles from Red Bank Church on August 1, 1809, two years after their marriage.[7] The middle name they gave him represented the prevalent English pronunciation of his grandfather Berwick's given name, just as their very name Travis itself had evolved from Travers over the centuries to a spelling that matched its sound.[8] His time in South Carolina was brief, leaving little impression on his memory. In later years he might have some dim recollections of the Red Bank Baptist Church, where his family attended services, and around which much of community life certainly revolved. There may have been a fleeting memory of some men going off to war with the British, though Edgefield was little touched by the War of 1812. Of course there were glimmers of childhood days with the Stallworth cousins and with children of neighbors. Not very far away, though a couple of steps up the social stair, lived James Bonham and his wife, Sophia, and their children, Julia and James Butler. The daughter would one day marry a Bowie. Brother James, though two years older than young William Travis, may well have met him at church or play, and in the way of children, the differences of age and station could easily disappear when playmates were few and opportunities to frolic even fewer.[9]

There would not be time for young Travis to get better acquainted in the Edgefield area, for in the way of those restless young Americans of the age, Mark and Jemima looked to the west, though his younger brother, Alexander, led the way. Tall, dignified, grave in manner and speech, the younger of the brothers was the more adventurous, though he sought souls rather than prosperity on the western horizon. A frenzy called "Alabama Feaver" that followed the end of the war with Britain saw thousands of emigrants from the Carolinas take to the new Federal Road, largely opened by the military during the war. It commenced at Augusta, Georgia, on the Savannah River, scarcely thirty miles from the Mark Travis farm, and by 1820 the Great Migration saw more than one hundred thousand white settlers in the territory that became the states of Mississippi and Alabama. The land out there was not free, but it was cheap. In 1816 Crockett came to Alabama scouting for a likely setting, and the next year Alexander Travis did the same, only he found what he was looking for and settled in Conecuh County, near a place called Sparta—a name apt enough for the living conditions of the place. Yet there was great promise in the hilly red soil and the dense forests of hardwoods and evergreens. He sent word back to his brother, Mark, to follow his lead, just as he preached to guide souls to a better place.[10]

Mark Travis cleared his affairs in South Carolina in late spring of 1818, and by William's ninth birthday was ready to put his family on the road.[11] They would have made the journey on foot, their worldly goods in a wagon, driving their livestock before them. It was not a long trip, but a hard one in the summer heat and humidity of the Deep South. The Federal Road took them across central Georgia, through Milledgeville and Macon, past the Creek agency on the Flint River, where young William may have seen his first Native Americans, and on to the

Chattahoochee. Once across that river, they entered the Alabama Territory, and from there the road led them onward past a succession of frontier forts and battle sites to Burnt Corn in the heart of Conecuh. From there another few hours brought them to Alexander Travis's home.

While the federal surveyors were still at work making the township plats of the public-domain land, Mark Travis and his family lived with Alexander for a time until May 19, 1819, when the Sparta Land Office opened for business, and Mark stepped forward to purchase its very first certificate.[12] For $1.25 an acre, he bought title to eighty-two and a half acres near his brother, and there built his house about five miles from the future county seat, Evergreen.[13] A few years later he added more property to his original tract, but that seemed to satisfy any land hunger he may have felt. He stayed there for the rest of his days, and there Jemima gave birth to more children until 1829.[14]Alexander Travis, meanwhile, prospered spiritually in Conecuh. He preached every Sunday near a place called Evergreen, and the same year that his brother came, he organized there the Old Beulah Church. He had only one book, a Bible, and when not working his fields or preaching from it in the daylight, he read it in his cabin at night by the light of blazing pine knots. He also acted as a sort of backwoods judge in the absence of more formal justice at the time, and this literate and public-spirited uncle exerted a powerful influence on his nephew William.[15] Indeed, where it is difficult to find much of Mark Travis other than his own youthful irresponsibility in this, the first of his sons, the stamp of Alexander Travis was indelibly left on his nephew.

Nothing signified this more than Alexander's commitment to education. He would himself be a founder and trustee of the later Evergreen Academy, and probably played some role in the petition that led to the legislature of the new state of Alabama incorporating the Sparta Academy in December 1821.[16] Up to this time young William, when he went to school, probably attended one of the "blab" classes or the so-called old field schools, built on worked-out land, where students simply recited lessons over and over again mindlessly. The academy system, largely built on the Englishman Joseph Lancaster's "Lancastrian" method of older pupils helping to teach the younger ones, started to spread through the state at the same time as statehood itself, and though it would be realized too late to be of any use to this Travis, his younger brothers and sisters would benefit from Alabama's progressive efforts to establish public education.[17]

William Barret Travis's first encounter with formal education came at the Sparta Academy, where his uncle Alexander served as a superintendent. There were only two teachers, John McLeod and Murdock McPherson, yet the typical curriculum in such a school included Greek, Latin, French, philosophy, rhetoric, geography, history, mathematics, and more, all for anywhere from six to sixty dollars a term, and here in Sparta much more likely the former.[18] Then, too, just going into Sparta itself regularly could be educational, though it was not much of a frontier community. The Methodists and others had to hold their services in the courthouse, while the Freemasons used the second floor for their meetings. There were but two hotels, the Rankin House and the much rougher Gauf House, its dirt floor and log walls softened only slightly by calico curtains.[19] Yet to young Travis, just entering his teen years, this was his first taste of town life, of a way of living not tied to the ceaseless toil of the farm, a place where men with professions wore better clothes and talked of the world and not the soil.

With that taste of learning, and the backing of his father and uncle, Travis went on to the academy of Professor William H. McCurdy, a few miles west of Sparta in new Monroe County.[20] Here the introduction to classical learning that he got at the Sparta Academy was extended and rounded, so that twenty years later Bowie's friend William Wharton would speak of Travis being "collegiately" educated.[21] Travis must have proved an apt pupil, for when he finished at the academy, probably in 1827, aged nearly eighteen, he almost immediately took a job as a teacher himself, perhaps at this same school.[22] Though he held the position less than a year, he showed aptitude as a professor as well, judging by the considerable literacy and skill of expression of at least one of his students.[23] Of course that one student, Rosanna E. Cato, "the beautiful Miss Cato," as he called her, attracted more attention than his average pupil.[24]

Still Travis wanted to learn more. It did not take long at a schoolmaster's desk to learn that it would not bring him either the prosperity or the station in life that he craved. On this frontier, that kind of status went only to two kinds of men, the big planters and the lawyers. He had seen enough of the field and the plow to know that his future lay not in that direction, but he liked what he saw of that other profession.

There were only a few in Sparta, but his uncle Alexander sometimes preached to the Baptists in Claiborne, county seat of Monroe, on the bluff above the Alabama River, and if William went with him he saw there something far more stirring. This was a thriving community, growing rapidly, tied by the river to Mobile and the rest of the world, with an active and distinguished bench and bar. If he was to learn the attorney's trade, he would have to "read law" under a practicing lawyer for a year or more, and clearly Claiborne was the place to do it.[25]

Moreover, one man there stood above the others, and however he got the introduction, Travis sometime in 1828 presented himself to James Dellet.[26] Here was a giant of the frontier bar. A native of New Jersey, Dellet was not quite forty, a graduate of the University of South Carolina who came to Alabama at the same time as the Travises, and settled in Claiborne. Almost immediately he became a judge of the circuit court, then spent three terms in the state legislature, being elected its first speaker of the house in 1819.[27] He was a stout fellow, of seemingly careless bearing, by turns gregarious and taciturn, but the keen eyes in his round face flashed with brilliance. Given the mood, he always had an anecdote in the rich vein of his Irish ancestors, and could spellbind audiences or juries with pathos or convulse them with laughter. In politics he supported John Quincy Adams against Jackson, as would have been expected of a prosperous professional man who owned fifty-five slaves and a property in Claiborne valued at two thousand dollars.[28] When the Marquis de Lafayette visited Claiborne on his tour of America in 1825, Dellet headed the town's celebrations, as the undisputed head of the Claiborne bar. Travis might have been put off at first acquaintance, as was Benjamin Porter, who met Dellet a couple of years later and found him "so morose that I was driven from the idea of pursuing the law," but this was only the attorney's way of putting potential students on the defensive. On longer acquaintance he proved to be a frank, sincere friend and a man of unrivaled integrity.[29] This was the kind of man William Barret Travis wanted to become.

Once Dellet agreed to take Travis on as a pupil, the young student applied himself intensely, bent on learning as much as quickly as he could. It was the way he would go about everything in life.[30] Indeed, now, while only just nineteen and already training for one career, he actively commenced another. Aside from attorneys, no one in a booming town like Claiborne exerted more community influence than the editor of a newspaper. Yet frontier journalism was a risky business, with a high mortality rate. In the past Claiborne had seen no fewer than three weekly newspapers fail. The *Alabama Courier* commenced in 1819 and lasted three years. Christopher Dameron's *Gazette* began in 1824 and ran scarcely a year, while the *Alabama Whig*, published by Thomas Eastin, apparently enjoyed an even shorter life.[31]

Somehow young Travis managed to attempt to fill this vacuum. No doubt press and type were available from either Dameron or Eastin, though he could only have purchased them either by his note, which was unlikely, since he had neither property nor income, or else by means of a loan from his father or his uncle. Or he may simply have continued Eastin's defunct *Alabama Whig* under some private agreement to assume its liabilities but changed its name under his own editorship. In any case, on May 16, 1828, he brought from the press the first issue of his new *Claiborne Herald*, "Edited & Published by William B. Travis." To proclaim the independence and incorruptibility of the journal, he chose for his motto, "Thou shalt not muzzle the ox that treadeth out the corn," certainly to the point, if less than stirring.[32]

Every Friday the *Herald* appeared, its annual subscription rate the same four dollars that Dameron had charged for his defunct *Gazette*. Each of Travis's four pages stood twenty-two inches high by fourteen wide, and the five columns on each page had much the same content as every other rural weekly of the time. As with most small-town weeklies, the editorial matter was mostly borrowed from other newspapers that came into Claiborne—an account of a great storm in Norway, a visit to Niagara Falls, an anecdote from Brooklyn, a three-week-old notice of activity in the U.S. Senate. There was precious little in the way of local news, but then not much that was newsworthy happened in Monroe County. Of course there were the local civic events to be announced; lists of unclaimed letters to be collected at the post office; and always a number of announcements from Samuel McColl, clerk of the circuit court, more from James H. Draughton, clerk of the county court, and even some from neighboring Clarke County.

Those official notices brought revenue, for naturally the courts paid, though probably at a lower rate than regular advertisers. Advertising was the lifeblood of a sheet like the *Herald*, few publishers surviving

on subscription sales alone. Travis charged a dollar for the first insertion of each ten-line advertisement, and fifty cents for each subsequent
appearance. Moreover, like many editors, he included in each advertisement a little reminder to himself of how long it should run, with a
code in the lower corner showing the number of the first issue of
appearance and then, after a dash, the number of times he was to run
it, as in "35–6t"—start with issue 35 and publish six times. The best
orders, of course, were those few that he encoded "35-tf"—start with
issue 35 and run in every issue "'til forbid." After nine months he was
running ten columns of advertising, with a billing per issue in the
neighborhood of $16.50, or monthly revenue of about $65.00.
Considering the cost of paper and ink, the income was hardly princely,
especially when bills might go unpaid for months before any hard coin
came in. Some, no doubt, he simply took in trade from merchants who
advertised with him. Still, the income should have been enough for a
bachelor of nineteen to get by on.[33]

The problem was, he was not a bachelor any longer. During those
months of teaching, he had become irresistibly enamored of Rosanna
Cato, the daughter of local Monroe County farmer William Cato, and
she returned his interest passionately.[34] Travis later claimed that they
had agreed to marry as soon as he could acquire a profession and be
prepared to support a family, and perhaps they did.[35] Yet perhaps there
is just the possibility that their ardor got the better of their patience, a
trait for which young Travis would have to pay consequences more
than once, or that in fact it was their passion that led to the wedding.
When they married on October 26, 1828, it is entirely possible that
Rosanna, aged just sixteen, had already given birth to a baby boy
named Charles Edward two months earlier. If so, it was hardly uncommon then or later, and the postponement of the formality of a wedding
only awaited Travis's ability to make a home for his new family.[36]
    With two mouths to feed and possibly a third, however, that sixty-
five dollars a month did not go so far. In addition, the distractions of a
family robbed him of time needed on the newspaper. By February 1829
signs of haste and carelessness, showed all too evidently in the *Herald.*
He forgot to lock his type in place on the press, allowing letters to jump

out of place above their lines. His proofreading became sloppy, and misspelled words started to appear. Worse where income was concerned, he ran at least one advertisement upside down, and in one issue alone he included five that had already expired, in one case six weeks before. His own contribution to editorial content became marginal, no more than one or two local stories. Recognizing that he could not manage all this, the family, the newspaper, and the studies with Dellet, he advertised in his own pages for a journeyman printer to help him, even there committing a typographical error when he promised "liberal wages, and study employment." He meant "steady," of course, but there were no takers.[37]

All the while Travis studied his torts and contracts and criminal law, reading Blackstone, Chitty's *Pleadings*, and Harry Toulmin's *Digest of Alabama Law*, and the other texts in Dellet's library. Dellet himself, like most attorneys, would have taught Travis simply by assigning him extensive readings, then examining him orally, as well as allowing him to observe courtroom proceedings when the county and circuit judges sat. Dellet also set an example of industry, being himself a slave to his office. He let nothing distract him from business when he was working, and often seemed harsh and abrupt. "I was driven at first from cultivating an acquaintance with him by his stern and forbidding deportment," another young lawyer found on meeting Dellet in 1829, "but I soon learned to value the sterling qualities of his mind and soul."[38] Beyond question, just as Travis hungrily absorbed the law from Dellet, so he also modeled some of his manners after his mentor.

With all that crowded Travis's day, he hardly had time to participate much in Claiborne society, such as it was, yet certainly he craved to be a lion of the community. The town sat atop a bluff in a scenic spot with a beautiful view of the five-hundred-yard-wide Alabama 180 feet below. Though hardly a city, it was considerable by Alabama standards at the time, with 453 white men and women and another 382 slaves and free blacks. More important, it served as county seat for Monroe, whose 8,782 inhabitants must all at one time or another have walked its streets.[39] Settlers first appeared in 1816, and four years later planners laid out the town—one of its first citizens being Dellet, and another William Cato's friend Samuel DeWolf.

It was one of the five principal towns in the state by then. A steep slide allowed planters to shift cotton bales to the riverbank, from which boats carried the white gold downriver to Mobile. The steam ferry *Emaline* made regular passages to Mobile, while at least three full-size steamboats plied up and down the river making frequent stops below the bluff. Weatherford's ferry, just below Claiborne, allowed a crossing into Clarke County; another ferry operated north of town; and Monroeville, fourteen miles to the east, allowed connection with the stage road to Montgomery, the capital.[40]

The road from Monroeville came into town from the east and became Main Street, ending at the Masonic Hall on the bluff. Just south of Main Street sat the town commons, with the Methodist and Presbyterian Churches, while the Baptists—often led by Travis's uncle Alexander—had no building of their own and met in the Masonic Hall. The occasional stage deposited travelers at Ansel Erwin's Eagle Hotel or at George Medlock's Washington Hall on Main, while Edward Ellis operated a tavern on Monroe Street. H. Goldsmith promised that his was the "Cheapest Store Under the Sun" for general merchandise, though he had plenty of competition from James Colburn, Francis Pridgeon, and several more. Samuel Forwood recalled Claiborne as all "bustle and full of life" in those days. There were a jeweler, three tailors, a saddler, three carpenters, a combination tanner and Baptist minister, and more. And there were also the characters, and even a celebrity in the person of the famed Sam Dale, now in his late fifties. Some called him the "Daniel Boone of Alabama," though the local Creek and Choctaw regarded him as "Sam Thlucco" or "Big Sam." No one would ever forget his famed Canoe Fight, when he and three others defended themselves in their boat against eleven warriors in the middle of the Alabama. He was a sad figure now, though, almost destitute thanks to being a spendthrift.[41]

It was thanks in no small part to men in debt like Dale that a county seat such as Claiborne offered thriving ground for lawyers. Dellet may have led the bar, but he had distinguished company. There was Arthur Bagby, just thirty-four yet already once an elected legislator and youngest speaker of the state house in its history. An exciting orator, only he truly rivaled Dellet. Then there was the tall and lanky Enoch Parsons, noted as much for his huge nose and "Indian features" as for his skill as an advocate, and also currently sitting in the legislature. The one-legged Virginian Charles Tait was over sixty, just retired as judge of the U.S. District Court for Alabama, but still occasionally active as an attorney, devoting his idle hours to science and literature, and believed to have turned down an appointment as ambassador to Great Britain in 1828 when offered by Jackson. Henry Abney practiced law and also served as clerk of the circuit court, while Benjamin F. Porter, little older than Travis, had come to town in 1829, first as a physician, but was studying law as well.[42]

It was a crowded bar to be sure, yet on February 27, 1829, it made room for its newest member. Shortly before Travis went before Judge Anderson Crenshaw to be examined, and after scarcely a year of studies, he proved equal to the test.[43] Travis himself was proud of the intense application he made to learn from Dellet, and prouder still on that day in February when in his own *Herald* he announced to Claiborne for the first time that "WILLIAM B. TRAVIS has established his Office for the present at the next door above the Post Office, where he may be found, at all times, when not absent on business."[44] Schoolteacher, publisher, and now attorney at law, he had not yet turned twenty.

When he got his first legal business, almost certainly a suit for collection of debt, which constituted the great bulk of an attorney's efforts at the time, he filed his papers with Sheriff George Medlock first, then with Draughton if it was a county court matter, or Samuel McColl for circuit court cases. Since Claiborne remained without a separate courthouse, the ground floor of the Masonic Hall served as courtroom and courthouse combined, and there he would argue his cases when and if they came. Meanwhile, Travis waited for those clients to appear, and until then the overwork and distracted energies of the past months left him facing his own first real experience with debt. The newspaper cost money to run, and he had borrowed at least $90 at the beginning of the year. Just ten days before opening his law practice he borrowed another $55.37, probably for the expenses of setting up even a modest office.[45] Undoubtedly there were more debts, forcing Travis to undertake even more efforts to provide income. He did job printing at the *Herald* office, sold blank forms, business cards, even made book plates, including his own. He took subscriptions at the office for journals like the *National Souvenir* and the *Jackson Wreath*, and at home he apparently took in two or three boarding students to tutor. Having a middle-aged slave woman to help around the house, and a young slave male to assist with any heavy work may have eased the load on Rosanna, but it also added to the expense of a household already financially stressed.[46]

In order to attract the widest possible clientele, Travis stood ready to practice not just in the Monroe courts, but also in neighboring counties Clarke and Wilcox, but the customers had to come to him first.[47] Unfortunately, the clients never rushed to that office next to the post office. Years later when Samuel Forwood recalled Claiborne in 1829–30, he spoke of the town's many "able" attorneys and mentioned Dellet and Bagby and Parsons and several others. But he did not recall Travis. Worse, despite Travis's earnest efforts to take a prominent role in community affairs, Forwood could not even remember Travis being a resident.[48]

Certainly young Travis tried his best. He undoubtedly participated in the Euphemian Lodge, a debating club whose members included Samuel Cloud, his recently married near neighbor in town.[49] He promoted the efforts of the American Tract Society, no doubt helping in the formation of Claiborne's auxiliary group in March 1829, and at the same time assumed the secretaryship of the Claiborne Temperance Society, helping to disseminate its constitution and ideals to neighboring counties, all in keeping with his Baptist upbringing.[50] Even though few cases took him to the first floor of the Masonic Hall, he saw the second floor more frequently when in June he secured induction and initiation into Claiborne's Alabama Lodge No. 3, Free and Accepted Masons as an Apprentice, took the Fellowcraft degree a month later, and became a Master Mason in August, despite the fact that he was only twenty and regulations required a man to be twenty-one. Most likely he simply lied about his age, as he would do again in his life.[51]

And as any gentleman of spirit and patriotism should, Travis joined the militia. On January 3, 1830, he took a commission as adjutant of the Twenty-sixth Regiment, Eighth Brigade, Fourth Division, headquartered at Claiborne, an appointment that made use of his considerable writing and legal skills. Sheriff George Medlock commanded the local troop, also called the Monroe Cavalry, but it was only eighty men strong, many of them without arms.[52]

In short, William B. Travis—he always insisted on the inclusion of the middle initial in his name—did everything an ambitious young man was supposed to do to establish himself and become a success, to make himself another Dellet. But it all failed. The *Herald* went steadily down by the end of 1829. The leading men in Claiborne, such as Dellet and Tait, did not subscribe.[53] By the fall he actually failed to get out as many as six issues, and in December was down to publishing a single two-sided sheet along with the apology that "the disorganization of our office for some time past compells us to issue a half sheet this week, for which we would *beg to be excused.*" Advertising fell by more than a third, and most of his receipts now were for legal announcements, with less and less coming from business. After almost a year, no one suitable had responded to that advertisement for a journeyman printer, which meant that he was still doing the whole job virtually alone.[54] It cannot have lasted more than another few issues.[55]

And the debts continued to accumulate. The deadlines on the notes for those loans for $90.00 and $55.37 came and went without payment, and the holders turned them over to Dellet for collection. More unpaid notes joined them—$192.40 in May 1829, $50.12 in June, and another $50.00 in July, and so it continued. By August 1830 Travis's creditors turned increasingly to Dellet to file suit in the circuit court for collection. All of them went unpaid.[56] He could not even afford to buy a house or property, and most likely operated newspaper, law practice, book sales, and home all in the same rented building not far from Dellet's town home.[57] Including the slaves, nine people lived under his roof by the latter half of 1830, and feeding them became a trial. By the end of 1829 he even tried to get his hands on a large quantity of corn and half a ton of pork, obviously in hope of a resale.[58] There was a real question of him even being able to pay the modest county tax of $1.00 for himself and $2.00 for his slaves. Probably he could not afford even to pay the $1 tax for a gold watch, much less own one.[59]

When finally he did get cases, they promised little reward. His brother-in-law William M. Cato gave him a brief for collection of a $5.50 debt, but Travis's fee at the usual 5 percent would only amount to 27.5 cents. When Cato had larger business, moreover, he took it to

Dellet instead, which must have hurt. In August 1830 Travis undertook collection of debts to the estate of Ansel Erwin, but when he spent hours filing subpoenas for collecting $4.77 due for tavern meals, $1.77 for drinks, 31.25 cents for glassware, and so on, he must have felt shaken when he considered that his fee would be barely 60 cents, and measured that against all the effort it had taken him to come to this. The largest case he got for collection in the fall 1830 term of the Monroe court promised a fee of less than $2.50. Just like the newspaper, his law practice was a dismal failure.[60]

And then there was the marriage. Relations may have been strained from the day of the wedding if not before, especially if young Charles arrived a year earlier than the 1829 that Travis or Rosanna later altered in their family Bible. With Travis trying to manage so many things at once, there could be little time to be a husband to his teenage wife or a father to the baby boy. Mounting debt certainly caused a strain, especially since some of it may have been unnecessary. Travis liked fine clothing, and he also liked to gamble, while three slaves in the household certainly showed a penchant for living beyond his means, even if they were only on loan from parents. As for Rosanna, she was strong-willed and perhaps flirtatious, as the circumstances of her youthful marriage would suggest, and Travis, too, may well have given cause for jealous discontent, for he would soon show an immature young man's cavalier attitude toward fidelity in matters of the heart. It can hardly be denied that all the frustrations and disappointments of his thwarted dreams of career success and social position made Travis an unhappy, even brooding man, hard to live with, and harder perhaps to love. The mounting pressure of debt and the impending humiliation of being sued in court, himself a lawyer, surely put froth on an already poisoned domestic cup.

"Choose wisely the wife of thy bosom," Travis wrote in the *Herald* early in 1829, quoting an essay no doubt borrowed from a book or some other newspaper. A man should avoid the gaudy and preening in a woman, as well as the proud, for all that would wither. More to the point, a wife should be subservient and obedient. "She must be the unspotted sanctuary to which wearied men may flee from the crimes of the world, and feel that no sin dare enter there."[61] With all his troubles, that was the kind of wife Travis needed, but Rosanna was independent, perhaps even accusing, and at only eighteen hardly mature enough herself to be dealing with a son, heavy debt, a distracted and morose husband, and late in the year another child on the way when she was scarcely out of childhood herself. She may even have sought comfort from their friend Samuel Cloud, who lived in town next door to her brother William, and who though a few years older than Travis, probably knew him from their younger days at Sparta or through the Euphemian Lodge.[62] He had a wife and two children by 1830, but an old friend could still be a friend, though if he was, Travis might well have seen it as something else. For her part, Rosanna protested: "I endeavoured to preform my duty as a wife with the most undeviating integrity and faithfulness and if any thing occured to dissatisfy him with me it was the result of my ignorances as to what was my duty as a wife, or I would have performed it to his entire satisfaction."[63]

It was not enough, and for all these reasons and more, the marriage was breaking down.[64] Travis himself would only say that "my wife and I had a feud which resulted in our separation."[65] But that was disingenuous, and Travis knew it. Disappointment, debt, fear, and humiliation finally tore them apart. The bills and overdue notes hung around his neck like a dead weight. He could not pay for the corn he fed his horse. A new creditor filed a suit with Dellet to collect $202.93. His brother-in-law Allen Cato did likewise for $55.06. As the spring 1831 term of the circuit court approached, Dellet alone held briefs for the collection of debts against Travis totaling $834, and certainly other attorneys held more.[66] Other men owed much greater sums. Poor old Sam Dale was in debt to a single creditor for $1,174, but Travis was just twenty-one, susceptible to the special pain that only youthful pride can feel. Even when he went to Clarkesville on the rare occasion that he got a case in that county, as like as not men at the court there simply used him as a courier to take their business letters back to Dellet in Claiborne.[67] Worse, the newcomer Benjamin Porter, just admitted to the bar in 1830, was now to be Dellet's partner and was already spoken of as a candidate for the legislature in the next year's election.[68] That was the success that should have been Travis's.

With the opening of the court and the hearing of the suits against him scheduled for March, William Barret Travis sank even lower within himself. Everyone saw it, even Porter, who scarcely knew him. "Never have I seen a more impressive instance of depression from debts," Porter recalled, sympathizing in the struggles to support his family that he felt had led Travis to this unhappy pass.[69] But Dellet had no such sympathy. When the court opened and the suits for those debts came up before Judge Taylor, Travis received the summons he knew must inevitably come. At least he managed to make himself go down Main Street to the Masonic Hall, the same building where he attended church, where he had become a Mason, where he had passed the bar on that proudest day of his life. But now he came to the rail as a defendant, and to act as his own counsel.[70]

Dellet was there, and Porter, and no doubt the other litigants that day, as well as a few loungers. When Travis arose to speak they saw a man slightly above average, perhaps five feet nine or ten inches tall, at 175 pounds a bit fleshy for his stature, with light brown hair, blue eyes, and a reddish-brown beard trimmed short over what Porter called "a fine Saxon face." Some thought his manner gentle, but that may have been merely his humble pose for the court on this most trying of days. His usual associates found him instead not unlike Dellet, brusque to the point of giving offense, and when someone took his manner for an insult, he simply turned his back. "He was unquestionably an honest man," said the onlooker Porter, "but debt will weigh down the loftiest soul, and humble the brightest intelligence."[71]

As Dellet brought to the bench one suit for debt after another, Travis had no answer until finally a possible means of escape came to him. Almost all these debts dated to the two years prior to his twenty-first birthday, now just seven months past. A minor, by custom and law in many jurisdictions, was not considered legally responsible either to incur or to redeem debts. The official plea in such a case was to dismiss the suit on grounds of "infancy." But Travis should have known Dellet better than to give him that opportunity. As soon as Travis offered his plea, his former mentor came to him and had him stand, then led him to the jury box, Travis apparently having no idea what his opponent was doing. Then, with all the theatrical sarcasm for which Dellet justly enjoyed fame, he pointed to Travis and said: "Gentlemen, I make 'proofest' of this infant." If the strange word confused the jury members at all, there was no mistaking Dellet's meaning. Porter found that "the effect was electrical, on account of Travis' size." With a tall, filled out, bearded man standing before them claiming to be an "infant," they

1. David Crockett as he preferred to be seen, a gentleman. This portrait, attributed to Boston artist Chester Harding, shows Crockett in 1834, probably during his northeastern tour sponsored by the Whigs. It may, in fact, have been intended for political use in the 1836 presidential contest. (*Courtesy of the National Portrait Gallery, Smithsonian Institution, Washington, D.C.; on loan from Katherine Bradford in honor of her mother, Dorothy W. Bradford*)

2. The man who dominated an age, seen as Crockett did by 1832—as the manifestation of corruption and autocratic power. Crockett's obsession with Andrew Jackson, whom he repeatedly called "King Andrew the First," virtually ruined him in politics and in the end drove him to Texas. Jackson played a large role in defining the culture that produced all three: Crockett, Bowie, and Travis. One way or another, his brooding presence loomed constantly in the background of their lives and deaths. (*Library of Congress*)

3. The mythical "Davy" whom Crockett cultivated and capitalized on and yet resented. When visitors came expecting to see a "bar," this is what they had in mind. The well-dressed if not urbane reality left them rather disappointed. This remained the prevailing image of him for generations, though it is in fact a depiction of the actor James Hackett as Nimrod Wildfire in Paulding's play *The Lion of the West.* (Davy Crockett's Almanac, *1837*)

4. For half a century after James Bowie's death, no likeness of him was known to the public. Then, in 1889, his brother Rezin's grandson John Seyborne Moore revealed a portrait—of which this is a detail—claiming that it was James, painted from life by an artist referred to simply as "West"—presumably William West. As with so much else about the always mysterious James Bowie, even his likeness remains overcast by shadows of uncertainty. See also chap. 22, n. 68. (*Center for American History, University of Texas, Austin*)

5. Probably the only surviving example of a forged Bowie *requéte* and order of survey for one of his bogus Arkansas claims. When Isaac T. Preston investigated these claims in 1829, he found that in the 124 documents he examined, the same common Spanish words were consistently misspelled, even though the *requétes* (the top half of the document) were

purportedly written by 124 different people, while the orders of survey (the bottom half) were supposedly written over a fifteen-year period by several clerks. See also chap. 10, n. 47. (*Entry 394, Record Group 49, National Archives, Washington, D.C.*)

6. The San Antonio home of Juan Vera-mendi and his family, including for a time James Bowie and his wife, Ursula. By the 1890s when this image was taken, it had become a saloon, souvenir shop, and the parlor of "Mme. Amanda, Palmist & Clairvoyant." (*Daughters of the Republic of Texas Library, San Antonio*)

AN INDIAN BATTLE.

7. The only known contemporary representation of the 1832 San Saba fight, this crude woodcut accompanied Rezin's account of the battle published in Philadelphia the following year. It depicts either Rezin or James in the center carrying the wounded Robert Buchanan to safety, while at the same moment a volley from friends in the thicket at left stops an assault by several Caddo at right. It is interesting to note that both Buchanan and his rescuer, whether James or Rezin, wear top hats. (Atkinson's Saturday Evening Post, *August 17, 1833*)

W.B. Travis
By Wiley Martin
Dec. 1835

8. The only presumed portrait of William Barret Travis made from life, drawn in December 1835 by his friend Wiley Martin in San Felipe, shortly before Travis left to raise his cavalry legion and go to San Antonio. It matches contemporary descriptions of him as being pleasant faced and somewhat robust. (*DeGolyer Library, Southern Methodist University, Dallas, Tex.*)

9. Travis might have recognized a few buildings in this circa 1860 view of Claiborne, Ala., though the town had grown considerably since he left it in disgrace nearly thirty years earlier. (*Alabama Department of Archives and History, Montgomery*)

10. The small house in Claiborne locally reputed to have been the home of Travis and his small family before he left for Texas. (*Courtesy of Joan F. Headley, San Antonio, Tex.*)

11. The man who taught Travis the law and served as the role model he sought to equal or surpass, attorney James Dellet of Claiborne. It fell to Dellet to attempt to collect on the debts that forced Travis to flee Claiborne, and later to help Rosanna Travis commence her divorce proceedings. (*Alabama Department of Archives and History, Montgomery*)

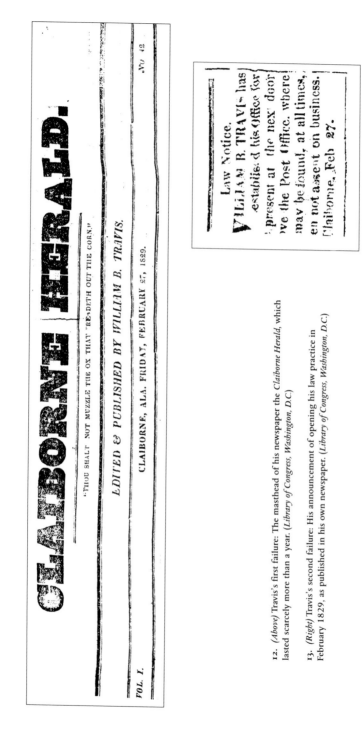

CLAIBORNE HERALD.

"THOU SHALT NOT MUZZLE THE OX THAT 'READETH OUT THE CORN.'"

EDITED & PUBLISHED BY WILLIAM B. TRAVIS.

VOL. I.   CLAIBORNE, ALA. FRIDAY, FEBRUARY 27, 1829.   NO. 42

Law Notice.

WILLIAM R. TRAVIS has established his office for present at the next door ve the Post Office. where may be found, at all times, en not absent on business. Claiborne, Feb 27.

12. *(Above)* Travis's first failure: The masthead of his newspaper the *Claiborne Herald*, which lasted scarcely more than a year. *(Library of Congress, Washington, D.C.)*

13. *(Right)* Travis's second failure: His announcement of opening his law practice in February 1829, as published in his own newspaper. *(Library of Congress, Washington, D.C.)*

The State of Alabama.

TO ANY CONSTABLE OF Monroe COUNTY—GREETING:

YOU are hereby commanded to summon Frances H. Gordin

to be and appear before me H. Mc. Alvey — a Justice of the Peace in and for said county, at my office within the county aforesaid, on the 28th day of August — 1830, at 11 — o'clock in the forenoon, then and there to answer to William B. Gains who sues for the use of William Mc. Cato

of a debt or demand, not exceeding fifty dollars.

H- REIN fail not, and have you then there this precept, with your doings.

WITNESS my hand and seal, the 14th day of August — in the year eighteen hundred and thirty.

Mc. Alvey J. P. (SEAL.)

14. The cruel evidence of failure: One of the rare cases that came the way of the young lawyer Travis, this one was on behalf of his father-in-law, William Cato. Few as they were, they were all for the collection of minor debts, providing fees as small as fifty cents, hardly enough to support his family, his ambition, or his taste for living. (*James Dellet Papers, Alabama Department of Archives and History, Montgomery*)

15. Travis's greatest failure of all: "the beautiful Miss Cato." Rosanna Travis appears here in an unpublished portrait, dating probably from the later 1830s after her marriage to Samuel Cloud. Despite dark and mythical stories of her infidelity, she seems more sinned against than sinner. Still, the marriage was undoubtedly troubled, certainly not strong enough to hold Travis in Claiborne to face up to his other, professional, problems. (*Courtesy of the Daughters of the Republic of Texas Museum, Austin*)

16. The scene of the final embarrassment. Here in the Claiborne Masonic Lodge No. 3, which also served as Baptist church and Monroe County courthouse, Dellet humiliated Travis in a suit over his mounting debts early in 1832. Within weeks Travis left for Texas, never to return. (*Courtesy of Joan F. Headley, San Antonio, Tex.*)

7. Perhaps some idea of Travis's features may be gleaned from this 1850s photograph of his son Charles, the boy he wanted so much to have with him in Texas. Travis did not live to make him the fortune he promised, and the ne'er-do-well son would likely have squandered it if he had. (*Center for American History, University of Texas, Austin*)

18. The "Father of Texas," Stephen F. Austin. After amicable initial relations, he never trusted Bowie and warned friends to be careful in their dealings with him. Austin found Travis more to his taste, and a mutual respect and admiration grew between them. As general of the revolutionary forces besieging San Antonio in late 1835, however, he proved vacillating and uncertain, causing widespread discontent in his army, especially with Bowie and other officers. (*Center for American History, University of Texas, Austin*)

19. Sam Houston, onetime friend of Crockett, newfound friend of Bowie, led the forces trying to wrest power in Texas away from Austin. In the end he won, but at a terrible price, for many believed that either through self-interest or simple neglect he sacrificed the garrison at the Alamo to his own ambition to solidify his hold over the new republic. (*Center for American History, University of Texas, Austin*)

20. Where all roads led, and where Crockett, Bowie, and Travis finally met, and died. The earliest known photograph of the Alamo church, a daguerreotype taken prior to 1850, and showing clearly some of the damage done during the fortifying of the place, and the subsequent bombardment. (*Center for American History, University of Texas, Austin*)

would send for her and the children when he established himself in Texas. Loving him, she believed him. "I had not lost confidence in his integrity to me," she explained, "however deficient he may have been to others I confided in his assurances to me."[80]

She had little choice but to accept, and to keep his plan a secret as well, for surely he told no one that he intended to leave his family and run away from his debt.[81] He no doubt did tell her, quite sincerely, that he intended to repay those debts when he could, but that was small comfort.[82] Somehow he managed to gather a little hard cash to cover the expense of his journey. Hardly able to afford steam passage—and besides, all of Claiborne could see him if he boarded a steamboat for the trip to Mobile—he almost certainly readied his horse for a long trip.[83] Sometime in the first two weeks of April 1831 he made his farewells, mounted, rode down to the ferry, and crossed the Alabama River, never to return.[84]

It had all started so well in Claiborne, and if ever a young man deserved to succeed for his energy, intelligence, application, and pure hard work, then surely it was William Barret Travis. But there was something lacking in him, as evidenced by the manner of his leaving. He was not yet a whole man. Ambition and brains were no guarantee of character. Only years and experience produced that, and of years he had scarcely enough to qualify as an adult, and a streak of impulsiveness, immaturity, and irresponsibility that argued against even that modest title. He wanted too much too fast and finished with nothing. When he came up against an angry man he preferred not to face, he turned his back on him, just as now he turned his back on his troubles, responsibilities, and even his wife and child. A much greater journey awaited him within himself than this long road to the Sabine, however. Travis needed to grow up. That being the case, what lay ahead was just what he most needed, for Texas in the days to come would have a way of making men.[85]

could do nothing but break out in howls of derisive laughter,
that they promptly found against him.[72]

Certainly it had an effect on Travis. "He was very ambitiou
close friend; "he hungered and thirsted for fame—not the kin
which staisfies [sic] the ambition of the duelist and desperado
exalted fame which crowns the doer of great deeds in a good
Instead of that, here in Claiborne where he had hoped to be
much, he was laughed at, ridiculed, and disgraced.[74] Moreover,
court's judgments against him for his debts, the clerk would be
orders of arrest on March 31, the last day of the session. His bro
law William Cato had some experience with that sort of thi
Travis himself knew that Alabama still sent debtors to prison.[75]
days, perhaps even hours of the ruling, he knew what he would

Years later, Claiborne old-timers recalled that "when a man co
ted a crime, he fled to Texas as that was such a distant country
sure the law would not pursue him."[76] Certainly Travis knew
Texas. As a publisher he would have seen many of the same
Orleans newspapers that Bowie did, telling of the land and op
nity and amenable Mexican authorities. There were stories tha
could be had "with great facility" at Austin's colony, and at a c
less than four cents per acre, even that on credit.[77] Just weeks befo
trial, if Travis attended the regular meeting of the Masons, he w
have met José de la Garza, one of the most prominent landowne
Béxar, then visiting in the United States and on his way to
Alabama's governor.[78] De la Garza must have told them all muc
Texas, and the more he spoke, the more attractive it sounded—s
place new, where a man might start over, a place where those
came early, as Dellet did to Claiborne, might stand at the front of
community. And wherever there was a great deal of land chang
hands, there was always a need for lawyers.[79]

The news would not be welcome to Rosanna. Just as proud as
husband, she also felt the humiliation of their situation, only n
when he told her that he intended to leave her and go to Texas,
would be left behind with their toddler, Charles, and another child
the way, thrust on the charity of her family, to face the scorn of t
community on her own. He promised that he would return to h
when he had recouped his fortunes and could pay his debts, or else l

BOWIE

It was his habit to settle all difficulties without regard to time or place, and it was the same whether he met one or many.

WILLIAM H. SPARKS, 1881

Norris Wright's bullet gave James Bowie his first real encounter with mortality, though it would have been uncharacteristic of him to be sobered by his brush with death. If anything as he lay recuperating he thought only of finding his antagonist to finish the fight, and most likely without resort to the conventions of the *code duello*. He had no patience for a process so slow and deliberate as that. Bowie epitomized that species of American whom Tocqueville found "trusts fearlessly in his own powers, which seem to him sufficient for everything."[1] He would wade into Wright at first sight wherever he found him, and that would be an end to it. Wisely, once he learned that Bowie lived, Norris Wright kept his distance for the next several months, but in a small frontier community like Rapides, inevitably they must meet again, and Bowie would be ready this time.

While in bed he determined to make that leather scabbard to wear on his belt, and when Rezin visited him after the fight, he brought something to fill it. Some years earlier at his Avoyelles plantation, Rezin had stood at his forge and fashioned a hunting knife, perhaps using an old file for iron stock. He hammered out a straight blade one and one-half inches wide and just over nine inches long, put it to a grinder to hone a keen edge on one side, and then added a crosspiece separating the handle from the blade. Not at all ornamental and entirely utilitarian, it showed the stains and wear of long use. But with a good edge it made a deadly weapon all the same, and now he gave it to James. In the next encounter with Wright, if there was one, his

brother would lose no precious time on a misfiring pistol or opening a
clasp knife. When finally he arose to walk the streets of Alexandria
once more, James Bowie wore his brother's knife at his belt, where it
remained every day thereafter.[2]

Bowie had been lucky to survive Wright's bullet, but then James
seemed charmed by good fortune, and as he recuperated his luck held
elsewhere. Through a remarkable chain of misunderstandings and
oversights—aided perhaps by a forged letter from Graham written by
Bowie—George Davis went ahead and allowed the surveys of seven
claims in Terrebonne on the Harper report. By April 1827 Bowie
started registering transfers of the titles from the Martins to himself,
and once he had the surveys in hand, he owned clear title to at least
17,600 acres. When an incensed Graham learned of the error, he could
do nothing but start an investigation and threaten to ask President
Adams himself to issue a special executive order to stop Bowie. And
meanwhile, as usual, Bowie removed almost all of the original papers
from land office files by showing a power of attorney from Robert
Martin. His only slip was failing to do the same for the one claim on
file for William Wilson.[3]

At the same time affairs looked bright for Bowie elsewhere. On
January 28, 1827, old Reuben Kemper died at his home on the Calcasieu.
That removed him, at least, as an obstacle to Bowie pursuing his supposed de la Français heirs' claim to that forty thousand dollars or more
due to Kemper from the government.[4] As for more immediate availability
of money, prospects improved for everyone in the region that year. After
the depression of the early 1820s, planters in the western parishes sought
to shift capital control away from the usurious New Orleans banks.
Finally, in its 1826 session, the legislature approved a charter for the
Consolidated Association of the Planters of Louisiana. Since most farmers were land rich and cash poor, the Planters Bank, as it came to be
called, pioneered in accepting land as collateral for loans. The original
shareholders elected Hugh de la Vergne controller and sent him and an
associate to New York and England seeking two million dollars in
investment capital, which they finally got from the house of Baring
Brothers in London. Though Bowie was not an original shareholder, he
soon became one. A planter acquired shares by pledging land, and share-
holding in turn entitled him to apply for loans. Bowie used his newly

acquired Terrebonne property to gain him shares, and soon had need for a loan, as his spending habits had not changed.[5] With fall approaching he faced court action by Wilfred Dent for a $1,990 debt, and even his smooth tongue could not find a way to avoid confessing the validity of the judgment.[6] Thus he parlayed his fraudulently acquired land into a tool to work for him even before he found buyers.

On the horizon in Rapides, meanwhile, all the years of mounting frustration, resentment, jealousy, ambition, and more finally came to a head. Once more financial recession loomed. The wave of land speculation of the past several years left many overextended and indebted, their property, like the Martins', about to be seized in judgment. "The weight of debt must sooner or later force a change of owners of most of the property in the Parish," John Johnston warned his brother in July, "which will bear in its train distrust, hatred, malevolence, jealousy and all of the concomitant discord." This only exacerbated the personal animosities among the several factions in the parish, and now they gelled into two camps. On the one side stood the Wells brothers, chiefly Samuel and Montfort, and Bowie's old friend Warren Hall. General Cuny loosely allied with them as well, perhaps in part because of an $11,750 mortgage that he owed Montfort Wells.[7] On the other stood Robert Crain, Dr. Thomas Maddox, Alfred Blanchard, and Norris Wright. Chances were that by late summer of 1827 none of them knew the true origins of their feud. Crain and Cuny had a long-running disagreement.[8] The Wellses and Wright, of course, harbored grudges over recent and past elections. Hall and Wright were also enemies thanks to old insults and Hall's friendship for Bowie. Dr. Maddox, though long friendly with Samuel Wells, had recently been pulled by loyalties to his other friends, and Wright especially could be counted on to feed him poisoned information about his own antagonists. Bowie, of course, harbored his own feelings toward Wright.[9]

Ostensibly the final explosion began when friends on both sides urged the Wells brothers and Hall to meet Maddox, Wright, and Crain on the dueling field and finally settle their differences. The confrontations began when Montfort Wells and his second, Hall, met to fight Crain and his second, Wright. Rather than shoot, however, they shouted. Wells was so nearsighted that he demanded a distance of no more than ten paces between the duelists, but the two seconds, already enemies, grew so angry in the negotiations that they issued their own challenges, and Maddox and Wells left with no fight after all. Wells responded by simply aiming a shotgun at Maddox a few days later on an Alexandria street, but he missed, and the fact that his brother Samuel was sheriff saved him from arrest and prosecution. That only strained the Samuel Wells–Maddox friendship, though each tried to avoid an open break. John Johnston declared by July 13 that Rapides had become a "scene of constant warfare," with the end of the turmoil not in sight.[10]

This kind of violence was all too common on the southern frontier. A traveler some years later remarked that "the darkest side of the southerner is his quarrelsomeness, and recklessness of human life." Men fought duels over the smallest slight, real or imagined. Their ready resort to such violence may have been in part a cultural artifact from their Scottish and Irish ancestors, encouraged by the inability to accept questions or challenges to authority instilled in Southern men by slavery, and enhanced by a frontier society in which justice and retribution by officialdom could not be counted on to be either swift or appropriate, especially when lawmen themselves—like Wells and Wright—were often parties to feuds. Add competition in land speculation, ambition, and greed, and the mix inevitably led to crowded dueling fields and wayside ambushes.[11]

Meanwhile Wright and Hall announced their fight for July 26. The origins of their feud may have gone all the way back to 1821 and Hall's trial and acquittal, which almost led to a duel with the judge in the case.[12] In any event none of these men now seemed content to settle their differences one-to-one. Rather, they went in small gangs. When Wright left Alexandria on July 21 to meet Hall, he took Crain, Maddox, and six others with him, along with an arsenal of four rifles, one double-barreled shotgun, and seven braces of pistols. "What their intentions are I am unable to say," Samuel Wells cracked in droll and disingenuous fashion. He should have been more sobered just before their departure by a visit from Crain, who handed him a challenge from Maddox, proposing a meeting on August 5. Though Wells wanted to avoid fighting Maddox, he felt he had no choice but to accept. He suggested a more convenient date, however, privately hoping to delay until October, by which time he hoped they could have adjusted their differences. "It has been unnecessarily brought on," he lamented, and all grew out of public debate over the fault for the breakdown of the Maddox–Montfort Wells duel. "I regret exceedingly to be thrown in collision with Dr. Maddox, he is an honest upright peacable citizen—we had hitherto been on terms of extreme intimacy, and if he had been left to pursue his own feelings and disposition, we never should have fallen out." Now it was too late.[13]

The anticipated Hall-Wright fight became a spectator event, with some two hundred or more people turning up to watch. They saw no duel, however, but what one termed "a most farcical tragedy." Hall waited at the appointed place on time, with Bowie acting as his second, but never even saw Wright. After loading a steamboat with men, guns, knives, and surgeons and taking them all across to the Mississippi side of the river, Wright sent his principal second to settle the final details. There followed twenty minutes of discussion over the propriety of Bowie acting as Hall's second, no doubt objected to by Wright's second since Bowie and Wright had their own unfinished business, and he could not be counted on to act fairly under the circumstances. Hall looked increasingly nervous during it all, and when no resolution ensued, the fight fizzled, and Wright left claiming the victory though he had never set foot on the field. An enraged Hall demanded another meeting and issued a public challenge. "War has again been declared in Rapides," old Overton told Senator Johnston. Everyone awaited the Samuel Wells fight with Maddox, while the two principals began practicing their marksmanship. "They are both spending their time in killing trees," said a cynical observer. Soon enough their targets would have flesh.[14]

Throughout August, Rapides hummed with talk of the anticipated fight. Both antagonists and would-be spectators had been disappointed in two previous duels. Everyone banked on this fight really taking place, and at the same time the war talk inflated it to such proportions that most expected the fighting to spread beyond just Maddox and Wells. After some negotiating they agreed to meet in or near Natchez in mid-September, with no final agreement on place, date, or terms yet fixed. Gradually the antagonists traveled east. Maddox, accompanied by Wright and Crain, arrived in Natchez on September 16, lodging with Maddox's fellow physician John Nevitt.[15] Wells arrived the next day, with his second, Maj. George McWhorter, and his physician, Dr. Richard Cuny.

Rather than cross over to Natchez immediately, they lodged in the Alexander House at Vidalia, immediately on the west side of the Mississippi. James Bowie came with them, as did Gen. Samuel Cuny and Thomas J. Wells. Word of their arrival reached Maddox quickly enough, and that same evening in Natchez their opponents began to talk of the impending duel turning into a general melée.

Bowie remained in Vidalia the next day, when Wells went to Natchez and met with Maddox. They agreed to fight in the morning, Wells specifying a partially wooded sandbar on a bend a few hundred yards upstream from Natchez on the Mississippi side of the river. Because of the mutual fear of the meeting turning into a free-for-all, they also agreed that only three men on a side should be present on the field, the principals and their seconds and surgeons. By now more friends of Maddox—or more properly friends of Crain and Wright—arrived, including Alfred Blanchard and his brother Carey, and with the two parties growing larger, each man brought his own animosities to add to the mix, and the danger of the affair getting out of hand increased dramatically. In the negotiations for the meeting, Wright had made it clear that he did not wish to see someone from the other party on the field, meaning Bowie, while some believed they had heard Crain announce that he would shoot his old foe General Cuny on sight.[16] Boast and probably drink raised the blood of both camps, each man supporting and encouraging the determination of his partners. Only a miracle could prevent a tragedy on the morrow.

Bowie simply watched these preliminaries, being there in no official capacity but simply as one of the "friends" of Wells. Finally, on the late morning of September 19, he turned participant when he and the others stepped into a small skiff at Vidalia and rowed across the river. When they reached the sandbar they found that they had arrived before their opponents, and tied their boat to the beach and walked inland a bit to shade themselves in a stand of willows. The late summer day, already over eighty degrees, grew warm. The sky was clear, the humidity rising by noon, when at last Bowie saw Maddox and at least ten men with him, plus some of their servants, approaching on horseback. They stopped and dismounted some distance away from the Wells party, and then Maddox, Crain, and their friend Dr. James Denny walked down to the sandbar to join Wells, McWhorter, and Dr. Cuny.

Bowie stood in the willows no more than one hundred yards from the sandy beach where he saw Wells and Maddox look over the ground. He could see but not hear some urgent conversation as Drs. Denny and Crain tried to persuade the principals to settle the matter amicably. Then the antagonists took their places and exchanged a shot, neither taking effect. Once again Denny tried to get them to stop, arguing that honor was now satisfied, but Wells and Maddox insisted on a second round. Bowie kept to his place with his friends, while Wright and his party moved closer, though still in the woods, to get a better view of the next exchange. After the puffs of smoke and the reports, Bowie saw that again both men remained standing, and then Denny stepped between them, said a few words, and Wells and Maddox approached each other to shake hands. It was over, mercifully, without either suffering a scratch.

In a few moments the principals and their associates turned and as a group looked toward Bowie, Thomas J. Wells, and General Cuny, but then they started to walk toward Wright and his party. Bowie heard someone yell that they were all going to take a glass of wine together with Maddox's friends to celebrate the happy conclusion of the affair, and he and those with him started walking at a brisk pace toward them, Cuny ahead of him, catching up to them when they were about halfway to Wright's party at the edge of the woods. Then it happened.

He heard Cuny ask Wells how it had gone, and Wells replied that he and Maddox were friends again. Fired no doubt by the rumors that Crain intended to shoot him on sight, Cuny then turned to Crain and suggested that they go back to the beach to settle their own differences. He may have reached for his pistol. Seeing this, behind him Bowie did the same. Wells and Cuny's brother immediately stepped between the two and told the general that this was neither the time nor the place. Behind them, and without their seeing it, Crain also drew a pistol. Then Cuny agreed to back down, and Wells and Dr. Cuny stepped aside and began to walk on. Bowie and Crain still had guns in their hands, however, and within a second Crain fired his. Taking Bowie for the "Major General" of the group, as he put it, Crain aimed at him. He missed Bowie, and Bowie's answering bullet just clipped Crain's cravat. Instantly Crain drew another and fired, this time hitting Cuny in the thigh, severing an artery. Bowie saw the gen-

eral fall, and as Crain turned to run back toward his friends in the willows, Bowie drew his other pistol and fired but missed. Then he
reached to his belt and that new scabbard, drawing out the long knife
Rezin had given him.

This was the sort of moment for which James Bowie was made. "If
there ever lived a man who never felt the sensation of fear, it was James
Bowie," said his friend Sparks. Rezin would always avoid violence if
he could do so with honor, but his brother was quicker. "It was his
habit to settle all difficulties without regard to time or place, and it was
the same whether he met one or many." Caiaphas Ham averred simply
that "he was a foe no one dared to undervalue, and many feared. When
unexcited there was a calm seriousness shadowing his countenance
which gave assurance of great will power, unbending firmness of purpose, and unflinching courage." However, said Ham, "when fired by
anger his face bore the semblance of an enraged tiger."

In a transport of primal rage, the "tiger" followed Crain some small
distance, yelling out, *"Crain you have shot at me; and I will kill you if I can."*
Suddenly he found himself isolated and without a loaded weapon.
Crain turned and seeing what he called "his savage fury," threw his
own empty pistol at him, catching Bowie on the side of the head with
a force that almost sent him to his knees. Maddox rushed up to grab
Bowie but was thrown off; then Wright and the rest rushed down
from the woods to assist Crain. Bowie staggered over to a twelve-inch
driftwood tree trunk about five feet high, standing buried by one end
in the sand, and gripped it for support, when Denny and McWhorter
came up. Seeing Wright draw a pistol, Bowie yelled out: "You damned
rascal, don't you shoot." Wright yelled something back at him, and
just then McWhorter handed Bowie a pistol. He fired at the approaching Wright just as Wright fired at him. Again both missed, but then
Wright drew a second pistol. Unable to answer his fire, Bowie yelled
at him to shoot and be damned.

By now McWhorter held a drawn pistol, and he and Wright fired at
the same time. McWhorter's ball just barely penetrated Wright's left
side, and he yelled: "The damned rascal has killed me," but the wound
was hardly mortal. Denny came up to Bowie now, grasping him by the
coat lapel and urging that "this must be stopped, sir, this must be
stopped." When Wright fired, however, his bullet struck Bowie full in

the breast just where Denny had his left hand. The ball carried away Denny's middle finger, then passed through one of Bowie's lungs, staggering him. Freeing himself from Denny, Bowie lunged toward Wright, who had turned to flee. Bowie got about fifteen paces and was just in the act of grabbing his quarry when the Blanchard brothers opened fire on him. One bullet struck him in the thigh and brought him down. Seeing that, Wright turned around and drew his sword cane, as did Alfred Blanchard, and the two of them set upon the stricken man. They stabbed at him repeatedly, though neither got in a good strong thrust as Bowie flailed about, deflecting their blows with his free arm and his knife, giving them each some small cuts in the process and hitting Wright in the arm twice. Wright leaned forward and his sword pierced Bowie's left hand, and when he then turned the hand to fend off another blow, the blade tore through the flesh. One of the sword blows actually bent the blade as it hit Bowie's breastbone and then slid along one of his ribs.

By what Samuel Wells called "wonderful exertion," Bowie got himself up to a sitting position. Then in one lunge he reached up to grab Wright by the collar, and as Wright tried to straighten himself he inadvertently helped raise Bowie to a near standing position. As Bowie later told the story to Rezin and their friend Sparks, he said in Wright's ear: "Now, Major, you die!" With a single savage thrust, he drove the knife through Wright's chest, boasting afterward that he "twisted it to cut his heart strings." Wright pitched forward, dead instantly, falling on Bowie and pinning him to the ground. By this time the Wells brothers—Samuel and Thomas—who had been at the dying General Cuny's side, ran up to where Blanchard still stabbed at Bowie, now trapped on the ground with Wright's body above him. Thomas Jefferson Wells shot Blanchard in the arm, and at the same time Bowie finally threw off Wright's corpse and gave Blanchard a bad cut in his side with the knife.

With that last thrust of the blade, the brawl ended. Crain had already stepped away, as had Carey Blanchard, soon joined by his wounded brother. Maddox never participated, nor had any of the physicians or the other spectators who came with his party. As quickly as the fight began it was done, the whole explosion of violence taking scarcely more than ninety seconds. Dr. William Provan of Natchez, watching from the woods, came out to Wright, opening his vest to reveal the gaping wound, and pronounced him dead. While the physicians bandaged the several other wounds, Bowie called out to Crain nearby: *"For God sake; Crain assist me, give me some water, and help me to the shade."* There had never been antipathy between the two prior to the encounter this morning, and the bloodletting of the last few minutes seemed to take any hostility out of all of them. Crain quickly went to Bowie's side, and aided by McWhorter and others, carried him to the willows. On the way Bowie said: *"Col Crain* you ought not to have shot at me." Crain replied that Bowie should not have drawn his pistol on him, but Bowie protested that "I did not draw for you; it was to protect my friend." They laid Bowie in the shade beside Samuel Cuny, who died within a few minutes. Turning their attention to Bowie, the doctors found that one bullet had passed through his lung and another through his thigh. There were at least seven stab wounds on his body and a severe wound on his head from Crain's thrown pistol. If Bowie was still conscious at this point, and if they conferred within his hearing, then he heard all but Dr. Cuny conclude that he would not survive. Quickly they loaded Cuny and Wright into the boat, and Crain and Provan helped to carry Bowie, and within fifteen minutes from the firing of the first shots they were rowing back to Vidalia, there to bury the dead and nurse the wounded.[17]

Bowie's friends carried him to a room in the Vidalia House, and while the doctors tried their best to close his wounds, the story of the battle spread rapidly. The next day the Natchez papers first reported the affair. Town gossip and the papers said that Bowie was not expected to live. Bowie himself had other ideas, but confessed to his friends that after being hit by several bullets and multiple sword thrusts, he felt he was "d—d badly wounded." He asserted that Crain's bullet never really hit him, which prompted Crain, who stayed in the area for several days and apparently called on Bowie, to accuse him of lying, but Bowie did jokingly express gratitude that his foes had heavily charged their pistols with powder, for the bullets passed completely through his body rather than lodging inside to do added mischief. He expressed not a bit of remorse at the death of Wright, and asserted frankly that when he plunged his knife into him, he meant to kill.[18] The next day Wright was buried temporarily in Vidalia.

Bowie spent almost two months recuperating to the point at which he could move about and leave the Natchez area to return to Alexandria, and for fully half a year after the fight he was not himself. Indeed, those wounds, especially the puncture of his lung, troubled him for the rest of his life.[19] While in Vidalia, and in Natchez once he could move, Bowie found himself something of a curiosity as the much wounded survivor of the brawl. After all, once Cuny went down, Bowie became almost exclusively the object of attention of Crain, Wright, and the Blanchards, all of whom he equaled or bested practically single-handed. Men came to meet him as he lay in his sickbed, one finding him "cool and powerful, but generous and kind hearted." The violence over, Bowie quickly reverted to his normal cordial and winning manner, though obviously strained by the pain of his multiple wounds. New friends found him intelligent, suave, and deceptively gentle mannered. "He exhibited so much kindness of heart and mildness of manners that a stranger would have selected almost any other man in a crowd of strangers, if the eye and powerful frame were disregarded, as the renowned Jim Bowie."[20] He struck a friendship with the lawyer Angus McNeil, who would soon replace Quitman as his attorney in Natchez, and no doubt received visits from his brother Rezin, whom he could well thank now for that knife.[21]

Meanwhile the story of the fight and what John Johnston called "the feuds of our parishioners" soon became national news.[22] The Natchez press reported it extensively, a whole special edition of the *Ariel* appearing on October 19, and thanks to that the papers in Philadelphia and New York eventually picked it up. *Nile's Register*, the most widely read news weekly of the day, republished an article on it. Though Bowie himself did not figure prominently enough in most accounts even to have his first name appear, still, having been a participant, and the most active one at that, a mantle of notoriety inevitably attached itself to him above all the rest. It was no duel, but a small spontaneous riot. Borrowing from the old Anglo-French, Rezin called it a "chance medley," a onetime legal term for an accident that was not *completely* accidental, and typical of frontier hardscrabble scrapes in which the real fighters risked themselves only when they seemed to have the advantage and happily ran to cover otherwise—all except Bowie, that is. Impelled by the rage that blinded him to fear or self-protection, he stood his ground and simply kept fighting. That was the sort of thing that turned brutal, pointless brawling into legend.

Naturally a grand jury met in Natchez on the fight, since two deaths had taken place in the county. It sat on January 24, 1828, but did not call Bowie to appear, and in the event, the jury handed down no indictments. Meanwhile the atmosphere back in Rapides remained as charged as ever even after the release of all that animosity on the sandbar. Having survived his duel with Maddox and the free-for-all that followed, poor Samuel Wells succumbed to a fever three weeks later, and yet another Cuny brother seemed in line for the office of sheriff to replace him. "The fighting I am afraid is not done away," lamented a friend of Johnston's. "The animosity which exists still among the Parties must end somewhere." Crain himself simply went to New Orleans, resolved never to return to Rapides so long as any of the Cunys lived, though in fact he came back within the year, seeking a seat in the legislature.[23]

Though bedridden and in severe pain, Bowie wasted no time. Ever since learning of the death of Reuben Kemper, he intended to renew his campaign for the de la Français claim, especially since the prize now ran to more than forty thousand dollars. Originally he had expected to go to Washington in person that winter to press the matter with the Treasury and State Departments, but his wound now made that seem unfeasible. Recently he had taken on a partner, however, none other than Maj. Isaac Thomas of Rapides. Years before, Thomas had written several letters to the General Land Office on behalf of Bowie's Sutton report claims, in spite of the common knowledge of their fraudulence, and the previous year Thomas dealt with John Bowie, too. Before long he also entered a partnership with William Wilson, the front for Bowie in one of the Terrebonne claims, making it evident that despite his good reputation locally, Thomas probably was not wholly incorruptible.[24] Just how he acquired a one-half share in the Kemper claim is uncertain, but given Bowie's perpetual need for money, he probably simply sold Thomas an interest or gave him a share to redeem a debt.[25] Certainly Bowie owed Thomas money even after he took him on as a partner in the claim, for in January 1828 he allowed his brother Stephen by power of attorney to turn over one thousand *arpents* of his Terrebonne property to Thomas in fulfillment of a debt owed him jointly by James Bowie and Robert Martin.[26] The land turned over, of course, was part of the very ground that Bowie had gained through fraud and accident, with Martin as his front, and on behalf of which Thomas had written to the General Land Office. The land may have been a final payoff for Thomas's influence—though it had not worked the trick—or it may even have been part of a larger scheme of which the Kemper claim interest was only a portion. Certainly Thomas had influence: In 1830 he would be a candidate for the governorship.

At a meeting in early November, Bowie agreed that Thomas should go to Washington on their behalf during the coming winter. Through Bowie he already knew what he needed, including statements of evidence of the actual purchase of the arms during the West Florida rebellion, their possession by the infant republic and subsequent assumption by the United States, and the actual use of part of them in the Battle of New Orleans in 1815. He could get ample testimony from Gen. Fulwar Skipwith, Maj. Philemon Thomas, and other veterans of the West Florida enterprise, by all of which they hoped to persuade the government to reconsider its position on the claim. Indeed, Bowie may already have secured some or most of this on advice from Secretary of State Clay.[27]

Though hardly robust, Bowie moved to New Orleans in November and attended to some business in Rapides again late that month, and a few weeks later went to Terrebonne to sell another of his newly confirmed tracts on Bayou Caillou for a much needed twelve hundred dollars to support him when he wintered in New Orleans as usual.[28] The bulk of his attention, however, he turned to his next land campaign, the Arkansas grants. He and John had bombarded the authorities with hundreds of claims, all of which in that territory went to the superior court, which tried them for confirmation. The Bowies were clever. Prior to the trials they transferred many of the claims to some of Arkansas's most prominent men, and these men, perhaps acting as fronts like Martin and Wilson, engaged the territory's best lawyers in defense of "their" claims. If they succeeded in defending Bowie's spurious grants, then they would buy the property from John at a preferential price.

United States Attorney Samuel C. Roane found himself virtually alone and overwhelmed, with neither the time nor the wherewithal to mount a case against what he already believed to be fraudulent claims. He sought a postponement that he might learn enough Spanish to study the grant documents and go to Louisiana to talk with the General Land Office people there familiar with Bowie frauds, but on both counts the court denied him. As a result the court first passed favorably on thirty-six cases, and then in a Christmas Eve bonanza, the court on December 24 confirmed another 117 or more. The decisions covered between fifty and sixty thousand acres, of which the Bowies had already transferred a considerable portion to those influential associates. The success was stunning.[29]

James Bowie only knew of his Arkansas successes from afar. Too weak yet to travel that far, he went to New Orleans around the first of the new year, there to remain for the next two months continuing his recovery. While there he began selling his Bayou Black and Bayou Caillou tracts, receiving $2,500 in hand and a promissory note for the same amount a year hence.[30] He also bent his efforts to getting the necessary papers for the Kemper claim, without informing his partner Thomas, but in the main he rested. New Orleans was always exciting, especially this season of the year. He was there for Mardi Gras in February, and was surely in town for the great event of the month before when the city welcomed back its hero of 1815. It was no secret that Andrew Jackson wanted to seek the presidency again in that year's election, and the Louisiana legislature issued him an invitation to be the honored guest at an anniversary celebration of his victory on January 8. Jackson came down the Mississippi, stopping at Natchez on January 4, and then four days later made a somewhat triumphal landing at the Crescent City. For the next four days he was feted, especially at a Jackson Ball held on January 10, and while the Creoles and the Henry Clay people gave him a cool reception, his own supporters were warm enough.[31] Certainly James Bowie was no Jackson man, but he could not have avoided witnessing the outpouring of enthusiasm for this apostle of the "common man," and he would hardly have missed an opportunity to attend one of the balls and dinners, if only to see the beautiful ladies and cultivate the acquaintance of the wealthy and influential.[32] There is one social call that Bowie almost certainly did make while he was in New Orleans. Somehow he and Robert Crain each learned that the other was in town that season. Crain, already tiring of living with the fear that every hand in Rapides stood poised to kill him, invited Bowie to meet him in his hotel room and Bowie accepted, despite the advice of friends to keep his distance. There, behind a closed door and with no one to witness what they said, they ended their differences permanently and emerged as friends. In future years Bowie even spoke in endorsement of Crain's character. If the rest of the Rapides factions continued their hostility, at least one small peace broke out there in New Orleans.[33]

Bowie stayed in the Crescent City until late in February, but though still feeling the effects of his wounds, he could not remain idle. That winter he started making substantial land sales, and by April had realized more than $33,000, seeing at last the kind of money he had dreamed of, though his Sutton report claims remained stalled. He even started buying Caillou land legitimately, and signed over another parcel to settle a $4,000 debt of Stephen's. He had $25,000 or more remaining in hand, though given his lifestyle, much of that was committed in debts. Still, he must have had more cash in his purse than ever before in his life.[34]

Naturally he only wanted more. "One usually finds that love of money is either the chief or a secondary motive at the bottom of everything the Americans do," said Tocqueville just a few years later. "It is odd to watch with what feverish ardor the Americans pursue prosperity and how they are ever tormented by the shadowy suspicion that they may not have chosen the shortest route to get it."[35] That was James Bowie to the life. Rezin often complained of his brother's impetuosity, saying that "James is too impatient to wait for events; he will hurry them before matters are ripe for action."[36] James tired of waiting for action on the Kemper claim. Now, even though he had previously agreed with Thomas that his partner should make the Washington trip instead, he changed his mind. On his own and with the assistance of Montfort Wells, he secured the necessary testimony and affidavits— some of which may have been forged, since the government seemed to have satisfactory evidence that the Spanish arms were never received or used—and as many of the supporting documents as he felt he needed. Then, without even consulting Thomas, he left his power of attorney with Rezin and Stephen to handle the March and April land sales, and around the first of March took ship once more from New Orleans.[37]

When he heard that Bowie had left without telling him, Thomas took the news badly. It is evident that he never fully trusted Bowie, a feeling based as much on knowledge of his partner's dealings as on the fact that the two shared some similarities of character. As soon as he heard, Thomas shot a quick letter to Senator Johnston, enclosing one to be handed to Bowie when he arrived in the capital. Scolding Bowie for going on without telling him and, he feared, without proper preparation of the documents in the case, Thomas went on to specify that if his partner should still be successful in getting the $40,000 or more out of the government, he did not want Bowie to bring his share back with him. Rather he wanted it left with Johnston as his authorized agent.[38]

In accompanying correspondence to Johnston, however, Thomas became far more candid. He knew thanks to the assurances of men of high standing that the material facts of the Kemper claim were quite provable, but Thomas did not trust "the precipitancy of Mr. B. and his loose manner of doing business." Worse, he suffered a mounting fear that Bowie might just be successful and have the entire settlement turned over to him on behalf of both partners. He implored Johnston to receive his half if Congress appropriated the money. "I have my motives for making this request," he said, adding that "they will suggest themselves to you, without the necessity of my mentioning them." He asked emphatically that his money should not come south unless in Johnston's keeping, and finally dropped any attempt at subtlety for his reasons, saying frankly that "I fear if he gets the possession of it it will be more difficult to get it out of his hands than those of the government." Preferably Johnston should insist on calling in person with Bowie to receive the payment, and if Bowie mounted any objection to Johnston receiving his half, then Thomas begged Johnston to get the State or the Treasury Department to suspend and hold his payment until he could come to Washington in person to collect.[39]

Johnston never gave Bowie the letter from Thomas.[40] In all probability the occasion to do so did not arise, because no approval was forthcoming on the Kemper claim during Bowie's visit to Washington. Moreover, by mid-April, with Bowie apparently still in the city, Johnston received a warning from a representative of Kemper's heirs that "a person has gone on to Washington with a view to obtain payment of this claim under a pretended transfer of it from de la Français." Having looked into the matter, the attorney told Johnston that "in my opinion there is no genuine transfer." Indeed it was not genuine. The problems that the late Kemper thought he saw in Bowie's power of attorney from the fictional Jose de la Francia were all too apparent, and typical of the careless mistakes he made in his land grant forgeries. For a start, there was no Jose de la Francia, and Kemper had apparently known it, and now so did Kemper's heirs' attorney. The man who appeared on Bowie's behalf before De Armas in New Orleans was an impostor paid by Bowie to pretend to be someone he was not. Most people, including Kemper who actually knew Henri de la Français, referred to him by the French version of his name, suggesting that de la Français himself did so as well. Bowie's man, however, appeared with a Spanish name, but then unwittingly gave himself away as being neither Spanish nor French. The man did not write out the recorded power of attorney himself but rather dictated it to the notary, and De Armas, being himself the son of a Spanish Creole, used the proper acute accent over the *e* in the deponent's name when he wrote "José." However, when the presumed de la Francia himself signed the document, he omitted the accent, a mistake that not even a semiliterate Spaniard or Spanish Creole would make in his own name. And if he were really French instead, and stating and signing his name on a Spanish form for some reason, there was still a problem, for a Frenchman would have written a cedilla beneath the *c* in Francia, making it França. Yet there was none, again a mistake a real Frenchman would not make in his own name. Consequently, whether the government allowed it or not, the original de la Français claim still legally belonged to Kemper, meaning that whatever remained of the $40,000 after paying the de la Français debt, belonged rightfully to Reuben Kemper's family.[41] In that case Johnston would hardly act for Thomas in a fraudulent claim, nor would he even need to see Bowie, for whom he must by this time have entertained a considerable distaste.

Bowie himself left Washington disappointed but not defeated. Though unable to convince the State or Treasury Departments to authorize Congress to recognize the Kemper claim and appropriate the money to pay him, his tenacity in this scheme matched his determination on his land deals, and after all, they were starting to pay off. He simply must wait, muster more testimony, and gain more influence in the capital.[42] If he made more efforts on behalf of his Sutton report claims north of Red River, there, too, he came away with nothing to show. But what probably disturbed Bowie most of all was Brent. After all but promising him two years earlier that he would back Bowie for his congressional seat in the 1828 election, the slippery Brent had now determined to run again himself.

Worse yet, when Bowie got back to Louisiana sometime in late April or early May, he found that none of the support he had—or thought he had—in 1826 still backed him. No men of influence came forward to endorse his candidacy. His best friends and strongest supporters, such as Kemper, Samuel Wells, and General Cuny, were all dead. Even Isaac Thomas would hardly support him, being in the first place a Jacksonian and in the second highly distrustful of Bowie. Two years earlier, men like Kemper declared that only Bowie could defeat Brent and even urged him to declare himself, while Brent seemingly promised his own support. But by the time the campaign opened in 1828 Brent had gone back on his word—as usual. Moreover, the notoriety of the Sandbar brawl could not have helped his reputation, and the continuing and expanding stories of his land frauds proved even more damaging among the honest voters. Being so closely tied to Brent may even have worked against Bowie, for disgusted as voters were with the congressman, they would not be likely to support one who was seen as his ideological protégé. As a result all of Bowie's support either died or evaporated.

It rankled even more that Brent proved so vulnerable this time. The presidential contest dominated the campaigning as never before. Now it was Jackson against Adams, and Brent came out against him back in December, charging that Old Hickory was no friend to the planters, with his stands in favor of a heavy duty on the bagging needed for cotton bales, and against a high duty on imported sugar.[43] Brent predicted Adams's reelection, moreover, in the face of the widespread rise in support for the people's candidate. In the coming election all states but two would vote by actual popular ballot, rather than leaving their electoral votes to be committed by their legislatures. All that boded well for Jackson, and Brent failed to see it.[44] Worse, Brent joined those who stooped to personal slurs against Jackson, including the charge of immorality because he had unwittingly committed bigamy when it turned out that his wife Rachel was not yet divorced when they wed. As usual Brent decided to campaign from Washington, but only wounded himself the more that summer when he sold his Louisiana plantation and thus became virtually a nonresident. As a result, when the election came, Johnston's friend the old crippled rheumatic Gen. Walter Overton defeated him handily, garnering nearly as many votes from Brent's former supporters as from the Jackson camp.[45]

Bad as the result was for Brent, it seemed worse for Bowie. Where Brent had been a useful ally in Washington, Overton openly disliked and distrusted Bowie and stood far too close to Johnston. Thus Bowie's ties to influence in Congress substantially diminished. But that was nothing compared to the disappointment he felt at not having been in the contest himself. He could have beaten Brent, of that he was certain. Indeed, that year almost anyone could have beaten Brent, and with the prize seemingly so easily within his grasp—with all the attendant influence and chance for profit that it promised—Bowie's denial of the chance to take it must have mortified him. It did not help that his brother John resigned from the legislature in order to attend to the Arkansas business, and Rezin gave up his seat as well, thus dramatically diminishing even his ties to influence in Baton Rouge.[46]

It left James Bowie feeling bitter and disillusioned. He was through with Alexandria and the feuding cliques of Rapides. His involvement with them had gotten him shot once by Wright. He had risked his life out of loyalty to them on the sandbar, and still carried the pain of his wounds every day. When he needed their loyalty they either let him down or betrayed him. His brother saw it eating at him when they met. "He had not been well used, or properly treated by some of his political friends," said John.[47] Bowie needed steady excitement, challenges, changes of scene. Even though a heavy motive for gain certainly inspired the land swindles, still they carried about them an added element of adventure, not unlike the Laffite slave enterprise, the thrill of challenging the authorities and besting them. Election to Congress would have opened whole new vistas, some of them for profit, undoubtedly, but also thrusting him into the highest society, placing him next to real power and influence. He had seen New York, Philadelphia, Baltimore, and Washington, and in his imagination he had seen himself walking their fashionable thoroughfares and looking very much at home.

If the betrayal of his supposed friends denied him new horizons in the East, so be it. He could look in other directions. The unquenchable appetite for cheap or free land had already drawn his attention west to Texas two years before, in 1826, and there things changed rapidly. The Mexicans actively encouraged North American settlers, and their congress passed successive laws in 1823 and 1825 to stir immigration. The requirements were few: A settler must embrace Catholicism and obey the laws of Mexico. With slavery officially outlawed in the country, Americans presumably would have to leave their slaves at home, though both immigrant and native Texians circumvented the law with little difficulty. In return every settler could have one league—4,428 acres—of grazing land for cattle, and one *labor*—177 acres—for farming, as an outright grant, not subject to taxation for six years. The first grants went to *empresarios* like Stephen Austin, who themselves brought in settlers, but after 1825 the government sold grants directly to immigrants. Marital status also influenced grants, as subsequent laws provided that a single man would get only one-fourth of a league, a married man the full league and one *labor,* and a man who married a Mexican woman would get an extra quarter league in addition to the rest. The cost for a grant was only $30 plus expenses, and not payable until four years later. As for the *empresarios* like Austin, they received eleven leagues for every 200 families they brought in, to a maximum of nearly forty-two leagues, of which the *empresario* himself could keep up to eleven. In short, out of the vastness of Texas, a man might acquire enough land on long-term credit that he could sell it for more than enough to satisfy the debt and then some, well before the debt came due. And if a man had real ambition, he could become an *empresario* and get his land entirely free of charge by bringing in other settlers.[48]

Even without his penchant for land speculation, James Bowie could not have been unaware of the situation in Texas. For several years past the local press carried articles on Texas colonization. Men from the colony frequently passed through Rapides on business, and accounts "by a gentleman direct from Austin's settlement" frequently appeared in Alexandria papers. Bowie could hardly fail to pay attention when such articles declared that "land certainly can be readily obtained."[49] The Natchez and New Orleans press published the successive colonization laws, including the clause about men who married Mexican nationals receiving extra land.[50] Moreover, a fair volume of the letters coming into Rapides either came from or talked about Texas. Friends like Littleton Bailey talked of relocating west of the Sabine, and already the cry went abroad that debtors in the Southwest ran out on their bills. "Whenever an individual becomes somewhat embarrassed," complained a friend of Johnston's, "he crosses the Sabine with all his property & then remains in perfect security."[51] As far away as Kentucky, the ledgers in counting houses and the dockets in courts revealed entries beside unsettled cases of debtors that they had "gone to Texas." James Bowie himself may have gone to Texas in the spring or summer of 1826 just to investigate, once he learned of the new land laws.[52] It would have been like him to cast his eye west.

With his Louisiana schemes finally on the verge of paying off, and with the Arkansas frauds still to oversee, he did not contemplate actually moving to Texas then, but now everything changed. He was not yet done with Louisiana, though he had finished with Rapides, but for an adventurer and speculator like "Big Jim Bowie," as some called him, a new horizon always lay in the offing. For a man living on the edges of violence and the law, it was almost a necessity.

He left from Natchez in late May or early June after spending some time with his brother Stephen, perhaps a few hands of cards with Nevitt and the other gamblers at the Natchez Hotel, and withdrawing enough money to cover the journey.[53] If he thought of making the trip entirely overland by horseback, recent rains put that out of the question. Ordinarily the route would have been due west on horse from Natchez to the mouth of the Ouachita, and then straight on to Natchitoches. But a major flood inundated the whole region now. Avoyelles lay underwater, and people left many towns deserted. Even Alexandria was a ghost town at the moment, reachable only by steamboat on the Red.[54] That, then, was the way he would have to go. Ordinarily a huge raft of driftwood trees blocked the Red to navigation from Alexandria, but with this flood vessels could get all the way to Natchitoches.

Natchitoches—called "Nackitosh" by its inhabitants—had been a frontier outpost for more than a century, the conduit through which flowed most of the goods and raw materials, much of them contraband, between Louisiana and Texas. The Spaniards once came there to buy their supplies, and stories still passed across its tavern tables of the Dons paying with bars of silver from long lost mines. This was the jumping off place for Texas, a haven of rough characters fleeing from the law or poverty who could lose themselves in a polyglot society of American frolics, Spanish fandangos, French balls, and Indian pow-wows.[55] It was the kind of society that James Bowie relished, and though he had been there before, he probably stayed a few days this time, easing the aches that travel aggravated in his wounds, outfitting himself for the rest of the journey, and resting before an arduous overland trek. Besides, he could learn much in "Nackitosh" from eastbound travelers—where the inns would be on the road, where he could find water, where to go to look into land and settlement, perhaps even vague stories about where those silver mines might be found.

When he left Natchitoches, Bowie rode a well traveled frontier road with mile markers and signs apprising him of the distances to places ahead. Frequent houses and occasional log cabin villages along the way offered refreshment in the pleasant, undulating country, much of it through dense pine forest as he approached Cantonment Jessup, where two companies of scruffy frontier regulars occupied the last U.S. Army outpost.[56] Then he crossed the Sabine at Gaines's Ferry and set foot in Texas. Once across, he reached first San Augustine, the place he chose years before for the mythical purchase of many of his forged land grants. Then he proceeded on the La Bahía Trace, passing through Lorenzo Zavala's grant lands, past Peter Ellis Bean's sawmill, to Nacogdoches, the first real town in Texas.

All along the way he met other Americans. "A person may travel all day; and day after day, and find Americans only," wrote a fellow traveler. "He can hardly make himself believe that he is not still in the United States."[57] Bowie may well have known some of the others he met on the road. Certainly he had some acquaintances in Nacogdoches, or at least friends of relatives. Thomas F. McKinney was one of the town's more prominent traders and citizens, and he and his uncle Stephen Prather living nearby were, by a complex set of relationships, connected to John Bowie. James did not neglect striking an acquaintance with them.[58] Once he left Nacogdoches he crossed the Angelina and Neches Rivers, rode along the fringes of Kickapoo land and then across the Trinity to Trinidad, just at the edge of Austin's colony.

At Trinity he had his choice. He could take the Camino Real—the King's Highway—southwest for another two hundred miles or more to San Antonio, or he could turn south on the La Bahía and onto the Coushatta Trace and across the Brazos, about eighty miles to Austin's settlement at San Felipe. Bowie chose the latter. The little community was unimpressive. Another visitor found it "a wretched, decaying looking place," with only five stores, two "mean" taverns, and twenty to thirty unpainted log houses. There was about the place "no appearance of industry, of thrift or improvement of any kind."[59] Yet San Felipe, after all, was not just Austin's home and headquarters but the administrative center of his colony. Bowie could find lodging at Jonathan Peyton's inn and learn from local leaders of the ruling council, or *ayuntamiento*, how to go about acquiring and choosing land. He knew a few people in the small community, most notably Dr. James Long's widow, Jane, who had lived for a time in Alexandria a few years before; and he made friends with at least one, young Noah Smithwick, a gunsmith recently emigrated from Tennessee, during his visit.[60] Austin himself Bowie did not meet, for Austin was often absent doing the colony's business, but from others he learned that he would be best advised to go on to the Mexican administrative capital, San Antonio de Béxar.[61]

San Antonio dated back to 1718, its roots lying in the presidio of San Antonio de Béxar and the village of San Fernando de Béxar. In 1773 it became the capital of Spanish Texas, its houses rough one- and two-story adobe buildings on a few streets clustered about the military plaza on which sat the governor's palace. At first sight little recommended the place. With a population of somewhere over 2,000 Spaniards, Mexicans, indigenous natives and a few blacks, plus mixtures of all of them, it struck visitors as poor, dirty, and unpleasant. Worse, it suffered repeatedly during the revolts leading up to Mexican independence. Now, with Texas part of a state with Coahuila, its capital, south of the Rio Grande at Saltillo, San Antonio was reduced to being a provincial center for Mexican administration and a small military outpost. Its most prominent citizen was Juan Martín de Veramendi, an old friend of Austin's who had held a number of minor offices including that of *alcalde*, or mayor. He had also tried to get a colonization grant of his own and so had some interest in land speculation.

Naturally Bowie sought Veramendi on his arrival. By now he already knew some of the requirements for getting land grants in Texas, the first and foremost being that the settler must accept Mexican citizenship. Prior to that, however, he either must be confirmed in the Catholic church or else swear that he intended to do so. Whatever religious instruction James Bowie had received came from his parents, a mixture of the Scots Presbyterian and the Methodist, though the Church of Rome was hardly unknown to him. After all, his father Rezin had faced the same conversion requirement when he settled in Missouri many years before, and his brother Rezin had married a Catholic and actually converted. Denominational allegiance was always loose on the frontier, simply because worshippers often settled for any church at hand, regardless of doctrine. The bloody rift with Rome three centuries earlier, not to mention religious wars and Inquisition to follow, still left most Protestants with a special suspicion of Catholicism, but not James Bowie. While he felt some degree of respect for religion and those who believed, he gave no evidence of any deeply held convictions of his own. Thus it would have involved no great struggle with his conscience to decide to take the first step toward acquiring Texas land by swearing an intent to convert to Catholicism.[62]

Just how long Bowie stayed in San Antonio is unknown, though he took the time to acquaint himself rather thoroughly with the town and the surrounding countryside. It looked like fertile land, good for cotton, though at the moment there was no way of processing it in the province. Any fiber grown had to be shipped at some trouble and expense east to Louisiana, just as manufactured cotton goods had to be imported back from the East, again at some expense. Bowie witnessed the trade in operation in Nacogdoches, where McKinney especially did a thriving business. It did not escape him that this abundant fertile land could be made very profitable indeed by a man with capital and enterprise.

He may have stayed in Béxar a little longer because of an entirely different opportunity. Veramendi had a comely daughter named Maria Ursula, soon turning seventeen. Though he may still have been paying court intermittently to Cecilia Wells or other women back in Louisiana, nothing serious awaited him there. But James Bowie hardly felt indifferent to women. His friend Ham saw that he was "attentive to ladies on all occasions, and seemed to entertain a devotion for them which might be appropriately termed chivalrous." Ever the "clever, polite gentleman" with female company, he may well have charmed the girl with his smooth manners, just as he won over her parents.[63] Nothing serious necessarily developed with Ursula on this first visit, for that matter, but he did not forget her, despite the difference in their years. And undeniably he could not forget that her father was a rising man in the government, already spoken of for high office, or that a settler who married a Mexican woman received an extra bonus of free land. Such things were worth remembering.

By mid-July it was time to return to Louisiana, though he may have chosen a different route back from San Antonio. At San Felipe a poor road could take him on a three-day trip through forests on the west side of the Brazos, south to Brazoria, just a few miles inland from the Gulf of Mexico, and not far from Laffite's old haunts on Galveston Island. There were numerous houses along the way, some operating as inns where one dollar bought a night's lodging and supper and breakfast.[64] His old friend Warren Hall had moved to Brazoria not long before, himself tiring of the endless feuding and broils of Rapides, and it would have been unlike Bowie to miss a chance to meet with this figure who kept flitting into and out of his life at pivotal moments.[65] From Brazoria Bowie could ride back toward San Felipe until he struck the Atascosita Trace, then follow it east until he made Balew's Ferry on the Sabine, thence overland to Opelousas, and so on to home. Or he could have ridden back to Nacogdoches and home via San Augustine, or even taken Trammel's Trace north from Nacogdoches into southwest Arkansas to look at his claims business there.

However he traveled, he was back in Terrebonne by the middle of August.[66] Once there he had much to ponder. Texas looked good to him, and so did Ursula. It offered limitless opportunity and the advantage of a much looser rein for his kind of business than the oppressive scrutiny of men like George Graham and Josiah Johnston. On the other hand, despite his disillusionment with former political friends in Rapides, Louisiana still offered much. He was selling land now, and for big money. Moreover, Rezin and Stephen were about to build a major plantation on Bayou Lafourche. Naturally they wanted him in on the deal, and the Arkansas scheme with John still looked good, though some trouble loomed on that horizon. It was too soon yet to turn his back irrevocably on his old life, but at least with his baptism and his contacts with the Veramendis, he had taken important steps toward a new one. For a little while yet he would have to be content with keeping one foot in each of two worlds.

BOWIE

If there has been fraud committed, it is not chargable upon Arkansas, *but on the* Bowies *of Louisiana.*

LITTLE ROCK, *Arkansas Advocate,* FEBRUARY 9, 1830

Bowie returned to Louisiana in late summer 1828 just in time to see the Arkansas scheme take fire. John Bowie actually moved from Louisiana to Chicot County in the southeast corner of the territory in order to manage it more closely, and in October commenced selling more of the claims in Hempstead and elsewhere. On October 22 alone he took in $5,200 for fifteen of the confirmed grants.[1] Previously he sold a plot to none other than the same Hugh White who had sworn years earlier that Bayou Tensas was really Bayou Maçon.[2] In July he entered more of the claims in the Batesville district, yet others at Helena and Little Rock in the first half of the year, and he would put more on record at Clarkesville the coming December.[3] Nevertheless tremors came from Washington, where Attorney General William Wirt suspected the manner in which all those claims had been stampeded through the territorial superior court. Wisely John Bowie sold what he could now in case legal obstacles arose in future.

For James, however, the chief attraction on his return lay to the south, along the lovely Bayou Lafourche. James always seemed to trust Rezin's judgment implicitly—even Stephen's at times, which was less wise—and while James was off socializing in San Antonio, Rezin had turned his eyes south.[4] The disastrous flood that summer all but drove Rezin and Stephen from their Avoyelles land anyhow, and just before his brother's return from Texas, Rezin bought on his behalf 260 *arpents*, or about 220 acres, on the right bank of the bayou just one and one-half miles downstream from Thibodeauxville.[5] But that was to be only the beginning. Rezin had plans for the place—plans that he and James may have discussed fleetingly months before, when James decided to leave Rapides, but that more likely came to the latter as something of a surprise.[6]

The whole region had once been called simply the Lafourche Interior, but then in 1822 all of the parish south of Bayou Lafourche became Terrebonne Parish, and there James located his now profitable claims on the Harper report. A sparsely settled region prior to 1817, valuable only for its timber, the Lafourche suffered almost yearly inundation by the Mississippi. But in that year workers finally completed the levees along the banks from Donaldsonville south, protecting the parish from all but the worst floods, and acts by the legislature requiring inhabitants to maintain those levees thereafter ensured that Lafourche could be settled and exploited.[7] It flowed roughly parallel to Bayou Teche to the west, anywhere from twenty to fifty miles distant, and a number of south-to-north bayous flowed in between that made east-west travel a nightmare. A resident on the Lafourche could go two hundred miles to Natchez faster than he could get the fifty miles through the bayous to New Orleans. Only now, in 1828, had a canal been constructed connecting the two bayous so that planters in Terrebonne could get their produce to the Lafourche, and thence up to the Mississippi at Donaldsonville, and so down that river to New Orleans.

The inhabitants by 1828 were still mostly Acadians, about whom opinions varied. Some outsiders described them as "lazy vagabonds, doing but little work, and spending much time in shooting, fishing, and play," and Sergeant S. Prentiss, who visited the area in 1829, called them "the poorest, most ignorant, set of beings you ever saw—without the least enterprise or industry."[8] Yet others, like William Sparks, found them "amiable, law-abiding, virtuous, and honest." They spoke little English but a rich French patois, and were uncommonly trusting. Rarely did their affairs ever come into court, and when they did a judge could be hard put to find one who was literate enough to act as jury foreman. They lived in sparse settlements strung along a single road on either side of the bayou, making in effect a "street" almost thirty miles long. The men wore blue cotton twill pants and striped shirts, while the women wore no adornment other than an occasional colored kerchief about their heads when they went to church. Both sexes often as not clomped about in wooden shoes, and one resident swore there were not half a dozen proper ladies' bonnets in the parish. There was only one pleasure carriage in the whole Lafourche—and only the one road anyhow. Poling up- and downstream in their *bateaux*; their sail-powered, flat-bottomed skiffs; and their even smaller paddled *pirogues*, chiefly the bayou itself was their highway.[9]

Moving at a sluggish three miles an hour when its source, the Mississippi, ran at high water, and almost stagnant when the river ran low, the bayou measured no more than one hundred yards wide in places. On both sides the land was wonderfully fertile—built up along the banks, then gradually sloping away to swampland a mile or so distant—ground full of oak, magnolia, ash, and cypress. Alligators flourished in the swamps as well as on the bayous, and residents constantly worked to keep them under control. "The leisure time of every day was devoted to their extermination, until the cold of winter rendered them torpid," said one resident, and the locals became somewhat ingenious in their ways of killing the reptiles.[10] Miraculously that summer's huge flood did not touch the Lafourche, but the extensive damage it did to the parishes north actually drove many planters there from their land, thus encouraging the settlement in Lafourche, and that in turn drove the price of land upward, all of which attracted the Bowies.[11]

No more than a half dozen Anglo-Americans lived there at the time, and with the exception of one cotton planter, the rest grew sugarcane. The cane brought the Bowies. The Jesuits first harvested it in 1751, and by 1795 Etienne Boré produced granulated sugar commercially in Louisiana. Twelve years later Evan Hall commenced the commercial cultivation of sugarcane, and by 1811 planters on Bayou Teche ground sometimes two or three barrels a day of syrup.[12] Then in 1820 came a new variety of cane that provided a bigger crop, and the business expanded rapidly, though always hampered by the cost of harvest and shipment.[13] "A sugar establishment is necessarily a very expensive one," wrote Timothy Flint in 1824, noting that "the great capital that it requires to commence the business profitably" deterred many.[14] But as the prices for sugar steadily rose, more planters took the gamble. The Lafourche produced an enormous crop in 1826, some of the stalks running six inches in circumference, and the wholesale price at the New Orleans market hit twenty-two cents a pound. Moreover, cotton prices fell dramatically just then, whereas a three-cent-a-pound tariff actually protected the cane industry and supported the price of domestic sugar. No wonder that between 1825 and 1828 the number of sugar plantations doubled.[15]

And no wonder the Bowies came. It helped that the trusting Acadians, unused to hard currency or to financial dealings in general, often proved willing to sell their holdings for very small sums.[16] For a mere $4,200 Rezin bought that first tract from Jean Maronges on August 12. On paper it looked like a lot of money for just 220 acres, but what the title did not show was what sat on his property. Maronges only purchased it himself on July 5, from André Candolle of Assumption Parish, a Creole who was one of the first to see the way to high production. Until then slaves had put cut bundles of cane in stone bins, and teams of mules or oxen then pulled a heavy grindstone around and around over the cane, crushing out the syrup that ran in rivulets into scuppers for collection. The syrup then went into the *perjurie*, a long low building where fires burned constantly under several kettles, reducing the liquid.[17] It was slow and tedious work, with an output of only two or three barrels a day. But eastern manufacturers could now build steam-driven mills that crushed many times the old daily output, and as early as 1826 merchants in New Orleans solicited orders for their purchase.[18] Two planters on Bayou Teche already used steam crushers, but to date no one on the Lafourche had made the investment.[19] The property that Rezin bought had a crusher, but it may have been animal powered and slow. Certainly the plantation had virtually bankrupted Candolle. In November 1826 creditors started trying to foreclose, and finally a district court judgment against him put the property in Maronges's hands. Candolle was forced to sell to satisfy judicial mortgages and loans totaling $31,659.48, the largest due to Candolle's own father. What Maronges paid satisfied none of the debt, but in buying the property for James, Rezin refused to recognize that the mortgages were binding on him. That remained for a court to settle, and he ran some risk as a result. Meanwhile, having acquired it all for a mere $4,200, he could hope to make enough by installing a steam crusher to cover his risk if a court should decide in favor of the creditors.[20]

James Bowie was apparently delighted with the new prospect offered by the Lafourche, and with Rezin's going ahead on his behalf even without his power of attorney. Here was a chance to start something big, profitable, and legitimate for a change. Moreover, a prosperous planter could become a man of influence. The eyes of Louisiana were turning to these sugar lands southwest of New Orleans. A success here could win him far more than he would ever have achieved in faraway Alexandria. Thanks to his large sales in Terrebonne the past winter and spring, James had substantial cash to lay out in order to expand on the start made by Rezin. First he bought out his brothers' holdings in Avoyelles and elsewhere, to give them sufficient cash to invest in the new plantation on the Lafourche. He resold the land but kept the slaves that went with their property, for sugar planting and harvesting was labor intensive even with the crusher. Then he started building the new plantation with purchases in November and December that brought it up to more than 800 acres and seventy blacks.[21]

Candolle may not have had the steam crusher operating yet when Maronges took over the land and sold it to Rezin, and in any case the harvest and grinding season had passed before James assembled the full plantation. They would have to wait for the 1829 crop to start producing syrup, and that would not come until October. Of course there was plenty to do in the meantime, but James virtually left the running of the plantation to Rezin, whose first task was to order $874.09 worth of machinery, including a steam boiler and all the shafts, bearings, journals, and a gear box and pump, to run the crusher—all of it on credit from the Massachusetts firm of Cushing and Ames.[22] Instead he may have mixed a little in local society, but such as it was, it offered few attractions. Cecilia Wells was 150 miles away, well out of sight, and probably long out of mind. The local Creole women rode about in old *caleches* made of wood and rawhide, hardly better than a farm wagon, and the Acadian women were mostly noted for "blowzed, uncombed hair" that hardly turned his head. Ursula Veramendi must have seemed all the better in recollection. The local planters lived well, were polished and somewhat educated yet without snobbery, and most shared Bowie's sentiments in support of Henry Clay as opposed to the new President Jackson. They sometimes gave lavish afternoon dinners at 2 P.M., starting with gumbo and ending with black coffee and champagne, not to mention wine and cards. But it

was still a provincial life for a man of Bowie's tastes. Half the population
were slaves, and the best entertainment available was their singing in the
caneyard at night while cooking syrup, or the wild Acadians at their carnival time.[23]

He preferred New Orleans, and as had been his custom, he left the
Lafourche to winter in the Crescent City. Indeed, for the future he made
only occasional visits to the plantation, usually when he needed Rezin's
advice. Their friend Sparks noted that James "had implicit faith in the
wisdom and abilities of his brother."[24] Building something suited James's
temperament, but the humdrum of running it was another matter.
Besides, in New Orleans he could attend to some of the plantation's
business, including placating the creditors whose debts were tied to his
property. He may even have investigated obtaining a charter from the
state for the construction of a short-line railroad connecting the
Lafourche with a convenient shipping point on the Mississippi. It was
the era of a sudden explosion of interest in the new iron horse, with
innumerable charters being sought and fortunes dreamed of. Indeed, it
would have been unlike the Bowies not to consider attempting to cash
in on the growing mania. Louisiana had no railroads as yet, but the legislature granted charters right and left, and with the growing volume of
sugar from the Lafourche, the carrying trade promised a handsome
profit, and also could open the interior to further development, making
their holdings only the more valuable.[25]

There were also new friends to cultivate, especially Benjamin Z.
Canonge, a former interpreter of the city criminal court not long ago dismissed for killing a man in a duel. Canonge was now a broker and auc-
tioneer on St. Louis Street, who could be helpful in the Bowies' sugar
dealings. Perhaps more important, he stood in line soon to become the
new registrar of the land office in New Orleans, and James Bowie could
use his help in the continuing battle over some of his claims. On
December 22 James visited James Erwin, whom he may have known
years before as one of the planters buying and smuggling Laffite's slaves.
He paid Erwin $275 for an eleven-year-old boy named Charles, and that
same day deeded him as a gift to Canonge's minor son Dawson.[26] James
Bowie understood bribes well enough, and rarely gave away anything
without expecting something in return. Canonge would be a good man
to have in his debt.

Someone else was in New Orleans that winter. In January 1829 George Graham stopped there, having visited his plantation in Rapides. He and Bowie would hardly have called on one another, but his presence punctuated the fact that Bowie still faced a formidable foe in Washington. Without needing the help of Canonge, over the winter Bowie successfully sold almost all of his remaining property in Terrebonne from the Harper report. He profited from the generally rising land prices in the region, and got more than $18,000 from property sold to his attorney Quitman and, more importantly for future events, from a sale to rising Natchez attorney and politician Robert J. Walker. By now he realized in all from the Harper report claims at least $51,250, a good payoff for eight years of waiting. Most of the new cash probably went to retire old debt, and for equipment for the new sugar plantation.[27]

Yet the success of his Terrebonne sales only emboldened Bowie to try to bully through his fraudulent claims north of Red River. Late in February he took a boat to Natchez and then rode the few miles to Washington, Mississippi, to confront the new man in the land office there, James Turner. In polite but increasingly belligerent tones he vented his dissatisfaction at the delays in providing locations and certificates of his claims. Turner replied that he had recent instructions from Graham that henceforth on all suspicious claims a claimant must first prove that the survey about to be located for him on the official township plats was precisely the land specified in the original grant. Of course, none of Bowie's spurious grants specified anything other than a certain bayou, since it had been his intention to choose the best land available for surveying, but now that part of his plan wrong-footed him, and Turner saw through him. He protested that his claims should be treated and located just the same as those in which there was no suspicion of forgery. Turner stood firm. He told Bowie that he would advise Graham to proceed immediately with surveying all the areas covered by Bowie's claims as if they were unquestioned public lands, and then offer them for sale, at which time Bowie might take his case to court and prove the legitimacy of his claims if he could. Turner was blunt, both with Bowie and Graham. "My own opinion is, that

four out of five of all the claims reported by Mr. Sutton, are fraudulent," he said, and that Bowie and other forgers "who are so noisy
about their rights, are no more entitled to the land they claim on the
principles of justice and equity, than the inhabitants of Hindostan."[28]

Worse, Turner now started to extend his gaze to the Harper report
claims in Terrebonne. When Bowie learned of that, or perhaps even in
anticipation of a problem, he remembered that he might have
neglected to get all of his original papers out of Harper's office in
Donaldsonville back in 1827, and indeed he had. There were still the
papers and survey of the tract on Bayou Black for which he had used
William Wilson as a front. He could not afford to have Turner scruti-
nizing any of his self-created originals.[29] Bowie went to James Allison,
the pliable surveyor whom he had paid to locate the erroneous surveys
in the first place, and told him to get into the land office in
Donaldsonville, find out if the Wilson papers were still there, and if so
to get them out before Turner saw them.[30]

Bowie asked Allison to get the papers in part because he would
cause less suspicion, but also because Bowie was leaving. By the spring
he was ready to travel once more, his imagination fired by memories of
Ursula, of the empire awaiting in Texas, and of those stories of lost silver mines. Before going he bought for a mere $350 a twenty-two-year-
old runaway mulatto slave named William Ross, so light-skinned he
could pass for a Cherokee. Accompanied by him, and perhaps by
Caiaphas Ham or another friend or two, and maybe even Rezin, Bowie
set off not long after his visit to Turner in Washington. He made the
long trip up the Red River, and so on once more through
Natchitoches and across the Sabine into Texas.[31]

Certainly Bowie went to San Antonio to visit with the Veramendis
and to see Ursula again. She would be eighteen that coming fall.[32]
Sometime during his visit Bowie broached the subject of marriage to
her father, and did not meet with an unencouraging response. By now
he had enough money—or the promise of it—that he could talk in
earnest of the idea of building a cotton mill somewhere in the province
of Coahuila y Tejas, probably in partnership with Veramendi, and what
better way to seal their financial alliance than with one between their
families? Besides, Bowie had developed some genuine romantic feeling
for Ursula, so matrimony did not seem so onerous, and at thirty-three it

was time for him to wed. Just what plans were made Bowie kept to himself, but undoubtedly by the time he left San Antonio that summer there was an understanding at least of his interest.

While in Béxar Bowie also met José Antonio Menchaca, a locally born native Mexican, or *tejano*, and friend of the Veramendis with whom he struck up a close acquaintance.[33] Indeed, Bowie found that the *tejanos* and the local *bexareños* made good company. Just as he could ingratiate himself with the influential civil leaders, so did he win friends among the middle class, like Menchaca. They could tell him about the countryside, take him hunting the bison that ranged the prairies, advise him where the best land was to be had, and provide wonderfully convivial companions of an evening in the *cantina* or at one of their festive fandangos. Some of them could also tell him more about those stories of lost Spanish silver mines, especially the legendary Los Almagres mine in the San Saba country. Somewhere more than 120 miles northwest of San Antonio, in an unsettled wilderness ruled only by the Comanche, lay a forgotten shaft that led to a rich vein once worked by the local natives for the Spaniards. No one had seen it for a century. That alone provided a challenge to James Bowie.

The possibility of new riches only added stimulus. Accompanied by a few companions, he rode out across the trackless hill country, probably following the Colorado River to the mouth of the San Saba, then up its course until he reached the ruins of the old Presidio de San Saba and the nearby abandoned mission. There they spent untold days scouring the countryside looking for a closed shaft, or the tell-tale pile of crushed rock from which ore had been extracted, but without success. He could not know that the whole story was a myth, and that in any event he was looking in the wrong place. Los Almagres lay seventy miles away and had never been an operating mine, its ore assaying too thin to merit the effort required to extract it from the earth. In the end he left with nothing to show, but at least he could leave a sign of his passing. On the wall of the main entrance to the ruined presidio earlier visitors had carved their names. One was a "Padilla" in 1810. Another had passed through that very year, etching the name "Cos" nearby. Beside them, before leaving, the latest visitor engraved "Bowie con sua tropa 1829." His Spanish grammar was not yet what it should be, but the words conveyed well enough the message that "Bowie with his troop" had passed that way.[34]

By early June Bowie was on his way home, and somewhere near Nacogdoches the runaway William Ross ran away again, only to be caught and sent to the jail in Alexandria to await his owner's sending for him, but Bowie did not interrupt his journey on that account.[35] The news awaiting him in Louisiana was not good. He found James Allison and discovered that when Allison called at the Donaldsonville land office, Turner just happened to be there and immediately turned suspicious when Allison asked if the Wilson survey plat he had done was still there. He even made the mistake of calling it one of "Mr. Bouyes" claims. The official said that it was still there, which was not what Allison hoped to hear. Allison began acting restless—which Turner took as suspicious—then said he wanted to remove the document to make some further notes on the back of the survey. Turner flatly refused, and Allison lost his composure, saying first that he thought he had destroyed it, that it should have been destroyed, and that he suspected someone of concealing it from him when he had removed the rest of Bowie's surveys.[36] There was nothing else he could do, and now Bowie knew that not only was he suspect, but that Turner had documents by which he might prove forgery.

His reaction was typical. Confronted by the mounting weight of evidence and prejudice against his claims, he assumed the offensive. Late in June he went to Natchez for a few days, collected some debts, played some faro, and spent at least an evening or two in the local taverns.[37] In one of them he must have had rather more to drink than was good for him, for he began to brag of his plans. He was going to go east to Washington and pull every string he could find to get George Graham dismissed from his position as commissioner of the General Land Office. That would solve his problems and get his land speculations back on course. On June 27 he boarded a steamboat for the trip up the Mississippi, unaware that someone less sympathetic to Bowie's scheme overheard his injudicious boasts and passed them along to Turner. On another boat, just two days behind Bowie, a letter from Turner was on its way to apprise Graham of what was coming.[38]

In fact the letter may have reached Washington before its subject, for Bowie stopped at Lake Providence to visit with his brother John and no doubt look into the progress of the Arkansas scheme.[39] He would not have reached Washington until well into July, and whatever efforts he made there failed to live up to his boast. He could no longer look to Brent for support. Indeed, he had no friends in the Louisiana delegation now, and Congress was in recess until December in any case. With Andrew Jackson in office as president, Graham had a new superior in office as secretary of the treasury, a Pennsylvanian whom Bowie did not know and with whom he could have no influence. What Bowie really expected to accomplish, or how he thought he would do it, is a mystery, the whole trip being another example of that impetuosity that Rezin often decried. At best Bowie may have thought he could somehow resurrect an attempt to unseat Graham that had been set in motion two years before when the dismissed and disgruntled surveyor John Wilson filed charges against him with Congress.

Wilson was not unknown to Bowie, of course, and possibly played some hand in getting part of his Sutton report claims surveyed before his termination. On January 31, 1827, Wilson filed charges with the Speaker of the House on twelve different counts, most of them wholly frivolous, and after several days of testimony the committee on public lands dismissed all of them.[40] That ended the matter, and if Bowie hoped to revive it, he was disappointed. He cut a fine figure on the streets of Washington as he went from office to office, dressed "finely but not gaudily," but that was his only success.[41]

Bowie may have gone on to Boston after finding his Washington mission a failure. Concerns there like the Boston Manufacturing Company could produce the kind of machinery necessary for the cotton-milling factory that he had in mind for Texas. The cost would be high, at least $20,000 initially, with shipping and assembly probably a substantial additional expense, but it was not out of the question for a man of his resourcefulness at raising money. And even if all his talk of the mill was only a ruse to win over Veramendi, still it would serve him well to have as much firsthand information as possible in order to make him the more convincing. He left no later than mid- or late September for the journey home, this time going by coach to the Ohio River, then down it to the Mississippi. Traveling the last leg down the Mississippi by steamboat, he practiced his old craft of impressing the influential, this time Gen. J. E. Jefferson, with whom he played cards on the boat, and who found him "high as a citizen and a gentleman" and of "incorruptible integrity."[42]

He stopped at Natchez before going on to Lafourche to see the progress of the plantation.[43] If he hoped to find good news awaiting him, he met even more disappointment than in Washington. Any lingering attachment to Cecilia Wells—if indeed there had ever been one—ceased for eternity. The summer of 1829 proved to be one of the worst for fever in several years, and on September 17 she died of it, having suffered the onset while attending the wedding of the late General Cuny's brother.[44]

But far worse was what he learned of the land business. Not only had Allison failed to secure the Wilson papers from the Washington land office, but he had thrown additional suspicion on the whole enterprise, and in his absence Bowie's associates exacerbated the problem. Turner investigated Allison after the May visit to his office, and found that Allison had made all of Bowie's surveys and approved the plats—the final step to confirmation—against his superior's specific orders. "We are left to conjecture," said Turner, as to why Allison did it, but then he learned that Bowie may have bribed Allison with the promise of a share of the proceeds from the sale of the Wilson tract. Since Bowie knew that the Wilson parcel was under suspicion as far back as 1827, he risked very little in any case, and may have been buying Allison's cooperation for a share of what he knew to be nothing. Regardless of that, Turner was onto Allison now. "All his acts as an officer are becoming public without investigation," Turner told Graham. And there was more.

When Allison visited the office in May he told Turner that all the papers supporting the certified plats for Bowie's other Terrebonne claims had been destroyed. Certainly Turner could not find them in the office of the deputy surveyor in Donaldsonville. But then, while Bowie was in the East, his sister Martha's husband Alexander Sterrett paid a call at the Donaldsonville office and produced a stack of documents that proved to be certified copies of those now destroyed originals. He told the surveyor there that such documents properly belonged in his office, of course, and Sterrett was only doing his duty as a citizen by delivering them to be placed in their proper files. But the surveyor knew all about the Bowie claims and refused to allow Sterrett to leave them in the office without first securing a satisfactory explanation from Allison as to their original absence. He saw Sterrett's obvious intent on Bowie's behalf. He wanted to "plant" the certified copies in the hope that once on file they would support the validity of the claims—though not being "originals," they could be of no use to those suspecting forgery. Instead his visit only aroused further suspicion, as if any more were needed. Turner gave the surveyor at Donaldsonville direct orders thereafter to protect his files from unauthorized intrusion or interference.[45]

As if Bowie did not already feel the authorities closing in on him, it now looked as if statute law might join his enemies. All this time he had continued pressing his forgeries with impunity thanks to the fact that neither the state nor Congress had happened to enact legislation proscribing his activities as crimes. But in the past spring and summer the indefatigable James Turner had been chipping away at that last barrier. He had talked to enough men so that he knew he could get certified statements testifying "how those Spanish orders of survey came into existence," and promised Graham that he would have them in time for the next session of Congress, starting in December. Moreover, he was working with the "Court for the Parish of the Interior of Lafourche" on two or three cases that he hoped to bring to trial there, revealing the "manner of obtaining transfers for those illegal claims."[46] In short, Turner assembled a dossier to document every step of Bowie's procedure, and if trying to steal public domain land in Louisiana by fraud was not a violation of a statute, still Bowie had broken enough other laws covering forgery, bribery, suborning public officials, and perhaps even extortion or intimidation. Even if it never came to prosecution, still Bowie had to realize that for him the land game in Louisiana was all but up.

No sooner was he home than he found that the Arkansas enterprise stood nearly as compromised. Graham had employed a virtual counterpart to Turner, Col. Isaac T. Preston of New Orleans, to go to Little Rock to investigate the Bowie claims in that territory. On October 10, the same day that James Bowie arrived in Natchez, Preston filed his first report, and it was devastating. "I regret to inform you that the impositions practiced on the United States have been much more extensive than you supposed," he told Graham. The commissioner sent him a list of suspicious claims to check out, and on them Preston found 63 of "what are called *Bowie* claims," but he then told Graham that in fact the superior court two years before passed on 117 such claims, covering "upwards of 60,000 acres." Worse, and seemingly playing right into the Bowies' hands, the following year the court allowed claimants to withdraw their original documents from the files. However, through oversight or overconfidence, the brothers left original papers from 58 of their claims in the land offices, and now Preston had examined them. "I can prove them, by a great many witnesses of the highest character and standing," he said, "to be forgeries."

Though he hoped to send these papers and others to New Orleans, where a commission might take testimony, it would be pointless unless somehow the government obtained a revision of all the confirmed claims, and the Act of Congress on Arkansas claims made no provision for rescinding bogus claims. All the time for appeal in the courts had lapsed long since, and the U.S. attorney for the territory thought it hopeless to try. Arkansas was about to become a state, and the territorial courts would not have jurisdiction long enough to bring cases to trial, he feared. Once again it looked as if James Bowie might fortuitously slip through unwitting gaps in the legal system.

Preston felt uncertain of just how the government should proceed. "Men of the deepest thought, as well as the Bowies, are embarked in this business," he warned (seeming to suggest thereby that the Bowies were not themselves "men of the deepest thought," as evidenced by the carelessness of their forgeries). "I fear they are meditating something to increase and sanction their claims," he added, and suggested that the problem merited Congress itself taking a hand. He made quite certain that the pattern was familiar. He knew of James's other activities. "The government were, in like manner, at the land office in New Orleans, defrauded out of 60,000 acres of as good lands as are in Louisiana." Reflecting on "the insatiable character of successful fraud," he asserted that "forgery creates no rights," and that the Bowies must be stopped, and soon.[47]

How much James or John Bowie knew just yet of Preston's investigation is uncertain, though it became common knowledge in Arkansas, and John would have picked up the news quickly enough. Within a few weeks the Little Rock press carried rumors about Preston's report and its repercussions on the "*Bowie Claims*," expressing concern over the fate of those who innocently bought the land from James and John. "If there has been fraud committed," said one editor, "it is not chargable upon

Arkansas, but on the *Bowies* of Louisiana, who had them presented to the Court. *They* received the benefit of the Claims, and if the fraud which is charged exists, it rests on them, and on them alone."[48]

Moreover, when the land office called an immediate halt to further location and confirmation of surveys of any of the claims, James and John knew that their problem was serious and perhaps insurmountable. Confirmations already in hand covered just under 28,000 acres, but that left the majority of the land they sought in limbo. Worse, bills of review were about to be introduced that could set aside some of the confirmations already in hand, even though John had sold them to others by now.[49] Then it came out that the drunken extortioner John Wilson also had some involvement with the Bowie claims, making their odor only the stronger.[50]

By November President Andrew Jackson himself saw Preston's report and took an interest in what he termed "the case of claims called Bowie's." He instructed Graham and the U.S. attorney for Arkansas Territory to start taking depositions and testimony in the matter, suggesting that possible legal action would be the result, and soon thereafter the Judiciary Committee of the House of Representatives agreed to an investigation of the Arkansas land business.[51] Their findings could conceivably see the whole matter referred to the Supreme Court itself.

Surely James Bowie thought that his homecoming could not possibly get any worse, but then it did. When he met Rezin he learned that the creditors holding notes totaling $30,860 against the tract on the Lafourche that he got from Maronges had gone to court. At the same time Jean Baptiste Montez, from whom he had purchased the adjacent tract, also went to court for the $3,000 still due him on the purchase price. The court decided in favor of the petitioners and issued a writ of *fieri facias* directing the seizure of the Maronges parcel, that it might be sold at sheriff's sale on September 26. Conveniently for the family, Stephen bought it at the auction, paying a mere $599.86, and at that simply paid with his note for twelve months. That kept the property in the family, but it did not relieve the creditors, who still considered their mortgages outstanding and would be ready to contest their case and obstruct clear title should the Bowies ever sell the plantation. On top of all that, smallpox broke out on the Lafourche that year, killing twenty-seven of the Bowie slaves. The steam crusher was not yet working, and the mechanic brought in to set it up was put to making coffins instead.[52]

•

No wonder James had little stomach for staying in Louisiana. Everything had turned to dross, all his schemes stymied or exploded. Of course he still owned more land on the Lafourche, but the creditors could go after that next, and either he was simply too stubborn to pay off those huge notes, or more likely no longer had any of the windfall in cash that he realized the year before. He wintered in New Orleans as usual, but took no interest in the harvest on the plantation that now belonged to himself and Stephen.[53]

Besides his impatience and tendency to rush affairs without careful forethought, Bowie also usually revealed a tenacity bordering on the stubborn, a refusal to see that the odds were against him and move on. But he simply could not ignore all that had occurred in the last few months. He had run out his string in Louisiana; it offered him nothing more except debt and failure, and perhaps eventual prosecution. Even the partnership in the plantation held few attractions. Just as the harvest and grinding season began, sugar prices started to fall, and if their steam machinery was not yet in operation, that placed them far behind others as the new technology spread into Rapides and elsewhere.[54] Money tightened again. Stephen was always impecunious, and now even Rezin was forced to write to James's old foe Josiah Johnston in hopes of getting an agency to oversee timber cutting on the Louisiana coast.[55]

Everything suggested that his tentative exploration of the possibilities of Texas had been well advised, and that he should close the book on Louisiana. Tocqueville had seen how "every American is eaten up with longing to rise, but hardly any of them seem to entertain very great hopes or to aim very high." In their rush for property, reputation, and power, he thought that "few conceive such things on a grand scale."[56] Obviously the French visitor had never heard of James Bowie. He had made a stunningly bold play at exploitation here, in all laying fraudulent claim to 80,000 acres in Arkansas, and between 73,000 and 80,000 more in Louisiana. If it had succeeded he would have been whole or part owner of 250 square miles of bayou and riverfront property, and possibly another 200 square miles in 188 other Arkansas claims he had withdrawn, making him the largest landowner in the region, and in his time very possibly the largest private landholder in the United States.

James Bowie was never a prudent man with money. If he had been, he could well have parlayed all that into a fortune that would have made him the first American millionaire west of the Mississippi. He may not have thought things through very carefully, but he certainly thought big. Now, instead, he was apparently all but broke. When one of his Terrebonne buyers made a timely installment payment of $3,333.33 on January 11, 1830, the money was welcome, but not enough.[57] He had one or two legitimate properties in the state, but nothing of significance, and no prospect of deriving anything from the vast acreage claimed under the stalled Sutton report. All that he could sell to fund a move to Texas was the balance of his land in the Lafourche plantation. On January 15, at Rezin's home on the Lafourche, he transferred his land and thirty-four slaves to Rezin and Stephen in return for $42,000, and at the same time left his power of attorney with Rezin to handle any further sale of his Terrebonne hold-ings, and with Stephen for any affairs in New Orleans. Even then they only paid $10,000 in hand, while they would apply the balance of $32,000 to the mortgages still owed on some of the slaves, and the debts due to Montez and the other creditors who had taken James to court.[58] At that, what they agreed to pay James in hand was probably really just a note, for Rezin and Stephen were sufficiently short of cash themselves that a month later they mortgaged sixty-five slaves for $15,000 to cover debts of their own.[59] James told them to have his $10,000, or as much of it as possible, forwarded from Natchez to Saltillo, Mexico. He was leaving.[60]

In the end, when Bowie left Rezin's on his way to Texas, he may have had no more than $1,000 in his purse, little enough to show for a decade of energetic fraud.[61] His friend Caiaphas Ham agreed to go with him, and they left Thibodeauxville late in January for the long trip up the Lafourche to Donaldsonville, then up the Mississippi to the mouth of the Red, and so on to Natchitoches.[62] If he bought a horse there it could have cost him $95, but at least he knew he could turn around and sell it in Texas for up to $300 if necessary.[63] Then it was horseback on the old trail to Texas, less a road than a track marked by notched and blazed trees, but still with traffic so heavy that one observer said "we saw them marching in shoals" for Texas.[64] Once into Texas they would have stopped at one of the two large taverns in San

Augustine, perhaps finding as did other travelers that the fare on the table was poor but not as bad as the beds.[65]

Mexican law required that prospective colonists must bring with them a reference either from their former homes or else from a man of respectable stature in Texas.[66] James Bowie might have had something of a problem getting a good reference from someone in Louisiana other than his brothers just now, and thus his acquaintance with Thomas F. McKinney became useful. The merchant was one of the biggest traders in Texas, widely known and respected, and moreover just at the moment commencing a partnership with Jared Groce to transport Groce's cotton by mule train to Mexico. Thus he and Bowie might well look to a mutually beneficial future association, and when Bowie reached Nacogdoches, one of his first stops after taking a room, probably at John Hyde's notoriously "quite inferior" Emigrants Hotel, was at McKinney's, where on February 13 he secured the requisite recommendation.[67] It may have been rather more effusive than their slight acquaintance justified, and probably reflected McKinney's own interest in Bowie's success. Nevertheless he affirmed that "James Bowie is a gentleman who stands highly esteemed by his acquaintances and merits the attention particularly of the citizens of Texas as he is disposed to become a citizen of the country and will evidently be able to promote its general interest." Bowie got not just the recommendation that he needed, but McKinney made it serve as well as an introduction to Stephen Austin himself, with McKinney's expressed wish that when they met the two "may concur in sentiments" and that Austin might help to further Bowie's plans.[68]

When Bowie and Ham left the Nacogdoches mixture of shabby old Spanish chinked log cabins and new crisp American frame homes, they rode into the monotonous pine woods of the Great East Texas Forest again, and followed the sandy soil along the La Bahía Road until they came to Groce's store on the Brazos, not far from Robinson's ferry and the small settlement then called La Bahía, though soon to be renamed Washington.[69] Now and again they came out of the forest onto wide prairies, sometimes dotted with moss-hung live oaks and cottonwoods. Bison, deer, and wild horses seemed abundant, and when they camped at night by the road the howling of wolves disturbed their sleep. A man on a horse could cover easily one hundred miles in three days, and if he stayed the night at one of the occasional "stands," or private homes that let beds, it cost him one dollar a night for his bed, coffee, supper, breakfast, and some corn for his horse. "The whole catalog of luxuries has been erased from their cooking books," one traveler lamented. The invariable fare was cornbread and pork, beef, or venison, with rarely either butter or milk. Often it was simply "hog and hominy."[70]

Jared Groce was another good man to know, by some accounts the richest in the region. Here they remained well into March, Bowie and Groce talking of the cotton potential and meanwhile exploring the countryside. Bowie and Ham rode on south the thirty miles to San Felipe more than once while staying at Groce's, and now he finally met Austin for the first time.[71] The *empresario* was only a year older than Bowie, university educated, with a career full of business and politics before he came to Texas in 1821 to assist his father in colonization under a grant from Mexico. He had been quite successful, virtually ruling the colony until he turned over much of his power to an elected council or *ayuntamiento*, and thereafter concentrated much of his time on encouraging immigration and business and overseeing land affairs in his colony. Most of all he tried to insulate his *norteamericano* settlers from the continuing factional politics in Mexico, which seemed constantly fluctuating from anarchy to military despotism and back again. As the population in Texas swelled, and as more *empresarios* brought in settlers with no allegiance to Austin, it became increasingly difficult to attempt to maintain control and quell dissent. Certainly Bowie and Austin met each other politely and established what appeared to be cordial personal relations, though it is just possible that stories of Bowie's Louisiana and Arkansas activities may have reached Austin. There were many coming to Texas now who knew of Bowie's reputation, and Austin himself felt a growing aversion to land speculators. Nevertheless, if Bowie's cotton mill scheme came to fruition, it would be wonderful for Texas, and on that basis he certainly had Austin's support.

While in San Felipe, Bowie and Ham also met with other locals, such as Austin's principal assistant, Samuel May Williams, secretary of the *ayuntamiento*. Jane Long was there from time to time, too, and though society was slim, such as there was the people enjoyed. Very few single women lived in the village, making thoughts of Ursula all the sweeter and Bowie the more anxious to move on to San Antonio.

When a "ball" was held, it often as not involved no women at all, with the result that "stag parties were a bit convivial." Godwin Cotton sometimes simply gathered several men at his home, gave them a dinner, and required each to provide a few minutes of entertainment to the rest in whatever manner he could manage.[72]

Bowie stayed sometimes at Peyton's inn, but may well have frequented James Whitesides's as well, for that was where the land hunters seemed to congregate. Of a piece with Bowie in the main, they were well limned by Tocqueville, who observed the exemplar of such men being fearless either of native arrows, wild beasts, or the hundred solitary dangers of the wilderness: "A passion stronger than love of life goads him on," he found. "An almost limitless continent stretches before him, and he seems in such a hurry not to arrive too late that one might think him afraid of finding no room left."[73] The Frenchman might almost have been portraying Bowie in particular. Most were Louisianians like himself, some of them men of intelligence, but not a few fugitives from justice. At the breakfast table one morning a visitor counted four murderers, and Texas brag said that eleven such broke bread at the same board on one occasion. They all blamed their misfortunes on others, presenting themselves as victims of circumstances "in which it was necessary to violate the laws, while they admitted no criminality in their conduct." Among the most common questions after a stranger sat down to eat were where had he come from, and why had he come.[74] "There may be 'murderers and outlaws' among them," said another visitor about now, "and some few perhaps, who, tired of waiting for a general jubilee, fled their country to shake off the burden of debt." But none of them were idlers. No one had any time for the lazy or for the tinhorn sharper, "and this class of emigrants either reform from necessity, or leave the country in disgust."[75] Certainly there were men here whose pasts were a match for James Bowie's, and many a one whose criminal deeds far exceeded his in violence if not enterprise. Yet for any who had heard of that increasingly well known battle on the Natchez sandbar thirty months earlier, and who saw now that same long knife sheathed at his belt, they knew that this new man among them had the grit to make his way in Texas, and even to bend Texas to his way.

Before leaving San Felipe Bowie gathered to himself a number of other people either interested in his cotton enterprise or else simply anxious for his company and protection during their own anticipated journey deeper into Mexico. Groce's son Jared junior of course could represent his father's interests in negotiation for the cotton deal, and may well have represented some of his father's money that Bowie expected to attract to the enterprise. Groce's daughter and son-in-law William Wharton decided to come along. Being an attorney, he, too, could look after Groce's interests, and Bowie himself was always comfortable in the company of lawyers. As it happened, Wharton was also one of the more outspoken proponents for taking an aggressive stand with the Mexicans, and if anyone spoke of eventual Texian independence, Wharton listened sympathetically. There was also Isaac Donoho, a Tennesseean just arrived in Texas who had some capital to invest, and to whom Bowie paid speedy and earnest attentions. Since they all wanted to go to the provincial capital at Saltillo, they needed passports, which Austin provided, along with letters of introduction to Veramendi and to another influential *tejano*, Juan Erasmo Seguín.[76]

The journey to San Antonio took them from the flat landscape around San Felipe westward, where after a few miles the country started to take on contour and gentle rolling rises that continued all the way to Béxar. The forest was gone now, and it was all one continuous prairie, a sea of waving grass with occasional small islands of trees offering shade and a spring.[77] San Antonio itself was still rather a squalid looking log-and-adobe town when they arrived, at least to eyes that had seen New Orleans and Boston, but its hospitality proved nonetheless generous.[78] Veramendi welcomed Bowie and his companions, and Ursula certainly welcomed James in particular. This time there was more concrete discussion of the cotton mill plan, and Veramendi lent it his hearty endorsement, providing Bowie with an introduction and recommendation to one of the leading senators in the congress in Saltillo. Seguín also proved to be hospitable, and would be a friend second only to Veramendi in furthering Bowie's hopes for Texas. The *alcalde* of San Antonio had formerly been a congressman and was now a leading merchant, enjoying widespread respect in the area. His son Juan Nepomuceno Seguín was also an alderman in town, making them one of the most influential families in Béxar. Bowie met Moses Foster and Peyton Splane, who agreed to join his party.[79]

Here, too, Bowie probably got the first news of what must have seemed a setback. However sincere he may or may not have been with the cotton mill idea, there is no question that he also intended to become a major landowner and speculator. But President Anastasio Bustamente in Mexico City grew wary of the growing numbers of *norteamericanos* and the way they were taking over. Mexico was a republic now, a federation of states—Coahuila y Tejas being one of them—with a constitution based heavily on the one drafted nearly half a century before in Philadelphia. Yet in adopting the letter of the Constitution, the Mexicans had not yet caught the spirit of the document, and even in their infancy as a republic suffered one of the strains that even then had started opening cracks in the Union east of the Sabine. Mexico City seemed constantly caught in conflicts between state sovereignty and national authority, and the most pressing example at the moment was the disposal of public lands. The 1824 constitution left it to each of the states to control its own immigration and land policy. As a result the 1825 colonization law that first attracted Bowie's interest was quite liberal, but as the balance of *tejanos* and immigrants shifted more and more in favor of the latter in Texas, Bustamente feared that someday there might come an attempt to wrest Texas away from Mexico and align it with the United States. He did not need to be reminded that such had been the intent of more than one of the filibusters who invaded the territory in the past three decades.

It was time to stop the immigration and make firm Mexico's grip, and on April 6, 1830, Bustamente overrode state sovereignty and issued an edict that closed Texas's borders to more settlers from the United States, though Europeans were still welcome. Moreover, he decreed that Mexican soldiers were to garrison posts at Nacogdoches, Béxar, Goliad, Velasco, Anahuac, and elsewhere, and one of their duties would be to ensure that customs houses to be established received their proper excise. Until now Texians had simply ignored customs duties on their imports, and Mexico City let them get away with it, but no more. As for the soldiers, thirteen hundred of them, their very presence rankled, being redolent of the British occupation of the old colonies that so disturbed their grandfathers, and it did not help that many of the soldiers to be sent north would be released convicts.[80] Bowie missed the initial uproar over the April 6 law because he was on his way out of Texas by late May, his party now grown to sixteeen, including a few slaves. The country proved much rougher going now, some of it across virtually

unsettled territory, and a large party promised mutual protection. Mules
were the animals for this sort of trip, and aboard them they rode southwest 130 miles on the Camino de la Pita to the Presidio de Rio Grande.
There they remained for a few days before crossing the Rio Grande to
Piedras and moving deeper into Coahuila, following the de la Pita to
the Sabinas River and then to Santa Rosa. There the road ran beside the
mountains southward until they reached Monclova, the first real town
since they left San Antonio. There they added another merchant to their
party, before they left again after several days for the last 100 miles to
Saltillo. It was not an easy journey. They went 60 miles before they
found the first well by the road, whose rawhide bucket gave the water
such a foul taste that even their mules would not drink. Bowie boiled
the water first and then made it into coffee in order to keep it down.
Then, too, a notorious bandit prowled the Camino de la Pita, but
Bowie and his companions kept careful watch, and their number discouraged any assault.[81]

When finally they reached the mountain town of Saltillo, they
rejoiced, Ham confessing that he and Bowie "indulged freely" in
drinking and bathing away the dust of the road. That done, Bowie
found a two-story house to rent for a few months, and then set about
the old business of winning friends. There were members of congress
to call on and show his letters from Veramendi and others, and here he
immediately had to summon his best resources. Only one member
from Coahuila y Tejas was a *norteamericano*, all the rest being Mexican
nationals, which meant that Bowie must polish his Spanish as well as
his charm, and it was prudent of him to have bought a Spanish-
English grammar and dictionary, not to mention a text on mechanics
that would help explain the mill machinery itself.[82] There were merchants and men of finance who might be investors in the cotton mill to
cajole. By the beginning of August he saw himself making progress. "I
am driving along tolerable well amongst these people," he wrote to
Samuel Williams, and added with some of his accustomed boast that
he had "become something of a favourite at last."[83] At the same time,
though, other Mexicans were not won over, and some circles came to
regard him as simply a common braggart.[84]

Bowie came to Saltillo with more than one agendum. The public
reason was his cotton project, and by the time he wrote Williams,

Bowie had made an intimate friend of Donoho and sent him back to San Felipe with news of the progress on that front. All parties in Saltillo welcomed the proposal, so there would be no trouble in gaining the charter he needed from the congress. But beyond that, and much less public, lay his old passion for land. The avenue to a large grant was cut off now, at least for the time being, by the April 6 law. Austin and other *empresarios* could get around that within their established colonies, but in any event a mere league of land was too small for James Bowie. He would have learned from Veramendi, if not others, that eleven-league grants for Texas land had been given to Mexican citizens on application during the past five years, Veramendi himself receiving one. They sold for one hundred to two hundred dollars per league depending on the nature of the ground, but few Mexicans had the money to apply, and of those who bought them, fewer still did anything with the property. If he could simply purchase some of these he would have more than enough land to start speculating, and this time legitimately.

Williams took an interest in the scheme with him, and also Donoho, as well as S. Rhoades Fisher, a recently immigrated Pennsylvanian who scarcely knew Bowie, yet whom he so impressed that Fisher told Austin that "the most valuable emigrant you have ever had is James Bowie. I consider him of the first order of men."[85] Bowie and Fisher had discussed their land hopes with Austin and apparently gotten his blessing, suggesting that Austin, too, had fallen under Bowie's spell. The expectation seemed to be that at least two of the current eleven-league grant holders would sell out cheaply, and that was enough to make a start.[86]

Inevitably Big Jim Bowie found a way to step between the laws. It developed that there were no grants to be had for sale in Saltillo, but having become a "favourite" with some of the Mexicans, he persuaded them to apply for the eleven-league awards, at the same time agreeing to buy them once awarded.[87] Thus his lengthy stay in Saltillo, for it took time first to make friends, then more time to come to terms with them, and yet more for them to apply for and receive their grants. Meanwhile, one by one all the rest of his original party left except Ham and Donoho, and on August 1 he sent Donoho back to San Felipe to bring Williams news of his progress. In the end Bowie secured commitments to buy fifteen or sixteen new grants, and once again he was looking at a small empire. One square league contained 5,760 acres; all the grants combined totaled close to one million acres or more, and at a total cost of around $25,000. Moreover, it was not necessary for the grantees to pay all at once, and so with only a few thousand dollars Bowie could simply buy leases on the grants and make the actual purchase after he sold enough land himself to raise the necessary money. He was back in the land business again, and this time on a scale that dwarfed his Louisiana enterprise. Though perhaps a bit shady at the edges—some of the grants would just "happen" to fall on property already occupied by earlier settlers on prior Mexican grants—the enterprise was on the whole legitimate.[88] But then Bowie was stymied when the large sum of money he expected Rezin to send from Natchez did not arrive.[89] There seemed to be nothing to do but ask Ham to return all the way to Louisiana to get the money in person and bring it back to him.[90]

Now Bowie stayed in Saltillo by himself on into the fall. Welcome relief came in early September when the Veramendi family arrived, for Juan Veramendi had been chosen lieutenant governor of the state and—though he would still spend much of his time in San Antonio—went to the capital to take his oath and assume office. Bowie enhanced the growing friendship, and passed most agreeable time with Ursula for the next several weeks, the interest between them clearly growing into open courtship. He might have been stymied in his suit late that month when a warrant for his arrest was issued, but it soon proved to be a mistake and did him no harm with the Veramendis.[91] At the same time others of his plans came to fruition. On September 30 the congress granted his application for Mexican citizenship, making it conditional on fulfillment of his promise to build the mill.[92] Five days later the congress granted him a concession to establish a cotton and woolen mill under the title Compania de Manufacturas de Coahuila at Monclova, with an authorized capitalization of one million pesos, to be raised through the sale of two thousand shares at five hundred pesos each. Once he sold one thousand shares, or raised five hundred thousand pesos, he could commence business.[93]

That decree was the last to be heard officially of the cotton and woolen mill, though no doubt he continued to promote the idea. Bowie may have been feigning all the time, using the plan as a means of impressing Veramendi and others, or as a tool to secure his citizenship so that he could pursue his real interest in land. He may even have conceived it as a way of raising a fortune from investors by share sales, with no actual intent to spend the money on machinery. And of course it is possible that he really intended to establish the mill. Within a few months he would have a couple of machinists with him in Texas, presumably to set up the mill, and six months after getting his charter he did claim to have twenty thousand dollars in the hands of Angus McNeil in Natchez for "the buying of one machine and all the utensils necessary to a manufacturing plant of cotton goods and wool" from a Boston supplier. Bowie even kept with him a manual on mechanics. But it is just as probable that he made the claim only for the purpose of impressing Governor Veramendi.[94] Besides, industry and manufacturing were not in James Bowie's temperament. They required too much careful preparation and long-range planning. His goals were always short term, exploiting a quick opportunity, and employing "confidence" in many meanings of the word. He may never have sold a single share in the new company, and the only loom he would ever operate in Mexico was the one on which he wove his own tangled webs.[95]

With all of his business completed, or as complete as it could be until Ham returned with his money from Natchez, Bowie accompanied the Veramendi family on their return journey to San Antonio in October. Along the way, if not before, James made a formal proposal to Ursula and she accepted. Equally important, her father agreed to the marriage, though with a proviso.[96] Perhaps he was not entirely convinced by Bowie's talk of his wealth back in Louisiana or of his bold plans for Texas. The man's interest in the San Saba mine made him a treasure hunter, and a treasure hunter could just as easily be a fortune hunter. As a condition of the union, Veramendi demanded to see a statement of Bowie's real assets, and at the time of the wedding he wanted Bowie's written pledge of a portion of those assets to Ursula for her protection and security. James and Ursula planned to be wed in the spring. That would give him time to return to Louisiana and close out all his remaining holdings there. He was making two commitments, now, one to Ursula, and the other to Texas. Whatever else might be said of James Bowie, when he fixed his mind on a purpose, like Crockett he went ahead.

TRAVIS

1831–1833

> *Mexicans have learned a lesson, Americans know their rights*
> *and will assert and protect them.*

WILLIAM BARRET TRAVIS, JULY 8, 1832

Blooming dogwood and purple wisteria grew wild along the road from the Claiborne ferry. It would have brightened the spirits of the ordinary traveler, but William Travis, running away from his failure, probably failed to notice. As his horse's hooves kicked up the red-orange earth of Clarke County, he set his eyes on the future and redemption. Along the way the great tufts of Spanish moss hanging from the trees offered at least a taste of Texas to come. The well-traveled road led straight across Mississippi to Natchez. With his taste for gambling he was fortunate if he escaped falling into one of the gaming dens on the bluff, or down in the notorious waterside area called Under-the-Hill. After Natchez he went overland to Alexandria, then on to Natchitoches, and so on into Texas by early May, only a few weeks behind the now newlywed Bowie.[1]

Travis knew enough to go first to San Felipe. Though he felt no urge to be a farmer, still if he could get a piece of cheap land merely for the asking, he would be wise to do so. Men respected other men who owned land, and besides, it would be something to use as collateral if he needed to borrow money or to sell if he must. And to get land he had to see Stephen Austin. Knowing and caring little for the soil himself, he probably did not bother to scout property before he showed up in San Felipe in the first week of May.[2] Undoubtedly, like so many before him, his introduction to Texian society came at Peyton's or Whiteside's, where others at the supper board eyed the newcomer and asked the inevitable questions: "What have you come to

Texas for?" or, "What did he do that made him leave home?"³ Some
may even have read the real answer in his face, regardless of what he
said, for they knew the look of those immigrants who, as one traveler
said, "fled their country, to shake off the burden of debt."⁴

Though Travis may have evaded their curiosity, he found immediate
signs for hope. Within just a few days of his arrival he already did his
first business, surely brought to him by word of mouth, for there had
been no time to make his presence and purpose known, and in any case
he did not intend to settle in San Felipe. On May 11 he was engaged to
make out a petition over a contested note involving, among others,
William H. Jack. When he finished with it he made the acquaintance of
the *alcalde*, Frank Johnson, and presented the document for signature. It
seemed an auspicious beginning.⁵ At the same time he introduced himself to Austin and Williams. He told them he was a lawyer from
Alabama, which was true in principle, however little he had been able
to make it a reality in practice, but prevaricated a bit when he listed
himself as twenty-two instead of twenty-one, and rather a lot when he
declared that he was not married as he filled out application number
588 for the standard quarter-league grant for single men.⁶ That done,
on May 23 he gave Austin his promissory note for ten dollars, due in
one year. He was paying less than one cent per acre.⁷

Based either on what he had been told by de la Garza or had read in
Alabama, or advice he got once in Texas, Travis turned his reins west
from San Felipe, on the old trace that led to Harrisburg. There, as he
crossed Buffalo Bayou, he could inspect his new property, the first he
ever owned, though he had no intention of settling on it then. He was a
town man, a professional. Another few miles east brought him to the
San Jacinto River, where it flowed into the great Galveston Bay, and
skirting the northern rim of the bay he came to the mouth of the
Trinity. Once across that and it was not much farther to Turtle Bayou,
and then, on a low rise on the eastern side of Trinity bay, to Anahuac. It
was an old Attacapan word that locals pronounced "anawack," but its
meaning lay forgotten in the dim past. A man who came just two
months before Travis found it a pleasant village, bordered by poor soil
called "pig-bed" prairie behind, and a thirty-foot bank down to the bay
in front. About twenty log houses and another seven rather crude shops
made up the town. Spanish moss hung from the trees, and redwing

blackbirds nested in their branches, while out over the waters of the bay the graceful egrets and white herons and pelicans pressed their ceaseless quest for food. Alligators were numerous in the bay, where the locals joined the birds in dining off redfish, catfish, drum, and perch, not to mention crabs and oysters. Now and then they even pulled from the water a prehistoric-looking monster called the alligator gar, appearing to be half fish and half reptile. Ducks, wild turkeys, deer, and wild hogs also contributed to make the area a cornucopia, while the bears, wolves, wildcats, foxes, and more filled the nearby forests that dotted the prairie. Morning and evening the cacophony of the wild geese overhead could be heard for miles.[8]

Much as he might admire the wildlife and enjoy the edible bounty, what brought Travis to Anahuac was its establishment as one of the customs points of entry for Texas. It began in 1821 as a port for settlers, and late in 1830 the Mexican government sent a garrison there in the wake of the April 6 decree to collect excise and prevent smuggling. Customs meant paperwork, and that meant work for lawyers. Moreover, in the wider area around Anahuac—communities like Liberty and even Harrisburg—attorneys were in short supply just then. A visitor noted that "the country needs more professional men. It opens a fine field for enterprising men in any profession."[9] There was only one other lawyer in Anahuac, William Jack's brother Patrick, and he may actually have arrived with Travis, who was just a year his junior. Together they boarded at William Hardin's inn, where they found a warm welcome, as they received from the other fifty *norteamericanos* living in the village.

There was much to do, but it always suited Travis to immerse himself in work and challenge. He soon learned that though court transactions might be done in English, all the land records were written in Spanish, and so he set about teaching himself the language, and at the same time began studying Mexican law.[10] Then he had to get acquainted with the rest of the bar. Jack he already knew, a Georgian with whom he found much in common, and who had himself moved from Alabama to Texas only the year before. Then there was James Woods, an attorney living in Liberty, some ten miles up the Trinity. In fact this area was known as the Liberty District, and though Travis kept his rude office in Anahuac, most of the legal practice would be in Woods's village. In time Travis's growing practice required him to look beyond the immediate vicinity to engage cocounsel, acquainting him with other ambitious men, such as lawyer and entrepreneur David Burnet.[11]

When he went to Liberty for court, Travis often stayed at the Hugh Johnson home outside town on the Nacogdoches road. There was no courthouse, but the weather was usually fine, and Travis and the other attorneys handling cases generally met under the shade of a large live oak that served as well as public meeting hall and polling place.[12] And before many months in Anahuac, Travis began to find the kind of standing that had been denied him in Claiborne. John Linn at Lavaca Bay, some distance along the Gulf Coast, became acquainted with Travis at Anahuac, and found that he "enjoyed the respect, confidence, and love of the colonists in general."[13]

While "love" may have been a bit extravagant for this abrupt and sometimes difficult young lawyer, certainly the community did come to respect him, and at least some of his closer friends called him by the nickname "Buck."[14] By the fall of 1831 people spoke favorably of Travis to Austin, testifying to their respect and esteem. And certainly Travis wasted no time in trying to advance himself. The United States maintained a consulate at Brazoria, where most of the business with Texas was conducted, but Austin believed that establishing a consulate at Galveston Bay would serve both American and Texian interests, and in November he recommended Travis after learning that the attorney expected to apply for such a position.[15] In the event, Travis never received the appointment, and perhaps thought better of applying, but without doubt he was not letting the prairie grass grow beneath his feet as he sought to rebuild his hopes for a career in this new land.

The only source of friction seemed to be another building in Anahuac. When Mexico City decided to enforce the customs laws, it sent a garrison to build a barracks and enforce the duties. To command it sent none other than Bowie's old comrade in arms John Davis Bradburn, now a colonel in the Mexican army and called Juan. Having helped Mexico secure its independence, his reward was this outpost in Texas, though when first he arrived in late October 1830 the Brazoria *Texas Gazette* met the news with "great pleasure."[16] Perhaps the editor felt that Bradburn, being a Virginian by birth, would be a sympathetic commander. If so, he proved to be mistaken, for Bradburn took his oath and uniform very seriously, and his brusque, condescending, and occasionally brutal manner often put him at odds with the locals. He told the land agents that they must leave the country in the wake of the decree, and though he continued to be kind and courteous to arriving would-be immigrants who came ignorant of the prohibition, still he was adamant in not allowing them to go inland. Instead, they stayed on their ships, lived in small tent camps, or went back to New Orleans. To enforce his presence, and protect his small garrison, Bradburn set the command to work building a stone barracks 150 feet long by 20 feet wide, with his own quarters at one end and a guardhouse at the other.[17]

By the time Travis settled there, Bradburn was all but shunned, and his *soldados* the more so. "The common soldiers at this post were men of a most depraved character," wrote a visitor in 1831, "while they were believed to be as cowardly as they were wicked and ignorant." Many were convicts who had been given the option of enlisting in the army or going to prison. And when an epidemic struck Anahuac, killing a dozen or more citizens, rumor said that Bradburn personally seized the effects of the dead and sold them at auction for the benefit of his garrison or the government.[18] Any lawyer was almost destined to come to a confrontation with Bradburn, and Travis and Jack certainly did.[19] Travis, priggish where his concept of rights and civil liberties were concerned, found himself in one confrontation after another. The chief causes of conflict between Bradburn and Travis were slavery, land, and customs, but just as likely any issue would have served to put two such antagonistic personalities in collision. In fact Travis evidenced no difficulty with Mexicans in their own right, and little if any of the prevailing prejudice against them. He even established at least formally cordial relations with Bradburn's executive officer, Col. Domingo Ugartechea, in the spring of 1832. But Bradburn's attitude, especially where rights of property and person were concerned, naturally raised his ire. When it achieved its independence from Spain, Mexico stopped just short of a positive prohibition of slavery in its constitution, but still by edict it prohibited the practice of black servitude for life. In opening Texas to settlers from the United States, however, the authorities in Mexico City had to recognize that there were already many in Austin's colony who had come there with their slaves before the abolition. The owners thereafter got around the prohibition by claiming that their blacks were not slaves but "lifetime indentures," presumably being paid a pittance in return for a ninety-nine-year labor commitment, a slippery semantic trick that fooled few, but with which Mexico City seemed able to live equably. As more settlers came into Austin's colony, up to the time of the April 6 law, they continued to bring their "indentures" with them, and by 1832 the flaunting of the prohibition was becoming simply too flagrant.

Bradburn, meanwhile, refused to recognize the practice, since Anahuac and Liberty were outside Austin's colony. An especially nagging problem arose when Louisiana slaves ran away from their masters, as Bowie's young man William fled from him. Anahuac sat a mere forty miles from the Sabine, and inevitably slaves fleeing Louisiana ended up in Bradburn's hands seeking sanctuary. Bradburn, in fact, used them as laborers on his barracks and the masonry fort he started to build that spring. Travis came into the equation when the owners engaged him or Jack to file claims for the return of the runaways. Anahuac being a port, there were more of these cases there than in most of Texas, and Bradburn's refusal to return blacks to masters quickly offended the lawyers' senses of justice and property rights.[20] During Gen. José Manuel Mier y Terán's visit the previous fall to enforce collection of customs and other Mexican law, a William Logan from Louisiana appeared to claim two of his runaways, and Mier y Terán told him he would have to apply through the Mexican embassy in Washington. The owner hired Travis to try to settle the situation, but after Mier y Terán's departure, Bradburn proved even more prickly in the matter, and told Travis that the blacks had enlisted in his command and applied for Mexican citizenship.[21]

That alone would have been enough to outrage the lawyer. Travis had kept his politics to himself until then, but there was no question that he came from a family that believed in and practiced slavery, and which regarded slaves as property, recognized as such by the Constitution. In Claiborne he had held slaves himself, though they may have been hired or on loan. The coming fall his father, Mark Travis, would be a firm supporter of South Carolina's attempt to nullify a federal tariff that it felt violated its rights of property and sovereignty. In the pages of his own *Herald* he had editorialized against government interference with the rights and business of the people, even to such things as a ban on carrying the mail on the Sabbath.[22] What Bradburn was doing violated a sacred right of property, and in common with most other Texians, Travis either did not recognize—or refused to recognize—that the Constitution of the United States meant nothing on Mexican soil.

As for the land problems, Anahuac became a visible bottleneck in the Mexican land policy in Texas. The number of immigrants stalled there continued to grow, while even those who had secured their grants prior to the April 6 law were still awaiting the necessary surveys before they could claim their titles. Bradburn interpreted his instructions to prohibit even the latter, which only further outraged new Texians, and then went beyond that to try to interfere in local Texian *ayuntamiento* politics. Being a highhanded martinet was not the way to deal with these volatile immigrants, especially thanks to events in Mexico at the moment. A power struggle was under way between the ruling faction, the centralists, who sought to concentrate and hold power in Mexico City, and a growing group of liberal federalists coalescing around former general Antonio López de Santa Anna, urging national reform and greater local autonomy in the several states. Such unrest only seemed to undermine the centralist Bradburn's backing. At the same time that he looked ever more autocratic, he also looked that much weaker and more vulnerable.

Meanwhile some of his *soldados* outraged the citizenry, getting drunk, insulting the citizens, and even assaulting them, including one rumored rape. A Texian witnessing the last assault refused to come to the victim's assistance, and his fellow Texians were so outraged that on April 26 they tarred and feathered him and paraded him through Anahuac until Bradburn sent *soldados* to stop the disturbance. As such things do, the confrontation escalated until Bradburn had a good portion of his garrison trying to quell a small riot. Gunshots rang out, men struck each other, and in the end the citizens backed away, leaving the punished Texian in Bradburn's protection. Bradburn determined to arrest those he thought to be behind it all, and he immediately suspected Pat Jack and Buck Travis.[23]

Bradburn already harbored a festering grievance against Travis. On May 1 the citizens in Anahuac met to organize a local militia, even though they knew that Mexican law prohibited any such organizations. They declared that the fear of raids from the Comanche and Tawakoni and other bands required that they organize for their own defense, but Bradburn easily saw through the guise. The nearest hostile natives were a good two hundred miles north, and would never raid as far south as the Gulf Coast. The militia was intended to protect the colonists from Bradburn and his *soldados*, especially after the result of the riot, and its members chose Pat Jack as its captain. With Santa Anna leading his uprising in Mexico, Bradburn and other Mexican commanders in Texas felt very vulnerable, fearing that colonists would take the opportunity—as they did—to identify themselves with the *santanistas* and move against the garrisons. Bradburn immediately arrested Jack. In the days ahead he received repeated calls from Jack's friends, especially the lawyer Robert M. Williamson and undoubtedly Travis, and though Bradburn soon released him, he marked Jack down as a leading troublemaker, and anything involving Jack surely had Travis behind it.[24]

Then came the last insult. Despite Travis's repeated entreaties, Bradburn remained adamant about not releasing the two runaway slaves. Suddenly there came to his ears rumors that armed slaveowners from Louisiana were gathering at the Sabine, their purpose to raid Anahuac and take the runaways by force. The colonel immediately put his garrison in readiness to be attacked, and when he learned that the rumor was untrue, he continued to keep the garrison on the alert just the same. Then one night, under cover of darkness and rain, a "tall man, wrapped in a big cloak," approached one of Bradburn's sentries. "*Quien es?*" asked the sentry, wanting to know who was there. "*Amigo,*" came the reply. When the sentry allowed the cloaked man to approach, the stranger handed him two letters, then disappeared. The letters were for Bradburn, and when he read them he found a renewed warning that one hundred men on the Sabine were coming to take the runaways by force. One letter was simply signed "McLaughlin" and the other "Billew," but having been fooled by such a rumor once, Bradburn immediately suspected a hoax. In his current state of agitation, he decided to make an arrest, and given his suspicions with regard to the recent riot, as well as the steady agitation over the slaves from a certain Anahuac lawyer, Bradburn decided that Travis was behind the trick.[25]

On May 17 Travis and Jack were together in their office when a noncommissioned officer and a dozen *soldados* halted before their door and demanded that Travis surrender himself for arrest.[26] Suddenly it was no longer a prank. Jack joined him for the walk to Bradburn's office in the barracks, and once there got into a heated argument with Bradburn over the arrest, which only resulted in the colonel arresting him too, not forgetting his suspicions about who lay behind the April 26 incident. Bradburn ordered the two of them confined in the guard-house at the end of the barracks building.

Suddenly Travis found himself in something deadly earnest, but given his temperament, by now almost certainly he had already crossed an inner line. The almost certain arrest that he fled in Claiborne would have been an ultimate humiliation. This arrest in Anahuac, however, cemented his standing as a respected member of the community, a spokesman for the rights of Texians, and perhaps even a martyr—if only figuratively—in the struggle against Bradburn's tyranny. It hardly mattered if the issues involved were a teapot tempest. Very small things could become very big in a village like Anahuac. Yet he and his friends saw beyond their parochial concerns, a vision that placed them in the immensely wider context of the Texian struggle for justice from its rulers, and the *santanista* revolution in Mexico itself. Widely read as he was, Travis knew that sometimes great movements emerged from just such minor events as this.

For the next fifty days Travis had little choice but to wait while events unfolded around him. At first the arrest proved not too onerous, and despite Bradburn's orders he and Jack were able to communicate with the outside. On their first or second day of confinement Travis managed to speak to a friend through a window in their cell, but the punishment of the guard on duty put an end to that. Bradburn did allow them clean clothes, though, and their friend Monroe Edwards soon had a slave named Hannah collecting their soiled linen, and bringing letters from Edwards to them in the clean laundry. Shortly after his arrest Travis "by great efforts" tried to get a message to his friend—and leading dissident—David Burnet on the San Jacinto, but a guard found the missive and gave it to Bradburn, who read in it their plea to the people of Austin's colony to "*come and rescue them from the claws of thirsty, ra[s]cally and convict soldiers.*"[27]

Nevertheless Bradburn allowed the laundry run to continue until a week later, when in the outgoing clothing a guard found another letter addressed simply "O.P.Q." In the previous week Travis and Jack had found a way to get themselves out of their confinement, either by bribing a guard or perhaps by breaking through the door. In either case they had decided not to risk Mexican military justice. Edwards knew, and could have informed them, that Bradburn, "a damned insignificant Military despot," intended to send them to Matamoros for trial.[28] They may also have known by then that Bradburn's judge advocate believed that they planned to foment a separation of Texas from Mexico.[29] Bradburn was taking depositions from his soldiers and some unfriendly citizens without their being able to question or confront the deponents themselves. They even believed that he was suborning and intimidating perjured testimony, and that "all sorts of villainy has been practiced" to condemn them. They could hardly afford to remain there idle, to be sent south into what they expected would be a rigged trial and perhaps indefinite imprisonment. Already they had gotten out to Edwards a plea for him to send word of their plight to Austin's colony and entreat friends to come to their aid. No succor had appeared, however, and now they must act on their own. The "O.P.Q." letter asked Edwards to have a horse ready for them at an appointed hour on the next Thursday night.[30]

When Bradburn saw the letter, he suddenly anticipated anew that a small army of colonists would come to release the prisoners. At that very moment Bradburn's men were in the process of building a small masonry fortress mounting two cannon, and the kiln they had used to make the bricks sat empty. To make certain there would be no breakout, he decided to move Travis and Jack to the kiln, then train his cannon on the approaches to the new *calabozo*.[31] The entire garrison mustered in line on the day that Travis and Jack emerged from the guardroom and walked under heavy escort to the kiln. A few citizens gathered to watch, and Travis recognized the local physician, Nicholas D. Labadie, standing on a fence waving to him. He heard Labadie bid him to stay cheerful, that help would soon come. Travis managed a brief bow in response before being hurried onward.[32]

Ever since the arrest, Edwards had been trying to arouse the people to muster in defense of the prisoners and force their release, but only five men responded, and even they refused actually to attack the guard to free Travis and Jack. Word of his efforts reached Bradburn, who in any case suspected Edwards of being the mysterious "O.P.Q.," and two days after the prisoners entered their new cell, Edwards suddenly joined them.[33]

Colonel Bradburn felt in no mood to pamper his prisoners further now. On one occasion they went for more than a week eating nothing but boiled beans and stale bread, though Lt. Juan Cortina of the garrison and their friend James Morgan in Anahuac managed to see that some variety of diet found its way into the kiln, though some of it never reached them, being consumed by their guards instead.[34]

Most unsettling of all, however, was being completely cut off from outside news. Travis had no way of knowing that Bradburn's commander, General Mier y Terán, envisioned attacking him from another quarter, advising Gov. José Maria Letona that "men with the title of lawyers" were making trouble at Anahuac. He called them a "plague of locusts," and suspected they might be practicing without licenses, and if that was the case, he could put them out of business. The men he had in mind were Travis and Jack, and he soon gave Bradburn orders that any attorney seeking to practice in the Liberty District must first present a license obtained at the state capital in Saltillo. Travis probably had no such license and probably never got one, but if he managed to win his freedom from this cell, the authorities could make it very difficult for him to practice law again.[35]

As the days went on, Bradburn arrested more local leaders, while word spread throughout the colony of the happenings at Anahuac. Jack's brother William Jack left his San Felipe law office and came to see Bradburn, and when he remonstrated that Mexican military law did not extend to civilians, the colonel gave him fifteen minutes to leave town or face arrest himself. When he got back to San Felipe, Jack spread the word of Bradburn's tyranny, and soon emissaries went out to all points in the colony to rouse the settlers. Meanwhile the pleas from the prisoners began to work. Travis's new friend Williamson, a jolly fellow called "Three-legged Willie" because a childhood illness had left one leg permanently bent and he attached a wooden limb to the knee for walking, issued a call on June 4 to men in Brazoria and elsewhere in Austin's colony to gather at Lynch's Ferry on the San

Jacinto a few miles west of Anahuac. Frank Johnson was already there recruiting, and soon others arrived, including Robert Wilson, a would-be capitalist, and the man always present when there was tension in Texas, Bowie's old friend Warren D. C. Hall. Soon Williamson joined them with thirty men from Brazoria, led by their *alcalde,* John Austin.[36] The volunteers elected Johnson their leader, with Hall second in charge, and in the next few days even more men assembled, until the force swelled to well over one hundred. Meanwhile Colonel Ugartechea in Velasco urged John Austin to be cautious, and, heeding the plea, he agreed to press Bradburn for a peaceful turnover of the prisoners, abetted by a petition from Ugartechea himself. Overreacting—understandably, given his isolated situation—Bradburn took the Lynch's Ferry gathering for an expedition intent not just on freeing his captives but on revolution, and that only spurred him to even greater conviction that Travis and Jack were behind it all. "We may anticipate serious evils from forbearance towards men who are insult-ing us even within the walls of our prisons," he declared. They must not tolerate that kind of insolence. In his imagination he swelled Johnson and Hall's numbers to six hundred or more, with the Comanche now joining in the plot, and begged for relief for his piti-ful eighty-man garrison.[37]

Travis may have been unaware of the approach of Johnson's volun-teers into Anahuac's outskirts on the morning of June 10. Certainly he must have heard or sensed some commotion outside the brick kiln, but he would have known nothing of the parlay between John Austin and Bradburn until guards burst into the cell. They tied the prisoners down to the ground and then stood over them with muskets poised. Travis himself had his hands tied over his knees. Negotiations had broken down, even though Ugartechea had sent his own plea to Bradburn to turn Travis and Jack over to civil authorities, and when Austin threat-ened to reduce the fort to rubble, Bradburn replied by giving orders that the prisoners were to be bound and shot at the first sound of an attack.[38] When he heard what had happened, and sensed that Austin and some of his men might be within hearing of his voice, Travis shouted to them to forget about him and "blaze away upon the fort." He was willing to die if he must, and preferred it to seeing the tyrant Bradburn get away unchastened for his crimes. Outside the kiln the

Texians found his words moving, impressed that Travis "never shrunk but called on his friends to witness that he would die like a man."[39]

The heat of the moment cooled, fortunately. The Texians retreated to the outskirts of Anahuac, and that afternoon Travis heard some desultory firing that betokened a skirmish, but Bradburn made no sign of carrying out his threat. There was more firing the next day, and then silence, and the following day Travis may have learned that Bradburn and the colonists had come to an agreement. The Texians would withdraw to Turtle Bayou and give up some Mexican prisoners, and in return Bradburn would free his captives within twenty-four hours. Travis could not have known, however, that Bradburn had no intention of honoring the agreement. Instead the colonel used the time to continue fortifying his position and call in all of his several outposts, boosting his strength to about 160 men. He looted the houses of Anahuac for anything that could be of use to the garrison, including carrying away some of Travis's clothing from his room in town.[40] The next morning he sent word to Austin and Johnson that if they wanted the prisoners, they were welcome to try to take them.[41]

Travis probably knew little of this, though again he would have heard the renewed sounds of firing when the Texians made a tentative advance on Anahuac, this time drawing blood. Only later would he learn that Austin and the others then withdrew and decided that they had better identify themselves with the *santanista* movement in Mexico in order to give some legitimate aim to their uprising. They adopted resolutions, listed grievances, and circulated them throughout the colony, a virtual declaration of war. And only later, too, would Travis learn that Father Michael Muldoon, friend of Mier y Terán and the only non-Mexican practicing priest in Texas, came forward on June 21 and unsuccessfully offered himself as a hostage for the freedom of the prisoners.[42] Colonists fought a skirmish with Ugartechea at Velasco that resulted in his agreement to withdraw to Matamoros, Travis and Jack and the others all the while languishing in their cell. They probably did not even know that Austin's force grew steadily to up to three hundred men, now cutting off all supply and communications to the garrison in Anahuac.

Finally, on July 2, Travis saw the door of the kiln open at last.[43] Col. José de la Piedras, commanding the garrison in Nacogdoches, marched to Bradburn's relief, but on encountering Austin's rump militia halted and decided to negotiate instead. After a few days of discussions, they came to an agreement on June 29 that Travis and the others would be released to civil authorities at Liberty to be tried by civilian law, if trial there should be, and that Bradburn should be relieved of his command, while the colonists would immediately return to their homes and private pursuits. Two days later Piedras and Hugh Johnson, *alcalde* of Liberty, presented themselves to Bradburn, who had no alternative but to yield to his superior's orders, though another day passed before the prisoners walked free.[44]

Buck Travis had been more than fifty days imprisoned, and for a few hours in danger of instant death, and all because of Bradburn. The novelty of being a martyr had long since worn away, and though he certainly relished his status as a cause célèbre, he bore an unrelenting grudge against Bradburn for his ordeal, not to mention the loss of his personal effects from his office and hotel room. There was never any question of Travis being tried in Liberty, for there were no concrete charges for him to face. Even the prank letter, if he wrote it, hardly constituted a crime, and there was no evidence at all that he contemplated the overthrow of the existing government and a separation from Mexico, though his ordeal may well have started him thinking in that direction. Given the opportunity, even the normally noncombative Travis might have confronted Bradburn, but the colonel, after relinquishing his command to Lieutenant Cortina, kept a low profile in Anahuac.

Yet the upheaval was not over just yet. Piedras stayed to keep peace until July 8, but then he had to leave quickly for Nacogdoches, for he feared a similar *santanista* uprising there, and he was right. Within a few weeks he would be surrendering himself to another rabble of upstart militia, this one led by James Bowie. Meanwhile, in Anahuac, Bradburn feared for his life. Believing that Travis intended his assassination, Bradburn begged a guard from Cortina to stand outside his door, and Cortina afterward told Labadie that the colonel was so fearful of Travis that he "ran to him like a *benau* (a deer) to be protected." Murder was a bit out of Travis's line, of course, but he may well have taken perverse delight in allowing Bradburn to fear such, perhaps even following up his letter prank by sending terrifying rumors in the colonel's direction. Certainly his friend Labadie saw that Travis "felt no great friendship toward Bradburn." Much as he appreciated Cortina for his respectful treatment, Travis also bore a lasting grudge against Lt. Manuel Montero, who bound him and held him at the edge of death on that terrible day in June.[45]

Travis got his revenge on July 11, three days after Piedras left. He and Jack and others came back from Liberty, brought a barrel of whiskey to the plaza in Anahuac, and invited members of the Mexican garrison to drink with them, no doubt on the pretext of cementing the resumption of civil relations. The drinking lasted long into the evening, moving indoors, and as the convivial mood spread, the Texians played on incipient dissatisfaction that the *soldados* already felt with the centralist regime for abandoning them at this outpost. Eventually, at the urging of the Texians and feeling the freedom of the *aguardiente*, the soldiers declared themselves for Santa Anna and called for Col. Félix Subarán, a *santanista* who outranked Cortina but did not hold the command. Subarán himself appeared and got drunk, and the mutiny was complete. The soldiers refused to obey Cortina's orders and demanded that Subarán take charge, while the officers remaining loyal to the old regime asked Bradburn to resume command. Bradburn was at least wise enough to know that this situation was out of hand, better escaped than confronted. He could not even get himself and his loyal men and officers away by water, since Texian vessels loyal to Santa Anna blockaded Trinity Bay. In the end Bradburn and a few others slipped away through the bayous on July 13, closely pursued by angry colonists who may have included Travis himself.[46]

The Texians felt more than a little full of themselves. "The blow has already been struck," one wrote while the prisoners still languished in the brick kiln. "Now or never is the time to sever all ties."[47] Travis himself was scarcely out of his cell before the editorialist in him began to write for public consumption. On July 8 he penned a stirring account of the whole episode, taking the high ground by asserting—and exaggerating—that he and Jack had been imprisoned not for pranks or for stirring civil unrest, but because of their political views. Bradburn was a tyrant and a coward, but the Texians had beaten him. "Mexicans have learned a lesson," he crowed; "*Americans know their rights and will assert and protect them*" and would not see constitutional guarantees "trampled under foot." That the guarantees of the American Constitution held no force in

Mexican territory seems not to have bothered Travis or the others. In his view, when the colonists came to Texas, they brought their sacred rights as Americans with them. It was a short mental leap from that notion to the idea that if *norteamericano* civil rights rather than Mexican justice should rule in Texas, then maybe Texians ought simply to rule themselves. "The Americans have gained every thing which they claimed," he boasted. "There is every prospect that this happy state of things will have a long and prosperous duration."[48] Certainly the Mexican authorities did not necessarily see it that way, and feared not an end but a beginning to their troubles. Even Tocqueville, now visiting the United States, saw the inevitable direction of events. "Daily, little by little, the inhabitants of the United States are filtering into Texas, acquiring land there, and, though submitting to the country's laws, establishing there the empire of their language and mores," he observed. "The province of Texas is still under Mexican rule, but soon there will, so to say, be no more Mexicans there."[49] So it appeared to some Mexican authorities after Anahuac, and moreover they clearly believed that Travis was party to the scheme. Ugartechea, having met Travis cordially enough, concluded from the papers shown him by Bradburn that Travis, Jack, "and other accomplices" were a part of a plan "to separate the territory from the Govt of the state and the federation."[50]

For the moment Travis only intended to separate himself from Anahuac. He had good friends there, his practice had prospered enough to support him, and certainly the events of the past two months had given him a celebrity that he could hardly have acquired otherwise. But the scope of Anahuac was simply too limited. Indeed, it may be that this very notoriety given him by Bradburn persuaded Travis that he could capitalize on his fame if he relocated to a more lucrative market. In August he added a small tract with a house and other improvements to his Buffalo Bayou property, but he never had any intention of living there. He would simply rent it or hold it for resale.[51] A man with prospects and ambition—and a reputation to exploit—could only go one place: San Felipe.

Sometime in August he packed his baggage and set out for Liberty, thence to go west on the Atascosita Trace until a side road took him to the bank of the Brazos. There on the low bluff on the other side sat San Felipe. A flatboat ferry took him across the stream, and once up

the sandy, steep forty-foot bank he saw anew this rude capital of
Austin's colony, the acknowledged center of Texian political and business activity. It was a young town, started by Austin in 1824 at the
head of navigation of the river, and from it keelboats and flats made
the passage down to Brazoria and Velasco on the Gulf, the town's
chief link with New Orleans and the rest of white America. There
were perhaps fifty clapboard-roofed, unhewn-log houses and buildings by now, with only one more imposing frame dwelling. Yet the
street seemed busy, wagons and carriages moving about on their owners' business, most of it concerned with the land and the law.

The village offered some amenities for its size. San Felipe had a billiard room, of all things, its table heavily used, though Cooper and
Chieves's comparatively elegant frame establishment saw as much use
for gambling as more gentlemanly sport. There was one weekly newspaper, Three-Legged Willie Williamson's *Mexican Citizen*, formerly the
Texas Gazette. Several merchants maintained establishments, notably
Walter White, Thomas Gay, Silas Dinsmore, and Seth and Ira Ingram,
and there were the inns and hotels of the Peytons and James
Whitesides, not to mention a couple of taverns. To minister to other,
more spiritual needs, a Baptist preacher with the wonderfully apt name
of Thomas Pilgrim taught an informal Sunday school and gave sermons, careful not to violate the letter of the Catholic law.[52]

Few families lived in town, most of them dwelling out on their
farms, but Stephen Austin could be an interesting host, though it was
simple fare at his typical dogtrot home and office. It sat half a mile
back from the river, and it offered nothing more imposing than the
rest of the town. Visitors stood on dirt floors and breathed air redolent
with the woodsmoke from fireplaces that sent as much smoke into the
rooms as up the chimneys. He did his business in one cabin and slept
in the other, tended by an old black cook named Mary, but took most
of his meals at Samuel Williams's cabin another half mile back from
the village. Travis found Austin slender and wiry, graceful, dark curly
hair framing a fair face set alight by green eyes. Austin had the habit of
pacing back and forth in his office, hands behind his back, when in
deep thought or conversation. He could seem distant and preoccupied,
but—to Travis's taste—he was neither profane nor intemperate, and
he shared Bowie's taste for a neat appearance.[53]

Of special interest to Travis, of course, was the bar in San Felipe. A contemporary visitor found in the town "several persons of some education who perform the part of advocates, much on the principles of the laws of the United States."⁵⁴ His friend David Burnet practiced there with his partner, Hosea League, as did Samuel Williams and his partner, Luke Lesassier, who had been one of those on Turtle Bayou who came to rescue Travis. Lesassier currently served as prosecuting attorney before the *ayuntamiento*, which met in a cheerless, floorless unfinished log cabin that began as a hotel but was never finished. Since no one ever got around to chinking the gaps between the logs with mud, the wind whistled through the building as it pleased, convincing the community fathers that it would be superfluous to cut windows for ventilation, and so there were none.⁵⁵ Certainly San Felipe offered Travis something much closer to Claiborne than did Anahuac, and the decision to stay came easy, especially since everyone in town now knew who he was and regarded him as a patriot, if not a hero. He engaged a room at Peyton's inn for one dollar a night for bed and board for himself and his horse, rented quarters from one of the merchants, and on September 1 announced that "WILLIAM B. TRAVIS, Attorney & Counsellor at Law," was available for business.⁵⁶

At the same time Travis threw himself into such social life as there was in a community in which most of the men dressed in buckskins.⁵⁷ Much of it centered at Peyton's, where the impish Williamson was always a source of fun when in town. Jonathan Peyton's wife set two tables for the main meal, one with rather rough fare for the men, and another with some dainties for the ladies who dined with her. One night Williamson, a natural wit, diverted the women with a fund of amusing stories in another room, while other men, perhaps including Travis, switched all the dishes at the tables and then sat down to a far-better-than-average repast.⁵⁸ Of course there was a risk in aggravating Mrs. Peyton overmuch, for, being one of the matrons of San Felipe society, she could make trouble for the likes of Travis and Williamson with the local young ladies. There were few enough single women, and when one arrived she was likely not to remain unmarried for long. During the previous three years Bowie's acquaintance Noah Smithwick lamented that "there was not a ball or party of any kind in which ladies participated." There were only the stag parties at Godwin

Cotton's home.[59] Now and then an open-air fandango offered dancing to some poor fiddle tunes, attended chiefly by the Mexican population, but the *norteamericanos* sometimes joined with reels and jigs.[60] Certainly Travis reestablished his Masonic connections. Hosea League had convened the first Masonic meeting in Texas back in 1828, and they still met in San Felipe from time to time, though they had no lodge charter and were still officially members of the Grand Lodge of Louisiana. And of course in his free hours Travis read widely as he always had. He continued studying Spanish and the civil law of Mexico and Texas, devoured the newspapers, both local and imported, and took on a book when he could find one. By this time there were already a few copies of a new title floating about Texas, having been announced in the Brazoria press while Travis was in the brick kiln: *The Life and Adventures of Col. David Crockett of West Tennessee.* As sample anecdotes in the newspaper suggested, it would make for spirited reading.[61]

Even while establishing his practice, Travis could not help but be engaged by the political swirl around him. Just a month after he opened his office, the convention met in San Felipe to frame its set of resolutions, including the call for Texian separation from Coahuila, and he must at least have followed its progress in the tavern and hotel conversation of an evening, if he did not actually listen to the debates themselves. The conclusion to recognize Santa Anna in preference to Bustamente would have appealed to Travis, who was himself the living embodiment in San Felipe of the abuses of the centralist regime. He would have approved of its creation of a standing committee in San Felipe, with subcommittees in other districts, to maintain correspondence and communication with one another for mutual interest, rather like the Committees of Correspondence in the American colonies before the Revolution. If Travis felt any disappointment at the convention's result, it was that the absence of Béxar representatives, and the reluctance of some others to go too far too fast, meant that the delegates selected to carry the resolutions to Coahuila and Mexico City never went.

Certainly an assertive mood was all around him. The reactivated *Texas Gazette* moved to Brazoria in July, immediately after the Anahuac uproar, and changed its title to the not insignificant *Constitutional Advocate & Texas Public Advertiser.* The message was everywhere that Texians wanted the civil rights and guarantees that they had enjoyed at home in the United States, and most of them believed that Santa Anna sympathized in their interest. When Stephen Austin returned to San Felipe in the fall, called there by the turmoil in Texas, he was so disturbed by the situation he found that he decided not to return to his seat in the Saltillo legislature.[62] Travis himself stood in the advance guard in his sympathies. Caiaphas Ham, who knew him—but not nearly so well as he knew Bowie—maintained that Buck Travis was an early advocate of separation from Coahuila at least, and perhaps even from Mexico.[63] Reuben Potter in Matamoros knew Travis by reputation, if not personally, and found him "not backward in revolutionary movements."[64] And there is no question that Travis enjoyed and cultivated the acquaintance of men who acted as leaders in the march to Anahuac and the October convention. By December, when elections were held for delegates to the April 1833 convention, he actively supported Pat Jack and others who left no doubt of their support for Santa Anna and the secession from Coahuila.[65]

With the convention and the December election done, the fate of Texas lay in other, distant hands, and Travis could concentrate the bulk of his attention on his practice. He remained in his rented office space at Walter White's store, next door to Dinsmore's, for more than a year.[66] With gratifying alacrity, the clients began to come through the door, some of them no doubt to see the center of the Anahuac disturbances, and others referred by Travis's growing network of prominent friends. Not only were there court days in San Felipe to attend, but also in Brazoria, and Travis traveled back and forth to represent briefs at both, drawing and witnessing wills, filing for collection of notes, and even arguing maritime law and the extent of territorial limits at sea.[67] Influential men like Eli Holly, a fellow Alabamian émigré, engaged him to administer their estates, and some of Austin's original settlers—called "the Old Three Hundred"—gave him their briefs. After a year of practice in Claiborne he had scarcely half a dozen cases on his desk; after a year in San Felipe there were sixty or more, the number growing steadily.[68] In October 1833 Samuel Williams engaged Travis to handle all legal affairs for his land business, and as well to counsel him on colonization law. At the end of the year Travis even did a small job for James Bowie.[69]

Soon the variety of work expanded even more. He defended in criminal cases of theft, wrote mortgages, accepted debts for clients in every form from cash to oxen, wrote petitions, took depositions in estate settlements, prepared powers of attorney, acted for defendants in civil suits, made out warrants and subpoenas, and even wrote some official papers for the *ayuntamiento*. Firebrand William Wharton came to him to act on his behalf in a mortgage dispute with the late John Austin, just deceased in the cholera epidemic, and Travis had to make a public speech in the matter, perhaps his first of note in his new home. When he spoke well he took rather a lot of pride in the fact, just as he did not easily forget when an opponent at the bar embarrassed him (the memory of Dellet and the "infancy" fiasco still stung). The volume of business grew to the extent that by late 1833 he was going back and forth to Brazoria once a month, dividing himself between the courts. In Brazoria he generally stayed at the inn kept by Jane Long, widow of James, and became such a regular customer that she commenced charging him the same daily rate paid by her permanent boarders. Indeed, the volume of his Brazoria business grew to the point that in September he actually considered relocating there, and found an office he could rent for five dollars a month.[70]

He decided instead to stay in San Felipe. Even though more lawyers vied for its business, it was the center of political, social, and legal affairs, and the most logical place for him to be. A move to Brazoria would not have ended his necessity to be in Austin's capital on a regular basis anyhow. Instead, facing his expanding needs, he gave up his office at White's and made a substantial step up in November by renting an entire house and grounds for home and office from Dr. James Miller for one hundred dollars a year, with the proviso that the landlord make some improvements. In an expansive mood in celebration of the event, Travis paid a *tejano* fifty cents to move his office contents, while he spent the afternoon and early evening playing faro with friends, losing thirty-four dollars. The change in his circumstances over the day seventeen months before when he left Claiborne was intoxicating. Then he could not afford to pay debts as small as thirty-seven dollars for his horse's fodder. Now he could lose that much in an evening's gambling and still feel jolly enough to continue celebrating with something else that may have been in short supply at Claiborne those last days: He spent the night in the arms of a woman named Susana.[71]

In the days ahead Travis only improved the outlook for his practice.
He bought a case to keep his papers organized, though he had to confess that he was not the tidiest of record keepers. While many of his
clients paid with promissory notes, which Travis himself often used to
make his own purchases from others, still he was getting enough hard
currency and banknotes on New Orleans banks and the Bank of the
United States that he could actually start to choose his cases rather
than take all comers. He did more real estate law, handling house and
lot sales, and in something that would have shocked the struggling
Claiborne lawyer, he turned down one client's offer of a fifty-dollar-
per-year retainer, quite possibly more money than he actually earned
in his last year in Alabama.[72]

In fact Travis had never seen so much money in his life. His business
receipts for September were $104.75, and more than double that in
October at $260.00. In the last four months of 1833 in all he took in at
least $519.25, with some of his relatively simple tasks like preparing a
title now bringing him $25 fees.[73] One client paid him $210 in cash for
a single fee in April 1834.[74] With his new-found liquidity, Travis
bought more land, including a house and 100 acres a few miles east of
San Felipe, though he continued to live in town and must only have
rented the place.[75] He even became an investor, in his own future and
the future prosperity of Texas.

Robert Wilson, one of those who volunteered to help release Travis
at Anahuac, was a thirty-nine-year-old steam engineer from Maryland
who first came to Texas in 1828. Two years later, in partnership with
David Harris, he built and commenced operating a steam saw mill at
Harrisburg, forty miles east of San Felipe. He also took an interest in
shipping, and it was aboard his own sailing vessel that Bradburn and
his garrison first came to Anahuac in 1830.[76] Texians thought well of
Wilson, calling him "Honest Bob," and for his part he thought very
highly of Travis, in time taking pride in their friendship.[77] Their political views certainly brought them together, for Wilson sat in the
October 1832 convention and held advanced ideas like those of
Wharton and others, and now Travis. He also looked forward commercially. Not content with running a sailing vessel, he wanted to bring
steamboats to Texas and brought Travis into his scheme. On November
27, 1833, a group of subscribers pledged sufficient funds for Wilson and

William Harris to purchase a boat in New Orleans and bring it to ply the waters of the Brazos between Velasco and San Felipe. The commercial impact could be enormous, and significantly William B. Travis was one of the three largest subscribers, pledging five hundred acres of land to help fund the project. At the same time he also secured virtually all of Wilson's and the Harrises' legal business.[78]

With Travis's growing prosperity came a steady maturing in his attitude toward debt. Never would he forget those awful days in Claiborne. He still frequently borrowed small amounts from friends, often to pay an evening's gambling debt when he had no cash, and to be repaid quickly enough in the following days. In that month of September 1833, when his practice really took hold, he borrowed $55.55 from friends, but paid back all but $1.05 that same month, while himself loaning others some $23.00. In the last four months of 1833 he borrowed all told $254.55 and paid back every cent, plus helping others with out-of-pocket loans of $104.00.[79] He would always have a carefree attitude toward money, in one case borrowing $5.00 from the desk of his landlord Dr. Miller without asking, but six months later he paid it back. And finally, in September, he decided it was time to erase those other debts from his memory. He engaged a friend who was traveling back to Alabama to go to Claiborne and redeem all those outstanding notes, a step on the road to regaining his reputation. William B. Travis was growing up.[80]

Yet there was still much of the proud gay youth about him—and no wonder since he was still just twenty-four in 1833. His prosperity allowed him to indulge some of the whims that Claiborne's poverty forbade, and a slight taste for ostentation that made ready employment for spare cash. He liked horses, and in October bought a new one, then soon traded up for a little bay that took his liking.[81] While waiting for Dr. Miller to make the improvements in the house he rented, Travis boarded at the widow Jane Wilkins's house, where he could find the company of her two daughters, aged twenty and twenty-nine, entertaining. Both to attract the attention of the less-than-plentiful ladies as well as suiting his own taste, he began spending money on his wardrobe: $30.00 for a frock coat, $7.00 for a hat, $1.00 for stockings, $6.00 for a waistcoat, $9.00 for boots, shoes at $2.25, and even dancing pumps for $2.65. He bought bolt linen to have shirts made and a neck stock to wear for a collar, and in November spent nearly $30.00 on brown linen and black bombazine for a coat and vest. A week later he took a pair of red pants to a tailor and paid him to remake the fabric into a coat with a long hood and a decorative gold braid, beyond question the most colorful attire in San Felipe.[82] He now paid a barber twenty-five cents to cut his hair, and bought vials of scents of lavender and bergamot to anoint his hair and clothes. For his correspondence he spent thirty-seven and one-half cents on a quire of "fancy writing paper."[83] In short counsellor Travis was becoming a bit of a fop, and clearly loving it.

Happily, with this new prosperity, there was still enough of the Baptist in him to keep some temptations beyond arm's reach. Travis never had much interest in liquor. Now and then he spent four bits for brandy or wine, but often as not to add spirit to a gathering rather than for his own consumption.[84] But he made up for that restraint when it came to gambling, a taste no doubt acquired—to his distress—in Claiborne, and never since lost. In the latter part of 1833 he gambled several times a week, sometimes nightly, and like most players never proved to be as good as he thought. In October he won $88.25, in November he lost $104.31, neither an inconsequential sum. In seven straight months he won more than he lost only in two, and by March 1834 his cumulative losses outweighed his winnings by $53.46.[85] It was not a large sum to him now, perhaps, but it was money he could have been sending back to Rosanna in Alabama, but apparently did not. The process of maturing still had some distance to go.

As befitted a man of Buck Travis's new standing in the community, he tried anew to assume the role that eluded him in Claiborne. Despite being a Baptist, he gave $25.00 with others to raise a fund of $300.00 to bring a Methodist, Rev. John Wesley Kenney, and his family, to the Brazos to preach to them in spite of the law authorizing only Catholicism.[86] When men with a racing bent established the Planters & Farmers Jockey Club of Mill Creek not far from town, Travis wrote their articles of incorporation.[87] He bought a rifle, for every man should have a gun, though he loaned it to others more than he used it himself, and he also kept a slave, a twenty-year-old black named Joe, whom he only rented for the time being.[88] He threw himself into what literary society San Felipe offered, and found a surprising variety of books available to borrow and read. Luke Lesassier, newly elected *alcalde*, lent him a book of anecdotes, and another friend gave him four volumes of *The Spectator* and one of Bolingbroke's histories. His tastes ran from popular novels like *Roderick Ransom* to the histories of Herodotus, which he used to pass the hours on Christmas Eve. He borrowed the two volumes of James Kirke Paulding's 1832 novel *Westward Ho!* to read over the 1834 New Year's holiday, and could not have helped but be amused by its picture of a frontier not unlike his own, where any time three men were seen talking together "it is ten to one the subject is politics, five to one religion, and three to one making a speculation."[89]

And the young lawyer about town did more than read for the holidays. Travis partook of every bit of amusement that poor San Felipe could offer, and helped in planning the merriment. He joined Spencer Jack, the lawyer brother of Patrick and William, in making the arrangements for a Christmas subscription ball, and on the evening itself dined first at Thomas Gay's, where he contributed two bottles of wine to the meal, and then went on to the ball for what he called a "fine enjoyment." The next day he attended a party at the home of Maj. Ira Lewis, and on December 30 he joined others in the mock trial of a fiddler who gave them "much fun," then went to an auction where he bought a bottle of whiskey that he gave to local natives for their own celebration. New Year's Eve itself he spent attending a wedding celebration. If there was an ounce of fun to be had in San Felipe, Travis was sure to seek it out.[90]

He did not neglect the ladies. Regardless of what he had told Rosanna, Travis's intentions toward her may have been equivocal at best from the moment he left Claiborne. He promised to come for her or send for her as soon as he established himself and could support his family, now grown by the birth of a daughter, Susan Isabella, born August 4, 1831.[91] During the ensuing two years he regularly wrote to Rosanna and her brother William Cato, who looked after her affairs, and during all that time he continued to profess his love and his intentions. It

would have been unlike him to conceal his pride in how well his practice progressed, and certainly he could not conceal the fancy paper he
used now for his correspondence. Yet he did not send for her. Worse,
word of his prosperity undoubtedly got back to Claiborne, especially
when Henry Sewell appeared in late September or early October and
word got out that he was redeeming all of Travis's debts.

Meanwhile Rosanna's letters betrayed her increasing frustration. Even
though he could gamble away more than $30.00 in a day for his own
entertainment, he rarely sent her any money to support herself and the
children. The entire fall of 1833 he may have sent no more than $10.00.
Her friends advised her to petition the legislature for a divorce on
grounds of abandonment. They had a daughter that Travis had never
even seen. She wanted the family reunited, and her brother William, too,
tired of Travis's delays and evasions. Finally that fall, probably after
Travis's friend Sewell appeared with evidence that for months now
Travis could have sent for them anytime he wanted, William Cato sent
him a peremptory demand to state his intentions unequivocally.

At last Travis faced what he had been trying to ignore for so long
and replied that he did not want a reunion now or in the future, and
that he wished the separation to be permanent. All he wanted was his
son and his freedom. Crushed but probably not surprised, Rosanna
agreed. At Travis's suggestion, she consented to bring the children to
Natchez that coming winter, and he would meet them there. But once
she was there he did not appear, instead sending word that she should
send Charles on to Jane Long's in Brazoria. Then he changed his mind
again and asked his friend Monroe Edwards to go to Alabama to get
the boy for him. Though he might have redeemed his legal debts,
Travis was still too proud and immature to go back to Claiborne in
person to pay his moral obligations and meet face to face those whom
he had ill used—family, creditors, and Rosanna. In the end Rosanna
went to Natchez for nothing, and Edwards never went to Alabama,
and Charles for the time being remained with his mother. And
Rosanna, mortified that she would have to bear alone the odium of
being an abandoned and divorced woman, set about rebuilding her life
by learning the millinery trade. Perhaps, too, she still entertained a
glimmer of hope, if only she could see Travis in person, for she did
nothing about the divorce.[92]

Like many a young man with more libido than conscience, Travis may even have found it convenient to have a wife back in Alabama, for she presented an automatic impediment to any young lady in Texas trying to force him to the altar. Certainly he did not let marriage inhibit his romantic life. Women were scarce enough in San Felipe that when an opportunity presented itself, Travis did not stand on ceremony. Sometimes he paid for sex, mostly with native and *tejana* prostitutes or Texian washerwomen supplementing their meager income. Occasionally the daughter of one of the settlers was in an agreeable mood. With the callow pride of youth, Travis even numbered his conquests. On September 26, 1833, using his still evolving grasp of Spanish for recording more delicate matters he noted in the diary that he used mainly for business notes, he wrote that "*chingaba una mujer que es cincuenta y seis en mi vida*": "I fucked a woman who is the fifty-sixth of my life."[93] If by that he meant that this was only the fifty-sixth time he had enjoyed sexual congress in his life, then the two and one-half years of marriage and living with Rosanna may well have been troubled from the start. On the other hand, if he meant that the lady involved was the fifty-sixth partner in his lifetime, then Travis had been a busy fellow in Texas indeed, and the eight weeks in Bradburn's brick kiln might have provided a welcome bit of rest.

An opportunistic attitude toward casual sex hardly meant that Travis was immune to romance, of course, even more indication that when he left Alabama, not much affection for Rosanna left with him. In December he courted Miss E. Henry in competition with two other suitors, one of them his friend A. C. Westall, and good-naturedly admitted defeat by attending her wedding to Westall on New Year's Eve. Perhaps he took it with equanimity because he had other interests simultaneously, one of them an acquaintance perhaps just starting to blossom into romance. Early in September, on his way home from a business trip, he had stopped at Mill Creek outside San Felipe and dined at the inn kept by John Cummings, meeting there his sister, Rebecca, who acted as hostess. Thereafter he made Cummings's a not infrequent stop.[94]

After scarcely more than two years, Texas had been awfully good to William B. Travis. When he came he arrived like so many others that Tocqueville had seen "at the extreme edge of the confederated states,

where organized society and the wilderness meet." They were bold
and adventurous, leaving poverty in their homes behind them as they
"dared to plunge into the solitudes of America seeking a new homeland." They came with little or nothing. "All his surroundings are
primitive and wild, but he is the product of eighteen centuries of labor
and experience," said the Frenchman. "He wears the clothes and talks
the language of a town; he is aware of the past, curious about the
future, and ready to argue about the present; he is a very civilized man
prepared for a time to face life in the forest, plunging into the wilderness of the New World with his Bible, ax, and newspapers."[95] Property
and prosperity, fine clothes, influential friends, as good a home as anyone in San Felipe, an end to debt and apparently no end of compliant
women, and a seemingly boundless future, all lay before him. No
stranger to pride and self-regard, Travis wore his success quite literally
on his sleeve. In September, just past his twenty-fourth birthday, he sat
down with a pen and his "Common place Book." At an age when most
American men had not yet lived or experienced enough to warrant
more than a footnote, Travis wrote what he called "a short memorandum of the principal events of my life up to 1832."[96] Nothing could say
more for his opinion of himself at that moment than that he should
feel his life to date important enough for an autobiography, however
brief. By ending it in 1832, with his rise to celebrity at Anahuac, he
also revealed that he was hardly indifferent to the role that his recent
past might play in his immediate future. Far from merely equaling his
old mentor's success, Travis could already see hope of surpassing
Dellet. If his maturing kept pace with his material progress, Travis's
prospects in Texas appeared limitless.

BOWIE

> *The pages of history record few such achievements. The valorous men who*
> *bared their breasts . . . who fought without fear and without hope . . . should*
> *be remembered and honored as long as civilization endures.*
>
> CAIAPHAS HAM, CA. 1880

Bowie rode back to Louisiana in the fall of 1830, the monotony of the trip broken only by a chance meeting with Caiaphas Ham when he passed through Gonzales, seventy-five miles east of San Antonio. The faithful friend had gone to Natchez to collect Bowie's money, and was now on his way back, almost certainly empty-handed. He turned around and rode as far as Jared Groce's with Bowie, then left him to proceed on to Nacogdoches, the Sabine, and eventually the Lafourche once more in November.[1] A lot of news awaited Bowie on his return. For one thing his old nemesis George Graham had died the previous August, one of his last statements a reiteration of his determination that "all claims founded upon fraud should never be confirmed."[2] For another, Rezin had been elected to another term in the legislature, this time representing Lafourche Parish, where he made his principal residence on the brothers' plantation.[3]

Of most immediate interest, however, was the impending reduction of the import duties on sugar. If that came to pass, the price on domestic sugar would fall more, and the value of the Bowie cane plantation could plummet as well. On this issue the planters lined up regardless of party behind Henry Clay and his nascent Whig organization, but for the Bowies what these events suggested was that the time to sell their plantation was nigh. The timing could not have been worse. Once Rezin got the steam crusher into operation, the machinery proved to be defective and it ruined half the 1830 crop, a loss of up to five thousand dollars.

Then a heavy frost ruined another hundred acres of cane. Even using the steam engine to saw lumber failed.[4] If this just happened to coincide with James's need to sell his remaining assets in Louisiana, so much the better. This time James's more deliberate brother Rezin agreed. He did not receive James's announcement of moving permanently to Texas too well, however. "James is too impatient to wait for events," he complained. "He will hurry them before matters are ripe for action."[5]

James and Stephen, and probably Rezin as well, went to Natchez in January 1831 to try to close out their holdings. James unloaded one of his last Terrebonne properties for $3,900 and then met with one of his other former buyers to discuss something much bigger.[6] Robert J. Walker walked with a severe stoop, making his diminutive stature seem even smaller, and leading one friend to call him "a mere whiffet of a man." His voice wheezed when he spoke, while his face remained entirely expressionless, yet behind it lurked a vaulting ambition backed with great ability and no small cunning. He enjoyed a lucrative legal practice in Natchez, while close contacts with such prominent bankers as James C. Wilkins, cotton gin merchant and president of the Planters Bank of Natchez, gave him access to more than enough money to indulge a taste for land speculation. The word was out that he was buying big, spending hundreds of thousands of dollars of his credit on cane land and slaves, and that he was willing to take risks on land with questionable titles.[7] James Bowie thought Walker made to order even if he—like his brother, Duncan, and his investment partner Wilkins—was a firm Jacksonian. Both Walker and Wilkins had political ambitions as well.

Whether the Bowies approached the Walkers and Wilkins or the other way around, in February they came to terms that saw the sale of the remnant of James's Harper report claims, the Lafourche sugar plantation and eighty slaves, and almost all of the four brothers' other Louisiana land, including twenty-four of James's bogus Sutton report claims. In all the deals covered nearly 70,000 acres and a total purchase price of $192,000. At last it seemed that James had beaten his old enemy Graham. He never got clear title to more than 56,000 of those acres, but now that would be the buyers' problem. Yet the Walkers and Wilkins were no fools. They paid very little outright cash and required that James sign over all of his shares in the Consolidated Association of

Planters, acquired when he had used his property as collateral to borrow money from the association. In fact, for most of the sales Bowie
only received the buyers' notes, due at intervals, and which they could
refuse to pay if trouble arose with titles. If James had any cash in hand
after it was all done, it amounted to no more than $20,000, and proba-
bly much less.[8] There is no question that Robert Walker knew that the
Sutton report properties were problematic at best, though the ever-
persuasive James managed to convince the buyers that he and his
brothers were selling at "great sacrifice" because the surveyor George
Davis had spitefully ordered all the evidence of approvals for James's
land claims to be destroyed, and thus he could not prove title. Even an
eventual appeal to Walker's friend President Jackson did not help him
secure clear title. Though he could not know it then, James Bowie
would never see most of the rest due him on the buyers' notes.[9]

Whatever cash he received, Bowie spent $6,000 of it immediately
on February 23, when he bought from Stephen two speculative tracts
on the Lafourche some twenty-two miles below Thibodeauxville, next
to property of his friend Angus McNeil.[10] Most or all of the balance he
put in the hands of McNeil in Natchez. Then he went downriver to
New Orleans, and there on February 25 made out the formal transfer
of his shares in the Consolidated Association to Robert Walker, advising the directors that "as I am about leaving this state for Mexico," he
hoped the transfer could be made speedily.[11] There was also other family business to take care of. Nothing good was happening in Arkansas.
The previous June a decree came down allowing the courts to try all
previously allowed Spanish claims, along with the announcement that
the United States would file suits against the several claimants. The
newspapers published a list of the suits to be prosecuted, and of course
the overwhelming majority of them were the Bowies'. That meant the
Supreme Court, and they could expect little good to come of that.
James had never had any luck in Washington.[12]

As for brother John, his personal life, as usual, seemed to be a mess.
He was living in Chicot County now. Sometime after his first wife,
Nancy, left him he had taken another named Lucinda, and in September
he filed for a divorce from her, immediately thereafter marrying a
widow whose daughter by her first husband would one day marry
Stephen Bowie's son James.[13] Seeing the Arkansas scheme playing out,

John may have turned his hand to trying to lay claim to some land back near New Madrid, Missouri, that their father once owned, but it was a small-time affair compared to the enterprise of the last decade, a faint echo of the great land grabs that James and John attempted.[14]

Then there was brother Stephen, always the weakest link in the tight Bowie chain. In Rezin's family it was said that Stephen "had more good looks than practical sense," and Rezin's wife, Margaret, frankly claimed that he was the "least bright" of the Bowies. Certainly he felt a lesser brand of loyalty to his brothers than they gave in return, James and Rezin having bailed him out of financial trouble more than once. When he won appointment as sheriff of Lafourche Parish in February 1830, Rezin posted part of a $9,560 bond for his good feasance in office, and just that past November, after returning from Texas, James signed another $7,500 bond for him. Nevertheless, on the very day in 1826 that Rezin sold Stephen a piece of land in St. Martin Parish at a very low price, Stephen turned around and filed suit against his brother for the collection of a $50 debt. And on February 23, when Stephen sold James those two new tracts on the Lafourche, one of which Stephen himself had bought only the day before for $1,000, he then demanded $2,000 from his brother. It was even rumored that Sheriff Stephen Bowie walked out of his office leaving a substantial sum of money on his table, and that when he returned it was gone, and James and Rezin had to make it up out of their own pockets before the theft was discovered. Despite the land sales to the Walkers and Wilkins, he was almost broke.[15] Six months later his land in Terrebonne would be seized for his debts, and in another few weeks he would be arrested on the streets of Natchez for debt and vagrancy. Typical of him, he blamed his insolvency on his brother James, claiming that he had left for Texas owing him $12,000. By the end of the year he was apparently actually hiding to try to avoid an arrest order being served by the U.S. marshal for eastern Louisiana.[16]

When James left Natchez early in March 1831, moving to Texas for good, he gave Rezin his power of attorney to sell his few remaining bits of land in Louisiana, as well as in Arkansas and the "province of Texas, in Mexico."[17] Clearly he still had some hopes for more Arkansas sales, and just as clearly, he asked Rezin to start selling tracts in his new eleven-league grants to potential immigrants. Then, after taking in hand

$600 in a cash payment due from the Walkers and Wilkins, he set out once again.[18] Behind him there was almost nothing left to sell. Rezin would take $7,340 for parcels on the Red River and Bayou Black in June and July, and another $2,000 a year later, but even then the payments would come in installments, and one tract was encumbered with $1,990 in debt that James had never satisfied.[19] As for what cash he actually took with him when he left Natchez, Bowie may well have lost some of it in gambling on the way. He met Noah Smithwick somewhere in western Louisiana, where he was in virtual banishment after helping a friend escape from the San Felipe jail, and the gunsmith recalled that "Jim was prodigal with his money, though he was no gambler, and soon let his share slip away from him."[20] But James *was* a gambler, enough so that he was reputed to play faro in a tavern where the dealer was a known cheat, simply because it was the only game within fifty miles.[21] It would have been unlike him to hold on to much money for long.

As usual the road back to Texas took him up the Red River, through Alexandria of ill memory, and there he could note with grim satisfaction that the inhabitants were still killing one another, the most recent being the murder of a retired general during the recent election: "We are here now so effectually divided that society does not exist for any one except with those of his side," wrote a friend of Senator Johnston's. "The line of demarcation is traced with blood."[22] Quite happily James Bowie passed right on through to Natchitoches, and so on to the Sabine.

These long journeys could be lonely affairs. The only companion Bowie brought from Natchez was a twenty-five-year-old slave named Ned, on loan from his brother Stephen. Bowie had spent part of the money he had received on what Ham called "some fine stock" of china and porcelain, carpenter's tools, and more, that he hoped to sell at a tidy profit in San Antonio, and Ned would be of help with the pack animals.[23] As a result men like Bowie often struck acquaintances with other travelers and banded together for company and mutual protection. On this journey, however, two of his newfound companions almost brought him trouble. One was an itinerant preacher bound for Nacogdoches to pitch his tent and save souls. Rudeness, loud talk, and obscene banter during a church service was fairly common in the Southwest, and even more so out there.[24] Religion was not a man's business on that frontier. They left faith to the women and children, and a circuit preacher often found himself harassed and even threatened by the men.[25] When Bowie's companion reached his destination and held his first service, rowdies tried to break up the meeting by braying like asses and hooting like owls. Despite his own apparent indifference to religion, James Bowie was always faithful to a friend, even one of short acquaintance, and now he threatened to thrash any man who further disturbed the proceedings. The sight of his supreme self-confidence, remembered stories of the Sandbar, and the knife at his belt, were all that it needed to ensure silent worship.[26]

The other companion Bowie picked up along the way proved far more controversial. Col. Martin Parmer fought in the ill-fated Fredonian rebellion in 1826, in which he led a small group of men against Nacogdoches to arrest and try the town officials on charges of corruption. Soon thereafter he and others proclaimed the independent republic of Fredonia near Nacogdoches, but in January 1827 the appearance of Mexican troops put them to flight, and Parmer himself escaped to Louisiana. He was still under proscription by the Mexican authorities, but decided now to try to return. Parmer was the sort of adventurer who always appealed to Bowie, and whether by accident or previous acquaintance, they rode into Texas together. It was spring, and as they approached San Antonio they rode through prairies exploding in wildflowers, the bluebonnets and the brilliant orange- and persimmon-colored Indian paintbrush. But the new season brought no forgiveness for Parmer's transgressions of four years before. The *tejanos* and the Mexican authorities deeply resented him as the kind of troublemaker who attracted unwanted attention from Mexico City, and Bowie quickly discovered that by arriving in his company he jeopardized his own standing with the Veramendis and others. "Popular as Bowie was at that time with the Mexicans," his friend Frank Johnson noted, "he could not disabuse them of the jealousy and fears of Parmer." Parmer left to go back to Louisiana before he was arrested, and Bowie quickly set about mending fences.[27]

He could not afford to alienate anyone now that everything was coming together for him. Stopping in San Felipe in mid April, he met with Williams who gave him letters to take to the influential member of the Saltillo congress José Navarro, at Gonzales, probably recommendations for Bowie's mercantile ambitions or his eleven-league grant enterprise.[28] Now that he was a citizen, he also obtained on April 20 his grant of a league of land on the East Navidad, forty miles west of San Felipe, as a colonist under *empresario* Austin.[29]

And then in San Antonio there was Ursula. They appointed April 25 for the wedding, but first there was the matter of the prenuptial contract that Veramendi wanted. Bowie had probably been working over this in his mind for some time, deciding what to include, and just how to state his assets. On April 22 he appeared before acting *alcalde*, José Maria Salinas, and dictated easily the most unwittingly revealing document of his life. He stated that he was thirty-two now, shaving three years from his age, and offered to Ursula as his pledge in recognition of her "virtue, honesty and other laudable gifts," the sum of $15,000 to be drawn from "the most select of his estate or property" should he for any reason back out of the marriage before the vows were taken, or should they in future divorce. He then appended a virtual statement of net worth, starting with 60,000 arpents of land in Arkansas worth $30,000. Then there were the notes due him from the Walkers and Wilkins, one set totaling $45,000, and the other $20,000. Following this came $32,800 acknowledged as due him from the United States government, then $20,000 that he said he had left with McNeil in Natchez to buy the cotton mill machinery, and finally various unstated properties in Texas that he had bought or was buying, and which could not yet be estimated. Of course, none of this property or money was in Texas, since he had only just immigrated, so he pledged to redeem the contract in coin within two years after the marriage was consummated. Moreover, he gave his oath not to otherwise pledge, mortgage, attach, or spend those assets prior to paying the dowry. Then, almost as an afterthought, he appended to the statement another 15,000 arpents of land on the Red River and in Ouachita Parish, Louisiana, worth an estimated $15,000.[30]

On the face of it, James Bowie stated his fortune at $162,800, not counting his new Texas property. Yet at every turn he either lied or stretched the truth. The sixty thousand *arpents* in Arkansas were the forged claims, never his in the first place, shared equally with John if realized, and in any case virtually a dead issue by now, as he well knew. There were no assets there. The total of $65,000 due from the Walkers and Wilkins in notes may have been genuine, but given Bowie's other exaggerations in the document, they could just as easily have been greatly inflated, and were always subject to cancellation anyhow if or when Bowie's titles were rejected. The $32,800 due from the United States represented the $11,850 plus interest from Bowie's bogus Kemper–de la Français claim, with Isaac Thomas now out of the picture, but contrary to what he said, the government had never allowed the de la Français claim, the balance genuinely due to Kemper remained unappropriated, and in any case Bowie's title to it was fraudulent and worthless. As for the $20,000 left with McNeil, that may have been genuine, but since so much of the rest of the document was falsehood, this could just as easily be at best an exaggeration. And the 15,000 *arpents* on the Red River and in Ouachita were in fact land already covered in the February sales to the Walkers and Wilkins, and thus part of the $65,000 in notes due him. In short, he was listing the asset twice, once as real property, and again as a debt due him.

In fact James Bowie's real assets amounted to no more than some notes due from the Walkers and Wilkins, totaling something up to a possible $65,000, and whatever cash McNeil held for him. Almost half the total, at least $77,800, was a complete lie, money he knew he would never see, for property and claims that were forgeries and that he never owned. Two years later, when the dowry came due, there would scarcely be one dollar in this statement that he could call his own, especially after Walker discovered the problems with his titles. As for Bowie's promise not to mortgage or otherwise encumber this property, in fact some of the Arkansas and all of the Louisiana land had already been sold, while the de la Français claim may still have been half Thomas's. The document typified Bowie's aggressive and boastful manner, his confidence man's ability to oversell himself convincingly to others, and his stunning economy with the truth. Like the man himself, it was big, bold, and just over half dishonest.[31]

But the document achieved its goal with Veramendi. Three days later, on April 25, James and Ursula and her parents went into the San Fernando Parish Church, not far from the military plaza, and stood before Padré Refugio de la Garza. While Navarro and others looked on as witnesses, he made them man and wife.[32] The ceremony done, they moved at first to a rented house belonging to one Zambrano, dwelled there for two months, then moved again for another three months to a house rented from Señor Yturio. That fall they relocated again, this time to land given them by Veramendi near the Mission San José not far from town, and there they commenced housekeeping until the end of the year. Their furnishings were Ursula's, given her by her father, Bowie having none of his own.[33] One of their first visitors was Caiaphas Ham, who would virtually live with them from time to time, and before long they seemed to have established a comfortable and happy domestic life.[34]

Juana Navarro, Ursula's cousin and adopted sister, recalled the newly married Bowie as "a tall, well made gentleman, of a very serious countenance, of few words, always to the point, and a warm friend. In his family he was affectionate, kind, and so acted as to secure the love and confidence of all."[35] The Veramendis themselves lived a princely existence by San Antonio standards. Their one-story house on Soledad Street was a hollow square built around a central patio, well furnished, with paneled doors and a veranda. Being a leading merchant as well as a politician, Veramendi had plenty of money and enjoyed the best that could be had in Texas, and either for his daughter's sake or because Bowie's story of wealth and standing back in Louisiana had gained *his* confidence, Veramendi extended to him almost unlimited credit in money and supplies. "Bowie was treated like a son," the family friend Menchaca noticed. "His style of living was like a man who had plenty of money." The money was all Veramendi's. By the beginning of 1832 the Bowies simply moved in with the Veramendis on Soledad Street, there to remain.[36]

Menchaca would also note, with a note of veiled disapproval, that Bowie had "no regular occupation." Two months after his marriage Bowie did go to San Felipe, where he met recent immigrants Matthew Doyle, Thomas McCaslan, Daniel Baker, and a fellow named Mann. McCaslan, at least, was a mechanic whom Bowie had sent for to help with the cotton mill plan, and the others may have had a similar connection. He met them now by prior arrangement and assisted as they applied to the *ayuntamiento* for passports to go to Béxar. At the same time Bowie applied to Alcalde Frank Johnson for approval and paid the appropriate fees to sell the china and other goods he had brought.[37]

Thus at least he was making a start as a merchant, and showing some genuine intent on the textile factory, but within only a month the authorities in Béxar summoned him before them. He was suspected of engaging in contraband trade, meaning no doubt that he was selling goods on which he had not paid the required customs duties.[38] That, of course, only put Bowie in the mainstream of Texas merchants, most of whom still tried to get around the customs requirements, and all of whom harbored increasing resentment toward Mexico for imposing duties in the first place. This single incident, in what was probably no more than a passing mercantile enterprise in any case, would be James Bowie's first grievance against Mexico.

If the new Texian had not the temperament for industry, neither did he for trade. Both required too much time and effort for too small a return. Bowie always wanted the big transaction, quick and substantial wealth, and like so many who hunted for fortune, he could sometimes be gullible himself when gripped by the lure of riches. He never supposed that the 1829 trip to the San Saba would be his last. Perhaps he got stories from some of the friendly locals—or those who enjoyed misleading a white man—and perhaps he even saw one of the few spurious maps floating about the region, supposedly showing the mine's location.[39] Back in Louisiana he certainly told Rezin the stories he heard, what he had found and had not found, and before James returned to Texas to marry in 1831, the brothers probably agreed that Rezin would come west that fall and join him in another expedition. So strong was their inseparable bond from early childhood that despite the fact that Rezin had his own family and interests to look after, he would leave them for months when James called.[40] Besides, it was not hard for him to share the preoccupation with the mineral fortune that was ever on James's mind. "Bowie was occupied most of his time hunting for mines," said his friend Menchaca, "and mountains of gold or silver."[41]

Rezin arrived in Béxar late that fall, and joyful as the reunion must have been, it came at the price of bad news. The plantation continued to be a shambles. The steam machinery was worthless now, and the debt continued to mount. Rezin needed a bonanza even more than James did.[42] Affairs for brother Stephen got progressively worse. Creditors closed in on him. Arrested in Natchez in September, he had to give an oath of insolvency to be released, and even then one creditor filed a statement that, since Bowie did not reside in Mississippi, he could be expected to "leave the county . . . so as to prevent the recovery of the plaintiff's claim." He was arrested a second time on September 20, and once again discharged on the plea of bankruptcy. His only asset was land he owned next to James's new tract twenty miles below Thibodeauxville, and even on that he needed one thousand dollars to secure clear title from the seller. And there was also twelve thousand dollars that he said James still owed him, that and the slave Ned, and in a last act of fraternal disloyalty he had engaged an attorney to collect from his brother. The debt, if it ever existed, would never be repaid, and Stephen himself had disappeared.[43]

Then there was the news of Arkansas. The territorial supreme court reviewed the superior court's 1827 confirmation of the Bowie claims during its April 1830 term on a test case. One of the fictitious grants James and John created had been to a Bernardo Sampeyrac. Following the Arkansas superior court confirmation of the claims, John Bowie sold the Sampeyrac claim to Joseph Stewart, but now the United States attorney in Arkansas filed a bill charging that the confirmation of the claim was achieved "by fraud and surprise," moving to set aside the superior court's action in confirming the 117 Bowie claims. Further, the attorney charged that the original grant was a forgery, that Bernardo Sampeyrac was a fictitious person, and that the witnesses who testified to seeing him sell his claim to Bowie had perjured themselves. Since Sampeyrac could not be found, the court proceeded against him as an absent defendant, and since the innocent Stewart now assumed that he legally owned the property, he was made a codefendant, though the court granted that he had no part in or knowledge of the fraud. Finally on February 7, 1831, the court handed down its decree reversing and annulling the original decree in favor of the Sampeyrac claim. The innocent Stewart, faced with losing both his land and the money he had paid for it, filed an appeal to the next higher authority. It was now scheduled to be argued before the January 1833 term of the U.S. Supreme Court.[44]

Since no legal action was being threatened against James Bowie— only John's name actually appeared in any of the documents—he had nothing to fear personally from a Supreme Court decision, but it did mean that, whatever the finding, the Arkansas scheme was dead for good. No doubt he kept this virtual elimination of a significant chunk of his dowry assets concealed from Veramendi, especially since he had him interested again in another San Saba expedition, this time to be accompanied by Rezin. The combination of James's enthusiasm and bluff and Rezin's quiet intelligence must have persuaded the vice governor that they had as fair a chance of success as anyone.

Moreover, Caiaphas Ham had been living for the last five months among the Comanche near the San Saba country. When he first left, his friend Bowie urged him not to go, the Comanche being unpredictable, but in the end James helped Ham prepare for the trip, equipping him with trade goods and a packhorse, and sending him more supplies after a time. By late November, however, Bowie sent a message to Ham to return to Béxar as soon as possible. The always tenuous peace between Mexico and the Comanche was in danger of breaking down, and he feared Ham might lose his life if war erupted. An unspoken motive, which Ham spotted soon enough, was that Bowie also wanted him along on his own expedition thanks to what he had learned of the country.[45]

With Rezin and Ham as a nucleus, Bowie mustered his mechanics McCaslan and Doyle, who obviously were not in Monclova setting up any machinery, and for whom the professional pose may have been only a sham to secure them passports in spite of the tightening restrictions on immigration. Their goal may have been treasure hunting all along. Joining them were David Buchanan, Robert Armstrong, Jesse Wallace, James Coryell, and two servants named Charles and Gonzales. Bowie spoke with political chief Ramón Músquiz of his plan, and certainly there is no doubt of his goal, though when he reduced it to writing he couched it in euphemistic language, stating that he had received information "through different channels" inducing him to organize the expedition "expecting that some benefit might result therefrom both to the community and myself." Rezin was much more frank, as usual: They were bound, he said, "for the silver mines." On November 2, 1821, with the financial backing of Veramendi and his hearty endorsement, they rode out of San Antonio at first light, bound for the San Saba.[46]

They moved slowly northwest over one hundred miles for more than two weeks on a minor trail called the De la Bandera, until they crossed the Llano River. Beyond lay the San Saba Hills, and a few miles past the Llano on the morning of November 19 they met two

Comanche—one of them known to Ham—with a Mexican captive. Using the prisoner as an interpreter, they assured Bowie that they were friendly, and part of a party then driving horses stolen by another tribe back to San Antonio. Bowie gave them his own promise of friendship and that they would be welcomed in Béxar, and saw them on their way. But the next day at dawn, as his party ate their morning meal, the Mexican rode up to them in a lather. His captors had sent him, he said, to give them a warning. After leaving Bowie and the others, the Comanche continued south until they camped for the night, and just then a party of 124 Tawakoni, Waco, and Caddo came up with them and said they were on the Bowies' trail, intent on attacking and killing them to get their horses and equipment. The Comanche tried to talk them out of it, to no avail, and all the chief Isayune could do was to send the Mexican with the news. If Bowie's party could get to the Comanche, they would willingly help them defend themselves, but there were only sixteen of them, badly armed, and in any case the hostiles were now between them on the road. Isayune's only other advice was for the Bowies to push on hard to a brush-covered hill, where they could make a stand when attacked.

Always impulsive, James Bowie decided not to follow the chief's advice but to push on to the ruins of the fort on the San Saba instead. He would not be deterred from his goal by any number of marauders, and besides, the fort's walls offered better cover in an attack than chaparral. It was a hard twenty-five miles to the San Saba, the trace strewn with rocks that injured their animals' hooves, and when they reached the river they could not find the ruins of the fort, which lay some twelve miles away. Moreover, the ground around the river offered no good cover, so they pressed ahead another few miles on the other side until they came to a grove of thirty or forty mature live oaks that afforded some protection. It sat some forty yards east of a small stream, with another smaller grove of scrub oak fifty yards distant.[47] The Bowies decided to make camp there for the night, dividing themselves between the two clusters of trees so that each might protect the other in case of attack. As a further precaution they cleared a wide space around a nearby thicket, just to deny their pursuers cover in that quarter.

They passed a tense but undisturbed night, and the next morning, December 21, had just loaded the pack animals, and about 8 A.M.

mounted their horses to ride on in search of the old fort. But on gaining their saddles, the improved vantage from that height revealed to
them a lone Tawakoni following their tracks, not fifty yards from the
main grove. Behind him the rest of the band, well over one hundred
strong, followed, some 150 yards distant. The first of Bowie's party to
spy them yelled out "Indians," and immediately every man dismounted,
tied his animals fast to a tree, unloaded the packs, and readied his rifle.
Seeing the commotion in the trees, the pursuers let out a series of war
whoops, and themselves started to strip and prepare for battle, while at
least one mounted Caddo rode forward, brandishing a scalp.

The Bowie brothers may not have been acting with perfect accord
at this point, for Rezin and Buchanan walked to the smaller clump of
trees, which stood between the rest and the main war party. James
seemed not to know what his brother was about, but Rezin attempted
to speak to the Caddo, using either Spanish or some native dialect that
he hoped the Caddo would understand. He asked the man to send forward their leader, in order to talk. Instead, the Caddo and others
yelled back in a kind of mockery: "How de do?" and "How are you?"
Their evidence of concern proved somewhat less than sincere, since
their next action was to fire a volley of a dozen or more shots. All but
one of them missed, but that one broke Buchanan's leg, as Rezin emptied a pistol and a shotgun at them and then carried Buchanan back to
the small grove. In response to Rezin's fire, the rest of the attackers
withdrew a hundred yards or more to cover, obviously steeling themselves for a real assault, and in this lull James rushed over to Rezin and
urged them to rejoin the main party in the larger grove. As they hurried across, carrying the injured Buchanan, renewed sniping hit
Buchanan in two more places with slight wounds, while other bullets
clipped Rezin Bowie's hunting shirt, and then about eight of the
Tawakoni left their cover and came after them with tomahawks, only
to be stopped when covering fire from the main grove brought down
four of the attackers.

For perhaps five minutes James and Rezin caught their breath, while
they all hurried to reload their weapons. Then the whole party of
Indians came out of the cover of a small hill about sixty yards away
and rushed their position. Surely they would have been overrun but
for another stroke of that occasional but dramatic Bowie luck. Their

leader sat on horseback, unperturbed, the buffalo horns and other decoration on his head marking him as a chief. He moved at a walk as he rode along with his men, urging them to valor. James found his own rifle still empty. "Who is loaded?" he yelled. "I am," came a voice. It was Caiaphas Ham. Bowie told him to bring down the mounted man, and at once Ham fired. His aim was true. The bullet broke the chief's leg and killed his horse, and as he hobbled around on one leg, his rawhide shield raised before him, four of the prospectors finished reloading and sent out a volley that brought him down dead in an instant. When the rest of the war party saw him fall, a number of them rushed to carry him away, only to be shot down, and then more did the same, with like effect.

For fifteen minutes or more the skirmish raged, the attackers taking more casualties until they retreated to their hill and then began firing flights of arrows at the grove, along with occasional musket shots. About fifteen of them then advanced into yet another cluster of oaks along a creek some sixty yards northwest of the beleaguered explorers, and began a hard sniping fire that severely wounded Doyle in the chest and nicked Coryell. Soon a new leader appeared on horseback, and again James Bowie yelled to find who had a loaded rifle. No one answered, but then the mulatto servant Charles came running up to him carrying Buchanan's rifle. Bowie took it from him, fired, and brought down the rider, and once again the attackers suffered more casualties as they ran out and clustered around their fallen chief. But McCaslan also ran to his fallen comrade, yelling: "Where is the Indian that shot Doyle." Others screamed to him not to expose himself, that for the foemen on the creek to have hit Doyle they must have rifles rather than muskets. Just then McCaslan saw one of the Caddo arising from the ground, but as he raised his rifle to fire, the enemy moved quicker and shot him in the breast, killing him almost instantly. Armstrong lost his composure, shouted "damn the Indian that shot M'Caslan, where is he?" and then he, too, nearly lost his life when one suddenly appeared before him. He was lucky to escape with a bullet in his rifle stock.

By this time the balance of the war party had virtually encircled the oak grove where the Bowies, now reduced to ten including the servants, held out. From their cover behind rocks and bushes they poured a steady if ineffective fire in on the besieged Texians, and soon the whites decided that they were too exposed with only the trees to shelter them. They moved, under fire, to the nearby thicket, where they were better concealed, and where the clearing they had made the night before prevented any of the enemy from approaching unseen through the brush. To keep from being spotted by the puffs of smoke from their own muzzles, Bowie and the others immediately moved several paces away after firing, so that the enemy bullets whizzed harmlessly through the bushes. For another two hours, or until around 11 A.M. they continued to hold out, the warriors gaining nothing on them.

Finally on the western breeze the Bowies smelled smoke, then saw the black clouds and flames in the brush west of them. The enemy had decided to burn them out since they could not shoot them out of their hiding place. Once the blaze took hold, James heard them shouting war whoops behind the barrier of fire, apparently thinking to frighten the whites from their thicket as they advanced behind the wall of flames. The whites frantically scraped away the leaves and dry brush from around their pack animals and their wounded, to prevent the advancing fire from spreading through their position, but then the Bowie fortune held, and when the prairie-grass fire reached the creek and leaped across it, the blaze branched off north and south of their thicket but left them entirely untouched. Meanwhile Charles and Gonzales scrambled around their small perimeter piling rocks and boughs, and even their saddles and packs, into a rude breastwork. Being saved from fire once did not mean they would be again, so when the breastwork was done, the two servants went to work pulling up more dry grass inside the position, and piling rocks around the wounded to shield them from flames as well as arrows and bullets.

The attackers had withdrawn to their hill when they saw their first fire go out, and for several hours into the afternoon they kept up a desultory sniping that the Bowies and their companions answered as they could. Then around 4 P.M. the wind shifted, affording another opportunity to try to burn them out from a different direction, and a brave warrior stole out to the creek bed and started another prairie fire before Armstrong brought him down with his rifle. This time the fire looked as though it would burn them out in earnest. A wall of flames that Rezin thought reached ten feet high swept toward them, and they knew they could not stop it. As the Bowies saw it approach, they expected the Tawakoni and their confederates to attack, and seeing no prospect of escape, they huddled their band together and concluded that the best thing they could do was to stand in a tight circle around the wounded, place their backs together, and fire a single volley when attacked, then draw their knives and defend themselves as long as they could. Once more that sheath at Big Jim Bowie's belt might hold his life in its grip. If the foe did not attack them, though, they decided to stand as every man for himself until the flames reached their breastwork, and then they would turn all their effort to trying to put out the flames.

Fortunately the warriors seemed content merely to continue their sniping, and at the same time sent parties in under cover of the fire and smoke to collect their dead and wounded. Then the blaze actually reached the Bowie party. They all frantically pulled up the grass at their feet and used their blankets and bearskins and buffalo robes to beat out the flames. They managed to save most of their packs, but a few animals panicked and broke their tethers, running off into the prairie. They had survived the fire, but it brought down most of the brush that had been their cover, so now they all huddled within the rock breastwork and started building it even higher, using their knives to pry up more stones and even dirt. None had time to look at a pocket watch, but by the setting of the sun James knew it had to be well past 6 P.M. They had been fighting sporadically now for more than ten hours, and were exhausted, their eyes burning from the smoke, their throats parched by the heat of the fire and the tension of their perilous situation. Every one of them felt great relief when they saw the attackers withdraw some distance to camp for the night, obviously abandoning any intention of a further assault that evening. At least that gave them time to continue strengthening their defense, while one or two went out to the creek to fill their water skins. A lone rifle fired at the water party was the only hostile shot that evening, and well into the night the Bowies listened instead to the mournful wailing of the warriors as they sang over their dead. About midnight James heard a single shot in the enemy camp but did not know its meaning. Rezin surmised that, as was supposedly their custom, they were ending the misery of one of their mortally wounded.[48]

That evening the Bowies actually planned to attack the Indians in their sleep, thinking that pluck and surprise might overcome the disparity in numbers, but when James looked about and saw only six of them sufficiently fit to fight, and that they would have to leave the wounded completely defenseless, he abandoned the idea, and wisely. They took turns at guard during the night, and when Ham stood his watch he saw one of the panicked pack mules wander back to the camp, and he quickly grabbed and tethered it. Then, an hour or two before daylight, he heard sounds of movement off toward the enemy's camp and immediately woke the rest of his friends. They grabbed their rifles and took their places, each expecting a night attack that probably would be an end to them. What they heard, in fact, was the attackers leaving. They had given up the fight, not uncommon when casualties began to make any gains too costly.

Sometime after 8 A.M. two of the whites carefully walked out to where the hostiles had been camped and found the site abandoned. Though a dozen of the Tawakoni or their allies showed themselves a few hours later, they simply withdrew out of sight. Incredibly, it seemed that the Bowies had beaten them. By counting the bloody spots on the grass, they estimated that they had killed about forty and wounded another thirty, a count that was probably somewhat exaggerated. Their own losses were McCaslan killed and Buchanan, Coryell, and Doyle wounded, as well as five of their animals killed. But in fact, not a man among them failed to be touched by an enemy ball or arrow, and some of them bore several superficial wounds, as did other horses and mules. With a certainty, James Bowie knew they were in no condition to try to retrace their steps to Béxar, not knowing where or how many of their foes might be lurking along the trace. Instead they decided to stay put, better fortify their rock breastwork, and hope for help. With a typical show of bold defiance, James Bowie erected a slim pole and actually flew a small flag from its top "to intimidate them and show them that there were still men ready for a fight." Only James Bowie could think of six men intimidating a hundred.

There for the next eight days the Bowies and their friends stayed in their fort, sallying out only for water and keeping up a steady rifle fire at intervals in hopes of attracting the attention of any friendly Comanche within hearing. By the evening of November 29 they had seen no one. James personally attended to the wounded, and by this time they felt better and in a condition to move, and the injured animals could walk once more, so they decided it was time to try reaching safety. They rode all that night and into the following afternoon, until they stopped and fortified another likely spot, and halted for two days to rest and recuperate. Buchanan's broken leg by now showed signs of severe infection and possible gangrene, but all they could do for him was to boil some tree bark, thicken the brew with charcoal and ground meal, and stuff a buffalo skin with the poultice and tie it around his leg.

They traveled on for several more days. By the time they reached the Pedernales River, still sixty miles from San Antonio, they saw dramatic signs of recent Tawakoni activity, and a column of smoke on the river in the distance. That was enough to persuade Bowie to turn away from the trace that provided the most direct route, and instead to swing out to the west. Thereafter they saw no more hostiles. Buchanan's leg showed a dramatic improvement when, after five days, they removed the poultice, and finally on the night of December 6 came the best news of all: In the distance they saw the glimmering lights of San Antonio. Exhausted, most of them walked into the town, leading their weary animals. When someone recognized Bowie or one of the others, he sent up a shout that soon spread from house to house and street to street. Quickly men rushed to the returning prospectors and grasped their hands or hugged them joyfully. Before long Bowie learned that the Comanche they had met on their way to the San Saba had come into Béxar and reported his party attacked and almost surely killed. Lights went up in houses all along the way as shouts of "Bowie's party have returned" carried the news.

Of course it must have been a special homecoming for James, just like Crockett's after his reported death during his first bout with malaria. Ursula and the Veramendis would have heard the rumors of his death. Her anguish, believing herself a widow after only seven months as a bride, must have been wrenching, a sorrow shared by others. Stephen Bowie reached San Antonio after the expedition left, probably intending to join his brothers, but just as likely hoping to make a new start here after his disaster in Louisiana. It was pointless to go after them, not knowing the way, and then when he heard the Comanche's story of James's and Rezin's deaths, he began trying to raise a company of men to go after the Tawakoni to wreak revenge.[49]

Thus when Stephen and Ursula heard the shouts, or saw him walk through the door, the house on Soledad Street must have echoed mingled cries of gladness and relief.

James Bowie had been bold, as usual, and awfully fortunate, as usual. Certainly he had nothing to show for the ordeal. He did not find the mine (which of course was not there to be found in any case) and he lost McCaslan, the foreman of his mechanics. That was bound to set back the cotton mill establishment, and the sustained hardship cannot have helped with his old Sandbar wounds, which Ham saw continued to trouble him from time to time. Yet the party had done something that inevitably won the admiration of a frontier people. They had met an aboriginal foe that grossly outnumbered them, yet had killed several dozen—in true frontier fashion the figure steadily rose in the retelling—and wounded many more. Of course, sustained battle on an organized basis was not the Indians' way. The Tawakoni and their friends fought the kind of battle they usually fought, and when it showed signs of becoming too costly for too little gain, they simply walked away from it, as was their custom. But so far as the Bowies and the *bexareños* were concerned, a party of less than a dozen Americans had defeated odds greater than 10 to 1.

"The pages of history record few such achievements," Ham himself boasted of the San Saba fight. "It stands almost alone upon the scenic walls of Fame's grand temple. The valorous men who bared their breasts to the assaults of a savage enemy, in overwhelming numbers, who fought without fear and without hope, and rolled back the tide of barbaric aggression, should be remembered and honored as long as civilization endures, and gratitude has a place in the human heart." To Ham, as to others, an isolated frontier skirmish became suddenly a milestone victory in the age-old fight against the tide of barbarism. The Bowies and their friends had not just saved themselves, they had seemingly helped to save Texas from some unstated menace. Men forgot the fact that James and the others had gone silver prospecting solely for their own benefit. Somehow Western civilization now owed them gratitude for their selfless stand. It was the way that frontier myths were created.

More important for James Bowie, it was the kind of episode that turned people into living legends, and thus he made some profit by the expedition after all. Until now he had been Veramendi's son-in-law, a big-talking *norteamericano* who lived high and had the land hunger and promised much, and about whom there clung some vague stories of dark dealings and a vicious fight east of the Sabine. The San Saba battle transformed him in the eyes of *tejanos* and Texians alike into a leader of men, someone to look up to and count on in a moment of peril. So far as his future in Texas was concerned, and as pointless in its origins as it may have been preordained in its conclusion, the San Saba scrape made James Bowie.

CROCKETT

1831–1834

Well!—they came to see a bar, and they've seen one—hope they like the per-formance—it did not cost them any thing any how.

DAVID CROCKETT, 1834

"The people of my district were induced to take a stay on me," said Crockett, using quaint gamblers' slang for deciding not to risk a bet, but he said it two years after his 1831 defeat.[1] At the time, though the voters merely decided to keep Crockett in Tennessee for awhile, so far as he was concerned he had been sent to Coventry, and it rankled and festered within him long after the fact of having been beaten sank in. Only in Congress had he been someone of importance. People there paid attention to him and treated him as a man to reckon with, even if many regarded him with hostility. He could even feel flattered at the extraordinary efforts from outside his district to see Fitzgerald win. In election there was more than public victory: It gave him repudiation of that part of himself that he never liked, the humble, ignorant, impoverished failure from the canebrakes. More than anything he hoped to do for his fellow West Tennesseans, Crockett needed victory for himself.

Before in his life when fate defeated him, he moved away from the bitter memory, whether it was after a failed farm or a flooded mill. Crockett may well have thought of leaving Tennessee in the wake of this defeat, so much worse than those other losses because of the humiliation and resentment he no doubt felt at every encounter with one of the voters. This had been no rejection by nature, but by his people. There was no malice or pity or triumph in nature, but Crockett could imagine these feelings in the faces of his constituents. It must have been very difficult for a time for him to face them. Perhaps the tears that came so readily to the ruddy-cheeked boy came again to the forty-five-year-old man.

If Crockett did think of abandoning West Tennessee, he soon found that he could not. "An election costs a man a great deal in my Country," he told friends, and at the end of his campaign he was once more heavily in debt.[2] He had borrowed everywhere he could, including from the Bank of the United States, whose Whig managers were only too happy to help him with his campaign, but now he could not repay his loan and had to ask for an extension, reminding the managers that during his canvass he came out in support of renewal of their charter, and promising to vote on their behalf if he won back his seat in 1833. In the end Nicholas Biddle simply canceled the note.[3] If a Jacksonian had taken such a loan and made such promises, Crockett would have seen it as evidence of corruption. If the government had no business using public funds for the private relief of individuals, then surely the government-chartered bank had no business writing off loans that came out of the interest the government allowed it to charge. It simply never occurred to him that he could be doing anything unethical.

"Times is hard in this country," he told his bank friends. "I will do the best I can."[4] Sadly, his best would not get him out of debt. Cajoling from a friend a very favorable six-year lease with option to buy on another property on the south fork of the Obion, he moved to the lease tract in January 1832 and began to clear twenty acres there to live on, build a small cabin and smokehouse and cribs for his corn, and plant a small orchard.[5] He would stay there for the next two years, trying to build that home and rebuild his personal fortunes, without success. If she ever moved there with him, Elizabeth soon departed again. She had endured enough of Crockett, and moved with the children to Gibson County to live with her Patton family. Relations with David remained amicable but distant. Perhaps it seemed fitting. His constituents had abandoned him, and now so had his wife.[6]

Crockett himself passed the next eighteen months largely in seclusion, scarcely seen or heard, and leaving almost no trace of his comings and goings. No doubt he went back to the long hunt, as much from necessity as to find anew that personal victory in the killing that evaded him on the stump. He saw a few friends, of course, including the equally impoverished young Ben McCulloch, who lived in Dyersburg.[7] Sometime in 1832 he also managed a trip east to Washington and Philadelphia. After four years as a congressman, enjoying the bustle and excitement of the cities, he simply could not sit and stagnate on a hard-scrabble patch on the Obion. Besides, he needed to deal with his friends at the bank, to discuss both his past loans and possible future notes to finance his 1833 campaign. He would need Whig support to help counter all that the Jacksonians would throw at him, and this trip afforded an opportunity to enlist such assistance, which the Whigs would be only too willing to offer, for their benefit more than his. Either on his way to or from the East, he joined Matthew St. Clair Clarke for some of the journey, regaling him at length with stories of his life in the backwoods and on his hunts. Clarke very likely pumped Crockett consciously for recollections, and it is quite possible that the two came to an understanding of how that information was to be used.[8]

Soon enough the spring of 1833 arrived, and with it the anticipation of another canvass. Crockett did not wait to be importuned to seek election: It had been his determination since the day of his defeat in August 1831. Fitzgerald was his opponent, of course, but by a mutual pact both candidates agreed to conduct the campaign on a higher plane than last time.[9] When David took the stump he tried to address the questions facing Congress in the next term—and much had happened in his time out of office. The rift between Jackson and former Vice-President John C. Calhoun grew ever greater, especially over the tariff, and when Jackson reneged on earlier promises and supported a permanent tariff that seemed unfavorable to the agrarian South, Calhoun's South Carolina met in a state convention that proclaimed a policy of nullification. They asserted that the Union was a compact of sovereign states, and that any state could nullify the acts of president and Congress within its own borders. Jackson denounced nullification as anarchy and disunion and threatened force to impose the rule of federal law everywhere. Compromise at the winter 1833 session of Congress averted outright crisis at the last minute, but the whole issue remained hot in the minds of the people.

Then there was the Bank of the United States. Jackson never liked the bank, thanks largely to its perceived Whig leanings, and his own prejudice against anything savoring of monopoly, which the government charter of the bank certainly implied. Biddle unwisely allowed the bank's recharter to become an issue in the 1832 election. Even though Congress passed the recharter, Jackson successfully vetoed the measure, and then when he defeated Henry Clay and won a second term, the bank's unqualified support of Clay doomed it forever. By July 1833, even as Crockett and Fitzgerald stumped the district, it became known that Jackson intended to bleed the bank dry by removing the government's deposits to meet operating expenses, and instead of replenishing them to place deposits in selected state banks. He would kill the bank even before its charter expired in 1836.

And, of course, for Crockett himself, Andrew Jackson was a campaign issue, and everything that had happened in his time out of office only further convinced him that Old Hickory had become a tyrant, abetted now by having Van Buren as vice-president, obviously the hand-chosen successor. On the stump now Crockett spoke out strongly for rechartering the bank and holding onto its deposits. Speaking at Brownsville, Crockett accused Jackson of seeking to close the bank in order to take control of the deposits himself to use for the purpose of ensuring Van Buren's succession.[10] Should they be a nation of laws "or have a despot," he asked them. As he later put it himself, his constituents told him to "go ahead, Crockett."[11]

Predictably the Fitzgerald forces once more sought to ridicule Crockett for his ignorance, but he had no problem with that question. "It is objected to me that I want learning. Look to your President. Look to your President I say. What does he know." Harking back to the "blab" school lessons he learned, he boasted that "I will spell with him all the way from AB—ab up to Crucifix and beat him at that." The reference to the cross suggested that Crockett still associated his defeat in 1831 with martyrdom.

There was another reason for his reference to the Crucifixion. Wisely his opponents did not play the bumpkin card too strongly this time. Paulding's *The Lion of the West* was an enormous success wherever it played now, and the public appetite for the backwoodsman only grew. Calling attention to Crockett in that idiom would only help him. Instead the Democrats engaged Adam Huntsman to attack Crockett with a biblical satire called *The Book of Chronicles, West of the Tennessee and East of the Mississippi Rivers*. The pamphlet appeared in the district in June and was extensively distributed. Huntsman, known locally as Blackhawk, burlesqued Crockett as a would-be savior of the poor whites of the district. "And it came to pass in those days when Andrew was chief Ruler over the Children of Columbia, that there arose a mighty man in the river country, whose name was David," and so it went. Huntsman accused Crockett of falling into the clutches of Clay, Adams, and Daniel Webster, and making a bargain with them that he would join them if they supported his land bill.[12] The vehicle and satire were crude but made an effective point, and Crockett himself saw no humor in it. He thought Huntsman unprincipled for writing such a document, and suspected that his motive was to achieve notoriety in order to run against Crockett himself in 1835. "I have no confidence in him," said David.[13]

If the Jacksonians knew that the Nimrod Wildfire weapon was a weak one in their hands, there is no doubt that Crockett recognized it for all its power and used it to the full. Paulding had followed *The Lion of the West* with a novel in 1832 called *Westward Ho!*, once again populated with colorful frontier characters, one of whom echoed Crockett's own growing trademark when he said: "I do just what I think right." Crockett now used the phrase liberally himself, though typically it varied before he found its final form. Daniel Webster, whom Crockett certainly knew and might well have met in Washington the year before, said that Crockett told him that his watch phrase was "*If for the right*, go a-head."[14] By the end of the year he refined it to its permanent form, "Be always sure you're right—THEN GO AHEAD."[15]

Crockett's recognition of the potential of exploiting his frontiersman image was further confirmed by what had been appearing in the press around the nation, and of which he could not be entirely unaware. As far away as New York's spas at Saratoga Springs, visitors that summer read stories in their newspapers, not about this campaign but tales of "the notorious Davy Crockett."[16] The reason those tales were there was the next step in the progression of the literary exploitation of the Crockett idiom. In January 1833 a new book came from the presses, *Life and Adventures of Colonel David Crockett of West Tennessee.* The book made an immediate hit, sold out rapidly, and appeared the same year in another edition titled *Sketches and Eccentricities of Colonel David Crockett of West Tennessee.* No author's name appeared on the book, but Matthew St. Clair Clarke almost certainly wrote it, and was probably even composing it at the time of his travels with Crockett, and possibly without Crockett's knowledge.[17]

The appearance of Clarke's book was enormously propitious timing for Crockett, and given his Whig connections, Clarke may have meant it to be so. His close relationship to Biddle certainly afforded both a motive, and even raised the possibility that Biddle paid Clarke to write it, since the actual royalties went to someone else.[18] While it contained much of truth that he could only have gotten firsthand from Crockett himself, the book contained as much of Jeremiah Kentucky and Nimrod Wildfire. It employed every cliché of the frontiersman, and then took the backwoods vernacular already so closely associated with Crockett and exaggerated it even more into something so ignorant and ungrammatical that Crockett himself was angered at the caricature. "I'm that same David Crockett, fresh from the back-woods," it pro-claimed, and then added the by-now-obligatory "Half-horse, half-alli-gator, a little touched with snapping turtle." In places it did little more than lift phrases from *The Lion of the West* and combine all manner of frontier stories to present them as though lived or told by Crockett. Clarke even included the notion that Crockett could "grin" wild crea-tures into giving themselves up to him without being shot, or that he once funded a campaign party by selling the same coon skin to a tav-ern keeper over and over again without being caught.[19]

That buffoon image was one that Crockett struggled in his personal life to avoid. He wanted to be a gentleman. Yet he could not help but realize how potent the Clarke book's popularity was in his favor. Then, too, it may have upset him that someone was making money from his life story—or a parody of it—when it had been *his* life and *he* needed the money.[20] But as he traveled the stump during this canvass he encountered time and time again people who had read the book, or seen extracts from it in the newspapers, or merely heard about it. Moreover, when he told them repeatedly that he had nothing to do with the book and that it was full of fiction, they invariably suggested that he should write his own story. It would set matters straight. Better yet, they would buy it to read.[21] That got his attention.

So did the newspaper letters of Maj. Jack Downing. Seba Smith, a New Englander, recognized the literary potential of the new common man and tried to stretch the definitions of the idiom by inventing a bumpkinish Maine character who wrote letters to the editors commenting on current political topics. He was, said Smith, "a green, unsophisticated lad from the country," who happened to blunder into the legislature.[22] Like Crockett, Smith was a Jacksonian in the midst of shifting allegiance, though Crockett was considerably ahead of him in his move to the Whigs. By the time of this campaign, the Jack Downing letters had appeared throughout the nation's press, and despite his speaking in a Down East vernacular, people still associated him with the Crockett of the Clarke *Life*, and both of them with the living Crockett. Seba Smith may even have been influenced by Crockett in his writing, for in Downing's August 4, 1833, letter commenting on Jackson and the bank question—a letter that appeared in the same issue of *Atkinson's Saturday Evening Post* with an account of the San Saba fight by Rezin Bowie— Downing very pointedly used the expression "go ahead," putting it in quotation marks to signify not only that it was borrowed but also that it was coming to be an Americanism.[23]

Unwittingly, all this literary output, and the public celebrity it gave to Crockett (or characters seen to be based on Crockett), worked to his advantage. He needed the help, for the Jackson-dominated legislature even engaged in a sort of passive gerrymandering to help in his defeat. Prior to the election it planned to divide his enormous district in two, the Twelfth and Thirteenth Congressional Districts, with Crockett running in the former, where he lived. But as originally intended, Madison County—the one that ensured his defeat in 1831—would have gone into the Thirteenth. Now, to try to defeat him again, the legislature attached Madison to the Twelfth. "It was done to make a mash of me," he complained, pointing out that the resultant redistricting produced a bizarre Thirteenth District that almost encircled the Twelfth. He used the obvious electioneering trick to good advantage in campaigning against Fitzgerald, who he believed lay behind the plan, and told the voters not to let themselves be shifted around like hogs and horses.[24]

It all worked. On election day in August, Crockett narrowly squeaked past his opponent by 3,985 to 3,812. Gleefully he sent a friend the sparsest of victory announcements: "Dear Sir—Went through—tight squeezing—beat Fitz 170.—Yours, D.C."[25] His actual margin was 173 rather than 170, but the import of the message remained the same, and it was not lost on the Jacksonians. Polk's friend Clement Clay of Alabama heard the news and sent a condolence to Polk over the victory of "the notorious Davy Crockett."[26]

The Whigs felt even more pleased than the Jacksonians did chagrined. In a half-admiring, half-condescending quip a few years later, an English editor remarked that "Democracy and the 'farwest' made Colonel Crockett: he is a product of forests, freedom, universal suffrage, and bear-hunts."[27] He was right. All that popularity of Crockett and his distorted image on the stage, in books, and the press coincided precisely with the burgeoning power of the common voter. In this election every state but one finally countenanced universal white male suffrage, and the more common the voter—and the more there were of his kind—the more electable became the real David Crockett. The Whigs learned the lesson the moment they heard of his election. Suddenly one of their major national journals, *Nile's Weekly Register*, published in Baltimore, began to sing his praises. Crockett, said its editor, was "just such a one as you would desire to meet with, if any accident or misfortune had happened to you on the high way." There was the Robin Hood aspect of the Trickster—the honest, dependable, strong, brave, and gallant defender. As for Crockett the statesman, *Nile's* asserted boldly that when he gave his vote in Congress, "whether right or wrong, *the vote is his own*."[28] Seba Smith authored a special letter after Crockett's election, addressed to him, and inviting him to come to Washington to observe Congress as Major Downing observed his state legislature.[29]

This attention from the Whig press and writers may have had a special motive. Sensing the sudden dramatic power of the frontier hero in politics, they felt all the more the want of anyone in their own ranks who could capitalize on the enthusiasm. A party still led by the privileged and the affluent, and primarily serving a like constituency, it had no "common men" that could be groomed to resist Van Buren for the presidency in the coming 1836 election. Yet that was exactly the time they would most need such a candidate, for in the eyes of much of the nation, "Little Van" looked and acted more like a Whig, well-to-do, professional, educated, and cunning. He utterly lacked any of the common-man antecedents of his sponsor Old Hickory.

Ironically, then, the best way to beat Van Buren would be to find someone like Jackson to run against him, to turn the tables and pit a

Whig common man against a Democratic candidate of the eastern establishment. Henry Clay was no spent force, but he no more fitted the image needed than did Webster or Adams. Since the Whigs would use onetime Jacksonian stereotypes against the Jacksonians in 1836, why not use one of their own disaffected men against them in the process? That being considered, only one man fitted the bill, and to stunning perfection. For perhaps the first time in U.S, history, the popular media had created a genuine celebrity. By giving Crockett attention far beyond the significance of one distant Tennessee district, and completely out of proportion with his utter failure to date as a congressman, that same attention gave its object a potential power of unfathomed depth. The longer Clarke's book sold, the more performances of *The Lion of the West* that toured the country, the more letters Maj. Jack Downing wrote, the greater that power must become. And now, bathed in the light of the focus of public gaze, every move the real David Crockett made, however trivial, would only increase public awareness and provide ever more fuel for the scribblers molding public opinion and interest. Suddenly, out of the chance juxtaposition of the man and the times, the real Crockett stood in danger of being swallowed by the jaws of his own folk image.[30]

That was the kind of power that could make a president. The frontier dragon slayer must be a western man, for the stereotype so demanded. Kentucky could offer only Clay, clearly an impossible fit, and none of the other states then comprising the West and the Old Southwest—Alabama, Mississippi, Louisiana, and Missouri—had any Whig favorite sons with national appeal. But they could do what the other western state could not. The Whigs in Tennessee were simply too weak and cowed by the Jackson machine to expect anything but ridicule if they tried to propose their favorite son as a potential 1836 nominee. However, neighboring Mississippi could do it for them, and within a few months of his election Crockett received an inquiry from a state convention asking if he would be willing to allow them to put his name forward as a possible candidate.[31] There was a dramatic turnaround in the very best American tradition—a downcast failure in a rude log cabin in West Tennessee that summer, and a candidate touted for the presidency in the fall.[32]

Crockett may not have taken the presidential business all that seriously. After all, the election would not come for another three years, and he of all people knew how a man's fortunes could change in that time. Still, the contact made an impression on him and at least planted the idea of higher office in his mind. It gave him the taste of possibility, and with it the ultimate revenge against Jackson and even more the hated Van Buren. More than that, it would make him incontestably a gentleman, and above everything else, a success.

Crockett must have champed to get to the capital to start the new term. The euphoria over his win, the approach of the Mississippi convention, that fact that his favorite son John was himself successful now as a court clerk and teacher at a local academy—all seemed to signal a complete reversal of his fortunes.[33] There were still the inevitable debts, however, including one to the bank that he could not settle.[34] But in the back of his mind Crockett already had the solution to that problem developing, a solution that could as well advance his fortunes in ways not at all financial. He may have started work on the project right after his election, or could have been working out its details as he traveled east. In either case, by the time the first session commenced on December 2, 1833, and Crockett took his seat for the opening, he stood ready to get started. He was going to write his own memoirs.

Constituents had suggested the idea to him again and again during the canvass. He resented the farcical caricature of the Clarke *Life*, and grew weary of meeting people for the first time to find them amazed, as he put it, "at finding me in human shape, and with the *countenance, appearance,* and *common feelings* of a human being."[35] Moreover, by the time Clarke's *Life* came out again as *Sketches*, Crockett fully realized the income someone else was making on his story. "Justice demands of me to make a statement of facts to the american people," he told a friend. "I consider no man on earth able to give a true history of my life."[36] Being largely the beneficiary of a false image, he wanted now to straighten the mirror, to give a truer reflection of himself. Crockett arrived in Washington a week before the first gavel, and may have been surprised to find that even people who knew him seemed not to recognize him. On the Capitol steps he encountered John Quincy

Adams, now a representative like himself, and he had to identify himself to Adams before the ex-president knew who he was, even though Crockett had dined at his table in the White House but a few years before. When Adams congratulated him on his election, Crockett revealed just how much he appreciated the power of public information and opinion. His first call had been on Joseph Gales, urging him to announce his arrival in the city, and to publicize his address at Mrs. Ball's. Moreover, Crockett told Adams that he was going to share his rooms now with "Major Jack Downing, the only person in whom he had any confidence for information of what the Government was doing."[37] Within only a few days, Crockett went to the Washington Theater to see *The Lion of the West* for himself, with Hackett as Nimrod Wildfire, and when the audience learned that he was present, Crockett stood for a bow and applause alongside the actor.[38] The influence of the Downing letters that he was reading, and the presentation of Paulding's play, was powerful. Moreover, while Crockett rejected the Clarke book's caricature, he openly chose to associate himself with Nimrod Wildfire by accepting bows with Hackett. Wildfire was eccentric, to be sure, but he stopped short of lampoon, and the audience's reaction to the character was not lost on David.

He took all this back to his rooms with him as he worked on his memoir. People who called on him in Washington that season found a man who "rarely, if ever, exhibited either in conversation or manner, attributes of coarseness of character that prevailing popular opinion very unjustly assigned to him," said the noted painter John Chapman. "There was an earnestness of truth in his narrations of events, and circumstances of his adventurous life, that made it obvious," Chapman continued, "and with all gentle and sympathetic play of features, telegraphing, as it were, directly from the true heart, overflowing with kind feeling and impulse, irresistibly dispelled suspicion of insincerity and braggartism."[39] But that was not the Crockett that the public wanted, and so he consciously decided to caricature himself just enough to suit popular taste, without offending his own. He would exaggerate his stories somewhat, use understatement and in some cases even fabrications and omissions, to mold his own image.

The appeal of the vernacular in the Downing letters impressed him with the need to consider the style of his writing as well as his substance, and he already had an impetus to try a hand at that kind of writing when Smith addressed that Downing letter to him after his election. Crockett had actually written a reply for the press in which he agreed to publish his observations on Washington, and moreover said he would write them in dialect to give them an appearance of "authenticity," as he put it, though Crockett had gone on to joke that, of course, a backwoods vernacular was foreign to him.[40]

Nothing could have been more distant from the truth. In breaking down the old social distinctions, observed Tocqueville, "the continual restlessness of a democracy leads to endless change of language as of all else." New words came into usage and old ones went out. "Democracies like movement for its own sake," he believed, and that went for language as well as politics. "Even when there is no need to change words, they do so because they want to." They used words indiscriminately. "The rules of style are almost destroyed," the Frenchman saw, but though he would have abhorred such chaos in his own language, he saw it as rather charming in America. "Hardly any expressions seem, by their nature, vulgar, and hardly any seem refined." Writing at the same time that Crockett began his composition, Tocqueville could have been describing the Tennessean himself when he went on to say that "individuals from different strata of society have brought along with them, to whatever station they may have risen, the expressions and phrases they were accustomed to use; the origin of words is as much forgotten as that of men, and language is in as much confusion as society."[41]

Crockett had to be blind and deaf not to grasp the appeal of that sort of style. Almanacs, dramas, newspapers, traveling performers—all exploded into this new idiom by now. Anxious for their own distinctive characters and literature, American writers and readers wanted their own language as well. Having no native tongue, they turned American English into something new by their spellings, which represented backwoods pronunciation and idioms. Already publishers issued glossaries of "Americanisms," virtual dictionaries of American English.[42]

Crockett had a few other aids as he contemplated his task. One of the books he owned was Franklin's *Autobiography*.[43] Of course Franklin wrote without dialect, but in his story of a poor boy making good through humility, hard work, ingenuity, and honesty, Crockett could see a framework for his own book. If he needed help with the actual composition, his friend Thomas Chilton lived at Mrs. Ball's as well, and he was an experienced writer. The effect of the whole enterprise should be to present himself as he thought the public ought to see him, "as I really am, *a plain, blunt, Western man*, relying on honesty and the woods, and not on learning and law, for a living."[44] But already he was a bit disingenuous, for Crockett intended the work to be a commercial success and thus shaped himself to suit the popular appetite. For a man whose image rested heavily on the notion of his ignorance, David Crockett proposed to undertake a truly intimidating task. Having decided that he wanted to do it, however, he had to "go ahead."

He worked steadily at his desk, and by early January 1834 was already well into the book. He expected to finish by the first week of February, promising friends a book that would be "just like myself, a plain and singular production." He also believed it would be amusing, but most of all he knew it would sell. That, and repudiating the Clarke *Life*, occupied his mind uppermost. "I am poor," he wrote a friend, "with a large family; and as the world seem anxious for the work, I know they would want me to have the profits of it." He sent letters, some written for him by Chilton, to several cities to solicit interest from publishers for the copyright to the book, asking friends to "get your book-sellers and book-printers to send me their propositions." By January 9 he already had several on his desk, but wisely he shopped around for the best offer.[45]

The work went quickly, though Crockett found himself busy enough with the affairs of the House. Still, he could miss a session from time to time, and must have worked many a long evening with his pen. He seemed preoccupied with the book's length, at first wanting it to run to 150 published pages, and then changing his mind and striving for 200 or more. The actual story he confined to little more than fifty thousand words, but still, unpracticed as he was at narrative writing, he must have taken two full months to complete the task, meaning he might have started as soon as he reached Washington. Throughout the writing he kept friends informed of his progress, expressing the hope that his book "may be of little prophit to me." Once he started, he found that it went faster than expected, and moreover that he felt some natural flair for the work, with the result that by mid-January he revised his deadline and expected to finish in another ten days.[46]

When done with the manuscript, Crockett may not have realized exactly what he had achieved. To be sure, he had told his story. Pretending not to understand why the public so wanted to know about his life, he set about casting himself as almost the perfect delineation of the people's notion of the western common man. He grew out of poverty thanks to some inner strength of character that had nothing to do with the wealth and position of the East. He dwelled on his youthful hardship and determination, on overcoming one obstacle after another. He gave a third of the book to his life before the Creek War, presenting an unending portrait of confrontation with adversity. Another fourth of the book described the war itself, for the frontiersman had to be a military man, and there more than anywhere else he bent the truth. He said nothing about having risen above the rank of private. The common man should not be an officer, even in the non-commissioned ranks. He included fabricated accounts of the Battles of Emuckfau Creek and Enotachopco Creek, and said he missed the climactic Battle of Horseshoe Bend while on furlough, when in fact he missed them all when he was between his two enlistments, for the yeoman volunteer must not be safely at home when his fellows met the foe in action. In describing the mutiny of some volunteers that Jackson put down, Crockett included himself among the mutineers, even though he was home at the time. Yet it served his purpose to show himself standing up against Old Hickory even in youth.

Another third of the book he gave over mainly to his long hunts and adventures between the war and his first election to Congress. But then his entire service of two terms in the House of Representatives received only one long paragraph, and not surprisingly since he had nothing to show for it and had achieved nothing for his constituents. The less said about his inept land bill management the better. Instead he simply presented himself in the pose he liked best, the lone warrior standing up against the evil combinations of Jackson and his henchmen. He finished writing on January 28 with a brief account of his recent election victory, and proclaimed that he was still a free man, ready to vote his conscience, and no tool of any party. "Look at my arms, you will find no party hand-cuff on them!" he declared, and then unable to resist his favorite invention, he wrote, "look at my neck, you will not find there any collar, with the engraving MY DOG. Andrew Jackson."[47]

To be sure, he filled the book with current political allusions, disparaging and often strained puns and comments about Jackson and his cronies, and more than a few thinly veiled indications of his interest in the presidency. But he went far beyond this. This was America's first *western* autobiography, no figment of a writer's imagination, but essentially the real story of a real man. Unlike Seba Smith and Clarke and Paulding, all easterners, he did not have to strain and resort to caricature to write in the genuine vernacular, because he was himself the genuine article. Certainly he included phrases and folk expressions that did not originate with him—a few may have been borrowed from Clarke, who borrowed them from Paulding—but if not, still they were the sayings of his people, real even if exaggerated. Moreover, he wrote as he and the western people spoke, spelling phonetically just as he did in his private correspondence, with only a little exaggeration for effect. Throughout he made it evident that he wanted to be seen as a character, not a clown. What he succeeded in doing was capturing on paper the essence of the new national personality. By the illustration of himself in two hundred pages, he achieved what Tocqueville took two volumes to accomplish.

He gave everyone what they wanted: The East got a legitimate representation of the literary figure that so fascinated them, while the West got the pride and attention it craved, manifest in the story of one westerner who mirrored them all and rose to become a national figure without compromising their dearly cherished simple values. He took Franklin's *Autobiography* and moved it west, placed it in the new language of the new generation of Americans, mixed genuine events with the popular culture of current literature, and created a wholly fresh character in native literature, part man, part legend. And he did it with a species of ironic, self-deprecating wit that combined political satire with broad—but never bawdy—tavern-room storytelling. Regardless of how much of his wit originated with him and how much he simply absorbed from the people of his region, the fact that he set it down so effectively in his book was destined to have a profound effect on American humor. Amusing as they were, the exaggerated portraits of Smith and Clarke and Paulding and others were destined to last only as folklore, while their idiom itself would die in a generation as tastes changed. But Crockett's humor would last indefinitely, long after the public craze for the man himself waned, and take a prominent place in the evolution of distinctive American humor, and all for the simple reason that it was genuinely funny.[48]

On February 2 he got the offer he was looking for from the firm of Carey and Hart of Philadelphia, and he wasted no time in accepting the next day. Perhaps from overwork in the rush to finish the book, or maybe a recurrence of the old malaria, Crockett found himself almost incapacitated when he received their January 31 offer. Indeed, he had to have his friend Chilton draft his reply, as the Kentuckian did much of Crockett's correspondence during his illness. Like all first-time authors, he had no idea of the author-publisher relationship, confessing: "I am too ignorant of the business of printing, to pretend to give you any instructions about the manner of executing it." But he then went on immediately to specify that the type must be large, with good leading and margins, in order to stretch the text to that seemingly magical two hundred pages or more. Chilton went over the manuscript for him making some corrections, and the final draft that Crockett sent to Carey and Hart was entirely in Chilton's hand, but Crockett insisted that the editors were not to change either spelling or grammar, "as I make no literary pretension." Equally to the point, though unsaid, he realized that the book needed at least a little of the quaint spelling and speech of his people in order to appeal to the public demand. Moreover, if the publishers cleaned up his text, then it would not be *him* speaking. He already had the copyright, and sent that off along with his only copy of the manuscript.[49]

From the moment he heard of the publishers' offer, Crockett suffered the anxiety and impatience of the new author. Indeed, in his letter of acceptance he already began to ask earnestly when he would get his printed copies. Of course, part of his anxiety was purely monetary. He knew hundreds wanted to buy this book. A dealer in Louisville told him that over five hundred copies of the Clarke "counterfeit" had sold there, and Crockett felt those sales should have been his. He believed he could sell five hundred to the trade in Washington on his own. Moreover, even before having a signed contract—if there was one—he began calculating his receipts. He demanded copies of the printing and binding bills so he could estimate what the gross margin per copy would be, and received from Carey and Hart the generous offer of 62.5 percent of that margin as his share. He urged them to keep the manufacturing cost of the book low, so that the margin would be high. This new book was more than literature or vindication—it was income desperately needed.[50]

Further, Crockett could not in conscience take all of that promised percentage, making it the more important to him personally that the profits be high. Chilton gave him a lot more assistance than just copying the manuscript and correcting some errors and omissions. He helped some with the structure, "to clarify the matter," as Crockett put it, though the style remained entirely David's own. Chilton also owned half of the copyright that Crockett sent with the manuscript, meaning that David most probably had sold a half interest in the proceeds of the book in return for Chilton's assistance, and quite probably some much needed cash in hand. Crockett now insisted that the publishers amend their agreement to guarantee Chilton a full half share in the royalties that would be due. In a revelation of just how sensitive David felt about anyone else being seen to speak on his behalf to the public, however, he also made certain that Chilton's name was not to appear anywhere in the book.[51]

With the good sense to promote his work before it appeared, Crockett wrote a preface to tease readers' interest and gave it to the press in February, and Carey and Hart, with the good sense to strike while interest soared, rushed the manuscript through press. In fact, within hours of receiving Crockett's acceptance of their offer, the publishers issued an advertising broadside on February 7 announcing that "it may interest the friends of this genuine Son of the West to learn, that he has lately completed, with his own hand, a narrative of his life and adventures, and that the work will shortly be published."[52] Apparently in the interest of time they bypassed the customary procedure of having Crockett read galley proofs to catch errors, but it may have been because they made changes they did not want him to see. There were not quite enough of his natural misspellings, and so they added some more. At the same time they toned down some of his account of the slaughter of the Creek women and children at Tallusahatchee in 1813, perhaps anxious not to allow Crockett to seem too violent or bloodthirsty. Carey and Hart may even have run the manuscript by some leading Whigs such as Sen. Thomas Ewing of Ohio, or Biddle, to get

326 ⚜ THREE ROADS TO THE ALAMO

their views on changes or additions that might further the book's utility as a campaign biography, for that it certainly was in addition to everything else. If the Whigs did run Crockett against Van Buren in 1836, this book could be a major weapon in the fight.[53]

It might almost seem that in the rush to finish the book, Crockett had forgotten what it was that brought him to Washington, however, he started his political duties even before the House assembled.[54] Of course as soon as Congress convened, he went back for another try at the land bill, but the Democrats were not very amenable to resurrecting Crockett's bill, backed as it was now by many Whigs' wishes. Undaunted, Crockett told a friend that "I will go a head."[55] Finally, on December 17, Crockett successfully got a motion on the floor to appoint himself the head of a select committee to investigate disposal of the public lands in Tennessee, and his optimism began to grow. "I have but little doubt of its passage during the present Session," he wrote in January.[56] He sent a copy of his land bill to his son John to show in the district, certain that "this will secure every occupant in the district and that will effect the object that I have been So long and So anxious to effect." He expected the whole Tennessee delegation to stand with him this time. "My prospects is much brighter than ever it was at any former Session."[57]

He reckoned without the personal animosity of his old Jacksonian foes and the equivocal support of his new Whig friends, who faced two mutually exclusive goals—the advancement of Crockett and the sale of public lands at high prices for the federal treasury. When he succeeded in getting the select committee approved, the Jacksonians groaned. "I notice that the *Immortal 'Zip Coon'* has called up his old land relinquishing bill," a friend wrote Polk in derision.[58] There was still plenty of opposition, and now his foes were using his new image increasingly to ridicule him. They derided him as "Zip Coon," "the Western David," "David of the River," and even simply "Davy," and they frustrated his every attempt to get a bill on the floor. By late May he still had hopes. "I know of no opposition to it if we could get to act on it," he said, failing to grasp that his inability to get it to debate revealed powerful opposition.[59] By mid-June he still tried, and still failed, finally accepting the fact that he would not succeed that session.[60]

Part of the reason was another issue that even Crockett had to admit took up much of his time. The battle was on over Jackson's policy of denying the bank a renewal of its charter, and he had taken advantage of the recess between sessions of Congress to remove its deposits. "The old man is in much trouble," Crockett gloated five days into the session, and thereafter he speedily made the issue an obsession, delighted that Jackson had done something that fixed the attention of the nation on his abuses of power. His correspondence for the next several months dripped with venom, self-righteous indignation, and glee at the uproar. "It will sink the administration in the mind of all honist men," he predicted, maintaining that Jackson's opposition proved that his animosity toward the Bank stemmed from its failure to lend its aid to sustaining his regime and Van Buren's prospects. "I do believe the old chief is in a worse drive then he ever was before and he is begining to find it out."[61]

For weeks to come Crockett harped on Jackson's "kingley powar," especially when Jackson declared that he would stand fast even if his entire party deserted him. "By this you see we have the government of one man that he puts forward his will as the law of the land," Crockett crowed. In his mind, the nullification crisis of 1832 paled in comparison. "I consider the present time one that is marked with more danger than any period of our political history," he said. The "ambition of King Andrew" would destroy the country. "He is surrounded by a set of imps of famin that is willing to destroy the best intrest of the country to promote their own intrest," he continued. "I write the truth and the world will see sense I hope before it is too late."[62] He expected Congress to order the deposits returned, though the House seemed soft on the issue, but then believed that Jackson would veto any such order, only deepening the crisis. If so, he expected Congress to teach him a lesson with an unequivocal override.[63] "The truth is if he had been dead and at the devil four years ago it would have been a happy time for this country," Crockett told one friend.[64] Privately he predicted that in two years' time it would be hard to find any man who would admit ever having been a supporter of Old Hickory.[65]

The battle lasted through most of the session, and as evidence of Crockett's spreading cultural influence despite his practical failures in the House, even Jackson's supporters on the bank issue advised the administration with what one called "one of Davys expressions," to "go a head."[66] As spring approached Crockett sent a number of political documents under his frank to inform his district of his views of what he saw as "political war," and meanwhile issued ever darker predictions that if Jackson succeeded, the people would be trading democracy for despotism.[67] He saw signs all across the country of public opposition to Jackson's course, which made Old Hickory's stubbornness seem even more dictatorial. People left their work; factories stopped their manufactures, or so he believed; the monetary system of the nation faced disruption with the loss of the stabilizing influence of the bank; and the commercial community predicted depression, "all for the vengeance of Jackson on the Bank because it would not aid him in upholding his party." The result might well be civil war.[68]

When he could, Crockett opposed the campaign against the bank from his seat on the House floor, sometimes letting his near monomania over Jackson get the better of him. "The people can't stand it, sir," he almost shouted one day in April. "I can't stand it. I won't," slapping his hands down on his mahogany desk so vehemently as he sat down that the gallery broke into laughter.[69] "This is a new seen in our political history," he lamented to a friend. Gradually his hopes of Congress forcing Jackson to back down evaporated as he realized that many Democrats in the House, though opposed to the removal, would not break with party policy in favor of principle. If anything, the business only reinforced Crockett's thorough disgust with the growing force of political parties in American politics.[70] When Congress proposed raising a Bank Committee to investigate all of Jackson's charges against the institution, Crockett vehemently opposed the idea, believing it to be a sham, since the committee, packed by the Speaker with Jacksonians, would inevitably whitewash Old Hickory's actions.[71]

Slashing at Jackson was simply a reflex now, and one that made David rather a bore. However original he may have been as a character, or in his literary construction in the autobiography, when it came to style itself Crockett was anything but original. The same phrases and aphorisms appeared over and over again. "King Andrew the First," "imps of famin," "this political Judeas Martin Vanburan," and more. Just as with "go ahead" and other expressions in the book, when he found a phrase that he liked, he used it too often. He derisively called the President "Dr. Jackson," after Harvard gave Old Hickory an honorary degree.[72] He took to referring to Washington as "head quarters," implying that Jackson was now a military dictator.[73] "We may say with propriety that we have the government of one man," he declared. "Andrew Jackson holds both the sword and purse." Then he began to accuse Jackson of being more tool than tyrant. "They have prompted the poor old man by Singing glorification to him until he believes his popularity is able to brake down the constitution and laws of the country," he said, and he knew where the real manipulation came from. "If I can put Back this political Judeas Martin Vanburan I will do so for I think him a perfect scoundral."[74] Over and over Crockett repeated the refrain that he had been one of the first to enlist under Jackson in the Creek War, that he had never abandoned the president but that Jackson abandoned him and his principles. "I do consider him a greater tyrant than Cromwell, Caesar or Bonaparte," David ranted near the end of the session. "I hope his day of glory is near at an end!"[75]

Yet there may have been more to Crockett's endlessly repetitive harangues than simply obsessive ranting. By the end of the session the next presidential election lay just two years in the future and no clear candidate led the Whig field. Indeed, the Whig Party itself was still amorphous, comprised as it was of old Clay-Adams Republicans, disaffected Jacksonians like himself, and even a burgeoning "Anti-Masonic" movement. The eventual choice of nominee might just as likely be determined by his own efforts as by any unified decision of the nascent party. By his constant and strident attacks on Jackson and Van Buren, unimaginative as they were, Crockett established himself as one of the most outspoken opponents of the administration. In addition he may just have been subtle enough to see that if those boastful frontier expressions so identified with him—things like whipping wildcats and riding lightning bolts—could take such deep hold in the public imagination, then why not other expressions more to his purpose? Even now "go ahead," which probably was his creation, began to sweep the country, entering the speech even of his enemies. Why not, then, other sayings like "King Andrew" and "political Judeas" and "one man rule"? If those caught fire with the public, their association with Crockett would only make him a stronger contender and keep him prominently in the public mind as the election approached. As the session came to an end, he spoke frequently of the 1836 contest, and he actually started making plans for a summer trip through the Northeast as far back as January.[76] Of course he disclaimed any purpose other than purely vacation. "I have no object in view more than to injoy myself," he told a prospective host. "I am electioneering for no boddy in the world."[77] That was all but a formal declaration of candidacy.

Nothing, then, could have been better timed than the appearance early in March of *A Narrative of the Life of David Crockett, of the State of Tennessee*. Crockett's anxiety mounted in the days approaching publication. He chafed at the delay when his manuscript, being somewhat longer than anticipated, held up typesetting and perhaps resulted in some of those cuts. A British firm's representative called on him to ask about foreign rights to publish the book, sight unseen, and Crockett repeatedly referred inquiries from anxious wholesalers to Carey and Hart.[78] In the latter part of February and early March he wrote to his publishers every three or four days with more suggestions, more questions, and usually wanting to know when he would see the finished book "for my own private satisfaction." He also anxiously awaited having ten author's copies to distribute to his close friends, to share that moment of pride and joy of the new author.[79]

When the package finally arrived, Crockett felt first the burst of pride of a father holding his newborn, and then some disappointment as he turned the pages and noted the changes in his orthography, and the omissions.[80] That mild chagrin stayed with him for some time, but was quickly overshadowed by the book's public reception. Priced at sixty-five cents each when purchased in quantities of a dozen or more, the book's first printing sold out in no more than three weeks.[81] One book dealer in Washington told the congressman that his *Narrative* "was the only Book that he could Sell." Crockett immediately predicted a brisk trade for the book in the Ohio and Mississippi Valleys, where Clarke's "counterfeit" work first appeared in Cincinnati. Perhaps realizing his vernacular's appeal to the boatmen from whom it in part derived, he believed it would do especially well in the river towns like Memphis, Natchez, and Louisville.[82] Within a few months the *Narrative* went into its sixth printing, and Crockett himself seemed never to tire of talking about the book, an acquaintance noting that "he did not affect indifference to the popular notoriety it had brought upon him."[83]

He took an avid interest in the sales, to the point of objecting when Carey and Hart wanted to reduce the wholesale price to fifty cents per copy for a bulk order of five hundred. "I know mighty little a bout such matters," he confessed, but then shrewdly noted that the result of such a reduction could lead to a reduction in his royalty. But his way to make up the difference was to secure an agreement from the publishers to sell up to a thousand copies to him personally at the same price. He would get a small share of that sale, of course, and then be free to retail the books himself, pocketing all of the difference between cost and retail price himself. Throughout he dealt fairly and openly with Carey and Hart and placed an implicit trust in their honesty that was almost touching. "I am hard pressed in money matters," he told them in April before another printing. He needed to "form some opinion of the aid I may expect from this sourse."[84] Within days of the end of the session and his anticipated departure, he talked of taking up to fifteen hundred copies with him for friends in Tennessee to market.[85] Just how much Crockett did in fact derive from the *Narrative* is difficult to judge. Even at fifty cents per copy wholesale, Carey and Hart still certainly made some profit on the title, if no more than ten or fifteen cents. The book must have sold between five and ten thousand copies that first year, at an average wholesale price of about fifty-eight cents. If the margin on that was only twenty cents a copy, still Crockett's 62.5 percent share must have brought him between $875 and $1,750, and probably more. It was no fortune, but enough to relieve much of the strain of debt.

He could hardly fail to be gladdened and impressed by the attention the *Narrative* brought him. People accosted him in the House and on the city streets begging for his autograph, and in signing he could not resist making again the point that he used in his opening preface to attest to the authenticity of his account. "I David Crockett of Tennessee do certify that this Book was written by my self and the only genuine history of my life that ever has been written," he inscribed in one copy. "The first work is a counterfit and was written with out authority."[86] Even some of the literati noticed the popular reaction to the book, if not in the most glowing terms. Harriet Martineau, an English journalist just then visiting in America, encountered the *Narrative*, and perhaps even observed Crockett in Washington. "Persons have made up their

minds that there is very little originality in America, except in regions
where such men as David Crockett grow up," she observed. She disagreed, thinking him not truly original but merely a popular aberration,
arguing that the New England that much more suited her refined tastes
produced just as many original men as Crockett "or any other self-
complacent mortal who finds scope for his humours amid . . . the canebrakes of Tennessee."[87]

Martineau's opinion of Crockett's book mattered far less than the
phenomenon she perceived—that it produced a popular sensation that
only enhanced his image as *the* western man and the embodiment of
the new character of America. Tocqueville was closer to the mark on
the impact and import of Crockett's book, though not writing about it
specifically. "In democracies a writer may hope to gain moderate
renown and great wealth cheaply," he wrote the same year that the
Narrative appeared. "For this purpose he does not need to be admired;
it is enough if people have a taste for his work. The ever growing
crowd of readers always wanting something new ensures the sale of
books that nobody esteems highly."[88] Crockett's book got him much
more renown than wealth, of course, but it hit at exactly the right
time, when more and more Americans of the common classes were
reading, and their tastes ran far less to the classics and the works of the
literati than to small books that spoke for and about their own kind.
Coming as it did at the same time that Crockett attracted more and
more attention as the leading and most vocal foe of the Democratic
regime, this substantially enhanced his prospects for a presidential
nomination in 1836. If he could keep his name and his image in front
of the people in the interim, it must inevitably place him among the
top Whig contenders. Happily attention begat more attention, and
another medium stepped in now to fill out the word portrait he had
made of himself with a likeness on canvas.

Probably within no more than two months of the appearance of the
Narrative, the painter John G. Chapman asked Crockett to sit for him
to produce a bust portrait. This in itself presented nothing new to
David. Two or three other painters had done likenesses of him in previous years, none of which he found very impressive. They tended to
make him look like what he called "a sort of cross between a clean-
shirted Member of Congress and a Methodist Preacher." Still he gave

Chapman his sittings, but felt no hesitation in expressing his displeasure with the result. Almost in passing he told the painter that "if you could catch me on a bear-hunt in a 'harricane,' with hunting tools and gear, and team of dogs, you might make a picture better worth looking at." Chapman liked the idea, though feared that he knew nothing of the outdoors kind of scene needed, let alone anything of "harricanes," but David promised to give him all the technical advice necessary. Chapman made a rough sketch that pleased the congressman. "That's the sort of thing to start with," said David. "I'll show you how to have all right. We'll make the picture between us, first rate, mind if we don't So *Go ahead!* just as soon and fast as you like."[89]

Of course Crockett may simply have been caught up in the spirit, not to mention the flattery, of being painted. Yet certainly there was more to it than that, and Crockett, who so despised manipulation in his foes, now consciously or unconsciously manipulated Chapman. The bust portrait had been fine, but it looked like all the others he had seen, and for that matter was of a piece with standard portraiture throughout the country. There was nothing original in it, and moreover it depicted the man Crockett had been, not the man the public now wanted. No one reading the *Narrative* wished or expected to see the head and shoulders of a man in a broadcloth suit, cravat at his neck, sitting in the obligatory three-quarters view with some dim and indistinct background behind him. Those readers, and all Americans, wanted the Crockett that David persuaded Chapman to paint, on the hunt in the wilderness where every man was a lord. Having just published what could well be his campaign biography in 1836, Crockett now cajoled Chapman into producing the perfect companion piece, a Crockett that even the illiterate could absorb, the living likeness of "the gentleman from the cane."

No point in the developing canvas seemed too small for Crockett's attention. He scoured Washington and the Potomac suburbs for just the right gear, the proper shirt, leggings, and moccasins. He wanted a butcher knife that was practical rather than ornamental, despite the fact that already Philadelphia cutlers were starting to produce what people called Bowie knives, some of them enormous almost grotesque blades fitted more for Wildfire and Edwin Forrest than a real backwoodsman. The hunting dogs must be mongrels, their tails showing signs of having been bitten off, as if in a fight with a bear. The rifle presented something of a problem until he found nearly the right weapon, plain and unadorned, but a bit too short, in the hands of an old Potomac hunter. Crockett and the rifleman became great friends after he loaned David the weapon, and eventually the man simply gave it to him. "A grand old fellow that," Crockett said of him, and then with a veneer of humor that scarcely concealed what must have been chiefly on his mind as he posed for this painting, Crockett added that "when I'm President, I'll be shot if I don't put him into the War Department."

Crockett even helped direct the pose. After several days of sittings he looked at the result and found it static. He simply stood on the canvas, his hat on his head, his right arm dangling unoccupied at his side. It seemed all wrong, and for some days he brooded over the matter, until one day he strode into Chapman's studio in full costume, lifted the hat from his head and held it out at arm's length, and gave a shout that alarmed people several doors away. This was the right pose: Crockett poised on the hunt, just about to set the dogs and himself on the trail of the next quarry—a bear in the portrait, but rather larger game in his imagination. When Chapman adjusted the portrait, Crockett wholeheartedly approved, and it was done. The artist suggested painting Crockett's name and "go ahead" maxim in the scene, and David suggested the knife handle for his name and the rifle for the quotation, but the handle proved too short to fit in all the letters. Crockett's solution was to spell his name "Croket," saying "there'll be enough left to tell who the 'butcher' belongs to, and three letters saved." It would only save two letters, actually, but by now the illiterate pose was second nature to David.[90]

Never one to pay scrupulous attention to attendance in the House, or to issues that did not interest him, Crockett must have given less heed than usual this session, with all the distractions of the book, the painting, and the new demands of celebrity. "I am well and hanging on to the true faith like a puppy to a root," he told a friend in January, but he was out of touch.[91] He had seen no Tennessee newspapers after he left home for Washington, but when he heard rumors that there would be another gerrymandering attempt, this time in the legislative districts, he told a friend and potential candidate that "let it be laid off

as it may I go the whole hog for you against any person whatever."⁹²
He determined to use his free franking privilege liberally—thereby
raising the postal deficit, though that seemed not to trouble him—in
order to keep his constituents informed. "I am determined to enliten
the people if it costs me my salary," he declared, though in fact it
would cost him only the printing. "I will trust to an honist comunity
hereafter for reward."⁹³ His Jacksonian opponents saw what he was
doing, of course, and denounced "our Sham representative" for flood-
ing the district with speeches, but then went on to add that it would
do him little good since most of his voters could not read, as evidenced
by their election of a man like him.⁹⁴ Still, despite the carping, most of
what Crockett heard from home sounded good. Hearing that the voters of one region approved his course, he defended it, saying "I never
did know any mode of legislating only to go and do what my con-
scince dictated to me to be wright."⁹⁵ He needed to make sure that his
constituents stood behind him now more than ever, for any attempt at
a nomination in 1836 must hinge on him being reelected to his seat in
1835. The "bug" for higher office had seized him. "Among the evils of
a new country is the rage for political life," an editor would write two
years hence, "and Crockett was infected by this mania."⁹⁶

There was even a little time for society this session, especially once
his health improved and he finished the book. Visitors frequently
called at his rooms on Pennsylvania Avenue, opposite Brown's Hotel,
though when they did he often felt obliged to perform for them,
putting on a hunting hat, throwing one leg over the arm of his chair in
a careless pose. He welcomed one group of the curious by bidding
them to "take seats, gentlemen—make yourselves at home—glad to
see you—hope you find yourselves well," and more such meaningless
pleasantries, his visitors all the while staring at him in curiosity. He
entertained them with a few stories, and once they left stood distracted
for a moment, and then quickly went out of character, the act ended.
Putting his hat back on the table, he forthrightly confessed to a friend
that "well!—they came to see a bar, and they've seen one—hope they
like the performance—it did not cost them any thing any how—Let's
take a horn."⁹⁷ Almost without his realizing it, the character he had
created out of his own experience and the personality of his people
was starting to control him. He profited from being the embodiment

of a legend, but in the Faustian bargain he risked the submergence of his own true character as a gentleman.[98] It was a bargain that never rested in complete comfort on his conscience.

Yet he could not deny or resist the attention. The Whig press continued its campaign of lionizing him. "There are some men whom you cannot report," said *Nile's Register* shortly after the *Narrative* appeared. "The Colonel is one. His leer you cannot put upon paper—his curious drawl—the odd cant of his body and his self-congratulation. He is an original in every thing, in the tone and structure of his sentences, in the force and novelty of metaphors, and his range of ideas."[99] Chapman found Crockett's speech irresistible. "Say what he might his meaning could never be misinterpreted. He expressed opinions, and told his stories, with unhesitating clearness of diction, often embellished with graphic touches of original wit and humor, sparkling and even startling, yet never out of place." As for his backwoods vernacular, now perhaps a bit exaggerated for popular effect, "it was to him truly a mother-tongue, in which his ideas flowed most naturally and found most emphatic and unrestrained utterance."[100] In the most casual encounter people expected wit from him, and others challenged him at their peril. A Massachusetts representative met him on Pennsylvania Avenue one day just as a farmer drove a small herd of cattle down the street. "Hello, there, Crockett," he said, thinking to get the best of David. "Here's a lot of your constituents on parade. Where are they going?" Without hesitation Crockett responded: "They are going to Massachusetts to teach school."[101]

Invitations came in from all across the East as the demand to see this phenomenon in the flesh grew, and Crockett was wise enough to capitalize on the opportunity to go before a wider constituency. He thought of going into the northern states as early as January, and perhaps even earlier, from the time that the Mississippi convention raised the presidential question. By late April he had a double impetus, for not only would the exposure enhance his prospects, but also it would sell more books, and his debts were slow to disappear. In late March he asked Carey and Hart for an advance of $150 to $200 on his share of sales, and so desperate was he for money that two weeks later he almost violently demanded payment of another $200 that someone owed him, an uncharacteristic act for his gentle nature.[102] Unwisely, perhaps, he decided not to wait for the end of the long session, especially since there was no movement on the land bill, and that was his chief interest. He would hardly be missed for the three weeks the trip would take, and if anything, it would be a relief to escape Washington for awhile. Moreover, many of his Whig friends urged him to make the trip, no doubt promising that it would be something in the way of a triumphal procession. They would make all the arrangements, probably even cover his expenses, and he would sell books and get a much-needed rest. Most of all—and this was the overriding reason for the trip in the first place—he would venture into the large metropolitan areas where the Whigs still reigned, showing himself to voters and managers alike. He was already a regional phenomenon in the West and upper South. If he could win favor in the Northeast, he might be unchallengeable for the nomination in two years' time.

In a political career marked by naïveté, miscalculations, and simple blunders, it would be the biggest mistake of all.

BOWIE

Whether they liked him or not, they all knew that he was absolutely brave,
and that they could depend upon his being fair to foe and loyal to friends.

JUAN SEGUÍN, APRIL 10, 1874

A few days after his return from the San Saba expedition, James Bowie addressed to the political chief in Béxar, Ramón Músquiz, a long account of his recent journey, most of it taken up with the events of the battle. He was under no requirement to do so, since this had not been an official or military venture, but with the rumblings of native unrest on the frontier, the authorities appreciated hearing from anyone with information on the state of affairs there.[1] For a man known to be boastful and self-consciously larger than life, Bowie showed great restraint. True, he said nothing at all about the purpose of the expedition, evidence that though he had discussed it with Músquiz beforehand, he did not want all and sundry knowing what he was about. Yet in his report of the fight, he said nothing that would glorify himself, rather paying a compliment to the stamina and bravery of all of the men with him. Nevertheless his report itself soon became well known, only adding to his reputation as a result of the fight. Músquiz forwarded a copy of it to Governor José Letona, who returned his thanks to Bowie, and Músquiz himself meanwhile wrote to Bowie to compliment him on his bravery. José Antonio de la Garza, one of the largest landowners in the Béxar region, and the same man who visited Claiborne shortly before Travis left for Texas, also wrote to Bowie offering his thanks. Clearly James did not have to exaggerate his role in the fight for these influential men to conclude that he was a man of rare courage and leadership ability.[2]

Músquiz must have spoken with Bowie about leading another, stronger party out again to strike the Tawakoni hard and put an end to their frequent raids on outlying settlers, and certainly such an expedition would be to his purpose as well, giving him ample opportunity to survey the region for mines, and this time with enough force not to be driven away. But a combination of factors induced Bowie to turn briefly from his fixation on silver mines. Even though Ursula certainly deserved some time with him after her ordeal of uncertainty, that old loyalty to his brothers that so strongly governed his motives induced him instead to accompany Rezin and Stephen back to Louisiana on a brief trip. Rezin was starting to look into a new means of capitalizing on old Spanish land grants, this time legitimately, and Stephen may have brought news of more trouble with the land dealings in Louisiana and Arkansas. The Walkers and Wilkins were having second thoughts, and now President Jackson heard frequently from his cabinet officers of what one called "the far famed 'Bowie claims.'"[3] Perhaps most important, an installment of money that James expected from his share of the sale to the Walkers and Wilkins was due. A quick trip to Louisiana could serve several interests.[4]

James rushed back to Texas at the end of the year, in the company of several other friends by ship from New Orleans to Galveston.[5] What he found there disturbed him. For all the notoriety his San Saba exploit gained him, it also got him a reputation as a fortune hunter, and now when several "foreigners" came back to Texas with him, and he started putting together another, larger expedition supposedly to strike the Tawakoni and teach them a lesson, rumors flourished that his real intent was to "further the views of speculators in mines." The fact of his plans being so promiscuously broadcast actually impelled him to publish an announcement in the Brazoria Texas Gazette, on January 10, denying any such intention, but he probably fooled few if any. At the same time the slaves accompanying the Louisianians that Bowie brought caused concern. Some of them took the opportunity of entering a province that outlawed slavery to run away. When authorities captured them, it led to some debate over whether they should be returned to Bowie's men.[6] All the old ghosts were catching up to him, it seemed. Certainly he was Bowie the hero, but land speculation, fortune hunting, and now the perhaps unwitting introduction of illegal slaves all attached themselves to his reputation as well.

By January 26 he had his company assembled, twenty-seven of them including himself this time, and he led them out of Gonzales northwest toward the Pedernales once more. When he reached that river, two friendly Indians joined the party as guides, and they moved on across the Llano to the San Saba, where nine more attached themselves to the expedition. Finally Bowie marched all the way to the headwaters of the Colorado River, then turned east and went on for several days until they reached the upper Brazos in the country of the Waco. All along the way, at Músquiz's request, he surveyed any signs of hostile activity, especially by the Tawakoni, yet in ten weeks of travel saw only six of them. It was "a fruitless search," he concluded. They would have no opportunity to strike a hard blow at the tribe, and Bowie decided that the well-armed Cherokee from Nacogdoches, long at war with the Tawakoni, must have succeeded in driving them to more remote country.

While fulfilling the official part of his mission, Bowie always kept one eye on another goal. He noted the abundant beaver along the Colorado. The country between the Llano and the Colorado looked splendid, and he believed that it would "afford large bodies of land not excelled in this or any other part of the country, & at some future day it will & must be of the greatest acquisition & importance to the agriculturist." And of course there was the matter of gold and silver. "I also spared no pains in extending my examinations to the mineral character of the country, in hopes that something might be discovered that should prove advantageous & beneficial to that section of country." He collected mineral samples to turn over to Músquiz, and no doubt kept his eyes alert for anything that promised to profit himself in the offing.[7]

It was a grueling two and one-half months in the wilderness, and Bowie did not get back to San Antonio until the middle of April, exhausted, and with no silver mine to show for his effort, though his report of the disappearance of the Tawakoni certainly pleased Músquiz. He returned, however, to find that there were problems fomenting for his other interests in his new home. Either at Bowie's behest or at Austin's, José Carbajal, who surveyed land titles for Austin, went to New Orleans while Bowie was on his expedition, his mission to collect from Rezin Bowie the money James had been unable to secure the previous December. He, too, failed, for the Walkers and Wilkins were parting with nothing now.[8]

Then there appeared to be trouble brewing with Austin himself. In March, just before leaving to take his seat in the legislature at Saltillo, Austin saw what he believed to be machinations by an unknown hand to "foment discord between Bowie and his connections and me."[9] Austin walked a delicate line in trying to mollify both the unruly and aggressive Texian settlers and the uneasy Mexican rulers in Saltillo and Mexico City. A man like Bowie could have upset things on any number of scores, but it was certainly land speculation that lay at the bottom of this incipient difference. Austin himself bought three of the eleven-league grants from native Mexicans in 1831. But the knowledge that Bowie had been in Saltillo buying more than a dozen of them under suspicious circumstances seemed to endanger the whole business by making the subterfuge of Texians buying through Mexicans public knowledge. Moreover, Bowie was a known speculator with no reputation for subtlety in Louisiana. If he pushed the sales of his grants too hard too soon, he could touch off a wave of speculation that would likely bring the Mexican authorities down hard on the whole colony, and from first to last it was always Stephen Austin's policy to keep the hand of Mexico City, and even Saltillo, as far removed as possible. At the very least, any untoward activity by Bowie could crush hopes of a repeal of the April 6, 1830, law prohibiting further immigration from the United States.

Then, too, the more the government tried to regulate or control the Texians, the more likely there would come an outbreak of the strong yet until then latent feeling for independence. "The true interest of Texas is never to separate from Mexico," Austin told Williams while Bowie was still out looking for Tawanoki and silver, but even if he was not a revolutionary himself, James Bowie was the kind of man whose intemperate actions could touch off an incident that would give the real revolutionaries all they needed to act.[10] Mary Austin Holley, Austin's observant young cousin, had recently visited Texas and saw only too well that "certain political changes are hastening on." As for the potential for an explosion of speculation, she surely reflected her cousin's views when she added that "the restrictions will be removed, & when the North Americans come pouring in without restraint, you can not imagine the value of these lands." James Bowie could.[11]

Bowie seems to have done nothing to push speculation at the moment, nor did he take part in any of the political rumblings that finally began to erupt into action that spring even without his involvement. Yet he cannot have been entirely unaware of the ferment in Texas when he returned from his latest expedition. The centralist government in Mexico City had never been a stable one. The Mexicans prized their hard-won freedom from Spain, but almost immediately found themselves plagued by factionalism from within that led to increased centralization of authority and the abrogation of some portions of their 1824 constitution. Moreover, theirs was a huge country, nearly as large as the United States, but without the transportation and communication links to make it manageable. Having been exploited by Spain for so long, it had no efficient infrastructure for supporting itself as a republic. Mexico City could scarcely see beyond its own internal difficulties, let alone give any kind of attention to the faraway province of Coahuila y Tejas, with the result that by 1832 the regime there was already disintegrating.[12] That same year Gen. Antonio López de Santa Anna precipitated an uprising in favor of a looser republic. Austin expected him to win power but advised his colonists to stay out of the turmoil, for any action on their part could work against Texas, regardless of how the power struggle ended.

As they did more and more often, the Texians decided not to listen to Austin. The unrest erupted at the settlement at Anahuac on Galveston Bay, frequently a trouble spot because of the customs house there, and the small garrison. In May the Mexican commander arrested Travis when he tried to follow the pattern of what Bowie had done that winter and raise a civilian militia to defend Anahuac from hostile Indians—who were, of course, well more than one hundred miles away. In the resulting uproar, Texians around Anahuac advanced against the garrison in June, laid bloodless siege to it, and finally forced its surrender. In the process they declared themselves in favor of Santa Anna, and soon other communities did the same. Yet Austin was opposed to this, and in San Felipe the *ayuntamiento* split over the issue. Sam Williams urged peace and passivity, while Bowie's new friend Wharton denounced the pacifists and called for resistance. The Texians themselves were being split by events in poor troubled Mexico.

Bowie left no record of his reaction to this growing turmoil, but his position is not hard to judge. His political interests in the past had always been closely allied with his personal fortunes. At the moment his ambitions were tied to his land speculation and possibly the cotton mill, and his most important personal alliance was with the Veramendis. All those interests argued in favor of maintaining the status quo. Governor Letona thought the April 6, 1830, prohibition on colonization was unconstitutional, and Vice Governor Veramendi would have been in accord thanks to his own interests in land speculation. This at least gave some hope of an eventual relaxation or abrogation of the policy. No one knew what Santa Anna would do if he came to power, and Austin actually feared that the republicans might make colonization even more difficult. As for his personal friendships, those bonds always so important and influential to James Bowie, he maintained close ties to men in both camps—Williams and Navarro on one side, and Wharton and Frank Johnson on the other. For the moment that was the best place for a man of business to be. As for the active participants in the gathering troubles, neither side seemed to regard Bowie as one of its own, suggesting that he kept completely out of the political discussion. But with his rising reputation as a man of action in the field, both may have viewed him as someone they might one day need, and soon.

Bowie himself had family matters to attend to just then. The depth and nature of the relations between him and Ursula is a secret that each kept to the grave. Ham found her "a most esteemed lady" who obviously adored her husband. As for Bowie, Ham saw that he was "kind and gentle—anticipating wants and wishes with great foresight and judgment."[13] Occasionally the Bowies stopped at Gelhorne's tavern in Gonzales, and there the keeper's daughter thought Ursula "a woman beautiful in person and character."[14] Capt. William G. Hunt, who sometimes accompanied Bowie on his wilderness rambles, recalled that "Mrs. Bowie was a beautiful Castilian lady, and won all hearts by her sweet manners. Bowie seemed supremely happy with and devoted to her, more like a kind and tender lover than the rough backwoodsman."[15] In his only known surviving reference to her, Bowie himself spoke of Ursula as "my dearly beloved wife."[16]

Certainly Bowie was a man with a sense of the romantic, and of romantic justice. The regulars at Jonathan Peyton's San Felipe tavern,

where Bowie boarded when in town, told the story of a young couple
who wanted to wed when the Catholic priest was not present to perform the service. In such circumstances settlers customarily held a
"constitutional marriage," a nonbinding ceremony after which they
would live as man and wife until the priest could arrive to make their
union formal—and legal, since no Protestant marriage was allowed or
considered legal under current restrictions. But Bowie recognized the
would-be groom as a horse thief who already had an abandoned wife
and children. He got a friend to pose as a Mexican priest whose unexpected arrival would allow a legal ceremony to take place. The ersatz
priest supposedly spoke no English, however, so Bowie offered to act
as interpreter, and while the priest gave the groom his catechism and
took his confession, Bowie repeated every sentence in a voice so loud
that others in the house, including the prospective bride, could hear.
At Bowie's prompting the priest asked the charlatan during confession
about his horse stealing and his abandoned family, and both questions
and answers were heard by the Peytons and the bride. When the priest
left to take her confession, she called off the wedding, and Mrs.
Peyton ordered the scoundrel out of the house.[17]

Yet, strangely, for all his concern for that young bride, and his supposed devotion to Ursula, Bowie repeatedly left his own new wife for
long periods, an abandonment that must have been very hard on a
young woman just turned twenty, especially the daughter of an aristocrat. Bowie barely got back from the second San Saba expedition in
time for their first anniversary, and during that first year was away
from her for almost five months in all. Such long absences were not all
that unusual among the wandering breed of frontier entrepreneurs and
adventurers like Bowie. Crockett often left his second wife for
extended periods as he scouted new lands and went on long hunts. A
wife could be more a luxury than a necessity to their kind, and the
routine of home and hearth hardly competed with the excitement of
exploration, treasure hunting, and the wilderness. Certainly Bowie
never found a spouse to be a necessity until he was thirty-five, in his
day rather old for a man to be marrying for the first time. And it could
not be denied that she was beyond question the very best match a man
of his inclinations could have made in Texas. Being Veramendi's son-
in-law would open to him every door in all of Mexico. This does not

mean that he did not love her when they were wed, or that he did not come to love her in his way while they were married. Many who knew James Bowie testified to his attentiveness and respect toward women, a requirement of the time in any man essaying to be called a gentleman, but his repeated absences for such long periods make it evident that lovely young Ursula was always secondary to him. To men of action like himself, male loyalties were always the strongest, as were his bonds to his brothers.

And so Ursula continued to wait for him. After a year of marriage she might have hoped to be expecting their first child, but his absences severely reduced the chances for that, and then sometime in June, after barely two months at home, he left her again, off once more to chase the silver rainbow on the San Saba. But this time he scarcely got into the interior as far as the Colorado before an urgent message from Austin caught up with him.[18] Political events were racing. Dissidents had captured a Mexican vessel at the mouth of the Brazos, declaring themselves for Santa Anna. In San Felipe Samuel Williams, in charge in Austin's absence, invoked the *empresario's* name in declaring that "this once happy and prosperous country is now a perfect charnal house of anarchy and confusion," and called on all Texians to "rouse up your neighborhood."[19] Then Austin himself arrived in San Felipe in mid-July to find his own community in turmoil, with men like Wharton and Johnson pushing for a declaration of unity with Santa Anna.

Austin needed someone he could count on, as his associate Williams had disappointed him by letting things get out of hand. Then there were rumblings of discord at Nacogdoches, and with a new community in Texas confronting Mexican garrisons and going over to the republicans almost weekly now, he was torn in too many directions. He had to remain in San Felipe to contain events there. What he needed was someone to send to Nacogdoches, the kind of man who could control events. He needed James Bowie. Whatever else he thought of Bowie, Austin knew by now that he was a leader born for such moments. Moreover, as a land speculator Bowie would have shared his view at this time that an uproar of any kind could damage hopes of a repeal of the April 6, 1830, decree. Austin sent a messenger to the Colorado with an urgent request that Bowie come immediately to San Felipe, where "his services were greatly needed."

The message reached Bowie sometime in mid-July, and he dropped his prospecting at once. By late in the month he was in San Felipe, where Austin asked him to go to Nacogdoches. Austin had no authority to give Bowie any sort of formal commission, but certainly he sent with him his endorsement and a request that the colonists listen to Bowie and follow his leadership in forestalling a confrontation.[20] By the time of Bowie's arrival there was no time to lose, for now San Felipe itself, led by Johnson, had declared for Santa Anna, and by late in July Nacogdoches was ready to erupt. Its Texian community knew that Colonel Piedras, commanding the Twelfth Permanent Battalion posted there, opposed Santa Anna and the republic and rigidly enforced the law against immigrants coming from the United States, almost all of whom would pass through Nacogdoches. Worse, it was rumored that he was inciting local Indians to massacre Texians if they declared for Santa Anna.[21] Inspired by the successful expulsion of the Mexicans from Anahuac, men from nearby settlements were known to be mustering to march on Piedras. Bowie left immediately, pausing only to send Ursula a letter that she would have to wait longer to see him again, for he could not predict how long this commission might last or where it would lead him.[22] No later than July 31 he rode out of San Felipe, pushing hard to reach Nacogdoches before an explosion.[23]

He was just a day too late. By July 31 some three hundred men had left their farms. They converged on Nacogdoches the next day, giving Piedras an ultimatum to surrender. He chose rather to resist, whereupon the unorganized Texians elected James Bullock their commander and the next day at noon marched into the town. When they reached the central square, Piedras attacked. It was not much of a battle, and after nightfall of August 2 Piedras decided to evacuate. Bowie arrived that same evening to find Bullock already in command.[24] During the night they heard sounds from the Mexican position as Piedras had his men throw all the arms and ammunition they could not take with them into wells. They interpreted the noise as preparations for a dawn attack, but the coming of light revealed instead that the Mexicans had gone.[25]

In the face of this revelation, Bullock either lost his control over the attackers or else he simply did not know what to do, for his men seemed leaderless.[26] Bowie stepped into the vacuum and apparently on his own authority took twenty men and mounted to pursue Piedras.[27] It was like Bowie to take twenty to attack two hundred. They raced toward the Angelina River, some ten miles south, on the road they believed the Mexicans had taken. Though Piedras enjoyed a several-hour head start, still he moved slowly, and Bowie easily rode around his line of advance to put himself in position south of the Angelina when the Mexicans approached the crossing. With his men in ambush, Bowie calmly watched as Piedras sent a mounted advance party down to the river to reconnoiter. While their horses drank, a shot rang out, and a Mexican sergeant fell from his saddle into the stream. Immediately the rest of the party galloped back to Piedras, while Bowie mounted his men and pulled them back prudently.

Having put fear into the Mexicans without revealing how small was his command, Bowie simply kept Piedras in sight for the rest of the day. The Mexicans crossed the Angelina but then, confused and appre-hensive, moved no farther, making camp there that night. Bowie camped his own men not far away, and the next morning he sent a man named Bolina to Piedras with a bold demand for his surrender, threatening that they would all be killed otherwise. Bowie's bluff did not ruffle Piedras, but it convinced some of his officers that they were in mortal peril. Capt. Francisco Medina was sufficiently persuaded that he drew his pistol, put it to Piedras's head and insisted that Bowie's demand be met. Piedras simply handed Medina his sword, and with it the command, telling him to do as he pleased.

When Medina sent word accepting the Texians' terms, Bowie him-self rode up at the head of the rest of his men and immediately disarmed the *soldados*. That done, he put them all on the march back to Nacogdoches, and no doubt a thundering welcome as his band of twenty came in with more than ten times their numbers as prisoners. It was even better than the San Saba fight. Once again Bowie had con-quered overwhelming odds. With twenty men he had achieved com-pletely what 300 disorganized Texians had failed to do a few days before. There was no Texas army or even militia in the summer of 1832, no commanders or officers or enlisted men. Yet no one could question that from this moment onward, James Bowie's was the first name to come to mind when any crisis arose that required a leader of men.[28]

Once the congratulations faded, the civil leaders in Nacogdoches sent Piedras to San Felipe under parole, and asked Bowie to take command of an escort to conduct the *soldados* to San Felipe, where they would be discharged.[29] The column left on August 7 or 8, but by the time they crossed the Angelina, Bowie was already concerned for the soldiers. "They are very destitute of necessaries," he reported. Even many of the officers were on foot without horses. He sent ahead to Austin asking for horses, and for the men some beefs and provisions. At the same time he announced, with wry humor, that the regiment "has been induced by certain American arguments to declare in favor of the Constitution of Sa[nta] Anna," and that it had, in fact, "put itself under my command."[30] Bowie also gave his personal receipt for seventy-four dollars' worth of supplies and a wagon for the sick and wounded.[31]

In the end Bowie took the soldiers all the way to San Antonio, where they would remain for months. He arrived sometime around September 17, and the next day received from Captain Medina himself a note of thanks for his kindness and consideration on their march. At the same time, perhaps as a reward, Alcalde Seguín gave Bowie a rifle.[32] Just how Bowie dealt with his celebrity is uncertain, but beyond doubt he both enjoyed it and determined to use it to his benefit. Regardless of where he had stood on political matters prior to the Nacogdoches episode, his capture of Piedras identified him with the *santanistas* at the very least, while men of even more ambitious views, those who dreamed of making Texas a province independent of Coahuila, saw in him a potential ally. And there were even those who wanted an early and complete separation from Mexico, an independent Texas. "Col Bowie was reputed to have entertained similar views," Caiaphas Ham said years later.[33] Bowie may not have crossed that particular line as yet, however. Indeed, as subsequent events revealed, he still saw the best interests of his own future lying in a Mexican Texas. Nevertheless, in those huddled tavern conversations and in meetings in the back rooms of San Felipe and elsewhere, when independence was the subject, men naturally assumed that Bowie would be in the vanguard when the time for action arrived.

News of interest awaited Bowie when he returned to San Antonio in September after an absence of at least three months. The disturbances at Anahuac and Matamoros and Nacogdoches were in no way coordinated with Santa Anna's uprising in Mexico, but coincidentally each worked to the benefit of the other, and the Texians were quick to imply for his benefit that their acts were done in the interest of his movement. The more they saw of the general's progress, the more they saw Santa Anna as a liberal whose rise to rule would benefit them. This alone troubled Austin. Back in March 1832 when he left for Saltillo, he extracted from his supporters the promise that they would not allow matters in San Felipe to get out of hand. But then, apparently immediately after his Nacogdoches triumph, Bowie joined with Wharton and others and used his newfound prominence to excite the citizens into calling for a convention to meet in October.[34] When the delegates from all the leading communities—with the notable exception of San Antonio—met, they drafted resolutions to Santa Anna asking for the repeal of the April 6, 1830, decree; a reduction of the tariff and some means of controlling their often corrupt customs officers; a reorganization of local government to speed the issuing of land titles; and permission to raise their own militia for protection against hostile Indians. Most dramatic of all, however, they asked for the separation of Texas from Coahuila and its admission as an equal state in the Mexican republic. It was everything that Austin had hoped to avoid. Shortly afterward he would lament that he had always wanted to keep Texas out of the revolutionary fervor then seizing Mexico, but that "the flame broke out in my absence from Texas."[35] This precipitous action could send a signal to Santa Anna that the Texians were too ambitious, and certainly Austin blamed Bowie in part. Only the strenuous efforts of his supporters in the convention kept the body from sending the resolutions on to Mexico City immediately. Instead the convention finally agreed to hold them for reconsideration and affirmation by another meeting set for April 1833.[36]

Bowie could play no active role in the convention itself, since his residence was San Antonio, and that municipality had chosen not to send representatives. But merely by speaking out in favor of the meeting, he showed that he was feeling his sudden influence in public affairs. It was the kind of role he had wanted to play in Louisiana before the perfidy of Brent and others ruined his chances for a seat in Congress. Just as Texas brought back to life his old dreams of wealth from land, so it also offered resurrection for his hopes of position and influence. Besides, the ideas reflected in the convention's resolutions all suited his business purposes, while its action suited his temperament. Patience, calculation, and biding time were for men like Austin. When Bowie had an idea or espoused a goal, he wanted it realized immediately, usually without thought of the consequences. He may not have felt great opposition to Austin's long-held policy of saying and doing nothing to challenge or upset the Mexicans, because that, too, had served Bowie's ends. But now, seeing the ease with which Mexican garrisons were being driven from Texas, Bowie was emboldened to take a more aggressive stance. If he was disappointed that the sending of the resolutions was postponed, he could still take heart from the fact that Austin himself had been forced to adopt the convention's views in order not to bring down on himself accusations of being a traitor to Texians' interests.

Other news was coming to San Antonio almost the same time that the convention met. Governor Letona had died in September, and now Veramendi would go to Saltillo to assume office in his place. When Veramendi reached Saltillo on November 11 he found the city in an uproar. Bustamente's government was all but toppled, and Santa Anna was taking power. Already he had proclaimed the return of the 1824 constitution and dissolved the former centralist legislature, calling for the election of new delegates. What this might result in was anyone's guess, but when the news reached Bowie, he realized soon enough that here might be an opportunity to further his own land interests and those of Texas. Saltillo was a seedbed of centralist sympathy, poor soil to nurture any *norteamericano* land speculator. But Monclova on the Rio Grande, a scant forty miles from the Texian border on the Nueces, was far more friendly to Texian concerns, and physically close enough that Texians could hope to exert much more influence there than in Saltillo. Perhaps he and Veramendi had already discussed the idea of trying to get the capital of Coahuila y Tejas moved before the new governor left. Certainly it answered the needs of both.

James Bowie decided that he could help, but he would have to go to Saltillo. On December 27 he appeared in San Felipe to leave his power of attorney with his friends Donoho and Thomas Gay to handle any of his land affairs in his absence, then made ready to depart.[37] Before leaving San Felipe, however, he made a new acquaintance who would come with him as far as San Antonio. Just then arrived on his first visit into

Texas was Sam Houston, the onetime governor of Tennessee, friend of Crockett, and once the presumed heir apparent to the presidency after his friend Andrew Jackson. Houston virtually self-destructed in 1829 when his new marriage broke down. He resigned his governorship, and for the next three years lived with the Cherokee in the territory west of Arkansas. There he earned the sobriquet "Big Drunk," and entertained the soldiers at Fort Gibson by telling them stories in return for drinks. One of them, young Lt. Jefferson Davis of the First U.S. Infantry, found Houston to be an "enigma," and elaborated by calling him "a worthless man with some good points."[38] Now, for reasons that may have ranged from land speculation to a desire to see the United States annex the province, or even to see it become independent, Houston had decided to remake himself in Texas, and his first stop was San Felipe.

It was not unnatural that Houston would attach himself to Bowie. A man of big ideas and bold talk, a man of action, he would naturally gravitate to Bowie, given his current reputation. For his part, Bowie found Houston a congenial companion and an eager listener on the road. They were men of the same stripe: always on the move, seeking something better—and quickly—bold and decisive if sometimes hasty, and occasionally intemperate. Houston listened intently to Bowie's stories. He came in part to report on the Comanche, who had been raiding north of Red River, and also to observe for himself the mood of the Texians toward independence. Bowie's San Saba explorations and Indian encounters could inform him on the former, while the Piedras capture, perhaps exaggerated in Bowie's storytelling style, helped convince Houston of the mistaken notion that Texians had already beaten and expelled all the Mexicans from the province.[39]

Bowie, Houston, the ever-present Caiaphas Ham, and another new friend, Gen. Sterling Robertson of Tennessee, left for San Antonio before year's end. Another would-be *empresario*, Robertson had been trying to get a grant to settle in Texas since 1822, then actually brought a number of families on a contract in early 1830, only to arrive after the April 6 decree. The government denied him permission to settle the families, instead turning his contract over to Austin and Williams, but now he was coming back to try again for a contract of his own, and his association with Bowie on this journey suggests that he may have been one of the causes of friction between Bowie and Austin, for a considerable enmity naturally developed between Robertson on the one hand and Austin and Williams on the other.

It was not an uneventful trip, though Bowie had traveled the road many times. Given the climate of unrest, they felt it wise to mount a guard every night, for the Comanche and other bands were occasionally raiding this far south again. One morning Houston came to the campfire laughing, saying that on his watch that night he believed he had heard an arrow whizzing past him every time he turned his head. Stand or stoop, look left or right, he heard the buzz of another shaft past his ear. Only by morning did his terror turn to amusement when he finally discovered that the noise came from his own hat rubbing against his collar.[40]

Houston left the party in San Antonio, but there at his home Bowie found an old face awaiting to join him—his recently arrived brother-in-law Alexander Sterrett. Just what brought Sterrett to Texas now is uncertain, but it may well have been bad news, perhaps even word of the death of Stephen Bowie. Just as likely, Sterrett came to advise Bowie of the family's financial situation in Louisiana. The whole Walker and Wilkins sale was falling through, thanks to James's bogus titles. On July 28 they had sold for thirty thousand dollars part of the land on Bayou Boeuf that Bowie secured through forged grants in the names of Antonio Pilboro and Julien Galbon, only to have to refund the money on September 11.[41] Moreover, when the Walkers and Wilkins sold other tracts to purchasers, they found on survey that the claims infringed on the lawfully located claims of others and that some of the land was already occupied.[42] Congress was passing renunciation acts, under which titles gained by forgery were being withdrawn, regardless of innocent purchasers who might own them, and the Walkers and Wilkins had no choice but to accept "all the renunciations and confirmatory acts for the plantation purchased . . . from Reason & James and Stephen Bowie."[43] With that avenue of future revenue cut off, it was all the more important for Bowie to press for an opportunity to start selling the eleven-league grants on which he held leases, and especially before those leases expired.

Thus the trip to Saltillo came at an opportune time. Bowie and his party reached the capital on February 7, 1833, and immediately called on Veramendi.[44] In a climate of dangerous uncertainty, Veramendi felt unsure of his own position, since he had been elected under the former regime. The centralist delegates recently turned out of office hid themselves in their homes for fear of some form of reprisal, and republicans felt unsafe in the city of the opposition. Veramendi himself thought it wise to keep sentinels on guard outside his Saltillo home. Bowie and Ham shared a room in the Veramendi house, and they kept a guard in the chamber with them. No one entered the house without giving the password "*como caballo*," which meant rather loosely: "I eat horse."[45]

Veramendi only held office briefly, serving out Letona's term, and when the new legislature met it did little but debate. Yet Veramendi would have his influence, and so too would Bowie. The day after his arrival in Saltillo, on February 8, Bowie met with Veramendi, who then introduced him to influential members of the new congress. In the days to come, Bowie unsheathed all of his old charm to ingratiate himself with the legislators. Even down here his capture of Piedras would be known, and applauded by the republicans and *santanistas*. Of course his connection to Veramendi gave him considerable clout, and so did his reputation from the San Saba fight. Bowie also took pains to look the part of an important man. However rough he dressed for the long trek across the interior, he always had a blue broadcloth suit in his baggage to change into once he reached civilization.[46]

Most important of all, though, was James Bowie's attitude. He lived in a time and place where some white Texian settlers felt—and all too often manifested—a condescending racial superiority to *tejanos* and Mexicans, regarding their brown-skinned neighbors as only a step or two removed from the black-skinned men whom they actually bought and sold. Moreover, being overwhelmingly Protestant, the Texians resented the virtual hegemony of the Catholic Church, while unquestionably the continuing spectacle of disorganization and instability in its public affairs gave all the immigrants a healthy disdain for Mexican political institutions when compared to government in the United States. Thus, being ruled by Mexicans carried with it an added element of distaste and resentment that contributed to the sentiments for complete independence. That this had actually been the Mexicans' land for centuries did not matter. White Americans were destined to have it by a kind of divine right that must inevitably see their eventual rule everywhere on the continent. Yet the *tejanos* and the Mexicans in Saltillo could see that Bowie was different. Whatever his private feelings may have been, publicly he showed nothing but courtesy and respect and every indication that he regarded them—the landed class, anyhow—as equals. His treatment of Piedras and his soldiers testified to that, and so did his marriage to Ursula. No doubt he felt the same superior attitude toward the landless *peons* that the aristocratic Veramendis would naturally have entertained, but still in meeting these legislators and others in Saltillo, he impressed them with his courtesy and consideration. Seguín's son Juan recalled that Bowie was "known among the Mexicans from Saltillo to Béxar." Some loved him. Others loathed him, calling him "*fanfarrón Santiago Bowie*"—"James Bowie the braggart."[47] But whether they liked him or not, said Seguín, "they all knew that he was absolutely brave, and that they could depend upon his being fair to foe and loyal to friends."[48]

Thanks to the respect that he earned in legislative circles, Bowie soon began to call on individual congressmen, as no doubt did Veramendi, with their plan to move the capital to Monclova. The idea was probably already in the minds of many of the new delegates anyhow. Firmly in the hands of republicans, Monclova offered a much more congenial atmosphere for Texian interests, and for Bowie's. Such a move would certainly serve Veramendi as well, and his voice and Bowie's were heard in the taverns and drawing rooms of Saltillo during the following days, encouraging the new delegates to their vote. From two of the leading delegates, in particular, he secured promises of assistance, and they came through, for when finally the congress met on the issue, it cast a decisive ballot to move to Monclova. Veramendi's family friend Menchaca believed that Bowie himself bore the greatest influence in effecting the change. If so, it most likely involved more than his charm. If the land and immigration restrictions could be relaxed, there was money to be made in renewing the old eleven-league-grant policy. In the friendly atmosphere of Monclova, these legislators could easily arrange the grants for themselves and their friends, and men like Bowie and Williams and Robertson could buy them. With the capital on the waters of the Rio Grande, one hand could wash another.[49]

•

His goal accomplished, Bowie returned to Béxar and was in San Felipe in time to participate in the convention that met on April 1, the very same day that Santa Anna finally took power in Mexico.[50] Bowie's friend Houston sat as a delegate from his new home near Nacogdoches, and William Wharton took the chair to preside, guaranteeing that the more radical faction would be in charge. By the time it adjourned on April 13, the meeting had not only affirmed all the resolutions of the previous October but now taken the additional step of drafting a constitution for the proposed new Mexican state of Texas, reminding Mexico City that in the 1824 constitution, to which Santa Anna professed loyalty, Texas was only provisionally attached to Coahuila until its population grew sufficiently to merit its being a state in its own right. Certainly its population now justified separation.[51] They selected James Miller, Erasmo Seguín, and Austin as emissaries to take their petition to Mexico City. When it came to it, the first two refused to go, but by the end of the month Stephen Austin was on his way—hopeful, apprehensive, and somewhat disillusioned at the way Texas had gotten away from him. Yet he seemed resigned. "No one can be blamed in any manner for what has happened since June 1832, in Texas," he would say shortly. "It was inevitable."[52]

While in San Felipe, Bowie did a final service for Piedras's *soldados* when he secured from merchant John Brown supplies valued at 101 pesos for them to make their final return to Mexico.[53] Then he turned his attention to his own affairs. It was time to prepare for speculating in earnest. Immediately after the adjournment of the convention, he went south to Brazoria in company with a powerful host of men anxious for land. There were Archibald Hotchkiss and Gen. John Thompson Mason, agents of the Galveston Bay and Texas Land Company of New York, which had been stymied for some time in settling families; Bowie's new friend Houston; Samuel Sawyer, to whom Bowie had sold one of his eleven-league grants; Sterrett; Thomas J. Chambers, who had been the official surveyor for land titles in Texas and was now a paid representative at Saltillo for residents of eastern Texas; Henry S. Brown, who had been a delegate from Brazoria; and others.[54] They kept their purpose well cloaked, but so many men with a hunger for speculation could hardly have been on a pleasure trip.

Not only did he have those leases on eleven-league grants that he

and Donoho had bought in Saltillo back in 1830, but now he was taking advantage of the growing rift between Austin and Williams to get
close to the latter. Bowie had already sold at least one of his leased
grants to Sawyer prior to March 1833. The leases cost him as little as
seventy-two dollars, whereas the property could be sold for at least
two thousand.[55] As for Williams, he was branching out into selling
merchandise in partnership with McKinney, and at the same time was
promoting a second colony thanks to an *empresario* grant to himself
and Austin jointly. It allowed him to settle eight hundred families
north of the original Austin colony, in a large tract between the
Navisota and the Colorado that had originally been the Robertson
grant prior to the April 6, 1830, law. Stephen Austin became disenchanted with the proposed colony and sold his interest to his cousin
John Austin. Now, standing to profit considerably by this, Williams
turned most of his attention away from the San Felipe colony.

Instead, apparently on advice from Bowie, he started selling "location privileges" in the area, essentially a device to raise money from
would-be settlers by giving them the right to squat on certain land,
though under current law they could not actually purchase title.[56]
Stephen Austin was already distressed over what Williams was doing
when he left for Mexico, and it troubled him enough that when he
stopped in Matamoros at the end of May, he wrote to Williams, chiding him strongly: "Keep clear of land jobbing," he warned. "Keep clear
of all speculations for the future." Austin feared that he might be
ruined himself by his own second small colony just above the
Colorado. As for Williams and his cousin and their much more ambitious venture, he warned sternly that "such men [as] Bowie etc will led
[*sic*] you and John too far into speculations."[57] In fact, Texas was about
to experience a boom in speculating that many then and later would
date from the first sales of Bowie's eleven-league grants.[58] That boom
would play no small role in the increasing tensions between Texas and
Mexico.

As summer approached, Bowie decided that it was time to return to
Louisiana, with a variety of business at hand. The news Sterrett
brought required that he see for himself what remained, if anything, of
his prospects of realizing any money from his sales there. Rezin was
planning a trip to the East on business of his own, and James might

accompany him, both for pleasure and to make one more approach in Washington on the Kemper–de la Français claim. Finally Veramendi, possibly at Bowie's coaxing, sent ten thousand dollars to Músquiz in July, with instructions that it be sent to New Orleans, for an unknown purpose most likely connected with the proposed cotton mill. Since Bowie's sources of large cash from Louisiana land sales had dried up, the governor may have decided to risk his own capital to buy the machinery to get started.[59] It was only natural that Bowie himself actually transport the money, especially if it was to be involved in one of his schemes.

Accompanied by Caiaphas Ham, Bowie left San Antonio and Ursula one more time.[60] Married just over two years, they had actually spent at least eleven months of that time apart, with now the prospect of at least another three or four months' separation as Bowie traveled the East. For poor Ursula, now just twenty-one, still childless though possibly expecting at last, there was nothing to do but accept her lot as his wife, keep her complaints to herself, and like a woman of her class restrain her tears and assure her husband that wherever he went, her heart was with him.

The ground was well traveled by now, and the trip to Louisiana seemingly got shorter as the years passed. Once he reached Natchitoches, Bowie could get to New Orleans by steamboat in a mere three days, and from New Orleans to Natchez in only five. There was small cause for rejoicing when he arrived, however. By now Stephen was definitely dead, aged scarcely thirty-five, with a widow and two orphans left behind. Worse, from John—if not from the press—came word that at its January term, the Supreme Court of the United States had passed down its ruling in *Sampeyrac and Stewart* v. *the United States*, finding against the plaintiffs. In the argument Stewart's attorney admitted that the original grant to Sampeyrac was a forgery, and that the deed from Sampeyrac to John Bowie was also a forgery, and that the witnesses who testified to having seen Bowie make the purchase had lied. Stewart's whole case rested on his being an innocent good-faith purchaser, but the court found that no right of title could be claimed by any buyer of a forged grant, whether knowingly or unknowingly. Since Bowie never had any title to sell, Stewart could not buy it from him.[61] In a single stroke the Court overthrew all of the

Bowies' Arkansas claims. Their past sales could be revoked at any time, leaving them very unpopular in the area, while regardless of the confirmation of their claims by the superior court of the territory, they would certainly be unable to sell any more. And in an infuriating irony, the *Sampeyrac and Stewart* v. *United States* decision would henceforth be used by the U.S. Treasury and the General Land Office to deny title or compensation to innocent buyers of James's Louisiana lands, men like the Walkers and Wilkins. The day of what Commissioner of the General Land Office Ethan Brown called "the numerous fraudulent Bowie land claims" was over at last.[62]

About the only good news awaiting Bowie was of the misfortune of another. His old foe Josiah S. Johnston had been killed in May while traveling from Alexandria to Natchitoches when a boiler exploded on the new steamboat *Lioness*. It was a hollow pleasure, if any, given that it came at the same time as the ultimate destruction of Bowie's land speculations east of the Mississippi. To be sure, over the years he had realized no small sum in actual cash in hand, perhaps as much as fifty thousand dollars over a decade, but it was a small and disappointing reward in his grasp, compared to the scope of his reach. He still owned one or two small properties on genuine title, but they could hardly excite his interest now.

Thus a trip east with Rezin offered the prospect of welcome relief from the scene of failure. Of the Bowie brothers, only James seems to have been spared the curse of failing eyesight, and by now Rezin's had reached a stage at which he felt he needed to consult specialists in New York and Philadelphia. Having originally intended to return to Texas that season, he scarcely got beyond Donaldsonville on his way upriver when his vision all but gave out, forcing him to cancel his plans. James's coming may even have been partially in response to a call for help from Rezin, a summons that he would never refuse, and together in late July or early August they set off for New York, probably taking ship from New Orleans. Rezin needed to get away if for no other reason than to escape his oppressive financial situation. By April 1832 his debts had mounted above $38,000. The frost that killed part of a crop, the faulty steam machinery that ruined more, the smallpox that killed slaves, and a host of other calamities had left him in ruinous shape. With the creditors closing in on him through the courts, he had no choice but to file a declaration of insolvency and surrender all his possessions except his clothing, his blacksmithing tools, and his militia arms and equipment. Everything else had to go, and even an attempt to shelter some of his property by turning it over to his wife, Margaret, and claiming her as a creditor did not work.[63]

In New York, Rezin called on a doctor, while James may have had a chance—and amicable—encounter with his onetime foe at the Sandbar, Robert Crain. The visit included a trip to Niagara Falls before they headed south to Philadelphia in mid-August.[64] In that city Rezin submitted to treatment from Dr. Valentine Mott that resulted in the partial recovery of sight in one eye, at least.[65] While there he also indulged a whim that had taken him sometime before—to write and publish an account of the San Saba fight, and having James along with him allowed him to check his memory against his brother's. He gave it to the editor of *Atkinson's Saturday Evening Post and Bulletin: A Family Newspaper, Devoted to Literature, Morality, Science, News, Agriculture and Amusement*, and had the pleasure of seeing it appear in the August 17 issue while he and James were still in the city. Accompanied by a crude woodcut showing the besieged whites defending themselves against a horde of Tawakoni, it allowed the brothers to relive again the most desperate hours they ever shared.

If they tore their eyes from Rezin's article to peruse the rest of that issue, they also read "Major Downing's Official Report on the United States Bank," one in a series of satirical letters by Seba Smith that he wrote in the exaggerated vernacular of the backwoodsman. Another close reader of those letters was a man Bowie might not have heard of: U.S. Representative David Crockett, who at that very moment was preparing to start writing his *Autobiography*, employing and perfecting that same style, and much influenced by Smith's Downing letters. This very one, in the issue with the Bowie article, showed that Smith, in turn, had been influenced by Crockett. Though Crockett's name was not mentioned in the letter, still here James Bowie probably saw for the first time the phrase that so characterized not only the Tennesseean, but himself and his generation—"go ahead."

Finally they reached Washington, and another fruitless attempt to cajole or bully something out of the Treasury and State Departments on the Kemper claim. Bowie met Archibald Hotchkiss there, perhaps

by accident, and possibly by design to further their speculating interests, but with nothing else to accomplish, he and Rezin took ship for
New Orleans once more, arriving sometime near the end of
September.[66] Awaiting him he found letters from Ursula speaking of
family matters, visitors coming to San Antonio, and her father's wish
to consult with him, no doubt about that ten thousand dollars that
Bowie was to invest.[67] Ursula herself may have felt some concern about
her husband's handling of the money, reminding him that Veramendi
had given him unsecured funds for investment and that James must not
use the money as if it were his own. "Here they have another way of
thinking," she prompted. But, as always, her last words were for him
to "receive thou the heart of thy wife."[68] She must have had at least
some of his heart as well, for while here in New Orleans Bowie
bought her a splendid set of emerald jewelry, looking forward to seeing her wear it upon his return.[69]

But now some doubt arose as to when Bowie would go back to
Texas, and even *if* he would return. He went to Natchez after reaching
New Orleans, and there cultivated old friends like McNeil and new
ones like Dr. William Richardson. His stories of Texas land sparked the
interest of new friends, too. Dr. Samuel Gustine loaned him four thousand dollars to spend in Texas on land speculation, and Dr. Addison
Dashiel covered Bowie's notes for up to another four thousand, McNeil
all the while marveling at and admiring Bowie's "extraordinary
Capacity in getting money from his friends." Even Richardson parted
with some cash, McNeil observing that "Bowie could easily have
obtained from him any reasonable amount of money." If the several
physicians had paid more careful attention to the lavish way Bowie
spent money, they might have been a bit more judicious in entrusting
theirs to him, but his manner was, as usual, irresistible.[70]

Yet something sinister, and far more irresistible than even Bowie's
charm, visited Natchez that same summer. The whole Mississippi
Valley was hit—first by cholera in Arkansas, and then by the malaria
that so often ravaged Mississippi and Louisiana.[71] That summer proved
to be one of the worst, and the innocuous mosquitoes that carried the
virus did not discriminate great men from small. One of them bit James
Bowie while he was in Natchez in October, and within days he was
deathly ill. All the symptoms were there—the fevers and chills, the ache

in the back, the delirium. It did not help that his body had never fully recovered from the bullets and blades of the Sandbar. By the end of the month he lay near death at McNeil's house, cared for by his friend Richardson. Perhaps at McNeil's urging, he decided that it was time to make out his will. He dictated it to his friend attorney Felix Huston, and kept it simple. He wanted Gustine to be repaid his loan, and Dashiel secured from having to pay any of the notes that he guaranteed. To Ursula, "my dearly beloved wife," he left her new jewels and nothing else, since she was provided for in his prenuptial agreement. Apparently Bowie was sufficiently disoriented that he did not remember that between all the outright lies and exaggerations, and the evaporation of the money due him for his Louisiana land, there might not be fifteen thousand dollars' worth of estate left to satisfy his obligation to her unless his eleven-league grants could be confirmed and sold. Instead, all of his estate after his debts he left to Rezin and Martha Sterrett, stipulating that he wanted them to ensure that they used some of the money to educate Stephen's orphans, and that his executors, Rezin and Alexander Sterrett, should heed Veramendi's advice in liquidating his Texas holdings. When it was done, Huston read it aloud to Bowie, who approved and falteringly affixed his signature.[72]

Having settled his affairs and prepared himself for death, Bowie and his iron constitution proceeded to defeat the malarial parasites in his blood, just as he turned back the Tawakoni on the San Saba. Within a few days his fever broke, and Richardson told him that he was on the mend. But then, while he recuperated at McNeil's, came devastating news. There had been a death in the Bowie family after all. Ursula was gone. The cholera outbreak in Arkansas was not isolated, but quickly spread via travelers into Texas. John Austin died of it in September, and in Béxar Bowie's friend José Navarro confessed that he was "very much upset with the danger of this damned cholera." A worried Veramendi took his family, including Ursula, to Monclova to get away from the epidemic.[73]

They left too late. If the infection was not already with them, it appeared on the way, for no sooner did they reach Monclova than the dying commenced. As Menchaca and others watched helplessly, Josefa Navarro de Veramendi went down with cramps, then the violent vomiting and diarrhea, physical collapse, and finally death, all in the space of a day. In terror, each of the others in turn felt the onset of the symptoms, and faced their ends, first Governor Veramendi, then his adopted son, Santiago, and at last Ursula. By about September 23 they were all gone.[74] Three days later the word reached Navarro in Béxar, and he wrote off to Samuel Williams, who had himself nearly died of the epidemic in San Felipe. "Bowie is already a widower," said Navarro. He should get word of the tragedy to Natchez.[75] Perhaps because of Williams's own illness, he did not send the word at once. Moreover, it would take time for a letter addressed to Bowie to find him. More than five weeks passed before the black day, early in November, when McNeil handed the recuperating Bowie the letter with the news. Having nearly beaten the microbes in his body, Bowie almost relapsed, leaving McNeil worried at how "very low" he sank with the news.[76]

But nothing, it seemed, could kill him. Realizing now how much he had missed in all those months away from Ursula, and perhaps as well realizing that she meant more to him than he had thought, he may have fought a losing struggle with his conscience, but his body won its battle and he recovered. Always, it seemed, his prospects brought him to the brink of success, and then his hopes were dashed. The land schemes in Louisiana and Arkansas had come so close, then dissolved. His plans for Congress and high position had looked so bright, then evaporated. Now, in this dreadful 1833, with the finest marriage to be made in all of Texas fairly begun, it ended in tragedy, taking from him not only his wife but his intimate tie to great influence through the dead Veramendi. There was nothing to do but go back to Texas when he was able, of course. Sobered, even shattered, he still never gave up. Defeat simply was not in him. On his way back he encountered on the road his acquaintance Noah Smithwick. When Bowie spoke of Ursula's death, Smithwick saw tears in his eyes.[77]

TRAVIS

1833–1834

*We must wait patiently for the moving of the waters. The course of events will
inevitably tend to the right point, and the people will understand their rights;
yea, and assert them, too.*

WILLIAM BARRET TRAVIS, NOVEMBER 13, 1834

The cholera that killed Bowie's wife and in-laws missed Buck Travis,
but it hit San Felipe and Brazoria hard enough. John Austin died of it.
Travis's friend William Eaton came down with it and luckily survived.
On September 6, 1833, Travis and Thomas McQueen sat up much of
the night with their dying friend Eli Holly from Alabama, and the next
day attended to arrangements for his funeral and burial. Travis dosed
himself with salts and vials of patent nostrums on sale at the local merchants, but in the end his survival came down to pure good fortune.[1]

The diseased bodies of Texians, *tejanos*, and Mexicans from the
Brazos to Saltillo seemed to speak for the unrest in the body politic as
well. Travis was a close observer of the April convention that met in
San Felipe, especially since by then he was so well acquainted with
many of its delegates. He knew Bowie by now. He met new faces, too.
Travis would have encountered Houston for the first time, who sat as a
delegate from Nacogdoches; and if he did not know William Wharton
already, he saw much of him now as leader of the convention. Of
course Travis knew Stephen Austin, and beyond question wholeheartedly endorsed the mission of the convention that sent him to Mexico
to seek separation from Coahuila. If anything, Travis may have wished
by this time for more: separation from Mexico itself.

That is what some of the Mexicans in San Felipe feared. A correspondent of the new secretary of war in Mexico City wrote as the con-

vention met that "lately your Honor what I feel is the state of Texas is very soon to be lost if the steps necessary to save it are not taken."[2] Yet the Texians went rather quiet after Austin left, awaiting with hope the result of his mission, while the instability in Mexico continued. By July, Travis was warning a friend that "there is war and rumors of war in the interior," and sending open letters on the subject to Daniel Anthony, editor of the Brazoria *Constitutional Advocate and Texas Public Advertiser*, showing that he clearly felt he should voice his opinions on public matters.[3] There were no real parties in Texas politics as yet. Some men favored the old centralist regime with power concentrated in Mexico City, while others backed the republican movement that called for more local and regional autonomy, with affairs controlled through the legislature in Saltillo, or else at San Felipe in a separated Texas. Yet most men crossed these lines on other issues, severely blurring the edges of loyalty, so that by now many simply adhered to one leader or another, chiefly the conservative Austin or the growingly popular Houston, who favored a more aggressive stance. Certainly Bowie stood with Houston by late 1833, along with Wharton and others. But Travis kept a foot in both camps. His youth, enthusiasm, and passionate impulse drew him to the dynamic leaders, yet an incipient sense of prudence kept telling him that this was not yet the time to push too hard. If he hoped eventually to see an independent Texian nation, he seems intellectually to have understood that it would best be accomplished in stages, with independence from Coahuila the first step.

Unfortunately Austin met too many delays in Mexico City. He did get a commitment to withdraw the April 6 law on immigration, in itself a major concession, and officials at least promised to address other reforms, but by October, when he saw no movement on the issue of separation from Coahuila, he wrote to the *ayuntamiento* of Béxar suggesting that they go ahead and form a provisional state government. Perhaps presenting the Mexicans with an accomplished fact would spur them to action, he reasoned. In November the government did at last repeal the April 6 law, but then Santa Anna finally took power and suspended the repeal for six months. In frustration Austin left for Texas, only to be arrested and charged with sedition for his suggestion to the Béxar *ayuntamiento*.

Through all this time Travis, like the rest of the Texian leaders, remained an observer. He really did not enter the political arena actively until the late fall, when the time came for elections for a new *alcalde* in San Felipe. He had become increasingly close by now to men like Gay and Johnson, and especially Williamson. He dined with the latter two at Peyton's from time to time, and Williamson called frequently at Travis's office when in town. When Williamson announced himself a candidate, running against Silas Dinsmore, Travis promptly electioneered on his behalf, going into the *tejano* section, which he called "Spanish Town," to cajole or bargain votes. So confident was he of Three-Legged Willie's success that Travis bet ten dollars and a new hat on the outcome, and a pair of boots that his choice for sheriff would triumph. On December 8, after Williamson's victory, Travis spent the whole day buying drinks to celebrate the triumph—and perhaps to pay for a few votes.[4]

Then things started to happen. On January 13, 1834, Travis first heard word of the repeal of the April 6 law. "Joyous intelligence!" he called it, but the news was dampened by word of Austin's arrest.[5] At almost the same time Travis slipped into a more active political role, thanks in part to his growing skill with Spanish, and also to his friendship with Williamson. He had done some translating of letters for the *ayuntamiento* by now. Then Samuel Williams's term as secretary to the *ayuntamiento* expired, and, no doubt prompted by the new *alcalde*, Williamson, the body chose Travis to replace him. At first Travis thought to decline the position, but a stipend of four hundred dollars a year changed his mind, and on February 19 Williams turned over to him the official records of the *ayuntamiento*, though Travis actually commenced his duties several days before. It was not exciting work— some translation, lots of copying of letters and resolutions, filing reports with the department political chief in Béxar, compiling vital statistics for Austin's colony, and the like. But the secretarial pen put him at the center of what was happening, where he saw every incoming letter and wrote or copied almost all outgoing correspondence and reports. Moreover, being present at all the meetings of the *ayuntamiento*, and its members being his friends, he could by mere conversation exert almost as much influence as a voting member.[6]

Travis had to be careful about his friends, though, for sometimes his new position put him at risk of conflict of interest. He still served privately as attorney for Samuel Williams in his land dealings, and now the subject of the old Sterling Robertson *empresario* grant came before the *ayuntamiento*. Robertson brought his claim to their attention in the wake of the announcement of the revocation of the April 6 law. Travis had previously advised Williams to meet informally with Williamson and others to try to settle the matter out of court, but now the council met formally and on February 6 concluded that Robertson's contract should still be valid and that he by rights ought to be recognized as head of the colony that Williams had been trying to develop.[7] In fact, copying the resolution was Travis's first task as secretary, the very day that he accepted the position. Given the fact that he was not yet officially secretary when the council made its decision, Travis's personal and business relationship with Williams could not likely have influenced its decision, but Williams decided not to accept the finding without a fight. The next day he spoke with Travis, now officially secretary, and promised to give him certificates for land in the colony that had been taken away from him. The implication that he expected Travis's assistance when the issue came before the *ayuntamiento* again is unmistakable, but in the end the congress in Monclova settled the case by finally revoking Austin and Williams's claim to the grant.[8] If Travis took any note of the possible intention of a bribe, he kept it to himself.

Scarcely two months later, when congress decreed the establishment of Austin's colony as a separate administrative jurisdiction from Béxar by creating the Department of Brazos, the *ayuntamiento* had to submit nominees for the position of political chief. Alcalde Williamson's name naturally came forth. So did that of James H. C. Miller, not to be confused with James B. Miller, Travis's landlord. The surprise was the third nominee, William B. Travis. It would have been a considerable elevation to go from mere secretary in February to head of a whole territorial department a few months later. It must have been both a mark of esteem on the part of most of the *ayuntamiento*, and a political move evidencing the divisions within the council. Miller was a centralist, thoroughly loyal to the old regime, and so despised by Travis that when he wrote of the nominations in his diary that night, he declined even to mention Miller by name.[9] Reflecting Stephen Austin's hesitant stance, San Felipe was always diffident about stepping forward or backward, and the best the aggressive faction, headed by Williamson, could do was to put two of its own on the slate.[10]

The next day Travis as secretary sent a copy of the nominations, as well as those for several other new positions in the Brazos Department, to political chief Músquiz in Béxar. Two weeks later he did not hesitate to send a private letter. In it he first informed Músquiz that Miller was a "foreigner," not a colonist, and had not become a naturalized citizen of Mexico, thus disqualifying him. Having attempted to undermine his opponent, and whether or not he had a sound basis for making that claim, Travis then went on to add the line that established him then and forever as a politician: "I have no desire to be employed in the position of Chief," he said, "but if I were named I should comply with all the laws and orders of the Government according to the best understanding thereof." In short, he very much wanted the position.[11] At the same time, when he learned that his friend David Burnet would be appointed a district judge at San Jacinto, Travis could not help crowing to Burnet about how he had been "instrumental in promoting your appointment." A bit full of himself in his new influence he may have been, but Travis would not have been a politician if he did not also want recipients of his favors to know what he had done for them, for favors could be returned one day. He urged Burnet to accept, as they were of like mind, and Travis wanted to see as many of the hawkish Texians in office as possible.[12]

Interested as he was in his possible elevation, Travis had even more important things to pass along to Músquiz. Williamson wrote a personal address to the *ayuntamiento* expressing his views on the question of Texian independence from Coahuila. "We still continue our unnatural connexion with Coahuila," he said. The petition taken by Austin had been ignored, Austin arrested, and the Mexican congress apparently intended to ignore their pleas. In such a situation, they must act: "Desertion by *us* then, of this *Our own cause, would be worse than political apostacy,*" he declared. He proposed that San Felipe and the other *ayuntamientos* in Texas draft a "respectful memorial" on independent statehood. "*Let us try it,*" he pleaded. At the same time he attached a petition to the congress in Mexico City begging for Austin's release, and stating, in words borrowed rather significantly from the Declaration of Independence, that Texians would pledge "their lives, their fortunes and their sacred honor" to uphold the constitution and the laws of Mexico. He reminded Mexico that Texians had risen in support of Santa Anna, and the outbursts at Anahuac and Nacogdoches had been forced on them by necessity. Travis copied the two documents for transmission to Béxar, and may well have had some small hand in their composition, given his close alliance with Williamson.[13] In the months ahead, as one or another of the other *ayuntamientos* followed suit with memorials, Travis forwarded them to Béxar as well. The one from Nacogdoches came, ironically enough, on Bastille Day.[14] The leaders of the aggressive faction were becoming more bold, and Travis with them.

Momentous news came on May 14, the same day that Travis tried to undercut Miller's chances for the Brazos leadership, when he received the announcement that the state congress now in Monclova had passed a law opening virtually all the public land in Texas and Coahuila for sale at auction in eleven-league tracts. It was, of course, part of Bowie's work, though Travis may have known nothing more than rumors of his involvement. Still, Travis regarded the act as "the most important law ever passed by the state govt."[15] From his point of view, in tandem with the abolition of the April 6 law, this move would allow the influx of thousands of new settlers from the United States. To buy their land they would have to become citizens, which would give them the vote, and the prospect of shifting the seesaw struggle between the centralists and the republicans decisively to the left. And should that struggle turn ugly, or even become a struggle with Mexico itself, then their arms would be needed in defense of Texas.

Travis did not get the political chief's portfolio in the Brazos department. It went to the schoolteacher Henry Smith, but if Travis felt any disappointment he kept it to himself. More likely, he enjoyed sufficient success elsewhere that he could weather a disappointment now with a maturity that had been foreign to him in Claiborne. The daily routine of the *ayuntamiento* kept him busy enough translating documents, finding translators when his skills proved insufficient, preparing passports, and the like.[16] When Williamson was absent, as he was for a time in July, Travis actually conducted the dealings with Béxar on his own, most of it routine transmission of documents and reports. When illness forced Músquiz to resign as political chief in San Antonio, Bowie's friend Juan Seguín replaced him, and Travis dealt with him thereafter. On occasion all of San Felipe's elected officials were absent, leaving Travis to act as *alcalde*, alderman, and everything else.[17]

The appointment of Henry Smith was a significant event, for he was the first *nortemericano* to win such a high office in Mexican Texas. It showed goodwill on the part of the new governor, Augustín Viesca, and also gave promise of a greater Texian voice in Texian affairs. Travis congratulated the new appointee, expressing the "hope that you may be the means of great good to Texas." Since the new Department of Brazos was to be headquartered in San Felipe, it would have been most efficient if political chief Smith had moved there, but he kept his home in Brazoria and seldom even visited Austin's village. That only meant the more work for Travis, for the *ayuntamiento* there had to work in tandem with Smith, and its secretary was his secretary. When Travis notified Smith of his appointment on July 24, he sent along a plea to come to San Felipe to preside at forthcoming elections, and to deal with correspondence awaiting him. Smith would keep to Brazoria for the most part, however, and as the summer wore on, Travis found the paperwork accumulating. It was especially frustrating when a large bundle of documents arrived in the *ayuntamiento* office directed specifically to Smith. Only he could open them, but Travis confessed that "we are anxious to know" the contents.[18]

Their anxiety for information reflected the uncertainty of events in Mexico. By August, Travis lamented to a friend that there was still no word of the prisoner Austin's fate.[19] Coahuila itself reeled in turmoil following the election of the new legislature and the removal of the capital to Monclova. Once Santa Anna took power it became painfully evident that people had been mistaken about his liberal sentiments. Faced with unsettled conditions, largely the result of his own uprising, he began concentrating more and more power in Mexico City, essentially becoming the very sort of centralist that he had rebelled against. Seeing this, the Monclova legislature in May condemned him and called for a special session to meet and address the situation. That was all the old centralists in Saltillo needed. They reconstituted themselves as a rump legislature, chose their own governor, creating a virtual state of civil war in Coahuila as each capital vied for power, as well as for the profits to be made from the anticipated boom in land speculation set off by Bowie and others the year before. In August the Monclova congress failed to gather a quorum, as many members feared to appear, and a military-led centralist coup seized power, deposed the sitting governor, and officers of the army installed their own governor. When the two competing capitals referred their dispute to Santa Anna, he decided in favor of Monclova but ordered the election of a new congress in December, with a postponement of the special session until the following March. Perhaps most foreboding of all, Santa Anna sent Gen. Martín Perfecto de Cós and a garrison to Saltillo to keep order. With all that happening, it was even worse for Travis and his friends in San Felipe that it could take nearly four weeks for documents from Monclova to reach San Felipe. No wonder they fussed at unopened mail when Smith stayed in Brazoria.

Based on what they did know, Travis and the *ayuntamiento* were worried. The Texian delegation in the Monclova congress sent them an address early in September detailing the chaotic conditions there, warning of a military overthrow of civil government, and two rival legislatures, both of questionable legitimacy. Texas should recognize neither, they advised. In the political power vacuum then existing, they advised that Texas call a convention to create its own provisional government headquartered at Béxar. With two cities in Coahuila fighting each other to be capital, "is not Texas as much entitled to a government?" the delegates asked.[20] Hearing this, the new political chief in San Antonio, Seguín, promptly agreed, condemning Santa Anna in the process. In San Felipe, Williamson condemned the rise of a military despot at Monclova "whose ignorance is alone equaled by his arrogance."[21]

By mid-September in San Felipe affairs seemed to calm, and Travis could actually tell his friend Burnet that "there is no news of much importance." There were rumors of Austin being released, though unconfirmed, San Felipe had voted for Viesca's reinstallation as legitimate governor, and there was a movement to unseat Thomas J. Chambers, one of the Texian delegates to the Monclova congress. Travis offered to have Burnet nominated if he wished, another example either of Travis's genuine influence with the *ayuntamiento* by now, or else of his belief in his influence.[22] But then came news of a threat that the military in Béxar might overthrow the outspoken Seguín for his declaration against Santa Anna, and once more the unrest emerged. The threat took Henry Smith by surprise, and even if Travis did not have the clout he had thought with the rulers in San Felipe, he certainly enjoyed great influence with the political chief of their department, for now Smith turned to the secretary. Frankly—and incredibly—he confessed that he did not know what to do, and begged for Travis's advice.

"We are all at a loss," Travis admitted, but then hammered home his repeated theme that "one thing is certain, never has there been a time when your presence was so much needed as now." Smith must come to San Felipe and act rather than stay at home and allow events to pass around him. For his own part, however, Travis was as decisive as Smith was diffident. "Texas is forever ruined unless the citizens make a manly, energetic effort to save themselves from anarchy and confusion," he said. The central committee, created in the wake of the Anahuac disturbance, must meet with Smith and the *ayuntamiento* and issue a call for a convention, and the delegates sent to the proposed meeting in Béxar must be sent with "*absolute powers*" to act and to "dispose of the destinies of the country."

"We are virtually and *ipso facto* without any legal government in the state or nation," he declared. "We are subject legally and constitutionally to no power on earth, save our *sovereign selves*. We are actually in a situation of revolution and discord, when it becomes the duty of every individual to protect himself." If Texians did not act for themselves now, he said, the rule of law and order would be crushed everywhere. "The fact is, something *must* be done to save us from our inevitable fate, and the sooner the better." Through circumstances, Smith was now the highest ranking legal *norteamericano* official in all of Texas, and he should take the lead. "Let all party animosities drop. Let us march like a band of brothers to the same saving and vitally important point." Whatever the majority in their convention decided, they must support it, and as for Smith, he could dally no longer. "*Come! Come! Come!*"[23]

It was a remarkable statement, certainly saying more than Smith expected, and perhaps even more than Travis realized. Not only did he refuse to recognize the legality of either legislature in Coahuila, but he also maintained that there was now no legitimate government in

Mexico itself. Moreover, Texians now owed allegiance to no one. They were, in the underscored word he used himself, "*sovereign.*" Every man must step forward, and they must all act now, for revolution was upon them. It was William B. Travis's personal declaration of independence, not just from Coahuila, but from Mexico itself. If there had ever been any lingering doubt as to his sentiments, he ended it with this clear, bold alignment with the most hawkish of the Texians, now aligning into a group whose origins traced to the original uprisings at Anahuac and Nacogdoches. Travis had been in at the beginning, if only as a passive participant in his prison cell. Now in advising the uncertain Smith, he made a bid to assume leadership.

In evidence either of his trust in Travis or his inability to fix his own mind, Henry Smith adopted every one of Travis's suggestions. On October 25 he published a call to the *ayuntamientos* in the Brazos district "and the Citizens of Texas Generally," calling for the selection of delegates to a convention to declare Texas independent from Coahuila and establish its own constitutional government. At the same time came word—probably from Travis—that in Béxar the *tejano* leaders under Seguín were taking the same step, proposing November 15 and Béxar as the venue.[24] Meanwhile, in San Felipe, Travis distributed handbills sent by Smith conveying the same call, and their reception took him a bit by surprise. Especially troubling was the dissent from Frank Johnson and William Jack, important members of the central committee. He hoped that a spontaneous approval by the people would overrule his colleagues, especially as he had opened a package addressed to Smith—no more waiting anxiously for him to come and open his own mail—and found the plan of the people in Béxar. It looked good, and he believed the people would give their accord to the convention. "Let us meet their advances," Travis declared. "It is all important to our success now and in future to have them with us. Now is the time to secure them & their influence in our favor."

Indeed, Travis regarded cooperation with Béxar as sufficiently important to justify engaging in a little political maneuvering. He found to his surprise that he was virtually alone on the central committee in favoring the convention call. Johnson and Jack, his new friend Wylie Martin, the odious Miller, and others all felt it was going too far too soon. Faced with their opposition, Travis advised Smith that he should bypass the committee. "I think it has never done any good," Travis complained. "To succeed we must act through the legal authorities," and that meant the *ayuntamiento*, where there was a safe majority in favor of a convention. He advised Smith to write to Jack and Miller only to mollify them and observe the forms of consultation, but to go around their committee entirely and communicate directly with the movement's leaders in Béxar. Indeed, in San Antonio, Travis happily saw that both the native *tejanos*—whom he, like others, still called Mexicans—and the immigrant Texians seemed of one accord. The Mexicans, he said, had "thrown themselves into our arms & upon our protection." Common decency dictated that Smith "improve the golden opportunity & send commissioners to meet them."[25]

Significantly, and to his credit, Travis shared little if any of the common prejudice against Mexicans, either *tejanos* or their brothers in the rest of the nation. If anything, he saw them as allies in their common cause against anarchy in Coahuila, and possible dictatorship in Mexico City. He enjoyed good relations with Juan Seguín, though theirs was as yet a passing association, and he counted a fair number of *tejanos* among his clients and professional acquaintances. Certainly he had no reluctance to sleep with a *tejana*. Like Bowie, and like the *tejanos* themselves, he probably accepted much of the prevailing Mexican social distinction between the *pobres*, the landless poor, and the families like the Veramendis and the Seguíns, but as subsequent events would show, he looked on even the *peon* class as people entitled to respect if deserved. Hence his anxiety to meet the *bexareños* halfway.[26]

Unfortunately, Travis could not control events as he seemed to control Henry Smith. At the political chief's request he spoke with Johnson, Jack, and the others and found an almost unanimous resistance. "Public opinion runs so high against any change that I doubt whether anything can be done towards an organization of Texas at this time," he wrote in disappointment on November 1. Regardless of his suggestion that it be bypassed, the central committee met formally on the proposition late in October, and over Travis's objections decided against calling for the convention. Immigrants were coming to Texas again, and they did not want to precipitate another closure of their borders. Santa Anna had made good on a few other reforms. Most of all, Austin still languished in a Mexican jail, and any precipitous act on their part might endanger his life. Severely disappointed, Travis told Smith that "I knew it was useless to oppose them." Consequently, much as Travis may have choked on the words, he joined with the majority in issuing a broadside stating their opinion that the revolt in Coahuila did not justify Texas in violating the 1824 constitution. Conditions in Texas had improved. They enjoyed most of the advantages of being an independent state without having to bear the additional expense. For Austin's sake they must stay tranquil.[27]

That callow youth from Claiborne who was always in a hurry for everything had come a long way. He was only twenty-five now, and yet he had learned restraint, patience, and most of all discretion. "Unless the people were more favorable to the plan than they are here," he wrote Smith from San Felipe, "I should say let us remain quiet. For unless we are all united Texas can never sustain herself alone." He may have gone along with the majority on his committee for the sake of unity, but he still favored a separate state government for Texas, as he always had, "provided we can be united and get it on peaceable terms." In addition, while a few days before he spoke of "revolution" and sovereignty, now he tempered his aspirations and linked them only to what could be obtained by "peaceable" means. His own goals remained the same, but he was mature enough now to know that he could not have it all at once, and that the situation called for patience rather than petulance. Better not to attempt a separation at all, he reasoned, than to try it prematurely and fail, especially given the possible repercussions for Austin. Having discovered a political truth as old as government itself, he told Smith that "as long as people are prosperous they do not desire a change." Nothing could be done for Texas now, of that he was certain. "I am, however, for Texas, right or wrong, and never will oppose anything for her benefit," he concluded, but in the absence of unity on a vital issue like separation, "it would only be to make confusion doubly confounded to attempt to do anything." He had learned one of the lessons that divided democrats from demagogues: The opinion of the people was more important than his own.[28]

It was a lesson that Henry Smith never learned. Sensing in the decision of the central committee a criticism of his own conduct—which, after all, had been but to do as Travis advised—he proceeded to ignore both the voice of the committee and of the people. Unable to make up his own mind at first, once he set it on a course he could not change, and so he went ahead and called a referendum for November 8 on sending delegates to Béxar. The result humiliated Smith. Few even bothered to vote, and those who did soundly rejected the convention. It did not help that the committee issued a broadside condemning the idea, and privately Jack wrote to Austin that the hasty move would "kill Smith and his friends and check this present exertion for a state."[29]

At least Smith did not begrudge Travis going along with the majority, and after the debacle the younger but now much wiser lawyer tried to calm his agitated friend. "I am extremely sorry the people could not harmonize on the State question," he told Smith, "but so it is." Liberty and Nacogdoches delivered even greater majorities against the issue than did San Felipe. Travis confessed that the committee report had been unfair to Smith personally, but he tried without avail to prevent that. "My voice in the committee was only one against six," he said. "I found myself almost alone. All my friends were opposed to my views." Travis even began to offer fatherly advice, of the sort he had probably received himself not so many years before: "We must wait patiently for the moving of the waters. The course of events will inevitably tend to the right point, and the people will understand their rights; yea, and assert them, too."[30]

Attorney Travis could attest personally to the general prosperity now, for his own business seemed to explode in 1834. February and March had been busy months, and then by May his cases rose to the point that accounts due him totaled $4,860.99.[31] Of course hard cash was still scarce in 1834, and barely one debt in ten was actually paid in coin.[32] In fact, Travis the onetime debtor now found himself using the courts to collect debts owed to him—a happy, if ironic, turnaround.[33] One client alone owed him as much as $2,400.00.[34] His duties with the *ayuntamiento* took much-needed time away from his own paperwork, and in early May he employed a bookkeeper to make sense of his accounts. He bought two hundred writing quills and new ledger books for his practice accounts, and paid to have the front of his log office covered with clapboard siding. He even hired a French gardener, Pierre Blanchet, to work for $1.25 a day plus meals to plant a vegetable garden and dress up the ground around the rented house. By the end of May, considering that his business net now spread to Brazoria and Harrisburg and communities on the Colorado, he even toyed with taking on a partner, the brother of Benjamin Fort Smith, Bowie's possible childhood playmate.[35]

The partnership did not materialize for the moment, but Travis did take on another sort of person in the practice. On May 7 he added a new link in the chain of comparisons with his own mentor Dellet when Travis accepted a student to read law under him. Jonathan H. Kuykendall was the nineteen-year-old grandson of Adam Kuykendall, one of the elder Rezin Bowie's neighbors back in Logan County, Kentucky, a very intelligent (though almost cripplingly morose) young man just now glad to be alive. He started reading law with Luke Lesassier, but when that attorney fell ill, he agreed in February to go on a journey with Travis's friend Thomas McQueen. McQueen himself was an ill-fated fellow. He was taking to Monclova a commission from Samuel Williams to carry his petition for keeping the Sterling Robertson grant, but he and Kuykendall had scarcely gotten forty miles from Béxar when a party of Tawakoni or Comanche attacked. An arrow in his side knocked McQueen from his saddle, and as he was falling his own pistol discharged and shot him in the hip, while another arrow struck Kuykendall beneath his left eye, leaving its point lodged beneath the skin in an ugly wound. Kuykendall got McQueen back to Béxar just in time for him to die, and then "moody, restless and discontented," he struck the bargain to read law under Travis for three years and receive room and board in return for helping in the practice.[36]

It did not prove to be a well-made match, though Travis tried to meet his end of the bargain. With the arrow point causing Kuykendall's left cheek and throat glands to swell grotesquely, Travis paid his friend Dr. Robert Peebles, a member of the central committee, to operate on the boy and remove the barb. He paid fifteen dollars a month for Kuykendall to eat his meals at Connell's inn, where Travis himself frequently dined, and where he also paid for his new gardener to eat.[37] He spent money for new pantaloons and shoes for Kuykendall, whose mood did not improve when, a month after the glum young fellow moved into Travis's home, Joseph Clayton settled an old feud by murdering his father, Abner Kuykendall, in the street in San Felipe.

Clayton's conviction and hanging did not lift Kuykendall's spirits, as he found himself "driven to distraction" by his health and depression.[38]

Young Kuykendall's tastes actually leaned more to poetry than the law, which he only agreed to take up when his father threatened to turn him out if he did not. Thus he was hardly the kind of apt pupil that Travis had been. He read Blackstone's *Commentaries*, just as Travis had for Dellet, and studied Spanish law as well, but he lacked his teacher's liking for the work. The boy's dark attitude must have grated on Travis from the first, and he complained about the quantity of office work that Travis gave him: It interfered with his preferred reading of Ovid and the other classical authors. Travis's practice was too big, and besides his mentor also set him to doing some of the work of copying documents for the *ayuntamiento*. "I soon found I had made a bad bargain," Kuykendall recalled. If anything, his experience with Travis left him with a prejudice against the law that he never lost, though when he left Travis after only a couple of months, he continued to read under William Jack in Columbia for a time.[39]

Still Kuykendall did not leave without gaining some respect for Travis, however much their personalities may have clashed. He confessed that he found his mentor "a laborious student, a good scholar, and a very brainful young man." Moreover, he was a good speaker at the bar, though more fluent than pleasant, for his voice seemed loud and his manner often harsh, like Dellet's.[40] Yet he gained enough success that the clients kept coming, and those whom he worked for in the past returned. Eli Holly's widow continued giving him the family's legal work, and Isaac Donoho engaged him to defend himself and Bowie in a suit. Though not often thrown together with Bowie, Travis had other business that occasionally called for him to see the land speculator on those now rare occasions when he was in San Felipe. Bowie's old friend Warren Hall engaged Travis in Brazoria to oversee the purchase of twenty-three slaves from Peyton Splane, a $12,450 transaction that paid Travis a handsome fee, and may have told him of the early days with Bowie as well, since Travis occasionally stayed the night with Hall. In fact Travis did a fair bit of business for those who bought and sold "lifetime indentures." Business came from San Antonio and even as far away as New Orleans.[41]

Since he lived on what was still a rugged frontier, Travis also more than once had to clean up the legal mess after a quarrel ended in murder, as with Abner Kuykendall. Feuds over a variety of issues were not at all uncommon. Morris Mays and Rawson Alley feuded for some time in the spring of 1834, Alley accusing Mays of stealing and rebranding one of his yearling calves. In April, Alley took the matter to J. W. Moore, the *alcalde* in Harrisburg, and four lawyers came into the case, Travis leading for Mays, and Pat Jack for Alley. They held court outdoors under the live oaks, with quite an audience present for the entertainment, as Ben Fort Smith volunteered to roast a couple of calves for lunch for the crowd. Travis entered a plea of not guilty for Mays, and then Jack helped Alley state his case, his best evidence being that one of his own cows was letting the yearling suckle. Despite Travis's best efforts at defense, the judge found for Alley. Travis promised an appeal, and the judge, his friend David Burnet, obliged by granting him a second hearing right after lunch. During the meal, and apparently at Travis's instigation, Smith took Alley to one side and actually bought the cow and the yearling, then sent Alley on his way home. When Burnet reconvened the court, there was no plaintiff, no evidence, and no case. Burnet decided that the branding had been a mistake and discharged the defendant, and the whole party enjoyed a chuckle at a dance that evening. Yet if Alley was temporarily mollified, it did not last, and in November he took his revenge and stabbed Mays fatally.[42]

The trick Travis played typified his idea of fun, though not everyone appreciated his sense of humor, especially when it often came at the expense of someone else. Kuykendall saw how much Travis liked his own brand of prank, though adding that with the rest of the community in San Felipe, Travis was "not noted for either wit or humor." He especially practical jokes like the one with Alley's calf. In the summer of 1834, not long after the Mays trial, a stranger appeared in Travis's office with a plan to build a steamboat to run the Brazos and asked the lawyer for his help. Obviously he had learned of Travis's leading role in the Wilson and Harris plan and expected the attorney to do the same for him. Unfortunately the current steamboat deal was bogged down in problems in New Orleans. It was supposed to start construction in April, but then the failure of a major banking house caused delays with their credit, and by May 18 William Harris told Travis dejectedly that "our prospects are more gloomy now," and that the land that Travis and others had pledged might have to be sold just to satisfy debts to date, with no promise of the boat being finished. Even now he was under instruction to sell land for Wilson and the Harrises in order to raise more money.[43] Consequently, Travis had little interest in another scheme that would only compete with his own, and when the visitor came back day after day, Travis decided to get rid of him entirely.

Knowing a tall young fellow in the area who was otherwise unemployed, Travis hired him to start a quarrel with the annoying caller and then challenge him to a duel. When the fight had been picked and the challenge issued, the victim called on Travis as the only lawyer he knew to ask what he should do. Travis, of course, told him to accept, and suggested having the fight at once. "I will be your second," he said, "and you must fight with pistols across this very room." The dupe protested that he had no experience with pistols, while his antagonist was most certainly a rugged fellow who had cut his teeth fighting the local natives. Travis comforted him that such men always stood behind trees when shooting at the Comanche and Tawakoni, "but bring one of them face to face with his antagonist without a protecting tree, and he will ingloriously back out." That was enough to reassure the man, but when the time for the duel came, and Travis had secretly loaded the pistols only with powder, the man's nerve broke down as he stared across the office at the Texian. He dropped the pistol and refused to fight, pleading that he was a mechanic, not a killer, and asked Travis, as his second, to fight in his place. Travis harshly scolded him for his cowardice, and the man promptly left not only the office but San Felipe.[44]

In that instance Travis's practical joke amused everyone, because it was directed at an outsider. When he turned his eye toward his friends, though, he met with less agreement as to just what was and was not funny. He could be prickly, too, and sometimes stood rather too much on ceremony, traits that combined with his sometimes unappreciated pranks could have led him to serious trouble of his own. In April he gave testimony that William Jack had grossly overcharged a client with a $5,000 fee, when $200 would have been more appropriate, not an act calculated to keep a friend or repay him for his efforts at Anahuac, and one that in some could have led to violence.[45] Moreover,

Travis could lose his temper, and was not yet so mature that prudence always governed his tongue. Late in 1833 he had a serious argument with his friend and landlord at the time, John R. Jones, and moved out in anger, though when his temper cooled they became close once more.[46] At almost the same time that he defended Mays, Travis actually spoke so intemperately in front of the *ayuntamiento* that Williamson fined him twenty-five dollars for contempt, and a few weeks later his own client and friend Robert Mosely filed suit against him for eighty dollars, which Travis thought "rascally." In May his friend B. L. Burks actually became so angry with him that he cursed Travis to his face.[47]

Undoubtedly much of the trouble lay in Travis's personality, though some of his manner may well have been modeled after Dellet's. "Though generally recognized as both able and honest, Travis was not a very popular man," thought Kuykendall during their time together. "His brusque manner often gave offense and some times provoked insults upon which he turned his back."[48] Ephraim Roddy, an attorney at the new village of Washington, thirty miles up the Brazos from San Felipe, found Travis "very irascible," and not very well disposed to take in good humor having a joke turned on him. When Roddy turned some particularly effective sarcasm on him while they argued a case in Washington, Travis became visibly irritated, indicated the knife in his belt, and banteringly—but with some temper—suggested that he might like to use it on his opponent. Roddy reached into his pocket and drew out his only weapon, a small pen knife for carving quills, and addressed the judge. "Your Honor, owing to the discrepancy of our weapons I cannot do opposing counsel much bodily harm, but if he insists upon it, I will try." The explosion of laughter among the witnesses defused the tension at once, and Travis apparently saw the foolishness of the situation well enough to back down in good grace and stand a round of drinks afterward. The two remained friends, and Travis even did a fair bit of business for the man who made him look foolish, but when they met again in court and this time Travis won, he could not help gloating in his diary that "I whipped old Roddy."[49]

In fact, if anything Travis had a reputation for walking away from confrontations, evidence enough that he became involved in at least a few. Reuben Potter knew him slightly, but knew others of long acquaintance with the lawyer, and he recalled a prevailing impression that Travis "had been in civil life habitually cautious in avoiding broils and personal collisions, so much so that the rougher class of his contemporaries took for signs of timidity what I believe merely indicated a cool temper and guarded deportment."[50] Kuykendall agreed. "He certainly was not a man of impulsive physical courage," he said of Travis. "It required a strong moral stimulus to rouse his combativeness."[51]

Yet his friends and associates also saw another side of his nature, a touching generosity that few forgot. He consistently encouraged religion, whether he tried to find a Bible for the wife of a friend, sent a Sunday School book to two little girls, personally attended the preaching of a new Cumberland Presbyterian minister, Sumner Bacon, or gave a visiting priest a borrowed cot and a place to sleep in his house and personally paid the padre's board at Connell's.[52] The product of a better-than-average education himself, Travis actively supported efforts to educate the children of Texas. He encouraged the establishment of a new "classical and English" school at Columbia, opening in October 1834, and lent his name as a character reference for the proprietor.[53] With touching regularity he gave small sums of money to children, even to a slave boy named Jared and a local native child, for them to buy candy. He gave donations to local charities.[54] He sent books to some children, and bought shoes as a gift for the child of Jonathan Peyton.[55] Beyond question he saw in those little ones the son, Charles, he had not seen for more than three years, and the daughter he never saw at all. When community organizations tried to start in San Felipe, he proved an eager participant, whether it was the San Felipe Club, a men's group that sometimes let its debates turn violent, or the jockey club, whose members as often as not relived the local horse races in lively discussion in Travis's office while the lugubrious Kuykendall looked on.[56] More than once he sat up through the night with a sick or dying friend. Texians did not forget that.[57]

Even if they found him abrupt and humorless—or his idea of wit not to their taste—none could deny that Travis was a member of the community of whom they could be proud. He kept his house and office neat, a nice little patch of potatoes, cabbage, and peppers growing in his garden outside. He made a good impression when seen on the streets. He almost always wore new boots and pantaloons—Travis was partial to pantaloons and treated himself to several pairs—a colorful coat set off by a black cashmere shawl, and a sparkling white hat. He ate at the best boardinghouses in town, such as they were, and rode a hand-some new bay horse named Shannon that cost him eighty dollars.[58] Like any affluent professional gentleman of property, Travis also had slaves, though he hired as often as he bought, and generally looked on his blacks as an investment to provide lease income. Besides Jared, Travis bought a fifty-year-old man named Jack from Eli Holly's estate, another named Simeon, and a young girl named Eliza, whom he would hire out to others. Jack, at least, gave him trouble by getting drunk, and Travis had no compunction about whipping him for his behavior. After renting Joe for quite some time, Travis eventually bought him, and this slave he kept to himself, though early in the year he did briefly consider selling him.[59]

Few now were Travis's creditors, though he was still paying off debts from 1832 as late as February 1834.[60] Instead he became increas-ingly an investor, more recently in land, though never on the Bowie scale. He picked up a tract on the west side of the San Bernard River, twelve hundred acres or more in the Caney Creek and New Year's Creek vicinity, took Williamson's promise of a full league of land in return for representing him in his own speculating interests, and con-tinued working with Sam Williams, including an agency to sell nearly twenty leagues in the still-disputed Robertson grant.[61] Though he occasionally borrowed small sums from friends, in the first half of 1834 he paid back all but $9 of what he borrowed, and at the same time himself loaned others more than $260.[62]

"I do just what I think right." So said a character in Paulding's *Westward Ho!* obviously modeled on David Crockett, borrowing even on his trademark phrase "be always you are right, then go ahead."[63] William B. Travis did the same, though until this period of his life it appeared more that he did what he pleased. He continued to indulge his appetite for reading, moving from *Vivian Grey* to *Court and Camp of Bonaparte, The Scottish Chiefs,* a good spate of Sir Walter Scott, including *Guy Mannering* and *Rob Roy,* as well as most of the Texas newspapers from San Felipe and Brazoria.[64] If there was a party or a fandango on offer, he was sure to go, especially now that the lawyers and politicians invariably made speeches on the latest turn of events with Mexico, and when the mood took him, he still parted with fifty cents or a peso for a night with a woman, though the encounters were less frequent, and apparently less satisfying for him. He stopped numbering his conquests in his diary.[65] Moreover, in April he all but quit gambling.

The cause was Rebecca Cummings. John Cummings had opened his inn at Mill Creek crossing in February 1832, a modest place where he impressed some callers as shrewd if illiterate. His sister Rebecca, however, seemed to be responsible for the good running of the place. "Everything is in plenty, and of good kind," wrote one diner.[66] Travis probably met her for the first time at fellow lawyer Maj. Ira Lewis's Christmas season party on December 27, 1833, and since he paid for the fiddler for the party and a fair bit of its liquid cheer, she was certain to notice the gregarious young counselor. Courtship moved quickly, and on February 16, 1834, Travis made at least a firm expression of his interest, if not a conditional proposal, at the same time telling her of his situation with Rosanna. From then on the trips to Mill Creek came frequently, weather allowing. When high water forced him to give up crossing the boggy prairie early in March, he returned to San Felipe dejected, complaining to his diary that it was *"the first time I ever turned back in my life."* He seems not to have considered running out on Claiborne, debt, and his family as giving up.[67]

The courtship was not without its difficulties. Rebecca took some persuading. If his rather indiscriminate relations with women of the past two years had become known to her, the knowledge could have given her pause, and the equivocal nature of his marital situation created some definite problems. Travis may in fact have told her that he was already divorced, for in March he spoke to Rebecca about Rosanna, whom he called "my former wife," even though they were still very much married. But by late March her doubts disappeared, and Travis delighted in visit after visit to meet "many caresses" in "the company of my beloved." On March 31 they came to what he called "a simple understanding," and soon agreed that they would be married as soon as his divorce could be effected. Giving up gambling must have been one of Rebecca's conditions, for after March 31 he gambled only twice in the next three months, losing all of $1.75.[68]

Still there were problems, with Travis himself to blame. Just five days after first expressing his love for Rebecca, he went to a prostitute, though he found he could not perform, perhaps from a guilty con-

science. Yet again, five days before their "understanding," he went to
another woman and paid the tariff, though he commented that the experience was "*malo*"—bad—another pang of conscience perhaps. Some
word of this must have reached her, for on May 31 she gave him a cold
reception, and Travis spoke bitterly of someone repeating slanders about
him. Well into June the see-saw continued. On June 21–22 he may have
engaged in some kind of flirtation with two young women that got to
Rebecca, for she was cool to him yet again three days later. Yet Travis
always seemed to calm her anger or fears, and there was an inevitable
reconciliation. While they may not have made a general announcement,
the rumor soon spread through the colony that Travis and Rebecca were
to wed.[69]

Of course there remained the problem of Rosanna, the wife he
already had. Travis kept up a steady correspondence both with her and
her brother William, on one occasion even using him as a reference,
suggesting that his estrangement from Rosanna did not entirely extend
to the rest of her family. Then, too, it is just possible that Travis himself may have wavered in his determination to separate from her, even
though she was pliant enough to his demands to agree to let him have
Charles. The arrangement with Monroe Edwards to go to Brazoria in
January 1834 to collect him fell through, and so did a subsequent plan
for William Huff to go to New Orleans in March, where Rosanna was
to have taken the children. Either through confusion, or out of willful
revenge, she went to Natchez instead, and once again the exchange
failed to happen. This, and perhaps information from Claiborne of her
liaison with Samuel Cloud, if it had started yet, enabled Travis to go to
Rebecca on March 20 and explain his situation by portraying Rosanna
as the culprit, which helped in persuading her to accept his suit.[70]

Not until September did final action commence, and then it was
Rosanna who initiated events. She had finally given up on any reconciliation with Travis, and the fact that she waited this long suggests
that she clung to hope long after he had given every assurance of
wishing to be free of her, unless he did, in fact, fluctuate afterward in
his expressions. Having heard that her husband's old mentor Dellet
had actually volunteered his services in procuring her a divorce—
which gave some idea of Dellet's opinion of Travis's behavior—she
now accepted, asking him to institute the legal proceedings as soon as

possible, hoping that it could start at the spring 1835 term of the court in Monroe County. It now became evident, too, that she was learning a trade, because she received no support from Travis either for herself or her children, despite his considerable prosperity. Evidence suggested that by now, in the natural progression of things, Travis had gone from regarding Rosanna as an inconvenience to seeing her with some animosity.[71] The divorce would not be easy, for the state legislature had to pass on such acts. Only Rosanna could initiate the matter, because a complainant had to have been a resident of Alabama for more than three years, and she could only claim a divorce on three grounds—abandonment for three years or longer, adultery, or "cruel, barbarous, and inhuman" conduct. Abandonment would do. If her trials with Travis included either of the others, she kept it to herself.

Yet now at last the divorce would start to put an end to a marital situation that had festered for more than three years. More than just Travis's love life headed toward a resolution that fall. Like him, Texas too faced the prospect of separation. Already thousands of Texians had made the break in their hearts, few earlier or more completely than Travis himself. The months ahead would reveal what sort of break it was to be. On November 30 that year the moon passed between the sun and the earth, and most of Texas was in a solar eclipse. As events around them picked up speed once more, few Texians, even Travis, knew what would await them on the other side of the darkness.[72]

CROCKETT

1834–1836

> *I am rejoiced at my fate Do not be uneasy about me I am with my friends*
>
> DAVID CROCKETT, JANUARY 9, 1836

The trip north must have been the most enjoyable experience of David Crockett's life, despite a nagging chest pain that may have been a very mild recurrence of his old ailment.[1] Just before leaving he met his old friend Sam Houston, now finished with his years of seclusion with the Cherokee, and in the East pursuing several agenda. He looked into securing the agency for a land speculation firm that hoped to get a grant in Texas. He also met with his old friend Jackson, who had been trying to manage either the cession or purchase of Texas for years. Even now Jackson's emissary continued the negotiations, and no doubt Houston fed the president—and Crockett—with stories of the vastness of the place and the temper of its inhabitants. Listening to his old friend, Crockett must have liked the sound of what he heard, especially the opportunity for huge tracts of land at almost no cost.

Perhaps now, for the first time, Crockett heard the name of James Bowie. Perhaps he had heard dim accounts of the fight on the Natchez sandbar, though most of those in the press omitted Bowie's name. Maybe, too, he connected the name with the new Bowie knife rapidly occupying the nation's cutlers. From Houston he would have heard of the man's reputation for daring and for his remarkable influence with the Mexicans where land grants were concerned. Certainly Houston knew Travis, if only passingly, but there was no occasion to talk about one more lawyer. Whatever Houston told his friend, it impressed Crockett. Never before in either speeches or correspondence did David mention Texas even once. Within months it stole into his sentences repeatedly. If Crockett entertained any serious thoughts about the province, they remained unformed, but Houston passed the germ there in Washington in April, 1834.[2]

Crockett left Washington on April 25 for a whirlwind tour that included his first trip by sailing vessel and his first ride on a railroad train, taking in Baltimore, Philadelphia, New York, Newport, Boston, Lowell, and then back via Providence and Camden. With his itinerary carefully planned and publicized by his Whig friends, he met enthusiastic crowds at every stop. In New York he finally met and dined with Seba Smith, an interesting meal for four—two men and two legends—requiring a table only for two. No doubt Crockett boasted that just a few days before, while in Philadelphia, he visited his publishers and arranged for them to do another printing of at least two thousand copies of the *Narrative* to meet the demands just from his own district.[3] For his part Smith revealed his growing disenchantment with Jackson, and the two may well have discussed a collaboration in which Jack Downing and Crockett would "correspond" on the issues of the day. That same evening Crockett dined with Verplank, the congressman who defended his behavior at the Adams dinner years before, and Augustin Smith Clayton, a Georgian who backed John C. Calhoun and therefore loathed Jackson and Van Buren. Apparently amid all the conviviality Crockett gave up on his pledge to abstain from liquor, if it had lasted even that long. One of his hosts suggested that the guest help himself to the decanter on the sideboard in his drawing room, then turned his back while Crockett poured, which Crockett took as a sign that he could drink as much as he wished, pronouncing his host "the most through and through gentleman, to the very backbone."[4]

Crockett went everywhere there were people, acting the tourist that he truly was in part, and yet every visit was orchestrated by local Whig committees. He attended theaters, flag raisings, factories, museums, and more, and at each stop either made a speech that castigated the administration or at least offered a few quips that both amused the people and made his single-minded point about Jackson. In New York he visited Peale's Museum to see a ventriloquist, something entirely new to him, and watched intensely, even as others in the audience studied Crockett. "He is wholly different from what I thought him," a woman present noted. "Tall in stature and large in frame, but quite thin, with black hair combed straight over the forehead, parted from the middle and his shirt collar turned negligently back over his coat. He has rather an indolent appearance and looks not like a 'go ahead' man." When the ventriloquist did a few sleight-of-hand tricks, one of them involved magically moving money from one closed box to another, and as he performed the feat the artist joked that he was "about to remove the deposits." The trick accomplished, Crockett said in a voice loud enough for all to hear that "he can remove the deposits better than Old Hickory," winning himself cheers and applause.[5]

All along the way there were the gifts, a new suit of plain clothes from a Lowell cotton mill, a watch fob engraved with "go ahead," the promise of a fine custom rifle from the Philadelphia Whigs, a hunting coat, and more. At every dinner Whig hosts and audiences treated him as a conqueror, laughed at his stories, and applauded his increasingly harsh pronouncements on Jackson. In the euphoria at his reception, Crockett may not even have realized that in part his journey was designed as a parody of a similar trip made by Jackson the year before while on his way to collect his Harvard degree.[6] Indeed, he most probably never grasped the extent to which his new friends were using him. This whole tour was a trial that could not fail. Even if the voters did not see a likely 1836 prospect in him, still the attention and the press all served to embarrass the administration with Crockett, the tame Democrat, denouncing Old Hickory and pouring hot oil into the cracks in his party to sear the breaches. If the Whigs did, indeed, make a successful presidential candidate of him, so much the better, for he seemed malleable enough, though if ever in the White House that independent and honest streak in him would have served them a hearty disappointment. Crockett would not have been a good chief executive, but he would have been his own president.[7]

David returned to Washington on May 13, exhausted and somewhat ill tempered from the trip, no doubt weary of having to compromise his sense of dignity by posing for all those who came to see him. The news that his son John had gotten religion ordinarily would not have troubled him, especially given his own flirtation with conversion a few years before, but now when his son sent him a letter with the news, Crockett turned morose. "Thinks he's off to Paradise on a streak of lightning," grumbled his father. "Pitches into *me* pretty considerable."

Crockett was not accustomed to being chastised, especially by his children. He lost his patience in the House at the endless speeches that seemed to accomplish nothing, and more and more often he simply left. The painter Chapman met him on the Capitol steps one day "looking very much fagged," and obviously on the way home or to a tavern. "You look tired, Colonel, as if you had just got through a long speech in the House," he said. "Long speech to thunder, there's plenty of 'em up there for that sort of nonsense, without my making a fool of myself at public expense," Crockett growled. "I can stand *good nonsense*—rather like it—but *such nonsense* as they are digging at up yonder, it's no use trying to—I'm going home."[8]

When he did sit through the sessions, he became more and more vitriolic in his attacks on Jackson.[9] Crockett lost any sense of propriety or proportion in his mounting attacks on Old Hickory, and yet through it all he may have been following a conscious plan, however ill advised. Maintaining the attack on the president furthered the growing impression that there was a battle between himself and Jackson alone for the future of the country. On top of his celebrated trip through the Northeast, maintaining and enhancing such an impression ought only the more to establish him in the minds of the nation's opposition as the right man to trounce Van Buren in 1836. Thus he unreservedly used his final blasts of the brief session to advance that cause.[10] When a measure was introduced to censure Jackson, Crockett heartily approved, and fought against Polk's tabling motion so strenuously that Speaker of the House Andrew Stevenson had to call him to order several times. "Let members stand up to the rank and say to their constituents that we have supported the laws and constitution," he cried. They must give evidence of whether "we have a government or not." Repeatedly Crockett's temper, and the aroused growls and cheers of the Whigs, forced the Speaker to reprimand him. In what must have appeared more petty spite than policy, he even voted against the customary resolution of thanks to the Speaker at the end of the session, apparently solely because Stevenson was a Jacksonian.[11]

Crockett could not wait to get out of Washington. "I now look forward to our adjournment," he said on June 15, "with as much interest as ever did a poor convict in the penitentiary to see his last day come."[12] In fact, convinced that this long session had accomplished nothing for

the good of the country, he decided not even to wait for the adjournment on June 30.[13] Originally he had intended to go straight back to
Tennessee at the adjournment, but now he changed his plans to capitalize on the success of his recent tour by returning to Philadelphia
and a few other cities.[14] Traveling by stagecoach to Baltimore, he made
Philadelphia his first stop, there to remain nearly a week to include an
invitation for a July Fourth celebration. Since the time of his last visit
in late April, a local gunsmith had completed the presentation rifle and
sent Crockett targets that displayed the weapon's accuracy. He had
already given some instructions on adjusting its sight to correct a tendency to shoot too low, and shortly before leaving Washington sent
an order for several canisters of fine rifle powder to be sent to Carey
and Hart so they could pack them in his shipment of books.[15]

He had not actually seen the rifle himself, though descriptions of the
finished weapon went throughout the nation's press in June. "A superb
tool," one sheet called the gun. A silver plate in the stock depicted a
rampant alligator, jaws agape, a possum and a deer, seemingly all the
metaphors associated with Crockett, though one journalist decried the
absence in the engraving of "the slight touch of an earthquake." The
smith inlaid a gilded arrow into the barrel near the muzzle, with the
motto Go Ahead near the front sight. To accompany the rifle, the
young Whigs gave him a shot pouch, a tomahawk, a knife, and a liquor
canteen in the form of a bound and gilded book. The volume represented, significantly enough, was *The Spirit of the Times*, the New York
journal that more than any other publication collected and disseminated
tall tales of Crockett and the West.[16] On July 1 they gave him the rifle in
a small ceremony, during which he promised ever to use it in defense of
his country, and then the next day he and the gunsmith took it to New
Jersey for a test. Its firing mechanism used the relatively new cap-and-
ball system, far faster and more reliable than the old flintlock, and
Crockett felt well pleased with the result. His old well-worn hunting
rifle he called "Betsey," an especially favored name with him for rifles,
apparently, for now he dubbed this new work of art "Pretty Betsey."[17]

The chief political purpose of the trip was the Fourth of July
speeches, and Crockett made several, all of them in the company of the
true big Whigs, Daniel Webster heading the list. "I love my country,"
he told them. "If I don't I wish I may be shot!"[18] He trotted out once

again all of the old arguments, the by-now tired aphorisms about King Andrew and one-man rule and the removal of the deposits. Despite the enthusiasm, he was tired, and not a few of his auditors wearied of hearing the same old litany. After resting a day, he boarded a train and set off across Pennsylvania for Pittsburgh, and a steamboat down the Ohio. Along the way he made one or two stops to let people "see a bar," though some instead found themselves looking at a stoutly built man approaching six feet who had hands and feet that seemed too small for his body, and long curly hair that needed to make the acquaintance of a comb. He accepted a few toasts and made some of his own, and unfurled all the old quips they expected to hear. His appearance sometimes disappointed, for they assumed he would be in buckskins, whereas he appeared in anything from a broadcloth suit to the incongruous combination of fashionable pantaloons and calico hunting shirt with ruffles at the collar and cuffs, an ensemble that one observer said "set off his person as the rough and untutored woods-man, to peculiar advantage." Still he gave satisfaction. "God bless you," he told them in Columbia, Pennsylvania, "for I can't."[19]

Home in Weakley County at last by mid-July, he heard the first sound of criticism of his tour. Some of the Democratic press attacked him for leaving his seat for those three weeks, and again for the few days at the end of the session. They accused him of "playing the buf-foon" in order to delight the Whigs, and of conduct unseemly for a member of Congress. With the next summer's congressional race in mind, they suggested that he should be "kept at home" hereafter. "He may be an honest man," said one editor, "but he is a very foolish one."[20] Crockett's claim that his trip had been solely for his health fooled no one, for the Whig management behind it was impossible to overlook. To his protest that he only missed one appropriations vote, his critics could answer that a congressman was paid $8.00 a day. What had Crockett done to earn the $100.00 or more the government paid him while he was making himself the darling of the Northeast?[21]

His critics would have jumped him even more if they knew how he intended to capitalize on his tour. His money problems did not disap-pear with the sales of the *Narrative*, though certainly his debts dimin-ished. His few months at home seem to have been spent chiefly in try-ing to clear the affairs of his father, John Crockett, who died in late summer, and forestalling yet more suits for debt, one of them more than six years old. Shortly before he left for the second session of the House, he had to borrow $312.49, and even then, when he reached Washington, he was still unable to make good on a debt to the bank now nearly two years overdue. He wrote urgently to Carey and Hart a week after the opening gavel, asking for a full accounting on sales. "I am anxious to know how we stand I expect to be hard pressed," he explained. "I can never need money worse than at present."²²

There seemed only one way out of the money crunch. During the late fall Crockett discussed with his old boardinghouse mate William Clark collaborating on a book about the triumphal Northeastern trip, and David broached the subject with his publishers. Nothing more came of the idea until he reached Washington, but in December he and Clark quickly came to an arrangement.²³ Crockett would gather documents, chiefly newspaper accounts of his travels and speeches, add some notes and probably bits of narrative, and then turn it all over to Clark to arrange, edit, and flesh out into a book. There would be less of Crockett's own prose in the effort, chiefly because he was in a dreadful hurry. When Carey and Hart agreed to publish it, Crockett then made arrangements with them to send portions as completed, to get the typesetting started, and speed the publication date. Three weeks after the opening of the session he handed the first thirty-one pages to Clark for editing revision, with another twelve ready to turn over. Clark himself seemed pleased with Crockett's work, and told him that he could turn the raw material into "the most interesting Book you ever had." Crockett actually believed he could finish his part of the work by New Year's, but feared Clark might not keep up with him. Clark himself would do the preface this time, while Crockett concentrated on the material for the main text. All through December, Crockett pushed his collaborator, making no secret of the reason for the hurry. He needed $300.00 to settle a debt due on January 1, and asked Carey and Hart for an advance. It would not be the last time.²⁴

For the next few weeks Crockett wrote to friends and asked them to send him newspaper accounts of his travels and speeches, and as before kept the publishers apprised almost daily of his progress.²⁵ In his anxiety to complete the job he even worked on Christmas Day and New Year's. By January 1 he had finished much of the work, and it all lay in Clark's hands, while he sent to Carey and Hart a proposed title page for what would become *An Account of Col. Crockett's Tour to the North and Down East in the Year of Our Lord One Thousand Eight Hundred and Thirty Four.* At the same time he reiterated his request for money, this time reducing it to $150.00–$200.00 "so that I can get myself out of this tite place."[26] A week later he had the money, and with it some temporary relief, but Clark's sudden preoccupation with the continuing investigation of the deficit in the Post Office Department kept him from keeping pace on his part of the work.[27] His sense of truth troubling him a bit, Crockett suggested that instead of his being credited as the book's actual author, it would be more accurate for the title page to state that it was "written from notes furnished by my self," so long as the publishers did not think that would hurt sales. He realized that some critics might challenge him on the correctness of the account when they knew he had not in fact written all of it, but that troubled him only a little. Besides, from the very first he saw the book as far more burlesque than his *Narrative*, intending it to be "as amusing as posable."[28]

By January 21 Crockett announced the completion of his part of the job, but the sixty-one-year-old Clark fell so ill that he could scarcely sit up in bed, which delayed the sending of the final manuscript to Carey and Hart. Meanwhile Crockett continued gathering other materials to append to the book, including newspaper articles, statements of manufactures from textile mills to bolster his arguments against Jackson's tariff policy, and public letters and short essays he intended to write.[29] It would take until April for him to secure the copyright, but by then Clark had finished his task, and in late March the book was already on the shelves.[30] It was a work in every way inferior to the *Narrative*, chiefly because it lacked Crockett's spark of authenticity in its style, and because of its obvious nature as a loosely strung together compilation. The Whigs touted the book, but the public seemed little impressed, and Carey and Hart would find themselves with copies left on their hands, and Crockett with not enough money to make a serious dent in his debts.

Yet he continued to see in writing a two-edged sword to advance his political fortunes on the forward thrust, and cut down his poverty on the backstroke. Even while compiling accounts for the Clark book in January, he already had another in mind. To Carey and Hart he pro-

posed that the next dragon he slay with his pen should be none other
than the man he might well face in an election little more than a year
later—Martin Van Buren.[31] The publishers felt wary, for they knew
Crockett's temper toward the "fox," and frankly feared that he might
produce something libelous. "I am not going to give him a chance at
me for a libel," Crockett reassured them. "What I write will be true."
And then for the moment he dropped the subject.[32]

Crockett virtually repeated his behavior of the first session in the second. Instead of attending wholeheartedly to the business of the House,
he spent a great deal of his time working on his book, and the rest of it
carping about the administration. When he did take the floor, predictably it was to raise one more variation on the land bill, and then
his own deportment prejudiced his chances. He tried four times to get
it on the floor without success, and in the votes on his motions he saw
many of his former Whig supporters reverse themselves. They were no
longer willing to bolster the promotion of David Crockett by risking
denying the sale of public lands to boost the U.S. Treasury.[33]

Meanwhile Crockett never let up in his ranting about Jackson, only
now he increased the heat on Van Buren as well.[34] He accused Jackson
of trampling the Constitution underfoot and telling the "Judicial powar
to go to hell."[35] The presumption by Jackson that he could simply
anoint his own successor made Crockett apoplectic. "The time has come
that men is expected to be transferable and as negotiable as a promissory note of hand," he declared on Christmas. "Little Van sits in his
chair and looks as sly as a red fox," he went on, and worst of all, recent
elections in some of the northern states appeared to sustain the administration. "There is more slaves in New York and Pennsylvania than there
is in Virginia and South Carolina," and the shame of it was that they
were "Volunteer slaves." He felt so agitated that he began to tell friends
in December that "I have almost given up the ship as lost." Faced with
the grim prospect of more years of corrupt rule, he declared openly: "If
Mr *martin vanburen* is elected that I will leave the united states for I never
will live under his kingdom." Before he would submit to Little Van's
rule, said Crockett, "I will go to the wildes of Texes." The Mexican rule
there would be "a Paradice to what this will be."[36]

Crockett never quailed at hyperbole. He accused Jackson of fomenting
a debt crisis with France in order to divert attention from the corruption

of his regime, for if the nation learned what Old Hickory and his min-
ions were about "it would Blow them all to the devil."[37] He may well
have seen just such a phenomenon in operation when Richard
Lawrence, a deranged house painter, attempted to assassinate Jackson
in the Capitol on January 30, and Crockett could not refrain from comment, probably to express sorrow that the insane assailant's two pistols
misfired.[38] As for Van Buren, Crockett vowed never to speak to him,
and within a few months would be telling a story that may have been
true or that may have been his own invention to illustrate his disdain.
Attending the Washington Theater one night, Crockett found himself
sitting directly in front of the Little Fox and overheard Van Buren
whisper to a friend, "Now is a favourable opportunity to introduce
me." The friend tapped Crockett's shoulder and said, "Colonel
Crockett, allow me to take the liberty of introducing to you the future
president of the United States." Crockett turned around, his eyes flashing, and replied, "Really, my friend, anything in reason, but by heaven
I cannot permit anyone to take such a liberty with me."[39]

Inevitably the coming presidential contest colored everything. By
the end of 1834, despite the success of his tour and his *Narrative*,
Crockett sensed the waning Whig support for his candidacy.
Prominent party leaders like Biddle and Poindexter had to be concerned about his repeated appeals to them to help with his debts, not a
good sign for a potential chief executive, and gradually they distanced
themselves.[40] His constant attacks on Jackson and Van Buren became
tiresome and repetitive, while his increasing stridency took an embarrassing turn. Some of the Whigs who had voted with him in the House
abandoned him in the last session; and moreover, in looking at his
record as a congressman, there was not a single achievement on which
they could run him. In almost three complete terms he had failed to
achieve a single piece of legislation that he promoted, and the Jackson
press adeptly highlighted his shortcomings as a statesman.

The same Mississippi convention that had approached him about the
presidency toward the end of 1833 contacted Missourian Thomas Hart
Benton late in 1834 about the vice-presidency, but he turned them down,
suggesting instead that the country would be best served by Van Buren in
the White House. Crockett took the occasion in January 1835 to ghost-
write—or more likely coauthor—several satirical letters calling for the

publication of Benton's own answer to the Mississippi convention, which response never saw light of day in 1833.[41] In the sham response now published he said that he declined to seek the office in 1836, thinking it proper that a northern man should be elected. That was Crockett's parody of Benton's refusal. But then he—or his coauthor—went on to say that of course if a Yankee got the White House in 1836, then in 1840 it should go to a man from the Southwest, "and that president shall be myself."[42]

Though he may have been writing satirically, it is apparent that Crockett had all but given up his presidential hopes for 1836 by the time of the Benton letter. On December 27, 1834, he told a constituent that he saw no hope at all for anyone beating Van Buren in the coming election.[43] Thus he may have been more serious than not in the parody letter when he said that he expected 1840 would be his turn, for certainly in the preparation of the book about his tour, and in the projected Van Buren biography, Crockett still saw potential for advancing his possible candidacy. But if Van Buren was, as he believed by late December, unbeatable, then far better that David not be the Whig nominee in 1836. Consequently on December 29 he joined with all the rest of the Tennessee delegation except Polk, Grundy, and Cave Johnson in signing a letter to Sen. Hugh Lawson White asking him to seek the Democratic nomination against Little Van. White already enjoyed widespread Whig support, and as a Tennessean his candidacy would hurt Van Buren and humiliate Jackson. Strangely, having been at odds on so many other issues, Crockett and most of the delegation united this time because they all disliked the Fox, objecting to Jackson's regal assumption that he could name his own successor. On December 30 White accepted the proposal, and a few days later Crockett called on him personally, and thereafter wrote an open letter to his home district saying—disingenuously, considering his declaration of a few days before—that he thought White "the only man in the nation able to contend against little Van."[44]

In short Crockett knew more than enough not to challenge Van Buren for the Democratic nomination, and knew as well that no Whig nominee was likely to beat him in the general election. Standing that beside the evidences of softening Whig support for himself, the path of wisdom called for him to step out of the path to the presidency for the time being. However, if there was even a little of the calculating about him, Crockett might also have reasoned that his supporting White would win him some favor where he most needed it, among Democrats. Even if White lost the contest for the nomination, it would be a bloody fight that might weaken Van Buren going into the election, at which time a strong Whig candidate—himself—could attract those disaffected Democrats and perhaps deny the Fox his quarry at the polls in November. If Crockett actually viewed the situation that way, it was a clever, even shrewd strategy. Either way his own prospects seemed still very much alive.

Among other things, of course, any presidential hopes now or in the future depended upon retaining his seat in the House in the coming election. Some of his constituents wrote to him expressing their pleasure with his conduct as their representative, which much gratified Crockett. For his part he sent occasional circular addresses or open letters to the press to explain his positions and actions, and used the frank liberally to keep constituents supplied with reading material showing his efforts—such as they were—and more to send anti-Jackson materials through the post.[45] By the end of 1834 he suspected that "Blackhawk," Adam Huntsman himself, would be his opponent, though he thought he could beat him. Yet he was not entirely confident. "I cannot tell," he confessed. "I am determined to do my duty if I should niver See another Congress."[46]

Huntsman believed that he detected signs justifying that same uncertainty felt by Crockett. On New Year's day Blackhawk told Polk that he wanted to run against "Davy of the River country." He saw signs that the people were tiring of and even offended by the quantity of anti-Jackson literature coming into the district. "Crockett is evidently losing ground," he thought, "or otherwise he never was as strong as I supposed him to be." Either way Huntsman believed he could beat him unless Crockett succeeded in getting his land bill passed during the remainder of the term.[47] Certainly that was impetus enough, as if he needed any, for Polk to continue to do his best to keep the land bill from reaching the floor. And no one thought the Hugh White approach a greater betrayal than did Old Hickory himself. He already regarded Crockett as a traitor, but now saw him as the agent of the treason of the others on the Tennessee delegation who turned against Van Buren. He spoke of "Crockett and Co." as destroyers of Democratic unity—which he long since crippled himself—and accused Crockett of being the "tool" of his enemies. He was an apostate, and he and the others should be "hurled, as they ought, from the confidence of the people." Even in loathing David, though, Jackson could not resist being in some measure affected by the growing pull of the folk hero. Now he called him "Davy Crockett."[48]

Others commented on what appeared to be a waning in Crockett's novelty, at least to the people in the East. When Chapman's portrait went on display at the National Academy of Design in New York that year, visitors paid it a great deal of attention that could do him no harm, though when one viewer said Crockett had misplaced the tomahawk in his belt, Crockett shot back a snarl to Chapman. "Don't you go to altering my picture for any body's nonsense," he snapped. "If any man in New York says that I do'nt know how, or where, to stick my hatchet, send him to me and I'le show him."[49] Yet another New Yorker perceived more than "Davy of the West's" shortening fuse. "As he picked up a few more words of English, and softened some of his bold sayings, in fact the more he lost of the man of the woods the less interesting he became as a curiosity," remarked a man who had seen and heard Crockett over the years. "The last time we saw him he reminded us of the savage who had lost the energy and pantomime grace of the war dance, in taking lessons from a French master to figure in a cotillion."[50] George W. Terrell, a friend of Houston's currently sitting in the Tennessee legislature, thought Crockett "a strange man—a mighty hunter, but rather 'smart' than good," charging him with a lack of political consistency, and even asserting that Crockett's friends doubted his political bravery, fearing that he was "wanting moral courage."[51]

Of course, these commentators were Jackson–Van Buren men, but that did not change the fact that Crockett seemed to have lost his focus. He and the publishers and the Whig politicians had conceived among themselves a creature that they no longer controlled. The public could not tell David from Davy, and sometimes now neither could Crockett. In his private moments his ironbound honesty must have plagued him for allowing himself to act a role for which he was born, yet in which he was always chiefly just a player, not an incarnation. In order to become what he thought he was and wanted to be, he had to pretend to be what he was not, and the years of increasing sham told on him.

THREE ROADS TO THE ALAMO

•

Still he kept trying. Despite Carey and Hart's early reluctance, they eventually agreed to publish the Van Buren book, and by spring Crockett had engaged Augustin Clayton to do the actual writing, while he furnished bits and pieces and lent his name to the title page.[52] In June *The Life of Martin Van Buren, Hair-apparent to the Government and the Appointed Successor of General Jackson* appeared in the stores and stalls, Carey and Hart still fearing it sufficiently libelous that they left their firm's name off the title page. Crockett's contribution, if any, was minimal, and neither did he apparently exercise any control—or perhaps show any real interest—in the presentation, for anyone expecting a Crockett book was immediately disappointed. Gone were the exploits and tall tales, and absent, too, was the wonderful vernacular. The book read as if written by the man who in fact wrote it: an erudite, college-educated lawyer. The only vestige of David was its bitterness toward Van Buren.[53]

With reelection in mind, Crockett may have had a bit more to do with a series of letters that appeared in Seba Smith's new magazine, the *Downing Gazette*. Smith came out strongly in opposition to Jackson at last, and one of the features of his tabloid was a weekly exchange of letters between Downing and Crockett. The series began just as Crockett was on his way home to start his campaign, coincidentally, and continued until the August election, a clear indication that Smith tied the letters to the purpose of supporting Crockett's campaign. Crockett himself had nothing to do with actually writing the letters, for their orthography and grammar, while studiedly quaint, hardly matched his own, but he may have discussed them during his meeting with Smith, or in subsequent private correspondence. Certainly they contained some of the themes that continually occupied his speeches and letters, and even approximations of some of his better known aphorisms.[54]

So far as Crockett's reelection efforts were concerned, the *Downing Gazette* probably did him little good, since few copies would reach West Tennessee. The Van Buren book and the narrative of the eastern tour exerted little more influence, if any. In the end that decision came down to David and Blackhawk, both skilled campaigners, each adept at appealing to the people in their own speech, and both able with the

pen. As soon as he got home, David took the stump, and after canvass-
ing three of his counties felt that he had nothing to dread, even thinking that his popularity might force Huntsman to withdraw. "If he does
not I have no doubt of beating him with ease." Moreover, Crockett
saw signs that White's candidacy was strong in the district, "and I go
for him."[55] But White would balk in the end and decide not to challenge Van Buren for the Democratic nomination, which Little Van got
unanimously in May. Instead, White ran along with Webster and others as the candidate of one or two states, the Whigs hoping that they
might take enough electoral votes among several candidates to throw
the election into the House of Representatives. Though the Democrats
had a majority there at the moment, that might change after the election, and there were already enough Southern Democrats opposed to
Van Buren that they could join with the Whigs in sending someone
else to the White House.

No doubt White's decision not to run as a Democrat, but to change
stripes and become a Whig instead, must have hurt Crockett with
some of his voters, for attached as many were to him, they were
equally if not more attached to the Democratic Party. By supporting
White, Crockett had backed a defector, even though he was one himself in all but name. Huntsman ran quite clearly as an administration
Democrat, and one with the endorsement of Polk and Jackson. A year
before Crockett thought Blackhawk was politically dead and ready to
be laid "away among the unfinished business."[56] Now he found him
very much alive, and quite his match on the stump. Huntsman
thumped him for abusing the franking privilege in his own behalf, and
also for refusing to frank pro-Jackson documents requested by his constituents. Crockett threw the accusation right back at him, charging
that the Jackson forces sent copies of the administration paper, the
Washington *Globe*, to every post office in the district. Huntsman
harped on Crockett's most vulnerable spot, his failure to achieve anything in three terms in the House, and to that there was no effective
reply. At the same time constituents started to complain about
Crockett's about-face on one aspect of the land bill, when he changed
his position and allowed that West Tennessee land was quite fertile. By
so doing he tacitly accepted that it was more valuable than he originally asserted, and that in turn could make it more expensive if ever

put on the market, possibly pricing it out of reach of the very people he was supposedly trying to help. It had been simply one of the several compromises that Crockett made for the greater good of getting a bill passed, but now it came back to bedevil him.[57]

By early July, with a month of the campaign still to go, Crockett remained supremely confident. "I have him bad plagued for he dont know as much as me about the Government," he wrote his publishers after two straight weeks of daily stump meetings. "I handle the Administration without gloves," he boasted, and continued his prediction that the Jacksonian wave was on the ebb. He would double Huntsman's vote, he said. Moreover, he felt so sure of victory that he adapted his old threat about Van Buren's election, and promised that if he did not beat Blackhawk he would leave the country and go to Texas.[58]

Crockett bedeviled him as he had every past adversary, and once almost got Blackhawk into very serious trouble indeed. Huntsman had lost a leg during the War of 1812, making him as much a war hero as Crockett, if not more, and now had to wear a wooden leg on campaign. The two candidates spent one night during the canvass with a farmer who happened to be a Jackson man, and who, like the ubiquitous farmer of the old stories, had a daughter. He put the two men in one cabin of his dogtrot, while she slept in the other. When Huntsman, who had a reputation for philandering, fell soundly asleep, Crockett stole out of their cabin, picked up a chair, and walked across the boarded breezeway between the cabins and made a purposefully loud attempt to open her door. When she awakened and cried out, he put one foot on a rung of the chair, held onto its back, and used it as a noisy crutch to stamp back to his own room. The effect was to sound just like a man with a wooden leg, and so the farmer took it, threatening Huntsman with bodily harm before being calmed, and changing his vote thereafter.[59]

The Democrats played their own tricks in return, chiefly in the press, where Crockett found himself accused of saying that former Governor Carroll was corrupt and had been bribed to come out in support of Van Buren, in return for administration support in his bid for reelection to the governorship. Even in denying the accusation, Crockett could not help giving it some foundation when he went on to state that Carroll had been seen walking arm in arm with Van Buren, and riding with him in his lavish carriage. This and other newspaper charges took their toll with the voters.[60] Jackson forces also published charges that he cheated on his mileage expenses for going to and from Washington for the sessions, and Crockett could only respond that he put in for the same mileage as Felix Grundy, an administration pet, who lived in Nashville. It may have been true, but that did not alter the fact that he claimed one thousand miles of travel for a trip that was really seven hundred.[61]

David remained as animated on the campaign as ever. "His voice was loud, and well suited to stump oratory," wrote a listener a few months later. "If his vocabulary was scanty, he was master of the slang of his vernacular, and was happy in his coarse figures. He spurned the idle rules of the grammarians, and had a rhetorick of his own."[62] Crockett never missed a barbecue, a house raising, or a logrolling fete where there might be votes. Nor did he let pass any chance for a jape at Huntsman's expense. Late in the campaign, when Blackhawk tried to emphasize Crockett's rude backwoods bumpkin image by handing him a coonskin to ask if it was good fur, David's own hair remained unruffled. He blew into the fur, examined the pelt carefully, then handed it back saying: "No, sir, 'tis not good fur; my dogs wouldn't run such a 'coon, nor bark at a man that was fool enough to carry such a skin."[63]

When it came down to the last days in early August, Crockett repeatedly said that he had been a good steward, looking out for the interests of his people, and that he was the same man he always was, only now better qualified thanks to experience.[64] But he could not disguise the fact that he had accomplished nothing for his voters, abandoned Jackson and the Democrats, and that the district had paid the price for the administration's punishment of him. That hurt him more than any outside accusations or tricks by Huntsman.

On election day itself Crockett went to McLemoresville, midway between two forks of the Obion. There he cast his own vote and tried to muster a few others. When he encountered one eighteen-year-old he asked him if he had voted, and hearing that he had not, Crockett marched him to the polls despite his being underage.[65] At the same time he saw, or heard, that the Jackson forces had promised twenty-five dollars to every man who would vote for Huntsman. The officials supervising the polling places also appeared to be thoroughly in the Jackson camp, and some he heard rumored to have placed heavy bets on Blackhawk to win. With or without chicanery, the count ran close,

406 ᗓᗉ THREE ROADS TO THE ALAMO

and no one knew the result until August 9. It showed Crockett with 4,400, but 4,652 for his opponent. "The great *Hunter* one Davy has been beaten by a *Huntsman*," one voter crowed to Polk, while another exulted that "we have killd blacguard Crockett at last."[66] Even in far-away Little Rock, Arkansas, the Jackson press celebrated Huntsman's victory over "the buffoon, Davy Crockett."[67]

Predictably, David did not accept the defeat gracefully. Not only was it the sort of rejection that always sent him into a reverie of self-pity, it also virtually brought an abrupt end to any hopes he had for the presidency in 1836, especially since White would be running as a Tennessee favorite son for the Whigs. As soon as he knew the results, Crockett charged corruption over the vote-buying rumors. Now he knew why Jackson had removed the deposits. It was to use the money to buy elections to sustain his support, and perhaps especially to defeat Crockett. The old irrational suspicion completely took hold as he imagined the President and all the government having as its sole aim the destruction of this one lone honest man. "I have no doubt that I was compleatly Raskeled out of my Election," he grieved to his publishers, then heaped self-righteousness onto self-pity when he protested that "I do regret that duty to my self & to my country compels me to expose such viloney."

He felt vindicated that he had spoken the truth in the canvass, his truth anyhow, and more pride than ever that he refused to bow to Jackson's power and party. "I have suffered my self to be politically sacrafised to save my country from ruin & disgrace," said the reemerged martyr, "and if I am never a gain elected I will have the grattification to know that I have done my duty." Yet, in a tantalizing phrase, he also noted that "I have no doubt of the time being close at hand when I will be rewarded for letting my tongue Speake what my hart thinks." He meant, of course, that when White beat Van Buren in 1836, he could expect a prominent appointment in the new administration as reward for having been for so long the lone voice of truth in Tennessee. To make certain that the Whigs would know he was available, he suggested to Carey and Hart that they might want to publish his letter.[68] Ironically, Huntsman saw more clearly to the essential truth of Crockett's defeat. Advocacy of the tariff and internal improvements, his fight on behalf of the bank, and above all his fanatical and highly personalized animosity toward Jackson were what really beat him. He also lost, quipped Huntsman, "because he did not get votes enough."[69]

The depth of the hurt that Crockett felt at his defeat is evident in his announcement through the press in September that "I never expect to offer my name again to the public for any office."[70] Time and time again during the campaign, and as far back as late 1834, he made those boasts about leaving the country if Van Buren won, and then brought the threat closer to home when he made it with reference to his own reelection. The eastern press, commenting on his frequent remark about going to Texas, noted in his defeat "strong *premonitories* of which event he now begins to see."[71] Just as he took off into the wilderness for the long hunt after defeat before, he needed to get away now, to conquer some new beasts or new territory to relieve the ache of failure in his heart. Moreover, having made that boast so often, he may have felt honor bound to live up to it, to "stand up to his lick log." The prospect of remaining an impoverished hardscrabble farmer without even his own land in West Tennessee seemed intolerable. A fellow Tennesseean remarked of Crockett that "his life had been a wayward one, and he could not tie himself to routine."[72] A New Yorker who heard him during the 1834 tour, and who recognized the infection of politics, understood David at this moment perfectly. "He could not live without being before the public," he said. "He had been half inebriated with distinction for eight or ten years, and inglorious seclusion would not answer for David Crocket."[73]

It did not help that some of Elizabeth's relatives charged him that summer with malfeasance in administering her father's will, an embarrassing though eventually inconsequential matter that only further soured him on staying in Gibson County. Never apparently deeply involved with his family, now estranged from Elizabeth entirely, and rejected by the voters of his district, there was nothing to keep him here any longer. He could always return, of course, and nothing in his threats of going to Texas included a promise to *stay* there. At least the trip would be an adventure. He could spend a few months scouting the land, hunting the game, including the buffalo now long disappeared from Tennessee, and mixing with old friends like Sam Houston. Surely he knew of the growing uproar out there, and that the colonists were virtually in rebellion now, but that was their fight, not his. On the other hand, he also knew that politically Tennessee might be played out for him, whereas Houston assured him that one day Texas must be a state in the Union. If David liked the look of the place and decided to stay, Texas might just provide a base for getting back into politics in case Van Buren won next year, or if the Whigs did not come through with the reward he expected. The trip promised much to gain and nothing to lose.

The prospect of the adventure buoyed his spirits, making up for his humiliation at defeat, and Crockett decided to give himself a sendoff with a large barbecue at his Gibson County farm. He dug a pit one hundred yards south of the cabin, and there the cooks tended the meats while he and most of the men played at a logrolling, the object being for a man to roll a barkless and heavily greased log some distance. Through the day Crockett dipped a gourd into the barrel of liquor, and the more he drank, the more he talked of Texas. It commenced raining, but still the frolic continued, and well into the afternoon the logrolling began. Crockett took the first turn at the black, sticky poplar trunk, and in two minutes was black from head to toe, to the great mirth of his friends. He swore that he would move the log, and good-naturedly promised to change the color of every one of them to red from embarrassment for laughing at him, and so he did. That done, he took his fiddle and played a merry tune for them all, and regaled them with stories and quips, including a new variation on his threat to leave. He had done his best to get elected, he said, but the voters had rejected him. In that case, the voters could go to hell, and he would go to Texas.[74]

By October 31 he was ready. His nephew William Patton decided to join him, and that pleased the uncle who regarded him as "a fine fellow." Two of his neighbors also made up the party, Lindsay Tinkle, and Abner Burgin. "We will go through Arkinsaw and I want to explore the Texes well before I return," he told Elizabeth's brother.[75] Though he did not live with Elizabeth any longer, there seems to have been no animosity between them, and he went first to her family's place to say his farewells to her and their minor children. Their son Robert was just turned nineteen now, and David left him in charge of watching out for the other children and their mother.[76] To the rest of the family he showed the old confident air on the morning of November 1 when he stepped outside, clad in his accustomed hunting suit for the ride, and bid them farewell. He told them that if he liked what he saw in Texas he would send for them to come and join him, but mentioned nothing at all about any interest in the uprising out there, which even as he spoke sputtered into violence.[77] Then he mounted a large chestnut horse with a white star on its forehead and, joined by his friends, rode off into the woods to follow a star of his own.[78]

The road took them south, and on to Bolivar, where Crockett picked up the main road west to Memphis. Wherever he went people noticed his passing, and he called on numerous friends along the way. Word of Crockett's trip had spread before his departure, and several men determined to join him along the way, most apparently expecting, unlike Crockett, to involve themselves in the Texas uprising, for those who saw them pass through West Tennessee observed them to be "well armed and equipped." By the time Crockett rode through Jackson, witnesses claimed to count thirty men with him, though most were only along for a lark, and would return home before he crossed the Mississippi, or else separated from him to travel to Texas by other routes.[79] In Bolivar he stayed with Calvin Jones, from whom he leased his Gibson place, and met a warm greeting from the citizens. Many men passed through Bolivar these days, most of them armed and on their way to Texas, and Jones regarded them as little better than filibusters. But David was different. In his coming there was something out of the ordinary, as sensed by everyone. "Crocket who cannot blow his nose without a queery remark or observation, was regarded as a passing comet, not to be seen again," he wrote a few weeks after David's visit, "and every hand extended either in courtesy or regard. This occasion proved him to be more of a Lion than I had supposed."[80] Jones chose an apt metaphor, for just as Crockett rode through West Tennessee, the night sky overhead thrilled its people with the slow passing of Halley's Comet. Well might they wonder when either of those celebrated phenomena would be seen again.

Crockett reached Memphis on November 10, to be reunited once more with old friends like Winchester. Entering the city early one morning, David and his friends walked the streets for much of the day looking for acquaintances and fun, and finding both. In time quite a following gathered at his heels, and that evening they began a real party at the Union Hotel. When the tavern there became too small for the crowd, they moved to several succeeding establishments. Inevitably, as they took one "horn" after another, some got out of hand and unruly, and Crockett himself had to stop a fight over the bill. When the revelers moved on to Neil McCool's saloon, they carried Crockett on their shoulders into the bar and stood him on the counter to make a speech. Naturally he repeated the "go to hell, I am going to Texas" refrain, then ended by saying "I am on my way now." McCool became somewhat angered to see Crockett standing on the new oilcloth he had just placed on his counter, and another brawl almost ensued before Crockett suggested that it was time for all of them to go to their homes. Still they wound up at one more saloon before the night ended, with Crockett giving yet more impromptu speeches. With an early start to make on the morrow, they were all far too late to bed, and one of them recalled that "we all got tight—I might say, yes, very tight."[81]

At least some of Crockett's friends in Memphis got the idea that he intended to join the Texian forces then besieging San Antonio, though that may simply have been the natural assumption since so many other Tennesseans passed through Memphis now with that object.[82] Yet that was far from Crockett's mind as, with no doubt aching head, he arose early in the morning and walked down to the ferry landing near the mouth of Wolf Creek, where it emptied into the Mississippi. Winchester and other local friends accompanied Crockett and his party to the flatboat ferry run by an old black man named Limus. Their good-byes said, Crockett stepped into the bow, Limus slipped his mooring, and they rowed off down the Wolf and out into the Mississippi.[83]

Once across, they set out overland on the 120-mile ride to Little Rock. On a well-traveled road, they covered the distance in two days, coming in sight of the town on the banks of the Arkansas on the evening of November 12.[84] He intended to stay only the one night but reckoned without his celebrity. Not many famous people passed through Little Rock, and the town's fathers would not be denied their chance to fete the famous man. Crockett and his party took rooms at Charles Jeffries' City Hotel, but when the delegation came to invite him to a supper in his honor, they found him behind the hotel skinning a deer he had shot on the day's ride.

In the same breath, Crockett recognized the head of the delegation, then boasted about the two-hundred-yard shot he made in bagging the deer.

At first Crockett acted reluctant, but he agreed to attend the dinner, and once there entertained the crowd with the usual speech, blasting Jackson and his administration, telling the "go to hell" story, and quipping that he hoped there were no federal deputies in the house, since Jackson had declared a policy of neutrality toward the Texas revolution, and Crockett and his boys might be violating that if they got involved.[85] Since his hosts were themselves largely Whigs and anti-Jackson Democrats, they delighted in what one called "the sport of hearing him abuse the Administration, in his outlandish style."[86] He dwelled more on his recent defeat at the polls than the events in Texas, though one reporter swore that Crockett boasted that he would "have *Santa Anna's* head, and wear it for a watch seal."[87] Whatever he said, the audience stamped and applauded in approval.[88] One local thought his remarks "few, plain, moderate and unaffected—without violence or acrimony," and that instead of forced eloquence, his talk was "simply rough, natural, and pleasant." He intended to end his days in Texas, he told them.[89] A young man in the audience never forgot the evening. Having expected Crockett to act the clown, he found the Tennessean instead to be a gentleman, his speech flashing with wit, but never vulgar or buffoonish.[90]

The next morning the editor of the local *Times* called at the City Hotel, but instead had to go to a local carpenter's shop, where he found Crockett sharpening a small ax on a grindstone, preparing to take the road once more.[91] Several young men of the town became so enthused that they hoped to join his party for the ride to Texas, and perhaps a few did, as he seemed ever to pick up people along the way. Having left home with three companions, and then up to thirty, now he had six or eight remaining with him by the time he reached Little Rock. One of the young men hoping to join him was John Ray, who, as it happened, also knew the Bowies in Louisiana, but sudden ill health forced him to stay behind.[92] Another who may have attached himself to the party was Martin Despallier, Bowie's onetime partner in Opelousas land fraud.[93]

His ax sharpened, Crockett mounted his party late that morning and departed heavily armed to the south, a considerable crowd cheering them on.[94] They rode southwest, probably passing through Washington, finally reaching the Red River in the very southwest corner of the state, probably at McKinney's Landing. Crossing to the Mexican side near a place called Lost Prairie, Crockett set foot in Texas at last. He accepted the hospitality of Isaac Jones for the night, and while there confessed his financial embarrassment, and arranged to trade his engraved, buckskin-wrapped pocket watch, the same one given him by the citizens of Philadelphia in 1834, in return for Jones's timepiece, plus thirty dollars. It was a symbolic closing of a door, perhaps. The relic of a time when everyone spoke his name no longer had meaning to him now, and in this place. Like the whole trip that it represented, the watch was only a means to a future end. "With his open frankness, his natural honesty of expression, his perfect want of concealment," said Jones a few months later, "I could not but be very much impressed." Finding Crockett a most congenial companion, he treasured the watch as a memento "which would often remind me of an honest man."[95]

Leaving Lost Prairie, Crockett rode a few miles over the level prairies to Big Prairie.[96] There he passed the night with a settler family whom Crockett told he had come to Texas to indulge "his favorite propensity for fighting," more boast than fact since it had been fully twenty years now since Crockett heard a hostile shot. His hostess showed concern for his family back in Tennessee without him, but Crockett revealed that the watch and memories of the old political life were not all that he was breaking with. "I have set them free—set them free," he said of Elizabeth and the children. "They must shift for themselves."[97]

By early December, Crockett had passed through Clarksville, and then decided to set off across country to the west on a hunt. The land here was completely wild, not a white settlement in the region, and the Kickapoo could be unfriendly, yet Crockett had sufficient men with him now to feel safe enough. Here was his first real chance to take the bison, the Texas bear, and the measure of the landscape as well. He rode more than eighty miles west and found the land between the Bois d'Arc Creek and Choctaw Bayou, both flowing into the Red, particularly pleasing. No sooner did he see it than he decided that he might not return to Tennessee at all. He could file for a headright claim and settle right there where he found abundant fertile soil, lush forest, clear spring water, good open prairie to range cattle, and game aplenty. He also found that the stream would certainly support the inevitable gristmill. Best of all, the great herds of bison migrated north and south on their annual treks right through the area. He could enjoy a magnificent hunt twice a year. Local swarms of bees produced abundant honey, sweet for man and a good lure for bears.[98] Before setting off he agreed to rendezvous with others of his party on Christmas at the falls of the Brazos, but when he did not show up for several days after the appointed time, a rumor went out that he had been attacked and killed by the Kickapoo. By New Year's, however, word reached his friends that he was quite alive and just enjoying the hunt so much that he ignored the approaching deadline. By February the stories of his death reached the eastern press, and no doubt his family, but they were used to hearing exaggerated reports of his demise and this one, like those before, they probably realized to be "a whapper of a lie."[99]

By January 5 Crockett found his way down the old Trammel's Trace to Nacogdoches, and there a welcome awaited him. His old friend Ben McCulloch, who may have been with him in Arkansas but skipped the hunt, greeted him.[100] Townsmen, delighted at seeing the celebrity, and taking it for granted that he had come to join their struggle for independence, gave him the inevitable dinner, and he responded with the inevitable speech. "I am told, gentlemen, that, when a stranger, like myself, arrives among you, the first inquiry is—what brought him here?" David said. "To satisfy your curiosity at once as to myself, I will tell you all about it. I was, for some years, a member of Congress. In my last canvass, I told the people of my District, that, if they saw fit to re-elect me, I would serve them as faithfully as I had done; but, if not, *they might go to hell, and I would go to Texas.* I was beaten, gentlemen, and here I am." Inevitably it brought a roar of applause, but especially here, where he delivered the little set piece for the first time.[101]

Crockett found more than enough in Texas to persuade him that his future, at least for the time being, lay there. He enjoyed wonderful health on his trip so far, and the distraction of the adventure had erased any depression as a result of his defeat in August. He found the country itself exhilarating—"the garden spot of the world," he called it. Any man could make his fortune there, with so much land available, and at such a small price that he could pay off the purchase price of his three-quarters of a league from its own produce. More than that, after seeing the Choctaw–Bois d'Arc country, he contracted a bit of the land fever himself, and thought he might be able to secure an appointment as land agent to settle the territory. "I would be glad to see every friend I have settle there," he said. "It would be a fortune to them all."

Perhaps most of all, the warm enthusiastic welcomes that met him wherever he went in Texas convinced Crockett that the men there appreciated him. There was no taint of being pro- or anti-Jackson here. American politics stopped at the Sabine, for Texians cared only about what was happening in Texas, and so far prospects looked bright. After a few minor skirmishes and a desultory siege at San Antonio, the Mexicans had been pushed south of the Rio Grande. Their supreme general, Santa Anna, was rumored to be on the way with another army, but if the Texians had beaten them once they could do it again, and every day more volunteers passed through Nacogdoches from the States. No one could tell the outcome. U.S. troops might even intervene, but whatever happened, Texas seemed destined not just to be free of Coahuila, but from Mexico itself. He could be a part of a "bran fire" new country.[102]

After a few days in Nacogdoches, and with the invitation to return for a grand dinner given by the ladies of the town, Crockett and about ten followers rode east a day to San Augustine where the same welcome awaited on January 8. The town fathers fired their one little cannon to celebrate his arrival, Crockett made a speech from a street corner, and again there was the bountiful dinner fete afterward. Judge Shelby Corzine hosted Crockett at his home, where no doubt they reminisced about their service in the Creek War, and civic leaders approached him to suggest that he become a candidate to represent their community in the coming constitutional convention on March 1.[103] Crockett assumed from the moment of his arrival that he could take a leading role in Texian politics almost at once if he wished. He could win a seat merely by putting his name forward. Having no property or residence as yet, he had no constituency, but now San Augustine offered itself. During the fete for him that evening he responded to their offer with the obligatory protest of disinterest. He had come to Texas to fight, not to seek office, he told them disingenuously, for getting involved in the rebellion formed no part of his original intention. Nevertheless, just so that San Augustine would not be offended by his apparent demur, he went on to add that he would "rather be a member of the Convention than of the Senate of the United States."[104] His audience understood him well enough. The next day a man in San Augustine wrote to Lt. Gov. John Robinson to tell him that Crockett "is to Represent them in the Convention."[105]

"I have but little doubt of being elected a member to form the Constitution of this province," David wrote soon after the offer. Yet the lure of an adventure tugged at him as well. In giving his very equivocal denial of the town's offer, he had committed himself for the first time publicly to going into the volunteer forces, though he must have made the decision some days earlier, perhaps in part because of the assumption that there would be generous land bounties for volunteers once the hostilities ceased. Two decades had passed since his last campaign of the military sort. He was forty-nine now, perhaps graying a bit, the firm frame starting to show a little flesh after the soft years in Congress. He would enjoy the excitement of a fight or two, and more the camaraderie of the camp and field. It would be his last chance to be a boy again. Moreover, Crockett always knew enough to go where the votes were, and in the current crisis, with or without property, every volunteer serving in the Texian forces got a vote. He had but to volunteer, which would automatically put him among hundreds of voters. He could serve Texas a little while, electioneer at the same time, and win the volunteers' convention seat or the one from San Augustine perhaps. Either might start him back on the road of political fortune, its terminus not yet imagined in the unknown territory of Texas's future. Echoing what he told the men of San Augustine, he wrote his daughter that "I had rather be in my present position than to be elected to a seat in Congress for Life." He would make his fortune here in Texas. "I am rejoiced at my fate."[106]Crockett and friends returned to Nacogdoches in a day or two, and there David went before Judge John Forbes on January 12 to take his oath of allegiance to the provisional government of Texas. In talking with Forbes, Crockett and those with him gave their promise to sustain Robinson and the General Council that took power in November 1835 in their resistance to the speculators like Bowie and Mason, who backed Henry Smith. Crockett balked, however, when he noted that the oath included the words "or future other government that may be thereafter declared." The unsaid clause, of course, was that there might be an independent *national* government in time, but David objected to such a blanket promise of fealty. He insisted that the word "*republican*" be inserted before "government" before he would sign.

Forbes, already greatly flattered at giving the oath to such a celebrity, gladly agreed, and so Crockett became a volunteer with a six months' commitment.[107] More than that, he committed his future to Texas. Thereafter he told those he met that he intended never to return to Tennessee again.[108] In keeping with the militant spirit of the times, and his new status as a mounted volunteer, Crockett trotted out all the old clichés that the people wanted to hear. When Nacogdoches' ladies regaled him with another dinner, he boasted that Texian men would "*lick up* the Mexicans like *fine salt.*" Better than that, he promised personally "to *grin* all the Mexicans out of Texas."[109]

In the days following his enlistment, Crockett saw a loose band of other volunteers form under his assumed leadership, though he held no rank. Tinkle and Burgin appear to have left him before now, but his nephew William Patton was still at his side, and with him McCulloch, Peter Harper, Jesse Benton, Daniel Cloud, and B. Archer Thomas of Kentucky, Crockett's cousin John Harris, Micajah Autry, and a dozen others.[110] They were all delighted with the addition of the distinguished Tennessean, and partially in his honor began to call themselves the Tennessee Mounted Volunteers. Perhaps too, in recognition of the kind of service David performed in the Creek War, they regarded themselves as "spies," meaning scouts.[111] As evidence of the common assent that "Colonel" Crockett should lead them, they left much of the official detail of their outfitting to him, and he spent a busy January 15 getting ready to leave for the seat of expected action. Always in need of cash, he sold two extra rifles to the provisional government for $60.00, though he only got $2.50 on the spot, the balance to be paid later. He also allowed his tall chestnut horse and its equipment, plus the rifle he kept for himself, to be absorbed into the government service, for another voucher for $240.00 to be collected thereafter.[112]

By January 16 they were ready, though their orders, if any, were loose. The Rio Grande lay 300 miles away, and San Antonio, a probable point of defense, nearly 280. Governing authorities lay divided themselves as to the next move, whether to await Santa Anna's coming, or send an expedition to Matamoros. In the absence of specific orders, Forbes no doubt simply suggested that Crockett take his small company toward San Felipe, where the consultation of (now) Gen.

Sam Houston could decide where to send them. Expecting to spend not a few days out in the open now, and with the rain and cold blasts of winter expected, Crockett drew a small tent from the local military supplier, bid farewell to Nacogdoches, and set off on the La Bahía.[113] Those of them who could write sent letters back to their old homes in the United States before they left, for hereafter mail service would be increasingly chancy. Young Daniel Cloud sent home what amounted to an assertion of American manifest destiny. "The tide of emigration will be onward and irresistible," he said. Inevitably Americans must have Texas, and spread on west, even beyond the Rocky Mountains. "The prospect is grand, too much so for my feeble power of description to compass," he continued. "We go with arms in our hands, determined to conquer or die."[114]

David Crockett, too, sent a letter home to Tennessee, though only one, for time did not allow him to write more, and he had been working on this one desultorily for days. He said nothing of conquest, but spoke only of his prospects. "I am rejoiced at my fate," he wrote. All his bad fortune was about to turn around. He would achieve wealth and renewed station here in this newer world, and promised to do the best he could. "Do not be uneasy about me," he said before he rode off toward the revolution. "I am with my friends."[115]

BOWIE

Bowie, and others cry, "wolf wolf, condemnation, destruction, war, to arms, to arms!" to deceive many persons and make them believe that an army is coming.

JAMES KERR, JULY 5, 1835

Whatever Ursula Bowie's death took from the heart of her husband, one overriding thing still drove his life: his passion for land. When he returned to San Antonio in March 1834, he began settling her estate, or at least claiming what was due him as her survivor. The fact was that, despite his earlier promise not to encumber his assets with mortgages, Bowie had almost completely entangled their community property, and though he owed no substantial debts in Texas thanks to his late father-in-law's generosity, still the fact remained that he had no ready source of income.[1] He owned only the league of land on the Navidad, and that was hardly worth much at the moment. With Veramendi dead, access to his wealth ceased, though he left an estate worth around one hundred thousand dollars, some of which should surely be Bowie's as Ursula's inheritance. Yet that would take time and remained uncertain, for Ursula's grandmother survived and could claim all of her son's estate.[2]

For the first half of 1834 Bowie largely wandered, and may have surrendered to drink more than he should as he tried to regain his personal and financial balance. His old temper flared again, and there were fights. After one supposed brawl in San Antonio he asked a friend why he had not come to help in the scuffle. The man answered that, so far as he could tell, Bowie had been in the wrong in the encounter. "Don't you suppose I know that as well as you do?" replied Bowie. "That's just why I needed a friend. If I had been in the right, I would have had plenty of them."[3] The fact was, with Ursula and Veramendi gone, with Caiaphas Ham and brother Rezin back in Louisiana and Stephen dead,

Bowie did need friends just now. Houston came back to San Felipe in December 1833, and the two may have passed a few convivial evenings in the taverns, but then Houston left on his trip to Washington, where he would meet Crockett and others, and perhaps New York, to look into yet another colonization and land company.[4]

During much of the late winter and early spring of 1834 Bowie simply went on a long hunt, scouting land on the upper waters of the Trinity River as far as the Cross Timbers region two hundred miles north of San Felipe. William Lacy, his companion for much of the time, found Bowie "a roving man," unattached to any steady way of life, yet "he was like Barnum's show, wherever he went everybody wanted to see him." Bowie kept to himself much of the time, seldom laughed, and frequently did not speak at all. Occasionally he reminisced, however, and once even recounted for Lacy the story of the Sandbar scrape, opening his shirt to show the ugly scars left by the sword canes and bullets. Lacy found to his surprise that Bowie rarely if ever swore.[5]

Yet it was unlike Bowie to stay reclusive for long. By late spring he returned to the more settled parts of Texas, and at the same time felt the old instincts rising once more to find or make an opportunity in his favorite currency, land. His timing, though accidental, proved perfect. For some time, now, he had been unable to sell the eleven-league grants that he and Isaac Donoho acquired from Mexicans the year before, because it was up to Samuel Williams actually to make the location of the grants. Resenting the way Bowie got them in the first place, Williams consequently delayed.[6] But on March 26 all those efforts to encourage moving the capital from Saltillo to Monclova, and to relax land policies, finally paid off, and it looked as if Bowie would not have to wait on Williams to start making land money again. The Monclova legislature, undisguisedly corrupt from its first convening, realized that the movement to separate Texas from Coahuila might soon be successful and hit upon the means of subsidizing itself at no real cost by capitalizing on its remaining time in jurisdiction over the northern province. The legislature passed an act opening vacant Texas land to foreigners in quantities up to eleven leagues per buyer, to be sold at auction, with a ten-dollar minimum for each 177-acre plot. If no one bought, then a supplementary act allowed the land to be sold subsequently to anybody for the ten-dollar minimum fee on application.

Moreover, the act decreed an end to further colonization contracts so that *empresarios* would no longer receive profits that could not go to the legislature. Then, on April 19, another measure authorized the sale of up to four hundred leagues of vacant Texas lands to raise money for defense against the marauding Indian tribes on the frontier, though again the real intent of the act was simply to sell Texas land to all comers in order to enrich Monclova.[7]

As design would have it, Mason, agent for the Galveston Bay and Texas Land Company, was in Monclova at that very moment, and may have had something to do with encouraging the more pliable of the legislators to vote for the land acts. The moment the measures passed, he sent his resignation to his company and then started negotiating as a private investor for the purchase of hundreds of nonauction leagues in a personal contract with the governor.[8] Almost as soon as they heard of the legislation, would-be speculators like Bowie, his friend Archibald Hotchkiss, and William Wharton hurried to Monclova to take advantage, not knowing that Mason was ahead of them all. Travis himself prepared the passports for Bowie, Wharton, and several others on June 4, and Bowie probably left for Monclova immediately after borrowing $790 from Frank Johnson, part of it to cover the cost of the journey, but the bulk to be spent on land.[9]

Bowie and Mason had been at least casual acquaintances since the year before, and Mason no doubt discovered that their association could be to his advantage. Bowie enjoyed the goodwill and esteem of several in the legislature, knew who could and could not be bribed if necessary, and perhaps still carried some influence as the late Veramendi's son-in-law. As it happened Bowie had other business here anyhow, for late in the month he engaged Oliver Jones, a Texas delegate to the legislature, to act as his agent with power of attorney to collect from Veramendi's administrators all of his property left in Ursula's hands.[10] There could not have been much of value to be collected, but a few months earlier Bowie's friend Angus McNeil managed to raise $750 for him by selling a slave man named Abner, whom Bowie had left behind in Natchez, and that added to the residue of the Johnson loan at least gave him the start of some investment money.[11]

Once more the old charm and bold talk came out, and within days Bowie gained Mason's trust and at least a promised share of the land deal. Mason himself would have to return to New York soon to raise the money to pay the governor, and while he was away he left Bowie's friend Hotchkiss in charge, though the hand of Bowie himself was seen everywhere.[12] By June 10 they had their first ninety-five leagues, most of it in eleven-league parcels.[13] Initially Mason transferred them to another agent of the company, George Nixon, on June 25 purely for title purposes, until Bowie, acting as sales commissioner in Texas, could actually make the sales. Eventually Mason would gain title to up to three hundred or more leagues of Texas land, and Williams would buy another three hundred himself.[14]

By late summer more hopeful entrepreneurs reached Monclova, including the noted abolitionist Benjamin Lundy, who thought all of the agitation in Texas merely part of a plot to separate it from Mexico in order to create another slave state. His mission here was to combat that, rather frontally it has to be said, by trying to get a colonization grant to settle free blacks in Texas. He did not succeed, but on September 22 he did encounter Oliver Jones on the street in Monclova, and with him "the noted Bowie."[15] Frank Johnson, Samuel Williams, Dr. James Grant, and several others arrived in December, and still Bowie was there, apparently continuing his efforts through Jones and others to encourage even more land concessions from the legislature.[16] Grant, a Scot most recently from Nacogdoches, had also held a seat in the legislature, and would take office in March 1835 as the body's secretary. He and Bowie became somewhat close as the fall turned into winter, and when James's money ran out Grant started advancing him rather considerable sums, no doubt for living expenses and, perhaps, a little sweetening to hurry legislation. In return Bowie promised him 100 leagues of Texas land when he finally secured possession.[17] Yet another old friend from Louisiana joined Bowie at some point, Blaz Despallier, a part of the Alexandria family so involved in his forged Spanish grants in the Opelousas district.[18]

Unfortunately government always impeded Bowie's schemes. The continuing unrest in Mexican politics worsened through 1834 and into 1835, and the situation rapidly disintegrated. Augustín Viesca took office as governor of Coahuila y Texas in April, and soon thereafter Vice-President Valentín Farías arrived from Mexico City with news that Santa Anna had ordered the Congress there to dismiss him. Virtually a dictator now, Santa Anna—at last openly revealed to be anything but republican—intended to put down all opposition to his regime. He directed drastic reduction of local militia, and all other arms surrendered to the central authority. Already the state of Zacatecas rebelled, and faced a harsh punishment. In the former capital of the province, Saltillo, the ruffled ousted legislators fed military commander Martín Perfecto de Cós with rumors that Farias and Viesca planned a revolt of their own. Fearful of being attacked by Cós, Monclova's legislature passed its March 14 land act to raise money for defense.

All the politicking and cajoling, and probable bribery, had been a waste of time, it seemed, but the result was the same when the legislature passed the measure to sell an additional four hundred leagues in Texas, and followed that with an April 7 act for more. Mason and Williams, hovering in anticipation of the legislation, swooped on the opportunity immediately, and then the congress began to appoint commissioners to oversee the actual sale of the land in the grants. It appointed Bowie to act for Mason's 400 leagues, and almost immediately he began issuing titles for eleven-league parcels.[19] Moreover, Bowie obtained as payment for his services a grant of his own, ninety-five leagues not far from Nacogdoches. It seemed stunning. "Col. Bowie was the rightful owner of thousands of acres of land in Texas," his friend Ham later remembered, but his recollection hardly met the case.[20] Bowie suddenly held in his hand a title to more than half a million acres, some 850 square miles, four times his known Louisiana and Arkansas frauds, and all at a fraction of the trouble, and nothing more illegal than cozening a few legislators.[21] One Texian estimated that "within a year every league will be worth 40,000$."[22] That was certainly an exaggeration. Still, if Bowie sold at a good price, that old elusive fortune would finally be his.

Unfortunately for Bowie, the nature of the land sale was so obviously corrupt—Williams and others got their parcels for a fifth of the going rate, and before any property was put up for public sale—that when Santa Anna heard of it his congress annulled the legislature's acts. Word of that suggested to Cós that this was the time to make a military march on Monclova to clean out the speculators infesting the place and exert some control over the irresponsible legislature and plotting governor. On April 7 Bowie and others learned of Cós's approach, and a few days later the Monclova militia confronted the Mexican regulars outside the city. Typically, his instinct always to go on the offensive, Bowie himself was out with the militia, and according to Spencer Jack "did every thing in his power to bring on a battle."[23] Fortunately Cós kept a cool head, no one started shooting, and then the Mexican soldiers retired. Fortunately too, after putting down the Zacatecas rebellion rather brutally, Santa Anna went back to Mexico City instead of going on to Monclova. The speculators and their legislature were a nuisance, but apparently not yet sufficient to warrant an outright attack.

The respite allowed Mason and Bowie to leave on or after May 3 to make the trip to Matamoros, a three-hundred-mile ride along the south bank of the Rio Grande. Once they reached the port city early in May they received $40,000 in specie sent from New York for Mason to pay the balance due on his 1834 contract, and then set off once more for Monclova. By May 25 they were close to Monclova when they heard terrible news: Cós had come back.[24] Issuing a proclamation that charged "two or three designing and naturally turbulent foreigners, somewhat crafty in their machinations," with engineering the land grab, he blamed the upheaval in the state on them and their kind, hinting that their ultimate goal was to bring about Texas's secession from Coahuila.[25]

Indeed, even in Texas, when news of the land deal arrived, there was some considerable outcry. The Brazoria *Texas Republican* hammered Viesca for having "bartered our public lands for a mere song," and in San Felipe the *Telegraph and Texas Register* referred to them as "unjust and fraudulent claims." When the buyers of those eleven-league grants started trying to locate and survey their claims, they inevitably had to displace hundreds of squatters and occupants who had made improvements to land in anticipation of being able to buy it one day. It would be a repeat of the dislocation that Bowie's Louisiana frauds caused years before, and the injustices brought about by the North Carolina warrants in Crockett's west Tennessee.[26]

Certainly Cós thought of Mason as one of those "designing and turbulent foreigners," and most likely Williams and Bowie were also on his mind. In spite of that, they went on toward Monclova, to find that the legislature had adjourned on May 20 just as Cós and his command from Saltillo approached. Bowie and Mason found Governor Viesca and some of his followers encamped outside the town, and joined them when they began to move to the Rio Grande, intending to cross into Texas to reconvene the legislature in Béxar. But within a few days Cós caught up with them and arrested almost the whole lot.[27] Oddly enough Bowie allowed himself to be captured, though it may be that he did not want to be separated from Mason and his forty thousand dollars. Nevertheless Mason and the money soon disappeared.[28]

The Mexicans sent Bowie to Matamoros along with several others, including his friend Despallier, but their confinement was not so strict that Bowie could not see events unfolding in the town near the mouth of the Rio Grande. Mexican authorities impounded every vessel in the port, ostensibly for the purpose of convoying troops and munitions to points on the Texas coast, obviously to strengthen garrisons and quell any spread of the Zacatecas and Monclova resistance. He heard that three thousand soldiers were in Saltillo even then, on their way over-land, dire news indeed. Fortunately for Bowie the authorities relaxed their guard and on June 12 he and Despallier managed to escape, and in the ensuing ten days traveled overland 240 miles along the Atascosita road to the Lavaca River, 50 miles south of San Felipe. There they stopped at Sylvanus Hatch's plantation, near Texana. Despallier felt too sick from fever to continue without several days' rest, and Bowie himself perhaps wanted to dally awhile with Clara Lisle of Texana, who may have rekindled some romantic interest in the widower now that Ursula was nine months gone.[29]

Bowie sent a note to James Miller of the *ayuntamiento* at Nacogdoches with news of what he had learned in Matamoros, and soon it spread through the Texas settlements, leading to calls for militia to turn out.[30] Williams and Johnson also made their escapes from Matamoros, and as they arrived in Béxar and San Felipe, the alarm took on even more urgency. A few days later Bowie, and perhaps Despallier, continued on to Brazoria, but already some looked skeptically at the news he brought. Bowie now stood clearly identified with those soon to be called the War Party, yet many saw them and the speculators as one and the same, and their interests suspiciously intertwined.[31] James Kerr protested to Thomas Chambers that "Williams, Johnson, Carbajal, Bowie, and others cry, 'wolf wolf, condemnation, destruction, war, to arms, to arms!'" when their only real objective was "to deceive many persons and make them believe that *an army is coming to destroy their property and annihilate their rights in Texas.*"

The fact was, he charged, that they stirred up trouble, even rebellion, in hopes of protecting their massive illegal land purchases. Santa Anna had repudiated the Monclova land actions. If Bowie and others could deny Mexican rule in Texas, then they had a chance of making their titles hold. [32] Of course self-interest guided Bowie's actions, but within a few weeks Texians would realize that Santa Anna had more things than land titles on his mind as Mexican soldiers marshalled to come to Texas. [33]

Puzzled Mexican authorities believed that after his escape Bowie went all the way to Mississippi to raise troops to bring back to Texas. [34] They were mistaken. He made his way to Nacogdoches by early July, along the way meeting his old friend Caiaphas Ham who was just returning from a visit to Louisiana. In fact, he certainly had it in mind to go to Louisiana and Mississippi, but more for money and investors in the Mason grants than to enlist volunteers. But now events began to control him just as they directed everyone else in Texas. Travis and others expelled the garrison at Anahuac a few weeks before, and now Mexican activity intensified at the garrisons along the frontier. The political chief at Nacogdoches, Henry Rueg, reacted to the Anahuac affair with fear that there would be a general clamping down on Texas by the Mexicans, and decided within days of Bowie's arrival to urge the citizens to form a militia.

By July 13 nearly one hundred men gathered in the public square, and either by election or common assent they elected Bowie their "colonel." In a crisis men seemed naturally to turn to him. With the celebrity gained by his escape, not to mention his prior reputation, he naturally seemed the right man when they needed a commander. Though there was no official sanction, he would naturally have been given, or assumed, the title of colonel, not so much as a recognized rank but as a title of command customary among southerners for more than a generation now whenever any number of them gathered for an armed enterprise.

Either by his direction or as a spontaneous act, they marched to the Mexican warehouse where local commander Pedro Bean kept a small armory. Without actual violence, but most certainly by the threat of it, Bowie and his men broke into the warehouse and removed enough muskets and accoutrements to arm themselves. The act had the double advantage of arming the militia and removing weapons that the

Mexicans might use against them. Bean was outraged. He believed that Bowie intended to foment rebellion, and immediately reported the offense to his commander Ugartechea, asking instructions on what to do about Bowie. The only good news seemed to be that the majority of the people in the Nacogdoches area did not seem inclined to countenance or join with the upstarts. Convinced that Bowie planned to lead a revolution, Bean concluded within a few weeks that the lack of local support had forced him to abandon the project.[35]

Bowie was not all that passive, though. Just a week after taking the muskets, he learned from a mail carrier passing through Nacogdoches that a sealed packet of dispatches addressed to the Mexican consul at New Orleans had been left at a house just east of San Augustine. The packet awaited an eastbound courier to take it on its journey, but Bowie decided to change its destination. "Col. Bowie ever alive to the true interests of Texas," said John Forbes, spoke with a few men in town and among them they decided to intercept the packet. He sent word to two friends near San Augustine to get an authorization from their *alcalde* to take the packet, and soon they sent it back to Bowie in Nacogdoches. He called a meeting of the townsmen in the public square, and there they read aloud the Mexican dispatches, detailing as they did their accusations against the Texians for treason and plotting, orders for the arrest of Travis and others involved in the Anahuac capture in June, and news that the Mexicans were considering a military occupation of Texias.[36] If Nacogdoches needed anything to arouse its ire, this performance "moved their deep wrath and indignation." For a member of the war party, it was a wise stroke of opinion molding, especially at a time when many in Texas were reacting strongly against the taking of Anahuac as reckless and inappropriate. Bowie may have sensed this in the aftermath of apathy that followed his seizure of the muskets, and within a few days he would hear from Travis much the same, as he realized now that the time was not right, that public sentiment did not yet support the war party, and anything that could be done, such as the revelation of these dispatches, would help to fan the guttering flame of revolt into life.[37]

Bowie's standing grew rapidly now. First the escape from Matamoros—forgetting his involvement with the despised Mason—then the taking of the armory, and now the capture of the dispatches.

When Rueg received information that several groups of renegades were starting trouble among the Indian tribes on the northern border of Texas, he recognized at once that with the prospect of Mexicans perhaps invading from the south, the Texians could not handle a war with the Comanche and others in their rear. He asked Forbes to send the town's sheriff to drive the renegades away and try to establish peaceful relations. Significantly, however, Rueg directed that Forbes should put the mission, including the sheriff himself, "under the direction of Col Bowie." Once again, when the prospect of a crisis loomed, people looked instinctively toward James Bowie.[38]

Those instructions from Rueg mark the first time that someone in an official capacity referred to Bowie as a colonel. He had exhausted his horse on the long ride from Matamoros, and with the animal not yet refitted, he looked for another in company with Ham. Sam Houston lived in town at the time, and Bowie knew that he had a fine animal, fresh and strong. "Houston, I want your horse," Bowie told him, no doubt in a tavern. When Houston good-naturedly refused, Bowie typically said: "I am going to take him," and left the room to get the animal. Houston turned to Caiaphas Ham and asked him if he thought he ought to lend Bowie the horse. Ham, who knew Bowie's determination far better than most, replied that it might be a good idea under the circumstances. "D—m him," said Houston, "let him take the horse."[39]

On July 31 or August 1 Bowie and his small party rode north into the Cherokee country along Trammel's Trace. Several villages on the way were all having drinking frolics, which could make them dangerous, and so he bypassed them and went about forty miles north of Nacogdoches on to the Caney Creek settlement of Chief Bowl, head man of the Cherokee in Texas. Bowl agreed to bring some of his own men with Bowie on his mission, and sent couriers to the Shawnee and other Cherokee to rendezvous at his village in early August to help in the expedition. Meanwhile Bowie moved on to the west another forty miles or more until he came to the Neches River on August 3, and there he met a man who told him that 250 Texians from San Felipe had also gone on an expedition to calm the northern border, and that they were well ahead of him in their march north. There being no chance of catching up with them to act in unison, Bowie decided to go straight north himself. The informant on the Neches told him that large groups of Waco, Towashi, and Tawakoni had joined with some Comanche at the Coffee's Station trading house north of Crossed Timbers on the Red River. Holland Coffee was reported to be encouraging the natives to kill Mexicans and bring their livestock to him for purchase, and when some Tawakoni told him they had killed some Texians, he even said it did not matter and encouraged them to continue, with the promise that he would buy all their plunder.

Having learned that Coffee also had some two hundred Tawakoni and twenty-five renegade whites protecting him and his establishment, Bowie knew there was no point in his going ahead with his small party. He sent a report south to Nacogdoches with a recommendation that Rueg raise a party of fifty or more and send them to join with Bowie and Bowl's men to march for Coffee's Station. They ought to be able to link with the Texians from San Felipe, and together they could break up Coffee's establishment and disperse his allies.[40] Bowie needed to decide what to do next while he waited for Rueg to act, and typically he apparently determined to go on in advance of any men who might be coming from Nacogdoches. Just how far he got, though, is a mystery, and so is his intent, for within a few days he changed his destination once more. Word may have reached him that the natives and Coffee were not in fact as menacing as rumored and that he need not go farther. He may have decided to go west on his own to check into the activities of the Comanche. He may have decided that his recent confrontations with Mexican authority called for him to disappear for a time, or even concluded that with the people of Texas not yet in a temper for active resistance, he should take advantage of the doldrums to make that trip he had planned for some time.

Whatever the case, without returning to Nacogdoches, Bowie set off for Louisiana, leaving behind him a mystery as to his disappearance and, within a few weeks, rumors that the Comanche attacked and killed him early in August.[41] He may have passed through Arkansas on his way, to visit with John Bowie at his new home in Helena on the Mississippi, where he had just been elected to the legislature and was still trying to dabble in the land business, though now legitimately.[42] If James met with him, he undoubtedly impressed on his brother the

mounting state of urgency in Texas, and perhaps asked him to help
encourage volunteers to hurry to the province to help in resistance to
the feared Mexican invasion. Certainly John Bowie did what he could.
A few weeks later he hosted a grand barbecue, ostensibly in honor of
the Bowies' friend Littleberry Hawkins, and within a few days a party
formed to take the road for Texas.[43]

By that time James had gone ahead. There might be more land deals
to look after in Louisiana now. McNeil would have informed him by
March that Robert Walker had given up his attempt to secure title on
the Sutton report claims purchased from Bowie. That made the claims,
bogus as they were, available for James to attempt to pursue once
again, though he should have learned more than enough by now to
realize that he was never going to get them approved.[44] Still, there was
always the possibility of selling them to someone who might not yet
have heard of the famous "Bowie claims," and so James got someone to
register copies of the spurious conveyances in Natchitoches a few
months earlier, on May 26, by his power of attorney.[45] As much as his
dishonesty in land dealings invited the harshest condemnation, James
Bowie's determination, once set, was a true marvel.

Looking into all this required a visit to Natchez, where he called on
his friend and attorney Angus McNeil. Besides starting anew the
Louisiana land efforts, Bowie had something even bigger to discuss.
With his commission to handle the Mason grants, he could offer the
lure of vast expanses of cheap land. He went to work at once on his old
physician William Richardson, whom McNeil found to be "very much
under his influence, as was most of his other friends." Richardson had a
considerable fortune, "and Bowie could easily have obtained from him
any reasonable amount of money." He promised the doctor his own
league of land on the Navidad, his original settlement grant, in return
for $5,000. But that was to be only the start. McNeil marveled anew at
Bowie's ability to sell himself and his ideas, and to persuade his friends
to hand over their money. Before he left he had raised close to eighty
thousand dollars, most of it apparently in Richardson's hands to invest
in Bowie's Mason grants. Richardson and McNeil also decided to come
with him on the return journey to Texas to look over the property for
themselves.[46] It was Bowie's last visit to the storied city on the river that
figured so strongly in the making of his reputation as a fighter, and

even more prominently in the tall tales soon to be told of him. No doubt he enjoyed the entertainments Natchez provided, so much more varied and refined than what Texas could offer. If he read the local press while he was there he might have seen a review of a new book that the editor praised as "decidedly the best thing we have met with for many a day." It was Crockett's blast at Van Buren.[47]

By late September or early October, Bowie and his party, which may have grown to include several besides McNeil and Richardson, recrossed the Sabine into eastern Texas. No sooner were they there than Bowie encountered the Presbyterian missionary Sumner Bacon, who had traveled the traces of Texas for several years now trying to counter the enforced—and increasingly ignored—Catholic faith. In what seemed an old story at camp meetings, a few rowdies threatened to break up Bacon's service near Nacogdoches until Bowie told him to go ahead, and himself walked around the crowd with a double-barreled shotgun in hand. It was almost a repeat of that Good Samaritan act several years before.[48]

Bowie got back to Nacogdoches to find that much had happened in his absence, with dramatic shifts in sentiment. The Mason grants that he represented were more unpopular than ever, and there was talk that the permanent council might recommend to a forthcoming consultation, to gather on October 16, that it declare all of the Monclova legislature's 1834 and 1835 land laws in Texas null. Nevertheless, once in Nacogdoches Bowie managed to execute transfers for nine of the eleven-league parcels, no doubt to Richardson's investors, once the doctor had a chance to see what the land looked like. Unfortunately, given the state of political upheaval, there would be no hope of gaining actual title until the situation calmed, and the same applied to securing a proper title for the league that Bowie sold personally to Richardson.[49] In that case, Richardson very probably held onto the eighty thousand dollars he carried for the investors, and most likely also the five thousand due Bowie, especially if he learned on seeing it that the property was really worth no more than five hundred. McNeil apparently did not like what he saw and remained only a short time before returning to Louisiana, there to start founding the town of Shreveport.[50]

In fact Bowie found the land speculators like himself being charged with fomenting the current disturbances. Seeing this, and fearing the effect it could have on the genuine war party movement, Houston may have told him that he intended to suggest the grant nullification measure to the permanent council, news that would not make Bowie happy.[51] Houston also feared that the speculating demoralized men who might otherwise volunteer for the growing militias, particularly as leaders like Williams made no move to take up arms. Indeed, of the speculators, the only one to have risked himself actively was Bowie, which saved him from some of the odium attaching itself to the others.[52]

Waiting for him too, when Bowie reached Nacogdoches, was a July 30 letter from Travis. Bowie knew the young lawyer, though not well. Travis had handled a small land transaction for him several months earlier, and of course Bowie knew of Travis's June adventure at Anahuac, the act that really ignited the current unrest.[53] Beyond that the two had nothing in common, and their different temperaments probably would not have encouraged close friendship. Yet after his recent Anahuac experience, and when he heard of Bowie's exploits with the Nacogdoches armory and the captured dispatches, Travis seemingly sensed some kindred sympathy in Bowie, and on July 30 wrote him some encouragement in the face of the dominant influence of the peace party at the moment. Indeed, what Bowie read seemed to contain both encouragement, and advice, with possibly a hint of something else. "Unless we could be united, had we not better be quiet and settle down for a while?" asked Travis. It seemed to be a suggestion that Bowie do nothing more, rather presumptuous of the lawyer from San Felipe. But then, in speaking of those favoring a policy of submission, he suggested that if the people had "a bold and determined leader" they might rise up and defeat the Peace Party. Was he suggesting that Bowie should be that "bold and determined" leader?[54]

Of course much had changed by mid-October, when Bowie finally saw Travis's letter.[55] Stephen Austin, released from imprisonment, returned to Texas on August 30, at last resolved on a more aggressive policy, but following rather than leading events now. Fearful of an armed outbreak, especially in the wake of Bowie's seizure of the muskets and other small provocations, Ugartechea ordered the citizens of Gonzales to hand over a cannon in September. They refused, Cós sent soldiers, and on October 2 shots were fired. The revolution so long hoped for and feared had begun. Meanwhile General Cós had landed at Copano in mid-September with a small force and soon marched on San Antonio. Militia captured Goliad, a vital point on Cós's supply link to the coast, and soon volunteers began mustering from all over the region to form an army to drive the Mexicans out of Béxar. They elected Austin commander of the "Volunteer Army of the People" on October 11, and soon the three-hundred-man army set out from Gonzales, its numbers growing every day. Overhead in the night sky on October 14 they first saw that same comet that Crockett followed. It seemingly blazed a quarter of the way across the heavens, pointing the way to San Antonio.

Bowie had no intention of missing this action. Ham and Donoho and a few other Louisiana friends, including Richardson, were with him in Nacogdoches when word of the outbreak came. They rushed off to find the nascent army, stopping briefly in San Felipe on October 15, where Bowie and Richardson registered the conveyance of the Navidad league.[56] By the time they got to Gonzales, Austin had left, and Bowie finally caught up with the army on the evening of October 19 in its camp at Cibolo Creek, forty miles west, and only twenty miles from San Antonio.[57] Austin got there two days before, but halted his progress to allow more volunteers to arrive, bringing his numbers up to 366 in eight companies. With men arriving daily, by October 21 there would be eleven companies, totaling 453 or more, with 25 to 30 men joining every day.[58]

Bowie's arrival meant more than just the small number who came with him. "Bowie's prowess as a fighter made him doubly welcome," said Noah Smithwick, and the Louisianians like Ham and Richardson who came with him seemed "spoiling for a fight."[59] He arrived too late to attend a war council that Austin held that evening, and it was just as well, for Austin conducted the meeting more as a negotiation, mindful of the fact that all these men were volunteers who could come and go as they pleased. He may have been general in charge, but he put every decision to a vote of his officers. The day before they had voted to stay on the Cibolo for the time being, but this evening they voted to rescind their decision of the day before, leaving future movement to Austin's discretion. Running an army, even this one, in such an indecisive way, would have enraged Bowie. It would in fact soon enough.[60]

Bowie knew all or most of the officers he met when he reached headquarters. Austin made his old friend Warren Hall adjutant, and William Jack inspector. Edward Burleson and John Moore held commissions as lieutenant colonels, William Wharton acted as major, and James Fannin and others commanded the several companies as captains. Travis was here, too, now a lieutenant. Thanks to having lived in San Antonio for some time at Veramendi's, Bowie already knew something from his friends of the state of Cós's preparations for its defense, and when he told Austin of this it only made the hard-pressed commander even more hesitant. Ill as well as uncertain, Austin sat in his tent with his head in his hands much of the time, burdened with the knowledge that he—and perhaps he alone—was keeping this army together and that a wrong move on his part could see it dissolve. Moreover, the army formed much faster than his ability to care for it, and the volunteers found themselves short of bread and other necessities, with only his promise of imminent action holding some men in the ranks.[61]

It was the sort of situation made for Bowie. Austin immediately appointed him a volunteer aide on his staff, but recognized his brief militia rank as a colonel, and acknowledged even more his surpassing fitness for such a crisis. While the army stayed on the Cibolo for a few days, Bowie managed to get a letter into San Antonio on October 21 to his old friend Menchaca, who passed it along to some influential *bexareños*. He wanted information of the Mexicans' preparations, and also encouraged his *tejano* friends to come and join Austin. The next day a few dozen *tejanos* stole out of the city and came to the Texian camp, and brought with them information of the Mexicans' fortifying of the old Alamo mission, emplacing cannon on the roofs of some of its buildings, and the division of their forces between the mission and the town.[62]

There also came news of an expected wagon train of supplies, something that interested the Texians very much. Moreover, it was believed that some stores of corn and other provisions were left at the missions San Juan Espada, San Juan, and San José, a few miles south of San Antonio. On the morning of October 22 Austin gave Bowie orders to take Fannin's company to the missions, send any corn and beans found there back to the main army, and reconnoiter the surrounding country. The missions lay right on the La Bahía road, the route by which any supply train headed for Béxar must come, and thus if one of the missions seemed suitable for fortifying, the Texians could command the road and cut off further supplies to Cós, and make good use of the provisions themselves. Bowie should also determine the sentiments of the local people, and keep an ear cocked for any news of the Mexicans' *caballado*, the horses that could not be foraged in San Antonio and had to be kept out on the open prairie to feed.[63]

Bowie and Fannin covered twenty miles, much of it off the road, to reach the mission Espada by 4:30 that afternoon. The guard of five Mexican soldiers fled with no resistance, and Bowie soon found some corn and beans, but it belonged to local tenant farmers who would only sell for cash. There would be no Mexican military stores at the San José or nearby San Juan missions, but there was abundant corn belonging to *tejanos* who lived in town, and Bowie dispatched a scout to infiltrate through the Mexican defenses of San Antonio to try to negotiate a purchase from the owners. Most of the crops still in the fields were not yet ripe, unfortunate for the Texians, but equally bad for the Mexicans in the city.

Indeed, Bowie's knowledge of San Antonio and its people proved a great asset now, for he made contacts that brought information out of the fortified town. Repeated messages told of citizens being forced to work on the Mexican defenses, and many of them resolving to escape to Austin's army instead. The Mexican engineers were fortifying the housetops at every street entrance, cutting firing holes in the walls of homes, and stationing soldiers throughout. So far Cós had eight small four-pounder cannon and one larger gun mounted, with his powder and ammunition stored at the Alamo itself.[64] He proposed conducting a reconnaissance himself above the town the next day, at the same time suggesting that Austin move from the Cibolo and occupy a position north of San Antonio on El Camino Real, while Bowie held Espada. That would isolate Cós from any communications, "alarm and intimidate the enemy, and inspire our friends with renewed confidence." If Austin could send him fifty more men, Bowie even boasted that he could take and hold any position desired. He believed that the foe numbered about six hundred, with no recent reinforcements, and most of his horses sent off to Laredo, only two to three hundred being with the command, grazing outside the city during the day, and brought in for protection at night. The only real failure in his intelligence gathering came when faulty information led him to believe that, despite their apparent strength, the Mexicans were desperately low on provisions. "In *five days,* they can be *starved* out," Bowie reported to Austin, a wildly inaccurate estimate.[65]

It was on the whole an excellent report, giving Austin copious detailed information more than sufficient to formulate a campaign plan taking advantage of Mexican weakness without risking enemy strength, and virtually all of it must have been due to Bowie, for Fannin had no connections in this area. Wisely Austin conformed his decision to Bowie's suggestions. He gave orders for them to go ahead to the other missions, and on October 23 Bowie and Fannin went to San José and San Juan. As expected they found only a very little corn and peas, much of it unripe, and even that Bowie could not just take, and having no public money he could not buy. In order to forestall the mounting complaints in their command over hunger, he and Fannin decided to spend their own money to buy corn and beef for the men that night. But he warned Austin that "our private resources are quite limited, and cannot be expected to last beyond tomorrow." They must have food or money to continue. "You know the materials we have," they said. "They will fight—and fight desperately; but must *Eat.*" There also came word from Béxar that a reinforcement of thirty Mexican soldiers got into the city the night before, and Bowie's regular communications with friends in the town informed him that more and more sympathetic *tejanos* were leaving.[66]

Suddenly the Mexicans took the initiative. Shortly after dawn the next morning Bowie heard firing, and soon found himself attacked at Espada by an unknown number of the foe. He saw about fifty, but the dust cloud from their column on the road in the distance looked like one made by two hundred or more, and one witness mistakenly thought he saw Ugartechea leading them. Before long the Mexicans retired with no damage done on either side, but Bowie started putting Espada in shape to be defended, and asked Austin what his plans were, and if he could not spare a reinforcement of fifty men. He and Fannin agreed that Espada offered an important strategic point and should be held. Moreover, he suggested that with thirty minutes' notice he could advance to timber within three-quarters of a mile of San Antonio itself, further harassing Cós. But he must have men and orders, not to mention food or money. Bowie recognized the sagging morale of the volunteers.

These men had left their homes expecting a few days' service, a fight or two, and then a return home. But now they had been in the field for two weeks and more, ill fed, unpaid, and with no action. Moreover, Bowie saw some of his men starting to look uneasy at being so far in advance of the main army. Austin must come up and they must act. Bowie and Fannin sent an emphatic plea at 7:00 A.M., shortly after the Mexicans retired, saying that they "suggest—*nay urge*, the propriety—the *necessity* of some movement, which will bring us *nearer together, and shut in the enemy*, and either starve them out, whip them out, or dishearten and beat them in small parties."[67] Unsaid in the message there appeared to be a growing impatience with Austin's apparent caution and indecision.

That afternoon Warren Hall arrived bringing a message from Austin, and also newly commissioned Capt. Juan Seguín, whom Austin wanted to raise a cavalry company from among the loyal *tejanos*. Hall was to give Bowie instructions on movements, but apparently Austin had not been sufficiently specific for them to do anything but consolidate the position they already held.[68] Hall did say that Sam Houston had joined Austin, however, and that results were coming in from the recent election of delegates to the consultation. Bowie sent Hall back with a fresh statement of the situation, and now increasing the requested reinforcement to 150, since he learned from Hall that more men had come into the Cibolo camp. This would allow him to cover the lower roads to the Rio Grande, and also to enhance defense, for he had a report from a friend in San Antonio that the foe intended to attack that night. "He *knows* our numbers," Bowie warned. Bowie had to have specific orders as to what Austin wanted done, and specific information of what he intended, and whether they would combine for an advance on San Antonio on the morrow. In a cryptic note at the end of their dispatch, Fannin added a comment about the possibility of Bowie being superseded in command.[69]

That night Austin sent a reply that said nothing about future movements, but at least informed Bowie that 50 men would be coming as soon as they caught their horses. However, he could send no money for buying supplies at the missions. Instead, he offered his own personal obligation for compensation for any food Bowie bought, and if the owners would not accept that, then he gave Bowie authority to invoke the "Law of necessity" and impress the grain.[70] While Austin's previous messages addressed "Colonel James Bowie," this last one he sent to "James Bowie Esq." Perhaps it signified nothing at all, or a great deal. Having no formal commission, his "colonelcy" could not have expired, nor, for that matter, would Austin have the authority to revoke a title bestowed by the volunteers of Nacogdoches when they elected Bowie their colonel months before.

More likely Austin's mode of address represented the anticipation of something else. In early October the several jurisdictions held their elections for delegates to the new consultation to meet in San Felipe in November. Nacogdoches ran nine candidates on its ballot, and even though Bowie probably left before the election—he was in San Felipe on the day of the vote—he must have known that his name was one of the nine. Austin may well have expected that Bowie would be one of those elected, just like the recently arrived Houston. As it happened, a number of men in the army were candidates, and as election results filtered in, their absence meant that no quorum was possible when the consultation met on October 16. They adjourned until November 1, or whenever a quorum should be present.[71] Austin now faced the prospect of seeing several men, especially from his officer corps, leave to assume other duties in San Felipe. The expectation that Bowie would be among them is probably what lay behind both Fannin's otherwise unexplained comment, and Austin's suddenly addressing Bowie by a civilian honorific usually reserved for attorneys and public officials. But Bowie had not been elected. Houston led the field in the Nacogdoches balloting, and he and six others won seats, but Bowie received just sixty-eight votes and came in ninth.[72] When Austin found out, he immediately dropped the "Esquire" and went back to addressing Bowie as "colonel."

Bowie probably did not get the news for another day or two, and in any case likely received it without much disappointment. The real excitement would be out here with the army, if Austin ever made up his mind to do something. Unfortunately, the difficulty over all the newly elected delegates who might have to leave delayed the general for two days on the Cibolo, revealing as much as anything the state of Austin's debilitated health and its effect on his ability to think and act. On October 25 Austin mustered the entire army, calling in Bowie and perhaps Fannin, to put the question before the men, yet more than just the leaving of delegates seemed to be in the balance. A strong contingent, led by Houston, maintained that the army itself should retire toward San Felipe, being too weak to accomplish anything in the face of Cós's forces. Houston spoke to the men in terms that bordered on defeatism, and when he finished others took the stump to counter all his arguments except those in favor of the elected delegates being sent to the consultation. Some all but denounced him for demoralizing the men, and Houston may already have been drinking when he made his unwise appeal.[73] When Austin finally put it to a vote, the army decided to remain, but that the delegates should go to their new duties in San Felipe. Houston, who no doubt hoped to lead most of the army away under his command, was so downcast that he took refuge in his tent and the bottle, and by midnight was so drunk he was shouting for a pistol with which to shoot himself. Bowie actually restrained him, remaining with him long enough for sleep or calm to remove any danger.[74] Houston and most of them left on October 26, though a few, including Travis, now elected from San Felipe, volunteered to stay.[75]

That same day events started to move at last. The Mexicans were seen emplacing a large sixteen-pounder cannon on the roof of the Alamo church in San Antonio, and then Bowie and Fannin withdrew from Espada in the face of a strong force of skirmishers sent out to cover the arrival of a reinforcement.[76] Meanwhile Austin finally put the army in motion toward Espada, arriving the next morning to find Bowie and Fannin in their former position. At last this looked like something promising to Bowie. He also probably took a little pleasure in finding out that a few days earlier Austin had appointed his friend William Richardson surgeon of the army, meaning, if nothing else, that Bowie would have two close allies on the general's personal staff, Richardson and Hall.

Austin wanted to move cautiously, as always, and was still waiting for large cannon of his own to lay siege, yet now he seemed to be in the mood to make an offensive, perhaps in part because Houston had argued so strongly against it before he left for San Felipe. Espada sat eight miles south of San Antonio on the La Bahía Road. Six miles north of them lay the mission Concepción, just below the San Antonio River. He wanted to occupy that spot, where the river would protect his front,

preparatory to moving against Cós himself, and called on Bowie and
Fannin once more on the morning of October 27. They would take
Fannin's "First Division," which consisted only of Fannin's company
and that of Andrew Briscoe, ninety-two men in all, and move cautiously
forward toward the river to select the best place for the army to follow
and camp that night. If possible, they should also reconnoiter the outskirts of Béxar, but in any event they were to report back to him "with
as little delay as possible." Austin wanted to have time to get the rest of the
army on the road and in position before nightfall, not relishing having
his army divided in the immediate presence of the enemy.[77]

Bowie's column passed cautiously up the La Bahía, through country
well timbered, and by noon he saw the mission Concepción ahead,
and beyond it the tree-lined bank of the San Antonio. There was more
than enough time now to send word back to Austin to bring up the
rest of the army, but Bowie delayed. A small party of Mexican cavalry
came out and skirmished briefly in the afternoon, but then withdrew,
to take word of the Texians' arrival to Cós. Carefully Bowie chose his
ground in the bend of the river about five hundred yards from the mission, and put his men in the woods skirting the stream, with the river
at their backs. He divided the command into two wings, placing
Fannin's company on the south flank of the river bend, and the balance, about forty men under Bowie himself, on the upper flank. The
timber and the riverbank gave them good cover, with a clear field of
fire onto an open plain leading to the mission. To reach them the
Mexicans would have to come down the other side of the river, cross
below them, and then approach across that plain. The positions
selected, Bowie finally sent a courier back to Austin around sunset.[78]

Of course that was not what Austin had in mind. His instructions
were for the entire party to return to him. All through the afternoon
and into the evening he nervously waited to hear from Bowie. One of
his aides saw that "this disobedience of orders gave the Comr in chief
great discomfiture." Austin became almost obsessed with the fear that
the Mexicans would attack before he could get there, but since he only
received Bowie's dispatch after dark, he could not put the army on the
road until the morning, and in the best of conditions his leading elements would take two hours to reach Concepción. Austin sat awake all
night, too anxious to sleep.[79]

For his part, Bowie slept quite well. During the evening a Mexican arrived in the camp, sent by the padre of a mission in San Antonio with a bag of sugar candy and a bottle of mescal as a present for Austin. The Texians suspected that he might be a spy, trying by his gift to learn if the general himself was actually present, meaning presumably that his whole army would be with him. Some spoke of killing the man, but Bowie thought otherwise and apparently just held him overnight.[80] Instead, serenaded by the mournful calls of the whippoorwills and the occasional distant howls of coyotes and wolves, Bowie passed the evening drinking mescal and chewing on the candy sticks called *pilancillos*. Finally he lay down, expecting a fight on the morrow. "I stayed all night with James Bowie," a companion that evening later recalled. "On the night before the fight was to take place I never saw a man sleep more soundly than he did."[81]

Bowie kept strong pickets out during the night, and also put seven men in the bell tower of the mission. Unfortunately, after a quiet night, the first glimmers of dawn revealed a dense fog that made chances of detecting any approaching Mexicans very slim. About an hour after first daylight Henry Karnes, doing picket duty, suddenly saw beneath the fog the legs of a Mexican horse carrying a cavalry scout at the same time that the mounted man discovered him. Each fired at the other, awakening Bowie's command to the imminent prospect of a fight. Thanks to the fog, he could not see the Mexicans, either their numbers or their positions, but as the mist gradually cleared it became evident that he was in a terrible spot he had not anticipated. Mexican infantry, with one cannon, had crossed the river below them undetected and were now advancing toward them, with a fair opportunity to surround them in their bend of the river, while enemy cavalry were on the La Bahía on the other side, cutting off any chance of escape.

Bowie's men rushed to their arms and simply sat out the desultory firing from the foe as they waited for the fog to lift. "When the fog rose it was apparent to all that we were surrounded and a desperate fight was inevitable," he said a few days later. He shifted Fannin's company downstream slightly, and moved his own wing as well, increasing the advantage they would have of a crossfire if the Mexicans advanced into their bend on the stream, as well as making it possible for one wing to reinforce the other more readily if necessary, without having to run directly across the open ground between the wings. Once in position he set the men to clearing the low brush and vines along the foot of the riverbank so they could move back and forth without hindrance, and at the same time had them cut steps into the earth on the six-to-ten-foot bank so they could stand on them to fire out into the plain, and then step back down to reload. Fortunately the enemy commander seemed in no hurry to press the attack and gave them plenty of time to make their preparations. For Bowie it was the San Saba fight all over again, hurriedly preparing the ground for a desperate defense while surrounded.[82]

Finally Fannin saw infantry supported by artillery approaching the right of his line at about 8:00 A.M. A single Texian rifle fired toward the line, and at once the firing became general. The Mexicans gave well-disciplined volleys, while Bowie's Texians fought largely as individuals, each man choosing his target and firing as he felt sure, then stepping below the brow of the bank to reload in safety while another man stepped up the bank to take his place. After no more than ten minutes the Mexicans brought up their brass cannon and sent a charge of canister—a scatter load—toward their line, and then sounded the assault. "As if by magic," said Bowie, a Texian volley turned back the infantry and brought down or dispersed the gunners at the cannon. Twice more the Mexicans tried again, only to be turned back, Bowie all the while walking along his line steadying the men, telling them to stay cool and choose their targets carefully.[83] As the canister loads flew through the trees overhead, clipping pecans and sending them falling among the Texians, some men actually stopped to eat them, as Bowie kept pacing back and forth, calling out for them to keep under cover and reserve their fire.[84] Between each attempted enemy charge, Bowie had his men moving secretly to their right beneath the bank, every step bringing them closer to the cannon. After the third repulse, as the infantry regrouped in the distance and a brave party of artillerymen tried to reload the gun for another discharge, Bowie decided the Texians were close enough and urged the men on to "the cannon and Victory." The Texians went up and over the bank and rushed forward, taking the field piece in an instant and turning it around and loosing a charge of canister at the Mexican infantry that put them to flight. Mexican cavalry brought up another cannon at some distance and loosed a few ineffective rounds, but the fight was done for that day. Incredibly, having started the morning surrounded, Bowie, by his coolness and timing, his men's marksmanship, and their excellent choice of position, finished as the victor on the field, with a cannon as a trophy.[85]

Bowie was nothing if not boastful. A few days later he would proclaim that "thus a detachment of ninety two men gained a most decisive Victory over the main Army of the Central Government—having at least an advantage of numbers in their favor of four to one." In a way he was right, for the Mexicans had about 475 men on the field, but really only the two hundred infantry and a smattering of cavalry actually took part. Still they outnumbered the Texians just about 2 to 1, but Bowie's excellent position and the greater range of the Texians' hunting rifles over the Mexican brown Bess muskets made all the difference. The Mexicans suffered at least sixty casualties, with more than a fourth of them killed or mortally wounded. Bowie lost only one man wounded, and poor Richard Andrews—once a client of Travis's— dead. That night they buried him under the pecan trees and fired a volley over his grave, including a shot from the captured cannon.[86]

There was no denying that it was a great moment. James Bowie had won the first real battle of the revolution.

TRAVIS

1835

> *God knows what we are to do! I am determined, for one, to go with my countrymen; "right or wrong, sink or swim, live or die, survive or perish," I am with them.*
>
> WILLIAM B. TRAVIS, JULY 30, 1835

"There are two things which a man particularly guards in this world," William Barret Travis wrote on April 11, 1835. "Himself & his hobby horse. And you had as well attack the one as the other."[1] Texas had become Travis's "hobby horse" by the end of 1834, and yet he all but disappeared from public view during the first two seasons of 1835, as if he had joined the sun in its trip behind the moon during that eclipse and simply never came out. Certainly he stayed out of active politics, having learned that public sentiment did not match his own, and being wise enough to wait until it did before he tried to shine again. Instead, for a time he concentrated on that alternative to the hobby horse— himself. His post as secretary of the *ayuntamiento* expired at the end of 1834, freeing him to fix all his energies on his practice, though he closely watched local elections just the same, supporting what he called the "Austin Ticket," those candidates supportive of Stephen Austin.[2]

In fact, with business prospering, he formed a partnership with T. Willis Nibbs in January, 1835, in order to extend the practice to the court in Columbia as well as San Felipe, and devoted much of the next several months to his trade. When he looked at the announcement of the new partnership, he could hardly miss in the same issue of the Brazoria *Texas Republican* one of the current popular anecdotes about David Crockett, borrowed from the eastern press.[3] Travis's friend and business associate Robert Wilson finally got the steamboat built, and on January 8 the *Cayuga* made its first trip up the Brazos to San Felipe, an event redolent with promise for investors.[4] Travis also expanded his personal land holdings when he went to Mina, also known as Bastrop, on the Colorado, about seventy miles west of San Felipe, and applied for and received a headright for a league of land in Ben Milam's colony north of San Antonio. Williamson gave him the papers for the land on April 9, and the next day Travis took the required oath, attesting that "my station is that of a widower, and that with my family I have entered the country for the purpose of locating myself therein permanently." He promised to put his league under cultivation, and attested also that he was a lawyer, a Christian, and aged twenty-six.[5]

At least part of that was true. Travis was a Christian and a lawyer, but he was twenty-five that April and certainly lacked either the temperament or the inclination to become a farmer on his new league of land. He must have acquired it simply because it was available and cheap, with an eye to possible future sale. As yet there was not so much as a settlement in Milam's colony, most of it wild country traversed by Bowie in his San Saba adventures. And Travis was no "widower," as apparently he had been claiming for years. He and Rosanna were still very much married. Yet by April 10 he expected to be able properly to speak of intentions for his "family" very soon, for the land application was surely only a prelude to a long ride to Brazoria. Arriving there around April 13 or 14, he met his family. Rosanna came to Brazoria, possibly to visit friends but more likely to have a final face-to-face settlement of affairs with her husband, and most probably Travis knew in advance of her coming. He went there to meet her and found that the years of separation had softened the rancor on both sides. They talked amicably, agreed finally that Rosanna should go ahead and commence the divorce proceedings, and Travis probably gave her an unequivocal written statement that he intended never to return to her, for her lawyer to use in filing the case. Then they discussed the children, both of whom Rosanna had brought with her. It was the first time Travis ever saw his daughter, Susan Isabella, now approaching four years old, and the first time in four years that he had seen his boy, Charles, a lad Kuykendall described as "a lively, prattling little fellow." Now Rosanna honored her agreement to let Travis have their son to raise. That done, little remained to be said. On April 16

Travis lifted little Charles up behind him on his saddle and rode back to San Felipe, never to see Rosanna or his daughter again.[6]

Having his son with him now made Travis think even more about his responsibilities. He purchased another piece of land south of San Felipe and bought a slave couple, no doubt to run his household and tend Charles while Travis was absent at court. He did what so many attorneys overlooked doing and made out his own will on May 25, providing that all of his estate go to his two children, to be managed by their guardians, Rosanna's brother William Cato for Susan, and James Butler of Alabama for Charles. Moreover, he stipulated that Charles be sent to college, and that his daughter receive an "ample and complete English education." His friend Henry Smith would act as executor.[7]

Having brought order to his own house, Travis inevitably could not stay out of Texas's family affairs for long. His friend David Burnet approached him late in January about seeking elective office, no doubt as a member of the *ayuntamiento*, or perhaps even *alcalde*, and Travis was self-aware enough to admit that the possibility tempted him. "I have never professed an indifference to the honors of official station," he said, "and were I to do so now I should only make myself ridiculous." In fact "in the republican cause there is no higher aim than that of office." Moreover, as he remembered his studies of history and the evolution of the law, he drew from them the lesson that great changes in society took a long time and only came about because the men who advocated them sought and obtained offices from which to launch their movements.

Certainly Travis saw a cause before him even as he wrote, and the lesson that history taught him there was that "the higher object of this contest" might not be obtained within the lifetime of a single man like himself.[8] The cause, of course, was freedom for the imprisoned Austin, Texian independence from Coahuila, a return to the Constitution of 1824, and as an ultimate alternative, complete independence from Mexico. He stayed quiet these months in part in order not to damage prospects for Austin's freedom, but he remained ever alive to the rest of that "higher object." Viewing events in Mexico, he all but abandoned Austin's continuing adherence to the country. The two peoples of Texas and Mexico simply differed too much, and as Texas continued to grow in population and wealth, it must inevitably resent the more being a vassal to Mexico City. At the least Texas must soon have its own legislature, "or she must take over of herself," especially if they were to prevent the speculators from stripping the province of all its most valuable land.[9]

It had come as wonderful news to Travis when the Mexican authorities finally released Austin from prison the previous December, but he remained on his bond not to leave Mexico City until the end of July. Meanwhile, though Travis tried to keep himself out of overt politics until Austin was safely away, he involved himself assiduously in those efforts to increase Texian prosperity that he foresaw would encourage a spirit of independence. Ironically, and probably inevitably, those efforts led him right back to politics. Never one of the speculating faction, he still inadvertently tied his name to theirs when he lent a new carriage from New Orleans to Sam Williams for a journey to Monclova that turned out to be part of the general speculating frenzy involving Bowie, Gen. John Mason, Frank Johnson, and others.[10]

Travis involved himself directly in the affairs of Robert Wilson, his mill at Harrisburg, and his steamboat, however. Wilson's mill sat idle, thanks to the interference of Mexican customs authorities, whose rigid enforcement of the law led them to seize Wilson's goods from the ship bringing his supplies from New Orleans. "I am vexed and contrite," Wilson complained to him. Speaking for himself and his partners and others in Harrisburg, he added that "if something is not done Texas is gone." Nor did he stop there. "We are determined not to stand It," he declared, even if it meant a clash with the Mexicans. "A few we can kill and that with a fine good will."[11]

The seizure by the ship *Montezuma* of the goods of several Texians besides Wilson, as well as holding up incoming passengers for indefinite periods, caused an uproar throughout Texas. Travis himself shared Wilson's outrage, and did not need to hear his threats to have similar thoughts of resistance. The acts of the customs officers at Anahuac who controlled the vessel he called nothing more than "piracies and robbings." Texians should not and would not accept it passively. He had seen nothing in his four years in Texas that so much aroused the people. "All are for energetic resistance to the oppressions of a govt. that seems determined to destroy, to smash & to ruin us," he told Burnet on May 21, and added that there was "not a dissenting voice as far as I know in this place." While some put the seizures down to the arbitrariness of the Anahuac customs official, José Gonzales, backed by a company of soldiers commanded by Capt. Antonio Tenorio, Travis saw beyond the immediate to realize that the real problem lay in Mexico City. Having allowed the customs issue to lie dormant for some time now, the centralist regime of Santa Anna needed money and was determined to collect it. The days of relaxed smuggling or paying duties voluntarily were at an end. Moreover, Travis read in the Mexican press that the Mexican congress might soon consider acts to abolish citizenship for residents of Texas, and perhaps even to abrogate once more the April 6, 1830, law allowing immigration.

It was definitely too much. "These are alarming circumstances," he told Burnet. "Indeed we stand or fall now by ourselves." While he prayed for unity, he also pondered the wisdom of calling for a convention, which could be seen as provocative, which might hurt Austin. Increasingly in private conversation with friends he argued that Texians ought to be more forceful in asserting their rights, but other heads responded that Austin could solve all their problems when he was among them once more. Yet by late April, Travis believed that Austin would never be allowed to leave Mexico so long as there was unrest. He was virtually a hostage to ensure good Texian behavior, and Travis wearied of that. In frustration he even suggested "let them [kill] him if they dare. A thousand of their contemptible *red* skins [would] be sacrificed" if Austin were slain. Never before did Travis exhibit anything suggesting any ethnic disdain for Mexicans, nor did he really now. His reference to "contemptible *red* skins" applied not to all Mexicans, but only to those who would injure Austin. Yet even that expression revealed his temper. "I have as much to lose by a revolution as most men in the country," he told Burnet. "Yet, I wish to know, for whom I labor—whether for myself or a *plundering* robbing, autocratical, aristocratical jumbled up govt. which is in fact no govt. at all—one day a republic—one day a fanatical heptarchy, the next a military despotism—then a mixture of the evil qualities of all." Even as he sought the views of others, his own were transparent.[12] A visitor to Texas now found that in the troubled atmosphere "the inhabitants have a strong belief that Texas will at some future day become one of the United States," but he disagreed. "It is more probable, that it will in time become an independent sovereignty."[13]

All it needed to ignite the seething cloud of unrest was a spark, and in a rare repetition of history, it came at Anahuac. The tension mounted there from the moment that Gonzales and Tenorio arrived. Resentful colonists withheld supplies from Tenorio's small command and sabotaged the soldiers' attempts to construct a fort, and that only made the Mexicans the more resolute in performing their duty. Travis's and Bowie's friend Andrew Briscoe, a merchant in Anahuac, especially felt their severity, as Gonzales expected him to pay full taxes based on the kinds of articles he imported, whereas other Mexican customs collectors simply charged a lesser tonnage duty. When Gonzales left office in May and his successor arrived in early June, the policy did not change, and Briscoe's appeals for support, on top of the seizure of Wilson's mill equipment, finally brought some action.[14]

On June 4 Travis, DeWitt Clinton Harris, and seventeen others joined Briscoe at Harrisburg for a meeting to determine what should be done. "We have come to the cool determination to submit to no more imposition of the kind that will prove ruinous to the country," they resolved, "by destroying the commerce and stopping the emigration." In a resolution that Travis himself probably drafted, they decided to "discharge" Tenorio and his soldiers and customs officials and send them back to Mexico. Unless something arose to alter their determination, they appointed June 6 at Harrisburg as the time and place for them to gather again, elect their officers, and march on Anahuac. The resolution did not necessarily imply violence, but the fear of it must have been sufficient that two days later many of those attending had changed their minds, though not Travis.[15]

During the next several days other matters diverted Travis's attention momentarily. On June 9 he got a report that Austin was finally released and expected to have left Mexico on May 25. Williams, Johnson and the rest had been arrested when General Cós and the Saltillo forces dispersed the Monclova faction and cracked down on the speculators, and the Monclova legislators themselves tried unsuccessfully to move their capital to Béxar. Meanwhile, Travis turned his hand to an attempt to publish the laws of Texas and Coahuila in a combined English and Spanish edition, no doubt assuming that it would be useful in future attempts to justify the actions of himself and his discontented countrymen, though he warily tried to keep his own involvement with the project from being known.[16]

"Let us wait with patience, the issue of things," he counseled Smith on June 9. "The time will come when we shall be called upon to act."[17] It came soon enough. Travis did not need to be told by his friend Wilson that "Santa Ana is not our friend"—he knew that already—but the warning to "look well to windward and see he does not surprise the Boys" was well timed.[18] Wilson's partner Harris came to Anahuac June 10 to buy goods from Briscoe, and in a confused incident that evening a Mexican soldier shot a Texian, and Tenorio arrested Briscoe and Harris. Briscoe remained in custody, but the Mexicans released Harris the next morning, and he raced back to Harrisburg, sending word of the affair to Travis in San Felipe. Then, on June 21, a Mexican courier carrying dispatches for Tenorio came to San Felipe and indiscreetly let his mission be known, the result being that the Texians seized his letters and in them read news that strong reinforcements were to be sent from Mexico to enforce the customs laws. There was also word that Governor Viesca had been arrested.

In sum, the political situation seemed to disintegrate precipitately, and political chief J. B. Miller had already called a meeting of delegates in San Felipe for June 22 to take some action. Unfortunately the majority could decide on nothing more than doing nothing, and Travis and others stamped the streets in outrage. That same evening, those about to be dubbed the war party gathered again, and with Miller in the chair they resolved that "feeling the necessity of disarming the military of Anahuac," they pledged to meet on June 27 to form themselves into an armed militia company, elect officers, and march on Anahuac. Travis was the second to sign the resolution, directly beneath Miller, a sign of the prominent role he played in the meeting.[19]

Travis himself left for Harrisburg June 25, probably shortly after Bowie's note to Miller arrived, detailing his escape from Matamoros and warning of three thousand or more Mexicans marching north past Saltillo. That only heightened the sense of emergency. David Harris there owned the sloop *Ohio*, then sailing the bay, and with the help of a few men and some borrowed wheel trucks from the Wilson mill, they loaded a small cannon aboard the vessel. By June 28 the *Ohio* sat moored at Lynch's Ferry at the northwestern tip of Galveston Bay, and there Travis and his friend David Burnet awaited. Some twenty armed volunteers assembled in the following several hours, and they promptly elected Travis their commander. The next day the *Ohio* convoyed them across the bay to Anahuac but ran aground half a mile from the shore. Travis ordered a shot from the deck gun fired to alert Tenorio to their coming, an imprudent move perhaps, and as a prelude to his demand for a surrender, and then his small company lowered the cannon into one of two small boats and rowed ashore, Travis himself in the bow of the lead boat.

As they approached the shore about 3 P.M., Travis saw the bank lined with men, and at first was uncertain if they were friends or Mexicans but soon found them to be sympathetic villagers. When Travis stepped out of the boat he received a note from Tenorio demanding to know his intentions and immediately sent back a demand for surrender. The Mexican commander asked for a delay until the next morning for his response, but Travis, conscious that he was outnumbered and fearful that Tenorio might use the time to good advantage, refused. He promised a grace of only one hour before he attacked. Even at that Travis decided not to let the full hour elapse. Rather than have the time expire after darkness fell, he launched an advance, placing six men in front as skirmishers, and then himself leading the main line with the cannon back on the wheel trucks. In the gathering twilight, they lit their way with a blazing torch, but on reaching the Mexican quarters found them deserted. Tenorio had taken to the woods some two hundred yards or more distant. Travis immediately ordered the cannon fired into the trees to intimidate the Mexicans, and soon enough Tenorio sent another note, this time asking to meet Travis at the water's edge to discuss terms for a surrender. Not entirely trusting the captain, Travis agreed, but had three of his volunteers follow him out of sight, ready to act if they saw any sign of treachery.

Travis stepped to the shore, bathed now in moonlight, and called out in Spanish for Tenorio, only to hear him answer from a clump of trees, for he was equally fearful of coming to harm. Travis himself walked to the spot where he heard the voice, and in a few minutes' conversation again refused Tenorio's request to take until morning to give an answer. Going considerably beyond the case of the moment, Travis apparently said that this was only the beginning, that the Texian colonists intended to force the release of Viesca, and set up the

Monclova legislature once more either at San Felipe or some other spot in the Texas interior safe from Mexican invasion. Travis may only have been boasting, though every point was one with which he was in accord, but he had neither the authority nor the power to make any of that happen.

He had twenty men and a small cannon, and when it came to the business at hand, he only gave Tenorio fifteen minutes and then, in an attempt to bluff the Mexican, threatened that after the time expired he would "put every man to the sword." The Mexican commander put the proposition to his officers and shortly returned to Travis with his assent. Travis also demanded the surrender of all public property, and that Tenorio and his command should leave Texas and never return again. It was a bloodless beginning to a bloody revolution. Yet one matter was troubling. Even if only a bluff, Travis's threat to take no prisoners was unusually bloodthirsty for a group of citizens supposedly just making a stand for constitutional rights. It might come back to haunt him.[20]

The next day Tenorio signed the formal surrender, and Travis loaded his own party and the Mexicans into the *Ohio* and took them back to Harrisburg. On the approach to the town he imposed the rather evocative password "*Victory or death*" in approaching the town, no doubt to make certain no one mistook the large party of Mexican soldiers as hostile.[21] If there was any doubt that William Travis now stood as a leader in the War Party faction, his arrival in Harrisburg with these trophies of war removed all question. He stood now on a par with Bowie, Frank Johnson, and the few others regarded as being ahead of the rest in the dispute with Mexico.[22]

He was not prepared for the degree to which Texians did not want to be led in that direction just yet. When Travis got back to San Felipe late on July 5, he sent Smith a quick account of what happened, adding that "this act has been done with the most patriotic motives, and I hope you and my fellow citizens will approve it, or excuse it," and then apparently tried to return to his legal work as if nothing had happened.[23] "Excuse" was more like it, for just as he noted the dissension in town over how to react to the wholesale arrests of the government officials,

now he found people sharply divided on his action. There and elsewhere people who saw in his expedition an attempt to foment a revolution against Mexico reacted sharply, passing community resolutions
condemning his action. "He was headstrong and precipitated the war
with Mexico," his friend Dilue Harris believed.[24] Leaders of the Peace
Party excoriated Travis, as well as Bowie and Williams and others seen
as too radical, and James H. C. Miller, a leading Peace Party member,
gleefully noted that "Travis is in a peck of troubles."[25] In a public proclamation another member of the peace faction warned the people of San
Felipe to "listen not to men who have no home, who have no family,
who have nothing to lose in case of civil war."[26] James B. Miller, the
political chief, publicly disavowed Travis's action, saying that the meeting of June 22 that produced the resolutions for volunteers to gather
had no such object in mind, though that was a trimming protest at best.
"The war and speculating parties are entirely put down," James H. C.
Miller declared, and went on to suggest that the *ayuntamientos* should
put out arrest orders for Travis and the other leading War Party men.
"Till they are dealt with," he said, "Texas will never be at quiet."[27]

So shocked was Travis by this response that on July 18 he issued a
notice in the Brazoria *Texas Republican* asking "a suspension of public
opinion in regard to the Capture of the Fort of Anahuac" until he
could publish his own account and an explanation.[28] He asked too late.
Besides, the matter was not in the hands of the people, but at the
moment in control of the War Party. On July 25 James H. C. Miller
suggested that Travis be arrested, along with Johnson, Williamson,
Lorenzo Zavala, and their fellow radical Moseley Baker, and called for
alcaldes in other jurisdictions to do so. There was some wisdom in this,
for if the Texians themselves arrested the troublemakers, then it might
forestall General Cós from sending troops into Texas.[29]

Travis himself did not see the arrest order coming. On July 26 he
worked peacefully in his San Felipe office, finishing the draft of his
defense, which he sent to Henry Smith asking him to go over it and
then see to its printing. Indeed, noting that the Peace Party seemed
fully in sway, he only added that "there is no news of importance stirring."[30] He realized by now that any general popular uprising was out
of the question, and on July 30 sent a letter to Bowie, most recently
known to be in Nacogdoches after himself helping to disarm a

Mexican garrison and send it on its way home. "The truth is, the people are much divided here," he told Bowie, whom he must now have regarded as a kindred spirit. The Peace Party was ascendant, and "unless we could be united, had we better not settle down and be quiet for a while," he asked. "God knows what we are to do! I am determined, for one, to go with my countrymen; 'right or wrong, sink or swim, live or die, survive or perish,' I am with them."[31] Despite the peaceful tenor of his advice to Bowie, there was no question of Travis having given up. Already he counseled Henry Smith on how they should conduct themselves when the final break came. "Let us be firm and united in defending Texas to the last extremity," he told him. "In offensive war we can do nothing, in defensive everything."[32] He resolved now only to go quiet while waiting for events and opinion to catch up with him.

Meanwhile Tenorio remained in San Felipe before taking his men back to Mexico, and now he peppered his superiors with requests to get back his weapons, only keeping alive the insult to Mexican arms.[33] Travis himself tried to calm the Mexicans' unrest by addressing a letter to Ugartechea the day after he wrote Bowie, reminding the colonel of their brief acquaintance—at Anahuac, ironically—three years before. He wrote in English, protesting disingenuously that "I do not know how to express myself" in Spanish, even though he had been translating documents for the *ayuntamiento* for all of the previous year. "I am confident that I have acted from pure motives," he said. All the statements about him being a revolutionary were untrue, and he wanted now to make a full statement of the case to the governor, if only Ugartechea would counsel him on how to go about it. "I am extremely anxious to bring all our difficulties to a happy and peaceable termination," he went on. He wanted a firm government established, and did not care what form of government Mexico should adopt "so that we are guaranteed in the security of person and property." He even offered to help in bringing about such an end, and bordered on obsequiousness when he begged that Ugartechea would "condescend to open a correspondence with me."[34] Ugartechea never replied.

Travis obviously lied in the hope of buying time, time to calm the outrage at his act, and time for the Mexicans to cool down short of starting arrests. His contrition came too late. On August 1 General Cós

issued an order from Matamoros to the political chief Miller to arrest
Travis, and at the same time followed it with a similar order to
Ugartechea, then in Béxar. They were to detain "the ungrateful and
bad citizen W. B. Travis who headed the revolutionary party," and
bring him to Béxar. His excesses had been tolerated long enough, said
Cós. "He ought to have been punished long since."[35]

Travis did not yet know it, but now he was in considerable danger of
becoming yet another indefinite prisoner like Austin. Ugartechea
received Cós's order on August 4, and immediately sent it on to San
Felipe, where it could not arrive until two days later.[36] Meanwhile, on
August 5 Travis was still in San Felipe, and now regretting that he must
make a public explanation. He drafted a document, did not like it,
rewrote it, then gave it to Wharton to work over, and in fact it was
Wharton who published the promise of an explanation in the first
place, apparently without Travis's permission. He felt as resolute as ever
in his rectitude in the Anahuac affair. "I know my motives were pure,"
he said. "I know I acted by the consent & approbation of the political
authorities. I know that the people here all favored the measure." He
had been but one actor on the stage, and never solicited command of
the volunteers. "Most men in this part of the country are satisfied with
my course," he went on. "Conscious that I have not intentionally erred,
I bid defiance to any who may be disposed to persecute me." As for his
explanation of his conduct, he still preferred that it not be published,
but left that in Smith's hands, only insisting that it be short "& not in
the tone of apology, as I feel like I have none to offer."[37]

It may only have been hours later that he learned he was to be taken
into custody. Rather than suffer that, he and his friend Three-Legged
Willie Williamson stole out of town and rode north to Horatio
Chriesman's place on the La Bahía Trace, near Washington. They
remained there for several days and then moved on, and thus were not
there when riders came to Chriesman's to tell them it was safe to return.[38]
In a marvelous reversal of fortune, the mobilization of opinion that
Travis could not achieve by his own act, Cós and Ugartechea brought
about by trying to arrest him. Whatever even men of the Peace Party
felt about Travis's actions, they did not want to see another Texian
political prisoner languish indefinitely in a Mexican jail. When they
learned moreover that Santa Anna intended to establish larger military

garrisons in Texas, their civil authorities openly refused to cooperate with the arrest orders.[39] Indeed, Moseley Baker believed that "this military order may justly be regarded as the final success of the war party."[40]

For the rest of August, Ugartechea and Cós continued to try to have Travis arrested, and the commander of a Mexican ship at Anahuac even offered a thousand-dollar reward, promising that he "would swing said Travis at his yard arm in less than half an hour after his delivery."[41] But Texian political authorities only stalled and delayed.[42] Then outraged citizens held meetings in places like Columbia, calling for a consultation of delegates from all of Texas as "indispensable" and setting up committees of safety and correspondence.[43] Soon it became clear to Travis that he had nothing to fear and could return to San Felipe, and when he did he came in triumph. "Huzza for Texas!" he crowed. "Huzza for Liberty, and the rights of man!"[44] The word of the call for a consultation delighted him. Weeks before he pleaded for unity of action, believing that a consensus of all the people in Texas needed to determine their course, and now that seemed about to be realized.[45] To encourage matters, he began writing articles for publication in the press though, wary thanks to his recent experience, he wanted their authorship kept secret lest his name cause a backlash with those so recently won over from the Peace Party. That they must act, and quickly, he never doubted, especially if Santa Anna sent troops to places like Béxar and San Felipe. "Let the towns be once garrisoned," he warned, "and we are slaves."[46]

In his elation at the turnaround of events, Travis spent almost the entire day August 31 writing letters to such friends as Briscoe, Henry Smith, Burnet, and more, bristling with renewed pride and defiance. "Principle has triumphed over prejudice," he proclaimed. "Texas is herself again." He crowed over the withering of the Peace Party in San Felipe in such a short time. "They are routed horse and foot," he declared. "I feel the triumph we have gained, and I glory in it." With the convention scheduled for September 12, he urged everyone who could to attend. "The Tories are dying a violent death, and their last expiring struggle will be made on that day." Fortune favored the brave, he exhorted them, "and now let *Tories, submission men,* and Spanish invaders look out." Even as Travis finished his letters, a messenger arrived in San Felipe with news that the Mexicans intended to have two hundred soldiers garrisoning the town by mid-September. "We shall give them hell if they come here. Keep a bright lookout to sea," he continued. "Secure all the powder and lead. Remember that war is not to be waged without means. Let us be men and Texas will triumph." There were rough waters ahead, of that he was certain. "It is time to be on the qui vive." They must of necessity act defensively, as he told Smith weeks before, and be prepared "for the scenes that are to be enacted." "If we are encroached upon, let us resist until our bodies & our property lie in one common ruin, ere we submit to tyranny."[47]

Already starting anew to act as publicist of the revolution, Travis turned his attention to another weapon in the Texian arsenal that needed honing. He recognized the power of religion in molding and sustaining public spirit, and knew as well the longtime resentment at the enforcement of Catholicism on the colonists. Now that Texians might be about to meet Santa Anna with rifles and muskets, they should confront him with ideology as well. Back in August, when still in danger of arrest, he had written to New York to subscribe to the *Christian Advocate and Journal,* and informed the publishers that Texas stood almost destitute of proper religious instruction. Texians had few preachers, and some denominations such as the Methodists, known for their itinerant preachers, like Lorenzo Dow and his own uncle Alexander, neglected the country entirely. He wanted the journal to publicize their need in the hope that it would stimulate preachers to cross the Sabine. "In sending your heralds to the four corners of the Earth," he implored, "remember Texas."[48]

As good as his word, Travis supported Protestant missionaries and ministers when they took the risk of coming to Texas. On September 3 Rev. John W. Kenney, a Methodist whom Travis helped bring to Texas in 1833, came to San Felipe and camped in the woods nearby for a several-day meeting. People came from some distance, covering the field with their tents and wagons until the congregation numbered some four hundred. Kenney himself felt some trepidation at holding such a large and public Protestant meeting, for fear that Mexican authorities would attempt to break it up, but Travis himself assured Kenney that he and his friends would attend and stand guard to assure no interruptions. Of course Travis could also see in the meeting an opportunity to press his call for assertion and organization for political as well as spiritual rights. They appointed early October for another meeting, but by then events were moving too rapidly, and at too much peril, for it to be held. Indeed, now any gathering, even a friendly barbecue that fall at James Pevehouse's farm south of San Felipe, could be turned into a political meeting when Travis attended. Conscious of the danger, Travis and his friends began to look suspiciously on any unknown Mexican visitors.[49]

Travis no longer felt he had to explain his Anahuac affair defensively. Immediately before the camp meeting he gave Smith a brief matter of fact account, with few details, and more than a little self-conscious flattery. "Time alone will shew whether that step was correct or not," he said, "and time will shew that when this country is in danger, that I will shew myself as patriotic & ready to serve her as those, who to save themselves have disavowed the act & denounced me to the usurping military."[50] It no longer mattered that Cós continued to call for his apprehension, and would even appeal to Austin himself when the *empresario* finally returned to Texas.[51] Arresting Travis was a dead issue.

And within days Austin was back in Texas. He reached Brazoria on September 8, to be met by a public dinner in his honor, during which he finally abandoned his conciliatory policy. With Santa Anna sending troops to garrison Texas, their rights under the 1824 constitution were destroyed, and the constitution itself must be considered as abrogated. He would turn all of the states of Mexico into centrally ruled provinces. "Something must be done, and that without delay," said Austin. Four days later he arrived in San Felipe, where Travis and the other leaders had called a public meeting. Privately Austin declared to friends that he was for "no more doubts—no submission. *I hope to see Texas forever free from Mexican domination of any kind.*" Yet it was too soon to say so publicly. They must still be a bit cautious if they wanted to hope for anything like unanimity. At Johnson and Winburn's tavern on September 12 Travis and others chose Austin chairman of their meeting, and then listened as he read aloud several of the military orders for Travis's arrest, and suggested that a consultation of all Texas was imperative. They then formed resolutions reaffirming loyalty to the 1824 constitution and suggesting that each jurisdiction send five delegates to San Felipe on October 15 for the convention. They, too, formed a committee of correspondence to maintain constant communication with the other municipalities. Travis supported every measure and concluded the meeting with a motion of thanks to Austin.[52]

Travis turned his attention immediately to the forthcoming consultation. He wanted to sit as a delegate, and as the man who had largely stirred up the current situation, he no doubt felt he had a right. He also encouraged his friend Henry Smith to make efforts to be elected to represent Brazoria. "I want to see that body composed of men talented, firm and uncompromising," he told him. In other words, men like Travis, and his emphasis on their being "uncompromising" left no doubt of the kind of result he hoped to see from that consultation.[53] So enthusiastic did Travis feel that he even presumed to give Austin very pointed advice on the conduct of the elections and the meeting itself. Ailing from his long confinement, and emotionally drained by the stress of events, Austin was easily swayed, and Travis may well have seen and taken advantage of his suggestibility—and perhaps of his susceptibility to flattery, which Travis did not stint in offering. "All eyes are turned towards you," he told Austin ten days after the San Felipe meeting. "Texas can be wielded by you & *you alone*; and her destiny is now completely in your hands." The people felt the spirit of war, he said, and Austin could assemble numbers of volunteers merely by asking. "This is not the base flattery of a servile mind," he explained. "It is the reasoning of one ardent in his country's cause, & who wishes to un[ite] his feeble efforts with those who have the power & inclination to lead us in safety to the desired end."[54] It was also the none-too-subtle effort of a revolutionary to guide events by guiding the one man whom most Texians most admired.

In part Travis's advice to Austin was a response to Austin's September 21 call for volunteers to come forward, organize themselves into companies, and mobilize on September 28 on the Colorado or the Lavaca. Immediately Texians began to volunteer for military companies, organizations far more formal than the loose town militias like the one that had made Bowie its colonel earlier in the summer. Travis visited with Rebecca Cummings for a few days after the Austin meeting but was back in San Felipe on September 28 to enlist.[55] The company did not organize immediately, however, and for Travis it was just as well, for he needed to press upon the citizens his candidacy for the consultation, and early in October they rewarded his efforts.[56]

Events moved quickly. On October 3 Travis learned that a few days earlier Mexican troops had appeared outside Gonzales in a threatening posture, and that 150 Texian volunteers stood there to meet them, with more arriving daily. He expected a Texian attack on the Mexicans momentarily, and had already received a plea from Gonzales for more men. Travis saw one friend after another leave for Gonzales every day, and would have gone himself but for a bout with influenza. He hoped to be able to go in a few more days, and meanwhile exhorted his friend Randall Jones that "our frontier is attacked & who says now that we shall not fight." The metal of Texas was hot enough at last. "Let us go at it heart & hand," he said. "Stand up like men & we have nothing to fear."[57]

Then came the news of the actual outbreak at Gonzales, the firing on October 2 that ignited the revolution. San Felipe would have gotten word of the outbreak on October 4, and it only added impetus to getting the local company formed. Randall Jones came in from Fort Settlement, and the volunteers elected him their captain, and when Travis could arise from his sickbed they made him their lieutenant. On October 5 they hurriedly prepared for the journey, Travis impressing a horse for a man without a mount, and then took the road for Gonzales, probably accompanied by Austin. By October 11 or earlier they reached the scene of the skirmish.[58]

There was little to do there at first. The assembled volunteers overwhelmingly elected Austin their general-in-chief, and had hoped to move on Goliad, occupied by Cós's main contingent of a few hundred *soldados*, but word that he had withdrawn to Béxar gave them a pause, and time to regroup. Jones and Travis's company had left San Felipe so hurriedly that they had not taken time to prepare statements of the horses and equipment that their volunteers brought into the Texian service, and now Austin directed them to do so. Travis had good friends in this company, some of them men he had known ever since settling in San Felipe, including several of Kuykendall's close relations.[59]

The same day that Travis and Jones handled their paperwork, they got Austin's order to commence the march to Béxar. Exciting as it was to be on a campaign, even with this scruffy "army" of barely three hundred men, Travis must have felt some small regret. He had been elected to the consultation. So had his friend Henry Smith, and a number of other leading men including Wharton, Williamson, Hall, and more who shared his views. But the consultation was to meet on October 15 or the next day, and there was no way he could go to Béxar and take his seat. At least he would not be alone. Most of the elected delegates were with the army, and Travis knew well that his duty must keep him there for the moment. Overhead, pointing the way, Halley's Comet inflamed the heavens. Crockett saw it, leading him west from Tennessee. Bowie saw it as he raced to catch Austin's army. But of the three of them, probably only Travis had read Shakespeare's *Julius Caesar*. Only he could wonder knowingly at the portent: "When beggars die, there are no comets seen," said Calpurnia. "The heavens themselves blaze forth the death of princes."

The army made slow progress to the vicinity of Béxar, and only reached the banks of the Cibolo on October 16, and there a council of war decided to wait for more volunteers to arrive. Three days later, however, Travis went to Austin's headquarters in place of Jones for another council, and this time cast his vote with the rest in favor of an immediate advance on Béxar.[60] The next morning they resumed the march, accompanied now by Bowie, who had joined them on the Cibolo, and within a few days Travis waited with the rest of the command while Bowie took Fannin's company and some others off to scour the missions Espada, San Juan, and San José for food and to establish a position on the main road south from Béxar.

While waiting for Bowie and Fannin, Travis and the other elected delegates to the consultation met to decide what course they should follow. Travis argued for remaining with the army, but most thought they should leave to take their seats. The convention had already been postponed on October 17, when no quorum assembled. If they left immediately, they could be there for the opening, now scheduled for November 1. Because of their own inability to form a consensus, and no doubt fearful that they might be regarded as self-serving or cowardly for leaving the army almost in the face of the enemy, they decided to put the question to the whole army. On October 25 Travis stood with his company when Austin paraded the command in review to hear speeches on the issue. When the volunteers voted that the delegates ought to go to San Felipe, Travis declined, volunteering to remain at the post of danger, especially after hearing Houston give a defeatist address that urged the entire army to retire. Several other elected delegates declared their intention to remain as well, and then when Austin and others rebutted Houston, Travis no doubt joined the volunteers in their cheers of "on to San Antonio."[61]

Perhaps it was Travis's unqualified support that won him a special assignment from Austin, but more likely Travis himself had been taking advantage of his influence with the commander to urge a project of his own. The idea of the cavalryman held a special appeal for Travis. He liked horses himself and had owned several, even encouraging the formation of a local jockey club. Moreover, his taste in fiction tended toward the kind of romantic novel that glorified the man on horseback. Out there with the army, seeing it spending days of immobility, his instinct for quick, even impetuous action no doubt rebelled at the inactivity. They were in a vast countryside, with much open ground, ideal for the off-road travel of the horseman, and with the ever-present danger of Mexican supplies and reinforcements coming from unexpected quarters, they needed rapid intelligence and competent reconnaissance. No organized mounted force was with the army as yet, and Austin and Travis both could see that it needed one.

As a result on October 27 Austin authorized Travis to raise from among the existing companies a command of fifty to eighty volunteer cavalrymen, each to be armed with a double-barreled shotgun or carbine, and a brace of pistols. In no case was he to accept more than one-tenth of the volunteers from any one company, so as not to dangerously deplete Jones's or any other captain's command.[62] Since there were a good number of horses with the army already, Travis had no difficulty in raising the nucleus of his company that same day, and by the next morning they were mounted and ready to ride north in advance of the rest of the army. Austin had sent Bowie and Fannin out the day before to find a bivouac for the army near Concepción, just two miles from San Antonio, and he was anxious that they might be attacked while isolated from the main army.

As Travis and his men galloped up the road, they crossed the San Antonio River and were the first to hear the sounds of firing in the distance, including the booming of a cannon, which only hurried them on. But then Travis received an order from Austin to halt at the river until the army could catch up. He needed Travis's mounted command to cover and protect the crossing, and did not want Travis isolated from him on the other side. Only when he was allowed to press on did Travis finally come in sight of Concepción, and then just in time to see the beaten Mexicans making their retreat. Without even thinking of sending word back to Austin, or asking permission, he ordered his men forward at the gallop to harass the foe, adding to the panic that already infected some of the *soldados.*[63]

If Austin felt irritation at Travis for taking an unnecessary risk, he showed less inclination to scold than he revealed to Bowie and Fannin. With Travis commanding his own company now, Austin recognized him as a captain, though he would be the only company commander in the army at the moment not elected by his own men.[64] Then, when he received a report that Cós had sent up to nine hundred surplus horses on the road to Laredo on October 30, Austin ordered Travis and his company out after them the next day. The new captain took fifty men with him, and a few good guides, and Austin sent him on his way with an expression of confidence in his success.[65]

Not long after setting off on the southwest road toward Laredo, Travis learned that the herd and its guards enjoyed enough of a head start that he expected the expedition to take him perhaps three days.[66] Austin, ever mindful of the absent cavalry, already had another task escorting a cannon awaiting him even before he returned from hunting the *caballado.*[67] But Travis returned without the horses—and not surprisingly, since the original report Austin received was almost certainly false. Cós only had about six hundred men in San Antonio, most of them infantry, and nine hundred horses, plus the two hundred more believed still to be inside the Mexican fortifications for his cavalry, were far more than he needed for his baggage and artillery wagons.[68]

Travis returned to find the army in turmoil, the volunteers insubordinate over their inactivity, and other officers resigning in alarming numbers, including Bowie. On November 6 Travis himself sent Austin his resignation, without explanation other than that he felt he could not serve longer without giving rise to complaint.[69] Perhaps Austin personally reprimanded him on his return for his impetuosity at Concepción, or maybe Travis himself only now saw Austin's October 28 edict to arrest any officer disobeying orders, and assumed that it was a veiled criticism of his conduct.[70] Then, too, Travis may have had trouble with his volunteers during the chase for the horses. It was his first experience in independent command, and as several could attest, he was not always the most popular of men. More likely the men in his company may have raised complaints at Austin choosing him as their captain rather than their being allowed to elect their own officer as did all the other companies. As bad as the rot of jealousy was in Austin's army, Travis may even have found himself complained of by his fellow captains for his close relationship with the general. If his face-to-face relations with the commander were as flattering and occasionally fawning as his letters, others might well have seen him as a syco-phant—an atmosphere in which he no longer wished to serve.

Austin had just written an order for another assignment for Travis when he received the resignation. He crossed out his name and instead gave the mission to Travis's friend Briscoe, who would now command the cavalry company. But having resigned his captaincy—Travis had no commission, nor did any of the other officers—he did not leave the army. Rather he became simply another private cavalryman in the ranks, and now followed Briscoe out of camp when Austin sent them off west of Béxar with orders to go as far as the Medina River some twenty miles distant to intercept mail riders, supply trains, and even a rumored shipment of silver coin for Cós's troops. Austin also believed that the enemy sent its horses out at night to graze west of town, and made forays to collect beefs for the men, and this too Briscoe was to disrupt. Austin did not want them to be gone more than two nights, however, so it was to be a short patrol.[71]

Some of the men in the cavalry company were *tejanos*, and while Travis certainly knew a number of *tejanos* prior to his service in the army, this may have been his most intimate association with them to date. They dressed much the same as the Texians, since they shopped in the same stores, most of which catered to *norteamericano* tastes, but being experienced men of the range, they no doubt wore Mexican-style boots and wide *sombreros*. Having grown up on horseback in this country, they had much to teach Travis of how cavalry could operate, and he made an apt pupil. Despite his angry comment about "*red* skins," when discussing invading Mexicans, Travis entertained cordial and apparently unpreju-diced friendships with *tejanos* like Don Manuel Del Moral, and Juan

Seguín, and pronounced any *tejano* who aided Austin's attempt to take Béxar as "a good man." Some won his continuing respect when they voluntarily contributed their cattle to help feed the undernourished army, and his service on this scout would do even more to impress Travis with the fact that not all the patriots in this cause were whites.[72]

Briscoe left that same evening, and by early November 8 had ridden completely around San Antonio from the north to the west, and now to the south, arriving on the Medina where the road to Laredo crossed the stream. He encountered nothing along the way, and at that point decided to return to Austin's camp, his mission done. Travis thought it might prove worthwhile to stay out a bit longer and perhaps scout farther south to the Atascosa River, some twenty miles distant. His friend Briscoe disagreed, but then in the excessively democratic spirit that was practically the ruination of this army, they decided that Travis could ask for volunteers to leave Briscoe and accompany him on such a mission. A dozen men came forward, one of them the colorful scout Erasmus "Deaf" Smith, and unanimously chose Travis their captain, and Travis sent Briscoe back with a message to Austin that he expected to be at the Sabinas *rancho* on the Atascosa that evening.[73]

Leading his small company south, Travis in fact reached the Atascosa that evening. The next dawn he crossed over and went on south another five miles before he suddenly came on the unmistakable signs of a large herd of horses that had come onto the Laredo road at that point. Obviously this was a *caballado*, probably the very one that false rumor said had left San Antonio back in late October. This herd could only be about eight days out of Béxar, and clearly had been led off to the west and then south to pick up the road in order to evade Austin's scouts. Travis led his men on the trail for several miles until they found the site where the Mexican herders had camped, surely no more than two nights before.

Now he was on a fresh trail, and with each succeeding mile Travis could see from the signs that he was getting closer. "With renewed confidence of success," he said, he pressed on briskly. When he reached Macho Creek, fifty miles south of Béxar, he found the *caballado's* previous night's camp. Knowing the quarry to be close now, he dispersed his small command to either side of the road and thereafter moved forward cautiously until twilight stopped them two or three miles above San Miguel Creek. The *tejanos* with Travis who knew this country told him that the creek would be the only water for some miles around. The Mexicans must camp there.

Now for the first time Travis faced the real prospect of a fight. Tenorio had offered no resistance at all, and Travis had a cannon to support him at Anahuac. At Concepción he arrived to find the Mexicans already in flight, and his chase after them had been as much a lark as anything. Now, however, there were armed Mexican soldiers ahead. He did not know how many, though the report of a *tejano* passed along the way suggested there might be twenty. The prospect of being outnumbered did not daunt him, for he counted on the superior range and accuracy of the rifles his men carried as opposed to the weapons of the foe. But if he made an attack after dark he gave up that advantage and might also lose the strength of surprise, since in the dark he, too, could be taken unawares. Besides, too much blind firing might spook and stampede the herd, his real objective. With a maturity and prudence not characteristic of the Travis of Anahuac, he decided to wait, bed his men down where they were for the night, and attack in the morning. Cold and miserable though they were that night, he had made the wise decision. They camped without fires in the rain, with no fresh water and their only fare the unsalted dried meat on which they had subsisted for days past.

At the first glimmers of dawn on November 10, Travis mounted the command and they raced down the road to the San Miguel. As he approached, he first saw two Mexicans out collecting the horses to start the day's trek, and took advantage of their being away from their companions by ordering a charge right into the Mexican camp, hoping to surprise and divide them in order to eliminate their advantage of numbers. Travis himself rode at the head of his volunteers and dashed into the camp, so stunning the *soldados* that they gave up without a shot being fired. It turned out that instead of being twenty, they were only seven, and the two Travis passed initially made their escape. Far more important, though, he captured—besides the five soldiers, six muskets, and two swords—a total of three hundred or more horses and mules. Only now did Travis have a little trouble with his men. Unused to military usage, they assumed that what they captured would belong to them, in the manner of privateers. Their captain, however, "whose only thoughts were for his countriees welfare," as one volunteer said, persuaded them that the horses must go to Austin for the benefit of the army, and the men acquiesced.[74] Immediately he sent a rider off to Austin with the news, then collected the horses, and started the herd back to the north, reaching the San Antonio River, a short ride from the Texian army, on November 13.

Austin had been worried about Travis for some time after Briscoe brought word of his continuing to the Atascosa. Now that Travis was leading his own party of men, though only a dozen, Austin at once recognized him again as a "captain." By November 9 he had Fannin looking for him, in the hope that Travis could help with an expedition after another Mexican pack train supposedly headed for Laredo, but Fannin never found him.[75] Two days later Austin sent an order to Travis himself, telling him to link with Fannin, but no sooner did he write the message than Travis's rider came in with the report of the capture of the *caballado*. A delighted Austin wrote another dispatch immediately. "I have to thank you and express my approbation of your conduct and that of your men in this affair," he said. "It has been creditable to yourselves and usefull to the service." Learning that most of the horses were in poor condition, he ordered Travis to leave them to graze on the Seguín *rancho*, and then hurry himself back to get orders for a new mission. The reward for success was to be no rest.[76]

Travis rejoined the army late November 15, and thereafter Austin kept him out almost constantly on scouts, usually accompanied by "Deaf" Smith. They burnt the grass along roads leading out of San Antonio to deny the Mexicans the grazing. They joined with Capt. Juan Seguín and his company to guard routes into and out of the city, and ranged widely around the countryside, vigilant for more horses and reinforcements.[77] On those days when Travis stayed with the main army, he witnessed the laxity and poor coordination that made it such a troubled command, with discipline in short supply and too great an abundance of individual independence. The men fired their guns promiscuously in camp, wasted food, and came and went as they pleased, and Travis could not have been blind to the fact that many of Austin's directives took on more the aspect of requests than orders. It taught him a lesson in command. "A mob can do wonders in a sudden burst of patriotism or passion," he would say in a few days, "but cannot be depended on as soldiers for a campaign." If ever he had a substantial company of his own, he saw object lessons here in how not to command.[78]

When Austin planned on November 21 to storm Béxar at last, there would naturally be no role for Travis's small company of mounted men, and so he and the others attached themselves to the infantry companies, Travis himself joining Fannin's Brazos Guards.[79] But then the continuing problems of this troubled mob of men—it could hardly be called an army—led to an almost universal refusal to make the attack just hours before it was to go. For some it was too much. Fannin resigned, and a number of other disheartened men decided simply to go home. Two days later, when Austin gave up and announced his departure to undertake a mission to the United States decreed for him by the consultation, and an election was held to choose his successor, only those men electing to continue the siege were allowed to vote.

Travis did not vote. He, too, had seen enough. Some men in his own company had simply gone home without leave.[80] It was time now for him to return to San Felipe, though he went from different motives than those animated by simple disgust.[81] Even though the consultation had adjourned on November 14 and thus he could not now take his seat, there was still good work for him to do, especially since the permanent council continued to sit, and in its hands now rested the organization of the country for a more systematic and extended resistance. Besides, his personal affairs needed tending. In the face of the volunteers' unwillingness to attack now, he had better uses for his time— better for himself and for Texas. Travis remained with the army a few more days, and his reconstituted company of scouts no doubt went out on another reconnaissance or two. Austin's confidant Moses Bryan maintained that "no one was more efficient in this line of service than Travis."[82] His friend "Deaf" Smith brought in the word on November 26 of a Mexican pack train that resulted in Bowie going out for what became known as the Grass Fight, and Travis and his men may have joined in the general rush. If so, it was his last action with this troubled army. Within a few hours, or a day or two at most, Travis was riding back to San Felipe.[83]

He arrived to find himself one of the lions of the hour. On November 18 Austin had written to the permanent council to report the capture of the *caballado* and compliment Travis on his action.

About the time Travis left the army, on November 27, the military committee of the permanent council reported a commendation of "citizen Capt. Wm. B. Travis for his personal worth and distinguished service."[84] By that time Austin's announcement of the *caballado* capture was already in the San Felipe newspaper.[85] Travis at last had everything he had wanted: His practice flourished, the leading men of the community looked up to him, he enjoyed widespread influence, he had a cause that was worthy of his talents as a political firebrand, and now he was a celebrity. Even James Dellet had never been a war hero.

BOWIE

1835–February 2, 1836

> *We will rather die in these ditches, than give it up to the enemy. Public safety*
> *demands our lives rather than evacuate this post to the enemy.*
>
> JAMES BOWIE, FEBRUARY 2, 1836

Even with the elation that came at the moment of seeing the Mexicans
retire from Concepción to San Antonio, Bowie felt as well frustration,
and perhaps some regret that he had not followed his orders more
carefully the day before. If only Austin and the rest of the army had
been with him this morning, or in immediate supporting distance, he
believed that they could have pursued the foe and taken Béxar itself by
noon.[1] Austin felt the same frustration. He had his army on the road at
first light, with Lieutenant Travis and his small company of mounted
volunteers in the advance, and Travis and his men were the first to
hear the sounds of the firing ahead at Concepción. Before long Bowie
could see Travis's horsemen on the other side of the San Antonio
River, riding after the Mexicans, but to no useful end other than
harassing the withdrawal. An hour after the fighting ended Bowie saw
Austin himself ride up at the head of the main column. Without dis-
mounting, Austin began issuing orders for a full pursuit and general
attack on Béxar itself.

Bowie ran over to Austin and immediately remonstrated with him to
rescind the order. He had learned more than enough from his friends
sending information out of the town to know that its defenses were
now too strong. The Mexicans who attacked that morning would by
now be well inside their own works again, and without artillery Austin
was no match for them. He would simply suffer as the foe had suffered
that morning. Fannin joined Bowie in his argument, and finally Austin

yielded, believing that Cós would have to surrender before long anyhow as the Texians tried to starve him out. The general ordered Bowie
to direct the distribution of the army in the position selected around
Concepción, and dismounted to send a quick dispatch to await the
meeting of the consultation. In it he complimented "colonel Bowie and
captain Fanning" on "the brilliancy of the victory," and included
Bowie's count of thirty muskets and the brass field piece as spoils. He
would add to that in a few days that he thought Bowie and Fannin
fought "in the best Manner."[2]

Austin's health plagued him now, leaving him physically too debilitated to be equal to his duties and mentally too fatigued to think and
plan with clarity. Having accepted Bowie's advice on assaulting San
Antonio and its works, he feared there must inevitably be a long siege
ahead, for which he had little stomach. Moreover, without decisive
action soon, he knew he could not hold the army together. The volunteers would simply disappear as quickly as they came. Already the
desertion of one company had delayed his march to Concepción on
the morning of the fight. His only hope was to instill some sense of
discipline, and for all his compliments for Bowie's and Fannin's conduct of their fight, he could not forget that the two had disobeyed
express orders in not immediately reporting finding a position for the
army. Had they done so, Austin would have brought up the army on
the afternoon of October 27, and the victory of the next morning
might have seen them in possession of San Antonio itself. Now Austin
issued an order that "any officer who disobeys orders, shall be immediately arrested and suspended from his command, until a court martial
decides his case."[3] Undoubtedly he had Bowie in mind, and certainly
Bowie must have seen it that way.

Meanwhile Austin slowly made his preparations for a siege. Learning
that three hundred volunteers were on their way to join him, he felt more
confident, and early on October 30 sent Bowie in command of three to
four hundred men, nearly half the army, across the San Antonio and into
the outskirts of Béxar itself in a clear invitation to Cós to come out and
fight, but the Mexicans wisely stayed within their fortifications. Bowie
remained there all day, retiring only at dusk.[4] The attempt to lure the
Mexicans out may have been Bowie's idea, quite possibly with the intent
of falling back to lead the foe on to the rest of the army in ambush. Or it

may as well have been to divert Cós's attention to the south, for the next day, October 31, Austin led his half of the army north to a position on the Alamo Canal, a ditch a mile above Béxar, taking Travis with him and sending him off on a raid to find the enemy *caballado*.

Before putting his men in motion, Austin directed that he and Bowie would send their commands in to harass the foe that evening as soon as Austin had his men in place.[5] But that night in his camp at Concepción, Bowie got a message from Austin. He canceled the planned skirmish, yet in typically equivocal fashion gave Bowie permission to go ahead with his part of it if he wished. He also wrote that Refugio de la Garza, the very priest who had married Bowie to Ursula, sent word from town that two companies of the Mexican cavalry wanted to defect to the Texians and needed only a demonstration on the south side of Béxar to act as a pretext for their being ordered out. Austin told Bowie to make a diversionary movement the next morning, and went on to ask his opinion on what their future operations ought to be, including the possibility of an all-out assault on the city.[6]

Of course Bowie had an opinion, and an aggressive one. He doubted the accuracy of Garza's information, for he had been getting similar rumors himself, but so contradictory that he did not believe them. Nevertheless he knew that Cós's supplies of corn were short, and in a close siege the Texians could force him to give up or come out and fight. In case the two companies did defect, Bowie urged that he and Austin be prepared to rush the town immediately in a coordinated attack to take advantage of Mexican confusion. He advised waiting no more than five days for the defectors to come out, and if they did not, then the Texians should storm Béxar. "We cannot doubt for a moment the result." To be certain that his and Austin's movements coordinated well, he suggested that each send a courier to the other twice a day, morning and evening, and at the same times, so that each would know the situation of the other simultaneously.[7] It was wise policy, indeed, though it also revealed how little Bowie knew of military history. For centuries commanders had had exactly the same idea, only to find that the exigencies of the battlefield almost invariably defeated simultaneity.

•

Bowie made his demonstration the next morning, taking his division within eight hundred yards of the town, and finding the position so advantageous that he determined on his own to occupy it rather than returning to Concepción. But no deserters came out to him, and he firmly believed now that none would. Bowie then did something typical of his independent instinct to act on the whim of the instant. Taking advantage of Austin's absence, and almost certainly without his permission, Bowie assumed one of his commander's prerogatives by sending a message into San Antonio to the Mexican commander. He proposed that Cós enter into negotiations with him for the surrender of his garrison and "to close the war." Bowie wrote the note hurriedly, and as usual without thinking it through carefully beforehand, for no sooner did he finish than he started making additions, mostly boast. Between the lines he scrawled that "I fought you on the 28th inst with only a small detachment of ninety two men," obviously rubbing Cós's nose in it a bit, but also implying that with several hundred he could inflict even greater damage. Then as a postscript, he elaborated further, mentioning the large reinforcement just received, and how difficult it was to restrain his men from attacking on their own, especially—he could not refrain from boasting again—as they were "nearly flushed with victory, purchased with no loss on their part."

At the same time, however, he also maintained that they were not revolutionaries. He and his men were pledged to defend the constitution of 1824. "They hold to that as their sheet anchor, and will sooner part with life, than abandon it."[8] Perhaps, though more likely Bowie was being disingenuous again. The sentiment for a declaration of independence, not just from Coahuila but from Mexico itself, was growing, and everyone expected the consultation to discuss the issue. Certainly for Bowie's personal land interests, full-scale independence offered more promise than did remaining in the Mexican federation with its renunciation of the Mason grants. But it would be unwise to say anything like that to Cós now. Better to present themselves in the guise of loyal Mexican citizens, simply defending their constitutional rights. That would soften the sting if Cós agreed to negotiate.[9]

Cós's reply, when it came, stated that his duty allowed him only to obey his orders, and those were not to communicate with the "rebels," consequently he returned Bowie's message unread. Apparently no one in San Antonio had informed him who his antagonist was, and Cós must not have kept much abreast of recent events elsewhere in Texas, for he knew his antagonist only as "an individual Bery Bowie who is called Colonel."[10] Privately, however, he sent Garza out with a verbal message that he had been told to fortify and hold Béxar at all costs, and would do so. "Every thing seems to wear the appearance of resistance," Bowie consequently wrote to Austin that afternoon. Good as his new position was, he found it sufficiently exposed that Cós must surely know his numbers, and that made him vulnerable. Bowie had already asked for a reinforcement once before. Now he reiterated his request, perhaps unwisely underlining his suggestion of "a more *equeal* division of forces," and then repeating it once again in a postscript, asserting that it was necessary to keep his men satisfied.[11] Throughout, though polite, Bowie could not help underlining words to emphasize his need for more men, which could well have had the appearance of an attempt to lecture Austin.

During the day Bowie heard four cannon shots fired at Austin's position above town, nothing more than an annoyance, really; then that evening came word from Austin, who somewhat defensively explained that the division of forces between them was not as unequal as Bowie thought. He had to send Travis out with his cavalry company, and send Hall with a detachment to occupy another position between the two divisions. He had to detail soldiers to guard the growing number of Mexican prisoners they had taken in the past few days, many men were down sick, and Austin expected to occupy one or two other spots on the periphery of San Antonio, all requiring men. Still, he promised to try to send some reinforcement "compatible with the service," saying that "everything shall be done on our part possible for the service & to keep up harmony." It was not so much a communication from a commander to a subordinate as a negotiation between rivals. Austin may well have felt that Bowie was trying to undercut him and assume de facto command of the army. Certainly, in the face of Austin's ill health and indecision, Bowie had no question as to which of them was better suited to the task.[12]

The next morning, by now unwilling or unable to take a decision without a vote, Austin held a council with his officers on the question of storming Béxar or laying siege, and the majority opted for the latter.

Within an hour Bowie read Austin's message with the result, asking him
to hold the same vote among his own officers. He had four companies
with him, Fannin's, Briscoe's, Robert Coleman's, and the recently arrived
company led by Thomas J. Rusk, along with a small artillery company.
Bowie called all their officers—twenty in all—together, and put Fannin
in charge of holding the council. In the end only two voted for an immediate attack, and the rest for a siege. Bowie himself did not vote.[13]

In fact he had resigned. Several factors may have influenced his
decision. His growing impatience with Austin's indecisiveness had
been apparent for several days. The implied censure of the general
order about officers disobeying orders must have stung. Or he may
have found Austin's other suggestion that morning so stunning that he
wanted to disassociate himself completely from the scheme. The commanding general proposed that the two divisions divide themselves
into some twenty or more small groups of twenty to twenty-five men
each, and then start circulating the parties around the periphery of San
Antonio, having them sleep on alternate nights either above or below
the town, though he failed to explain what purpose that was to serve
other than to spot any foragers or reinforcements.[14]

Yet, far more likely, Bowie simply saw that his command would
evaporate away from him. In addition to voting on the attack or siege
question, his officers also balloted by a 2 to 1 majority to unite their
division with Austin's above the town, deeming it necessary for security and morale. Bowie wholeheartedly endorsed that idea. However,
he knew full well that there was no formal organizational structure in
Austin's army. There were just eleven independent volunteer companies, and two of artillery, all commanded by captains who reported
directly to Austin. Bowie held no command of his own, for his old
Nacogdoches militia was not there. His leadership of the "First
Division" was a temporary expedient, an assignment given him by
Austin as an aide, to exercise while those companies were separated
from the main army. But once the army was united again, as it was
now to be, Austin would likely exercise direct overall control again as
he had before. Thus Bowie would be superfluous, with not even his
own company to command. He would still be an aide on Austin's staff,
but the idea of being a headquarters functionary or errand boy held no
charms for him. Consequently he quite courteously wrote to Austin a

"resignation of the nominal command I hold in the army," and expressed the hope that the general would appoint someone more suited to a staff position in his stead.[15]

Later that day or the next morning Bowie went to Austin and discussed with him in person his reasons for the resignation, yet there is nothing to suggest that Austin found anything objectionable in Bowie's motives, or that the interview did not end amicably—at least, as amicably as it could be, given these two very different men, with quite divergent attitudes toward land speculation.[16] By November 4, however, a rumor did come out of the Texian camps and find its way into Béxar that Austin and Bowie were at odds, part of a wider unrest in the army.[17] Certainly there was trouble in the ranks. The bivouac presented more the aspect of a mob than an army. When drums called the morning muster, the volunteers either stumbled out of their tents and huts half dressed or simply stayed in their blankets, while those at the roll call often as not continued eating their morning meal with not even the show of an attempt to stand at attention. During the day they wandered about the countryside, often venturing toward Béxar to a redoubt where two field pieces occasionally fired at the town.[18] Discipline was utterly lacking, and poor Austin simply had neither the health, the personality, nor the experience to whip an assembly of volunteers into an army.

Bowie, on the other hand, for all his faults, personified the leader. Men instinctively followed his standard. Austin would not have been human if he did not feel some tinge of resentment at that, the more so since some no doubt lionized Bowie as the hero of Concepción. Already Bowie's name appeared in the press as the victor, and on November 3, in the very first act of the newly convened consultation, Houston read a brief account of Bowie and Fannin's fight and offered a resolution giving the thanks of the convention to them both, as well as to Austin.[19] Then, too, Austin had to resent Bowie's presumption, and there was no secret of the good relations Bowie enjoyed with Houston, fast becoming an archrival of Austin's. Moses Bryan, traveling with Austin, saw more than once how Bowie managed to overawe the general. "I have seen him yield his own opinions and adopt those of the impetuous Bowie and others," said Bryan, "for the sake of order and to prevent agitation." Bryan himself regarded Bowie as one of several "ambitious, self asserting men among them, each believing himself capable of commanding."[20] Bryan was not alone in his view, even some civilians not with the army sensing the exploding ambition of a few. "Every man seemed to think he could command an army," one of them lamented, and there is no reason to doubt that Bowie believed he could, certainly more ably than Stephen F. Austin.[21]

It is just possible that land had something to do with Bowie's resignation beyond the immediate military situation. By November he may well have heard that on October 27 the permanent council had passed a resolution closing all the land offices in Texas during the emergency, their express object being to halt sales of land in the Mason and similar Monclova grants.[22] That was not good news for Bowie, certainly, and he may have thought to leave the army at once and return to San Felipe in hopes of influencing the council to reconsider. A man who would go to Washington, D.C., to beard cabinet officers and congressmen, would not be put off by a few rustics in a drafty log meeting hall.

Bowie remained with the army, however, though he spent November 3 and 4 in a private capacity until November 5, when Warren Hall left for San Felipe and Austin appointed Bowie temporary adjutant general in Hall's absence.[23] Yet that was to Bowie's temperament a pointless position, involving nothing more than acting as a conduit of orders from general to army, a clerk's job at best. Meanwhile the unrest throughout the army reached such a stage that Fannin doubted that all of the men would voluntarily remain, and Frank Johnson and some of the other captains sent petitions to Austin in protest at some actions. William Wharton had a grievance with the general that he rather ostentatiously settled that same day with a public letter, indicating that Austin had in some manner backed down, and Travis submitted his resignation in response to grumblings in his command and a possible implied slight from Austin.[24]

It seemed to Austin that everything was collapsing around him, and in his physical and mental state he could not face remaining any longer. On November 5 he issued orders through Bowie as adjutant that all the companies then in the army form on review at dawn the next morning, though he did not immediately reveal his intent. When he faced them he announced that he would resign his command, or at least intimated an intention to do so, and said he would take those who no longer wished to remain back to San Felipe. Those choosing to stay and continue the siege were to be organized into a regiment and choose their own regimental commander, though he would leave Bowie behind as his representative in overall command with orders to collect as much provender as they could, burn the grass in the area to prevent the Mexicans grazing their horses, and then retire toward the Rio Grande, burning the grass along the way, whenever Cós should force him to retreat. He was giving up on the siege.[25]

In the balloting that day the 517 men volunteering to remain overwhelmingly chose Edward Burleson as their colonel. Five men were mentioned in all in the voting, with Bowie himself polling last at a mere five votes. There seems to have been no "campaigning," and it is possible that nominations were not even put forth. The soldiers simply voted spontaneously, naturally choosing from among the more outstanding leaders in the army, including Fannin, Joseph Wallace, and Frank Johnson. Yet Bowie's showing of a paltry five votes, all in John Bird's company, is still surprising given his prominence in the field thus far. Despite what appears to be Bowie's dominance over Fannin in their joint command, it is possible that in the army as a whole the perception prevailed that Fannin was really in charge. Wallace had jointly led the forces that expelled the Mexicans from Gonzales, and had a large following, and even Johnson at least held an elected command as a company captain. By contrast Bowie still wore no real rank other than his informal appointment as colonel by Austin, and now on November 6 was a mere adjutant. He had no constituency since he did not have a company of his own as did Fannin and Johnson, and on top of that, news of his resignation a few days before may have persuaded the men in the ranks that he would be leaving, making votes for him pointless.[26]

But then Austin changed his mind and decided to stay with the army after all.[27] In fact, it may all have been a clever ruse to quell the dissatisfaction while still saving face. He would let Burleson exercise operational command, thus removing himself from having to have routine dealings with the company commanders, while at the same time his announcement of his own resignation had initiated those of others he might just as soon be rid of. His nephew Moses Bryan, who noted the "aspiring men" his uncle had to deal with, found the day after the election that the situation was dramatically better at head-quarters and in the army.[28]

And so Bowie thought he was to have the army command, even if only for a short time, and perhaps of a depleted army at that; but then, considering what he did with only 92 men at Concepción, the 517 men remaining would still be a lot. The news that Austin changed his mind proved simply too much disappointment, and not just to Bowie. Soon after learning of Austin's reversal, Warren Hall sent his own res-ignation as adjutant, obviously unhappy, and quite possibly because he had been counting on his friend Bowie having the army command.[29] Wallace decided to leave, as did William Wharton. That same November 6 Bowie resigned again, and this time with evident temper, out of pique at losing his chance at army command, as well as chagrin at his miserable showing in the vote for regimental colonel. "I have declined farther action under the appointment given to me by your-self," he notified Austin. "I will be found in Captn Fannins Company where my duty to my country and the principles of human rights shall be discharged on my part to the extent of my abilities as a private."[30]

That resolution to serve with Fannin lasted scarcely thirty-six hours, for almost immediately he decided to leave the army and go to San Felipe as soon as Frank Johnson could replace him as adjutant. Bowie departed on November 8, along with other disaffected men like Wharton and Wallace, and accompanied by Alexander Hotchkiss and Richardson, who bore dispatches from Austin to the consultation.[31] Bowie could not have reached San Felipe before late on November 13, with nothing to indicate why a three-day trip had taken him five, though he may have made a detour by way of the mission Refugio near Copano, to move some four hundred head of cattle, one of his few gen-uine assets, to the old *rancho* of Veramendi, combining them with the Veramendi stock so that they would appear to be part of his late father-in-law's herd, and thus secure from confiscation by Mexican forces.[32]

When Bowie did reach San Felipe, Houston startled him at first by congratulating him on taking command of the army at San Antonio. A letter had come in a day or two earlier with the now obsolete news of Austin's resignation and Bowie's elevation, but Bowie soon brought Houston up to date on affairs in Austin's camps.[33]

•

A lot had happened in San Felipe. A week earlier the consultation by a heavy majority declared its adherence to the constitution of 1824, and defeated a motion to make a declaration of independence. However, they definitely chose to separate themselves from Coahuila, and formed a provisional government, choosing Henry Smith as governor and James Robinson as lieutenant governor. They elected Houston major general to command their "army," and decided that Austin should go to the United States as an emissary to seek assistance. They also decreed that all *empresarios* and land commissioners such as Bowie were to cease operations immediately. Then on November 14, just hours after Bowie's arrival, the consultation adjourned until March 1, 1836, having created an advisory council to sit indefinitely to oversee the continuing formation of the army and government.[34] That same day Bowie saw a little bit of celebrity come his way when the local *Telegraph and Texas Register* published the report of the Concepción fight jointly submitted by himself and Fannin.

Bowie and Houston undoubtedly met during the day on November 14, and among other things Houston gave Bowie the news that Austin was being sent to the United States. That would finally leave his army without a commander. Houston himself had to remain in San Felipe and thereabouts to organize the raising of volunteers and the creation of several forces to defend vital points from invasion. He could not go to that army, and therefore it would be up to the soldiers there to elect a new commander for themselves. Suddenly Bowie's prospects brightened. If he were present, and especially if he came with Houston's blessing, he might stand a chance of winning the ballot, and it is apparent that Houston preferred him to have the command. Sam Houston did not forget that Bowie may have saved his life—and his future—just a few weeks before.

To have a chance at election Bowie needed to return to the army. Houston told him that clerks were even then preparing copies of dispatches from the consultation for Austin, including notification of his ambassadorial appointment. Bowie could return to San Antonio with the couriers. He passed the rest of the afternoon and evening at Peyton's inn, where the family of the proprietor usually found him "refined and courteous."[35] Unfortunately on this occasion he had considerably too much to drink. Anson Jones arrived in San Felipe that evening and, on being introduced to Bowie, found him "dead drunk" and talking loudly with Houston and abusing Austin mercilessly in their drunken chatter.[36] Thus when the packet of letters was finally ready around midnight, the couriers had to wait with horses saddled for an hour before Houston could get Bowie outside, and then it took help to mount him on his horse. Turning to one of the other riders, George Patrick, Bowie good-humoredly said, "now Patrick you have been kind enough to wait for me and I guarantee to make up the lost time." Riding hard through the night, they changed horses at DeWees' Crossing on the Colorado, and pressed on. "Good as his promise," said Patrick, "he made things quite lively enough for me."[37]

They reached Austin's camps above San Antonio early in the afternoon of November 18 and immediately turned over the dispatches to Austin, who may have been a bit suspicious to see Bowie return.[38] Certainly Patrick thought he understood his riding companion's motive. "Col. Jas. Bowie wanted to be in Camps, yea and present when Genl. Austin resigned the command of the army," he said later. The unrest had broken out again after Bowie's departure, and Austin finally had to combine the two wings of the army, which he delayed doing in spite of the vote on November 6.[39] As a result he did not feel that he could leave the army immediately, for fear the discord would make it disintegrate in his wake. It was a wise decision, for even Fannin feared the "depressed feelings & ardour of the men" might lead to a dissolution. Having seen far too much of indecision, he wrote to Houston with the recommendation that there be more decisions and fewer councils of war. Warren Hall wrote to Austin resigning his position as adjutant general for much the same cause, and the only good news was that Travis, rethinking his resignation, had actually captured the Mexican *caballado*. When Austin tried to order an assault on Béxar for the morning of November 22, no doubt thinking it would inspire the men, his commanders reported to him that the volunteers declared themselves unwilling to make the attempt, and that same day Fannin asked for a discharge to leave the army. Concluding that "this army has always been composed of discordant materials," Austin decided on November 22 that he himself should stay no longer.[40]

Austin ordered the election of the new commander for November 24. By now the army had dwindled from a high of 600 or more early in the month to just 405 who said they would stay. Limiting the balloting to those remaining, Austin proceeded with the election. Patrick, at least, believed that Bowie hoped to win the command for himself, though the suggestion seems thin, for Bowie's miserable showing in the November 6 election would hardly have encouraged such expectations. Any prospect he might have had he sabotaged himself, for unfortunately James brought some refreshment with him from San Felipe, and the night before the election he became once again quite publicly drunk, considerably diminishing his standing with the soldiers.[41] By the morning of the balloting, Burleson, destined to win all along, emerged victorious with no real opposition.[42]

In any case Houston had probably already given Bowie an assignment even before sending him to Austin's army. Since Bowie held no position under Austin, and was not in fact an enlisted volunteer, Austin could give him no orders of any kind anymore; neither did his authority extend beyond his own army. Yet almost immediately after the election Austin sent word to Goliad that Bowie would be on his way there in a few days to oversee the preparation of its defenses, and the direction for Bowie to do so could only have come from Houston.[43] No doubt Bowie would have been pleased to get away, yet he lingered with the army a few days, taking an appointment as adjutant on Burleson's staff, and it was good that he did.

For a day or two rumors came into the Texian camp that Ugartechea would attempt to reinforce Béxar, and Burleson kept one of his best scouts, Smith, on the lookout to the west. On the morning of November 26 Smith came galloping into camp with word that he had seen a pack train with 150 Mexicans about five miles from Béxar. Intending to prevent the presumed supplies from reaching Cós and his hungry garrison, Burleson immediately sent Bowie and nearly forty cavalrymen off to skirmish and delay the train's progress, while William Jack led one hundred infantry after him. With his usual impetuosity, Bowie led his party at a gallop off to the west, and finally came in sight of the train only about a mile outside San Antonio. As it happened, some of the Texians had heard rumors of a convoy of silver bullion on its way to San Antonio, and some of Bowie's men—perhaps including Bowie himself—concluded that the mules in this train might just be carrying treasure.[44]

Despite being outnumbered perhaps 4 to 1, Bowie let his instinct for aggression take over, and he ordered his cavalrymen to charge the startled Mexicans just as they were crossing the dry Alazan creekbed. The move disconcerted the foe, and then Bowie quickly dismounted his party, took cover below the bank of another dry bed, and opened a steady skirmishing fire. The Mexicans themselves dismounted to take shelter in the dry creek, while a messenger dashed away to Béxar to ask Cós to send aid. Meanwhile Jack and the infantry, Burleson now in command, rapidly approached from the rear, hearing the firing in their front. By the time they were within a mile of Bowie's position, they went into a streambed themselves, hearing reports that Mexican cavalry were coming out of Béxar.

The Mexicans with the pack train tried to rush Bowie's position, but his men turned them back, while Burleson tried to find his way forward to join Bowie, but instead managed to advance to a spot between Bowie and San Antonio just as Cós sent out a reinforcement. As a result Burleson turned his attention to the new arrivals, while Bowie continued to battle the pack guard—triple his numbers—on his own. In places the antagonists were separated by not much more than a few yards in their respective dry beds, and unable to see what was happening elsewhere, Bowie had to rely on one brave fellow who stood on the high ground where he could see all the contending parties and signal which way to move.[45]

Finally Bowie reunited his dismounted men with the main body of Texians and rushed forward in a charge that dislodged the Mexican line, even though it was then being reinforced. The enemy opened fire with a cannon, but evidently only to cover the withdrawal into town, which then commenced. The Texians pursued for some distance but gave up when they saw the Mexicans pull into the San Antonio fortifications, and when Mexican cannon in town began to fire on them.[46] The Mexicans left behind many of their mules, but the Texians who now scampered hurriedly across the prairie to collect the silver found the packs filled with nothing but grass freshly cut and on its way to feed the animals in the town. "This ludicrous affair," one of them complained, "was then dubbed and is since known in our history as the 'Grass Fight'."[47]

Truly it did not amount to much. When the Texians collected their booty, they found animals and equipment worth perhaps $2,000 when later auctioned. They lost four men wounded and one by desertion themselves, and counted fifteen dead Mexicans on the field, though Bowie believed that the total enemy casualties ran to sixty or more.[48] Some of the men involved firmly believed that Bowie "was the hero of the occasion," yet significantly, when Burleson filed his report the next day, he complimented every one of his officers by name *except* Bowie.[49] Perhaps he resented the way Bowie had impetuously lunged into action. Perhaps, too, he simply resented Bowie, having seen enough of the ambitious fellow's dealings with Austin to prefer to keep him at arm's length, and distrustful of Bowie's obviously close relationship with Houston, now supreme commander of all Texas forces.

Shortly after the Grass Fight, Bowie finally left on his mission to Goliad, about eighty miles southeast of Béxar. Austin had expected the army to spend the winter there, and if so, the Texians must commence building defenses for protection, fortifying the houses and streets as the Mexicans had done in San Antonio.[50] It was also believed that Cós might be grazing some of his command's horses along the San Antonio River, so Burleson sent part of a company along with him in case an opportunity arose to capture or disperse the herd. Some of those accompanying him were *tejanos* who had served in the company now commanded by Benjamin Fort Smith, born within a few miles and days of Bowie back in Logan County, Kentucky. Bowie never saw the animals, but he did meet with a Mexican who said he knew another man who had tended the herd and would know where it lay. Bowie soon arrested the man, but he refused to give away the location.

Then something happened. One of Smith's volunteers, Plácido Benavides, suggested that they tie the man, put a rope around his neck, and raise him by a tree branch, strangling him until he agreed to talk. There was nothing surprising in that for Benavides. He was one of the *ricos*, the wealthy landed local aristocracy, like the Veramendis, who felt an ancestral cultural contempt, or at best disdain, for the *pobres*, the poor. Thus for Benavides there was no dishonor in torturing a *peon* for information, especially if he was working for the enemy. Bowie, who came from an entirely different culture that generally frowned on such brutality, agreed to the suggestion. Perhaps his marriage into the Veramendis had brought him not just family affluence but also family attitudes.[51]

The brutality, once commenced, almost got out of hand. Bowie ordered a fire started near the tree, and then some of his men hauled the unfortunate man up over it, adding the double torture of burning—or at least extremely uncomfortable proximity to the blaze—to the strangulation. At the same time eight of his company stood with cocked rifles beside the fire, pointing them at the poor man. When the victim stopped kicking and appeared near unconsciousness, they let him down and then threatened to shoot him. He refused to talk, and the whole business was repeated twice more, even though one of Bowie's men rebelled at the cruelty and refused to participate further. After the third time the Mexican revealed the whereabouts of a herd of horses, though Bowie's one rebel suspected they might have belonged to the man himself instead of the enemy army, but he gave them up simply to save his life. Even then, it seems, Bowie was not done, announcing that he intended to continue the torture the next morning, though what there was left to gain is a mystery, and in the event he failed to make good on the threat. With the rumors of a silver train still flying about, it is just possible that Bowie thought the man might know something of that as well. As for the rebel, Bowie punished him for his insubordination by making him sit up all night guarding the prisoner.[52]

The fact that one volunteer refused to engage in the torture suggests that Bowie did not have so secure a hold on them as he did in battle. Fighting was one thing, and men would follow him blindly into certain death. But barbarity, even toward a Mexican, was something else, at least for one man. As for Bowie, who usually stood up for the defenseless, his behavior seems inexplicable, yet perhaps it is not. When Bowie wanted something he let nothing stand in his way. He wanted the horses—and maybe something more, if the silver rumors were involved—and this *peon*, defenseless or not, was an obstacle.

Bowie must have reached Goliad in the first week of December, and what he saw there looked bad. Capt. Philip Dimitt commanding its volunteers attempted to rule with a hand so arbitrary that complaints against him circulated widely. He interfered with judicial authorities, made unlawful arrests, and eventually was ordered to relinquish his command, yet refused to do so. His was the sort of personality born to clash with Bowie's, yet nothing suggests that any sparks flew at their meeting. Bowie simply observed Dimitt's management of affairs, and surveyed the condition of the post, which was not good. Dimitt's volunteers needed winter clothing, his supplies of provisions and ammunition dwindled, his sick list grew, and the command's horses were unfit for service. By December 2 he believed he could not defend the place if attacked.[53]

Rather than attempting to do anything with Goliad's defenses with the limited and weak manpower available, Bowie saw as much as he needed, and then returned to Burleson's army, no doubt hopeful of being present for the taking of Béxar. In his absence Burleson hesitated for several days, then finally ordered an assault for December 5. It made some initial success, taking a foothold in the city streets, and the fighting continued for several days, though at the cost of Ben Milam, shot December 7 right in the courtyard of the Veramendi home, which some in the army called "Bowies house."[54] After two more days of desultory fighting, Cós finally decided that he could not continue, and sought terms. Two days later the formal surrender took place.

Just when Bowie arrived is uncertain, but it was a few days after the fighting had ceased. He reported conditions at Goliad to his friend Frank Johnson, who assumed command when Burleson left on December 15, and then agreed to take Johnson's dispatches back to San Felipe. Before going, however, Bowie saw an old friend, Antonio Menchaca, who had left Béxar a refugee when the Mexican army came, and now returned. Seeing him brought back a flood of gentle memories for Bowie, who threw his arms around Menchaca and wept bitterly as he confessed his grief that Ursula had died alone, without him to give her comfort. "Are you still my companion?" Bowie asked almost pitifully.[55]

On December 17 Bowie left, accompanied by William B. Scates, a veteran of Travis's recent Anahuac adventure, and rode hard for San Felipe.[56] He arrived two days later and took up his old lodging at Peyton's.[57] He found the provisional government already in a mess. Governor Henry Smith struck some as "too illiterate, too little informed, and not of the right *calibre*" for his post, too burdened with conceit and stubbornness. Robinson enjoyed scarcely better opinions, and the members of the consultation had treated him rather coolly even though they elected him. The divisions in San Felipe were obvious. Smith and Houston favored the radical step of proclaiming full independence, while Robinson and the majority of the permanent council still clung to the 1824 constitution.[58] Smith also stood opposed to the land-speculating interests, which should have included Bowie, and since some on the council had their hands in the land business, that only added to the unwholesome ferment. He complained of his opponents in San Felipe that "there was nothing of patriotism" in their actions. "It was all sordid self interest," yet if ever a man was destined by temperament to alienate others it was Smith.[59]

Bowie also discovered on his arrival that Brown and Houston had a job for him that would throw him right into the middle of the mess. His old friend James Grant had been for some weeks promoting the idea of a military expedition to Matamoros at the mouth of the Rio Grande. He interested Dimitt in the notion, and Dimitt may well have discussed it with Bowie during his visit to Goliad. The port there took in one hundred thousand dollars or more in monthly revenue from shippers, they believed, and that would go a long way to finance their movement. Taking a position on what was uncontestably Mexican soil, even if only across the river from Texas, would also send a strong message to Mexico City, some thought, as well as inviting those in Coahuila who supported their cause to enlist. The Matamoros idea took on an additional attraction because it would be a means of employing the army now freed by the surrender of Béxar. The government had to feed and clothe those volunteers, and might as well have them doing something for their pay.

Yet there was another dimension to the plan, and the reason for James Grant's consuming interest. The capture of Matamoros would inevitably mean that loyal Mexicans living there and in the rich Rio Grande Valley would likely be willing to sell their homes and farms and livestock to Texians for very favorable prices, in order to leave for some safer location in the Mexican interior. Grant himself had extensive grant property in Coahuila, and saw the expedition as a way of protecting his own investments. Despite his blatant self-interest, he still exerted considerable influence, both with the army at Béxar and with Frank Johnson, and in San Felipe as well.[60] Henry Smith liked the idea, seeing in it an act that would, by capturing Mexican soil, propel this conflict from an uprising into a revolution for independence. The council, largely because of the speculative advantages, also backed the plan. Houston objected to it, at least so far as the motive of protecting Grant's interests was concerned.[61] Moreover, his own position as general-in-chief was not secure, and he knew that Grant had called for his replacement by Johnson. Thus Houston could not afford for an expedition like this to make a rival into a hero. If it had to go, and on December 16 Smith gave him a positive order to launch the expedition, then either he must command it himself, or entrust it to someone strong within his own faction.

Houston chose Bowie. On December 17 he drafted an order to Bowie and sent it to Goliad, where he believed his friend still to be working on defenses. He told Bowie to raise as many volunteers as necessary, march on Matamoros, capture and occupy the place until further orders. If he could not take the town, then he should at least go as far toward the Rio Grande as safely possible, and certainly to Copano, north of Corpus Christi Bay. From that position he was to harass any Mexican movements that must necessarily use the nearby Atascosita Trace, all the while "using the precaution which characterizes your mode of warfare." Beyond that, he left all of the details to Bowie's discretion, with the proviso that he and his command must deal with the enemy "conformably to the rules of civilized warfare."[62] Houston told Smith that he chose Bowie for the task thanks to his familiarity with the country and its people, and because "there is no man on whose forecast, prudence, and valor, I place a higher estimate than Colonel Bowie."[63] Only a man who had never seen James Bowie in action would call him "prudent," but of Bowie's prowess as a leader and fighter there was not a scrap of doubt. Yet Houston apparently intended that *he* would in the end himself command the expedition. Bowie was only to get things in motion while Houston fought the political battles raging in San Felipe.[64]

Just when Bowie himself actually learned of the order is uncertain, though the rumor that he had been selected was abroad in San Felipe the same day he arrived, on December 19, and by that time Houston was in Washington, thirty miles up the Brazos.[65] Meanwhile, to thwart Smith, the council acted on its own, approaching Johnson and Fannin both about raising and commanding the expedition, either unmindful of the order Houston had given Bowie or more likely simply ignoring it. Grant, meanwhile, made preparations of his own, and it was obvious that neither governor nor general-in-chief had any real control. But James Bowie's loyalty to Houston was strong, and had he gotten his orders, he undoubt-

edly would have proceeded to put them into effect regardless of what the
council or other would-be commanders said or did.⁶⁶ Somehow Bowie
either did not learn of his orders or unaccountably took no action on
them for fully a week after reaching San Felipe, though his delay may
have been in recognition of the command vacuum there. Learning of
Smith's order to Houston, the council maintained that it was invalid since
the council believed itself to be the supreme authority. Only on October
27 did the council endorse a Matamoros expedition.⁶⁷ Then, and only
then, it asked Smith to appoint someone to command.

Apparently Bowie did not stay in San Felipe for long after his arrival,
and Houston only learned of his being in the area on December 26,
hearing a report that he would show up either at Washington or San
Felipe the next day. He sent instructions that Bowie was to come to him
in Washington immediately in order to receive a copy of the December
17 order, and apparently he did, for armed with a copy of the order,
Bowie was back in San Felipe by late afternoon, December 28.⁶⁸ At 7
P.M. that evening he walked into the council chamber, no doubt at the
request of its members, and with their leave offered his observations on
the condition of their volunteers at Béxar and elsewhere. He stressed
"the necessity and importance of active operations," and then submitted
a proposal for carrying out the Matamoros expedition. He would raise a
new force of "auxiliary volunteers," no doubt meaning temporary militia
as opposed to the enlisted volunteers at Béxar, and rendezvous them at
Goliad preparatory to moving on Matamoros. It was Houston's orders
to the letter.⁶⁹ The manner of Bowie's presentation impressed some of
the council with his forcefulness, and perhaps even the earnestness of
his commitment to the cause. He could always unleash those old powers of persuasion, the ability to sell himself and his ideas, on command.⁷⁰
The council deferred a decision until the next morning, when the military affairs committee reported a resolution calling on the council to ask
Smith to authorize Bowie to raise his volunteers.⁷¹ Of course this was
not an order but merely a resolution to the council for its consideration,
and so action must await a council decision, and in ensuing days the
confusion only worsened. The council had already recommended sending Fannin to the west to take command of regularly enlisted men, and
then also asked Travis to be sent to the frontier with all the cavalry he
could raise for a move on Matamoros. It was all an uncoordinated mess,

with no firm hand in charge, and Bowie and his orders remained hostage in San Felipe until the council should approve the military committee's resolution. Then on January 3, 1836, Frank Johnson brought word that on his own authority he had already started his volunteers, under command of Grant, on the road south to Matamoros, leaving only one hundred men under Capt. J. C. Neill to hold San Antonio. Moreover, Johnson and Grant had almost emptied the town of its military provisions, leaving Neill in danger of starving. Presented with an accomplished fact, and sympathetic with the speculative motives of Johnson and Grant, the council dropped consideration of the resolution about Bowie and formally authorized Johnson to command the expedition.

It only got worse. Seeing his authority being usurped by the council, Smith now tried to cancel the whole operation, and then on January 6 Johnson himself withdrew his application for authority to command the expedition when he learned that the council was not going to adopt his recommendations for commissions for some of his officers. Learning of that, Bowie went before the council that evening around 7 P.M., and this time exhibited his direct orders from Houston to take the command.[72] Apparently curious about the nature of the order from Houston, since the council had not authorized it, they sent a delegation after Bowie to get from him a copy of the document, and were lucky to catch him as he was already packing his saddlebags at Peyton's to leave for Goliad.[73] The next day the council appointed Fannin to the command, but Houston began giving orders of his own for a concentration of the army near Copano, and on January 8 left himself to assume command. Bowie, meanwhile, was on his way, and by January 10 was a day's ride from Goliad, when he learned that James Grant had passed through the town a few days before and appropriated for his command all of the army horses there.[74] Hearing that, Bowie left at once for Goliad, determined to assume his responsibilities in spite of Johnson, Grant, or anyone else. He sent a quick message to Houston before leaving: "Some dark scheme has been set on foot to disgrace our noble cause," he said. He expected to ride all night and reach Goliad by dawn to "put a stop to Grant's movements."[75]

Behind him affairs deteriorated. The feud between Smith and the council broke into open war on January 9, and the next day Smith severely upbraided the council, when he learned how destitute Johnson and Grant had left the San Antonio garrison under Neill. Smith now blamed the Matamoros expedition that he had once championed, and he used such intemperate language in lecturing the council that it responded in kind. Smith tried to dissolve the council, and it tried to impeach him, setting up Robinson in his place. Then, in a move to strike against Smith by undermining Houston's authority, on January 11 the council issued a proclamation stating that it did not recognize Bowie as an officer in the Texian army, and that therefore Houston had no authority to give him orders, and Bowie had none to organize or lead volunteers.[76] In fact the council was quite correct. Bowie held no commission either by election or appointment. His "colonelcy" referred only to the honorific title of command of the Nacogdoches militia the previous summer. Johnson, Fannin, and even Grant actually held acknowledged commissions, either as elected commanders of companies or by appointment. Bowie rather had been a knight errant, serving as a volunteer aide to Austin, then briefly on his staff, and afterward as a roving troubleshooter. Ironically the one Texian who to date had seen more action in independent command than any other held no official rank whatever.[77]

Reaching Goliad on January 11, Bowie found matters in a shambles. Grant and Johnson—for Johnson had once again changed his mind and was now with Grant—were raising their force in absolute defiance of orders from anyone now. Fannin appeared to be the current holder of the council's authority for the Matamoros expedition, yet Grant and Johnson acted as if he did not exist. Bowie did what he could, but the opposing forces were clearly in the majority. Since he had himself no formal commission, and since Grant and Johnson simply ignored Houston's order of December 17, there was nothing for Bowie to do but wait until Houston himself arrived on January 14, and by then new exigencies arose that, mercifully, removed him from the Matamoros morass.

While Houston began to deal very diplomatically with the volunteers currently adhering to Grant and Johnson, he also turned his eyes northwest to San Antonio. Even before learning of what Johnson and Grant had done there—destroying many of the fortifications, and leaving Neill with a hundred men to hold a position that Cós could not sustain with seven hundred—Houston made plans for its safety. On December 15 he suggested sending a new field commander and several commissioned officers to the town to take over the army, and at the same time wanted a good engineer to go to work on its fortifications. He left no doubt of his intention. He maintained that the necessity of occupying and holding Béxar was so "manifest" that his reasons did not bear repeating.[78] Now within two days of reaching Goliad, Houston got a letter from Neill detailing just how bad his situation was. His men had been in the field for four months and were broken down, some nearly naked, and none of them had been paid in some time. Desertions mounted, and Neill expected more, reducing his strength in a day or two to no more than eighty. Reports of up to 3,000 Mexicans massing at Laredo, 140 miles south on the Rio Grande, only heightened the crisis. "We are in a torpid, defenseless condition," he said, warning that he could be overrun in as little as eight days.[79]

Here was a new crisis, and one made for Bowie. Houston would have to deal with the Johnson-Grant problem himself, as only he had the legal or moral authority to do so. But a mission to Béxar was perfect for his friend of the roving portfolio. On January 17, shortly after he received Neill's urgent plea, Houston met with Bowie and outlined the situation to him. He asked Bowie—he could not really order him—to go to Béxar immediately, taking thirty to fifty men with him, if they agreed to go. Once he reached Béxar he was to start tearing down the remainder of the fortifications not already demolished, and if threatened by the enemy presumably withdraw men and munitions into the Alamo church compound. But before that could happen, Houston continued, he hoped to have permission from Smith for Bowie to blow up the Alamo entirely and remove all the artillery and remaining munitions to Gonzales and Copano. He simply did not believe that volunteers could hold such a place if besieged by Mexican regulars.[80]

Houston remembered that Bowie undertook his mission "with his usual promptitude and manliness."[81] First Bowie unleashed again his most persuasive eloquence to persuade the necessary number of volunteers to accompany him. "He used every means in his power to effect this object," recalled one man in Goliad, but in the end he only influenced about thirty to accompany him.[82] Even though Bowie was going voluntarily, Houston still gave him written instructions, no

doubt so that Neill would take any order coming from Bowie as having the force of coming from Houston himself.[83]

It was a hard ride to cover the eighty miles in a day, but on January 18
Bowie saw the mission Espada ahead, then the familiar ground of San
José, San Juan, and Concepción, and beyond them San Antonio itself.
For all of his travels these last few years, and despite the personal
tragedy that emptied the Veramendi house of the joy he had once
found there, this town was still the only real home Bowie had known
in Texas. Yet he helped besiege it once as an attacker several weeks
before, and now he came as a potential destroyer.

Bowie arrived to find Neill briefly absent, and felt no hesitation in
immediately assuming temporary command of the motley garrison on
the strength of his written orders from Houston.[84] He was nothing if
not decisive. When Neill returned, Bowie found him a capable man, an
Alabamian who came to Texas nearly the same time as Travis. The first
shot of the revolution from that cannon at Gonzales was his, and
Bowie probably already knew him at least in passing from their being
at the siege of Béxar together in November and December.[85] Now he
held a commission as a lieutenant colonel of artillery. One of his
artillerymen, Lt. Almeron Dickenson, had also been at Gonzales, and
Bowie may have heard of another officer present, his own distant
cousin by marriage, James Butler Bonham.[86] There were old friends
there, too. Toribio Losoya, a *tejano* in the garrison, was of the family of
José Domingo Losoya, who had served with Bowie in Johnston's
Louisiana volunteers back in 1815.

In fact Neill had far more guns than he had men to serve them.
When Cós surrendered Béxar, he left behind some twenty bronze and
iron cannon of sizes ranging from two- to twelve-pounders, and perhaps one or two of larger bores. A few were in such bad shape that
they could not be fired, but most of the remainder Neill now had
emplaced in and around the old Mexican works. The Texians also captured from Cós powder, solid shot, and canister totaling more than
twelve hundred rounds, though some of the powder seemed of poor
quality. The Mexicans also gave up four hundred or more British
brown Bess muskets, and even after Johnson and Grant ransacked the

arsenal, there were still sixteen thousand or more rounds of ammunition in hand for them.[87]

Neill had recently divided his small command, stationing part of it
in the town, with his own headquarters in a house at the end of
Potrero Street on the Civil Plaza, while the balance occupied the
Alamo itself, commanded by Lt. William R. Carey, and including most
of the cannon.[88] He also had an excellent amateur engineer officer in
Green B. Jameson. Just the day of Bowie's arrival Jameson counted a
total of 114 men and officers present, though nearly a third of those
were either sick or wounded, leaving just 80 fit for duty, and some of
them had to divert attention to deal with the 50 or more sick and
wounded Mexicans left behind by Cós.[89] Jameson knew there to be
Mexican spies in town, and feared that almost every night someone
left town to take information south to the enemy. He tried to catch
them, but Johnson and Grant had taken virtually all of their horses, so
patrols had to go out on foot and were usually officers at that. In fact
the officers steadily performed more and harder duty than the enlisted
men, including standing guard at night. It was not an enviable situation.[90]

About the only good news awaiting Bowie was that discipline
among the volunteers had improved somewhat with the renewed
rumor of a thousand or more Mexicans somewhere south toward the
Rio Grande, gathering to invade. Moreover, Jameson and Neill were
energetic, and the engineer especially seemed anxious to strengthen
rather than destroy the fortifications. He fully believed that if attacked,
his artillery could repulse odds of 10 to 1. Of course Bowie had to
await receipt of Governor Smith's approval before he could carry out
Houston's demolition instructions, but until then—and on the chance
that the Mexicans might advance—he prudently allowed Neill and
Jameson to go ahead with emplacing the guns and strengthening the
works as manpower allowed.

Once more politics in San Felipe intervened. By the time Houston's
request for approval of his plan to destroy the Alamo and abandon
Béxar reached San Felipe, Smith and the council were at open war.
There was no one there to deal with Houston's communication
because council members had taken all official papers away from
Smith and refused to allow him to give any orders, supporting

Robinson instead. Houston, meanwhile, tamely stayed with Johnson and Grant, trying by persuasion to win back his army, and all but forgot the Béxar command for several days. Bowie, quite unwittingly, had stepped into a vacuum. In a situation like that, his own instinct was to take charge and act on his own initiative.

The more he studied the defenses of Béxar, especially the Alamo compound, the more Bowie's initiative suggested to him that this post was too promising to yield without a fight. After all, if Cós and his superiors thought it significant enough to endure a siege of more than a month, then the position meant something and should not be abandoned. Certainly only two principal roads made paths of invasion into Texas. The post at Goliad blocked one, and Béxar the other. Whether the forces of Johnson and Grant took Matamoros, or stopped at Copano as Houston wanted, or even remained at Goliad, no invasion by way of the Atascosita could get past them without a fight. But if their forces did advance to Copano or below, and San Antonio were abandoned, then a Mexican army coming into Texas by the Presidio de Río Grande could easily pass Béxar and suddenly be at Gonzales or even San Felipe, in their rear, cutting them off from supply and communications, and with unfettered opportunity to range about the Texian interior at will. San Antonio was the only place to stop such an invasion south of the Colorado, and maybe even south of the Brazos.

Besides, with Grant taking all the horses and draft animals when he left, Bowie and Neill had no means of hauling away all those prize cannon, and considering that the Alamo's complement of artillery was at that moment the largest west of the Mississippi, they could not afford simply to abandon the guns or disable them. Late on January 22 Neill and Bowie got a report that Santa Anna himself was coming, with three thousand men at Saltillo, while he had sixteen hundred more at Presidio de Río Grande. Faced with that news, Neill wrote to Smith saying that if he only had the teams, he would haul away the guns and evacuate at once to Copano. But then, as if to add more force to the logic of holding the place instead, Bowie got a report from Padre Garza that same day.

Immediately on coming back to San Antonio, Bowie reestablished the old relationships he had enjoyed in better days, and as the son-in-law of the respected and lamented Veramendi, he still commanded some respect in the town. Garza repeatedly confided in him, and a number of the townspeople became sources of information, though it is also possible that some hid their Mexican sympathies and intentionally gave him false intelligence. But not Garza, and now the priest told him that *tejanos* coming from the Rio Grande reported that the enemy intended to send its main advance against Copano and Goliad, where the principal Texian army would be found. The foe would send only a few hundred cavalry against San Antonio. Thus Béxar faced relatively little immediate danger. If its works were strengthened, and only a few reinforcements sent, one hundred or more men and those twenty cannon could certainly hold the Alamo against a few hundred mounted Mexicans.[91]

Inevitably politics inserted itself into the formula. San Antonio was a divided town, the Texians and many of the *tejanos* favoring the resistance, and even the almost inevitable declaration of independence, while the other *tejano* inhabitants remained loyal to the old Mexican regime, even if disturbed by Santa Anna's autocratic leanings. That alone provided cause for concern, and a deplorable weakness of internal security. But political dissatisfaction also gripped the garrison. Then, feeling isolated and forgotten, yet in danger as a forward outpost of the resistance, the volunteers realized that by being away from their homes, they would have no votes or voice in the coming election for delegates to the consultation to meet at Washington on March 1. On January 23 Neill wrote to Smith again asking for a writ of election to allow the volunteers to elect two representatives of their own to attend the convention, making it clear that "they are all in favor of Independence." Moreover, most of the citizens of Béxar asserted that they, too, wanted a break from Mexico, he said, and they all supported the beleaguered Smith himself as the properly constituted head of the provisional government.[92]

There is no question that by now Bowie, too, had come over to independence. His protest of loyalty to the 1824 constitution back in October may have been genuine at the time, but the persuasions of Houston and Smith must have exerted some influence on him in the meanwhile, encouraging his naturally independent leanings. Besides that, he had fought and risked his life for Texas now, and somehow that sort of thing demanded a higher cause than a return to some previous state of affairs. Then, too, by friendship and chance, he stood allied with Smith and Houston. If their side won the internal power struggle, and independence followed, James Bowie enjoyed the high regard of both and could expect it to accrue to his benefit in the future. He probably crossed the line by December, if not before. Bowie's own sense of self-interest surely contributed a full share to his decision, as it did with many of these men. But by now a species of budding patriotism motivated him as well. For all his scheming and avarice, he was not immune to more altruistic impulses. In 1815 he had enlisted in the Louisiana militia, prepared to risk his life in battle when he had as yet no property in land or slaves to defend, or at that time any prospect of future material gain to protect. He can only have been answering then the twin calls of youthful enthusiasm for adventure and the desire to protect his homeland—be it Louisiana or the United States—from an invader's heel. There is no reason to believe that those same engines did not drive him now, only fueled the more by his dreams of personal empire. There are few absolutely pure patriots, and few indeed among the leaders of the Texian uprising. But by any mature measure, James Bowie was a patriot nonetheless.

As if to punctuate Neill's expression of support, he called a meeting of the volunteers and interested citizens on January 26, Bowie among them. Calling attention to the political chaos at San Felipe, Neill suggested that they express their views, and appointed Bowie, Bonham, Jameson, Dr. Amos Pollard, Juan Seguín, and two others a committee to draft resolutions for discussion and a vote. They retired to deliberate, and then returned with a report that condemned the act of the council in trying to unseat the governor and abrogate his acts when they had no constitutional authority to do so, there being, of course, no constitution. Their originally mandated role was purely advisory. Moreover, the council had countenanced Grant's attempted usurpation of Houston's command. They had misappropriated money donated for the succor of the Béxar garrison, and "private and designing men" among them were seeking to reopen the land offices in order to continue speculating while other brave men ran the risks of the field. Bowie no doubt felt a special interest in that last charge.

In response to these grievances, the committee resolved that they should reaffirm their support for Smith as governor, that all of the usurpatory acts of the council were null, "anarchical assumptions of

power to which we will not submit," that they should call on
Houston's army to adopt similar resolutions, that the council had been
"in the highest degree criminal and unjust" in misappropriating money
intended for Béxar, that they repudiated Grant and all the officers of
his illegal expedition, and that Smith himself accept their thanks. In so
doing, said the resolutions, "yet under treatment however illiberal and
ungrateful, we cannot be driven from the post of Honor and the sacred
cause of freedom." Certainly Bowie's influence was apparent in the
forceful, even intemperate language used against the council and
Grant. And in that last sentiment about the "post of Honor" could be
read his own position on the most important issue of all. These were
more than resolutions. They were Béxar's declaration of independence
from the false authorities that ignored and abused the garrison. They
were also the irrevocable announcement of Bowie and the rest that so
long as this internal discord plagued the provisional government and
the rest of its forces, they intended to stay there, come what may.[93]

So Bowie decided to stand. He quartered in his old home at the
Veramendi house, where Ursula's adopted sister, Juana, lived with her
new husband, Horace Alsbury, and her sister Gertrudis. Bowie, though
quite literate, was not facile with a pen, and Alsbury acted as secretary,
writing his letters and passing the idle hours with him in conversation.[94]
Bowie stored his few belongings there for the time being. He also had
four mules to stable in town, and at least one and maybe two slaves
with him who had probably been in Béxar all along, including a cook.[95]
As soon as he arrived he began cultivating the *tejano* community again.
Some suspected him, the old braggart they remembered from earlier
days, and one or two at least believed that he really came only to prepare for another try at the San Saba treasure.[96] In fact, however, most
readily welcomed him back. Garza quickly became a main support in
the town, and Bowie began politicking with other leading *bexareños* to
bring them over to the revolutionary side, including Alcalde Francisco
Ruiz.[97] Within two weeks of his arrival, Bowie had cajoled the citizens
and their leaders sufficiently that he commented on their cooperative
attitude to Smith. In fact, there was no one else in Texas better
qualified to get cooperation from them than Bowie.[98] By January 30
Houston still had no answer to his suggestion of destroying the Alamo
and evacuating San Antonio, and now spoke of the possibility instead

of its being maintained.⁹⁹ In any event the volunteers at Béxar had all but taken the matter out of his hands so long as he could not enforce his orders. By February 1 they had held their election, choosing Samuel Maverick and Jesse Badgett to represent them in the coming consultation.¹⁰⁰ Now they were a political entity, one more encouragement to remain. Neill and Bowie pushed the work of the fortifications rapidly, and Bowie paid tribute to Neill's energy, saying that no other man in the army could have kept the command together as long as he had under the hardships it faced. The two of them used their imaginations in trying to raise funds to pay "the small but necessary expenses of our men," with no success. They pleaded with Smith to send some money if he could. Bowie assumed from the outset that if the enemy did approach, then they would be besieged, and so they all worked long hours laying in as much of corn and beans and other foodstuffs as possible.

To that end Bowie wrote to Smith on February 2 to implore that "relief at this post in men, money and provision is of *vital* importance." He could not stress the point enough. "The salvation of Texas depends on keeping Béxar out of the hands of the enemy," he said. He had good reports that the foe was marshaling in strength on the Rio Grande, and now his latest intelligence suggested that more than just a few hundred might move on San Antonio. He kept small parties of mounted volunteers out as far as the Rio Frio, fifty miles southwest, to keep watch. They brought no word of an advance as yet, but it might only be a matter of days before his scouts spotted the van of an advancing army.

Bowie and Neill decided by now what they must do. "We will rather die in these ditches, than give it up to the enemy," Bowie told Smith. "Public safety demands our lives rather than evacuate this post to the enemy." He expected a few volunteers to be coming in within a few days, but he needed a large reinforcement with ample provisions. The muster that day showed only 120 men and officers. "It would be a waste of men to put our brave little band against thousands," he pleaded. "Again we call loud for *relief.*" Until such reinforcements arrived, he and Neill would continue encouraging the men, scavenging for supplies, and watching for the enemy. Just before Bowie closed the letter a scout brought him fresh news that the enemy at the Presidio de

Río Grande now numbered 2,000, with up to 5,000 more marching north through Mexico to join them. "There is no doubt," he added, that their objective was Béxar.

For a man who never before showed a sense either of understatement or irony, Bowie revealed a sudden inspiration of both when he closed his letter to Smith. "We have no interesting news to communicate," he said. But then maybe it was not so ironic after all. For James Bowie, the man who single-handedly fought several at the Sandbar, who drove away perhaps 100 on the San Saba, who led 92 against 200 or more at Concepción and faced even greater odds in the Grass Fight—for Bowie, the man who tried to steal a kingdom in Louisiana and Arkansas, then tried to buy an empire in Texas—for Big Jim, who dreamed of a seat in Congress and who thought nothing of confronting the mighty in Washington when they stood in his way—for a man like James Bowie—the prospect of 120 ragged volunteers and twenty cannon facing 2,000 or more well-fed and -equipped Mexican soldiers, many of them seasoned professionals, simply may not have been enough to make what he called "interesting news."[101]

TRAVIS

1835–February 23, 1836

I am determined to defend it to the last, and should Bejar fall, your friend will be buried beneath its ruins.

WILLIAM BARRET TRAVIS, FEBRUARY 12, 1836

Travis had no sooner unpacked his saddle bags in San Felipe than Texas claimed him again. On December 1 or 2 a member of the permanent council approached him with a question. The military committee needed advice on the organization of a proper army for the defense of Texas. Austin was gone, most of the other experienced company commanders were either resigned and gone home, or still with the army in Béxar, and Travis may have been the only experienced officer from the army readily at hand, or the only one trusted. Nevertheless, with the caveat that "my military experience is so limited," he drafted on December 3 a comprehensive organizational plan to go before the council.

Travis knew that Fannin had already sent in a proposal for a "regular," or professional force, and thus since he wholeheartedly endorsed Fannin's outline, Travis confined himself to the volunteer forces, those to be raised during the time of emergency, and then released. Texas must have a *dependable* volunteer army ready and equipped to take the field at a moment's notice. He suggested enlisting 1,000 to 1,600 men for a brigade, and one battalion of cavalry numbering 160 to 180, plus officers. The cavalry should be armed with broadswords, pistols, and double-barreled shotguns. A lieutenant colonel ought to command them, and he should report directly to Houston rather than through any intermediary officer. "I consider that such a Battalion as I have indicated, is indispensible to the service of Texas during the present struggle," he said. "Do you wish to get information of the movements of a distant enemy? Cut of[f] supplies of the enemy? Harrass an invading army by hanging upon his rear, or forming ambushcades in his front? Do you wish to carry the war into the enemie's country as has been indicated?" If so, they needed cavalry. "In an word, all the brilliant military exploits which have ever been performed in time & which we read of in the history of nations, have been accomplished by celerity of movement, promptness of action."

Travis made little attempt to conceal his own enthusiasm for the cavalry, and the unexpressed message in his report fairly screamed that he wished to be its commander. "A storm is impending over us," he warned. "The time that is 'to try men's souls' is yet to come."[1] The council shared his sense of urgency, and within two weeks deliberated on a bill incorporating substantially his recommendations for the "permanent" volunteer army, men to be enlisted and serve not for a specified time, but for the duration of the war. Even before that, however, the council revealed its other plans for Travis. It had been some time since he had seen Rebecca Cummings, and shortly after sending his ideas to the council, he rode out to Cummings Mill to stay several days. He was with her on December 17 when news of several events reached him at the same time. Along with seemingly everyone else, he favored the idea of an expedition to take Matamoros, and now news of impending plans—Houston assigned Bowie to the operation that very day—persuaded him to reiterate to Lieutenant Governor Robinson his support. "I intend to join the expedition if one is gotten up," he said, "and I will execute to the best of my ability any command which the council may see proper to confer on me."

Travis knew he could expect a command because of the other news that came that day. Even while deliberating on the volunteer forces, the council organized the regular army of Texas, and that included a regiment of artillery. It chose Fannin as colonel, James Neill for lieutenant colonel, and Travis learned that he had been commissioned its major. Flattered though he was, he did not welcome the news. "I could not be so useful in the artillery as elsewhere," he explained.[2] Indeed, appointing Travis to the artillery did seem an ill-conceived idea, since his sole experience with cannon was loading one aboard the *Ohio* for the Anahuac raid. Moreover, he certainly had more practical field experience—limited though it was—than Fannin, while Neill out-stripped both of them in artillery expertise.

More than anything else, these appointments represented compro-mises in the council. There were better commissions to be had, but some members felt that if they gave out all the best ranks in the regu-lar services now, it might discourage experienced officers from the U.S. Army from resigning and coming to Texas to take commands, and they counted heavily on attracting such men of proven military education and talent. At the same time, the council was bitterly divided between Austin and Houston adherents. Fannin, at the moment, was a Houston man, also heavily identified with Frank Johnson and James Grant and the speculating faction that seemed to command a slight majority in the council. Neill, the most qualified, had no such base of support on the council, and Travis must in part have owed his appoint-ment to the need of the majority on the council to appease in some measure the Henry Smith—Austin faction.[3]

But it did not matter in any case, for Travis immediately wrote to Robinson with a polite but firm refusal of the post. Beyond question, he was holding out for a cavalry command, and since the regular army did not include a mounted arm, he wanted the company of volunteers that he had suggested to the military affairs committee. In the end he got it. On December 19 the council created the Legion of Cavalry, and the next day unanimously selected Travis to hold commission as lieu-tenant colonel in command. The act mandated a force of 384 men and officers, divided into six companies, and the council also appointed the captains, including Robert Wilson and Juan Seguín, though Seguín never accepted his appointment. An appointment as first lieutenant went to James Butler Bonham, the South Carolinian born near Travis's boyhood home, who may possibly have known him, or at least who he was, during their childhood.[4]

This appointment Travis accepted as quickly as offered. The act even specified the uniform of his legion, suits of cadet gray, cowhide boots, black cloth neck stocks, and fur caps, though uniforms were a long way in the future just then. The only adjustment the council made in Travis's recommendation was to call for six rather than four compa-nies, with nearly double the number of men, and only half of them armed with shotguns, while the rest were to carry rifles. The result was the creation of a much larger unit, combining the mobility of cavalry, with the firepower of infantry. If Travis ever raised the full complement of his command, he would lead a force nearly as large as Austin's army when it first approached the Cibolo.

Travis's commission was confirmed on December 24, and on that day he took his oath, and at a time when so much was being done in a communications vacuum, that some seemed uncertain of just what Travis's command involved.[5] Houston called the new unit the "First Regiment of Cavalry," and thought it was in the regular army rather than the volunteers. At the same time, he seemed to be under the impression that Travis's new commission was as a colonel, and in the infantry.[6] Meanwhile, down in Matagorda, on the coast one Texian official thought Travis might be available as a lawyer to settle a shipping dispute.[7] The confusion for many only disappeared early in January when the *Telegraph and Texas Register* actually published the roll of officers of the legion.[8]

There was little time to lose on confusion and cross-purposes. On Christmas Day San Felipe got information from San Antonio, dated December 18, of an advance toward Texas by a large contingent of Mexican *soldados*, on its way both to relieve and avenge Cós's loss of Béxar. At once the military committee ordered Fannin to go to the west and take command of the volunteers until recently commanded by Burleson, and at the same time gave Travis instructions to go immediately to the frontier with all the volunteers he could gather.[9] The weeks of confusion over the ill-fated Matamoros expedition ensued, but happily Travis stayed out of that, for he had more pressing matters.

He may have been lieutenant colonel of the mounted legion, but it was a unit in name only until he could recruit the men to fill its ranks. There was no recruiting service. Each commander had to raise his own volunteers, and the council made no appropriation for recruiting expenses until December 21, when it voted for forty thousand dollars, which mostly it did not have.[10] Houston gave Travis orders on December 23 to make his headquarters in San Felipe and immediately start recruiting, directing further that Travis send his captains off into the countryside to recruit, and even that he send one or more of them to Louisiana and Mississippi to raise their companies, all to return and rendezvous by March 1, 1836.[11] Travis quickly sent Bonham to San

Antonio to try to recruit among the informal volunteers there, and then to proceed to Goliad.[12] Travis himself would stay in San Felipe.

The work of raising his men tasked Travis more stressfully than anything he had done since moving to Texas. The council did at least allow him some enlistment inducements, including a 640-acre land bounty, plus a bonus of an additional 160 acres and twenty-four dollars, though only half of the money was to be paid in hand on signing up, and the land itself would not be forthcoming until—and unless—Texas won its independence.[13] Feeding and clothing the men once they did take their twelve dollars and give their oath presented an equal challenge. In January he personally initiated ordering the uniforms and equipment for his men through Thomas McKinney, and met with McKinney personally to place an order for his own military clothing, which he apparently designed himself in the absence of any legislation covering officers' uniforms.[14] As the number of his volunteers slowly grew, he had to purchase food and gear for them personally, furnishing merchants an order against the provisional government, and sometimes the necessary articles proved hard to find, as everyone was scouring the shops and countryside.[15] When forced to, he used his own credit to buy what he needed.[16] Travis himself arrived back from the Béxar siege to find that one of his own horses had been impressed by the military in his absence, and now he resorted once more to impressment himself to get at least one of his men mounted.[17]

The worst challenge of all was finding the men. They simply did not come forward. "Volunteers can no longer be had or relied upon," he complained to Smith, and by late in January he began to believe that only an enforced conscription could raise the men needed to defend Texas. "In consequence of dissentions between contending and rival chieftains, they have lost all confidence in their own govt. & officers," he lamented, thinking in part of the controversy over the Matamoros expedition, but also of the battle within the provisional government.[18] The situation had become bad enough that Travis actually resorted to deception to persuade enlistees. He told Edward Wood that "the surest chance for a commission in the army was to enlist in the Cavalry Corps," and promised that if Wood signed up with him he would have a priority claim on promotion, actually promising him elevation within a few days. Wood gullibly enlisted under those terms, but two days later when Travis roused him from slumber to drill under what Wood called "some Corporal Sergeant or other inferior officer," the recruit rebelled. He reminded Travis of his promise of speedy promotion, and insisted on being released from service if Travis could not keep the bargain. Travis simply refused. He needed every man, and apparently did not scruple at how he got them.[19]

All the while, with the prospect of a long campaign ahead of him, Travis also had to pay some attention to his personal affairs. The partnership with Willis Nibbs had not worked out, and it expired on January 20.[20] Unattended business accumulated. He had an inventory of notes he had been engaged to collect, and not yet seen to. Suits needed investigation. There were wills and estates to look after. Travis certainly knew even before the partnership expired that he could not handle this himself while absent with his command.[21] He needed another partner, and happily found one just in time. Franklin J. Starr had come from Georgia in 1834, looked around Texas, then returned home again, only to leave in November 1835 for the Brazos area once more, arriving in January 1836. He had been unable to resist the lure of the new country, though he wavered for a time until his friends told him to go. "Your ruling passion is avarice," one told Starr playfully, borrowing Crockett's idiom. "Well, go ahead! for that is the only true philosophy which teaches that to be continually active in *endeavoring* to acquire that which we do not possess is the road to happiness." Even as Starr and Travis formed their partnership, his brother in Georgia wrote to remind him that "Crocket's motto is the best that can be devised."[22]

Starr brought much to the practice, including a nice store of new law texts, including Archbold's *Pleadings*, Crabbe's English law, *Peake on Evidence*, and other references on criminal and civil law, Louisiana statutes, a Spanish legal digest, and more.[23] That alone was helpful, but Starr's energy proved even more useful, as he went to work quickly settling the accumulated unfinished business.[24] It would have been a boon if Starr could have addressed some of Travis's own personal business as well, for his debts and other affairs had been just as much neglected. He owed a fair bit of money, $850 here, $100 there, his $80 house rental, another $112 for board for himself and a Mexican he employed, and more. He owed a little to Moseley Baker, had accepted responsibility for a debt of Noah Smithwick's, and even gave his note for $600 for the purchase of a slave woman, perhaps to help in caring for Charles and his house. He also owned other slaves. One named Joe he kept with him as a personal servant, but there was the man John, who needed to be hired out. The total of his financial affairs was not too great for a man of Travis's means by now, but he could not afford to neglect such things.[25] The oldest piece of unfinished business on his personal docket finally reached resolution now, and he possibly learned of it this month while still in San Felipe, or else he certainly knew it was in train. The previous November 27 his former colleague the lawyer Arthur Bagby in Claiborne, now in the Alabama legislature, arose and presented the record and proceedings in the "case of Rosanna E. Travis against William B. Travis." It went to the committee on divorce and alimony, and they shortly reported a bill to effect the divorce. On January 8, 1836 the senate passed the bill, and the next day the house did likewise. As of January 9, 1836, by Act no. 115, five years of matrimonial limbo came to an end with the decree that "said Rosanna E. Travis be henceforth divorced from her husband."[26]

Certainly Travis knew it was coming, as he and Rosanna no doubt continued to correspond insofar as necessary because of the children, and Travis also kept in touch with William Cato. If he felt any delight or relief at the prospect of final divorce, whenever or if ever he got the news, there was no time for celebration other than a brief visit to Rebecca to assure her that soon they could wed. There was too much else to do. Indeed, with the demands of his official duty, he largely had to forgo his personal life. As opportunity afforded he continued to encourage Protestant preachers coming to San Felipe, and actually came out and denounced the enforced Catholicism of the past as part of the tyranny of a "bigotted clergy."[27] He still promoted education in Texas, gladly providing public endorsements of Miss L. A. McHenry's Montville Boarding School for Young Ladies.[28] It helped that the academy shared quarters about forty miles northwest of San Felipe in the home of David Ayers, a good friend whom Travis recommended on January 3, 1836, to be appointed comptroller of the treasury in the provisional government.[29] Moreover, Miss McHenry taught more than just young ladies. She taught the Ayers children, too, and Travis now enrolled his son, Charles, under her tutelage. Travis even found time, perhaps one evening at Peyton's or Winburn's, to sit quietly for a few minutes with his friend Wiley Martin, currently political chief for the Brazos department but keeping his office in San Felipe. Martin had a Tennessee gazetteer, and on one of its empty flyleaves he sketched a rough, but not unpleasant portrait of Travis, the only likeness from life ever made.[30]

The inevitable politics certainly attracted some of Travis's fleeting attention, and almost ensnared him in the most divisive issue of the day. On January 22 the council issued orders that all official papers be forcibly taken from Smith's possession as part of the attempt to impeach him. It named twelve men to perform the task, but nine of them, Travis included, refused, and that greatly reduced what little regard he still felt for the council or any of its pet projects.[31] Much as he loved political life, the unseemly infighting in San Felipe just now must have made him yearn to take the field.

Time and events conspired to force Travis to leave long before he was ready, regardless of his wishes. On the same day that the announcement of his new partnership appeared in the local press, the *Telegraph and Texas Register* published a January 14 letter from Neill at Béxar with the news that the Mexicans were certainly going to advance on San Antonio.[32] Meanwhile Houston had advised Governor Smith of the growing crisis on January 17, intimating the necessity of concentrating all available troops on the frontier, and a few days later San Felipe received Green Jameson's January 18 statement of the condition of the garrison at Béxar. Travis already had orders from the council to leave as soon as he raised his company. No specific destination had been stated, but the intent was Matamoros, and on January 9 the council rescinded those instructions. On January 21, however, Smith gave him a definite order to collect one hundred volunteers and leave for Béxar as soon as possible. In fact he had a mere twenty-six men, but he must leave now, and he must go to the relief of San Antonio.[33]

As soon as Travis got his orders that day he began buying whatever he could for the trip: flour, tin pans, twine, a pair of leggings and spurs, a powder flask for his pistols, a new bridle, blankets and a tent, and even a flag.[34] He had expected to be able to leave in two days, but delays in securing provisions detained him until January 24 before he finally packed his own necessaries in old leather saddlebags with "Wm Barret Travis" on the flaps in his own handwriting, and put the command on the road. Riding along with him as a personal aide was young Charles Despallier, the brother of Bowie's old associate from Opelousas. They got only as far as Beeson's Ferry on the Colorado, twenty miles west of San Felipe.[35] There for the next few days he halted his men, while he and perhaps a few others rode some distance through the countryside visiting every available merchant to buy more provisions, a horse for one of his men, and even saddles and bridles. Along the way he also forcibly took into the service one animal without payment, and then virtually impressed a man into the company to ride the beast, paying the enlistment bounty out of his own pocket. Travis had received only $100 from the government to cover expenses for the journey, and as a result charged much of what he bought to his personal credit, totaling at least $143.[36]

By January 28 Travis was still on the Colorado, having moved twenty miles upstream to Burnham's Ferry, where he made much more substantial purchases.[37] He seemed to be delaying, in part perhaps because of exhaustion, for he had not gotten a full night's sleep since leaving San Felipe. His spirits sank deeper and deeper as the days passed, and he would have given much to be free of this assignment. Then no sooner did he reach Burnham's than eight of his men deserted, taking three horses and two guns with them. "I have done every thing in my power to get ready to march to the relief of Béxar," he groaned in a letter to Smith that morning. Shortages of animals and equipment, desertions, everything seemed to conspire to retard his progress. Even with last-minute enlistments and impressments, he only counted thirty men in his command. He gave strong hints that he would prefer to be ordered to return to San Felipe, for he could accomplish nothing for the good of Béxar with this little command. Indeed, it may have been as much the fear of looking foolish—a lieutenant colonel leading a "legion" of thirty—that lay behind his disillusionment. "I shall however, go on & do my duty, if I am sacrificed," he said. "Our affairs are gloomy indeed. The people are cold & indifferent. They are worn down & exhausted with the war." Without money to enlist men and equip them properly, he feared the cause might be hopeless. "The patriotism of a few has done much; but that is becoming worn down." Hoping that Houston might be persuaded to call a halt to his seemingly pointless expedition, Travis asked Smith to show him the letter if the general was in San Felipe.[38]

Travis intended to press on that afternoon but seemed unable to get the command or himself moving, and was still there the next day. He wrote to Smith yet again, this time making his wishes unmistakable. This expedition was pointless. "I must beg that your excellency will recall the order for me to go on to Béxar in command of so few men," he pleaded. "I am unwilling to risk my reputation (which is ever dear to a soldier) by going off into the enemie's country with such little means, so few men, & them too badly equipped." And now he revealed just how much of his displeasure turned on his own pride and dignity, pleading that this little command only merited a captain, not a lieutenant colonel. If Smith or Houston so desired, he would be happy to "visit" Béxar or any other post to consult with the officers in command, "but I do not feel disposed to go to command a squad of men, & without the means of carrying on a campaign." He would be more useful back in San Felipe recruiting than on this fool's errand. If Smith did not give him orders relieving him of this assignment, he threatened to resign, and to emphasize the gravity of the situation he sent his quartermaster to Smith to explain in person.[39]

Travis's attitude did not do him credit. In his exhaustion and frustration, there reemerged that other part of his personality that he had done so much to outgrow—the petulant, priggish, even self-pitying and decidedly immature Travis. Now, for all of his months of patriotic exhortations to everyone else that no sacrifice was too great for the cause of Texas, he found his own pride more important to him than his duty, and even presumed to bargain with his superiors. To ease his frustration, while here at Burnham's he took the opportunity to make the twenty-five-mile ride north to Montville to see his son. It was a brief visit, perhaps, but a pleasant one. Travis read for a time in the Ayers home, until little Charles came up to him and whispered into his father's ear that he wanted fifty cents. "My son, what do you want with four-bits?" asked Travis. "To buy a bottle of molasses from Mrs. Scott to make some candy," the six-year-old replied. Travis handed him the coin, but it fell to the floor and rolled away, Charles running after it until it was safely in his palm. That evening, after Travis rode back to Burnham's, Charles and the other children had their candy, and his father had at least one pleasant memory from this dispiriting journey.[40]

Travis left Burnham's about February 1 and moved south to the main road for Gonzales. He had formed the men with him now into a company under Capt. John Forsyth, and originally intended to keep them pressing on toward Béxar, while he would himself wait at Gonzales or some other point on the road to receive orders. But then he apparently changed his mind and actually left the command to ride ahead independently, a lone rider being able to move faster than a company with its impedimenta. Perhaps he decided to proceed to Béxar to see the situation for himself, without waiting for Forsyth and the men. Travis may have met a courier from Neill along the way, carrying the Béxar commander's January 28 dispatch with the news that two thousand Mexicans were seen massing on the Rio Grande, preparing to invade. Neill certainly needed Travis and his company to reconnoiter south along the anticipated route of invasion, as well as to harass the Mexican supply lines.[41] Learning this from the courier could have induced Travis to hurry ahead to see the situation. Before leaving Gonzales he sent Despallier back to San Felipe with a dispatch presumably telling Smith where he would be.[42] When Forsyth reached Gonzales on February 2, Travis had probably already left. Indeed, traveling that evening under a full moon, by then he was only hours away from Béxar.[43]

When Travis rode into San Antonio on February 3 he got his first look at the town from the other side of the Mexican fortifications.[44] Indeed, he may never have set foot in Béxar before now. What he found was a shabby place, all but denuded by Grant and Johnson of anything edible, rideable, or valuable, and a tired garrison of 120 volunteers remaining from the November–December siege, many of them not properly enlisted in the new volunteer forces and under no obligation to remain. The town's narrow streets ran crookedly back from the San Antonio River, lined on either side with plastered and whitewashed one-story stone and adobe houses, and a number of rude mud hovels. In the center of town sat the Plaza de Armas, between Potrero and Dolorosa Streets, and just east of it was the Plaza de Las Yslas, where Soledad Street crossed the other two. One block north on Soledad was the Veramendi house, where Bowie now stayed, its garden backing down to the San Antonio River. Potrero continued on from Soledad some distance to a deep bend in the river, and on the other side, several hundred yards from the stream, sat the Alamo.

Travis reported to Neill before doing anything else, learning the latest news of the Mexican army on the Rio Grande. Telling Neill that his company would not arrive for another day or two, Travis could do nothing about the reconnaissance work at the moment, and besides, Bowie or others may have been out doing the same work already. Travis took a room in the city, probably near headquarters on the Plaza de Las Yslas, and set about learning something of the post and the garrison.[45] Naturally the first lesson was one in politics. This garrison was just as intensely politicized as any other group of Texians at the moment, though for a change they enjoyed a wonderful unanimity. The discordant and speculating elements had left with Grant and Johnson, and almost all of those remaining stood behind Governor Smith in his struggle with the council. They sent a resolution to that effect to Smith on January 26, and just two days before Travis's arrival held their election for delegates to represent them in the coming consultation to meet at Washington on March 1. In fact one of Travis's very first acts on arriving was to append his name to the petition of citizens and soldiers that Neill sent out February 4, asking the convention to seat their elected delegates, Samuel Maverick and Jesse Badgett.[46] Travis himself signed almost at the very last, as lieutenant colonel of cavalry. Having neither rank nor command, Bowie signed immediately after him with just his name and nothing more.

Now at last Travis and Bowie were to serve more intimately together, and in the next few days they became truly acquainted, probably for the first time. No doubt Bowie told Travis of the letter he sent Smith on February 2, stating his resolve and Neill's that they would not abandon the post, but would take a stand there, hoping to force the governor and council to send more reinforcements. The arrival of Travis and the coming of Forsyth and the rest of the cavalry on February 5 were a start, but they needed far more, and Travis fully agreed.[47]

They got more a day or two after they prepared the petition for Maverick and Badgett. Someone brought Bowie a message that there were horsemen in the Mexican graveyard just west of town, and he and Menchaca immediately rode out in the rain to see who it might be. In fact it was David Crockett.[48] Like the course of his life, his trail from Nacogdoches to Béxar had been a wandering one, seemingly oblivious of the manpower emergency in Neill's garrison. He left Nacogdoches in a large company on January 16, and their path on the La Bahía naturally brought them to Washington in a few days. By the time they arrived, there were just Crockett and four others, the rest either going on faster, or more likely lagging behind to hunt. His cousin John Harris was with him, along with Micajah Autry, Daniel Cloud, and B. Archer Thomas. Crockett himself took his time, probably exploring a bit of the country looking for likely headright claims while making his way in a desultory fashion. Only during his stay in Washington on January 22–24 did he get word—as Houston did—of Neill's situation at Béxar and the anticipated Mexican advance.[49]

It may have been on learning this that Crockett himself left on January 24, leaving Thomas behind to catch up.[50] Late that afternoon he approached the James Swisher home at Gay Hill, not far from Montville, spending a convivial night talking of hunting with his host, and joking about a shooting contest with his son John Swisher. Crockett captivated both father and son. "Few could eclipse him in conversation," John remembered. "He was fond of talking, and had an ease and grace about him which, added to his strong natural sense and the fund of anecdotes that he had gathered, rendered him irrestible." Many of the stories he told seemed to have no point, "were common place and amounted to nothing in themselves, but his inimitable way of telling them would convulse one with laughter." Crockett stayed an extra night or two, and they rarely went to bed before midnight as he regaled his hosts with his tales. When Thomas caught up with him at last, they moved on toward Béxar.[51]

Crockett traveled in simple riding clothes, no buckskins or Nimrod Wildfire regalia, but he must still have looked a bit eccentric wearing an old top hat. The nights were cold in this season, and even the days occasionally, and an old beaver like that offered no warmth to the reddening ears of a man on horseback. He gladly traded the impractical headgear for a fur hat when he got the chance, and that kept him much the warmer on the balance of the ride.[52] Thereafter he continued his gradual progress, toward Mina at first, then south to the main road to San Antonio, passing through Gonzales.[53] He may have turned south for a time, thinking to join the volunteers gathering around Houston at Goliad, but ultimately spurred his horse toward Béxar until he arrived in a drizzle in that quiet graveyard.[54]

Bowie and Menchaca brought Crockett and his companions into the town and took him first to Don Erasmo Seguín's home, though thereafter he found quarters near the Plaza de Armas.[55] Naturally the garrison hailed the unexpected arrival of this genuine American legend, even if he only came with a handful of men instead of the army they needed. Simply for the sake of morale his arrival proved a boon. Before long Neill summoned the garrison and the citizens joined the party in the Plaza de Las Yslas, and Crockett stood atop a packing box to make the inevitable speech. He told yet again the now-dusty "go to hell" quip and many other "jolly anecdotes," as Dr. John Sutherland recalled from what he heard. In the end Crockett turned serious. "Me and my Tennessee boys, have come to Help Texas as privates," he said, "and will try to do our duty."[56]

In fact Crockett *was* no more than a private, a situation that some no doubt thought inappropriate to say the least. While the so-called Tennessee Mounted Volunteers with whom he rode naturally looked to him as their leader during their journey, the fact remained that they were not an officially organized unit. Indeed, at least one in the party had actually enlisted in another company after they left Nacogdoches, and so Neill was now at liberty to assign them within his command as he wished, and put Crockett and the others in the company of Capt. William Patton—no relation to Crockett's nephew of the same name.

Yet if Crockett did not hold actual rank, everyone recognized his symbolic importance. Green Jameson reported his arrival to Henry Smith, and Bowie introduced Crockett to his brother-in-law, Horace Alsbury.[57] And on February 10 the officers put together an impromptu fandango in his honor, inviting the ladies of the town to attend a dance that went on into the early hours of the next day. At 1 A.M., while the party still reveled to the fiddle and guitar, Bowie walked over to his friend Menchaca, whom he saw reading a letter. He gave it to Bowie, and while he read, Travis approached. When Bowie handed over the letter, Travis playfully complained that he had no time for reading, for he was just then dancing with the most lovely lady in San Antonio. Bowie suggested that the letter was important enough for Travis to forgo the dance, and when Travis took it he read it aloud, translating the Spanish for Crockett and others. Benavides, scouting near Camargo, nearly 200 miles south on the Rio Grande, sent confirmation that Santa Anna himself had his army at Presidio de Rio Grande, ready to advance. In two weeks the Mexicans could travel the

140 miles to San Antonio, and perhaps sooner. Benavides's dispatch was already four days old, which meant they might have only ten days. But there was nothing to be done then. "Let us dance to-night," said Travis, "and to-morrow we will make provisions for our defense."[58]

While Crockett served in the ranks, and Bowie held no real portfolio as yet, Travis had command concerns to consider even before the word arrived of the Mexicans's coming. He needed to get to know the other officers, though he knew Green Jameson, at least, since he once acted for a creditor to collect a debt from him.[59] Then after Forsyth and the rest of the legion arrived on February 5, he had to spend some time— and some of his own money—providing them with fodder for the animals and a little cash for the men.[60] Naturally he had to be concerned about what was happening back in San Felipe, for that would govern what he was to do here, and how long he must stay. On January 31 the council finally learned of Houston's request to have the Alamo blown up and the place evacuated, and immediately sent an express off to Béxar to countermand it, though Bowie and Neill clearly never regarded it as a direct order in the first place.[61] When that rider arrived, possibly the same day as Travis, Buck knew that now he was to stay here for awhile unless he followed through on his threat to resign.

By February 11 affairs started to change rapidly, and dramatically. The garrison still backed Governor Smith in his battle with the council, though now it was charging him with giving orders to Travis after it had unlawfully tried to remove him from office.[62] "Politics are all straight here," Jameson wrote to Smith that day, "and every man in the Army your friend." Unfortunately, some of those volunteers intended to start leaving on February 12, disenchanted from lack of pay and clothing and even provisions for the past two months. Recent additions brought their force up to 150 as of that day, but it would not last if the men began going home. Even worse, Neill left now, responding to an urgent message of illness in his family. He would be back in three weeks, he said, though the garrison urged him not to leave. At his departure he put Travis in command.[63]

Suddenly Travis went from near humiliation at the paltriness of his legion to command of Béxar, and from that moment on he dropped all

pressure to be relieved. As next ranking officer in the service, he naturally assumed command on Neill's departure, but almost immediately
he felt himself cast in a delicate situation. The only men by regulations
subject to him as an officer were those who had enlisted under the
December 1835 acts of the council creating the regular and volunteer
services. Yet perhaps half of the garrison or more were men simply
remaining from the old informal volunteer companies that besieged
Béxar, men who remained solely out of desire rather than legal obligation. They had stayed with Neill, no doubt, because he was a known
quantity, having been with them most of the time for months now.
Travis was new, however, and in the pleadings of some of the volunteers for Neill to stay, he interpreted their dissatisfaction at his being the
colonel's replacement. He could show them his commission, which he
had brought with him, as evidence of his right to command, but that
would hardly matter to these men.[64] Moreover, Travis took command
by Neill's request—though military procedure of course dictated that as
next in seniority of rank he would do so anyhow—and he feared that
the volunteer portion of the garrison might not accept him unless some
positive order came from Smith or Houston for him to command.[65]

It was a delicate situation, and it soon became even more so. While one
company said they would accept him as their commander, two others
made it clear that they objected to his commanding them because he was
a regular, while they had served from the previous October in an army
that had popularly elected its commander—first Austin, then Burleson.
They had a point, frustrating though it was, and Travis took the only reasonable expedient available at the moment. He told them that they could
elect their own commander, and Travis and their choice would share the
command in Béxar. Any other option risked a confrontation that would
see scores of the men simply leave, with Travis powerless to stop them
short of arrest. At least if they chose their own commander, they would
be appeased, and might stay on until the mess in San Felipe was cleared
and some genuine direction could come from Smith. Houston was no
good to Travis in this situation either, for he had given up on his Goliad
mission and was now off on a near-pointless trip to see the Indian tribes
to conclude treaties to keep them out of the war.[66]

So there would be an election. There were only two obvious candidates. Some of the volunteers wanted Crockett to accept the post. After

all, he was "Colonel" Crockett, and he had war experience, which most of them no doubt had heard greatly exaggerated versions of in recent years. When they approached him, however, he refused. "I have come to assist Travis as a high Private," he said.[67] He made a wise choice, whether he knew it or not, because there were undercurrents here he knew nothing about. Then, too, having tried to conceal his elevation above private during the Creek War, he may well have thought it unseemly for him to accept any form of rank now. Moreover, a somewhat larger proportion of the volunteers preferred Bowie, and it was obvious from the first that he would be elected. He may even have politicked among the men for the position. Certainly he had their confidence as a fighter. When the ballots were cast, Bowie was "Colonel" Bowie once more, though of the four companies of volunteers present, possibly only two actually voted. Clearly this was no mandate.[68] Though Travis's solution to the problem seemed reasonable, it quickly foundered on problems inherent in the arrangement, exacerbated by Bowie's behavior. No one was completely in charge. Bowie would not obey Travis, and Travis certainly would not yield to Bowie, and so the garrison divided into somewhat unfriendly camps. On February 12 Adjt. J. J. Baugh saw that Bowie, "availing himself of his popularity among the volunteers seemd anxious to arrogate to himself the entire control." By the next day the situation had become intolerable, precipitated mainly by Bowie unfortunately choosing his election as an event worth celebrating with a two-day drunk. When he saw some of the citizens trying to leave the town with their belongings on their carts in fear of the advancing Mexican army, he forcibly detained them.

Then he fomented trouble with his old friend Judge Erasmo Seguín, when he ordered a convicted *tejano* thief to be released from jail, even though both Bowie and Travis had sat on the jury that convicted him. Seguín sent him back to the *calabozo*, but when Bowie learned of that he lost his temper and furiously confronted the judge. When Seguín refused to back down, Bowie sent for troops and ostentatiously paraded them in the main square in what Baugh called "a tumultuously and disorderly manner, Bowie himself, and many of his men, being drunk—which has been the case ever since he has been in command." Then Bowie ordered the release of a private from Travis's company of regulars, a man convicted of mutiny, and issued a general order that all prisoners were to be released and assigned to labor details instead.[69] That provoked Travis to go to Seguín himself in protest, and then to write to Governor Smith in exasperation, supported in part by a statement from Crockett.[70]

Travis actually sent his protest about Bowie to his old law partner Nibbs, to be handed to Smith, for fear that in being addressed directly to the beleaguered governor it might instead fall into the hands of the council, doing potentially considerable harm. "My situation is truly awkward & delicate," he complained. "I do not solicit the command of this Post," he said. Indeed, now he would be happy to yield it to any other artillery officer Smith could send, but he begged for some definite orders. Bowie had "been roaring drunk all the time," and "turning every thing topsy turvey." Travis only remained because honor required him to obey his orders, but he warned Smith that "I am unwilling to be responsible for the drunken irregularities of any man." He implored Smith to send more regulars as soon as possible. Otherwise Bowie and his volunteers might run roughshod indefinitely over his two companies of regulars, the legion and the artillery company.[71] Travis may have been disposed to be rather more intolerant of Bowie's behavior thanks to his own views on drinking. If he drank at all it was only moderately, while his prominence in the Claiborne Temperance Society several years earlier may have meant that he abstained altogether. But whether Travis was a teetotaler or not did not matter. Bowie's behavior was abominable.

Just what impelled Bowie so to misbehave is unclear. Maybe the celebration simply got out of hand. Then, too, he may have been on a long-term binge going back to his drunk in San Felipe in November. Perhaps already he did not feel well, not his usual robust self, and used the liquor to deaden his senses. Maybe he just felt like getting drunk. Whatever the reason, his timing could not have been worse, for his drunkenness encouraged it in the other volunteers. Some men even sold their rifles to get money for liquor, and Samuel Bastian maintained, perhaps not entirely hyperbolically, that "most of the garrison were drunk," adding that "there was a bitter feeling between the partisans of Travis and Bowie, the latter being the choice of the rougher party in the garrison."[72] The situation actually created sufficient animosity between the two factions in the command that Travis did the only sensible thing. He ordered the regulars to accompany him, and they left the town to camp a few miles southwest on the Medina to escape what Baugh called "this disgraceful business." Otherwise there seemed to be the very real risk of violent clashes between the factions.[73] But then as quickly as it arose, the problem seemed to evaporate, and that was probably due to Bowie. "It is well known that he sometimes drank too much," recalled William W. Fontaine, who was one of the little children at Montville with Charles Travis. "But it is not so generally known how quickly he hastened to make the *amende honorable*, so soon as he came from under the influence of liquor." On February 14 Bowie sobered and apparently sent for or went to see Travis, and gave an apology, for immediately Travis and his command returned to San Antonio, and all signs of friction between the two disappeared for good.[74] It may have helped that both were Freemasons, and Bowie quickly made his apologies to Erasmo Seguín, too.[75] They agreed to share a joint command of the post, Travis over the regulars and Bowie over the volunteers. It was perhaps the best that could be done under the circumstances, and while Travis probably maintained some private resentment at Bowie's uprising, publicly the two gave all appearances of having put the sad episode behind them.

It helped that the Mexicans distracted the attention of everyone away from such lesser matters. The day after Neill left, even while dealing with the Bowie embroglio, Travis received more intelligence that now put the enemy strength on the Rio Grande at 2,000 commanded by Gen. Joaquín Ramírez y Sesma, with another 2,500 at Saltillo personally led by Santa Anna, who reputedly issued a declaration of vengeance against Texas, promising extermination. Travis saw the obvious, that the roads from Saltillo, Laredo, and Presidio de Río Grande all led to San Antonio first. "This being the Frontier Post nearest the Rio Grande, will be the first to be attacked," he wrote to Smith this day. "We are illy prepared for their reception." With only now about 150 men—and those "in a very disorganized state" thanks to the Bowie uprising—he could offer no effective resistance.

Writing in the sure expectation that Smith would circulate or even publish his letter, the politician, publicist, and revolutionary in him went on to speak for the public eye. Only raising a large force of militia—and quickly—would save them, he said. The forces at Goliad and

Copano, which never got to Matamoros, should be sent to Béxar immediately for a concentration against the foe. Turn back Santa Anna here, and they might end the war. "For Gods sake, and the sake of our Country, send us reinforcements," he cried. He called for an end to the factional strife that crippled the provisional government and left his post isolated and ignored. "We hope that our Countrymen will open their eyes to the present danger," he went on. "I fear it is useless to waste arguments upon them.—*The Thunder of the Enemy's Cannon and the pollution of their wives and daughters—The Cries of their Famished Children, and the Smoke of their burning dwellings, will only arouse them.*" It was almost as if he were writing headlines for his newspaper, resorting even to the lurid imagery of interracial rape to arouse Texian manhood.

He said that he was determined to hold his post "as long as there is a man left because we consider death preferable to disgrace, which would be the result of giving up a Post which has been so dearly won." Travis may well have been criticizing Houston's desire to abandon and destroy the place, and when Houston saw the letter he may have taken it in just the same fashion. "Yet should we receive no reinforcements, I am determined to defend it to the last, and should Bejar fall, your friend will be buried beneath its ruins."[76] Travis wisely spent two dollars on writing paper that same day, knowing from now on until he received relief, he would be fighting his war with words as well as weapons.[77]

At least Travis knew that Neill's scouts had burned the bridge over the Rio Grande at Laredo, and that would delay the Mexicans a little.[78] Knowing that several men of the garrison were out looking at land, Travis sent riders to collect and hurry them back to Béxar.[79] Using his own legion and mounted men informally commanded by Capt. Juan Seguín, Travis maintained a constant stream of patrols and scouts to monitor the roads leading to the Rio Grande. His old friend Deaf Smith proved particularly useful, and so at least Travis could hope not to be taken by surprise. On February 13 he received an encouraging letter from Smith promising aid and soon, and despite the stormy weather read it to the assembled garrison to boost their morale. Their cheers for Smith encouraged Travis, and even better now was the help the people of San Antonio gave.[80]

Bowie's cooperative attitude made a great difference. Starting on February 14 they signed most of their orders and letters jointly, and now Buck saw the positive side of Big Jim. Bowie's contacts in the *tejano* community helped to bring forth provisions. Neill had negotiated a five-hundred-peso loan from the city council that was long spent, and now both Travis and Bowie used their personal credit to purchase goods for the garrison, but that was nearly exhausted. The local vendors would not extend much more credit, and the two pleaded with Smith to send them a substantial sum to continue their work. They had only a few days' provisions left, and scarcely a dollar in their purses. "It is useless to talk of keeping up the garrison any longer without money," they protested, "as we believe that unless we receive some shortly the men will all leave."[81]

Day after day they struggled on. By now Bowie and the volunteers seem to have been staying in the Alamo compound, while Travis and his command lodged in town. It was a time of rumors and routine, one day a spurious story coming in of a Comanche plan to send two hundred or more warriors to massacre the garrison and pillage the town, and the next Travis sending Deaf Smith to San Felipe with the latest report on the condition of the post.[82] Surveying his arsenal, Travis found a total now of twenty-one cannon of varying descriptions, some of them old and virtually useless. Most were already emplaced at the Alamo, and now he and Bowie put the men to work getting the rest that were serviceable put in position. Their only ammunition would be the powder and projectiles captured when Cós surrendered in December, and the quality of some of that appeared questionable. At the same time, he and Bowie put some of the other men to work digging ditches outside the walls of the Alamo complex, in the event that the Texians would need to man them for skirmishing.[83]

Living virtually in the midst of a people with whom there was no easily obvious way to tell friend from foe, Travis wisely cultivated increasingly better relations with the *tejano* community, even though he may have suspected that some of them, loyal to the centralist regime, sent information of his strength and plans to Santa Anna. He helped *tejano* cattle owners file their claims for animals taken by Austin's and Burleson's army during the siege, and seemed happily to attest to good behavior.[84] He got along well with both Seguíns, and by the third week of February, José Rodriguez thought that Travis was "a very popular man and was well liked by everyone." Travis walked daily from his headquarters on the Plaza de Las Yslas to the Alamo to oversee the work, and often stopped at the Rodriquez home, the last one he passed before crossing the San Antonio. The family there thought him a fine-looking fellow, and he sometimes passed an hour or so in conversation with them. The man of the house sometimes urged Travis to take his command and leave San Antonio, for everyone knew that Santa Anna was coming. That was no surprise, of course, but Travis told him what he had told Governor Smith: "Well we have made up our minds to die in the Alamo fighting for Texas."[85] None of them had any intention of dying anywhere if they could help it, of course, but the same bold and determined posture that might persuade some help out of San Felipe would also be useful in sustaining the support of that part of the *tejano* community loyal to Texas.

The garrison worked long days, and yet there were a few hours for some conviviality. While Travis cultivated the *tejanos*, Crockett visited frequently at the quarters of Almeron and Susanna Dickenson, and wherever he went he took mirth and cheer with him.[86] In the erratic weather of February, when one day it was just forty-six degrees, then two days later exceedingly hot, Crockett might be seen alternately in his hunting shirt, his traveling suit, or even under wraps in a caped overcoat, and probably still wearing that crude hat he traded for the beaver.[87] Bowie, staying for a while at the Veramendi house, fell right into the old society, though at least one of the *tejanos* thought that now he seemed to be "a sad man." He took a liking to young Gregorio Esparza, who came with his mother every day to the fortifications to sell tamales and beans to the working Texians, possibly saving the boy's life once when he pulled him out of the San Antonio after an accidental fall. "I was very fond of Señor Bowie after this," Esparza recalled. Bowie may even have spoken of helping to educate the boy one day. "I had to keep close to Señor Bowie," said Gregorio. "He knew my language and I could feel his strength."[88]

What he could not feel was that Bowie's strength was waning. He had led a hard life, much of it outdoors, pushing his system to the limits of its resilience. Then there were the wounds, a sword thrust through the lung, a bullet in the breast and yet others in the leg and chest. If the recent bouts of drinking were not just isolated incidents, then spirits, too, could be debilitating his body, especially the indifferent and sometimes extremely powerful liquor available on the frontier. Malaria less than three years before took an added toll, and though he was only thirty-nine, still he felt older.

Perhaps melancholy played its part. Living there in the Veramendi house he saw everywhere reminders of Ursula and what he had lost. If they had and lost a child, it explained his fondness for young Gregorio, seeing in him the son Bowie never had. He had his own possessions about him, but they were miserably few for a man who had lived the life he led, and made small fortunes. Moths dined on his black dress coat, and all but devoured another. He had a few books, a dictionary to help with his Spanish, a book on mechanics for the cotton mill he never built, and a few tools. The coach he once owned in Monclova was sold to pay debts he owed the Veramendi estate, and he had little else but a few of those eleven-league grant forms and some of the papers representing his land speculation efforts.[89] The other bundled papers in his room were debts. Once the owner of scores of slaves, now he had only his servant and cook.[90] No wonder he was susceptible. Even now, he began to feel the symptoms of something coming on.

Travis had crossed a domestic Rubicon of his own, though word of it never reached him. On February 14, Valentine's Day, the same day that Travis and Bowie agreed on a joint command, Rosanna married his old acquaintance and near neighbor Samuel G. Cloud.[91] Scarcely a month had passed since the divorce, and some in Monroe County no doubt whispered that she must not have waited for her freedom before letting Cloud come courting, but then Travis had pursued *his* amorous whims for nearly five years before the decree. He bore her no malice now, and if it had mattered at all, it might have relieved him to know that Rosanna's marriage meant that his daughter would have a father who could support her comfortably. Travis's more immediate concern was money. Having spent all he had and borrowed all he could, he needed more just for himself. He knew that his friend John R. Jones was in San Felipe, and so were his former partner Nibbs and his current partner Starr. When he spent probably his last $2 for corn on February 17, he decided to send an accounting of his expenditures since leaving San Felipe back to the council for reimbursement. It was only $143, but that could go a long way at the moment. He included in his dispatches that day the little red-morocco-bound book in which he recorded his expenses, directing it to one of those three who could see that he would be paid.[92]

Most of Travis's attention went to the work on strengthening the fortifications around the Alamo, though he left direct oversight of that to the would-be engineer Jameson, and Travis was unstinting in his praise of what the man accomplished. He dug wells to provide a water supply inside the compound, emplaced the cannon in spite of the lack of proper tools, and even envisioned quite ambitious extensions to the fort if given the time and resources. Travis sent Jameson's report out in the hands of Bonham, along with his usual request for assistance, and reiterated his suggestion that Fannin's command at Goliad be sent to Béxar, even though if Fannin arrived himself, being a full colonel, he would supersede Travis as commander. There would have been a logic to it not lost on Travis, for a fort was primarily an artilleryman's command, and Fannin was an artillerist. Besides, Fannin was well known to many of Bowie's volunteers, and his assumption of command might have helped morale. The men seemed to be getting along, but there were still those volunteers who felt entitled to leave at will, and on February 14 at least eleven of them were planning to depart to the Cibolo to stake out land headrights.[93]

Bonham carried other dispatches and letters, including probably Travis's statement of expenses, and also a letter to Houston—the first time Travis had written to the general since arriving.[94] Perhaps Travis only now got word that Houston was back from his diplomatic mission to the Indians and was starting to muster volunteers at Nacogdoches. He was brief. He needed at least five hundred more soldiers, and he wanted them to be regulars. "Militia and volunteers are but ill suited to garrison a town," he said from sad experience, and he desperately needed money. "Enthusiasm may keep up an army for a few days, but *money*, and *money* alone, will support an army for regular warfare."[95]

Travis's sense of urgency was well fed by the time he wrote to Houston, for now the reports of Mexican buildup and imminent advance were coming in repeatedly. The day before a cousin of

Rodriguez's arrived from Laredo and said that the enemy was on the move, and from February 18 onward more and more *tejanos* came into Béxar with the same news.[96] The next day, in response to the increasing threat, Travis sent Capt J. L. Vaughan on a wide recruiting sweep that would take him as far south as Matamoros. Travis hoped that Vaughan would be able to enlist several companies, and as he filled the quota of each he was to send it on to Béxar, meanwhile remaining vigilant for intelligence of enemy movements.[97] By sending Vaughan to Matamoros and Camargo, it is evident that Travis hoped to entice some of the men he believed still to be with Grant and Johnson into joining the regular service.

Meanwhile Travis tried another scouring of the countryside for provisions. He sent two men toward Gonzales to gather cattle, and employed a number of Seguín's cavalry in foraging.[98] But then on February 20 the intensity of the situation mounted. It was a Saturday, and Seguín came to Travis in the evening with a report just received from one of his cousins who had recently been on the Rio Grande. After a hard three-day ride, he reported that Ramírez y Sesma's forces had crossed and were on their way. At a hastily summoned council of war, Travis, Bowie, and the other officers discussed the report, as well as another saying that Ramírez y Sesma had fifteen hundred men and was making a forced march hoping to take Béxar by surprise. Some of the officers refused to believe it. After all, there had been so many conflicting reports in the past several weeks. Travis and Bowie may have been divided on it themselves, and the council adjourned without taking any decisive step.[99]

The scout's information was strikingly good. Ramírez y Sesma, at the head of the fifteen hundred men of the First Brigade, had crossed several days earlier, and at the very moment of the council was camped just a day's march from the Medina.[100] Even if some of the Texians were prone to disregard information brought by a *tejano* as suspect, Seguín and the *tejanos* in his company thought better. Later that night or early the next morning, Seguín approached Travis with a request to furlough some of his men whose families and farms lay in the path of the Mexican advance, and in the next day or two at least a dozen of them left the garrison with his permission.[101] Others clearly intended to go in time, yet Travis seemed to entertain no ill will toward them. His feeling toward native Mexicans he summed up in his recommendation of one of them, Antonio Cruz, who had fought well in the siege of Béxar. "I think a distinction ought to be made between those who lost property while in our service & those who were against us or were neutral," he said.[102] Travis could ill spare men now most of all, but he could hardly deny a faithful soldier's need to see to the safety of his family, and he made no distinction between Texians and *tejanos*.[103]

Perhaps in part because of the reduction of the strength of their best scouting company with these furloughs, Travis and Bowie seem to have gotten no further accurate reports of Mexican movements in the next forty-eight hours. Thus on the evening of February 22 they felt it safe enough to let the town and garrison stage a fandango on Soledad Street to celebrate the birthday of George Washington. The women of the town came wearing their *rebozos* drawn over their faces like bonnets, smoking their cigarettes, and joining the volunteers and regulars in both traditional reels and Mexican dances to the tune of fiddle and guitar. The local women prepared tamales and enchiladas, and the men bought small cakes to present to the young ladies with whom they danced. Crockett himself could play the fiddle, and may have helped with the music, and certainly Travis danced, though Bowie, feeling increasingly ill and feverish, probably stayed in bed.[104] In fact there were twenty-five or more men on the sick list now, and Dr. Amos Pollard was hard pressed to attend to all of them, especially since he still had the care of fifty or more Mexicans too seriously wounded to leave when Cós evacuated in December. Pollard exhausted his small stock of medicines, most of them ineffectual in any case, and asked Dr. John Sutherland to contribute his store of nostrums in helping the sick. One of those sick was Bowie, not yet confined to hospital but clearly unwell. Sutherland actually moved from his room at the Dickensons' to share a chamber with Bowie at the Alamo barracks, but he could not identify Bowie's problem from the symptoms, and therefore could not treat it even if he had sufficient medications.[105] On the morning after the fandango, February 23, with no fresh intelligence on the enemy, Travis prepared to conduct a court-martial of one of the soldiers for some infraction perhaps connected with the recent insubordination of Bowie's volunteers. Even before it got under way he noticed unusual activity in the streets of town. Many of the *tejanos* were loading their carts, hitching their teams, and starting to leave for the countryside. Somehow, it seemed, they knew something that he did not.

APOTHEOSIS

February 23–Dawn, March 6, 1836

*I feel confident that the determined valor & desperate courage, heretofore
exhibited by my men, will not fail them in the last struggle.*

WILLIAM BARRET TRAVIS, MARCH 3, 1836

From his headquarters on the Plaza de Las Yslas on Potrero Street,
Travis went among the milling *tejanos* and asked them what they were
about. Their answers that they were just leaving to prepare for the
spring planting seemed evasive. Travis and Bowie felt especially suspicious when they found the wife of Ramón Músquiz about to leave.
Her husband, once prominent in Béxar affairs, remained loyal to the
new Mexican regime and even now acted as a guide to the advancing
Mexicans. Suspecting that Músquiz somehow had gotten word to her
to leave, Travis ordered her arrest, even though she was pregnant, and
only the intervention of Capt. Philip Dimitt in her behalf secured her
release shortly thereafter. Travis meanwhile continued with his court-
martial, while his other officers continued to try to find the reason for
all the activity among the townsfolk. Nathaniel Lewis was just giving
his evidence in the case when a messenger came to Travis. He knew
why the *tejanos* were leaving: The Mexican army was almost in sight.[1]
A friendly *tejano* told Travis that Ramírez y Sesma and his column
had just been seen on Leon Creek, not five miles from San Antonio,
and marching fast in the hope of taking the garrison by surprise.
Somehow the word of his coming got into town during the night,
which was why so many of the citizens were trying to leave.[2] Travis
gave orders to stop the evacuation of the people, hoping that would
quell any panic, especially if the report proved to be untrue. Until
some confirmation came in, he put a man in the belfry of San Fernando
to keep an eye on the southwestern horizon. Then he waited.

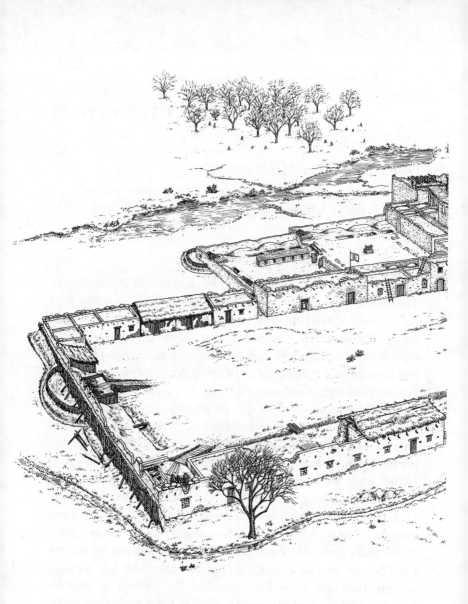

The Alamo compound as it appeared in February–March 1836. In the foreground the long west wall faces San Antonio. In the center of the north wall (*at left*), stands the north battery, where Travis fell. The south wall is to the right, with the main gate in its center. The rooms immediately east of the gateway were hospital quarters, and the best evidence places Bowie in the room next to the gate when he was killed. Crockett may have died anywhere in the compound, or even outside it with one of the breakouts. The most persistent tradition, based solely on the unreliable statements of

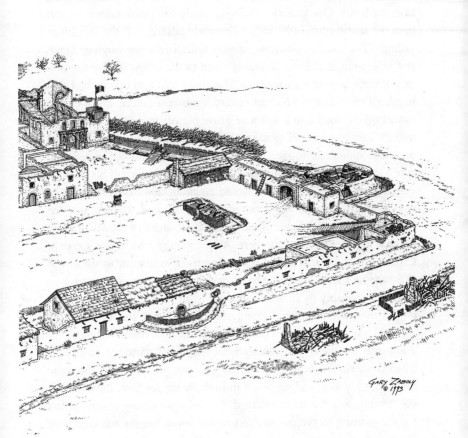

GARY ZABOLY
© 1993

Susanna Dickenson, has him dying somewhere in the small enclosure in front of the
church in the center rear. Yet Francisco Ruiz, who had the task of identifying the
bodies, said that he found Crockett in a small fort to the west of where Travis fell,
which would suggest either the fortified northwest corner that the Mexicans called
the Fortine de Condelle, or else the embrasure projecting from the middle of the
west wall. The nagging fact is that we will almost certainly never know for sure.

(Drawing by Gary Zaboly; courtesy of Stephen L. Hardin and the artist)

The hours passed slowly. Noon came, and no word, and nothing from the belfry. One o'clock. . . . Two o'clock. . . . Three o'clock . . . and then the sound of the bell in San Fernando pealing and the watchman yelling: "The enemy is in view," almost unheard for the ringing. Travis and others ran to the church and climbed to the belfry, but by the time he got there he could see nothing. The sentry told him that he had seen hundreds of mounted Mexican cavalry a moment before, but they just turned off the road into a mesquite grove out of view. One or two with him thought the sentinel mistaken, but the man insisted on what he had seen. Dr. Sutherland suggested that Travis should send out someone to take a look, and John Smith, called "El Colorado" because of his red hair, volunteered. Sutherland said he would go along, and Travis said that he would watch them as they moved down the road. If they saw the Mexicans, they were to wheel and gallop back, and that would be a signal that the enemy was truly there. A few minutes later Travis spoke to Crockett, who of course had wide experience as a scout in the Creek War, and he started preparing to go out on a more extensive survey.

Joined probably by Bowie, Travis stayed in the belfry and looked on as the two riders cantered down the road toward the Leon. As he watched, they got perhaps a mile and one-half from town to the crest of a low rise. Suddenly both horses spun about and started to race back. Then Sutherland's went down, falling across his legs, and they saw Smith quickly stop and dismount to help the doctor back into the saddle.[3] Even before the riders returned, Travis began yelling out the orders for the garrison to prepare to evacuate the town. Seguín was with him. "In the act of the moment," he said, "Col. Travis resolved to concentrate all his forces within the Alamo."[4] At the same time he ordered Dimitt and Lt. Benjamin Nobles to make a major reconnaissance.[5]

Crockett just heard Travis give the order for the move to the Alamo when he mounted and started out on his own scout, but at the end of town he met Smith and Sutherland returning, the doctor in pain from a bad sprain to his leg. He told them what was happening, then rode on out a little way before turning back to join them as they went to report that the Mexican cavalry had indeed arrived. As they turned their horses toward the Alamo, expecting already to find Travis there, they ran into Dimitt and Nobles on their way out. Everything seemed to be happening at once.

Crockett helped Sutherland dismount and assisted him in walking into Travis's headquarters room in the Alamo compound. They found him penning a hasty dispatch. "The enemy in large force is in sight," he wrote. "We want men and provisions. Send them to us. We have 150 men and are determined to defend the Alamo to the last. Give us assistance."[6] At the moment there was time for nothing more. Seeing Sutherland's injury, Travis realized he would be unable to do any good to the garrison just then, but if he could ride he might take the message to Gonzales, the nearest source of men. Even before Sutherland left the room, Crockett asked Travis to tell him where he and his Tennesseans should post themselves. They were ready to fight.[7]

Suddenly Travis and Bowie tried to manage a flurry of confused activity. The fifty or more sick and wounded Mexicans from Cós's command they would leave behind for their comrades to find and care for.[8] The rest of their own sick had to walk or be carried across the San Antonio, while the able-bodied men took with them everything they could carry that they might need. Seguín moved his company through town down Potrero Street, past weeping women crying out: "Poor fellows you will all be killed," hardly an encouraging send-off.[9] Most of the rest of the men ransacked every possible source of grain and meat to take into the fort. Bowie took a detachment and broke into several deserted houses, or *jacales*, in the vicinity of the fort, and found nearly ninety bushels of corn, and another small company of Texians quickly drove in thirty beefs belonging to a *tejano* willing to hand over his small herd. The volunteers who had sold their rifles ten days before to get drinking money now frantically tried to get them back, and through the streets of town a cacophony of shouts and swearing echoed from the adobe walls. But there was no panic, and no one sought to escape.[10] Nearly forty of the *tejano* citizens of San Antonio also decided to take refuge with the garrison, among them Bowie's sister-in-law and Horace Alsbury.[11] At least one man decided that it was time to leave, however. Jesse Badgett, elected delegate to the consultation, departed several days earlier, but Samuel Maverick had stayed on. Now he made ready to go. Travis was standing on the top of the outer wall of the Alamo, watching for the Mexican advance into the town, when he saw Maverick ride up below. He hailed him and they spoke for a few minutes, Travis urging

Maverick to spread the alarm through the country as he rode to Washington, and to implore Texians to send men and money.[12]

When Travis caught his first sight of the head of the Mexican column, which he could not know was Santa Anna himself with his staff, he ordered a flag raised from a makeshift staff, perhaps the very same flag he had bought for five dollars back in San Felipe. To the Mexicans it appeared to be their national tricolor, with two stars in the middle, denoting the two states of Coahuila and Texas.[13] It was late afternoon by the time the Mexicans occupied San Antonio, Travis and Bowie and probably most of the rest of the garrison watching from the west wall of the compound. They saw a red flag go up on the San Fernando belfry, where so recently they had stood, and took it to be a sign of no quarter. In defiance Travis ordered the big eighteen-pounder fired in return, and following that the Mexicans unlimbered their cannon and sent four shells in quick succession toward the fort, none doing any harm.[14]

Travis and Bowie, still sharing command, held a brief discussion, and immediately disagreed. Travis wanted simply to await the Mexicans' next move, while Bowie, always the talker, wanted to try a parley. He had persuaded so many people in the past that perhaps he thought he could sway Santa Anna, and as Veramendi's son-in-law, he would certainly be at least known to many of the officers in the enemy army. He and Travis came to an impasse on the matter, though not necessarily to a falling out. But then Bowie heard from someone that the cannon fire might have drowned out the sound of a bugle call, sounding a request for a meeting. True to form, Bowie simply went ahead on his own. He found the only piece of paper readily at hand, a blank page from a child's copybook. Not trusting his own Spanish for something this important, he dictated a note to Seguín, then called Jameson to take it out under a white flag. "I want to know if a parley has really been called," it said tersely. When Bowie looked at the note, he saw that the writer had out of habit ended it with the standard "God and the Mexican Federation," but Bowie crossed that out and in Spanish wrote instead "God and Texas." In the address he also crossed out the word "Federal" in Santa Anna's title, Bowie's way of stating that he did not recognize Santa Anna as holding a legitimate position under the federal constitution of 1824. That done, he affixed a shaky signature to the document, his hand probably unsteady thanks to the high fever he was running.[15]

When Travis saw Jameson ride out of the fortress with a white flag he became furious at Bowie's unilateral action.[16] No doubt there was something of a scene between them, punctuated by Jameson's return with a terse note from Santa Anna's aide José Batres refusing to discuss terms "with rebellious foreigners to whom there is no other recourse left, if they wish to save their lives, than to place themselves immediately at the disposal of the Supreme Government."[17] Travis interpreted this as a "surrender at discretion," meaning that Santa Anna would have their lives at his disposal and might well execute them.[18] He probably overreacted, for Batres clearly stated that they "may expect clemency after some considerations are taken up." Most likely some would be executed, such as Travis and Bowie, or there might have been incarcerations. Certainly, though, they would not be allowed to leave their post with the honors of war accorded to Cós when he gave up Béxar, and in the absence of equivalent terms, Travis would not continue the negotiations. Jameson said he had talked with Col. Juan Almonte of Santa Anna's staff, hinting at a desire for "some honorable conditions" for a proposed surrender, but obviously to no avail.

Just the same, unwilling to be entirely precipitous, Travis now sent out his own man, Albert Martin. With him Travis sent a verbal message that if Almonte, who was known and respected in Texas, wished to talk with him, he would be glad to open a discussion. From the wall, Travis could see the two men meeting on the foot bridge that spanned the San Antonio.[19] Almonte, of course, could not speak on behalf of Santa Anna, and the general's position was already on record in the reply to Bowie. There was nothing further to discuss except whether or not Travis would accept Mexican terms.[20] Almonte reiterated Santa Anna's conditional offer, and when Martin returned, Travis told him to tell Almonte that he would let them know if he accepted their terms. If not, he would fire another round from his cannon.[21]

It was no doubt what Travis had expected, but he needed to hear it for himself. Moreover, he needed now for the garrison to hear the enemy terms. Assembling the men, Travis gave them an impassioned speech, still fired by his anger at Bowie, and no doubt spoke of rights and liberty and Mexican perfidy, and perhaps even raised for them, too, the specter of rape and pillage in their own homes if they did not stop Santa Anna here. In the end his harangue stirred them to a pledge

never to surrender.[22] That was all he needed. He gave the order to his
gunners to send his reply with a cannon. Immediately a Mexican how-
itzer responded and commenced the bombardment.[23] Faced with what
he took to be a threat to put every man in his garrison to the sword,
Travis might momentarily have recalled that he made the same threat
himself with Tenorio back at Anahuac the year before. Had he been
serious then? Was Santa Anna serious now?

With the first concussions of the artillery ringing in his ears, Travis
sat down with Bowie to dash off a message to Fannin in Goliad. "We
will make such resistance as is due to our honour, and that of the
country," they said, but they expected assistance from Fannin, and
immediately. That morning's muster revealed just 146 men among the
regulars and volunteers, though they probably had a few more with
the *tejanos* who came into the Alamo with them, and this tally may not
have included 40 or more on the sick roll. If Fannin came, they could
hold out, but they were firm in their resolve "*never to retreat.*"[24] Travis
also wrote a similar dispatch to send by express to San Felipe. If Texas
answered his pleas, the Alamo garrison could hold on.[25]

That done, there was little else to do except keep the men out of the
way of the enemy shells, though the barrage did not last long and
proved ineffective in any event. Not knowing if there might not be an
assault even that evening, Travis and Bowie no doubt assigned the
companies to positions on the walls. Their fortress was never designed
for this use, certainly. The church had been built many years before—a
shield over the door read "1758"—and named for the Flying Company
of San José y Santiago del Alamo de Parras, but by 1835 everyone simply called it the Alamo. The main part of the compound was a large
rectangle of intermittent single-story adobe houses, connected by an
outer wall about eave height. The long west wall presented an unbroken face toward San Antonio, with a number of doors and windows
now closed and barred, and a semicircular earthwork redoubt jutted out
from the center. The shorter north wall was much the same, with
another center redoubt, and cannon mounted on a reinforced parapet.
The south wall, equal in length to the north wall, held in its center the
main gate, with a very substantial redoubt equipped with more cannon
to guard the entrance, and more guns emplaced in the courtyard, fixed
on the entrance to meet any attacker that broke through.

The east wall was more complex, however. A long row of one- and two-story buildings composed most of it, but about sixty feet before it would have joined the south wall, the buildings stopped, and there was only a crumbling chest-high mud wall to continue the connection. At the point where the row of buildings stopped, a long extension broke off to the east, finally linking with the north wall of the Alamo church itself. The line of the church facade ran to the south, and stopped some fifty or sixty feet from the east end of the south wall. To span that gap, the Texians expanded on defenses previously erected by the Mexicans, and now had a picket palisade, with a ditch on the outer side, and beyond that abatis, tree limbs buried in the ground with their sharpened branches pointing in the direction from which an attacker would come. Also outside the east wall, and connected to it, sat two outer enclosures, a cattle pen and a horse corral.

The Texians placed cannon at the southwest and northwest corners, another one in the palisade wall, and three atop the reinforced roof of the Alamo church, with two more in the outer horse and cattle corrals. The entire perimeter should have had 500 or more for a proper defense. With just 146–160 able-bodied men on hand, there was far too much for any one man to cover, and Bowie and Travis knew it. If hit from all sides at once, they must be overrun, and quickly. For now, though, with the Mexicans in San Antonio, most of the garrison would simply have stayed in the rooms lining the outer walls to avoid the enemy shells should they land in the center parade ground. Some even raised low earthen parapets outside the doors to the houses, to prevent any Mexican shells from rolling inside before exploding. No doubt Bowie and Travis kept a few men, themselves included, atop the walls to study the Mexican movements in the town, and placed sentinels at points around the perimeter to watch for an attack. Beyond that, they were well advised to stay under cover. Travis may have assigned Crockett and others of Patton's company to the palisade outside the church, though they, too, would stay indoors during the bombardment.[26]

That first evening twilight came on shortly after the Mexicans commenced firing, and they ceased at nightfall, though their engineers immediately went to work building a battery emplacement near the Veramendi house, and Bowie could most likely hear them at their work.[27] Travis meanwhile went about business as normal, not forgetting to give a *tejano* a receipt for the thirty cattle he allowed to be brought into the compound.[28] No doubt he wondered why Captain Dimitt did not return from his reconnaissance, and perhaps concluded the worst—that the Mexicans were already spreading out so that Dimitt could not get through.[29]

Perhaps it was that very first night that one of the buildings on the edge of the parade became especially important. The Texians established their hospital on the second floor of an old convent building, right at the corner where the east wall ended and then turned east toward the church, and the sick may actually have been there already before the rest of the garrison came into the fort. There were forty or more of them, all with unspecified maladies, and they may not have been included in the 146 that reported for duty.[30] Now there was to be another: James Bowie. For a couple of days he had probably felt ill, but not so much that he could not exercise his command, and take part in the withdrawal to the Alamo. But by now he ran a temperature of 101 or even up to 104 degrees. He felt lethargic, exhausted, and may have suffered his first bouts of vomiting and even bloody diarrhea, though if not, they would come. Something in the water he drank was in his system now, a bacterial infection, and though Dr. Sutherland had not been sure of its nature before he left, it was almost certainly typhoid. The onset may even have been sufficiently severe that the fever gave him chills and shakes, making his hand too unsteady even to hold a pen, for he would sign no more documents jointly with Travis. For the time being Bowie shared a room with the Alsburys and Juana's sister, where the two women could care for him.[31]

Now Travis held the entire command, though he and Bowie may have tried to keep Bowie's incapacitation secret for a time, in order to quiet the volunteers. They would know soon enough, however. Meanwhile, the presence of the Mexicans outside would be more than enough to keep them obedient. February 24 dawned warm and cloudy. A strong northerly wind blew cold drizzle in the faces of the men as they left their buildings, though they could feel that the day would only get colder.[32] Early in the morning they saw the Mexicans start putting up another battery near the river, about 350 yards distant, and by the afternoon it, too, opened fire on them. Travis and Crockett and the rest most probably saw Santa Anna himself riding up almost within musket range of the fort as he personally reconnoitered.[33]

On and off through the day and into the afternoon the Mexicans continued their fire, and all Travis could do was sit it out. He put the time to its best use by doing what he did so well, composing a stirring call to arms, designed for publication. He addressed it to "The People of Texas & All Americans in the World":

I am besieged, by a thousand or more of the Mexicans under Santa Anna—I have sustained a continual Bombardment & cannonade for 24 hours & have not lost a man.—The enemy has demanded a surrender at discretion, otherwise the garrison are to be put to the sword, if the fort is taken—I have answered the demand with a cannon shot, & our flag still waves proudly from the walls—*I shall never surrender or retreat. Then,* I call on you in the name of Liberty, of patriotism & everything dear to the American character, to come to our aid, with all dispatch—The enemy is receiving reinforcements daily & will no doubt increase to three or four thousand in four or five days. If this call is neglected, I am determined to sustain myself as long as possible & die like a soldier who never forgets what is due to his own honor & that of his country—*Victory or Death.*[34]

Travis gave the letter to Albert Martin to take out, then turned his attention to the condition of the fort, pleased to find that so far the Mexican shells and cannonballs had only caused some damage to the outer walls, but nothing serious. That evening he and the rest of the garrison heard a band playing in the Mexican camp, though hardly intended to lull them to sleep, for the foe augmented the music with the firing of several exploding shells toward the fort.[35] Apparently Travis spent a fair bit of time out on the parapet now, despite the enemy shelling, for Seguín saw him there and decided that his commander possessed "a high degree of constitutional bravery."[36]

The next morning the artillery started early, and the action suddenly escalated when Travis saw two hundred or more Mexicans of the *Permanente Matamoros* battalion crossing the San Antonio downstream, and then coming up within less than one hundred yards' range of the southwest corner of the fort, where they took cover in some *jacales* near the stream.[37] At once Travis ordered his riflemen to pin them down, while he got his artillerymen to train cannon on the houses and start firing scatterloads of canister and grapeshot. For the next two hours the skirmishing continued through a light rain, the Mexicans immobilized by the Texian fire. When they withdrew, Travis saw them carrying off eight or more dead and wounded. Through the whole action the bombardment from Mexican guns on the other side of the river continued, yet Travis was delighted to see that not a man in his garrison was hit. Moreover, he watched as his men withstood the fire, behaving well, especially Dickenson at the artillery. He saw another, too. "The Hon. David Crockett was seen at all points, animating the men to do their duty," he said later that day. This, of course, was the sort of moment for a man like Crockett, staying cool under fire, jolly even, his own devil-may-care air giving courage and confidence to the others. When the Mexicans withdrew, Travis called for volunteers to go out and burn the *jacales* to prevent the Mexicans using them for cover again, and the men got the job done.

The action convinced Travis that he faced a probable major assault soon, and he wrote another urgent appeal, this time addressed to Houston, whom he thought might be in Gonzales by now. Reporting the action of that morning, he reiterated that "I shall hold out to the last extremity," and then went on to try to shame Houston if he did not send succor. "If they overpower us, we fall a sacrifice at the shrine of our country, and we hope posterity and our country will do our memory justice. Give me help, oh my Country! Victory or death!"[38] Travis knew that he was writing for many eyes. Indeed, he hoped that his dispatches would be circulated or published.[39] It would not have occurred to him that Houston and others might take his melodramatic prose as hysteria or exaggeration—that the situation in Béxar was not as serious as he made it seem.

To date Travis had depended on volunteers to bear his messages, but today no one stepped forward to carry the dispatch to Houston. The morning's skirmish may have left them a bit stunned with the realization that there really was a battle in the offing. Some no doubt did not want to leave for fear of missing the time of trial, while others may have suspected that by now the Mexicans would have all the roads covered, making it impossible for a rider to get through. In the end the men of the legion and Seguín's company took a vote among themselves, since they were still the only companies unquestionably subject to Travis's command, and chose Seguín himself. Travis objected. He needed Seguín there. He spoke Spanish more fluently than most, and certainly better than Travis himself. He knew the customs of the Mexicans outside the fort, and more importantly those of the *tejanos* inside. But the rest of the men insisted that they wanted Seguín to go, and once again an excess of democracy had its way. Seguín left at eight o'clock, well after dark.[40]

Travis was right about another attack, for that evening there came noises and then shots in the dark, but it was only a feint on the east side, no doubt to test his strength there. A few loads of grapeshot drove them back, and at the same time let Santa Anna know that the Texians had cannon on that wall, too. Off in the distance Travis may have heard the sound of cavalry riding out to a position on the Gonzales road. Seguín had left just in time, it seemed. Along the river Travis either heard or saw two more batteries being erected, and perhaps to give himself a clear field of fire in any future engagement, he sent out another party in the darkness to set ablaze more of the huts and some piles of straw near the fort.[41] It was evident that the Mexicans were slowly trying to surround them, and almost leisurely getting things ready for the inevitable assault.

Off to the east Travis's and Bowie's first pleas finally reached San Felipe and Goliad, the couriers stopping frequently along the way to pass on the news. "The appeal of Cols. Travis & Bowie cannot however pass unnoticed," Fannin wrote today. "Much has to be risked to relieve the besieged." In San Felipe, Governor Smith immediately printed a broadside publishing Travis and Bowie's first February 23 appeal, exactly what Travis hoped would happen, and exhorted the people to "fly" to their aid. "The campaign has commenced," Smith proclaimed. Texians must not let their brothers be "massacred by a mercenary foe." At once a company of volunteers began to form in San Felipe, and no doubt Smith sent a dispatch back to Travis to tell him to hold on, they were coming.[42]

The next two days brought little change for either Travis or Crockett. It was cold and windy, with morning frost in the compound. On February 26 Travis answered some Mexican cavalry that came in to skirmish on the east side of the fort, no doubt just to test further the strength of his defenses. The cannonade from Santa Anna's batteries continued all day, and now and then Travis allowed his gunners to answer, though with some of his powder being of poor quality, he could not afford to waste what he had. Fortunately most of the Mexican pieces were of the same caliber as his own, and solid shot that landed inside the parade ground could actually be picked up and fired back. Travis ordered two more sallies during the day, one for wood and water, even though he had a well, and the other to burn more of the huts down along the San Antonio that might give shelter to the foe. Rain the next day eased the water problem—and also dampened the ardor of the Mexicans, for they relaxed their bombardment—and Travis took advantage of the lull to send a party to repair some of his damaged outer wall, especially on the north. In a hard north wind, he sent Bonham out with another plea for reinforcements, giving him Bowie's horse for the ride. Bowie would not be needing it now.[43]

Bowie's illness became dramatically worse, and his sister-in-law Juana Alsbury had no doubt whatever that it was typhoid. Bowie believed so as well, and knowing the disease to be contagious, he insisted on leaving her quarters rather than endanger her and her sister. Being herself a *tejana*, she no doubt feared some of the men in the garrison who might not distinguish between her and the enemy, and as well had to fear the Mexicans on the other side of the wall. Bowie had been her protector in San Antonio and now here, and the prospect of losing him frightened her. He summoned two soldiers to come and help him away, but before he left he tried to comfort Juana. "Sister, do not be afraid," he told her. "I leave you with Col. Travis, Col. Crockett, and other friends. They are gentlemen, and will treat you kindly." He promised to come back to see her occasionally, but she was not to go to his sickroom for fear of contagion. With the help of the soldiers, the weakening shell of a once mighty man made his way to a small room immediately to the left of the main gate, next to the officers' quarters, and there he would wait to see which of his twin enemies he must meet first, death from his fever or the Mexicans. But then, not everyone with typhoid died. About half recovered, though the disease took up to three weeks to run its course. He had beaten death before more than once, and no foe ever cowed Big Jim Bowie. Surely the man of the Sandbar and the San Saba could beat a few bacteria.[44]

Crockett, meanwhile, may have come close to visiting death on another of the more noted men in the vicinity. He had already engaged in target practice during the day, as Mexican artillerymen set up and then operated their forward battery in the bend of the San Antonio that came near the fort. The people in town became convinced that he killed the very first *soldado* to fall, with a two-hundred-yard shot from his long rifle.[45] Then, on the afternoon of February 27, Santa Anna himself rode forward to one of his batteries, only to be fired on by Texians from the Alamo, and the *tejanos* in Béxar swore that one of the bullets that sent him scurrying back to safety came from Crockett's rifle.[46]

Travis took a chance that night and sent a volunteer out of the fort to reconnoiter, probably because he heard the sound of enemy horses riding off on the Gonzales road. Could they be going out to meet advancing Texian reinforcements? Whatever else the scout found, he encountered and killed one *soldado* before he returned. At least there was still ample opportunity to get couriers through the Mexican forces, especially to the east. The next day the thunder of the bombardment started again early on a cold, drizzling morning, but there was no news of reinforcements on the way.[47] In fact Travis's heart would have sunk if he knew what was not happening back in the settlements. "The *vile rabble* here cannot be moved," a man in Washington complained.[48] A committee in San Felipe voted to print and distribute copies of his February 24 "All Americans in the World" letter, and passed resolutions calling on the men of Texas to arise from their lethargy and enlist, otherwise "Texas, and her citizens, and her liberties, and her hopes, are gone forever."[49] The message was clear that if the Alamo fell, Travis and his men would all die, and down in Goliad, Fannin expressed his fears that Santa Anna would get to make good his threat. "Hoping for the best, being prepared for the worst, I am in a devil of a bad humor," he said. But neither he nor anyone else seemed to make positive steps to relieve the garrison.[50]

This 1836 was a leap year, but for Travis, Crockett, and a now desperately ill Bowie, there was nothing special about February 29, just more bombardment and a little break in the cold after a hard west wind in the night pushed a warming front through. Travis saw more Mexican reinforcements arrive and take a position on the east of the fort.[51] He got another courier or two out, with more of the same urgent requests for assistance, and at the same time a message from Santa Anna somehow managed to get into the compound. In fact, for the

546 of the siege

first few days of the siege, some *tejanos* passed back and forth almost at will, and Seguín actually had his meals brought to him from town before he left.[52] Now Santa Anna wisely let it be known that he would offer amnesty to any *tejanos* in the fort who came out and made no further resistance. He could take the position that perhaps they had been coerced, or were simply misguided, but however he viewed them, their departure would weaken Travis. The Mexican commander offered them three days to decide.

That evening or the next day several *tejanos*, including his old friend Menchaca, came to Bowie. Weak as he was, they all still looked up to this man out of habit. They had known him for several years, and he had always seemed so much a larger-than-life figure in Béxar. Though he could scarcely rise to meet them, they wanted his advice. Bowie acted this time after consulting Travis. The *tejanos* were not soldiers. None of those before him had enlisted or taken an oath. They had families in San Antonio. "All of you who desire to leave here may go in safety," he told them from his cot. Travis approved as well. In the next few hours some of them would start to filter out as they came to their decisions, including Menchaca, who took his family south toward the Seguín ranch.[53] It was a miserable night. A terrible thunderstorm came out of the north, bringing lightning, hail, and heavy winds and rain, and driving the temperature down to thirty-three degrees by the morning of March 1.[54] But it could not dampen Travis's spirits, for something else came in the night, this time from the east. About 3 A.M. a sentinel awakened him, if he was not himself standing watch, and brought him to the main gate in time to see "El Colorado," John Smith, bring thirty-two men from Gonzales into the fort. By good fortune Ramírez y Sesma and much of the cavalry had been out of position looking for men reported elsewhere by false rumor, and that gave Smith the opening to get through.[55] At last the reinforcements were coming.

With daylight Travis could possibly see the Mexican cavalry returning to its former position to the east, near an abandoned powderhouse, and later in the day could not help but see a group of Mexicans at a mill northwest of him. Santa Anna was reconnoitering yet another position for a battery. Perhaps to celebrate the arrival of the Gonzales contingent, Travis gave the order for two of his twelve-pounders to be fired toward a building believed to be Santa Anna's headquarters, and one actually struck it, causing some damage but missing the absent general.[56] Even Bowie may have been buoyed by the reinforcements, for he had himself carried out of his sickroom on his cot by a couple of soldiers, and met with Juana and her sister for a time, and perhaps talked with some of the Gonzales men.[57] Yet there were also subtractions from the garrison, for that day more of the *tejanos* left, and there was every likelihood that others might go on the morrow before the deadline expired.[58]

In the outside world it seemed that Travis's appeals were finally going to bear fruit. This same day one Texian predicted: "A general and immediate turnout of a great majority of our citizens," while the next day one fellow with Fannin gloried in the news from Travis that two Mexican sallies had been repulsed, joking that "probably Davy Crockett 'grinned' them off."[59] On March 2 Travis's "Victory or Death" letter appeared in the Brazoria *Texas Republican,* just as he had expected, and he had to count on it impelling more men to follow those brave thirty-two from Gonzales.

But Travis would have been stunned if he could have seen into the mind of Sam Houston, who had done nothing to relieve the garrison. He arrived in Washington on February 29 for the convention to meet the next day, and almost immediately started a grand spree, chiefly on eggnog. He slept most of the daylight hours, and when confronted with Travis's frantic pleas for help, actually convinced some people that "a fraud had been practiced upon the people by the officers of the frontier, for party purposes; that there was not an enemy on our borders." Houston suspected that either Travis or Fannin or both wanted to take his command away from him by politicking. Certainly Fannin had challenged him in the Matamoros affair, and now Houston, his mind clouded by drink, may have seen in Travis's melodramatic letters, obviously intended for publication, a none-too-subtle attempt to draw attention to himself. A few days later he actually told one man that Travis's report of being besieged was "a damned lie, and that all those reports from Travis & Fannin were lies, for there were no Mexican forces there and that he believed that it was only electioneering

schemed [by] Travis & Fannin to sustain their popularity."[60] Certainly
Houston knew that Travis was an Austin man, and that worked against
him. Houston may even have sent a message to Bonham, when he
learned that Travis's messenger had reached Gonzales and was enlisting men to go to the aid of the Alamo. He wanted Bonham to urge
Travis to abandon the post, and retire to unite with the main army, and
by assuming that Travis could withdraw, he must have believed that
there was no Mexican army in Béxar.[61] Meanwhile Houston continued
to tell other delegates at the convention that Travis was exaggerating
his appeals, and that they were really political grandstanding, and
some even began to question whether Travis himself was writing
them. They might, after all, be false reports sent by Mexicans to disrupt the convention or lure Houston and his small but growing army
into who-knew-what.[62] While the ceaseless ferment of politics undercut the Alamo garrison in San Felipe, Travis and his men faced March
2 with more hope thanks to the recent reinforcement. He saw another
Mexican battalion take a forward position in a slightly protected spot
almost within pistol shot of the fort, and that night sent out another
sally of his own toward the new battery being established at the mill,
but the Mexicans drove his men back.[63] Travis was doing exactly the
right thing. He could hardly leave his fort and attack the Mexicans.
But he could send out small parties in the dark to try to undo some of
the enemy's daylight work, uncover their protected positions, and at
least try to keep Santa Anna uncertain of his intentions. He had to
expect that the enemy knew his strength, now close to 180, and really
more than that including the sick and the remaining *tejano* men. Loyal
Mexicans in San Antonio would have told him that. He also had to
assume that Santa Anna knew of the Gonzales contingent's arrival, and
could hope that Santa Anna might not know their number, or even
assume that they were but one of several reinforcements. Thus a little
show of bravado with these nightly sallies made good sense, and they
also helped to sustain the morale of the men, for whom the tedium of
siege could otherwise be demoralizing.

March 3 came in clear and slightly warmer, a few degrees above
freezing. As soon as the men were roused, he sent them back to the
work that had occupied them the past several days, chiefly now the
reinforcement of their walls with earth and timber abutments to shore

up weak spots and openings created by the enemy bombardment. He also put them to digging shallow trenches inside the compound, some of them outside the doors to the houses. Already he envisioned the possibility that if the Mexicans attacked and broke through the outer defenses, he and his men might have to fall back into those rooms and meet the foe at the windows and doorways. That such a pass might come seemed increasingly a possibility, for no more reinforcements had arrived after the Gonzales company, and meanwhile that morning the whole garrison could see a large addition to the Mexican army arrive as three new battalions approached from the southwest.[64]

But at 11 A.M. the shout of a sentry announced the coming of a rider, the familiar shape of James Butler Bonham. In broad daylight they saw him riding unmolested from the east, between the powderhouse and an enemy battery.[65] He brought some encouragement. From his saddle-bag he took a letter from Three-Legged Willie Williamson, written in San Felipe two days before, and it breathed encouragement and promise. He spoke of 60 volunteers leaving San Felipe, hoping they might have arrived by this time. Moreover, Williamson told Travis that Fannin was at last on the march, with 300 men and a battery of four cannon, and having left Goliad on February 28, he should be approaching any day now. At least 300 more volunteers were due to reach San Felipe the evening of March 1, and would be sent on their way as quickly as possible. "For God's sake hold out until we can assist you," Williamson pleaded. He would be coming soon himself.

That was the kind of news Travis had waited for. Undoubtedly he shared it with the entire garrison, for it offered the first positive encouragement in many days. With the 60 men now due, the 300 more with Fannin, and the promised additional 300 from San Felipe, if Santa Anna did not attack and overrun them in the next three or four days, the Texians could have more than 850 men and at least twenty-two serviceable cannon including the eighteen then working in the fort.[66] With that they could easily hold off twice their numbers and more to allow an even larger army to gather. But then Bonham handed Travis another letter dated March 1, and probably also told him of the urging from Houston to evacuate and join him to the east. Williamson had read this second missive, and made it clear that he regarded it as politically motivated. "*Let it pass*," he advised. "You will know what it meant; if the multitude gets hold of it, let them figure it out." It was probably either from Houston, reiterating what he had told Bonham, or from Governor Smith, detailing his continuing battle with the council and Robinson to maintain control. Robinson, too, sent a letter by Bonham, no doubt offering a mixture of encouragement, promises, and justification of his side of the squabble in San Felipe, especially now that he knew the garrison had come down squarely on the side of Smith.[67] Travis could be forgiven if the two other letters raised his ire. Here he and his men stood day after day, with nothing but a mud wall between them and Mexican bayonets, and the petty politicians in San Felipe and Washington—including Houston, it seemed—could only think to treat the Alamo as a constituency to be wooed, and perhaps even as a ball to kick back and forth between them, each using it to score his own points.

Thus Bonham's arrival brought him mingled hope and despair, and it came atop the discovery that more of the *tejanos* had gone out. Of the forty or more who had come into the fort on February 23, only a handful remained, and some of those were children.[68] Was everyone to abandon him? Thankfully the Texians in the garrison remained firm in their resolve, and the Williamson letter certainly must have given them encouragement that they would yet prevail, or at least survive. Travis kept the other two letters to himself, and perhaps even destroyed them, but he put Williamson's letter in his pocket, no doubt to show as a reminder to any who might waver in the next day or two.

The ease with which Bonham got through suggested that now was a good time for Travis to send out another courier himself. He took half an hour or so and composed something to address the several constituencies who now seemed to look to the Alamo, governors, would-be governors, councils, conventions, even generals. And he had no qualms about opening with a direct reference to "the present confusion of the political authorities of the country." Naturally he gave them a report of conditions in the Alamo since his last dispatch, glad to be able to report still the loss of not a single man. That in spite of at least two hundred shot and shells falling inside the compound. By now he faced an enemy reported to number between sixteen hundred and six thousand, though he mistakenly thought Santa Anna was not actually with them yet, and that Ramírez y Sesma commanded.

But then he got to the meat of his report. He confessed in this letter to the convention at Washington what he surely did not tell the men: He did not believe that Fannin was really coming. He had sent several expresses to Fannin himself, and yet not one word came from him in reply. If Fannin did not come, or if those other reinforcements promised in Williamson's letter should not arrive, he would have no choice but to await the enemy's pleasure, and he left no doubt of what would be the outcome. "I feel confident that the determined valor & desperate courage, heretofore exhibited by my men, will not fail them in the last struggle," he said with a greater hint of fatalism and less melodrama than before, and not without cause. For several days now he and his men had seen the red flag flying above San Fernando. When it first went up it may have been a ploy to intimidate them into giving up. Now its sanguine folds seemed more like a grim promise. "Although they may be sacrificed to the vengeance of a gothic enemy, the victory will cost the enemy so dear, that it will be worse for him than a defeat."

He needed powder, at least a quarter ton for his artillery, and pro-jectiles in four calibers, plus several kegs of rifle powder and enough lead for the soldiers to cast their own bullets, since the large store of captured bullets for the brown Bess muskets would not fit the volun-teers' rifles. With that, and the promised reinforcements, he would hold his fort, and they could still stop Santa Anna on this frontier. Without it, he and his men would meet their ends "with desperation, and that high-souled courage that characterizes the patriot, who is willing to die in defence of his country's liberty and his own honor."[69] Travis could not close without venting his anger at the *tejanos* who had left the garrison. He believed there were only three *tejano* men left in the Alamo. The rest he considered now as traitors, and promised to deal with them as such if somehow they came into his hands. He sug-gested that the government should declare them public enemies, and issue orders to confiscate their property. He did not mean that to apply to every *tejano* in Texas, of course, but only those who had abandoned him, yet his words contained a bitterness that only a sense of betrayal could inject. "I will visit vengeance on the enemy of Texas," he threat-ened this afternoon, "whether invaders or resident Mexican enemies."[70]

Shortly after Travis sent the courier out with his letter—it contained a comment that he did not feel entirely confident that the man would make it through the Mexican lines—Travis heard loud cheers of "Santa Anna! Santa Anna!" and the ringing of the church bells in San Antonio. Some suggested to him that it must betoken the arrival of Santa Anna himself, though he had been there all along. Rather, it celebrated a modest victory at San Patricio a few days before.[71] To dampen enemy spirits a bit, or at least to drown out the sound of the cheering, he used some precious powder and fired a few cannon and rifles at the town, to no effect other than perhaps to relieve some of his own pent-up frustration.[72] The relief was short lived, for he and his men saw the Mexicans that afternoon building scaling ladders, and there could be no mistaking their purpose.[73] Needing to do *something* to fight back, Travis used the weapon that always made him the strongest, his pen. He asked "El Colorado," who had already gone out and returned once, to make another try at the enemy lines. Travis had several letters for him. One he addressed to Jesse Grimes, a delegate to the Washington convention, and in it he urged the body to declare for full independence. "We will then understand and the world will understand what we are fighting for," Travis declared. Then, in the only comment about surrender that he made during the siege, he added that "if independence is not declared, I shall lay down my arms and so will the men under my command." It was only said for effect, for he knew by now that surrender was out of the question. They would only trade death in battle for dying standing against a wall. But he did not entirely despair. Give him just five hundred men, he said in a return of the old bravado, and he would take the offensive and drive Ramírez y Sesma back to the Rio Grande. "I shall have to fight the enemy on his own terms," he reiterated, "yet I am ready to do it, and if my countrymen do not rally to my relief, I am determined to perish in defense of this place, and my bones shall reproach my country for her neglect."

There were yet two more, brief letters to go out with Smith. One he asked Grimes to forward to Rebecca, possibly the first time he had been able to write to her with all that he had to do.[74] The other he sent to David Ayers at Montville. Smith was almost ready to go out in the darkness, before the rise of the moon made him too easily spotted, and Travis had to rush. Tearing a strip from some old yellow wrapping paper, he scrawled hastily an injunction to Ayers to "take care of my little boy." If Texas won its independence, he might yet make a name and a fortune for him to be proud of. "But if the country should be lost, and I should perish, he will have nothing but the proud recollection that he is the son of a man who died for his country."[75] Handing the letters to Smith, Travis told him that every day from now on he would fire a signal gun three times a day: morning, noon, and night. Any Texian hearing that gun would know that the men in the Alamo still held out. Then Smith crept away into the night.[76]

Still another blow had come that day, though by now many expected this one. Bowie took a dramatic turn for the worse. If the soldiers brought him out to see Juana and her sister on March 3 at all, it was his last visit. Several times before now they carried his cot to the barracks on the south side of the compound, where many of his volunteers messed together. Whatever the misunderstandings of the past, now he urged them repeatedly to regard Travis as their commander so long as they chose to stay. But those lucid moments came infrequently now, and only when his fever temporarily abated. Instead, his disease so debilitated him that he lay in intermittent delirium, scarcely able to rise from his cot when conscious, and so dehydrated from the diarrhea and vomiting that any movement at all was painful. He could not even lift his head from the pillow. The typhoid had held him in its grip probably ten days or more, and he either approached or was already suffering the critical period of its progression. Susanna Dickenson expected him to die, or at least others who saw him told her that he lay near death. All he could do for the cause now was to feed its soldiers, for unknown to him, other volunteers, including Fannin's—the men who were supposed to be coming to relieve the garrison—were even now confiscating his cattle with the brand "JB," and some of Veramendi's as well, from the *rancho* near Refugio.[77] When the soldiers carried Bowie back to his room by the gate, now poorer by the measure of a herd of beefs, Juana Alsbury did not even know who would tend to him thereafter. But then, other than trying to get him to drink and take some nourishment, there was little anyone could do for him. As he had so many times before, Big Jim Bowie would fight this battle alone.[78]Ironically, even then a report was gradually making its way eastward through the United States that Bowie had actually been relieved of his command.[79]

For the rest, fully conscious of the progress of the siege, March 4 brought a warmer wind and a renewed Mexican bombardment that started early and concentrated heavily on the north wall. Travis held his fire, knowing by now that he would probably need his powder for the actual battle, whenever it came.[80] Instead he kept the men indoors as much as possible, cutting loopholes in the walls of the buildings that lined the main rectangle. The situation hardly allowed for much of a plan of defense. All the advantages belonged to the enemy. Clearly Travis foresaw more and more the probability that if the enemy struck before reinforcements arrived, he would have to pull the men back from the walls when they were overrun, to make their last stand in these rooms. Perhaps he even gave instructions as to which companies were to occupy which rooms, though if that extremity came, organization would not matter in the scramble to reach cover. He may even have suggested that if the enemy breached their defenses, the men should resist as long as possible, then go over the east wall and try to get away as best they could toward Goliad.[81]

Indeed, Travis must have wondered why the Mexicans had not completely sealed off the route to the east past the powderhouse, as he sent out another messenger or two during the day. Some of the *tejanos* in town knew of this, and even speculated that Santa Anna ordered the east side loosely guarded intentionally, hoping that Travis would take advantage of it to get his garrison out in an escape.[82] But that was non-sense. Ramírez y Sesma's lancers could still have ridden down a band of Texians on foot almost at will. Santa Anna wanted a victory as an example, and that was why he took his time spreading his army and emplacing his batteries. If he really wished Travis to evacuate the fort, it was only so that he could overwhelm the Texians in the open, away from their artillery.[83]

By now it was too late for Travis to leave even if he wished. The Mexicans surrounded him. In fact the garrison could never have left as an organized unit from the first day of the siege. Ramírez y Sesma's lancers alone outnumbered the Texians, and Travis did not have enough horses to mount many—perhaps most—of his command, which meant abandoning those on foot or dooming the rest to a slow running fight in the open where they could be surrounded quickly. In short, despite his fiery—and sincere—proclamations about not giving up his post, Travis had no practical alternative but to stay and hope for reinforcements. The only option was to tell the men to try to slip out in the night like the couriers, every man for himself, but where one could get through undetected, two hundred or more must surely give themselves away, once again dooming the slow and the ill, and those without horses, to the point of a lance.

It was a stark reality made all the more frustrating for the fact that by now, and in the absence of relief or any likelihood of holding Béxar and repulsing Santa Anna, the garrison had accomplished all that it could hope to do. Travis had held the Mexican advance stalled here for eleven days, buying time that, sadly, Houston and Fannin had squandered. Indeed, for several days now—if not from the first— Travis had not *held* the Mexicans there. Santa Anna stayed because he *wanted* to, taking his time to set up an inevitable and total victory. An army the size of his could have marched around the Alamo and on to the Texas interior with no fear at leaving two hundred or so Texians in a mud fort in his rear. The Alamo was as much prison as fort. It kept the Mexicans out, but it kept the Texians in as well, and Santa Anna need only leave behind one of his regiments or a few companies of lancers to contain the garrison, thus eliminating them from any role in the campaign despite being in his rear and on his supply line. In short, so far as the campaign in Texas was concerned, the Alamo and its gar- rison ceased really to matter by March 1 if not before. From then on it was important only because Santa Anna chose to make it so.

And so did Travis. Still there were some hopeful signs. Though the bombardment did a lot of damage to the Alamo church walls, some of its architectural ornaments remained, even the statues of St. Anthony and St. Ferdinand standing in their wall alcoves on either side of the main door.[84] The spirits of the men still seemed high, thanks in large part to the perennial good humor of Crockett. When the shelling lulled, he brought out his fiddle and entertained the soldiers with jigs and reels he had known since he was a boy in East Tennessee. Maybe a speech or two helped. He could remember tight spots before, like that flatboat about to sink in the Mississippi with him on it until friends pulled him out. Well, his old friend Houston could still pull them out of this sinking ship, and Williamson's March 1 letter said men were on the way. They could arrive at any minute. Privately he felt less sanguine. "I think we had better march out and die in the open air," he told Mrs. Dickenson one day. "I don't like to be hemmed up."[85]

Travis fired only his signal rounds at the Mexicans on March 4, and the same three rounds the next day, in case there was anyone on the way who might hear them and know that he still held out.[86] Perhaps he noticed that now the Mexican batteries concentrated their fire heavily on the north wall, which was practically ruined. Travis and Jameson had to have the men build a timber revetment on the outside of it at night, and then pack earth in the space behind to shore up the crumbling facade. Ideally they needed to cover the horizontal exterior timbers of the revetment with earth as well, otherwise those logs would provide hand holds that could aid an attacker in scaling. But there simply was not time. Because of the need to keep the men sheltered during the daylight bombardment, Travis could only send them out to repair the damage done to the walls after dark, when the enemy ceased firing. That meant that by now the men were worn out, working late hours every night and unable to recover lost sleep during the day for the roar of the artillery. On top of that, Travis mounted extensive guards every night, fearing an attack in the dark, and he took his turn as sentinel like the rest. His servant Joe, with him now for more than two years, saw the toll the tension and fatigue took on the men. "The garrison was exhausted by incessant watching," he said a few days later.[87] Travis could see what the Mexicans had arrayed against him, mostly six- and eight-pounder field pieces, and by nightfall on March 5 they had fired some 334 cannonballs at the walls, and another eighty-six rounds of exploding shells.[88] The place was starting to crumble faster than the Texians could make their repairs.

As darkness fell on March 5 it was time to send another courier. By now Travis had sent out between fifteen and twenty men, and only one or two, like Bonham, had come back.[89] He could ill afford to lose even a single man now, but it was imperative to let the rest of Texas know that the garrison held out, and that the men were still up to the challenge before them. He called for a volunteer, and young James Allen stepped forward. He was a slight lad, with a very fast mare, and Travis sent him off toward Goliad with one more effort to make Fannin stop dithering and do something.[90]

There were other demands to be met. For some time now Travis kept the women and children in the sacristy, a room near the northeast corner of the church itself, about as far from any anticipated direction of attack as possible.[91] There they were to stay every night. Believing that Santa Anna would spare them if the garrison fell, he left his watch with Juana Alsbury for safekeeping about now, and handed other personal effects to some of the others, not because he believed the end was near but simply because it was prudent.[92] In the event that the enemy did attack before relief came, he would have no time in his last moments to be vouchsafing things to people. Meanwhile, the room on the southwest corner, the baptistery just to the right of the main church door, the Texians used as their powder magazine. It seemed an illogical choice, since the south wall of the baptistery formed part of the south wall of the fort itself, and a fortunate penetrating shot might well detonate the magazine and destroy them all. But the Mexicans showed relatively little interest in the south wall during the siege, probably because of those abatis and the heavily fortified main gate. Forced to consider the possibility that there would be an attack before help came, Travis finally gave orders that the last man alive or the last to evacuate the fort was to fire the magazine if possible.[93]

Travis and the men worked late into the night on March 5, probably not laying down their tools until after midnight. He put the sentinels out as usual, though seeing how exhausted everyone was by now, himself included, he should have wondered if they would be able to stay awake at their posts.[94] Asleep or awake, every man on the parapets had several loaded rifles, muskets, or pistols at his side, for that was one commodity of which Travis suffered no shortage. Many of the volunteers had brought more than one with them, as had Crockett, and a number of captured long arms taken in the surrender of Béxar in December came into his hands. As a result, there were 816 rifles, shotguns, pistols, and English brown Bess muskets on hand, and with his garrison now numbering more than two hundred men, that meant four apiece.[95] In the event of an attack, the Texians could deliver a deadly rate of fire in the first few minutes of a defense. Beyond that he had more than fifteen thousand prepared cartridges of powder and ball, most of them for the muskets, enough for sixty rounds or more per man, sufficient for a lengthy engagement, though loading would be slow after the initial volleys. He also had twenty-five exploding shells with fuses equipped to be used as grenades, to drop among attackers as they approached the walls, and if the Mexicans made it onto the walls themselves, they would meet two hundred bayonets that fit the brown Besses, though not the volunteers' rifles and shotguns.

In an attack he could hope that his artillery would keep the enemy from reaching the walls in the first place, but here he had some problems. His gunners had enough powder to fire more than twelve hundred rounds among the eighteen remaining operable guns, but in an attack his 686 solid shot offered little benefit, and it is just possible that he had run out of ammunition for his big eighteen- and sixteen-pounder guns. He really needed grapeshot and canister to beat back an infantry assault, and for the guns he had available with proper ammunition there were no more than five hundred loads, still more than enough to do great damage, and likely his gunners would not have time to fire all those before an attack either succeeded or failed.[96]

For Travis the last hours of that late March 5—really the earliest hours of March 6—passed no differently than any of the several nights before. He made his rounds in the cold night air, checked his sentries, and finally retired, perhaps no earlier than 3 A.M.[97] In the cold he probably slept in his clothes, as well to be ready in case of an alarm. Perhaps he wondered if the new uniform he ordered before he left San Felipe was there waiting for him now.[98] At least it would have comforted him to know that back in San Felipe that day the people were reading his stirring letter of February 24, now published in the *Telegraph and Texas Register.*[99] Maybe he could not expect reinforcements to come in time. But at least Texas and the world would know why he died. How much it would have comforted him this cold night to know that three days earlier, on March 2, the convention at Washington finally decided unanimously for a declaration of independence. And he and his men were among those whose voices were heard in that vote, for Sam Maverick and Jesse Badgett were there to affix their signatures to the document. By rights it should have been his name on the declaration, for no one had done more to bring it about. Yet he had gone far beyond that piece of paper. Out there in the Alamo, in the face of perhaps ten times his numbers, he and his garrison for the last twelve days had made of themselves a *living* declaration, a human document that Texians could not hold in their hands but must ever clasp in their hearts.

And they had given Texians—and Americans—a definition of bravery. Not the sort of courage that Bowie showed in a spontaneous battle at the Sandbar, or of the man who in the last seconds of his life dies well. Few, even the strongest and most resolute, could really control their deaths in battle, for that lay as much in the hands of chance and their slayers. The better bravery, the real courage, lay in the fact that for nearly two weeks Travis, Crockett, Bowie, and the rest knowingly placed and kept themselves in harm's way, aware each day that the Mexicans could overwhelm them at the next dawn, and yet they stayed. Regardless of their motives for enlisting in the revolution and coming to the Alamo, that alone made them heroes, though not a one of them had yet faced death as a certainty.

Dawn would come a few minutes before 7:00 A.M. on March 6. The exhausted sentinels inevitably dozed at their vigils. Travis placed a few men in picket posts outside the fort's walls, in order to detect any movement in the night, but they, too, slept. No one heard the distant sound of horses and the muffled jingle of sabers and spurs around 3:00 A.M., just as Travis fell into a deep slumber. No one heard mounted men slowly form a loose circle around the fort a hundred yards or less out in the night. No one saw the moonlight, no longer full but still bright, glinting off polished steel. No one heard the inevitable rustling and stumbling of more than a thousand pairs of feet, the clatter of bayonets rattling on their sockets, and the occasional thud as ladders banged together. It was just as well. The men in the Alamo needed their sleep.

The door to Travis's chamber in a house on the west wall burst open at about 5:30, just as the sound of not too distant shouts of "*Viva Santa Anna*" may have been awakening him.[100] Officer of the day J. J. Baugh rushed in, shouting: "The Mexicans are coming." Travis leaped from his cot, and even as he reached for his shotgun and saber and yelled to Joe to wake up to come with him, he heard the thudding of two axes and crowbars on the wooden doors and windows of the houses along the perimeter. Followed by Joe, he rushed out into the darkness, saw flashes of gunfire on the north wall, and ran the seventy yards to the earth ramp that led up to the gun emplacement.

By now men were coming alive from their slumber throughout the compound, but he could see they had been taken by surprise. His outer pickets must have been overrun, and by the time he got to the top of the parapet, the enemy Toluca Battalion was already near the foot of the wall on the other side. The gunners had opened on them with the cannon, illuminating the night scene with eerie flashes of yellow light followed by darkness, and at first did terrible damage, but by now the front ranks of the foe were so close that the artillery could not be depressed sufficiently to reach them. They had ten scaling ladders and were about to place them against the wooden revetment.[101] Travis yelled back into the compound, *"Come on Boys, the Mexicans are upon us, and we'll give them Hell!"*

Leaning over the edge of the parapet to take hasty aim, Travis gave the Mexicans both barrels of his shotgun. Out of the milling throng below a spotty volley came back at him. Flying at shattering velocity, a lead ball more than three-quarters of an inch thick struck him full in the forehead and sent him reeling back against one of the cannon. Joe thought his master was stunned yet still living, but did not stay to find out. He turned and raced for one of the barricaded houses to hide. Yet surely, with a missile as great as a brown Bess bullet plowing through his brain, Travis was dead as he hit the ground. Defiant even after the end, he still clutched his gun in his hand.[102]

It is just possible that someone got word of Travis's fall to Crockett. He may even have seen it or caught a glimpse of Travis's body, since Crockett could have been anywhere that morning. Travis may have assigned him to the picket palisade in front of the church back on February 23, but that was no surety that he would still be there thirteen days later. In any case, with the heaviest pressure coming on the north wall, men from several other positions no doubt ran there to try to stem the tide of *soldados* starting to swarm over. With Travis down, one of the captains would be next in line to assume command, but it hardly mattered, for there were no orders to give.[103] Men simply had to stand their ground where they were, rush by common instinct to where the newest danger arose, and slowly—but inevitably—fall back when Mexican numbers on the walls grew too great.

Down on the south wall a Mexican assault column skirted off to the left of the palisade rather than attack it, and passed around the emplacement guarding the main gate, heading for the southwest corner to try a lodgement. At least one Texian almost certainly heard nothing of their passage. By now Bowie was probably in a near-constant delirium, when not actually asleep. Somewhere in his third week of the typhoid, he lay shaking and sweating on his cot as the constant high fevers of the worst stage of the disease robbed his body of everything, even lucidity. He may have heard nothing at all of the fighting that went on at the opposite end of the parade, or of the firing and yelling that gradually, and then suddenly, drew very close to the south wall as the resistance everywhere gave way. Many of the remaining defenders went to ground in their fortified rooms along the perimeter. In full control of the parade ground now, the *soldados* took the Texians' own cannon and started blasting them out of their rooms, one by one.

It took no artillery to open the door to Bowie's room. He was alone. The night before someone had put a blanket over him to keep out the cold and help his wasting body's remaining warmth fight the racking chills. The covering still lay over him now, perhaps even shielding his face from the cold. If the terrible din outside did awaken him, he may have been too weak to pull the fabric from his eyes. Possibly he did not even hear the sound of feet stepping into his room. Confined for days now to this cot, he no longer wore the knife at his belt.

To the Mexican soldiers who warily entered the chamber, at first all they saw was a cot with a rumpled blanket covering something beneath. Perhaps they heard breathing or a cough. More likely in all the cacophony of sound outside, they heard nothing but saw a movement, a shiver. Or one of them simply poked at the blanket with his bayonet, or lifted back the corner to see Bowie beneath. If they had found him in the hospital with the other sick, they would have known that he, too, was incapacitated. But finding him like this, by himself, covered by a blanket, while his brave comrades fought bitterly and died hard outside, they could only suppose that this Texian was actually trying to hide from them. He may never have known what was happening. What the bayonets started, another massive bullet finished, leaving his blood and brains splattered on the wall behind him. In a cruel irony at the end of a remarkable life, one of the most fearless men of his generation died at the contemptuous hands of soldiers who mistook him for the worst sort of coward.[104]

•

There were simply too many Mexicans and too few Texians. Once the
initial breakthrough came on the north wall, the west wall and southwest corner gave way. The collapse came so quickly that the Texians
did not even have time to throw all their grenades over the wall into
the teeming mass of *soldados*. The men not now isolated in the houses
lining the parade ground, and grimly awaiting their turns to be blasted
or bayoneted, had pulled back over the east wall, either into the horse
and cattle corral, or the yard in front of the church. But the Mexicans
were pushing them, and another column started to come around from
the north to strike the upper half of the east wall. By instinct rather
than design they began to abandon the fortress.

First a good number of them came out through the gun emplacement at the northeast corner of the cattle pen. Leaping over the wall,
they raced for the brush lining a small ditch. Soon thereafter about
fifty Texians went over the wall of the horse corral farther along the
wall and almost beside the church. They, too, raced for the ditch and
chaparral, and then a third group went over the palisade and through
the abatis. In all perhaps eighty men, a third of the garrison, were outside the Alamo now. They had no plan and no hope. They had simply
been pushed out of the fortress by overwhelming numbers. It was
either go over the walls to fight and live a little longer, or else stand
and be swarmed where they were.

It might have been better for them if they had stayed. Now they
discovered for the first time the Mexican cavalry. Commanded directly
by Ramírez y Sesma, it was there patrolling precisely to prevent anyone getting away. When Ramírez y Sesma saw the first breakout, he
sent a company of lancers to ride them down in the brush. Even
though testifying to "the desperate resistance they posed," Ramírez y
Sesma saw that his mounted men made short work of them. The second group of fifty or more put up an even greater defense, as Ramírez
y Sesma himself saw that the Texians were "ready to sell their lives at a
very high price," and he had to send reinforcements twice before his
lancers finished them one by one. The last group to go over the wall
fared no better. The brutal lances killed all of them but one, a man
who took deep refuge in dense brush and had to be shot.[105] Perhaps
Crockett was one of them. He had told Susanna Dickenson he preferred to "die out in the open," not penned up like cattle. And if he was

still assigned to the palisade or its vicinity when the battle began, then he was right where the third group went out, and very close to the point of departure of the second, largest breakout. But maybe he did not get that far. If he ran to where the fight began and raged the hottest, he could have fallen anywhere from the north wall all the way to the south, or been trapped in any one of the rooms that lined the parade. There he could have been killed by a cannon's blast and a rush of bayonets, or captured and put to death out in the center of the compound, where several others met a similar fate. If he escaped that, and did not go out to face death at the end of a lance, then perhaps he did fall where Sutherland left him thirteen days before, somewhere in the dirty yard in front of the church. He may even have died very early in the battle in the redoubt that projected out of the center of the west wall.[106] No one who knew him saw him fall and lived to tell of it. "That Crockett fell at the Alamo is all that is known," a visitor concluded sadly a few months later; "by whom or how, no one can tell."[107] He was the most famous man in the Alamo, yet his death was just like his birth, an event shrouded in complete obscurity. Or perhaps the opposite was the case. His death, like his life, was simply too big to contain within the normal bounds of mortals. In the best heroic fashion of Nimrod Wildfire, Jeremiah Kentucky, Daniel Boone, and a whole generation of Americans searching for a new identity all their own, Davy Crockett, David of the River, Davy of the West, Loco Davy had died *everywhere*, because he was a host in himself.

Besides, his end fitted the life of a legend. For when no one *sees* a legend die, then the legend *lives*.[108]

ENSHRINEMENT

Dawn, March 6, 1836–Posterity

In some good cause, not in mine own,
To perish, wept for, honor'd, known,
And like a warrior overthrown.

J. HAMPTON KUYKENDALL, *Sketches of Early Texians*

They all died in the darkness. As the glimmers of dawn softened the shadows in the compound and out in the chaparral, they revealed a ghastly scene. Well over three hundred dead, Mexican and Texian, lay in scattered heaps. The victorious yet stunned *soldados* filled the Alamo searching every room, finding Susanna and Juana and the other women and children, even locating and sparing Joe because he was a slave. Some still stabbed at the corpses with their bayonets and here and there fired a shot, so overwrought by the fight or the loss of comrades that even vengeance against a dead foe seemed to help.

Santa Anna and his staff entered through the main gate, having watched from the near distance. He surveyed the carnage, perhaps ordered the execution of the few who had been taken alive, and issued instructions for the care and safety of the women and children. That done, he wanted to see the bodies of the men he had conquered, not the common soldiers, but Travis and Bowie. Joe led him to his dead master up on the gun platform of the north wall, and the word went through the Mexican army that this enemy had died well. Travis's old foe Gen. Martín Perfecto de Cós led one of the columns that hit this wall, and now perhaps he at last looked down on the bloody face of the man who had caused him so much trouble. Not surprisingly, the body showed signs of bayonet wounds, though the bullet certainly killed him almost instantly.[1]

Joe knew where Bowie stayed, and took the general to the little room to the left of the gate. There lay the emaciated hulk of a man

Santa Anna might conceivably have met some years before when
Bowie was in company with Veramendi. Certainly every upper-class
Mexican had heard of Santiago Bowie—*el fanfarrón*, as some called
him, "the braggart." What they saw now must somehow have seemed
not enough to have been such a man, especially with some of his
brains splattered on the wall behind his cot. It was a new vision of the
firmament: James Bowie, not just dead but defeated.[2]

Santa Anna probably did not ask about Crockett, not knowing that
he was in the garrison, and quite probably not even aware of who he
was or why the Texians attached such importance to him. But when he
heard Joe and some of the *tejanos* now filtering curiously into the
Alamo from San Antonio refer to Crockett as "colonel," he wanted to
see him, too. They had to look for him, and most likely Joe simply
pointed out the body when he spotted it in a general survey around
the entire scene of the battle. Joe never said where he saw him, but
Susanna Dickenson later thought she had seen him lying with many of
his Tennessee comrades somewhere in front of the church, when she
was led out of the sacristy, deep in shock. His cheeks were still red.

Less than two hours after the close of the battle, Santa Anna wrote a
hasty report of the action to send back to Mexico City. "The picture the
battle presented was extraordinary," he said. "Among the bodies were
found the first and second chiefs of the enemy—Bowie and Travis—
colonels as they called themselves—Crockett of the same title and other
chiefs."[3] Having seen them in death, he wanted to see them no more.
Moreover his soldiers could not spare the time for burial, for they had
their own dead and wounded to attend to. He gave orders for the *soldados* to collect most or all of the Texians into three piles, two smaller
ones probably composed of men killed outside by the lancers, and a
large pyre for the men who fell inside the compound. Then he sent
tejanos out into the countryside with their carts to gather dry wood, and
when they returned, they stacked the bodies and the wood in alternate
layers, poured combustible camphene on the pyres, and set them alight.
The fires burned and then smoldered for hours and on into the night.
The next day a *tejano* came to look at a pile of charred wood and ashes,
and saw mixed with it fragments of bones and even bits of charred
flesh. A darkened moist ring a foot or two wide surrounded each of the
pyres. It was the fat broiled out of the bodies by the flames.[4]

Texians in the distance, hoping to hear Travis's signal guns, heard nothing that day or in those following, though a few may have seen the thick column of smoke rising from the direction of San Antonio on March 6. That same day Travis's last dispatch, the one written March 3 and sent out with Allen, reached the convention in Washington, and the president called a special session to read it to the delegates. They voted to print a thousand copies to distribute. Houston thought it a "thrilling" document, patriotic and courageous, and yet couched in what he called "the language of despair."[5]

In Texas at large, everyone wondered and waited for more news from the Alamo. A rumor spread that Travis had turned back an enemy attack, killing five hundred Mexicans, and that he still held out; and Forbes in Nacogdoches, the man who gave Crockett his oath, wrote confidently that "the Alamo is bravely defended by Cols. James Bowie and Travis, and numbers are marching to their relief." Not Fannin, however. Having lost all nerve or resolution, he planted himself in Goliad and refused to move. By March 6 one member of the convention, after hearing the reading of Travis's letter, turned gloomy: "It is much feared that Travis and company are all massacred," he wrote. March 10 came in Washington, and still there was no news. "Much anxiety is felt for the fate of the brave men there," Col. William Gray wrote that day. "It is obvious that they must be surrounded." The next day, with still no word, he observed that "the anxiety begins to be intense." Yet a few remained confident. One man with Fannin at Goliad assured his father on March 10 that "Davy Crockett and James Bowy are fighting at San Antone like Tigers."[6] He seemed to have forgotten that Travis was at the Alamo. But then, so had Fannin.

Finally it came, the news that they had feared. On March 11 two *tejanos* from Béxar reached Gonzales with a garbled account that had Travis and Bowie and several others committing suicide rather than die at Mexican hands. Houston sent Travis's old friend Deaf Smith and others off toward San Antonio to ascertain the facts. Certainly they heard no signal guns. Then they came upon Susanna and Joe and the other survivors, on their way east after their release by Santa Anna. Now there was no doubt. Gradually the word spread, reaching the convention on March 15, and Nacogdoches within a week.[7] The news stunned men and women everywhere. Travis's old student Kuykendall was in

Gonzales when the survivors came in that evening. The "astounding intelligence" they brought inspired disbelief in him at first.[8] But the wives of Gonzales, who sent their husbands off in that thirty-two-man reinforcement that followed El Colorado to the Alamo, believed it sure enough. Their weeping and cries of anguish turned Gonzales into a town in mourning even as the people packed and hurried off to the east to escape Santa Anna's army.[9] Pleasant Rose's two girls, when they learned of their friend Travis's death, grieved for days even as they joined the exodus of Texians away from the path of enemy invasion.[10] David Ayers at Montville still had little Charlie Travis with him, and as he evacuated toward Harrisburg he had to break the news to the boy.[11] And at Cummings's Mill the word arrived late one evening. Others heard Rebecca screaming. Just a few days before a letter written by Travis on March 3 finally reached Rebecca, its contents then and forever an eternal secret between them.[12]

With the shock of the first news came exaggerated and unfounded rumors: Travis shot himself when he saw the garrison about to fall. No, he stabbed himself. Bowie was killed in his bed, or killed himself, or did he stand in the doorway of his room, pistols and knife in hand, and take several of the enemy with him before he went down? Crockett fell "fighting like a tiger." Seven men did surrender, only to be executed at Santa Anna's order, and there was even one report that mentioned the executions in such close juxtaposition to Crockett's name that it appeared he might have been one of those who sought quarter.[13]

No one took the news harder than Houston, for almost as much as Fannin, he bore the brunt of the responsibility for failing to relieve the garrison in time. His skepticism and disbelief, tinged by his political opposition to the faction Travis represented, and certainly influenced by a desire to stay at the convention to exert his influence there, meant that he had all but abandoned the Alamo to its fate. For a man with his ambitions that could be fatal, and so almost immediately he began covering his conduct. On March 7 he still expressed doubt that the Mexicans were even in San Antonio, despite all of Travis's dispatches and the certain eyewitness testimony of the couriers.[14] Then two days after definitive word of the fall of the Alamo reached him, he began the refrain that he would pursue for the rest of his life. He had given orders to blow up the Alamo and remove its guns, he claimed, but first the removal of all the draft animals by the Matamoros filibusters—"the author of all our misfortunes—and then the unwillingness of the garrison to leave, took the matter out of his hands.[15] "Our forces must not be shut up in forts," he proclaimed on March 15. Within two years the fault would be Travis's and Bowie's: "The fall of the Alamo," he declared, "resulted from disobedience."[16] Houston's excuse was sufficiently persuasive that by September some blamed Henry Smith for failing to approve the request to blow up and abandon the Alamo. He "had the blood of both Fannin and Travis on his hands," charged one critic.[17] By the time Houston got around to writing his memoirs, Bowie came to bear the blame for disobeying his order, though Houston would say at the same time that Travis, Crockett, and Bowie were all "brave and gallant spirits." They acted openly and boldly: "Their policy of warfare was to divide, advance and conquer."[18] He conveniently forgot that at the time, his policy had been to stay drunk on eggnog in Washington. "It was a bad business," he privately confessed then of his behavior. "I hated it."[19] As for his "order" being disobeyed, it was never an order in the first place, but only a suggestion to Governor Smith. When not blaming Travis or Bowie, he blamed the council for secretly countermanding his nonorder.[20] Henry Austin, a cousin of Stephen's, no doubt had Houston, among others, in mind when he wrote just three weeks after the disaster that "painfull as the event is in itself to me it came as the harbinger of Salvation to Texas—for I had long been convinced that some severe disaster alone could call the wretched set of men who have obtained the lead in public affairs to a sense of their duty to the people."[21] Whatever other emotions it produced in Texians, the fall of the Alamo did most certainly get their attention.

Back in San Antonio itself, the defenders of the Alamo held the attention of their foes long after they were dead. In the brief battle, and despite their disadvantages, Travis and his command inflicted terrible losses on Santa Anna's army. Of the sixteen hundred men involved in the attack, some four hundred fell wounded, including one general and twenty-eight officers, and seventy-five of them would die later.[22] The number actually killed outright in the fight is unclear. Santa Anna claimed only seventy when he reported the action that morning, but then he underestimated his wounded by fully one hundred, and other

570 Mexicans present would

Mexicans present would place the dead and mortally wounded closer to two hundred.[23] Regardless of the exact count, two hundred or more Texians inflicted at least 33 percent casualties on the attacking columns in the space of less than an hour. No one could say they did not give a good account of themselves. Six weeks later a Texian saw the wounded from the Alamo in their hospital. "A pretty piece of work 'Travis, and his faithful few' have made of them," he said.[24]

Meanwhile the campaign continued, the Alamo being just a stop for Santa Anna, not a goal. A few days after the fight more soldiers arrived, including Travis's old adversary from Anahuac, Juan Davis Bradburn. By June, with all the changes in the military situation, and with the Mexicans in Texas being supplied by sea, one commander reported to the secretary of war in Mexico City that "Bejar is almost insignificant," and some even argued for its evacuation.[25] By the end of April they were doing just that, for a partial Texian victory at San Jacinto on April 21, and the capture of Santa Anna the next day, virtually ended the revolution.

Well before the Mexicans left Béxar, in fact just four days after the battle, a new unit of lancers arrived. Santa Anna ordered them quartered in the Alamo, where no doubt the curious men ransacked the place for any remaining souvenirs, while their horses trod through and kicked about the three piles of dusty ashes outside the compound. By late May, when a Texian visited the spot, he saw only the vestiges of the piles. "The bones had been reduced to cinders, occasionally a bone of the leg or arm was seen almost entire," he wrote in his journal. "Peace to your ashes!"[26]

Yet nearly a year passed before those ashes met that peace, and in the meantime the wind and rain scattered and eroded the heaps, and small scavengers carried away the bits of bone. So preoccupied was newly independent Texas with other affairs that not until February 25, 1837, did it pay its proper respects to the Alamo's fallen. Fittingly, Capt. Juan Seguín brought his company of cavalry to San Antonio that day and examined what survived of the piles of charred remains. He gave orders that the bells in San Fernando should start to peal, and keep ringing throughout the day, then engaged a Béxar carpenter to build a coffin. They covered it with black cloth, then placed the ashes from the two smaller piles in the box. Though the contents reflected part of scores of men, Seguín caused to be inscribed on the inside of the lid just three names, Travis, Bowie, and Crockett. Laying a Texian rifle and sword atop the casket, his men carried it to San Fernando, and there it remained as a procession gathered in the street outside, the bell tolling all the while.

At 4 P.M. Seguín led the mourners back through the main street of town, across the San Antonio, and back toward the Alamo and the remaining pile of ashes. Setting the box down, his troopers fired three volleys over it, then did the same over the remaining larger pile. After his men gently laid the casket atop that heap, Seguín addressed the crowd in Spanish. "Even now the genius of liberty is looking down from her lofty seat, smiling with approbation upon our proceedings," he said, "and calling to us in the names of our departed brethren, Travis, Bowie, Crockett." When he finished, Maj. Thomas Western spoke to them in English, stating the obvious when he averred that "in those ashes before us we behold naught but the tangible remains of a Travis, a Bowie, a Crockett." That done, they buried the coffin and the remaining ashes on the spot and fired three more volleys. Then they marched back to the town with their banners flying and their musicians playing. They did not think to mark the spot, for who could forget the resting place of the immortal Alamo garrison. Within a few years a small grove of peach trees grew up above the grave site, yet within scarcely more than a generation, the spot was lost. Ironically the commander who gave Seguín the order to come and perform these last obsequies was Albert Sidney Johnston, younger brother of Bowie's old nemesis Josiah S. Johnston.[27]

Inevitably the word of the deaths reached relatives and friends far away from Texas, and in every instance prompted a desire for revenge. Travis's family in Alabama knew by late March 1836, and his brother Mark resolved to go to Texas to fight the Mexicans himself, though he never actually made it until the war between the United States and Mexico some ten years later, suffering a wound that afflicted him the rest of his life.[28] In Tennessee Crockett's widow Elizabeth was left to ponder the odds of a woman being twice married to men killed in massacres in forts, while his son Robert was working in the field when the horrible news came. He lost no time in rushing to Texas, where a captain saw him "so wrathy" for revenge that he wanted to kill all Mexicans. Afterward he led a small company of his own toward Matamoros, that eternal poisoned will-o'-the-wisp that had so prejudiced his father's chance of survival.[29] Three years later John Crockett won his own seat in Congress, and there took up his father's old lost cause. In 1841 he succeeded in seeing passed a bill to provide cheap land to Tennessee squatters.[30]

No one took it as hard as Rezin Bowie. Thomas J. Green went to Mississippi and Louisiana to raise volunteers for Texas immediately after the fall of the Alamo, and on April 9 offered Rezin the colonelcy of a new regiment to be raised. Bowie accepted, though he feared that his failing eyesight would keep him from active service. That did not matter to Green. Just the knowledge that Bowie held a commission would benefit Texas measurably.[31] Bowie went to New Orleans to enlist men in his regiment, and by April 12 was ready to take them upriver for the rendezvous. "From his known experience and skill in arms, together with his own and his brothers popularity," said Green, Bowie "will be able to carry many of the elusive spirits." Green could not mistake Bowie's motivation. "He longs to avenge his brothers murder." On May 5 they started for Texas, but not before a ceremony at Natchez in which citizens raised a cenotaph on the stage of the Natchez Theatre inscribed with the names of Bowie, Travis, and Crockett, among others.[32]

None of them arrived in time for the decisive battle on the San Jacinto. Through a combination of Santa Anna's overconfidence and Houston's good luck, an isolated portion of the Mexican army suffered a costly defeat, Santa Anna became Houston's prisoner, and the balance of the invasion force not captured left for the Rio Grande. Bowie's old lawyer friend Quitman missed the battle but was there immediately afterward, and actually saw the captured enemy general, who seemed to "cringe and cower" when interviewed. He also learned that when the Texians attacked at San Jacinto, they ran into battle yelling "Alamo! Alamo! Alamo!" and "Alamo! Travis! Crockett!" Others, he reported, "charged at a trot shouting 'Remember the Alamo.'" In that victory the friends of the dead found both hope and revenge. "I congratulate you sir on the ascendancy of your great cause," a man wrote to Travis's friend William P. Harris. "What can stop it now?" And back in Clarke County, Alabama, where men remembered the struggling lawyer with too few cases and the publisher with no subscriptions, the local press gloated that San Jacinto was "retribution for the savage butchery of his fellow soldiers who were massacred at the Alamo, whose blood cried aloud for vengeance on a lawless enemy."[33] San Jacinto did not end the revolution, however. In the months of inactivity and uncertainty after the battle, the old lethargy returned, and with it no little cynicism about Texian leadership. Late that summer, when the military authorities wanted to regarrison and fortify San Antonio, Green found volunteers reluctant to go. "We have to encounter the Travis, Bowie & Crockett prejudice with the soldiers," he complained.[34] Moreover, complaisance that the Mexicans would never invade again took over. "The same false logicts that prevailed last campaign is still in the country," complained one Texian, who feared they would not change their ways until "the texians are to meet with some *disastrous*."[35]

But there were no more disasters, and Texas became an independent republic. There was much to do for a new nation, though Texians did not forget their dead heroes. Before the end of 1836 Bowie's heirs began the long process of closing his estate, which proved to be surprisingly little after the near fortunes he had made and spent in his lifetime. They petitioned to collect $6,625.00 for the cattle used by Fannin's command, sold his moth-eaten coats and a few tools for a mere $47.13, and even then faced a considerable debt that he owed.[36] His only other property was his headright land, and most of that he sold to Dr. Richardson, yet more than forty years after his death the Veramendis would be trying to get it as due to them for Ursula's unpaid prenuptial settlement.[37] Crockett's estate started through probate on the same day as Bowie's, July 10, 1837, and was much simpler since he was entitled to bounties for his service and his death, and neither were encumbered. His son Robert was handed a warrant for $240.00 for Crockett's military service, then years later in 1854 settled permanently in Texas, taking up the headright his father was entitled to at his death.[38]

Travis left the most complicated estate, though chiefly because of the nature of his legal practice. There were small notes that he owed, totaling a few hundred dollars, rent due on his office in San Felipe, and papers on cases pending that needed to be turned over to his clients. John R. Jones, his executor, had to feed, clothe, and hire out his slave John and pay the proceeds into the estate, and would have done the same with Joe except that the young black ran away, all but disappearing forever. No doubt he believed that in risking a horrible death at the Alamo, he absolved himself of any need to do anything more for Travis, living or dead. Jones dealt with the joint assets of the new partnership with Starr, including the law texts. The notices of their new partnership were still running in the Texas press even after Travis's death. In the hurly-burly of the Alamo and the invasion, Starr never thought to take them out of the papers. William Cato came to Texas in November to look after the interests of Rosanna's children, and now in death Travis probably provided for Charles and Susan much more substantially than ever he had in life.[39]

Of course there was more left behind as their legacy than papers and debts and pieces of land. Partly from guilt, but chiefly out of veneration for their sacrifice, Texians soon began to memorialize them. In October 1836 Reuben Potter's poem "Hymn of the Alamo" spoke of "how Travis and his hundred fell amid a thousand foemen slain" in order to give Texas "freedom's breath of life."[40] In time counties bore the name of each of the three, Travis County being the first, when the legislature created it in November 1836. No sooner did the revolution end than the Alamo itself became an object of curiosity. "I never look into the ruins of the Church without shedding a tear," an old *tejano* woman told one of the mounting number of visitors in 1843: "I knew them all." Five or six years after the fight men still saw the dark spots on the wall of that room to the left of the gate, where Bowie's brains and blood spattered the mud. But then someone replastered the room and erased the stain, just as the winds and the small creatures all but obliterated the remainder of the piles of ashes outside. By the early 1840s many Texians smoked souvenir pipes or wore crucifixes made of stone from the crumbling walls.[41] Almost forty years after the siege, Travis's slave Joe reemerged in the new capital, Austin, in Travis County. A local editor proposed making him and Susanna Dickenson guests of honor for a celebration of the anniversary of San Jacinto, but then Joe disappeared once more. Hiding had saved his life at the Alamo, and he may have spent years hiding or running after he escaped from slavery. Not being seen had become for him virtually a way of life.[42]

Inevitably their fame spread beyond the bounds of Texas. Only Crockett had enjoyed a prior national reputation, and his death at the Alamo seemed almost tailored for his legend. Ironically, he quickly became the best known and remembered of the men in the Alamo pantheon, even though he could hardly have been said to be a Texian yet by the time of his death, and it had never been his intention originally to involve himself in the revolt. Crockett souvenirs became immediately prized. Nearly twenty horses were sold at varying times in and around Washington, and at highly inflated prices, all purporting to be the one he rode into Texas astride, despite the fact that the "large American horse" that bore him out of Tennessee was actually returned to Elizabeth Crockett within a few months, along with the watch Crockett sold in Arkansas. But then, the legendary Crockett, "Davy of the West," could have ridden twenty horses at once.[43] His threat to go to Texas if Van Buren won the White House soon became a catchphrase among Whigs and Calhoun Democrats. Even as Crockett visited Nacogdoches on his way to San Antonio, Bowie's old friend Quitman in Natchez felt so disgusted at the prospect of Van Buren as president that he threatened to "go to the wild woods of Texas."[44] In his sometimes counterproductive worship of absolute honesty, David became in the public mind a paragon. "I am a plain and anxious seeker for unsophisticated truth," wrote an Alabamian a few weeks after the Alamo. "I know very well that when this truth is presented, it is like the lone Davy Crockett battling with a hundred Mexicans. It is a lone truth against a hundred sophisms."[45] David would have liked that, and he would have loved the way the country at large seemed so reluctant to part with him. "Alas, poor Davy!" wailed a Nashville editor, "thine was a horrible fate; but like a man, and an *American*, you met it!"[46] Even the more sedate eastern press caught the spirit. "He was indeed a character," said a New York journal, "one that no other country but our own ever did or ever will produce." He was a pure through and through product of the frontier, it asserted, and in his death he, "in the flash language of the country, became a *steamboat*."[47] All across the country men read again his autobiography, and the other, spurious works that soon appeared. For the first time in American history, entrepreneurs began to capitalize by marketing books and products associated, if only by name, with a national celebrity. Even in the spurious works, however, there lived a spark of that distinctive American vernacular and humor that Crockett first so effectively utilized.

In fact, just as Crockett died in March 1836, an infant Samuel Clemens lay in his crib far to the northeast. When he grew to manhood he would use his pen to continue and expand the evolution of a distinctive brand of American literary humor that had its roots in Crockett. Huckleberry Finn would be but the young David Crockett, still on the road, still having adventures, and still amusing and charming generations. Americans were reluctant to let him die. In February 1840 when a letter came from Camargo with a report that Crockett survived the battle and now worked as a slave in a Guadalajaran mine, the public quickly felt renewed hope before the story proved to be spurious.[48]

Travis, by contrast, was a disembodied name to the nation outside Texas. No one had heard of him before the Alamo, and thus his inclusion in the listing of the heroes' names failed to resonate. He never became a folk hero, for he did not fit the mold of the time. He was educated, moved with no air of violence about him as did Bowie, nor had any of Crockett's legendary frontier exploits and eccentricities. As time went on, many outside Texas simply forgot him, never having known him in the first place, and only Crockett and Bowie would stick in the memories of the people at large. Yet those who knew Travis remembered "a man of transcendent talents," as one Texian said a few weeks after his death.[49] His old friend DeWitt Clinton Harris thought him "brave and Gallant," and another Texas editor concluded that he was "a man who was endowed with talents scarcely inferior to the bravery which has placed his name next to that of Leonidas on the List of heroes."[50] But there would be no growth of legend around his exploits as with Crockett. His memory did become entangled with its share of myths, but perverse ones that made him a murderer or a fool in Alabama, and a man with a death wish at the Alamo. Nearly a century after his demise a few men began a rumor that he left Claiborne to escape retribution for killing a man who had cuckolded him with Rosanna, and somehow Alabamians preferred to believe that rather than have a man now a hero be remembered as a fugitive from debt.

Decades after the Alamo, a second- or thirdhand claim emerged that a survivor said shortly before the final attack that Travis told his men they were all destined to die, and drew a line in the dirt with his sword, asking those who would stay to cross and stand with him. It, too, was entirely imaginary, but this legend caught the imagination of the nation, and with it Travis reemerged as a national hero, not just a Texian icon.

Sadly that did little to help his family. Cato took Charles back to his mother and her new husband, Samuel Cloud, who raised him until they both died in a fever epidemic in 1848. Young Travis went back to Texas and actually won a seat in the legislature at age twenty-two, showing some of his father's precocity. But he also had that irresponsible streak, would not stay with something when he started it, and in 1856, as a lieutenant in the Second U.S. Cavalry, then commanded by that same Albert Sidney Johnston who had buried his father's ashes, he was cashiered for dishonesty. He went on to get a bachelor's degree in law at Baylor University in 1859, but died the next year, barely thirty.[51] He left no children, but his sister Susan married and had a daughter. Alas Travis's granddaughter fared no better in life than had his son. She married a man named DeCaussey, but by 1895, almost sixty years after her grandfather's death, they were all but destitute, and selling family mementos like Travis's Bible and his famous February 24, 1836, letter to the State of Texas just to live. In desperation, they appealed to the William Barret Travis chapter of the patriotic descendants' organization, the Daughters of the Republic of Texas, who by then owned and operated the remains of the fort as a historic site. They wanted the Daughters to hire DeCaussey as a janitor at the Alamo.[52] As if that was not irony enough, many years later, in August 1939, an old and financially strapped Mark A. Travis, nephew of the hero, tried to secure the same job.[53]

Bowie fared somewhere in between Crockett and Travis in memory. His celebrity prior to the Alamo extended only to western Louisiana and Arkansas, Natchez, and of course Texas. Moreover, when men spoke of him at all, it was not in exaggerated myths and frontier stories, but all-too-factual discussions of his land dealings. His name appeared only twice in the eastern press, the first time in relation to the Sandbar brawl, and the second time in the publication of Rezin's account of the San Saba fight. There was no Bowie mythology before March 6, 1836. The reality of his immediate legacy was uncertainty in some quarters in Texas as to his real motivation in espousing the cause, and an overpowering sadness among his family in Louisiana. His mother took the news bravely, and supposedly only commented that she doubted any wounds would be found in his back. Of course, given the circumstances of his death, there was no question either of heroism or cowardice on his part, but she would never know that.[54] Caiaphas Ham was in Louisiana when the news came. It "almost crushed many hearts in that sunny land where Col. Bowie was best known and most appreciated," he remembered years later, though he may have been overstating the case a bit, considering that many chiefly knew and appreciated Bowie for his land frauds.[55]

Yet there is no room for doubt about how Rezin took the news. His involvement in raising volunteers for Texas did not at all relieve him of his anger and anguish. His friend William Sparks watched as, for the next five years, Rezin brooded over James's death. It sapped him of his vitality, and he lost all zest for the adventures and enterprises of yore. He sold out and moved to Iberville Parish, but the move affected no change, and the physician attending him in his melancholy told Sparks that "the death of James Bowie was killing Rezin."[56] Never before contentious, he now began to guard his brother's reputation, and especially against a growing number of fictitious stories placing James in duels and fights, generally in defense of the innocent. He wrote for publication in 1838 a denunciation of all such stories, emphasizing that James had only ever been in one fight, and that at the Sandbar. Revealing his hurt and his anger at seeing his beloved brother's memory beginning to fall into the hands of mythmakers, he even threatened to challenge to a duel himself those who created falsehoods about James. By January 18, 1841, he could fight his poor health and his sorrow no longer. He died in New Orleans, leaving John, the eldest, the only survivor of all the Bowie brothers.[57]

Before he went, Rezin had been at work on one more Bowie land deal, and one that no doubt would have appealed to James. Indeed, only months after his brother's death, Rezin made another trip to Cuba, to see the widow of Vicente Pintado. She had all of those land survey plat books from his days as principal surveyor before the

Louisiana Purchase. For some time before his death he made a little money by providing certificates of the surveys to grant holders and purchasers. These grants, of course, were all quite genuine, and in the continuing confusion over titles in the state, his documents were vital. If Rezin ever had any notion of copying James's claim techniques, knowing all the details and actual location of genuine grants would be an enormous advantage in any fraudulent scheme. If James had had access to Pintado's papers, he might never have made the errors that resulted in his being discovered. But Rezin was no fraud. With two other partners, John Wilson of Missouri and Judge Edward White of Louisiana, he bought the papers from Pintado for more than five thousand dollars, probably intending to do a fair business in continuing to provide certificates of survey, and nothing more. But when he died he had done nothing with them as yet, and efforts to sell them to the General Land Office failed. His brother would have found some much more imaginative use for the Pintado papers if he had gotten them.[58]

James Bowie's imagination in land dealings did continue to manifest itself long after his death. In Texas one of the first acts of the new constitution was the invalidation of most of the eleven-league grants he had held.[59] Far more important and far reaching, however, were his Louisiana frauds. Even before his death, their extensive number actually delayed the proper survey and sale of public domain property in Louisiana, to the injury of the U.S. Treasury. By 1838, two years after his death, the term "Bowie claims" became a euphemism in Washington for fraudulent titles. As the surveying of the state progressed, time and time again a genuine survey was found to conflict with a title already issued on the basis of one of Bowie's false grants, with the government forced to provide the innocent claimant property elsewhere at no benefit to the Treasury. Sutton's 1821 report achieved a remarkable notoriety by the late 1830s, most of it being Bowie's forgeries. By 1848 the popular press in Louisiana, discussing the decades-old problem of bogus grants, paid him a backhanded compliment when James B. D. DeBow declared in his influential *Commercial Review* that "none of these secured for themselves a greater notoriety as holders of fraudulent land claims than James Bowie, a man of courage and daring." The problems continued until March 13, 1844, when Senate Bill 110 passed Congress, attempting to clear up the confusion

caused by Bowie's activities. Even then the difficulties did not end. In
1882, nearly half a century after Bowie's death, his Antonio Vaca
forged grant was still sending litigants to court to decide the ownership of the land. His schemes may not have succeeded entirely, but
Bowie managed to leave the state of Louisiana and the U.S. government a legacy of fifty years or more of confusion.[60]

Perhaps it was fitting, then, that the imagination of others went to
work quickly on Bowie himself. A month after his death his old
friends in Natchez would read of "Gen'l Bowie" in their papers, as if he
had somehow been promoted from the colonelcy he never really held.[61]
Before long states in which he never once set foot began to claim him.
Some said he had been born in Georgia, South Carolina, or Tennessee,
and by the 1850s citizens in Travis's old Alabama home thought they
recalled Bowie living in a double log house on the road from
Claiborne to Burnt Corn, giving Monroe County claim to two Alamo
heroes.[62] People began confusing James with Rezin just two years after
his death, in 1838 speaking of "Col Bowie, the inventer of the celebrated knife that bears his name," and how he left behind two daughters who were excellent marksmen.[63] In July 1838 the noted actress
Charlotte Cushman claimed to have James Bowie's actual knife, taken
from his baggage left in the Alamo, and some years later Edwin
Forrest made claims that *he* had the famous eponymous blade, a gift
from James himself.[64] Both were obvious lies, but just as some found
they could cash in on Crockett's fame, so too did a few people attempt
to make capital from Bowie.[65]

Rezin at least tried to correct the record on the knife and its uses. In
1838 he published a letter in the press detailing exactly how he made
the first one, the one that James carried and used at the Sandbar fight,
and then forthrightly pointed out that his original differed considerably from the extensive variations of the 1830s as the rage for large
knives took over. He would take no credit for what he had not done
himself. So solicitous was Rezin of his beloved brother's memory that
if James actually had invented the design of the great blade then
sweeping the frontier imagination, surely he would have promoted
rather than discouraged such a claim. Similarly, he also denied the
growing body of legend that put James and himself in a number of
duels and "medleys" in the Mississippi Valley. Neither was ever in a

duel, he said, and James only took part in one, admittedly legendary, frontier brawl, and only ever used the knife in personal combat that one time, and then only after he had fired his pistols.

No one wanted to listen. By the 1850s the same craze for invention that created a mythical Davy Crockett alongside the real one took over James Bowie. His old friend Sparks saw it happen, commenting on how Bowie's undoubted notoriety as a violent man gave rise to "many an imaginary and ridiculous story of doubtful morality."[66] In time the real man was completely forgotten, not an altogether unfortunate circumstance in some respects, since forgotten, too, were his land frauds, the slave smuggling, the intimidation, and more. Instead, legend makers quickly engrafted onto his unquestioned bravery and spirit of adventure a host of new escapades. Yet, in an evolution from the frontier legend of Crockett of the 1830s, by the 1850s and later, the eccentricity and outlandish feats and boast were gone—ironic, since boasting was one unquestioned trait of the real Bowie. In their place this newer frontier society substituted increasing violence. The great majority of the Bowie stories that emerged involved him in fatal duels, often acting as the heroic protector of some victim or underdog, and even borrowing from old—and probably never used—dueling idioms like the participants being nailed by their trousers to a log, to ensure that they fought until one died. In these legendary fights Bowie killed the son of his old friend Jean Laffite, turned out unscrupulous gamblers in Natchez like Jack Sturdivant—who perhaps never lived—and more. After Rezin died in 1841 and was no longer able to refute them, they took over completely. Bowie was the Good Samaritan, helping a minister battle disruptive rowdies. He was the gentleman, defending ladies against ungentlemanly conduct. He was the invincible gambler, winning back small fortunes for dupes unwittingly cheated at cards. According to the growing legend, great men as far away as England, such as Thomas Carlyle, extolled Bowie's bravery and prowess.[67] Like Crockett, he was the Trickster at times, and yet at the root of all of the Bowie legend lay at least the hint of violence—and more often the fact. Whatever he did and wherever he went, there was always that knife. So completely did the legend take hold that after just two generations, Rezin's own grandchildren knew almost nothing of the reality of James's life, and firmly believed the legends instead, becoming themselves an influential source of misinformation.[68]

It was in that several inches of sharpened steel that lay the ultimate irony of Bowie to posterity. Innumerable legends made him, not Rezin, its designer, and the attachment of the family name to a weapon that caught public imagination ensured that the two would be inseparable. A big knife was practical, no mystery in that, and as more and more men came across the Mississippi to challenge the frontier, they needed one, more as a tool than a weapon. In 1834 a British visitor noted the growing craze for such knives—Rezin always said that others designed and made this new variety—and commented that they "got their name of Bowie knives from a conspicuous person of this fiery climate."[69] The next year they were being made in Boston and Cincinnati and elsewhere, and by 1841 James Black claimed to have made them in Arkansas. The year after Bowie's death, the Alabama legislature passed legislation decreeing that anyone carrying a Bowie knife who subsequently killed a person in a fight would be charged with premeditated murder. Mississippi prohibited it as a dueling weapon, and in 1838 Tennessee tried to ban its sale. By 1839 the name caught the imagination sufficiently that the Grenada, Mississippi, *Bulletin* changed its name to the *Bowie-knife*.[70] No one could ever say for certain just how the knife got its name, whether for Rezin who made the early prototype and apparently made others as gifts for friends, or for James, who only used it once in action. If James does deserve the credit, it is probably because after 1827 he was so often seen wearing the large knife at his belt, and that identified the blade with him.

That distinctive type of American frontier character was evolving from bumpkin and prankster, like Crockett and Mike Fink, toward a more sinister stereotype, surrounded by the ever-present danger and violence of the less civilized new West. At the same time a terrible weapon like a big knife seemed to symbolize the cold determination and occasional savage brutality of the new American, who in this generation would create aphorisms like "war to the knife, and the knife to the hilt." He was a far cry from Nimrod Wildfire, and unlike Crockett, there was no living man for the new icon's image to ride. The dead Bowie was perfect for this new folk hero, however. He was brave, he could be brutal, and he once killed a man with the big knife. That was enough. Ironically, he became ultimately the blade's most famous victim, for the rising legend attached to the knife and the mythology that put it repeatedly in James's hand in duel after duel all but killed the memory of the historical James Bowie.

As the craze for the knives spread, his fame and growing legend spread with them, until both were suddenly superseded a generation later by a newer and vastly more deadly weapon, the repeating pistol. When the "six-gun" came, it created a whole new dimension for the frontier hero, and the knife went back to being a utilitarian instrument, and the Bowie legend stopped growing. Yet he lived on in a way, for behind the new revolvers there was still the essential man of violence—fearless, quick to fight, yet a defender of the weak. American mythology simply took the Bowie of the knife myth and put a gun in his hand. And still beneath the myths and fables lay something fundamental. They all turned on an undeniable truth. This was James Bowie of the Sandbar and the San Saba and more. Even if he had not done all those legendary deeds, few doubted that he could have done them. Unsaid in every bit of the Bowie lore was the implicit feeling that if only he had not been confined to his cot by cruel fate and illness that March morning, then Santa Anna and his army might *still* be trying to get into the Alamo.

Travis's friend and pupil Kuykendall, ever the suffering poet, wrote some verse about them in 1849, calling it "The Valiant Dead."

> The trumpet's voice and war's alarms
> Shall summon them no more to arms;
> In Valor's ranks they've left a space
> And in our hearts a vacant place:
> But Sleep evokes in solemn night
> Their radiant forms to Fancy's sight,
> And waking thought, to sadness wed,
> Dwells mutely on the valiant dead.
> High Bards shall sing their deathless deeds,
> And Freedom's pilgrims, clad in weeds,
> Oe'r their cold graves warm tears will shed
> And Heaven reward the valiant dead.[71]

It was not a particularly good poem, and verse would present no challenge to legend for custody of their memory. Neither would fact.

Myth claimed them all by degrees: Crockett the most, Travis the least. Forgotten entirely was that they had been men of their times, yet somehow exaggerated, larger in life, than the types they represented. They all in a way stood for the aspirations of Jacksonian America, and yet not one of them was a true Jacksonian. Crockett was never a party man, and his personal aspirations were always to rise to property and standing, much more in tune with the Whigs. Bowie left no comment on national political affairs, but it is not hard to see that his sympathies, too, lay chiefly with the Whigs, for they were the men with whom he associated and who stood to further his ambitions. Travis was a Democrat at least, but by all evidence more attached to the school of John C. Calhoun than that of Jackson.

Certainly not one of them, not even Crockett, was the so-called "common man" so exalted in the Jacksonian era, and Bowie and Travis were not even typical Southerners, with their constant efforts at material and financial self-betterment. Indeed, each of the three came from what could have been called the middle class in the context of their time and place, even Crockett. Yet they were all self-made men, building on varying degrees of advantage and disadvantage at birth. The paths they took to "make" themselves varied widely, but they were the roads that all these new men took in building lives for themselves and in conquering the continent. Their roads just happened to lead them to the Alamo. Crockett's type would always be on the outer edge of the new land, living for the thrill of exploration and in the hope of finding that elusive free land on which to settle, though once obtained they almost always pushed on when a new horizon opened farther west. Bowie and his kind followed in the next wave, coming to capitalize and exploit the opportunities proffered by new and unlimited resources, and limited legal restraint. Neither could achieve his life's goal, for neither was capable of satisfaction. Crockett lived doomed to be "Davy," an original, perhaps, but not a gentleman in the eyes of America, and for him one horizon only led to another. Bowie never got rich because for him no fortune could ever be great enough.

It was the Travises who made the greatest mark, and only Travis truly realized his ambition before he died. They were the third wave of settlement—the professionals, doctors, lawyers, newspapermen, educators—who came to bring stability, learning, and the rule of law. They were the community makers who took what a Crockett would find and a Bowie exploit, and turned it into a state. Had he lived, Crockett might never have settled permanently until too old to keep going on the long hunt toward another sunset. Had he survived, Bowie would only have stayed in Texas as long as opportunity for big land deals afforded, and that drying up, he would have moved on. Unquestionably, if he had still been alive in 1848, a fifty-two-year-old Bowie would have been on his way to California in the first rush after the gold strike. Men like Bowie and Crockett were made to bestride continents. As for Travis, the Alamo got in the way of what almost certainly would have been a career leading to the presidency of the republic, or after Texas achieved statehood, a governorship or even a seat in the U.S. Senate.

Their critics then and thereafter would charge that these were no patriots. They were simply men bent on the main chance. If these three and the two hundred or more who fell with them undeniably died heroes' deaths for the way they put themselves in harm's way when they could have escaped, still they acted out of self-interest, not selfless devotion to a cause. Bowie especially seems susceptible to the accusation. All his involvement in the eleven-league grants gave him a tremendous motive for wanting to see Texas break away from a Mexican government that would repudiate those grants. Travis, though hardly in Bowie's class as a speculator, still evidenced some hope of land profit, and significantly in his very last message out of the Alamo he wrote of the "fortune" he hoped to make for his son, though he might just as well have been speaking in the classical sense of "making one's fortune," meaning to establish a standing in the world, a good name and reputation. But even those things are personal goals, with seemingly little or nothing to do with patriotism. As for Crockett, he was embracing Texas as a new home, and a new base from which to launch perhaps yet another political career. But would he have stuck with it any longer than he had any of his previous homes? Did he die at the Alamo because of a deep commitment to a cause, or would Texas have been in the end just one more tentative settlement like all the rest, a stop but not a terminus on his ceaseless quest to find his own fortunes?

They all sought their own ends in Texian independence, but to dismiss them as self-serving opportunists—even Bowie, the most opportunistic of all—is to be obtuse, and woefully ignorant of the history and nature of what men call patriotism. Tocqueville observed the struggles of millions like Crockett, Bowie, and Travis throughout America at the very moment that the revolt in Texas approached. He marveled at how an American could one moment devote himself single-mindedly to the relentless pursuit of his personal interests as if he were the only man on the planet, and yet the next instant immerse himself so deeply in the public interest that it might appear he had forgotten his own entirely. "Sometimes he seems to be animated by the most selfish greed and sometimes by the most lively patriotism," wrote the Frenchman, but he saw perceptively that "a human heart cannot really be divided in this way." The passions that Americans displayed alternately for their own welfare and then for their idea of liberty were so similar, he found, "that one must suppose these urges to be united and mingled in some part of their being." To an American, freedom for the body politic was the best and surest guarantee of the prosperity of the individual, and at the same time the best tool for levering that fortune from the continent. Americans loved freedom and prosperity equally "for the sake of each other." As a result "they think it their most important concern to secure a government which will allow them to get the good things they want and which will not stop their enjoying those they have in peace."[72]

Like their ancestors in the days of Elizabeth I, they faced a new world brimming with opportunity for the man with Crockett's spirit of adventure, Bowie's bold daring, and Travis's drive to succeed. Like those earlier men who discovered and exploited an earlier American frontier, Crockett, Bowie, Travis, and legions like them felt no hesitation in displacing others as they seized their new world in the relentless pursuit of personal gain and the spread of their civilization. In their coming together at the Alamo, they signified the combination of all the forces then in mutual contest with the continent. They thought and fought for the day, and not tomorrow. Like the Americans whom Tocqueville saw everywhere, they were ambitious, and "ambitious men in democracies are less concerned than those in any other lands for the interests and judgment of posterity," he found. "The actual moment completely occupies and absorbs them. They carry through great undertakings quickly in preference to erecting long-lasting monuments. They are much more in love with success than with glory."[73]

•

They had been in every way men of their time. It was only in death that they became unwittingly men for all time, only by their ends at the Alamo that they erected, in their own way, their lasting monument. The elegies came early and were many. William Wharton spoke within weeks of how "the gallant Travis was cut off in the flame of his life," and asserted that "Bowie is a name that was synonymous with all that was manly and indomitable in the character of man."[74] But it was another man, unknown, remembering Crockett a month after the Alamo, who spoke for each of them, and for their generation. "The bear, the wild cat, and the alligator, no longer tremble at the sound of his carabine," said the eulogist.

"He has 'gone ahead.'"[75]

NOTES

Abbreviations Used in the Notes

ADAH   Alabama Department of Archives and History, Montgomery

DRT   Daughters of the Republic of Texas Library, San Antonio

HSP   Historical Society of Pennsylvania, Philadelphia

Jenkins, *PTR* John H. Jenkins, comp. *Papers of the Texas Revolution, 1835–1836* (Austin, 1973)

LSU   Hill Library, Louisiana State University, Baton Rouge

NA   National Archives, Washington, D.C.

SHC, UNC   Southern Historical Collection, University of North Carolina, Chapel Hill

TSL   Tennessee State Library and Archives, Nashville

TXSL   Texas State Library and Archives, Austin

UT   Center for American History, University of Texas, Austin

Men and Legends

1. The background and sources for this fable, and an examination of its impossibility, are found in chapter 9, note 32.

2. The burial of the ashes is covered in the final chapter, including the statement of sources. Whether or not the coffin contained any part of Crockett, Bowie, or Travis, is entirely conjectural. It is supposed, with some foundation, that the large pile of dead burned were those killed inside the Alamo compound, while the two smaller piles were of those killed outside the walls, who would have had to be carried much farther to reach the main pile, hence the formation of two smaller ones. If this is the case, the certainty that Travis and Bowie were killed inside the compound would put their bodies in the large pile, and hence none of their ashes went into the casket. Crockett's place of death is uncertain, though he probably died inside the compound as well, and thus would have missed being included in the coffin.

3. New York *Times,* October 24, 1996.

4. Galveston *Daily News,* September 8, 1875. See also New Orleans *Times,* September 5, 1875.

5. Lucy Leigh Bowie manuscript, Lucy Leigh Bowie Papers, Maryland Historical Society, Baltimore; Elve Soniat to Mr. Bowie, March 11, May 12, 1896, Lucy

Leigh Bowie Papers, DRT; John S. Moore to W. W. Fontaine, May 14, 1890, William W. Fontaine Collection, UT; New Orleans *Times-Picayune,* March 24, 1976. Moore's sister-in-law who produced so much was Effie Harrison Snyder, one of her interviews appearing in the St. Joseph, La., *Tensas Gazette,* May 8, 1931.

6. J. De Stefani, "Handwriting Analysis of Jim Bowie," *Alamo Journal* 99 (December 1995): n.d.; Joseph Musso, untitled article on a Bowie knife, *Alamo II* 21 (February 1982): 1–7. Joe Nickell, ed., *Psychic Sleuths: ESP and Sensational Cases* (Buffalo, N.Y., 1995), 14, 17, 21–29, 237, exposes the falseness of Hurkos's claims to have helped police solve crimes, noting that even some believers in the questionable field of psychic detection have branded Hurkos "a psychic scoundrel." For an example of the way he worked, see Ronald A. Schwartz, "Sleight of Tongue," *Skeptical Inquirer* 3 (Fall 1978): 47–55.

7. Alexis de Tocqueville, *Democracy in America,* ed. J. Mayer (New York, 1966), 285.

8. Henry David Thoreau, "Walking," in Henry Seidel Canby, ed., *The Works of Henry David Thoreau* (Boston, 1937), 673.

Chapter 1   Crockett 1786–1815

1. There is some controversy about Crockett's ancestry, with some claims that he descended from a French line, but the true lineage remains uncertain.

2. David Crockett, *A Narrative of the Life of David Crockett of the State of Tennessee,* ed. James A. Shackford and Stanley J. Folmsbee (Knoxville, 1973), 14. Unless otherwise cited, all material on Crockett in this chapter is drawn from this source.

3. Stanley J. Folmsbee and Anna Grace Catron, "The Early Career of David Crockett," *East Tennessee Historical Society's Publications* 28 (1956): 59–60.

4. Crockett, *Narrative,* 15–16; Folmsbee and Catron, "Early Career," 60n.

5. David Crockett to Elizabeth Crowder, January 11, 1835, Barrett Box, Special Collections, Alderman Library, University of Virginia, Charlottesville.

6. Crockett, *Narrative,* 15.

7. James A. Shackford, *David Crockett, The Man and the Legend* (Chapel Hill, N.C., 1956), 6–7.

8. Crockett, *Narrative,* 18–21.

9. Ibid., 21–22; Folmsbee and Catron, "Early Career," 61–62. There is, in fact, some dispute about just where the tavern was located, as discussed in the Folmsbee-Catron article and in the notes of the Shackford-Folmsbee edition of Crockett's autobiography.

10. Shackford, *Crockett,* 6.

11. Crockett, *Narrative,* 22.

12. John L. Jacobs to the editor of the Morristown *Gazette,* November 22, 1884, Correspondence by Subject, David Crockett, TSL.

13. Crockett, *Narrative,* 22–23.

14. Ibid., 23.

15. Joseph Arpad, "David Crockett: An Original Legendary Eccentricity and Early American Character" (Ph.D. diss., Duke University, Durham, N.C., 1970), 171–72.

16. Typically in this time and place, when several youngsters of varying age started schooling at the same time, as Crockett and his brothers appear to have done, it meant that the school had just gone into operation, hence the conclusion that Kitchen had just opened his class.

17. Crockett, *Narrative*, 30.

18. Ibid., 33.

19. Ibid., 47.

20. William C. Davis, *A Way Through the Wilderness: The Natchez Trace and the Civilization of the Southern Frontier* (New York, 1995), 166–67; Arpad, "Crockett," 169–71.

21. Marriage license, October 27, 1805, in "Documents of the Texian Revolution," *Alamo Journal* 101 (June 1996), 17.

22. Crockett, *Narrative*, 53–54.

23. Folmsbee and Catron, "Early Career," 63.

24. Crockett, *Narrative*, 67–68; Jacobs to the Editor of the Morristown *Gazette*, November 22, 1884, Correspondence by Subject, David Crockett, TSL.

25. Folmsbee and Catron, "Early Career," 64; Crockett, *Narrative*, 69n.

26. Crockett, *Narrative*, 71–73.

27. Crockett to James Davison, August 18, 1831, David Crockett Vertical File, DRT.

28. Crockett, *Narrative*, 82.

29. Ibid., 89–90.

30. John Reid and John Henry Eaton, *The Life of Andrew Jackson* (1817; reprint, University, Ala., 1974), 90–98.

31. Compiled Service Record of David Crockett, Adjutant General's Office, War of 1812, Record Group 94, NA.

32. Ibid.; Crockett, *Narrative*, 101–24.

Chapter 2   Bowie 1796–1820

1. John Evans, "Bowie (Boo-wee) or Bowie (Bo-wee)? What's in a Name?" *Alamo Journal* 69 (December 1989): 6.

2. Savannah, *Georgia Gazette*, November 7, 1765; Allen D. Candler, comp., *The Colonial Records of the State of Georgia* (Atlanta, 1907), vol. 9, 632; vol 10, 132, 715; vol. 12, 174; Allen D. Candler, comp., *The Revolutionary Records of the State of Georgia* (Atlanta, 1907), vol. 2, 600; Georgia Records of Livestock Brands, March 6, 1769, copy in James Bowie Biographical File, DRT.

3. Walter Worthington Bowie, *The Bowies and Their Kindred* (Washington, D.C., 1899), 258–59; Martha Bowie Burns article, n.d., for the *News Sunday Magazine Supplement*, James Bowie Biographical File, DRT; Candler, *Revolutionary Records*,

vol. 2, 729. All these family sources for Bowie history in the eighteenth and early nineteenth centuries must be used cautiously and in large part be regarded more as family lore than solid documentary history.

4. Deed Book 1, 81–82, 125, 128, 160, Clerk of the Court, Sumner County Courthouse, Gallatin, Tennessee; J. Guy Cisco, *Historic Sumner County, Tennessee* (Nashville, 1900), 230; John J. Bowie, "Early Life in the Southwest—The Bowies," *DeBow's Review* 13 (October 1852): 379. Of all sources for the early years of the Bowies, the John Bowie article, skimpy as it is, remains the most reliable.

5. Deed Book A1, 28, 29, Clerk of the Court, Logan County Courthouse, Russellville, Ky. This is now the Turnertown Road, Terrapin is now known as Spring Creek, and the site is in Simpson County, which was split away from Logan in the next century.

6. Typical of the wild inaccuracy in much of the writing on James Bowie, his birth-place has been given as Tennessee, Georgia, South Carolina, even Mississippi—see for instance J. F. H. Claiborne, *Mississippi as a Province, Territory and State, with Biographical Notices of Eminent Citizens* (Jackson, 1880), vol. 1, 259. There has never been any real mystery that Logan County was the site, as his brother John Bowie definitely said that James was born there in the spring of 1796, and since he was eleven years old at the time, John should have been mature enough to have remembered the event accurately later, especially since he associated with his par-ents who could recall it for him to the end of their lives (Bowie, "The Bowies," 379). In addition to his *DeBow's* article, John Bowie also published substantially the same reminiscences in the Washington, Tex. *Lone Star*, October 23, 1852, in which he reiterates James's spring 1796 birth date. It should be noted that Raymond Thorp, *Bowie Knife* (privately published, N. Mex., 1948), n.p., states that uncited Logan County tax records revealed James Bowie's birth date to have been specifically April 10, 1796, and this has subsequently been picked up by Bowie students. This was apparently pure invention by Thorp, for no Logan County records even mention James, much less pinpoint the date of his birth. They only establish that the Bowies were living in Logan County during the years covering the period of James's birth, just as John Bowie said they were.

7. Survey of October 27, 1796, Survey Book A, 18, Land grant no. 1268, Order Book 1A, Deed Book A–1, 32, Logan County Courthouse; Bowie, *The Bowies*, 262–63, 277.

8. Louis Houck, *History of Missouri* (Chicago, 1908), 165n.

9. Bowie, "The Bowies," 379.

10. Tocqueville, *Democracy in America*, 55.

11. John Mack Faragher, *Daniel Boone: The Life and Legend of an American Pioneer* (New York, 1992), 278–79.

12. Deed Book A–1, 300, Logan County Courthouse.

13. G. Glenn Clift, "*Second Census of Kentucky, 1800*" (Frankfort, 1954), 29, shows "Reason," "Rhue," and "Alesy" Bowie on the Livingston County tax list for 1800. This should be Rezin, Rhesa, and Elsie.

14. Houck, *Missouri*, 162–63, 167.

15. Ibid., 151; *History of Southeast Missouri: Embracing a Historical Account of the Counties of Ste Genevieve, St. Francois, Perry, Cape Girardeau, Bollinger, Madison, New Madrid, Pemiscot, Dunklin, Scott, Mississippi, Stoddard, Butler, Wayne and Iron* (Boston, 1888), 109.

16. Walter S. Lowrie and Walter S. Franklin, eds., *American State Papers. Documents Legislative and Executive* (Washington, D.C., 1834), Public Lands Series, vol. 2, 497, 664. The *arpent* is, in fact, .84625 acres, though all surveys of the time were subject to variance.

17. Houck, *Missouri*, 151; Robert L. Ramsay, *Our Storehouse of Missouri Place Names* (Columbia, 1952), 39, 42–43.

18. William E. Foley, *A History of Missouri*, vol. 1, *1673 to 1820* (Columbia, 1971), 180–84; John Bowie in the (Washington, Tex.) *Lone Star,* October 23, 1852; Bowie, *The Bowies,* 265–67.

19. *History of Southeast Missouri,* 109.

20. Record Book 1, 41, 47, 57, Clerk of the Court, New Madrid County Courthouse, New Madrid, Miss.

21. Deed Book A, 300, Logan County Courthouse.

22. Bowie, *The Bowies,* 263. Walter Bowie, as always, is not to be relied on completely when dealing with this branch of the family. He is unclear on when and where David Bowie was born, and may even have confused him with Rezin and Rhesa's brother David. That David was a son of Rezin and Elve's does seem probable, however, in that he would make the eighth of their living children, and contemporary testimony states that the Bowies had eight children when they settled at Tywappity. *American State Papers*, Public Lands Series, vol. 2, 497.

23. *American State Papers,* Public Land Series, vol. 3, 342; Record Book 1, 47, 57, New Madrid County Courthouse.

24. Bowie, "The Bowies," 379; *American State Papers*, Public Lands Series, vol. 3, 247.

25. A. Kilpatrick, "Historical and Statistical Collections of Louisiana," *DeBow's Review* 12 (June 1852): 636.

26. Conveyance Book A, 11–12, Book B, 96, Book C, 488–89, Clerk of the Court, Catahoula Parish Courthouse, Harrisonburg, La.

27. John J. Bowie to Mr. Willis, November 12, December 19, 17, 1808, Bowie Family Papers, Natchez Trace Collection, UT.

28. Bowie, "The Bowies," 379; Bowie, *The Bowies,* 260; Kilpatrick, "Historical and Statistical Collections of Louisiana," 636; *American State Papers*, Public Lands Series, vol. 3, 204–5.

29. *American State Papers,* Public Lands Series, vol. 2, 823, 857.

30. United States Census, Catahoula Parish, La., 1810.

31. *American State Papers*, Public Lands Series, vol. 3, 204–5; Conveyance Record B, 17, Record C, 35, Catahoula County Courthouse.

32. Martha Bowie Burns article, James Bowie Biographical File, DRT; [Kilpatrick], "Historical and Statistical Collections of Louisiana," 640.

33. Bowie, *The Bowies*, 261–62. Walter Bowie cites this story as an oral tradition in the family and provides much more detail that involves Rezin killing one squatter, being jailed for manslaughter, and subsequently freed at pistol point by his wife. The detail of the story is highly improbable, like so much of the unsubstantiated Bowie legend, but the root of the tale in a problem with squatters is not at all unlikely.

34. Robert Bowie to the author, August 19, 1996; Elve A. Soniat to Walter Bowie, February 28, 1896, Lucy Leigh Bowie Papers, DRT. Robert Bowie, "Col. James Bowie and the Bowie Families of Early Louisiana" (n.p., n.d.), though a thoroughly bewildering document in places, as befits an attempt to figure out the identities and relationships of so many Bowie men with identical names, is still persuasive in its conclusion that Rhesa was the father of the black James Bowie. Rhesa's will, dated 1848 and in the Bowie Family Papers, UT, lists his only heir as his son James Bowie. For some of the dealings between John Bowie and his black cousin, see Conveyance Record C, 266, Catahoula Courthouse, Book A, 165, Clerk of the Court, Chicot County Courthouse, Lake Village, Ark., and Conveyance Record G, 240, Clerk of the Court, Ouachita Parish Courthouse, Monroe, La.

35. These tales come from Effie Harrison Snyder, whose sister married Rezin Bowie, John junior's grandson. She was thus not even a blood member of the family and quite certainly never met either Rezin or his brother James. This and the fact that her account was not written until 1931, appearing in the St. Joseph, La., *Tensas Gazette* on May 8 of that year—more than 120 years after the fact—makes everything she says highly suspect, the more so since almost all Bowie descendant recollections have proven to be ill-informed and unreliable. It is obvious that much of her account is influenced by the Bowie mythology of the latter nineteenth century. As a result, while she provides specific instances of James's relationship with Mandy and of other childhood events, they have not been used in the text. They could be inventions or even confused with Rezin's activities. Only the general suggestion that James had a friendly relationship with family slaves should reasonably be inferred from her account.

36. It must be emphasized that this story of the involvement of Rezin Bowie in the Kemper forces is based on only one source, and that a questionable one. Matilda E. Moore, "The Bowie Brothers and their Famous Knife," *Frontier Times* 19 (February 1942): 201, states that Rezin left home in 1810 and went to Texas with Kemper, then spent three years fighting Indians. Kemper went in 1812–13, not 1810, and Rezin could not have spent the ensuing three years there because he enlisted in the Louisiana militia in January 1815. Most troubling, Moore gives no sources for her statement about the Kemper episode. Nevertheless the article is accurate and detailed on other aspects of Rezin Bowie's life, and she was herself a great-granddaughter of Rezin's through his grandson John Moore. Such a filibustering adventure would have been in character for Rezin Bowie, and in later years he and James certainly had repeated and verifiable relations with Samuel Kemper's brother Reuben, who was also probably a participant. Consequently, with reservations, it seems reasonable to assume some kind of involvement on Rezin's part.

37. Marriage Record Book 1, 256, St. Landry Catholic Church, Opelousas, La. Her name is occasionally given as Marguerite.

38. John H. Carr to sheriff, February 6, 1812, Bowie Family Papers, UT.

39. Bowie, *The Bowies*, 263, is the only source for David's death, with no date given, only his age.

40. Philadelphia, *Pennsylvanian*, July 19, 1838. This is one of the earliest newspaper articles to deal with the Bowie brothers, yet already it is full of myth and misinformation. Nevertheless it is correct in some respects, and its author says that "Jim Bowie informed us" of some of the details therein sometime before his death. If James Bowie knew anything, it would be the behavior of the older brother to whom he was so attached.

41. Bowie, "The Bowies," 379.

42. James Bouyee [Bowie] Compiled Military Service Record, Josiah S. Johnston Compiled Military Service Record, War of 1812, Records of the Adjutant General's Office, Record Group 94, NA.

43. Compiled Military Service Records for Abraham Bird, John Davis Bradburn, John L. Bruard, Samuel Wells, War of 1812, Record Group 94, NA; William and Marjorie K. Walraven, *The Magnificent Barbarians* (Austin, Tex., 1993), 164; Margaret Swett Henson, *Juan Davis Bradburn* (College Station, Tex., 1982), 25.

44. Elve Soniat to Walter Bowie, March 31, 1896, Lucy Leigh Bowie Papers, DRT.

45. Compiled Military Service Record, Warren D. C. Hall, Josiah S. Johnston, War of 1812, Record Group 94, NA; H. Yoakum, *History of Texas from Its First Settlement in 1686 to Its Annexation to the United States in 1846* (New York, 1856), vol. 2, 508–9; Octavia Rogan, "Warren D. C. Hall," *Texas Grand Lodge Magazine* (July 1937): 274. It must be noted that there is no documentation of James Bowie and Hall forming a friendship while they served in the same unit. However, the fact that several sources indicate that Hall and James were intimately involved in repeated events starting just two years later suggests that they were certainly acquainted by 1817, though they lived far apart. Thus their military service is the only prior point at which they were both unquestionably in very close proximity, and in a small regiment of only a few hundred. It therefore seems reasonable to assume that their association commenced then.

46. Compiled Military Service Record, James Bouyee [Bowie], War of 1812, Record Group 94, NA.

47. Bowie, "The Bowies," 379–80.

48. Timothy Flint, *Recollections of the Last Ten Years in the Valley of the Mississippi* (1826; reprint, Carbondale, Ill., 1968), 231–32.

49. Ibid., 379–80; Washington, Tex., *Lone Star*, October 23, 1852. That Bowie squatted at first is speculation, based on the facts that his brother John in the sources here cited says that he went out on his own in 1814–15, and that no land purchases of any kind are recorded for Bowie prior to 1817. Squatting seems the only explanation that would bridge the two-year gap.

50. Bowie, "The Bowies," 379–80. Samuel Mims, *Trail of the Bowie Knife* (Homer,

La., 1967), 33, a strange and confused book, claims that James had a contract for fifty thousand feet of lumber at New Orleans, but gives no source.

51. Sales and Mortgages Book D–1, 1-B–2, 2, Clerk of the Court, St. Landry Parish Courthouse, Opelousas, La. That Bowie gave a note rather than cash for the slaves is a supposition. The transfer says payment was made "in hand," but does not specify cash. This terminology often did not differentiate between cash payment and payment by IOU. Since $1,700 seems an unlikely sum for Bowie to earn from timber cutting in less than two years, and since he was buying from his own father, a personal note seems the more likely means of purchase. It should be noted that Lucy Leigh Bowie, in the manuscript of an article found in her papers at the Maryland Historical Society, Baltimore, claims that Rezin Bowie Sr. gave James and Rezin Jr. horses, cattle, and ten slaves each to start them off in life. She gives no source, and considering the unreliability of much of the rest of her writing, it has seemed best not to incorporate this information here. Moreover, the St. Landry Tax Assessments for both 1817 and 1818 (MM 2017, 2168, St. Landry Courthouse, Opelousas) show James Bowie with only five slaves, not ten.

52. Conveyance Book C, 206, 211, Clerk of the Court, Avoyelles Parish Courthouse, Marksville.

53. Ibid., 241, 242, 253.

54. Ibid., Book B Bis, 189.

55. Ibid., 210.

56. Bowie, "The Bowies," 380.

57. Bennet Store Ledger, August 5, 1817, in Mary Ann Wells, *A History Lover's Guide to Louisiana* (Baton Rouge, 1990), 66.

58. Bowie, "The Bowies," 379–80. Effie Harrison Snyder told a story in the St. Joseph, La., *Tensas Gazette*, May 8, 1931, of James Bowie striking a trapper who had stolen his father's bloodhounds, and later of stealing them back. When brought before a local court for the offense, Bowie struck the judge, too, when he scoffed at Bowie's explanation. Like the rest of Snyder's stories, this one is related more than a century after the fact and is third- or fourth-hand information at best and therefore not to be relied on. Mims, *Trail*, 35, also carries a probably apocryphal story of Bowie fighting pirates who tried to steal his logs on their way to market.

59. Natchez, *Mississippi State Gazette*, June 16, 1819.

60. Dudley G. Wooten, ed., *Comprehensive History of Texas 1685 to 1897* (Austin, 1898), vol. 1, 97; W. B. [William Bollaert], "Life of Jean Lafitte," *Littell's Living Age* 32 (March 1852): 441n; Natchez, *Mississippi Republican*, August 18, 1819.

61. James Bowie's participation in the Long expedition has often been asserted, but with no sure foundation. Amelia Williams, "A Critical Study of the Siege of the Alamo and of the Personnel of Its Defenders, Chapter III," *Southwestern Historical Quarterly* 37 (October 1933): 91, places Bowie with Long, without authority, and so does Clifford Hopewell, *James Bowie, Texas Fighting Man* (Austin, 1994), 21–22.

The only roughly contemporary source that appears to be well informed is Bollaert's 1852 article "Life of Jean Lafitte," 435, 441n, which states that "the celebrated Jim Bowie, and W. D. C. Hall, were followers of Long's. Jim Bowie was a favorite with all; he was 'quiet as a lamb,' but aroused, or in a fight, 'he was a very devil.'" Bollaert states that his source for material relating to Long and Laffite (whose name Bollaert and many others misspelled "Lafitte") was "my friend, the late Colonel G., who visited Laffite in 1819" (441). This is a reference to Col. James Gaines, one of Long's chief lieutenants, who visited Laffite in company with Warren Hall sometime in July or August, a visit also attested by the early Texas historian John Henry Brown, *Long's Expedition* (Houston, 1930), p. 1. Bollaert was in Galveston collecting historical material from 1842 to 1845, and this is when he would have become acquainted with Gaines, though he is mistaken in his 1852 article in thinking Gaines deceased, for the latter lived until 1856. This discrepancy notwithstanding, Gaines had definitely been in a position to see and know Bowie if he was with Long, and the added association of Bowie's friend Hall lends further weight to Bollaert's statement of what Gaines told him being a trustworthy firsthand account. Thus Bowie is definitely placed with the Long expedition during the summer of 1819. Bowie appears to have been in St. Landry or Avoyelles in early June (Jesse Andrus v. James Bowie, April 24, 1820, James Bowie House Museum, Opelousas, La.), while court documents make it quite certain that Bowie was in Avoyelles on October 2 and 16, 1819, and therefore could not have been with Long later than mid-September (Conveyance Record D, 55, 96, Avoyelles Parish Courthouse). Thus his participation in the expedition was only brief before he returned home.

62. Donald J. Hebert, ed., *Southwest Louisiana Records* (Eunice, 1974), vol. 2, 16.

63. William H. Sparks, writing in 1879 for an unidentified newspaper, and quoted in Edward S. Ellis, *The Life of Colonel David Crockett* (Philadelphia, Pa., 1884), 213. The Sparks memoir of the Bowies is remarkably accurate and useful, despite a few errors.

64. Bowie, *The Bowies*, 265–67.

65. Genealogy notes compiled by G. M. G. Stafford, Mary E. Compton and Family Papers, LSU.

66. Martha Bowie Burns article, James Bowie Biographical File, DRT.

67. Richard Slotkin, *Regeneration Through Violence: The Mythology of the American Frontier, 1600–1860* (Middletown, Conn., 1973), 395.

68. Eugene Barker, "The African Slave Trade in Texas," *Quarterly of the Texas State Historical Association* 6 (October 1902): 149.

69. Barker, "Slave Trade," 145; Wooten, *Texas*, vol. 1, 87–89.

70. Manifest of the Cargo on Board the Ship *Patterson*, Record of Fees Paid, Cargo Manifests, Entry 1657, Record Group 36; Drawbacks for Brig *Devorador*, January, March 7, 25, April 4, 1817, Record of Drawbacks, Bureau of Customs, Entry 1656, NA.

71. W. B., "Lafitte," 440.

72. Wooten, *Texas*, vol. 1, 89.

73. Beverly Chew to William H. Crawford, August 1, 30, October 17, 1817, *American State Papers*, Foreign Relations, vol. 4, 134–36.

74. Sparks in Ellis, *Crockett*, 222–23.

75. Deed of Sale, February 13, 1821, Alonzo Snyder Papers, Hill Memorial Library, LSU; Joe Gray Taylor, *Negro Slavery in Louisiana* (Baton Rouge, 1963), 55.

76. Flint, *Recollections*, 6.

77. Sales and Mortgages Book E–1, 80, St. Landry Parish Courthouse; Jesse Andrus v. James Bowie, April 24, 1820, James Bowie House Museum, Opelousas, La.

78. Galveston, *Daily News*, March 16, 1920, March 21, 1930, January 13, 1935. These articles are written—or based on articles—by Joseph O. Dyer, who had interviewed men who knew Laffite at Campeachy. While the interviews took place many years after the fact and the articles were written even later, still they are the only authority with any connection to eyewitnesses to establish Bowie's visit to Campeachy. They also indicate that Rezin accompanied him, though this appears unlikely. They are also the source for Hall's connection in introducing the Bowies to the smuggler, which is entirely consistent with Hall's activities at the time. James's own relations with Laffite are attested in the information given to Bollaert in 1842–45 by James Gaines in Bollaert's "Life of Jean Lafitte," 435, in which he states in relation to Laffite that "Jim Bowie . . . and Razin Bowie . . . were connected with him." C. L. Douglas, *James Bowie: The Life of a Bravo* (Dallas, 1944), 13, 20, says without citing sources that James was selling lumber in New Orleans when he heard of the Galveztown operation, and that he and Rezin and John made their trip in mid-January 1818. This is almost certainly Douglas's own invention in what is a highly fictionalized biography.

79. Crawford to Chew, August 11, 1819, Letters Received, New Orleans Collection District, Bureau of Customs, Entry 1627, Record Group 36, NA.

80. Mims, *Trail*, 27, citing St. Landry Parish records.

81. Walter Pritchard, ed., "George Graham's Mission to Galveston in 1818," *Louisiana Historical Quarterly* 20 (July 1937): 643.

82. Wells, *Guide*, 129.

83. Bowie, "The Bowies," 380–81. Confirmation of John Bowie's description of the slave business is found in "Negroes Imported," *Nile's Register* 15 (December 12, 1818): 29, which describes precisely this form of operation, claiming that ten thousand slaves were thus imported in 1818 alone.

84. New Orleans *Times-Picayune*, August 22, 1937, quotes then recently discovered records of the U.S. District Court in New Orleans showing that on January 16, 1810, Pierre Laffite was a deputy marshal.

85. James Sterrett to Josiah S. Johnston, November 21, 1821, Josiah S. Johnston Papers, HSP; Joseph Anderson to Beverly Chew, March 14, 1820, Entry 1627, Record Group 36, NA.

86. Bowie, "The Bowies," 380–81; Washington, Tex., *Lone Star*, October 23, 1852. It is necessary to state here that dating the commencement and duration of the Bowie slave enterprise is conjectural. Laffite's presence at Galveston from April 1817 to sometime in early 1821 provides the extreme limits of their possible

involvement. The Joseph O. Dyer articles on Warren Hall in the Galveston *Daily News* (see note 78) state that he and James visited Laffite in 1818, though they are not to be relied on too heavily, while James's heavy activity in his subsequent land deals in 1820 would seem to restrict the time period to mid–1818 to early or mid–1820. John Bowie's statement that James sold his Bayou Boeuf property to fund the enterprise is the only potential clue to a more positive date, and James sold virtually all of that land in October 1819 (Conveyance Book D, 55, 96, Avoyelles Parish Courthouse). It is worth noting that in February 1819 James bought a slave for $1,200 at Opelousas, which would hardly make sense for him if he was already in the business of buying them from Laffite at $140 or less, and by September 1819 he still had not paid for the slave, an indication that he was not yet making the substantial profits from the slave business that brother John claimed in his article. Thus, the fall of 1819, though seemingly late, seems the best date to assume the Bowies' entry into the smuggling enterprise.

Amelia Williams, "Critical Study, III," 92, says that the Bowies practiced the enterprise from 1818 to 1821, but gives no source, and thus must be taken as supposition. John Bowie's statement in "The Bowies," 380–81, that they made $65,000 before quitting argues that, at an average profit of $300 per slave, they smuggled more than two hundred blacks into Louisiana. Further, he says they bought them forty at a time, which would mean no more than five expeditions, hardly requiring a two- or three-year period to carry out. Finally, John Bowie says at the same time that James used his money from the enterprise to start speculating in land, which James certainly commenced in late 1820. Considering that the article "Negroes Imported" in the December 12, 1818, issue of *Nile's Register* (15, 29) highlights the kind of operation that the Bowies ran as a current outrage, a period of mid- or late 1819 to early or mid-1820 seems to be a most logical time for the Bowie involvement, and is only gainsaid by the comment in the Hall articles that Bowie and Hall visited Laffite in 1818. It is possible, of course, that the Dyer articles are mistaken as to the date, being written a century after the fact, and it is equally possible that Hall and James did visit Laffite in 1818, but that the Bowie brothers did not respond to the opportunity until a year later.

87. Conveyance Book D, 96, Avoyelles Parish Courthouse.

88. Ibid., 55.

89. Andrus v. Bowie, April 24, 1820, Bowie House Museum, Opelousas.

90. Josiah Shinn to Walter Bowie, June 23, 1917, Walter Bowie Papers, Maryland Historical Society, Baltimore.

91. Homer S. Thrall, *A Pictorial History of Texas* (St. Louis, 1879), 502–3 tells a story of ninety blacks escaping and fleeing westward, and of Bowie following them as far as the Colorado River. It seems hardly likely, since John Bowie states that they never moved more than forty at a time. Moreover, the Colorado was at least 180 miles from the Sabine, and at this point entirely unknown to James Bowie. Thrall is probably simply repeating a garbled and embellished story that may have some germ of truth.

92. Galveston, *Daily News*, March 21, 1930. In fact, the source states that Bowie said the slaves feared his knife's "unerring aim," but this is certainly an after the fact assignment of knife prowess to Bowie based on the growth of the Bowie knife legend subsequent to James's death. There is no reason or evidence to suppose that at this or any other stage in his life James Bowie had any special prowess at *throwing* a knife, and in any event, contrary to popular fiction and film, a thrown knife simply does not have sufficient mass to leave more than a surface wound when it strikes pliable human flesh, especially when it has to penetrate clothing first. Only a hit on the skull would have any real possibility of being incapacitating.

93. J. G. Dyer to William Beer, February [no year], William Beer Papers, Tulane University Library, New Orleans. "The Bowie Knife," *American Notes and Queries* 2 (March 23, 1889): 251, states that a Juan Antonio Padillo who served with Laffite became a lifelong friend of Bowie's. Like so many such sources, its obsession with the Bowie knife makes it a less than reliable source about Bowie himself.

94. Pritchard, "Graham's Mission," 646–48.

95. Bowie, "The Bowies," 380–81. It should be noted that in 1820–22 the United States filed charges against at least a dozen Louisianans, all involved in illegal slave importation, and in all of those cases the buyer of the illicit black forfeited the chattel and also faced a fine of a thousand dollars or more per slave. A share of those fines may also have been part of the Bowies' proceeds from their enterprise. Works Project Administration, *Synopses of Cases in the U.S. District Court for the Eastern District of Louisiana, Cases #1 to #3000, 1806–1831* (Baton Rouge, 1941), pp. 203–5, 212.

96. Tocqueville, *Democracy in America*, 383.

97. At the time that Bowie sold his Bayou Boeuf property to his brother Stephen, he also owned two small parcels in Avoyelles on Elm Bayou that he bought on December 3, 1818, for $900 (Conveyance Book C, 241–42, Avoyelles Parish Courthouse). No subsequent disposition of this property has been found, nor can Elm Bayou be located today, its name having presumably changed over the years. If it was adjacent to the Bayou Boeuf property, which seems probable, then it should have been a part of the sale to Stephen Bowie, but it is possible that James still owned this tract after the sale.

Chapter 3   Crockett 1815–1824

1. Crockett, *Narrative*, 125–26. Crockett does not say what she died of, but he does speak of "her sufferings," making it evident that she did not die instantaneously by accident or seizure. Cholera would have taken about two days, and typhoid two weeks. Since she had just given birth to their daughter a few months before, it could not have been birth labor that killed her, though of course any of a number of internal problems not connected with disease might also have been the cause.

2. Ibid., 126–27; Shackford, *Crockett*, 34.

3. Jessie Arn Henderson, "Unmarked Historic Spots of Franklin County," *Tennessee Historical Magazine*, Second Series, 3 (January 1935): 117–18.

4. Shackford, *Crockett*, 34.

5. Crockett, *Narrative*, 127–32.

6. Shackford, *Crockett*, 37–38.

7. Arpad, "Crockett," 171–72.

8. Crockett, *Narrative*, 133–35; Court docket, May 5, 1818, August 3, 1819, copies in David Crockett Papers, UT; bill of sale, August 3, 1818, Daughters of the American Revolution Papers, East Texas Research Center, Stephen F. Austin State University, Nacogdoches, Texas.

9. Crockett, *Narrative*, 137–38.

10. Arpad perceptively identifies this self-image in "Crockett," 135.

11. Tocqueville, *Democracy in America*, 536.

12. Crockett to John C. McLemore, October 24, 1820, David Crockett Collection, DRT.

13. Crockett, *Narrative*, 138.

14. Shackford, *Crockett*, 42–43.

15. Crockett, *Narrative*, 139–43.

16. Ibid., 143–44, tells this story, implying that the discussion took place at a meeting in Pulaski. However, Crockett told the story early in 1836 to John Swisher and then said it happened while he and Polk were on their way to Washington to take seats in Congress in 1827, or so Swisher remembered it (John M. Swisher, *The Swisher Memoirs* [San Antonio, 1932], 19–20). Certainly Crockett embellished and varied his stories in the retelling. In this case the date of 1821 with the legislature the destination seems the more likely timing, as in the *Narrative*, but the venue is more likely the horseback ride to Murfreesboro, as in Swisher. Indeed, viewed in the light of the Swisher version, Crockett's statement in the *Narrative* that he and Polk spoke "in a large company," would mean a "company" of travelers rather than a meeting, as usually assumed.

17. Crockett to McLemore, October 23, 1820, Crockett Collection, DRT; James K. Polk to Samuel H. Laughlin, March 15, 1822, in Herbert Weaver and Paul H. Bergeron, eds., *Correspondence of James K. Polk*, vol. 1, *1817–1832* (Nashville, 1969), 13–14n.

18. Shackford, *Crockett*, 47–49; Folmsbee and Catron, "Early Career," 72–73.

19. Ellis, *Crockett*, 58–59, quoting the *Cincinnati Gazette* of unknown date in the early 1880s.

20. John L. Jacobs to the editor of the Morristown *Gazette*, November 22, 1884, Correspondence by Subject, David Crockett, TSL.

21. Crockett, *Narrative*, 144–45.

22. Shackford, *Crockett*, 50–52; Crockett, *Narrative*, 142n.

23. This episode comes from the Matthew St. Clair Clarke ghostwritten book *Life*

and Adventures of Colonel David Crockett of West Tennessee (Cincinnati, 1833), 51–53. Shackford, *Crockett,* 52–53, and 257–58, concludes that Crockett made at least passive contributions to this book by passing along recollections to the author, thus lending some authority to incidents such as the encounter with Mitchell, a conclusion that seems sound, as will be discussed later.

24. Galveston *Daily News,* January 27, 1895. This commentary on Crockett's hunting dress, and his comments on rifle and knife, are from John G. Chapman's account of conversations with Crockett in 1834.

25. Richard Slotkin, *Regeneration Through Violence: The Mythology of the American Frontier, 1600–1860* (Middletown, Conn., 1973), 412–13, 415. Admittedly this conclusion about the significance of hunting to Crockett—other than as recreation and a means of putting meat on the table—is purely speculative and will no doubt draw fire from those who object to so-called "psychobabble" in biography. Nevertheless a biographer has the duty at least to make an attempt at informed speculation on a subject's motives, using whatever sources are at hand, even if, as with Crockett, they are nothing more than recorded behavior. Measured against the whole of Crockett's life, this conclusion about hunting fits a broad pattern in the way he dealt with failure and defeat. It is thus, at least plausible and consistent with the evidence. However, it is certainly possible that other interpretations might be drawn from this same evidence. Slotkin's thoughtful work was of great help in addressing this whole subject.

26. S. H. Stout, "David Crockett," *American Historical Magazine* 7 (January 1902): 17.

27. Crockett, *Narrative,* 147–54.

28. Shackford, *Crockett,* 55–56.

29. Ibid., 58.

30. Ibid., 56–58.

31. J. V. Drake to the editor of the *News,* October 17, 1877, David Crockett Biographical File, DRT.

32. No evidence exists to provide any detail of the rifle Crockett used in these days. Jim Cooper, "A Study of Some David Crockett Firearms," *East Tennessee Historical Society Papers* 38 (1966): 62–65, states that on May 5, 1822, in Nashville he was given a presentation rifle, which his son John sold after Crockett's death, but that eventually it found its way back to John W. Crockett, David's great-grandson, who said he doubted that it ever belonged to his ancestor. Judging from the description of the embellishments on the rifle, and from the fact that Crockett had no known business in Nashville in May 1822, it seems probable that the story of this gun was a hoax.

33. Crockett, *Narrative,* 155–65.

34. Shackford, *Crockett,* 59.

35. Crockett, *Narrative,* 166–67.

36. Folmsbee and Catron, "Early Career," 74, misreads Crockett's statement in his *Narrative,* 169, about having a special shirt made for the tobacco and liquor. This is clearly only Crockett's brag and bluff, done for humorous effect in front of a crowd, not an actual shirt that he made and used. Shackford, *Crockett,* 65, gets it right.

37. H. S. Turner, "Andrew Jackson and David Crockett," *Magazine of American History* 27 (May 1892): 385–87; Stanley J. Folmsbee, "David Crockett and West Tennessee," *West Tennessee Historical Society Papers* 28 (1974): 6. Shackford, *Crockett*, 64, and Folmsbee, "West Tennessee," 6, are misled by their source on the matter of Crockett's giving Butler's speech for him. They accept at face value the statement by Turner that Crockett usually spoke last and on this occasion asked Butler to let him go first. Stump speaking did not work in this fashion. The candidates either alternated speaking first or else decided the matter by chance. Thus Crockett did not have to ask to be allowed to go first, though by the time Turner wrote his recollection of the event in 1892, he may have remembered it that way. Also, by making Butler the unwitting agent of his own embarrassment in letting Crockett go first, the story took on added irony.

38. A very good exposition of the Trickster in mythology will be found in Nikolai Tolstoy, *The Quest for Merlin* (Boston, 1985), 186ff.

39. Slotkin, *Regeneration*, 308.

40. Crockett, *Narrative*, 171.

41. M. J. Heale, "The Role of the Frontier in Jacksonian Politics: David Crockett and the Myth of the Self-Made Man," *Western Historical Quarterly* 4 (October 1973): 416–17.

42. Shackford, *Crockett*, 68–70; Folmsbee and Catron, "Early Career," 76–82.

43. Arpad, "Crockett," 169–73.

44. Speech of Col. Crocket [*sic*] on a resolution to remove the seat of the Legislature, n.d., Calvin Jones Papers, SHC, UNC.

45. Shackford, *Crockett*, 68–72; Folmsbee and Catron, "Early Career," 76–84.

Chapter 4   Bowie 1820–1824

1. Joseph G. Tregle, Jr., "Louisiana in the Age of Jackson: A Study in Ego-Politics" (Ph.D. diss., University of Pennsylvania [Philadelphia], 1954), 70–72. Tregle's brilliant study of the Byzantine workings of Louisiana politics in the 1820s is due to be published in 1998 by Louisiana State University Press.

2. John Millikin to Josiah Meigs, February 1, 1821, *American State Papers*, Public Lands Series, vol. 3, 609.

3. Ibid.

4. Johnston to Register and Receiver, March 15, 1814, *American State Papers*, Public Lands Series, vol. 3, 250.

5. Caiaphas Ham, Recollections, John S. Ford Papers, UT; Robert B. Ardoin, com, *Louisiana Census Records,* vol. 1, *Avoyelles and St. Landry Parishes 1810 & 1820* (Baltimore, Md., 1970), 17, 119. Since James Bowie does not appear in the 1820 Louisiana census by name, this argues further that his 1819 sale to Stephen included all of his Avoyelles property, including the two Elm Bayou parcels. However, in all his business dealings for the next four years, he is listed as being "of Avoyelles," and in 1824 he officially changed his residence from Avoyelles to

Rapides Parish. Stephen Bowie's census enumeration shows that there were living at his plantation four white males aged sixteen to twenty-six, one of them being Stephen himself. Since the age limit of twenty-six exactly matches James Bowie's age in 1820, since he officially resided in Avoyelles, and since he appears nowhere else in the census, it is rather conclusive that he lived with Stephen and was one of the other three males mentioned.

6. Stafford and Bowie v. Spencer and Lee, November 21, 1820, District Civil Suit no. 496, Spencer and Lee v. Stafford and Bowie, January 7, 1822, District Civil Suit no. 403, St. Landry Courthouse.

7. Sparks, in Ellis, *Crockett*, 214–15.

8. Tocqueville, *Democracy in America*, 54.

9. Ibid., 221–22.

10. Elijah Hayward to Andrew Jackson, January 16, 1832, Entry 404, Letters Sent Re: Fraudulent Bowie Claims in Louisiana, 1829–1873, Records of the Bureau of Land Management, General Land Office, Division D (Private Land Claims Division), Record Group 49, NA.

11. Sparks in Ellis, *Crockett*, 222–23.

12. Daniel J. Sutton Report, January 1, 1821, Report of Register North of Red River, La., 1821–1890, Entry 293, Record Group 49, NA (the Sutton report, minus some important notations, is published in *American State Papers*, Public Lands, vol. 3, 599–602); Bill of sale, November 3, 1823, John Bowie to Hugh Johnson, Bowie Family Papers, Natchez Trace Collection, UT. Stephen Bowie acquired some Bayou Boeuf claims that had been confirmed in an even earlier report in 1816, but since the name of the grantee actually appears in the 1820 Louisiana census, and since there is no evidence that the land office ever suspected his claim of being forged, it was probably legitimate. Still, with the Bowies what one brother did, they often all did, so it is at least possible that some other Spanish grants that Stephen put forward for confirmation may have been bogus, but never exposed (Old Index of Private Land Claims in Louisiana 1800–1880, Entry 273, Record Group 49, NA).

13. The texts of the deeds of transfer of the forged grants are entered in several parishes in Louisiana, but their earliest surviving record is in Avoyelles, where they were entered on February 23, 1826 (Conveyance Book E, 410–28). Bowie probably registered them even earlier in Rapides, but all those records were destroyed by fire in 1864. While there is no question of the fraudulence of the Bowie grants, it is worth mentioning as confirmatory that the Archivo General de Indias, Cuban Papers, at Louisiana State University, and the Library of Congress, Washington, D.C., fail to mention even one of the named grantees, and neither do the Pintado Papers at LSU.

14. Conveyance Book E, 413–22, Avoyelles Parish Courthouse.

15. Samuel H. Harper Report, January 6, 1821, *American State Papers*, Public Lands Series, vol. 5, 437.

16. Ibid., vol. 3, 599–602; vol. 5, 437.

17. Levin Wailes to John Millikin, January 1, 1821, *American State Papers*, Public Lands Series, vol. 3, 608–9.

18. Ibid., vol. 5, Edward Jones to Harper, February 7, 1824, 436, Harper to Crawford, March 9, 1821, 436, Harper to George Graham, May 24, 1827, 436–37, August 29, 1827, 437–38.

19. Testimony of Antonio Menchaca, March 1879, 127, testimony of Angus McNeil, 141, *Veramendi* v. *Hutchins et al.,* Documents Pertaining to James Bowie, UT.

20. Conveyance Book D, 194, Avoyelles Parish Courthouse.

21. John Sibley to Josiah S. Johnston, June 26, October 5, November 1, 1821, Johnston Papers, HSP. There is a story, most recently published in Mims, *Trail*, 36–38, of Bowie at this time risking his life to save a runaway slave from two bounty hunters and then thrashing the offenders. Given that slaves in general were property to Bowie, and that this one in particular could have meant profit, it is inconceivable that he would act to help the runaway. If anything it would have been more in character for him to thrash the bounty hunters and then turn in the slave for the reward himself, but given the nature of the source, it is safe to conclude that the episode is purely apocryphal.

22. Angus McNeil testimony, March 1879, *Veramendi* v. *Hutchins,* 141, Documents Pertaining to James Bowie, UT.

23. John Johnston to Josiah S. Johnston, May 25, 1821, H. A. Bullard to Josiah S. Johnston, November 13, 1821, John Brownson to Josiah S. Johnston, December 20, 1821, Johnston Papers, HSP.

24. John Johnston to Josiah S. Johnston, May 25, 1821, ibid.

25. R. H. Sibley to Johnston, January 18, 1822, H. A. Bullard to Johnston, February 2, 1822, ibid.

26. Bowie was in Alexandria on May 2, 1822, for instance, and the burned Rapides Parish records would likely have revealed many more visits (Conveyance Book D, 345, Avoyelles Parish Courthouse).

27. Tregle, "Louisiana," 162; William B. Chilton, com, "The Brent Family," *Virginia Magazine of History and Biography* 20 (October 1912): 434; John Sibley to Johnston, March 8, 1822, Johnston Papers, HSP.

28. Tregle, "Louisiana," 236–37; John Johnston to Josiah S. Johnston, November 29, December 27, 1822, Isaac Baker to Johnston, March 11, June 23, November 11, 1822, Johnston Papers, HSP.

29. Conveyance Record C, 247, Catahoula Parish Courthouse.

30. John Sibley to Johnston, June 26, August 14, December 24, 1821, Johnston Papers, HSP.

31. John Sibley to Johnston, February 26, March 8, 1822, ibid.

32. Flint, *Recollections*, 235.

33. Isaac Baker to Johnston, March 5, 1824, Johnston Papers, HSP. While no contemporary source puts Bowie in New Orleans during any of these winters, John Bowie, "The Bowies," 381, states that James always spent the winters in the

1820s in the city, and we may safely assume that being there at Mardi Gras time, he would not ignore the festivity.

34. Lawrence Estavan, ed., "Edwin Forrest," *San Francisco Theatre Research Monograph* 23 (San Francisco, March 1940): 25–26; William R. Alger, *Life of Edwin Forrest, the American Tragedian* (Philadelphia, 1877), 118–19. A lot of nonsense has been written about Bowie and Forrest, most of it generated by Forrest himself in the Alger book, which is really an autobiography. Forrest would claim in the book and afterward that he and Bowie became devoted friends until they fell out over a woman, and that Bowie so loved Forrest that he gave him his celebrated knife, "used by him awfully in many an awful fray." It was pure fiction, from an actor who also invented much of his life history.

35. [J. Madison Wells], "James Bowie. Something of His Romantic Life and Tragic Death," n.d., but post 1912, James Bowie Biographical File, DRT; Davis, *Way Through the Wilderness*, 245–46.

36. [Wells], "James Bowie. Something of his Romantic Life and Tragic Death," James Bowie Biographical File, DRT. Internal evidence establishes J. Madison Wells as the probable author of this brief article, and sometime after 1912 as its date of publication, though it was certainly written several decades earlier. As the younger brother of Bowie's good Alexandria friends Samuel and Montfort Wells, Madison Wells was in a position to know much about Bowie. In this article he gives details of a romantic involvement with a Miss Gibson of Natchez that would have taken place at about this time, when Bowie did not own a home of his own. Supposedly her father opposed her interest in Bowie because of his wildness, and at the same time the son of another wealthy local planter named Parker sued for her affections. It led to a fight between Bowie and Parker and his brother, in which Bowie killed them both, was tried for the killings, and acquitted, while Miss Gibson soon died of yellow fever. No Parker appears in the Natchez area in the 1820 or 1830 censuses for Mississippi or Louisiana, nor is there any hint in the Natchez press of such killings or a trial. Since Wells was writing probably half a century, if not more, after the fact, the whole episode must be considered too garbled and encrusted with myth and embroidery to be able to sift any substantial truth from the nonsense, other than to conclude that Bowie did have dimly remembered romantic affairs and that they were not successful.

37. Rezin's 1823 trip to Havana is confirmed by the registration of the property he bought while there, and entered in Conveyance Book D, 54, Terrebonne Parish Courthouse, Houma, Louisiana. The Baltimore *Commercial Transcript*, June 11, 1838 says that Rezin went to Cuba "many years since," even asserting that he engaged in a knife fight while there, though this is obvious hearsay, and probably an amalgamation of the association of both James and Rezin with the eponymous knife, and a confusion with James's growing mythical reputation as a fighter. That James went with him is almost wholly conjectural, though it would have been typically in character for the two to make the trip together. There are family stories that James went to Cuba, copied the Pintado papers, and used them to acquire his large Louisiana grant holdings. Of course, later members of the Bowie family knew nothing of James's forgeries, and naturally

assumed that he got his land through energy and ingenuity. In later years the tricks of hearsay and memory may simply have amalgamated recollections of his land dealings with other memories of Rezin's quite genuine trip and involvement with the papers. In any event, as in so many other instances, family recollections and traditions about James Bowie and Cuba are wholly inaccurate. Lucy Bowie in 1955 even asserted that James copied the Pintado papers, and that the copies in his handwriting were now in Louisiana's archives (Lucy Leigh Bowie to Mr. Palmer, March 9, 1955, Lucy Leigh Bowie Papers, DRT). In fact, it is the *original* Pintado Papers that are now housed at LSU, and as a result of Rezin's later purchase of them, which is dealt with in a subsequent chapter.

38. James Whitcomb to J. A. Bynum, February 11, 1839, Letters Sent, vol. 5, Entry 200, Record Group 49, NA.

39. Isaac Thomas to Johnston, November 25, 1822, Johnston Papers, HSP.

40. George Mason Graham, "The Autobiography of George Mason Graham," *Louisiana Historical Quarterly* 20 (January 1937): 43, 46.

41. George Davis to George Graham, October 29, 1824, Entry 404, Record Group 49, NA.

42. Ibid.

43. Conveyance Book C, 246–47, 275, Catahoula Parish Courthouse; Conveyance Book F, 286, 287, 307, Ouachita Parish Courthouse.

44. George Davis to Graham, October 1824, Statement of Hiram Burch, Statement of Hugh White, December 5, 1823, Extracts of Letters and Other Documents Relating to Fraudulent Land Claims in Louisiana, 1823–1832, M1385, Record Group 49, NA; Conveyance Record F, 286, 287, 307, Ouachita Parish Courthouse.

45. McCrummon to Johnston, February 1, 1824, Johnston Papers, HSP.

46. Graham to John Wilson, April 15, 1824, *American State Papers*, Public Lands Series, vol. 4, 35.

47. Davis to Edmund Wailes, October 16, 1824, ibid., 35.

48. Davis to McCrummon, October 17, 1824, McCrummon to Davis, October 18, 1824, Entry 404, Record Group 49, NA; Davis to Graham, October 23, 1824, *American State Papers*, Public Lands Series, vol. 4, 37.

49. Davis to Graham, October 29, 1824, Entry 404, Record Group 49, NA. The date on this document is smudged, and could possibly be October 9 or 19, but the twenty-ninth appears to be the most likely.

50. Davis to Graham, November 1, 1824, *American State Papers*, Public Lands Series, vol. 4, 37–38.

51. Wailes to Graham, October 28, 1824, Entry 404, Record Group 49, NA.

52. John Hughes to Graham, March 25, 1825, *American State Papers*, Public Lands Series, vol. 5, 438.

53. John Johnston to Josiah S. Johnston, October 11, 1822, May 20, 1824, Johnston Papers, HSP.

54. Conveyance Book E, 262, Avoyelles Parish Courthouse.

Chapter 5   Crockett 1824–1829

1. Indenture, April 14, 1824, *American Book Prices Current, 1991* 97 (Washington, Conn., 1991): 46.

2. Turner, "David Crockett," 387.

3. Shackford, *Crockett*, 74, 301n. Shackford tried to locate a copy of this circular, whose existence is confirmed, but without success. We know only that it was dated in 1824, nothing more.

4. Crockett, *Narrative*, 172. Shackford, *Crockett*, 73, says without any apparent source that Crockett had intended to seek reelection to the legislature but gave it up in favor of the congressional race. This is certainly possible, since campaigns for both offices would have been concurrent, and he could not run for both.

5. Crockett, *Narrative*, 173.

6. Jackson *Gazette*, June 18, 1825; J. M. Keating, *History of the City of Memphis and Shelby County, Tennessee*, vol. 1 (Syracuse, N.Y., 1880), 169.

7. Jackson *Gazette*, July 16, 23, 30, August 6, September 17, 1825.

8. Crockett, *Narrative*, 173.

9. Ibid., 174–94.

10. Arpad, "Crockett," 146.

11. Crockett, *Narrative*, 195–99; Keating, *Memphis*, vol. 1, 181; James D. Davis, *History of the City of Memphis* (Memphis, 1873), 146–49. Keating, likely just reiterating Davis, misdates this episode to 1823. Davis, while probably to some degree influenced by Crockett's *Narrative*, clearly appears to have had access to firsthand recollections of the event from Memphians of the time.

12. Crockett, *Narrative*, 201–2.

13. Arpad, "Crockett," 133; Folmsbee, "West Tennessee," 11.

14. Arpad, "Crockett," 163; Chapman in the Galveston *Daily News*, January 27, 1895.

15. Crockett, *Narrative*, 205.

16. David Mitchell Saunders to William A. Graham, September 15, 1827, J. G. de Roulhac Hamilton, ed., *The Papers of William Alexander Graham*, vol. 1 (Raleigh, N.C., 1957), 159.

17. Historians have conventionally dated the term "loco," when applied to a radical Democrat, to an 1835 convention in New York, when conservatives turned off the gas in the meeting hall to break up a gathering, but the participants continued by striking so-called locofoco matches, thus becoming known as "Locofocos." There is some indication that the term saw earlier use applied to Jackson supporters. Crockett's use of the term "loco" is clearly related in context, but predates the supposed origin of the usage by fully eight years. The only other known usage of the slang word means "crazy," and is a late-nineteenth-century derivation of "loco weed," much too late and the wrong context to apply here. He must have been referring to the match in some fashion and for some unknown reason, and certainly the usage did not seem to baffle his audi-

ence or Graham's correspondent in 1827, but the term apparently slipped from usage until resurrected in 1835.

18. Saunders to Graham, September 15, 1827, Hamilton, *Papers of William Alexander Graham*, vol. 1, 159.

19. Folmsbee, "West Tennessee," 9. Folmsbee questions the contemporary newspaper reports that have Crockett using these expressions, but the letter to Graham cited in note 16 above makes it clear from an eyewitness that he amalgamated the river boasts into his stump presentations. The Nashville *Republican* of March 18, 1828, indicates that Crockett made this boast when in the first session of Congress, but it is far more likely that the journalist was juxtaposing expressions commonly associated with Crockett in *Tennessee* with his conduct in Washington.

20. Christian Schultz recorded essentially these same boasts among flatboatmen in his *Travels on an Inland Voyage*, vol. 1 (New York, 1810), 145–46.

21. Crockett, *Narrative*, 203–4.

22. John W. Crockett to Charles Dunlap, March 6, 1827, in Shackford, "The Autobiography of David Crockett: An Annotated Edition" (Ph.D. dissertation, Vanderbilt University, 1948), 554–55.

23. Folmsbee, "West Tennessee," 9n.

24. Swisher, *Swisher Memoirs*, 19–20.

25. James Erwin to Clay, August 12, 1827, Mary W. M. Hargreaves and James F. Hopkins, eds., *The Papers of Henry Clay*, vol. 6, *Secretary of State* (Lexington, Ky., 1981), 892.

26. Erwin to Clay, September 30, 1827, ibid., 1098.

27. Crockett to James Blackburn, July 5, 1828, Crockett Letters, Correspondence by Author, TSL.

28. Shackford, *Crockett*, 84–86.

29. Lewis Williams to Clay, November 15, 1827, Hargreaves and Hopkins, *Papers of Henry Clay*, vol. 6, 1269.

30. Crockett to Blackburn, July 5, 1828, Correspondence by Author, Crockett, TSL.

31. Williams to Clay, November 15, 1827, Hargreaves and Hopkins, *Papers of Henry Clay*, vol. 6, 1269.

32. Crockett to James Blackburn, February 5, 1828, Crockett Letters, Correspondence by Author, TSL.

33. Undated notes in Calvin Jones Papers, SHC, UNC.

34. Charles Francis Adams, ed., *Memoirs of John Quincy Adams*, vol. 7 (Philadelphia, 1877), 361, November 27, 1827.

35. Arpad, "Crockett," 188.

36. Adams, *Memoirs of John Quincy Adams*, vol. 7, 361, November 27, 1827.

37. Polk to Alfred Flournoy, December 6, 1827, Weaver and Bergeron, *Correspondence of James K. Polk*, vol. 1, 101.

38. Crockett to Blackburn, February 5, 1828, Crockett Letters, Correspondence by Author, TSL.

39. Tennessee delegation to Clay, December 7, 1827, Weaver and Bergeron, *Correspondence of James K. Polk,* vol. 1, 103–4.

40. Crockett to James L. Totten, December 17, 1827, Shackford, "Crockett," 415.

41. Tocqueville, *Democracy in America,* Mayer edition, 497–98.

42. Ibid.

43. Ibid.

44. Crockett to Totten, February 11, 1828, Special Collections, University of Tennessee, Knoxville.

45. Chapman in Galveston, *Daily News,* January 27, 1895.

46. Walter Blair, *Davy Crockett: Legendary Frontier Hero* (Springfield, Ill., 1986), 110–11. This statement is quite possibly Blair's invention.

47. Chapman in Galveston *Daily News,* January 27, 1895.

48. Crockett to Totten, February 11, 1828, Special Collections, University of Tennessee; Crockett to Mr. Seal, March 11, 1828, Crockett Papers, UT.

49. Crockett to Seal, March 11, 1828, Crockett Papers, UT.

50. Crockett to Blackburn, July 5, 1828, Miscellaneous Collection, Tennessee Historical Society, TSL.

51. William Henry to Polk, February 20, 1828, 151–52, N. Steele to Polk, March 2, 1828, 158, Weaver and Bergeron, *Correspondence of James K. Polk,* vol. 1.

52. Alexander to Polk, January 26, 1828, Weaver and Bergeron, *Correspondence of James K. Polk,* vol. 1, 135–36.

53. Stanley J. Folmsbee and Anna Grace Catron, "David Crockett: Congressman," *East Tennessee Historical Society Publications* 24 (1957): 48.

54. Ibid., 48.

55. Crockett to Blackburn, July 5, 1828, Miscellaneous Collection, Tennessee Historical Society, TSL.

56. Nashville *Republican,* March 18, 1828.

57. Chapman in Galveston *Daily News,* January 27, 1895.

58. Walter Blair, "Six Davy Crocketts," *Southwest Review* 25 (July 1940): 454. Blair mistakenly dates the press attention to Crockett in 1824, when it should be 1828.

59. Slotkin, *Regeneration,* 5.

60. Arpad, "Crockett," 65.

61. Ibid., iv.

62. Arpad, "Crockett," 62.

63. Folmsbee, "West Tennessee," 11n; Crockett to George Patton, January 27, 1829, Miscellaneous Collection, Tennessee Historical Society, TSL.

64. Bond, September 5, 1827, *American Book Prices Current, Index, 1965–70* (Washington, Conn., 1970): 2227; Crockett to Dear Doctor, September 11, 1828, Miscellaneous Collection, Tennessee Historical Society, TSL.

65. Crockett to Patton, January 27, 1829, Miscellaneous Collection, Tennessee Historical Society, TSL.

66. Crockett to James Davison, August 18, 1831, Crockett Biographical File, DRT; Crockett to Blackburn, July 5, 1828, Miscellaneous Collection, Tennessee Historical Society, TSL.

67. Blair, "Six Davy Crocketts," 452–53; Crockett to James Clark, January 3, 1829, *American Book Prices Current Index, 1965–70* (Washington, Conn., 1970): 2226.
   The story appeared in the Nashville, *National Banner and Nashville Whig* on November 25, 1828. Verplank's and Clark's refutations appeared in the same journal on January 9 and 23, 1829. Shackford, *Crockett*, 124–25 interprets this to mean that between the November charge and the January retraction, Crockett made a deal with the opposition to aid in opposition to Jackson, in return for their support on his land bill. The accusation came before the deal was made, and the retractions followed once Crockett had changed sides. This seems a very flawed explanation, especially since Crockett's January 3, 1829, letter to Clark clearly establishes that the refutation came at Crockett's request, and not as a result of a spontaneous realization by the opposition that they had to remedy damage done to a man now on their side, as Shackford suggests.

68. Admittedly this entire scenario is hypothetical, as is Shackford's contrary interpretation cited above, but it seems much more to fit the known facts of the moment.

69. Crockett to Patton, January 27, 1829, Miscellaneous Collection, Tennessee Historical Society, TSL.

70. Crockett to the editor, December 13, 1828, Jackson *Gazette*, January 3, 1829.

71. Polk to Pryor Lea, February 17, 1829, Weaver and Bergeron, *Correspondence of James K. Polk*, vol. 1, 240–42.

72. Shackford, *Crockett*, 95–96.

73. Polk to Davison McMillen, January 16, 1829, Weaver and Bergeron, *Correspondence of James K. Polk*, vol. 1, 229–30; Crockett to the editor, January 14, 1829, Jackson *Gazette*, February 7, 1829.

74. Polk to McMillen, January 16, 1829, 229; Archibald Yell to Polk, February 14, 1829, 238; Weaver and Bergeron, *Correspondence of James K. Polk*, vol. 1.

75. Polk to McMillen, January 16, 1829, Weaver and Bergeron, *Correspondence of James K. Polk*, vol. 1, 230. Shackford, *Crockett*, 96, seems to interpret Polk's charge as meaning that Crockett may not have written the speeches he gave on the floor. This is possible, of course, but it is not what Polk *charged*. He quite explicitly says that what Crockett *said* in the House was not what Gales *reported* him as saying in his newspaper. In other words Gales was dressing up Crockett's speeches for publication after they were made, not writing them beforehand, a practice common then and later, down to the present.

76. Crockett to Patton, January 27, 1829, Miscellaneous Collection, Tennessee Historical Society, TSL; Chapman in Galveston *Daily News*, January 27, 1895.

77. J. J. B., "Davy Crockett's Electioneering Tour," *Harper's New Monthly Magazine* 35 (April 1867): 607–9.

78. Jackson *Gazette*, March 14, 21, 28, 1829.

79. Crockett to the "Mess at J. Davises," February 23, 1829, Manuscripts Collection, University of Rochester, Rochester, New York; Crockett to the "Mess at Dowson's," February 23, 1829, Columbia University Manuscripts Collection, Columbia University, New York, N.Y. Crockett has noted on the latter of these two documents that he received no reply.

80. Robert V. Remini, *Andrew Jackson and the Course of American Freedom, 1822–1832* (New York, 1981), 159.

81. Crockett et al. to Jackson, February 25, 1829, John Davis Batchelder Autograph Collection, Library of Congress, Washington, D.C.

Chapter 6   Bowie 1824–1826

1. Tregle, "Louisiana," 463–65.

2. Isaac Baker to Johnston, December 4, 1823, Johnston Papers, HSP.

3. Walter H. Overton to Johnston, May 10, 1824; John Johnston to Josiah S. Johnston, July 8, 1823 [misdated—should be 1824], ibid.

4. Tregle, "Louisiana," 100, 162, 257, 264–65; John Sibley to Johnston, April 20, 1824. John Johnston to Josiah S. Johnston, June 19, July 15, 1824, Johnston Papers, HSP.

5. John Johnston to Josiah S. Johnston, June 19, 1824, Johnston Papers, HSP.

6. Tregle, "Louisiana," 274; St. Martinville, La., *Attakapas Gazette*, January 15, 1825.

7. Tregle, "Louisiana," 275–76, 278, 286–87.

8. John Bowie receipt, 1823, Alonzo Snyder Papers, LSU; Sheriff's conveyance, February 6, 1822, Bowie Family Papers, UT; Conveyance Record F, 221, Ouachita Parish Courthouse.

9. Bill of sale, January 16, 1823, Bowie Family Papers, UT.

10. G. W. Lovelace to James G. Taliaferro, June 5, August 24, 1824, James G. Taliaferro Papers, LSU.

11. Taliaferro to John Bowie, July 30, 1824, Deposition, October 22, 1824, Petition, October 23, 1824, Taliaferro Papers, LSU. It must be stated emphatically that no documentary evidence links James Bowie with John Bowie's campaign, or suggests or implies that James might have been involved in voter intimidation. Such a possibility is based solely on James Bowie's character as it will continue to develop in this book, and on his later willingness to resort to heavy intimidation in pursuit of his goals, combined with his demonstrated burgeoning interest in politics.

12. Taliaferro to John Bowie, October 11, 25, 1824, John Bowie to Taliaferro, October 22, 1824, Taliaferro Papers, LSU.

13. Graham to Crawford, December 17, 1824, *American State Papers*, Public Lands Series, vol. 4, 32–33. It is as well to note here as anywhere that Williams, "Critical Study, III," 95, states that Bowie established an office in New Orleans for his land business. She offers no source for the statement, and there is no evidence to support it, her assertion being merely a garbled reading of the John Bowie article "The Bowies."

Bowie operated out of Alexandria alone until he moved to Lafourche.

14. Edward Jones to Samuel Harper, February 7, 1824, Harper to Crawford, March 9, 1824, *American State Papers*, Public Lands Series, vol. 5, 436.

15. Graham to Davis, December 26, 1824, Entry 404, Record Group 49, NA.

16. St. Martinville, La., *Attakapas Gazette*, February 19, 1825.

17. On Charges by a Deputy Surveyor Against the Official Conduct of the Commissioner of the General Land Office, *American State Papers*, Public Lands Series, vol. 4, 943, 947, 951–52.

18. Conveyance Book D, 33, 34–35, 155–56, 344–45, Terrebonne Parish Courthouse; Conveyance Book E, 412, 418–19, 425, Avoyelles Parish Courthouse.

19. Flint, *Recollections*, 239; John Sibley to Graham, August 6, 1825, Graham to Sibley, September 16, 1825, Entry 404, Record Group 49, NA.

20. Davis to Graham, November 16, 1825, Extracts, M1385; Davis to Graham, November 12, 1825, Davis to Milo Johnson, October 29, 1825, Johnson to Davis, November 12, 1825, Entry 404, Record Group 49, NA.

21. Valentine King to Graham, October 13, 1825, Reports on Private Land Claims, Southwest District, La., Act of May 11, 1820, 1820–1825, Entry 292; William Armstrong to R. C. Nicholas, January 23, 1839, Letters Received by the Commissioner of the General Land Office Relating to Private Land Claims in Louisiana, 1818–1881, M1385, Record Group 49, NA. It has not been either practical or possible to trace the extent of this third set of Bowie's frauds. That they were in some degree successful is evidenced by the fact that in 1839 the Despallier claim was still under active consideration and by then the property of either Montfort or J. Madison Wells, both friends of Bowie. Since no conveyances connecting Bowie with the properties specified in the two letters cited above have been found in any of the other Louisiana parish records, the transactions must have been confined to Rapides, and the complete destruction of its courthouse records by fire in 1864 effectively obliterated all evidence there. Consequently the fraud may have been confined to the 8,124 acres specified in the Despallier, De Leon, and Duran claims, or it may have covered the other three claims mentioned by King, whose acreage is not mentioned. If they were the same customary size, that would extend the fraud to 16,248 acres, always with the possibility that there were other claims that King did not catch.

22. Sibley to Graham, December 6, 1825, Entry 404, Record Group 49, NA; Sibley to Johnston, February 27, 1826, Johnston Papers, HSP. Sibley's handwriting is not always legible, and it is possible that his specific mention of what appears to be Bowie could in fact be another name entirely, possibly Nevin.

23. Conveyance Book C, 102, Terrebonne Parish Courthouse.

24. Conveyance Book E, 410–28, Avoyelles Parish Courthouse; McCrummon to Johnston, December 10, 1825, Johnston Papers, HSP; Hughes to Graham, January 6, 1826, Entry 404, Record Group 49, NA.

25. Conveyance Book D, 209, Terrebonne Parish Courthouse.

26. John Johnston to Josiah S. Johnston, February 13, 1826, R. Donaldson to Johnston, February 13, 1826, Johnston Papers, HSP.

27. C. Beaman to Johnston, August 23, 1826, ibid.

28. Graham to Johnston, March 5, 1826, ibid.

29. Isaac Baker to Johnston, December 4, 1826, ibid.

30. Isaac Thomas to Johnston, November 5, 1827, ibid., says that Clay's advice had been secured in the Reuben Kemper claim, and in a subsequent letter to Johnston, March 5, 1828, when Bowie was in the East again, makes reference to Bowie's "first trip" to Washington in the matter. The only other trip Bowie is definitely known to have made is this one in late winter 1826. It is possible that Bowie made an 1827 trip, but no evidence of one has been found to date. Thus he either got Clay's advice in person or subsequently by mail. It is worth noting that there is a persistent story, supposedly told by Jefferson Davis, that Clay told him of once meeting Bowie on a stagecoach, and that during the trip Bowie performed one of his customary acts of heroic chivalry ("The Bowie Knife," *American Notes and Queries*, vol. 3 [July 27, 1889], 155). The story itself is probably completely apocryphal. Certainly there is no evidence that Davis ever told such a story, and he and Clay were not on sufficiently cordial terms that the latter would have traded stories with him (William C. Davis, *Jefferson Davis: The Man and His Hour* [New York, 1991], 193ff). Nevertheless the juxtaposition of Clay's name with Bowie's even in myth may contain some germ of fact from a genuine meeting, and this 1826 trip to Washington, and an errand that would have taken Bowie to the State Department, seem the most likely opportunities.

31. W. H. Overton to Johnston, August 2, 1826, Johnston Papers, HSP.

32. Overton to Johnston, August 2, 1826, ibid.

33. Flint, *Recollections*, 232–33.

34. Edward Doney to Taliaferro, May 4, 1825, Taliaferro Papers, LSU.

35. Mims, *Trail*, 38–38, says without authority that Bowie established a steam sawmill on Bayou Boeuf in 1825, and that when he applied to the bank for a loan after he overextended himself, he was turned down. There is no contemporary evidence whatever to confirm the mill story or the loan. The former is probably a confusion with the mill that John and James's late father owned on Bayou Nezpique. The loan myth is connected to Norris Wright, who—so goes the story—had influence at the bank and ruined Bowie's chances for the loan, commencing the feud that led to him shooting Bowie sometime in 1826–27, and their subsequent fatal encounter in the Sandbar brawl.

36. Case #1780, *U.S.* v. *Charles Mulhollan*, General Case Files, 1806–1932, Entry 21, U.S. District Court for the Eastern District of Louisiana. New Orleans, Record Group 21, National Archives–Southwest Region, Fort Worth, Tex.; Stanley C. Arthur, *The Story of the West Florida Rebellion* (Baton Rouge, 1976), 13, 124.

37. Reuben Kemper to Johnston, March 18, 1824, December 1, 1825, Johnston Papers, HSP.

38. Reuben Kemper to Johnston, May 19, 1826, Henry Boyer to Johnston, March 30, 1828, ibid.

39. Notary Felix De Armas, Power of Attorney, Jose de la Francia to James Bowie, February 10, 1826, vol. 5, 72–73, New Orleans Notarial Archives; Kemper to

Johnston, March 18, 1824, February 7, 1825, Johnston Papers, HSP.

40. Bayou Sara is in Point Coupee Parish, where Charles Mulhollan had a land claim in 1820. Mulhollan's connection with Bowie is further established by an article in the Alexandria, *Red River Herald*, of June 1836, quoted in the Little Rock, *Arkansas Advocate*, February 3, 1837.

41. Kemper to Johnston, May 19, 1826, Johnston Papers, HSP. The precise nature of this deal is still uncertain. Mulhollan's role is unknown, but since Kemper says that Bowie told him "he had become the owner of this claim," it does not appear that Mulhollan had an interest in the claim. Nor is Isaac Thomas mentioned by Kemper, though he was later to be a co-owner of the claim.

42. Notary Felix De Armas, Power of Attorney, Jose de la Francia to James Bowie, February 10, 1826, vol. 5, 72–73, New Orleans Notarial Archives.

43. Kemper to Johnston, May 19, 1826, power of attorney, May 19, 1826, Johnston Papers, HSP.

44. L. Pleasonton to Reuben Kemper, April 15, 1820, vol. 1, 171; Statement of the Fifth Auditor to Henry Clay, April 20, 1826, vol. 2, 257–58, Fifth Auditor's Office, Letters Sent, 1817–1869, Record Group 217, NA.

45. Kemper power of attorney, August 3, 1826, Kemper to Johnston, December 14, 1826, Johnston Papers, HSP. It must be said that this construction of events is somewhat speculative, based on the few sources available. Bowie filed the perjured power of attorney on February 10, 1826. In July Kemper received a letter from Johnston that apparently ended the matter for Bowie. The fact that three months earlier Johnston secured a listing of $11,396.44 in payments due to Kemper from the U.S. Treasury represented some of his other claims due. Moreover, it is evident in Kemper to Johnston, December 14, 1826, that Kemper has assumed personal responsibility for the de la Français heirs' claim, hence the narration of this episode as written.

46. Bowie, "The Bowies," 380.

47. Flint, *Recollections*, 241–42.

48. Sparks, in Ellis, *Crockett*, 220.

49. Flint, *Recollections*, 242.

50. No definitive record of when or where Bowie became a Freemason has been found. Among his effects after his death was a Masonic apron, which is the only testimony to his having joined. The first active lodge in Texas formed in late December 1835, when he was too heavily engaged in the revolution to be joining fraternal organizations, and prior to his departure from Louisiana the closest lodges to Alexandria were at Natchitoches and Opelousas, both towns to which his business would have taken him on occasion. His frequent visits to Natchez also make it a possible location for his joining. The timing of his association with the Freemasons can only be guessed at, but considering the social and business advantages to membership, and Bowie's own drive in 1826 for social prominence, this seems the most likely period.

51. Bowie, "The Bowies," 380.

52. There is absolutely no contemporary evidence or authority for these rumored romantic alliances of Bowie's. They are to be found chiefly in Horace Shelton,

"Texas Heroes—James Bowie," *Under Texas Skies* 2 (November 1951): 27, and in 1989 letters from a very distant cousin of the Louisiana Bowies to Clifford Hopewell (*Bowie*, 139n). The Montejo reference comes from "James Bowie," an undated anonymous manuscript probably written sometime after 1912, in the James Bowie Biographical File, DRT. It should be noted that no families of the name Montejo, Bornay, or Cade appear in the Louisiana censuses for 1810–1830, though this is not conclusive that they did not exist. Catherine Villars certainly did exist, bearing Laffite a child in 1818, but being a quadroon with no property she would not appear in any census. She disappears from history after Laffite left Campeachy in 1821.

53. The story of the Cecilia Wells courtship rests on no better foundation than the stories of Bowie's other romances. The undated account by J. Madison Wells, "James Bowie: Something About His Romantic Life and Tragic Death," at DRT, was certainly written prior to 1900, by one who knew Bowie and who was Cecilia Wells's cousin and virtual foster brother, and yet does not mention Miss Wells at all in speaking of Bowie's romantic life. There is an undated indirect reference to it in the Virginia Berkeley Bowie manuscript, "The Story of James Bowie," in the Lucy Bowie Papers at DRT, wherein she says that "there is some dim tale of a young girl whom he loved in his youth, and who died before they could come to marriage." It is presumably on the basis of this that Lucy Bowie wrote the first published reference to Cecilia Wells, in the Doylestown, Pa., *Daily Intelligencer*, June 20, 1916, embellishing the story by having her die two weeks before their wedding. How she actually connected Cecilia Wells specifically with the story is unknown. Hopewell, *Bowie*, 28, 68, repeats this, in the process making Cecilia the sister rather than the cousin of the Wells brothers. Joseph Musso, "Jim Bowie's Sandbar Fight," *Alamo Journal* 60 (February 1988): 4, accepts the Lucy Bowie story, and further embellishes it by making her romance with Bowie a part of the Bowie-Wells bond that led to his involvement in the Sandbar fight. In fact Cecilia Wells died September 17, 1829, two years almost to the day after the Sandbar brawl, and at a time when Bowie had been living in Terrebonne Parish, 150 miles away from Alexandria, for fully a year and was already spending much time in Mexico and Texas preparatory to his move there. None of this suggests that he was engaged, or even involved in a romance that, at best, was extremely remote. Besides, it would have been much out of character for Bowie to endure a two-year engagement. George M. G. Stafford, *The Wells Family of Louisiana and Allied Families* (Alexandria, 1942), 129, gives no indication of having found anything connecting Cecilia to Bowie, and when John Johnston wrote to his brother Josiah on September 18, 1829, notifying him of her death, he made no mention of her being engaged to James Bowie, who by this time was very much a foe of Johnston's, which would have made the fact of such an engagement quite newsworthy (Johnston Papers, HSP). In the end, while Bowie may have paid some court to Cecilia Wells during 1826–28, it is virtually certain that there was never an engagement.

54. Tregle, "Louisiana," 85, 117–18; New Orleans, *Louisiana State Gazette*, October 16, 1826.

55. John Johnston to Josiah S. Johnston, May 4, 9, 1826, Johnston Papers, HSP.

56. Ibid., June 1, August 30, 1826.

57. Pierre Rost to Johnston, February 20, 1826, B. Leonard to Johnston, April 24, 1826, Isaac Baker to Johnston, May 6, 1826, ibid.

58. Chilton, "Brent Family," 434; Tregle, "Louisiana," 275–76, 278, 286–87; Henry Clay to John Quincy Adams, July 25, 1826, James F. Hopkins and Mary W. M. Hargreaves, eds., *The Papers of Henry Clay,* vol. 5, *Secretary of State, 1826* (Lexington, Ky., 1973), 568; John Johnston to Josiah Johnston, July 25, 1826, Johnston Papers, HSP.

59. Baker to Johnston, October 5, 1826, Johnston Papers, HSP.

60. Sparks, in Ellis, *Crockett,* 213–14.

61. Kemper to Johnston, December 14, 1826, Johnston Papers, HSP.

62. Samuel Bastian account, n.d. but circa 1887–92, in John Henry Brown, *Indian Wars and Pioneers of Texas* (Austin, 1896), 138. The Bastian account, when mentioned at all, has been dismissed as a hoax, first by Brown, who published it in his book, and subsequently by others, principally because of one or two small internal errors that are in fact entirely consistent with an eighty-year-old man's recollections of events that took place sixty years before, such as confusing Gonzales with Goliad, Texas. Bastian definitely did exist, was a member of a large and prominent family of French ancestry in Philadelphia, and his father Washington was definitely in Natchitoches Parish in the 1830s with a claim on the Red River (Report, Register & Receiver, Land Office, Opelousas, La., on Private Land Claims, Act of Feb. 6, 1835, 1836–1840, Entry 297, Record Group 49, NA). Moreover, a surprising amount of what he says in his account checks out independently, leading Alamo historian Thomas R. Lindley to conclude that Bastian was, as he claimed, a messenger from the Alamo, and probably the first one sent out by Travis on February 23, 1836 (Lindley to the author, July 1, 1996). More to the point for this study, Bastian's is the only early comment to be found in print connecting Bowie with land fraud in *Louisiana.* Bowie's later Arkansas activities are well known, but no one has ever even hinted that he might have done the same thing in Louisiana until this present study, yet it was the comment made by Bastian that led to a hunch to start checking the Louisiana land records, with the extensive results contained herein, all of which confirm Bastian's accuracy on the point. Williams, "Critical Study, III," 93n, attempted to verify Bastian's account of the Kaufman killing without success, and indeed nothing on it seems to survive, if it ever happened. The Dalton Bastian mentions may be Samuel Dalton, who lived in Rapides at the time according to the 1820 census, and there was one man named Kaufman living in the state, but he traveled on business between Natchitoches and Natchez, and in any event was still living as late as 1836. He did a lot of business with Bowie's attorney John Quitman, though this may be mere coincidence, as Quitman was the most successful attorney in Natchez at the time. The whole story of Bowie's connection to the death of Kaufman may be false recollection, an unwitting amalgamation of several discrete stories into one by an elderly man, or it could

be a genuine story that was lost without trace when the Rapides courthouse records were burned in 1864. In the absence of any shred of corroborating evidence, it must be treated only as unsubstantiated rumor, though it may reasonably be added to the body of evidence showing that Bowie had a reputation for instilling fear and intimidation in those who crossed him. Unfortunately, in quoting the interview with Bastian, Brown was very imprecise as to where it came from. He cites an October 3 issue of the Philadelphia *Press* without giving the year. Internal evidence suggests either 1887 or 1891–92 as the proper year. However, October issues for both the Philadelphia *Press* and the more likely *Weekly Press* have been checked for every October for the inclusive years 1887–92, without finding the article. Probably with sufficient time the article could be found, but in any case it appears that Brown has quoted all that is relevant to Bowie.

63. Kemper to Johnston, December 14, 1826, Johnston Papers, HSP.

64. Overton to Johnston, August 2, 1826, ibid.

65. Baker to Johnston, October 5, 1826, Overton to Johnston, December 7, 1826, ibid.

66. Overton to Johnston, August 2, December 7, 1826, ibid.

67. R. H. Sibley to Johnston, October 4, 1826, ibid.

68. Overton to Johnston, December 7, 1826, ibid.

69. Samuel Wells to Johnston, December 15, 1826, Bullard to Johnston, January 26, 1827, ibid.

70. Douglas, *Bowie*, 33, actually says that Bowie opposed Wright, and that this was part of the background of the Sandbar fight. He is undoubtedly right, but in fact there is no contemporary documentation that says Bowie supported Wells. It can only be inferred from the general alliance between them relative to Bowie's congressional candidacy.

71. William S. Speer and John Henry Brown, eds., *The Encyclopedia of the New West*, vol. 1 (Marshall, Tex., 1881), 436.

72. Conveyance Book C, 151–52, 154, Terrebonne Parish Courthouse.

73. C. Beaman to Johnston, August 23, 1826, Johnston Papers, HSP.

74. In the previous couple of years James engaged in a few transactions with his brother John, including the joint sale of some of the as-yet-unconfirmed property on Deer Creek claimed in the Sutton report. John himself actively traded in land and occasional slaves in the Catahoula region, but, typical of the Bowies, he seems not to have managed his money well and fell heavily in debt by the end of 1826. As a result he sold more property than he bought, and in December 1825, when he acquired some two thousand *arpents* of undesignated land from James, he paid with three slaves rather than cash. Much more significant, though, is that John had to know of his brother's false titles—everyone else seemed to know—and yet, on the face of it, he allowed James to cheat him. But there was much more to it than that. This was no case of one brother defrauding another, but rather the beginning of a partnership destined to extend the reach of James Bowie's land appetite beyond the borders of Louisiana. Conveyance Record C, 331, Catahoula Parish

Courthouse; various debt judgments against John Bowie for 1826–28, Bowie Family Papers, UT; Conveyance of December 8, 1825, recorded with Clerk of the Court, Chicot County Courthouse, Lake Village, Arkansas, and cited in George Kelley, "John J. Bowie, 1787–1859," Arkansas History Commission, Little Rock.

75. Josiah Hazen Shinn, *Pioneers and Makers of Arkansas* (Little Rock, 1908), 87–88. It is not possible to recreate the nature of James Bowie's involvement in the Arkansas scheme in any greater detail because he successfully kept his name almost entirely out of it. His name does not appear on any of the conveyances, yet his authorship of the titles is confirmed in Reuben Kemper to Johnston, December 14, 1826, Johnston Papers, HSP, while by his own hand he connects himself with the scheme as at least a full partner, if not the prime mover, by his 1831 marriage dowry in which he lists the Arkansas property among his assets. Furthermore, when the Arkansas claims became controversial, they were universally spoken of as claims by "the Bowies," making it clear that though only John's name was on the documents, still everyone knew that James was in the shadows behind him.

76. Isaac T. Preston to Graham, October 10, 1829, *American State Papers*, Public Lands Series, vol. 6, 5–6.

77. Conveyance Record B, 231–32, Clerk of the Court, Hempstead County Courthouse, Washington, Arkansas.

78. Kemper to Johnston, December 14, 1826, Johnston Papers, HSP.

79. Bowie Claims, Cleland List, St. Augustine, Fla., Locations Under Arkansas Court, Decrees Act of 1824, Private Claims Division, General land Office, Entry 215, Record Group 49, NA.

80. Bowie, "The Bowies," 381.

81. J. Madison Wells account, James Bowie Biographical File, DRT.

82. There are, of course, the numerous stories of Bowie's duels and fights that can be regarded as nothing more than frontier myth, and they will be dealt with subsequently. Prior to the encounter with Norris Wright of about December 1826, however, not a shred of reputable evidence survives of any Bowie fight or duel.

83. Kemper to Johnston, December 14, 1826, Johnston Papers, HSP.

84. Receipts and Expenditures of the United States, 1818, 88–89; 1819, 85; 1820, 62–63, Record Group 217, NA.

85. Kemper to Johnston, December 14, 1826, Johnston Papers, HSP.

86. *Journal of the House of Representatives During the First Session of the Eighth Legislature of the State of Louisiana* (New Orleans, 1827), 3, 4.

87. Flint, *Recollections,* 242.

88. Alexandria, *Louisiana Messenger,* October 31, 1826, quoted in New Orleans, *Louisiana State Gazette,* November 13, 1826.

89. The episode of the Wright-Bowie fight is difficult to pinpoint, there being virtually no directly contemporaneous sources. This account is drawn chiefly from Caiaphas Ham's "Recollections of Col. James Bowie," 1887, in the John S. Ford

Papers, UT. It has all the earmarks of considerable circumstantial accuracy, and Ham himself must either have witnessed the affair or more likely heard Bowie tell about it. There is no question that they were well acquainted in Avoyelles, as court documents establish, and Ham frequently spent time with Bowie at least until 1833. On April 10, 1827, Ham signed an Avoyelles document as witness for Rezin Bowie, and thereafter crops up from time to time in legal proceedings as an associate of the Bowies. Thus his account—which is remarkably accurate in most other events as well—may be regarded as very reliable. Ham says nothing about Bowie having any weapon other than the clasp knife.

John Bowie in "The Bowies," 381, says of the event only that the fight took place "about the year 1826," that Wright shot Bowie while he was unarmed, and that James responded with his fists. This is also the authority for the statement that as a result of the fight, Bowie decided to make the scabbard to keep his hunting knife with him at all times. Rezin Bowie also referred briefly to the episode in an August 24, 1838, letter published in "The Bowie Knife," *Nile's Register* 55 (September 29, 1838): 70. In it he states only that "James Bowie had been shot by an individual with whom he was at variance." A report in the Baltimore *Commercial Transcript*, June 11, 1838, gives a very garbled account of the affair, making it Rezin who had come off a steamboat, and further making him a participant in the fight. Rezin himself repudiated this account in his letter (above) but it may at least confirm that the brawl occurred shortly after James arrived in Alexandria. There is also a very garbled account of a Bowie duel in Alexandria in the Houston, Tex., *Petrel* April 4, 1860, but it is too heavily embellished to be trusted. John S. Moore to W. W. Fontaine, April 25, 1890, W. W. Fontaine Papers, UT, is the source for the statement that Wright's bullet may have been deflected by a coin, and the only source that gives Bowie a pistol that misfired. Moore was Rezin's grandson and James's great-nephew, but born too late to know either of them, and therefore everything he had to say about James came to him thirdhand at best, and much of it is unreliable.

As for the dating of the fight, Ham states that it took place immediately upon James's arrival after "the absence of Col. Bowie in the North." Kemper to Johnston, December 14, 1826, Johnston Papers, HSP, establishes that James had returned a day or two previously, yet says nothing about the altercation, indicating that it probably had not happened yet. Unfortunately, for all that Josiah S. Johnston's Rapides correspondents kept him informed of the gossip and the violence in the parish, none made any mention of this fight in his surviving correspondence. Moreover, a search of several Louisiana newspapers for the period failed to find any mention of such an event, though many of them, especially those from Alexandria, no longer survive. Thus the only logical placement of the event that fits all the evidence is sometime soon if not immediately after Kemper's December 14, 1826, letter, and it may be significant—and more than coincidental—that the Alexandria *Louisiana Messenger* of December 15, 1826, cited in Tregle, "Louisiana," 85, speaks out against renewed violence with pistols and knives in the streets. Thus, until better evidence should surface, a date of December 13–14 seems the most likely.

Chapter 7   Crockett 1829–1831

1. Promissory note, February 24, 1829, Panhandle-Plains Historical Museum Research Center, Canyon, Tex.
2. Crockett letter to the editor, January 14, 1829, Jackson *Gazette*, February 7, 1829.
3. Folmsbee, "West Tennessee," 9.
4. Crockett to William Seat, January 26, 1829, Crockett Letters, Correspondence by Author, TSL.
5. Crockett to Joseph Gales and William Seaton, April 18, 1829, Personal Miscellaneous Papers, New York Public Library, N.Y.
6. Jackson *Gazette*, March 7, 1829.
7. Scrapbook Number 4, 19–21, June 20, 1848, Cooper Family Papers, TSL. This account was related by Sam Houston on the date cited, aboard the steamboat *Peytona*. Essentially the same story, with minor differences, appeared in 1873 in Davis, *Memphis*, 150–51. Shackford, *Crockett*, 83, cites this account from Davis but places it during the 1827 campaign. This is most unlikely. There is no evidence that Crockett "backed out" any candidates in that canvass, whereas by his own statement in his April 18, 1829, letter to Gales and Seaton, he had backed out three by mid-April. He does not name them, but Cooke was almost certainly one of them. Moreover, Houston related the story in 1848 as having been told to him by Crockett, and Crockett's very same April 18 letter also states that he had been with Houston and spoken with him a few days before.
8. Alexander to Polk, April 25, 1829, Weaver and Bergeron, *Correspondence of James K. Polk*, vol. 1, 258.
9. Keating, *Memphis*, vol. 1, 175–76.
10. J. J. B., "Crockett's Electioneering Tour," 610.
11. Jacobs to the Morristown *Gazette*, November 22, 1884, Correspondence by Subject, TSL.
12. J. J. B., "Crockett's Electioneering Tour," 608–9.
13. Crockett to Gales and Seaton, April 18, 1829, Personal Miscellaneous Papers, New York Public Library.
14. Crockett to John H. Bryan, May 26, 1829, John H. Bryan Papers, East Carolina University, Greenville, N.C.
15. Jackson *Gazette*, August 15, 1829.
16. Stout, "David Crockett," 18–19.
17. Quoted in Heale, "Self-Made Man," 405.
18. Arpad, "Crockett," 85–86.
19. Shackford, *Crockett*, 127; Receipt, September 2, 1829, Christie's Auction Catalog, May 17, 1996 (New York, 1996): 170.
20. Shackford, *Crockett*, 102.
21. Crockett to Hugh D. Nelson, January 24, 1820, Miscellaneous Collection, Tennessee Historical Society, TSL.

22. Keating, *Memphis*, vol. 1, 178.

23. Jackson *Gazette*, May 22, 1830.

24. Ibid., May 15, 1830.

25. Shackford, *Crockett*, 110, argues that this relationship was "too complex for David's reasoning," which seems clearly unwarranted, and not a little uncharitable.

26. Keating, *Memphis*, vol. 1, 176, 178.

27. Jackson *Gazette*, March 27, 1830. With what seems to be wholly inadequate support, Shackford, *Crockett*, 126, concludes that Crockett did not write this letter. Certainly it shows much better grammar, syntax, and spelling than his holograph documents, but it would have been quite commonplace for an editor to clean up that sort of thing without changing the sense of the document at all. In general Shackford is far too prone to conclude that letters that were *published* displaying good grammar did not therefore *originate* with Crockett. Had he known more of the journalistic practices of the time he might not have leaped to this conclusion so easily.

28. Shackford, *Crockett*, 123–25, dates Crockett's defection from Jackson somewhat earlier, to the fall of 1828. This is too early, and he confuses Crockett's defection from Jackson's Polk-led supporters with Crockett's disavowal of Jackson himself.

29. The May 24 dated text appears in the Jackson *Gazette*, June 26, 1830, the May 19 dated text in *Speeches on the Passage of the Bill for the Removal of the Indians Delivered in the Congress of the United States, April and May 1830* (Boston, 1830), 251–53. Folmsbee, "West Tennessee," 16, speculates that Crockett might actually have delivered the speech in Congress, but persuaded Gales and Seaton to leave it out of their published *Register of Debates*. This is impossible, not least because Gales and Seaton did not become official publishers of the House debates until February 1833. But more immediately, if Crockett had made such a speech, it is inconceivable that Polk and his other Jackson foes who were present to hear it would not have leaped on it and promoted it extensively to injure Crockett. Yet such was not the case, and other than appearing in the Jackson *Gazette*, in Crockett's own district, it was entirely overlooked by the national press, lending further support to the notion that Crockett himself sent it to the *Gazette*.

To his credit, Crockett showed little selectivity in his charity. He spoke up for the Indians because Jackson was their foe, but undoubtedly also out of some sympathy. When Jackson forces, with Old Hickory's backing, introduced a bill to appropriate a large sum for the relief of the widow of the naval hero Stephen Decatur, Crockett joined those opposing the measure, stating that respect for the dead and sympathy for the survivor should not lead them into an injustice to the majority of the taxpayers. Decatur had been paid his salary during his lifetime, and the government owed him no more. Further, Congress had no power to appropriate public funds for an act of individual charity. It was a position he had taken in his first term regarding a pension for another military widow. But in both instances, immediately after helping defeat the bills, he offered to contribute himself to a private subscription on behalf of the widows. "I do not wish to be rude, but I must be plain," he said. "I am the poorest man on this floor," he said, and as he told the House repeatedly, the poor were "the very class upon whom I should delight to bestow a benefit." But Mrs. Decatur was no more entitled to a huge benefit than the poor widow in his own district who had lost a husband in war, like Elizabeth for instance. If he introduced a bill for several thousand dollars on behalf of such a person, he suggested, the House would laugh him out of the chamber. He would always do what he could for the needy. Not long after helping defeat the Decatur measure, he recommended a young man for an appointment in the Navy, stressing that he was the son of a "widow lady of good character." (Crockett to William B. Lewis, May 31, 1830, *Philpott Collection Catalog*, Item no. 223).

30. Shackford, *Crockett*, 89, 118; J. J. B., "Crockett's Electioneering Tour," 606–607.
31. J. J. B., "Crockett's Electioneering Tour," 606.
32. Quoted in Heale, "Self-Made Man," 406.
33. Crockett to Gales and Seaton, April 18, 1829, Personal Miscellaneous Papers, New York Public Library. Shackford, *Crockett*, 123–24, makes far too much of this mention of Clarke in the letter, extrapolating from a mere "Pleas tender my Best Respects" a scenario in which Clarke visited Crockett in Tennessee in 1828 and planted the seeds of Crockett's supposedly unwitting defection to the Whigs.
34. Johnston to Clay, August 24, 1830, Robert Seagur and Melba Porter Hay, eds., *The Papers of Henry Clay*, vol. 8, *Candidate, Compromiser, Whig, March 5, 1829–December 31, 1836* (Lexington, Ky., 1984), 257.
35. J. A. McClung to Johnston, n.d. [docketed 1830 on verso], Johnston Papers, HSP.
36. Yell to Polk, December 1, 1830, Weaver and Bergeron, *Correspondence of James K. Polk*, vol. 1, 349.
37. Crockett to Henry McClung, December 21, 1830, Miscellaneous Collection, Tennessee Historical Society, TSL.
38. Crockett to Daniel Pounds, January 6, 1830, U.S. Manuscripts, J. K. Lilly Library, Indiana University, Bloomington.
39. Ibid.
40. Crockett to A. M. Hughes, February 13, 1831, Miscellaneous Collection, Tennessee Historical Society, TSL.
41. Shackford, *Crockett*, 120, suggests that Crockett may not have been the author of the dog-collar expression, but that it and others to follow were possibly the work of Matthew St. Clair Clarke, Shackford's completely unsubstantiated supposition being that Clarke was "feeding" Crockett sayings that he would later include in his 1833 *Life* of Crockett. It is far more logical to assume that this and most other similar expressions originated with Crockett, and that Clarke got them from him in their conversations in 1832–33 that helped produce the *Life*. Certainly in this instance, if Clarke had fed Crockett the collar aphorism, it would have been unlike David to wait more than two years to use it publicly, satisfying himself with this private usage in a personal letter. Shackford seems in general to be unwilling to grant Crockett much originality.

42. Crockett to Pounds, January 6, 1831, U.S. Manuscripts, Lilly Library, Indiana University, Bloomington.

43. Quoted in Shackford, *Crockett*, 112, and Heale, "Self-Made Man," 416–17. With a view to his bid for reelection, Crockett followed his House announcement four days later with a circular letter to the press in West Tennessee. Quite possibly with some help in composition from friends in Washington, most likely his messmate at Ball's, Thomas Chilton, Crockett laid out in clear detail the course of his falling out with Old Hickory. He charged him with hypocrisy for his promise of retrenchment, whereas the cost of government was increasing—or so Crockett thought. He railed against the cruel Indian Bill, accusing Van Buren of being Jackson's manipulator, and also blamed the "fox" for Jackson's turnaround on internal improvements, seeing in the design an attempt to aid Van Buren's chances of being Jackson's successor when Old Hickory left office. There was another betrayal, by the way, for Jackson always said a president should serve only one term, yet now he had all but announced that he would seek a second. Moreover, Jackson gave high appointments to a host of Van Buren's friends from Congress, despite his earlier stand that a constitutional amendment should be passed, if necessary, to put a stop to presidents giving appointments to congressmen.

44. Shackford, *Crockett*, 128–30; Folmsbee and Catron, "Congressman," 60.

45. Crockett to Pounds, January 6, 1831, U.S. Manuscripts, Lilly Library, Indiana University, Bloomington.

46. Turner, "Andrew Jackson and David Crockett," 386.

47. Alexander to Polk, December 15, 1830, Weaver and Bergeron, *Correspondence of James K. Polk,* vol. 1, 361.

48. Folmsbee and Catron, "Congressman," 65; Jackson *Gazette*, December 4, 1830.

9. Jackson to Samuel J. Hays, April 1831, Emma Inman Williams, *Historic Madison: The Story of Jackson, and Madison County, Tennessee* (Jackson, Tenn., 1946), 403.

50. Promissory note, March 29, 1831, RWA Inc. Auction Catalog no. 39 (Np., July 1, 1996): 16; Promissory note, May 3, 1831, *American Book Prices Current, 1979* 85 (New York, 1979): 908.

51. Crockett to Michael Sprigg, May 5, 1830[1831], Philpott Collection Catalog Item no. 222. This letter is headed 1830 by Crockett, and has been so treated by Shackford and others, but it was beyond doubt an inadvertent error on Crockett's part. On May 5, 1830, he was still sitting in the first session of the Twenty-first Congress, which did not adjourn until May 31 of that year, making it impossible for him to go home to Tennessee in early May and still be back for votes he cast at the end of the session. Since he is known to have stayed in Washington until at least March 29, 1831, after the close of the second session, this makes 1831 the more likely date of the writing, and no sources have been found that place him in Tennessee earlier than late May. Nor can this be from 1834 or 1835, when he returned from sessions of the Twenty-third Congress, for the first session lasted until June 1834, and his own letters already place him back home in Tennessee by April 1835. Thus only 1831 will fit.

52. J. J. B., "Crockett's Electioneering Tour," 611.

53. Ben Perley Poore, *Perley's Reminiscences of Sixty Years in the National Metropolis* (Philadelphia, 1886), 152.

54. Crockett to Davidson, August 18, 1831, Crockett Biographical File, DRT.

55. Heale, "Self-Made Man," 406–9, 414; Arpad, "Crockett," 48, 73.

56. Arpad, "Crockett," 36; James K. Paulding to John Wesley Jarvis, n.d. [1829–30], Ralph M. Aderman, ed., *The Letters of James Kirke Paulding* (Madison, Wis., 1962), 113.

57. Arpad, "Crockett," 112–13; Crockett to Paulding, December 22, 1830, Philpott Collection Catalog Item no. 224. Shackford, *Crockett*, 254–55, maintains that the Crockett letter is spurious because of its better than average composition, and supposedly strained attempts at quaint misspellings. Shackford, it has to be said, was starting to go off the deep end here, for he concluded that the letter was part of an elaborate Whig literary hoax played on Paulding, somehow designed to make Crockett "a more powerful anti-Jackson weapon" on behalf of the Second United States Bank. Crockett's own paranoia may have been rubbing off on him, for he was seeing conspiracy and forged letters almost at every turn after 1830. Unfortunately Shackford only had access to a printed version of the letter. Had he seen the original, cited above, he might have come to a more prosaic—and logical—conclusion, simply that it was genuine.

58. Crockett, *Narrative*, 207.

59. Ibid.; Crockett to Davidson, August 18, 1831, Crockett Biographical File, DRT.

60. Shackford, *Crockett*, 136, 306n.

61. Crockett to Richard Smith, January 7, 1832, Conarroe Autograph Collection, HSP.

62. Crockett to Davidson, August 18, 1831, Crockett Biographical File, DRT.

63. Crockett to Jones, August 22, 1831, Jones Papers, SHC, UNC.

64. Crockett, *Narrative*, 207–8.

65. Crockett to Davidson, August 18, 1831, Crockett Biographical File, DRT.

66. Jackson, Tenn., *Southern Statesman*, June 18, 1831.

67. Arpad, "Crockett," 175.

68. Moses Green to Polk, July 23, 1831, Weaver and Bergeron, *Correspondence of James K. Polk,* vol. 1, 414.

69. Crockett to Jones, August 22, 1831, Jones Papers, SHC, UNC.

70. Folmsbee, "West Tennessee," 18.

71. Crockett to Davidson, August 18, 1831, Crockett Biographical File, DRT; Folmsbee and Catron, "Congressman," 67.

72. Crockett to Smith, January 7, 1832, Conarroe Autograph Collection, HSP; Crockett to Davison, August 18, 1831, Crockett Biographical File, DRT.

73. Crockett to Jones, August 22, 1831, Jones Papers, SHC, UNC.

Chapter 8   Travis, 1809–1831

1. The ancestry of William Barret Travis beyond his grandfather Berwick is uncertain at best. This account draws largely on Archie McDonald, *William Barret Travis, A Biography* (Austin, 1976), 21–24, and to a lesser extent on Robert J. Travis, *The Travis (Travers) Family and Its Allies* (Decatur, Ga., 1954), 6–30.

2. McDonald, Travis, 24–25; *Travis, T*ravis Family, 30–31.

3. As with so much of the Travis ancestry, sources disagree on Mark's birthdate. Travis, *Travis Family*, 32, says February 2, 1783, while information furnished by his son James C. Travis in 1916 gave the date as September 6 (Statement in Mark B. Travis Surname File, ADAH). According to McDonald, *Travis*, 27, the latter date agrees with the date in the Travis family Bible, which this author has not seen, but as this appears to confirm James Travis's statement, it is adopted here.

4. Thomas M. Owen, *History of Alabama and Dictionary of Alabama Biography* (Chicago, 1921), vol. 4, 1681.

5. The date of the Travis-Stallworth marriage comes from the James C. Travis statement in 1916 in the Mark B. Travis Surname File, ADAH, and it is presumed that he based this on his father's family Bible, which was then in his possession.

6. There has been considerable debate about the number of Mark and Jemima's children, but since ten can definitely be identified by name, that number seems the most likely. There may have been an eleventh. Rayburn Fisher Jr., "William Barret Travis in Alabama," master's thesis, Howard College—now Sanford University (Birmingham, Ala., 1929), 1.

7. The birthdate has varied widely according to sources. James B. Boddie, *Historical Southern Families*, vol. 2 (Baltimore, 1958), 257, claimed to have seen the Mark Travis family Bible many years before his book appeared and said that it gave the date as August 9, 1809. The Bible has not been seen since to verify this, and there is always the possibility that Boddie's recollection was faulty or that he mistook the numeral 1 for a 9, something not uncommon with early-nineteenth-century handwriting. Far more convincing are statements by William Barret Travis's youngest brother James and a niece that the date was August 1 (James C. Travis to anonymous, April 2, 1907, Samuel Asbury Papers, UT; Evergreen, Ala., *Conecuh County Record,* October 5, 1899; M. E. Travis to Fannie J. McGuire, ca. 1925, Ruby Mixon Papers, UT). Moreover, at the time of his statements, James C. Travis owned the family Bible.

    Disagreement also extends to William's birthplace, some even placing it in North Carolina, but the same family sources cited above agree on Edgefield County (now Saluda), and several sources suggest the vicinity of Red Bank Church, where Mark Travis had his farm. John A. Chapman, *History of Edgefield County from Its Earliest Settlements to 1897* (Newberry, S.C., 1897), 188.

8. Numerous apocryphal stories appeared late in the nineteenth century to explain the name Barret, and as well suggesting that William was born out of wedlock

before Mark and Jemima wed. It is also said that young Travis was a foundling, left at Mark's gate in a basket hanging from a fence bar, leading to his middle name being "Bar," later lengthened to "Barret." They are all nonsense and folklore. Chapman, *Edgefield*, 76; Milledge L. Bonham to Asbury February 2, 1923, Asbury to E. W. Winkler, n.d., Asbury Papers, UT; Daisy Burnett to Ed Leigh McMillan, "Monday Afternoon," 1936, Ed Leigh McMillan Papers, ADAH; Ruby Mixon, "William Barret Travis, His Life and Letters," master's thesis, University of Texas (Austin, 1930), 12.

9. There is absolutely no evidence of a friendship in childhood between Travis and Bonham. The 1810 census for Edgefield does show the Travis family separated from the Bonhams by thirty-one names, which suggests that they were in the same vicinity, though certainly not neighbors. Milledge L. Bonham Jr., great-nephew of James Butler, told Samuel Asbury on February 2, 1923 (Asbury Papers, UT), that Travis and his great-uncle were childhood friends, though this could only be hearsay or family tradition no doubt influenced by the later relationship between the two. Williams, "Critical Study, I," 248, states without a source (though it is obviously a Milledge L. Bonham Jr. statement) that the two went to school together, which is hardly likely. Walter Lord, "Myths & Realities of the Alamo," Stephen B. Oates, ed., *The Republic of Texas* (Palo Alto, Calif., 1968), 18–19, concluded that no reliable evidence connected Travis and Bonham as childhood friends or even acquaintances. The best that can be asserted is that they might have known of each other, but no more.

10. Owen, *Alabama*, vol. 4, 1680–81; B. F. Riley, *History of Conecuh County, Alabama* (Columbus, Ga., 1881), 33–35.

11. McDonald, *Travis*, 31, citing records of Red Bank Baptist Church.

12. *Alabama Territory. A List of Taxable Property Taken in the County of Conecuh. In the Year 1818* (N.p., n.d.), 2, shows that as of October 26, 1818, even though Mark Travis must have been in Conecuh for several weeks by that time, he owned no property, leading to the conclusion that he lived with Alexander.

13. Marilyn Davis Hahn, comp. *Old Cahaba Land Office Records & Military Warrants, 1817–1853* (Birmingham, 1986), 27; Will T. Sheehan, "Commander of the Alamo Alabama Reared and Bred," clipping based on interview with Mark Travis, brother of William, in William Barret Travis Surname File, ADAH.

14. Marilyn Davis Hahn, *Old Sparta & Elba Land Office Records & Military Warrants, 1822–1860* (Birmingham, 1983), 1.

15. Owen, *Alabama*, vol. 4, 1680–81; Riley, *Conecuh*, 35; B. F. Riley, *Makers and Romance of Alabama History* (N.p., 1951), 98.

16. Riley, *Conecuh*, 35; *Acts of Alabama 1818–1975, Schools and Academies*, 84, ADAH.

17. William C. Davis, *A Way Through the Wilderness* (New York, 1995), 169–70.

18. William Letford, *The Story of William B. Travis As Told by Phillip Alexander Travis*, William B. Travis Surname File, ADAH. There is no contemporary source establishing that William Travis attended the Sparta Academy, but substantial local oral history, and this one account by a cousin of his—plus the fact that Travis was certainly well educated, and this was the only primary academy around—

argue strongly that he must have attended, especially with his uncle a school superintendent.

19. William Letford, "Sparta—Little Remains of this Once Thriving Community," Brewton, Ala., *Brewton Standard*, July 13, 1967.

20. Zachary R. Fulmore, *History and Geography of Texas, As Told in County Names* (N.p., 1951), 140–41; 1830 United States Census, Conecuh County, Alabama. McDonald, *Travis*, 44–45, concludes that McCurdy's establishment was, in fact, the Claiborne Academy, which was incorporated December 21, 1823. This is possible, but there is no firm evidence to support the assumption. Classes did not actually commence at this academy until 1825, when Travis would have been sixteen, and if he did attend, it would have been for no more than two years.

21. New York, *United States Telegraph*, May 19, 1836.

22. Fulmore, *History and Geography*, 141; Clarence R. Wharton to Ruby Mixon, March 27, 1929, Mixon Papers, UT. Jonathan H. Kuykendall, *Sketches of Early Texians*, referring to Travis's 1833 autobiography, says that he started teaching school at age eighteen or nineteen "for some months" (Kuykendall Family Papers, UT).

23. Rosanna Travis to James Dellet, September 6, 1834, James Dellet Papers, ADAH. Allowing for her time and place, Rosanna's letter is very well constructed and expressed.

24. Autobiography of William Barret Travis, 1833, quoted in Kuykendall, *Sketches of Early Texians*, Kuykendall Family Papers, UT.

25. McDonald, *Travis*, 49, says without authority that Alexander Travis and James Dellet were well acquainted, and that this is how William was introduced to his mentor. There is no evidence for this, though it is possible.

26. The assumption that Travis started reading under Dellet in early 1828 is based solely on the fact that Travis commenced his own practice in February 1829 and would have had to read for at least a year beforehand, though Kuykendall, *Sketches of Early Texians* (UT), says that Travis was a precocious student. Since Kuykendall also says that "at age 18 or 19 he taught school for some months," presumably basing this on Travis's autobiography then in Kuykendall's possession, it would appear most probable that Travis ceased teaching at some point after his nineteenth birthday, which would likely be sometime around the beginning of 1828.

27. Sketch of James Dellet, Dellet Papers, ADAH.

28. James Dellet tax list, September 16, 1831, Dellet Papers, ADAH.

29. Benjamin F. Porter Reminiscences, Porter Collection, Auburn University, Auburn, Ala. Travis biographers have persistently tried to suggest that Travis himself witnessed Lafayette's welcome in Claiborne, or even that he assisted Dellet in preparations for the visit, but the fact is that there is not an atom of evidence that Travis was even in Claiborne at the time. He would not have been there studying with Dellet until at least two years later. This is not to say that he could not have gone to Claiborne to witness the festivities, only that it is unwar-

ranted to assume that he did. Mixon, "Travis," 7; McDonald, *Travis*, 44; Martha Anne Turner, *William Barret Travis, His Sword and His Pen* (Waco, Tex., 1972), 6.

30. While there seems to be no reason to doubt the fact, it is worth noting that there is no firm contemporary evidence to support the claim that Travis read law under Dellet. The earliest reference to his legal education is in Kuykendall's 1857 *Sketches of Early Texians*, and he only says that "Travis commenced the study of law," with no mention of Dellet (Kuykendall Family Papers, UT). Travis's cousin Phillip Travis—who never met him—said at an unknown time that Travis studied under Dellet, as did Travis's nephew Mark Travis, who also never met him. It has long been a local Alabama tradition that he did so. Fulmore, *History and Geography*, 140–41, says that he studied under Dellet and Enoch Parsons, and James K. Greer told Samuel Asbury on January 17, 1934 (Asbury Papers, UT), that an old former probate judge of Monroe County told him that Travis had read with Dellet. Ed Leigh McMillan, Memoranda with Regard to William Barret Travis, May 26, 1940, McMillan Papers; Letford, *Story of William B. Travis,* William B. Travis Surname File, ADAH.

31. Rhoda C. Ellison, *History and Bibliography of Alabama Newspapers in the Nineteenth Century* (University, Ala., 1954), 37; Claiborne *Gazette*, March 19, 1825; Woodville, Miss., *Republican*, October 27, 1827. Only one issue of the *Gazette* is known to exist, at the American Antiquarian Society in Worcester, Mass. No issues of the *Alabama Whig* are known to survive, and its existence is only known from its being quoted in the *Republican*.

32. Claiborne *Herald*, February 27, 1829. Only two issues of this newspaper survive, both at the Library of Congress. Since it was a weekly, and the February 27, 1829, issue is volume 1, number 42, that would make the date of the first issue May 16, 1828, though since Travis certainly did not maintain a precise schedule after February 1829, it is possible that he had not prior to that time.

33. All the above is deduced from the February 27, 1829, issue of the *Herald.*

34. M. J. DeCaussey to William B. Travis Chapter, Daughters of the Republic of Texas, January 31, 1895, Asbury Papers, UT.

35. Kuykendall, *Sketches of Early Texians*, Kuykendall Family Papers, UT.

36. William Barret and Rosanna E. Travis Bible, TXSL. The speculation that Charles may have been born on August 8, 1828, instead of a year later, is based on the fact that the entry for his birth is apparently in Travis's handwriting, while all other birth and death entries are in other hands, and at some time someone altered the year in the entry for Charles by using a dark ink to write "1829" over what Travis had originally written. Also, the last numeral of the year in the entry for Travis's wedding is illegible, yet has always been assumed to be 1828, with which there is no quibble. The point is that when children appeared before a marriage made them legitimate, or when the firstborn came less than nine months after the wedding, the most common means of "sanitizing" the record for future generations was either to backdate the wedding by a year or to postdate the birth by a year, and such alterations are to be found in probably half of the extant family Bibles of the eighteenth and nineteenth centuries. In this particular instance, putting the baby before the wedding would

have been entirely in keeping with Travis's known impulsive—and libidinous—nature, and also with what some suspect of Rosanna.

37. Claiborne *Herald*, February 27, 1829.

38. Porter, Reminiscences, Porter Collection, Auburn, lists the books he was required to read when studying law in Claiborne in 1830, presumably under Dellet, and therefore Travis would have read the same texts.

39. United States Census, Monroe County, Alabama, 1830.

40. Peter A. Brannan, "Claiborne," *Alabama Historical Quarterly* 19 (Summer 1957): 241; Harry Edgar Wheeler, *Timothy Abbott Conrad* (Ithaca, N.Y., 1935), 14; Claiborne, Ala., *Herald*, December 5, 1829; Claiborne, Ala., *Gazette*, March 19, 1825; Caroline G. Hurtel, *The River Plantation of Thomas and Marianne Gaillard, 1832–1850* (Mobile, 1946), 2–8.

41. Hurtel, *River Plantation*, 8; *Claiborne Herald*, February 27, 1829; Claiborne *Gazette*, March 19, 1825; Samuel Forwood to Isaac Grant, December 4, 1888, "Samuel Forwood's Letter Concerning Old Claiborne," *Clarke County Historical Society Quarterly* 5 (Spring 1981): 29–30; Riley, *Makers and Romance*, 5–7; fragment, January 22, 1830, Samuel Dale Papers, ADAH.

42. Riley, *Makers and Romance*, 18–19; Porter, Reminiscences, Porter Collection, Auburn; Claiborne, Ala., *Gazette*, March 19, 1825; *Monroe County* (N.p, n.d.), 441–43.

43. Porter, Reminiscences, Porter Collection, Auburn, states that in 1830 he took the examination from Crenshaw, so it is assumed that Crenshaw would have administered it to Travis the year before, especially since the *Herald*, February 27, 1829, states that Crenshaw was presiding at the court then in session.

44. Kuykendall, *Sketches of Early Texians*, Kuykendall Family Papers (UT), states that "Travis commenced the study of law and so intense was his application thereto that he was admitted to the bar before he was twenty-one years of age." Kuykendall had just prior to this quoted from Travis's autobiography, which he obviously had in front of him, so it is reasonable to suppose that this information, too, came from that now lost document, including the testimony to his application and precocity. Travis announced his practice in the *Herald* on February 27, 1829, and Travis's code on the advertisement is also dated February 27, indicating that this was its first insertion and therefore must have come immediately after his passing the bar.

45. *B. F. Hampton* v. *William B. Travis*, Practice Docket, 1828–1830, note of William B. Travis to W. H. Simpson, February 16, 1829, Dellet Papers, ADAH.

46. Claiborne, Ala., *Herald*, February 27, 1829. The conclusion that Travis took boarding pupils is derived from the 1830 United States Census, Monroe County, Alabama, which shows in addition to Travis himself and Rosanna and their infant son, one teenage female, one teenage male, and another male between twenty and thirty. While there is no way of identifying who they were, boarding pupils seems the most logical explanation, given Travis's financial straits.

47. There has long been a prevailing belief that Travis actually lived in Clarke County, in or near Gosport, and that he commuted to Claiborne. Probably the

earliest such recorded statement is Timothy H. Ball, *A Glance Into the Great South-East, or, Clarke County, Alabama, and Its Surroundings, from 1540 to 1877* (Grove Hill, Ala., 1882), 196, which states that Travis practiced out of Clarkesville. This would appear to be the foundation for all subsequent statements. Letford, *Story of William B. Travis*, Travis Surname File, ADAH, says that he opened his office in Gosport but only stayed a short time before moving to Claiborne. John S. Graham, *History of Clarke County* (Birmingham, 1923), 131, merely reiterates Ball. Travis J. Benson, a distant cousin, wrote to Ruby Mixon on March 22, 1929 (Mixon Papers, UT), that Travis had his office in Clarkesville. Clarke County Historical Society, *Illustrated Sketches of Clarke County, Alabama* (Huntsville, 1977), 102, says that Travis was a member of its bar, and 103 refers to "Travis, a lawyer at Clarkesville."

Travis biographers, starting with Mixon, have accepted this story. Mixon, "Travis," 9, did so, and so did Turner, *Travis*, 6, while McDonald, *Travis*, 48, reiterates the Gosport office story. There is no support at all for it, and much to argue against it. Travis's own first announcement of his practice clearly states that his office is in Claiborne. The next year, in the 1830 Monroe census, he is quite clearly a resident of Claiborne, despite the statement of Peter Brannan, "Claiborne," 281, that he could find no evidence that Travis ever lived in that community, and that "it is generally concluded that he lived across the river in the neighborhood of Gosport and commuted back and forth every day for the meetings of the court." The loss of the Monroe County court records in a fire in 1834 neatly erased much evidence that might have shown more Travis activity in the town, but the Clarke County Courthouse records in Grove Hill are extant. County Court Minutes, Book A, 1824–1833, and Minutes of the Commissioners Court, Book A, 1813–1832, Clerk of the Court, Clarke County Courthouse, Grove Hill, Alabama, have been scanned for every page, and not a single mention of Travis as either resident or practicing attorney appears in any of its suits, court minutes, or subpoenas issued or in any indexes of conveyances. Moreover, given his heavy debts in Monroe, and the resulting court actions against him, he would undoubtedly have borrowed in Clarke as well, yet there are no records of judgments for collection of debt against him there. All the Claiborne lawyers occasionally practiced before Clarke court when it sat, and surely so did Travis on at least one occasion early in 1831. But any idea that he lived anywhere other than Claiborne simply does not survive scrutiny.

48. Forwood to Grant, December 4, 1888, "Forwood's Letter," 29–30.

49. Brewton, Ala., *Standard,* July 13, 1967; Deed Book A, 33–34, Clerk of the Court, Monroe County Courthouse, Monroeville, Alabama.

50. Claiborne, Ala., *Herald,* February 27, 1829; W. A. Stewart to Travis, May 13, 1829, W. A. Stewart Letterbook, quoted in Theodore B. Pearson, "William Barrett [sic] Travis," *Clarke County Historical Society Quarterly* 18 (Summer 1993): 15.

51. George A. Beauchamp to Mixon, March 28, 1929, Mixon Papers, UT; Gordon Evatt to Archie McDonald, February 27, 1969, cited in McDonald, *Travis*, 49; Pearson, "Travis," 13–14.

52. Military Roster of Alabama, vol. 2, 1820–1832, ADAH; Peter Brannan to Asbury, February 10, 1932, Travis Surname File, ADAH; George Medlock to

Gabriel Moore, February 17, 1830, Militia Correspondence, Governors' Papers, Gabriel Moore, ADAH.

53. Dellet's papers and the Tait Family Papers, ADAH, contain receipts for numerous publications to which these two men subscribed in this period, but none for the *Herald.*

54. Claiborne, Ala., *Herald,* December 5, 1829; William B. Travis receipt, November 8, 1829, *American Book Prices Current 1979* 85 (New York, 1979): 1037.

55. McDonald, *Travis,* 49, states without authority that Travis published the *Herald* until he left Claiborne in early 1831. Considering its faltering condition in December 1829, and Travis's increasingly dire financial straits throughout 1830, this hardly seems possible.

56. *B. Hampton* v. *Travis,* January 1, 1829, *James Colburn* v. *Travis,* October 1829, *N. N. B. Hays* v. *Travis,* January 1, 1830, *Francis Pridgeon* v. *Travis,* January 1, 1830, *D. L. Weakley* v. *Travis,* July 17, 1829, *Joseph Lindsey & Co.* v. *Travis,* August 13, 1830, Practice Docket 1828–1830, J. Emanuel to Dellet, July 14, 1831, Dellet Papers, ADAH.

57. Long tradition in Monroe County says that Travis lived in a one-story, two-room house with attic, with probably no more than three hundred square feet in all. This building has been restored and is today open to the public at Perdue Hill, Ala., under the auspices of the Perdue Hill–Claiborne Historic Preservation Foundation, which also maintains the Claiborne Masonic Hall, both structures having been moved from their original sites since Claiborne essentially no longer exists. Joan Headley, who has overseen the Perdue Hill restorations, confirmed to me in a letter of October 25, 1996, that there is absolutely no documentary basis of any kind to connect this house with Travis. "We are indeed dealing with local oral tradition," she said. Given the grotesque inaccuracy of Monroe local tradition relating to Travis's departure from Alabama, as will be seen, it would be unwise to put much credence in it where this house is concerned. Moreover, as the 1830 census taken between June 1 and December 1 lists nine people living under Travis's roof, this small cottage hardly seems sufficient. The conclusion that Travis lived near Dellet, but in town, comes from the census listing, which quite distinctly segregated Claiborne residents from those of the rest of the county, and Travis's enumeration appears just six names from Dellet's, suggesting possibly that they even lived on the same street and block.

58. Claiborne, Ala., *Herald,* December 5, 1829.

59. Claiborne, Ala., *Gazette,* March 19, 1825.

60. Summons to Francis Farrar, August 14, 1830, Receipt to William M. Cato, August 24, 1830, William B. Travis as administrator of estate of Ansel Erwin, summons, August 14, 1830, Subpoena to G. R. Holland, August 26, 1830, Dellet Papers, ADAH.

Local folklore and Travis biographers have left the impression that he was a very successful lawyer. Turner, *Travis,* 6, says that "although it is believed that the young attorney achieved more than indifferent success during these years, no records are available to confirm it." McDonald, *Travis,* 46–47, goes much farther, concluding that "Travis established such a strong association with Dellet that he may almost be thought of as a junior partner," and moreover that "Dellet's papers indicate that he was active in the affairs of the county" and that "several cases in which he was an attorney are listed in the dockets of the Claiborne courts" (48). These are misconceptions based on a fundamental misunderstanding of the nature of the Travis documents in the Dellet Papers. With the exception of a single passing reference in one letter, Travis's name does not appear in any correspondence by or to James Dellet. Travis appears on only two kinds of documents, those in which he is representing someone trying to collect a debt, and the much greater number in which he is being sued for debt, usually by Dellet. The presence of these documents in Dellet's papers is explained by the fact that they are court documents, not his practice papers, and in 1830–32 Dellet served as judge of the local court. Moreover, by 1830–31 Dellet already had another partner, Benjamin F. Porter.

61. Claiborne, Ala., *Herald,* February 27, 1829.

62. United States Census, Monroe County, Alabama, 1830.

63. Rosanna Travis to Dellet, September 6, 1834, Dellet Papers, ADAH.

64. A common story suggests that Rosanna was unfaithful, though like virtually all stories connected with Travis's life in Alabama, this one did not surface until almost a century after he left, and as usual came second- or thirdhand from people who never knew him. Travis's nephew Mark Travis told Samuel Asbury, April 17, 1929 (Mixon Papers, UT), that his father, James C. Travis, had told him that in the marriage "his brother William put up with things tha[t] he never though[t] he would, but he always say it was best, maybe, for him to have done as he did." At the same time Mark Travis told Rayburn Fisher on March 23, 1929, that James told him that but for "family troubles," William might not have left (Mixon Papers, UT). On April 4, 1929, Mark Travis told Fisher that William had "charged Infidelity" against Rosanna (Fisher, "Travis," 10), and later that month, on April 20, 1929, told Fannie J. McGuire (Fisher, "Travis," 10) that a court determined that Rosanna was an "unfit" mother, the inference being that she was an adulteress. There is more of this, but the important point is that Mark Travis's father James never knew his brother William, and therefore got nothing from him firsthand. As will be shown subsequently, all the stories he apparently told Mark about Travis suing Rosanna for divorce and winning, having her declared unfit by the court, and being granted custody of their children were completely false. Certainly Rosanna would not have told anyone this sort of thing. The most logical explanation is that after Travis abandoned Rosanna and the two children, his family in later years—especially after he became a hero—dealt with the unpleasant fact by concocting this myth, especially when she married Samuel Cloud immediately after the divorce was final in February 1836, suggesting that they had become quite close before she was officially single once more. Of course she had been alone five years at that point, and Travis himself certainly did not hesitate to form new romantic liaisons while still married, and apparently even while protesting his love to Rosanna and promising to return to her. But any suggestions that she was found culpable by a court are completely false.

65. Travis Autobiography, 1833, quoted in Kuykendall, *Sketches of Early Texians,* Kuykendall Family Papers, UT.

66. Executions unsettled on the docket 1828 to 1832, Dellet Papers, ADAH.

67. James Savage to Dellet, January 21, 1831, Dellet Papers, ADAH.

68. Porter, Recollections, Porter Collection, Auburn.

69. Ibid.

70. Petition, December 1831, Conecuh Trial Cases, March 1831, Dellet Papers, ADAH. Dellet's papers confirm that the session of the Monroe court commenced in March 1831.

71. Porter, Reminiscences, Porter Collection, Auburn.

72. Ibid.

73. Kuykendall, *Sketches of Early Texians,* Kuykendall Family Papers, UT.

74. Mixon, "Travis," 9, argues that Travis was "a respected and responsible citizen" in Claiborne, obviously an erroneous conclusion.

75. Arrest orders, March 31, 1831, arrest order for William M. Cato, October 10, 1831, Dellet Papers, ADAH; Benjamin F. Porter, The Porters in America, biographical notes, Porter Collection, Auburn.

76. Monroeville, Ala., *Journal* December 22, 1966.

77. A. Mead to Austin, February 15, 1830, Eugene C. Barker, ed. *The Austin Papers,* Vol. 2, (New York, 1919–26), 332.

78. Dellet to John Murphy, February 12, 1831, Dellet Papers, ADAH.

79. Marquis James, *The Raven: A Biography of Sam Houston* (New York, 1929), 180, makes the absurd claim that in late 1830 Travis was in correspondence with Sam Houston in regard to the conquest or purchase of Texas by the United States, the inference being that this had something to do with Travis leaving Alabama. There is, of course, absolutely no authority for such a statement, or for the myth that two years earlier, in January 1828, Travis attended the Jackson dinner in New Orleans and made a speech.

80. Rosanna Travis to Dellet, September 6, 1834, Dellet Papers, ADAH. It should be pointed out that several writers have perpetuated a myth that Travis was well off when he left for Texas. Williams, "Critical Study, III," 81, says that "it is generally stated that Travis left Alabama in financial straits, but this is probably not true, since he is known to have left a bank account of a considerable amount for the support of his wife and child. It is true, however, that he left all he had for the support of his family." To support this she cites a Travis family tradition told her by D. W. Stallworth, a distant Travis cousin, in February 1930. John Myers, *The Alamo* (New York, 1948), 117, says that Travis "left his very comfortable bank balance," and Virgil Baugh, *Rendezvous at the Alamo* (New York, 1960), 143, is even more imaginative. "Clients began to pour in," he said of Travis' practice. "They established a fine house, made friends, became quite prominent in the social life of the town," and when Travis left he did so "after making provision to turn over to his wife most of his worldly wealth, including a sizable bank account." All are complete nonsense. Travis was broke and left Rosanna with

nothing but debts that were still on Dellet's docket, unpaid, two years after Travis left.

81. The tone of Porter's *Reminiscences* makes it quite clear that he is writing to mitigate an impression left by the manner of Travis's departure from Claiborne, and this combined with Rosanna's comment about her husband's "deficient" integrity to others, adds up to establish that he fled town without telling his creditors that he was leaving. Further, the absence of any listings or summons for Travis in the Dellet papers after June 1831 indicates that by then his creditors had given up on collecting from him, circumstantial evidence that they regarded him as having run out on his bills.

82. Robert E. Davis, ed., *The Diary of William Barret Travis, August 30, 1833–June 26, 1834* (Waco, Tex., 1966), 9, the entry for September 8, 1833, indicates that Travis is arranging for a man to return to Claiborne to "buy my paper for me," meaning to redeem his notes.

83. McDonald, *Travis*, 58, says that Travis left on horseback. While he offers no authority for the statement, it is probably correct. The last document in Claiborne bearing Travis's name is a note in the Dellet papers dated February 5, 1831, for fifty bushels of corn, undoubtedly for his horse, and among the unpaid bills he left behind was a blacksmith's account for shoeing a horse, establishing that he certainly had one such animal. Blacksmith account book, Dellet Papers, ADAH.

84. The date of Travis's departure is conjectural. No document places him in Claiborne later than February 5, 1831, and he first appears in Texas on May 11. Such a trip would not take him three months, however, and since the court did not sit until March, and its arrest orders did not start to go out until March 31, an early April departure is far more likely. As for his route, all is conjecture, but if he went by horse, his most direct route was across the Alabama, on to Fort Stephens, then across Mississippi to Natchez, and so on to Texas. The only roughly contemporary source, Porter in his *Recollections*, merely says that Travis left "soon after" his embarrassment by Dellet in court, which would again argue for April.

85. Of all the myths surrounding Travis in Alabama, the majority—and the most ridiculous—relate to the reasons for his leaving. One maintained that he was caught in a land fraud (Clarence R. Wharton to Mixon, April 12, 1929, Mixon Papers, UT). Another suggested that while a resident of Clarke County—which he was not—he objected to moving the courthouse from Clarkesville to Grove Hill, and when he lost the argument, left in a huff. Even more ridiculous is that some prankster clipped his horse's tail, so angering Travis that he refused to live in Alabama any longer (Travis J. Benson to Mixon, March 22, April 6, 1829, Mixon Papers). More accounts state that he left because of the breakup of his marriage, though the evidence of his repeated expressions of his affection and his intent to come back to Rosanna for two years after he left, casts very serious doubt on this (Rosanna Travis to Dellet, September 6, 1834, Dellet Papers, ADAH). Travis himself, in his 1833 "autobiography," stated that "my wife and I had a feud which resulted in our separation," though a man as proud as he could hardly be expected

to write that he really left to evade debt (Kuykendall, *Sketches of Early Texians*, Kuykendall Family Papers, UT). His nephew Mark Travis, who never met or knew him, and who got his information from Travis's brother James, who also never knew him, repeatedly said that Travis left because of marital discord (Mark Travis to Samuel Asbury, April 17, 1929, Mark Travis to Rayburn Fisher, March 23, April 4, 1929, Mark Travis to F. J. McGuire, April 20, 1929, Mixon Papers, UT). An undated clipping circa 1920 in the Mixon Papers also quotes Milda Stewart, supposedly a Travis cousin, as saying that he left Alabama "a broken hearted crushed man as a result of trouble in his own family." Mixon, "Travis," 10–11, has accepted marital problems as the primary reason for his departure. At the time she wrote, the Dellet papers and the Porter *Recollections* were not yet available.

The most ridiculous of the myths concern Travis killing a man who had seduced Rosanna. The stories seem to originate with Dabney White and M. M. Fountain of Alabama, and first appeared in 1928, though White supposedly was telling the story many years earlier. These were expanded upon in 1936 by a Daisy Burnett and collected, first by Ruby Mixon in 1929 for her thesis on Travis, and later by Alabama historian Ed Leigh McMillan. Basically Travis caught a gambler or man about town dallying with his wife and waylaid and shot him. When an innocent man—in one version a black—was charged with the crime, Travis defended him, and when he lost the case and the man was to be hanged, Travis confided to Dellet the real story, and Dellet told Travis that he would keep his secret long enough for Travis to pack and leave for Texas. The man was freed surreptitiously and told to disappear. There are variations in the story, such as that Travis believed that the child Rosanna was pregnant with at the time was not his own, that Dellet was the judge in the case, that Travis was really just a spectator at the trial, and suddenly jumped up and confessed his own guilt to save the accused, and that the accused was white rather than black (M. M. Fountain to Marian B. Owen, December 19, 1928, Daisy Burnett to Ed Leigh McMillan, 1936, Ed Leigh McMillan, Memorandum, May 26, 1940, Memorandum with Regard to William Barret Travis, August 24, 1957, Travis Surname File, ADAH; Mixon to Asbury, 1929, Samuel E. Miller to Mixon, March 17, 1929, Mixon Papers, UT).

Interestingly, when these stories were presented to Mark Travis, he maintained that he had never heard anything of them either from growing up in the region, or from his father, James C. Travis. The only explanation circulating in the family for William's departure was marital discord. Historian Samuel Asbury regarded the murder stories as false and hoped to disprove them, but subsequent biographers have been less critical (Asbury to Marie Owen, January 29, 1932, Travis Surname File, ADAH). Mixon, "Travis," 488 takes no firm position on the question, and Turner, *Travis*, 7–12, 15, is equivocal, though suggesting that the legends were probably just that. McDonald, *Travis*, 50–54, suggests that Travis knew Rosanna too well before they were married to trust her afterward, but offers no support for this, nor for the statement that "ample evidence" suggests that Travis suspected her of infidelity. He concludes that Travis suspected that she was pregnant with another man's child, even though in his subsequent will

Travis acknowledges Susanna Travis as "my daughter." In the end he concludes that "what seems indisputable is that Travis killed a man because of his wife's amorous involvement or suspected involvement." Yet the sources he cites—all listed above—are all third-, fourth-, even fifthhand stories, originating with people who never knew Travis personally and never set down on paper until 100 years after his departure from Claiborne. McDonald reiterates this conclusion in his "Travis: The Legend and the Legend Makers," *Journal of the American Studies Association of Texas* 13 (1982): 42, saying that "the truth is he killed a man who was suspected of intimacy with Rosanna and left for Texas to forget the mess."

For a start, all the Mark Travis testimony is tainted by derivation from his father, who knew nothing of his brother firsthand. The claims that Travis divorced Rosanna are incorrect; she divorced him, as the laws of Alabama and the surviving record make clear, to be cited subsequently. Moreover, as revealed in her September 6, 1834, letter to Dellet, and in Travis's own diary, no court awarded custody of the children to Travis; Rosanna agreed to give up Charles to him of her own accord long before the divorce proceedings commenced.

Then there is the murder story, and this, interestingly, may contain a grain of truth, that gossip and fading memory engrafted onto the Travis story. As reported in Travis's own newspaper, the Claiborne *Herald*, December 5, 1829, William Foster was assassinated at his home in November, and a slave was charged with the crime, tried, and convicted. A year later, but more than four months before Travis left Claiborne, someone slipped the black a key to his cell and he escaped (Dellet to Moore, December 4, 1830, Reward Files, Governors' Papers, Gabriel Moore, ADAH). As Travis himself stated in his editorial on the Foster murder, it was particularly shocking since it had been two years since there had been a murder in that vicinity, and the escape of the presumed killer would make it even more memorable.

The story bears some superficial resemblance to the Travis legends. Putting the two together suggests that the tricks of memory and sanitizing took over in later years. Once Travis became a hero, the people of Claiborne would remember the way he left the community by night, in disgrace, five years earlier, yet no one but Porter ever left a recollection of his reason for leaving, his debt. As time went on, and with the tendency of memory to confuse chronology and to compress time, the four months between the disappearance of the black murderer and the disappearance of Travis—the two most memorable Claiborne happenings of 1830–31—could easily be reduced until the two became virtually simultaneous. If there really were contemporary rumors about Rosanna's fidelity, then this added to the other two events could produce cause and effect. And what community—or even family, for that matter—would prefer that its most famous son be remembered as leaving it because of escaping debt, versus taking manly action to avenge an insult to the sanctity of his home. In short, the legend actually enhances Travis's reputation as a man of action and honor and spirit, even if hasty. What the legend ignores, of course, is the established fact that in that time and place, if a man killed someone who had cuckolded him, he faced not a trial but the approbation of his fellow citizens. Moreover, it is evident that

Travis repeatedly told Rosanna he intended to come back to Claiborne for her, evidence that he felt he had nothing to fear from the law so far as a murder was concerned, and therefore no reason to run away in the first place on that count.

In short, all of this murder business is an invention, not malicious certainly, and perhaps not even conscious. Even some in Travis's family by 1929 were beginning to accept it, having long since forgotten the matter of debt and desertion. It is worth noting, by the way, that murders were sufficiently uncommon that they gained wide circulation in the press. Reports of Claiborne's last murders, in 1827, appeared in newspapers as far away as Woodville, Mississippi (*Republican*, October 27, 1827), yet a search of all available Alabama newspapers for the period of Travis' last months in Claiborne, January-May 1831, has failed to reveal a single mention of any Claiborne murder or trial in that period. Sadly, the destruction by fire in 1834 of almost all of Monroe County's records makes it impossible to consult documents that almost certainly would have put the lie to this story once and for all. Asked by Raymond Fisher about the murder story, Mark Travis told him in a letter on April 4, 1929, "I am sure that this is false" (Fisher, "Travis," 12). He was right.

Chapter 9   Bowie 1827–1828

1. Tocqueville, *Democracy in America*, 95.

2. More nonsense has been written over the last century and a half about James Bowie and the Bowie knife than any other episode in his heavily mythologized life. No attempt will be made in this study to deal with the history of the knife itself, simply because in relation to the life of James Bowie it is of peripheral importance at best. James Bowie did not design it, nor did he make it. Perhaps the earliest known account of its invention comes from the Little Rock, *Arkansas Advocate* February 3, 1837, quoting a June 1836 issue of the Alexandria *Red River Herald*. It says that the knife was made on Charles Mulhollan's plantation on Bayou Boeuf in Rapides around 1820 on instructions from "Big Jim Bowie." However, there is no verifiable account of him ever using any knife in a fight except once, in the Sandbar brawl, and there is no reason at all to doubt the statement of Rezin Bowie in his August 24, 1838, letter (*Nile's Register* 55 [September 29, 1838], 70) that he made this first knife himself, that he gave it to James after the Wright shooting, and that it was this knife that James carried several months later on the famed Sandbar. Rezin also states that the later so-called Bowie knife, with a much wider blade, a curved sharp edge along one side, and a concave indentation leading to the tip on the other, was not his design but done by what he termed "experienced cutlers." Innumerable stories appeared in later years, most of them long after both James and Rezin were dead and could not gainsay them, assigning the design to James and others, and the actual manufacture to a dozen or more different claimants. The literature on this subject is too confused, contradictory, and often amateurish to merit discussion here, and again as relates to James, it is unimportant in any case. James may himself have had another knife or two made subsequent to the one given him by

Rezin, but no evidence exists that he ever used them for more than conventional outdoor purposes. Both Mims, *Bowie Knife*, and Raymond Thorp, *Bowie Knife* (N.p., 1948), are largely devoted to the history of the blade, and can be consulted as compendia of most of the several accounts of the knife's origin, though they should not be relied upon for any details on the life of James Bowie himself.

Among the numerous stories relating the origin of the knife are: J. Madison Wells account in the James Bowie Biographical File, DRT; Sparks in Ellis, *Crockett*, 217–18, 230–31; Mrs. Eugene Soniat to David F. Boyd, September 14, 1885, David F. Boyd Papers, LSU; San Antonio *Daily Express*, July 8, 1888; John S. Moore to W. W. Fontaine, April 25, 1890, Fontaine Papers, UT; Philadelphia *Pennsylvanian*, July 19, 1838; Baltimore *Commercial Transcript*, June 9, 11, 1838; James L. Goodloe to Lucy L. Bowie, April 23, 1917, Lucy Leigh Bowie Papers, DRT, and Andrew J. Sowell, *Rangers and Pioneers of Texas* (San Antonio, 1884), 126–27. William B. Worthen, "The Term 'Bowie Knife,'" *Knife World* 21 (November 1995): 1, 15–17, is a useful and sensible addition to this history of the blade after Rezin Bowie.

3.   Graham and Johnston discussed the bogus land claim issue frequently, and as far back as December 1824 the commissioner had expressed his anxiety to get the public lands surveyed and on the market. On January 9, 1827, he wrote to Johnston again referring to fraudulent claims, specifically Bowie's Martin and Wilson applications; then elsewhere in the letter Graham addressed another applicant and expressed his desire that this one might be approved. Two months later he enlisted Brent's aid in dealing with surveys, and Johnston, meanwhile, went on the record for a year, now promoting confirmation of claims in another district of the state.

Bowie himself told potential buyers that positive orders had arrived from Washington to survey his claims, that the surveys were done and in the files of the land office in New Orleans. Samuel Harper, who in May 1827 finally brought to Washington's attention the full details of his lost 1821 letter about Bowie's forgeries, believed conclusively that Bowie lied. Yet in this instance Bowie may have been telling the truth for a change. Somehow a confusion took hold in the local land office—a combination of Bowie's statements, Johnston's, and the January 9 letter from Graham to Johnston. The result was that George Davis, about to resign, came under the impression that Graham wanted Bowie's claims surveyed and certificates of survey issued, virtually confirming his possession of the property. Early in 1827 he allowed the claims to be surveyed at Bowie's expense.

Bowie wasted no time in starting his transactions. Indeed, perhaps even before the final surveys came through, he commenced selling. In April and May he began the formal transfers from the Martins to himself, on paper showing a purchase price of nineteen thousand dollars for six of the nine claims, whereas he may have paid nothing at all except a fee to the notoriously corruptible Martins for the use of their names. The amounts in the transfers meant nothing, other than perhaps an attempt to establish a benchmark for future asking prices. As for the Martins themselves, they certainly needed money, for in July a judgment against them for debt led to seizure of some of their own property, including slaves. The holder of the judgment was none other than Josiah S. Johnston.

The news of the issue of surveys and certificates to Bowie stunned George Graham. He commenced an investigation at once and discovered that once again Bowie had benefited from fantastic luck. All approvals on his claims had been withheld since Graham first discovered the possibility of fraud. But then that spring James Turner in the Donaldsonville land office had resigned and left, and several weeks passed before his successor, James Allison, arrived. Before Turner left, however, he turned over certificates of approval on Bowie's plats of survey. Most infuriating of all, it appeared that Bowie or his agent had actually showed Turner a letter from Graham to Johnston authorizing him to issue the approvals. Precisely what the letter said no one seemed to know, but Graham himself knew that he never wrote such a document. Turner somehow may have mistaken Graham's January 9 letter for an authorization, but in any event no one could see how that document came into Bowie's hands. Graham himself believed that the "pretended letter" was nothing but "an imposition," meaning a forgery. He demanded from Turner's superior, George Davis, an explanation of how this could have happened, and declared that he would take the matter to President Adams himself. He would ask for an executive order directing that Bowie's surveys be declared void, instead ordering the land surveyed and sold at public auction immediately. At the same time he asked Davis's superior, Harper, for his explanation and for copies of all of the documents on file in the matter. Harper replied that he had never ordered or authorized Davis or Turner to conduct the surveys, and that after Congress approved his original report recommending the claims—his later letter having been lost—he assumed that he had nothing more to do in the matter and gave all the documents back to Bowie when he called at the office and displayed Robert Martin's power of attorney. Since Bowie did not have a power of attorney from William Wilson, the papers for that one single claim still lay in the office. Turner, meanwhile, tried to put the responsibility on George Davis, finding him "highly culpable" in the matter, and an associate blamed Turner. Kenneth McCrummon to Johnston, December 8, 1824 [misdated 1823], Graham to George Davis, November 1, 1827, M1385; Harper to Graham, May 24, 1827, Davis to Graham, July 18, 1827, Graham to Harper, August 16, 1827, James Turner to Graham, April 23, 1829, Graham to Davis, August 16, 1827, Harper to Graham, August 29, 1827, Entry 404, Record Group 49, NA; Graham to Davis, March 2, 1827, *American State Papers*, Public Lands Series, vol. 5, 440–41; New Orleans *State Gazette*, April 11, 1826; Conveyance Book D, 154, 344–45, Terrebonne Parish Courthouse; Wells to Johnston, July 26, 1827; McCrummon to Johnston, December 23, 1827, Johnston Papers, HSP.

4. Stanley C. Arthur, *The Story of the Kemper Brothers* (St. Francisville, La., 1933), 13, says that Kemper died in 1828. However, Wells to Johnston, February 12, 1827, Johnston Papers, HSP, mentions Kemper's recent death, obviously placing the event in January 1827.

5. Tregle, "Louisiana," 157–58; Commission, March 24, 1827, Nathaniel Lockhart to Finlay Hodgson & Co., July 16, 1827, De La Vergne Family Papers, LSU.

6. *Dent* v. *Bowie*, November 30, 1827, Judicial Mortgage Record A, 54, Natchitoches Parish Courthouse.

7. Wells to Johnston, July 26, 1827, Johnston Papers, HSP.

8. Sparks in Ellis, *Crockett*, 215.

9. John S. Moore to Fontaine, April 25, 1890, Fontaine Papers, UT, asserts that the ensuing duel grew out of an argument over the recent election, but that would only apply to the disagreement between Wright and Bowie.

10. John Johnston to Josiah S. Johnston, July 13, 1827, Johnston Papers, HSP.

11. Grady C. McWhiney, *Cracker Culture: Celtic Ways in the Old South* (Tuscaloosa, Ala., 1988), 148ff.

12. H. A. Bullard to Johnston, November 13, 1821, Johnston Papers, HSP.

13. Wells to Johnston, July 26, 1827, Johnston Papers, HSP; Thorp, *Bowie Knife*, 10, states that in 1927 James O. Wells, a member of the family, said that the origin of the Maddox-Wells duel was that a female patient of the doctor's told him some gossip on Wells, and Maddox spread it injudiciously.

14. Overton to Johnston, August 18, 1827, Robert Sibley to Johnston, September 2, 1827, Johnston Papers, HSP.

15. John Nevitt Diary, September 16, 1827, Southern Historical Collection, University of North Carolina, Chapel Hill (SHC, UNC).

16. It has been suggested that Wright did not want to meet Bowie on the dueling field because this would imply social equality with him, whereas if Bowie was really a fraud then he was no gentleman. This could also explain why the two had not settled their differences after the earlier shooting incident before this. However, given Wright's own behavior in shooting an unarmed Bowie, he could hardly lay claim to being a gentleman himself. His real reason for not wanting to encounter Bowie on the ground now was probably prudence, knowing that Bowie would be well armed this time and ready for him.

17. The contemporary first-person sources on the Sandbar brawl are numerous, and all have been used in compiling this account. They include: letters and statements by Crain, Wells, Denny, Provan, Maddox, and others in the Natchez, *Ariel*, October 19, 1827; Samuel L. Wells to Johnston, September 20, 1827, Johnston Papers, HSP; Samuel L. Wells letter, September 24, 1827, in the Woodville, Miss. *Republican*, October 13, 1827; Robert A. Crain "To the Public," October 1827, Miscellaneous Collection, LSU; Crain to Joseph Walker, October 3, 1827, in Stafford, *Wells Family*, 23–24; an account by "An Eye Witness" that is probably Crain, published in the New Orleans *Argus*, October 2, 1827; and the statement of Thomas J. Maddox, ca. 1880, Thomas J. Maddox Papers, SHC, UNC. Also useful is an account from a March 1860 issue of the Concordia, La., *Intelligencer*, of which a transcript is in the James Bowie Vertical File, UT. It is only signed "W. M.," but is clearly written as either an eyewitness account, or else an extremely well informed one, as it speaks of conversations with Bowie the night before the fight and in the days that followed. The author was probably William Minor of Concordia, who appears there in the 1830 census. It should be noted that there are several minor discrepancies in these accounts, as

would be expected in a number of views of an event that lasted no more than a minute or two, under great stress and excitement. The account offered in the text is an amalgamation of them all.

Additional but probably not eyewitness sources survive from men who would have gotten their accounts directly from Bowie as close friends. These include Caiaphas Ham's "Recollections," UT, and the William Sparks account, which appears to have been published first in the Philadelphia *Times* in late 1880 or early 1881, and reprinted in the San Francisco *Chronicle*, February 23, 1881. The article is not signed but is repeated verbatim in a lengthy Sparks account of the Bowies that appears in Ellis, *Crockett*, 215–18. Sparks moved from Georgia to Natchez in the mid-1820s, and was certainly a resident of Assumption Parish in 1830, just a few miles from the Bowie plantation in Terrebonne (1830 Census, Assumption Parish, La.), and his comments on the Bowies, as stated previously, are so accurate and perceptive on many vital points that he must have been well acquainted with them, as he claimed. William H. Sparks, *The Memories of Fifty Years: Containing Brief Biographical Notices of Distinguished Americans, and Anecdotes of Remarkable Men* (Philadelphia, 1870), is disappointing in that it only mentions James Bowie twice in passing, but much of the rest of it confirms what he wrote in his 1880 article on other points.

There are several obviously spurious supposed eyewitness accounts or ones written so long after the fact, and so muddled by confused memory and the influence of legend, as to be virtually useless. These include accounts in the San Francisco *Chronicle*, February 28, 1881, by an unidentified "L. H.," and an even more confused rendering in the New York *Times,* January 15, 1893.

A full compilation of almost all of the genuine Sandbar sources is James L. Batson, *James Bowie and the Sandbar Fight: Birth of the James Bowie Legend & Bowie Knife* (Madison, Ala., 1992), while the best and most complete recent narrative account of the affair is J. R. Edmondson, "James Bowie, First Blood," *Knife World* 21, October, November, and December 1995 issues, and 22, January 1996 issue. Less useful is Joseph Musso, "Jim Bowie's Sandbar Fight," *Alamo Journal* 60 (February 1988).

18. Woodville, Miss., *Republican,* September 29, 1827, quoting the Natchez *Statesman,* September 20, 1827; Concordia, La., *Intelligencer,* March 1860, in Bowie Vertical File, UT; Maddox statement, 1880, Maddox Papers, SHC, UNC; Nevitt Diary, September 19, 1827, SHC, UNC.

19. Ham, "Recollections," UT.

20. Concordia, La., *Intelligencer,* March 1860, Bowie Vertical File, UT.

21. *Veramendi* v. *Hutchins et al.,* 140, Documents Pertaining to James Bowie, UT.

22. John Johnston to Josiah S. Johnston, September 30, 1827, Johnston Papers, HSP.

23. John Bails to Johnston, October 25, 1827, ibid., HSP.

24. Whitcomb to Bynum, February 11, 1839, Entry 200, Record Group 49, NA; Conveyance Book F, 125–26, Terrebonne Parish Courthouse; Bill of Sale, May 12, 1827, Bowie Family Papers, UT; House Bill 474, 22nd Congress, 1st Session, March 16, 1832.

25. Thomas to Johnston, November 5, 1827, Johnston Papers, HSP.

26. Conveyance Book D, 158, 216–17, Terrebonne Parish Courthouse.

27. Thomas to Johnston, November 5, 1827, Johnston Papers, HSP.

28. Conveyance Book D, 133–34, Terrebonne Parish Courthouse.

29. Shinn, *Pioneers and Makers*, 88; Frederick W. Cron, "The Bowie Land Frauds in Arkansas," James Bowie Vertical File, UT; Samuel C. Roane to Graham, July 16, 1830, Benjamin Desha to Graham, March 1, 1828, Records of the Bureau of Land Management, General Land Office, Division D (Private Land Claims Division), Records Re. Bowie Claims, Fraudulent Claims in Arkansas, 1827–1843, Entry 394; Bowie Claims, Cleland List, St. Augustine, Fla., Locations Under Arkansas Court, Entry 215, Record Group 49, NA. John Bowie retained in his own name roughly one-fourth of the acreage, but Roane knew that regardless of the names on the claims, "John Bowie pretended to be the owner." John Bowie speedily worked to capitalize on their good fortune. He went to Arkansas in January and began selling the grants already in his name, while at the same time transferring those claims confirmed to fictitious persons over to himself for equally fictional nominal sums. "The original claimant or confirmee, was a fictitious person," land office officials later discovered, "and a part of the fraud perpetrated on the government and the innocent purchasors of those claims, consisted in the forged assignment of those claims from such fictitious persons to John J. Bowie." Several months later, on October 16, 1828, he appeared in Clark County, where he entered the transactions with the local clerk of the court, and his witnesses came with him and signed their affidavits that they had seen Bowie purchasing the grants from the fictitious grantees. A week later he appeared at Washington, Arkansas, in neighboring Hempstead County, where he entered copies of the records made in Clark but did not have to produce his witnesses, and there he located his actual claims. Thus, in his brother James's standard practice, he had erected a structure of supposed documentary evidence elsewhere, while in the county where he would claim the land no original documents or witnesses could cause problems (Conveyance Book B, 143, 144, 221–45, Hempstead County Courthouse; Samuel Wheat and D. T. Walton to Thomas H. Blake, November 22, 1842, Entry 394, Record Group 49, NA).

30. Bowie's presence in New Orleans as early as January 12 and as late as February 14 is definitely confirmed by these sales in Conveyance Book D, 247, 214–16. However, Isaac Thomas to Johnston, November 5, 1827, and March 5, 1828, Johnston Papers, HSP, indicate that Bowie was in the city by early November, as Thomas speaks of their having a meeting there that was apparently prior to the writing of his November 5, 1827, letter.

31. Nevitt Diary, January 4, 1828, SHC, UNC; New Orleans *Bee*, January 10, 11, 1828.

32. A preposterous story gained wide currency in the late 1800s and on into this century that not only did Bowie attend the principal Jackson dinner, but also that it was hosted at the American Theater by none other than Stephen Austin, and that other guests included Crockett, Travis, James Fannin, and a man identi-

fied only as Wright, probably Claiborne Wright who later died at the Alamo, all of them a committee being sent to Texas on behalf of would-be settlers in Kentucky and South Carolina. Variants of the story have Bowie sitting next to Austin in honor of his being a veteran of the Battle of New Orleans, and he, Crockett, and Travis all making speeches, Crockett praising Jackson inordinately, and Bowie declaring prophetically that they were off to Texas to fight the Mexicans and might even die in defense of freedom.

The origin and earliest appearance of this fable is unknown. A handwritten note by Lucy Bowie in her papers (DRT) states that she found the story in a scrapbook belonging to Francis Xavier Martin, former chief justice of Louisiana. She does not say if it was a newspaper clipping or an account written by Martin himself. Attempts to locate such a scrapbook among the few remaining Martin papers have failed, and in any case Martin was a known crank, avoided by most of New Orleans society (Tregle, "Louisiana," 180–81). If such a scrapbook did exist with Martin's account of the Jackson dinner, then it would probably be the origin of the story. John Henry Brown does not have it in his 1881 *Encyclopedia*, but it appears in his later books in the 1890s, and so it had gained some currency by then. Lucy Bowie published it in her article on Bowie in the Doylestown, Pa., *Daily Intelligencer*, June 20, 1916, and by 1935, when it appeared in the March 3 San Antonio *Express*, it was a common part of the Bowie and Texas canon and has since been passed on by Hopewell, *Bowie*, 60.

It is, of course, complete nonsense. In January 1828 Crockett was at his seat in Congress a thousand miles away in Washington (Shackford, *Crockett*, 87–88). Stephen Austin was in Texas, and James Fannin was in Georgia. As for Travis, he was at that time an eighteen-year-old student at Claiborne, who hardly had the wherewithal even to get to New Orleans, two hundred miles distant. That unknown nobodies like Fannin and a teenage Travis would be invited to come and make speeches in front of Jackson is ridiculous. As for Bowie, his ardent associations with pro-Clay supporters make it clear that he was no Jackson adherent, and in any event he could not have been invited to attend as an honored guest for his participation in the Battle of New Orleans because, of course, he was never anywhere near the battle. Moreover, as of January 1828 he had exhibited no intentions to locate in Texas, and his stirring words about giving his life if need be to defend it against the Mexicans are an obvious projection of future events that reeks of fiction. The entire story can be safely put down as a myth, possibly created by Martin himself in his later irrational years.

33. There is more than sufficient testimony to this meeting to establish that it did take place, though the details are muddled, as usual. Placing it in the winter of 1827–28 is conjectural. Crain's grandson, N. C. Blanchard, wrote on September 29, 1875, that the reconciliation took place "a short time after the Sand Bar fight" (undated clipping from the New Orleans *Times*, attached to T. Alexander to Taliaferro, October 10, 1875, Taliaferro Papers, LSU). The following year Crain took a seat in the legislature in early January 1829 and thus would not have been in New Orleans, where all sources agree the meeting took place, and later years seem less likely, though the meeting could have happened any time up to Bowie's last known trip through Louisiana in the fall of 1833. The earliest

account of the meeting is in the "W. M." article in the March 1860, Concordia, La., *Intelligencer* in the James Bowie Vertical File, UT. It states that Crain asked Bowie to his room, closed the door, and placed two pistols on the table, saying they should settle things finally there and then, either by taking the pistols or by shaking hands. Interestingly, this is almost exactly the manner in which Bowie supposedly settled a difference of his with the Natchez editor Andrew Marschalk, though that episode is certainly apocryphal (San Francisco *Chronicle*, February 28, 1881). The "pistols on the table" theme, in fact, is a common one in the mythology of dueling in the Old Southwest.

In 1880 Thomas Maddox, Crain's friend, said that Bowie invited Crain to his room, and that they there settled things (Maddox statement, SHC, UNC). Finally, William H. Sparks, friend of both Bowie and Maddox, related in his 1879–80 account in Ellis, *Crockett*, 219–20, that the reconciliation actually took place several years afterward in New York, where Bowie helped save Crain from a mob. This version seems highly fanciful, though Sparks was not given to making up stories in his Bowie account, and is generally quite accurate, allowing for the vagaries of aging memory. Bowie was in the East in 1828, again in 1829, and perhaps in 1832, so it is just barely possible that there is some germ of truth in the Sparks account, which in any event he most likely would have gotten from his intimate friend Maddox, Crain's close associate. Nevertheless, it has seemed most likely that the reconciliation took place sooner rather than later, as Blanchard indicated.

34. Conveyance Book D, 134–38, 208, 214–26, 227–28, 234–35, 237–38, 247–48, 258–63, 293–94, Terrebonne Parish Courthouse. John Bowie, "The Bowies," 381, said in 1852 that his brother went into land speculation "and soon made $15,000." The sum is reasonably close to what James derived from these sales, though brother John is quite indefinite as to when James realized this $15,000. It could even refer to James's share of the Arkansas speculations, with which John would have been more familiar than with the Terrebonne sales.

35. Tocqueville, *Democracy in America*, 536, 615.

36. Sparks in Ellis, *Crockett*, 224.

37. Conveyance Book D, 227–28, 237–38, Terrebonne Parish Courthouse.

38. Thomas to James Bowie, March 5, 1828, Johnston Papers, HSP.

39. Thomas to Johnston, March 5, 9, 28, 1828, ibid.

40. This conclusion is based on the fact that Thomas's letter is in Johnston's papers at HSP and is apparently not a copy but the original.

41. Henry Boyer to Johnston, March 30, 1828, ibid.; Notary Felix De Armas, Power of Attorney, Jose de la Francia to Bowie, February 10, 1826, vol. 5, 72–73, New Orleans Notarial Archives. Interestingly, there is no further correspondence from Isaac Thomas on the subject in the Johnston Papers. The ultimate fate of the Kemper claim has eluded discovery, but Thomas's sudden silence, after writing repeated and highly excited letters, suggests at least that nothing was done at the time, and perhaps that Boyer's letter and Johnston's investigations may have revealed the scheme at hand. If Johnston refused to be involved, that

would silence Thomas so far as he was concerned. Or Johnston may have demonstrated to Thomas that Bowie's title to the claim was forged, causing Thomas to desist from further efforts. In the absence of further evidence, one can only speculate.

42. Evidence that Bowie still believed the Kemper claim to be an open issue is the fact that he listed $32,800 due him "for quantities that the government of the said United States has given me according to documents already granted" in the dowry statement dated April 22, 1831 (transcript in the James Bowie Vertical File, UT); this statement suggests that the government had admitted the claim and agreed to pay him, but the Bowie dowry statement is so riddled with half-truths and deceptions that this should not be taken too literally. It is just as likely that Bowie's reference to "documents already granted" deals with the several Treasury warrants issued in Kemper's behalf, but for which Congress failed to appropriate funds for payment). No claim of Bowie's against the United States has been found except the Kemper–de la Français matter, and while the $32,800 mentioned is considerably different from the $40,000 plus interest that was due Kemper, it should be born in mind that Kemper's figure was an approximate one.

Receipts and Expenditures of the United States 1818, 88–89; 1819, 85; and 1820, 62, RG 217, NA, reveal that in those years the Treasury approved warrants in Kemper's name totaling $31,948.05. Not found there, but located by Josiah S. Johnston in 1826, was an additional August 5, 1819 warrant for $1,000.00, making a total genuinely due of $32,948.05, dramatically close to the $32,800 that Bowie would list on his dowry statement. No statement of "settled account" can be found for these warrants, indicating that they were almost certainly never paid, either to Kemper or Bowie or Kemper's heirs. Furthermore, adding the $11,850 due the de la Français heirs to this $32,948 totals $44,798, well in the realm of Kemper's statement in his December 14, 1826 letter (Johnston Papers, HSP), that he was owed "over" $40,000 plus "several years back interest." Therefore the later Bowie figure of $32,800 would apparently represent the approximate figure of what he felt was due him if he had by then abandoned the de la Français claim or perhaps turned it over to Isaac Thomas, thus deducting the $11,850, but possibly including an unknown amount of interest.

43. New Orleans *Bee,* December 17, 1827.

44. Brent to Taliaferro, May 9, 1828, Taliaferro Papers, LSU.

45. Tregle, "Louisiana," 334–35, 345–46, 350–51, 356.

46. *Journal of the House of Representatives During the Second Session of the Eighth Legislature of the State of Louisiana* (New Orleans, 1828), 3.

47. Bowie, "The Bowies," 381. John Bowie, as usual, is not specific about the date of this. He says it as a prelude to James moving to Texas permanently, which did not happen until 1831. However, James Bowie does go to Texas in the summer of 1828, just after it is evident that he will not be sent to Congress as he had expected, so this seems the most likely time to which John Bowie could refer with his statement about his brother's disappointment with "his political friends."

48. Thomas L. Miller, *The Public Lands of Texas, 1519–1970* (Norman, Okla., 1972), 15–16, 18; Eugene C. Barker, "Land Speculation as A Cause of the Texas Revolution," *Quarterly of the Texas State Historical Association* 10 (July 1906): 76–77; Eugene C. Barker, "The African Slave Trade in Texas," *Quarterly of the Texas State Historical Association* 6 (October 1902): 150.

49. Woodville, Miss., *Republican*, September 23, 1826; New Orleans, La., *State Gazette,* October 2, 1826; Alexandria, La., *Messenger,* July 28, 1826.

50. Natchez *Newspaper and Public Advertiser,* November 22, 1826.

51. Littleton Bailey to Johnston, April 22, 1824, Benjamin Morris to Johnston, November 24, 1827, Johnston Papers, HSP.

52. There is no contemporary evidence of Bowie visiting Texas in 1826–27. Speer and Brown, *Encyclopedia,* vol. 1, 434, says he first came in 1826 and maybe as early as 1824. Fifteen years later Brown, *Indian Wars,* 136, says only that Bowie first came to Texas in 1824. Neither source gives any authority for its statement, and neither Speer nor Brown ever met Bowie, so their statements must be considered as conjecture at best. Still, it is not unreasonable to suppose that Bowie would have looked over Texas after the land laws were published, but prior to his decisive trip of 1828.

53. Nevitt Diary, May 31, 1828, SHC, UNC; Check on the Bank of the State of Mississippi, May 1828, Bowie Family Papers, Natchez Trace Collection, UT. The check, in the amount of $245, is signed by Stephen Bowie and made payable to himself and James Bowie. This may have been expenses for James's trip, or something else entirely, but it does place James in Natchez that month.

54. John Johnston to Josiah S. Johnston, June 8, 1828, Johnston Papers, HSP.

55. Flint, *Recollections,* 264–65.

56. Ibid., 267.

57. Amos Parker, *A Trip to the West and Texas in 1834* (Concord, N.H., 1836), 185–86.

58. The Bowie-Prather-McKinney connection is complicated but important. John J. Bowie supposedly married Nancy Scoggins in 1806. Walter Bowie in *The Bowies,* 264, states that she died in 1816, and John's daughter Martha Burns, by his second wife, states that Nancy Scoggins Bowie died "a few years" after their last child, Rezin, was born in 1815 (Martha Burns, "Eventful Lives of the Bowies," undated newspaper clipping in the James Bowie Biographical File, DRT; internal evidence dates the article no earlier than 1896). Both are in error, and Martha Burns, at least, may have been concealing a minor family scandal. While no divorce records are extant, it is clear from Catahoula Parish records that by 1818 Nancy Bowie was not dead but was living apart from John right under his nose in Harrisonburg, and calling herself the "Widow Bowie," even though John was very much alive. Moreover, sometime during that year she had married Blassingame W. Harvey, who abandoned her by 1820 and went to Texas, after which she lived with his brother John Harvey and eventually married him as well. Blassingame Harvey, meanwhile, married again in 1826 in San Augustine, this time to the daughter of Stephen Prather (Margaret Henson to

the author, July 11, 1996). Thus, while James Bowie had no blood or legal relationship to Prather, still he certainly either knew or at least knew of
Blassingame Harvey, and also may have known Prather himself from the days
when Prather lived in Catahoula. His brother John would have known both
men, and may have born Blassingame no ill will if Nancy was herself the reason
for their parting, and could have provided an introduction to either. With
Prather as McKinney's uncle, and Blassingame married to the merchant's first
cousin, an introduction to McKinney for Bowie would then have been quite natural.

Whether John Bowie abandoned Nancy, or she abandoned him, or whether
theirs may have been only a common-law marriage without benefit of clergy, is
unknown, and of no importance here, though judging from her history it would
appear that she was not adept at keeping husbands and moved rather easily
from man to man. It is even possible that their parting was quite amicable, as
John Bowie witnessed a document for Nancy on March 9, 1819, well after she
had taken up with Blassingame Harvey (Bowie Family Papers, Natchez Trace
Collection, UT).

59. William Gray, *From Virginia to Texas, 1835: Diary of Col. Wm. F. Gray* (Houston,
    1909), 111.

60. Noah Smithwick, *The Evolution of a State* (Austin, 1900), 135–36. Smithwick is
    notoriously suspect in many details, his recollections being written down at the
    age of ninety, some sixty-seventy years after the fact, and then heavily embel-
    lished by his daughter as editor, including some outright inventions of her own.
    Thus it was thought best not to incorporate his stories of making a knife for
    Bowie during this visit. Mention of his meeting Bowie in San Felipe in 1828 is
    only included because Bowie definitely did visit Texas that summer.

61. That Bowie did not actually meet Austin on this trip may be inferred from the
    fact that two years later, when he came to Texas to settle, he brought with him
    an introduction to Austin from McKinney. Had they met previously, such an
    introduction would obviously have been unnecessary.

62. It has frequently been claimed that while in San Antonio, Bowie accepted bap-
    tism into the Catholic Church, a first step to Texas citizenship—and marriage to
    Ursula. Nothing at all survives connecting Bowie with religion, other than a few
    stories, to be dealt with subsequently, that show him defending ministers
    against unruly crowds. These may be entirely apocryphal, however, since such
    stories are not infrequent in the literature of frontier heroes, including Travis.

    Stories of Bowie's being baptized are erroneously based on a misreading of
    the baptismal record of "Santiago Rox," June 26, 1828, Book of Baptisms of San
    Fernando Parish Church, San Antonio, Texas.

    Research by Robert L. Tarin Jr. of San Antonio concludes that the baptism
    entry is actually for James Ross, the surname spelled "Rox," and that students
    have misread the calligraphy as "Buy," a frequent Mexican spelling of "Bowie."
    Further research by Tarin shows a Texian James Ross who was born in South
    Carolina, which agrees with the statement in the baptismal certificate, whereas
    Bowie was born in Kentucky. Moreover, the baptism records the man's parents

as James and Juana, a far cry from Bowie's parents, Rezin and Elve. Thus it is virtually certain that this baptism is not that of Bowie. Probably at some time he simply swore that he *intended* to be baptized, as did many other colonists, and on the basis of that oath he was later granted citizenship.

63. Ham, "Recollections," UT.

64. *A Visit to Texas, Being the Journal of A Traveller Through those Parts Most Interesting to American Settlers* (New York, 1836), 16, 208–20.

65. Rogan, "Warren D.C. Hall," 274.

66. Conveyance Book D, 349–50, Terrebonne Parish Courthouse. Jeff Long, *Duel of Eagles: The Mexican and U. S. Fight for the Alamo* (New York, 1990), 31, makes the completely unsubstantiated claim that "shortly after his baptism" Bowie returned to Louisiana via Arkansas, and that on the way he met Sam Houston in Arkansas and recommended Texas to him. Like most of what Long says about Bowie, this is utter nonsense. In the summer of 1828 Houston was still in Tennessee serving as governor, and would not set foot in Arkansas until late Spring of 1829. John Hoyt Williams, *Sam Houston: A Biography of the Father of Texas* (New York, 1993), 72, places the meeting on a steamboat in spring 1829 (and also misses the fact that Stephen Austin is the man called: "father of Texas"!), and Hopewell, *Bowie,* 62, also puts the encounter in 1829, though this time ashore in Helena, Ark.

There is nothing at all to substantiate any of these statements, and they all seem to derive from two works, James, *The Raven,* 90, and Llerena Friend, *Sam Houston: The Great Designer* (Austin, 1954), 92. Neither of these authors provided a source for the claim. Friend probably borrowed it from James, and James apparently simply made it up. Speaking of making things up, it is worth noting that Long in *Duel of Eagles,* 26–27, also states that Bowie and Houston met "floating upriver on a flatboat" just after James's baptism. When Houston did go to Arkansas in the spring of 1829, he went up the Arkansas River to Fort Gibson. In no wise was the Arkansas a river that Bowie or anyone else would use to go to or from Texas. Moreover, unless Long has reinvented the laws of hydrography, nothing, especially a flatboat, floats *upriver.* A flatboat could not even be propelled upstream, and was used exclusively for a single downstream voyage, after which it was broken up and sold for lumber. As for the first Bowie-Houston meeting, it cannot be dated any earlier than 1832, as will appear subsequently.

Chapter 10   Bowie 1828–1830

1. Conveyance Book B, 233, 241–42, 244, 246, Hempstead County Courthouse.

2. Deed Book A-B, 38–42, Chicot County Courthouse.

3. Bowie Claims, Cleland List, Entry 215, Record Group 49, NA.

4. The power of attorney is registered in Conveyance Book D, 227–28, Terrebonne Parish Courthouse.

5. Conveyance Book D, 505, Clerk of the Court, Lafourche Parish Courthouse, Thibodaux, La. It is assumed that James had not yet returned from the fact that

Rezin made the purchase rather than James. It is not clear from the copy in the conveyance book that Rezin was buying this for James, but a year later this parcel is spoken of as being the property of James Bowie, and no formal conveyance from Rezin to James has been found, leading to the only alternative conclusion that Rezin actually bought it for him in the first place. Since no power of attorney has been found from James authorizing Rezin to make purchases in Lafourche, as was the practice, Rezin had to act on his own and recover from James later, with a transfer that presumably did not get registered. Deed Book G, 256–57, Lafourche Parish Courthouse.

6. The supposition that the Lafourche purchases were not discussed between Rezin and James prior to the latter's Texas trip rests on the absence of any power of attorney from James to his brother for such purchases. It was the custom for powers of attorney to state specifically those parishes and kinds of transactions that were authorized.

7. Helen M. Bowie, "Bayou Lafourche" (master's thesis, Louisiana State University, Baton Rouge, 1935), 23–26.

8. Harnett T. Kane, *The Bayous of Louisiana* (New York, 1944), 158–62; Prentiss to William Prentiss, April 9, 1829, G. L. Prentiss, ed., *Memoir of S. S. Prentiss*, vol. 1 (New York, 1856), 94–95.

9. Sparks, *Memories*, 374–77.

10. Thomas B. Thorpe, *The Mysteries of the Back-Woods* (Philadelphia, 1846), 140–41.

11. Sparks, *Memories*, 374–75.

12. Joseph C. Guild, *Old Times in Tennessee* (Nashville, 1878), 107.

13. Bowie, "Bayou Lafourche," 18.

14. Flint, *Recollections*, 233–34.

15. New Orleans *Louisiana State Gazette*, November 29, 1826; New Orleans *Price-Current and Commercial Intelligencer*, September 15, 1827; Notes, 1829, in John Quitman Diary, John Quitman Papers, SHC, UNC.

16. Kane, *Bayous*, 159.

17. F. D. Richardson, "The Teche Country Fifty Years Ago," *Southern Bivouac*, n.s., vol. 1 (March 1886): 594.

18. New Orleans *Louisiana State Gazette*, July 16, 1826.

19. Richardson, "Teche Country," 594. One of the persistent Bowie myths is that he and Rezin were the first to introduce steam to the sugar industry in Louisiana. See, for instance, Williams, "Critical Study, III," 92. Hopewell, *Bowie*, 11, says without citing a source that they installed the machinery in 1827, fully a year before James and Rezin first bought the property!

20. Conveyance Book D, 505, 527, Lafourche Parish Courthouse. Clerk of the Court, Assumption Parish Courthouse, Napoleonville, La., has an index listing a judgment against Candolle in favor of Maronges from the November 1826 judicial term, but the document itself could not be found.

21. Conveyance Book D, 427–28, 430–31, 433–35, Terrebonne Parish Courthouse; Conveyance Book F, 9–10, 129–30, Book G, 29–31, Lafourche Parish

Courthouse; Conveyance Book E, 439–40, Avoyelles Parish Courthouse. On November 25 James bought Stephen's extensive Bayou Boeuf plantation and slaves for $20,000 in hand—the same plantation he had sold him nine years before for $17,000—and then the next day sold some of the land for a mere $4,000. That same day James bought a large plot from Rezin on Bayou Caillou for $7,000, then immediately sold it again for $9,300. On November 25 he paid Rezin $7,000 for another twelve arpent frontage on the bayou that had belonged to Maronges, and about the same time took legal possession of the old Candolle tract. There was a subtle advantage to his actually buying it from his brother. The practice of the courts was to attach mortgage obligations to property rather than owners. When Candolle lost the land, the obligation for the mortgages went to Maronges, and from him to Rezin Bowie, and now on to James. The money Rezin had paid Maronges had left the family, and should the court foreclose on the mortgages while he held title, they would lose the land, too. But by James buying it from Rezin, they inserted one more layer of legal barrier against foreclosure, and sheltered James's cash from seizure by transferring it to Rezin. This done, James went on in December to buy another adjacent parcel for $2,000 and a slave in the bargain, and the following April yet another four-*arpent* frontage for $4,000, of which he only paid a fourth down. Now he had just over twenty-four *arpents* of frontage on the right bank of the Lafourche, a total of about 830 acres. He also acquired more slaves, three in November, added to at least four that he had owned for two years now, plus the ones that came from Stephen. As stated before, the transfer from Rezin to James on the Candolle property has not been found, but must have taken place prior to December 15, 1828, when Bowie bought property from Nicholas Laine that is described as bordering on this tract, now belonging to James Bowie (Deed Book E, 555, Lafourche Parish Courthouse).

22. Sparks in Ellis, *Crockett*, 223–24; case #3040, *Cushing and Ames* v. *Rezin P. and Stephen Bowie*, General Case Files, Entry 21, U.S. District Court for the Eastern District of Louisiana, New Orleans, Record Group 21, National Archives—Southwest Region, Fort Worth, Tex.

23. Richardson, "Teche Country," 593, 594–97; Sparks, *Memories*, 376–77.

24. Sparks in Ellis, *Crockett*, 223–24.

25. Charles Robert Goins and John Michael Caldwell, *Historical Atlas of Louisiana* (Norman, Okla., 1995), 67. Mims, *Bowie Knife*, 26 says—without source, as usual—that the Bowies chartered "'The Bowie, Lafourche & Northwestern' on which the principal shipping point was a town called 'Bowie.'" No source of any kind for this statement has been found, and it is probably merely the sort of local hearsay that informs much of Mims's strange booklet. Certainly no railroad was ever built by the Bowies. There is an intersection in the parish called Bowie Junction not far from Raceland, on what is now the Southern Pacific line. Nearby there is also the Bowie Canal, which by a complex interchange of canals and bayous connects the Lafourche with the Mississippi. It is possible that both named features are artifacts of some planned railroad that never came to be, but more likely they simply take their names from the much later—and uncon-

nected—Bowie Lumber Company. Seeing the name "Bowie Junction," Mims
may well have simply dreamed up the idea of a Bowie railroad.

26. New Orleans *Louisiana State Gazette,* July 25, August 8, 1826; *Michel's New Orleans
Annual and Commercial Register* (New Orleans, 1833), 38; Report, Register and
Receiver of Land Office, New Orleans, Louisiana on Private Land Claims 1833,
Entry 296, Record Group 49, NA; Conveyance Record 4, 496, Clerk of the
Court, Orleans Parish Courthouse, New Orleans.

27. Joseph Fenwick to Johnston, May 10, 1829, Johnston Papers, HSP; Conveyance
Book D, 389–90, 425–29, Book E, 27, 79–80, Terrebonne Parish Courthouse;
Conveyance Record F, 157, Lafourche Parish Courthouse. Rezin also sold seven
of James's slaves in Lafourche for $4,300

28. Later that month Turner notified Graham specifically of some of the grants that
he "considered spurious claims," almost all of them Bowie's, and announced that
he would do nothing on them. He also secured testimony from old Judge
Bullard, no friend of Bowie's anyhow, that after living in the area for over
twenty years, he had never heard of one of the supposed grant recipients. In
fact, rather, it was discovered that the locations Bowie had chosen for some of
his claims were actually on property already confirmed to genuine grantees
years before, further confirmation of the fraudulence of his forged grants.
Graham soon replied endorsing Turner's policy, and directed him not to proceed on any claim without the *original* papers and all suspicion of fraud elimi-
nated. Turner was delighted, though he predicted that Graham's instructions
would "give rise to considerable clamour amongst the claimants, they have been
so long indulged in the practice of fraud and imposition on the Government,
that they are ready to contend, that they are priviledges in which they are war-
ranted by Law and common usage, let their cases be ever so absurd and ridiculous" (Turner to Graham, March 4, 23, April 15, 1829, Graham to Turner, March
27, 1829, Entry 404, Ethan A. Brown to Levi Woodbury, September 18, 1835,
Letters Sent Relating to Private Land Claims, Records of the General Land
Office, vol. 2, 235–37, Entry 200, Record Group 49, NA).

29. If Turner had ironclad proof of forgery in his hands, it could jeopardize title to
all the tracts Bowie had sold, and cost him a fortune since in many cases he had
pledged his personal bond in high amounts that clear title would be forthcoming, and in any event all of the purchasers would come after him for the refund
of their money when the land office negated their titles.

30. Harper to Graham, August 29, 1827, Graham to Rush, December 14, 1827,
Turner to Graham, June 29, 1829, Entry 404, Record Group 49, NA.

31. Conveyance Record 3, 586, Orleans Parish Courthouse; Certificate of Adolphus
Sterne and William Garret, June 8, 1829, Nacogdoches Archives, Archives
Division, TXSL. The capture of William Ross is the only known means of dating Bowie's 1829 trip to Texas with any precision. Adolphus Sterne delivered
him to Alexandria, suggesting that the slave ran away and was caught in Texas
near Sterne's home in Nacogdoches, and his delivery to Alexandria on June 8
suggests that Bowie must have passed through Nacogdoches sometime earlier in
late May or very early June, and probably on his way back rather than out. The

suggestion that Rezin may have gone with James is only supposition, based on several stories that Rezin also visited the San Saba around this time. Since Rezin did not undertake any transactions for several months after April 1829 in Louisiana, a trip to Texas with James *could* explain his absence from the conveyance books.

32. Baptismal certificate, Ursula de Veramendi, November 1, 1811, San Fernando Cathedral, San Antonio.

33. Testimony of Menchaca, *Veramendi* v. *Hutchins*, 126, Documents Pertaining to James Bowie, UT.

34. Adele Looscan, "The Old Fort on the San Saba River as Seen by Dr. Ferdinand Roemer in 1847," *Quarterly of the Texas State Historical Association* 5 (October 1901): 139, cites Roemer's journal as stating that he saw the Bowie inscription on February 18, 1847. This will also be found in Robert S. Weddle, *The San Saba Mission* (Austin, 1964), 208, and "Old Fort San Saba, Part IV," Ben C. Stuart Papers, Rosenberg Library, Galveston, Tex. Of course the inscription does not give a first name, and one could conclude that it was Rezin who went, and some accounts suggest that he made the first exploration looking for the silver. Or it could simply be a bit of early hoax graffiti. Nevertheless, given James Bowie's confirmed visit to Texas in 1829, it seems most reasonable to assume that he was responsible. In the Kuykendall Family Papers (UT) there is an account of an 1829 expedition to the San Saba, but Bowie is not mentioned, and it was probably an entirely separate venture.

35. This is admittedly something of a surmise. It is possible that the slave ran away at the beginning of Bowie's trip, and was only just caught and returned as he was concluding the journey in June.

36. Certificate of James Turner, September 22, 1829, Entry 404, Record Group 49, NA.

37. Nevitt Diary, July 1, 1829, SHC, UNC.

38. Turner to Graham, June 19, 1829, Entry 404, Record Group 49, NA.

39. Ibid.

40. On Charges by a Deputy Surveyor Against the Official Conduct of the Commissioner of the General Land Office, February 27, 1827, *American State Papers*, Public Lands Series, vol. 4, 922–57.

41. Archibald Hotchkiss quoted in Speer and Brown, *Encyclopedia*, vol. 1, 436. Hotchkiss says he saw Bowie in Washington in 1832, but as there is no certain proof that Bowie made a trip east that year, 1829 is the more likely time.

42. Speer and Brown, *Encyclopedia*, vol. 1, 436. The Jefferson statement says he met Bowie in 1829, was with him on a steamboat, and knew him in Natchez, and this October arrival in Natchez from his eastern trip would be the only time that fits. Jefferson's memory was hardly infallible, however, for he also said that Bowie had a plantation called "Sedalia" near Natchez on the west side of the river, whereas Bowie had no property there at this time, and his only plantation, the Lafourche cane operation, is believed to have been called "Acadia," though there is no evidence that Bowie called it that during his ownership.

43. John Nevitt Diary, October 10, 1829, SHC, UNC. It must be noted that Nevitt's handwriting is difficult at times, allowing for the misconstruing of names, so the apparent mention of Bowie in the entry cited here as evidence of Bowie's being in Natchez in October is not an absolute certainty.

44. Montfort Wells to Johnston, November 15, 1829, John Johnston to Josiah S. Johnston, September 18, 1829, Johnston Papers; HSP. Musso, "Sandbar Fight," 4, erroneously says that Cecilia Wells died of pneumonia two weeks before her scheduled wedding to Bowie. His source is Lucy Bowie, and as noted before, she is entirely in error. Montfort Wells makes it clear that she died of fever, undoubtedly malaria. Moreover, if they had had a wedding date two weeks hence, that would have meant on or around October 1, and surely her death just short of her nuptials would have called for comment in John Johnston's letter.

45. Turner to Graham, September 22, 1829, Entry 404, Record Group 49, NA. Meanwhile, following Bowie's visit to Washington, Graham reiterated his own positive order that henceforth any claims founded on supposed Spanish titles believed to be forged were to be considered void, and further that on any claims where fraud was suspected, survey must not proceed until presentation of the *original* papers, and only the originals (Graham to Turner, August 4, 1829, Entry 404, ibid.).

46. Turner to Graham, June 29, 1829, ibid.

47. Isaac T. Preston to Graham, October 10, 12, 1829, ibid. These documents are also in *American State Papers*, Public Lands Series, vol. 6, 4–8.

Yet Preston found some cause for encouragement. Originally the Bowies filed more than 300 claims. But in the fall of 1828 they gave up on 188 of those because they could not, or would not, post a cash security with the land office covering the costs of surveys. Of the remainder, the 117 had been confirmed, but there were still seven unsettled, covering another 20,000 acres, and at least these could be delayed. Moreover, Preston looked into the manner of presentation of the Bowie claims, and found a familiar system at work. In every one of the 124 claims that they pursued, they submitted depositions from the same three men testifying that they had known the original Spanish grantees. In the other 188 abandoned cases, Preston found that the depositions came from quite a number of men, yet all proved nearly identical in wording, in itself a statistical miracle. The claims they supported just happened to fall on what in 1827 was land appropriated as public domain by the United States, not conflicting at all with any confirmed private property or the land settled on the future state for its own purposes. That "ought to have excited surprise," said Preston, while the fact that all of the depositions came from men in Louisiana in 1827 who yet somehow had known Spaniards getting grants as much as forty years earlier between 1785 and 1798 was, he suggested, "impeached by nature."

Moreover, Preston possessed the original journals of the orders of survey of Governors Miró and Gayoso, and none of the Bowies' appeared in them. He recognized the signatures on the *requétes* as clumsy forgeries, especially Miró's, and then Preston found that in the 124 *requétes* there were only about four different handwritings, and perhaps as few as two, even more miraculous. He spotted the unconvincing attempt to age some of the documents, the failure to use distinctive Spanish calligraphy, and the signatures by men notorious as illiterate hunters and itinerants. *Tiera* is used instead of *tierra, ordiniaria* rather than *ordinaria, profondidad* instead of *profundidad,* and even *Nueva Orleans* (New Orleans) is spelled *Nueva Orlieans.* Besides these and more crippling anomalies, the signature of Gov. Esteban Miró is wrong. "Miró wrote a free, careless, quick hand," said Preston; "the counterfeiter has invariably written slowly, with great care, and generally pointed." All the mistakes that the Bowies made he found. In addition he noted that the Bowies tried to locate some of these claims in areas completely unknown to the Dons, adding wryly that "it is almost as notorious that the Spanish governors never made consessions in those countries as that they never granted lands in the District of Columbia."

Genuine Spanish grants all carried the regulation statements that the grant could only be located on land already vacant, that the grantee was not to seek in any way to injure adjacent landholders, that he must make a good road in one year from settlement, and that the grant would be void if not settled within three years. The last two requirements automatically nullified grant claims presented decades after the fact, while the first interfered with locating the grant on the best possible land. As a result the Bowies simply omitted those clauses from their forgeries. But now Preston noted that their claims, and only their claims, contained such omissions, while every undeniably genuine grant carried the full wording. He hardly needed any more evidence of their fraudulence, but could not help telling Graham that "an individual came here some time ago with one hundred similar claims," but refrained from filing them when he learned of the suspicion attached to the others. He did not say that the man was either of the Bowies or someone acting on their behalf, but he went on to say of them that "the fact that 188 of those claims filed have been abandoned proves the falsity of the whole." Even while Preston made his investigation in Little Rock, John Bowie employed an agent in town charged with trying to renew the 188 abandoned claims, offering now to post the necessary security against the costs, and Preston only saw in that additional proof that they were not genuine, or Bowie would not have abandoned them in the first place.

48. Little Rock *Arkansas Advocate,* February 9, 1830.

49. Cron, "Bowie Land Frauds," James Bowie Vertical File, UT.

50. Little Rock *Arkansas Gazette,* March 9, 1830.

51. Jackson to Graham, November 9, 1829, Entry 394, Record Group 49, NA.

52. Deed Book G, 256–57, Lafourche Parish Courthouse; Notary William Boswell, *Rezin P. Bowie* v. *His Creditors,* vol. 18, #505, statement of Rezin P. Bowie, April 27, May 12, 1832, New Orleans National Archives, Civil Courts Building, New Orleans.

53. Bowie, "The Bowies," 381. Henry Clay was in New Orleans in February and March of 1830, so it is just barely possible that the rumored meeting between the two took place as Clay arrived and Bowie departed for Texas. It should also be noted that the Nevitt Diary for December 21, 1829, shows Nevitt playing cards with a man whose name appears to be "Bown," and which in Nevitt's

handwriting could mean Bowie, so he might have made an early winter trip north for a few weeks or less.

54. Statement regarding sugar prices 1818–1830, John Johnston to Josiah S. Johnston, November 17, 1829, Johnston Papers, HSP.

55. Rezin Bowie to Johnston, January 28, 1830, Johnston Papers, HSP.

56. Tocqueville, *Democracy in America*, 627.

57. Conveyance Book E, 223–24, Terrebonne Parish Courthouse.

58. Deed Book F, 380–81, Lafourche Parish Courthouse; Notary L. T. Caire, Mortgage, February 20, 1830, vol. 4, #144, New Orleans National Archives.

59. Deed Book G, 249–50, Lafourche Parish Courthouse.

60. Ham, "Recollections," UT. Ham states that in the summer of 1830 Bowie expected to find a large sum in Saltillo, having been shipped to him from Natchez. The only large sum due him at this time seems to be the ten thousand dollars from his land sale, and the assumption that Fisk would have sent it simply comes from his role then as virtually a private banker, and the fact that Rezin and Stephen had credit with him up to fifteen thousand dollars. Indeed, the mortgaging of the slaves may have been to cover money to be sent to James, but it seems unlikely, since according to Ham the money was not in Saltillo when he arrived.

61. Bowie, "The Bowies," 381, and the John Bowie article in the Washington, Ark., *Lone Star*, October 23, 1852, both state that James left for Texas with "only about a thousand dollars."

62. Ham, "Recollections," dates their departure as January 1, 1830, but since James was in Thibodeauxville in person on January 15 for the sale to Rezin and Stephen, his departure cannot have been earlier than January 16, and probably a few days later.

63. John H. Jenkins, ed., *The General's Tight Pants* (Austin, 1976), 7. In common with most travelers of the time, Bowie almost certainly did not take a horse with him on the steamboat up the Mississippi and Red Rivers, but would have bought a mount in Natchitoches.

64. *A Visit to Texas*, 225; Flint, *Recollections*, 269.

65. Parker, *Trip to the West*, 150.

66. Miller, *Public Lands*, 21.

67. J. H. Starr Memoranda Book 1836–1837, February 17, 1837, James H. Starr Collection, UT.

68. McKinney to Austin, February 13, 1830, Barker, *Austin Papers*, vol. 3 (Austin, 1919–26), 331–32. It is possible that McKinney also knew Bowie from dealings in Rapides, as a Thomas McKenney was a correspondent of Josiah Johnston's, though any friend of Johnston was unlikely to be recommending Bowie (McKenney to Johnston, May 14, 1824, Johnston Papers, HSP). Bowie also owned property next to a McKinney on Bayou Black in Terrebonne, and this could have been some relation.

69. Parker, *Trip to the West*, 151, 154.

70. Jenkins, *Tight Pants*, 6–7, 13.

71. Ham, "Recollections," UT.

72. Smithwick, *Evolution*, 69–70.

73. Tocqueville, *Democracy in America*, 283.

74. *A Visit to Texas*, 214.

75. John M. Niles and L. T. Pease, *History of South America and Mexico; . . . to Which is Annexed A Geographical and Historical View of Texas*, vol. 1 (Hartford, Conn., 1839), 226.

76. Ham, "Recollections," UT.

77. Jenkins, *Tight Pants*, 5.

78. Parker, *Trip to the West*, 196.

79. Ham, "Recollections," UT.

80. Miller, *Public Lands*, 23.

81. Ham, "Recollections," UT.

82. Statement of effects of James Bowie, 1837, James Bowie Vertical File, UT.

83. Bowie to Williams, August 1, 1830, Samuel May Williams Papers, Rosenberg Library, Galveston, Tex.

84. Mexico City *El Mosquito Mexicano*, April 5, 1836, carries a letter written after the fall of the Alamo in which the writer refers to "the braggart Bowie," and other Mexican accounts occasionally state that he was known chiefly for his boastfulness and bullying.

85. Fisher to Austin, August 14, 1830, Barker, *Austin Papers*, vol. 2, 465.

86. Austin to Fisher, June 17, 1830, ibid., 428, Fisher to Austin, August 14, 1830, ibid., vol. 3, 465.

87. Francis W. Johnson, *A History of Texas and Texans*, vol. 1 (Chicago, 1914), 186. Johnson's narrative, which is virtually a memoir, is the only authoritative source for Bowie's purchases in Saltillo. Johnson was intimately involved with Williams and others in the land business, and since Williams himself had some interest in Bowie's dealings, Johnson would surely have known of them. He states that Bowie bought fifteen or sixteen in all. J. Frank Dobie, "Fabulous Frontiersman: Jim Bowie," *Montana, The Magazine of Western History* 9 (April 1958): 48, misstates Samuel Williams's 1840 testimony into saying that Bowie got these grants in 1831, after his marriage to Ursula. Dobie may have been an excellent folklorist, but here and elsewhere in the Bowie literature he repeatedly shows himself to be a poor historian at best.

88. Samuel Williams statement, 1840, *Journal of the House of Representatives of the Republic of Texas, Fifth Congress, 1840–1841* (Austin, 1841), 369.

89. Ham, "Recollections," UT, says that on the Saltillo visit "Bowie speculated in Texas lands. He made many purchases."

90. Ham, "Recollections," UT.

91. Extracto, September 25, 1830, Béxar Archives, UT.

92. James Bowie Citizenship Decree No. 159, October 5, 1830, Nacogdoches Archives, TXSL.

93. Decree No. 160, October 3, 1830, James Bowie Vertical File, UT.

94. Promissory Note of the Dowry concerning the Nuptials, April 22, 1831, copy in James Bowie Vertical File, UT.

95. Sources disagree on the fate of the cotton mill project, and none of them seems to be well informed. Edward Sears, "The Low Down on Jim Bowie," in Mody C. Boatright and Donald Day, eds., *From Hell to Breakfast* (Austin, 1944), 196, says that Bowie never operated his mill in Mexico, and that when one finally opened it was run by someone else, but the Sears article is a dreadful piece of misinformed muckraking that is not to be taken seriously. Williams, "Critical Study, III," 97, says that Bowie got the mill running but left the operation of it to Veramendi, who was his partner, and later sold the business at a loss following Ursula's death in September 1833, but gives no source for these claims. Yet this is hardly likely, as Veramendi soon assumed the governorship and hardly had time to manage a business. Dudley G. Wooten, ed., *Comprehensive History of Texas 1685 to 1897*, vol. 1 (Austin, 1898), 131, is the closest thing to an authoritative contemporary source, being a virtual reiteration of H. Yoakum's Texas history of 1846, and he states that nothing was ever done on the cotton mill project.

It is also worth mentioning here that several sources claim that while in Saltillo Bowie was made a "colonel" and appointed leader of the San Antonio "Texas Rangers." Williams says this in "Critical Study, III," 99, as does Mims, *Trail*, 53, and Hopewell, *Bowie*, 65, all without authority. In fact the Texas Rangers did not come into being until November 1835, in addition to which there is no evidence of Bowie ever receiving any kind of commission or official appointment prior to the fall of 1835, though he exercised informal command of volunteers on a few occasions in the interim, but only for specific duties, and he certainly had no roving commission.

96. Menchaca, *Memoirs*, 20–21; Menchaca testimony, *Veramendi* v. *Hutchins*, 126, Documents Pertaining to James Bowie, UT.

Chapter 11   Travis 1831–1833

1. Williams, "Critical Study, III," 81, says on no authority that Travis went to Texas with an emigrant train from New Orleans to Nacogdoches. There were no such trains.

2. Mixon, "Travis," 12–13, speculates that Travis actually spent his first several days in Texas scouting land before going to San Felipe. She may be right, though it does not seem to conform to his interests or impatient temperament.

3. *A Visit to Texas*, 215. It should be noted that the adjective "Texan" did not appear in common or official use until statehood came. Prior to that time the inhabitants universally referred to themselves as Texians.

4. Niles, *History of South America*, vol. 1, 226.

5. [William B. Travis], petition, May 11, 1831, *Frontier America Rare & Unusual Americana Catalog* no. 37 (N.p., 1996): 72–73. This document is listed as being

dated May 10 in John H. Jenkins, *The Texas Revolution and Republic Catalog* no. 188 (Austin, 1986), item 48. It is not signed by Travis, but Jenkins and others are satisfied that it is in his handwriting.

6. Application no. 588, Spanish Archives, General Land Office, TXSL.

7. Promissory note, May 23, 1831, Stephen F. Austin Papers, UT.

8. *A Visit to Texas*, 90–91.

9. Parker, *Trip to the West*, 199.

10. N. D. Labadie, "Narrative of the Anahuac, or Opening Campaign of the Texas Revolution," in James M. Day, com, *The Texas Almanac, 1857–1873: A Compendium of Texas History* (Waco, 1967), 30–31.

11. Miriam Partlow, *Liberty, Liberty County, and the Atascosito District* (Austin, 1974), 273, 277; William Barret Travis to David Burnet, April 15, 1832, *Philpott Texana Collection Auction Catalog*, Dallas, October 16–17, 1995, item no. 203.

12. Partlow, *Liberty*, 173, 277.

13. John J. Linn, *Reminiscences of Fifty Years in Texas* (New York, 1883), 16.

14. Phillip E. Pearson, ed., "Reminiscences of Judge Edwin Waller," *Quarterly of the Texas State Historical Association* vol. 4 (July 1900): 42; J. M. Morphis, *History of Texas* (New York, 1874), 68. The origin of Travis's nickname "Buck" is unknown. Most references to it are in recollections, but at least one contemporaneous use of the name appears in a statement by Hiram M. Thompson, n.d., in the Hiram M. Thompson pension claim file, TXSL.

15. Austin to Thomas Hart Benton, November 25, 1831, Barker, *Austin Papers*, vol. 2, 711.

16. November 6, 1830.

17. *A Visit to Texas*, 90–91, 95–96, 258.

18. Ibid., 260.

19. G. M. Patrick to Moses A. Bryan, May 17, 1879, Texas Veterans Association Papers, UT.

20. Stanley Siegel, *Political History of the Texas Republic* (Austin, 1956), 12.

21. Labadie, "Anahuac," 129–30.

22. Owen, *Alabama*, vol. 4, 1681; Claiborne, Ala., *Herald*, February 27, 1829.

23. Músquiz to Antonio Elosua, June 19, 1832, Músquiz to Letona, June 18, 1832, Nacogdoches Archives, TXSL. Later Texian recollections do not mention this episode.

24. Labadie, "Anahuac," 128.

25. Ibid., 129–30; Monroe Edwards to Robert M. Williamson, May 24, 1832, Mirabeau B. Lamar Papers, TXSL. Margaret Swett Henson, *Juan Davis Bradburn* (College Station, Tex., 1982), 95, concludes without citing an authority that Warren D. C. Hall was involved with Travis in the false letters. Certainly this is possible. Labadie only mentions one letter, but he was writing a quarter century later. Monroe Edwards, writing at the time, and on the scene, says two letters were delivered. Assuming Travis to be smart enough not to write both in the

same handwriting, but sign them with different names, he could well have had help Hall likely would have known an old Laffite hand named Ballou who lived some distance away, and thus could have written the letter signed "Billew," while Travis wrote the McLaughlin letter.

26. The date of the arrest is established by an unsigned letter dated July 8, 1832, and published in the New Orleans, *Louisiana Advertiser*, July 26, 1832. Content makes it clear that either Travis or Jack wrote it, and the general tone and emphasis on constitutional liberties are most consistent with Travis' later writings, making it probable that he was the author.

27. Lindsay to Williamson, May 18, 1832, Lamar Papers; Francisco Medina to Elozua, June 22, 1832, Nacogdoches Archives, TXSL.

28. Edwards to Williamson, May 24, 1832, Lamar Papers, ibid.

29. John Davis Bradburn to Military Commander of Coahuila y Texas, June 1, 1832, Nacogdoches Archives, ibid.

30. Labadie, "Anahuac," 130.

31. James Lindsay to Williamson, May 18, 1832, Edwards to Williamson, May 24, 1832, Lamar Papers, TXSL.

32. Labadie, "Anahuac," 130.

33. Edwards to Williamson, May 24, 1832, Lamar Papers, TXSL.

34. Patrick Jack, Notes Regarding Disturbances at Anahuac, Williamson to the Citizens of Brassoria and its vicinity, June 4, 1832, ibid.

35. Mier y Terán to Letona, May 21, 1832, General Land Office, Applications, Austin's Colony, Volume 53, 163, ibid.

36. Wanda Louise Roark, "Robert Wilson: Letters to His Son" (master's thesis, Stephen F. Austin State College [University], Nacogdoches, 1966), 12; Rogan, "Hall," 274.

37. Medina to Elozua, June 22, 1832, Nacogdoches Archives, TXSL.

38. Elozua to Músquiz, July 18, 1832, ibid.

39. Jack, Notes, Spencer Jack to Lamar, n.d., M. B. Lamar, Notes Upon the Taking of the Martha, etc., Lamar Papers, TXSL; Notes Made by Mrs. Holley in Interviews with Prominent Texans of the Early Days, Mary Austin Holley Papers, UT.

40. Labadie, "Anahuac," 133.

41. Miguel Aeciniega to Músquiz, June 17, 1832, Nacogdoches Archives, TXSL. Though flawed and dated in many respects, Edna Rowe, "The Disturbances at Anahuac in 1832," *Quarterly of the Texas State Historical Association* 6 (April, 1903): 286ff, is a good account of this affair.

42. Michael Muldoon to Members of the Expeditionary Force, June 21, 1832, Nacogdoches Archives, TXSL.

43. Other accounts say July 3, but the Travis account written on July 8 must be presumed to be more authoritative, and it says July 2.

44. James Whiteside to Anthony Butler, August 2, 1832, Barker, *Austin Papers*, vol. 2, 829.

45. Labadie, "Anahuac," 136; Memorial of Colonel Juan Davis Bradburn concerning the Events at Anahuac, 1831–1832, in Henson, *Bradburn*, 141–42.

46. Memorial of Colonel Juan Davis Bradburn, Henson, *Bradburn*, 141–42.

47. James B. Bailey to David Shelby, June 27, 1832, Nacogdoches Archives, TXSL.

48. New Orleans *Louisiana Advertiser*, July 26, 1832.

49. Tocqueville, *Democracy in America*, 409.

50. Ugartechea to Colonel Guerra, July 27, 1832, Ex XI/481.3/801, Archivo Historico Militar Mexicano, Secretaria de la Defensa Nacional, Mexico City.

51. Francis J. Haskins to Austin, August 15, 1832, Williams Papers, Rosenberg Library, Galveston, Tex.

52. *A Visit to Texas*, 213, 220; Parker, *Trip to the West*, 214; Smithwick, *Evolution*, 55–57.

53. Moses A. Bryan, Recollections of Stephen Austin, 1889, Moses A. Bryan Papers, UT.

54. *A Visit to Texas*, 217.

55. Smithwick, *Evolution*, 55–57, 69.

56. Brazoria *Constitutional Advocate & Texas Public Advertiser*, September 5, 1832.

57. Moses A. Bryan, Reminiscences, Bryan Papers, UT.

58. Duncan W. Robinson, *Judge Robert McAlpin Williamson, Texas' Three-Legged Willie* (Austin, 1948), 16.

59. Smithwick, *Evolution*, 69–70.

60. *A Visit to Texas*, 217.

61. Brazoria *Constitutional Advocate & Texas Public Advertiser*, July 15, 1832.

62. Bryan, Reminiscences, Bryan Papers, UT.

63. Ham, "Recollections," UT.

64. Reuben M. Potter, "The Fall of the Alamo," *Magazine of American History* 2 (January, 1878): 18.

65. Travis to Burnet, December 5, 1832, *Philpott Texana Collection Auction Catalog*, Dallas, October 16–17, 1995, item no. 204.

66. Davis, *Travis Diary*, 68, November 7, 1833.

67. Ibid., 29n, September 14, 1833, 49, October 18, 1833, Robert E. Davis, ed., "Travis Draws a Will," *Manuscripts* 22 (Spring 1970): 113; Travis to O. H. Allen, July 15, 1833, Lamar Papers, TXSL.

68. Davis, *Travis Diary*, 8–9, September 18, 1833, 43, October 6, 1833; Agreement, December 19, 1833, Jenkins, *Texas Revolution Catalog*, item no. 67.

69. Davis, *Travis Diary*, 45, October 9, 1833, 93, December 27, 1833.

70. Ibid., 7–41, September 1833, 71, November 14, 1833, 75, November 29, 1833.

71. Ibid., 68, November 7, 1833.

72. Ibid., 68–73, November 1833; Parker, *Trip to the West*, 210.

73. These figures are compiled from Davis, *Travis Diary*, and should be considered approximate because it is impossible to separate some of Travis's business receipts from repayments of personal loans.

74. Draft, April 13, 1833, Williams Papers, Rosenberg Library, Galveston, Tex.

75. Mixon, "Travis," 66n; McDonald, *Travis*, 92–93.

76. Roark, "Robert Wilson," 2–6, 10; Brazoria *Texas Gazette,* March 13, 27, September 25, 1830;.

77. DeWitt Clinton Baker, *A Texas Scrap-Book* (New York, 1875), 289; Robert Wilson to James Wilson, November 9, 1853, in Roark, "Robert Wilson," 148.

78. Proposals for Introducing a Steam Boat into Texas, November 27, 1833, Benjamin C. Franklin Papers, UT; Roark, "Robert Wilson," 18–20.

79. Totals derived from Davis, *Travis Diary,* for the months of September–December 1833.

80. Davis, *Travis Diary,* 9, September 8, 1833; 49, October 19, 1833.

81. Ibid., 46, October 10, 51, October 24, 85, December 2, 1833.

82. Ibid., 13, September 18, 15, September 25, 50, October 20, 68, November 6, 75, November 28, 86, December 3, 87, December 9, 1833.

83. Ibid., 11, September 15, 74, November 25, 88, December 10, 1833.

84. Ibid., 91, 1833.

85. Figures compiled from Davis, *Travis Diary,* for the months of September 1833–March 1834.

86. Homer S. Thrall, *History of Methodism in Texas* (Houston, 1872), 30; Wilma H. Moore, "A History of San Felipe de Austin, 1824–1836" (master's thesis, University of Texas, Austin, 1929), 84.

87. Davis, *Travis Diary,* 45, October 9, 1833.

88. Ibid., 45, October 9, 1833; "The Reminiscences of Mrs. Dilue Harris, Part 1," *Quarterly of the Texas State Historical Association* 4 (October 1900): 88.

89. Davis, *Travis Diary,* 8, September 6; 10, September 10; 48, October 15; 94, December 24, 30, 1833; James Kirke Paulding, *Westward Ho!* vol. 1 (New York, 1832), 104.

90. Davis, *Travis Diary,* 90, December 16; 92, December 23; p 92–93, December 25; 94, December 30, 31, 1833.

91. Travis Family Bible, TXSL.

92. Davis, *Travis Diary,* 7, September 3, 46, October 11, 53, October 31, 67, November 1, 1833; Rosanna Travis to Dellet, September 6, 1833, Dellet Papers, ADAH.

93. Davis, *Travis Diary,* 15, September 26, 85, December 2, 1833.

94. Ibid., 7, September 2, 92, December 14, 92–93, December 25, 94, December 31, 1833.

95. Tocqueville, *Democracy in America,* 303.

96. Ibid., 10, September 12, 1833.

Chapter 12   Bowie 1830–1831

1. Ham, "Recollections," UT. Interestingly, Ham does not say whether or not the money he went to Natchez to fetch was there, but it seems reasonable to assume that it was, and that he had it with him when he came back to Texas. Otherwise such a lengthy journey on a wasted errand ought to have been memorable enough that he would have mentioned it in his "Recollections."

2. Sibley to Johnston, December 29, 1830, Johnston Papers, HSP.

3. United States Census, Lafourche Parish, Louisiana, 1830.

4. Tregle, "Louisiana," 393; Notary William Boswell, *Rezin P. Bowie* v. *His Creditors*, vol. 18, #505, statements of Rezin P. Bowie and others, April 27, May 12, 1832, New Orleans Notarial Archives.

5. Sparks in Ellis, *Crockett*, 224.

6. Conveyance Book F, 125–26, Terrebonne Parish Courthouse.

7. Claiborne, *Mississippi*, 415.

8. On February 12 James, Rezin, and Stephen accompanied by Sterrett, met the buyers in Natchez and transferred to them some 14,000 *arpents* in scattered tracts in Terrebonne, almost all of it the remnant of James's fraudulent Harper report properties, in return for $42,000. The buyers agreed to take James's titles at their own risk. Moreover, James had borrowed money against his property as collateral from the Consolidated Association of Planters. Consequently the Walkers and Wilkins required that he sign over to them all his shares in the association acquired as a borrower, and in return they would satisfy the mortgage, paying him whatever—if anything—remained. That same day the Bowies sold the partners the sugar plantation on the Lafourche for $90,000.00, including all the machinery, the defective steam mill, boilers, coolers, and even a carriage. With the property went eighty slaves, almost all of them in their teens and twenties. Once again, however, there were those old mortgages that had cost James his Maronges parcel the year before. Rezin and Stephen had failed to pay them off, and that $30,860.49 was still outstanding, even though the sellers continued not to recognize their validity. The Walkers and Wilkins did not require withholding of an amount to cover the mortgages, however. A few days later the Walkers and Wilkins met Rezin in Catahoula, and there he gave them a schedule listing all of the remaining Bowie property in Louisiana, his own, James's, Stephen's, and even John's, for John was now removing entirely to Arkansas. For $40,000.00 he allowed them to take their pick of 40,000 *arpents* from some 67,240 arpents in Rapides, Ouachita, and Catahoula Parishes, and then sold the remaining 27,240 arpents for a flat $20,000.00. Of the twenty-six plots listed and sold from Ouachita and Rapides, all but two were James's fraudulent claims from the old Sutton report. Of some 56,900 acres covered in the sale, all but 320 were James's. He never got confirmation or clear title to these properties, but now it would be Robert Walker's problem, and he already had good enough ties to President Jackson that he might succeed where Bowie had failed, especially with Graham out of the way.

The Walkers and Wilkins knew they were accepting a large risk in buying James Bowie's land, and as a result parted with very little money in hand. From the first sale involving the shares in the Planters Association, Bowie probably was due no more than $4,000.00 after his mortgage. On the sale of the Lafourche plantation, James really owned none of the land, and only a portion of the slaves, and even then he may still have owed Stephen and Rezin considerable money for the plantations he bought from them in 1828 and 1829. His final share of the $90,000.00 sales price may have been as small as $16,000.00. As for that final omnibus sale of the remaining land from the Sutton report, his share of the $60,000.00 total was about $45,000.00. But for most of these sales Bowie only received notes from the buyers, due at various intervals (and which, of course, they could refuse to pay if they encountered trouble with titles). If he had any cash in hand after it was all over, it amounted to no more than $20,000.00, and may have been considerably less (Conveyance Record E, 1837, 205, Clerk of the Court, St. Mary Parish Courthouse, Franklin, La.; Deed Book R, 512, Book H, 205–7, Lafourche Parish Courthouse; Conveyance Book G, 38, Terrebonne Parish Courthouse; Conveyance Record G, 399–401, Ouachita Parish Courthouse; Notary Felix De Armas, "Hypothètique par James Bowie en favr de l'Association Consolidé," June 16, 1829, vol. 33, #751, New Orleans Notarial Archives).

James Bowie's share of these sales is almost impossible to calculate, since the brothers sold their property jointly, the transfers giving no hint as to how much each was to receive. The only hint lies in the Bowie Promissory Note of the Dowry, April 22, 1831, James Bowie Vertical File, UT. It lists two debts to him, one notes from the Walkers and Wilkins for $45,000.00, and the other due in notes from the same parties totaling $20,000. Bowie's largest part of the sales were his numerous Sutton report claims, which made up at least seventy percent of the total land being conveyed, and thus would suggest that of the $60,000.00 purchase price, this $45,000.00 could be his share. The other $20,000.00 on the dowry, then, could only be notes due for his Terrebonne property after his mortgages were satisfied, and his share of the proceeds from the Lafourche plantation. The dowry statement also lists $20,000.00 in cash left with Angus McNeil in Natchez. This *might* be cash realized as money down on these sales, but knowing Bowie, it is also possible that it was chimerical, as a subsequent analysis of the full dowry to follow will show to be quite possible.

9. Notary William Boswell, *Rezin P. Bowie* v. *His Creditors*, vol. 9, #505, statement of Duncan Walker, May 30, 1832, New Orleans Notarial Archives. Walker appealed to Jackson after he found that many of Bowie's spurious claims had been surveyed as public domain and would be sold at auction. Jackson refused to interfere, but only referred it to Graham's successor, who told the president that the respectability of the Walkers and Wilkins as the present owners of these claims "does not in the least affect their validity or clear them from the imputation of being base attempts to defraud the Government." Ten years later Walker was still trying to sell the properties that everyone now knew as "Bowy claims," and still running into an inability to secure clear title. The term crossed the river to Mississippi, too, for with the Terrebonne land from the Harper report, it was soon known that Robert Walker had gotten stuck with what one of his friends

in the state called "the famous Bowie claims." Even the Lafourche plantation caused him problems. By 1834 Walker was calling it "Acadia," but after he won a seat in the U.S. Senate in 1836 he started selling his property, and in 1840 disposed of Acadia for $220,000, only to have the buyer find that the title was unsound even there, though this time, for a change, it appears to have had nothing to do with James Bowie. The story persists that the Bowies themselves named the Lafourche plantation "Acadia" or "Arcadia," or even "Sedalia." It is possible that they did so, but the earliest recorded reference to the name comes three years after the sale, in Quitman's April 1834 letter. (Elijah Hayward to Jackson, January 16, 1832, Entry 404, James Whitcomb to John Henderson, January 22, 1841, Letters Sent, Volume 6, 293, Entry 200, Record Group 49, NA; Claiborne, *Mississippi*, 415n; Quitman to Eliza Quitman, April 19, 1834, Quitman Papers, SHC, UNC; Robert and Duncan Walker to William Givens, March 7, 1840, Conveyance Book R, 22, Lafourche Parish Courthouse).

10. Conveyance Book 7, 232, Orleans Parish Courthouse; Deed Book H, 237–38, Lafourche Parish Courthouse.

11. Bowie to the President and Directors of the Consolidated Association of the Planters of Louisiana, February 25, 1831, J. Fair Hardin Collection, LSU.

12. Little Rock *Arkansas Gazette,* June 8, 1830.

13. Ibid., September 8, 1830; Bowie, *The Bowies*, 264. This second wife of John J. Bowie's was not discovered by Walter Bowie in *The Bowies*, and apparently was completely unknown to John's children by his third wife, Americus Watkins Kirkland. At least, Martha Bowie Burns makes no mention of her in her article on "Eventful Lives of the Bowies" in the James Bowie Biographical File, DRT.

14. James Whitcomb to William Wright, May 9, 1838, vol. 4, 227, Entry 200, Record Group 49, NA. This New Madrid business is uncertain, speaking only of the "representatives" of Rezin Bowie, which could be any one, or a combination, of James, John, Rezin, or Stephen, and their sister Martha Sterrett. They do not appear to have gotten the property.

15. Elve Soniat to M. S. Bowie, October 19, 1896, July 26, 1897, Lucy Bowie Papers, DRT; Deed Book G, 242, 245, Lafourche Parish Courthouse; W. L. Martin to Barnes F. Lathrop, June 19, 1958, citing a November 30, 1830, bond seen in the Lafourche Parish Courthouse but not there now, Barnes F. Lathrop Papers, UT; Conveyance Record Book 7, Old Series, 207–208, St. Landry Parish Courthouse; Conveyance Book E, 407, Avoyelles Parish Courthouse. The statement about Stephen Bowie losing money while sheriff is in the two Elve Soniat letters, the amount stated being $20,000. This sounds like an exaggeration, and she is probably confusing the bonds posted by Stephen's brothers for money they actually had to pay out.

16. Conveyance Book F, 228–29, Terrebonne Parish Courthouse; Stephen Bowie, Oath of Insolvency, September 26, 1831, *Harris & Marsh* v. *S. Bowie*, Box 7, Adams County Circuit Court Records, Historic Natchez Foundation, Natchez, Mississippi; Arrest order for Stephen Bowie, May 14, 1831, Case #3040, *Cushing and Ames* v. *Rezin P. and Stephen Bowie,* General Case Files, Entry 21, Record Group 21, National Archives—Southwest Region.

17. Conveyance Book 21, 59–60, Natchitoches Parish Courthouse.

18. Conveyance Book F, 135, Terrebonne Parish Courthouse.

19. Deed Book F, 396, Lafourche Parish Courthouse; Conveyance Record 18, 40, Natchitoches Parish Courthouse; Conveyance Book F, 179, H, 424–45, Terrebonne Parish Courthouse.

20. Smithwick, *Evolution*, 137–38. Smithwick's recollections are muddled here, for he says that James and Rezin Bowie had just won a famous case over their Louisiana claims "and had a fortune," and that it was his share of this money that Bowie lost. Smithwick's memory has confused the 1827 court confirmation of the Arkansas claims, in which Rezin had no part, with the large sale of the Louisiana lands to the Walkers and Wilkins. Nevertheless this appears to be a genuine recollection of Smithwick's, and not one of the fabrications included in his memoir by his daughter who edited the book.

21. San Antonio *Light*, May 4, 1917; "James Bowie," undated manuscript in James Bowie Biographical File, DRT.

22. Henry Bry to Johnston, December 24, 1830, Johnston Papers, HSP.

23. Stephen Bowie, Oath of Insolvency, September 20, 1831, Box 7, Adams County Circuit Court Records, Historic Natchez Foundation.

24. McWhiney, *Cracker Culture*, 189–90.

25. Richardson, "Teche Country," 595.

26. There are at least three variant accounts of Bowie defending a minister during a service. The earliest is William H. Sparks's unlocated 1879–80 newspaper narrative later quoted in Ellis, *Crockett*, 229–30, in which he recounts a story told him "some years ago" by a Methodist preacher, and substantially this account has been used in the text. The San Francisco *Chronicle* of February 28, 1881, repeats Sparks almost verbatim, and John Henry Brown repeats this last version in August 1881, though misquoting the date of the article as February 22, and includes it in Speer and Brown, *Encyclopedia*, vol. 1, 438. Thorp, *Bowie Knife*, 131–32, concludes that the unnamed minister was Charles Wesley Smith. Some years later, and certainly after 1901, a clipping from an unidentified issue of the Washington *Herald*, in the James Bowie Biographical File, DRT, says the event happened in Mississippi, again with a Methodist, and that Bowie, a "small man," threatened to cut the throats of any who disturbed the service. Finally, A. J. Sowell, in the San Antonio *Light*, May 4, 1917, tells the story, placing it in Nacogdoches, but this time the minister is the early Baptist missionary Z. N. Morrell, and when the rowdies start Bowie makes a speech, threatening them to "be quiet, leave the room or fight me."

    None of the sources date the occurrence. If it had happened on Bowie's 1830 trip, Caiaphas Ham would probably have noted it. Thus it would have to be on one of Bowie's 1831–32 passages from Louisiana through Nacogdoches, and this trip is as likely as any other, and he is known to have had another road companion on this journey, Martin Parmer. Quite possibly all these stories are apocryphal, however, and the later ones may well be derivative from the earliest Sparks account. As usual Thorp is completely off base, for Charles W. Smith was not even born until 1855, nineteen years after Bowie's death! Morrell, of course, did not set foot in Texas until December 1835, at which time Bowie was more than two hundred miles away from Nacogdoches at San Antonio, San Felipe, and Goliad, deeply engaged in the preliminaries that led him to the Alamo. If the event took place at all, it more likely involved the Methodist Henry Stephenson in 1834, but this is pure conjecture. Significantly, it should also be noted that there is at least one similar story about Travis defending a Texas minister from rowdies, suggesting that this kind of heroic defense of the faith may have been simply an idiom of frontier myth applied to several heroes.

27. Johnson, *Texas*, vol. 1, 163.

28. José Navarro to Williams, April 14, 1831, Williams Papers, Rosenberg Library, Galveston, Tex.

29. "A List of Titles made under the Contract with the State of Coahuila & Texas for settling 500 Families By Stephen F. Austin 1827–1833," 35, Benjamin C. Franklin Papers, UT.

30. James Bowie Dowry Obligation, April 22, 1831, copy and translation in Fontaine Papers; Promissory Note of the Dowery, April 22, 1831, James Bowie Vertical File, UT. Two sources of the contract are cited because the translations differ, and each should be used to draw the full sense of the document.

31. There have been several analyses of the Bowie dowry contract, all of them deeply flawed either by blind acceptance of every statement as fact, or by quite defective background research on the part of its critics. Of the falsity of the claimed land in Arkansas and Louisiana there is no doubt. The $32,800 mentioned is not stated to be the de la Français claim, but that is the only known claim that Bowie ever filed with the United States government, and at 10 percent simple interest per annum, the original $11,850 claim would have grown to $32,060 by August 1828, when Bowie returned from his first trip to San Antonio, at which time he dropped further pursuit of the claim and, presumably, stopped bothering to keep up to date with interest calculations he was unlikely to collect anyhow. The remaining question on the dowry lies only in the notes due from the Walkers and Wilkins, and the supposed $20,000 left with McNeil. As will be seen, the Walkers and Wilkins in 1832 will cease payments on these notes when their titles are rejected. As for the money supposedly left with McNeil, the fact that almost everything else in the document is a lie or a half truth does not argue in its favor.

32. James Bowie Marriage Record, April 25, 1831, San Fernando Parish Church, San Antonio. Elve Soniat to Lucy Bowie, n.d. but in the 1890s, states that James gave Ursula a set of emeralds as a wedding gift. This is of course possible, but since in his 1833 will, made out in Natchez, he mentions his wife's jewelry, then in the hands of his sister Martha Sterrett, it is more likely that James bought her the jewelry during his 1833 visit to Louisiana, as he would hardly take jewelry she already owned with him on a journey to Louisiana to leave with his sister.

33. Testimony of Menchaca, 126, *Veramendi* v. *Hutchins*, Documents Pertaining to James Bowie, UT.

34. Ham, "Recollections," UT; Edward Rohrbaugh, "James Bowie and the Bowie Knife in Fact and in Fancy" (master's thesis, University of Texas, Austin, 1938), 31.

35. Juana Navarro Alsbury Account, ca. 1880, in John Ford Papers, UT.

36. Testimony of Menchaca, 127, *Veramendi* v. *Hutchins*, Documents Pertaining to James Bowie, UT.

37. James Bowie passport, June 23, 1831, Petition to sell goods, June 22, 1831, Béxar Archives, UT.

38. James Bowie statements of testimony, July 27, 31, 1831, UT. Bowie identified McCaslan as "the foreman of my mechanics" in his December 10, 1831, statement on his fight on the San Saba expedition, Nacogdoches Archives, TXSL.

39. John Warren Hunter, *Rise and Fall of the San Saba Mission* (Bandera, Tex., 1905), 53–56, repeats an old myth that James had befriended a Lipan chief named Xolic, and through him was adopted into the Lipan tribe, and that he learned the location of the San Saba mine from them. This account states that he lived with them for eleven months, despite the fact that there is no such period for which Bowie cannot be shown to be elsewhere. The narrative also places the November-December 1831 expedition sometime in 1834. Moreover, it is evident from James's report that he was *looking* for the mine, not going after a location he already knew. Mims, *Trail*, 51ff., adopts this myth and, of course, so does Hopewell, *Bowie*, 72–73. The earliest source for this story is unknown, but it probably does not predate the 1880s.

40. Martha Bowie Burns article, James Bowie Biographical File, DRT.

41. Menchaca testimony, 127, *Veramendi* v. *Hutchins*, Documents Pertaining to James Bowie, UT.

42. Rezin's passport to visit Texas has not been examined, but was given to the Alamo in 1889 by his grandson John S. Moore, and supposedly carries the date 1831. Certainly he arrived no later than December. San Antonio *Daily Express,* October 11, 1889.

43. Arrest order, September 8, 1831, *Stephen Duncan* v. *Stephen Bowie*, September 8, 1831, Arrest order September 10, 1831, *William Harris and Marsh* v. *Stephen Bowie*, September 20, 1831, Summons, November 8, 1831, *Duncan* v. *Rezin Bowie*, Box 7, Adams County Circuit Court Records, Historic Natchez Foundation. The date of Stephen Bowie's death is currently unknown. Until now it has been assumed to have been sometime in 1830 (Bowie, *The Bowies*, 278), but the Natchez records clearly have him living as of late September 1831. He was dead when James Bowie made out his will on October 31, 1833. He may have died in late 1831, from the fact that on September 8, 1831, Stephen Duncan was claiming a debt against Stephen and Rezin combined, but that on November 8 the debt only mentioned Rezin. This could mean simply that Stephen was no longer party to the debt in Natchez because of his insolvency, or it could mean that he was no longer living and action could only be sought against Rezin. Only Ham, "Recollections," UT, has him alive past this time, in December 1831, and this could be in error. Further research, hardly germane to this narrative, could probably pinpoint Stephen Bowie's death with much greater accuracy.

44. Order November 3, 1831, Court Record Relating to Arkansas Land Claims, 1824–1832, Entry 214, Record Group 49, NA; *Bernardo Sampeyrac and Joseph*

Stewart v. *the United States,* Richard Peters, cop., *Reports of Cases Argued and Adjudged in the Supreme Court of the United States. January Term 1833* (Philadelphia, 1833), 223–25. There has not, to date, been an adequate study of the Bowie Arkansas case. Frederick Cron's brief essay in the James Bowie Vertical File, UT, is little more than an outline. Sears, "Low Down," 175–91, provides perhaps the fullest examination in print, but like the rest of his article, it is snide, sophomoric, and packed with misinformation, including the ridiculous assumption that Bowie invented the name Sampeyrac really intending it to represent the French *sans payer rien,* which would then translate to "Bernardo who pays nothing." Though unusual, the surname was genuine enough. Senator Johnston did frequent business with a Natchitoches merchant named Ambroise Sampeyrac. Sears's chronology of Bowie's life is topsy-turvy; Sears says that Angus McNeil was probably a fictitious person, that it took months for letters to go from New Orleans to Little Rock instead of barely more than a week by steamboat, and so on, and so on.

45. Ham, "Recollections," UT.

46. The account of the expedition that follows is drawn, unless otherwise noted, from three participants' narratives: James Bowie to Ramón Músquiz, December 10, 1831, Nacogdoches Archives, TXSL; Rezin Bowie, "An Indian Battle," *Atkinson's Saturday Evening Post and Bulletin; A Family Newspaper, Devoted to Literature, Morality, Science, News, Agriculture and Amusement* 13, August 17, 1833; and Ham, "Recollections," UT. It should be noted that the two accounts by the Bowie brothers were much reprinted in the late 1800s, though not in their entirety, and very inaccurately. Only the originals cited above have been used here.

47. While it is nearly impossible to locate this spot exactly, it would seem to be in the vicinity of Calf Creek, not far from the small town of the same name.

48. A. J. Sowell, *Early Settlers and Indian Fighters of Southwestern Texas* (Austin, 1900), 406–7, tells a fanciful story supposedly given to Sowell's father by James Bowie, that has his black servant being asked to go for the water, and refusing until Bowie threatened him, after which one of the Indians came after the slave and was brought down just in time by Armstrong. The story is either apocryphal or else a gross exaggeration due to poor memory. Sowell has the slave's name as Jim instead of Charles, the attackers Comanche instead of Tawakoni, and the location one hundred miles southwest of San Antonio, about two hundred miles from where it actually took place.

49. Ham, "Recollections," UT, is the only source that locates Stephen Bowie in Texas at this time, and it could be mistaken. Certainly Stephen's last appearance in any known contemporary record was in September 1831. Given Ham's usual surprising accuracy in spite of his age when he wrote his "Recollections," it seems probable that Stephen's being in San Antonio on his brothers' return is correct, the more so since the brothers very soon went back to Louisiana, which might suggest that Stephen came with some important news that called them back.

Chapter 13   Crockett 1831–1834

1. Crockett, *Narrative*, 208.

2. Crockett to Carey and Hart, March 25, 1834, in Shackford, *Crockett*, 152.

3. Crockett to Biddle, January 2, 1832, Nicholas Biddle Papers, Crockett to Richard Smith, January 7, 1832, Conarroe Autograph Collection, HSP.

4. Crockett to Smith, January 7, 1832, Conarroe Autograph Album, HSP.

5. Crockett to Jones, August 22, 1831, Jones Papers, SHC, UNC.

6. Arpad, "Crockett," 186.

7. J. V. Drake to the editor of the *News*, October 17, 1877, Crockett Biographical File, DRT.

8. Christopher Baldwin, "Diary of Christopher Baldwin," *Transactions of the American Antiquarian Society* 7 (1911): 239–40.

9. Arpad, "Crockett," 182–83.

10. Crockett to T. J. Dobings, May 27, 1834, U.S. Manuscripts, Lilly Library, Indiana University, Bloomington.

11. St. Martinville, *Attakapas Gazette,* April 26, 1834.

12. Arpad, "Crockett," 36; Folmsbee, "West Tennessee," 19; Shackford, *Crockett*, 140–41.

13. Crockett to Thomas Henderson, March 10, 1834, in Shackford, *Crockett*, 151.

14. William Kennedy, *Texas: The Rise, Progress, and Prospects of the Republic of Texas* (London, 1841), 557n. Crockett's acquaintance with Webster at this time is established by Crockett to Webster, December 18, 1832, *American Book Prices Current 1987–1991, Index* (Washington, Conn., 1992), 167–68.

15. Richard B. Hauck, *Crockett: A Bio-Bibliography* (Westport, Conn., 1982), 66–67, and Shackford, *Crockett*, 26–27, 296n, give some discussion of the aphorism's origin, and while not coming to an actual conclusion, both seem to favor the notion that it was not original to Crockett. Of course, one cannot prove or disprove the origin of a colloquialism like this, but no instance of anyone else using the expression has been found prior to Crockett's May 1831 notations cited in Shackford, 136.

16. Hauck, *Crockett*, 57ff; Heale, "Self-Made Man," 406.

17. Controversy continues over the authorship. See Hauck, *Crockett*, 3–4, and Shackford, *Crockett*, 258–64, for well reasoned arguments in favor of Clarke as author.

18. Heale, "Self-Made Man," 407–8.

19. Hauck, *Crockett*, 83ff.

20. Paul A. Hutton, "Introduction," in David Crockett, *A Narrative of the Life of David Crockett of the State of Tennessee* (Lincoln, Nebr., 1987), vii.

21. Crockett to Carey and Hart, February 3, 1834, J. S. H. Fogg Collection, Maine Historical Society, Portland.

22. Arpad, "Crockett," 179.

23. Philadelphia *Atkinson's Saturday Evening Post*, August 17, 1833.

24. Crockett, *Narrative*, 209–10.

25. Undated newspaper clipping, August 15, 1833, Jones Papers, SHC, UNC.

26. Clay to Polk, August 19, 1833, Herbert Weaver and Paul H. Bergeron, eds., *Correspondence of James K. Polk,* vol. 2, *1833–1834* (Nashville, 1972), 101.

27. *London and Westminster Review* 32 (1839): 139.

28. *Nile's Register* 45 (September 7, 1833): 20.

29. Jackson, Tenn., *Southern Statesman*, September 14, 1833.

30. Heale, "Self-Made Man," 409.

31. Crockett to Carey and Hart, January 8, 1835, David Crockett Vertical File, Maryland Historical Society, Baltimore.

32. There is only Crockett's word for this presidential offer, but there is no reason for it not to be genuine. It is dated to late 1833 because in late 1834 the Mississippi convention made the same approach to Thomas Hart Benton, and in the letter Crockett makes it clear that the offer to him had come previously. Meeting only once a year, the convention could only have made the Crockett approach the previous fall (1833).

33. Crockett to G. W. McLean, January 17, 1834, Miscellaneous Manuscripts Collection, Library of Congress.

34. Crockett to Biddle, December 8, 1834, Simon Gratz Collection, HSP.

35. Crockett, *Narrative*, 4–5.

36. Crockett to McLean, January 17, 1834, Miscellaneous Manuscripts, Library of Congress.

37. Allan Nevins, ed., *The Diary of John Quincy Adams, 1794–1845* (New York, 1928), 444–45, November 26, 1833.

38. Arpad, "Crockett," 113; Shackford, *Crockett*, 256. Shackford commits an error either in his text or in the supporting note, for he says Crockett saw the performance on December 30, 1833, but then cites a source published on December 13, 1833, seventeen days *before* the event, which is hardly possible. The original source has not been examined for this narrative.

39. Chapman in Galveston *Daily News*, January 27, 1895.

40. Jackson *Southern Statesman*, September 14, 1833.

41. Tocqueville, *Democracy in America*, 478, 480–81.

42. Arpad, "Crockett," 60–61.

43. Ibid., 182.

44. Blair, "Six Davy Crocketts," 456–57.

45. Crockett to Dear Friend [believed to be Henry Slorrs], January 9, 1834, Buffalo & Erie County Historical Society Archives, Buffalo, N.Y.

46. Crockett to McLean, January 17, 1834, Miscellaneous Manuscripts Collection, Library of Congress.

47. Crockett, *Narrative*, 210–11.

48. There are several examinations of the literary impact of Crockett's book. The

best are probably Arpad, "Crockett," and Hauck, *Crockett.*

49. Crockett to Carey and Hart, February 3, 1834, Fogg Collection, Maine Historical Society.

50. Ibid.; Crockett to Carey and Hart, February 20 [or 23 or 28], 1834, Mellen Chamberlain Collection of Autographs, Boston Public Library, Boston, Mass.

51. Crockett to Carey and Hart, February 20 [23 or 28], 1834, Chamberlain Collection, Boston Public Library; Arpad, "Crockett," 189.

52. Blair, "Six Davy Crocketts," 456–57; Paul Hutton, ed., *A Narrative of the Life of David Crockett of the State of Tennessee* (Lincoln, Nebr., 1987), vi.

53. Chapman in Galveston *Daily News,* January 27, 1895.

54. With the Indian Removal Bill an accomplished fact, he tried to help secure the appointment of a competent agent to help the Florida Seminole with their move (Crockett to Lewis Cass, November 28, 1833, Ford Collection, Pierpont Morgan Library, New York).

55. Crockett to A. M. Hughes, December 8, 1833, Miscellaneous Collection, Tennessee Historical Society, TSL. Jackson preempted him for a time with the furor raised by his veto of a land bill passed at the end of the previous session. It had been Clay's measure, and one not dear to Crockett either, for it provided for the government retaining public lands in the several states and selling it to raise revenue to support internal improvements and other "American System" measures. In his veto Jackson said such a policy would naturally keep land prices high, out of the reach of the poor. The land should be sold at the lowest possible prices and at liberal terms to the people, said Old Hickory, and what remained should go to the states for their own uses.

   Had it been anyone but Jackson saying such things, Crockett might have cheered, for the president's policy did not stand at a great remove from his own, and it seemed to bode well for getting his bill back on the floor and passed at last. But Clay lambasted Jackson on the Senate floor for the veto, and Crockett's friend George Poindexter of Mississippi was nearly as severe, which aroused the ire of Democrats who might otherwise have supported Crockett.

56. Crockett to William Rodgers, January 8, 1834, Miscellaneous Collection, Tennessee Historical Society, TSL.

57. Crockett to John W. Crockett, January 10, 1834, Thomas W. Streeter Collection of Texas Manuscripts, Beinecke Rare Book and Manuscript Library, Yale University, New Haven, Conn.

58. McKay W. Campbell to Polk, January 7, 1834, Weaver and Bergeron, *Correspondence of James K. Polk,* vol. 2, 222.

59. Crockett to Dobings, May 27, 1834, U.S. Manuscripts, Lilly Library, Indiana University, Bloomington.

60. Crockett to William Hack, June 9, 1834, Miscellaneous Collection, Tennessee Historical Society, TSL.

61. Crockett to Hughes, December 8, 1834, ibid.

62. Crockett to Rodgers, January 8, 1834, ibid.

63. Crockett to McLean, January 17, 1834, Miscellaneous Manuscripts Collection, Library of Congress.

64. Crockett to John O. Cannon, January 20, 1834, *Philpott Collection Catalog*, item no. 225.

65. Crockett to John W. Crockett, January 10, 1834, Streeter Collection, Yale.

66. Joel R. Smith to Polk, January 21, 1834, Weaver and Bergeron, *Correspondence of James K. Polk*, vol. 2, 269.

67. Crockett to Thomas Henderson, February 26, 1834, in Shackford, "Narrative," 474.

68. Crockett to John Drury, April 4, 1834, Gilder-Lehrman Collection, Pierpont Morgan Library.

69. St. Martinville *Attakapas Gazette,* April 26, 1834.

70. Crockett to Drury, April 4, 1834, Gilder-Lehrman Collection, Pierpont Morgan Library.

71. Crockett to Hack, June 9, 1834, Miscellaneous Collection, Tennessee Historical Society, TSL. At every turn Crockett detected Jackson's arbitrary usurpation and corruption. The shortfall in the Post Office Department now ran to $375,000, and he believed it might top $1 million. The true total, he said in December, "is yet unknown but they can hide it no longer and the thing has to come before the world in its true coulers." The postmaster general acknowledged having to borrow from some thirty or more banks to keep the department running, and risked defaulting on earlier loans. All this in the administration that had promised to clean house and set operations on a sound footing. "Glorious reforme and retrenchment under King Andrew the first," he sneered. "Will the people be blinded always to uphold a name destitute of principle." Crockett himself investigated the expenditures on printing jobs given to the administration organ the Washington *Globe*, and found it to be $42,000. At the same time he found ten other contracts by which $112,000 of public funds were paid to Jackson favorites. "This is Jackson retrenchment," he accused. "Jackson is determined to feed his pets out of a silver spoon." Everything now seemed to be a test of strength and will more than principle. The House spent most of the session trying to decide a contested election for a seat in Kentucky between Thomas Moore and Robert Letcher. In the previous Congress, Letcher had helped Clay outwit the Jackson forces in pushing through a tariff bill, and now they strove for revenge by backing Moore. Crockett, naturally, favored Letcher, if only to spite Jackson (Crockett to Hughes, December 8, 1833, Crockett to Rodgers, January 8, 1834, Miscellaneous Collection, Tennessee Historical Society, TSL; Crockett to Drury, April 4, 1834, Gilder-Lehrman Collection, Pierpont Morgan Library; Crockett to Cannon, January 20, 1834, in "Davy Crockett vs. Andy Jackson," *Confederate Veteran* 11 [April 1903]: 163; Crockett to Dobings, May 27, 1834, U.S. Manuscripts, Lilly Library, Indiana University, Bloomington).

72. Drake to the editor of the *News*, October 17, 1877, Crockett Biographical File, DRT.

73. Crockett to Drury, April 4, 1834, Gilder-Lehrman Collection, Pierpont Morgan Library.

74. Crockett to Joseph Wallis, May 26, 1834, Crockett Papers, UT.

75. Crockett to William Yeatman, June 15, 1834, in Davis, *Memphis*, 155.

76. Crockett to John W. Crockett, January 10, 1834, Streeter Collection, Yale.

77. Crockett to Wallis, May 26, 1834, Crockett Papers, UT.

78. Crockett to Carey and Hart, February 20 [23 or 28], 1834, Chamberlain Collection, Boston Public Library; Crockett to Carey and Hart, February 25, 1834, Edward Carey Gardiner Papers, HSP; Crockett to Carey and Hart, March 8, 1834, Miscellaneous Personal Collection, New-York Historical Society.

79. Crockett to Carey and Hart, February 20 [23 or 28], 1834, Chamberlain Collection, Boston Public Library.

80. Chapman in Galveston *Daily News*, January 27, 1895.

81. Hutton, *Narrative*, vi.

82. Crockett to Carey and Hart, March 25, 1834, quoted in Shackford, *Crockett*, 152.

83. Chapman in Galveston *Daily News*, January 27, 1895. Chapman only states that Crockett's sittings for him took place in 1834, but it is evident that they were during a House session. It seems more likely to have been the first session, which lasted until June 30, rather than the second, of which only the month of December was in 1834.

84. Crockett to Carey and Hart, April 10, 1834, Manuscript Vault File, Beinecke Library, Yale.

85. Crockett to Carey and Hart, June 1, 1834, *Philpott Collection Catalog*, item no. 227.

86. Inscription, March 19, 1834, quoted in John H. Jenkins, *Texas Revolution and Republic Catalog* 188 (Austin, 1986), item no. 71.

87. Arpad, "Crockett," 201.

88. Tocqueville, *Democracy in America,*, 475.

89. Chapman in Galveston *Daily News,* January 27, 1895.

90. Ibid.

91. Crockett to Slorrs, January 9, 1834, Buffalo and Erie County Historical Society.

92. Crockett to Hughes, December 8, 1833, Miscellaneous Collection, Tennessee Historical Society, TSL.

93. Crockett to Rodgers, January 8, 1834, ibid.

94. Ephraim Dickinson to Polk, February 16, 1834, Weaver and Bergeron, *Correspondence of James K. Polk*, vol. 2, 317.

95. Crockett to Dobings, May 27, 1834, U.S. Manuscripts, Lilly Library, Indiana University, Bloomington.

96. New York *Sunday Morning News*, May 1, 1836.

97. Chapman in Galveston *Daily News,* January 27, 1895.

98. Arpad, "Crockett," 216.

99. *Nile's Weekly Register* 46 (May 3, 1834): 148.

100. Chapman in Galveston *Daily News,* January 27, 1895.

101. Folmsbee and Catron, "Congressman," 71.

102. Crockett to Carey and Hart, March 25, 1834, in Shackford, *Crockett,* 152; Crockett to Jacob Dixon, April 11, 1834, *American Book Prices Current, Index 1960–1965* (New York, 1968): 1878.

Chapter 14   Bowie 1831–1833

1. Some writers have mistakenly assumed that Bowie's report indicates that he was on a mission for the political chief, or that he held some official command, an echo of the myth that he was made a captain of rangers in 1830. Such is not the case. His was purely a personal venture that neither had nor required official sanction, and other than Rezin and Caiaphas Ham and the two servants, most of the men with him were nominally his employees in the cotton mill enterprise.

2. Bowie to Músquiz, December 10, 1831, Músquiz to José Letona, December 18, 1831, Antonio Elozua to Músquiz, January 5, 1832, Músquiz to Bowie, December 19, 1831, Letona to Músquiz, January 20, 1832, José Antonio de la Garza to Bowie, February 6, 1832, Béxar Archives, UT.

3. Hayward to Jackson, January 16, 1832, Entry 404, Record Group 49, NA. Caiaphas Ham is the only authority for Bowie making this December 1831 trip to Louisiana, but since Rezin, and Stephen (if he actually came to Texas) would need to return home, and because of other stories placing Bowie in Arkansas in 1831, it seems reasonable to accept Ham on this. However, it is also possible that Ham was confused, and really was thinking of Bowie's probable December 1832 trip to Louisiana.

4. They probably went by way of Arkansas, traveling first to Nacogdoches, and then north on Trammel's Trace to the Red River, and beyond a few miles to Washington, in Hempstead County. It gave James a chance to look into the land sales there, as well as to take a reading on what had happened with the Bowie claims in the courts. On the way across the wild country he had lost the knife that Rezin gave him, and while in Washington he may also have called on local blacksmith James Black to have another one made. Then it was a hasty trip on down the Red to Natchitoches, and so on to Rezin's home once more, only to find that he would have to wait to collect the money due him, an unfortunate circumstance that delayed not only his own land speculations in Texas, but apparently some plans of Austin's as well.

The seemingly innumerable devotees of the Bowie knife would rise in rebellion if some acknowledgment were not made here of the pretensions of James Black to being the maker of one of Bowie's knives. According to the Washington, Ark., *Telegraph,* December 8, 1841, Black claimed at that time that he had made a knife for Bowie. The article says that it was *James* Bowie whom he made it for, but does not actually quote Black. The article states no more detail than that. Black does not claim to have made the *original* Bowie knife, nor does he claim that the knife he says he made was his own design or Bowie's. He supposedly elaborated on this considerably in later years when, while blind, he lived with the Jones family in Little Rock. According to Augustus Garland to William F. Pope, April 28, 1895, in the Little Rock, Ark., *Gazette*, June 11, 1908, the old and infirm Black told him that James Bowie brought him the pattern for a knife that he had whittled in soft wood and asked him to forge the blade. Pope used this information in his *Early Days in Arkansas* (Little Rock, 1895), 44–46, but then said that it was Rezin Bowie of Walnut Hills, in neighboring Lafayette County, who actually called on Black to have the knife made. This was not James's brother Rezin, but a much younger cousin, the son of John J. Bowie. No date for the event appears in any of the succeeding accounts until the March 14, 1920, Galveston, Tex., *Daily News*, in a story titled "True Story of the Bowie Knife," which says it happened in 1831. An undated typescript of an article by Dan Jones, son of the family with which Black lived, is in the Lucy Bowie Papers at DRT, and it states that Black made the knife for James. Thorp, *Bowie Knife*, 16–23, concludes that it happened in 1830. Virtually all subsequent accounts of the Black-Bowie connection are based on these sources.

There are many problems with the Black story. For a start, by 1841 James Black had been battling insanity and delusion at least since May 1836, and that was only when his father-in-law actually made the matter public in seeking to have Black declared incompetent, a judgment with which the court agreed, making him Black's legal guardian (Hopewell, *Bowie*, 53, citing Hempstead County Circuit Court records). Consequently, stories of Black's connection with any of the Bowies or of making a knife for any of them may have been pure lunatic fantasy. Then there is the problem of identity. James's brother Rezin Bowie never lived in Arkansas. Their cousin Rezin, mentioned above, did, though he lived in Phillips County, near Helena, on the other side of the state, and 150 miles from Lafayette County or Hempstead. It stretches credulity to think that he would have to travel that far to find a blacksmith to make him a knife. Everything that Garland and Dan Jones said, of course, was purely what Black told them. They knew nothing firsthand.

The Arkansas Territorial Restoration Museum at Little Rock has a photo purporting to be of Black and Jacob Buzzard, each holding pistols and knives. On August 18, 1966, Louise King appended a caption to the photo saying that Black is the man seated on the right and that Buzzard is seated on the left, and that in 1831 Black made a knife for James Bowie. She cites no authority either for the identification of Black himself, or for the dating of the purported forging of the knife. Joseph Musso, "A Bowie Knife," *Alamo Journal* 84 (December 1992): n.p., accepts the photo as genuine, identifies the pistols as 1840 and 1842 models, and cites the Washington, Ark., *Telegraph*, September 7, 1842, as saying that a daguerreotype photographer had recently visited Washington, and that thus the photo was probably made "circa 1842."

This is all wishful thinking, unfortunately. In the first place, while the photograph has not been examined in the original, it bears in reproduction none of the hallmarks of an 1840s daguerreotype, and looks much more like an ambrotype, a

NOTES TO PAGE 340

process not in use until 1855. Furthermore, the clothing on the two men pictured is not that of the 1840s, but that of the mid-1850s and later, and was still being worn well into the 1860s, for that matter. Then there is the problem of Black himself. He was born in 1800, and the 1841 *Telegraph* article about him said that as of that date he had been blind for several years. Those like Garland and Jones, who knew him when he was forty-one, referred to him then as "the old man," the inescapable inference being that he looked older than his years. However, the man identified as Black in the photograph is so fresh-faced and boyish that he can scarcely be more than twenty-four or twenty-five, if that, whereas Black would have to have been at least in his early forties when the photo was made, and more likely in his fifties. And the man in the photo has clear, unclouded eyes quite definitely focused on the camera taking his picture. In short, this is a photograph taken in the 1850s of a young man in his twenties or even late teens, and who apparently had perfectly normal eyesight. No amount of imagination can turn him into James Black. In all probability, the photo really shows two young Arkansans repeating a ritual taking place all over the South when, in 1861, their state seceded and they sat for a warlike pose with knives and guns before going off to war.

In the end, there is no direct contemporary evidence to establish that James Black made a knife for James Bowie, or that he did it in 1830 or 1831, or indeed at any time. The story rests solely on Black's claims made well after he had been adjudged mentally incompetent and, significantly, well after James Bowie had become a cultural hero and the knife whose origin was erroneously associated with him a cultural icon in its own right. Having been a blacksmith, James Black undoubtedly made many knives, and probably many to one of the Bowie patterns. He may even have seen or encountered James or John or one of the two Rezin Bowies. While it is possible that he did in fact fashion a blade for James, it is equally possible that his disoriented mind simply invented the story out of these elements in exactly the same way that the insane and the senile quite often confuse events and place themselves in proximity to the famous in their imaginings.

Nevertheless, on the assumption that it was possible for Black to have encountered James Bowie on one of his few trips through Washington during the Arkansas land fraud days, it seems worthwhile to include such an episode in the text, though no more than in passing. There is no way to date it, however, and placing it here at the end of 1831 simply seems slightly more likely than on other long journeys James is known to have made. And again, so far as the life of *James* Bowie is concerned, who designed or forged *any* knife for him is of monumental unimportance. As stated earlier, the only time he *verifiably* used a knife in a personal encounter was on the Sandbar in 1827, and Rezin gives a perfectly acceptable accounting for that one.

5. This is only supposition, based on the fact that a sea voyage would get him back to Texas much faster than an overland trip from Louisiana, and that in order for Bowie to have an announcement in the January 10, 1832 issue of the Brazoria *Texas Gazette*, he had to be in that town at least a day or two earlier. Brazoria would not be on the normal overland route from Louisiana, but it would be on

the customary route for someone who came by ship to Galveston, and was on the way to San Felipe or San Antonio.

6. Manuel Jiménez to Political Chief, January 17, 1832, Béxar Archives, UT.

7. Bowie to Músquiz, April 23, 1832, Secretary of State, Domestic Correspondence, Record Group 307, TXSL.

8. This involves a lot of surmise, based on the frustratingly brief statement in Nathaniel Cox to Austin, March 22, 1832, Barker, *Austin Papers*, vol. 2, 761, from New Orleans that Carbajal had "failed in making any collection from Mr. Bowie as contemplated." This says nothing about which Bowie, or how much money, or what it was for. Since James had been expecting a large sum from Natchez in 1830 and it did not arrive, and since installment payments from the Walkers and Wilkins on their notes were due each year, it seems probable that this is the money Carbajal hoped to collect. This would also explain James's quick trip to Louisiana in late 1831, in hopes of collecting it himself. Just how Austin was mixed up with money due to Bowie is a mystery.

   By the way, it may be significant that Cox speaks only of one Bowie in Louisiana. This could mean that Stephen was dead by March 1832.

9. Austin to Williams, March 21, 1832, Barker, *Austin Papers*, vol. 2, 759.

10. Ibid. The conclusion that the Austin-Bowie problem in this case was land is based on Austin's later clear break with Bowie over land policy, and on Austin's own concern in March 1832 with his own eleven-league grants.

11. Mary Austin Holley to William Brand, January 6, 1832, Mary Austin Holley Papers, UT.

12. Paul D. Lack, "In the Long Shadow of Eugene C. Barker: The Revolution and the Republic," Robert Calvert and Walter Buenger, eds., *Texas Through Time* (College Station, 1991), 138–39.

13. Ham, "Recollections," UT.

14. Williams, "Critical Study, III," 96n, cites an interview with Francis Gelhorne in the San Antonio *Express*, of May 21, 1905. Unfortunately, this must be a miscitation, because that issue contains no such interview, and so the original has not been examined. Hopewell, *Bowie*, 139n, cites the article in the paper of that date, but obviously never really saw it, since it is not in that issue.

15. John Henry Brown, *Indian Wars and Pioneers of Texas* (Austin, 1896), 137. Hunt gave this recollection around the 1880s, half a century after the fact, placing his encounter with James and Ursula at a party on Christmas Day in 1831 on the Colorado River, presumably at either Bastrop or Columbus. On the basis of this, some have stated that Bowie took Ursula to New Orleans in December 1831, but this is impossible, since he was certainly back in Brazoria by January 9 at the latest, and the mere fifteen days in between would not have been sufficient time for them to get to New Orleans, spend any appreciable time, and then return to Brazoria, even by sea.

16. Last Will and Testament of James Bowie, October 31, 1833, in *Heirs of James Bowie v. Houston & Texas Central Railway* Company, Documents Pertaining to James Bowie, UT.

17. John J. Linn, *Reminiscences of Fifty Years in Texas* (New York, 1883), 302–4.

18. Menchaca, *Memoirs*, 21.

19. Margaret Swett Henson, *Samuel May Williams, Early Texas Entrepreneur* (College Station, 1976), 39.

20. Menchaca, *Memoirs*, 21, is the only source for Austin's summoning Bowie, and gives few other details, but the context and timing suggest that it can only have been in response to these events, and Bowie's appearance at Nacogdoches on August 2 makes it evident that this was the mission Austin had given him.

21. Sibley to Johnston, August 13, 1832, Johnston Papers, HSP.

22. Menchaca, *Memoirs*, 21.

23. Mims, *Trail*, 53, states that Bowie was made "a captain of troops and sent to Nacogdoches to crush a rebellion that was led by Colonel Piedras," whereas, of course, it was Texians rebelling *against* Piedras. This is par for Mims, and again there is no authority for stating that Bowie was a captain or any other rank.

24. No contemporary source is specific about when Bowie arrived, but it is apparent from several that it must have been during the night, since he was present the next day. Brown, *Indian Wars*, 136, does state that he came during the night of August 2, but without indicating on what authority the statement is based.

25. Wooten, *Texas*, vol. 1, 145–46; Niles, *South America*, 262–63; Mirabeau B. Lamar, "Expulsion of Pedres from Nacogdoches," 1832, Charles Adams Gulick, Jr., and Katherine Elliott, eds., *The Papers of Mirabeau Bounaparte Lamar*, vol. 3 (Austin 1923), 269–71.

26. Lamar, "Expulsion of Pedres," 1832, in Gulick and Elliott, *Papers*, vol. 3, 271.

27. Yoakum, *Texas*, vol. 1, 298–99.

28. Sibley to Johnston, August 13, 1832, Johnston Papers, HSP; Wooten, *Texas*, vol. 1, 145–46.

29. Lamar, "Expulsion of Pedres," Gulick and Elliott, *Papers*, vol. 3, 271.

30. Bowie to Austin, August 8, 1832, Barker, *Austin Papers*, vol. 2, 832–33.

31. Receipt, November 16, 1832, Barker, *Austin Papers*, vol. 2, 1142.

32. Bowie to Antonio Etonia, September 17, 1832, Medina to Bowie, September 18, 1832, receipt, September 18, 1832, Béxar Archives, UT.

33. Ham, "Recollections," UT.

34. Austin to David Burnet, January 27, 1833, Jacqueline Beretta Tomerlin, com, *Fugitive Letters, 1829–1836: Stephen F. Austin to David G. Burnet* (San Antonio, 1981), 27.

35. Benjamin Lundy, *The War in Texas* (Philadelphia, 1837), 20.

36. Ibid.; William C. Binkley, *The Texas Revolution* (Baton Rouge, 1952), 8–9.

37. James Bowie power of attorney, December 27, 1832, *Gary Hendershott Catalog no. 87* (September 1995): 3.

38. William Preston Johnston to Rosa Johnston, May 22, 1862, Albert Sidney Johnston and William Preston Johnston Collection, Special Collections, Tulane University, New Orleans.

39. As noted previously, there is absolutely no contemporary or even after-the-fact evidence for any meeting between Houston and Bowie earlier than this. Ham, "Recollections," UT, is the source in this case, and though written fifty years after the fact, its timing and circumstances are perfectly correct, since both Bowie and Houston can be placed in San Felipe in December 1832. Wooten, *Texas*, vol. 1, 152, writing in 1898, also has them meet here and now, basing his statement on Yoakum's 1856 history. The assertion in James, *The Raven*, 90, that the two first met in Helena is almost certainly nonsense, as is Long, *Duel of Eagles*, 31, wherein it is Bowie who actually suggests Texas to Houston as a place to settle in 1829.

40. Ham, "Recollections," UT.

41. Conveyance Book F, 399–400, Conveyance Book G, 144, Terrebonne Parish Courthouse.

42. Ethan A. Brown to Woodbury, September 18, 1835, Volume 2, 235–37, Entry 200, Record Group 49, NA.

43. Conveyance Book G, 42–43, Terrebonne Parish Courthouse.

44. Menchaca, *Memoirs*, 21.

45. Ham, "Recollections," UT.

46. Bowie's mode of dress in Saltillo is assumed from his known taste for fine clothing, and also from the fact that a blue suit was found among his effects in San Antonio after his death.

47. Anonymous letter to "Brothers of My Heart," March 7, 1836, Mexico City *El Mosquito Mexicano*, April 5, 1836.

48. Juan Seguín to W. W. Fontaine, April 10, 1874, Fontaine Papers, UT.

49. Menchaca, *Memoirs*, 21, states that Bowie brought about the shift of capital. This is certainly an exaggeration, but Menchaca is so accurate in so many things, and had been in such a perfect position with the Veramendis and Bowie to be uniquely well informed, that his statement must at least be taken to establish that Bowie exerted a lot of influence.

50. Statement of Archibald Hotchkiss in Speer and Brown, *Encyclopedia*, vol. 1, 436.

51. Niles, *History of South America*, 262–63.

52. Lundy, *War in Texas*, 20.

53. Statement of James Bowie, April 17, 1833, Barker, *Austin Papers*, vol. 2, 951.

54. Statement of Archibald Hotchkiss in Speer and Brown, *Encyclopedia*, vol. 1, 436. The Little Rock *Arkansas Advocate*, June 12, 1835, confirms Hotchkiss's involvement in this trip to negotiate the land deal.

55. Samuel Williams statement, June 5, 1849, Williams Papers, Rosenberg Library; Samuel Williams statement, 1840, *Journal of the House of Representatives of the Republic of Texas*, Fifth Congress, 1840–1841, 369.

56. Miller, *Public Lands*, 17; Elgin Williams, *"The Animating Pursuits of Speculation." Land Traffic in the Annexation of Texas* (New York, 1949), 50–51.

57. Austin to Williams, May 31, 1833, Barker, *Austin Papers*, vol. 2, 984.

58. Johnson, *Texas*, vol. 1, 186; Barker, "Land Speculation," 77.

59. Menchaca, *Memoirs*, 21. This source does not say that Bowie took the money to New Orleans for Veramendi, but since this information is contained in a passage chiefly dealing with Bowie, such can be inferred, especially since Bowie definitely went to Louisiana at this time.

60. Ham, "Recollections," UT.

61. *Sampeyrac and Stewart* v. *United States*, Peters, *Reports of Cases Argued*, 222ff.

62. Brown to Woodbury, September 18, 1835, vol. 2, 235–37, Entry 200, Record Group 49, NA.

63. Moore, "The Bowie Brothers," 201; Notary William Boswell, *R. P. Bowie* v. *His Creditors*, vol. 18, #505, April 27, May 30, 1832, Insolvency Papers for Rezin P. Bowie, January 17, 1834, vol. 26, #69, New Orleans Notarial Archives.

64. Sparks in Ellis, *Crockett*, 219–20, tells the story, previously cited, of Bowie encountering Crain in a New York courtroom.

65. Moore, "The Bowie Brothers," 201; John Hollingsworth to Mrs. S. B. Tamplet, February 26, 1894, James Bowie Biographical File, DRT.

66. It needs to be said that having James Bowie accompany Rezin on this trip is speculation, based on very circumstantial evidence. There is no question that Rezin went, as the article in *Atkinson's Saturday Evening Post* places him in Philadelphia on August 17 and for some days past. William Sparks in his 1879–80 article in Ellis, *Crockett*, says that James and Crain met in New York and Niagara several years after the Sandbar fight, but does not date the event, which he would have heard of from Rezin most likely. Hotchkiss, cited above, stated that he saw Bowie in Washington in 1832, but his recollection, which is quite accurate in general respects, could have been off by a year, for there is nothing to indicate that James visited the East in 1832. And given Rezin's failing vision, it is probable that he needed a companion on the long trip, and with Stephen dead, James would be the most logical choice. On top of all this, James quite definitely disappears from the Texas record by May and does not verifiably appear again until October 31 in Natchez, as will be seen. Thus his five-month disappearance could be explained by his accompanying Rezin.

67. Leonardo de la Garza to Lucy Leigh Bowie, August 17, 1969, Lucy Bowie Papers, DRT, quoting an undated letter of Ursula Bowie. This letter quotes only fragments of Ursula's letter and does not make much sense, nor does it say where the original letter was at that time.

68. Quoted in Walter Lord, *A Time to Stand* (New York, 1961), 28. Lord unfortunately offers no attribution for these quotations, so the veracity of his source cannot be judged. Certainly he did not invent conversation or quotations elsewhere, so it is safe to assume that he did not do so in this instance, but in the absence of a definitive source, it must be said that this quotation by Ursula, however plausible it sounds, may or may not be reliable.

69. Elve Soniat to anonymous, no date but sometime in the 1890s, Lucy Bowie Papers, DRT. As stated in an earlier note, this letter maintains that Bowie gave Ursula the emeralds as a wedding gift. However, since his will, dated October 31, 1833, speaks of jewelry he had recently bought for her and which was with

his sister, it seems more likely that Mrs. Soniat merely confused a family story, and that the emeralds in fact were purchased at this time.

70. Angus McNeil testimony, *Veramendi* v. *Hutchins*, 141, Documents Pertaining to James Bowie, UT.

71. Natchez, *Mississippi Gazette*, August 17, 1833.

72. Last Will and Testament of James Bowie, October 31, 1833, *Heirs of James Bowie* v. *Houston & Texas Central Railway Company*, 38–40, Documents Pertaining to James Bowie, UT.

73. José Navarro to Williams, September 11, 1833, Williams Papers, Rosenberg Library; Menchaca, *Memoirs*, 21.

74. There has long been a debate on whether or not James and Ursula Bowie had children. The earliest known statement to that effect is John Bowie, "The Bowies," 381–82, in which he said in 1852 that they had one child. During the testimony in the long case of *Veramendi* v. *Hutchins*, one deponent stated in 1873 that Ursula died "without children" (p 82–83), but on June 3, 1874, another deponent stated that "James Bowie had lost his wife and child by Cholera" (pp. 108–9). Yet again in testimony taken in March 1879, Menchaca said that Ursula died leaving no children (p. 125). These last two statements, of course, can be read to mean that she had no children who *survived* her, meaning that there might have been a child or children born to the marriage, but which died prior to or coincident with Ursula's death.

William Sparks, in his 1879–80 newspaper article quoted in Ellis, *Crockett*, 231, said that Bowie had one child. Caiaphas Ham, writing circa 1880, maintained that the Bowies had two children "but they both died young" ("Recollections," UT). Lulu Nelson, of unknown origin or authority, but possibly the widow of Rezin's grandson John S. Moore, wrote a letter November 12, 1896, stating that the Bowies had one child (Lucy Bowie Papers, DRT), and Martha Bowie Burns, John's daughter, agreed in a November 6, 1900 affidavit (LaSalle County Deed Records, vol. L, 358–59, copy in Documents Pertaining to James Bowie, UT). In her later article on the Bowies she elaborated on this to state that their child was a girl (James Bowie Biographical File, DRT). Samuel Maverick at some indefinite time stated that the Bowies had two children who died with Ursula, but this can only be hearsay at best, since he did not come to Texas until 1835 (Rena Maverick Green, ed., *Samuel Maverick, Texan: 1803–1870* [San Antonio, 1952]).

Secondary authors have only obfuscated the debate. Amelia Williams, "Critical Study, III," 97n, confused the issue by publishing an imaginative mis-translation of Navarro's September 26, 1833, letter to Williams, making it say that Bowie's "children" died with Ursula, whereas the original says nothing of the kind. Then there is Clifford Hopewell. In his *Bowie*, x, 72, 94, 131–32, he maintains that the Bowies had two children, Maria Josepha Elve, born April 18, 1832, and James Veramendi, born July 18, 1833. His source is the International Genealogical Index of the Family History Center, Church of Jesus Christ of Latter-Day Saints in Salt Lake City, Utah. Unfortunately, Hopewell did not look into the nature of the information furnished him by the Family History Center. The International Genealogical Index is *not* a data base compiled and verified by the church's indefatigable researchers. It is, rather, simply a repository of information that people all over the world send in, and the center makes no attempt to verify what it receives, nor would it be practical for them to do so. In the case of the supposed Bowie children, the information was furnished by Mrs. Diane Deputy of Sandy, Utah, and the form she submitted (Entry 84–103–0314)—and confirmed by a discussion with her in 1996—clearly lists her source for the names and birthdates of the children as Paul I. Wellman, *The Iron Mistress* (New York, 1951)—a novel. She did examine Wellman's papers at the University of Southern California in the hope of finding some genuine documentation on which he based the fictional names and dates, but without success. Moreover, Wellman provides only months and years for the children, and not actual dates (p 335, 349). Where Hopewell came up with the actual dates is a mystery, but in any case it is all nonsense.

In the end this must simply be put down as an issue that cannot be resolved. For all the likelihood that John Bowie would have known if his brother had a child, or that Caiaphas Ham's intimate relations with Bowie would have put him in a position to know if Bowie had two children, or that Sparks might have heard of a child from Rezin, or that Rezin's granddaughter might have learned of one from her mother, there are still some insurmountable problems, the greatest of which is Bowie's will. Given his intense feelings of family loyalty, it seems inconceivable that if he had a child or children, he would make no provision for them in his will, while he did provide for his brother Stephen's orphans. Also, the San Fernando baptismal records in San Antonio show no entries for Bowie children, though as grandchildren of Veramendi they would certainly receive special attention from Father Garza. At the same time, in Monclova, while Ursula's death is recorded along with those of her parents and foster brother, there is no mention of any children. Hopewell speculates that the children might have been born in Monclova instead of San Antonio, and that they might have died and been buried on the road to Monclova in September 1833, thus missing the record books at the beginning and end of their lives. This is at best a feeble rationalization. If they were born in Monclova, then there should be a baptismal or christening record there, which there is not. If they died between San Antonio and Monclova in 1833, they would still appear in the burial records of the latter, for it was only a four-day trip, and a family like the Veramendis would almost certainly have brought the bodies with them for the kind of burial equivalent to their station. Finally there is no record of Ursula ever being in Monclova except in the last days of her life.

Probably the most logical and likely explanation is that Ursula was pregnant, but had not yet given birth, when she died. This would explain the absence of a burial record for the child, and would also explain the statements by John Bowie and others intimate enough with Bowie to have known about him losing one child. After all, John Bowie's is the first record, and it was nineteen years after the fact. That would be more than enough time for a statement by James that his wife had died *carrying* their child, to evolve into a recollection that they had actually *had* a child. The only serious challenge to this theory is the Ham recollection. He is usually very accurate, confusing only chronology at times, and no logical explanation of his claim for two children presents itself.

75. Navarro to Williams, September 26, 1833, Williams Papers, Rosenberg Library, Galveston, Tex.

76. Angus McNeil testimony, *Veramendi* v. *Hutchins*, 140, Documents Pertaining to James Bowie, UT.

77. Smithwick, *Evolution*, 137. Mims, *Trail*, 55, cites a supposed soldier with Bowie in the San Saba fight saying that on their way back to San Antonio a courier brought Bowie the news of Ursula's death. This is, of course, complete fantasy. Ursula died almost two years after the San Saba fight, and there is no question that Bowie was in Natchez when he got the news. As for the Smithwick account, while Smithwick is always subject to question, there is nothing to disprove his encounter with Bowie. Smithwick was living in western Louisiana at this time, and Bowie could well have met him on his return to Texas.

Chapter 15   Travis 1833–1834

1. Davis, *Travis Diary*, 8, September 6–7; 11, September 13; 87, December 9, 1833.

2. Sr. Gonzales to Secretary of War, April 11, 1833, Ex XI/481.3/817, Archivo Historico Militar Mexicano, Defensa, Mexico City.

3. Travis to O. H. Allen, July 15, 1831, Lamar Papers, TXSL.

4. Davis, *Travis Diary*, 10, September 12; 43, October 6; 44, October 6; 87, December 7; 87, December 8; 88, December 11, 1833.

5. Ibid., 106, January 13, 1834.

6. Ibid., 107, January 16; 124, February 5, 9; 129, February 19; 152, April 5, 1834.

7. Travis and Williamson to the Governor of Coahuila y Texas, February 6, 1834, John Henry Brown, *Texas*, vol. 1, 319.

8. Davis, *Travis Diary*, 124–25, February 7, 1834.

9. Ibid., 159, April 28, 1834.

10. Ibid., 159, April 28.

11. Travis to Músquiz, May 13, 1834, in Mixon, "Travis," 329.

12. Travis to David Burnet, May 14, 1834, *Philpott Collection Catalog*, item no. 206.

13. Address to Ayuntamiento, and Memorial to General Congress of Mexico, April 28, 1834, Béxar Archives, UT.

14. Williamson to the *Ayuntamiento* of Béxar, July 14, 1834, Nacogdoches Archives, TXSL.

15. Travis to David Burnet, May 14, 1834, *Philpott Collection Catalog*, item no. 206.

16. Davis, *Travis Diary*, 174, May 30; 179, June 1, 1834, Williamson document, June 2, 1834, Williamson to Músquiz, June 11, 1834, Béxar Archives, UT; Travis to Burnet, June 3, 1834, *Philpott Collection Catalog*, item no. 207.

17. Travis to Williamson, July 14, 1834, Williamson to *Ayuntamiento* at Béxar, July 14, 1834, Williamson to Travis, July 14, 1834, Nacogdoches Archives, TXSL; Travis to Músquiz, July 3, 8, 9, 24, 1834, Béxar Archives, UT.

18. Travis to Henry Smith, July 24, 1834, in John Henry Brown, *Life and Times of Henry Smith* (Dallas, 1887), 24–26.

19. Travis to James Perry, August 11, 1834, Barker, *Austin Papers*, vol. 2, 1075.

20. Brown, *Smith*, 31–33.

21. Williamson to Smith, September 11, 1834, in Brown, *Smith*, 26–27.

22. Travis to Burnet, September 12, 1834, *Philpott Collection Catalog*, item no. 208.

23. Travis to Smith, October 11, 1834, in Brown, *Smith*, 27–28.

24. Brazoria *Texas Republican*, October 25, 1834.

25. Travis to Smith, October 25, 1834, Thomas W. Streeter Collection of Texas Manuscripts, Beinecke Rare Book and Manuscript Library, Yale University, New Haven, Conn.

26. It has been common with Travis students to assume that he disliked Mexicans. Turner, *Travis*, 34, says without supporting the contention that Travis felt "a consuming animosity for Mexicans in general." McDonald, *Travis*, does not really address the issue, but Amelia Williams asserts in "Critical Study, III," 82, that "Travis distrusted and despised all Mexicans." This, too, is said without supporting evidence, and one does not have to read much of Williams' correspondence before coming to the conclusion that she was, in fact, projecting her own prejudice onto Travis. As revealed hereafter, her discussion of the testimony of Travis's slave Joe displays a similar attitude toward blacks.

27. Johnson, *Texas*, vol. 1, 181–82.

28. Travis to Smith, November 1, 1834, in Brown, *Smith*, 50–51.

29. Eugene C. Barker, *The Life of Stephen F. Austin, Founder of Texas 1793–1836* (Austin, 1949), 468–69.

30. Travis to Smith, November 13, 1834, in Brown, *Smith*, 56–57.

31. Davis, *Travis Diary*, 125–28, February 11–14; 168, May 5; 173, May 21, 1834.

32. Linn, *Reminiscences*, 103.

33. Davis, *Travis Diary*, 127, February 14; 168, May 6; 184, June 19, 1834.

34. H. C. Hudson Statement, November 7, 1837, James H. Starr Collection, UT.

35. Davis, *Travis Diary*, 167, May 1–2;, 169, May ;7, 171, May 16; 174, May 29, 1834.

36. Thomas McQueen letter, March 13, 1834, St. Martinville, *Attakapas Gazette*, May 10, 1834; Jonathan H. Kuykendall, "A Short Review of My Life," Bancroft Library, University of California, Berkeley. This memoir is written as a long letter to Dr. A. B. Castle of Lexington, Kentucky, and dated December 1, 1849. Internal evidence suggests that he recalled being only sixteen when he studied under Travis, but that is probably a false memory. A typescript of the Kuykendall memoir is in the Kuykendall Family Papers, UT.

37. Davis, *Travis Diary*, 169, May 7, 1834.

38. Kuykendall, "Short Review," Bancroft Library; Davis, *Travis Diary*, 171, May 15; 180, June 6; 181, June 8; 184, June 18, 1834.

39. Davis, *Travis Diary*, 170, May 12, 1834; Kuykendall, "Short Review," Bancroft Library; Kuykendall to A. Somerville, April 16, 1841, Kuykendall Family Papers, UT.

40. Kuykendall, "Sketches of Early Texians," Kuykendall Family Papers, UT.

41. Davis, *Travis Diary*, 112, January 30; 130, February 22, 137, March 1, 151, April 3, 180, June 4, 1834; bill of sale, November 10, 1834, *Philpott Collection Catalog*, item no. 210, Travis to Burnet, December 19, 1834; Travis to Perry, August 11, 1834, Barker, *Austin Papers*, vol. 2, 1075; Travis to Isaac Morehead, July 7, 1834, Mixon, "Travis," 66n; Gaspar Flores to Williams, June 19, 1834, Williams Papers, Rosenberg Library, Galveston, Tex.

42. Harris, "Reminiscences, I," 100–2, 115. Harris only identified the protagonists as "Mr. A." and Mr. M." but Davis, *Travis Diary*, 182, June 11, 1834, pretty certainly confirms that Alley and May were the men involved.

43. Brazoria *Extra*, March 27, 1834; William Harris to Travis, April 16, May 18, 1834; Robert Wilson to William Harris, May 8, 1834, Franklin Papers, UT; Brazoria *Texas Republican*, November 8, 1834.

44. Kuykendall, Sketches of Early Texians, Kuykendall Family Papers, UT.

45. Mixon, "Travis," 64.

46. Davis, *Travis Diary*, 50, October 20, 89, December 14, 1833.

47. Ibid., 156–57, April 17; 168, May 6; 184, June 19, 1834.

48. Kuykendall, Sketches of Early Texians, Kuykendall Family Papers, UT.

49. B. J. Fletcher to I. C. Main, May 15, 1907, quoted in Davis, *Travis Diary*, 24n. Being a secondhand account by Roddy's grandson, written more than sixty years after the fact, this story may be inaccurate or embellished, especially since it portrays Travis genuinely threatening to resort to violence by pulling out his knife in a courtroom, which is decidedly out of character. On the other hand, given Travis's temperament, if he had reached that stage of blind anger, it would also have been uncharacteristic of him to cool down almost instantly, as the story says he did. Travis's own statement of pride in his diary when he said, "I whipped old Roddy" certainly shows some degree of rivalry, though, hence it has seemed reasonable to include a somewhat less heated version of the affair in the text (Davis, *Travis Diary*, 71, November 14, 1833).

50. Potter, "Fall of the Alamo," 18.

51. Kuykendall, Sketches of Early Texians, Kuykendall Family Papers, UT.

52. Davis, *Travis Diary*, 172, May 20; p 182–83, June 13, 17, 1834; Harris, "Reminiscences, I," 104.

53. Brazoria *Texas Republican,* October 25, 1834.

54. Davis, *Travis Diary*, 168, May 3, 1834.

55. Davis, *Travis Diary*, 167, May 1; 174, May 28; 180, June 6; 182, June 10, 1834.

56. Whiteside to Anthony Butler, August 2, 1832, Barker, *Austin Papers*, vol. 2, 830; Kuykendall to Isaac M. Pennington, April 23, 1838, William B. Travis Biographical File, DRT.

57. Davis, *Travis Diary*, 179, June 2, 1834.

58. Ibid., 112, January 29; 131, February 27; 137, March 2; 138, March 4, 6; 139, March 8; 142, March 20; 158, April 25; 172, May 18, 1834.

59. Ibid., 107, January 17; 109, January 23; 127, February 13; 182, June 11, 1834;

Instrument of sale, April 16, 1834, William B. Travis Legal Documents, DRT;
Statement of William B. Travis, November 15, 1834, Streeter Collection, Yale;
Travis to Burnet, February 1834, quoted in David Drake, "'Joe', Alamo Hero,"
Negro History Bulletin 44 (April-June 1981): 34.

60. Davis, *Travis Diary*, 129, February 19, 1834.

61. Brazoria *Courier,* June 9, 1840; Houston *Telegraph and Texas Register,* March 21,
1837; Davis, *Travis Diary*, 152, April 6, 160, April 30, 183, June 16, 185, June 23,
1834; Malcolm D. McLean, "Tenoxtitlan, Dream Capital of Texas," *Southwestern
Historical Quarterly* 70 (July 1966): 34.

62. Figures calculated from Davis, *Travis Diary*, entries for January-June 1834.

63. Paulding, *Westward Ho!*, vol. 2, 181.

64. Davis, *Travis Diary*, 103, January 3; p 104–5, January 9, 11; 125, February 8; 129,
February 20; 180, June 6, 1834.

65. Harris, "Reminiscences, I," 102, 110; Davis, *Travis Diary*, 129, February 21; 144,
March 26, 1834.

66. Brazoria *Texas Gazette,* February 18, 1832; Gray, *From Virginia to Texas*, 110.

67. Davis, *Travis Diary*, 93, December 27, 1833; 128, February 16; 139, March 9,
1834.

68. Ibid., 140, March 12; p 142–43, March 21, March 20; 151, April 1; 154, April 11;
157, April 19, 1834. Travis's gambling habits are compiled from this source for
the months of March-June, 1834.

69. Ibid., 129, February 21; 144, March 26; 174, May 31; p 184–85, June 20–21; 186,
June 25, 1834; Amelia Williams to Asbury, March 15, 1932, Asbury Papers, UT.
The assumption has been common in recent years that Travis had picked up a
venereal disease from one of the women with whom he slept. This derives
entirely from the March 28, 1834, entry in his diary (Davis, *Travis Diary*, 145) that
states, with no explanatory context: "Venerao mala." The editor has translated
this as "Venereal (disease) bad." There are several references to Travis buying
vials of medicine, including mercury, in the diary, and these are taken as evidence
that he was dosing himself for the unspecified disease. It is entirely possible that
Travis did contract a venereal disease. However, it must be pointed out that "venerao mala" could mean something else entirely. Certainly it is incorrect Spanish.
It could also be a flawed transcription from the original, as there are many such
errors in the Davis edition of the Travis diary. Travis could have been writing
"veneno malo," for instance, which in his imperfect Spanish might refer to food
poisoning. Or, as Steve Hardin has pointed out, the "venerao" could in fact be a
reference to the goddess Venus, a classical allusion to romantic problems, and
certainly his next diary reference to Rebecca Cummings on April 1 says that he
met a "cold reception" from her. The phrase's being in Spanish definitely makes it
a reference to something in his love life, as those were the only occasions in
which he used Spanish. And again, it is certainly possible that he *did* mean venereal disease, but to conclude that on the basis of this single reference would be—
no pun intended—rash. The example does point up the need for an entirely new,
more accurate, better edited and indexed edition of the diary.

70. Davis, *Travis Diary*, 105, January 9; 10, 108, January 18; 112, January 29; 125, February 10; 127, February 14; 130, February 25; 137, March 2; 142, March 20; 143, March 24; 152, April 5; 168, May 5; 184, June 19, 1834. On March 20 Travis said of Rebecca Cummings that "I showed a letter to her about the conduct of my former wife." He gives no indication of what that conduct may have been. It could have dealt with the failure to hand over Charles, it could have been about her posited—but completely unsupported—romance with Cloud, whom she would marry immediately after her divorce. It may even have related to behavior of hers that led to, or helped lead to, the original breakup in the spring of 1831.

71. Rosanna Travis to Dellet, September 6, 1834, Dellet Papers, ADAH.

72. Parker, *Trip to the West*, 158–59; F. J. Starr Memo Book, November 30, 1834, Starr Papers, UT.

Chapter 16   Crockett 1834–1836

1. Crockett to Hack, June 9, 1834, Miscellaneous Collection, Tennessee Historical Society, TSL.

2. Shackford, *Crockett*, 308n, cites an autograph book of Octavia Walton signed by both Houston and Crockett, the latter on April 23, 1834, with information from an autograph dealer's catalog in April 1936 indicating that the book established that the two visited her together. Crockett's inscription no longer rests in the album but most recently appeared in the *Philpott Collection Catalog* as item no. 226.

3. Crockett to Carey and Hart, May 27, 1834, Carl H. Pforzheimer Collection, New York Public Library, N.Y.

4. Chapman in Galveston *Daily News*, January 27, 1895.

5. Helen Chapman to Emily Blair, May 1, 1834, William W. Chapman Papers, UT.

6. Arpad, "Crockett," 40.

7. Shackford, *Crockett*, 157–60 gives a basic capsule account of the tour.

8. Chapman in Galveston *Daily News*, January 27, 1895.

9. On May 17, just a few days after returning to Washington, he proposed an amendment to an appropriation bill to provide funds for improving navigation on the Forked Deer, Hatchie, and Obion Rivers, all in his district. It was one of those days when he could not make himself stay in his seat, and he went home for his dinner, only to discover that his amendment came up in his absence and was tabled. Thus he was in no mood to support anyone else's appropriations bills, especially one from Polk, and two days later when his old nemesis offered such a bill, Crockett rose to suggest that the House henceforth table all such legislation, arguing that it was useless for the them to pass these measures. "A majority of this House has determined, by their votes, that Andrew Jackson shall be the Government," he ranted. The only "honest face" he had seen in Jackson's government, he said, was Secretary of State Louis McLane, and he was resigning,

thought Crockett, because he could not stand his colleagues any longer. "Let us all go home," he declared. Maybe the outcry from the people would bring congressmen to their senses and return them to Washington "to make the gentleman in the white house take down his flag." The people would let him know that they wanted no autocrat. When a fellow Tennessee delegate answered, charging Crockett with sour grapes because his own amendment had failed, David only responded the more vehemently. They had no government now, he said. Only the Almighty could save the country from Jackson and tyranny.

10. The previous fall Jackson fired Treasury Secretary William Duane for refusing to remove the deposits, and replaced him with Roger B. Taney, who happily did the president's bidding. That so enraged the largely Whig Senate that Jackson did not dare submit Taney's name for confirmation, knowing it would be rejected. By June, with the end of the session approaching, he still had not done so, and on the floor of the House Crockett attacked Old Hickory vigorously for the delay.

11. Shackford, *Crockett*, 164–67.

12. Crockett to Hack, June 15, 1834, in Davis, *Memphis*, 155.

13. Crockett to Carey and Hart, May 27, 1834, Pforzheimer Collection, New York Public Library, N.Y.

14. Crockett to Wallis, May 26, 1834, Crockett Papers, UT.

15. Crockett to J. M. Sanderson, June 25 [or perhaps 15], 1834, Frederick Dreer Collection, HSP.

16. St. Martinville *Attakapas Gazette,* June 12, 1834; Cooper, "Crockett Firearms," 66.

17. Shackford, *Crockett*, 167–68, 309–10.

18. Gary S. Zaboly, "Davy Crockett: New Eyewitness Description—and More," *Alamo Journal* 105 (June 1997): 10; Philadelphia *Public Ledger*, April 5, 1836.

19. Folmsbee, "West Tennessee," 20.

20. St. Martinville *Attakapas Gazette,* July 5, 1834.

21. Crockett to Hack, June 9, 1834, Miscellaneous Collection, Tennessee Historical Society, TSL.

22. Shackford, *Crockett*, 169–71; Crockett to Carey and Hart, December 8, 1834, Autograph File, Houghton Library, Harvard University, Cambridge, Mass.

23. Crockett to Carey and Hart, Autograph Files, Harvard.

24. Crockett to Carey and Hart, December 21, 1834, Rosenbach Museum & Library, Philadelphia.

25. Crockett to Charles Schultz, December 25, 1834, Gilder-Lehrman Collection, Pierpont Morgan Library, New York; Crockett to Carey and Hart, December 24, 1834, *American Book Prices Current, 1993* 99 (Washington, Conn., 1994), 49. This document was originally in the Slack Collection at Marietta College, Marietta, Ohio, but the library sold it in 1993, and no text appears in either Shackford's dissertation or *Crockett*.

26. Crockett to Carey and Hart, January 1, 1835, "Documents of the Texian Revolution," *Alamo Journal* 97 (July 1995): 17.

27. Crockett to Carey and Hart, January 8, 1835, Crockett Vertical File, Maryland Historical Society; Crockett to Carey and Hart, January 12, 1835, Miscellaneous Personal Collection, New-York Historical Society.

28. Crockett to Carey and Hart, January 12, 1835, Miscellaneous Personal Collection, New-York Historical Society. Crockett's suggestion as to the credit of authorship offers further evidence that the writing in the *Narrative* was indeed mainly his own. Seemingly it offended his sense of honesty to present himself to the public in a false guise.

29. Crockett to Carey and Hart, January 22, 1835, Rosenbach Museum & Library, Philadelphia.

30. Crockett to Carey and Hart, April 11, 1835, Charles Roberts Autograph Collection, Haverford College Library, Haverford, Pa.

31. Crockett to Carey and Hart, January 16, 1835, in Shackford, *Crockett*, 186–87.

32. Crockett to Carey and Hart, January 22, 1835, Rosenbach Museum & Library, Philadelphia.

33. Shackford, *Crockett*, 189–93; Folmsbee, "West Tennessee," 21–22; Crockett to John R. Ash, December 27, 1834, University of the South Archives, Sewanee, Tenn. On December 9 he tried to get it on the calendar for the next day, without success. Still he predicted to a constituent that he would pass the measure this session. "I have no fears of passage," he said. "If so it will bless many a poor man with a home." He tried again in January, to no avail, and yet again early in February, with only a month of the session remaining. His frustration showed as he complained that all the long partisan speeches only delayed addressing the pile of bills sitting on the table, one of them his own. He accused the House of being "a better place to manufacture orators than to dispatch business," and continued fighting unsuccessfully, encouraged only by the fact that in his annual message Jackson had reiterated his own favorable position on settling public lands back on the states for sale to the poor. Crockett's sense of the ironic even returned briefly, when he suggested that he "began to think the President was almost turning a Crockett man." But still no action came on the land bill, not even the last time Crockett took the floor this session on February 20, 1835. Someone else actually made the motion to take up the bill, and when David stood to make a few remarks, others in the House simply beat him into sitting down with their objections. Moreover, in the votes on his several motions, many of the Whigs who had stood by him in the previous session reversed their positions. The same fate befell his attempt to revive his improvement measure for the rivers in his district.

34. The United States stood on the verge of a crisis with France for more than a year thanks to French repudiation of a substantial debt, and Jackson had threatened to commission privateers to take French shipping in reprisal. The crisis cooled short of war, but by the time this session of Congress opened, there were genuine fears in some quarters, fears shared by Crockett. "The western & southern men dare not sustain Jackson in his mad carear," he said, predicting that when they refused to back him, Old Hickory would loose on them "all the Blood hounds in the nation." To take advantage of the situation, Crockett began work in January on an essay proposing that he would himself go to France and

meet with the head of state and King William IV of England, to mediate a solution, the intent being to put the essay in the William Clark compilation (Crockett to Schultz, December 25, 1834, Gilder-Lehrman Collection, Pierpont Morgan Library, New York; Crockett to Carey and Hart, January 22, 1834, Rosenbach Museum & Library, Philadelphia).

35. Crockett to Dobings, May 27, 1834, U.S. Manuscripts, Lilly Library, Indiana University, Bloomington.

36. Crockett to Schultz, December 25, 1834, Gilder-Lehrman Collection, Pierpont Morgan Library, New York.

37. Crockett to Ash, December 27, 1834, University of the South.

38. Crockett to R. R. Waldron, February 2, 1835, *American Book Prices Current Index, 1965–1970*, 2226. Sadly, this letter has not been found, and only the catalog description indicates that it comments on the assassination attempt.

39. Swisher, *Swisher Memoirs*, 21.

40. Crockett to Biddle, December 8, 1834, Gratz Collection, HSP.

41. Crockett to Carey and Hart, January 8, 1835, Crockett Vertical File, Maryland Historical Society, says that as of that date he is writing "an answer to Bentons letter," and his subsequently published letter enclosing his parody 1833 letter to the convention is itself headed January 1, 1834, lending support to the idea that Crockett definitely took at least some role in writing the series of letters.

42. Shackford, *Crockett*, 179–83.

43. Crockett to Ash, December 27, 1834, University of the South.

44. Quoted in Shackford, *Crockett*, 179.

45. Crockett to Carey and Hart, January 1, 1835, *Alamo Journal* 97, 17.

46. Crockett to Ash, December 27, 1835, University of the South.

47. Huntsman to Polk, January 1, 1835, Herbert Weaver and Kermit L. Hall, eds., *Correspondence of James K. Polk*, vol. 3, *1835–1836* (Nashville, 1975), 3.

48. Jackson to Alfred Balch, February 16, 1835, 21, Jackson to Polk, May 12, 1835, 190–92, Weaver and Hall, *Correspondence of James K. Polk*, vol. 3.

49. Chapman in Galveston *Daily News*, January 27, 1895.

50. New York *Sunday Morning News*, May 1, 1836.

51. W. Eugene Hollon and Ruth Lapham Butler, eds., *William Bollaert's Texas* (Norman, Okla., 1956), 168.

52. Crockett to Carey and Hart, April 11, 1835, Roberts Autograph Collection, Haverford College Library, Haverford, Pa.

53. Shackford, *Crockett*, 186–88.

54. Ibid., 200–2.

55. Crockett to Carey and Hart, April 11, 1835, Roberts Autograph Collection, Haverford.

56. Crockett to Henderson, March 10, 1834, in Shackford, *Crockett*, 151.

57. Ephraim Dickson to Polk, May 7, 1835, Weaver and Hall, *Correspondence of James K. Polk*, vol. 3, 187.

58. Crockett to Carey and Hart, July 8, 1835, in Shackford, *Crockett*, 204. This is a reconstruction by Shackford of a letter Crockett almost certainly wrote at this date, and that could only have been addressed to his publishers.

59. Davis, *Memphis*, 151–52. Davis tells the story as if it took place in 1833, but misdates the tale. Keating, *Memphis*, vol. 1, 180 questions the story without saying why.

60. Crockett to the Truth Teller, July 20, 1835, Gilder-Lehrman Collection, Pierpont Morgan Library, New York.

61. Crockett to Carey and Hart, August 11, 1835, Crockett Vertical File, Maryland Historical Society.

62. New York *Sunday Morning News*, May 1, 1836.

63. Little Rock *Arkansas Advocate,* August 28, 1835.

64. Swisher, *Swisher Memoirs,* 21–22.

65. "Brazos," *Life of Robert Hall* (Austin, 1992), 15. It has been commonly assumed that the subject Hall was himself "Brazos," but the introduction by Stephen L. Hardin rather effectively demolishes this contention. For one thing, the 1850 Texas census establishes that Robert Hall was born in 1811 in Arkansas, and thus would have been about twenty-four, well above legal voting age, in 1835, and not likely to be voting in Tennessee anyhow.

66. Joel R. Smith to Polk, August 9, 1835, William Armour to Polk, September 7, 1835, Weaver and Hall, *Correspondence of James K. Polk,* vol. 3, 261, 286.

67. Little Rock *Arkansas Advocate,* August 25, 1835.

68. Crockett to Carey and Hart, August 11, 1835, Crockett Vertical File, Maryland Historical Society.

69. Folmsbee, "West Tennessee," 23–24.

70. Crockett to Committee of Invitation, September 30, 1835, in *R.M. Smythe Winter Autograph Auction* 175, February 26, 1998, item #380.

71. New York *Sunday Morning News*, December 6, 1835.

72. Keating, *Memphis*, vol. 1, 180.

73. New York *Sunday Morning News*, May 1, 1836.

74. Drake to the Editor of the *News*, October 17, 1877, Crockett Biographical File, DRT; "Brazos," *Robert Hall*, 19. There are numerous examples of Crockett's "go to hell" aphorism, but it is uncertain when he first used it, and whether he actually said it during the campaign—which would seem unwise—or only coined it afterward.

75. Crockett to George Patton, October 31, 1835, in Shackford, *Crockett*, 210.

76. Robert Crockett to Smith Rudd, December 30, 1879, Rudd Manuscripts, Lilly Library, Indiana University, Bloomington.

77. Margaret Crockett statement in Gary L. Foreman, *Crockett: The Gentleman from the Cane* (Dallas, 1986), 41; Stephen L. Hardin, "David Crockett," *Military Illustrated* 23 (February-March 1990): 32.

78. Robert Crockett to Rudd, June 15, 1880, Lilly Library, Indiana University, Bloomington.

79. Atlas Jones to Calvin Jones, November 13, 1835, Jones Papers, SHC, UNC.

80. Jones to Edmund D. Jarvis, December 2, 1835, ibid.

81. Davis, *Memphis*, 140–41.

82. New York *Transcript*, November 28, 1835, quoting the Jackson *Truth Teller*, November 13, 1835.

83. Ibid., 139–40. It has been commonly assumed that Crockett took a steamboat from Memphis down the Mississippi, then up the Arkansas River to Little Rock. See for instance Shackford, *Crockett*, 212; Stanley Folmsbee and Anna Grace Catron, "David Crockett in Texas," *East Tennessee Historical Society Publications* 30(1958): 50; and Hutton introduction in Crockett, *Narrative*, Lincoln, Nebraska edition, xxvii. This is quite incorrect, and probably derives from a misreading of the account in Davis, *Memphis*, cited here. William T. Avery, whose account Davis published, quite clearly says that they boarded a ferry to *cross the river*, moreover making the point that there was no *steam ferry* across the Mississippi at that time. Obviously Crockett was *crossing* the river, not going down it. This is further supported by simple common sense. If he were taking a steamboat downstream, there would be no need of the flatboat ferry at all, since the steamboats tied up at the foot of the bluff beneath Memphis, where they still do today. He would simply have walked down to the bluff and aboard a boat. Another source for this misconception is the spurious *Col. Crockett's Exploits and Adventures in Texas*, published after his death. In it he states that he took a steamboat down the Mississippi from Mill's Point (see the version published as *Davy Crockett's Own Story* [New York, 1955], 243). However, Crockett's son Robert repudiated that statement in his June 15, 1880, letter to Smith Rudd (Rudd Manuscripts, Lilly Library, Indiana University, Bloomington). In addition—as if more evidence were necessary—sources cited below establish that Crockett arrived in Arkansas broke, and on horseback, and with game he had recently killed. One did not shoot game from a steamboat and then expect the captain to pull ashore to collect the kill, especially going upstream. Besides, the one-hundred-mile distance overland from Memphis to Little Rock was only a good two days, and no slower—and probably slightly faster—than the route by water, since it required one hundred miles down the Mississippi, then a wait for an Arkansas River packet that might not be along for hours, even days, for the slower one-hundred-mile trip up to Little Rock.

84. Little Rock *Arkansas Advocate*, November 13, 1835.

85. Pope, *Early Days in Arkansas*, 183–84.

86. Little Rock *Arkansas Gazette*, November 17, 1835.

87. New York *Sun*, January 29, 1836.

88. Ibid., January 12, 1836.

89. Little Rock *Arkansas Advocate*, November 13, 20, 1835; Baltimore, *Nile's Weekly Register* 54, December 5, 1835, 225.

90. Pope, *Early Days in Arkansas*, 185.

91. New York *Sun*, January 12, 1836.

92. Monroe, La., *Ouachita Telegraph*, August 25, 1888.

93. *Biographical and Historical Memoirs of Northwest Louisiana* (Chicago, 1890), 309, states that Crockett and his party passed through Natchitoches, Louisiana, but this is hardly possible, since it would have been far out of their way and off the known path they took. It also lists a "Matthew Despallie" as being with them, a "villanous bully" from Alexandria connected with the Wells family. This must be a muddled reference to Martin, whose kinsmen—probably his brothers—Charles and Blaz Despallier had already come to Texas. Charles would die at the Alamo. J. Fair Hardin, *Northwestern Louisiana, A History*, vol. 1 (Louisville, n.d.), 137, also says that Crockett went from Little Rock to Fulton, Arkansas, then sold his horses and took a boat down the Red River to Natchitoches, where he bought more horses and continued overland into Texas. No source is given for this, and the route is completely incomprehensible, adding hundreds of miles to Crockett's verifiable journey for no apparent reason. There is no evidence for him setting foot in Louisiana at all. An article in the St. Louis *Globe-Democrat* in 1909 made the claim upon which the Hardin account is probably based, and that article in turn probably derives from the fictional account in *Col. Crockett's Exploits and Adventures*, as found, for instance, in *Davy Crockett's Own Story*, 263ff.

94. Little Rock *Arkansas Advocate*, January 1, 1836; Little Rock *Arkansas Gazette*, November 17, 1835.

95. Isaac Jones to Elizabeth Crockett, [April] 1836, in Baltimore, *Nile's Weekly Register* 50, August 27, 1836, 432–33; Pope, *Early Days in Arkansas*, 184; Dallas *Morning News*, October 22, 1933. Jones headed his letter Lost Prairie "Ark's," suggesting that he certainly thought he lived in Arkansas. However, Albert Pike, in a series of articles in the Little Rock *Arkansas Advocate*, in the fall of 1835, clearly placed Lost Prairie *south* of the Red River, and thus in country claimed by both Arkansas and Texas. Thus Pike's location does not really conflict with Jones's, establishing that this must be where Crockett first crossed into what became Texas.

96. Statement of —— Clark, May 21, 1920, James Clark Family Papers, UT.

97. Little Rock *Arkansas Gazette*, May 10, 1836. It should be noted that this was a Jacksonian newspaper, so it is possible that it exaggerated or even invented Crockett's comment.

98. Crockett to Wiley and Margaret Flowers, January 9, 1836, copy in Samuel Asbury Papers, UT.

99. Bangor, Me., *Advertiser*, March 19, 1836; New York *Morning Courier and New York Enquirer*, February 27, 1836; Little Rock *Arkansas Advocate*, February 19, 1836; Jenkins, *General's Tight Pants* [7].
    It should be noted here that the author is indebted to Thomas R. Lindley for his very thoughtful itinerary of Crockett's trip through Texas. It is based on the same sources used by the author, but has been very helpful in some of its insights and interpolations when it comes to filling the documentary gap.

100. Undated clipping, probably from Dallas *Herald*, provided by Thomas R. Lindley; Henry McCulloch to Henry McArdle, January 14, 1891, Henry McArdle San Jacinto Notebook, TXSL.

101. Crockett's speech appears in substantially the same version in a number of contemporary newspapers, the earliest being perhaps the Augusta, Me., *Age,* April 27, 1836. The version in the text is taken from the Little Rock *Arkansas Gazette,* May 10, 1836. Peter Harper statement, February 9, 1837, Peter Harper File, Audited Military Claims, Record Group 5926, TXSL, definitely places Crockett in Nacogdoches by January 8.

102. Crockett to the Flowers, January 9, 1836, Asbury Papers, UT.

103. Galveston *Daily News,* January 9, 1898.

104. *Morning Courier and New York Enquirer,* March 26, 1836.

105. James Gaines to John W. Robinson, January 9, 1836, John H. Jenkins, ed., *The Papers of the Texas Revolution, 1835–1836,* vol. 3 (Austin, 1973), 455 (Jenkins, *PTR*).

106. Crockett to the Flowers, January 9, 1836, Asbury Papers, UT. This letter has caused a bit of confusion in the Crockett chronology in Texas because in it he states under date of January 9 from San Augustine that "I have taken the oath of the Government and have enrolled my name as a volunteer for six months." However, as cited below, official records show him taking the oath in Nacogdoches on January 12, and actually apparently signing enlistment papers two days later. This has led some to conclude that Crockett enlisted twice, once on January 8 in either Nacogdoches or San Augustine, and again on the latter dates.

A more likely scenario involves the letter itself. Dated January 9 in San Augustine, the entire first half of it deals with his trip to date, and chiefly his land explorations. He then abruptly says that he has enlisted in the volunteers and will leave "in a few days" for the Rio Grande. In fact he did not leave Nacogdoches to join gathering forces to the south for a full week. Then he discussed his confidence in being elected to the convention, and follows with a virtual restatement of the announcement made to the San Augustine fathers, "I had rather be in my present position than to be elected to a seat in Congress for Life." What has likely happened is that Crockett *started* the letter in San Augustine on January 9, but then stopped after finishing the portion covering the land he liked. He then put the letter aside and did not take it up again until January 12 or 14 in Nacogdoches, after his enlistment, by which time it truly would be "a few days" to his January 16 departure south. Thus he enlisted only once, not twice.

107. Columbia *Telegraph and Texas Register,* April 28, 1838; John Forbes to Robinson, January 12, 1836, Gulick and Elliott, *Papers of Lamar,* vol. 1, 296.

Confusion also exists over the date of Crockett's enlistment. In his January 12 letter Forbes speaks in the past tense of having given Crockett the oath, presumably that day. However, in Jenkins, *PTR,* vol. 4, 13, there is the actual statement of enlistments with the oath, and Crockett's name is nineteenth in order of signing, dated January 14, at the *end* of the list. The most logical explanation is that Forbes kept the list open and undated. Crockett signed on January 12, but more men followed in the ensuing two days, and Forbes only completed and signed and *dated* the list on January 14 when he had enrolled all the volunteers then available. This is supported by Micajah Autry to Martha Autry, January 13, 1836,

Jenkins, *PTR*, vol. 3, 504, in which he states that "Col Crockett has just joined our company," a statement made the day *before* the January 14 enlistment list.

108. Swisher, *Swisher Memoirs*, 22.

109. New York *Sun*, May 10, 1836; New York *Sunday Morning News*, March 27, 1836.

110. Statement of enlistments, January 14, 1836, Jenkins, *PTR*, vol. 4, 13; Amelia Williams, "A Critical Study of the Siege of the Alamo and of the Personnel of its Defenders, Chapter IV," *Southwestern Historical Quarterly* 37 (January 1934): 167.

111. Micajah Autry to Martha Autry, January 13, 1836, in Jenkins, *PTR*, vol. 3, 504; Statement, February 9, 1837, Peter Harper File, Audited Military Claims, TXSL.

112. Affidavit, January 15, 1836, "schedule of articles belonging to Colonel Crockett," January 15, 1836, David Crockett File, Audited Military Claims, TXSL.

113. A. McLaughlin to Committee of Safety, January 18, 1836, Jenkins, *PTR*, vol. 4, 66.

114. Daniel Cloud to a friend, January 1836, Jackson *Mississippian,* May 6, 1836.

115. Crockett to the Flowers, January 9, 1836, Asbury Papers, UT.

Chapter 17   Bowie 1833–1835

1. *Veramendi* v. *Hutchins*, 88–89, Documents Pertaining to James Bowie, UT; Notary Felix De Armas, Sale of Slave, February 21, 1834. James Bowie to Anatole Cousin, vol. 41, item #70, New Orleans Notarial Archives, establishes that Bowie was in New Orleans as late as February 21, probably selling the slave for money for the return to Texas, meaning he could not have reached San Antonio before early March at best.

2. Testimony of Menchaca, 1879, *Veramendi* v. *Hutchins*, 126–27, Documents Pertaining to James Bowie, UT.

3. Smithwick, *Evolution*, 138. Given the frequent unreliability of the Smithwick memoir, it is possible that this story is either invented, or more likely embellished or borrowed from a recollection of some other Texian and passed off as having happened to Smithwick personally.

4. Travis, *Diary*, December 15, 1833, 90.

5. Speer and Brown, *Encyclopedia*, vol. 1, 436.

6. Williams to Spencer Jack, March 26, 1834, Williams Papers, Rosenberg Library, Galveston, Tex.

7. Barker, "Land Speculation," 78–80.

8. Kate Mason Rowland, "General John Thompson Mason," *Quarterly of the Texas State Historical Association* 11 (January 1908): 180–81, 193; Barker, "Land Speculation," 79–80; Williams, *Animating Pursuits*, 47.

9. Promissory note, July 17, 1834, Gilder-Lehrman Collection, Pierpont Morgan Library, New York. This note covers Bowie's original June 3, 1834, loan from Francis Johnson, done at San Felipe. Since Travis, *Diary*, June 4, 1834, 180, established that Travis made out passports at San Felipe for Wharton and four

others to go to Mexico, it is assumed that Bowie was one of the four. He and Bowie were not sufficiently acquainted at this point for Bowie's name necessarily to be worthy of mention in the diary.

10. Power of Attorney, June 29, 1834, Béxar Archives, UT.

11. Conveyance Record 14, 499, Orleans Parish Courthouse.

12. John T. Mason to Archibald Hotchkiss, June 24, 1834, Alexander Dienst Collection, UT.

13. Barker, "Land Speculation," 81–82.

14. Brazoria *Texas Republican,* July 25, 1835.

15. Benjamin Lundy, *The Life, Travels and Opinions of Benjamin Lundy* (Philadelphia, 1847), 146–49.

16. Johnson, *Texas,* vol. 1, 168; Barker, "Land Speculation," 86.

17. Harriet Smither, ed., "Diary of Adolphus Sterne," *Southwestern Historical Quarterly* 30 (October 1926): 149, January 3, 1839.

18. Bowie to James B. Miller, June 11, 1835, Nacogdoches Archives, TXSL.

19. Barker, "Land Speculation," 76; Holley, *Texas,* 329; Houston *Telegraph and Texas Register,* January 27, 1841.

20. Ham, "Recollections," UT.

21. *Journal of the House of Representatives of the Republic of Texas, Fifth Congress, 1840–1841* (Austin, 1841), 338.

22. Henry Austin to Mary Holley, September 10, 1835, Barker, *Austin Papers,* vol. 3, 119–20.

23. Spencer Jack, Notes Concerning Trip to Mexico in 1834, etc., Lamar Papers, TXSL.

24. Smither, "Diary of Adolphus Sterne," 307; Johnson, *Texas,* vol. 1, 195. Perhaps it should be noted here that Mims, *Trail,* 56, cites the *Dictionary of American Biography* as saying that Bowie was a member of the "Committee of Safety" at Bastrop on May 17, 1835. The *DAB* has not been checked for this, as it is not worth checking, since on May 17 Bowie was demonstrably somewhere on the road between Matamoros and Monclova, about 260 miles away. Not a shred of evidence has been found connecting Bowie with such a committee.

25. Cós to the inhabitants of the Eastern Internal States, n.d., Nacogdoches Archives, TXSL.

26. Brazoria *Texas Republican,* May 9, 1835; San Felipe *Telegraph and Texas Register,* April 14, 1836.

27. Johnson, *Texas,* vol. 1, 195.

28. Joseph E. Field, *Three Years in Texas* (Austin, 1935), 12–13.

29. I. T. Taylor, *Cavalcade of Jackson County* (San Antonio, 1938), 379. This Clara Lisle story is possibly nothing more than local legend, and therefore as suspect as any other folklore regarding Bowie. It is included here because it represents the only known indication of the possibility of a resumption of romantic life after Ursula.

30. J. H. Money to *Ayuntamiento* at Nacogdoches, June 26, 1835, Nacogdoches Archives, TXSL.

31. J. H. C. Miller to Juan W. Smith, July 25, 1835, Béxar Archives, UT.

32. James Kerr to Thomas J. Chambers, July 5, 1835, ibid.

33. Barker, "Land Speculation," 92.

34. Ugartechea to Cós, June 29, 1835, Béxar Archives, UT.

35. Pedro Ellis Bean to Ugartechea, August 11, 1835, Nacogdoches Archives, TXSL.

36. Brazoria *Texas Republican,* June 27, 1835.

37. John Forbes to James B. Miller, July 24, 1835, Domestic Correspondence, Record Group 307, TXSL.

38. Henry Rueg to John Forbes, July 26, 1835, Nacogdoches Archives, ibid.

39. Ham, "Recollections," UT.

40. Bowie to Rueg, August 3, 1835, Nacogdoches Archives, TXSL.

41. New Orleans *Louisiana Advertiser,* September 16, 1835. The conclusion that Bowie did not return to Nacogdoches is based on this press report, which says that the rumor of his death came from that town. Obviously, if he had come through on his way to Louisiana, people would know the Comanche had not killed him.

42. George Kelley, John J. Bowie, 1787–1859, Arkansas History Commission, Little Rock; Little Rock *Arkansas Gazette,* August 18, 1835.

43. Sparks, in Ellis, *Crockett,* 234–36. This account is rather indefinite as to time, and there is no statement that James had anything to do with it, or that he called on John. The two were both well acquainted with Littleberry Hawkins, however.

44. Statement of Angus McNeil, March 18, 1835, on deed of Bowie to Thomas and Eliza McFarland, May 9, 1827, Bowie Family Papers, UT.

45. Conveyance Book 10, 131–37, Book 21, 179, 364, Clerk of the Court, Natchitoches Parish Courthouse, Natchitoches.

46. McNeil testimony in *Veramendi* v. *Hutchins,* 140–42, warrant from Record Book B, 126–27, Records for Bonds &c of Colorado County, Texas, in *Veramendi* v. *Hutchins,* 128–29, Documents Pertaining to James Bowie, UT.

47. Natchez, *Courier & Journal,* September 25, 1835.

48. John S. Ford Memoirs, typescript, II, 332, UT. This, like the episodes covered in an earlier chapter, may be apocryphal, or all may derive from a single episode.

49. John Borden to Robert Potter, November 21, 1840, in *Journal of the House of Representatives of the Republic of Texas, Fifth Congress, 1840–1841,* 356; Houston, *Telegraph and Texas Register,* February 3, 1841.

50. "One of Shreveport's Founders Handles Business Deal for James Bowie, Texas Hero," Hardin Collection, LSU.

51. Barker, "Land Speculation," 92–93.

52. Williams, *Animating Pursuits,* 64–65.

53. Clipping in Bowie Biographical File, DRT.

54. Travis to Bowie, July 30, 1835, Yoakum, *Texas,* I, 343.

55. Travis wrote the letter July 30, at which time Bowie was already on the trip to Chief Bowl. Since Bowie apparently did not come back through Nacogdoches, as evidenced by the rumors there that he had been killed, he would not have seen the letter—addressed to Nacogdoches—until he returned from Natchez in October.

56. James Bowie bond to William Richardson, October 15, 1835, Deed Book B, 122–23, Colorado County Courthouse, Columbus, Texas.

57. William T. Austin, Account of the Campaign of 1835 by William T. Austin, Aid to Gen. Stephen F. Austin and Gen. Edward Burleson, UT.

58. Eugene C. Barker, "The Texan Revolutionary Army," *Quarterly of the Texas State Historical Association* 9 (April, 1906): 247–48.

59. Smithwick, *Evolution*, 112–13. Any statement in the Smithwick memoir is subject to question, since that portion of the book attributable to him comes from the recollections of a ninety-year-old man more than sixty years after the fact, while other portions of the book are certainly the inventions or embellishments of his daughter and editor. Nevertheless, the muster roll of Thomas Alley's company, October 19, 1835, Austin Papers, UT, establishes that Smithwick was serving with the army on the Cibolo when Bowie arrived, and thus his comment can be taken as an authentic recollection, though perhaps hyperbolic.

60. Council of War, October 19, 1835, Jenkins, *PTR*, vol. 2, 162. The fact that Bowie is not listed as being present establishes that he had not yet reached Austin's camp.

61. William Austin, Account of the Campaign of 1835, UT.

62. Menchaca, *Memoirs*, 21–22; San Antonio *Daily Express*, January 15, 1905; Rena Maverick Green, ed., *Samuel Maverick, Texan, 1803–1870* (San Antonio, 1952), October 21, 1835, 31. In the *Express* article, quoting Samuel Maverick, the date October 21 is incorrectly stated as April 21.

63. Austin to Bowie, October 22, 1835, "General Austin's Order Book for the Campaign of 1835," *Quarterly of the Texas State Historical Association* 11 (July 1907): 22.

64. It has sometimes been assumed that Bowie brought this information with him when he joined Austin on the Cibola on October 19. William Austin, in Account of the Campaign of 1835, UT, states that as of October 28 "Col Bowie had left Sant Antonio but a very few days previously and he was fully informed as to the strength of the fortifications." Austin must be mistaken in saying this. Bowie was demonstrably in San Felipe on October 15, recording his land sale to Richardson. For him to have gone to San Antonio after that date, he would have had to go right past Austin's army, travel 160 miles in four days, manage to get around San Antonio undetected while surveying preparations, and get out of town once again. It is just barely possible, but highly unlikely. It *is* possible that he was in San Antonio *before* October 15, for no record of his precise date of arrival back in Texas survives, but this means Bowie could have been there no later than October 12–13, in order to be in San Felipe by the fifteenth, and as of that earlier date the Mexican preparations for defense were not as far advanced

as Bowie later reported. All elements considered, it simply seems more likely that what Bowie learned of the town's fortifications came from his many informants while he was at Espada.

65. Bowie and Fannin to Austin, October 22, 1835, Stephen F. Austin Papers, UT.

66. Bowie and Fannin to Austin, October 23, 1835, Barker, *Austin Papers*, vol. 3, 146–47.

67. Bowie and Fannin to Austin, October 24, 1835, ibid., 206–7.

68. Austin to Bowie and Fannin, October 24, 1835, "General Austin's Order Book," 26.

69. Bowie and Fannin to Austin, October 24, 1835, Barker, *Austin Papers*, vol. 3, 207.

70. Austin to Bowie and Fannin, October 24, 1835, "General Austin's Order Book," 29–30.

71. *Journals of the Consultation held at San Felipe de Austin, October 16, 1835* (Houston, 1838), 4–5.

72. Statement of returns for Nacogdoches, October 15, 1835, Election Returns, Secretary of State, Record Group 307, TXSL.

73. Frank Sparks account in San Antonio *Daily Express*, December 8, 1935.

74. Moseley Baker to Houston, 1844, Moseley Baker Papers, UT.

75. Moses A. Bryan to James F. Perry, October 26, 1835, Barker, *Austin Papers*, vol. 3, 211–12.

76. San Antonio *Daily Express*, January 15, 1905; Samuel Maverick Diary, October 26, 1835, UT.

77. Austin to Bowie, October 27, 1835, "General Austin's Order Book," 32–33.

78. Ham, "Recollections," UT; Wooten, *Texas*, 185–87.

79. Austin, Campaign of 1835; Moses A. Bryan, Reminiscences, Moses A. Bryan Papers, UT.

80. Ham, "Recollections," UT; James De Shields, *Tall Men with Long Rifles* (San Antonio, 1935), 37. It is apparent that these two sources, differing in details, are describing the same incident. Rohrbaugh, "James Bowie," 29–30, questions the Creed Taylor statement contained in De Shields, but having Ham as an additional, and earlier, source, would seem to confirm it.

81. Unidentified clipping in James Bowie Biographical File, DRT. This clipping is so vague that it does not identify what fight it describes, but only the night before the Concepción engagement seems to fit.

82. Except where otherwise cited, this account of Concepción is based on Bowie and Fannin's report, October 30 [misdated October 20], 1835, Adjutant General's Office, Army Papers, Record Group 401, TXSL.

83. De Shields, *Tall Men*, 38.

84. Smithwick, *Evolution*, 114, contains a description of the fight including his assessment that "Bowie was a born leader." However, Smithwick's company was not engaged in the battle, and thus what he—or his daughter—has to say about this phase of it is probably pure invention.

85. De Shields, *Tall Men*, 39–40; Sowell, *Rangers and Pioneers*, 130–31.

86. Davis, *Travis Diary*, 71, 79n; De Shields, *Tall Men*, 41.

Chapter 18 Travis 1835

1. Travis to Burnet, April 11, 1835, Jenkins, *PTR*, vol. 1, 63.

2. Travis to Burnet, January 20, 1835, *Philpott Collection Catalog*, item no. 212.

3. Brazoria *Texas Republican,* February 14, March 14, 21, 1835.

4. Roark, "Robert Wilson," 18–20.

5. Oath, April 10, 1835, Oaths of Colonists, Milam's Colony, 1835, 21; Contract, April 10, 1835, Mina, Spanish Archives, vol. 14, 185, General Land Office records, TXSL.

6. Kuykendall, Sketches of Early Texians, Kuykendall Family Papers, UT. Kuykendall's is not only the earliest authority for this episode, being written about twenty years after the fact, but it is also the only authoritative account, for he encountered Travis and Charles on their way back to San Felipe, in Columbia. Family stories, handed down no doubt from Rosanna, told many years later that she took both children with her, and that she demanded of him then a clear statement of whether or not he intended to return to his family, and that if not she demanded a written statement of his intention. This is obviously a false recollection, since by the time of her September 1834 letter to Dellet it was already plain that Travis had given her such a statement previously. However, it is possible that her attorney did ask for such a statement in writing to use in the proceedings. M. J. DeCaussey to William B. Travis Chapter, Daughters of the Republic of Texas, January 31, 1895, Asbury Papers; Clarence R. Wharton to Mixon, March 27, 1929, Mixon Papers, UT. McDonald, *Travis*, 96, relying on Travis's diary, incorrectly states that Travis got Charles in March 1834. Travis engaged somebody to pick up the boy then, but it never happened.

7. Bill of sale, May 29, 1835, William B. Travis Legal Documents, DRT; Travis title bond, May 16, 1835, *Philpott Collection Catalog*, item no. 215; Will of William Barret Travis, May 25, 1835, Domestic Correspondence, TXSL. It may be worth noting that in his will Travis specifies that his estate is to go to "my two legitimate children." Possibly nothing should be read into this, since it may have been simple pro forma wording. If not, though, then it suggests that much later rumors that he suspected Susan was not his are unfounded. And/or it could also suggest that he might have fathered an illegitimate child by one of his numerous sexual liaisons in Texas, or anticipated the possibility of it happening in future.

8. Travis to Burnet, February 6, 1835, *Christie's Catalog* no. 844K (May 1996), n.p.

9. Travis to Burnet, April 11, 1835, Jenkins, *PTR*, vol. 1, 63.

10. Mary A. Holley, Notes, Austin Papers, UT.

11. Wilson to Travis, May 13, 1835, Franklin Papers, ibid.

12. Travis to Burnet, May 21, 1835, *Philpott Collection Catalog*, item no. 216; Clarinda Pevehouse Kegans Memoirs, Nita Stewart Haley Library, Midland, Tex. The

quotations from the letter to Burnet are based upon a transcription from the illustration of the letter, and differ from the incomplete and inaccurate text appearing in the same catalog.

13. Parker, *Trip to the West*, 207.

14. Barker, "Public Opinion," 222; José María Tornel, *Tejas y los Estados-Unidos de America un Sus Relaciones con la Republica Mexicana* (Mexico City, 1837), in Carlos E. Castañeda, com, *The Mexican Side of the Texas Revolution* (Dallas, 1928), 334–35.

15. Agreement to Meet at Harrisburg, June 4, 1835, Lamar Papers, TXSL.

16. Travis to Smith, June 19, 1835, Gulick, *Lamar Papers*, vol. 1, 204.

17. Ibid.

18. Wilson to Travis, June 9, 1835, Franklin Papers, UT.

19. Agreement, June 22, 1835, Lamar Papers, TXSL.

20. The above account of the Anahuac affair is based on Travis to Smith, July 6, 1836, Brown, *Smith*, 59–61; Travis to the Public, September 1, 1835, [William Harris], Account of the ejection of Tenorio, 1835, Lamar Papers, TXSL; Eugene C. Barker, "Difficulties of A Mexican Revenue Officer in Texas," *Quarterly of the Texas State Historical Association* 4 (January 1901): 198–200; Antonio Tenorio to Ugartechea, July 1835, in Eugene C. Barker, ed., "William Barret Travis, The Hero of the Alamo," *Publications of the Southern History Association* 6 (September 1902): 416–17.

21. Anonymous account of Anahuac, June-July 1835, Lamar Papers, TXSL.

22. Yoakum, *Texas*, vol. 1, 343.

23. Travis to Smith, July 6, 1835, Brown, *Smith*, 60–61; James Cox to Col. Barrett, July 11, 1835, Jenkins, *PTR*, vol. 1, 149.

24. Harris, "Reminiscences, II," 160.

25. James H. C. Miller to John W. Smith, July 26, 1835, Domestic Correspondence, Record Group 307, TXSL.

26. Thomas Thompson, proclamation, July 26, 1835, Brown, *Smith*, 63.

27. James H. C. Miller to John W. Smith, July 25, 1835, Domestic Correspondence, Record Group 307, TXSL.

28. Brazoria *Texas Republican,* July 18, 1835.

29. Miller to John W. Smith, July 25, 1835, Domestic Correspondence, Record Group 307, TXSL.

30. Travis to Smith, July 26, 1835, Streeter Collection, Yale University, New Haven, Conn.

31. Travis to Bowie, July 30, 1835, Yoakum, *Texas*, vol. 1, 343.

32. Travis to Smith, July 6, 1835, Matagorda *Bulletin,* October 11, 1837.

33. Tenorio to Ugartechea, July 15, 1835, Béxar Archives, UT; Tenorio to Commissioner at San Felipe, July 15, 1835, Tenorio to Committee of San Felipe and Columbia, July 19, 1835, Tenorio to Miller, July 26, 1835, Nacogdoches Archives, TXSL.

34. Travis to Ugartechea, July 31, 1835, Barker, *Austin Papers*, vol. 3, 95.

35. Cós to Political Chief in Department of Brazos, August 1, 1835, Cós to Ugartechea, August 1, 1835, Béxar Archives, UT.

36. Ugartechea to Political Chief Department of Brazos, August 4, 1835, Nacogdoches Archives, TXSL.

37. Travis to Smith, August 5, 1835, Streeter Collection, Yale University, New Haven, Conn.

38. Johnson, *Texas*, vol. 1, 240.

39. Barker, "Public Opinion," 226-27.

40. Moseley Baker to Houston, October 1844, Austin Papers, UT.

41. Ugartechea to Chief of Department of Brazos, August 8, 1835, Ugartechea to Cós, August 8, 1835, Cós to Ugartechea, August 20, 31, 1835, Béxar Archives, UT; Affidavit, August 29, 1835, Brown, *Smith*, 67.

42. Wiley Martin to Ugartechea, August 16, 1835, Béxar Archives, UT.

43. Brown, *Smith*, 71-72.

44. Travis to J. W. Moore, August 31, 1835, Houston *Morning Star*, March 14, 1840.

45. Travis to Smith, August 4, 1835, Brown, *Smith*, 62; Travis to Smith, August 5, 1835, Streeter Collection, Yale University, New Haven, Conn.

46. Travis to Smith, August 24, 1835, Brown, *Smith*, 72-73.

47. Travis to J. W. Moore, August 31, 1835, Houston *Morning Star*, March 14, 1840; Travis to Burnet, August 31, 1835, Jenkins, *PTR*, vol. 1, 379; Travis to Briscoe, August 31, 1835, Mixon, "Travis," 409-10; Travis to Smith, September 1, 1835, Lamar Papers, TXSL.

48. Travis to New York *Christian Advocate and Journal*, August 17, 1835, in Texas *Christian Advocate*, April 4, 1861.

49. A. J. Lee, "Rev. J. W. Kenney," *Texas Methodist Historical Quarterly* 1 (1884-1885): 48-49; William Smith account of camp meeting, transcript in Mixon Papers, UT; Macum Phelan, *A History of Early Methodism in Texas* (Nashville, 1924), 44-46; Kegans Memoirs, Haley Library. The Clarinda Kegans reminiscence, obviously girlhood recollections written many decades after the fact, is at best confused. The barbecue she mentions took place "the fall before the war began," she says, suggesting autumn of 1835, and this is probably accurate. She has James Bonham attending as Travis' friend, however, even though Bonham did not come to Texas until November 1835, and Travis spent all of that month away with Austin's army at Béxar, and December organizing his cavalry command. Bonham and Travis were in San Felipe briefly at the same time in December, but since hostilities had been going on since October, this would hardly qualify as being "before the war began," and besides Travis would hardly have been attending parties at the Pevehouse place south of San Felipe with all he had to do getting his cavalry together. Besides, with the war in full sway, there was hardly any need for the men at any party in December to disguise their politics from suspected spies, as Kegans suggests. Kegans also has Mexican Colonel Juan Almonte attending the barbecue as a spy, but this is surely a false

recollection based on Almonte's visit to Texas in the spring and summer of 1834. Obviously she was unconsciously embellishing a recollection of a single event in which Travis is the central character, and which probably did take place in fall 1835. The addition of Bonham reflects persistent Texan folklore in her time and later that make the two childhood friends, even though there is no evidence at all to establish a connection between them prior to 1836. The addition of Almonte either confuses and condenses the Mexican's genuine 1834 trip into an 1835 recollection of Travis, or else reflects some now lost folk tale having Almonte traveling in Texas incognito as a spy. These are common characteristics of elderly reminiscences involving noted persons and events. One thing is certain: On no occasion were Travis, Bonham, and Almonte, all in the same place at the same time except during the siege of the Alamo in February-March 1836.

50. Travis to the Public, September 1, 1835, Lamar Papers, TXSL.

51. Cós to Austin, October 4, 1835, ibid.

52. Eugene C. Barker, *The Life of Stephen F. Austin* (Austin, 1949), 483; Minutes of San Felipe Meeting, September 12, 1835, Barker, *Austin Papers*, vol. 3, 122–140.

53. Travis to Smith, September 18, 1835, Brown, *Smith*, 74–75.

54. Travis to Austin, September 22, 1835, Barker, *Austin Papers*, vol. 3, 133–35.

55. Barnard E. Bee affidavit, December 18, 1839, William Barret Travis Certificate of Service, Miscellany File, TXSL.

56. Travis to Randall Jones, October 3, 1835, Travis Papers, UT. In this letter Travis did not address Jones as "Captain," nor did he sign it as "Lieutenant," which Travis, a stickler for formality, and a man somewhat bedazzled by military titles, would surely have done if they had been elected to their future positions prior to that time. Also the content of Travis's letter includes nothing to suggest that he felt himself as yet a part of an organized company, leading to the conclusion that Jones's company did not organize until after October 3, and perhaps not until word came of the Gonzales emergency on October 4.

57. Travis to Jones, October 3, 1835, Travis Papers, UT.

58. William B. Travis voucher to "Mrs. Kenner," October 5, 1835, Michael D. Heaston, *Texas in the Nineteenth Century*, catalog no. 27 (Austin, 1997), item 298. This document does not establish that Travis and his company were actually on the road to Gonzales on October 5, when he impressed the horse, but it is possible.

59. General Order, October 11, 1835, Jenkins, *PTR*, vol. 2, 93; Muster roll of Captain Jones Company, October 20, 1835, Austin Papers, UT. Austin was in San Felipe as late as October 5, and on that date was writing of volunteers leaving that day and the next. Most likely Jones's company was among them. October 11 is the earliest date that Travis can be placed at Gonzales, and is confirmed by "Reminiscences of Sion Bostwick," *Quarterly of the Texas State Historical Association* 5 (October 1901): 87.

60. Council of War, October 19, 1835, "General Austin's Order Book," 18–19.

61. Moses Bryan, Personal Recollections of Stephen F. Austin, 1889, Bryan Papers; Moses Bryan to James and Emily Bryan, October 26, 1835, Stephen Austin Papers, UT; Moses Bryan to Perry, October 26, 1835, Jenkins, *PTR*, vol. 2, 222.

62. Austin to Travis, October 27, 1835, "General Austin's Order Book," 31. The assumption that Travis himself may have urged the mounted company on Austin derives from his great interest in cavalry as shown in December, with the organization of the regular forces of Texas.

63. Austin, Campaign of 1835, UT; William Pettus Statement, n.d., William B. Travis Audited Military Claims file, Army Papers, Record Group 5926, TXSL.

64. It is not certain that the men of the company did not hold an election and formally choose Travis as their captain, but the fact that Austin ordered Travis to raise the company would suggest to the men that it was Austin's *intent* that Travis be its commander, and if the men who volunteered had that understanding when they volunteered, no election would have been necessary. Nevertheless, it is, of course, possible that an election was held as a formality.

65. Austin to Bowie and Fannin, October 31, 1835, Army Papers, Record Group 401, TXSL.

66. Ibid.

67. Austin to Bowie and Fannin, November 1, 1835, ibid.

68. The speculation that this October 28 report of a herd was false is supported by the fact that a genuine report of a different herd came in a few days later. Certainly there was a limit to just how many herds of horses Cós would have.

69. Jenkins, *PTR*, vol. 2, 341.

70. Michael R. Green, "'To the People of Texas & All Americans in the World,'" *Southwestern Historical Quarterly* 91 (April 1988): 489, supports this interpretation of Travis' resignation. Mixon, "Travis," 180 argues that he resigned because of trouble and complaints *within* his company.

71. Austin to Travis/Briscoe, November 6, 1835, Jenkins, *PTR*, vol. 2, 334.

72. Stephen L. Hardin, "'Efficient in the Cause," in Gerald E. Poyo, ed., *Tejano Journey 1770–1850* (Austin, 1996), 49–52, 57; Travis to Burnet, September 1, 1835, Jenkins, *PTR*, vol. 1, 384; Travis statement, February 19, 1836, Felipe Xaimes File, Republic Payments for Service, Record Group 304, TXSL.

73. Except where otherwise stated, this account of Travis's expedition comes from Travis to Austin, November 16, 1835, Army Papers, Record Group 401, TXSL.

74. In his forthcoming *Alamo Traces: Backtracking the Historiography of the Siege and Storming of the Alamo,* Thomas Ricks Lindley cites a statement of two of Travis's volunteers to be found in the Siege of Béxar File, TXSL, which provides this information.

75. Austin to Fannin, November 9, 1835, Army Papers, Record Group 401, TXSL.

76. Austin to Travis, November 11, 1835, "General Austin's Order Book," 37–38.

77. Bryan, Recollections of Stephen F. Austin, 1889, Bryan Papers; Guy Bryan to Fontaine, June 10, 1890, Fontaine Papers, UT; Jesús F. de la Teja, *A Revolution Remembered: The Memoirs and Selected Correspondence of Juan N. Seguín* (Austin, 1991), 78–79.

78. Morphis, *Texas*, 114; Barker, "Texan Revolutionary Army," 249.

79. Roll of Brazos Guards, November 21, 1835, Austin Papers, UT.

80. Morning Report of Captain Travis, November 26, 1835, Austin Papers, UT.

81. List of men who have this day volunteered to remain before Béxar, November 24, 1835, Austin Papers, UT.

82. Bryan, Recollections of Stephen F. Austin, Bryan Papers, ibid.

83. Judge Edwin Waller, a friend of Travis's, later claimed that when Austin left the Béxar army, he temporarily gave the command to Travis. This must certainly be a false recollection, for no contemporary source mentions such an event, and Austin did not leave until Edward Burleson was firmly in charge. Waller must have confused a correct memory that Travis stayed behind a few days when Austin left, and inadvertently embellished it into a turnover of command. Philip E. Pearson, ed., "Reminiscences of Judge Edwin Waller," *Quarterly of the Texas State Historical Association* 4 (July 1900): 42; Philip E. Pearson, *Sketch of the Life of Judge Edwin Waller* (Galveston, 1874), 10.

84. Austin to the Consultation, November 18, 1835, Army Papers, Record Group 401, TXSL; Report of Special Committee of the Council, November 27, 1835, in William C. Binkley, ed., *Official Correspondence of the Texan Revolution, 1835–1836*, vol. 1(New York, 1936), 124–25.

85. San Felipe *Telegraph and Texas Register*, November 21, 1835.

Chapter 19 Bowie 1835–February 2, 1836

1. Bowie and Fannin Report, October 30 [misdated October 20], Army Papers, Record Group 401, TXSL.

2. Austin, Account of the Campaign of 1835, UT; Austin to the Convention, October 28, 1835, "General Austin's Order Book," 33–34; Austin to Dimmit, November 2, 1835, Jenkins, *PTR*, vol. 2, 298.

3. Austin, Account of the Campaign of 1835, UT.

4. Austin, Account of the Campaign of 1835, Maverick Diary, October 30, 1835, ibid.; San Antonio *Daily Express*, January 22, 1905.

5. Austin to Bowie and Fannin, October 31, 1835, Army Papers, Record Group 401, TXSL.

6. Ibid.

7. Bowie and Fannin to Austin, October 31, 9 P.M., 1835, ibid.

8. Bowie to Martín Cós, October 31, 1835, ibid.

9. Ibid. Though Bowie's surrender demand is dated October 31 from Concepción, it is almost certainly a mistake in dating, and should be November 1, for in his letter of that date to Austin, cited below, he says that "I sent a demand today for a surrender."

10. Cós to José Tornel, November 2, 1835, Jenkins, *PTR*, vol. 2, 298–99.

11. Bowie and Fannin to Austin, November 1, 1835, Barker, *Austin Papers*, vol. 3, 226.

12. Austin to Bowie and Fannin, November 1, 1835, Army Papers, Record Group 401, TXSL.

13. Fannin to Austin, November 2, 1835, Jenkins, *PTR*, vol. 2, 301.

14. Austin to Bowie and Fannin, November 2, 1835, Jenkins, *PTR*, vol. 2, 294-95.

15. Bowie to Austin, November 2, 1835, Army Papers, Record Group 401, TXSL. Hopewell, *Bowie*, 104, explains Bowie's resignation as stemming from impatience with Austin's tactics—which may have had some bearing—and then invents an entirely unsubstantiated grievance because Austin was withholding a formal commission out of disapproval of Bowie's speculating interests. This is nonsense. There were no commissions in Austin's power to withhold. His own and all others above the rank of captain came by authorization of the permanent council and the consultation. Alwyn Barr, *Texans in Revolt* (Austin, 1990), 29, offers the much less imaginary, and more reasonable, conclusion that Bowie resigned because he regarded the vote to combine the wings of the army as evidence of unrest in his command, the implication being that he took the vote as a reflection on himself. This is possible, but weakened considerably by the fact that in his resignation Bowie himself goes strongly on the record in favor of joining the forces. No one to date has considered the fact that the only actual position that Bowie had to resign was as an aide, his command of the First Division being by its very nature temporary.

16. Austin to Bowie and Fannin, November 2, 1835, Jenkins, *PTR*, vol. 2, 294-95.

17. Maverick Diary, November 4, 1835, UT.

18. Ehrenberg, *With Milam and Fannin*, 43-44, 47-48.

19. Brazoria *Texas Republican,* October 31, 1835; *Journals of the Consultation*, 9.

20. Moses A. Bryan, Recollections of Stephen F. Austin, September 25, 1889, Moses A. Bryan Papers, UT.

21. "The Reminiscences of Mrs. Dilue Harris," *Quarterly of the Texas State Historical Association* 4 (January 1901): 185.

22. *Journals of the Consultation*, 11.

23. Memorandum, November 5, 1835, "General Austin's Order Book," 34.

24. Jenkins, *PTR*, vol. 2, 338-39, 341.

25. Thoms Rusk to Bowie, November 5, 1836, Jenkins, *PTR*, vol. 2, 333-34, Robert B. Irvine to Houston, November 7, 1835, 349-50.

26. Election Return, [November 6], 1835, Jenkins, *PTR*, vol. 2, 496. This return is improperly dated November 24 by Jenkins, who borrows the error from Gulick, *Lamar Papers*, vol. 1, 259. The return includes votes from companies such as F. Whitis's [probably Francis White] and Frank Johnson's, that do not appear to have been with the army, on November 2 at least, which is something of a problem, though they could have joined in the next four days. However, Capt. William Scott's company is listed, but Scott was discharged on November 18, and thus would not be exercising command or voting on the 24th. Even more significant, William Wharton appears as voting, yet he left the army November 8, and so did Joseph Wallace (Jenkins, *PTR*, vol. 2, 356, 362). Thus it would be

impossible for Wallace to have come in second in balloting on November 24, more than two weeks after he departed, while Wharton was in or near Brazoria on November 26, making it clear that he had been away from the army for some time, and therefore could not have been present to vote on November 24 (Wharton to Branch Archer, November 26, 1835, Jenkins, *PTR*, vol. 2, 518–20). Also, though Capt. Robert C. Morris's company of the New Orleans Greys joined the army on November 21, it does not appear on the voting list, arguing further that the document does not reflect the November 24 election (Jenkins, *PRT*, vol. 2, 489). Finally, on the very day in question, November 24, Capt. M. R. Goheen resigned command of his company, complaining that it numbered only eighteen men on that date, yet the number of men voting in his company in the misdated document is twenty-two, making it obvious that he is not writing on the same day as the vote (Jenkins, *PTR*, vol. 2, 496–97). More evidence could be added, but surely this is enough to establish that the document should be dated November 6 and not November 24.

27. Austin to President of the Consultation, November 8, 1835, Jenkins, *PTR*, vol. 2, 355.

28. Bryan to James Perry, November 7, 1835, Barker, *Austin Papers*, vol. 3, 244.

29. Hall to Austin, November 18, 1835, Austin Papers, UT.

30. Bowie to Austin, November 6, 1835, Army Papers, Record Group 401, TXSL. The document is misdated October 6, but "General Austin's Order Book," 34, confirms that the resignation took place on November 6. What may be the original, dated October 6, is in the Gilder-Lehrman Collection, Pierpont Morgan Library, New York.

31. Speer and Brown, *Encyclopedia*, 436. It is evident from Austin to the President of the Consultation, Jenkins, *PTR*, vol. 2, 355, that Richardson did not leave until sometime on November 8, or more likely the next morning. Speer and Brown state that Bowie was with him.

32. Affidavit of Horatio Alsbury, November 7, 1836, Petition of Administrators of James Bowie, Memorial No. 451, TXSL.

33. Houston to Fannin, November 13, 1835, Amelia Williams and Eugene C. Barker, eds., *The Writings of Sam Houston*, vol. 1 (Austin, 1938–1943), 306. Houston's statement in this letter that he had heard of Bowie assuming command of the army, sending his congratulations, is proof that Bowie had not reached San Felipe as yet, or Houston would have known otherwise.

34. *Journals of the Consultation*, 18, 21–22, 36.

35. Peytona Barry statement, May 31, 1903, Walter W. Bowie Papers, Maryland Historical Society, Baltimore.

36. Anson Jones, *Memoranda and Official Correspondence Relating to the Republic of Texas, Its History and Annexation* (New York, 1859), 12–13.

37. George M. Patrick to Moses A. Bryan, August 8, 1878, Texas Veterans Association Papers, UT.

38. The timing of Bowie's arrival is established by the fact that at 3 P.M. on November 18 Austin wrote to Henry Smith stating that since noon he had

received Patrick's dispatches. Austin to Smith, November 18, 1835, Jenkins, *PTR*, vol. 2, 450.

39. Austin to Edward Burleson, November 14, 1835, "General Austin's Order Book," 40–41.

40. Austin to Smith, November 18, 1835, Jenkins, *PTR*, vol. 2, 450, Fannin to Houston, November 18, 1835, 458, Hall to Austin, November 18, 1835, 462, Burleson to Austin, November 21, 1835, 480, Philip Sublett to Austin, November 21, 1835, 486, Austin to Perry, November 22, 1835, 487.

41. Patrick to Bryan, August 8, 1878, Texas Veterans Association Papers, UT.

42. The actual record of the voting in this November 24 election seems not to have survived, but it should be reiterated that the result appearing in Jenkins, *PTR*, vol. 2, 496, and Gulick, *Lamar Papers*, vol. 1, 259, is erroneously dated November 24, whereas abundant internal and external evidence dates it as November 6.

43. General order November 24, 1835, Austin's Order Book for the Campaign of 1835, Series 4, Austin Papers, UT.

44. William Taylor in Day, *Almanac*, 1868, 534; De Shields, *Tall Men*, 47.

45. Hunter, *Narrative*, 25.

46. Thomas Rusk, An Account of the Grass Fight, n.d., Thomas J. Rusk Papers, UT; Edward Burleson to the Provisional Government, November 27, 1835, William H. Jack to Burleson, November 27, 1835, Army Papers, Record Group 401, TXSL.

47. De Shields, *Tall Men*, 47–48.

48. Rusk, Grass Fight, UT; Yoakum, *Texas*, vol. 2, 18; Burleson to Provisional Government, November 27, 1835, Army Papers, Record Group 401, TXSL.

49. Brown, *Texas*, vol. 2, 409.

50. Austin, Account of the Campaign of 1835, UT.

51. Stephen L. Hardin provides important insights into the cultural background of this incident in his chapter "Efficient in the Cause," in Poyo, *Tejano Journey*, 68–69.

52. Reminiscences of Samuel C. A. Rogers, August 18, 1891, UT. Being written almost fifty-six years after the fact, this reminiscence may well be exaggerated or inaccurate, but it places the event where Bowie is known to have been at this time.

53. Dimitt to Henry Smith, December 2, 1835, Jenkins, *PTR*, vol. 3, 75–76. The tone and content of Dimitt's letter suggest that Bowie had not yet arrived.

54. San Antonio *Daily Express,* May 21, 1905; Stiff notes, November 8, 1835, Jenkins, *PTR*, vol. 3, 390.

55. Menchaca, *Memoirs*, 22.

56. William B. Scates, "Early History of Anahuac," Day, *Almanac*, 689. That Bowie returned from Goliad to Béxar, and left there December 17 is confirmed in Johnson to Smith, December 18, 1835, Jenkins, *PTR*, vol. 3, 244. Brown, *Smith*, 214–15, also confirms that while Houston believed Bowie to be in Goliad as of December 17, he was in fact in Béxar.

57. Inventory of Notes given for captured property by Volunteer Army, December 19, 1835, Army Papers, Record Group 401, TXSL; Peytona Barry statement, May 31, 1903, Walter W. Bowie Papers, Maryland Historical Society, Baltimore.

58. Gray, *From Virginia to Texas*, 111–12.

59. Henry Smith, "Reminiscences of Henry Smith," *Quarterly of the Texas State Historical Association* 14 (July 1910): 50.

60. James W. Robinson to Thomas J. Rusk, December 19, 1835, Thomas J. Rusk Papers, UT; Brown, *Smith*, 214–15. See Stephen L. Hardin, *Texian Iliad: A Military History of the Texas Revolution* (Austin, 1994), 105ff, for a good general view of the Matamoros expedition.

61. Williams, *Animating Pursuits*, 68.

62. Houston to Bowie, December 17, 1835, Williams and Barker, *Writings*, vol. 1, 322–23.

63. Ibid., Houston to Smith, January 30, 1836, vol. 1, 347.

64. Houston to Smith, January 6, 1836, Jenkins, *PTR*, vol. 3, 425–26.

65. Robinson to Rusk, December 19, 1835, Rusk Papers UT.

66. Ham, "Recollections," UT.

67. Ralph Steen, "Analysis of the Work of the General Council, Provisional Government of Texas, 1835–1836," *Southwestern Historical Quarterly* 14 (April 1938): 342–43.

68. Houston to Smith, December 26, 1835, Williams and Barker, *Writings*, vol. 1, 325.

69. *Journal of the Proceedings of the General Council of the Republic of Texas, Held at San Felipe de Austin, November 14th, 1835* (Houston, 1839), 166.

70. Speer and Brown, *Encyclopedia*, vol. 1, 435–36, and Brown, *Indian Wars*, 136, contain variant accounts supposedly deriving from James Robinson, of an impassioned speech of an hour or more by Bowie before the consultation, during which he referred to his dead wife and children, his neglect of his personal affairs on behalf of Texas, and his overweaning desire to serve his new country in the field by raising a regiment. "Pathos, irony, invective, and fiery eloquence" supposedly characterized his speech, as he even recounted his past life before coming to Texas.

   The consultation, of course, was not in session at this time. Bowie went before the *council*, and its minutes give no indication of any impassioned panegyric. Moreover, both of the above accounts say that when Bowie left, he went to San Antonio, whereas in fact he was still in San Felipe for more than a week afterward. Probably Bowie's manner made at least enough impression on Robinson that he remembered Bowie saying *something* before the council, and the passage of more than fifty years simply embellished in recollection what was probably a matter of fact report into something more. Bowie's known persuasive powers may well have accounted for some of that.

71. *Journal of the . . . General Council*, 166.

72. Ibid., 165ff.

73. Ibid., 192.

74. Dimitt to Smith, January 10, 1836, Jenkins, *PTR,* vol. 3, 465.

75. Bowie to Houston, January 10, 1836, quoted in Ham, "Recollections," UT.

76. *Journal of the . . . General Council,* 166ff.

77. It has been argued that the reference to "Col. James Bowie" in the proceedings of the council constituted a recognition of his rank, but it was simply a common usage, just like "Colonel" Crockett, and with no more authority in this context.

78. Houston to D. C. Barrett, December 15, 1835, Samuel Asbury Papers, SHC, UNC.

79. James C. Neill to Houston, January 14, 1836, Jenkins, *PTR,* vol. 4, 14.

80. Houston to Smith, January 17, 1836, ibid., 46.

81. Ibid.; Brown, *Smith,* 210.

82. Thomas R. Lindley, "Drawing Truthful Conclusions," *Journal of the Alamo Battlefield Association* 1 (September 1995): 27–28. This perceptive analysis is quite convincing on the point that Houston did not *order* Bowie to go to Béxar, but that it was a request, a decision reached mutually between them. Lindley may go too far, however, in suggesting that Bowie's going was entirely of his own volition.

83. This set of instructions does not survive, but reference to it is made in Orders of Gen. Houston, n.d., Jenkins, *PTR,* vol. 9, 144.

84. James Bowie receipt, January 18, 1836, in Jenkins, *Texas Revolution and Republic Catalog* no. 188, item no. 130. This receipt, by its date, established the day of Bowie's arrival, and since he signed it as commandant of the post at Béxar, it must mean that Neill was not present.

85. Stephen L. Hardin, "J. C. Neill: The Forgotten Alamo Commander," *Alamo Journal* 66 (May 1989): 5–11.

86. L. W. Kemp to John W. Dickinson, August 19, 1939, Williams Papers, UT, asserts that Dickenson had at this point changed his name to Dick*er*son, but there is no contemporary evidence to support this.

87. *Estado a manif'ta la Art'a, armes, municiones y armas efectos . . . ,* March 6, 1836 (copy dated April 29, 1836) Ex XI/481.3/1655, Archivo Historico Militar Mexicano, Mexico City. The figures in the text represent what is included in this March 6 statement of what was captured from the Texians at the Alamo, plus one additional cannon added after Cós left, and an allowance for the ammunition expended by the Texians during the siege. It does not include the 400 or more small arms brought in by the Texian defenders, that raised the total of rifles, pistols, shotguns, etc., captured on March 6 to 816.

88. John Sutherland, "Fall of the Alamo," typescript of a document written in 1860, Williams Papers, UT; William R. Carey to William F. Oppelt, January 12, 1836, in "A Letter from San Antonio de Béxar in 1836," *Southwestern Historical Quarterly,* 62 (April 1959): 516.

89. Green B. Jameson to Houston, January 18, 1836, Army Papers, Record Group 401, TXSL; Mariano Arroyo, Report of Military Hospital at Béxar, August 1,

1836, EX XI/481.3/1151, Archivo Historico Militar Mexicano; Testimony of Mrs. Hannig Touching on the Alamo Massacre, September 23, 1876, TXSL. Mrs. Hannig—Susanna Dickenson—said there were fifty to sixty Mexican sick and wounded in San Antonio.

90. Jameson to Houston, January 18, 1836, Army Papers, Record Group 401, TXSL.

91. Neill to Smith, January 23, 1836, Jenkins, *PTR*, vol. 4, 127.

92. Ibid., 128.

93. Proceedings of a meeting at Béxar relative to the general council & Gov. H. Smith, etc., January 26, 1836, Communications Received, Secretary of State, Record Group 307, TXSL. Henry Smith, "Reminiscences," 52–53, 55, later claimed that the garrison actually wanted to come to San Felipe to forcibly reinstall him as governor, but this is almost certainly false. If they would not abandon their post in the face of the enemy, they would hardly do so just to protect him.

94. Affidavit of Horatio Alsbury, November 7, 1836, Memorial No. 451, TXSL.

95. Green, *Maverick*, 55; Government of the Republic of Texas to William[son] Oldham, n.d. [1836], Petition of Administrators of James Bowie, memorial No. 451, TXSL.

96. Day, *Almanac, 1868*, 559.

97. José Maria Rodriguez, *Memoirs of Early Texas* (N.p, 1913), 71.

98. Bowie to Smith, February 2, 1836, Army Papers, Record Group 401, TXSL.

99. Houston to Smith, January 30, 1836, Jenkins, *PTR*, vol. 4, 188.

100. Memorial of Citizens & Soldiers of Béxar, n.d., Consultation Papers, TXSL.

101. Bowie to Smith, February 2, 1836, Army Papers, Record Group 401, TXSL.

Chapter 20 Travis 1835–February 23, 1836

1. Travis to the governor and council, December 3, 1835, Army Papers, Record Group 401, TXSL.

2. Travis to Robinson, December 17, Lamar Papers, TXSL.

3. Barker, "Army," 230–33.

4. Ibid., 234; *Journal of the . . . General Council*, 65, 72–73. For more than a century people have claimed that not only were Travis and Bonham childhood playmates, but that Bonham came to Texas at Travis's urging. Not an atom of contemporary evidence exists to support this, and the only basis at all are Milledge L. Bonham to Mixon, June 16, 1929, Mixon Papers, and Bonham to Asbury, n.d. [February 1923], Asbury Papers, UT. Both letters are by the grandson of James Butler Bonham's brother, simply repeating family stories nearly a century after the fact.

5. Travis commission, December 24, 1835, copy in Travis Papers, UT. The original is indicated as being in the Mexican Military Archives, suggesting that Travis had to have had it with him in the Alamo, or else left it in Béxar on February 23, 1836.

NOTES TO PAGES 506-509 · 713

6. Houston to Wilson, December 28, 1835, Jenkins, *PTR*, vol. 3, 350, Houston to Travis, December 23, 1835, 301.

7. Charles Willson to R. R. Royall, December 24, 1835, Jenkins, *PTR*, vol. 3, 310.

8. San Felipe *Telegraph and Texas Register,* January 9, 1836.

9. *Journal of the . . . General Council,* 94.

10. Barker, "Army," 232.

11. Houston to Travis, December 23, 1835, Jenkins, *PTR*, vol. 3, 301.

12. James Butler Bonham to Houston, December 31, 1835, Daughters of the American Revolution Collection, East Texas Research Center, Stephen F. Austin State University, Nacogdoches.

13. Barker, "Army," 230.

14. Travis to W. G. Hill, January 21, 1836, Jenkins, *PTR*, vol. 4, 109.

15. H. Klone receipt, January 22, 1836, Auditor's Book of Claims Paid 1835–1840, TXSL.

16. Travis to Smith, January 28, 1836, Army Papers, Record Group 401, TXSL.

17. Travis statement, January 7, 1836, Military Service Records, Republic of Texas, Series 1, Section 52, Book B, TXSL; Travis voucher to "Mrs. Kenner," October 5, 1835, with endorsement by Travis January 20, 1836, Heaston, *Texas in the Nineteenth Century,* catalog no. 27, item 298.

18. Travis to Smith, January 28, 1836, Army Papers, Record Group 401, TXSL.

19. Edward Wood to Robinson, January 1836, Jenkins, *PTR*, vol. 4, 229–30.

20. San Felipe *Telegraph and Texas Register,* January 23, 1836.

21. Inventory of notes, June 8, 1835, Austin Papers, UT; Travis document, November 1835, unidentified autograph catalog, n., n.d., 66, copy in possession of the author.

22. Autobiographical Sketch of James Harper Starr, 1881, James H. Starr to Franklin J. Starr, January 8, 1836, R. H. Pinny to Franklin J. Starr, May 25, 1835, James H. Starr Collection, UT.

23. Account of the sale of personal estate of Franklin J. Starr, 1837, Receipt for books, n.d., Starr Collection, UT.

24. Receipt of Travis & Nibbs, March 1, 1836, H. C. C. Hudson receipt, November 17, 1836, ibid.

25. John R. Jones Account Book, Estate of William B. Travis, Claims filed against the estate of Wm. B. Travis, March 26, 1838, copy in Travis Biographical File, DRT; Inventory of Estate of William B. Travis, certified copy in Mixon Papers; James H. Starr receipt, November 7, 1837, Starr Papers, UT.

26. *Journal of the House of Representatives of the State of Alabama* (Tuscaloosa, 1836), 48; *Journal of the Senate of the State of Alabama* (Tuscaloosa, 1836), 164; *Acts Passed at the Annual Session of the General Assembly of the State of Alabama* (Tuscaloosa, 1836), 112.

27. Travis to Smith, December 3, 185, Army Papers, Record Group 401, TXSL.

28. San Felipe *Telegraph and Texas Register,* November 14, 1835, January 2, 1836.

29. Recommendation, January 3, 1836, Consultation Papers, TXSL.

30. The original of this is in the Texana Collection, DeGolyer Library, Southern Methodist University, Dallas, Tex.

31. J. H. Money to Wood, January 22, 1836, Jenkins, *PTR*, vol. 4, 118. Williams, "Critical Study, III," 84, speculates without authority that Travis tried to get out of his assignment to command at Béxar because he still wanted to lead the Matamoros expedition, but his January 28 letter to Smith makes it plain that he had lost all respect for those involved in that enterprise.

32. San Felipe *Telegraph and Texas Register*, January 23, 1836.

33. Barker, "Army," 236. No actual order to Travis can be found, but in Travis to Hill, January 21, 1836, Jenkins, *PTR*, vol. 4, 109, he states that "I am ordered off to the defense of San Antonio." Yet in Travis to Burnet, January 20, 1836, Jenkins, *PTR*, vol. 4, 6, Travis speaks of a note due for collection and says that he will take it to Brazoria in person to collect. Clearly he did not have his marching orders at that time, or he would have known that he could not go to Brazoria. Thus Travis must have received his instructions late January 20 or early January 21. It is clear from Travis to Smith, January 28, 1836, that Travis is moving in response to orders from Smith, and Travis to Smith, January 29, makes reference to an order to take one hundred men with him. Both letters are in Army Papers, Record Group 401, TXSL.

34. John R. Jones statement as executor of William Barret Travis, December 18, 1837, Comptroller's Military Service Records, No. 5926, TXSL. This document is missing from the State Library and Archives and has not been seen, apparently, since it was examined by Ruby Mixon when she researched her "Travis" thesis, and consequently the material here is taken from her transcription on pp. 439–42 of her thesis.

Thomas Ricks Lindley, the most indefatigable researcher to go through the Texas Revolution documents in the State Library, concludes that the item was a forgery, a conclusion with which this author cannot concur. It is important to understand the nature of this document. In the transcript Mixon quotes Jones as saying: "The foregoing is taken from the original entries in Col Travis hand writing made in a small blank morocco bound book with his name in it." Thus, the document missing from the archives is not the book itself, but a one or two page copy of information in it made by Jones. The document may simply be misfiled, which has happened with other Texas Revolution documents, or it may have been stolen, and the archives did suffer a number of unfortunate thefts in past decades.

Lindley's conclusion that it is not genuine is based on a) the fact that it cannot be found, and b) certain discrepancies between dates and vendors for purchases and their locations listed from the book, and actual invoices for claims due from some of these same vendors now to be found in the Audited Military Claims files in the archives. However, certain things need to be kept in mind. The invoices in the Audited Military Claims are for goods that Travis purchased on government credit, and for which the vendors subsequently submitted their claims. The expenditures listed in the Travis book transcribed by Jones are expenditures that Travis made out of his own pocket, and which Jones was submitting, as executor of his estate, for reimbursement to the estate after Travis's death. Thus the amounts would not agree between the two sources because they do not cover the same purchases. A couple of seeming discrepancies do still exist where Travis appears to be in two different places on the same date, but again, the Jones tabulation only lists the names of vendors, without stating locations of the purchase. The fact that Audited Military Claims place Travis at Beeson's Ferry on January 25, while the Jones tabulation has him buying goods from Jesse Burnham on January 25, does not necessarily mean that Travis bought those goods at Burnham's Ferry, where his command did in fact camp January 28–29. Burnham could have brought the goods to Beeson's on January 25, or Travis could have ridden from Beeson's to Burnham's, a distance of less than twenty miles. Furthermore, it is always possible that Travis made some entries in his morocco book from memory, getting a date or name wrong. In 1834 in his law practice he engaged a clerk to clean up the chaos he had made of his own book-keeping.

And finally, it should also be borne in mind that the Jones tabulation is a copy made by Jones himself, and therefore subject to inadvertent mistakes in copying that could innocently introduce seeming contradictions that would not otherwise exist. Travis's numerals are not always distinct, his 3s, 5s, and 8s being quite similar, as are his 1s and 7s. The one remaining mystery, of course, is how the morocco book escaped being lost or destroyed in the fall of the Alamo. This is not an insurmountable problem, but of course can only be addressed by hypothesis. The latest entry in it is dated February 17, six days before the commencement of the siege. Either Travis could have sent it off with one of numerous couriers along with other personal papers, probably addressed to his partner Starr, or it may have been left behind in the town of San Antonio when the Texians went into the Alamo, escaped notice by the occupying Mexicans, and subsequently was sent to Starr, who gave all of Travis's papers to Jones.

Lindley himself, in a letter to the author, June 4, 1996, testified to having found in the Audited Military Claims an entry stating that an amount exactly equal to the expenditures on the Jones tabulation, was submitted after Travis's death. This certainly seems conclusive of the document's authenticity, though Lindley speculates that a forger, finding that payment, could have used it to create the Jones tabulation, which seems like rather a lot of effort in order to produce a document of no monetary value, the customary motive for forgery. By its own testimony, the document was in Jones' hand, not Travis's, and while Travis documents are extremely valuable, Jones documents are not. The only other possible reason to forge such a document would be the entry of a purchase of wood on February 3 in San Antonio, which establishes the date of Travis's arrival. Lindley makes a good case for Travis not reaching San Antonio until February 5—with which this author still disagrees—but if he is right, it still does not invalidate the Jones tabulation, keeping in mind that what we have in Mixon is her transcription of Jones's transcription of Travis's handwriting. Jones could have misread a Travis 5 for a 3, or Mixon could have misread it in Jones, and a simple error like this seems a far more reasonable and persuasive explanation than a complicated and extended forgery for no discernible purpose.

35. W. B. Price to Zachary T. Fulmore, February 4, 1898, Zachary T. Fulmore Papers, UT; William Zuber, *My Eighty Years in Texas* (Austin, 1971), 84.

36. Receipt of C. B. Stewart, February 22, 1836, Accounts and Receipts Submitted for Approval, Record Group 307, TXSL.

37. Thomas Ricks Lindley has produced an invaluable itinerary of Travis's journey to San Antonio, based on his extensive research. It will appear in a forthcoming work tentatively titled *Alamo Traces: Backtracking the Historiography of the Siege and Storming of the Texian Alamo*. It is most inventive and effective in its interpretation of the slim evidence to locate Travis each day on the road, and with only a few exceptions, this author has accepted his conclusions. Travis's arrival at Burnham's Ferry represents one of those disagreements, however. Lindley notes that Burnham's was off the direct route to San Antonio from Beeson's Ferry, and then speculates—without supporting evidence—that Travis made the diversion, intending to go in person to Washington on the Brazos to meet with Houston and try to have his orders rescinded. This seems improbable at best. If Travis wanted to go to Washington, the best road and most direct route was back through San Felipe, not overland to Burnham's. Moreover, Travis certainly knew enough not to exhaust his entire command with unnecessary riding on what would have been a personal errand. It seems much more probable, considering the way Travis was scouring merchants for goods, that while at Beeson's he learned that Burnham had merchandise he needed—Travis charged $325.85 with Burnham on January 29—and took his command there to collect the goods. And he could have learned of that merchandise on January 25 when the Jones tabulation shows him buying blankets, sugar, and coffee from Burnham, but not necessarily at Burnham's Crossing. In other words Burnham could have encountered Travis on the road on January 25, sold him a few things, and told him that he had much more at his store, persuading Travis to make the side trip a few days later. Again this is hypothetical, but seems more logical than an imaginary trip to Washington for which no evidence exists. Finally, a personal visit to see Charles, as suggested in the text, could have been an additional motive for the diversion.

38. Travis to Smith, January 28, 1836, Army Papers, Record Group 401, TXSL.

39. Travis to Smith, January 29, 1836, ibid.

40. A. J. Lee, "Some Recollections of Two Texas Pioneer Women," *Texas Methodist Quarterly* 1 (January 1910): 209–10. McDonald, *Travis*, 130, places this event between Travis's illness on October 3 and his company's arrival at Béxar on or about October 18, a span of time which subsequent research would have to reduce to October 5 to 11, the period between his departure from San Felipe and his presence in Gonzales. Such a side trip then, in the urgency of the situation, is unlikely, but in any case it is virtually impossible for Travis to have visited Charles at the Montville school then for the simple reason that the school did not open until February 1, 1836 (San Felipe *Telegraph and Texas Register*, November 14, 1835). However, a visit in the last days of January 1836 would be consistent if Charles had been placed there shortly before its opening.

41. James C. Neill to Travis, January 28, 1836, Jenkins, *PTR*, vol. 4, 174–75.

42. Travis to Smith, January 29, 1836, Army Papers, Record Group 401, TXSL.

43. This departs considerably from Lindley's conclusion in *Alamo Traces*, and it must be said is an interpolative conclusion that is certainly subject to debate. Lindley concludes that the company with Travis reached Gonzales by February 2 and remained there through February 4, the date of arrival being based on an average distance that mounted men could cover per day, and his conclusion seems sound. The only documents placing them in Gonzales, however, are two orders for payment dated February 4, both headed Gonzales and signed by Forsyth. It is significant, however, that from the date the company left San Felipe, all such pay orders were signed either by Travis or his quartermaster Thomas Jackson, the two senior officers authorized to initiate such documents. Jackson left the company on January 29, which would mean that all such subsequent documents should have been signed by Travis if he was present. However, after that date all subsequent pay orders were signed by Forsyth until the company reached San Antonio. According to prior practice, Travis should have and would have signed them if he had been with the company. This suggests that he no longer traveled with the company from at least as early as February 1, the date of the first order signed by Forsyth. Consequently, even though Forsyth and the company were definitely in Gonzales on February 4, Travis was not, meaning that the February 3 date of arrival in San Antonio indicated by an entry in the John R. Jones statement as executor (Mixon, "Travis," 442) is quite probably correct. The payment orders referred to will all be found in Lindley's essay, and are taken from the files for Samuel Leeper, J. W. E. Wallace, W. W. Arrington, William D. Lacy, Joseph Ehlinger, William Brookfield, Jesse Burnham, Thomas Chadoin, William A. Matthews, William Newland, and C. B. Stewart, Audited Military Claims, TXSL.

44. As stated above, Travis's February 3 arrival is based upon a note of an expenditure that day in the Jones tabulation (Mixon, "Travis," 442). It is possible that this is an error in transcription and should read February 5, in which case Lindley would be right in his assertion of an arrival on that date. Any decision on the issue rests solely on interpretation of very scanty and incomplete evidence.

45. Rodriguez, *Memoirs*, 8–9.

46. Memorial of Citizens & Soldiers of Béxar, n.d., Consultation Papers, TXSL. This document is almost certainly written and signed prior to February 5, the date often assigned to it (see Jenkins, *PTR*, vol. 4, 263–65). It is signed by every officer present in the garrison, yet Forsyth did not sign it. Since Lindley has conclusively established that Forsyth was in Gonzales as late as February 4, and could not have reached San Antonio until sometime February 5, the absence of his name establishes that this document was drafted and sent prior to his arrival, and therefore almost certainly either February 3 or 4, the latter seeming more likely. This being the case, it also presents additional persuasive evidence that Travis arrived ahead of Forsyth and the company, and prior to February 5.

47. Bowie to Smith, February 2, 1836, Jenkins, *PTR*, vol. 4, 236–37.

48. Menchaca, *Memoirs*, 22. Menchaca, usually strikingly accurate, says that

Crockett arrived January 13, which is impossible, since he was still in Nacogdoches then, and the error cannot be simply the wrong month, because Crockett was definitely in Béxar prior to February 13. Consequently, his memory of dates has failed him here, but there seems no reason to doubt the essence of his statement about the circumstances of Crockett's arrival. Hutton, introduction to Crockett, *Narrative*, xxx, says that Crockett arrived February 3 but offers no source to support this, and it seems too early. Even though not an officer, a man of his political importance would certainly have been asked to sign the February 4 memorial. Stanley J. Folmsbee and Anna Grace Catron, "David Crockett in Texas," *East Tennessee Historical Society Publications* 30 (1958): 60, speculate that he arrived February 7 or 8, since the John Sutherland memoir says that Crockett came "in a few days—less than a week" after Travis's arrival. The first specific mention of him is Green Jameson's February 11, 1836, letter, cited below. Thomas Lindley has prepared a useful itinerary of Crockett's journey from Little Rock, and his conclusion is that he arrived in San Antonio probably on or around February 5. In the absence of any newer or more specific information, that is about as good a guess as is possible.

49. Certificate, January 23, 1836, David Crockett File, Audited Military Claims, Comptroller's Military Service Papers, TXSL.

50. Certificate, January 24, 1836 Crockett File, Audited Military Claims, ibid.

51. John M. Swisher, *The Swisher Memoirs* (San Antonio, 1932), 18–19.

52. "Life of Nathan Mitchell," San Antonio *Express*, August 31, 1897.

53. Smithwick, *Evolution*, 117. In fact, nothing certain is known of Crockett's itinerary after he left Gay Hill. Smithwick is highly unreliable at times, and even though there are several other sources citing traditions that Crockett passed through Mina (now Bastrop), they could be erroneous (for instance, Frank Brown, *Annals of Travis County and the City of Austin* [N.p., n.d.], 47). Lindley's itinerary maintains that Crockett was in the Goliad-Copano area, more than one hundred miles off the most direct route to Béxar. Lindley's evidence is a claim filed for an expense incurred by Peter Harper, who had been part of Crockett's contingent, the inference being that if Harper was near Goliad or Copano, then so was Crockett. This may be true, and it may not. Since the most direct road from Gay Hill to Béxar was the old Gotier Trace to its junction with the Medio road, then south across the Colorado to the San Antonio road and thence via Gonzales, this has been chosen as his most likely route.

54. It is worth noting that nothing survives to establish exactly what Crockett's orders were when he left Nacogdoches, or even if he had any. He was probably directed simply to move to Washington, where Houston had been, in the expectation of getting orders, but Houston was not there when Crockett passed through. Consequently, while Crockett may have received orders from someone else directing him to Béxar, he may just as possibly have been moving about entirely on his own initiative.

55. Menchaca, *Memoirs*, 22; San Antonio *Daily Express*, February 12, 1905.

56. Sutherland, "Fall of the Alamo," Williams Papers, UT. This is the original 1860

version of the Sutherland memoir, and is used in preference to the published version, John Sutherland, *The Fall of the Alamo* (San Antonio, 1936), 11, which puts a much more eloquent speech on Crockett's lips. It is proper here to address this document. No original has been found. The typescript in the Williams Papers is fragmentary, but it is obviously by Sutherland, written in 1860, intended as an article for the San Antonio *Alamo Express*, but never published as intended. It was to be a response to Reuben Potter's "The Fall of the Alamo," which was published that same year in the San Antonio *Herald*. John S. Ford apparently revised this memoir somewhat when he included it in the 1880s or 1890s in his *Memoirs*, vol. 1, UT, and this is the version that finally saw print in an edited version published by James T. DeShields in the Galveston *Daily News*, February 12, 1911, news magazine supplement, and then came out as a book, *The Fall of the Alamo*, in 1936. There are some inaccuracies and inconsistencies in the memoir, but nothing that its being written twenty-four years after the fact could not explain. There is some question as to whether Sutherland was still in San Antonio after February 19, which may call into question his statements about affairs after that date, but there is no just grounds for being skeptical of what he says relating to prior events.

57. Jameson to Smith, February 11, 1836, Jenkins, *PTR*, vol. 4, 303; Claim no. 1358, February 11, 1836, Crockett to the auditor of accounts, February 13, 1836, Crockett File, Audited Military Accounts, TXSL.

58. Menchaca, *Memoirs*, 22–23.

59. Davis, *Travis Diary*, October 18, 1833, 49.

60. John R. Jones statement, December 18, 1837, in Mixon, "Travis," 442.

61. D. C. Barrett to Robinson, January 31, 1836, Jenkins, *PTR*, vol. 1, 204–6.

62. Alexander Thomson and J. D. Clements to Smith, February 11, 1836, Jenkins, *PTR*, vol. 4, 316.

63. Jameson to Smith, February 11, 1836, Army Papers, Record Group 401, TXSL.

64. Travis commission, December 24, 1835, Travis Papers, UT. This is a copy of the original, stated to have been found in the Archivo Historico Militar Mexicano in Mexico City, and the only way the document could have gotten there would be for Travis to have had it with him in San Antonio at the time of the fall of the Alamo on March 6, after which it must have been among other papers captured and sent to Mexico City.

65. Travis to Smith, February 12, 1836, Army Papers, Record Group 401, TXSL.

66. Travis to Smith, February 12, 1836, J. J. Baugh to Smith, February 13, 1836, ibid.

67. Sutherland, "Fall of the Alamo," Williams Papers, UT. Sutherland is the only source for the claim that Crockett was offered a command. All he says is that "D. Crockett had been requested to take command but refused at the time of Col Travis accepted." Despite the poor wording, Sutherland's meaning is clear, that when Travis took command, Crockett turned down a proffered command, but Sutherland does not say that Crockett was offered the entire command of the garrison. In the version of Sutherland's memoir in the John Ford Papers, UT, this has been changed to say "Crockett was immediately offered a command by

Col. Travis," which is quite a different matter. Later writers have mistakenly interpreted this to mean that Travis actually offered Crockett command of the whole garrison, which is preposterous. Travis could not even offer Crockett command of a company, for Crockett held no commission, and Travis did not have the authority to promote him to be an officer. Thus, if Sutherland's original statement derives from any genuine original incident, it can only have been that of some of the volunteers approaching Crockett and offering to elect him. This would be perfectly natural, given his celebrity. Significantly, the Baugh letter of February 13 also states that not all of the volunteers voted in electing Bowie, who was apparently the only candidate. This suggests that those who did not vote did not want Bowie as their commander, leading to the speculation that they were the ones who approached Crockett, preferring him.

It should be noted that the Sutherland version in the Ford *Memoirs* also errs grossly in saying that Bowie took command when Neill left, but that he fell ill and then asked Travis to take over. However, he also states that he got this information from others, implying that he was not yet actually present.

68. Though no one mentions the actual election until Baugh's February 13 letter and Travis's of the same date, it is apparent that it took place on February 11 immediately upon Neill's leaving, for Jameson in his February 11 letter to Smith refers to "Col. Bowie in command of the Volunteer forces." William Groneman, "Jim Bowie—A Popular Leader" *Alamo News* 34 (January 1984): n.p., makes well the case for Bowie's popularity not being as great as has been supposed.

69. Baugh to Smith, February 13, 1836, Army Papers, Record Group 401, TXSL.

70. Travis to Smith, February 13, 1836, ibid.

71. Ibid.

72. W. W. Fontaine notes, n.d., of interview with Nat Lewis [1870s], Fontaine Papers, UT; Brown, *Indian Wars and Pioneers*, 138.

73. Baugh to Smith, February 13, 1836, Army Papers, Record Group 401, TXSL.

74. Fontaine to Guy Bryan, June 3, 1890, Fontaine Papers, UT.

75. Juan N. Seguín to Fontaine, June 7, 1890, Fontaine Papers, UT. Phil Rosenthal, "Masons at the Alamo," *Alamo II* 3 (October 1980): n.p., is correct in noting Travis's documented Masonic membership, and Bowie's at least by implication, since his effects after his death included a Masonic apron. However, Masonry would have been offensive to Crockett's prejudices against secret groups, representing a kind of attempt at aristocracy, and therefore Rosenthal is mistaken in saying that Crockett helped Travis start a Blue Lodge in Texas. Lord, "William Travis," 12, is mistaken in saying that Travis was a member of Holland Lodge no. 36 in Brazoria, for it did not come into existence until January 1836, when he was far from Brazoria, in San Felipe, and then on his way to Béxar.

76. Travis to Smith, February 12, 1836, Army Papers, Record Group 401, TXSL.

77. John R. Jones statement, December 18, 1837, Mixon, "Travis," 442.

78. Samuel E. Asbury, ed., "The Private Journal of Juan Nepomuceno Almonte, February 1–April 16, 1836," *Southwestern Historical Quarterly* 48 (July 1944): February 12, 1836, 14.

79. Susanna Dickenson statement, December 9, 1850, quoted in C. Richard King, *Susanna Dickenson, Messenger of the Alamo* (Austin, 1976), 67.

80. Reuben Potter to William Steele, July 14, 1874, Adjutant General's Office, Miscellaneous Papers, TXSL; Travis to Smith, February 13, 1836, Army Papers, Record Group 401, ibid.

81. Travis and Bowie to Smith, February 14, 1836, Texas Collection of Documents, Bancroft Library, University of California, Berkeley.

82. John H. Jenkins, ed., *The General's Tight Pants* (Austin, 1976), 12; Travis to Smith, February 15, 1836, Jenkins, *PTR*, vol. 1, 348.

83. Ramón M. Caro, "Verdadera Idea de la Primera Campana de Tejas" (Mexico City, 1837), in Castañeda, *Mexican Side*, 101–2.

84. Travis statement, February 19, 1836, Felipe Xaimes File, Republic Payments for Service, Record Group 304, TXSL.

85. José Rodriguez, *Memoirs of Early Texas* (San Antonio, 1913), 7.

86. King, *Dickenson*, 70.

87. Hardin, "David Crockett," 32.

88. Rohrbaugh, "James Bowie," 30–31.

89. Inventory of personal effects of James Bowie, Probate Court, Béxar County Court House, San Antonio.

90. Sears, "Low Down," 198; Juana Alsbury Account, John S. Ford Memoirs, UT.

91. Marriage Record A, Monroe County Court, 1833–1838, 11. Other sources, presumably using this record, actually cite the marriage date a day later. Rosanna's marriage so soon after the divorce, and the fact that Cloud and the Travises lived near and knew one another in Claiborne, may be the origin of the much later legend of Travis leaving her because of her infidelity, a story that probably began with the Travis family, who would naturally prefer to blame her rather than their son for the divorce.

92. This whole episode of Travis sending his expenses back to San Felipe is suppositional. The only known facts are that the last entry in it was February 17, that the book wound up in the hands of his executor Jones a year later, and that Texas honored the expenses and paid them to his estate. It seems unlikely that the book was with him in the Alamo, for no papers there at the time of the fall seem to have survived in Texas, and if it had been sent to Mexico with other captured documents, it would never have reached Jones. Travis could have left it in his quarters in San Antonio on February 23 when the garrison went into the Alamo, and someone subsequently finding it might have sent it to Jones. But given the shortage of money, and the fact that the almost daily entries stop on February 17, it seems more likely that Travis sent it out himself, hoping for a speedy reimbursement.

   The San Felipe *Telegraph and Texas Register,* March 5, 1836, establishes that Jones was in San Felipe at about this time.

93. Travis to Smith, February 16, 1836, Army Papers, Record Group 401, TXSL; David Cummings to his father, February 14, 1836, Jenkins, *PTR*, vol. 4, 334.

94. Travis to the convention, March 3, 1836, San Felipe *Telegraph and Texas Register*, March 12, 1836, states that Bonham left carrying dispatches on February 17.

95. Travis to Houston, January [February] 17, 1836, in Yoakum, *Texas*, vol. 2, 59. Turner and McDonald both accept this as January 17, as does Jenkins, but they are in error. The original of this letter is lost, but Yoakum quite certainly misquotes its date, for he says it is headed "Béxar," and of course on January 17 Travis was still in San Felipe. Moreover, Travis did not get the Béxar assignment until January 21, and his pleas for money and troops do not commence until February.

96. Rodriguez, *Memoirs*, 8–9; Travis and Bowie to Smith, February 14, 1836, Travis Papers, UT.

97. Travis to J. J. Vaughan, February 19, 1836, typescript in Williams Papers, UT.

98. Sowell, *Rangers and Pioneers*, 136; Rodriguez, *Memoirs*, 8–9.

99. Sutherland, "Fall of the Alamo," Williams Papers, UT.

100. Mexico City *El Mosquito Mexicano*, March 4, 1836; Asbury, "Almonte Journal," 16, February 21, 1836.

101. Seguín to the state comptroller, December 5, 1874, in de la Teja, Seguín, *Memoirs*, 190; Hardin, "Efficient in the Cause," Poyo, *Tejano Journey*, 57.

102. Travis statement, February 22, 1836, Antonio Cruz File, Republic Payments for Service, Record Group 304, TXSL.

103. Menchaca, *Memoirs*, 23; Asbury, "Almonte Journal," 16, February 21, 1836. Menchaca does not mention encountering the Mexican army in his memoir, but Almonte records his arrival in his journal, though says nothing about what, if anything, was done about him.

104. Julia Nott Waugh, *Castroville and Henry Castro, Empresario* (Castroville, Tex., 1986), 93; Kevin Young to the author, June 10, 1996; Rodriguez, *Memoirs*, 9. The Rodriguez account maintains that Santa Anna himself attended the fandango in disguise, which is of course ridiculous. Francisco Beccera, *A Mexican Sergeant's Recollections of the Alamo and San Jacinto* (Austin, 1980), 17–18, does say that the Mexican army knew of the fandango, which is certainly possible, and tried to take advantage of it by making a surprise attack that night, but the swollen Medina made a crossing then impossible. There is no contemporary support for this. It should also be noted that it is possible that the fandango described as being in Crockett's honor on February 10 could quite possibly have been confused by the sources with this February 22 affair, since all of the sources for both are considerably belated and may suffer from faulty memory.

105. Sutherland, "Dr. John Sutherland on the Alamo," Ford Memoirs, UT. This is the 1880s version of Sutherland. The incomplete 1860 "Fall of the Alamo" in the Williams Papers at UT does not contain a reference to Bowie's health, but that portion may have been missing from the original when Williams made her transcriptions.

Chapter 21 Apotheosis: February 23–Dawn, March 6, 1836

1. Sutherland, "Fall of the Alamo," Williams Papers, UT. At this point it is necessary to say that there is a division of opinion on the reliability of the Sutherland account. Sutherland's claim dated 1836, in his file in the Audited Military Claims, Record Group 401, TXSL, places him in San Antonio on February 19, and William Patton's claim, 1836, in his file in the Audited Military Claims, TXSL, confirms this. However, the next entry in Sutherland's account is February 25, in Gonzales, with no accounting for his whereabouts for the previous five days. In the three versions of his memoir, all state that he was in Béxar on February 23, and left as a messenger for Travis on that date, which is compatible with the claims records. However, when he submitted a claim for a headright of land to the legislature in January 1854 (Sutherland File, Memorials and Petitions Collection, TXSL), stating that among other things he had been in Béxar on February 23 and acted as a courier for Travis, the legislature denied his claim, stating lack of supporting evidence. This may have been simple carelessness on the applicant's part, the rejection having nothing whatever to do with Sutherland's statement of where he was on February 23, but possibly it did. On the other hand, since many other factors may have been involved, it is not deemed that the legislature's refusal necessarily repudiates Sutherland's claim, and so his account is used here, judiciously. However, anything in his memoirs on affairs in San Antonio after that date is, as he said himself, derived after the fact from others who were there.

2. Sutherland, "Fall of the Alamo," Williams Papers, UT.

3. Ibid.; John Sutherland to the Legislature of the State of Texas, January 1854, Sutherland File, Memorials and Petitions Collection, TXSL.

4. Juan N. Seguín to Fontaine, June 7, 1890, Fontaine Collection, UT.

5. Philip Dimitt to James Kerr, February 28, 1836, Jenkins, *PTR*, vol. 4, 453.

6. Travis to Andrew Ponton and the citizens of Gonzales, February 23, 1836, Streeter Collection, Yale.

7. Sutherland, "Fall of the Alamo," Williams Papers; Sutherland Memoir in Ford Memoirs, UT. It should be noted here that in the San Antonio *Daily Express*, February 12, 1905, Samuel Maverick said that it was actually Crockett who persuaded Travis to move into the Alamo. This is nonsense. It should also be noted that Mixon in her "Travis" thesis, and Turner, *Travis*, 205, and McDonald, Travis, 158, all unaccountably make use of the bogus Crockett "diary" published after his death. It is a pure fabrication, as exposed in Shackford, *Crockett*, 273ff.

8. Susanna Dickenson interview, September 23, 1876, quoted in King, *Dickenson*, 105; Mariano Arroyo, Report of Military Hospital at Béxar, August 1, 1836, Expediente XI/481.3/1151, Archivo Historico Militar Mexicano, Mexico City.

9. Seguín to Fontaine, June 7, 1890, Fontaine Papers, UT.

10. Fontaine notes, n.d. [1870s], ibid.; Travis to "The People of Texas and All Americans in the World," February 24, 1836, Army Papers, Record Group 401, Receipt to Ignacio Perez, February 23, 1836, Republic Payments for Service, Record Group 304, TXSL.

11. "Mrs. Alsbury's Recollections of the Alamo," Ford Memoirs, vol. 1; Sutherland, "Fall of the Alamo," Williams Papers, UT; Susanna Dickenson interview, September 23, 1876, King, *Dickenson,* 105; Chester Newell, *History of the Revolution in Texas* (Austin, 1935), 88.

12. Amelia Williams to Asbury, February 1, 1932, Asbury Papers, UT.

13. Asbury, "Almonte Journal," 16–17, February 23, 1836.

14. Bowie to Santa Anna, February 23, 1836, James Bowie Vertical File, UT. There is some debate over which side fired the first shot. Asbury, "Almonte Journal," 17, February 23, 1836; Carmen Perry, ed., *With Santa Anna in Texas: A Personal Narrative of the Revolution by José Enrique de la Peña* (College Station, Tex., 1975), 38–39; Manuel Loranca account, San Antonio *Express,* June 23, 1878, all differ. Almonte's journal, being the most immediate and almost certainly unaltered in later years, is probably the most accurate, and is relied on here for the chronology of the negotiations, but Bowie's letter is certainly the best source for the first gun and the opening of negotiations.

15. Bowie to Santa Anna, February 23, 1836, Bowie Vertical File, UT; Walter Lord, *A Time to Stand* (New York, 1961), 102.

16. Reuben Potter, "Fall of the Alamo," *Magazine of American History* 2 (January 1878): 6.

17. José Batres to Bowie, February 23, 1836, Jenkins, *PTR,* vol. 4, 415. Santa Anna would later claim that he offered to spare the lives of all those who would lay down their arms and take an oath not to take them up again. His secretary Ramón Caro said this was a lie, and that the general demanded a "surrender at discretion," raising a red flag as a sign of no quarter. Certainly Travis spoke of seeing a red flag on the first day of the siege. Both are partially correct, though it is clear from Batres's note that Santa Anna suggested they would "save their lives" by giving up. Castañeda, *Mexican Side,* 14, 154.

18. Travis to Houston, February 25, 1836, Little Rock *Arkansas Gazette,* April 12, 1836.

19. Sutherland, "Fall of the Alamo," Williams Papers, UT. Sgt. Manuel Loranca in a letter in the San Antonio *Express,* June 23, 1878, which is strikingly accurate in most respects, says that Travis offered to surrender the fort if his command could march out with their arms and leave unmolested to join Houston, as the Texians had allowed Cós to leave Béxar the previous December. Certainly this is possible, considering the fact that Travis sent Martin to parley at all, but Loranca can only have been repeating camp gossip in his army.

20. Asbury, "Almonte Journal," 17, February 23, 1836.

21. Antonio López de Santa Anna, *Manifesto* (Vera Cruz, Mex., 1837), 14.

22. Potter, "Fall of the Alamo," 6. Potter got this information from Juan Seguín, who was present.

23. Travis to Houston, February 25, 1836, Little Rock *Arkansas Gazette,* April 12, 1836.

24. Travis and Bowie to Fannin, February 23, 1836, Jenkins, *PTR,* vol. 4, 419.

25. Travis to Houston, February 25, 1836, Little Rock *Arkansas Gazette,* April 12,

1836; Robert Hunter, *Narrative of Robert Hunter* (Austin, 1966), 9–10.

26. Sutherland, "Fall of the Alamo," Williams Papers, UT. This is the only source we have for the assignment of any of the garrison, and it must be remembered that Sutherland only says that Crockett was assigned here on February 23. That does not mean that Crockett and others of Patton's company stayed there throughout the siege. Hutton, introduction to Crockett, *Narrative*, Lincoln, Neb., edition, xxxi, speculates that Crockett drew this assignment, presumably the toughest, because of his legendary reputation. Moreover, he states that Crockett was "trapped by his own legend" and could not leave San Antonio. This ignores the fact that Crockett was now an enlisted soldier, subject to orders, and did not have the option of leaving unless he wished to be a deserter, and nothing in his life suggests that he would do that in the face of an enemy.

27. Asbury, "Almonte Journal," 17, February 23, 1836.

28. Travis statement, February 23, 1836, Ignacio Perez File, Republic Payments for Service, Record Group 304, TXSL.

29. Dimitt to Kerr, February 28, 1836, Jenkins, *PTR*, vol. 4, 453.

30. Sutherland, "Fall of the Alamo," Williams Papers, UT.

31. "Mrs. Alsbury's Recollections of the Alamo," Ford Memoirs, vol. 1, UT, is the only eyewitness source that actually identifies Bowie's illness as typhoid. Mrs. Dickenson said only that Bowie "was sick before & during the fight, and had even been expected to die" (Testimony of Mrs. Hannig touching the Alamo massacre, September 23, 1876, TXSL). Samuel Maverick, who would have been aware of Bowie's state up to the time of his leaving on February 23, said that Bowie was "feeble," but nothing more (Green, *Maverick*, 55). While many theories have been propounded as to his malady, these are the only firsthand eyewitness statements we have. Combined with one or two other statements about his symptoms, they are certainly consistent with typhoid, though not sufficiently detailed as to rule out other possibilities. Since Mrs. Alsbury tended him during the siege, and would have seen the course of his disease firsthand, she would have been in the best position to know in the end what he had, assuming that she knew the symptoms and progression of typhoid.

32. Gray, *Virginia to Texas*, 119.

33. Asbury, "Almonte Journal," 17, February 24, 1836.

34. Travis to The People of Texas, February 24, 1836, Army Papers, Record Group 401, TXSL.

35. Asbury, "Almonte Journal," 17, February 24, 1836.

36. Potter, "Fall of the Alamo," 18.

37. Asbury, "Almonte Journal," 17–18, February 25, 1836.

38. Travis to Houston, February 25, 1836, Little Rock *Arkansas Gazette*, April 12, 1836.

39. Travis to Jesse Grimes, March 3, 1836, San Felipe *Telegraph and Texas Register*, March 24, 1836, reveals that he expected others to see his February 25 dispatch to Houston.

40. Seguín to Fontaine, June 7, 1890, Fontaine Collection, UT.

41. Travis to Grimes, March 3, 1836, San Felipe *Telegraph and Texas Register*, March 24, 1836; Asbury, "Almonte Journal," 18, February 25, 1836.

42. Gray, *Virginia to Texas*, 119; Harris, "Reminiscences, II," 160; Fannin to Robinson, February 25, 1836, Jenkins, *PTR*, vol. 4, 429; Brown, *Smith*, 298–99. Hunter, *Narrative*, 9–10.

43. Gray, *Virginia to Texas*, 119–20; Asbury, "Almonte Journal," 18–19, February 26–27, 1836; Williams, "Critical Study, vol. 4," 307.

44. "Mrs. Alsbury's Recollections of the Alamo," Ford Memoir, vol. 1, UT.

45. Joseph Field, *Three Years in Texas* (Boston, 1836), 17; Andrew F. Muir, ed., *Texas in 1837: An Anonymous Contemporary Narrative* (Austin, 1958), 113; Louisville *Journal*, July 11, 1836. No one can say with certainty what sort of gun Crockett had with him in the Alamo, though contrary to popular depiction, it probably was not a flintlock, since he certainly favored a cap-and-ball percussion rifle after the gift of "Pretty Betsey" in 1834. For a circumstantial account of claimed weapons used by him, see Texas Jim Cooper, "A Study of Some David Crockett Firearms," *East Tennessee Historical Society's Publications* 38 (1966): 68–69.

46. Asbury, "Almonte Journal," 19, February 27, 1836; Field, *Three Years*, 57.

47. Asbury, "Almonte Journal," 19, February 28, 1836; Gray, *Virginia to Texas*, 120.

48. Gray, *Virginia to Texas*, 120.

49. San Felipe *Telegraph and Texas Register,* March 5, 1836.

50. J. W. Hassell to Jesse Hassell, February 29, 1836, Hassell Family Papers, Fannin to Joseph Mims, February 28, 1836, Fontaine Collection, UT.

51. Asbury, "Almonte Journal," 19, February 29, 1836.

52. Seguín to Fontaine, June 7, 1890, Fontaine Collection, UT.

53. Timothy M. Matovina, *The Alamo Remembered: Tejano Accounts and Perspectives* (Austin, 1995), 81–82. This is the account of Enrique Esparza, given seventy-one years after the fact, and therefore may be highly inaccurate. However, Stephen L. Hardin, "Efficient in the Cause," in Poyo, *Tejano Journey*, 57–58, makes a convincing case for Esparza being in the main correct about the *tejanos* leaving, and there are other sources, to be cited hereafter. Hardin also suggests that it is at this point that Menchaca leaves, even though Menchaca, *Memoirs*, 23, places his departure before Santa Anna arrived at Béxar. Hardin's argument is convincing, though that leaves the problem of explaining Asbury, "Almonte Journal," 16, February 21, 1836, which speaks of "Menchaca" coming into the Mexican camp on the Medina. This could have been a different Menchaca, of course, or it may have been only a visit, after which Menchaca escaped to return to San Antonio, though he makes no mention of anything like this in his memoirs. Almonte records only Menchaca's arrival in his journal, though says nothing about what, if anything, was done about him.

54. Gray, *Virginia to Texas*, 121.

55. Travis to the President of the Convention, March 3, 1836, San Felipe *Telegraph and Texas Register*, March 12, 1836.

56. Asbury, "Almonte Journal," 19, March 1, 1836.

57. "Mrs. Alsbury's Recollections of the Alamo," Ford Memoir, vol. 1, UT.

58. San Antonio *Daily Express*, May 12, 1907.

59. James K. Greer, ed., "Journal of Ammon Underwood, 1834–1838," *Southwestern Historical Quarterly* 32 (July 1928): 142–43, March 1, 1836; John S. Brooks to his mother, March 2, 1836, Jenkins, *PTR*, vol. 4, 487.

60. W. W. Thompson affadavit, December 1, 1840, Home Papers, Box 2–9/6, TXSL. See also Thomas Ricks Lindley, "Drawing Truthful Deductions," *Journal of the Alamo Battlefield Association* 1 (September 1995): 31–33. The quotations come from statements made in 1837 and 1840 and are given in full in Lindley's perceptive article.

61. Milledge L. Bonham, Memorandum, Milledge L. Bonham Papers, South Caroliniana Library, University of South Carolina, Columbia. This memorandum states that Houston told Milledge Bonham this in 1838. The memorandum says that Houston talked with James Butler Bonham, but this is impossible, since Houston was in Washington, and Bonham in Gonzales, but he may have meant that he "told" Bonham this, and Bonham's surviving brother assumed that it meant face to face. It is possible that this message to Bonham, if indeed Houston sent it, is the "other letter" referred to cryptically in Williamson's March 1 letter to Travis, dealt with below.

62. This is based on an interesting and very logical conclusion reached by Thomas R. Lindley, and shared in a letter to the author, June 4, 1996.

63. Asbury, "Almonte Journal," 20, March 2, 1836.

64. Travis to President of the Convention, March 3, 1836, San Felipe *Telegraph and Texas Register*, March 12, 1836.

65. Ibid.

66. The total number of cannon in the Alamo was twenty-one, only eighteen of them actually in usable condition. The best study to date of this is Thomas Ricks Lindley, "Alamo Artillery: Number, Type, Caliber and Concussion," *Alamo Journal* 82 (July 1992): n.p. The total number of defenders, as stated below, is a matter of continuing debate, but it is here assumed that it numbered two hundred or more at this stage.

67. Williamson to Travis, March 1, 1836, translation of text in Thomas Ricks Lindley, "James Butler Bonham," *Alamo Journal* 62 (August 1988): 5.

68. Sutherland, "Fall of the Alamo," Williams Papers, UT; Stephen L. Hardin to the author, July 1, 1996.

69. Travis to President of the Convention, March 3, 1836, San Felipe *Telegraph and Texas Register*, March 12, 1836.

70. Travis to Grimes, March 3, 1836, San Felipe *Telegraph and Texas Register*, March 24, 1836.

71. Sutherland, "Fall of the Alamo," Williams Papers, UT; Asbury, "Almonte Journal," 20, March 3, 1836.

72. Asbury, "Almonte Journal," 20, March 3, 1836.

73. Sutherland, "Fall of the Alamo," Williams Papers, UT. Sutherland, who definitely was not in the Alamo at this time, carefully qualifies this statement and
others by saying that he was informed of this by John Smith, who did not leave
until late on March 3.

74. Travis to Grimes, March 3, 1836, San Felipe *Telegraph and Texas Register,* March
24, 1836; Mary Holley Manuscript Notes, Holley Papers, UT, says that "Miss
Cummins" received a letter from Travis that went out with the last courier, and
this must be the letter that Travis asks Grimes to send "to its proper destination
instantly."

75. Travis to Ayers, March 3, 1836, in Mixon, "Travis," 455.

76. Sutherland, "Fall of the Alamo," Williams Papers, UT. Again, Sutherland says
that he was told this by Smith after the fall of the Alamo. It should be noted that
Williams, "Critical Study, II," 21n, speaks of her being shown a scrapbook of
clippings collected by Smith's daughter, presumably dealing with her father,
who unfortunately seems never to have given for publication his own account of
the Alamo. This scrapbook has not been found to date.

77. Affidavits of V. Bennett, n.d., Lewis Ayers, November 8, 1836, William L.
Hunter, William Rosenberg, and Thomas Kemp, November 8, 1836, Williamson
Oldham statement, n.d., Petition of Administrators of James Bowie, Memorial
No. 451, TXSL.

78. "Mrs. Alsbury's Recollections of the Alamo," Ford Memoir, vol. 1; Sutherland
account, Ford Memoir, UT; Testimony of Mrs. Hannig, September 23, 1876,
TXSL. According to Williams, "Critical Study, II," 43n, Susanna Dickenson's
granddaughter said in 1929 that her grandmother had told her that on March 3
Bowie was taken from his sickroom and into the small room at the southwest
corner of the Alamo church. Enrique Esparza agreed, and so did the aged
Andrea Castañán Villanueva, called Madame Candelaria. But Candelaria probably was not even in the Alamo at that point—if ever at all—and Esparza's recollections are so belated, and wildly inaccurate and self-contradictory, that little
faith should be put in them on this point, as he was probably influenced by the
numerous, and equally confused and contradictory, Candelaria accounts. As for
Dickenson's granddaughter's supposed statement, in the first place it is second
hand at best. None of the reports of interviews with Susanna, from first to last,
make any mention of Bowie being brought into the church, though she did
mention him once or twice, in the 1876 interview cited above saying that "she
knew Col Bowee & saw him in the Fort, both before & after his death. He was
sick before & during the fight, and had even been expected to die." Given the
increasing inaccuracy of statements attributed to her in her later years, and the
unmistakable evidence that she incorporated other stories and rumors into her
accounts, no reliance can be placed on this supposed hand-me-down story.
Besides, Bowie had isolated himself because of his typhoid, and his contagious
condition was presumably well known in the fort. It seems incredible, then, that
Mrs. Dickenson and the others who occupied that room in the church would
choose to expose themselves to the same virus that was probably killing him.
Also, the southwest room in the church happened to be the baptistry, already

occupied by the magazine. So far as any reasonable conclusion may be made, Bowie remained in the room beside the gate until he died.

79. John Stuart to Houston, March 15, 1836, Jenkins, *PTR*, vol. 5, 86; Baltimore *Nile's Weekly Register,* March 19, 1836.

80. Asbury, "Almonte Journal," 20, March 4, 1836.

81. This is not asserted as a fact, but merely as a speculation based on the fact that in the final minutes of the battle, this is what the surviving defenders did, as described subsequently.

82. Potter, "Fall of the Alamo," 7; Matovina, *Tejano Accounts,* 27. It has to be said here that while the *tejano* accounts in Matovina and others are certainly interesting and often quite colorful, as historical documents they cannot be regarded as very trustworthy so far as the events in the Alamo are concerned. Of the thirty-seven accounts in the book, including the one cited, only seven were actually written within twenty years of 1836, none of whose authors were inside the Alamo, and only one was even in the vicinity. With the exception of the statements of Juana Alsbury, Brigidio Guerrero, and Enrique Esparza, all these accounts are by people who claim to have been in San Antonio. Only Juana Alsbury's 1880s statement is truly valuable for what went on inside the fort. Esparza's accounts are mostly useless, being written sixty-five to seventy-five years after the fact, highly imaginative, and contradictory. Madame Candelaria, who claimed to have been inside during the fight, was clearly either lying or senile, repeatedly changing her story, incorporating the recollections of others as her own, and contradicting herself. These accounts are not unreliable because they are by *tejanos,* it should be emphasized, but simply because they are by people who were for the most part quite aged when they made these statements, and who had become accustomed to being minor celebrities because of the stories they could tell, and therefore had considerable motive to exaggerate them in the retelling.

83. There is a question of whether Travis may have sent out an offer of surrender on the night of March 4 or 5. Gen. Vicente Filisola in his *Memoirs,* vol. 2, 176–77, wrote of a rumor that on March 5 Travis sent a woman out of the fort to Santa Anna with a proposal that the garrison would surrender its arms and the fort, if he would spare their lives, but that the general refused, demanding a surrender at his discretion. Similar to this is the statement by José de la Peña in his *Narrative,* 44, that on March 5 Travis promised the garrison that if no reinforcements arrived that day, he would surrender the next day or try to break out and escape in the night, and that the Mexicans learned of this from a woman in Béxar. Neither the Almonte "Journal" nor the memoir of Santa Anna's private secretary Caro makes mention of any such rumor. Both Filisola and de la Peña probably derived their accounts from a common source and camp gossip, and de la Peña most likely confused some of the genuine stories no doubt going about Béxar among the *tejanos* who had left the fort in the previous few days. Of the two, only Filisola would have been in Santa Anna's headquarters, and thus able to speak from any direct firsthand knowledge. Travis did say in one of this letters that if the convention in Washington did not declare independence, he

would lay down his arms, and such a statement, if made to the garrison or in hearing of the *tejanos* before they left, might easily have percolated into the version that appeared in de la Peña's memoir. There were a few stories in Texian accounts of a *tejana* woman going out of the fort that night and somehow betraying Travis to the Mexicans, but the fact is there is nothing such a person or persons could have known that would have benefited Santa Anna, who already had all the advantage on his side. The only thing Santa Anna might not have known was the extent of Travis's provisions and ammunition, and what word he had gotten about reinforcements. These rumors seem to originate with Susanna Dickenson in an 1874 interview cited in Morphis, *Texas*, vol. 1, 175, and she seemed to imply that the traitor was Juana Alsbury, which is entirely erroneous, since she was still in the Alamo as of March 6.

84. Ehrenberg, *With Milam and Fannin*, 101; Hollon and Butler, *Bollaert's Texas*, 224.

85. Morphis, *Texas*, 174–75. Another reinforcement, perhaps the sixty men from San Felipe mentioned by Williamson, may have come in that day, bringing the total garrison—including those in the hospital—to something approaching 250. However, this is only conjecture at this point.

86. Asbury, "Almonte Journal," 20, 22, March 4–5, 1836; Houston to Fannin, March 11, 1836, Jenkins, *PTR*, vol. 5, 52–53.

87. Port Gibson, Miss., *Correspondent*, April 23, 1836.

88. Report of munitions fired at the Alamo, March 21, 1836, Expediente XI/481.3/1655, Archivo Historico Militar Mexicano, Mexico City.

89. Williams, "Critical Study, III," 164.

90. Fort Worth *Star-Telegram*, February 28, 1932; B. N. Pittman to Eugene C. Barker, April 4, 1932, Williams Papers, UT.

91. San Antonio *Express*, May 12, 1907.

92. "Mrs. Alsbury's Recollections of the Alamo," Ford Memoir, vol. 1, UT. McDonald, *Travis*, 175, and Turner, *Travis*, 244–45, both carry the story of Travis giving a small cat's-eye ring to Angelina Dickenson. Neither gives a source for this old story, which in any case is probably myth.

93. Frankfort, Ky., *Commonwealth*, May 4, 1836.

94. Ibid. This is the account related by Joe, as taken down by William Gray and originally written in a letter to the Fredericksburg, Va., *Arena*. It has not been emphasized sufficiently in the past that this account and those of Mrs. Dickenson, the only survivors to give interviews after the battle, are not in their own words but are the reports of others who heard them and wrote down what was supposedly said. Consequently, even these early accounts may have some unintentional mistakes in them as a result of not being written by the eyewitnesses themselves.

95. Space does not allow here the extended discussion necessary to deal with the question of the Alamo's total manpower as of March 6, 1836, nor is it especially germane to the topic of this book. Suffice it to say that the traditional figure of somewhat over 180 has been revised upward steadily in recent years by scholars, and the best authorities expect that the number may eventually go well over

200, putting it in the range of the 250 or more reported by some. De la Peña, *Narrative*, 54, for instance, states that the Mexicans counted 253 bodies. See Austin *American-Statesman*, March 12, 1996, and note 105 below.

96. These figures are derived from the newly discovered "Statement and manifest of the Arty, arms, munitions and other effects taken from the Enemy," dated March 6, 1836, Expediente XI/481.3/1655, Archivo Historico Mexicano Militar, Mexico City. This listing is what the Mexicans captured after the end of the battle, and included a total of 1,118 artillery powder charges, 686 solid shot, and 449 grape and canister loads. Thus the figures stated in the text have been enlarged from this base to allow for usage by the Texians during the battle. The statement of eighteen usable cannon is based on Lindley, "Alamo Artillery," which shows eighteen functioning cannon. The statement that Travis may have been out of ammunition for the 18-pounder and the 16-pounder rests on the fact that the statement of captures shows no ammunition for those guns. It is possible that the Texians simply exhausted all of it in the battle on March 6, but not likely, since none of these weapons was really practical for defending against an infantry assault. It is also possible that, the bore sizes of 12-, 16-, and even 18-pounders being fairly similar, the Mexicans doing the inventory may simply have mistaken the calibers in their survey.

The statement of 60 rounds per man is derived from the statement of captures listing 14,600 rifle and musket rounds and 816 rifles, muskets, and pistols. That would equal roughly 18 rounds per gun after the fight. Given the brief duration of the battle—between thirty minutes and an hour—and the confusion and movement entailed, it seems likely that each Texian fired no more than 4 or 5 rounds on average. That times the number of men, not guns, would add roughly 1,000 loads to the number captured. It is interesting to note that de la Peña, *Narrative*, 47, states that every Texian had three or four loaded guns at his side, accounting for their high initial rate of fire. This matches perfectly the figure of 816 weapons reported as captured, if there were 200 to 250 defenders.

97. John N. Niles and L. M. Pease, *History of South America and Mexico* (Hartford, Conn., 1839), 327.

98. Hardin, "Volley," 4–5, effectively lays to rest the claims that Travis wore a coat of jeans (possibly denim). There is no credible evidence to indicate any of his apparel.

99. It will be apparent to all Alamo aficionados that no account has been given here of the episode of Travis supposedly drawing a line in the dirt on the parade on March 5, and telling those willing to stay and face certain death to cross. Since this is not a book about the Alamo, there are several questions like this that simply do not merit here the lengthy discussion necessary to treat them adequately. Suffice it to say that the only source for this story is William Zuber's account written May 7, 1871, and published in the *Texas Almanac* in 1873. Nothing in the story stands up to scrutiny, and none of the survivors made any mention of such an incident, except Mrs. Dickenson, and she only mentioned it after Zuber's account appeared in print, and at a time when her own accounts were becoming increasingly imaginative, inaccurate, and derivative.

Zuber later admitted that he invented the speech Travis supposedly made on the occasion, but adamantly insisted that a man named Rose—Lewis or Moses—did actually refuse to cross such a line and make his escape. A Lewis Rose did later testify to having been in the Alamo until March 3, and several times gave testimony to establish the presence of others in order that their heirs or executors could apply for the land bounty due to the families of all of the Alamo slain. But Rose could easily have been inventing his story, since there was no one alive to challenge him except Susanna Dickenson and the other women, none of whom ever spoke up either to support or refute him. He says nothing in his statements about Travis drawing a line or making a speech, and these are the only two questions of importance that come out of the episode. A letter dated March 5, 1836, and credited to an Isaac Milsaps (William B. Bates Collection, University of Houston Archives) appeared to confirm that Travis made some sort of speech to the garrison on that day, but the letter has subsequently been proved to be a forgery.

Turner, *Travis*, 239ff, discusses the controversy but does not take a firm position, while McDonald, *Travis*, 172–74, leans toward acceptance. For more discussion of the pros and cons, see: J. Frank Dobie, "The Line That Travis Drew," in J. Frank Dobie, Mody C. Boatwright, and Harry H. Ransom, eds., *In the Shadow of History* (Dallas, 1939), 9–16; R. B. Blake, "A Vindication of Rose and His Story," *In the Shadow of History*, 27–41; W. Zuber, "An Escape from the Alamo," *In the Shadow of History*, 17–27; Lord, "Myths & Realities," 22; and Lord, *A Time to Stand*, 201–4.

Ruby Mixon, the first Travis student to study the matter, remained skeptical in her "Travis," 272ff, though she later accepted the Rose story. So did Amelia Williams, but by this time readers will understand that Williams's acceptance of almost anything hardly constitutes reliable confirmation. So far as this present work is concerned, the event simply did not happen, or if it did, then something much more reliable than an admittedly fictionalized secondhand account written thirty-five years after the fact is necessary to establish it beyond question.

100. Mexico City *El Mosquito Mexicano*, April 5, 1836; Santa Anna, *Manifesto*, 14.

101. Hollon and Butler, *Bollaert's Texas*, 223; Order of assault, March 5, 1836, Jenkins, *PTR*, vol. 4, 519.

102. There are only two sources to be positively relied on concerning Travis's death. The first is Joe, whose account was recorded by at least two people several days later, and all versions substantially agree. One is by George Childress and appeared in the Columbia, Tenn., *Observer*, April 14, 1836, and the other is William Gray's letter to the Fredericksburg, Va., *Arena*, appearing in the Frankfort, Ky., *Commonwealth*, May 25, 1836. Will T. Sheehan, in an article titled "Commander of the Alamo Alabama Reared and Bred" (Travis Surname File, ADAH), stated that in an interview with Travis's brother James conducted around 1900, the surviving Travis said that many years after the Alamo he visited the place in company with Joe—whom he called Ben, no doubt influenced by many confused stories later published that said this was the name of Travis's

servant or Bowie's servant. The black told him that William Travis died early in the fight, and pointed out black spots on a wall that he thought were the bloodstains from Travis's wound. "He was struck by a rifle ball," said James, "but continued to fight." This sounds very much like a false recollection based on reading accounts like Susanna Dickenson's. Joe, it should be noted, disappeared from sight in the 1860's.

The other account, which confirms Joe's, is by an anonymous Mexican soldier in a letter written the day after the battle, March 7, 1836, and appearing in the Mexico City *El Mosquito Mexicano* on April 5, 1836. It states: "Their leader, named Travis, died like a brave man with his rifle in his hand at the back of a cannon." The Childress account says that when Travis was hit, he dropped his shotgun over the wall before he fell. The Mexican account is the earlier and possibly more accurate, since it speaks of seeing Travis in death still clutching his gun.

The placement of Travis's wound was established by Francisco Ruiz, the man forced by Santa Anna to identify the bodies of Travis and Bowie, in a statement given in 1860. He spoke in Spanish, and his words were translated and written for publication by someone else, so allowance must be made for the possibilities of mistranslation or an inattentive or careless listener, but still the statement certainly seems simple and unequivocal enough. Ruiz said he found Travis's body on a gun carriage "*shot* only in the forehead" (Matovina, *Tejano Accounts,* 44).

The best examination of the death of Travis is Stephen L. Hardin, "A Volley from the Darkness: Sources Regarding the Death of William Barret Travis," *Alamo Journal* 59 (December 1987): 3–4. Quite rightly Hardin dismisses as myth or embellishment all of the other stories about Travis's death, including the story attributed to Joe in the Childress account, but to Susanna Dickenson in the Gray letter, that before he died Travis killed a Mexican general named Mora with his sword. It is clear from the accounts that neither was telling this story as something that they saw, or claimed to see, but that it was told to them by a Mexican officer after the battle. Mrs. Dickenson would thereafter be the most frequent source of the Mora story (San Felipe *Telegraph and Texas Register,* March 24, 1836). The same sources that relate Joe's story also relate Mrs. Dickenson's, and Gray's letter says that she said Travis did live for a few minutes, and cheered on his men as the Mexicans swarmed past him. This, like the Mora story, is either invention or hearsay, for she was in the sacristy of the church and saw nothing at all of the fight outside. De la Peña gives an account supposedly of Travis's death in his *Narrative,* 50, but since it in no way agrees with either Joe's account or the anonymous Mexican soldier's March 7 letter, it must be hearsay, and part of what de la Peña added to his narrative from other sources. In later years Mrs. Dickenson also became more inventive, or forgetful, and in recollection moved Travis's body from the north wall to the top of the church with her dead husband (Morphis, *Texas,* 177). The stories that Travis shot himself are dealt with in a subsequent chapter.

Amelia Williams, in researching her "Critical Study" dissertation, found what she called "pretty good evidence that he died by his own hand." What she found was simply one of innumerable newspaper accounts repeating an initial report by two men who brought the first news of the battle to Houston, and neither was an eyewitness. "Wasn't it just like Travis to have done it that way," she told Samuel Asbury in a March 15, 1932 letter (Asbury Papers, UT). She knew of Joe's eyewitness account, of course, but did not believe it because, as she explained to Asbury, "I know negroes," a statement that says a lot more about Amelia Williams than it does about Joe or Travis's death.

103. Andrew Briscoe, visiting the Alamo after the Mexicans left, somehow came by a statement that when Travis fell, Adjutant Baugh assumed command, and that when he went down Crockett took over. Since there was no one alive who could tell him, and since Joe was in hiding after Travis went down and Susanna Dickenson saw nothing at all of the fight, Briscoe must simply have encountered the assumption of someone in San Antonio who knew nothing about what really happened, and just assumed that in the normal course of affairs, Baugh would take over when Travis went down, and that then "Colonel" Crockett would follow upon his death. Little Rock, *Arkansas Advocate*, April 4, 15, 1836.

104. There is no credible eyewitness account of Bowie's death, though there are two or three fantastic and wholly fictitious belated claims to have witnessed it. As with Travis, the very first accounts by two *tejanos* who definitely did not see Bowie die, claim that he took his own life. The most authoritative sources are Mexican, especially the March 7, 1836 letter in Mexico City *El Mosquito Mexicano*, April 5, 1836. In it the writer states that "the perverse and boastful James Bowie died like a woman, almost hidden by covers." The diary of José Sanchez-Navarro, José Sanchez-Navarro Papers, UT, concurs precisely, saying that "Buy [Bowie] the bully, son-in-law of Beramendi died as a coward." This latter source is questioned by some, but in this instance it is confirmed by the first Mexican account. Clearly Bowie was one of the "celebrities" in the fort, much better known to Mexicans than Travis, and thus the nature of his death became common knowledge. Both are supported by an article in the Philadelphia *Pennsylvanian*, July 19, 1838, in which the writer states that Almonte told him that Bowie was "sick and helpless, and was butchered in bed."

Together they confirm that (1) Bowie died in bed, covered, without putting up a fight and, therefore, was quite probably either already unconscious or too weak to offer even token resistance; (2) that he was alone, and certainly not in the hospital, otherwise the Mexicans would not have mistaken his prostration for cowardice; and (3), that almost certainly he did not die in the church as Susanna Dickenson's granddaughter later claimed. For Susanna to have seen him die, he would have had to be in the sacristy, with at least three women and several children who survived, none of whom claimed to have seen him killed until many years later. Typical of their long after the fact accounts is Enrique Esparza in the San Antonio *Express*, May 19, 1907, in which he says Bowie was actually out fighting with the others, but after being severely wounded he was brought into a small room on the north side of the church, where he kept on fighting until killed. The Mexican accounts put the lie to this. Moreover, in this same account, Esparza also places Travis on top of the church, just as Susanna Dickenson did in her later interviews. Clearly these people are all unconsciously borrowing from one another in filling out their own failing recollections. No one put Bowie in the church for forty years after his death, and we may safely assume that is because he was never there. Francisco Ruiz, in the same 1860 interview in which he said where he found Travis, stated that "Colonel Bowie was found dead in his bed, in one of the rooms of the south side" (Matovina, *Tejano Accounts,* 44). Manuel Loranca, in his remarkably accurate article in the San Antonio *Express,* June 23, 1878, says that he and others saw Bowie's body in a "room at the right," after they entered the compound. There was simply no way to enter the fortress and have the sacristy be on one's right, unless Loranca had miraculously walked through the back wall of the church. Sutherland, "Fall of the Alamo," Williams Papers, UT, stated in 1860 that Joe and Susanna told him that Bowie died in the same room he had shared with Sutherland in February 1836, and while Sutherland does not say where that room was, he certainly does not mention it being the tiny sacristy in the church. At the time Bowie initially took a room in the Alamo, he was healthy, and either actually in command of the volunteers or else recognized as a man of status without portfolio. It is unlikely that in either case he would thus choose to isolate himself in a dark back room.

The accounts taken from the initial interviews with Joe and Susanna merely state that Bowie was killed in his bed, and his body mutilated. Nothing more. In the Columbia *Observer* account, May 25, 1836, Gray wrote that Joe said he "saw him murdered," which could be taken as a claim to have witnessed the actual killing, but by his own admission elsewhere, Joe did not witness this, or any of the rest of the fight after Travis fell. The "murdered" statement must be taken either as Gray's misinterpretation of Joe's account, or else the word is used to suggest a state of being, in the meaning of having seen Bowie's body after he was murdered.

In all her early interviews the only man Dickenson speaks of actually seeing killed was a boy named Walker. In her Testimony of Mrs. Hannig Touching the Alamo Massacre, September 23, 1876, TXSL, her most detailed interview, she explicitly said that Walker was the only man she saw killed, and as to Bowie said only that she "knew Col Bowee & saw him in the Fort, both before & after his death." She fails to say where she saw him in death. Talking with Ira Ingram in March or early April 1836, Susanna changed her story to say that she saw two men killed in her presence, both of them "raised on the points of the enemies lances." (Natchez *Mississippi Free Trader and Natchez Gazette,* April 29, 1836). This would suggest that some of Ramírez y Sesma's lancers were in the compound by this time, since the *soldados* who made the attack did not carry lances. But she may have mistaken bayonets for lances—which would be understandable given the trauma she suffered—or not even have known the difference between the two. Sutherland, in the version of his memoir in the Ford Memoirs, vol. 1, UT, says that he talked with Joe and Susanna after the battle, and all they told him was that Bowie was killed in bed while "unable to lift his head from his pillow." He visited Bowie's room in 1837 or 1838 and still saw "the stain of his brains yet upon the wall," yet does not state that Bowie's room was in the church.

The fantastic accounts of Andrea Villanueva, called Madam Candelaria, do not merit discussion. At varying times she has him firing from a window with her help, bayonetted in her arms, dying in the night before the attack began, and more, and in all of them she is wounded in trying to protect him. Walter Bowie for some reason accepted her claim that he died in the night, and used it in his family history (Walter Bowie to Washington Bowie, September 10, 1931, Bowie Papers, Maryland Historical Society). Susanna Dickenson's granddaughter Susan Sterling appears to have been influenced by Candelaria, too, for in her October 29, 1909 statement in which she places Bowie in the baptistry along with her grandmother (who was actually in the sacristy on the opposite corner of the church), she also states that Bowie's nurse was with them and that the nurse was wounded when Bowie was killed (Evelyn Brogan, *James Bowie, A Hero of the Alamo* [San Antonio, 1927], 39). There are other equally far-fetched accounts, all of them far removed in years from the event, and second or third-hand. Green, *Maverick,* 55–56, stated that Mrs. Alsbury told Maverick that Bowie was in the upstairs hospital, and was carried out into the parade and bayonetted. One story even had Bowie being the only survivor until he got into an argument with a Mexican officer who had his tongue cut out before throwing him on the burning funeral pyre. For many of these accounts, see Edward Rohrbaugh, "How Jim Bowie Died," *In the Shadow of History,* 48–58.

105. There are perhaps a score of commonly known sources indicating that a number of men went over the walls and died outside the Alamo, though their import has been ignored in Alamo historiography. Santa Anna referred to them in his report written only hours after the fight (Expediente XI/481.3/1900, Archivo Historico Mexicano Militar, Mexico City), as does Asbury, "Almonte Journal," 23, and de la Peña, *Narrative,* 54. The only detailed account has been that of Manuel Loranca, San Antonio *Express,* June 23, 1878, which states that 62 Texians left the east side and were killed by lancers. This does not seem to have attracted much notice from historians.

However, research for this book has uncovered the previously unknown March 11, 1836 report of General Ramírez y Sesma himself, which is quite detailed and confirms Loranca's account. The narrative given here is based on the Ramírez y Sesma report, Expediente XI/481.3/1149, Archivo Historico Mexicano Militar, Mexico City. Also the forthcoming David McDonald and Kevin R. Young, eds., "Siege of the Alamo: A Mexican Army Journal," *Journal of the Alamo Battlefield Association* 3 (Fall 1998), which translates a diary by an unknown Mexican *soldado,* says that the lancers killed 68 Texians outside the walls. This closely matches Loranca and Ramírez y Sesma. Ramírez y Sesma's report suggests that Loranca's number may be a bit low, but any figure of 60 or more should possibly be added to the traditional count of 182 bodies that comes from Ruiz and others. The figure of 182 is those burned in the pyres in or near the compound. Logically the Mexicans might not go to the trouble of dragging the men killed outside some distance to where the bulk of the Texian dead were heaped, and thus this 60–80 may not have figured in Ruiz's count. A number of Mexican dead may have been dumped in the San Antonio River, and the same disposition could have been made of any number of Texian bodies as well. Thus adding 60 to 80 to the traditional 182 suggests a possible total of defenders of 240 to 260 or more, matching the roughly 250 stated by several Mexican eyewitnesses, and matching even more closely the 232 dead cited by the anonymous Mexican diarist in his March 6, 1836, entry in McDonald and Young, *Mexican Army Journal.*

106. Ruiz in 1860 was quoted as saying that he found Crockett's body "toward the west and in the small fort opposite the city." That would be the earthwork that jutted out from the west wall. Matovina, *Tejano Accounts,* 44. A thoughtful, though ultimately inconclusive examination of the merits of this as a possible death site is Robert L. Durham, "Where Did Davy Die?" *Alamo Journal* 104 (March 1997): 3–6.

107. Muir, *Texas in 1837,* 115.

108. The publications on Crockett's death form the single largest subsegment of Alamo literature, and are too extensive to examine here to any purpose. The author has dealt with all the supposed eyewitness accounts of his death in "How Davy Probably Didn't Die," *Journal of the Alamo Battlefield Association* 2 (Fall 1997): 11–37. In essence there are several accounts by Mexicans, most notably de la Peña, claiming that Crockett and four to six others were taken alive, either surrendered or captured, in one of the fortified rooms, and brought before Santa Anna with a request for clemency. Instead he ordered them executed immediately, and they were—depending on which account is in hand—shot, bayoneted, or sabered.

Certainly several men did attempt to give up or found themselves without weapons and simply raised their hands. There are so many separate statements about a few being executed after capture—many by Mexican soldiers—that there is no reason to question that this took place, nor is it necessary to cite such sources here, though it is interesting to note that many years later Santa Anna tried to absolve himself of responsibility for a massacre by complaining that "not one would surrender" (Antonio López de Santa Anna to H. A. McCardle, March 19, 1874, Fontaine Collection, UT). However, the accounts claiming that Crockett was one of them are all tainted by being written at least several weeks, and in some cases more than a year, after the fact, and the later ones show what appear to be signs of being derived from the earlier. Moreover, the earliest suggestions that Crockett died in this fashion came not from Mexican sources but Texian writers, starting within less than two weeks of the fall. Thus it is quite possible that Mexican soldiers and officers, who made up a number of fantastic stories designed to make a villain of Santa Anna after he abandoned them in the aftermath of San Jacinto, may actually have borrowed the idea of Crockett surrendering and being executed from Texian rumor. Everyone wanted to know how Crockett died. After all, they knew from Joe how Travis died, and they knew from several sources how Bowie met his end. But the mystery and uncertainty about Crockett's death demanded something to fill the void. In time Mrs. Dickenson would supply that with imagined stories of his being found surrounded by the bodies of dead *soldados,* and Joe would supposedly say that Crockett had the biggest pile of dead enemies around him of any of the Texians. Yet we cannot be certain that either of them even saw Crockett's body after the fight. Joe was terrified, and Susanna was traumatized, having just lost her hus band, seen one or two or men butchered right in front of her, and spent some time in uncertainty as to whether she might be raped or worse, and her infant daughter killed. In such a situation, none of the normal rules of memory and recall operate as usual. Moreover, neither her accounts nor Joe's come to us in their own words, but only as reported by others. Nor can we ignore the probability that she, like everyone else, soon came to realize that the Texian cause needed for these men to be not just heroes—their dying at the Alamo made them that—but heroes of outstanding stature. Given Crockett's legendary status before he came to Texas, his case required even more so a superheroic death. Imagination quickly began to fill the need. He may have died fighting at the palisade, or in the redoubt on the west wall, or out in the chaparral, or being brutally executed after he was disarmed. We simply do not know, and—unsatisfactory as it is for those impelled to have a definite answer—we probably never will.

Chapter 22   Enshrinement: Dawn, March 6, 1838–Posterity

1. Stories soon began to circulate that Cós mutilated Travis's body with his sword, even beheading him, but though they appear in context with a statement about Joe showing the Mexicans Travis's body, they do not assert that Joe claimed to have seen Cós do this. As a result, the stories are probably just early rumors and nothing more. Cincinnati *Daily Whig and Commercial Intelligencer*, April 13, 1836; Natchez *Mississippi Free Trader and Natchez Gazette*, April 8, 1836. Joe possibly did say that he saw Cós stab the body with his saber (Frankfort, Ky., *Commonwealth*, May 25, 1836). The ever-inventive Zuber, writing in the Houston *Daily Post*, March 1, 1882, quotes a presumed *soldado* named Apolinario Saldiga whose story has Santa Anna himself mutilating Travis's body, and an unidentified man whose "florid face" suggests Crockett. Then Zuber goes farther into fantasyland with a description that Bowie survived, got into a quarrel with a Mexican officer, and had his tongue cut out before the Mexicans threw him still living onto the blazing pyre. It is all nonsense.

2. Many sources also state that Cós mutilated Bowie's body as well as Travis's, though again none can certainly be linked positively with a statement by Joe, who would have been the only Texian to witness this. Within a month of the battle, rumors also circulated that Cós, instead of mutilating Bowie's body, allowed it the honor of burial, out of respect for his bravery or his having been Veramendi's son-in-law. These, too, are only rumors, though thanks to the repeated repetition and inadvertent alteration of Joe's one or two statements, some sources make it appear that Joe actually claimed to have witnessed this. He did not. New York *Transcript*, April 12, 1836; W. B. Dewees to Clara Cardello, May 15, 1836, Jenkins, *PTR*, vol. 6, 283; New Orleans *Commercial Bulletin*, April 11, 1836.

3. Santa Anna to Minister of War, March 6, 1836, Antonio López de Santa Anna Papers, UT. This is not the original of the report, which is in the Archivo Historico Mexicano Militar in Mexico City, but a translation.

4. The best accounts of the burning of the bodies are the *tejano* stories, especially those of Francisco Ruiz and Pablo Diaz. Matovina, *Tejano Accounts*, 44, 76.

5. General Convention at Washington, March 1–17, 1836, Jenkins, *PTR*, vol. 9, 311–13; Gray, *Virginia to Texas*, 125; Donald Day and Harry H. Ullom, eds., *The Autobiography of Sam Houston* (Westport, Conn., 1954), 99–100.

6. Selma, Ala., *Free Press*, March 26, 1836; Forbes to Millard April 2, 1836, Little Rock, *Arkansas Gazette*, April 5, 1836; Gray, *Virginia to Texas*, 128–30; E. Thomas to his father, March 10, 1836, Jenkins, *PTR*, vol. 5, 45.

7. Brown, *Smith*, 316–17; Columbia *Observer*, April 14, 1836; Gray, *Virginia to Texas*, 131; Little Rock *Arkansas Gazette*, March 29, April 12, 1836.

8. J. H. Kuykendall Diary, March 13, 1836, Kuykendall Family Papers, UT.

9. Sowell, *Pioneers and Rangers*, 138.

10. Harris, "Reminiscences, II," 163.

11. Ayers to Houston, April 8, 1836, Jenkins, *PTR*, vol. 5, 369.

12. Notes Made by Mrs. Holley in Interviews with Prominent Texians of the Early Days, Holley Papers, UT.

13. A. Briscoe to the editor of the Alexandria, La., *Red River Herald*, March 1836, Jenkins, *PTR*, vol. 5, 258; C. B. Stewart to Ira Lewis, March 13, 1836, Natchez *Mississippi Free Trader and Natchez Gazette*, April 1, 1836; Cincinnati *Journal and Western Luminary*, April 28, 1836; Muir, *Texas in 1837*, 115; New Orleans, *Louisiana Advertiser*, March 28, 1836.

14. Houston to James Collinsworth, March 7, 1836, Jenkins, *PTR*, vol. 5, 17–18.

15. Houston to Collinsworth, March 15, 1836, Jenkins, *PTR*, vol. 5, 82–83.

16. Houston to the Senate of Texas, April 30, 1838, Williams and Barker, *Writings*, vol. 4, 52.

17. James Morgan to Samuel Swartwout, September 5, 1836, James Morgan Papers, Rosenberg Library, Galveston, Tex.

18. Day and Ullom, *Autobiography of Sam Houston,* 119; Charles E. Lester, *The Life of Sam Houston* (New York, 1855), 82, 85.

19. Holley, Notes, Holley Papers, UT.

20. Lindley, "Truthful Deductions," 19–21, 25. Lindley's is the best interpretation of Houston's noninvolvement in the Alamo story.

21. Henry Austin to Mary Austin Holley, March 29, 1836, Holley Papers, UT.

22. These figures are derived from the newly discovered Mariano Arroyo Report from the Military Hospital at Béxar, August 1, 1836, Expediente XI/481.3/1151, Archivo Historico Mexicano Militar, Mexico City. The document actually lists a total of 456 men in the Mexican hospital from March 6 to August 1, but that included the remaining wounded who had been left by Cós when he evacuated the previous December. Arroyo made no statement of their number, but others like Susanna Dickenson estimated them at about 60, so a battle wounded from the March 6 fight of 400 seems reasonable. It is possible that a few of the 75 reported as dying of their wounds were also some of Cós's men, but it seems most likely that men with wounds that would cause complications leading to

death would already have died in the three months between Cós's departure and the fall of the Alamo. This figure of 400 wounded in the fight also agrees with what the surgeon told Dr. J. H. Bernard on April 21, 1836, as stated in J. J. Bernard, *Dr. J. H. Bernard's Journal* (Goliad, Tex., 1965), 29–30.

23. Santa Anna Report, March 6, 1836, Santa Anna Papers, UT.

24. Bernard, *Bernard's Journal*, 29–30.

25. Potter, "Fall of the Alamo," 17, 19; José Garcia to the Secretary of War, June 21, 1836, Expediente XI/481.3/1150, Archivo Historico Mexicano Militar, Mexico City.

26. Asbury, "Almonte Journal," 23, March 10, 1836; Bernard, *Bernard's Journal*, 35.

27. Seguín to Albert Sidney Johnston, March 13, 1837, Mason Barret Collection of Albert Sidney and William Preston Johnston Papers, Tulane University, New Orleans; Columbia, Tex., *Old Capitol*, May 5, 1838, clipping in Asbury Papers, UT; Marilyn McAdams Sibley, "The Burial Place of the Alamo Heroes," *Southwestern Historical Quarterly* 48 (October 1964): 272–73.

28. Nat G. Smith to Amelia Smith, March 1836, Jenkins, *PTR*, vol. 5, 268–69;

29. Robert Crockett to Rudd, December 30, 1879, Rudd Manuscripts, Lilly Library, Indiana University, Bloomington.

30. Captain Wheeler to Zephaniah Kittredge, May 24, 1836, "Documents of the Texian Revolution," *Alamo Journal* 99 (December 1995): 17; Mortimer Wiggington to Col. Lewis, n.d., Jenkins, *PTR*, vol. 6, 21, Bridges to ?, July 21, 1836, vol. 7, 511; Shackford, *Crockett*, 239.

31. Thomas Green to Rezin Bowie, April 9, 1836, Jenkins, *PTR*, vol. 5, 402; Rezin Bowie to Green, April 9, 1836, Thomas J. Green Papers, SHC, UNC.

32. Green to Burnet, April 13, 1836, Green Papers, SHC, UNC; Notice, April 28, 1836, Jenkins, *PTR*, vol. 6, 111, Edward Conrad to Houston, April 30, 1836, 126; Natchez *Mississippi Free Trader and Natchez Gazette*, April 1, 29, 1836.

33. John Quitman to Eliza Quitman, April 29, 1836, Quitman to Henry Quitman, July 31, 1836, Quitman Papers, UNC, SHC; Anonymous, May 1, 1836, Jenkins, *PTR*, vol. 6, 147; Stuart Perry to William Harris, May 16, 1836, Benjamin C. Franklin Papers, UT; Suggsville, Ala., *Clarke County Post*, May 9, 1836.

34. Green to Thomas J. Rusk, August 1, 1836, Jenkins, *PTR*, vol. 8, 94.

35. A. Dimmit to John Johnston, February 17, 1837, Johnston Papers, HSP.

36. Petition of Administrators of James Bowie, Memorial No. 451, TXSL.

37. Affidavit of Horatio Alsbury, November 7, 1836, ibid.; Sears, "Low Down," 198; *Veramendi* v. *Hutchens* papers in Documents Pertaining to James Bowie, UT.

38. Probate records, Béxar County, July 10, 1837, copies in Crockett Biographical File, DRT; Treasury Warrant to Robert Crockett, August 22, 1837, *Gary Hendershott Sale* 87, item 2; Army Service Warrant, February 6, 1837, Jenkins, *Texas Revolution Catalog* 206; Robert Crockett to Rudd, December 30, 1879, Rudd Manuscripts, Lilly Library, Indiana University, Bloomington.

39. Claims filed against the estate of Wm B. Travis, March 26, 1838, John R. Jones Account Book, Estate of William B. Travis, Travis Biographical File, DRT;

Receipt of November 7, 1837, on estate of F. J Starr, T. W. Nibbs to Mrs. Starr, March 18, 1836, Account of sale of personal estate of Franklin J. Starr, James H. Starr Collection, UT; Inventory of Estate of William B. Travis, transcript dated January 20, 1930, Mixon Papers, UT; San Felipe *Telegraph and Texas Register,* March 12, 1836; Columbia *Telegraph,* March 21, 1837.

40. Reuben Potter, "Hymn of the Alamo," October 1836, Dienst Collection, UT.

41. Hollon and Butler, *Bollaert's Texas,* 222, 224.

42. Ford Memoir, UT; Austin *Statesman,* April 7, 1877.

43. Swisher, *Swisher Memoirs,* 20; Robert Crockett to Rudd, June 15, 1880, Rudd Manuscripts, Lilly Library, Indiana University, Bloomington.

44. Quitman to Eliza Quitman, January 16, 1836, Quitman Papers, SHC, UNC.

45. Suggsville, Ala., *Clarke County Post,* June 13, 1836.

46. Nashville *Republican,* April 11, 1836.

47. New York *Sunday Morning News,* May 1, 1836.

48. Brazoria *Brazos Courier,* March 31, 1840.

49. Port Gibson, Miss., *Correspondent,* April 23, 1836.

50. Harris to Mary Jane Harris, March 28, 1836, Adele Looscan Collection, San Jacinto Monument, San Jacinto, Tex.; Matagorda, Tex., *Bulletin,* October 11, 1837.

51. Thomas Turner, "Living in the Shadow of the Alamo," *Baylor University Report* 3 (March 1983): 20–21.

52. M. J. DeCaussey to William B. Travis Chapter, January 31, 1895, DeCaussey to Rebecca Fisher, February 4, 1895, Asbury Papers, UT.

53. L. W. Price to City Manager of San Antonio, August 4, 1939, Travis Biographical File, DRT.

54. Bowie, *The Bowies,* 262.

55. Ham, Recollections, UT.

56. Sparks in Ellis, *Crockett,* 225.

57. Bowie's death is also reported as February 17, 1841.

58. H. D. Gilpin to Levi Woodbury, February 10, 1838, Ethan Brown to Woodbury, September 29, 1836, Correspondence Relating to Efforts to Acquire the "Pintado Papers," 1836–1883, Unbound Records of the General Land Office Relating to Private Claims in Louisiana 1805–1896, M1385, James Shield to James H. Moore, May 31, 1845, vol. 10, 366–67, Letters Sent, Entry 200, NA; Works Project Administration of Louisiana, Pintado Papers, 1941, Stanley J. Arthur, "A History of the Pintado Papers," iii-xvi. Rezin's partner White was the father of future Chief Justice of the United States, Edward H. White.

59. Miller, *Public Lands,* 27–28.

60. Hayward to Jackson, January 16, 1832, Entry 404, James Whitcomb to T. J. Williams, May 2, 1838, Entry 200, vol. 4, 208–9, Whitcomb to John Rothrock, May 3, 1838, 210–11, James Shield to John Moore, August 1, 1842, vol. 7, 487–89, William Armstrong to R. C. Nicholas, January 23, 1839, Memoranda of

letters relating to claims in Sutton's Reports, Records Relating to the Private Land Claim of Antonio Vaca to Land in Louisiana, 1881–1882, M1385, NA; James D. B. DeBow, "Public Lands acquired by Treaty, etc.," *Commercial Review* 5 (February 1848): 117–18.

61. Natchez *Mississippi Free Trader and Natchez Gazette*, April 8, 1836.

62. Porter, *Reminiscences*, 42.

63. Houston, *Telegraph and Texas Register*, July 28, 1838.

64. Philadelphia *Pennsylvanian*, July 19, 1838; James Rees, *The Life of Edwin Forrest: With Reminiscences and Personal Recollections* (Philadelphia, 1874), 451; "The Bowie-Knife and its Inventor," *American Notes and Queries* 1 (June 2, 1888): 49–50.

65. The fate of James Bowie's actual knife remains a subject of hot debate, and is of no real importance to this study. Family sources—that may be misinformed—maintained that Rezin's grandson lost the knife, it obviously having been given back to Rezin prior to the Alamo. Other sources claim that James lost the original, and had a copy—perhaps with some of his own refinements—made. Of course, no knife found at the Alamo by the Mexicans would have been likely to find its way back to the hands of Cushman, nor is there any solid evidence of Bowie giving anything to Forrest. Like any man who lived outdoors and traveled extensively, Bowie probably had several such knives in his life. Currently there are at least two claimants for being knives that belonged to him, neither worthy of being taken seriously. One owner even engaged the services of the discredited "psychic" Peter Hurkos to support his belief, though Hurkos revealed his obvious prompting or prior research by reportedly "reading" as he held the knife a number of tales that are only part of the Bowie myth, for instance the story that Bowie was injured in a fall from a gun platform in the Alamo. See Joseph Musso, "A Bowie Knife," *Alamo Journal* 84 (December 1992): n.p.

66. Sparks in Ellis, *Crockett*, 221.

67. Houston, *Telegraph and Texas Register*, June 20, 1850. The Carlyle statement is almost certainly pure fiction. Nothing in Carlyle's papers or biographies gives any indication that he ever even heard of Bowie.

68. No attempt will be made here to list every known story of a Bowie fight or duel, but an examination of the more prevalent ones demonstrates the nature of them all. Moreover, as will be seen, all but one are exaggerations or embellishments based very loosely on only two original stories, both first appearing long after Bowie's death, and all highly questionable.

The earliest known written or published account of a Bowie duel other than the Sandbar fight, was published by Nicholas D. Maillard in his *The History of the Republic of Texas* (London, 1842), 102–4. The book is a viciously anti-Texian work condemned by most historians, and clearly attempted to portray Texians as drunken, violent, dishonest, and brutish. Maillard confuses James with Rezin Bowie, calls him "a reckless drunkard" who came to Texas as a fugitive from a duel, and even states that "Razin" (James) Bowie fought a duel in the Alamo a few nights before its fall. His first duel, we are told, was in Natchez in 1834, when, in a dispute over gambling, Bowie and a man named Black drew their knives and fought each other for twenty minutes while seated at a table, each being badly cut up before Bowie rose and killed the other in a rage.

Though written just six years after James Bowie's death, and only fifteen years after the Sandbar, the Maillard account has clearly garbled several stories that he heard while in Texas, and embellished them with his own imagination. He has James and not Rezin inventing the first knife, then has Rezin being the duelist who dies in the Alamo. The first duel at Natchez—the Sandbar—took place in 1827, not 1834, involved no one named Black, and of course did not take place at a card table. It is faintly possible that the reference to Black is a very garbled echo of the stories just reaching print the year before about James Black of Arkansas being the maker of a knife for Bowie. As for Bowie fighting a duel a few nights before March 6, he was too ill to walk, and so would hardly be getting into fights with fellow defenders. The business of the knife fight while seated at a gaming table is almost certainly an exaggerated variant of stories common about riverboat gamblers who whipped out knives and cut off the fingers of men caught cheating. Maillard also may have incorporated stories he could have heard of a bloody game sometimes played by boatmen in Natchez called "snick-a-snack," in which men sat around a table and on a signal started hitting each other on heads, shoulders, and hands with their knives, and kept at it until the first one cried to stop (Davis, *A Way Through the Wilderness*, 124–25, 249). There is no evidence that Bowie ever played such a game.

The Maillard account may reflect a commonly garbled version of the Sandbar fight circulating in Texas in the early 1840s, for William Bollaert in October 1843 heard an account that made Rezin, not James, a participant, and that has him killing Norris Wright with "a small couteau de chasse or Bowie Knife made for him by one of his brothers" (Hollon and Butler, *Bollaert's Texas*, 246n). Bollaert's informant, apparently an unidentified Dr. Wooster, confused James with Rezin just as did Maillard's sources, though without the character sleights. If anything, these confused versions of the Sandbar affair so soon after Bowie's death show how little real factual information of his early life was known in his adopted home, a situation ideal for the creation of myth to fill the vacuum.

The next story to surface, and the one with the most variations, appeared first in the Houston *Democratic Telegraph and Texas Register*, June 20, 1850. It states that on June 4, 1835, Bowie was on the steamboat *Rob Roy* going from St. Louis to New Orleans, where he saw a large gambler entice a young Natchez merchant into a game in which the card sharp cheated the innocent of everything he had, while the victim's wife watched, weeping. When it was finished, Bowie challenged the gambler to another game, identifying him as John Laffite, the son of the pirate and smuggler. In the play Laffite cheated again, but Bowie still beat him, after which he and Laffite fought a duel on the deck and Laffite fell dead. This same article is also the origin of the legend that Thomas Carlyle expressed some kind of admiration for Bowie's exploits, as it happens, a story that in all probability is equally spurious.

Three years later the Marshall *Texas Republican*, June 18, 1853, repeated the story, now calling Bowie "the Napoleon of Duelists," and attiring him in a red calico shirt and buckskins ornamented with tassels and beads. Thereafter the embellishments continued. Thirty-one years later Ben C. Truman, *The Field of Honor* (New York, 1884), 290–96, has the affair take place in June 1832, and this time on the steamboat *Orleans* near Vicksburg. Sometime around 1900 or later Martha Bowie Burns, daughter of John Bowie and niece of James, referred to this story in an article titled "Eventful Lives of the Bowies," in an unidentified newspaper (James Bowie Biographical File, DRT), and said that her father, John, told her about it and was an actual witness, and that it happened on the *Orleans* in 1831 or 1832. She does not name Laffite. After another decade or more A. J. Sowell, in the San Antonio *Light*, May 4, 1917, placed the Laffite fight in 1830, did not name the steamboat, but identified the victim as Harry Richardson and his newlywed wife as Milly Musgrove, both of Natchez, and said the money lost was five hundred dollars they were taking to New Orleans to get merchandise for starting a store in Natchez.

Some time after the appearance of the Martha Burns article, another appeared by an anonymous writer in an unidentified issue of a newspaper called the *Illustrated American* (clipping in Bowie Biographical File, DRT). It borrows from the Burns article in several places, including the erroneous statement that the Bowies built the first steam sugar mill in Louisiana. It then gives a further embellished version of the encounter on the steamboat *Orleans*, this time placing it in 1832, and now having the victim be a young Natchez newlywed who had collected a load of debts in New York due to Natchez merchants while on his honeymoon. He is fleeced by a gambling syndicate on the boat, but Bowie gets in the game, the stakes rise to a hundred thousand dollars, and Bowie wins. In the fight that follows he kills the lead gambler and returns the money to the victim. This account also borrows obviously from the February 28, 1881, San Francisco *Chronicle* article dealt with below, since it reiterates the nonsense that in the Sandbar fight six men were killed and fifteen wounded.

The original form of the story is riddled with problems, and none of the subsequent changes and elaborations make it any more plausible. For a start, in June 1835 Bowie was in Monclova, Mexico, not on the Mississippi or anywhere near a steamboat. While the smuggler Laffite did have a son, he was named Pierre, not John, and he was born in 1816, making him only nineteen in 1835, when the story would have him being an accomplished gambler and dangerous duelist. The Truman version, happening in 1832 on the *Orleans,* would make the Laffite son a mere sixteen, while the Sowell version placing the event in 1830 faces the problem that Laffite would now be just fourteen, and the *Orleans* was not built until 1831! Martha Burns's article is full of inaccuracies and stories she picked up from other sources (recall that she was apparently unaware of her father's abandonment by Nancy Scroggins, and thought he had been widowed, and knew nothing at all about his having a second wife prior to marrying her mother). Internal evidence dates it sometime after 1896, when she would have been at least sixty-three, and probably older and possibly approaching senility, for she mistakes the names of two of her three married sisters' husbands, and anything told her by her father would have been about a forty-year-old recollection, since he died in 1859.

The next duel story known to have appeared reportedly saw print sometime prior to 1861 in the New York *Spirit of the Times*, the nation's leading repository of humor and folklore, and the source of a great deal of the early Crockett legend. The actual issue has not been found, but the article was reprinted in the Jacksboro, Tex., *Echo,* May 25, 1877, and cited in Rohrbaugh's thesis "James Bowie and the Bowie Knife," 44–45. In it Bowie fights with a Spanish planter, using rifles, each standing back to back and then marching a certain number of paces before being given the word to turn and fire. Bowie is the faster and kills his opponent. Rohrbaugh regards the story as only a legend, and suggests that it is an early variant of a story to appear in the June 2, 1888, issue of *American Notes and Queries* 2, 49–50. In that an unidentified writer cites Charles Durand's "History of the Philadelphia Stage" for a story about a Spanish neighbor of Bowie in Terrebonne goading him into issuing a challenge. The Spaniard named knives and specified that they were to fight facing each other seated astride a trestle. Bowie easily killed his adversary, and later gave the knife to the actor Edwin Forrest. William F. Pope in his 1895 *Early Days in Arkansas*, 46, says that a year or two before publishing his book he met a descendant of Bowie's (of course there were none, so he must have meant a descendant of one of Bowie's brothers) who told him of a duel James fought with a Mexican, sitting on a log, nailed to it by their leather pants so that neither could get away. The descendant was probably Martha Bowie Burns, who retells this episode in her "Eventful Lives of the Bowies" (DRT) post 1896, starting with a nearly verbatim lifting from the *American Notes and Queries* article, which was obviously her source, but to it she adds the variation of the leather breeches, and the men being nailed by them to the log. Presumably she did not invent this, but no doubt heard it somewhere and added it to the story. The idea of nailing a pair of duelists to a log by their pants while they fought to the death with knives was an old frontier cliché, as stated earlier in this work, and may never have actually happened.

The myth of Bowie presenting a knife to Forrest has been dispensed with earlier as well, and the Durand work has been thoroughly scanned without finding any reference to Bowie or his knife. The whole episode may have been the invention of Forrest, who created the story of Bowie giving him a knife, and may just as likely have invented a duel tale to go with it that would lend added interest to the knife he owned. Though the pre–1861 variant of the story had Bowie and his opponent using rifles, and the later versions make it knives, both are tied by the fact that they are the only duel stories in which Bowie's opponent is a Spaniard, and the only ones in which the formalities of issuing challenges and the naming of weapons and places occur. All of the other Bowie duel stories are impromptu fights on the spur of the moment, growing out of cheating at gambling.

The most influential account, in terms of its numerous and highly exaggerated offshoots and variants, comes from an unidentified writer signing himself only as "L.H.," in the San Francisco *Chronicle*, February 28, 1881, and provides a small compendium of such stories. It is the chief—usually the sole—source for them in subsequent Bowie literature. The author began with what purported to

be an eyewitness account of the Sandbar brawl. "I stood by the side of my father
. . . and witnessed the fight in question," he claims. If that was true, then he was
describing events witnessed probably as a child, some fifty-three years earlier,
and in 1881 must have been at least in his sixties. Everything in the account is
wrong. He says that James and Rezin Bowie were natives of Maryland, rather
than Kentucky and Tennessee; that they moved to Mississippi in 1821 rather
than Louisiana many years earlier. He says that James Bowie and Robert Crain
had a long-standing feud prior to the fight, of which there is no evidence, and
places the actual brawl on the west bank of the river rather than the east. In the
battle itself, Crane attacks Bowie with a sword cane rather than pistols, and then
Bowie actually kills Crain—instead of Wright—with a sword cane instead of
the big knife. All told, according to "L.H.," six men were killed and fifteen
wounded, whereas only two were really killed, and the whole number involved
did not equal fifteen. There is more in a similar vein, but this should be more
than sufficient to establish that "L.H." had not the slightest clue of what he was
writing about, and was either indulging in fiction for its own sake, or else was
hopelessly senile by the time of writing.

Thus it should be no surprise that none of the several other duel and fight
stories he relates bear scrutiny. They are:

Bowie finding a master brutally whipping a slave. "He seemed to have a natural disposition to protect the weak from the strong," says the writer. Bowie
took the whip from the brute and lashed him with it, and a duel ensued in
which Bowie badly wounded the slave owner. In the end, Bowie paid for the
man's medical treatment, and bought the slave from him at twice its value, then
freed the black. Since no names are mentioned, there is no way to verify any
aspect of this tale, though anyone familiar with Bowie the businessman and
slave dealer will find it unlikely that he would ever pay a premium for a black,
and even more so that he would emancipate a slave. The story is repeated almost
verbatim by an anonymous writer in *American Notes and Queries* 2 (June 2, 1888),
50. Effie Harrison Snyder, in her wildly inaccurate 1931 St. Joseph *Tensas Gazette*
article, offers a garbled variant of this in which Bowie finds a white man whipping an Indian woman, and saves her. Thorp, *Bowie-Knife*, 133, gives a heavily
embellished version of this episode.

Bowie finding the son of Mississippi Governor William Lattimore being
cheated of his father's cotton crop money by a Natchez gambler named
Sturdivant. Bowie enters the game, detects Sturdivant cheating and confronts
him, then wins back all of the Lattimore money and returns it to him. The
aggrieved Sturdivant demanded a duel with knives with the two men bound
together by their left hands. In the fight Bowie disabled the gambler but
refrained from killing him. For a start, William Lattimore was a Mississippi congressman, but never governor. Secondly, no record of a Sturdivant appears in
any of the Mississippi or Louisiana censuses for 1810–1830, nor in Natchez
property tax records or county title records, even though embellishments to the
story date the event in 1829 and have him owning and operating several taverns
and brothels. He may have been a genuine character named John or Jack
Sturdivant, but of this there is no certainty. The same embellishers make

Lattimore the elder a neighbor of Bowie's, though Lattimore according to cen-sus records and other documents lived in Amite County, Mississippi, more than one hundred miles from Lafourche Parish, Louisiana, where Bowie then lived. There was a David Latimore who lived near Natchez in those years, and also held property across the river in Condordia, but no evidence connects him with William Lattimore or with this spurious story. John Evans, "The Bowie-Sturdivant Duel," *Alamo Journal* 65 (February 1989): 3–5, accepts all of the embellished accounts of the story uncritically, adds nothing to the story, and does not even consult the original source in the "L.H." article. It must be empha-sized that though this tale is widely published in many versions, all are based on the "L.H." article, which has already been shown to be heavily fictionalized or else so inaccurate of memory as to be dismissed out of hand. It should also be noted that the theme of Bowie detecting a card cheat, winning back from him ill-gotten gains, returning them to the victim, and then fighting the gambler, is a recurring theme, quite probably based on the original 1850 Houston *Democratic Telegraph and Texas Register* story about the spurious Laffite encounter. Quite probably this Sturdivant story derives from that 1850 article.

Andrew Marschalk, editor of a Natchez newspaper, publishing an unflatter-ing article about Bowie, and the aggrieved subject appearing in his office with a whip and two pistols and giving the editor the choice of being horsewhipped, or else fighting a duel. Marschalk immediately retracts his story, and the two amicably settle the affair over a brandy. Marschalk was quite definitely a very real character who edited five different newspapers in or around Natchez, and was known to be contentious. However, Marschalk was all but out of the news-paper business by the late 1820's when Bowie would have acquired sufficient notoriety to be the subject of any editorials, and none of the surviving issues of his papers—nor any of the many Natchez newspapers—carry a single article about Bowie. Indeed, the only time his name is known to have appeared in a Natchez newspaper was in the few references to him as "Mr. Bowie" in the *Ariel* and others when they reported on the 1827 Sandbar fight. The Bowie story in "L.H." is almost certainly a confusion of a real incident in 1815—when Bowie was just nineteen—when George Poindexter caned Marschalk in his office for a libelous article.

A. J. Sowell in the aforementioned May 4, 1917, San Antonio *Light* gives another duel story that takes place on an unnamed steamboat, in which a Major Ryan and wife were on their way to New Orleans when two gamblers plied him with drink and cheated him out of his money. Bowie enters the game and wins it all back, and when he catches the two sharps cheating, a fight ensues, and he kills both of them with his knife. This is an obvious variation on the original Laffite story, interesting in that Sowell goes on to tell the Richardson/Musgrove varia-tion in the same article, both myths having a common origin. The original 1850 newspaper article has now led to two different strains of descendant myths, with the names of the victims engrafted onto the legend, and a host of other details, including extensive conversation, that were not a part of the original story.

In the James Bowie Biographical File (DRT) there is a peculiar typewritten manuscript narrative of twelve pages, author and date unknown. Internal evidence indicates that it is a revision done in 1936 or later of an earlier version written sometime after 1911, and titled "Lure of the Frontier." The first three pages are almost verbatim drawn from a newspaper account identified by internal evidence as being by James Madison Wells, "James Bowie: Something of His Romantic Life and Tragic Death," published post 1912 but obviously written many years earlier (Bowie Biographical File, DRT). However, the balance is certainly not written by Wells, for the author speaks of moving to San Antonio in his boyhood in company with his father, and there getting acquainted with the aged Madame Candelaria, whereas Wells remained in Louisiana all his life. The Wells account, both in the post-1912 newspaper article and in the post-1936 typewritten version, includes an account of a fight during a card game between Bowie and twins named Parker, one of whom was his rival for a young woman. Bowie killed them both and was tried and acquitted. This has been discussed in chapter 4, note 36, and largely dismissed, since none of the characters mentioned in the story can be found to have been living in Louisiana or Mississippi during the years 1810–30, when such an event would have taken place. The "Lure of the Frontier" manuscript also contains a story, attributed to Perry Barksdale, the source of Wells's account of the above fight, that does not appear in the post-1912 Wells account, and thus may be an addition by the unknown author of the balance of the post-1936 account. It has Bowie engaging in a duel with a Frenchman, the "Count de Wantein," over the daughter of a Spanish nobleman named Montejo of New Orleans. Bowie dangerously wounded the count and was painfully injured himself, but lost the woman, who decided to enter a convent. Again, no Montejo appears in any of the Louisiana censuses for the years 1810–30, nor is it possible to identify any Barksdale in Louisiana at the time, even thought he was supposed to have been close friend of Bowie's for many years. The supposed Barksdale told the anonymous writer and/or Wells these stories in San Antonio sometime after the writer moved there as a boy, which would date the original telling of the stories to around the 1880s, since Madame Candelaria is spoken of as an old woman at the time. Thus they were told fifty years or more after the fact—if they were based on genuine events. The facts that they survive only in thirdhand accounts, written as much as another fifty years or more after being heard, were supposedly told to a boy by a man whose existence cannot be verified, and involve several other people who cannot be found in any records, all mitigate against their having any validity.

One other near-fight story should be mentioned, and this is the supposed episode on a stagecoach somewhere in the East when Bowie and Henry Clay shared the coach with a young woman and a rude brute who refused to quit smoking his cigar when the woman asked him to. Bowie intervened, drawing his knife and threatening violence until the other man threw out his cigar. Speer and Brown, *Encyclopedia*, vol. 1, 436–37, published the story in 1881 as told by William McGinley of Kansas, who claimed to be the only other passenger on the same coach. The story was supposedly told by Clay to many people, including Jefferson Davis, and eight years later someone identified only as "Collector" of Butte, Montana Territory, sent the supposed Davis version of the story to *American Notes and Queries*, which published it in vol. 3 (July 27, 1889), 155. This version says that the offending smoke was a pipe rather than a cigar, and that the only passengers were Clay, Bowie, the woman, and the brute—McGinley has somehow disappeared. There is no contemporary record in the papers of either Clay or Davis, or the recollections of their associates, to verify that either ever told this story, and its suspect nature has already been discussed earlier in this work.

Once more, it needs to be remembered that Rezin Bowie, the one person in the world closest to James, stated unequivocally in his August 24, 1838, letter ("The Bowie Knife," *Nile's Register* 55, September 29, 1838, 70) that "neither col. James Bowie nor myself, at any period of our lives, ever had a duel with any person soever." Moreover, he also stated that the only occasion on which James Bowie ever used a knife as a weapon was in the Sandbar brawl. While James Bowie may have been cavalier with the truth, no evidence has surfaced to indicate that his brother Rezin was anything other than truthful. More to the point, if James ever had been in a duel, the ethic in the South at the time would have made it something to burnish rather than tarnish his reputation, and Rezin, so watchful of his brother's memory, would have had no conceivable reason to try to deny any such feats of heroism. And certainly, if James Bowie was ever in a fight or duel, the one person guaranteed to know of it would be his most intimate confidant and friend, his brother Rezin. Consequently, in the complete absence of verifiable and directly contemporary evidence to the contrary, it has to be concluded that all the above duel and fight stories, as well as others omitted, are false, either the result of mistake and exaggeration, or of the conscious frontier myth-making prevalent in the 1840s–1870s. This is not to say that James Bowie was not capable of being in a duel, or other spontaneous "chance-medleys" like the Sandbar, nor that he may not have been in one or even several for which reliable record has not survived. If ever there was a man willing to fight, it was him. But if he was in any such encounters, all record remains lost to history, while all of the accounts that have been, and continue to be, published are myths and fabrications.

Similarly hard to pin down are the facts about the West portrait—purportedly of Bowie—revealed by his grandnephew John S. Moore in 1889. The identification is probably correct, but problems exist, not least the fact that Moore was born in 1846 and never saw his granduncle. Almost everything members of Rezin's family wrote about James from the 1870s onward has proved to be chiefly based on erroneous stories they gleaned from newspapers, showing that they had no real oral tradition passed down in the family. Yet it can only be from family members—or his own assumption—that Moore derived his identification of this portrait. His mother, Matilda, or her sister Elve might have told him, but they saw James infrequently after 1826, and were in their early and mid-teens at the latest when they last possibly saw him, probably in 1833. The only *reliable* source would have been Rezin's widow, who certainly knew James well, and who lived until 1876, long enough to pass identification on to her grandchildren. Thus it seems most likely that this is indeed James.

However, in the full portrait the man holds the hilt of a militia officer's sword in his right hand. There is no record of James ever serving as an officer in any

Louisiana militia, while his brief service in Texas with the honorific title of "colonel" was too hectic, and too brief, for him to have had the portrait painted in late 1835. Moreover, despite contemporaneous references to him carrying a pistol and the knife, no source puts a sword in his possession. If he did own one, it would have been a sword *cane* of the kind affected by civilian men of his time and place, such as the one with which Norris Wright nearly killed him in the Sandbar brawl. Significantly, his brother Rezin had been an officer of the Avoyelles Mounted Rifles in the 1820s. He still had what he called his "arms & militia accoutrements" in 1832, and certainly these included a sword. As of this writing, Rezin's descendants still own not only this portrait—and one identified as Rezin—but also a militia officer's sword they believe to have been James's. In light of the above, however, it seems more likely that the sword belonged to Rezin. In some features it resembles the one in the portrait, and if it is, then logic suggests at least the possibility that it is Rezin in the painting, not James. Keeping in mind the misinformation about James and Rezin unwittingly disseminated by the latter's grandchildren, none of whom ever met either of them, it has to be considered possible that family tradition included a confusion about the identity of this and other portraits. In fact family tradition later attributed this and two more paintings to G. P. A. Healy, which is all but impossible in the case of the others, and highly improbable with this one. The Healy attribution has also been questioned by the National Portrait Gallery.

69. William B. Worthen, "The Term 'Bowie Knife,'" *Knife World* 21 (November 1995): 15.

70. These statements come from Thorp, *Bowie Knife*, 44, 70–71, a notoriously unreliable source on Bowie himself, and have not been verified by the author.

71. Kuykendall, "A Short Review of My Life," December 1, 1849, Bancroft Library.

72. Tocqueville, *Democracy in America*, p. 541.

73. Ibid., p. 631.

74. New York *United States Telegraph*, May 19, 1836.

75. New York *Evening Star*, April 22, 1836.

BIBLIOGRAPHY

The published literature on these three men, and especially on the last days of their lives, is extensive, though of vastly varying quality. Only one previous book-length attempt has been made to produce a combined biography of them, Virgil A. Baugh's *Rendezvous at the Alamo: Highlights in the Lives of Bowie, Crockett, and Travis* (1960). It is throughout a careless and inaccurate work, casually researched at best, and mainly a reiteration of the tired old myths and legends, especially in the case of Bowie and Travis. J. Milton Nance's "Rendezvous at the Alamo: The Place of Bowie, Crockett, and Travis in Texas History," *West Texas Historical Association Year Book* 63 (1987), is almost equally unsatisfactory, and unduly critical of Travis in particular.

For David Crockett the starting place must be his own *A Narrative of the Life of David Crockett of the State of Tennessee*. There are two excellent modern editions, probably the more useful being that edited by James A. Shackford and Stanley J. Folmsbee in 1973, though a 1987 edition with an introduction by Paul A. Hutton is also good. The standard biography is still James A. Shackford's *David Crockett, The Man and the Legend*. The book is rather dated now after more than forty years, and has always suffered from a professorial and discursive writing style, but it is the current starting place for all serious study of Crockett. The articles by Stanley J. Folmsbee and Anna Grace Catron in the *West Tennessee Historical Society Papers* and *East Tennessee Historical Society Publications* make valuable additions and corrections to Shackford's earlier work. James W. Burke's *Davy Crockett: The Man Behind the Myth* and Gary L. Foreman's *Crockett: The Gentleman from the Cane* add little that is new, while among the much older biographies none is very worthwhile. Edward S. Ellis, *The Life of Colonel David Crockett*, published in 1884, is interesting, not for its content on Crockett but for a very valuable recollection of Bowie by William H. Sparks, published as an appendix. A much-anticipated work in progress by Paul A. Hutton promises to be the most definitive Crockett biography to date.

There are many significant special studies and monographs on Crockett as a frontier icon and folk character, the best of which are Joseph Arpad's 1970 Ph. D. dissertation, "David Crockett: An Original Legendary Eccentricity and Early American Character"; Walter Blair, "Six Davy Crocketts," in the July 1940 *Southwest Review*; Richard B. Hauck, *Crockett: A Bio-Bibliography*; and the works of Michael Lofaro, including *Davy Crockett: The Man, the Legend, the Legacy*, a fine anthology of recent scholarship, and *Crockett at Two Hundred*, edited with Joe Cummings. For an excellent though flawed examination of Crockett's controversial death, see Dan Kilgore, *How Did Davy Die?*

Much less attention has been paid to James Bowie, and the quality of what there is does not invite compliments. Evelyn Brogan's *James Bowie: A Hero of the Alamo*, published in 1922, is typical of the uncritical and superficial treatment given to his life. C. L. Douglas's 1944 *James Bowie: The Life of a Bravo* has been as much the standard life as any, yet it is heavily fictionalized, utterly uncritical of the sources used, and passes along a life that is largely mythical, being based on a few published

Texas histories, a smattering of archival research, and a preponderance of secondary sources. Raymond Thorpe's *Bowie Knife*, privately published in 1948, is a dreadful work, prejudiced, self-congratulatory, and utterly unsophisticated as regards sources. It, like Douglas, indulges in invented conversation and blind acceptance of old myths. Its citations are confused or erroneous, genuine quotations have been altered, and some material apparently simply invented. Equally bad is Sam Mims, *Trail of the Bowie Knife*, privately published in 1967. Contentious, packed with mythology, invented conversation, and such, it is typical of what has passed for Bowie biography. The most recent attempt, and little better than the above, is Clifford Hopewell, *James Bowie, Texas Fighting Man: A Biography*, which appeared in 1994. It is chiefly a repository of myth and legend, with some facts in between, though often either misstated or misunderstood. Its inventions and unsupported statements and assumptions are too numerous to deal with.

The only family history is Walter W. Bowie's *The Bowies and Their Kindred*, published in 1899. It is not reliable for the Louisiana Bowies, who were not his branch of the family or a chief concern. The numerous articles of J. Frank Dobie—"Bowie and the Bowie Knife," "Fabulous Frontiersman: Jim Bowie," "James Bowie, Big Dealer"—and his essays in such volumes as *In the Shadow of History* are interesting but reveal less about Bowie than they do about Dobie, who may have been an excellent folklorist but was no historian. In the same category is Edward S. Sears's unwarrantedly influential "The Low Down on Jim Bowie," in *From Hell to Breakfast*. It is iconoclastic without understanding of the subject matter, and completely misinterprets most of the data used. Somewhat more useful, if occasionally quirky, are some of the several articles on Bowie by J. De Stefani, Joseph Musso, and others that have appeared in *Alamo Journal*.

For Bowie's second most famous escapade, the Sandbar fight near Natchez, the best sources are James L. Batson, *James Bowie and the Sandbar Fight: Birth of the James Bowie Legend & Bowie Knife*, and J. R. Edmondson's four-part series, "James Bowie: First Blood," appearing in *Knife World* in 1995–96. Joseph Musso's article, "Jim Bowie's Sandbar Fight," in the February 1988 *Alamo Journal* is a fair overview in brief compass.

While Travis has been far less studied than the other two, he has certainly been better served than Bowie, at least. A starting point is his own diary, edited by Robert E. Davis as *The Diary of William Barret Travis: August 30, 1833–June 26, 1834*. The editing is careless and inconsistent, and the book is further marred by numerous errors in transcription from the original and an all-but-useless index, but it remains an indispensable source until a better edition appears. The best biography is Archie P. McDonald's 1976 *Travis*, a sympathetic yet not uncritical work that does an excellent job of evoking Travis's world. Its only serious weakness is in its handling of Travis's Alabama years. Martha Anne Turner's *William Barret Travis: His Sword and His Pen* appeared in 1972 and is considerably less satisfying than McDonald's book. Though very dated, Ruby Mixon's master's thesis "William Barret Travis: His Life and Letters" remains an essential source, and contains some primary material no longer available elsewhere. Robert J. Travis, *The Travis (Travers) Family and Its Allies* is only marginally useful as a family history, there being considerable disagreement about Travis's ancestry.

Archie P. McDonald's article "Travis: The Legend and the Legend Makers," in the *Journal of the American Studies Association of Texas* is the best short version of Travis's life, though it perpetuates a couple of legends. Robert H. Williams, Jr., "Travis—A Potential Sam Houston," in the *Southwestern Historical Quarterly*, is a largely unsuccessful attempt at psychobiography.

As for the Alamo, the literature is enormous, and of a widely varying quality. The best modern study of the political background is Paul D. Lack, *The Texas Revolutionary Experience: A Political and Social History, 1835–1836*, while the most able account of the campaigns and battles of the revolt is Stephen L. Hardin, *Texian Iliad: A Military History of the Texas Revolution*. The earliest serious study of the Alamo itself, and one that still dominates much thinking on the subject, was Amelia Williams's Ph.D. dissertation, "A Critical Study of the Siege of the Alamo and of the Personnel of Its Defenders," subsequently published in four parts in the *Southwestern Historical Quarterly* in 1933–34. It is a deeply flawed work, though useful, and must be approached carefully. Walter Lord's 1961 *A Time to Stand* remains after thirty-seven years the ablest account, and always worthy of reading for sheer pleasure. New information may have dated some of its conclusions, but it remains the definitive treatment until something better comes along. The most recent substantial effort is Jeff Long's 1990 *Duel of Eagles: The Mexican and U.S. Fight for the Alamo*. It is glib, marred by unseemly iconoclasm, misuse or ignorance of pertinent sources, and conclusions and inventions unwarranted by its evidence—when any is cited. It does not in any respect supplant Lord's earlier work

As a final note it should be added that only sources from which material has actually been drawn are listed below. Scores—perhaps hundreds—of others were consulted without contributing anything to this study.

PRIMARY SOURCES

Manuscripts

Alabama Department of Archives and History, Montgomery
Acts of Alabama, 1818–1975, Schools and Academies
Samuel Dale Papers
James Dellet Papers
Governors' Papers, Gabriel Moore, Reward Files.
Letford, William. "The Story of William Barret Travis as told by Philip Alexander Travis." Travis Surname File.
McMillan, Ed Leigh. Memoranda & Papers with Regard to William Barret Travis.
Benjamin Porter Letters
Secretary of State, Lands Division, U.S. Cahaba Land Office—Register of Lots Sold in the Towns of Claiborne, Jackson, and Wetumpka, 1820–1836
Territory of Alabama, List of Taxable Property Taken in the County of Concecuh in the Year 1818
Tait Family Papers
Travis Surname File

Arkansas History Commission, Little Rock
    Kelley, George P. "John J. Bowie, 1787–1859." Kelley Vertical File.
Auburn University Archives, Auburn, Ala.
    Benjamin F. Porter Collection
Stephen F. Austin State University, Nacogdoches; East Texas Research Center
    Daughters of the American Revolution Papers
Bancroft Library, University of California, Berkeley
    Kuykendall, J. Hampton. "A Short Review of My Life."
    Texas Collection   .
Boston Public Library, Boston, Mass.
    Mellen Chamberlain Collection of Autographs
Buffalo & Erie County Historical Society, Buffalo, N.Y.
    David Crockett Letter
Columbia University Rare Book and Manuscript Library, New York, N.Y.
    Columbia University Manuscripts Collection
    David Crockett Letter
Daughters of the Republic of Texas Library, San Antonio, Tex.
    James Bowie Biographical File
    Lucy Leigh Bowie Papers
    David Crockett Biographical File
    David Crockett Collection
    William Barret Travis Biographical File
    William Barret Travis Legal Document
Duke University Library, Durham, N.C.
    Gaylord G. Goodell Papers
East Carolina University Library, Greenville, N.C.
    John H. Bryan Papers
Nita Stewart Haley Library, Midland, Tex.
    Clarinda Pevehouse Kegan Memoirs
Haverford College Library, Haverford, Pa.
    Charles Roberts Autograph Letters Collection
Houghton Library, Harvard University, Cambridge, Mass.
    David Crockett Letter, Autograph File
Houston Public Library, Houston, Tex.
    Green B. Jameson Letter
University of Houston Library, Houston, Tex.
    William B. Bates Collection
J. K. Lilly Library, Indiana University, Bloomington
    Latin American Manuscripts, Mexico
    Rudd Manuscripts
    U.S. Manuscripts
Library of Congress, Washington, D.C.
    Archivo General de Indias, Cuban Papers
    John Davis Batchelder Autograph Collection
    Miscellaneous Manuscripts Collection
Louisiana Section, Louisiana State Library, Baton Rouge

James Bowie Vertical File
Hill Library, Louisiana State University, Baton Rouge
  Bowie Family Portraits
  David F. Boyd Papers
  Mary E. Compton and Family Papers
  Robert A. Crain Letter
  De La Vergne Family Papers
  J. Fair Hardin Collection
  Pintado Papers
  Alonzo Snyder Papers
  James G. Taliaferro Papers
Maine Historical Society, Portland
  J. S. H. Fogg Collection
Maryland Historical Society, Baltimore
  Lucy Leigh Bowie Collection
  Walter Worthington Bowie Papers
  David Crockett Vertical File
Archivo Historico Militar Mexicano, Secreteria de la Defensa Nacional, Mexico City
  Expediente XI/481.3/1149
  Expediente XI/481.3/1151
  Expediente XI/481.3/1655
  Expediente XI/481.3/1900
National Archives Southwest Region, Fort Worth, Tex.
  General Case Files, 1806–1932, Entry 21, U.S. District Court for the Eastern
  Region of Louisiana, New Orleans, Record Group 21
    Case #1780, *United States* v. *Charles Mulholland*
    Case #2628, *Warren Price* v. *Rezin P. Bowie*
    Case #2668, *Boyd McNairy* v. *Rezin P. and James Bowie*
    Case #3040, *Cushing and Ames* v. *Rezin P. and Stephen Bowie*
National Archives, Washington, D.C.
  Record Group 36, Bureau of Customs, New Orleans Collection District
    Entry 1627: Letters Received, 1818–1822
    Entry 1656: Record of Drawbacks 1795–1849
    Entry 1657: Record of Fees Paid, Cargo Manifests 1809–1821
  Record Group 49, Records of the Bureau of Land Management
    Entry 197: Index of Letters Sent
    Entry 200: Letters Sent Relating to Private Land Claims
    Entry 214: Court Records Relating to Arkansas Land Claims, 1824–1832
    Entry 215: Bowie Claims, Cleland District, St. Augustine, Fla., Locations
      Under Arkansas Court Decrees, Act of 1824
    Entry 273: Old Index of Private Land Claims in Louisiana, 1800–1880
    Entry 292: Reports on Private Land Claims, Southwest District, La., Act of
      May 11, 1820, 1820–1825
    Entry 293: Report of Register North of Red River, La., 1821–1890
    Entry 296: Report, Register and Receiver of Land Office, New Orleans,
      Louisiana on Private Land Claims, 1833

Entry 297: Report, Register & Receiver, Land Office, Opelousas, La., on Private Land Claims, Act of Feb. 6, 1835, 1836–1840

Entry 394: Records Re Bowie Claims, Fraudulent Claims in Arkansas, 1827–1843, Division D (Private Land Claims Division)

Entry 404: Letters Sent Re Fraudulent Bowie Claims in Louisiana, 1829–1873, Division D (Private Land Claims Division)

M1385: Letters Received by the Commissioner of the General Land Office Relating to Private Land Claims in Louisiana, 1818–1881

M1385: Correspondence Relating to Efforts to Acquire the "Pintado Papers," 1836–1883, Unbound Records of the General Land Office Relating to Private Land Claims, Louisiana, 1805–1896

M1385: Records Relating to the Private Land Claim of Antonio Vaca to Land in Louisiana, 1881–1882

Record Group 94, Adjutant General's Office, War of 1812. Compiled Service Records

    Abraham Bird

    James Bouyee

    Rezin Bouyee

    John Davis Bradburn

    John L. Brouard

    Warren D. C. Hall

    Josiah S. Johnston

    Coleman A. Martin

    Samuel Wells

Record Group 217, Accounting Offices of the Department of Treasury

    Fifth Auditor's Office, Letters Sent, 1817–1869, Vols. 1 and 2

    Receipts and Expenditures of the United States, 1818, 1819, 1820

New Orleans Notarial Archives, Civil Courts Building, New Orleans

    Notary William Boswell

    Notary Felix De Armas

New-York Historical Society, New York

    Miscellaneous Personal Collection—David Crockett

New York Public Library, New York

    Personal Miscellaneous Papers

    Carl H. Pforzheimer Collection

Southern Historical Collection, University of North Carolina, Chapel Hill

    Samuel Asbury, Papers

    Thomas Jefferson Green Papers

    Calvin Jones Papers

    Thomas F. Maddox Papers

    John Nevitt Diary

    Quitman Family Papers

Panhandle-Plains Historical Museum Research Center, Canyon, Tex.

    David Crockett Promissory Note

Historical Society of Pennsylvania, Philadelphia

    Nicholas Biddle Papers

Conarroe Autograph Collection
Frederick Dreer Collection
Edward Carey Gardiner Papers
Simon Gratz Collection
Josiah Stoddard Johnston Papers
Society Miscellaneous Collection
Pierpont Morgan Library, New York
Ford Collection
Gilder-Lehrman Collection
Rosenbach Museum & Library, Philadelphia
David Crockett Letters
Rosenberg Library, Galveston, Tex.
David Crockett Letter
James Morgan Papers
Ben C. Stuart Papers
Samuel May Williams Papers
San Fernando Parish Church, San Antonio, Tex.
Baptismal Record
San Jacinto Monument, San Jacinto, Tex.
Adele Looscan Collection
University of the South, Sewannee, Tenn.
University Archives
De Golyer Library, Southern Methodist University, Dallas, Tex.
Texana Collection
Tennessee State Library and Archives, Nashville
Cooper Family Papers
David Crockett Correspondence by Author
David Crockett Correspondence by Subject
Adam Huntsman Papers
Tennessee Historical Society Miscellaneous Collection
Special Collections, University of Tennessee, Knoxville
David Crockett Letter
Texas State Library and Archives, Austin
Alamo Vertical File
Samuel Asbury, Papers
Auditor's Book of Claims Paid 1835–1840
William Barret Travis
James Bowie, Vertical File
James Bowie, Petition of Administrator of Estate of
Comptroller's Military Service Papers
Consultation Papers
General Land Office Papers
Applications
Muster Book
Records of Milam's Colony
Testimony of Mrs. Hannig Touching the Alamo Massacre, Sept. 23, 1876

A. J. Houston Papers
Mirabeau B. Lamar Papers
McArdle San Jacinto Notebook
Memorials and Petitions Collection
    John Sutherland File
Miscellaneous File
    William Barret Travis
Nacogdoches Archives
Pension Claims
    Hiram M. Thompson File
Records of the General Council
Record Group 304
    Republic Payments for Service
        Antonio Cruz File
        Ignacio Perez
        Felipe Xaimes
    Accounts and Receipts Submitted for Approval
Record Group 307: Secretary of State
    Accounts and Receipts Submitted to General Council
    Communications Received
    Domestic Correspondence
    Reports of Treasurer and Auditor to Governor
Record Group 401: Adjutant General's Office
    Army Papers
    Miscellaneous Papers
Record Group 5926, Audited Military Claims
    David Crockett
    Peter Harper
    Samuel Leeper
    William H. Patton
    C. B. Stewart
    John Sutherland
Arthur E. Thomas Collection
William Barret Travis article, n.d. (probably by Ruby Mixon)
William Barret Travis Bible
William Barret Travis Collection
William Barret Travis Military Service Record
William Barret Travis Vertical File
Center for American History, University of Texas, Austin
    Samuel E. Asbury Papers
    Stephen F. Austin Papers
    Austin, William T., Account of the Campaign of 1835
    Moseley Baker Papers
    Béxar Archives

Biographical and Historical Files
Bowie Family Papers, Natchez Trace Collection
James Bowie, Documents Pertaining to
James Bowie Vertical File
John Henry Brown Papers
Moses A. Bryan Papers
William W. Chapman Papers
James Clark Family Papers
David Crockett Papers
David Crockett Vertical File
Frederick Cron Papers (Bowie Vertical File)
Alexander Dienst Collection
William W. Fontaine Collection
John S. Ford Memoirs
Benjamin C. Franklin Papers
Zachary T. Fulmore Papers
Warren D. C. Hall Vertical File
Caiaphas Ham Recollections (John S. Ford Memoirs)
Hassel Family Papers
Mary A. Holley Papers
Kuykendall Family Papers
Barnes F. Lathrop Papers
Nathan Mitchell, Life of
Ruby Mixon Papers
Samuel C. A. Rogers Reminiscences
Thomas J. Rusk Papers
José Sanchez-Navarro Papers
Antonio López de Santa Anna Collection
Henry Smith Papers
James H. Starr Collection
Texas Veterans Association Papers
William Barret Travis Papers
William Barret Travis Vertical File
Amelia W. Williams Papers
Tulane University Library Special Collections, New Orleans, La.
Juan Almonte Journal 1836
Albert Sidney Johnston and William Preston Johnston Collection (Mason Barret Papers)
Whittington, G. P. *Rapides Parish: A History.*
University of Virginia, Alderman Library, Charlottesville
Barrett Box
Beinecke Library, Yale University, New Haven, Conn.
David Crockett Letter
Thomas W. Streeter Collection of Texas Manuscripts

Court Records

Adams County, Miss., Circuit Court Records, Historic Natchez Foundation, Natchez
Avoyelles Parish Court House, Marksville, La.
    Conveyance Book E
Cameron Parish Court House, Vidalia, La.
    Conveyance Records
Catahoula Parish Court House, Harrisonburg, La.
    Conveyance Records
Chicot County Court House, Lake Village, Ark.
    Conveyance Book A
    Deed Book A-B
Clarke County Circuit Court Case Files, Alabama Department of Archives and History, Montgomery
Clarke County Court House, Grove Hill, Ala.
    County Court Minute Book A, 1824–1838
    Minutes of Commissioners Court, Book A, 1813–1832
Colorado County Court House, Columbus, Tex.
    Deed Book A
    Records for Bonds &c, Book B
East Carroll Parish Court House, Lake Providence, La.
    Deed Books B, C, F
Hempstead County Court House, Hope, Ark.
    Conveyance Book B
Lafourche Parish Court House, Thibodeaux, La.
    Conveyance Books D, E, F, G, H, I, R
Logan County Court House, Russellville, Ky.
    Deed Book A–1
    Survey Book A
Monroe County Court House, Monroeville, Ala.
    Deed Book A
    Order Book 1
Natchitoches Parish Court House, Natchitoches, La.
    Conveyance Books
    District Court Docket Books
    Judicial Mortgage Records
New Madrid County Court House, New Madrid, Mo.
    Record Books 1, 2
Orleans Parish Court House, New Orleans, La.
    Conveyance Records
Phillips County Court House, Helena, Arkansas
    Deed Book D
Point Coupee Parish Court House, New Roads, La.
    Conveyance Records
St. Landry Parish Court House, Opelousas, La.
    Conveyance Book D–1

Debaillon Acts Book B
District Civil Suits
Sales and Mortgages Book D, E
Tax Assessments 1817, 1818
St. Mary Parish Court House, Franklin, La.
Conveyance Records
Sumner County Court House, Gallatin, Tenn.
Deed Book 1
Terrebonne Parish Court House, Houma, La.
Conveyance Records C, D, E, F, G, H, K
Wilcox County Circuit Court, Bar Docket, 1828, Subpoena Docket, Alabama
Department of Archives and History, Montgomery

Newspapers

Austin *American-Statesman* , 1996
Baltimore *Nile's Weekly Register*, 1827, 1836
Brazoria (Tex.) *Brazos Courier*, 1840
Brazoria (Tex.) *Texas Gazette*, 1830, 1032
Brazoria (Tex.) *Texas Republican*, 1834–1836
Brewton (Ala.) *Brewton Standard*, 1967
Cincinnati *Daily Whig and Commercial Intelligencer*, 1836
Cincinnati *Journal and Western Luminary*, 1836
Claiborne (Ala.) *Gazette*, 1825
Claiborne (Ala.) *Claiborne Herald*, 1829
Columbia (S.C.) *State*, 1934
Columbia (Tenn.) *Observer*, 1836
Columbia (Tex.) *Telegraph*, 1837
Columbia (Tex.) *Telegraph and Texas Register*, 1838
Dallas *Dallas Morning News*, 1929, 1933
Evergreen (Ala.) *Conecuh County Record*, 1899
Evergreen (Ala.) *Evergreen Courant*, 1967
Fort Worth *Star-Telegram*, 1932
Frankfort (Ky.) *Commonwealth*, 1836
Galveston *Daily News*, 1875, 1878, 1885, 1893, 1895, 1898, 1920
Galveston *Weekly News*, 1861
Houston *Chronicle*, 1908
Houston *Daily Post*, 1882
Houston *Democratic Telegraph and Texas Register*, 1850
Houston *Morning Star*, 1840
Huntsville (Tex.) *Item*, 1858
Jackson *Mississippian*, 1836
Jackson (Tenn.) *Gazette*, 1828–1829
Jackson (Tenn.) *Southern Statesman*, 1833
Little Rock *Arkansas Advocate*, 1835–1837
Little Rock *Arkansas Gazette*, 1830, 1835–1836, 1908

Louisville *Journal*, 1836
Marshall *Texas Republican*, 1853.
Matagorda (Tex.) *Bulletin*, 1837
Mexico City *El Mosquito Mexicano*, 1836
Monroe (La.) *Ouachita Telegraph*, 1888
Monroeville (Ala.) *Monroe Journal*, 1966
Montgomery (Ala.) *Advertiser*, 1920
Nashville *Republican*, 1836
Natchez *Courier & Journal*, 1835
Natchez *Mississippi Free Trader and Natchez Gazette*, 1835–1836
Natchez *Mississippi Gazette*, 1833
Natchez *Mississippi Republican*, 1819
Natchez *Mississippi State Gazette*, 1819
Natchez *Mississippi Statesman*, 1827
Natchez *Natchez Newspaper and Public Advertiser*, 1826–1827
Natchez *Southern Galaxy*, 1828
New Orleans *Abeille*, 1827
New Orleans *Argus*, 1827
New Orleans *Bee*, 1827–1828
New Orleans *Commercial Bulletin*, 1836
New Orleans *Louisiana Advertiser*, 1832, 1836
New Orleans *Louisiana State Gazette*, 1826
New Orleans *Price-Current and Commercial Intelligencer*, 1827
New Orleans *Times*, 1875
New Orleans *Times-Picayune*, 1937, 1976
New York *American*, 1836
New York *Evening Post*, 1836
New York *Sun*, 1835
New York *Sunday Morning News*, 1836
New York *Times*, 1836, 1893, 1996
New York *Transcript*, 1836
New York *United States Telegraph*, 1836
Philadelphia *Atkinson's Saturday Evening Post and Bulletin . . .*, 1833
Philadelphia *Pennsylvanian*, 1838
Port Gibson (Miss.) *Correspondent*, 1836
San Antonio *Express*, 1878, 1889, 1900, 1905, 1907, 1935
San Antonio *Light*, 1917
San Felipe (Tex.) *Telegraph and Texas Register*, 1832, 1835–1836
San Francisco *Chronicle*, 1881
Savannah *Gazette*, 1765
St. Joseph (La.) *Tensas Gazette*, 1931
St. Martinville (La.) *Attakapas Gazette*, 1829–1832
Selma *Free Press*, 1836
Suggsville (Ala.) *Clarke County Post*, 1836
Tuscaloosa *Flag of the Union*, 1836
Vidalia (La.) *Concordia Intelligencer*, 1860

Washington (Ark.) *Telegraph*, 1841
Washington (Tex.) *Lone Star*, 1852
Woodville (Miss.) *Republican*, 1826–1827

Official Publications

Acts Passed at the Annual Session of the General Assembly of the State of Alabama. Tuscaloosa, 1836.

American State Papers . . . The Public Lands. Washington, 1859–1860. 6 vols.

Compendium of the Enumeration of the Inhabitants and Statistics of the United States, as Obtained at the Department of State, from the Returns of the Sixth Census. Washington, 1841.

Journal of the House of Representatives During the First Session of the Eighth Legislature of the State of Louisiana. New Orleans, 1827.

Journal of the House of Representatives During the Second Session of the Eighth Legislature of the State of Louisiana. New Orleans, 1828.

Journal of the House of Representatives of the Republic of Texas. Fifth Congress, 1840–1841. Austin, 1841.

Journal of the House of Representatives of the State of Alabama. Tuscaloosa, 1835.

Journal of the Proceedings of the General Council of the Republic of Texas, Held at San Felipe de Austin, November 14th, 1835. Houston, 1839.

Journal of the Senate of the State of Alabama. Tuscaloosa, 1836.

Journals of the Consultation, Held at San Felipe de Austin, October 16, 1836. Houston, 1838.

Lowrie, Walter S., and Walter S. Franklin, eds. *American State Papers: Documents Legislative and Executive . . . ; The Public Lands.* Washington, 1834.

———. *American State Papers, Documents, Legislative and Executive, of the Congress of the United States . . . ; Foreign Relations.* Washington, 1834.

Military Register of Alabama 1830–1832. Tuscaloosa, n.d. 2 vols.

Peters, Richard. *Reports of Cases Argued and Adjudged in the Supreme Court of the United States: Vol. 7, January Term 1833.* Philadelphia, 1833.

Printed Acts of Alabama 1818–1864. Montgomery, n.d.

United States Census
  Alabama
    Concecuh County, 1830, 1840
    Monroe County, 1830
  Arkansas
    Chicot County, 1830
    Phillips County, 1830, 1840
  Louisiana
    Assumption Parish, 1830
    Avoyelles Parish, 1820
    Catahoula Parish, 1810, 1820, 1830
    Lafourche Parish, 1830
    St. Landry Parish, 1820
  Mississippi
    Adams County, 1820, 1830
    Warren County, 1830

PUBLISHED WORKS

Books

Aderman, Ralph M., ed. *The Letters of James Kirke Paulding*. Madison, Wis., 1962.

Ardoin, Robert B., comp. *Louisiana Census Records*. Vol. 1, *Avoyelles and St. Landry Parishes 1810 & 1820*. Baltimore, 1970.

Baker, DeWitt Clinton. *A Texas Scrap-Book*. New York, 1875.

Ball, Timothy H. *A Glance into the Great South-east, or, Clarke County, Alabama, and its Surroundings, from 1540 to 1877*. Grove Hill, Ala., 1882.

Barker, Eugene C., ed. *The Austin Papers*. 3 vols. Washington, 1919–26.

Becerra, Francisco. *A Mexican Sergeant's Recollections of the Alamo and San Jacinto*. Austin, 1980.

Bernard, J. H. *Dr. J. H. Bernard's Journal*. Goliad, Tex., 1965.

Binkley, William C., ed. *Official Correspondence of the Texan Revolution*. 2 vols. New York, 1936.

"Brazos." *Life of Robert Hall*. Reprint, Austin, 1992.

Bryan, J. P., ed. *Mary Austin Holley. The Texas Diary, 1835–38*. Austin, 1965.

Canby, Henry Seidel, ed. *The Works of Henry David Thoreau*. Boston, 1937.

Candler, Allen D. *The Colonial Records of the State of Georgia*. 25 vols. Atlanta, 1907.

————. *The Revolutionary Records of the State of Georgia*. 3 vols. Atlanta, 1907.

Caro, Ramón M. *Verdadera Idea de la Primera Campaña de Tejas*. Mexico City, 1837.

Castañeda, Carlos E. *The Mexican Side of the Texas Revolution*. Dallas, 1928.

Claiborne, J. F. H. *Mississippi as A Province, Territory and State, with Biographical Notices of Eminent Citizens*. Jackson, Miss., 1880.

Clift, G. Glenn. *Second Census of Kentucky 1800*. Frankfort, 1954.

Colson, Lucy Wiggins. *Monroe and Conecuh County, Alabama, Marriages 1833–1880*. Easley, S.C., 1983.

Crèvecoeur (J. Hector St. John). *Letters from an American Farmer*. Gloucester, Mass., 1968.

Crockett, David. *A Narrative of the Life of David Crockett of the State of Tennessee*. Introduction by Paul A. Hutton. Lincoln, Nebr., 1987.

————. *A Narrative of the Life of David Crockett of the State of Tennessee*. Edited by James A. Shackford and Stanley J. Folmsbee. Knoxville, 1973.

Davis, Robert E., ed. *The Diary of William Barret Travis: August 30, 1833–June 26, 1834*. Waco, Tex., 1966.

Day, Donald, and Harry H. Ullum, eds. *The Autobiography of Sam Houston*. Norman, Okla., 1954.

Day, James M., comp. *The Texas Almanac, 1857–1873: A Compendium of Texas History*. Waco, 1967.

De la Peña, José Enrique. *With Santa Anna in Texas: A Personal Narrative of the Revolution*. College Station, Tex., 1975.

De la Teja, Jesús F., ed. *A Revolution Remembered: The Memoirs and Selected Correspondence of Juan N. Seguín*. Austin, 1991.

The Devil's Comical Texas Oldmanick. New York, 1836.

Dewees, William B. *Letters from an Early Settler of Texas*. Louisville, Ky., 1852.

Ehrenberg, Herman. *With Milam and Fannin: Adventures of a German Boy in Texas' Revolution.* Dallas, 1935.

Family Adventures. *Early Alabama Marriages, 1813–1850.* San Antonio, 1991.

Field, Joseph E. *Three Years in Texas.* Boston, 1836.

Filisola, Vicente. *Memoirs for the History of the War in Texas.* 2 vols. Austin, 1986–87.

Flint, Timothy. *Recollections of the Last Ten Years in the Valley of the Mississippi.* Reprint, Carbondale, Ill., 1968.

Ford, John S. *Origin and Fall of the Alamo, March 6, 1836.* San Antonio, 1895.

Gray, William. *From Virginia to Texas, 1835: Diary of Col. Wm. F. Gray.* Houston, 1909.

Green, Rena Maverick, ed. *Samuel Maverick, Texan: 1803–1870.* San Antonio, 1952.

Groneman, William, comp. *Eyewitness to the Alamo.* Plano, Tex., 1996.

Guild, Joseph Conn. *Old Times in Tennessee.* Nashville, 1878.

Gulick, Charles Adams, Jr., and Katherine Elliott, eds. *The Papers of Mirabeau Bounaparte Lamar.* 6 vols. Austin, 1923.

Hamilton, J. G. de Roulhac, ed. *The Papers of William Alexander Graham.* 7 vols. Raleigh, N.C., 1957.

Hargreaves, Mary W. M., and James F. Hopkins, eds. *The Papers of Henry Clay.* Vol. 6, *Secretary of State, 1827.* Lexington, Ky., 1981.

Herbert, Donald J., ed. *South Louisiana Records, I.* Cecilia, La., 1978.

———. *Southwest Louisiana Records, II.* Eunice, La., 1974.

Holley, Mary Austin. *Texas.* Lexington, Ky., 1836.

Hollon, W. Eugene, and Ruth Lapham Butler, eds. *William Bollaert's Texas.* Norman, Okla., 1956.

Hopkins, James F., and Mary W. M. Hargreaves, eds. *The Papers of Henry Clay.* Vol. 5, *Secretary of State, 1826.* Lexington, Ky., 1973.

Hunter, Robert Hancock. *Narrative of Robert Hancock Hunter.* Austin, 1966.

Jenkins, John H., ed. *The General's Tight Pants.* Austin, 1976.

———. *The Papers of the Texas Revolution 1835–1836.* 10 vols. Austin, 1973.

Johnson, Frank W. *A History of Texas and Texans.* 5 vols. Chicago, 1914.

Jones, Anson. *Memoranda and Official Correspondence Relating to the Republic of Texas, Its History and Annexation.* New York, 1859.

Kennedy, William. *Texas: The Rise, Progress, and Prospects of the Republic of Texas.* London, 1841.

Lester, Charles E. *The Life of Sam Houston.* New York, 1855.

Linn, John J. *Reminiscences of Fifty Years in Texas.* New York, 1883.

Lundy, Benjamin. *The Life, Travels and Opinions of Benjamin Lundy.* Philadelphia, 1847.

———. *The War in Texas . . . .* Philadelphia, 1837.

Maillard, Nicholas D. *A History of the Republic of Texas.* London, 1842.

Matovina, Timothy, ed.. *The Alamo Remembered: Tejano Accounts and Perspectives.* Austin, 1995.

Menchaca, Antonio. *Memoirs.* San Antonio, 1937.

Michel's New Orleans Annual and Commercial Register. New Orleans, 1833.

Morphis, J. M. *History of Texas.* New York, 1874.

Muir, Andrew F., ed. *Texas in 1837, An Anonymous Contemporary Narrative.* Austin, 1958.

Nevins, Allan, ed. *The Diary of John Quincy Adams, 1794–1845.* New York, 1928.

Niles, John M., and L. M. Pease. *History of South America and Mexico, . . . to Which is Annexed A Geographical and Historical View of Texas*. Hartford, Conn., 1839.

Parker, Amos A. *A Trip to the West and Texas . . . 1834*. Concord, N.H., 1836.

Paxton, John Adams. *The New-Orleans Directory and Register*. New Orleans, 1823.

Percy, S. E. *The New-Orleans Directory*. New Orleans, 1832.

Poore, Ben Perley. *Perley's Reminiscences of Sixty Years in the National Metropolis*. Philadelphia, 1886.

Pope, William F. *Early Days in Arkansas*. Little Rock, 1895.

Porter, Benjamin F. *Reminiscences of Men and Things in Alabama*. Tuscaloosa, 1983.

Potter, Reuben M. *The Fall of the Alamo*. N.p., 1860.

Prentiss, G. L., ed. *Memoir of S. S. Prentiss*. 2 vols. New York, 1856.

Rees, James. *Life of Edwin Forrest, With Reminiscences and Personal Recollections*. Philadelphia, 1874.

Reid, John, and John Henry Eaton. *The Life of Andrew Jackson*. Philadelphia, 1817.

Rodriguez, José Maria. *Memoirs of Early Texas*. N.p., 1913.

Santa Anna, Antonio López de. *Manifesto*. Vera Cruz, 1837.

Schultz, Christian. *Travels on an Inland Voyage* 2 vols.. New York, 1810.

Seager, Robert, and Melba Porter Hays, eds. *The Papers of Henry Clay*. Vol. 8, *Candidate, Compromiser, Whig, March 5, 1829–December 31, 1836*. Lexington, Ky., 1984.

Shinn, Josiah Hazen. *Pioneers and Makers of Arkansas*. Little Rock, 1908.

Smithwick, Noah. *The Evolution of a State*. Austin, 1900.

Sowell, Andrew J. *Early Settlers and Indian Fighters of Southwest Texas*. Austin, 1900.

————. *Rangers and Pioneers of Texas*. San Antonio, 1884.

Sparks, William H. *The Memoirs of Fifty Years: Containing Brief Biographical Notices of Distinguished Americans, and Anecdotes of Remarkable Men*. Philadelphia, 1870.

Sutherland, John. *The Fall of the Alamo*. San Antonio, 1936.

Swisher, John M. *The Swisher Memoirs*. San Antonio, 1932.

Thorpe, Thomas B. *The Mysteries of the Back-Woods*. Philadelphia, 1846.

Tocqueville, Alexis de. *Democracy in America*. Edited by J. P. Mayer. New York, 1969.

Tomerlin, Jacqueline Beretta, comp. *Fugitive Letters, 1829–1836: Stephen F. Austin to David G. Burnet*. San Antonio, 1981.

A Visit to Texas, Being the Journal of A Traveller Through Those Parts Most Interesting to American Settlers . . . . New York, 1836.

Weaver, Herbert, and Paul H. Bergeron, eds. *Correspondence of James K. Polk*. Vol. 1, *1817–1833*. Nashville, 1969.

————. *Correspondence of James K. Polk*. Vol. 2, *1833–1834*. Nashville, 1972.

Weaver, Herbert, and Kermit L. Hall, eds. *Correspondence of James K. Polk*. Vol. 3, *1835–1836*. Nashville, 1975.

Wharton, Clarence. *Remember Goliad*. Houston, 1931.

Williams, Amelia W., and Eugene C. Barker, eds. *The Writings of Sam Houston*. 8 vols. Austin, 1938–43.

Wilson, Robert. *Memorial of Robert Wilson to the Legislature of the State of Texas*. Houston, 1858.

Wooten, Dudley G., ed. *Comprehensive History of Texas 1685 to 1897*. 2 vols. Austin, 1898.

Yoakum, H. *History of Texas from Its First Settlement in 1685 to its Annexation to the United States in 1846*. 2 vols. New York, 1856.

Zuber, William P. *My Eighty Years in Texas*. Austin, 1971.

Articles

"A Letter from San Antonio de Béxar in 1836." *Southwestern Historical Quarterly* 62 (April 1959): 523–28.

Asbury, Samuel E., ed. "The Private Journal of Juan Nepomuceno Almonte, February 1–April 16, 1836." *Southwestern Historical Quarterly* 48 (July 1944): 10–32.

Austin, William T. "Account of the Campaign of 1835 by William T. Austin, Aide to Gen. Stephen F. Austin & Gen. Ed Burleson." *Texana* 4 (Winter 1966): 287–322.

B., J. J. [full name unknown] "Davy Crockett's Electioneering Tour." *Harpers' New Monthly Magazine* 35 (April 1867): 606–11.

B[ollaert], W[illiam]. "Life of Jean Lafitte." *Littell's Living Age* 32 (March 1852): 433–46.

Baldwin, Christopher. "Diary of Christopher Baldwin." *Transactions of the American Antiquarian Society* 7 (1911): 249–50.

Bowie, John. "Early Life in the Southwest—The Bowies." *DeBow's Review* 1 (October 1852): 378–83.

Bowie, Rezin. "An Indian Battle." *Atkinson's Casket; or Gems of Literature, Wit and Sentiment* 7 (September 1833): 422–25.

———. "The Bowie Knife." *Nile's Weekly Register* 55 (September 29, 1838): 70.

Connelly, Thomas L. "Did David Crockett Surrender at the Alamo? A Contemporary Letter." *Journal of Southern History* 26 (August 1960): 368–76.

Davis, Curtis Carroll. "A legend at Full Length: Mr. Chapman Paints Colonel Crockett—and Tells About It." *Proceedings of the American Antiquarian Society* 69 (October 1959): 155–74.

Davis, Robert E. "Travis Draws a Will." *Manuscripts* 22 (Spring 1970): 113.

DeBow, James D. B. "Public Lands Acquired by Treaty, etc." *Commercial Review* 5 (February 1848): 117–18

"Documents of the Texian Revolution." *Alamo Journal* 99 (December 1995): 17.

"General Austin's Order Book for the Campaign of 1835." *Quarterly of the Texas State Historical Association* 11 (July 1907): 1–55.

Graham, George Mason. "The Autobiography of George Mason Graham." *Louisiana Historical Quarterly* 20 (January 1937): 43–57.

Green, Michael Robert. "'To the People of Texas & All Americans in the World.'" *Southwestern Historical Quarterly* 92 (April 1988): 483–508.

Greer, James K. "Journal of Ammon Underwood, 1834–1838." *Southwestern Historical Quarterly* 32 (July 1928): 124–51.

Hardin, Stephen L. "The Felix Nuñez Account and the Siege of the Alamo: A Critical Appraisal." *Southwestern Historical Quarterly* 94 (January 1991): 65–84.

Holt, David. "Reminiscences Then and Now of the Quaint Little City of Claiborne." *Montgomery Advertiser*, July 5, 1920.

Kilpatrick, A. R. "Historical and Statistical Collections of Louisiana." *DeBow's Southern and Western Review* 12 (June 1852): 631–46.

Lee, A. J. "Some Recollections of Two Texas Pioneer Women." *Texas Methodist Historical Quarterly* 1 (January 1910): 207–13.

McDonald, David, and Kevin R. Young, eds. "Siege of the Alamo: A Mexican Army Journal." *Journal of the Alamo Battlefield Association* 3 (Fall 1998).

"Negroes Imported." *Nile's Weekly Register* 15 (December 12, 1818): 269.

Pearson, Philip E. "Reminiscences of Judge Edwin Waller." *Quarterly of the Texas State Historical Association* 4 (July 1900): 33–53.

Potter, Reuben M. "The Fall of the Alamo." *Magazine of American History* 2 (January 1878): 1–21.

Pritchard, Walter, ed. "George Graham's Mission to Galveston in 1818: Two Important Documents Bearing Upon Louisiana History." *Louisiana Historical Quarterly* 20 (July 1937): 619–50.

Pugh, W. W. "Bayou Lafourche from 1820–5." *Louisiana Planter and Sugar Manufacturer* (September-October 1888): 12–24.

"Reminiscences of Mrs. Dilue Harris." *Quarterly of the Texas State Historical Association* 4 (October 1900): 85–127, (January 1901): 155–89.

"Reminiscences of Sion R. Bostwick." *Quarterly of the Texas State Historical Association* 5 (October 1901): 85–96.

Richardson, F. D. "The Teche Country Fifty Years Ago." *Southern Bivouac,* n.s., 1 (March 1886): 593–98.

Smith, Henry. "Reminiscences of Henry Smith." *Quarterly of the Texas State Historical Association* 14 (July 1910): 24–73.

Smither, Harriet, ed. "Diary of Adolphus Sterne, Part I." *Southwestern Historical Quarterly* 30 (October 1926): 139–55; part 3 (April 1927): 305–24.

Snow, Elliott, ed. "A Visit to Lafitte." *Louisiana Historical Quarterly* 11 (July 1928): 434–44.

"Texas—A Province, Republic and State." *DeBow's Review* 23 (September 1857): 239–62.

Zuber, W. P. "The Escape of Rose from the Alamo." *Quarterly of the Texas State Historical Association* 5 (July 1901): 1–11.

Autograph Catalogs

American Book Prices Current 88 (New York, 1982)
————. 90 (Washington, Conn., 1984)
————. 91 (Washington, Conn., 1990)
————. 97 (Washington, Conn., 1991)
————. 98 (Washington, Conn., 1993)
————. 99 (Washington, Conn., 1994)
Christie's Catalog. New York, May 17, 1996.
Christie's Auction Catalog no. 8444K. May 1996.
Frontier America Catalog no. 37. N.p., n.d.
Heaston, Michael D. *Texas in the Nineteenth Century Catalog* no. 27. Austin, 1997.
Jenkins, John H. *The Texas Revolution and Republic Catalog* no. 188. Austin, 1986.
Morrison, W. M. *Catalog* no. 322. Waco, 1975.
Philpott Texana Collection Auction Catalog. Alterman Gallery, Dallas, October 16–17, 1995.
RWA, Inc. *Auction Catalog* no. 39. N.p., June 1, 1996.
Smythe, R. M. *Winter Autograph Auction* 175. New York, February 26, 1998

SECONDARY SOURCES

Theses and Dissertations

Arpad, Joseph. "David Crockett, An Original Legendary Eccentricity and Early American Character." Ph.D. dissertation, Duke University, 1970.

Bowie, Helen M. "Bayou Lafourche." Master's thesis, Louisiana State University, 1935.

Bowie, Robert. "Col. James Bowie and the Bowie Families of Early Louisiana." Monograph on file at the Arkansas History Commission, Little Rock.

Fisher, Rayburn J. "William Barret Travis in Alabama." Class thesis, Howard College (now Sanford University), 1929.

Mixon, Ruby. "William Barret Travis, His Life and Letters." Master's thesis, University of Texas, 1930.

Moore, Wilma H. "A History of San Felipe de Austin 1824–1836." Master's thesis, University of Texas, 1929.

Roark, Wanda Louise. "Robert Wilson: Letters to His Son." Master's thesis, Stephen F. Austin State College, 1966.

Rorhbaugh, Edward. "James Bowie and the Bowie Knife in Fact and in Fancy." Master's thesis, University of Texas, Austin, 1938.

Shackford, James A. "The Autobiography of David Crockett: An Annotated Edition." Ph.D. dissertation, Vanderbilt University, 1948.

Tregle, Joseph G. "Louisiana in the Age of Jackson: A Study in Ego-Politics." Ph.D. dissertation, University of Pennsylvania, 1954.

Williams, Amelia. "A Critical Study of the Siege of the Alamo and of the Personnel of its Defenders." Ph.D. dissertation, University of Texas, 1931.

Books

Adair, A. Garland, and M. H. Crockett, Sr., eds. *Heroes of the Alamo.* New York, 1957.

Alger, William R. *Life of Edwin Forrest, the American Tragedian.* Philadelphia, 1877.

Arthur, Stanley C. *The Story of the West Florida Rebellion.* Baton Rouge, 1975.

Bancroft, H. H. *History of the North American States and Texas.* 2 vols. San Francisco, 1889.

Barker, Eugene C. *The Life of Stephen F. Austin, Founder of Texas 1793–1863.* Austin, 1949.

Barr, Alwyn. *Texans in Revolt. The Battle for San Antonio, 1835.* Austin, 1990.

Batson, James L. *James Bowie and the Sandbar Fight: Birth of the James Bowie Legend & Bowie Knife.* Madison, Ala., 1992.

Baugh, Virgil A. *Rendezvous at the Alamo: Highlights in the Lives of Bowie, Crockett, and Travis.* New York, 1960.

Binkley, William C. *The Texas Revolution.* Baton Rouge, 1952.

Biographical and Historical Memoirs of Northwest Louisiana. Chicago, 1890.

Boddie, John Bennett. *Historical Southern Families.* 2 vols. Baltimore, 1958.

Bowie, Walter Worthington. *The Bowies and Their Kindred.* Washington, 1899.

Brady, Cyrus Townsend. *Conquest of the Southwest.* New York, 1905.

Brewer, W. *Alabama. Her History, Resources, War Record and Public Men, from 1546 to 1872.* Spartanburg, S.C., 1975.

Brogan, Evelyn. *James Bowie, A Hero of the Alamo.* San Antonio, 1922.

Brown, Frank. *Annals of Travis County and the City of Austin.* N.p., n.d.

Brown, John Henry. *History of Texas from 1685 to 1890.* St. Louis, 1892. 2 vols.

———. *Indian Wars and Pioneers of Texas.* Austin, 1896.

———. *Life and Times of Henry Smith.* Dallas, 1887.

———. *Long's Expedition.* Houston, 1930.

Burke, James Wakefield. *Davy Crockett: The Man Behind the Myth.* Austin, 1987.

Calvert, Robert, and Walter Buenger, eds. *Texas Through Time.* College Station, 1991.

Carter, Hodding. *Doomed Road of Empire.* New York, 1963.

Chabot, Frederick C. *With the Makers of San Antonio.* San Antonio, 1937.

Chapman, John A. *History of Edgefield County from Its Earliest Settlements to 1897.* Newberry, S.C., 1897.

Chariton, Wallace O. *Exploring the Alamo Legends.* Plano, Tex., 1990.

———. *One Hundred Days in Texas: The Alamo Letters.* Plano, Tex., 1990.

Cisco, J. Guy. *Historic Sumner County, Tennessee.* Nashville, 1900.

Clarke County Historical Society. *Historical Sketches of Clarke County, Alabama: A Story of the Communities of Clarke County.* Huntsville, 1977.

Davis, James D. *History of the City of Memphis.* Memphis, 1873.

Davis, William C. *A Way Through the Wilderness. The Natchez Trace and the Civilization of the Southern Frontier.* New York, 1995.

———. *Jefferson Davis: The Man and His Hour.* New York, 1991.

DeShields, James. *Tall Men with Long Rifles.* San Antonio, 1935.

Dobie, J. Frank, et al. *In the Shadow of History.* Dallas, 1939.

Douglas, C. L. *James Bowie. The Life of a Bravo.* Dallas, 1944.

DuBose, Joel C., ed. *Notable Men of Alabama.* Atlanta, 1904.

Durand, Charles. *History of the Philadelphia Stage, Between the Years 1749 and 1855.* N.p., 1868.

Elfer, Maurice. *Madam Candelaria.* Houston, 1933.

Ellis, Edward S. *The Life of Colonel David Crockett.* Philadelphia, 1884.

Ellison, Rhoda Coleman. *History and Bibliography of Alabama Newspapers in the Nineteenth Century.* University, 1954.

Estavan, Lawrence, ed. *Edwin Forrest: San Francisco Theatre Research Monograph XXII.* San Francisco, 1940.

Farragher, John Mack. *Daniel Boone, The Life and Legend of an American Pioneer.* New York, 1992.

Foley, William E. *A History of Missouri. Volume I, 1673 to 1820.* Columbia, Mo., 1971.

Foreman, Gary L. *Crockett: The Gentleman from the Cane.* Dallas, 1986.

Francis, M. E. *Bowie's Lost Mine.* San Antonio, 1954.

Friend, Llerena. *Sam Houston, the Great Designer.* Austin, 1954.

Fulmore, Zachary T. *The History and Geography of Texas as Told in County Names.* Austin, 1915.

Goins, Charles Robert, and John Michael Caldwell. *Historical Atlas of Louisiana.* Norman, Okla., 1995.

Graham, John S. *History of Clarke County.* Birmingham, 1923.

Groneman, William. *Defense of A Legend: Crockett and the de la Peña Diary.* Plano, Tex., 1994.

Hardin, J. Fair. *Northwestern Louisiana, A History.* 3 vols. Louisville, Ky.

Hardin, Stephen L. *Texian Iliad. A Military History of the Texas Revolution.* Austin, 1994.

Hauck, Richard B. *Crockett: A Bio-Bibliography.* Westport, Conn., 1982.

Helm, Mary Sherwood. *Scraps of Early Texas History.* Austin, 1884.

Henson, Margaret Swett. *Juan Davis Bradburn.* College Station, Tex., 1982.

————. *Samuel May Williams, Early Texas Entrepreneur.* College Station, Tex., 1976.

History of Southeast Missouri, Embracing A Historical Account of the Counties of Ste. Geneviève, St. François, Perry, Cape Girardeau, Bollinger, Madison, New Madrid, Pemiscot, Dunklin, Scott, Mississippi, Stoddard, Butler, Wayne and Iron. Boston, 1888.

Hopewell, Clifford. *James Bowie, Texas Fighting Man. A Biography.* Austin, 1994.

Houck, Louis. *History of Missouri.* Chicago, 1908.

Houston, Andrew Jackson. *Texas Independence.* Houston, 1938.

Hunter, John Warren. *Rise and Fall of the Mission San Saba.* Bandera, Tex., 1905.

Hurtel, Caroline G. *The River Plantation of Thomas and Marianne Gaillard 1832–1850.* Mobile, 1946.

James, Marquis. *The Raven. A Biography of Sam Houston.* Indianapolis, 1929.

Jenkins, John H. *Basic Texas Books: An Annotated Bibliography of Selected Works for A Research Library.* Austin, 1990.

Kane, Harnett T. *The Bayous of Louisiana.* New York, 1944.

Keating, J. M. *History of the City of Memphis and Shelby County, Tennessee.* 2 vols. Syracuse, 1880.

Kilgore, Dan. *How Did Davy Die?* College Station, Tex., 1978.

King, C. Richard. *Susanna Dickenson, Messenger of the Alamo.* Austin, 1976.

Lack, Paul D. *The Texas Revolutionary Experience: A Political and Social History, 1835–1836.* College Station, Tex., 1992.

Lofaro, Michael A. *Davy Crockett: The Man, the Myth, the Legacy, 1786–1986.* Knoxville, 1985.

Lofaro, Michael A., and Joe Cummings, eds. *Crockett at Two Hundred.* Knoxville, 1989.

Long, Jeff. *Duel of Eagles.* New York, 1990.

Looscan, Adele. *Micajah Autry: A Soldier of the Alamo.* Austin, 1913.

Lord, Walter. *A Time to Stand.* New York, 1961.

Marks, Paula Mitchell. *Turn Your Eyes Toward Texas: Pioneers Sam and Mary Maverick.* College Station, Tex., 1989.

McDonald, Archie P. *Travis.* Austin, 1976.

Miller, Thomas L. *The Public Lands of Texas, 1519–1970.* Norman, Okla., 1972.

Mims, Sam. *Trail of the Bowie Knife.* Homer, La., 1967.

Nickell, Joe, ed. *Psychic Sleuths: ESP and Sensational Cases.* Buffalo, N.Y., 1995.

Oates, Stephen B., ed. *The Republic of Texas.* Palo Alto, Calif., 1968.

Owen, Thomas M. *History of Alabama and Dictionary of Alabama Biography.* Chicago, 1921.

Partlow, Miriam. *Liberty, Liberty County, and the Atascosito District.* Austin, 1974.

Paulding, James K. *Westward Ho! A Tale.* 2 vols. New York, 1832.

Phelan, Macum. *A History of Early Methodism in Texas.* Nashville, 1924.

Pierce, Nicholas H., and Nugent E. Brown, eds. *The Free State of Menard.* Menard, Tex., 1946.

Poyo, Gerald E., ed. *Tejano Journey 1770–1850.* Austin, 1996.

Ragsdale, Crystal S. *The Women and Children of the Alamo.* Austin, 1994.

Ramsay, Robert L. *Our Storehouse of Missouri Place Names.* Columbia, Mo., 1952.

Remini, Robert V. *Andrew Jackson and the Course of American Freedom, 1822–1832.* New York, 1981.

Riley, B. F. *History of Conecuh County, Alabama.* Columbus, Ga., 1881.

———. *Makers and Romance of Alabama History.* N.p., 1951.

Robinson, Duncan W. *Judge Robert McAlpin Williamson, Texas' Three-Legged Willie.* Austin, 1948.

Saxon, Lyle. *Lafitte the Pirate.* New York, 1930.

Schoelwer, Susan P., and Tom W. Glaser. *Alamo Images: Changing Perceptions of a Texas Experience.* Dallas, 1985.

Shackford, James A. *David Crockett: The Man and the Legend.* Chapel Hill, N.C., 1956.

Siegel, Stanley. *Political History of Texas Republic.* Austin, 1956.

Slotkin, Richard. *Regeneration Through Violence:The Mythology of the American Frontier, 1600–1860.* Middletown, Conn., 1973.

Speer, William S., and John Henry Brown, eds. *The Encyclopedia of the New West.* 2 vols. Marshall, Tex., 1881.

Stafford, George M. C. *The Wells Family of Louisiana and Allied Families.* Alexandria, La., 1942.

Taylor, I. T. *Cavalcade of Jackson County.* San Antonio, 1938.

Taylor, Joe Gray. *Negro Slavery in Louisiana.* Baton Rouge, 1963.

Thorp, Raymond. *Bowie Knife.* N.p., 1948.

Thrall, Homer S. *A Pictorial History of Texas.* St. Louis, 1879.

———. *History of Methodism in Texas.* Houston, 1872.

Travis, Robert J. *The Travis (Travers) Family and Its Allies.* Decatur, Ga., 1954.

Truman, Ben C. *The Field of Honor.* New York, 1884.

Turner, Martha Anne. *William Barret Travis. His Sword and His Pen.* Waco, 1972.

Tyler, Ron, Douglas E. Barnett, Roy R. Barkley, Penelope C. Anderson, and Mark F. Odintz, eds. *The New Handbook of Texas.* 6 vols. Austin, 1996.

Walraven, William and Marjorie K. *The Magnificent Barbarians: Little-told Tales of the Texas Revolution.* Austin, 1993.

Waugh, Julia Nott. *Castro-ville and Henry Castro, Empresario.* Castroville, Tex., 1986.

Weddle, Robert S. *The San Saba Mission.* Austin, 1964.

Wellman, Paul I. *The Iron Mistress.* New York, 1951.

Wells, Mary Ann. *A History Lover's Guide to Louisiana.* Baton Rouge, 1990.

Wheeler, Harry Edgar. *Timothy Abbott Conrad.* Ithaca, N.Y., 1935.

Wilbarger, J. W. *Indian Depredations in Texas.* Austin, 1935.

Williams, John Hoyt. *Sam Houston. A Biography of the Father of Texas.* New York, 1993.

Williams, Elgin. *The Animating Pursuits of Speculation. Land Traffic in the Annexation of Texas.* New York, 1949.

Articles

Albers, June. "The Romances of William Barret Travis." *The Junior Historian* (January 1947): 9–10.

Barker, Eugene C. "The African Slave Trade in Texas." *Quarterly of the Texas State Historical Association* 5 (October 1902): 145–58.

―――. "Difficulties of A Mexican Revenue Officer in Texas." *Quarterly of the Texas State Historical Association* 4 (January 1901): 190–202.

―――. "Land Speculation as A Cause of the Texas Revolution." *Quarterly of the Texas State Historical Association* 10 (July 1906): 76–95.

―――― "Public Opinion in Texas Preceding the Revolution." *Annual Report of the American Historical Association for 1911* I (1912): 219–28.

―――. "The Texan Revolutionary Army." *Quarterly of the Texas State Historical Association* 9 (April 1906): 227–61.

―――. "William Barret Travis, the Hero of the Alamo." *Publications of the Southern History Association* 6 (September 1902): 417–21.

Blair, Walter. "Six Davy Crocketts." *Southwest Review* 25 (July 1940): 443–62.

"Bowie Knife, The." *American Notes and Queries* 2 (March 23, 1889): 251.

"Bowie Knife, The." *American Notes and Queries* 3 (July 27, 1889): 155.

"Bowie Knife and Its Inventor." *American Notes and Queries* I (June 2, 1888): 49–51.

Bowie, Lucy Leigh. "Famous Bowie Knife, Its History and Origin." *Bucks County Historical Society Papers* 4 (1917).

Brannan, Peter A., ed. "Claiborne." *Alabama Historical Quarterly* 19 (Summer 1957): 211–355.

Calhoun, Robert Dabney. "A History of Concordia Parish, Louisiana." *Louisiana Historical Quarterly* 15 (October 1932): 618–45.

Chilton, William B., comp. "The Brent Family." *Virginia Magazine of History and Biography* 20 (October 1912): 433–34.

Cooper, Jim. "A Study of Some David Crockett Firearms." *East Tennessee Historical Society Papers* 8 (1966): 62–69.

Costleloe, Michael P. "The Mexican Press of 1836 and the Battle of the Alamo." *Southwestern Historical Quarterly* 91 (April 1988): 533–43.

Crisp, James E. "A Reply: When Revision Becomes Obsession. Bill Groneman and the de la Peña Diary." *Military History of the West* 25 (Fall 1995): 143–56.

―――― "Back to Basics: Conspiracy, Common Sense, and Occam's Razor." *Alamo Journal* 100 (March 1996): 15–23.

―――. "Davy in Freeze-Frame: Methodology or Madness?" *Alamo Journal* 98 (October 1995): 3–8.

―――. "The Little Book that Wasn't There: The Myth and Mystery of the de la Peña Diary." *Southwestern Historical Quarterly* 98 (October 1994): 259–96.

―――. "Trashing Dolson: The Perils of Tendentious Interpretation." *Alamo Journal* 99 (January 1996): 3–14.

"Crockett's Height." *Alamo Journal* 102 (September 1996): 13.

Davis, William C. "How Davy Probably Didn't Die." *Journal of the Alamo Battlefield Association* 2 (Fall 1997): 11–37.

"Davy Crockett vs. Andy Jackson." *Confederate Veteran* 11 (April 1903): 162–63.

"Death of David Crockett." *Century Magazine* 32 (October 1886): 968.

De Stefani, J. "Handwriting Analysis of Jim Bowie." *Alamo Journal* 99 (December 1995): n.p.

Dobie, J. Frank. "Bowie and the Bowie Knife." *Southwest Review* 16 (April 1931): 351–68.

―――. "Fabulous Frontiersman: Jim Bowie." *Montana: The Magazine of Western History* 9 (April 1958): 43–55.

————. "James Bowie, Big Dealer." *Southwestern Historical Quarterly* 60 (January 1957): 3–23.

Drake, David. "Joe—Alamo Hero." *Negro History Bulletin* 44 (April-June 1981): 34–35.

Durham, Robert L. "*Where* Did Davy Die?" *Alamo Journal* 104 (March 1997): 3-6.

Edmondson, J. R. "James Bowie: First Blood. Part One." *Knife World* 21 (October 1995): 13–17, 29.

————. ". . . Part Two." *Knife World* 21 (November 1995): 27–30.

————. ". . . Part Three." *Knife World* 21 (December 1995): 13–17.

————. ". . . Part Four." *Knife World* 22 (January 1996): 13–17.

Evans, John. "Bowie (Boo-wee) or Bowie (Bo-wee)? What's in a Name?" *Alamo Journal* 69 (December 1989): 6.

————. "The Bowie-Sturdivant Duel." *Alamo Journal* 65 (February 1989): 3–5.

"Fall of the Alamo." *The Knickerbocker* 8 (September 1836): 295–98.

Folmsbee, Stanley J. "David Crockett and West Tennessee." *West Tennessee Historical Society Papers* 28 (1974): 5–24.

Folmsbee, Stanley J., and Anna Grace Catron. "David Crockett, Congressman." *East Tennessee Historical Society Publications* 29 (1957): 40–78.

————. "David Crockett in Texas." *East Tennessee Historical Society Publications* 30 (1958): 48–74.

————. "The Early Career of David Crockett." *East Tennessee Historical Society Publications* 28 (1956): 58–85.

"Genealogical and Historical Register." *Quarterly of the Texas State Historical Association* 5 (April 1902): 347–51.

Groneman, William. "A Rejoinder: Publish Rather than Perish—Regardless; Jim Crisp and the de la Peña Diary." *Military History of the West* 25 (Fall 1995): 157–66.

————. "The Controversial Alleged Account of José Enrique de la Peña." *Military History of the West* 25 (Fall 1995): 129–42.

————. "Jim Bowie—A Popular Leader?" *Alamo News* 34 (January 1984): n.p.

————. "Some Problems with the Almonte Account." *Alamo Journal* 90 (February 1994), n.p.

Hardin, Stephen L. "J. C. Neill: The Forgotten Alamo Commander." *Alamo Journal* 66 (May 1989): 5–11.

————."A Volley from the Darkness. Sources Regarding the Death of William Barret Travis." *Alamo Journal* 59 (December 1987): 3–10.

————. "Gallery: David Crockett." *Military Illustrated* 23 (February-March 1990): 28–35.

Heale, M. J. "The Role of the Frontier in Jacksonian Politics: David Crockett and the Myth of the Self-Made Man." *Western Historical Quarterly* 4 (October 1973): 405–23.

Henderson, Jessie A. "Unmarked Historic Spots of Franklin County." *Tennessee Historical Magazine*, 2d s., 3 (January 1935): 111–20.

Hunter, Mary Kate. "David Crockett of Tennessee and Texas." *East Texas Magazine* 2 (n.d.): 23, 39.

Huthmacher, Ned A. "What was Bowie's Ailment?" *Alamo II* 2 (September 1980): n.p.

Lee, A. J. "Rev. J. W. Kenney." *Texas Methodist Historical Quarterly* 1 (July 1909): 45–55.

Lindley, Thomas Ricks. "Alamo Artillery: Number, Type, Caliber and Concussion." *Alamo Journal* 82 (July 1992): n.p.

———. "Drawing Truthful Deductions." *Journal of the Alamo Battlefield Association* 1 (September 1995): 19–42.

———. "James Butler Bonham." *Alamo Journal* 62 (August 1988): 3–11.

———. "Killing Crockett: It's All in the Execution." *Alamo Journal* 96 (May 1995): 3–12.

———. "Killing Crockett, II: Theory Paraded as Fact." *Alamo Journal* 97 (July 1995): 3–16.

———. "Killing Crockett: Lindley's Opinion." *Alamo Journal* 98 (October 1995): 9–24.

Looscan, Adele B. "The Old Fort at Anahuac." *Quarterly of the Texas State Historical Association* 2 (July 1898): 21–28.

———. "The Old Fort on the San Saba River as Seen by Dr. Ferdinand Roemer in 1847." *Quarterly of the Texas State Historical Association* 5 (October 1901): 137–41.

Lord, Rylance A. "William Travis, Defender of the Alamo." *The Northern Light* 9 (September 1978): 12–13.

Lord, Walter. "Myths & Realities of the Alamo." In Stephen B. Oates, ed., *The Republic of Texas* (Palo Alto, Calif., 1968): 18–25.

McDonald, Archie P. "Travis: The Legend and the Legend Makers." *Journal of the American Studies Association of Texas* 13 (1982): 40–47.

McLean, Malcolm D. "Tenoxtitlan, Dream Capital of Texas." *Southwestern Historical Quarterly* 70 (July 1966): 23–43.

Moore, Matilda E. "The Bowie Brothers and Their Famous Knife." *Frontier Times* 19 (1942): 199–205.

Musso, Joseph. "A Bowie Knife." *Alamo Journal* 84 (December 1992): n.p.

———. "James Bowie's Portrait." *Alamo News* 26 (December 1982): n.p.

———. "Jim Bowie's Sandbar Fight." *Alamo Journal* 60 (February 1988): 3–9.

———. Untitled article on a Bowie knife. *Alamo II* 21 (February 1982): 1–7.

Nance, J. Milton. "Rendezvous at the Alamo: The Place of Bowie, Crockett, and Travis in Texas History." *West Texas Historical Association Year Book* 43 (1987): 5–23.

Pearson, Theodore Bowles. "William Barrett [*sic*] Travis." *Clarke County Historical Society Quarterly* 18 (Summer 1993): 12–18.

"Perdue Hill-Claiborne Historic Preservation Foundation, Inc." *Southwestern Historical Quarterly* 99 (January 1996): 404.

Rosenthal, Phil. "Masons at the Alamo." *Alamo II* 3 (October 1980): n.p.

Rowe, Edna. "The Disturbances at Anahuac in 1832." *Quarterly of the Texas State Historical Association* VI (April 1903): 265–99.

Rowland, Kate Mason. "General John Thompson Mason." *Quarterly of the Texas State Historical Association* XI (January 1908): 163–98.

Schwartz, Ronald A. "Sleight of Tongue." *Skeptical Inquirer* 3 (Fall 1978): 47–55.

Sears, Edward S. "The Low Down on Jim Bowie." Mody C. Boatright and Donald Day, eds., *From Hell to Breakfast* (Austin 1944): 175–99.

Shelton, Horace. "Texas Heroes—James Bowie." *Under Texas Skies* 2 (November 1951): 27.

Sibley, Marilyn McAdams. "The Burial Place of the Alamo Heroes." *Southwestern His-torical Quarterly* 48 (October 1964): 272–80.

Smith, Ruby C. "James Walker Fannin, Jr., in the Texas Revolution." *Southwestern Historical Quarterly* 23 (January 1920): 171–203.

Smith, W. Roy. "The Quarrel Between Governor Smith and the Council of the Provisional Government of the Republic." *Quarterly of the Texas State Historical Association* 5 (April 1902): 269–346.

Steen, Ralph. "Analysis of the Work of the General Council, Provisional Government of Texas, 1835–1836." *Southwestern Historical Quarterly* 41 (April 1938): 324–48.

Stout, S. H. "David Crockett." *American Historical Magazine* 7 (January 1902): 3–21.

Turner, H.S. "Andrew Jackson and David Crockett." *Magazine of American History* 27 (May 1892): 385–87.

Turner, Thomas. "Living in the Shadow of the Alamo," *Baylor University Report* 3 (March 1883): 20–21.

Williams, Amelia. "A Critical Study of the Siege of the Alamo and of the Personnel of Its Defenders, Chapter I." *Southwestern Historical Quarterly* 36 (April 1933): 237–312.

———. ". . . Chapter II." *Southwestern Historical Quarterly* 37 (July 1933): 1–44.

———. ". . . Chapter III." *Southwestern Historical Quarterly* 37 (October 1933): 79–118.

———. ". . . Chapter IV." *Southwestern Historical Quarterly* 37 (January 1934): 157–84,

Williams, Martha M. "A Man and His Knife. Passages from the Life of James Bowie." *Harper's New Monthly Magazine* 56 (July 1898): 223–29.

Williams, Robert H., Jr. "Travis—A Potential Sam Houston." *Southwestern Historical Quarterly* 40 (July 1936–April 1937): 154–60.

Worthen, William B. "The Term 'Bowie Knife.'" *Knife World* 21 (November 1995): 1, 15–17.

Zaboly, Gary S. "Crockett Goes to Texas: A Newspaper Chronology." *Journal of the Alamo Battlefield Association* 1 (Summer 1995): 5–18.

———. "Davy Crockett: New Eyewitness Description—and More." *Alamo Journal* 105 (June 197): 10–11.

INDEX

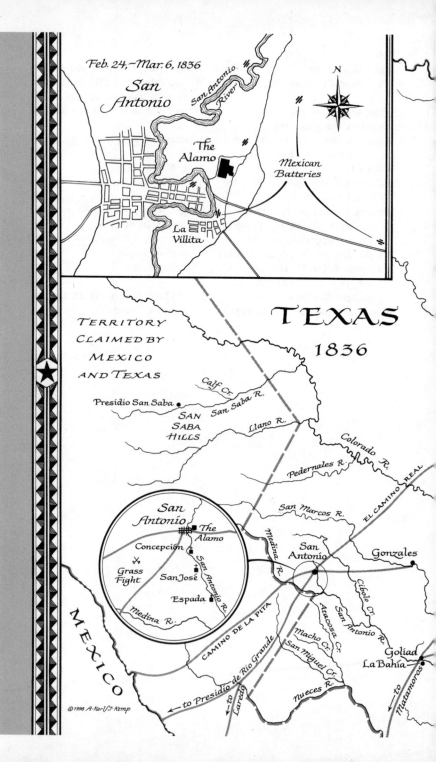

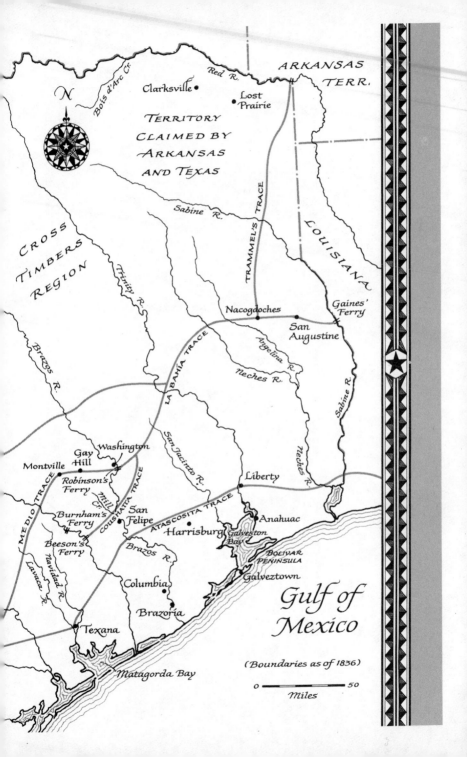

ABOUT THE AUTHOR

WILLIAM C. DAVIS is the author or editor of thirty-five books on the Civil War and Southern history, most recently *A Way Through the Wilderness*; *"A Government of Our Own": The Making of the Confederacy*; and the prizewinning biography *Jefferson Davis: The Man and His Hour*. For many years a magazine publisher, Davis now divides his time between writing and consulting for book publishers and television.